INTELLECTUAL PROPERTY
THE LAW OF
COPYRIGHTS, PATENTS
AND TRADEMARKS

By

Roger E. Schechter

Professor of Law,
George Washington University

John R. Thomas

Professor of Law,
Georgetown University

HORNBOOK SERIES®

Mat #11575277

West Group has created this publication to provide you with accurate and authoritative information concerning the subject matter covered. However, this publication was not necessarily prepared by persons licensed to practice law in a particular jurisdiction. West Group is not engaged in rendering legal or other professional advice, and this publication is not a substitute for the advice of an attorney. If you require legal or other expert advice, you should seek the services of a competent attorney or other professional.

Hornbook Series, WESTLAW and West Group are registered trademarks used herein under license.

 TEXT IS PRINTED ON 10% POST CONSUMER RECYCLED PAPER

For Craig

– R.E.S.

For Sayuri

– J.R.T.

*

Acknowledgments

Only other authors of similar books really understand the large number of people who make a work like this possible. I am deeply grateful to several remarkable law students at George Washington University who helped in the research for this work, including Michael Alter, John Donboli, James Gallagher, Mark Glaze, John Moran, Douglas Rettew and Wayne Stacy. Thanks are also due to David Colletti and Paul M. Levine for meticulous help in proof-reading under great time pressure.

Leonard Klein, a research librarian at the Jacob Burns Law Library was, as always, masterful, in finding just the right resource at just the right moment. My colleague Robert Brauneis offered many useful observations on several chapters, rescuing the reader from much ambiguity.

There are many others whose contributions were one step removed from the preparation of this book, but who laid the foundation that made it possible. I am greatly indebted to Professor J. Thomas McCarthy of the University of San Francisco, not only for his extraordinary contribution to trademark law through his definitive treatise, but for his many thoughtful observations and kindnesses over the years. He is one of the true gentlemen and scholars in our business. I would not be in law teaching if not for the confidence and support of Professor Glen E. Weston, my emeritus colleague at George Washington, who illustrated for me what a teaching book should look like. I am grateful as well to Jerome A. Barron, the Dean who hired me, and to Michael K. Young, my current Dean, for doing so well the hardest thing a Dean can do—namely to leave a faculty member unmolested to pursue a large project. The forbearance, patience, and grace of several at West Group, notably Tom Berreman, Doug Powell, Pam Siege, Heidi Hellekson and Roxy Birkel, has been remarkable.

This volume would have been simply impossible without the collaboration and encouragement of my co-author Jay Thomas, whose enthusiasm and amazing hard work kept me moving through many hard patches. Finally, there are no sufficient words of thanks for my students. So many teacher-authors have said it before that it may take on the trappings of a cliche, but the intellectual curiosity, probing questions, good humor, excitement and energy of two decades worth of G.W. law students have been, more than anything, what got me out of bed each morning and what made this book possible.

Roger E. Schechter

My participation in this project would not have been possible without the efforts of many mentors and colleagues. The late Chief Judge Helen

W. Nies gifted me with two unforgettable years of training in the work of the remarkable court on which she served. I miss her dearly. I shall always be grateful to Professors Martin Adelman and Rebecca Eisenberg for igniting my interest in intellectual property, Harold Wegner for first placing me in front of a law school classroom and Professor Hugh Hansen for proposing a full-time career in law teaching. I also acknowledge Professors Rochelle Dreyfuss, Jerome Reichman and Pamela Samuelson, distinguished senior colleagues who have inspired a new generation of intellectual property scholars. The thoughful commentary of Professor Douglas Lichtman improved the patent portions of this text and was of immeasurable help. My thanks also to Peter Corcoran, Jyotsna Gautam and Brian McMahon for their invaluable research assistance.

I was pleased to attend Roger Schechter's classes as a student and delighted to enter academia as his colleague; now I am honored to serve as his co-author. Roger's insight and eloquence of expression is apparent from the pages of this text, but I also admire his collegiality and extraordinary commitment to his students. The original vision of this treatise was his, and I am grateful to have shared in the work of fulfilling it.

JOHN R. THOMAS

Preface

Writing a book about intellectual property at the dawn of the twenty-first century is like trying to hit a moving target while riding in the bow of a speedboat. Dizzying political, economic and technologic changes have prompted the Congress to undertake massive revisions to all three major branches of intellectual property law over and over again in the past few years. Those new enactments, along with problems not addressed by legislation, have led to a cascade of decisional law on a stunning range of highly complicated issues. That in turn leads to circuit splits, law review articles, more legislation, and still more cases. Anything that one endeavors to say on the subject runs the risk of being obsolete before the ink has dried or the toner has cooled on the page.

We have done our best in this legal typhoon, to offer up a coherent survey of both basic principles and emerging issues. Our goal is to provide, in a single volume, a reasonably thorough introduction to the field that will be helpful to students, practitioners and judges alike. We have tried to summarize what is clear, identify what is unsettled, and sometimes to offer brief thoughts as to how some sticky issues might be resolved or why some existing rules seem poorly though through. We have attempted, above all, to make the text lively and readable and to leaven it with numerous examples and occasional humor. As always, our readers will determine if we have succeeded.

While there are many common themes that pervade the different branches of intellectual property law, the law of copyrights, patents, and trademarks still remain fairly discrete fields. Each is governed by its own separate, and fairly elaborate federal statute, and the cases dealing with problems in one of the areas rarely cite cases from the others. Our organizational scheme reflects this segregation of topics. After an introductory chapter exploring some of the unifying themes in all intellectual property disputes, we have divided this work into three principal parts dealing respectively with the three branches of the law. We have tried, however, through cross-references in both text and notes, to alert the reader to overlap or even conflict between the various branches of intellectual property law.

We have sought to steer a middle ground with the citation of authority. In order to keep the book to a manageable size, we did not attempt to follow the law review practice of supporting every statement with a citation, nor did we attempt to gather complete lists of authorities for various propositions. That such a task would have been impossible in a single volume is evidenced by the existence of huge multi-volume works in all three branches of intellectual property law. On the other hand, we have tried to provide at least some support for most major points, and sufficient information to allow the curious reader to get a head start on further research.

Intellectual property issues are unusually engaging and stimulating. The excitement of this area of the law reflects the excitement of living in a technologically advanced, culturally diverse, economically robust time and place. As more and more authors develop more and more ways to express themselves and to disseminate their work; as more and more technologists conjure more and more ways to make our lives longer, healthier, easier and more fun; and as more and more merchants conjure more and more varieties of goods and services to cater to our needs and wants along with appealing symbols to identify them; the law has been in a mad scramble to keep up. The Internet and globalization have thrown down extraordinary challenges to the legal system. For the student of intellectual property, there is never a dull moment.

Even more significantly, we believe that thoughtful legal rules in these areas can facilitate amazing progress and much good for the citizens of the United States and the world, while rules crafted to advance special interests hold the potential of doing great harm to large numbers of people. Our hope is that this book will help a wide variety of actors in the legal system to gain the kind of introduction to copyright, patent and trademark issues that will enable them both to distinguish between sound and unsound legal regimes and to become champions of the former. A teaching book can aspire to no more and should aspire to no less.

ROGER E. SCHECHTER
JOHN R. THOMAS

Washington, D.C.
March, 2003

WESTLAW® Overview

Intellectual Property: The Law of Copyrights, Patents and Trademarks offers a detailed and comprehensive treatment of the complex issues involving intellectual property. To supplement the information contained in this book, you can access Westlaw, West's computer-assisted legal research service. Westlaw contains a broad array of legal resources, including case law, statutes, expert commentary, current developments, and various other types of information.

Learning how to use these materials effectively will enhance your legal research abilities. To help you coordinate the information in the book with your Westlaw research, this volume contains an appendix listing Westlaw databases, search techniques, and sample problems.

The instructions and features described in this Westlaw overview are based on accessing Westlaw via westlaw.com® at **www.westlaw.com**.

THE PUBLISHER

*

Summary of Contents

Table of Contents

―――――

*

INTELLECTUAL PROPERTY
THE LAW OF
COPYRIGHTS, PATENTS
AND TRADEMARKS

*

Chapter 1

INTRODUCTION TO INTELLECTUAL PROPERTY

Table of Sections

§ 1.1 Forms of Intellectual Property

The term "intellectual property" may sound pretentious, but it is an apt description for the subject matter of the laws that give rise to proprietary interests in creations of the mind. The principal legal intellectual property disciplines are copyright, which concerns artistic and literary works; patent, pertaining to pragmatic innovations; and trademark, relating to commercial symbols. These three core fields are complemented by a number of statutes and common law doctrines in fields ranging from trade secrets, to the right of publicity, to false advertising. Although copyright, patent, trademark and related disciplines share much in common, they arose from distinct traditions and often operate

1

in different ways. A brief overview of the primary forms of intellectual property should assist the reader in tackling the remainder of this text.

1.1.1 Copyright and Related Rights

Copyrights provide protection for original works of authorship.[1] The types of creations addressed by copyright range from traditional works of art, including literature, music and visual art, to such modern forms of artistic expression as sound recordings, motion pictures and even computer software.[2] Copyright protection arises automatically, as soon as the work has been fixed in tangible form.[3] Authors may register their works with the Copyright Office, however, and obtain certain procedural and substantive advantages during copyright enforcement.[4] The copyright law affords authors the exclusive right to reproduce, adapt, and publicly distribute, perform, and display the protected work, subject to certain limitations such as the fair use privilege.[5] A variety of more specialized rights are provided to certain types of works or in certain specific situations. The term of copyright is ordinarily the life of the author plus seventy years.[6]

Congress has supplemented the federal copyright statute with some related statutes. The Semiconductor Chip Protection Act provides copyright-like rights for the circuitry designs of semiconductor chips.[7] The Audio Home Recording Act established a royalty payment system for manufacturers of digital audio home recording devices.[8] Also notable is the Digital Millennium Copyright Act, which prohibits the circumvention of anti-piracy measures built into computer software and limits the copyright infringement liability of Internet service providers.[9]

A number of intellectual property rights originating from state law are conveniently taken up alongside the federal copyright law. The right of publicity gives individuals control over the commercial use of their identities.[10] In addition, the common law has also developed principles for protecting individuals who submit ideas to others from the uncompensated use of those ideas.[11]

1.1.2 Patents, Trade Secrets and Related Rights

Patents provide exclusive rights to inventors of new, useful and nonobvious inventions.[12] The patent law concerns hard technologies, including chemical, electrical and mechanical products and processes, as well as other pragmatic innovations in fields ranging from biotechnology

§ 1.1

1. 17 U.S.C.A. § 102(a) (2000).
2. *Id.*
3. *Id.*
4. 17 U.S.C.A. § 408–412 (2000).
5. 17 U.S.C.A. § 106, 107–122 (2000).
6. 17 U.S.C.A. § 302 (2000).
7. Pub. L. No. 98–6209, 98 Stat. 3347 (1984).
8. Pub. L. No. 92–140, 85 Stat. 391 (1971).
9. Pub. L. No. 105–304, 112 Stat. 2863 (1998).
10. *See* RESTATEMENT (THIRD) OF UNFAIR COMPETITION §§ 46–49.
11. Nadel v. Play–By–Play Toys & Novelties, Inc., 208 F.3d 368 (2d Cir.2000).
12. 35 U.S.C.A. §§ 101, 102, 103 (2000).

to business methods.[13] An inventor may obtain a patent by filing a patent application with the United States Patent and Trademark Office ("PTO"). Such an application must completely describe and precisely claim the invention.[14] Issued patents confer the right to exclude others from making, using, selling, offering to sell or importing into the United States the patented invention.[15] The term of a patent is 20 years from the date the application was filed.[16]

In addition to the usual sort of patent, technically known as a "utility patent," the intellectual property laws also provide for other sorts of patents and patent-like rights. Design patents are available for new, original and ornamental designs.[17] A plant patent may be issued for a distinct and new variety of plant that has been asexually reproduced, through grafting, budding or similar techniques.[18] Plant variety protection certificates are available for sexually reproduced plants, including most seed-bearing plants, provided they are stable and clearly distinguishable from known varieties.[19]

The principal intellectual property alternative to patents is trade secret law.[20] Valuable information that is not publicly known and that is subject to measures to preserve its secrecy may be granted trade secret rights under state statutory or common law. Unlike patents, no formalities are required to maintain trade secret protection. Trade secret protection is more limited than that offered by the patent law, however. Trade secret law does not prevent reverse engineering or independent discovery of the protected information, for example, while patent rights would. Trade secret rights endure for as long as the protected information is not known to the public.

1.1.3 Trademark and Related Rights

Trademarks consist of any word or symbol used by a merchant to identify its goods or services, and to distinguish them from those of others.[21] To be subject to protection under the trademark laws, a mark must successfully distinguish the origins of its associated goods, and not be confusingly similar to marks used by others or merely describe the characteristics of those goods.[22] Trademark rights arise under state law as soon as the mark is used on goods in commerce.[23] However, trademarks may be registered with the PTO, a step that affords significant substantive and procedural advantages.[24] Trademark law also protects the appearance of product packaging and, in some cases, the actual physical configuration of the goods, if these serve as brand identifiers. A trademark owner may prevent others from using any mark that creates

---

13. 35 U.S.C.A. § 101 (2000).

14. 35 U.S.C.A. § 112 (2000).

15. 35 U.S.C.A. § 271 (2000).

16. 35 U.S.C.A. § 154(a)(2) (2000).

17. 35 U.S.C.A. § 171 (2000).

18. 35 U.S.C.A. § 161 (2000).

19. 7 U.S.C.A. § 2321 *et seq.* (2000).

20. *See* RESTATEMENT (THIRD) OF UNFAIR COMPETITION §§ 39–45.

21. *Id.* at § 9.

22. *Id.*

23. *Id.* at § 18.

24. 17 U.S.C.A. § 1051 (2000).

a likelihood of confusion as to the source or sponsorship of the associated goods or services.[25] Trademark rights persist so long as the mark continues to be used and retains its distinctiveness.[26]

Trademarks form one arm of the common law of unfair competition, a collection of principles that encourage the maintenance of honest practices in commercial affairs. A number of other doctrines are grouped under this heading, including passing off, reverse passing off, dilution and false advertising.[27]

§ 1.2   Norms of Intellectual Property

By now it should be apparent that "intellectual property" is an umbrella term. It concerns a variety of disciplines with important historical, theoretical and operational differences. There are, however, common themes that unite these diverse fields of law and a sense of some of these will provide a useful point of departure.

1.2.1   Intangible Property

Intellectual property law does not address the tangible, material object in which the creation of the mind has been embodied. It instead creates more abstract proprietary interests in the intangible.[1] For example, suppose a reader sends a letter to the co-authors of this text, offering a critique of our efforts. We are entitled to retain the document sent through the mails—the tangible pieces of paper on which the correspondence was physically written. However, the words of the letter constitute a work of authorship. Reproduction of that letter without the author's permission may implicate the copyright laws.

Ironically, although intellectual property law concerns abstract creations, it does insist that the intellectual creation be embodied in something tangible at least once. In copyright, works must be fixed in tangible form to be protected;[2] the patent law requires the inventions be "reduced to practice";[3] trademarks must, sooner or later, be subject to actual use in the marketplace.[4] These principles ensure that abstract ideas remain free from intellectual property rights. Intellectual property rights are instead allowed for the embodiment of that idea in a particular work of authorship, invention or commercial symbol. Put differently, intellectual property laws concern downstream products, not upstream ideas.

25. *See* Restatement (Third) of Unfair Competition § 20.

26. *Id.* at § 30.

27. *See generally* Restatement (Third) of Unfair Competition.

§ 1.2

1. *See* White–Smith Music Pub. Co. v. Apollo Co., 209 U.S. 1, 19, 28 S.Ct. 319, 52 L.Ed. 655 (1908) (Holmes, J., concurring) ("But in copyright property has reached a more abstract expression. The right to exclude is not directed to an object in possession or owned, but is *in vacuo*, so to speak.").

2. 17 U.S.C.A. § 102(a) (2000).

3. 35 U.S.C.A. §§ 102(g), 112 (2000).

4. *See* Restatement (Third) of Unfair Competition § 18.

One consequence of the abstract nature of intellectual property is that a single product may embody several intellectual property rights. Consider, for example, a can of a soft drink or "soda pop." The name of the soft drink, as well as any advertising slogans associated with marketing it and the overall design of the can itself are likely subject to trademark protection. The label on the can may well include some drawings or other pictorial work that may be subject to copyright protection. The can itself may be made out of a special rust-proof metal, the composition of which has been patented. Last, the method of making the soft drink, or the chemical composition of the drink, may be maintained as a trade secret.

1.2.2 The Right to Exclude

Intellectual property confers the right to exclude others from exploiting the protected intangible subject matter. It does not affirmatively provide a marketing right that allows an author, inventor or merchant to exploit a particular good.[5] Suppose, for example, that an inventor develops a new pharmaceutical. Procuring a patent upon that pharmaceutical does not allow the inventor to start dispensing the drug to patients. Approval of the food and drug authorities must first be obtained. The patent would, however, allow its owner to prevent competitors from marketing the protected drug. Similarly, public distribution of copyrighted works of authorship and of products bearing trademarks may be subject to laws governing defamation and obscenity, among others.

1.2.3 Exhaustion of Rights

Intellectual property rights are ordinarily subject to the concept of exhaustion.[6] Once an intellectual property right holder has sold a physical product to which its intellectual property rights are attached, it cannot prohibit the subsequent resale of that product. Any intellectual property rights in that specific physical product are said to have been "exhausted" by this first sale. The exhaustion doctrine allows, among others, law students to purchase used casebooks at the campus bookstore without further compensation to the book's authors and home owners to sell used toasters at a garage sale without fear of patent infringement liability. It also allows goods to move through the stream of commerce unhindered by multiple claims to intellectual property rights.

1.2.4 The Public Domain

In addition to creating proprietary interests, well-balanced intellectual property laws also account for the rights of consumers and other members of the user community. Out of recognition that one person's incentive can form another's limitation, various intellectual property doctrines strive to maintain a flourishing public domain. Free from the proprietary interests of others, the public domain provides a body of

---

5. *See* EMERSON STRINGHAM, OUTLINE OF PATENT LAW AND GUIDE TO DIGESTS § 4050 (1937).

6. *See, e.g.,* 17 U.S.C.A. § 109(a) (2000).

works that supports further creative expression, promotes effective communication, and ultimately allows each of us to experience our culture.[7]

The requirement that protected works exhibit an "intellectual step" is among those promoting the public domain. This standard is most apparent in the patent law, where an invention must be new and beyond the ordinary abilities of the skilled artisan to quality for protection.[8] A more lenient requirement applies to the copyright law, where the protected work of authorship must be original to the author and display a modicum of creative authorship.[9] In trademark law this requirement is yet more relaxed: the mark must be capable of distinguishing the source of the goods or services with which it is associated, rather then identifying those goods or services themselves.[10] These standards ensure that intellectual property rights do not extract subject matter from the public domain.

The limited duration of intellectual property rights also contributes to the public domain. Patent rights ordinarily endure for twenty years from the date of filing;[11] copyright for the life of the author plus seventy years.[12] When these rights expire, the subject matter is no longer proprietary and becomes free for others to use. Trademark law provides something of an exception to this principle: these rights endure for so long as the mark is used in commerce and remains capable of distinguishing the source of its associated goods or services. But if a mark is abandoned or, through public usage, becomes a generic term, it too will cease to be a proprietary term and will enter the public domain.[13]

1.2.5 Territoriality

The nations of the earth have yet to agree upon a unified legal regime governing intellectual property rights. There is no global copyright, patent or trademark. Innovators must secure and enforce these rights within the particular jurisdiction where they desire protection. Further, the reach of a particular intellectual property right extends only so far as the nation or region recognizing the right. A trademark recognized in the United States, for example, cannot be the basis of infringement litigation in Japan.[14]

The intellectual property laws of the United States and its trading partners are nonetheless linked through a modest number of international agreements that, together, comprise the international intellectual property regime. The foundational treaties, the Berne Convention (con-

---

7. *See, e.g.,* Jessica Litman, *The Public Domain,* 39 Emory L.J. 965 (1990).

8. 35 U.S.C.A. § 103(a) (2000).

9. 17 U.S.C.A. § 102(a) (2000).

10. *See* Restatement (Third) of Unfair Competition § 9.

11. 17 U.S.C.A. § 302 (2000).

12. 35 U.S.C.A. § 154(a)(2) (2000).

13. *See* Restatement (Third) of Unfair Competition § 30.

14. *See, e.g.,* Opinion of the Comptroller General, 159 USPQ 298, 301 (1968) ("It is a fundamental concept that territorial limitations of sovereignty preclude a country from giving extraterritorial effect to its patent laws.").

cerning copyright)[15] and the Paris Convention (concerning patent and trademark),[16] established the basic principle of national treatment: the requirement that signatories treat nationals of other signatory states no worse than their own citizens in intellectual property matters. More recently, the World Trade Organization Agreement on Trade–Related Aspects of Intellectual Property Rights,[17] the so-called TRIPS Agreement, required its signatories to provide minimum substantive standards of intellectual property protection and enforcement. Along with other treaties, these international agreements have eased the ability of innovators to enjoy intellectual property protection in foreign countries.

§ 1.3   Intellectual Property Policy

Intellectual property law has been with us for many years. Yet debate over the propriety of granting protection in intangible works has never been more vigorous. Two principal justifications for intellectual property law have emerged from these exchanges: instrumental rationales, which view intellectual property in terms of its benefits to society as a whole, and natural rights, which stresses the inherent authority of innovators to control works they have created. Intellectual property law has also attracted a range of dissenting views that are introduced below.

1.3.1   Instrumental Rationales

Like other products, information goods may be analyzed in terms of two economic characteristics.[1] The first is whether the benefits of the good are excludable. The owner of a bottle of wine may prevent others from drinking, but the producer of radio signals broadcasts for all to hear. The second trait is whether consumption of the good is rivalrous. If one person's use of the good necessarily diminishes the benefits of another's use, then it is said to be a rival good. For nonrival goods such as pleasing parkway scenery, all may profit from the good without diminishing the benefits of others.

Goods differ in their degrees of excludability and rivalrousness. Those that are fully nonexcludable and nonrival are termed public goods. The production of public goods is subject to market failure, for their nonexcludable and nonrival traits suggest that they will be underproduced relative to social need. This follows because potential producers of public goods are uncertain whether they will benefit from the good sufficiently to justify their labors. To put the matter bluntly, they might conclude that there is no point in producing something if they have no

15. Convention of Paris for the Protection of Industrial Property, 13 U.S.T. 25.

16. Convention of Berne Concerning the Creation of an International Union for the Protection of Literary and Artistic Works, 828 U.N.T.S. 221.

17. Agreement on Trade–Related Aspects of Intellectual Property Rights, Apr. 15, 1994, Annex 1C, 33 I.L.M. 1197 (1994).

§ 1.3

1. *See generally* William M. Landes & Richard A. Posner, *An Economic Analysis of Copyright Law*, 18 J. LEGAL STUD. 325 (1989).

assurance of being paid for their effort. Individuals will therefore tend to produce goods with greater excludability and rivalrousness and to under-produce public goods.

The production of desirable public goods is thus said to present a problem of collective action. Society as a whole favors the development of certain public goods, ranging from military defense to flood control projects. Private citizens may lack sufficient incentives to produce them, however, leading to suboptimal social outcomes. Government is uniquely suited towards solving collective action problems by modifying individual incentives to engage in desirable behavior.

Intellectual property laws are good examples of this sort of market intervention. The subject matter of the intellectual property laws—information products, inventions, works of authorship and commercial symbols—exhibit the characteristics of public goods. They are nonexcludable, for whether the work consists of a new song, a sculpture or a software program, others may easily become imitators. The cost of developing a new movie or pharmaceutical may run in the millions of dollars, but such works may be copied extremely cheaply. Information goods are also nonrival, for competitive uses do not impact an innovator's personal ability to exploit the invention. Individuals can sing a song repeatedly, for example, without exhausting the song or depriving another of its use. These externalities are said to discourage innovation. As a result, absent legal intervention, few inventors would invent, few authors would write and few artists would paint. In such a world consumers would have access to few new innovative works.

The intellectual property law ameliorates this market failure by allowing individuals to obtain proprietary rights in their innovative works. This property rule entitlement creates excludability, allowing innovators to prevent free riders from benefitting from their efforts. By diminishing the public goods aspects of inventions, the intellectual property system encourages individuals to increase their investment in creative activities. This rationale for the intellectual property system is sometimes termed the "incentive theory."

1.3.2 Natural Rights

In contrast to the incentive theory, where innovator's rights are but a necessary means to an end, the "natural rights" school places the innovator front and center. The most celebrated proponent of natural rights, John Locke, posited that persons have a natural right of property in their bodies.[2] Reasoning further, Locke asserted that individuals enjoyed a property entitlement on the products of their labors. Lockean theory suggests that innovators too should be entitled to enjoy the fruits of their labors, in terms of an exclusive rights in their works.[3]

2. JOHN LOCKE, TWO TREATISES OF GOVERNMENT (Peter Laslett, ed., 2d ed. 1967).

3. *See* Wendy J. Gordon, *A Property Right in Self Expression: Equality and Indi-*

vidualism in the Natural Law of Intellectual Property, 102 YALE L.J. 1533 (1993).

Natural rights theories hold most sway in the context of the copyright laws. Some natural rights theorists take one step further in this context, additionally stressing the dignity and worth of authors when rationalizing the copyright law.[4] Under this approach, the relationship between authors and their works of authorship is viewed as much more personal and intimate than the ordinary associations between individuals and objects. Creative works are seen as virtual extensions of the author herself, allowing others to view her consciousness and emotional, intellectual, or spiritual being. As such, authors possess the fundamental right to control, and should be compensated for, uses of their works.

1.3.3   Criticism of Intellectual Property Law

The regime of intellectual property has been subject to criticism throughout its long history. These critiques have seemingly become more withering in recent years. As innovative industries continue to play a more significant role in the U.S. economy, awareness of intellectual property has grown, along with the diversity of perspectives troubled by the intellectual property law's implications. In an era where information can be immediately disseminated in infinite quantities around the globe, the notion that an innovation can be an object of possession has been challenged. To such critics, the concept of property in information is little more than a bad metaphor.[5] Others commentators are troubled that intellectual property extends the values of the marketplace to ideas, and, in their belief, ultimately to knowledge and thought.[6] Some view intellectual property as a one-way ratchet ever favoring the expansion of rights. In recent years, for example, the term of copyright protection has significantly increased;[7] the scope of patent protection has expanded to include business methods and other post-industrial innovations;[8] and trademark law has embraced the expansive dilution doctrine.[9] Against these developments, there seems to be little on the balance sheet favoring consumers.[10]

Among proponent and critic alike, there is little dispute that the significance of intellectual property continues to grow. As innovators continue to develop new technologies, new forms of personal expression and new business strategies, the intellectual property law will continue to recreate itself. Although the pace of change in the information environment has become relentless, the fundamental challenge for intellectual property policy remains the same: achieving a balance between the encouragement of the labors that lead to creative expression on the one hand, and insuring that a sufficient amount of these products of the mind remain freely available as building blocks for the future, on the other.

4. *See generally* Alfred C. Yen, *Restoring the Natural Law: Copyright as Labor and Possession*, 51 OHIO ST. L.J. 517 (1990).

5. John Perry Barlow, *The Economy of Ideas*, WIRED 2.03 (March 1994).

6. Philippe Quééau, *Who Owns Knowledge?*, LE MONDE DIPLOMATIQUE (Jan. 2000).

7. *See infra* § 8.2.

8. *See infra* § 14.10.

9. *See infra* Chapter 30.

10. Pamela Samuelson, *The Copyright Grab*, WIRED 4.01 (Jan. 1996).

Chapter 2

INTRODUCTION TO THE
LAW OF COPYRIGHT

Table of Sections

Once an obscure specialty, copyright has become one of the more popular electives in the law school curriculum. For good reason: whether your background lies in the liberal arts or engineering, your reading preferences run towards speculative fiction or statutory compilations, or your practice focuses on personal liberties or international commerce, copyright has become a significant topic for every lawyer. Copyright is the law of text and of the arts, and also of computer software, digital technology and the Internet. Copyright is of extraordinary economic importance to U.S. information industries, including Hollywood, Silicon Valley and Big Media; but it also fundamentally impacts our personal expression, our right to read, and our ability to remain informed citizens within the public discourse.

At some earlier time, a legal commentator could claim that although copyright was the most conceptually difficult of the intellectual property regimes, its governing legislation was relatively straightforward. At present the conceptual difficulties remain, but have been augmented by increasingly complex statutory provisions. The sophistication and economic importance of those U.S. industries for which copyright is a principal concern have caused the Copyright Act to become more intricate, more regulatory in character, and at times an extremely perplexing read. Understanding the "metaphysics of the law" presents many challenges.[1] Yet it offers considerable rewards. Copyright necessarily is the study of the creative works it encompasses, ranging from humanity's greatest artistic achievements to its most humble entertainments and petty imitations. Individual judicial opinions leave the reader sometimes elevated, sometimes amused or saddened, but ultimately immersion in this most humanist of disciplines is an exceptionally rewarding experience.

§ 2.1   Brief Overview of the Copyright Law

Copyright today is an exclusively federal, statutory subject. The governing law is the Copyright Act of 1976, effective for works created on or after January 1, 1978.[1] Works created before this date may be governed in part by the predecessor statute—the Copyright Act of 1909[2] —in part by the common law of the various states, and in part by selected provisions of the 1976 law.

Under the 1976 Act, copyright may extend to any work of authorship.[3] Among the works of authorship amenable to copyright protection are literary, musical, dramatic, choreographic, graphic, audiovisual, and architectural works, as well as sound recordings.[4] Such works are eligible for copyright protection as soon as they are memorialized in a sufficiently stable form, or, in the words of the copyright law, "fixed in any tangible medium of expression."[5] No formalities are necessary to secure protection. However, authors that register their works with the Copyright Office,[6] and that place a notice of copyright on copies of their works,[7] are provided certain advantages when enforcing their copyrights.

A work must be original to be protected under the copyright law.[8] The originality requirement is a lenient one, requiring that the work was created by that author and was not copied from another, and that there be a minimal amount of creative authorship. Importantly, copyright protection extends only to the expression of an idea, not the idea itself.[9] For example, no author can obtain copyright protection on the abstract

1. Folsom v. Marsh, 9 F.Cas. 342, 344 (C.C.D.Mass.1841) (No. 4,901).

§ 2.1

1. 17 U.S.C.A. § 101–810 (2000).

2. Copyright Act of 1909, Ch. 320, 35 Stat. 1075.

3. 17 U.S.C.A. § 102(a) (2000).

4. *Id.*

5. *Id.*

6. 17 U.S.C.A. §§ 408—412 (2000).

7. 17 U.S.C.A. § § 401—406 (2000).

8. 17 U.S.C.A. § 102(a) (2000).

9. 17 U.S.C.A. § 102(b) (2000).

idea of a human changing into an insect. But the expression of that idea in a particular work of authorship with its own characters, plot, mood and setting—be it Franz Kafka's *The Metamorphosis* or the horror movie *The Fly*—may be accorded copyright protection.

Copyright confers a number of exclusive rights on the author or, in some circumstances, on the employer of the author under the "works made for hire" principle.[10] The copyright proprietor has the exclusive right to make copies of the protected work and to distribute it to the public. The 1976 Act also awards copyright owners the right to control derivative works, such as translations or screenplay adaptations, that are based upon the protected work. The proprietor further enjoys the exclusive right, with respect to most kinds of works, to display and perform the protected work publicly.[11] As we shall see, certain specific categories of works are also granted a variety of narrow or more specific rights.

The exclusive rights of copyright owners are limited by a number of exceptions and defenses, the most important of which is the fair use privilege. The fair use privilege allows the unauthorized use of copyrighted works in such contexts as educational activities, literary and social criticism, parody and news reporting under certain circumstances.[12]

Each copyright ordinarily enjoys a term of the life of the author plus seventy years.[13] The copyright proprietor may file a suit in federal court in order to enjoin infringers and obtain monetary remedies.[14] Criminal penalties may also apply to copyright infringers.[15] A copyright, or any of the exclusive rights under a copyright, may be assigned or licensed to others.[16] Individual authors possess the right to terminate such transfers after 35 years, although the transferee may continue to exploit derivative works produced under the transfer prior to its termination.[17]

§ 2.2 Historical Development

2.2.1 Early Origins

In many legal texts, a brief historical overview of the field is provided almost as a pro forma part of the introduction. In the field of copyright, however, familiarity with some basic history is more than mere background. Rather it is a valuable tool which can aid in the understanding of many of the ambiguities and controversies that confront copyright law to this day.

Copyright has evolved largely in response to the development of new and more efficient means of recording and reproducing the products of human expression. No copyright law existed in medieval Europe prior to the invention of the printing press, when few persons other than the

10. 17 U.S.C.A. § 201 (2000).

11. 17 U.S.C.A. § 106 (2000).

12. 17 U.S.C.A. § 107 (2000).

13. 17 U.S.C.A. § 302(a) (2000).

14. 17 U.S.C.A. §§ 501–505 (2000).

15. 17 U.S.C.A. § 506 (2000).

16. 17 U.S.C.A. § 201(d) (2000).

17. 17 U.S.C.A. § 203 (2000).

clergy were literate and when manuscripts had to be copied out by hand. The invention of the printing press and the possibility of mass production of the books led to a desire to regulate in this area.

The earliest versions of what we now know as copyright emerged in England in the 1500's.[1] Only a few skilled craftsmen had the know-how and resources to print books. These printers were organized in a guild known as the Stationers' Company. The members of the company agreed among themselves that whenever one of them printed a particular book, all the others would refrain from printing any copies of that book. They devised a system of record keeping to keep track of which member was entitled to print which books. Once a given printer's rights were memorialized in the records of the Stationers' Company, that printer had the "copyright" in the book. Obviously, this system did not reflect any effort to promote the larger good of society. Rather it was a self-interested arrangement that today would almost surely fall afoul of the antitrust laws if nothing else.

Of course there was a problem with the Stationers' Company system. Any non-member of the guild could buy a printing press and begin printing any books he or she wished, including those for which a Stationer member had purportedly exclusive rights. So, much like the lobbyist of our own era, the Stationers appealed to the government—in this case the crown. In 1534, a royal decree issued stating that it would be unlawful to engage in publishing activity without a government license. A system of censorship was also implemented as part of this decree. Within a few decades—in 1557, to be precise—the King granted monopoly publishing rights to the Stationers' Company. This grant, combined with the Stationers' own practices, now meant that only the publisher with the Stationers' "copyright" could publish a given book. Once again, however, none of this had the least bit to do with the public interest. Rather the situation reflected the combination of the economic self-interest of the Stationers with the political self-interest of the crown in suppressing dissent.

2.2.2   The Statute of Anne

Experience with the Stationers' Company was mixed. When monopoly publishing rights expired in 1694, they were not renewed. Independent printers soon commenced publication and left the Stationers vulnerable to competition. Following a concerted lobbying effort—during which the publishers shifted tactics to stress the plight of authors, rather than themselves—Parliament in 1710 enacted the renowned Statute of Anne.[2] The Statute of Anne marked a paradigm shift from its predecessor licensing statutes. Rather than offering rights to the publishers of new works, it protected the authors that created them. As such, the

§ 2.2

1. *See generally* L. RAY PATTERSON, COPYRIGHT IN HISTORICAL PERSPECTIVE (1968).

2. 8 Anne, ch. 19 (1710).

enactment of the Statute of Anne is broadly recognized as a foundational event for copyright in the common law world.

The Statute of Anne granted a term of 14 years of exclusivity for authors and their assigns, starting with the date of first publication. Authors enjoyed a second term of 14 years if they survived until its commencement. Infringement occurred when an individual printed, reprinted or imported a book without authorization. To enjoy these rights, the copyright proprietor had to register the title of the book at the Stationers' Hall and deposit nine copies of the book at official libraries.

2.2.3 Colonial Copyright and the Constitution

The Statute of Anne inspired twelve of the individual colonies to enact copyright statutes following the American Revolution.[3] Subsequently, the Framers of the Constitution recognized the need for a uniform federal law for both copyrights and patents. The result was Article 1, Section 8, Clause 8, which provides:

> The Congress Shall have Power ... To Promote the Progress of Science and useful Arts, by securing for limited Times to Authors and Inventors the exclusive Right to their respective Writings and Discoveries.[4]

This constitutional provision reveals a number of interesting features about the U.S. copyright law. First, the clause refers to "Authors" and their "Writings." While Congress might protect persons other than Authors or material other than constitutional Writings under other provisions of the constitution, such as the commerce clause, the subject matter of copyright appears to be limited to the writings of authors. Indeed, the Copyright law of 1909 defined the subject matter of copyright as "all the writings of an author."[5] The full implications of this constitutional limitation are best considered in the context of the present statutory language, and are taken up in the sections that follow. It is useful to note however, that from an early point, Congress and the courts have interpreted "writings" to include much material other than words written or printed on a page. Even the earliest copyright statutes provided protection for maps and prints.[6] More recent enactments have included materials ranging from photographs to computer programs.[7] When confronted with the question, the courts have found materials of this sort to be within the scope of the constitutional term "writings" and thus appropriate subject matter for copyright law.[8]

3. *See generally* Francine Crawford, *Pre-Constitutional Copyright Statutes*, 23 BULL. COPYRIGHT SOC'Y 11 (1975).

4. U.S. Const. art. 1, § 8, Cl. 8.

5. 17 U.S.C.A. § 4 (1909 Act).

6. Copyright Act of 1790, Ch. 15, 1 Stat. 124. ("An Act for the encouragement of learning, by securing the copies of maps, charts, and books, to the authors and pro-

prietors of such copies during the times therein mentioned.")

7. 17 U.S.C.A. § 101 (1988); 17 U.S.C.A. § 5(j) (1909 Act).

8. Burrow–Giles Lithographic Co. v. Sarony, 111 U.S. 53, 4 S.Ct. 279, 28 L.Ed. 349 (1884) (holding a photograph of Oscar Wilde copyrightable).

A second feature of the constitutional language worthy of note is that it contains not only a grant of power, but a statement of purpose as well. The clause indicates that the justification for copyright is the promotion of the "progress of science and useful arts." This raises the question of whether copyright must be further limited to those works that have cultural significance or are adjudged to be a significant addition to the national artistic heritage. Here again, the prevailing interpretation has been broad, rather than narrow. Thus, in an early case, the Supreme Court held that posters prepared as advertisements for a circus were copyrightable subject matter, and that their protection was consistent with the constitutional language.[9] Indeed, the notion that copyright should be content-neutral has even lead courts to uphold the copyrightability of obscene material.[10]

Congress quickly took advantage of its constitutional authority by passing the Act of 1790. Reminiscent of the Statute of Anne, the 1790 Act also featured an initial 14–year term with the possibility of a 14–year renewal if the author survived. The 1790 Act offered protection to any "map, chart or book," but only if the copyright proprietor complied with certain formalities, including registering title with a district court and depositing a copy with the Secretary of State. General statutory revisions in 1831 and 1870, along with additional amendments in other years, continued the development of U.S. copyright law.

2.2.4　The 1909 Act

Animated by a sense that the copyright laws required modernization, Congress enacted the Copyright Act of 1909.[11] The 1909 Act remained in place until the current copyright statute, the 1976 Act, took effect on January 1, 1978. The 1909 Act is of considerable contemporary importance because a large number of economically and culturally important works created before 1978 are still under copyright and are governed to a large degree by the provisions of the 1909 Act. Familiarity with both the current and the former copyright statutes is thus often necessary to understand the nature of copyright protection in the United States.

Among the principal features of the U.S. copyright regime under the 1909 Act were: (1) state common law copyright of perpetual duration for unpublished works; (2) commencement of federal copyright protection at the time of publication, rather than at the time of registration as had previously been the case; (3) first and renewal terms of 28 years each, allowing a maximum possible copyright term of 56 years; and (4) formalities that were necessary to preserve copyright protection, includ-

9. Bleistein v. Donaldson Lithographing Co., 188 U.S. 239, 23 S.Ct. 298, 47 L.Ed. 460 (1903).

10. See Jartech, Inc. v. Clancy, 666 F.2d 403, *cert. denied,* 459 U.S. 879, 103 S.Ct. 175, 74 L.Ed.2d 143 (1982); Mitchell Bros. Film Group v. Cinema Adult Theater, 604 F.2d 852 (5th Cir.1979), *cert. denied,* 445 U.S. 917, 100 S.Ct. 1277, 63 L.Ed.2d 601 (1980).

11. Copyright Act of 1909, Ch. 320, 35 Stat. 1075.

ing the placement of notice on all copies of published works and registration at the Copyright Office.

2.2.5 The 1976 Act

The 1909 Act began to show its age as new means of presenting works of authorship, including the phonograph, motion picture, radio and television, altered the copyright landscape. Congress also grew increasingly concerned over the ability of U.S. authors to protect their works abroad. Serious law reform efforts began as early as 1955 and eventually resulted in the passage of the Copyright Act of 1976. Among the core features of the 1976 Act are:

(1) All works of authorship are protected under the federal copyright law from the moment they are fixed in a tangible medium of expression.[12] State common law protection is expressly preempted.[13]

(2) A single term of copyright protection. At the time the 1976 Act was enacted, the term ordinarily consisted of the life of the author plus 50 years. (Congress subsequently increased this copyright term by an additional twenty years.)[14]

(3) Individual authors generally possess the inalienable option of terminating transfers after 35 years, although the transferee may continue to exploit derivative works produced under the transfer prior to its termination.[15]

(4) The fair use privilege was for the first time expressly recognized in the statute.[16]

(5) Ownership of copyright is divisible, in that a copyright owner can separately license or enforce the different exclusive rights associated with the copyright.[17]

(6) A number of compulsory licenses allow individuals access to copyrighted works, provided that they comply with certain payment schemes and formalities. An entity known as the Copyright Royalty Tribunal was established to review or establish rates under such licenses, as well as to distribute royalty payments. (The Copyright Royalty Tribunal was subsequently abolished in favor of ad hoc arbitration panels formed by the Librarian of Congress.)[18]

(7) The 1976 Act continued to require formalities, including notice, recordation, deposit and registration, as a condition of copyright protection or enforcement. Congress did provide for more lenient curative provisions for notice deficiencies.[19] Subsequent amendments have relaxed or abolished many of the previously required formalities

12. 17 U.S.C.A. § 102(a) (2000).
13. 17 U.S.C.A. § 301 (2000).
14. 17 U.S.C.A. § 302 (2000).
15. 17 U.S.C.A. § 203 (2000).
16. 17 U.S.C.A. § 107 (2000).
17. 17 U.S.C.A. § 201(d)(1) (2000).
18. 17 U.S.C.A. §§ 801–803 (2000).
19. 17 U.S.C.A. §§ 401–412 (2000).

2.2.6 Subsequent Legislative Developments

Congress has frequently amended the 1976 Act since its enactment. Most notable among these amendments was the Berne Convention Implementation Act, which in 1988 brought U.S. law into compliance with the leading international copyright agreement.[20] The most significant of these changes involved a relaxation of the copyright formalities of notice, recordation, deposit and registration.

Two major statutory developments occurred in 1998. The Sonny Bono Copyright Term Extension Act extended the usual term of copyright to life plus 70 years.[21] The term of anonymous and pseudonymous works, as well as works made for hire, increased to 95 years from publication or 120 years from creation, whichever is less. Congress also enacted the Digital Millennium Copyright Act, which, in part, made it illegal to circumvent technological measures controlling access to various works and which also prohibited altering or deleting certain identifying information that the statute refers to as "copyright management information."[22]

§ 2.3 International Copyright Harmonization

There is no global copyright system. Property rights in works of authorship must be recognized and enforced in each jurisdiction where protection is sought. A number of international agreements nonetheless establish international copyright relations, allowing nonresident authors to enjoy intellectual property overseas. Although the international copyright landscape receives deeper coverage later in Chapter 12 of this volume, two of the more significant copyright treaties, the Berne Convention and TRIPS Agreement, are worthy of note at this early juncture.

2.3.1 The Berne Convention

The International Union for the Protection of Literary and Artistic Works, known as the Berne Union or Berne Convention, remains the foundational multilateral copyright agreement. The Berne Convention requires that signatory states observe the principle of national treatment and provide minimum standards of substantive protection, including specified exclusive rights and a copyright term consisting of the life of the author plus fifty years. The Berne Convention also rejects formalities, such as registration of the work of authorship with the government, as conditions of copyright protection. Works first published in the United States or other Berne signatory state—or first published in a non-Berne country, followed by publication within 30 days in a Berne member state—are eligible for protection in all Berne member states.

20. Pub. L. No. 100–569, 102 Stat. 2853 (1988).

21. Pub. L. No. 105–298, 112 Stat. 2827 (1998).

22. Pub. L. No. 105–304, 112 Stat. 2860 (1998).

2.3.2 The TRIPS Agreement

The Agreement on Trade–Related Aspects of Intellectual Property Rights, or TRIPS Agreement, forms one component of the international agreement establishing the World Trade Organization (WTO). Joined by an impressive number of signatory countries, the TRIPS Agreement affirms and extends the Berne Convention. The TRIPS Agreement requires that WTO member states comply with much of the Berne Convention, recognize computer programs as subject to copyright and provide certain protections for data compilations and cinematographic works. Disagreements between signatories over TRIPS Agreement compliance are subject to dispute resolution before the WTO.

§ 2.4 Rationales for Copyright Law

2.4.1 Instrumental Rationales

The copyright law has often been rationalized in terms of the "incentive theory" discussed previously.[1] Under this view, the proprietary rights afforded through copyright are needed to prevent free riders from undermining the market for works of authorship. In addition, the copyright system is said to facilitate market mechanisms by creating discrete, well-defined property interests that decrease transaction costs and encourage commercial exchanges. Copyright is also believed to encourage individual expression on matters of interest to civil society, encouraging the discourse that is essential to democratic values.[2]

The Supreme Court has often invoked the incentive theory and declared it to be the basic animating purpose behind copyright law. For instance in *Twentieth Century Music Corp. v. Aiken*[3] the Court said "the immediate effect of our copyright law is to secure a fair return for an author's creative labor. But the ultimate aim is, by this incentive, to stimulate artistic creativity for the general public good." The Court reiterated the same themes in *Feist Publications, Inc. v. Rural Telephone Service Co.,*[4] when it observed that "the primary objective of copyright is not to reward the labor of authors, but 'to promote the Progress of Science and useful arts.' To this end, copyright assures authors the right to their original expression, but encourages others to build freely upon the ideas and information conveyed by a work."

2.4.2 Natural Rights

As mentioned previously,[5] natural rights theories are most resonant in the context of the copyright laws. Under these views the interests of authors in their works exceeds the economic. Authors are instead seen as bearing a personal relationship with their creative expression. By providing individuals with the right to control uses of their works of author-

---

§ 2.4

1. *See* § 1.3.1, *supra.*

2. *See* Neil W. Netanel, *Copyright and a Democratic Civil Society*, 106 YALE L.J. 283 (1996).

3. 422 U.S. 151, 156, 95 S.Ct. 2040, 45 L.Ed.2d 84 (1975).

4. 499 U.S. 340, 349–50, 111 S.Ct. 1282, 113 L.Ed.2d 358 (1991).

5. *See* § 1.3.2, *supra.*

ship, the copyright law acknowledges the dignity and worth of these individuals themselves.

The most noteworthy manifestation of natural rights theories within the copyright law is the doctrine of moral rights. Moral rights laws generally include three principal components. The integrity right allows authors to prevent objectionable distortions, mutilations or other modifications of their works. The attribution or paternity right allows authors to claim authorship of their works. Finally, the right of disclosure allows authors to decide when and in what form a work will be distributed to the public. Moral rights theories play a central role in many foreign copyright laws and have been recognized to a more limited degree in the United States.

2.4.3 Criticism of the Copyright Law

Copyright has been subject to increasingly vitriolic criticism during this era of the Internet. Some commentators assert that strenuous enforcement of copyright can result in the elimination of parody and satire, the curtailment of free speech and the suppression of creativity. Copyright law can indeed still voices, darken stages, and shut down presses; and as more individuals gain access to means for creating and disseminating sophisticated creative materials, the grasp of the copyright law seems to strengthen. Observers further note that Congress has recently augmented the scope of copyright in terms of such factors as the works subject to protection, the term of protection and the scope of exclusive rights, leading to perceived imbalances between the rights and responsibilities of content providers and consumers.[6] Still others suggest that however noble the theoretical justifications for intellectual property, copyright law has in practice been corrupted by publishers, record companies and media enterprises that exploit individual authors and have little regard for the interests of the user community.[7] Apparent from the vigor of this debate is that copyright has become an increasingly important discipline in the Information Age.

---

6. Pamela Samuelson, *The Copyright Grab*, WIRED 4.01 (Jan. 1996).

7. Johan Söderberg, *Copyright: A Marxist Critique*, FIRST MONDAY (26 Feb. 2002).

Chapter 3

THE SUBJECT MATTER OF COPYRIGHT—BASIC REQUIREMENTS

Table of Sections

Article 1, Section 8, Clause 8 of the Constitution authorizes Congress "To Promote the Progress of Science and useful Arts, by securing for limited Times to Authors and Inventors the exclusive Right to their respective Writings and Discoveries."[1] Although the Intellectual Property Clause suggests some vague outlines about the kinds of material that may be protected by copyright, it operates like most constitutional clauses—reserving to Congress the power to define the limits with greater specificity. Congress exercised that power in the current copyright statute—the 1976 Act—by providing a general definition of the subject matter of copyright in section 102. Because that section is so fundamental to understanding the structure of the copyright act, its full text is worth a close look at the very outset. The first sentence of section 102 provides:

> Copyright protection subsists ... in original works of authorship, fixed in any tangible medium of expression, now known or later developed, from which they can be perceived reproduced or otherwise communicated, either directly or with the aid of a machine or device.

_____

1.   U.S. Const. art. 1, § 8, Cl. 8.

The second sentence of the section goes on to itemize eight particular categories of works that are encompassed by the term "works of authorship." The list includes literary, musical, dramatic, choreographic, pictorial, graphic, sculptural, audiovisual, and architectural works, as well as sound recordings.[2]

This definition is open-ended. It reflects a congressional desire to protect not only those types of intellectual works that were known in the mid-seventies when the statute was drafted, but also the desire to protect new forms that capture the products of human creativity as they are developed.[3] This congressional command for flexibility and responsiveness to technological change is, in a sense, a reaction to a historical judicial reluctance to afford copyright protection to new types of works.

Parsing the language of section 102 reveals a number of separate requirements that an artistic creation must satisfy before becoming protectable under the statute. Specifically, the work must be (1) original; (2) a work of authorship; (3) fixed in a tangible medium of expression. Each of those requirements is discussed in the subsections that follow.

§ 3.1 Originality

In order to be protected by copyright, a work must be "original."[1] Interestingly, this term is nowhere defined in the text of the copyright statute. This was by design. Congress indicated in the accompanying legislative history that its failure to offer a definition of this crucial term was meant to incorporate the case law definition of originality that had evolved during decades of construing the 1909 Act.[2] Under that case law "originality" implicates two rather distinct concepts, both of which must be satisfied before a work can be assured of copyright protection.[3] First, the work in question must be the product of independent creative effort of the author. In this sense "original" is used as the opposite of "a

---

2. *Id.*

3. "Authors are continually finding new ways of expressing themselves, but it is impossible to foresee the forms that these new expressive methods will take. The bill does not intend either to freeze the scope of copyrightable subject matter at the present stage of technology or to allow unlimited expansion into areas completely outside the present congressional intent." H.R. Rep. No. 94–1416, 94th Cong., 2d Sess., p. 51 (1976). *See also* Lotus Dev. Corp. v. Paperback Software Int'l, 740 F.Supp. 37 (D.Mass.1990) ("[T]he designation 'works of authorship' is not meant to be limited to traditional works of authorship such as novels or plays. Rather, Congress used this phrase to extend copyright to new methods of expression as they evolve. . . .").

§ 3.1

1. Section 102 of the 1976 Act defines the subject matter of copyright as "*original*

works of authorship . . ." 17 U.S.C.A. § 102 (2000).

2. H.R. Rep. No. 94–1474, 94th Cong. 2d Sess. 51 (1976) ("the phrase 'original works of authorship,' which is purposely left undefined is intended to incorporate without change the standard of originality established by the courts under the present copyright statute.")

3. The Supreme Court aptly summarized the dual nature of the originality requirement when it remarked that: "Original, as the term is used in copyright, means only that the work was independently created by the author (as opposed to copied from other works), and that it possesses at least some minimal degree of creativity." Feist Publications, Inc. v. Rural Telephone Service, 499 U.S. 340, 111 S.Ct. 1282, 113 L.Ed.2d 358 (1991).

copy". Secondly, the work in question must have at least a modicum of creativity. In this sense "original" is used as the opposite of "mundane" or "routine". Both of these requirements are a bit more complicated than may appear at first blush.

3.1.1 Independent Creation

A work is only considered original if the author created it, or at least parts of it, "from scratch"—that is, without copying it from a pre-existing source. Since copyright provides an exclusive right of reproduction over the works it protects, any other rule would permit persons to withdraw works from the public domain merely by copying them. For instance, if someone copied Shakespeare's Hamlet by typing it into his own word processor and printing out a copy, it would be absurd to permit that individual to claim copyright in the resulting text. Not only has this person contributed nothing new to our literary inventory, but he might then try to exact a payment from every school teacher who sought to hand out photocopies of Hamlet to his or her students. The requirement of independent creation helps avoid this sort of result.

The independent creation requirement is also constitutionally required. The constitution only empowers Congress to protect the writings of *authors*. To author something means to be the originator or progenitor of it. One who merely copies pre-existing work is the very antithesis of an author, and thus such rote copying should be constitutionally ineligible for protection under the copyright law. As Justice O'Connor, speaking for a unanimous Supreme Court, put it, "[t]he *sine qua non* of copyright is originality.... Originality is a constitutional requirement."[4]

There is an interesting theoretical consequence to this focus on independent creation. If two authors each were to conceive of, and fix, the exact same work without knowledge of the other's activities, each would be entitled to an independent copyright on the resulting work.[5] This situation is sometimes referred to as *parallel independent creation.* Of course, the more elaborate the works in question, the more difficult it will be to believe that the second party actually created the work "from scratch" without referring to the first party's efforts. As an evidentiary matter, the strong similarity between the two works may give rise to an inference that the second of the two was necessarily copied from the first.[6] Nonetheless, the idea of parallel independent creation—and the consequence that two identical works could *both* be copyrightable—is an important part of the structure of our copyright law. Moreover, this is one of the major distinctions between the scope of patent law and that of copyright. As we shall later on in this text, once a patent issues to an

4. Feist Publications, Inc. v. Rural Telephone Service Co., 499 U.S. 340, 346, 111 S.Ct. 1282, 113 L.Ed.2d 358 (1991).

5. Sheldon v. Metro–Goldwyn Pictures Corp., 81 F.2d 49, 54 (2d Cir.1936) ("[I]f by some magic a man who had never known it were to compose anew Keat's *Ode on a Grecian Urn,* he would be an 'author,' and

if he copyrighted it, others might not copy the poem, though they might of course copy Keats's."); Arnstein v. Edward B. Marks Music Corp., 82 F.2d 275 (2d Cir.1936); Alfred Bell & Co. v. Catalda Fine Arts, 191 F.2d 99 (2d Cir.1951).

6. *See infra* § 9.2.

inventor, he or she may prevent others from creating the invention, even if they do so entirely independently. In other words, to be patentable, an invention must be "novel" in the sense of never having existed before. In contrast, there is no novelty requirement for copyrights.[7] Correspondingly, the author of a copyrighted work has a more limited privilege than a patent holder—only the right to prevent copying of his or her work.

There are, of course, many intermediate possibilities between exactly copying a pre-existing work and creating a new work entirely from scratch. Many authors might start with someone else's work and then modify it to a greater or lesser extent. For instance, someone might copy the first four acts of Hamlet verbatim, but write an entirely new Act Five; or might copy the painting of Whistler's Mother but do it in bright neon colors instead of the blacks and grays of the original. These works, which are neither wholly original nor wholly copied are usually called "derivative" works. These works are considered in detail in the following chapter of this treatise.[8]

For now, however, it is profitable to consider whether such works satisfy the requirement of "independent creation" The answer is that they do, to the extent—and only to the extent—that new material has been added. Thus the author of the revised version of Hamlet can use the copyright laws to prevent others from duplicating the text of his new Act Five, or of the entire play including his new Act Five, but obviously could not prevent anyone from copying Shakespeare's original Acts One through Four. This is because he created Act Five from scratch, thus satisfying the requirement of independent creation.

The problem of independent creation and derivative works has often been litigated in connection with reproductions of two and three dimensional artistic works. By definition, such reproductions are not the products of completely independent creation. The courts have struggled to determine when there is sufficient independent creation to justify copyright protection. In one celebrated copyright case, *Alfred Bell & Co. v. Catalda Fine Arts*[9] it was held that mezzotint reproductions of oil paintings were independently copyrightable. The court found that the mezzotints contained more than trivial variations from the original oil paintings, and that those distinctions made them separately copyrightable. Note, however, that the protection afforded to the mezzotints would not prohibit others from making their own copies of the original oil paintings.

Initially some courts read *Alfred Bell* to stand for the notion that virtually any slight variation from an underlying work would be enough to afford copyright protection.[10] These courts, however, were rewarding not the "from scratch" contribution of the reproducer, but rather the skill of that author in executing an effective copy. More modern cases

7. Alfred Bell & Co. v. Catalda Fine Arts, 191 F.2d 99 (2d Cir.1951).

8. *See infra* § 4.9.

9. 191 F.2d 99 (2d Cir.1951).

10. *See e.g.,* Alva Studios, Inc. v. Winninger, 177 F.Supp. 265 (S.D.N.Y.1959).

have insisted on at least a "distinguishable variation" from the underlying work before originality will be found and copyright protection rendered available. Thus, in *L. Batlin & Son, Inc. v. Snyder,* the Second Circuit held that a duplicate of a nineteenth century Uncle Sam mechanical bank that differed from the version in the public domain only in a number of trivial details was uncopyrightable.[11]

3.1.2 Minimal Creativity

The fact that a work was created "from scratch" will not, by itself, suffice for copyright protection. The work in question must also evidence a minimal degree of creativity.[12] Without this further requirement for protection we might run the risk of removing large quantities of material from the public domain without any offsetting benefit to the public. Alternatively, we might find ourselves engaged in unnecessary litigation over the originality of pedestrian creations. For instance, assume that you were to take out a blank piece of paper and write the words "the sun rises in the east" on the paper. Seemingly you have authored those words "from scratch." Nonetheless granting you copyright in the words would be most unwise. First, your contribution to the stock of creative work in the world is virtually zero—there seems to be little reason to reward or encourage you with the grant of exclusive rights. Second, you might attempt to prevent others from using similar phrases, which could hinder the production of creative work by others. Finally, the people you sued could argue that you must have seen those words elsewhere and subconsciously copied them rather than created them from scratch. The court would have no effective way to resolve such a claim. Thus the requirement of creativity seems amply justified based on both pragmatic and policy considerations.

The amount of creativity required, however, is not particularly great. As the Supreme Court has stated in its most recent declaration on the subject, "[t]o be sure, the requisite level of creativity is extremely low; even a slight amount will suffice. The vast majority of works make the grade quite easily, as they possess some creative spark 'no matter how crude, humble or obvious' it may be."[13] For example, in one recent case, a district court held that a jury could find that the words "Hugga–Hugga" and "Brr," used as lyrics in a rap song, were sufficiently creative to warrant copyright protection,[14] though to the authors of this volume, this seems virtually to read the creativity requirement out of the law. Somewhat more convincingly, a picture of a cake on the label of a

---

11. 536 F.2d 486 (2d Cir.1976). The court cited with approval, the observation in the leading copyright treatise that "[o]ne who has slavishly or mechanically copied from others may not claim to be an author." 1 NIMMER, COPYRIGHT § 6 at 10.2 (2002).

12. Feist Publications, Inc. v. Rural Telephone Service, 499 U.S. 340, 362, 111 S.Ct. 1282, 113 L.Ed.2d 358 (1991).

13. *Id.* at 345. See also Atari Games v. Oman, 979 F.2d 242 (D.C.Cir.1992); West Publishing Co. v. Mead Data Central, 799 F.2d 1219, 1223 (8th Cir.1986).

14. Tin Pan Apple Inc. v. Miller Brewing Co., 30 USPQ2d 1791 (S.D.N.Y.1994).

box of cake mix was also held copyrightable, the court remarking that
"[t]he pictures of the cakes used by plaintiff on its labels although
possibly not achieving the quality of a Leonardo 'Still Life' nevertheless
have sufficient commercial artistry to entitle them to protection...."[15]

On the other hand, some works fail even this minimal test. For
instance, titles and short slogans have traditionally been denied copyright protection, largely on the grounds that they are incapable of
reflecting the necessary creativity.[16] An envelope with a horizontal black
stripe on the middle, pre-printed with the words "Priority Message:
Contents Require Immediate Attention" was held insufficiently creative
to warrant copyright protection,[17] as were a professional sports team logo
consisting of four lines forming an arrow, with the word "arrows" in
script below,[18] and a 4–page booklet containing use and care instructions
for a pizza cooking stone.[19]

Thus far the courts have not articulated a general rule that can be
used to determine with precision whether a work meets the creativity
test. The decisions have an ad hoc quality to them. It would seem that
the best that can be said is that the creativity requirement should be
applied with an eye towards its purposes. If a phrase or image is so
pedestrian that it is probable that others will independently use it in
their own work, copyright protection of that particular image or phrase
would likely create a risk that innocent authors could be subjected to
harassing claims of infringement. Moreover, if the material is so pedestrian that no incentive, in the form of copyright protection, is required to
call forth its creation, that also militates in favor of a denial of copyright.

Regardless of how the creativity requirement is interpreted, the
decision is not supposed to involve the courts in an assessment of the
artistic merits of the work in question. The classic articulation of this
principle is found in *Bleistein v. Donaldson Lithographing Co,*[20] where
the Court had to decide whether an advertising poster depicting circus
performers was eligible for copyright. Justice Holmes rejected a claim
that the work was insufficiently "artistic" to deserve copyright by
observing that:

15. Kitchens of Sara Lee, Inc. v. Nifty Foods Corp., 266 F.2d 541, 545 (2d Cir. 1959).

16. Takeall v. Pepsico, Inc., 29 USPQ2d 1913 (4th Cir.1993) (slogan "You got the right one, uh-huh" as part of an advertise-ment for Pepsi–Cola not copyrightable); Pelt v. CBS, Inc., 30 USPQ2d 1639 (C.D.Cal.1993) (slogan "Listen Up, It's More Than Talk, It's Feeling" not copy-rightable); Alberto–Culver Co. v. Andrea Dumon, Inc., 466 F.2d 705 (7th Cir.1972) (slogan "most personal sort of deodorant" not copyrightable). Regulations promulgat-ed by the Copyright Office which govern the registration of claims of copyright specifical-ly provide that "[w]ords and short phrases such as names, titles and slogans ..." are not subject to copyright. 37 C.F.R. § 202.1(a).

17. Magic Marketing v. Mailing Services of Pittsburgh, 634 F.Supp. 769 (W.D.Pa. 1986).

18. John Muller & Co., Inc. v. New York Arrows Soccer Team, Inc., 802 F.2d 989 (8th Cir.1986)

19. Sassafras Enterprises Inc. v. Rosh-co, Inc., 889 F.Supp. 343, 36 USPQ2d 1194 (N.D.Ill.1995).

20. 188 U.S. 239, 23 S.Ct. 298, 47 L.Ed. 460 (1903).

It would be a dangerous undertaking for persons trained only to the law to constitute themselves final judges of the worth of pictorial illustrations, outside of the narrowest and most obvious limits. At one extreme some works of genius would be sure to miss appreciation. Their very novelty would make them repulsive until the public had learned the new language in which their author spoke. It may be more than doubted, for instance, whether the etchings of Goya or the paintings of Manet would have been sure of protection when seen for the first time. At the other end, copyright would be denied to pictures which appealed to a public less educated than the judge.... [T]he taste of any public is not to be treated with contempt.[21]

Thus, issues of artistic worthiness simply do not enter into the determination of whether a work is sufficiently creative to warrant protection.

Finally, it is necessary to appreciate that the requirement that work must reflect a modicum of creativity before becoming eligible for copyright protection has lead to a measure of terminological confusion among the courts and commentators. Some courts have merely treated this requirement as a component of the statutorily required "originality"[22] Others, however, refer to a separate "creativity" requirement, reserving the term "originality" to mean "not-copied."[23] Finally, still others use the rubric of "authorship" to designate the requirement of a modicum of creativity.[24] The difference is purely semantic. There appears to be little difference between these courts over the substance of the requirement. This book follows the practice of using the term originality in the dual sense of "not-copied" and "minimally creative."

§ 3.2 Fixation

The current copyright statute also requires that a work be "fixed" in order to receive copyright protection.[1] The statute defines fixation as the embodiment of the work in a tangible means of expression that is sufficiently permanent or stable to permit it to be perceived, reproduced or otherwise communicated, for a period of more than transitory duration.[2] In other words, the work has to be written down, taped, filmed, or otherwise captured in some way before federal copyright protection can attach. Once an original work is fixed, it is immediately protected by the copyright laws. There are no formalities required of an author—no application to an administrative agency, no act of publication, nothing other than the mere fixation.

21.   188 U.S. at 251–52

22.   Feist, 499 U.S. at 346.

23.   *See e.g.,* Folio Impressions, Inc. v. Byer California, 937 F.2d 759 (2d Cir.1991); John Muller & Co. v. N.Y. Arrows Soccer Team, 802 F.2d 989, 990 (8th Cir.1986).

24.   Atari Games v. Oman, 888 F.2d 878 (D.C.Cir.1989), *appeal after remand,* 979 F.2d 242 (D.C.Cir.1992).

§ 3.2

1.   17 U.S.C.A. § 102 (2000).

2.   17 U.S.C.A. § 101 (2000).

The fixation doctrine can be put the other way around—there is no federal copyright protection for unfixed creative works such as an extemporaneous speech, a brand new poem that the poet can recite from memory but has never written down, or a jazz improvisation performed spontaneously at a night club. These "unfixed" works might, however, be eligible for protection under state law, either under the misappropriation doctrine, or some other principle.[3] This means that the moment of fixation of a work is the dividing line between potential common law protection under state law and federal statutory protection.[4]

Because the statutory definition of fixation requires permanence or stability, a variety of temporary or short-term fixations probably fail to satisfy the statutory test. For instance a sculptural work fixed in a block of ice probably would not qualify as a copyrightable work because of the transitory duration of the icy work product.

While a work must be fixed to be entitled to federal protection, there is an important distinction between the work itself, and the object or objects in which it is fixed, or embodied. Works can be embodied in two types of objects, which the statute labels "copies" and "phonorecords." Phonorecords are material objects in which sounds are fixed, and thus would include objects such as compact discs and audio cassette tapes. All other material objects in which a work might be fixed are classified as "copies." Thus, computer floppy discs, books, photographic negatives, bronze statuettes, sheet music and architectural drawings would all be examples of copies. A given work might be embodied in only a single copy—as would be true of a handwritten letter or a one-of-a-kind oil painting,[5] or in multiple copies as would be true of a best selling novel. These physical objects can be transferred or destroyed without affecting the ownership of the copyright in the work.[6] Indeed, copyright in a work

---

3. *See e.g.* Metropolitan Opera Ass'n v. Wagner–Nichols Recorder Corp., 199 Misc. 786, 101 N.Y.S.2d 483 (1950) (Common law remedy available for unauthorized recording of live opera performances); Hemingway's Estate v. Random House, Inc., 23 N.Y.2d 341, 296 N.Y.S.2d 771, 244 N.E.2d 250 (1968) (Court assumed, without deciding, that in a proper case common law protection in certain limited kinds of spoken dialogue might be recognized if the speaker indicated that he intended to mark off the utterance in question from the ordinary stream of speech and to exercise control over its publication). California has codified protection for unfixed works. *See* Cal. Civ. Code § 980(a) (West 1982).

4. *See* H.R. Rep. No. 94–1476, 94th Cong. 2d Sess. 53. State law protection analogous to copyright is explicitly pre-empted by the federal copyright statute. *See* 17 U.S.C.A. § 301 (2000).

5. The statute provides that the "term 'copies' includes the material object, other than a phonorecord, in which the work is first fixed." 17 U.S.C.A. § 101 (2000). Thus, what we might call "the original" in common everyday speech is considered a "copy" under the copyright act, and when a work is embodied in only a single unique physical object, such as a one-of-a-kind art work, the physical object is similarly considered a "copy" in the terminology of the statute.

6. "Ownership of a copyright, or of any of the exclusive rights under a copyright, is distinct from ownership of any material object in which the work is embodied. Transfer of ownership of any material object ... does not of itself convey rights in the copyrighted work embodied in the object." 17 U.S.C.A. § 202 (2000).

will endure even after all physical copies of that work have been destroyed.[7]

Although the requirement of fixation was not explicit in federal copyright law prior to the 1976 act, it was a necessary adjunct of the scheme established by the prior laws. Under those statutes, federal protection did not attach until the work was either published with notice, or registered with the Copyright Office.[8] Both publication and registration necessarily presuppose that the work has been fixed in some fashion. Indeed, the Constitution may require a fixation requirement because it gives Congress power to protect only the *writings* of an author.[9]

On the other hand, the kinds of fixation that were considered adequate by the courts under earlier copyright statutes were considerably narrower than they are today. In *White-Smith Music Publishing Co. v. Apollo Co.*,[10] the court held that copyright in certain musical compositions had not been infringed by the unauthorized production of perforated piano roll encoding those compositions. The Court reasoned that the disputed piano rolls were not capable of being read and deciphered by the unaided human eye, and as a result were not "copies" of the protected musical compositions. Since they weren't copies it followed that the defendant did not infringe! The opinion reflects judicial reluctance to extend the scope of copyright protection to works embodied in new technologies. If the *White-Smith* ideology prevailed today, copyright protection might be denied to computer programs recorded on floppy discs, motion pictures recorded on videotape and music recorded on CD's on the grounds of inadequate fixation, because none of the objects can be read by the unaided human eye. Congress sought to end any judicial hesitation of this sort by providing in the 1976 Act that the fixation of the work would be acceptable so long as it permitted the work to be "perceived, reproduced, or otherwise communicated, either directly or

7. For instance, in Pacific & Southern Co. v. Duncan, 744 F.2d 1490, 1494 (11th Cir.1984), a television station routinely erased videotapes of previous broadcasts after seven days. In infringement litigation against another firm that had sold unauthorized videotapes of the same broadcasts, the plaintiff prevailed despite the fact that all of its copies of the work had been destroyed. As the leading treatise puts it "once a work is fixed for a period of more than transitory duration, it does not lose its copyright protection because thereafter all authorized copies are destroyed." NIMMER, COPYRIGHT § 2.03[B] (2002). *See also* H.R. Rep. No. 94–1476, 94th Cong. 2d Sess. 52 ("It is possible to have an 'original work of authorship' without having a 'copy' or 'phonorecord' embodying it.").

8. Copyright Act of 1909, §§ 10, 11. The House Report to the 1976 Copyright Act states that "[a]s a basic condition of copyright protection the bill *perpetuates the existing requirement* that a work be fixed in a

'tangible medium of expression,' . . .," H.R. Rep. No. 94–1476, 94th Cong. 2d Sess. 52 (1976), further illustrating the long-standing pedigree of the "fixation" requirement. *See also* Letter Edged in Black Press v. Public Building Com'n of Chicago, 320 F.Supp. 1303, 1310 (N.D.Ill.1970) ("It is settled that a copyright can exist only in a perceptible, tangible work.")

9. See Goldstein v. California, 412 U.S. 546, 561, 93 S.Ct. 2303, 37 L.Ed.2d 163 (1973) ("By Art. I § 8, cl. 8, of the Constitution, the States granted to Congress the power to protect the 'Writings' of 'Authors'.... [A]lthough the word 'writings' might be limited to script or printed material, it may be interpreted to include any *physical* rendering of the fruits of creative intellectual or aesthetic labor." [emphasis supplied]).

10. 209 U.S. 1, 28 S.Ct. 319, 52 L.Ed. 655 (1908).

with the aid of a machine or device," and regardless of whether the medium of expression chosen is "now known or later developed."[11]

Modern technologies have posed other problems for the fixation requirement. One of these problems concerns works that are created on a computer and displayed on a computer screen without being permanently embodied in another medium such as on a computer disk. The statute requires that a work is fixed only when its "embodiment in a copy or phonorecord . . . is sufficiently permanent or stable to permit it to be perceived . . . for a period of more than a transitory duration" in order to satisfy the statutory fixation requirement.[12] This lead to a spate of litigation in the early eighties concerning arcade-style computer video games. These games are operated by computer programs and there is no dispute that the programs are themselves "fixed" usually in silicon on a chip inside the game cabinet. However, the games' authors also sought to protect the screen displays from copying by claiming a separate copyright in those displays as an "audiovisual work." Of course the images on screen change constantly throughout the play of the game, and, more importantly no two consecutive games are likely to be the same because of the role of player input. In *Midway Mfg. Co. v. Artic Int'l, Inc.,*[13] the Seventh Circuit recapitulated the difficulty:

> Strictly speaking, the particular sequence of images that appears on the screen of a video game machine when the game is played is not the same work as the set of images stored the machine's circuit boards. The person playing the game can vary the order in which the stored images appear on the screen by moving the machine's control lever. That makes playing a video game a little like arranging words in a dictionary into sentences or paints on a palette into a painting. The question is whether the creative effort in playing a video game is enough like writing or painting to make each performance of a video game the work of the player and not the game's inventor.

Despite these conceptual difficulties, the *Midway* court found that the screen displays were sufficiently "fixed" to qualify for protection under the statute, commenting that

> Playing a video game is more like changing channels on a television than it is like writing a novel or painting a picture. The player of a video game does not have control over the sequence of images that appears on the video game screen. He cannot create any sequence he wants out of the images stored on the game's circuit boards. The most he can do is choose one of the limited number of sequences the game allows him to choose. He is unlike a writer or a painter because the video game in effect writes the sentences and paints the painting for

---

11. 17 U.S.C.A. § 102 (2000).

12. 17 U.S.C.A. § 101 (2000).

13. 704 F.2d 1009, 1011 (7th Cir.), *cert. denied*, 464 U.S. 823, 104 S.Ct. 90, 78 L.Ed.2d 98 (1983).

him; he merely choose one of the sentences stored in its memory, one of the paintings stored in its collection.[14]

Other courts that have considered the issue have also come to the same conclusion.[15]

Another potential problem posed by the fixation requirement involves the broadcast of live events. When a television network broadcasts a football game, the game itself is not protected by copyright since it is a live event and thus, by definition, not a work fixed in a tangible medium. Moreover, the broadcast itself does not satisfy the fixation requirement because it is merely an ephemeral transmission of the images on the TV screen and lacks the "permanent embodiment" required by the statute. Thus, it would seem that one who captured the broadcast images and either retransmitted them or recorded them could not be charged with copyright infringement. To deal with this problem, Congress added an additional sentence to the definition of "fixed" in the current copyright statute. It provides that a "work consisting of sounds, images, or both, that are being transmitted, is 'fixed' for purposes of this title if a fixation of the work is being made simultaneously with its transmission."[16] In other words, if a television network broadcasts a live telecast of an NFL football game, and at the exact same time also makes a videotape of that broadcast, the network will have satisfied the fixation requirement and will have copyright protection in the broadcast.

Finally, it is important to note that the fixation which the statute speaks of is one made "by or under the authority of the author."[17] Thus, if a comedian were to launch in a series of ad libbed jokes during a performance, and an unauthorized audience member were to tape the routine, that would not constitute a fixation under the 1976 Copyright Act. This means that the comedian would have no copyrightable work and could not rely on copyright law to prevent the audience member from duplicating and selling the tapes. Of course, the comedian would not be entirely without a remedy, as he or she would likely have remedies under state common law.

Historically the fixation requirement posed a particular problem in the context of so-called "bootleg" recordings of live musical performances. All a bootlegger needed to do was to attend a live performance, covertly record it, generate a master tape and begin selling copies. Such tapes are easy and cheap to make, and can result in substantial profits. Because bootleg recordings are often of lower quality than legitimately produced recordings, their market presence can harm the reputation of the performer in addition to undercutting sales. Yet the fixation require-

---

14. 704 F.2d at 1012.

15. *See, e.g.,* Williams Elec. Inc. v. Arctic Int'l, Inc., 685 F.2d 870, 874 (3d Cir. 1982) ("Although there is player interaction with the machine during the play mode which causes the audiovisual presentation to change in some respects from one game to the next ... there is always a repetitive sequence of a substantial portion of the sights and sounds of the game, and many aspects of the display remain constant from game to game regardless of how the player operates the controls.").

16. 17 U.S.C.A. § 101 (2000).

17. 17 U.S.C.A. § 101 (2000).

ment of the copyright law put such conduct beyond the reach of federal copyright law.

Out of recognition of this problem, along with a desire to comply with U.S. obligations under the World Trade Organization agreements, Congress in 1994 enacted a special anti-bootlegging law.[18] Under this statute, one who makes unauthorized sound recordings and music videos of a live musical performance may be subject to both civil and criminal causes of action. Trafficking in—that is to say, transporting, transferring or otherwise disposing of—the unauthorized sound recordings and music videos is also illegal. Note that this provision does not apply to other, non-musical types of live performances such as comedy improvisations or ad hoc dance routines.

The anti-bootlegging statute is codified in 17 U.S.C.A. § 1101, near the Copyright Act but not formally a part of it. This choice of codification reflects the distinctions between this *sui generis* right and the traditional copyright law. Some have argued that the extent of these differences makes the anti-bootlegging law constitutionally suspect. The Intellectual Property Clause of the Constitution only authorizes Congress to protect *writings*, thereby connoting that protected works must take a tangible material form. The Constitution also calls for protection to endure only for "limited times." The anti-bootlegging statute, however, does not stipulate any durational limits upon the rights provided. Nonetheless, at least one Court of Appeals has upheld the statute in the face of constitutional challenge, relying upon the Commerce Clause rather than the Intellectual Property Clause.[19] It remains to be seen whether other courts will decide similarly, however, and also whether the anti-bootlegging law remains a special case or the start of a more wholesale rethinking of copyright's fixation requirement.

§ 3.3   No Protection For Ideas

Copyright in a work does not protect the underlying ideas expressed in that work. This simple concept is a fundamental tenet of copyright law. It is embodied in the very structure of section 102 of the current copyright act. While the first subsection of that provision affirmatively sets out the prerequisites for protection—fixation and originality—section 102(b) negatively provides that,

> In no case does copyright protection for an original work of authorship extend to any idea, procedure, process, system, method of operation, concept, principle, or discovery, regardless of the form in which it is described, explained, illustrated, or embodied in such work.[1]

18. Pub. L. No. 103–465, 108 Stat. 4809 (1994).

19. United States v. Moghadam, 175 F.3d 1269 (11th Cir.1999), *cert. denied*, 529 U.S. 1036, 120 S.Ct. 1529, 146 L.Ed.2d 344 (2000).

§ 3.3

1. 17 U.S.C.A. § 102(b) (2000).

This means that copyright protects only the *expression* contained within a work and not the underlying plot, or theme, or insight of the work. In other words, if an author writes a book explaining how to repair automobiles in an efficient way, he or she may not prevent others from describing the technique in their own words in another book. Similarly, if an author writes a novel based on the notion of a highly placed CIA agent who is actually a spy for a foreign power, he or she may not prevent others from using that concept as the basis for their own, separate novel.

There are several justifications for this limitation on the scope of copyright. First, copyright is, according to the Constitution itself, supposed to promote the progress of science and the useful arts. Progress requires that subsequent authors remain free to build on the works of their predecessors. If the first person to articulate a theory, divulge a principle, or lay out a plot line could prevent all others from using it for several decades, progress would be stymied rather than promoted.[2]

Second, there already exists a legal regime to reward innovation in the development of principles and procedures—namely patent law. Unlike the relatively easy criteria necessary for copyright protection, patent law has fairly rigorous prerequisites. The would-be patentee must show that his or her invention is both "novel" and "nonobvious"[3] If copyright protection extended to ideas, concepts and the like, it would provide an alternative to patent law that would undermine the many significant policy objectives of patent.

Third, extending copyright protection to the ideas contained in works might pose serious problems under the First Amendment. Others might be effectively forbidden from discussing the material contained in a first author's works. As Justice Douglas put it,

> The arena of public debate would be quiet, indeed, if a politician could copyright his speeches or a philosopher his treatises and thus obtain a monopoly on the ideas contained. We should not construe the copyright laws to conflict so patently with the values that the First Amendment was designed to protect.[4]

The idea-expression dividing line for protection is often traced back to the Supreme Court's decision in *Baker v. Selden*,[5] a surprisingly opaque and controversial opinion even today, more than 120 years after it was decided. Selden devised a new method of financial accounting for business. His new scheme made it possible to record the entire operations of the business for a given period of time on either a single page or on two facing pages. He published a short book explaining his new

---

2. For development of this argument and, more generally, for a justification of the idea/expression dichotomy from an economic point of view, see William M. Landes & Richard A. Posner, *An Economic Analysis of Copyright Law*, 18 J. LEGAL STUD. 325, 347–53 (1989).

3. *See infra* Chapters 16 and 17 of this treatise.

4. Lee v. Runge, 404 U.S. 887, 893, 92 S.Ct. 197, 30 L.Ed.2d 169 (1971) (Douglas, J., dissenting).

5. 101 U.S. 99, 25 L.Ed. 841 (1879).

system, along with accompanying forms that would be used in putting the system into operation. Baker subsequently prepared forms that were not identical to Selden's, but were similar to them and tailored for use with the Selden system.[6] Selden sued Baker arguing infringement. Since Baker's forms were not identical, the gist of the lawsuit could be viewed as a claim that Baker had impermissibly copied the underlying idea of Selden's accounting system. The Court rejected the argument, concluding that Selden's copyright did not give him an exclusive right in the system of accounting he had developed and revealed to the world. The Court illustrated its result with an example:

> Take the case of medicines. Certain mixtures are found to be of great value in the healing art. If the discoverer writes and publishes a book on the subject (as regular physicians generally do), he gains no exclusive right to the manufacture and sale of the medicine; he gives that to the public. If he desires to acquire such exclusive right, he must obtain a patent for the mixture as a new art, manufacture or composition of matter. He may copyright his book, if he pleases; but that only secures to him the exclusive right of printing and publishing his book. So of all other inventions or discoveries.[7]

If *Baker* said no more than this, it would be a straightforward declaration of the rule that copyright does not extend to the underlying ideas of a work. Other portions of the opinion, however, seem to imply a different basis for decision.

At various points in the opinion, the Court seems to assume that Baker took not merely the idea of the accounting system, but its expression as well. As already noted, however, Baker's forms were *not* identical to Selden's. The Court might have felt that such differences as did exist were relatively minor, and Baker's forms could be considered so substantially similar to Selden's as to be indistinguishable. Under that view, one might think that Baker would be held liable for copyright infringement. The Court, however, noted, that it was impossible to use the ideas of Selden's system without also borrowing the expression contained in the accounting forms. That being so, it suggested that the forms were dedicated to the public.[8] This goes beyond the basic idea-expression distinction to say that not only may one copy the ideas of another person's work without incurring infringement liability, but that

---

6. "The defendant uses a similar plan so far as results are concerned; but makes a different arrangement of the columns, and uses different headings." *Baker,* 101 U.S. at 100.

7. *Baker,* 101 U.S. at 102–03.

8. "The very object of publishing a book on science or the useful arts is to communicate to the world the useful knowledge which it contains. But this object would be frustrated if the knowledge could not be used without incurring the guilt of piracy of the book. And where the art it teaches cannot be used without employing the methods and diagrams used to illustrate the book, or such as are similar to them, such methods and diagrams are to be considered as necessary incidents to the art, and given therewith to the public; not given for the purpose of publication in other works explanatory of the art, but for the purpose of practical application." *Baker,* 101 U.S. at 103.

one may also copy the expression of the work *if doing so is necessary in order to use the ideas.* This will generally be true of any system that is implemented through the use of blank forms of various sorts. Thus, *Baker* is also considered to be the genesis for the prevailing rule today that blank forms are not copyrightable subject matter.[9] Professor Nimmer, among others, has criticized this aspect of the *Baker* holding, pointing out that many blank forms can contain much creative expression.[10]

Baker is a difficult case because of the close interconnection between the ideas of Selden's system and the expression that is incorporated into his accounting forms. Cases of this sort, where the ideas and expressions of a work are closely intertwined, often occur when a given idea can only be communicated in one, or a limited number of expressions. For example the idea of a "meatloaf" involves the combination of specific ingredients and a particular method of preparation. There are a relatively few ways to set out those ingredients and instructions. If the first author to publish a meatloaf recipe could prevent other authors from publishing similar recipes that would give a monopoly not only over the original expression, but over the very idea of a meatloaf itself. In cases such as this, the courts generally say that the idea and the expression in question have "merged" and they deny copyright protection to the expression at issue.

One of the more famous "merger" case is *Morrissey v. Procter & Gamble Co.,*[11] which held that a set of rules for a sweepstakes based on entrants' social security numbers was not copyrightable because there were only a limited number of ways to express the underlying idea of the sweepstakes instructions.

Another example is *Herbert Rosenthal Jewelry Corp v. Kalpakian,*[12] where the court permitted copying of a jewelry pin in the shape of a bee on the ground that the idea of a bee merged with the expression of that idea. The court in *Rosenthal* recognized that there are only a limited number of ways to make a jeweled pin that looks like a bee, and that any subsequent design of such a pin would bear a close resemblance to the plaintiff's pin. If everyone else's bee pins were found to infringe the plaintiff's, the plaintiff would be the only person allowed to make pins in the shape of a bee. As the court put it, "When the 'idea' and its 'expression' are thus inseparable, copying the 'expression' will not be barred, since protecting the 'expression' in such circumstance would

9. According to the regulations for registration of claims to copyright, "[b]lank forms, such as time cards, graph paper, account books, diaries, bank checks, scorecards, address books, report forms, mail order forms and the like, which are designed for recording information and do not in themselves convey information ..." are not subject to copyright. 37 C.F.R. § 202.1(c) (1994). *See e.g.,* Brown Instrument Co. v. Warner, 161 F.2d 910 (D.C.Cir. 1947); Bibbero Systems, Inc. v. Colwell Systems, Inc., 893 F.2d 1104 (9th Cir.1990) (Medical billing form not copyrightable); Sheplers Catalog Sales, Inc. v. Old West Dry Goods Corp., d/b/a Old West Outfitters, 830 F.Supp. 566, 28 USPQ2d 1555 (D.Kan. 1993) (Order form in mail order catalog not copyrightable).

10. NIMMER, COPYRIGHT § 2.18[C] (2002).

11. 379 F.2d 675 (1st Cir.1967).

12. 446 F.2d 738 (9th Cir.1971).

confer a monopoly of the 'idea' upon the copyright owner free of the conditions and limitations imposed by the patent law."[13]

None of the forgoing addresses the practical problem of how to distinguish the "idea" of a work from its "expression." This problem of classification is invariably controversial, because in many infringement cases the defendant will claim that he or she took only the unprotected ideas of the plaintiff's work, rather than any of the protected expression. Moreover, the distinction between ideas and expression is not really a sharp dichotomy. Rather, it is a continuum. The general idea of a work can be phrased more and more specifically until, eventually, a line is crossed and we are dealing with expression instead. Learned Hand said it best in a case involving alleged copyright infringement of a play:

> Upon any work, and especially upon a play, a great number of patterns of increasing generality will fit equally well, as more and more of the incident is left out. That last may perhaps be no more than the most general statement of what the play is about, and at times might consist only of its title; but there is a point in this series of abstractions where they are no longer protected, since otherwise the playwright could prevent the use of his 'ideas' to which, apart from their expression, his property is never extended.[14]

In other words, a given work does not have merely one "idea" behind it, but a multitude of ideas. That, unfortunately, does not make the task of separating protectable expression from unprotectable ideas any easier. As Judge Hand noted with some frustration in a different case, "no principle can be stated as to when an imitator has gone beyond copying the 'idea,' and has borrowed its 'expression,' .... Decisions must therefore inevitably be ad hoc."[15] In making these ad hoc decisions, however, it is important to remember the underlying purpose the distinction seeks to achieve. As the Ninth Circuit put it, "The guiding consideration ... is the preservation of the balance between competition and protection reflected in the ... copyright laws."[16]

This problem of distinguishing protectable expression from unprotectable ideas recurs with virtually every type of copyrightable subject matter. Cases involving alleged appropriation of the plot of novels and plays turn on the distinction, as do cases involving alleged appropriation of the structure of computer software. In the following chapter, as various types of copyrightable subject matter are taken up, we will

13. *Id.*, 446 F.2d at 742. *See also* Kern River Gas Transmission Co. v. Coastal Corp., 899 F.2d 1458 (5th Cir.1990) (Map of route of natural gas pipeline not copyrightable because maps express idea of the location of the pipeline in the only effective way); Hart v. Dan Chase Taxidermy Supply Corp., 152 F.3d 918 (2d Cir.1998) (Taxidermy mannequins of fish are not copyrightable because they consist of minimal expression which merges with the idea of depicting the appearance of the fish in question).

14. Nichols v. Universal Pictures Corp., 45 F.2d 119, 121 (2d Cir.1930).

15. Peter Pan Fabrics, Inc. v. Martin Weiner Corp., 274 F.2d 487, 489 (2d Cir. 1960).

16. Herbert Rosenthal Jewelry Corp. v. Kalpakian, 446 F.2d 738, 742 (9th Cir. 1971).

repeatedly return to the principle that copyright does not afford protection for ideas.

§ 3.4 Procedural Considerations

Issues of fixation and originality arise both in copyright litigation and at the Copyright Office in connection with an author's request to register the copyright.[1] Section 701(d) of the 1976 Act makes registration decisions reviewable as "agency actions" under the Administrative Procedure Act.[2] Courts will usually afford considerable weight to the determination of the Register of Copyrights on these issues, and the prevailing rule is that the determinations of the Register will be reviewed under an abuse of discretion standard.[3]

In litigation, infringement defendants frequently will put into issue the question of whether a work has been adequately fixed, whether it is original, and whether the appropriated material constitutes unprotected ideas rather than protectable expression. For this reason procedural concerns such as who bears the burden of proof are significant. Generally speaking, the plaintiff in an infringement action bears the burden of proof on all elements of the prima facie case. Thus, plaintiff will bear the burden on the issues of fixation, originality, and protectable expression.[4] This burden is made considerably lighter than might otherwise be the case by the current requirement that copyright registration is a prerequisite for filing an infringement suit for most copyright plaintiffs.[5] With the registration certificate in hand the plaintiff is entitled to the benefits of section 410(c) of the 1976 Act. That provision provides:

> In any judicial proceedings the certificate of a registration made before or within five years after first publication of the work shall constitute prima facie evidence of the validity of the copyright and of the facts stated in the certificate. The evidentiary weight to be accorded the certificate of a registration made thereafter shall be within the discretion of the court.

Since fixation, originality and protectable expression are all requirements for a valid copyright, possession of a registration certificate gives the plaintiff a rebuttable presumption of validity of the copyright, provided the plaintiff registered within five years of publication.[6] Furthermore, even in cases where registration follows publication by more

§ 3.4

1. Indeed, because registration is a prerequisite for an infringement suit for most domestic authors, the Copyright Office will almost always have passed on the questions of fixation and originality before the court has an opportunity to do so. *See* 17 U.S.C.A. § 411 (2000).

2. 5 U.S.C.A. § 101 *et seq.* (2000).

3. *See* John Muller & Co. v. New York Arrows Soccer Team, Inc., 802 F.2d 989, 990 (8th Cir.1986); Norris Industries, Inc.

v. International Tel. & Tel. Corp., 696 F.2d 918, 922 (11th Cir.), *cert. denied,* 464 U.S. 818, 104 S.Ct. 78, 78 L.Ed.2d 89 (1983).

4. NIMMER, COPYRIGHT § 12.11 (2002).

5. The requirement is found in 17 U.S.C.A. § 411 (2000). The requirement, however, only applies to "United States works."

6. *See* Flick–Reedy Corp. v. Hydro–Line Mfg. Co., 351 F.2d 546, 549 (7th Cir.1965), *cert. denied,* 383 U.S. 958, 86 S.Ct. 1222, 16 L.Ed.2d 301 (1966).

than five years, the certificate of registration will likely be afforded considerable weight within the judge's discretion. Thus, in the typical case, it falls to the defendant to produce evidence challenging the validity of the plaintiff's copyright if the defendant wishes to put that subject in issue.

For works created under the 1909 Act, infringement plaintiffs face a slightly different situation. The provision in that act which roughly corresponds to section 410 of the 1976 act provides that the certificate "shall be admitted as prima facie evidence of the facts stated therein."[7] Unlike the 1976 Act provision, this section does not create a general presumption of validity. Instead, it speaks only of the specific facts recited in the certificate. Thus, the plaintiff's benefit from the certificate might be somewhat more narrow for a pre–1978 work.

7. 1909 Act, § 209.

Chapter 4

THE SUBJECT MATTER OF COPY-RIGHT—SPECIFIC CATEGORIES OF PROTECTABLE WORKS

Table of Sections

After setting out the general requirements for copyrightability, section 102 of the current statute itemizes eight specific "works of authorship" that are potential subject matter of copyright. These are (1) literary works; (2) musical works; (3) dramatic works; (4) pantomimes and choreographic works; (5) pictorial, graphic, and sculptural works; (6) audiovisual works; (7) sound recordings and (8) architectural works. In addition, section 103 of the statute indicates that "derivative works" and "compilations" are also within the subject matter of copyright.

The previous statute, the Act of 1909, provided that copyright would be extended to "all the writings of an author."[1] Because this language so closely echoes that of the Copyright Clause of the Constitution, it was assumed by some to reach to the full extent of congressional authority. Congress changed the wording to "works of authorship" in 1976 in part to clarify that it was not legislating to the outer limit of its constitutional powers.

The list of subject matter in section 102(a) of the current law is not meant to be exclusive. That statute says that the subject matter of copyright "includes" the listed materials, plainly indicating that other forms of original authorship fixed in a tangible medium of expression will qualify for copyright as well.[2] Moreover, the categories of section 102 are not mutually exclusive. There are numerous possible overlaps. For instance, a play is both a literary work and a dramatic work. In addition, the section 103 categories—derivative works and compilations—will always overlap with one of the section 102 categories. For instance, a French translation of an English novel is a derivative work, but it is also a literary work.

As you might expect, the vast majority of copyrighted works fall into the specific categories mentioned in the statute. Each of these types of copyrightable material has its own peculiarities and can pose its own problems. Some have been copyrightable subject matter since the founding of the republic, while others were added only recently. Moreover, the category in which a work falls can significantly influence the rights belonging to the owner of the copyright in that work since not all statutory rights are afforded to every type of copyrightable work.[3]

§ 4.1   Literary Works

Most people probably first think of "literary works" when they think of the subject matter of copyright. The 1976 Act defines literary works as

> works, other than audiovisual works, expressed in words, numbers, or other verbal or numerical symbols or indicia, regardless of the nature of the material objects, such as books, periodicals, manuscripts, phonorecords, film, tapes, disks or cards, in which they are embodied.[1]

1. 1909 Act, § 4.

2. The legislative history makes the point explicit: "The use of the word 'include' . . . makes clear that the listing is 'illustrative and not limitative,' and that the . . . categories do not necessary exhaust the scope of 'original works of authorship' that the bill is intended to protect." H.R. Rep No. 94–1474 (94th Cong. 2d Sess.) at 53, 1976 U.S.Code Cong. & Ad. News 5659, 5666.

3. *See infra* Chapter 7. The Copyright Office has promulgated regulations specifying administrative classes for registration purposes, and makes determinations concerning classification for works submitted for registration. *See* 37 C.F.R. § 202.3(b). In the final analysis, however, any dispute over the proper categorization of a work would be for the courts to decide.

§ 4.1

1. 17 U.S.C.A. § 101 (2000).

As the words of that definition indicate, the current copyright statute does not protect "books" or "magazines." Items of that sort are merely types of material objects in which a literary work can be embodied. The literary work itself is the combination of words and numbers conceived of and fixed by the author, regardless of the form in which they may be fixed. Literary works can include works of both fact and fiction and works in both prose and poetic form.

4.1.1 Fictional Works

Fictional literary works are, of course, protected by copyright. A work of fiction is considered original, and therefore protectable, if it is expressed in an original way, even if the basic plot or theme of the work is a familiar one. Thus one is free to write a story about swashbucklers who protect their king against treachery notwithstanding that this story line is the basis for *Robin Hood*, *The Three Musketeers* and numerous other famous works of fiction.

The reverse is also true. If an author conceives of a wholly new idea for a work of fiction, that underlying idea will not be protected against appropriation by a later author who wishes to use it. Copyright only protects the expressive elements of a work. Expression includes not merely the literal words, however, but also the detailed structure of the plot. Discerning just where the general idea of the work leaves off and the specific expression of the author begins is, as has been previously noted,[2] one of the most vexing aspects in all of copyright law. As a general rule, the issue need only be confronted in the context of infringement litigation, where the defendant will assert that any similarities between the works relate only to unprotected ideas. This means that the court does not have to identify some precise point at which ideas shade over into expression. Instead, it only has to decide if the particular elements appropriated by the defendant fall on one side of the line or the other. That, nonetheless, can still be a daunting task. Additional aspects of how the courts have met that challenge appear in the chapter on copyright infringement.

Another major issue that recurs in connection with copyright in fictional work is the protection to be extended to the characters who appear in such works. This is merely a specific incarnation of the general idea/expression problem. Many novelists will populate a work with a large number of "generic" characters—the suave secret agent, the rumpled detective, the kindly old lady, and the like. These characters are common literary property, free for all to use. They are nothing more than mere ideas. However, if a character is sufficiently delineated, courts have been willing to extend protection to them.[3] The principle was summed up by Judge Learned Hand when he noted:

---

2. *See supra* Chapter 2.

3. *See generally* DOROTHY J. HOWELL, INTELLECTUAL PROPERTIES AND THE PROTECTION OF

FICTIONAL CHARACTERS (1990); Leslie A. Kurtz, *The Independent Legal Lives of Fictional Characters*, 1986 Wis. L. Rev. 429.

If Twelfth Night were copyrighted, it is quite possible that a second comer might so closely imitate Sir Toby Belch or Malvolio as to infringe, but it would not be enough that for one of his characters he cast a riotous knight who kept wassail to the discomfort of the household, or a vain and foppish steward who became amorous of his mistress. These would be no more than Shakespeare's 'ideas' in the play, ... It follows that the less developed the characters, the less they can be copyrighted; that is the penalty an author must bear for marking them too indistinctly.[4]

Ever since, courts have struggled to define the point at which a character becomes sufficiently delineated to warrant independent protection. In *Warner Bros. Pictures v. Columbia Broadcasting System*,[5] often referred to as the Sam Spade case, the court had to determine whether a grant to Warner Brothers of exclusive rights to make a movie version of the story *The Maltese Falcon* precluded Dashiel Hammett, the original author, from writing additional stories featuring the Sam Spade character. While the case turned, in large measure, on interpretation of the contract between the parties, the court took the opportunity to indicate when, in its opinion, a fictional character could be protected by copyright. According to the Ninth Circuit, a character would only be protected if "the character really constitutes the story being told, but if the character is only the chessman in the game of telling the story he is not within the area of the protection afforded by the copyright."[6]

The approach of the Sam Spade case has been criticized as overly restrictive, and apparently rejected by other circuit courts of appeal.[7] For example, in *Burroughs v. MGM*,[8] the court considered whether copyright existed in the well-known character Tarzan. In reaching an affirmative result, the court stated: "Tarzan is the ape-man. He is an individual closely in tune with his jungle environment, able to communicate with animals yet able to experience human emotion. He is athletic, innocent, youthful, gentle and strong. He is Tarzan." This analysis plainly concerns the delineation of Tarzan, rather than whether Tarzan was himself the story. This broader notion of the protection of fictional characters apart from the stories in which they appear seems the more appropriate course. Living in an era of prequels, sequels and movie adoptions, modern readers can appreciate that fictional characters ranging from Sherlock Holmes to Superman exist beyond the reach of any individual work.

4. Nichols v. Universal Pictures Corp., 45 F.2d 119, 121 (2d Cir.1930), *cert. denied*, 282 U.S. 902, 51 S.Ct. 216, 75 L.Ed. 795 (1931).

5. 216 F.2d 945 (9th Cir.1954).

6. *Warner*, 216 F.2d at 950.

7. *See e.g.*, Columbia Broadcasting Syst., Inc. v. DeCosta, 377 F.2d 315, 320 (1st Cir.), *cert. denied*, 389 U.S. 1007, 88 S.Ct. 565, 19 L.Ed.2d 603 (1967).

8. *Burroughs v. Metro–Goldwyn–Mayer, Inc.*, 519 F.Supp. 388 (S.D.N.Y.1981), *aff'd*, 683 F.2d 610 (2d Cir.1982).

4.1.2 Non–Fiction Works

The category of "literary works" includes works of non-fiction of all sorts, ranging from cookbooks to instruction manuals to catalogs to comprehensive and scholarly histories and biographies. Some of these types of non-fiction works, such as catalogs and directories, are actually forms of compilations, special types of works which are discussed further on in this chapter.[9]

Among the most common non-fiction literary works are prose works of history or biography. Such works are plainly copyrightable to the extent that they meet the requirements of fixation and originality. The copyright in such works does not, however, include protection for the facts or research revealed in the work. This is true, moreover, even if the discovery of those facts required a great deal of labor or ingenuity. Thus, if a biographer of Lincoln were to discover, after years of research in a dusty library in Springfield, Illinois, that Lincoln had held a heretofore unknown series of secret meetings with Robert E. Lee in an effort to end the Civil War, and had made disclosure of those facts the central aspect of his book about Lincoln, those facts could nonetheless be used in subsequent works without infringing any rights of the first author.[10] The justification for this approach is that the facts in question do not "originate" with the author. They are the products of research, not creative authorship. Professor Nimmer has also suggested that First Amendment concerns would be implicated if the first party to discover and publish a fact could prevent others from doing so.[11]

In a sense, of course, there are no such things as "facts." All attempts to reconstruct the past involve interpretation as well as research. Many of the most important non-fiction works go beyond merely setting out facts and attempt to weave them together in a theory. In a number of cases, courts have denied copyright protection to these historical theories along with the underlying basic facts. For instance, in *Hoehling v. Universal City Studios, Inc.,*[12] Hoehling published a book entitled *Who Destroyed the Hindenburg?* in which he developed the thesis that the famous airship was destroyed by the sabotage of a member of the crew named Spehl. Sometime later, another author prepared a book about the destruction of the Hindenburg that Universal Studios eventually made into a movie. The second book and the movie both used Hoehling's theory that Spehl had been a saboteur. Nonetheless the court concluded that there was no copyright infringement

9. *See infra* § 4.10.

10. *See, e.g.,* Miller v. Universal City Studios, Inc., 650 F.2d 1365, 1369 (5th Cir. 1981) ("since facts do not owe their origin to any individual, they may not be copyrighted and are part of the public domain available to every person."); Narell v. Freeman, 872 F.2d 907, 910–11 (9th Cir.1989) ("Historical facts and theories may be copied, as long as the defendant does not 'bodily appropriate' the expression of the plaintiff."). Certain earlier cases had held to the contrary, *see, e.g.,* Toksvig v. Bruce Publishing Co., 181 F.2d 664 (7th Cir.1950); Huie v. National Broadcasting Co., 184 F.Supp. 198 (S.D.N.Y.1960). Those cases have since been repudiated.

11. NIMMER, COPYRIGHT § 2.11[E] ("Would anyone seriously suggest that the *Washington Post* was entitled to a copyright on the facts of the Watergate incident because its reporters, Woodward and Bernstein, through considerable labor, expense and ingenuity, discovered such facts?").

12. 618 F.2d 972 (2d Cir.1980).

because "an historical interpretation ... is not protected by ... copyright and can be freely used by subsequent authors."[13]

Of course, subsequent authors may not take the precise expression used by the first author and any fictional details added to a basically factual work will also be protectable.[14] On the other hand, if a non-fiction work contains quotations from historical personages or other celebrities, those are not protected by the copyright and can be reproduced by others, since the author of the work is not the originator or author of the particular quote in question.

Some might argue that denying protection to facts, research and historical theory seriously undercuts incentives for authors to undertake such projects. On the other hand, readers of history and biography know that the expressive elements—the words chosen to recreate the past—are often the most memorable and distinguishing aspect of these works. Moreover, the Supreme Court has observed that leaving factual information unprotected by copyright is "neither unfair nor unfortunate. It is the means by which copyright advances the progress of science and art."[15] Consequently, limiting protection to the actual words and structure of a non-fiction work and leaving the facts and theories available for free copying by others may strike a reasonable balance between incentives to creativity and public access.

4.1.3 Computer Programs

From their very first appearance, computer programs proved to be a controversial and troublesome subject area in the law of copyright. Some of the issues that bedeviled the courts and Congress have been resolved, but others continue to percolate. In order to understand both the historic and the current controversies, it is necessary to know just a bit about computer programs.

Programs are sets of instructions for a computer. The 1976 Act defines a computer program as "a set of statements or instructions to be used directly or indirectly in a computer to bring about a certain result."[16] Typically, programs are first written in one of any number of "high-level" programming languages, like "C" or "Javascript" or "HTML." In this form the program will consist of several cryptic but intelligible phrases, like "SET X=Y+Z" or "IF X > Y THAN GO TO LINE 250." Programs of this sort are said to be written in "source code." Computers cannot directly use source code instructions since

---

13. *Hoehling*, 618 F.2d at 979. *See also* Rosemont Enterprises, Inc. v. Random House, Inc., 366 F.2d 303, 310 (2d Cir. 1966), *cert. denied* 385 U.S. 1009, 87 S.Ct. 714, 17 L.Ed.2d 546 ("We .. cannot subscribe to the view that an author is absolutely precluded from saving time and effort by referring to and relying upon prior published material.... It is just such wasted effort that the proscription against the copyright of ideas and facts ... are designed to prevent.").

14. *See* De Acosta v. Brown, 146 F.2d 408 (2d Cir.1944) (Fictionalized aspects in generally factual screenplay about the life of Clara Barton held protectable and infringed).

15. Feist Publications, Inc. v. Rural Telephone Service Co., 499 U.S. 340, 350, 111 S.Ct. 1282, 113 L.Ed.2d 358 (1991).

16. 17 U.S.C.A. § 101 (2000).

computers cannot read English, even the garbled English of these phrases. Computers really only understand pulses of electricity and their entire vocabulary is limited to the concepts of "on" and "off." This means that, in order to be usable, the program must be converted to a binary form consisting of strings of ones and zeros with the ones symbolizing "on" and the zeros symbolizing "off." Programs in this form are said to be written in machine language, or "object code." The process of converting source code into object code is known as "compilation." Compilation is usually accomplished by running the source code version of a program through a computer using software known, not surprisingly, as a "compiler."

Computer programs can be fixed in a wide variety of media. Either source code or object code versions can be written or typed out on paper. The object code can also be stored on CD's, floppy disks, tape or other magnetic or digital media. In addition, programs can also be embedded in the silicon of computer chips. When you buy a computer, some software is typically sold as an integral part of the machine since it is included on the chips inside the computer. Other software that you wish to use must be purchased separately and is typically distributed on disks or tape.

It is also important to note that there are two broad categories of computer programs. First are the application programs. These are the programs that allow you to directly use your computer. They include things like word processors and spreadsheets, personal and business accounting programs, and a huge variety of games. Rather distinct from these application programs are the "operating systems." These are the programs that control the internal operations of a computer and enable it to interact with particular application programs. The Windows program developed by the Microsoft Company is, of course, one such operating system.

Starting in the mid-sixties, long prior to the adoption of the 1976 Act, the Copyright Office began accepting computer programs for registration as copyrightable works, but doing so under circumstances that left the significance of the action unclear. With the adoption of the 1976 Act, the ambiguity seemed to be eliminated. Computer programs, after all, fall within the literal language defining "literary works" in the 1976 Act since they plainly are "expressed in words, numbers or other verbal or numerical symbols or indicia ... "[17] Moreover, Congress noted in the legislative history accompanying the 1976 statute that "literary works ... includes computer data bases and computer programs to the extent that they incorporate authorship in the programmer's expression of original ideas, as distinguished from the ideas themselves."[18]

Notwithstanding these legislative developments, Congress continued to harbor some uncertainties as to the workability of using copyright law to protect software. Consequently, Congress established the National

17. 17 U.S.C.A. § 101 (2000).   **18.** H.R. Rep. No. 94–1476, 94th Cong. 2d Sess. 54 (1973).

Commission on New Technological Uses of Copyrighted Works, or CON-TU, in 1974 to consider the appropriate scope of any copyright protection for software along with a variety of other issues.[19] CONTU submitted its final report in 1978, concluding that copyright law was indeed the appropriate legal mechanism to be used for software protection.

In response to the CONTU conclusions Congress ultimately adopted the Computer Software Copyright Act of 1980.[20] That statute added a definition of computer programs to the copyright statute,[21] and also revised section 117 of the statute to provide limited exceptions to the exclusive right of a software copyright owner to make copies of the program.[22] The legislative history of this 1980 statute along with these two provisions reflected Congress's final conclusion to leave programs under the ambit of copyright rather than to devise some alternative, *sui generis* form of protection for them.

This brief history might suggest that the post–1980 copyright status of software has been non-controversial, but nothing could be further from the truth. Controversy soon emerged over a variety of issues. Among the first problems to confront the courts were claims that Congress intended only to protect programs in their source code form, and/or that Congress only intended to protect application programs, not operating systems. Litigants, and some commentators, advanced several arguments in favor of these distinctions. First, they noted that object code versions of software, unlike most copyrighted works, are not intelligible to human users. In addition, unlike all other forms of copyrighted subject matter, the author's expression in object code is not meant ever to be communicated to human users. Even music on a compact disc, which is not immediately perceptible by you when you buy the disc, will communicate the very work that was composed and recorded by the musicians involved when you eventually play it on your CD player. When you buy software, you will never encounter the program as written by the programmers. You may play a video-game or use a word-processor *generated* by that program, but that, it was argued, is not the same as experiencing the actual work.

These arguments were rejected in a number of cases decided in the early eighties, shortly after adoption of the Software Copyright Act. One of the most notable of these is *Apple Computer Inc. v. Franklin Computer Corp.*[23] Franklin, the defendant in this case, wanted to manufacture computers that would run software originally written for Apple computers. In other words, it wanted to build an Apple-compatible clone. In order to do so, it copied the object code version of Apple's operating system software from computer chips contained within Apple computers. Without the Apple operating system, the Franklin machine would not be

19. Pub. L. 93–573, 88 Stat. 1873 (Title II).

20. Pub. L. 96–517 § 10, 94 Stat. 3015 (1980).

21. "A 'computer program' is a set of statements or instructions to be used di-rectly or indirectly in a computer in order to bring about a certain result." 17 U.S.C.A. § 101.

22. *See infra* Chapter 6.

23. 714 F.2d 1240 (3d Cir.1983).

able to run software that was designed for Apple computers and thus would not be marketable.

Given the fairly clear copying in this case, Franklin had to argue that the Apple operating system was not copyrightable. To do so, it argued that programs in object code and operating systems ought not to be copyrightable. In addition, it argued that no copyright could exist in a program embedded on a computer chip because the chips were "machine parts." The court rejected all three contentions. The fact that object code is unintelligible to human readers did not affect copyrightability since the 1976 statute specifically applies to works fixed in a form that can be perceived "with the aid of a machine...." In this regard, *Franklin* was merely following earlier decisions that had held to the same effect.[24] The court also held with little discussion that a computer chip was a perfectly adequate medium in which to fix a computer program.

The most novel aspect of the case was the argument over copyrightability for an operating system. Franklin claimed that the operating system for a type of computer was a "process," "system" or "method of operation," and thus not eligible for copyright under the express terms of section 102(b) of the 1976 Act. The Third Circuit rejected the argument, relying in part on policy and in part on statutory language. It noted that the statutory definition of computer programs was all-inclusive, making no distinction between application programs and operating systems. Moreover, it stressed that Apple "does not seek to copyright the method which instructs the computer to perform its operating functions but only the instructions themselves. The method would be protected, if at all, by the patent law,...."[25]

Nor was the court impressed by the related argument that protection of the operating system would be equivalent to granting copyright in an "idea." Since Franklin had taken not merely the idea of Apple-compatibility, but the actual expression contained within Apple's program, this argument effectively invoked the merger doctrine discussed in the previous chapter.[26] The court recognized that this would only be true if Apple's operating system program was the only way to "express" the idea of Apple compatibility. "If other programs can be written or created which perform the same function as an Apple's operating system program, then that program is an expression of the idea and hence copyrightable."[27] Thus the court rejected the argument that operating systems were per se uncopyrightable. It did, however, remand for further findings on that question.

The *Apple* case involved questions concerning copyright protection for the literal code of a computer program, and it clearly established that literal program code was copyrightable regardless of the form in which it was written, the function it was to perform, or the medium in which it

24. *See e.g.,* Williams Elec., Inc. v. Artic Int'l, Inc., 685 F.2d 870 (3d Cir.1982); Stern Elec., Inc. v. Kaufman, 669 F.2d 852 (2d Cir.1982).

25. *Apple,* 714 F.2d at 1251.

26. *See supra* § 3.3.

27. *Apple,* 714 F.2d at 1253.

was fixed. It did not consider, however, the degree of protection to be afforded to the non-literal elements of computer programs. Just as a novelist may claim protection not only for his or her words, but for the details of plot structure, a software author may seek to protect various aspects of a program beyond the actual code.

Courts have given considerable attention to two types of non-literal software attributes. The first of these is the "structure, sequence and organization" of a program, sometimes referred to as the "SSO." For example, complex programs often have sub-components called modules, that are designed to interact with each other in specified ways. The organizations of these inter-modular relationships would be one aspect of SSO. In the 1986 case of *Whelan Assocs. Inc. v. Jaslow Dental Laboratory*,[28] the Third Circuit held that copyright protection for software extended beyond the literal code of a program to embrace the SSO. In reaching that result, however, the court suggested that the sole idea of a computer program is the purpose the program seeks to achieve. In *Whelan* that was "to aid the business operations of a dental laboratory." According to the Third Circuit, anything more specific in the program would be considered protectable expression. This approach is quite sweeping in the amount of protection it grants to non-literal elements of computer programs, and the case has been criticized by various academic commentators for providing overbroad protection to software.[29]

More recent cases have attempted to articulate a more precise boundary line between protected SSO and the unprotected ideas of a program. In *Computer Associates Int'l, Inc. v. Altai, Inc.*,[30] the court faulted the *Whelan* opinion for an insufficiently sophisticated understanding of software, and articulated a test to distinguish between protectable and unprotectable components of a computer program, which it labeled the "abstraction-filtration" test. Citing *Baker v. Selden*,[31] the court pointed out that not only are the underlying ideas of the work not part of the owner's copyright, but that aspects of a work which must necessarily be used as an incident to employing those ideas are also unprotected. To give full scope to that doctrine the court set out the following approach

> [A] court would first break down the allegedly infringed program into its constituent structural parts. Then, by examining each of these parts for such things as incorporated ideas, expression that is necessarily incidental to those ideas, and elements that are taken from the public domain, a court would then be able to sift out all non-protectable material. Left with a

28. 797 F.2d 1222 (3d Cir.1986).

29. The Nimmer treatise notes that the "crucial flaw in this reasoning is that it assumes that only one 'idea,' in copyright law terms, underlies any computer program, and that once a separable idea can be identified, everything else must be expression. . . . [T]he broad purpose that the program serves . . . is *an* idea. Other elements

of the program's structure and design, however, may also constitute ideas for copyright purposes." NIMMER, COPYRIGHT § 13.03[F] (2002).

30. 982 F.2d 693 (2d Cir.1992).

31. 101 U.S. 99, 25 L.Ed. 841 (1879). *See supra* § 3.3.

kernel, or possible kernels, of creative expression after following this process of elimination, the court's last step would be to compare this material with the structure of an allegedly infringing program.[32]

The first portion of the process described by this language—the breaking down into structural parts—is the "abstraction." The examination referred to in the second sentence is the "filtration." Only the "kernel" or "golden nugget"[33] of material left after this process is protected by copyright. While some commentators have criticized this test, not least of all for being vague, other federal circuits have endorsed it.[34]

The second, and related, issue concerning protection of non-literal elements of software that has received judicial attention is the problem of protection for the "user interface" of computer programs. A program's user interface is essentially its "look and feel," in particular such elements as menu structures, layouts, text prompts, and the use of particular key combinations or mouse clicks to accomplish particular tasks. Thus, the fact that a word processing program will indicate in the lower right hand corner of the screen the number of inches the cursor sits from the left margin is a part of the user interface of that word processor, as is the fact that pressing the F6 key will permit you to mark text in bold face type.

In *Lotus Development Corp. v. Borland International, Inc.*,[35] the Court of Appeals for the First Circuit considered whether a software user interface was subject to copyright protection. The court specifically considered the command menu hierarchy of the then hugely popular Lotus 1–2–3 spreadsheet program. Accused infringer Borland had copied the Lotus menu tree so that former Lotus users could readily transition to Borland's competing Quattro software. The district court had held that the Lotus designers had made expressive choices in choosing and arranging the program's command terms and concluded that the command hierarchy was consequently a copyrightable aspect of the program.

On appeal, the First Circuit disagreed, concluding that the Lotus commands were a "method of operation" within the meaning of § 102(b), and therefore not copyrightable subject matter.[36] Analogizing the Lotus menu command hierarchy to the buttons on a VCR machine, the Court of Appeals concluded that just because the functions of the

---

32. *Computer Associates,* 982 F.2d at 706.

33. Elsewhere in the opinion the *Computer Associates* court notes "[o]nce a court has sifted out all elements of the allegedly infringed program that are 'ideas' or are dictated by efficiency or external factors, or taken from the public domain, there may remain a core of protectable expression. In terms of a work's copyright value, this is the golden nugget." 982 F.2d at 710.

34. See e.g., Sega Enterprises Ltd. v. Accolade, Inc., 977 F.2d 1510, 1525 (9th Cir.1992) ("the Second Circuit's approach is an appropriate one"); Atari Games Corp. v. Nintendo of America, Inc., 975 F.2d 832, 839 (Fed.Cir.1992); Gates Rubber Co. v. Bando Chemical Ind., Ltd., 9 F.3d 823 (10th Cir.1993). The Nimmer treatise on copyright law also endorses the same approach under the name "successive filtering." See NIMMER, COPYRIGHT § 13.03[F] (2002).

35. 49 F.3d 807 (1st Cir.1995), *aff'd by an equally divided Court,* 516 U.S. 233, 116 S.Ct. 804, 133 L.Ed.2d 610 (1996).

36. *See supra* § 3.3.

Lotus program were arranged and labeled did not make them copyrightable expression. At best the menu command hierarchy was structured so that individuals could quickly learn and efficiently use the Lotus program—matters outside the scope of protection of the copyright laws, at least since the Supreme Court decision in *Baker v. Selden*.[37]

Judge Boudin's concurring opinion in *Lotus v. Borland* suggested additional policy issues at stake in the decision. Computer users had invested considerable time and effort, Judge Boudin recognized, in order to obtain the expertise needed to use Lotus 1–2–3. If that investment could not be transferred, then users would be discouraged from switching even to superior spreadsheet software. The effect of providing robust copyright protection for user interfaces that control the operation of a program would be to lock consumers into potentially inferior products—an aim wholly antithetical to the goals of the copyright system.

This legal and policy discussion of *Lotus v. Borland* does suggest that where elements of the user interface are not necessary to operate a program, copyright protection may be appropriate. The content of help screens, for example, or an animated figure offering suggestions during the operation of the program, such as an incredibly annoying paper clip that raps on the screen whenever it wants to get your attention, would not seem to bring the concerns of the *Lotus v. Borland* court into play and therefore ought to be subject to the copyright laws.

Another potential controversy concerning the copyrightability of computer software is the question of who owns the copyright in a "computer-generated work." For instance, software can be imagined which would permit a computer to generate elaborate works of music without any human input. The difficulty in such cases is whether the work itself qualifies as a "work of authorship" if it was not created through direct human involvement, and if so, who should be considered the author. While there is little law thus far on these problems, the CONTU Report suggested that such works should be protected and that the copyright owner should be the person using the program, rather than the author of the underlying program which generates the contested output. That is also the solution that has been adopted under British law.[38]

As the foregoing review of contemporary issues illustrates, computer programs have proven to be controversial subjects under the copyright law because they have utilitarian features uncommon for most other works. They don't just instruct users in how to perform tasks, they actually perform those tasks by themselves. Nonetheless, they are crea-

---

37. 101 U.S. 99, 25 L.Ed. 841 (1879).

38. *See* Copyright, Designs and Patents Act, 1988, ch.48 § 9(3) (United Kingdom) ("In the case of a literary, dramatic, musical or other artistic work which is computer-generated, the author shall be taken to be the person by whom the arrangements necessary for the creation for the work are undertaken."). For a thorough discussion of the issues involved in the copyrightability of computer-generated works, *see* Arthur R. Miller, *Copyright Protection for Computer Programs, Datatbases and Computer–Generated Works: Is Anything New Since CONTU?*, 106 Harv. L. Rev. 977, 1042–72 (1993).

tive products of human intellect and it would appear that the courts are succeeding in applying existing doctrines such as the idea/expression distinction and the merger rule to strike a proper balance between protection and productive borrowing.

Another notable development concerning computer-related works was the advent of the Semiconductor Chip Protection Act.[39] This legislation is housed in Chapter 9 of Title 17 of the U.S. Code, next to the 1976 Copyright Act but not formally part of it.[40] Congress enacted this legislation in response to the concerns of manufacturers of semiconductor chip products.[41] These products consist of thousands of miniaturized electrical circuits housed on small pieces of semiconductor material, such as silicon. In combination, these circuits are engineered to function as microprocessors, memories and other devices. Once limited to computers and other expensive machinery, chips are now employed in automobiles, cameras and all manner of common household appliances. The integrated circuit layouts on which chips are based are expensive to design but, thanks to a process known as photolithography, quite easy to copy.

Existing forms of intellectual property did not present a good fit with integrated circuit layouts. Because integrated circuit layouts are functional, utilitarian products, the copyright law was not a suitable form of protection. In addition, as will be discussed later in this hornbook, functional inventions must exceed the abilities of skilled artisans in order to be patented.[42] Although integrated circuit layouts are sophisticated products that are difficult to design, they nonetheless may be considered obvious variations of known circuit layouts.[43]

With neither the copyright law nor the patent law applicable, Congress enacted the Semiconductor Chip Protection Act (SCPA) in 1984 to afford some legal protection to chip designs. The SCPA creates a 10–year term for protection of integrated circuit layouts, provides exclusive rights to proprietors to reproduce these layouts and manufacture chips embodying them, and allows others to reverse engineer the layouts to analyze or evaluate them. In order to obtain protection, chip designers must register the work with the Copyright Office, depositing four chips embodying the mask work, and submit drawings or plots of each layer of the mask work.

§ 4.2 Musical Works

The second category of work of authorship specifically itemized in section 102 are "musical works, including any accompanying words." Although there is no statutory definition of "musical works" in the act,

---

39. Pub. L. No. 98–260, 98 Stat. 3335 (1984).

40. 17 U.S.C.A. §§ 901–914 (2000).

41. *See* Leon Radomsky, *Sixteen Years After the Passage of the U.S. Semiconductor Chip Protection Act: Is International Protection Working?*, 15 Berkeley Tech. L.J. 1049 (2000).

42. *See infra* § 17.1.

43. *See, e.g.,* Carl A. Kukkonen, III, *The Need to Abolish Registration for Integrated Circuit Topographies Under TRIPS*, 38 IDEA 105, 107 (1997).

the copyright office has defined music as "a succession of pitches or rhythms, or both, usually in some definite pattern."[1] Musical works typically consist of combinations of melodies, harmonies and rhythms. Courts rarely find sufficient originality in the rhythm of a work to warrant protection because, as one court explained, it "is simply the tempo in which the composition is written. It is the background for the melody. There is only a limited amount of tempos; these appear to have been long since exhausted; originality of rhythm is a rarity, if not an impossibility."[2] The requisite originality of a musical work is therefore most often found in the melody.[3] Because of the constraints involved in writing music, courts find that musical works lack the requisite originality somewhat more frequently than is true for other categories of works.

Of course, musical works must be "fixed" in order to be protected. In *White–Smith Music Pub. Co. v. Apollo Co.*[4] the Supreme Court considered the alleged infringement of musical compositions based on defendant's reproduction of those works in player piano rolls. The songs at issue were protected by copyright, and had unauthorized copying of the sheet music occurred there would have been no question of infringement. In the case of the musical compositions encoded on a piano roll, however, the Court was troubled by the fact that one could not readily deduce the tune from visual examination of the piano roll itself. The Court therefore required "a written or printed record in intelligible notation," before it would find that defendant had made a "copy" of the plaintiff's protected songs. Because piano rolls could not be read by the naked eye, the Court denied relief. This rule effectively meant that a musical composition could not be protected until it was reduced to the form of sheet music, and that was the rule that prevailed under the 1909 Act. Congress, however, wisely overruled the *White–Smith* doctrine when it enacted the 1976 Act. It is now clear that fixation on tape or compact discs is perfectly sufficient under the law, despite the fact that one cannot visibly interpret the music by looking at the tape or disc.

The copyright in a musical work includes both the music and the lyrics, if any. Use of either the words alone or the music alone are just as much forbidden as would be use of the words and music together.[5] While much important music is in the public domain—such as the vast body of works by composers such as Beethoven and Mozart—it is worth noting that an original "arrangement" of a musical work[6] will be separately

§ 4.2

1. Compendium II of Copyright Office Practices § 402 (1984).

2. Northern Music Corp. v. King Record Distrib. Co., 105 F.Supp. 393, 400 (S.D.N.Y. 1952).

3. *Id.* ("It is in the melody of the composition—or the arrangement of notes or tones that originality must be found. It is the arrangement or succession of musical notes, which are the finger prints of the composition and establish its identity.")

4. 209 U.S. 1, 28 S.Ct. 319, 52 L.Ed. 655 (1908).

5. *See, e.g., Mills Music, Inc. v. Arizona,* 187 USPQ 22 (D.Ariz.1975).

6. The Copyright Office defines an arrangement as "a work that results from the addition of new harmony to a preexisting work." *Compendium II of Copyright Office Practices* § 408.1 (1984) Harmony, in turn, is defined as "the combination, simultaneous, or nearly so, of different pitches. These tones are spaced at certain pre-

copyrightable as a derivative work. Thus there may be a number of versions of Beethoven's Fifth Symphony in existence, each of which is independently copyrightable as a separate arrangement of that symphony.

§ 4.3 Dramatic Works

Dramatic works, including any accompanying music, are protectable works under the 1976 Act.[1] The statute does not define "dramatic works" because the Congress felt that the concept was well settled under previous law.[2] Indeed, the 1909 Act did not contain a definition of dramatic works either. The Copyright Office has promulgated its own definition of dramatic works to guide it in making registration decisions. It provides that:

> A dramatic composition is one that portrays a story by means of dialog or acting and is intended to be performed. It represents all or a substantial portion of the action as actually occurring, rather than merely being narrated or described.... If the narrator is to devise or improvise his or her own action, the dramatic content is not fixed and thus the work is not a drama.[3]

In resolving whether a primitive film version of *Ben Hur* was a "dramatization" of the book of the same name, Justice Holmes gave us another, more pithy definition of drama. "The essence of the matter ... is ... that we see the event or story lived."[4] Professor Goldstein has suggested that these definitions may be unduly narrow in their insistence upon a story. He notes that non-narrative forms of drama are widely recognized as part of the dramatic arts by contemporary audiences and thus he advocates a definition including any work "in which performed actions, speech, or incident, or all three, convey theme, thoughts or character to an audience."[5]

Thus stage plays, screenplays and teleplays are all examples of typical dramatic works, as are opera and operettas, along with their accompanying music. Of course all of these works also fall within the definition of literary works, as they are expressed, at least partially, in words.[6] There can be similar overlap with the "musical works" category for those dramatic works that contain musical portions such as a Broadway musical, and with the "audio-visual works" category for dramatic works captured on film. For clarity's sake, therefore, other

scribed distances from one another in related progressions." *Id.* at § 403.1.

§ 4.3

1. 17 U.S.C.A. § 102(a)(3).

2. H.R. Rep. No. 94–1476, 94th Cong. 2d Sess. 53 (1973).

3. COMPENDIUM II OF COPYRIGHT OFFICE PRACTICES § 431 (1984). The compendium goes on to itemizes various features that

are characteristic of drama, namely plot, characters, dialog, and directions for action. *Id.* § 432.

4. Kalem Co. v. Harper Bros., 222 U.S. 55, 61, 32 S.Ct. 20, 56 L.Ed. 92 (1911).

5. 1 PAUL GOLDSTEIN, COPYRIGHT § 2.9.1 at p. 140 (1989).

6. *See supra* § 4.1.

sections of the statute occasionally refer to "nondramatic literary works" and "nondramatic musical works" when drama is meant to be excluded.[7]

Although original dramatic works as a whole are protected by copyright, individual stock scenes, jokes and gags are not by themselves copyrightable subject matter. Under a rule usually called the "scenes a faire" doctrine "sequences of events which normally follow from a common theme,"[8] are not protectable elements of a dramatic work. Thus, in *Walker v. Time Life Films, Inc.,*[9] the court considered whether the movie *Fort Apache: The Bronx* infringed the copyright in a book entitled *Fort Apache*. Both the book and the movie concerned the trials and tribulations of New York City police officers working in the 41st precinct of the South Bronx. In refusing to find infringement, the court remarked, "[e]lements such as drunks, prostitutes, vermin and derelict cars would appear in any realistic work about the work of policemen in the south Bronx. These similarities therefore are unprotectable as 'scenes a faire,' that is, scenes that necessarily result from the choice of a setting or situation."[10] While not a glowing endorsement of life in the South Bronx, this analysis is both widely accepted and, in our view, sound. It would surely hinder subsequent authors if they could only portray the South Bronx as populated by the sober, the law abiding and the chaste.

General plot outlines of dramatic works may also be denied copyright protection through application of the idea/expression principle. While the actual details of a dramatic work like *West Side Story* may not be appropriated without permission, the general idea of the work—young lovers who belong to opposing groups and come to grief because of the group conflict—is freely available for others to use. Deciding just where the line falls between general plot outline and expressive detail is, of course, a vexing and uncertain process. Nonetheless, it is well established as an abstract proposition that the copyright in a dramatic work only covers the expressive elements of that work.

§ 4.4   Pantomimes and Choreographic Works

Although the current copyright statute explicitly mentions pantomimes and choreographic works as a category of protectable subject matter,[1] it does not define those terms. According to the legislative history, the omission was deliberate because the terms have settled, generally accepted meanings.[2] The Copyright Office has, however, de-

7. For instance certain sections providing exceptions to the right to perform a work are limited to nondramatic literary and musical works. *See* 17 U.S.C.A. § 110(2),(3),(4) and (8).

8. Reyher v. Children's Television Workshop, 533 F.2d 87, 91 (2d Cir.), *cert. denied* 429 U.S. 980, 97 S.Ct. 492, 50 L.Ed.2d 588 (1976). *See generally* Leslie A. Kurtz, *Copyright: The Scenes A Faire Doctrine,* 41 FLA. L. REV. 79 (1989).

9. 784 F.2d 44 (2d Cir.1986).

10. *Walker,* 784 F.2d at 50.

§ 4.4

1. 17 U.S.C.A. § 102(a)(4).

2. H.R. Rep. No. 94–1476, 94th Cong. 2d Sess. 53 (1973).

fined each of these terms for its own purposes in handling applications for copyright registration. It defines a pantomime as

> [T]he art of imitating or acting out situations, characters or some other events with gestures and body movement. Mime is included under this category. Pantomimes need not tell a story or be presented before an audience to be protected by copyright.[3]

Choreography is defined quite similarly, as

> [T]he composition and arrangement of dance movements and patterns, and is usually intended to be accompanied by music. Dance is static and kinetic successions of bodily movement in certain rhythmic and spacial relationships. Choreographic works need not tell a story in order to be protected by copyright.[4]

Prior to the copyright act of 1976, U.S. copyright statutes made no explicit reference to either pantomime or choreography. Nonetheless, since a very large number of works of this sort are dramatic in nature, there is considerable overlap with the "dramatic works" category and protection for works of this type that could be labeled "dramatic" was available under earlier statutes.[5] On the other hand, protection for abstract dance would be problematic at best under the 1909 law. Professor Nimmer observes in his treatise that the inclusion of the separate category of pantomime and choreographic works in the current statute implies that non-dramatic renditions of this sort are now also eligible for protection,[6] and that view is reflected in the administrative definitions quoted above which note that the works "need not tell a story." Case law dealing with works of choreography and pantomime is meager.

Of course pantomime and choreography, like all other works of authorship, are only protected when they are original. Thus, while non-dramatic dance steps generally qualify for copyright protection, the legislative history makes it clear that " 'choreographic works' do not include social dance steps and simple routines."[7] Thus one could not claim copyright for the waltz or the tango. One can, however, combine social dance steps in an original fashion and the resulting work would be copyrightable.

Pantomimes and choreographic works must also be "fixed in a tangible medium of expression" in order to qualify for copyright protection. Fixation might be in the form of a motion picture of the dance or pantomime, in the form of a detailed verbal description, or in the form of special choreographic notation which can be used to record the movements of a dance. Any other fixation acceptable under the statute would

3. Compendium II of Copyright Office Practices § 460.01 (1984).

4. *Id.* at § 450.01

5. *See, e.g.* 37 C.F.R. § 202 (1959), which provided that "choreographic works of a dramatic character" would be eligible for copyright registration. *See also* Kalem Co. v. Harper Bros., 222 U.S. 55, 61, 32 S.Ct. 20, 56 L.Ed. 92 (1911), where Justice Holmes noted that "[i]t would be impossible to deny the title of drama to pantomime as played by masters of the art."

6. Nimmer, Copyright § 2.07[B] (2002).

7. H.R. Rep. No. 94–1476, at 54 (1976).

suffice for these works as well. The form of fixation need not rigidly specify every single movement of the dance. The Copyright Office takes the position that "registration will not be refused simply because there is room for improvisation, or because some improvisation is intended."[8]

§ 4.5 Pictorial, Graphic and Sculptural Works

The current copyright statute defines pictorial, graphic and sculptural works as "two-dimensional and three-dimensional works of fine, graphic and applied art, photographs, prints and art reproductions, maps, globes, charts, diagrams, models, and technical drawings, including architectural plans."[1] The range of works covered by this statutory category is quite broad, reaching from the most sophisticated works of fine art to such things as the labels used on various types of consumer goods. Regardless of the type of work at issue, artistic merit is not a requirement for protection. Under the long-standing principle of artistic non-discrimination, neither the courts nor the Copyright Office will deny protection to a work merely because they believe it to be "ugly" or "commercial" or "simplistic."[2] Several types of works in this category deserve special comment.

Maps are one of the many types of works subsumed under the heading of pictorial and graphic works. They have been included as a category of copyrightable subject matter since the very first American copyright law was adopted in 1790, evidencing their importance to the exploration and settlement of the then undeveloped regions of the United States. Much of the content of the typical map is not, however, protected by the copyright. For instance, the place names indicated cannot be monopolized by the first cartographer to prepare a map, and subsequent authors have the right to use those names without any fear of infringement. The key to originality in a map, and hence the key to copyrightability, tends to be the selection of the materials to be included. While there are some cases holding that a map cannot be sufficiently original for copyright purposes unless the author has made direct observation of the geographic features depicted,[3] that view is now widely regarded as unduly restrictive. A cartographer who inspects a variety of textual sources and then selects and arranges the data obtained from them in order to prepare a wholly new map has plainly created an original work of authorship notwithstanding the absence of direct observation of the terrain.[4]

---

8. COMPENDIUM II OF COPYRIGHT OFFICE PRACTICES § 450.07 (1984)

§ 4.5

1. 17 U.S.C.A. § 101.

2. Bleistein v. Donaldson Lithographing Co., 188 U.S. 239, 23 S.Ct. 298, 47 L.Ed. 460 (1903).

3. See Amsterdam v. Triangle Publications, Inc., 189 F.2d 104 (3d Cir.1951).

4. Cases rejecting or questioning the direct observation rule include United States v. Hamilton, 583 F.2d 448 (9th Cir.1978); Andrien v. Southern Ocean County Chamber of Commerce, 927 F.2d 132 (3d Cir. 1991). *See generally* the discussion on compilations in § 4.10 below.

Another type of work falling within the scope of "pictorial" is photographs. Because photographs are produced with the aid of a machine, and because they typically capture some existing reality, like scenery or the image of a group of people, one might doubt whether there is sufficient originality in photographs to justify copyrightability. In *Burrow-Giles Lithographic Co. v. Sarony,*[5] the Supreme Court confronted the issue of whether a photographic portrait could qualify as copyright-protected material. The statute then in effect expressly listed photographs as copyrightable subject matter, but the defendant argued that this provision exceeded the constitutional power of Congress because photographs could not be considered "writings" of "authors" as required by the relevant constitutional clause. The Court rejected that argument and found sufficient authorship in the photographer's posing of the subject, selection of costume and accessories, and arrangement of lighting. Although there is language in *Sarony* suggesting that an "ordinary" photograph might not qualify for protection, cases under both the 1909 Act and the 1976 Act have provided copyright protection for all manner of photographs.[6] Perhaps the most celebrated of these cases is *Time, Inc. v. Bernard Geis Associates,*[7] a district court opinion which held the famous Zapruder film of the the Kennedy assassination to be protected by copyright. The necessary originality in all these cases is thought to inhere in the photographer's choice of subject, camera, film and position from which to shoot, among the many other variables that go into producing a photograph.

Considerably more complex issues of copyrightability are raised by works of "applied art." This subcategory encompasses "all original pictorial, graphic, and sculptural works that are intended to be or have been embodied in useful articles, regardless of factors such as mass production, commercial exploitation, and the potential availability of design patent protection."[8] In other words, these are works that have an artistic or attractive appearance, but that also have a practical purpose. Examples might include such items as candlesticks, salt and pepper shakers, lamps, ash trays, stylized kitchen appliances and the like. The reason these items pose difficulties is that copyright protection does not extend to the utilitarian features of a work.

The policy justification for denying protection to utilitarian works flows from the very nature of copyright. Copyright protection attaches automatically. Under the present statute, protection arises as soon as the work is fixed in a tangible medium of expression. Under the 1909 Act the protection generally arose upon publication with notice. There is no requirement of government examination of the "worth" of the creation before copyright protection becomes available. This is exactly opposite of

5. 111 U.S. 53, 4 S.Ct. 279, 28 L.Ed. 349 (1884).

6. See e.g., Pagano v. Chas. Beseler Co., 234 Fed. 963 (S.D.N.Y.1916) (upholding copyrightability of photography of a library building).

7. 293 F.Supp. 130 (S.D.N.Y.1968).

8. H.R. Rep. No. 94–1476, 94th Cong. 2d Sess. at 54.

the approach used in patent law, where no government protection is available until a patent examiner has determined if the proposed invention meets the statutory standards. If useful objects could be protected by copyright, technology might be withdrawn from the public domain, hindering the commercial activities of others without affording the public any benefit.

For instance, assume that a manufacturer developed a toaster with extra wide slots, to accommodate bagels, thick slices of bread and the like. If a patent were sought on such a toaster it might well be denied on grounds of obviousness.[9] If the appearance of the toaster could be protected by copyright, however, there would be no inquiry into the question of obviousness. There would be no determination of "how good" a technical advance is represented by this wide-slotted toaster. Protection would be automatic. The result is that others would be hindered in their ability to make wide slot toasters.[10]

The evolution of the rule that utilitarian objects cannot be protected by copyright is a bit convoluted. Prior to 1870, the subject matter of American copyright law was sufficiently limited so that the issue did not come up. Even after 1870, when protection was extended for the first time to "statuary" and other three dimensional works, the statute spoke exclusively of the "fine arts."[11] That limitation effectively ruled out any possible controversy over protection for works of applied art. It was only with the elimination of references to "fine arts" in the 1909 Act that individuals began attempting to secure copyright on utilitarian objects.[12]

On its face the 1909 statute did not disqualify an otherwise eligible work from copyright merely because it had "utility." Copyright Office regulations interpreting the 1909 Act, however, contained language suggesting that productions of "industrial arts, utilitarian in purpose and character" would not be accepted for registration.[13] Over time the relevant regulations evolved and by the late 1940's they provided that registration would be permitted for "works of artistic craftsmanship, insofar as their form, but not their mechanical or utilitarian aspects are concerned."[14] By the middle decades of the 20th century, the Copyright Office routinely accepted numerous utilitarian objects for registration because of their artistic "form."

9. 35 U.S.C.A. § 103(a).

10. Others could make wide slot toasters independently without violating any copyright interests, since parallel independent creation is not forbidden under copyright law. But if the first manufacturer's toasters were widely distributed, there would be an inference that a second firm had access to them and thus had copied the design. The risk of litigation would be considerable and there would be a strong deterrent to use of the technology.

11. Act of July 8, 1870, ch. 230 § 86 16 Stat. 198.

12. For a more detailed exposition of this history, *see* Robert C. Denicola, *Applied Art and Industrial Design: A suggested Approach to Copyright in Useful Articles,* 67 Minn. L. Rev. 707, 709–11 (1983).

13. Rules and Regulations for the Registration of Claims to Copyright, Bulletin No. 15 (1910), as quoted in *Mazer v. Stein,* 347 U.S. at 212 n.23.

14. 37 C.F.R. § 202.8(a) (1949).

The story continues in 1954, when the Supreme Court handed down its opinion in *Mazer v. Stein*.[15] The plaintiff in that case had obtained copyright protection for certain statuettes depicting male and female dancing figures. These figures were then used as bases for table lamps. The defendants in the case made copies of the figures to use in their own, competing lamps. In the resulting infringement suit, the defendants argued that where a work of art or artistic craftsmanship is ultimately incorporated into a useful object, the work should not be copyrightable because the exclusive form of protection should be a design patent. The Court rejected the argument, concluding "[w]e find nothing in the copyright statute to support the argument that the intended use or use in industry of an article eligible for copyright bars or invalidates its registration."[16] In other words, the fact that an author intends to, and ultimately does, make a utilitarian use of a work of art does not deprive that work of copyright, assuming that it qualifies as a work of art in the first place. In reaching this conclusion, the Court approved the approach of the Copyright Office regulations mentioned above. It also declared that the presence or absence of a design patent should have no effect on the availability of copyright protection.

In the years immediately following *Mazer* a huge variety of useful articles were presented to the Copyright Office for registration. In response, the Copyright Office yet again modified its regulations. Under the version that came into effect in the mid–1950's:

> If the sole intrinsic function of an article is its utility, the fact that it is unique and attractively shaped will not qualify it as a work of art. However, if the shape of a utilitarian article incorporates features, such as artistic sculpture, carving or pictorial representation, which can be identified separately and are capable of existing independently as a work of art, such features will be eligible for registration.[17]

As tends to be the case in stories of this sort, this solution merely led to further problems. Determining whether the "sole intrinsic" function of an object is utilitarian, or instead whether there were artistic features that could be "identified separately," remained a puzzling challenge. Representative of these difficulties was the decision in *Esquire v. Ringer*,[18] which considered the copyright registrability of a nontraditional, decorative, outdoor lighting fixture. The Copyright Office held that the sole purpose of the fixture was utilitarian and denied registration. Esquire, the designer of the lamp, sued to compel registration. The district court granted the requested relief, reasoning that the useful aspects of the fixture were not its *sole* function, since it also served the function of enhancing the decor of the parking lots where it was mounted. On appeal, the D.C. Circuit reversed, concluding that the

15. 347 U.S. 201, 74 S.Ct. 460, 98 L.Ed. 630 (1954).

16. *Studio,* 347 U.S. at 218.

17. 37 C.F.R. § 202.10(c) (1959).

18. 591 F.2d 796 (D.C.Cir.1978), *cert. denied,* 440 U.S. 908, 99 S.Ct. 1217, 59 L.Ed.2d 456 (1979).

regulation barred registration because "the overall design or configuration of a utilitarian object, even if it is determined by aesthetic as well as functional considerations, is not eligible for copyright."[19] Essentially, the *Esquire* court held that the overall design of a utilitarian object could never be protected by copyright as a sculptural work.

Although the *Esquire* case arose under the 1909 Act, that court opted to consult the text and legislative history of the newly adopted 1976 law for guidance. The drafters of the 1976 Act had attempted to directly confront the question of how to protect the aesthetic elements of pictorial, graphical and sculptural works without protecting utilitarian objects. The 1976 Act ultimately provided:

> the design of a useful article . . . shall be considered a pictorial, graphic, or sculptural work only if, and only to the extent that, such design incorporates pictorial, graphic, or sculptural features that can be identified separately from, and are capable of existing independently of, the utilitarian aspects of the article.

The legislative history of the 1976 Act elaborated on the theme of artistic elements that exist "independently" of utilitarian aspects.[20] It specified that a showing that artistic elements were *either* physically *or* conceptually separable from the utilitarian features of the object would suffice for copyrightability.

At least one part of this test is straightforward. The notion of physical separability is fairly easy to apply in practice. The classic example is the hood ornament of a car. While a car is a "useful article," the hood ornament in the shape, perhaps, of a jaguar, has sculptural features that can be identified separately and can exist independently of the utility of the car. The problem is with the notion of "conceptual" separability.

In the years since the adoption of the 1976 Act several courts have struggled to define the notion of conceptual separability. At the outset, it is important to remember that the issue only arises if we are dealing with a "useful article." These are defined in the statute as articles "having an intrinsic utilitarian function that is not merely to portray the appearance of the article or to convey information."[21] Thus, a sculpture in the shape of a toaster that does not function to actually toast bread has no function except to portray the appearance of a toaster. Hence it is not a useful article, and there is no need for further analysis—it is non-utilitarian and fully copyrightable. On the other hand, if the object

19. *Esquire,* 591 F.2d at 804.

20. The relevant passage of the House Report states "although the shape of an industrial product may be aesthetically satisfying and valuable, the Committee's intention is not to offer it copyright protection under the bill. Unless the shape of an automobile, airplane, ladies' dress, food processor, television set or any other industrial product contains some element that, *physically or conceptually*, can be identified as separable from the utilitarian aspects of that article, the design would not be copyrighted under the bill." H.R. Rep. No. 94–1476, 94th Cong. 2d Sess. 55 (1973) (emphasis supplied).

21. 17 U.S.C.A. § 101.

serves a utilitarian purpose, even in part, only the conceptually separate artistic elements will be protected.

For aesthetically pleasing objects that also serve an intrinsic function, the law is in disarray. Professor Nimmer has suggested that "conceptual separability exists where there is any substantial likelihood that even if the article had no utilitarian use it would still be marketable to some significant segment of the community simply because of its aesthetic qualities."[22] This test has been criticized however, because certain works may incorporate unpopular, but nonetheless legitimate aesthetic elements. Because of their unpopularity presumably no one would buy them and and they would thus fail Nimmer's "marketability" test, despite meeting the criteria for copyright.

In the courts, divergent tests of conceptual separability have been articulated, particularly by the Second Circuit. In *Kieselstein-Cord v. Accessories by Pearl, Inc.,*[23] that court sustained the copyrightability of certain ornate belt buckles made of precious metals. The *Kieselstein* court was influenced by the fact that some owners of the belt buckles used them not to keep their pants up, but as jewelry. The court concluded that the artistic aspects of the buckles, though not physically separable from the utilitarian aspects, were "conceptually" separable.

Later, in *Carol Barnhart Inc. v. Economy Cover Corp.,*[24] the Second Circuit confronted the question of whether to allow copyright protection for various male and female human torso forms with hollowed backs, designed to permit them to be used to display clothing. The court concluded that there was no conceptually separable aesthetic elements to these mannequins. The majority opinion noted that the aesthetic features of the disputed mannequins were "inextricably intertwined" with their utilitarian features, and thus seems to suggest that the aesthetic elements must be wholly unnecessary to the utilitarian function of the object before they can be protected. Judge Newman, in dissent, proposed an alternative test which lead him to the opposite result. In his view "[f]or the design features to be 'conceptually separate' from the utilitarian aspects of the useful article that embodies the design, the article must stimulate in the mind of the beholder a concept that is separate from the concept evoked by its utilitarian function."[25]

Just two years later, a different panel of the judges on the Second Circuit took another stab at this thorny area in *Brandir International, Inc. v. Cascade Pacific Lumber Co.*[26] *Brandir* involved the copyrightability of a curvilinear bicycle rack fashioned from bent tubing. The test in this case seems to focus on the creative process, and the subjective thought processes of the *artist* rather than the *observer*. As the court put it, "where design elements can be identified as reflecting the designer's artistic judgement exercised independently of functional influences, con-

22. NIMMER, COPYRIGHT § 2.08[B] (2002).
23. 632 F.2d 989 (2d Cir.1980).
24. 773 F.2d 411 (2d Cir.1985).
25. *Carol Barnhart,* 773 F.2d at 422.

26. 834 F.2d 1142 (2d Cir.1987). This opinion was written by Judge Oakes, who had also authored the opinion in the *Kieselstein-Cord* belt buckle case.

ceptual separability exists.''[27] Of course, by the time of any litigation, the artist or artisan who designed the disputed object will have more than a little incentive to claim he was influenced by artistic judgment even if that is not the unvarnished truth. This may be a fatal shortcoming of the *Brandir* test.

It should be apparent from these loose standards that conceptual separability analysis remains rather muddled, and that much room for good lawyering exists when arguing such cases. It would seem that many of the close cases can and should be resolved by asking whether granting copyright protection would subvert core values of patent law. If there is any risk of such an outcome, we would think the better course would be to deny the sought-after copyright.

§ 4.6   Motion Pictures and Other Audiovisual Works

Audiovisual works are specifically defined in the 1976 Act. They are "works that consist of a series of related images which are intrinsically intended to be shown by the use of machines or devices such as projectors, viewers or electronic equipment, together with accompanying sounds, if any, regardless of the nature of the material objects, such as films or tapes, in which the works are embodied."[1] All forms of audiovisual works are itemized as copyrightable subject matter under the current statute.

Although an audiovisual work must consist of multiple images that are "related" there is no implication in the statutory language that those images must be shown in a specific sequence. Several courts reached exactly this conclusion in determining that a video game is an audiovisual work. Because of player involvement, each time the game is played, the precise series of images appearing on the screen will differ. There is no set sequence. Nonetheless, all of the images are related, as they depict the same characters or background and integrate with each other to produce the effect of the game. Given this circumstance, they qualify as audiovisual works.[2] The same would be true, of course, for a series of still photographic images arranged to be shown together, as in the case of the usual "slide show." Note that in such a case, each individual image might be separately copyrightable as a pictorial work, while the assemblage of all the slides would qualify for a distinct copyright as an audiovisual work.

The second requirement for an audiovisual work is that it must be "intended to be shown by the use of machines...." Thus, a series of related photographs, mounted in a museum to form a coherent and unified exhibition does not constitute an "audiovisual work" because no machine or device is necessary to show the images.

27. 834 F.3d at 1145.

§ 4.6

1. 17 U.S.C.A. § 101 (2000).

2. *See e.g.,* Midway Mfg. Co. v. Arctic Int'l, Inc., 704 F.2d 1009 1011 (7th Cir.), *cert. denied,* 464 U.S. 823, 104 S.Ct. 90, 78 L.Ed.2d 98 (1983).

Motion pictures are a subtype of audiovisual work, defined in the statute as "works consisting of a series of related images which, when shown in succession, impart an impression of motion, together with accompanying sounds, if any."[3] Since an "impression of motion" is required, certain audiovisual works, like the slide show mentioned in the previous paragraph, do not qualify as motion pictures.

The references to "accompanying sounds" in both of these definitions are important. Combined with language in the definition of sound recordings excluding "the sounds accompanying a motion picture or other audiovisual work," they make it clear that motion picture sound tracks are parts of audiovisual works. This means that several of the limitations on the rights granted to sound recordings do not apply to motion picture sound tracks. For example, the copyright owner will have a performance right in a motion picture soundtrack, where he or she would not have one in a sound recording.[4] Several other important distinctions between these two categories of works are discussed in the chapter dealing with the exclusive rights of copyright owners.

Like all other copyrightable material, audiovisual works must be fixed in a tangible medium of expression. As the statutory language reveals, there is no restriction on the type of objects in which the work may be fixed. Not only are photographic film and videotape adequate, but so are computer chips and other objects that may be developed for this purpose in the future. A pair of controversial cases went so far as to hold that a mechanical teddy bear with its accompanying cassettes that enabled the bear to "move" and "talk" was an audiovisual work, though that result has been criticized by Professor Nimmer.[5]

The creativity requirement for audiovisual works is often satisfied by the underlying material being captured on the film or videotape. The lines spoken by the actors and their inflection and bodily movement are surely creative in a copyright sense. On the other hand, copyright is available for audiovisual works even when the underlying material is not at all creative. For instance, a film of traffic passing by a busy intersection, or of wild buffalo stampeding through the prairie would also qualify for copyright. The creativity in works of this sort lies in decisions made about what types of cameras and films to use, where to place those cameras and a host of other related decisions. It is largely on this basis that the famous Zapruder film of the assassination of President Kennedy was found to constitute a copyrightable audiovisual work.[6]

§ 4.7 Sound Recordings

Copyright protection for sound recordings is a relatively new feature of the American copyright law. Over time, protection for sound record-

3. 17 U.S.C.A. § 101 (2000).

4. *See* § 7.4.1, *infra.*

5. Worlds of Wonder, Inc. v. Vector Intercontinental, Inc., 653 F.Supp. 135 (N.D.Ohio 1986); Worlds of Wonder, Inc. v.

Veritel Learning Sys., Inc., 658 F.Supp. 351 (N.D.Tex.1986).

6. Time, Inc. v. Bernard Geis Assocs., 293 F.Supp. 130, 143 (S.D.N.Y.1968).

ings became essential because of the ease with which record pirates could make cheap unauthorized duplicates of legitimate recordings. Pirates, of course, can undersell legitimate producers because they need not incur expenses for recording studios or for payments to performers. As the problems of piracy became more severe, Congress was moved to act in the early 1970's in advance of the general revision that led to the Copyright Act of 1976. Under the legislation adopted at that time, only those sound recordings first fixed on or after February 15, 1972 are protected by copyright.[1] Recordings fixed prior to that date may be protected under state law, but are not covered by federal copyright.[2] This continues to be true under the current statute.

The current copyright law defines sound recordings as "works that result from the fixation of a series of musical, spoken, or other sounds, but not including the sounds accompanying a motion picture or other audiovisual work, regardless of the nature of the material objects such as disks, tapes, or other phonorecords in which they are embodied,"[3] and provides for their protection by copyright. Sound recordings can include such items as instructional materials in foreign languages, recordings of bird songs or the comedy routine of a popular stand-up comic. Most of the time, however, they consist of captured performances of musical works. By statutory definition, sound recordings can only be fixed in material objects called "phonorecords."[4] Phonorecords include such objects as vinyl records, compact discs, cassette or reel-to-reel tapes, and any other material object that can be used to capture sounds.

The copyright interest in a sound recording is distinct from both the ownership of the physical objects in which it is embodied, and from the separate copyright that might exist in any underlying musical work captured in that sound recording. For instance, assume that Smith writes a musical composition called the Copyright Ballad. Thereafter, Acme Recording hires The Jones Band to make a recording of the Copyright Ballad, after obtaining permission to do so from Smith, the composer. Acme ultimately produces compact discs containing the Jones Band version of the song and sells them to the public. Green buys one of these CD's for her collection. Smith owns the copyright in the musical

§ 4.7

1. Sound Recording Amendment, P.L. 92–140, 85 Stat. 391 (1971).

2. The 1976 Act provides that "[w]ith respect to sound recording fixed before February 15, 1972, any rights or remedies under the common law or statute of any State shall not be annulled or limited by this title until February 15, 2047. The preemptive provisions of [section 301(a)] shall apply to any such rights and remedies pertaining to any cause of action arising from undertakings commenced on and after February 15, 2047.... [N]o sound recording fixed before February 15, 1972, shall be subject to copyright under this title before, on, or after February 15, 2047." Under this provision, pre–1972 sound recordings continue to receive whatever state protections may be available until the middle of the next century. Thereafter those state protections are pre-empted and the recording are effectively injected into the public domain.

3. 17 U.S.C.A. § 101 (2000).

4. Phonorecords are defined in the statute as "material objects in which sounds, other than those accompanying a motion picture or other audiovisual work, are fixed by any method now know or later developed and from which the sounds can be perceived, reproduced or otherwise communicated, either directly or with the aid of a machine or device." 17 U.S.C.A. § 101.

composition called the Copyright Ballad. Acme owns the copyright in a sound recording consisting of the Jones Band's aural version of that song. Green owns the individual disc, which is a type of "phonorecord" in copyright parlance. If Green were to start making "bootleg" copies of the CD and selling them to her friends, she would infringe two separate copyright interests—that of Smith in the musical work and that of Acme in the sound recording.

Like all categories of protected works, sound recordings only qualify for protection when they are original. Indeed, the legislative history points out that no protection will be available when "sounds are fixed by some purely mechanical means without originality of any kind...."[5] Originality can flow from either the contributions of performers, whose performance is captured in the sound recording, or from contributions of the party who sets up the recording session and makes the decision about how to capture the sounds, and then compiles and edits them into a final work. While two singers may sing the exact same song note for note, each will bring to it their own vocal stylings and thus each would possess "originality" in the copyright sense. The same point applies to sound recordings of works other than musical compositions. For instance, consider "books on tape." Two different actors—say William Shatner and Sir Lawrence Olivier—might both record versions of a novel. Because of differences in inflection and dramatic intonation, each version would be original and both would qualify for a sound recording copyright. Similarly, while two sound engineers or recording companies may decide to record the same song, the placement of microphones, the choice of acoustical setting, and decisions about how to capture and edit the results will yield two different, and original, sound recordings, each entitled to copyright protection.

As is developed elsewhere in this text, sound recordings receive more limited protections under copyright law than do most other types of works.[6] Most notably, the owner of a copyright in a sound recording does not have the right to prevent others from publicly performing the work.[7] This feature of the law is controversial, however, and the law is otherwise in most other nations of the world. There is a not insubstantial chance that Congress will eventually extend a performance right to sound recordings. Another significant limitation upon copyright in sound recordings is that these works are protected only against duplication of the work through mechanical means, such as a tape recorder. No matter how closely one band tracks a protected sound recording by imitating the earlier rendition, an independently fixed second version does not infringe the copyright in the first sound recording.[8]

---

5. H.R. Rep. No. 92–487, 92d Cong., 1st Sess. 6 (1971).

6. *See supra* § 4.7.

7. Recent amendments to the 1976 Act have granted the owners of copyrights in sound recordings a limited exclusive right to publicly perform the work by digital means. *See* 17 U.S.C.A. §§ 106(6), 114 (2000).

8. 17 U.S.C.A. § 114.

§ 4.8 Architectural Works

An architectural work is defined in the current version of the copyright act as "the design of a building as embodied in any tangible medium of expression, including a building, architectural plans, or drawings."[1] This definition did not appear in the original text of the 1976 copyright act, nor were architectural works among the listed types of protectable works of authorship when Congress adopted the current law. Congress added the definition and the category "architectural works" to the list of protected subject matter in 1990, in partial response to the decision of the United States to ratify the international copyright treaty known as the Berne Convention.[2]

Prior to the 1990 amendments, there was a crucial distinction between architectural plans and models on the one hand, and actual structures on the other. Plans, such as blueprints, were considered "pictorial" works, and thus fully eligible for copyright protection.[3] The same was true for three-dimensional scale models of buildings and other architectural works. Actual buildings, however, were considered "utilitarian" because they functioned to shelter humans, animals or equipment.[4] Thus, it was not considered an infringement of the copyright in architectural plans to erect a building corresponding to those plans, so long as no copies of the plans themselves were made. Similarly, it was not infringement to inspect an already existing building, take measurements, and then duplicate it by building an identical building elsewhere.

During this pre–1990 period, courts did grant copyright protection to full-size, three-dimensional works of architecture that served purely decorative or aesthetic purposes, such as monuments or funeral markers, precisely because they did not have any "utility" other than their aesthetic purposes.[5] It was also true, prior to 1990, that individual decorative elements on a building could be protected, as they were effectively nothing more than sculptural works. The classic example is a gargoyle, placed on a building for purely ornamental effect. Nonetheless, the bottom line remained that no protection would be afforded for the overall appearance of a building, no matter how striking or aesthetically pleasing.

Effective in 1989, the United States decided, at long last, to adhere to the Berne Convention, an international copyright scheme that had been in existence since 1886. Article 2 of that Convention requires the

---

§ 4.8

1. 17 U.S.C.A. § 101 (2000).

2. The Architectural Works Copyright Protection Act is Title VII of the Judicial Improvements Act of 1990, P.L. 101–650, 104 Stat. 5089, and it became effective on December 1, 1990.

3. *See e.g.,* Imperial Homes Corp. v. Lamont, 458 F.2d 895, 899 (5th Cir.1972); Herman Frankel Org. v. Tegman, 367 F.Supp. 1051 (E.D.Mich.1973); Aitken, Haz-

en, Hoffman, Miller P.C. v. Empire Constr. Co., 542 F.Supp. 252 (D.Neb.1982); Demetriades v. Kaufmann, 680 F.Supp. 658 (S.D.N.Y.1988). *See also* H.R. Rep. No. 94–1476, 94th Cong. 2d Sess. 53 (1976).

4. For discussion of the reasons for, and the history of, denial of protection to utilitarian works, *see supra* § 4.5.

5. *See e.g.,* Jones Bros. v. Underkoffler, 16 F.Supp. 729 (M.D.Pa.1936).

participating member states to afford protection to, among other things, architectural works.[6] Though certain changes in U.S. law were made in 1988 in anticipation of U.S. adherence to Berne, no action was taken concerning architectural works at that time, pending the results of a review of the subject by the Copyright Office. That review was completed in mid–1989, and shortly thereafter Congress adopted the Architectural Works Protection Act of 1990. As noted, this legislation extended copyright protection to completed buildings and provided a new, comprehensive definition of architectural works. Under that definition, "[t]he work includes the overall form as well as the arrangement and composition of spaces and elements in the design, but does not include individual standard features."

The legislative history clarifies a number of points about this new category of works. First, it makes it clear that buildings include not only habitable structures, but also "structures that are used, but not inhabited by human beings, such as churches, pergolas, gazebos, and garden pavilions." On the other hand, structures such as bridges, dams, cloverleafs, overpasses and the like are not meant to be included within the ambit of protectible subject matter.[7] The legislative history also states explicitly that the separability test, which has caused so much difficulty in defining the limits of copyright for most works of applied art,[8] is inapplicable to architectural works, and that "the aesthetically pleasing overall shape of an architectural work could be protected...."[9]

This new, expanded protection for works of architecture applies to any works first created after December 1, 1990, and to any works that were unconstructed on that date and embodied in unpublished plans or drawings. In the latter case, however, protection expired on December 31, 2002, unless the work had been constructed by that date.[10]

§ 4.9 Derivative Works

The Copyright Act also acknowledges so-called "derivative works" as within the subject matter eligible for copyright protection. A derivative work is defined in the statute as "a work based upon one or more preexisting works, such as a translation, musical arrangement, dramatization, fictionalization, motion picture version, sound recording, art reproduction, abridgment, condensation, or any other form in which a work may be recast, transformed, or adapted. A work consisting of editorial revisions annotations, elaborations or other modifications which, as a whole represent an original work of authorship is a deriva-

---

6. More specifically, Article 2(6) provides that "works mentioned in this Article shall enjoy protection in all countries of the Union," and Article 2(1) provides that "the expression 'literary and artistic works' shall include...illustrations, maps, plans, sketches and three-dimensional works relative to geography, topography, architecture or science."

7. H.R. Rep. No. 101–735, 101st Cong. 2d Sess. at 19–20.

8. *See supra* § 4.5.

9. H.R. Rep. 101–735, 101st Cong., 2d Sess. 20–21 (1990).

10. § 706, Pub. Law 101–650, 104 Stat. 5089 (1990).

tive work.''[1] As a result, the Copyright Act provides that a work that is based in substantial part upon a pre-existing work may itself obtain independent copyright protection, provided that the derivative work fulfills the requirement of originality. In addition, for a valid copyright in a derivative work to exist, the derivative work author must either base his work upon a public domain source, or obtain permission from the owner of the copyright of the underlying work on which it is based.[2]

In some sense, of course, almost every work borrows to some degree from the cultural traditions in which the work originated.[3] Not all works of authorship are derivative works within the meaning of the Copyright Act, however. Use of the term "derivative work" implies a substantial copying of expressive material (not just ideas) from a particular prior work. As explained by Professor Nimmer, a work is considered a derivative work only if it would be judged to infringe the original work on which it was based if that first work were not in the public domain and there was no permission to use it. What allows the derivative work to obtain copyright protection, and simultaneously protects the derivative work author from infringing another's copyright, is that the original work was used with permission or had already entered the public domain.[4]

The scope of protection in a derivative work copyright extends only to the additional materials created by the creator of the derivative work.[5] The derivative work copyright implies no exclusive right in the pre-existing material employed in the work.[6] Nor does the derivative work copyright "affect or enlarge the scope, duration, ownership, or subsistence of, any copyright protection in the pre-existing material."[7]

The Copyright Act also stipulates that "protection for a work employing pre-existing material in which copyright subsists does not extend to any part of the work in which such material has been used unlawfully."[8] This provision establishes a relationship between the copyrightability of a derivative work and the copyright associated with pre-existing work. A "second generation" work only obtains copyright protection as a derivative work if the later work was used with permission of the copyright holder, or if the later work was part of the public domain.

Consider, for example, the novel *Alice in Wonderland*, first published by Reverend Charles Lutwidge Dodgson under the pseudonym Lewis Carroll. As *Alice in Wonderland* was first published in 1865, its copyright expired long ago. Any movie studio can produce a feature film based upon Dodgson's novel without running afoul of the copyright laws. Such a film would be considered a derivative work of the public domain novel

§ 4.9
1. 17 U.S.C.A. § 101 (2000).
2. 17 U.S.C.A. § 103(a) (2000).
3. *See* Emerson v. Davies, 8 F.Cas. 615 (C.C.D.Mass.1845).
4. Nimmer, Copyright § 3.01 (2002).

5. 17 U.S.C.A. § 103(b) (2000).
6. 17 U.S.C.A. § 103(b) (2000).
7. 17 U.S.C.A. § 103(b) (2000).
8. 17 U.S.C.A. § 103(a) (2000).

because it would closely track the plot details of the book and maybe even use exact language from the book as part of the film's dialogue. While a distinct copyright would exist in this movie, Dodgson's novel retains its public domain status. Another studio would be free to consult the public domain source in order to produce its own independently copyrighted movie, but could not copy the original elements in the first movie, such as original dialogue.

As with other sorts of protected works of authorship, derivative works must fulfill the standard of originality in order to quality for copyright protection. In the context of derivative works, originality will be assessed in terms of the contribution the additional material makes to the pre-existing work. The additional material must recast, transform or adapt the pre-existing work.[9] If the additional material makes only a trivial contribution to the pre-existing work, then no separate derivative copyright will be established.

In *Lee v. A.R.T. Company*,[10] the Court of Appeals for the Seventh Circuit considered the originality standard with regard to derivative works. Lee created certain works of visual art that were embodied in notecards and small lithographs. A.R.T. Company purchased Lee's works, mounted them on ceramic tiles, and resold them. Lee contended that the ceramic tiles were derivative works within the meaning of the Copyright Act. Because the Copyright Act provides the copyright owner with the exclusive right to make derivative works—the so-called adaptation right of § 106(2)—then A.R.T. Company would have been an infringer.

The Seventh Circuit rejected Lee's contention. Judge Easterbrook reasoned that merely mounting copyrighted notecards and lithographs did not recast, transform or adapt them. Although the art was bonded to a ceramic slab, it depicted the same image without alteration. To accept Lee's position would seemingly lead to the result that anyone who wrote on one of the notecards, or placed a frame on a lithograph, would require Lee's permission and, even more curiously, would have a separate copyright in the item if they had acted with Lee's permission. Judge Easterbrook acknowledged that a prior decision of the Ninth Circuit, *Mirage Editions, Inc. v. Albuquerque A.R.T. Co.*,[11] had reached a contrary result on similar facts. The Seventh Circuit nonetheless refused to extend the concept of derivative works to provide a means for authors to block any modification of their works of authorship of which they disapprove.

If tile mounting does not yield a separate copyright as a derivative work, what steps would? An original arrangement of a traditional song has been held to be subject to copyright protection as a derivative work.[12] So has "panning and scanning" of a public domain film, a technique that alters the rectangular, widescreen version of a cinema film so that it was

9. 17 U.S.C.A. § 101 (2000).
10. 125 F.3d 580 (7th Cir.1997).
11. 856 F.2d 1341 (9th Cir.1988).

12. Plymouth Music Co. v. Magnus Organ Corp., 456 F.Supp. 676 (S.D.N.Y.1978).

more readily viewed on a square TV display.[13] Some courts have spoken of the standard of originality for derivative works as one of "distinguishable variation" from the underlying work. Under this standard, a trivial variation will not fulfill the originality standard, but a difference that renders the derivative work distinguishable from the original in any meaningful manner suffices.[14]

§ 4.10   Compilations

A compilation is a "work formed by the collection and assembling of preexisting materials or of data that are selected, coordinated, or arranged in such a way that the resulting work as a whole constitutes and original work of authorship."[1] Compilations are specifically listed as copyrightable subject matter under the 1976 statute.[2] The pre-existing materials that are gathered together to form the compilation can consist of either items that are independently copyrightable as well—such as poems, for instance—or of material that is not within the subject matter of copyright—such as population data for every city in the world with over 10,000 inhabitants. In other words, one might think of compilations as encompassing works such as anthologies, almanacs and even computerized data bases. Compilations of the anthology type are also known as "collective works," a term separately defined in the statute as a "work, such as a periodical issue, anthology or encyclopedia, in which a number of contributions, constituting separate and independent works in themselves are assembled into a collective whole."[3] Thus the typical issue of a law review and the typical law school casebook are "collective works."

Naturally, if one wishes to prepare a compilation consisting of copyrighted works, it is necessary to obtain permission to use each of those works first. Thus if one put together a volume of newspaper stories concerning the terror attacks of September 11, 2001, without obtaining permission from the copyright holder of each story, copyright in the compilation would be unavailable and the compiler would be liable for infringement. The statute makes this plain by providing, "The subject matter of copyright ... includes compilations ... but protection for a work employing preexisting material in which copyright subsists does not extend to any part of the work in which such material has been used unlawfully."[4] If only small portions of pre-existing works are included in the compilation, however, the use of those small portions might not be "unlawful" because of the availability of the fair use doctrine, and thus the validity of the compilation copyright would remain unaffected.

It follows from the foregoing that the copyright interest in a compilation is separate from any copyrights that might exist in the individual

13. Maljack Prods. v. UAV Corp., 964 F.Supp. 1416, 1426–28 (C.D.Cal.1997), *aff'd on other grounds*, 160 F.3d 1223 (9th Cir. 1998).

14. Alfred Bell & Co. v. Catalda Fine Arts, 191 F.2d 99 (2d Cir.1951).

§ 4.10

1. 17 U.S.C.A. § 101 (2000).
2. 17 U.S.C.A. § 103 (2000).
3. 17 U.S.C.A. § 101 (2000).
4. 17 U.S.C.A. § 103 (2000).

works that comprise it. However, in order for the compilation to qualify for this separate copyright protection, it, like all other works must satisfy the statutory requirement of originality. The historical difficulty with works of this sort has been determining what is original about a work that consists entirely of either pre-existing materials or of non-copyrightable facts.

For a number of years, some courts found the requisite originality for compilations in the fact that the author had invested effort in putting the compilation together. This was frequently referred to as the "sweat of the brow" or "industrious collection" test. In older cases this was the basis upon which copyright in directories, particularly phone directories had been sustained.[5] Indeed, those cases often extended copyright to forbid not only the reproduction of the compilation as a whole, but also the use of component pieces of data in the protected compilation despite rearrangement of that data into a new format. The courts apparently felt that the only way to preserve incentives for parties to invest effort in creating such works was to force others to return to original sources rather than "piggy-back" on the work previously done by the first author.[6]

It was only in 1991 that the Supreme Court addressed the nature of the originality requirement for compilations in *Feist Publications, Inc. v. Rural Telephone Service Co.*[7] Rural, the original plaintiff in that case, was a local telephone company that had published a white pages telephone directory, as it was required to do under Kansas law. Rural was able to obtain the name, address and phone number information for its directory from its own customer listings. Feist was a publisher of "wide-area" telephone directories that aggregated into a single volume the telephone listings for consumers in a large number of separate service areas. When it sought to produce a directory that included Rural's service area, Rural refused to grant Feist permission to use its listings. Feist then went ahead and used Rural's information anyway. A total of 1300 listings were copied verbatim, four of which were actually fictitious listings that had been inserted by Rural to detect copying.

The Court ultimately held that Rural's directory lacked sufficient originality to be copyrightable. The Court noted that the individual facts in the directory could not, in and of themselves, be protected by copyright. According to the Court any originality in a factual compilation must be found in the selection, coordination, and arrangement of the facts in that compilation, and protection extends only to those elements and not the underlying facts themselves. The Court specifically repudiat-

---

5. *See e.g.,* Leon v. Pacific Telephone & Telegraph Co., 91 F.2d 484 (9th Cir.1937); Jeweler's Circular Publishing Co. v. Keystone Publishing Co., 281 F. 83, *cert. denied,* 259 U.S. 581, 42 S.Ct. 464, 66 L.Ed. 1074 (1922).

6. *See e.g.,* Illinois Bell Tel. Co. v. Haines and Co., Inc., 683 F.Supp. 1204

(N.D.Ill.1988) ("a compiler commits copyright infringement if he copies the original compiler's information without conducting an independent canvass"), *aff'd,* 905 F.2d 1081 (7th Cir.1990).

7. 499 U.S. 340, 111 S.Ct. 1282, 113 L.Ed.2d 358 (1991).

ed the "sweat of the brow" test, holding that the work invested in compiling the data could not, by itself, warrant copyright protection.

Regarding Rural's directory, the Court found the "selection" unoriginal because Rural simply included every single name within the designated service area. The "arrangement" was similarly unoriginal because, as the Court put it, "there is nothing remotely creative about arranging names alphabetically in a white pages directory. It is an age-old practice, firmly rooted in tradition and so commonplace that it has come to be expected a as a matter of course."[8] Hence, the Court concluded that Rural's directory was "a garden-variety white pages directory, devoid of even the slightest trace of creativity,"[9] and was not eligible for copyright.

Feist, of course, does not mean that all or even most factual compilations are not copyrightable. To the contrary, most such works should be able to demonstrate the requisite creativity. In post-*Feist* litigation, for instance, a yellow pages directory was found protectable because of the creativity involved in the categorization and arrangement of the listings.[10] What *Feist* does is to eliminate any remaining confusion over the status of the ill-founded sweat of the brow doctrine, and ground compilation copyright analysis in the same concepts of originality as govern all other types of work.

§ 4.11   Non–Copyrightable Subject Matter

4.11.1   Works Prepared by the U.S. Government

Copyright protection is not available for any work of the U.S. government. As specified in § 105, the U.S. government cannot claim copyright in works prepared by government employees in the course of duties of their employment. Statutes, judicial opinions, regulations, reports, manuals and similar works prepared by federal government employees within the scope of their official duties will therefore fall within the public domain. Section 105 does, however, allow the U.S. government to receive and hold copyrights transferred to it by assignment, bequest, or otherwise.

By its own terms, section 105 does not apply to state and local governments. On the theory that what is not denied is permissible, some state and local government entities have sometimes asserted that works created by their officials are subject to copyright.[1] The courts have often been hostile to such claims, however, reasoning that citizens must have

8. 499 U.S. at 363.

9. 499 U.S. at 362.

10. *See, e.g.,* Key Publications, Inc. v. Chinatown Today Publishing Enterprises, Inc., 945 F.2d 509 (2d Cir.1991).

§ 4.11

1. *See* Va. Code Ann. § 9–77.8 (A) (1998) (providing that "[a]ll parts of any code published or authorized to be publish-

ed ... including statute text, regulation text, catchlines, historical citations, numbers of sections, articles, chapters and titles, frontal analyses and revisor's notes, shall become and remain the exclusive property of the Commonwealth...."). *See generally,* Irina Y. Dmitrieva, *State Ownership of Copyrights in Primary Law Materials,* 23 Hastings Comm. & Ent. L.J. 81 (2000).

access to the laws governing them.[2] Moreover, works prepared by state and local government employees acting in the scope of their employment would be work made for hire, and thus any copyright would belong to the state or locality as an entity. In a democratic society, these entities both represent and serve the people. It thus strikes your authors as entirely appropriate that citizens should be free to reproduce such governmental works without having to pay an economic toll to do so.

4.11.2 Fonts and Typefaces

A House Committee Report accompanying the 1976 Act addressed typeface designs as follows:

> The committee has considered, but chosen to defer, the possibility of protecting the design of typefaces. A "typeface" can be defined as a set of letters, numbers, or other symbolic characters, whose forms are related by repeating design elements consistently applied in a notational system and are intended to be embodied in articles whose intrinsic utilitarian function is for use in composing text or other cognizable combinations of characters. The committee does not regard the design of a typeface, as thus defined, to be a copyrightable "pictorial, graphic, or sculptural work" within the meaning of this bill and the application of the dividing line in section 101.[3]

Copyright Office regulations are in accord with this statement, expressly disallowing registration of typeface as well as "mere variations of typographical ornamentation, lettering or coloring."[4] The Court of Appeals for the Fourth Circuit upheld these regulations in *Eltra Corp. v. Ringer*.[5] The court squarely held that "typeface had never been considered entitled to copyright" and refused to issue a writ of mandamus compelling the Register of Copyrights to register the plaintiff's copyright claim.[6]

Although this *per se* rule seems clear enough, commentators have cast doubt upon it.[7] The proposition that a typeface design may constitute a work of art seems beyond reasonable dispute. Any user of a modern word processing program also knows that a choice of typeface is often based upon aesthetic considerations. Although Congress and the Copyright Office may be motivated by concerns that typeface is utilitarian, the statutory definition of the phrase "useful article" is "an article having an intrinsic utilitarian function that is not merely to portray the appearance of the article or to convey information."[8] Typefaces would seem to fall directly within this latter exception. Despite this logic, the rule denying typefaces a place within the copyright system is of long standing and will likely be retained for the foreseeable future. Moreover

---

2. *See* Veeck v. Southern Building Code Congress Int'l, 293 F.3d 791 (5th Cir.2002).

3. H.R. Rep. No. 94–1476, 94th Cong., 2d. Sess. 56 (1976).

4. 37 C.F.R. § 202.1

5. 579 F.2d 294 (4th Cir.1978).

6. *Id.* at 298.

7. NIMMER, COPYRIGHT § 2.15 (2002).

8. 17 U.S.C.A. § 100 (2000).

it does not seem to have greatly impeded creativity in the development of new and appealing font designs.

4.11.3 Titles and Short Phrases

It is a traditional rule that copyright may not be claimed in words and short phrases, including names, titles and slogans.[9] Given that words such as "Supercalifragilisticexpialidocious"[10] and titles such as "Chew Toy of the Gnat Gods: Reflections on the Wildlife of the Southeast Coast"[11] appear to be original writings within the meaning of the Constitution, this result may appear surprising. Still, the courts and the Copyright Office have apparently reasoned that such writings are too minimal to constitute works of authorship.[12] Protection for titles and short phrases may, however, be available under the "passing off" theory of the unfair competition law.[13] In addition, short phrases that qualify as trademark slogans may be registered under the Lanham Act.[14]

4.11.4 Blank Forms

Both the regulations of the U.S. Copyright Office and various judicial decisions indicate that blank forms are not copyrightable subject matter. Thus, the Copyright Office will not register claims for "blank forms, such as time cards, graph paper, account books, diaries, bank checks, scorecards, address books, report forms, order forms and the like, which are designed for recording information and do not in themselves convey information."[15]

The basis for this view is rooted in the celebrated case of *Baker v. Selden*[16], discussed in section 3.3 of the previous chapter in connection with the rule that copyright does not protect ideas. The defendant in that case was making use of certain accounting forms similar to those that were included in plaintiff's book about a new accounting system. The *Baker* Court reasoned that while the text of the book was clearly protected by copyright, the forms themselves were not, because without the forms no one could use the accounting system disclosed by the book. As the Court put it, "[t]he description of the art in a book, though entitled to the benefit of copyright, lays no foundation for an exclusive claim to the art itself. The object of the one is explanation; the object of the other is use."[17]

Cases down to the present have continued this approach. For instance, in *Bibbero Systems, Inc. v. Colwell Systems, Inc.*[18] the plaintiff claimed copyright infringement of a type of medical insurance claim

---

9. 37 C.F.R. § 202.1(a).

10. RICHARD M. SHERMAN AND ROBERT B. SHERMAN, SUPERCALIFRAGILISTICEXPIALIDOCIOUS.

11. BRUCE LOMBARDO, CHEW TOY OF THE GNAT GODS: REFLECTIONS ON THE WILDLIFE OF THE SOUTHEAST COAST (1997).

12. *See* Russ VerSteeg, *Rethinking Originality*, 34 WILLIAM & MARY L. REV. 801, 881 (1993).

13. *See* § 29.5, *infra*.

14. *See* § 27.2.1, *infra*.

15. 37 C.F.R. § 202.1(c).

16. 101 U.S. 99, 25 L.Ed. 841 (1879).

17. 101 U.S. at 105.

18. 893 F.2d 1104 (9th Cir.1990).

form called a "superbill." The bulk of the forms consisted of lengthy lists of medical diagnoses and treatments, corresponding to categories specified by the American Medical Association, along with accompanying code numbers. There were about two dozen different forms corresponding to different areas of medical specialization. Although the plaintiff had been granted a copyright registration on the forms by the Copyright Office, the Ninth Circuit held that these forms were not copyrightable, noting that "[t]he purpose of Bibbero's superbill is to record information. Until the superbill is filled out, it conveys no information about the patient, the patient's diagnosis, or the patient's treatment.... The superbill is simply a blank form which gives doctors a convenient method for recording services performed. The fact that there is a great deal of printing on the face of the form—because there are many possible diagnoses and treatments—does not make the form any less blank."[19]

19.   893 F.2d at 1107–08.

Chapter 5

PUBLICATION AND FORMALITIES

Table of Sections

---

§ 5.1 Publication

Under the Copyright Act of 1909, publication formed the crucial dividing line between protection under state common law and protection under the federal statute. Before publication, an author whose work was reproduced without his or her permission could maintain a cause of action for infringement of "common law copyright" under the law of his or her home state. There was no time limit on this right. The "common law copyright" was perpetual—it endured as long as the author kept the work unpublished. Moreover, federal law simply did not apply to unpublished works in most cases. After publication *with proper copyright notice* federal protection of the work replaced the common law remedy.[1] It is for this reason that common law copyright under the regime of the 1909 (and previous) copyright acts was sometimes also referred to as a "right of first publication."[2]

Under the 1909 Act system publication *without* notice was considered "divestitive" and injected the work into the public domain.[3] The

§ 5.1

1. 1909 Act, § 10.

2. *See, e.g.,* Stanley v. C.B.S., 35 Cal.2d 653, 221 P.2d 73 (1950).

3. In the U.S. law, the rule was first laid down in the landmark opinion of Wheaton v. Peters, 33 U.S. (8 Pet.) 591, 8 L.Ed. 1055 (1834). For a more recent example of divestitive publication see Bell v. Combined Reg-

rationale for this doctrine was that once an author forgoes the privacy of the work in favor of commercial exploitation, that author should be forced to enter into the tradeoff of federal copyright law—statutory protection, but only for a limited term—rather than continue to enjoy the indefinite protection of common law copyright.[4]

Two observations about this scheme seem to leap out. First, it constituted a very severe trap for the unwary, because of the extreme consequences of publishing a work without notice. Second, by virtue of those extreme consequences, it suggests that significant judicial time would be devoted to developing and refining the concept of "publication." As we shall see, the courts did indeed struggle to formulate such a definition, but it is not at all clear that they succeeded. This left the law both draconian and confused.

Not surprisingly, the authors of the 1976 Act decided to drain the publication concept of some of its importance. They did this by moving the dividing line between common law and federal statutory protection backwards, from the moment of publication to the moment of fixation of the work. Under the current statute, once a work is written down or otherwise fixed, federal protection attaches regardless of whether the work is published or not. State common law copyright for *fixed* works is explicitly pre-empted.[5]

Despite this change, publication continues to remain an important concept under the 1976 Act. First, a work first published prior to 1978 without the legally required notice does not regain any protection under the new act. Having been injected into the public domain by a divestitive publication, it cannot be withdrawn from the public domain. Consequently, controversies continue to arise today concerning the copyright status of older works, which turn on whether those were "published" without notice.

Second, even after Congress enacted the 1976 Act, publication without notice could still work a forfeiture of copyright. The new statute did, however, liberalize matters somewhat by providing several methods for "curing" the deficiency and thus avoiding the forfeiture.[6] It was only when the U.S. adhered to the Berne Copyright Convention and adopted the Berne Convention Implementation Act of 1988[7] that this pitfall was entirely eliminated. For works published after March 1, 1989, the absence of a copyright notice will not affect the validity of the copyright.

istry Co., 397 F.Supp. 1241 (N.D.Ill.1975) (distribution of copies of poem *Desiderata* to members of U.S. military held to work a forfeiture where copies lacked notice). *See generally* Howard B. Abrams, *The Historic Foundations of American Copyright Law: Exploding the Myth of Common Law Copyright,* 29 WAYNE L. R. 1119 (1983).

4. As Professor Nimmer puts it, "upon an author receiving the rewards that flow from the exploitation of his work he must make his treaty with the public by subjecting his work to the limited monopoly of statutory copyright." NIMMER, COPYRIGHT § 4.07 at 4–39 (2002).

5. 17 U.S.C.A. § 30 (2000). States can continue to protect unfixed works (such as impromptu speeches or musical improvisations) through their common law. See the discussion of fixation at § 3.2 *supra.*

6. 17 U.S.C.A. §§ 405–406 (2000).

7. Berne Convention Implementation Act, Pub. L. No. 100–568, 102 Stat. 2853 (1988).

Finally, publication still remains of significance in the post–1989 era for a variety of other reasons. Professor Nimmer itemizes over a dozen features of the current, post–1989, American copyright regime where publication remains important.[8] Moreover publication is also important in the international context. Under the major international copyright treaty, the Berne Convention, it is *publication* of a work in one participating state that triggers the obligations of other states to afford the work the same copyright protection as it would to works published in its own territory.[9]

Despite its central importance to the scheme created by the 1909 Act, that statute did not contain a definition of publication, leaving it to the courts to work out the notion on a case by case basis—something they were able to do with only partial success. Professor Nimmer attempted to synthesize this pre–1978 case law in his well-know treatise on copyright law. His oft-quoted[10] formulation is that publication occurred "when by consent of the copyright owner, the original or tangible copies of a work are sold, leased, loaned, given away, or otherwise made available to the general public, or when an authorized offer is made to dispose of the work in any such manner even if a sale or other such disposition does not in fact occur."[11]

One of the key aspects of the law of publication as it evolved under the 1909 act was the distinction between a "limited" and a "general" publication. A limited publication is one "which communicates the contents of a manuscript to a definitely selected group and for a limited purpose, without the right of diffusion, reproduction, distribution or sale."[12] For example, if a law professor were to prepare a draft of a law review article on the law of publication under the 1909 Act, and to circulate that manuscript to 10 colleagues at a variety of other schools for comment, with the implicit understanding that no further copies would be made, that would be merely a limited publication. Consequently, even under the strict rules of the 1909 Act, dissemination of that law review article manuscript *without notice* would not cause a forfeiture of copyright. In other words, only a general publication could be divestitive. The distinction was no doubt developed to ameliorate the harshness of consequences when authors inadvertently omitted notice from publicly circulated copies.

---

8. Nimmer, Copyright § 4.01[A] at 4–4 and 4–5 (2002). Among the situations in the statute where publication remains important are the measuring periods for terminating certain transfers, the durational period for works made for hire and certain other works, limitations on performance rights in certain dramatic works, and rules concerning the availability of statutory damages for infringement of unregistered works. These various publication-dependant rules are developed elsewhere in this text, in the sections that cover the relevant topics.

9. *See* Berne Convention, Art. 5(1).

10. *See e.g.* Bartok v. Boosey & Hawkes, Inc., 523 F.2d 941, 945 (2d Cir.1975); Bell v. Combined Registry Co., 397 F.Supp. 1241 (N.D.Ill.1975) *aff'd*, 536 F.2d 164 (7th Cir. 1976).

11. Nimmer, Copyright, § 4.04 at 4–14 (2002).

12. Intown Enters., Inc. v. Barnes, 721 F.Supp. 1263, 1265 (N.D.Ga.1989). *See also* White v. Kimmell, 193 F.2d 744 (9th Cir.),, *cert. denied*, 343 U.S. 957, 72 S.Ct. 1052, 96 L.Ed. 1357 (1952).

The key aspects of the limited publication doctrine were the requirements that distribution be limited to a "selected group" and that it be for a "limited purpose." As one court put it, for publication to be limited the distribution must be "restricted both as to persons and purpose."[13] Because general publication without notice could have such serious consequences, however, courts often stretched to find the foregoing requirements satisfied. Perhaps the best known example of this is *King v. Mister Maestro, Inc.,*[14] concerning the copyright to Dr. Martin Luther King's famous "I Have A Dream" speech given at the Lincoln Memorial during the 1963 March on Washington. Prior to delivering the speech, Dr. King delivered a copy of it to the press liaison personnel for the March on Washington. The speech was mimeographed and the copies, lacking notice, were put into a "press kit" which was distributed to reporters covering the march. Dr. King testified that this distribution was without his knowledge or consent, but there was nothing to indicate that he had expressly forbidden such reproduction. The defendant in the case had begun marketing phonograph records of the speech without Dr. King's permission, and he sued them for copyright infringement.

The defendants argued that King had lost his copyright interest in the speech because the distribution of copies lacking notice amounted to a divestitive publication.[15] The court, however, disagreed, stressing that copies had been only given to the press and that "there is nothing to suggest that copies of the speech were ever offered to the public."[16] This result has been criticized because there was no limitation on the further use that the press could make of the speech and some newspapers did, in fact, reproduce the entire text verbatim. Indeed, in the subsequent case of *Estate of Martin Luther King, Jr., Inc. v. CBS, Inc.,* a different district court held on summary judgment that Dr. King had engaged in a general publication of "I Have a Dream,"[17] only to be reversed by the Court of Appeals for the Eleventh Circuit.[18] Although the appeals court remanded the matter for further factfinding, the parties settled, leaving the copyright status of "I Have a Dream" unresolved.

In the pre–1978 legal regime, publication proved to be controversial not only for works such as books, poems and speeches. A number of other problems periodically arose in the cases. One of these was whether the public distribution of phonograph records constituted a publication of the musical composition recorded on the records. If it was, and if the records lacked notice (which they usually did), that would inject them into the public domain. However, under the doctrine of *White-Smith Music Pub.Co. v. Apollo Co.,*[19] unless a work was visually perceptible

13. White v. Kimmell, 193 F.2d 744 (9th Cir.),, *cert. denied,* 343 U.S. 957, 72 S.Ct. 1052, 96 L.Ed. 1357 (1952).

14. 224 F.Supp. 101 (S.D.N.Y.1963).

15. The defendant also argued that the oral delivery (or "performance") of the speech in front of 200,000 was also a publication. As to the question of whether oral performance of a work constitutes a publi-

cation, see the discussion in the text in the balance of this section.

16. 224 F.Supp. at 107.

17. 13 F.Supp.2d 1347 (N.D.Ga.1998).

18. 194 F.3d 1211 (11th Cir.1999).

19. 209 U.S. 1, 28 S.Ct. 319, 52 L.Ed. 655 (1908).

from the object in question, the object was not a "copy." Thus, litigants argued that records were not copies of the underlying musical compositions, and that therefore the distribution of such records could not be a publication. Some courts, including the Court of Appeals for the Ninth Circuit in its 1995 decision in *La Cienega Music Co. v. ZZ Top*,[20] rejected this argument and held that the public distribution of phonorecords constituted a publication of the musical or other works recorded.

Congress endeavored to overturn *La Cienega* in 1997 when it enacted § 303(b) of the Copyright Act. That provision specifies that the "distribution before January 1, 1978, of a phonorecord shall not for any purpose constitute a publication of a musical work embodied therein." Whether this legislative amendment will achieve its intended effect remains to be seen, however. Some commentators have suggested that after-the-fact changes to the 1976 Act cannot effectively alter judicial interpretations of the 1909 Act. Nonetheless, the courts that have considered the question have followed § 303(b) and concluded that the statute applies to cases pending at the time of its enactment.[21]

Another problem area involves the exhibition of a one-of-a-kind work of art. If an artist makes such a work available for viewing by the public at large, and if the work lacks a copyright notice, the usual question arises as to whether the work has been injected into the public domain. On general principles the answer should be no. The artist has not really relinquished control of the work, nor has he or she taken the final steps toward exploiting the work economically—namely the preparation of the multiple copies for sale. The Supreme Court endorsed only a modified version of this proposition, however, when it considered the issue in 1907. In *American Tobacco Co. v. Werckmeister*,[22] the Court held that public exhibition did not constitute publication *provided that there was an express or implied condition imposed on the public not to copy the work.* This, of course, leaves open the possibility that certain exhibitions might be found to be divestitive publications, and that is exactly what happened in some subsequent cases.[23] This created both ambiguity in the law and yet another trap for the unwary artist. In drafting the 1976 Act Congress eliminated the ambiguity and made it clear that mere public exhibition or display of the work does not constitute a publication.[24]

20. *See* La Cienega Music Co. v. ZZ Top, 53 F.3d 950 (9th Cir.),, *cert. denied*, 516 U.S. 927, 116 S.Ct. 331, 133 L.Ed.2d 231 (1995).

21. *See* Mayhew v. Allsup, 166 F.3d 821 (6th Cir.1999); ABKCO Music, Inc. v. LaVere, 217 F.3d 684 (9th Cir. 2000).

22. American Tobacco Co. v. Werckmeister, 207 U.S. 284, 300, 28 S.Ct. 72, 52 L.Ed. 208 (1907) ("We do not mean to say that the public exhibition of a painting or statue, where all might see and freely copy it, might not amount to publication within the statute, regardless of the artist's purpose or notice of reservation of rights which he takes no measure to protect.").

23. *See e.g.*, Letter Edged in Black Press, Inc. v. Public Bldg. Com'n of Chicago, 320 F.Supp. 1303, 1310–11 (N.D.Ill. 1970) ("In the case at bar there were no restrictions on copying and no guard preventing copying. Rather every citizen was free to copy the maquette for his own pleasure and camera permits were available to members of the public.... The activity in question does not comport with any definition of limited publication. Rather, the display of the maquette constituted general publication.").

24. Section 101, the definitional section of the 1976 Act, provides that "public performance or display of a work does not of

A closely related issue in the law of publication concerns the legal significance of the performance of a work such as a play, movie, musical composition or a speech. Here, the pre–1976 case law was a bit more uniform, holding fairly consistently that public performance was *not* a publication that forfeits copyright and dedicates the work to the public domain.[25] This result obtained even if the public in attendance was permitted to make notes on the performance. This solution is carried forward in the language of the 1976 Act which explicitly declares that public performance of work does not constitute publication.

What is curious about this doctrine is that it seems at odds with the underlying rationale of the publication rule in the first place. As noted above, courts treated publication without notice as divestitive because it represented an act of economic exploitation of the work, obligating the author to enter into a bargain with the public for statutorily defined and time delimited rights. Surely, the performance of a dramatic or musical work is a form of economic exploitation—indeed, in the case of drama it is perhaps the chief form. Nonetheless, the rule grew up that a performance would not be treated as a publication for largely practical reasons.

A further observation is useful concerning publication of motion pictures. The mere projection of a motion picture, being a performance, is quite plainly not a publication. It has long been the custom in the motion picture industry for companies to lease rather than sell prints of their films to distributors for exhibition to the public. Since this practice does not involve the transfer of ownership of copies to members of the general public, one might think that it too would not amount to publication. However, the case law interpreting the 1909 Act indicates that once a movie is placed in general commercial distribution, there has been a general publication, with all the attendant consequences.[26] Of course, where the movie has been placed on videocassettes and those videocassettes are sold directly to members of the public, a general publication occurs under the conventional analysis.

By the time of the 1976 Act, Congress decided to include an explicit definition of publication in the statute. In doing so its goal was substantially to codify the approach that had emerged in the earlier cases, and that is discussed above. The current statute provides that a publication is:

> the distribution of copies or phonorecords of a work to the public by sale or other transfer of ownership, or by rental, lease or lending. The offering to distribute copies or phonorecords to

itself constitute publication." 17 U.S.C.A. § 101 (2000).

25. *See, e.g.,* Ferris v. Frohman, 223 U.S. 424, 435, 32 S.Ct. 263, 56 L.Ed. 492 (1912) ("The public representation of a dramatic composition, not printed and published, does not deprive the owner of his common-law right, save by operation of statute. At common law, the public performance of the play is not an abandonment of it to the public use"); Nutt v. National Inst., 31 F.2d 236 (2d Cir.1929); Heim v. Universal Pictures Co., 154 F.2d 480 (2d Cir.1946); King v. Mister Maestro, Inc., 224 F.Supp. 101 (S.D.N.Y.1963).

26. American Vitagraph, Inc. v. Levy, 659 F.2d 1023 (9th Cir.1981).

a group of persons for purposes of further distribution, public performance, or public display, constitutes publication. A public performance or display of a work does not of itself constitute publication.[27]

The language referring to distribution to a group for purposes of public performance codifies the rule that treats general distribution of a motion picture as a publication. This language also eliminates any ambiguity over display of works where there are no restrictions on copying, as it makes it quite plain that such display does not constitute a publication in any event.

In the years since the 1976 Act was adopted, technological evolution has raised a new problem in the area of publication. Today authors may widely disseminate their works electronically, for example by making them available on the internet or other electronic bulletin boards. This form of dissemination can also indicate economic exploitation because the author may limit electronic access to only those who have paid a fee. For all the purposes for which publication is still relevant under the copyright laws, then, electronic dissemination might usefully be treated as a form of publication. It is clear, however, that under the statutory language now in effect there has been no *distribution of copies or phonorecords ... to the public* and hence no publication when a work is disseminated electronically. Whether legislation will alter this anomalous result remains to be seen.

§ 5.2   Notice

Historically, general publication of a work without proper notice had grave consequences for an author attempting to claim copyright. As discussed in the foregoing section, such a publication was "divestitive" of copyright, and it injected the work into the public domain. That rule has been relaxed over time, however, and it is important to determine the date a work was first generally published in order to ascertain the precise consequences of the publication. To be more precise, there are three separate eras in American copyright law insofar as notice is concerned—the pre–1978 period; the period from January 1, 1978 through February 28, 1989; and the post-March 1, 1989 period. The state of the law in each of these eras is discussed in the subsections that follow.

Before addressing the legal particulars, competing views on the worth of the notice requirement should be noted. Proponents have pointed to several benefits of affixing copyright notice upon works of authorship. Notice is said not only to inform the public of an intellectual property right, but to identify the copyright owner and the publication date. In addition, a notice requirement was also claimed to have the beneficial effect of instantly injecting into the public domain works that the author did not wish to copyright.[1] On the other hand, the technicali-

---

27. 17 U.S.C.A. § 101 (2000).

§ 5.2

1. H.R. Rep. No. 94–1476, 94th Cong., 2d Sess. 143 (1976).

ties of the notice requirement undoubtedly deprived worthy authors of the benefits of copyright protection over the years. A requirement of notice also in part prevented the United States from acceding to the Berne Convention. The permissive notice regime of the present U.S. copyright law attempts to profit from the perceived benefits of copyright notice without incurring too many of its costs.

5.2.1   Prior to 1978

The 1909 Act details the notice requirements in sections 19 through 21. Section 19 generally provides that the notice consist either of the word "Copyright," the abbreviation "Copr.", or the symbol ©, along with the name of the copyright proprietor. If the work was a printed literary, musical, or dramatic work, the notice must also include the year of the work's first publication. In a concession to artistic integrity, section 19 allows for a "short form" notice that may be placed on pictorial, graphical and sculptural works. For such works, the initials or mark of the copyright proprietor, along with the symbol ©, would suffice, provided that the proprietor's full name also appears on the margin, base, pedestal or other accessible portion of the work. The mandatory location of this notice is provided in section 20. For example, for a book or printed publication, notice had to be given on the title page or the page immediately thereafter.

Section 21 of the 1909 Act sets forth certain circumstances where the omission of notice will be excused. Section 21 is narrowly worded and was construed strictly by the courts. As a result, most would-be copyright proprietors found that this provision did little to ameliorate the harsh consequences of publishing without notice. In particular, section 21 operates only where an omission occurred by "accident or mistake." Mechanical difficulties encountered by the printer, such as a damaged printing plate, were the prototypical incident within the meaning of this provision.[2] In contrast, courts reasoned that negligence did not amount to the type of accident or mistake contemplated by the 1909 Act.[3] As well, section 21 states that notice must have been omitted only on "a particular copy or copies." Judicial opinions read this language to mean that the omission of notice must have occurred in only a limited number of copies for section 21 to apply.[4]

5.2.2   Between 1978 and 1989

Special rules apply to works published in the ten-year period between 1978, when the 1976 Act came into effect, and 1989, when Congress enacted the Berne Convention Implementation Act. Professor Nimmer termed such works "decennial works" because of the ten-year

---

2. Leon B. Rosenblatt Textiles, Ltd. v. M. Lowenstein & Sons, Inc., 321 F.Supp. 186 (S.D.N.Y.1970).

3. Puddu v. Buonamici Statuary, Inc., 450 F.2d 401 (2d Cir.1971).

4. Wabash Pub. Co. v. Flanagan, 14 USPQ2d 2037 (N.D.Ill.1990).

window in which a distinct legal situation will control.[5] As initially enacted, section 401(a) of the 1976 Act provided:

> Whenever a work protected under this title is published in the United States or elsewhere by authority of the copyright owner, a notice of copyright as provided by this section shall be placed on all publicly distributed copies from which the work can be visually perceived, either directly or with the aid of machine or device.

Section 401 further specifies that notice of copyright consists of three elements: (1) the familiar symbol ©, the word "Copyright," or the abbreviation "Copr."; (2) the year of first publication; and (3) the name of the copyright proprietor. For phonorecords, copyright owners must use the symbol ℗ .[6] The statute does not specify the relative locations of these elements, suggesting that any order creates effective notice. Unlike the 1909 Act, the 1976 Act does not specify the precise position where notice is to be fixed on particular sorts of works, but rather instructs the Register of Copyrights to prescribe by regulation the proper form and position of notice.[7] The Copyright Office regulations are expressly stated not to be exhaustive.[8] As compliance with them ensures that the 1976 Act requirements have been fulfilled, however, many publishers choose to follow them exactingly.

In contrast to works published under the 1909 Act, for decennial works the absence of notice upon copies of published works does not necessarily lead to forfeiture of copyright. First, copyright is not affected if the notice is removed without the authorization of the copyright owner.[9] Similarly, copyright is retained if a distributor fails to comply with an express written agreement that the distributor observe the notice requirement as a condition of the copyright owner's grant of permission to distribute.[10] Third, an omitted notice is wholly excused if the omission occurred in "no more than a relatively small number of copies or phonorecords distributed to the public."[11] In interpreting the phrase "more than a relatively small number," courts have tended towards a percentage test, rather than focusing on the absolute number of copies on which notice was not given. For example, in *Ford Motor Co. v. Summit Motor Products, Inc.,* the U.S. Court of Appeals for the Third Circuit excused the omission of copyright notice on four million out of 100 million works, concluding that under these facts four million constituted "a relatively small number."[12]

Even if the author cannot claim one of these three exceptions, the 1976 Act provides an additional curative mechanism for authors of

---

5. Nimmer, § 7.02[c][2].

6. 17 U.S.C.A. § 402(b) (2000).

7. *See* 37 C.F.R. § 201.20.

8. 17 U.S.C.A. § 401(c) (2000).

9. 17 U.S.C.A. § 405(c) (2000).

10. 17 U.S.C.A. § 405(a)(3) (2000).

11. 17 U.S.C.A. § 405(a)(1) (2000).

12. 930 F.2d 277 (3d Cir.1991), *cert. denied,* 502 U.S. 939, 112 S.Ct. 373, 116 L.Ed.2d 324 (1991).

decennial works to avoid forfeiture of copyright. Under § 405(a)(2), omission of notice is excused if "registration for the work has been made before or is made within five years after the publication without notice, and a reasonable effort is made to add notice to all copies or phonorecords that are distributed to the public in the United States after the omission has been discovered...."[13] The level of efforts considered reasonable, as well as the moment at which an omission can be discovered, remain somewhat ambiguous concepts.

The issue of a "reasonable effort" involves the extent of efforts a would-be copyright proprietor must make to attach notice to existing copies and phonorecords. Plainly a copyright owner is obliged to affix notice to all remaining copies within her possession in order to effectuate a valid cure. The obligation of the copyright owner regarding copies held by wholesalers, retailers and other distributors is less certain. The Court of Appeals for the First Circuit in *Charles Garnier, Paris v. Andin International, Inc.* adopted a strict stance on this issue.[14]

In the early 1990's, Garnier claimed copyright in earrings, copies of which it had been distributing without notice since 1988. Garnier attempted to cure the absence of notice in part by supplying retailers with "story cards"—written statements explaining that each earring embodied "a copyrighted design." Garnier instructed its retailers to include a story card with each purchased earring. Garnier also contended that its curative efforts need only relate to earrings distributed prior to March 1, 1989, the effective date of the Berne Convention Implementation Act (BCIA). Because most, if not all of these earrings had already made their way into the hands (and ears) of consumers, Garnier's view would have significantly limited its responsibilities.

The First Circuit disagreed with Garnier, however, holding that § 405(a)(2) imposed a cure requirement for all copies of a work that was first published prior to the effective date of the BCIA, regardless of when the individual copies were distributed. The result is a debatable one because it appears to perpetuate the difficulties that led to the loosening of the notice requirement. The First Circuit went on to hold that Garnier's efforts were insufficient to constitute reasonable efforts under § 405(a)(2), noting in particular that its "story cards" were not physically attached to the earrings. Although the determination of whether a copyright plaintiff made a reasonable effort or not is a question of fact,[15] *Charles Garnier* suggests that courts will apply this standard strictly. In the wake of this opinion copyright owners can only be confident that their cure efforts will be found adequate if they provided retailers and wholesalers with a label or other means for affixing notice to each copy or phonorecord in their possession.

Determining the moment at which the absence of notice was discovered presents no special complexities in cases of accidental omissions.

---

13. A similar provision governs errors in the name or the date provided in the notice. *See* 17 U.S.C.A. § 406 (2000).

14. 36 F.3d 1214 (1st Cir.1994).

15. *See* Princess Fabrics, Inc. v. CHF, Inc., 922 F.2d 99, 103 (2d Cir.1990).

Cases of deliberate omissions of notice present more difficulties. One possibility is that § 405(a)(2) does not apply to such cases. Under this view, a deliberate omission cannot be "discovered" in the sense of the statute because it was never hidden. Both the case law[16] and the legislative history of the 1976 Act[17] reject this position, the latter expressly stating that even deliberate omissions can be excused if the statutory conditions are met.

When, however, does a party who knowingly distributed copies lacking notice "discover" its "omission"? One position, with some support from the judicial decisions,[18] is that deliberate omissions are discovered when a copyright proprietor learns of a copyist. An alternative, even more lenient, view is that the moment of discovery occurs when the copyright proprietor learns of the legal significance of the failure to provide notice.[19] A difficulty with these extremely tolerant stances is that it eliminates incentives for copyright owners to place notice on copies of their works. Professor Marshall Leaffer has advocated what, to us, seems the most sensible solution: that the discovery of deliberate omissions occurs automatically when the work is first published.[20]

The case law does not clearly embrace any of these various positions on the question of when a deliberate omission of notice on copies of a decennial work should be deemed to be discovered. As we move further and further away from the decennial period, moreover, the issue is likely to come up less and less often. There can, of course, still be disputes over the copyright status of works first distributed in the decennial period, and the diligence and timing of cure efforts will be dispositive in resolving that question. Nonetheless, it is likely that the majority of such disputes would have already lead to litigation if the work in question had any significant economic value. Since copyright notice has been optional for well over a decade, the need for courts to invest energy in solving open issues in this area seems minimal, and we would predict that we will see few, if any, additional opinions.

Section 404 of the 1976 Act also stipulates notice requirements for collective works. Recall that not only may the individual elements of a collective work be amenable to copyright protection, the compiler of a collective work may also be entitled to a separate copyright.[21] Under section 404, a single notice covering the entire collective work is deemed to satisfy the notice requirement for not only the collective work, but each of its elements. Notice of copyright for an individual element was not required but was—and continues to be—advisable. Absent a separate notice on a given contribution, if an infringer mistakenly obtained permission to use an element of the collective work from the owner of

16. *See* Hasbro Bradley, Inc. v. Sparkle Toys, Inc., 780 F.2d 189 (2d Cir.1985).

17. H.R. Rep. No. 94–1476, 94th Cong., 2d. Sess. 147 (1976).

18. *See* O'Neill Devs., Inc. v. Galen Kilburn, Inc., 524 F.Supp. 710, 714 (N.D.Ga. 1981).

19. *See* Charles Garnier, Paris v. Andin Int'l, Inc., 36 F.3d 1214 (1st Cir.1994).

20. MARSHALL LEAFFER, UNDERSTANDING COPYRIGHT LAW § 4.11[D] (3d ed. 1999).

21. 17 U.S.C.A. § 103 (2000).

the copyright in the collective work, that infringer may be entitled to a defense of good faith infringement. This defense would exempt him from damages until such time as he received actual notice of infringement.[22]

5.2.3   After 1989

The Berne Convention Implementation Act (BCIA) of 1988 abolished the notice requirement for works distributed on or after March 1, 1989. Section 401(a) of the 1976 now merely states that notice "may be placed" on publicly distributed copies of works of authorship, as compared to its earlier mandate that such notice "shall be placed" on published works. This step was considered necessary to bring U.S. copyright law into compliance with the Berne Convention, which bars notice and other formalities from serving as conditions of copyright protection.[23] Although the proper affixation of copyright notice is no longer a predicate for copyright, the BCIA acts only prospectively. Works published prior to the BCIA must be judged as to the notice requirements prevailing at that time.

Although Congress eliminated notice as a requirement, it offered a significant incentive to copyright proprietors that affix notice to copies of their published works. Section 405(b) allows defendants in copyright infringement suits to claim that they are innocent infringers. If an infringer demonstrates that he was misled in reliance upon an authorized copy of the work that lacked notice, the statutes renders him immune from actual or statutory damages. (Such a party does, however, remain subject to an injunction against further acts of infringement.) The infringer retains this immunity until he receives actual notice of the claim to copyright. Post–Berne publishers that wish to retain the full range of remedies should therefore abide by the notice provisions of the 1976 Act.

§ 5.3   Registration

While copyright ownership arises immediately upon the creation of a work, without the necessity of any governmental examination or approval, copyright owners have the option of registering their claim of ownership in the Copyright Office of the United States. One might think of this as similar to the registration of an automobile. You own your car as soon as you pay for it and receive the title from the seller. Thereafter, you can—and in most states you must—register that claim of ownership by filing at the department of motor vehicles, but whether you register or not, you are still the owner of the car.

The difference between auto registration and copyright registration, however, is that copyright registration under the present law is not mandatory.[1] That observation may itself be misleading, though, because

22. 17 U.S.C.A. § 405(b) (2000).

23. Berne Convention, Art. 5(2).

§ 5.3

1. 17 U.S.C.A. § 408(a). This subsection is entitled "Registration Permissive." The last sentence of the subsection reads "...

there are numerous incentives in the current statute designed to encourage prompt registration of copyright claims, and registration remains a prerequisite to the filing of an infringement suit for many copyright owners.

Registration was not always optional under American copyright law. Under the earliest copyright statute in the United States, the law required the filing of the title page of a work with the clerk of the U.S. district court in the district where the claimant resided as a formal condition of copyright protection.[2] Without the filing, copyright protection under federal law would be lost. By the time of the 1909 act, however, registration was to be made with the Copyright Office rather than with the district courts, and was no longer an essential condition of copyright protection.[3] Registration of the claim of ownership was, however, a prerequisite to the filing of any infringement suit.

The current statute largely continues that pattern. Under the original version of the 1976 Act, registration continued to be permissive, and, as under the former statute, no infringement suit could be filed until registration was made. After the United States signed the international copyright treaty known as the Berne Convention in 1989, that requirement was amended to exempt works originating in Berne countries other than the United States. The statute was amended yet again after the United States signed the treaty that led to the creation of the World Trade Organization in late 1998.[4] As a result, the obligation to register in advance of an infringement suit now only applies to "United States works."[5] This term of art is defined differently depending on whether the work in question is published or unpublished. A published work will be deemed a United States work if it was (1) first published in the U.S.; (2) simultaneously published in the U.S. and in another nation that is a party to one of the major copyright treaties, provided that other nation has a term of copyright at least as long as the U.S. term; (3) simultaneously published in the U.S. and in another nation that is *not* a party to a major copyright treaty; or (4) first published in a foreign nation that is *not* a party to a major copyright treaty if all of the authors are U.S. citizens or residents. An unpublished work is declared to be a U.S. work if all the authors are U.S. citizens or residents.[6]

A few examples will illustrate. If an American citizen with a home in the South of France were to write a novel and first publish it in France, the novel would *not* be a U.S. work. France is a member of all major copyright treaties, so the fourth numbered definition in the preceding paragraph would not apply. The other three definitions are not applicable because they require either first publication in the U.S., or, at a

registration is not a condition of copyright protection."

2. Act of May 31, 1790, 1 Stat. 124 (1790). *See* WILLIAM F. PATRY, COPYRIGHT LAW AND PRACTICE 408 (1994).

3. *See* 1909 Copyright Act, §§ 11, 13. *See also* Washingtonian Pub. Co. v. Pearson, 306 U.S. 30, 40, 59 S.Ct. 397, 83 L.Ed. 470 (1939).

4. *See* Pub.L. 105–304, Title I, § 102(d) (1998).

5. 17 U.S.C.A. § 411(a) (2000).

6. 17 U.S.C.A. § 101 (2000).

minimum. simultaneous publication in the U.S. and abroad. Since this hypothetical novel is *not* a U.S. work, if the copyright owner ever needs to bring infringement litigation in the United States he or she will not have to register before filing suit. On the other hand, let us assume that the American novelist had his or her hypothetical second home in a fictional country that is not party to any copyright treaties—a country we can call Nimmerland. The author's novel would now be considered a U.S. work under the fourth numbered definition, since the author is a U.S. citizen. Any copyright lawsuits in the U.S. would thus have to be preceded by proper registration.

Finally, note that if the novel was written by the American living in France, but was never published, it *would* be considered a U.S. work, and registration *would* be required before the author could sue for infringement of that unpublished work in an American court.

All this complicated business is designed to simultaneously achieve certain domestic law objectives while still keeping the U.S. in compliance with its treaty obligations. The U.S. has traditionally mandated registration in advance of litigation because administrative scrutiny of copyright claims can simplify lawsuits, saving time and money. For instance, the Copyright Office will only register a work if it concludes that the work has sufficient originality to warrant copyright protection. Once registered, a presumption arises that the work is original and that issue need not be proved by the plaintiff in court unless the defendant chooses to make an issue of it.

On the other hand, however, the Berne Convention and other treaties are quite clear that copyright protection cannot be conditioned on "formalities." Conditioning access to the courts on the observance of an administrative obligation is widely considered to be exactly the kind of formality that is forbidden by these treaties. So where the treaties are arguably applicable, the U.S. law abandons its preference for registration. This approach is frequently been labeled a "minimalist" approach to U.S. obligations under international law, because it does not abolish the registration requirement across the board.

One aspect of this rule might seem particularly troubling. While most applications for copyright registration are approved by the Copyright Office, a non-trivial number are denied. With registration a prerequisite to infringement litigation, that might leave a copyright owner in the position of being unable to even gain access to the courts to press a claim of infringement. The statute deals with that contingency by providing that

> In any case, however, where the deposit, application and fee required for registration have been delivered to the Copyright Office in proper form and registration has been refused, the applicant is entitled to institute an action for infringement if notice thereof, with a copy of the complaint, is served on the

Register of Copyrights.[7]

Thus, the owner of a copyright in a U.S. work must at least attempt to register before filing an infringement suit, but if the effort to register is unsuccessful, the copyright owner will still be allowed to go forward.

Under this scheme, one might think that the best course would be for a copyright owner to dispense with registration—thus saving expense and inconvenience—until he or she learned of infringing activity. At that point, registration could be sought, and thereafter, a complaint could be filed. While such a course of action is certainly permissible under the statute, it would be rather inadvisable. This is because the statute contains a number of incentives for prompt registration and, effectively, a number of penalties for a tardy registration that is deferred until the eve of an infringement suit.

Before considering these statutory incentives in detail, it is worth pausing to consider why Congress adopted this type of scheme—optional registration with incentives. One might wonder, on the one hand, why, if registration is not important enough to be mandatory, should we have it at all? After all, most other countries of the world do not have such an elaborate system.[8] On the other hand if it is important enough to encourage with incentives, why not go all the way and make it a mandatory pre-condition of copyright protection?

The virtues of a copyright registration system are similar to those of any other form of organized record keeping. It establishes a system of public records that aids would-be users of copyrighted material in locating the owners of the material so that they can secure the necessary permissions. The economically minded might say that the system reduces transaction costs.

On the other hand, for certain authors, the registration process might prove unduly burdensome or expensive. Unlike large publishing houses or record companies that can hire personnel whose entire function is prosecution of copyright registration applications, the local garage band, the independent commercial photographer and the fledgling film maker may not have the resources to devote to compliance with a registration system, yet it seems unfair in the extreme to declare the copyright in these works forfeited merely because the authors find it difficult to comply with the registration system. Thus, the statute can be seen to represent a compromise—encouraging registration to the maximum extent possible, in order to secure its benefits, without imposing draconian consequences on those who fail to register.

So what, then, are the legal benefits of registration to copyright proprietors? The first benefit of prompt registration is found in section 410(c) which makes a registration prima facie evidence of the validity of the copyright and of all the other facts stated in the registration

7. 17 U.S.C.A. § 411(a) (2000).

8. *See* Ralph Oman, *The United States and the Berne Union: An Extended Courtship,* 3 J. L. & Tech. 71 (1988).

certificate, if the registration is made before or within five years after the first publication of the work.[9] If the registration is made after the prescribed time limit "the evidentiary weight to be accorded the certificate of a registration ... shall be within the discretion of the court." In the event of litigation, the evidentiary significance of the registration certificate can be a significant advantage to the copyright owner, thus making registration desirable.

The second important incentive for registration is that prompt registration is a prerequisite for some of the more important remedies under the current law. Under section 412

> no award of statutory damages or of attorney's fees ... shall be made for (1) any infringement of copyright in an unpublished work commenced before the effective date of its registration; or (2) any infringement of copyright commenced after first publication of the work and before the effective date of its registration, unless such registration is made within three months after the first publication of the work.[10]

Thus, in order to insure that the powerful remedial tools of attorneys fees and statutory damages are available, a copyright owner is well advised to register as soon as possible. Moreover, this provision applies both to U.S. and non-U.S. works alike. Consequently, although registration is not literally a prerequisite to suit for non-U.S. works, the owners of copyrights in such works still have strong reason to get their works registered and to do so promptly.[11]

Note that for published works there is a three-month "grace period." That means that if a work is published on June 1st, an infringer makes unlawful copies on June 20th and the owner does not register until August 10th, the owner will still be able to claim statutory damages and attorneys fees because even though he did not register until after the infringements began, he did register within three months of publication. On the other hand, if an unpublished work, having been created on June 1st, is infringed on June 20th before any registration is made, the owner of copyright will not be able to claim the enhanced remedies.

There are a few other positive consequences of registration scattered throughout the 1976 Act. For instance, the recordation of a transfer of

9. 17 U.S.C.A. § 410(c) (2000). Congress also included comparable benefits for prompt registration of claims to renewal interests for works first published after 1964 when it made renewal of copyright in those works automatic in 1992. *See supra* § 8.3.1.

10. 17 U.S.C.A. § 412. The "statutory damages" referred to are those provided for by section 504(c). That provision permits an infringement plaintiff to waive a claim of actual damages and instead to claim "a sum of not less than $750 or more than $30,000 as the court considers just."

11. Some have question whether conditioning certain remedies on prompt registration is consistent with U.S. treaty obligations under the Berne Convention and other copyright treaties. Berne forbids making copyright protection dependent on the observance of "formalities" and a registration requirement is plainly a formality. For a discussion of this issue *see*, Shira Perlmutter, *Freeing Copyright From Formalities*, 13 Cardozo Art & Ent. L.J. 565, 575 (1995).

ownership in a copyright will give constructive notice of the facts surrounding that transfer, but only if registration has also been made for the work in question.[12] Also, for works published without notice after 1978 but before March 1, 1989, registration within a five year period was one step in effecting a "cure" so as to avoid loss of rights because of that publication without notice.[13] These are bit less important than the prima facie effect of the certificate and the enhanced remedies for infringement that were discussed above, but they reinforce the general statutory approach of encouraging as many claimants as possible to make registration.

Assuming a copyright owner, in the face of these incentives, wishes to register a work—or, in the case of a non-U.S. work is required to do so in order to commence an infringement suit—how is registration accomplished? The actual registration process is not particularly complex. Registration may be made at any time during the life of the copyright by any party holding any exclusive right in the copyright. (In other words, not only may the owner of copyright in a novel register the claim of copyright to the novel, but the holder of the exclusive movie rights to that novel may register as well). The applicant for registration must submit three items to the Copyright Office. First is an application. Section 409 specifies some of the categories of data that such an application must include[14] and the Register of Copyrights has promulgated further requirements by regulation.[15] Under these provisions, parties seeking registration for a derivative work must identify the preexisting works upon which it is based. In actual practice, the Copyright Office has developed different forms for different categories of works, such Form TX for non-dramatic literary works and Form VA for works of the visual arts. This permits the Office to solicit information that is specific to particular categories of works.

The second item required for registration is the registration fee. The schedule of fees is set out in section 708 of the statute and currently provides for a registration fee of $30.[16] While that is certainly a modest sum, the registration process can become oppressively expensive for creators who generate large numbers of works in a short period of time, such as commercial photographers. To deal with that problem the regulations allow registration of certain groups of related works for a single fee.[17] The statute provides that the Register of Copyrights may increase fees to keep pace with the Consumer Price Index.[18]

---

12. *See infra* § 6.4.

13. 17 U.S.C.A. § 405(a)(2) (2000). *See supra* § 5.1.

14. Among those listed are the name and address of the copyright claimant; a statement that the work was made for hire if that is the case; the title of the work; the year in which the work was completed; and the date and nation of first publication. For the full list, see 17 U.S.C.A. § 409 (2000).

15. 37 C.F.R. § 202.3 (2001).

16. The schedule of fees for all Copyright Office services can be found at 37 C.F.R. § 201.3 (2001).

17. *See, e.g.,* 37 C.F.R. § 202.3(b)(9) (2001), allowing group registration of published photographs.

18. 17 U.S.C.A. § 708(b) (2000).

The third requirement for a proper copyright registration application is a "deposit." The subject of registration deposits is dealt with in sections 408 (b) and (c) of the present act, and the requirements differ depending on whether the work in question is published or unpublished. In the case of unpublished works, the application for registration must be accompanied by one complete copy or phonorecord of the work. If the work has been published, then two complete copies or phonorecords of the "best edition" of the work are required, unless the work was first published outside of the United States, in which case only one copy will be required.[19] The "best edition" of a work is statutorily defined as that edition that the "Library of Congress determines to be most suitable for its purposes."[20] The Copyright Office has issued detailed regulations specifying the attributes of a best edition.[21] For example, for printed textual matter, a best edition features a hard cover rather than a soft cover, library binding rather than commercial binding and is a trade edition rather than a book club edition. Those regulations also contain extensive clarifications and embellishments of the deposit requirements and provide that in certain cases—such as where the work is very large—"identifying material" may be submitted in lieu of a deposit copy of the actual work.

Once these materials have been submitted they will be examined by the Copyright Office, which must grant the registration if "the material deposited constitutes copyrightable subject matter and ... the other legal and formal requirements ... have been met."[22] Of course, if the examiner determines that the material is not copyrightable, registration will be denied, and such findings are often, but not always subsequently upheld by the courts.[23] Where registration is initially denied, the registration applicant can pursue an internal appeal within the copyright office to the Board of Appeals, and thereafter can seek judicial review.

§ 5.4   Deposit

As noted in the preceding section, if an author chooses to register a claim of copyright, he or she will have to submit copies or phonorecords of the work as part of the registration process. This "registration deposit" enables the Copyright Office to examine the work so that it can determine if the work in question meets the standards of copyrightability. There is, however, a second and entirely separate deposit requirement in the statute. This requirement applies to all works published in the United States regardless of whether the copyright owner chooses to

---

19. 17 U.S.C.A. § 408(b) (2000).

20. 17 U.S.C.A. § 101 (2000).

21. 37 C.F.R. §§ 202.20 (b) (1), 202.19 (b) (iii).

22. 17 U.S.C.A. § 410(a) (2000).

23. *Compare* Norris Indus., Inc. v. International Tel. & Tel. Corp., 696 F.2d 918 (11th Cir.), *cert. denied,* 464 U.S. 818, 104 S.Ct. 78, 78 L.Ed.2d 89 (1983) (upholding Copyright Office determination that wire-spoked wheel covers were utilitarian objects not eligible for copyright protection) *with* Atari v. Oman, 979 F.2d 242 (D.C.Cir.1992) (reversing copyright Office determination that video game was not eligible for copyright because of lack of originality).

file for copyright registration. The requirement appears in section 407 of the 1976 Act, which provides:

> the owner of copyright ... in a work published in the United States shall deposit, within three months after the date of such publication—(1) two complete copies of the best edition; or (2) if the work is a sound recording, two complete phonorecords of the best edition, together with any printed or other visually perceptible material published with such phonorecords.[1]

This deposit of materials called for by this section is sometimes referred to as "archival deposit" because its chief purpose is to ensure that the collections of the Library of Congress are both comprehensive and maintainable without undue cost to the government. As is the case for the "registration deposit," the archival deposit must be of the "best edition" of the work in question. The Register of Copyrights is empowered to promulgate regulations exempting certain types of works from the archival deposit requirement and has done so.[2]

Failure to make the archival deposit called for by section 407 does not affect the validity of the underlying copyright. The statute specifically declares that the section 407 deposit is not a condition of copyright protection. Rather, failure to make the deposit will subject the party involved to liability for fines. No liability will be incurred until the Register of Copyrights first makes a written demand for the materials in question. Thereafter, failure to deposit incurs a $250 fine for each work plus the cost of acquiring the copies of the work on the open market. The fine escalates to $2500 if the failure to deposit is either willful or repeated.[3]

If a copyright owner of a registered work opts to make voluntary registration, the copies submitted as part of that registration application will also be deemed to satisfy the archival deposit requirement under section 407.[4] In effect, this functions as another incentive for registration. After all, if authors must deposit two copies shortly after publication anyway—on pain of a fine—they might as well fill out the short registration form, pay a modest fee, and obtain the benefits of registration at the same time.

§ 5.4

1. 17 U.S.C.A. § 407(a) (2000).

2. *See* 37 C.F.R. § 202.19(c) (2001).

3. 17 U.S.C.A. § 407(d) (2000).

4. Section 408, dealing with registration, provides that "[c]opies or phonorec-ords deposited for the Library of Congress under section 407 may be used to satisfy the deposit provisions of this section if they are accompanied by the prescribed application and fee...." 17 U.S.C.A. § 408(b) (2000).

Chapter 6

OWNERSHIP AND TRANSFER OF COPYRIGHT INTERESTS

Table of Sections

§ 6.1 Initial Ownership

One might reasonably assume that the initial ownership of any copyrightable work would belong to the person who created the work—its author—and this is indeed the law. As the current statute, the Copyright Act of 1976, puts it, "copyright in a work protected under this title vests initially in the author or authors of the work."[1] Interestingly, the term "author" is itself left undefined in the statute, but is commonly understood to refer to the actual individual person or persons who created the work. As the Supreme Court explained, "the author is the party who actually creates the work, that is, the person who translates an idea into a fixed, tangible expression entitled to copyright protection."[2]

While this straightforward approach resolves the issue of copyright ownership in many cases, there are a number of situations that require

---

§ 6.1

1. 17 U.S.C.A. § 201 (2000).

2. Community for Creative Non–Violence v. Reid, 490 U.S. 730, 737, 109 S.Ct. 2166, 104 L.Ed.2d 811 (1989).

special consideration. For instance, a work may be created by an employee on the job, raising the question of whether the actual creator or the employer of that person should be deemed the legal owner. In other cases, multiple parties might collaborate to create a work, leading to ambiguity over which of them owns the copyright interest. Finally, an original owner of copyright might want to transfer the copyright to someone else, but such transfers may require the observance of certain formalities. These various situations are considered in the following sections.

§ 6.2   Works Made For Hire

For almost 100 years, U.S. copyright law has treated the copyright in works prepared by employees not as the property of the individual creator but rather as that of the creator's employer. The principle—known as the works made for hire doctrine—can be traced back to Justice Holmes' 1903 opinion in *Bleistein v. Donaldson Lithographic Co.*[1] Congress subsequently codified it in the 1909 Act[2] and, with substantial changes, carried it forward into the 1976 statute as well. The current law provides:

> In the case of a work made for hire, the employer or other person for whom the work was prepared is considered the author for purposes of this title, and unless the parties have expressly agreed otherwise in a written instrument signed by them, owns all of the rights comprised in the copyright.[3]

A number of significant consequences follow from classifying a work as a work made for hire, over and above the obvious consequences of deeming the employer the owner of the copyright. First, the duration of copyright in such works is not defined as the life of the author plus 70 years, but instead as either 95 years from publication or 120 years from creation, which ever comes first.[4] Second, while transfers of copyright interests initially owned by individual authors can sometimes be "terminated," permitting the original author to recapture copyright ownership, no such termination rights are available in the case of works made for hire.[5] Third, although individual creators of "works of visual art" have certain protections against the mutilation or destruction of their work, such protections are not available for works made for hire.[6] Consequently, determining whether a work is a work made for hire is quite important. Unfortunately, that characterization process raises numerous theoretical and mechanical questions.

§ 6.2

1. 188 U.S. 239, 248, 23 S.Ct. 298, 47 L.Ed. 460 (1903) (Because works were "produced by persons employed and paid by the plaintiffs in their establishment to make those very things," copyright belonged to plaintiff-employer).

2. 1909 Act, § 26.

3. 17 U.S.C.A. § 201(b) (2000).

4. 17 U.S.C.A. § 302 (2000).

5. 17 U.S.C.A. §§ 203(a), 304(c) (2000).

6. 17 U.S.C.A. § 101 (2000) (defining "work of visual art").

The initial question is whether the work made for hire doctrine is consistent with the congressional power under the copyright clause of the Constitution. That clause gives congress the power to secure exclusive rights in writings to "authors." One might wonder whether a corporate employer with dozens or even hundreds of employees preparing copyrightable works such as computer programs or greeting cards or wallpaper designs can legitimately be considered a constitutional "author."

Of course the Constitution itself is silent on this point. However, in a constitutional sense we might think of an "author" as someone who takes the necessary steps to bring an expressive work into being. In many cases, if an employer did not raise the funds to pay the salary of the creative employee, the work in question would never be created. At least in that sense, works created on the job "owe their origin" to the employer, and the employer could be considered a constitutional "author." Moreover, the courts have shown no particular willingness to question the constitutionality of the work made for hire doctrine, although their analysis of the issues has been terse at best.[7] Against this background, the constitutional status of the doctrine at this point seems fairly secure.

In addition to the constitutional question, there is also the issue of the policy justification for the works made for hire doctrine. It might be constitutionally permissible to treat employers as the copyright owners of works created by employees, but is it a good idea to do so? This question becomes particularly interesting when we realize that no comparable rule exists in the law of patents.[8] The usual justification for the work made for hire rule is that it places the legal incentive where it will likely do the most good—in other words where it will be most effective in inducing the creation of intellectual works. If employers know that they will control the copyright to works created on the job, they have the motivation to hire the right people and give them the right resources to engage in the creative endeavor. Without the incentive of copyright, those works might never be created. In addition, the employer may also be in the best position to disseminate the work once it is actually created. Thus, there seems to be considerable plausible policy support for the work made for hire doctrine.[9]

7. As the Second Circuit put it, without further elaboration, "Though the United States is perhaps the only country that confers 'authorship' status on the employer of the creator of a work made for hire ... its decision to do so is not constitutionally suspect." Childress v. Taylor, 945 F.2d 500, 506 n. 5 (2d Cir.1991).

8. Employees own the patent rights to inventions developed on the job. *See* United States v. Dubilier Condenser Corp., 289 U.S. 178, 53 S.Ct. 554, 77 L.Ed. 1114 (1933). Under certain circumstances the employee may have an obligation to assign those patent rights back to the employer, and in any event, if employer resources are used in the inventive process the employer will have the right to make and use the invention under the so-called "shop right" doctrine, Wommack v. Durham Pecan Co., 715 F.2d 962 (5th Cir.1983). *See infra* § 21.2.

9. For an article developing some of these themes *see* I. Trotter Hardy, *An Economic Understanding of Copyright Law's Work–Made–For–Hire Doctrine*, 12 COLUM.-VLA J. L. & ARTS 181 (1988).

Beyond these somewhat theoretical concerns is a more mechanical issue—which works should be considered as works made for hire under this doctrine? Particularly, what is the copyright status of works created by individuals who we might normally consider "independent contractors" because they are hired only for short periods and for the sole purpose of creating only one or a few works. For instance, one might hire a portrait artist to do an oil painting of the family dog, or retain a sculptor to prepare an abstract work for the plaza in front of a corporate headquarters building. In cases of "commissioned works" such as these, the actual creator is not a conventional employee, so resolution of the work-made-for-hire issue becomes a bit more ambiguous.

Under the 1909 Act, Congress dealt with the issue in a rather cryptic fashion. Section 26 of that act provided that "the word 'author' shall include an employer in the case of works made for hire." Nowhere, however, did the 1909 Act define "work made for hire" which left the problem to the courts. The cases interpreting the 1909 Act on this issue held that *both* works created by conventional full-time employees and commissioned works prepared by independent contractors were presumptively works made for hire, unless there was an agreement providing to the contrary.[10] Absent such an agreement, the creator had the burden of proving that work made for hire characterization was contrary to the intent of the parties. This pro-employer case law continues to be relevant today because the 1976 Act is not retroactive. Thus, the work made for hire status of works created prior to January 1, 1978, is determined under the standards of the 1909 Act.[11]

The current statute deals more explicitly with the problem by laying out a two-part definition for a work made for hire. Under the current statute a work made for hire is defined as follows:

(1) a work prepared by an employee within the scope of his or her employment; or

(2) a work specially ordered or commissioned for use as a contribution to a collective work, as a part of a motion picture or other audiovisual work, as a translation, as a supplementary work, as a compilation, as an instructional text, as a test, as answer material for a test, or as an atlas, if the parties expressly agree in a written instrument signed by them that the work shall be considered a work made for hire.[12]

10. *See, e.g.*, Murray v. Gelderman, 566 F.2d 1307 (5th Cir.1978); Scherr v. Universal Match Corp., 417 F.2d 497, 500 (2d Cir.1969), *cert. denied*, 397 U.S. 936, 90 S.Ct. 945, 25 L.Ed.2d 116 (1970); Brattleboro Publishing Co. v. Winmill Publishing Corp., 369 F.2d 565, 568 (2d Cir.1966).

11. Roth v. Pritikin, 710 F.2d 934 (2d Cir.), *cert. denied,* 464 U.S. 961, 104 S.Ct. 394, 78 L.Ed.2d 337 (1983), reasoned that a retroactive application of the 1976 Act provisions might run afoul of the constitutional provisions concerning the taking of property without compensation, because commissioning parties prior to the adoption of the new law would have had an expectation that they would own the copyrights in the resulting works.

12. 17 U.S.C.A. § 101 (2000). The provision goes on to define a "supplementary work" as "a work prepared for publication as a secondary adjunct to a work by another author for the purpose of introducing, concluding, illustrating, explaining, revising,

It would appear from the structure of this statutory definition that Congress meant to address the situation of the full-time or conventional employee in the first provision, and the situation of the independent contractor in the second. In the former case, works prepared on the job would clearly be works for hire, and the employer would be the owner of the copyright. In the independent contractor situation, however, the definition seems to strongly favor the creator. First only certain itemized types of works can ever be treated as works made for hire when prepared by a non-employee—namely the curious set of nine itemized in the statutory text (contributions to collective works, parts of motion pictures, translations, supplementary works, compilations, instructional texts, tests, answer material for test, or atlases).[13] These nine works are of a sort usually created at the instigation of an organizing entity and sometimes require the joint efforts of multiple parties, thus making them seem especially appropriate for work-for-hire status. Moreover, even with these nine types of works the parties must clearly specify their agreement on work made for hire status in writing. In every other case, it seems that Congress meant for creators who were not conventional employees to own the initial copyright in works they create under commission.

Notwithstanding the seeming Congressional desire to shift to a more "creator-friendly" version of the work made for hire doctrine, in the years immediately following the adoption of the 1976 Act, some courts began to interpret the word "employee" in the first prong of the definition more and more broadly so as to encompass a number of situations beyond the full-time salaried nine-to-five employee. That, of course, had the effect of broadening the range of works within the work made for hire definition, and depriving certain creators of copyright in favor of the commissioning parties.

For instance in *Aldon Accessories, Ltd. v. Spiegel,*[14] the court held that an independent contractor could be considered an "employee" under the first prong of the statutory definition where the commissioning party directed and supervised the work of that independent contractor.[15] That case involved the copyright ownership of a unicorn statuette.

commenting upon, or assisting in the use of the other work, such as forewords, afterwords, pictorial illustrations, maps, charts, tables, editorial notes, musical arrangements, answer material for tests, bibliographies, appendixes, and indexes...." It also specifies that an "instructional text" is "a literary, pictorial, or graphic work prepared for publication and with the purpose of use in systematic instructional activities."

13. This listing of nine appears to be the result of a legislative compromise. Various industry representatives were able to persuade Congress that in cases involving the nine itemized categories, the works were typically prepared only at the instigation of the hiring party and that the availability of work for hire status was something of a commercial necessity. Nimmer, Copyrights. § 5.03[B][2][a][i], n. 116.

14. 738 F.2d 548 (2d Cir.), *cert. denied,* 469 U.S. 982, 105 S.Ct. 387, 83 L.Ed.2d 321 (1984).

15. Other courts refused to follow this approach, and interpreted the term "employee" in the first prong of the work for hire definition narrowly, as covering only those who would be employees under the law of agency. *See, e.g.,* Easter Seal Society for Crippled Children and Adults of Louisiana, Inc. v. Playboy Enterprises, 815 F.2d 323 (5th Cir.1987).

An Aldon executive named Ginsberg worked closely with a model maker in Japan on the development of the statuette, but there was no plausible argument that the model maker was a full-time or conventional employee of Aldon. Nonetheless, the second circuit, found it significant that "[w]hile [Ginsberg] did not physically wield the sketching pen and sculpting tools, he stood over the artists and artisans at critical stages of the process, telling them exactly what to do." Some courts went even further than *Aldon* and held that the creator was an "employee" within the first prong of the definition if the hiring party merely retained the right to control the work, regardless of whether that control was actually exercised.[16]

Of course, these approaches had the effect of blurring the distinction between employees and independent contractors, since they permitted those who hired painters or sculptors for single projects to argue that those painters or sculptors were nonetheless "employees" under the particular circumstances in question. If a court agreed, that would give the hiring party ownership of the copyright under the first prong of the work made for hire definition.

Ultimately, the Supreme Court stepped in to clarify the meaning of "employee" in *Community for Creative Non–Violence v. Reid.*[17] In that case, Reid, a sculptor in Baltimore, was asked by the Community for Creative Non–Violence, or CCNV, a Washington-based charitable organization, to prepare a sculpture that would depict a "modern day nativity scene" of a homeless family on a steam grate. There were numerous consultations between the parties as the work progressed, CCNV supplied plans and sketches to Mr. Reid and also supplied the base or pedestal upon which the statue was to be mounted. Eventually, Reid and the CCNV had a falling out when CCNV wanted to take the statue on a fund-raising tour, and Reid objected. Litigation ensued over the ownership of the copyright in the statue.

The CCNV argued that Reid was an employee, and that the work was thus a work made for hire because they had the right to control his work, and because they had actually exercised such control as the work progressed. The Supreme Court disagreed. It criticized the actual control test by noting that since "it turns on whether the hiring party has closely monitored the production process, the parties would not know until late in the process, if not until the work is completed," whether the work was a work made for hire. It held that employee status should be determined instead by application of the law of agency. The Court was influenced by the structure of the definitional provision of the statute which seems to draw a sharp distinction between "employees" and "independent contractors." To assist the lower courts in applying its test, the Court identified several factors relevant under agency law in

16. *See, e.g.,* Peregrine v. Lauren Corp., 601 F.Supp. 828, 829 (D.Colo.1985); Clarkstown v. Reeder, 566 F.Supp. 137 (S.D.N.Y. 1983).

17. 490 U.S. 730, 109 S.Ct. 2166, 104 L.Ed.2d 811 (1989).

classifying a party as an employee. In a key passage, the Court instructed lower courts to consider:

> the hiring party's right to control the manner and means by which the product is accomplished [including such factors as] the skill required; the source of the instrumentalities and tools; the location of the work; the duration of the relationship between the parties; whether the hiring party has the right to assign additional projects; the hired party's discretion over when and how long to work: the method of payment; the hired party's role in hiring and paying assistants; whether the work is part of the regular business of the hiring party; whether the hiring party is in business; the provision of employee benefits; and the tax treatment of the hired party.[18]

Applying this test to the facts of the case before it, the Court found that Reid had not been an "employee" of CCNV. That meant that the sculpture could only qualify as a work made for hire if it fell under the second prong of the statutory definition. Because no written agreement stipulated that the work would be a work made for hire and because sculptures are not listed as one of the nine types of commissioned works for which such status is available, the Court found that the second prong of the statute was also unsatisfied. The end result was that the work was not a work made for hire and that Reid, as the individual author, owned the copyright.[19]

Of course, the use of agency law factors by the *Reid* Court does not mean that future decisions in this area will be easy or mechanical. As the Second Circuit put it in a post-*Reid* opinion:

> *Reid* established that no one factor was dispositive, but gave no direction concerning how the factors were to be weighed. It does not necessarily follow that because no one factor is dispositive all factors are equally important, or indeed that all factors will have relevance in every case. The factors should not merely be tallied but should be weighed according to their significance in the case.[20]

Indeed, because the *Reid* test is so fact-specific some commentators have criticized *Reid* as perpetuating all the uncertainty that existed under the former law.[21]

Regardless of ease of application, however, the thrust of the CCNV test is to more sharply distinguish between the classic full-time employee situation, where work made for hire status is the rule, and independent

---

18.　490 U.S. at 751.

19.　Actually, there was a further issue in the case. CCNV argued that it was also a "joint author" of the work with Reid. This issue was not addressed by the Supreme Court and was left for consideration on remand. The parties settled before the joint authorship issue could be judicially re-

solved. For a discussion of joint authorship *see* Section 6.3 *infra*.

20.　Aymes v. Bonelli, 980 F.2d 857, 861 (2d Cir.1992), *aff'd*, 47 F.3d 23 (2d Cir. 1995).

21.　Goldstien, COPYRIGHT: PRINCIPLES, LAW AND PRACTICE 1994 Supplement, at p. 84.

contractor situations, where work made for hire status will be available only in limited circumstances, and only if the parties have explicitly contracted for it.

§ 6.3   Joint Works

Quite often, multiple parties collaborate with each other to produce copyrightable works. Typical examples include the efforts of a composer and lyricist, such as Rogers and Hammerstein or Gilbert and Sullivan, who work together to develop one or more songs or the efforts of a screenwriter and a cinematographer who cooperate to produce a motion picture. These collaborative efforts raise a number of questions under the copyright laws concerning ownership of the copyright in the resulting work.

Under the current copyright statute the products of most of these collaborations are considered "joint works." More specifically, the 1976 Act defines a joint work as one "prepared by two or more authors with the intention that their contributions be merged into inseparable or interdependent parts of a unitary whole."[1] Elsewhere, the statute tells us who the owners of such "joint works" will be, and the answer is predictable—when multiple parties work together to create a "joint work," they are treated as co-owners of the copyright in that work.[2]

Authors need not contribute equally to the creative process in order to be considered co-owners of a joint work, although some courts have found that where one party has only contributed to the work in a minimal fashion that there is at least a presumption against joint authorship.[3] It also does not matter which of the collaborators does the "fixation" of the work, so that if one party merely dictates lines of prose which are physically incorporated into a play by his co-author sitting at a computer keyboard, the resulting work is plainly a joint work. It is essential, however, that each party contribute copyrightable expression to the collaboration.[4] In other words, if one party develops only the general idea for the plot of a novel or a play, and reveals it to another party who then executes the idea by crafting the actual prose, there is no joint work. The same would be true if one party supplied merely non-copyrightable facts or research.

This situation is illustrated by *Childress v. Taylor*,[5] where Taylor, an actress, conceived of the idea for a play about the renowned black

§ 6.3

1. 17 U.S.C.A. § 101 (2000). Joint creation is not the only situation that can lead to joint ownership of a copyright interest. For instance, a copyright could be assigned jointly to two or more individuals or multiple parties might inherent undivided interests in a single copyright. The situation of joint ownership resulting from collaborative creation is, however, the situation raising the most intriguing legal questions.

2. The statute provides that "the authors of a joint work are coowners of copyright in the work." 17 U.S.C.A. § 201(a) (2000).

3. *See e.g.* Eckert v. Hurley Chicago Co., Inc., 638 F.Supp. 699, 704 (N.D.Ill.1986).

4. Professor Nimmer argued for a contrary rule in his treatise, *see* 1 Nimmer on Copyright § 6.07, but his view does not seem to have persuaded the courts.

5. 945 F.2d 500 (2d Cir.1991).

comedienne Moms Mabley. She did considerable research about Mabley's life, including interviews with Mabley's friends and family, and then turned over her materials to Childress who was to write the actual play. As Childress worked, Taylor discussed with her the "inclusion of certain general scenes and characters in the play."[6] Unfortunately, the two artists ultimately could not agree over the ownership of the copyright interest in the play.

In the ensuing litigation concerning ownership of the copyright, the Second Circuit held that Taylor was not a joint author because she did not contribute copyrightable material.[7] In reaching the conclusion that a copyrightable contribution was required to achieve the status of joint author the court commented

> [T]he person with non-copyrightable material who proposed to join forces with a skilled writer to produce a copyrightable work is free to make a contract to disclose his or her material in return for assignment of part ownership of the resulting copyright.... It seems more consistent with the spirit of copyright law to oblige all joint authors to make copyrightable contributions, leaving those with non-copyrightable contributions to protect their rights through contract.[8]

One consequence of this rule requiring copyrightable contributions from each co-author is that parties who commission independent contractors and ask them to create copyrightable works cannot claim the status of joint authors merely because they provided the idea for the work or general instructions about how it was to be accomplished. In other words, the patron of the arts who hires a painter and instructs him or her to paint "a still life consisting of two apples, a peach and a white rose" will not be able to claim join ownership of the resulting painting. Similarly, one who hires an architect and provides instructions concerning the number and sizes of rooms to be included in the structure is not a co-author, as numerous cases have held.[9]

There is another, equally crucial requirement for a work to be categorized as a joint work. All of the would-be joint authors must share an intention to create a joint work at the time that the work is created. This requirement is clear both from the face of the statutory language and from the legislative history.[10] Thus, if a composer writes a song in 2003 with the notion that it will be a purely instrumental work, and

6. 945 F.2d at 502.

7. *See also* S.O.S., Inc. v. Payday, Inc., 886 F.2d 1081 (9th Cir.1989).

8. 945 F.2d at 507. To the same effect is Erickson v. Trinity Theatre, Inc., 13 F.3d 1061 (7th Cir.1994), where the Seventh Circuit quoted the following passage from Professor Goldstein's treatise with approval: "[A] collaborative contribution will not produce a joint work, and a contributor will not obtain a coownership interest, unless the contribution represents original expression that could stand on its own as the subject matter of copyright" 13 F.3d at 1070, quoting Paul Goldstein, COPYRIGHT: PRINCIPLES LAW AND PRACTICE § 4.2.1.2 at 379 (1989).

9. *See e.g.* M.G.B. Homes, Inc. v. Ameron Homes, Inc., 903 F.2d 1486, 1496 (11th Cir.1990); Aitken, Hazen, Hoffman, Miller, P.C. v. Empire Const. Co., 542 F.Supp. 252, 259 (D.Neb.1982).

10. H.R. Rep. No. 94–1476, 94th Cong. 2d Sess. 120 (1976).

then in 2004 asks a lyricist to write words for that song, the resulting work (song plus lyrics) is not a joint work.[11] Of course it is often difficult to reconstruct the actual intent of the parties by the time the case winds up in court. Courts thus often rely on a variety of circumstances surrounding the publication of the work. For instance it is at least some evidence that the crucial intent was lacking when one party has promulgated copies of the work listing only himself, or herself as the author.[12] Similarly a court would probably find the requisite intent lacking when one of the litigants has registered a claim of copyright in the work naming only himself as the sole author.

Assuming the requirements of a joint work are met, the several authors are, effectively, tenants in common of the copyright in question.[13] This means that each owns an undivided and equal fractional interest in the copyright. Thus, any one of the coowners of the copyright in such a work is free to exercise any of the rights of a copyright owner without the permission of the other joint owners, and to license others to exercise those rights as well. However, there is a duty to account to the other coowners for any profits realized from either direct use or licensing.[14] Thus, if a composer and lyricist collaborate on a song, the composer may enter into a license with a record company to produce the song on compact discs and sell them to the public without consulting with or getting the permission of the lyricist. The composer would, however, have to split the royalties earned from the license with the lyricist.

Things can get a little more complicated when one of the joint authors individually prepares a derivative work based on the previously created joint work. For instance, assume Alice and Bob jointly author a travel guide to New England in 2003, with numerous listings of charming country inns and fine restaurants. By 2005, such a book might be out of date, so Alice, acting on her own, prepares a new edition. She adds numerous entries, she deletes others, and rewords the descriptions of some that are retained. On the other hand, a good portion of the text is carried forward from the joint work verbatim. Bob might attempt to

11. At least one court came out the other way under the 1909 statute. In Shapiro, Bernstein & Co. v. Jerry Vogel Music Co., 221 F.2d 569 (2d Cir.1955), a case commonly called the *Twelfth Street Rag* case, a composer wrote an instrumental tune and then assigned away the copyright. Four years later the assignee of the copyright commissioned a lyricist to write words for the song. The Second Circuit held that the resulting song was a joint work even though it assumed that the composer had no intention of creating a joint work at the time he wrote the music. The Second Circuit retreated from the position in *Twelfth Street Rag* even before the enactment of the 1976 Copyright Act, and the position of that case seems to be clearly rejected by both the text and legislative history of the current statute.

12. *See Childress*, 945 F.2d at 508 ("'[t]hough 'billing' or 'credit' is not decisive in all cases and joint authorship can exist without any explicit discussion of this topic by the parties, consideration of the topic helpfully serves to focus the fact-finder's attention on how the parties implicitly regarded their undertaking.").

13. *See* H.R. Rep. No. 94–1474, 94th Cong. 2d Sess. 121 (1976). The use of the "tenant-in-common" analogy has led courts to look to cases dealing with real estate to resolve issues concerning the ownership rights to jointly authored works.

14. *See, e.g.* Oddo v. Ries, 743 F.2d 630 (9th Cir.1984); Shapiro, Bernstein & Co. v. Jerry Vogel Music Co., 221 F.2d 569 (2d Cir.1955), *modified* 223 F.2d 252 (2d Cir. 1955).

assert a copyright interest in this new edition, but if he tries to do so he will be unsuccessful. In *Weissmann v. Freeman*,[15] the Second Circuit addressed substantially this situation and held that the preparer of the derivative work was the sole owner of copyright in that derivative work. The court reasoned that any other rule

> would convert all derivative works based upon jointly authored works into joint works, regardless of whether there had been any joint labor on the subsequent version. If such were the law, it would eviscerate the independent copyright protection that attaches to a derivative work that is wholly independent of the protection afforded the preexisting work.[16]

This means that in our hypothetical case Bob cannot exploit the derivative work without Alice's permission and if he does so, he is guilty of infringement.

Weissmann did not address, however, the question of whether the preparer of the derivative work owes any financial recompense to the other joint author of the underlying work if the derivative work is exploited for profit. In other words, in the preceding hypothetical, does Alice have to share profits from the second edition of the guide-book (the one she prepared all by herself, and for which she owns the sole copyright) with Bob? After all, there is still some material from the joint work carried forward in that new edition. While there appears to be no definitive resolution of this question in the law as of yet, equitable considerations seem to argue for some form of compensation. The making of a derivative work is just as much a form of "exploitation" of the work as is reproducing and selling copies, or licensing third parties to perform the work, and in all of those cases the duty of an accounting is recognized. Moreover, an alternative rule might encourage joint authors who contributed relatively little to a first edition to immediately make minor revisions and attempt to market the resulting second edition without having to share the proceeds with the co-author. The exact amount of compensation owed under these circumstances might be difficult to calculate, but in our view the most plausible guideline should be the amount an independent licensee would have paid in an arms length transaction for the right to prepare the derivative work in question.

§ 6.4 Transfer of Copyright

Copyrights are freely transferable, just like all other types of personal property. They can be transferred outright, in a transaction usually denominated as an assignment, or the owner can merely give another party the right to exercise certain rights of copyright ownership by granting either an exclusive or non-exclusive license. These transfers can

---

15. 868 F.2d 1313 (2d Cir.1989). The case did not involve travel guides, but rather study guides prepared for medical stu-dents studying for licensing exams in radiology.

16. 868 F.2d at 1317.

be for compensation or can take the form of a gift. Moreover, copyrights will be treated as part of the owner's legal estate upon his or her death, and thus can be transferred by provisions in a will, or under the relevant provisions of state intestacy laws.

Because of the intangible nature of the copyright interest, however, a number of issues concerning transferability of ownership call for clarification.

6.4.1 Copyright Ownership Independent of Ownership of Copy

Under the Copyright Act of 1909, there was some ambiguity about copyright ownership in situations where the creator of a one-of-a-kind work of art, such as a painting or sculpture, sold or otherwise disposed of the sole copy of the work. At least some cases held that such a transfer also constituted a transfer of the underlying copyright interest.[1] This meant that the artist, having sold the work, could no longer control subsequent exploitation of the work in further copies or other media—for instance, he couldn't prevent the purchaser from making posters or postcards, nor could he make such reproductions himself, without running the risk of a charge of copyright infringement. This was, to say the least, a trap for the unwary.

The authors of the 1976 Act sought to prevent this result and eliminate any ambiguities in situations such as the one described above. Thus the present statute makes it absolutely plain that the sale or other disposition of a tangible copy of a work by the author does not in anyway affect or diminish that author's continued ownership of the copyright interest in the work. In other words, the ownership of any particular copy of a work and the ownership of the copyright are entirely independent. This principle is codified in section 202 of the current act, which provides:

> Ownership of a copyright, or of any of the exclusive rights under a copyright, is distinct from ownership of any material object in which the work is embodied. Transfer of ownership of any

§ 6.4

1. Perhaps the leading case reaching this holding was Pushman v. New York Graphic Society, Inc., 287 N.Y. 302, 39 N.E.2d 249 (1942). The precise scope of *Pushman* is somewhat uncertain. Since a one-of-a-kind work is, by definition, unpublished (*see supra* Chapter 3), the *Pushman* court was not actually addressing the ownership of federal copyright, since such unpublished works generally did not have federal copyright under the 1909 act. Rather, the court was concerned with the ownership of the *common-law copyright*, and it held that the unrestricted sale of the physical object was presumed to also convey the common-law copyright. Of course, once the transferee was determined to own the common law copyright, that gave him the right of publication, and the right to secure federal copyright upon such publication. The rule of the *Pushman* case was never popular—a few states even adopted legislation attempting to overrule it. Nonetheless, others courts followed it and the doctrine continues to have some importance, because in order to analyze the copyright status of a work where there was a transfers of unpublished copies prior to the effective date of the 1976 Act, *Pushman* may still be applicable. The House Report concerning the 1976 Act cited *Pushman* by name and indicated that the new statute would reverse the rule of the case. H.R. Rep. No. 94–1476 at 124 (1976).

material object, including the copy or phonorecord in which the work is first fixed, does not of itself convey any rights in the copyrighted work embodied in the object; nor, in the absence of an agreement, does transfer of ownership of a copyright or of any exclusive rights under a copyright convey property rights in any material object.[2]

6.4.2 Divisibility of Copyright Interests

Copyright owners seeking to maximize the economic value of their rights may often be motivated to deal with a variety of different people. An author of a novel, for instance, might wish to grant one publisher hardcover publication rights, another publisher paperback rights, a movie studio the right to make a derivative work in the form of a motion picture, and a record company the right to produce and market recording of the book on audiocassette tapes. Such a strategy is only possible if the copyright interest in the novel is "divisible"—permitting the copyright owner to transfer or license each right separately. The current copyright law provides for such divisibility in section 201, which states

> Any of the exclusive rights comprised in a copyright, including any subdivision of any of the rights specified by Section 106, may be transferred . . and owned separately.[3]

As a consequence, the assignee or exclusive licensee of any right has standing to sue for infringement where that transferee's rights are being violated.[4] For instance if a playwright were to grant an exclusive license to a theatre company to perform a particular play in New York City, during the month of September 2004, that theatre company could sue anyone else who attempted to perform the play in New York during the month in question. It could not, of course, sue someone for performing the play in Los Angeles or for preparing a derivative work based on the play (such as a movie). A non-exclusive licensee, however, does not have standing to sue for infringement. For instance, if a movie theatre receives a non-exclusive license to exhibit a particular motion picture, it anticipates that others may be showing the same movie in the same town at the same time. Even if some of those other exhibitors are infringing by showing the movie illegally, the copyright owner could have licensed them, and thus the non-exclusive licensee is no worse off than it bargained for.

The "divisibility" approach of the current statute represents a shift from the rule that prevailed under the 1909 statute. Under the 1909 Act, a copyright was an indivisible interest. The most important consequence of that rule was that a licensee lacked standing to sue for infringement, since a licensee did not "own" the copyright.[5] Over time, courts came up with several doctrines to make it possible for licensees to enforce their

---

2. 17 U.S.C.A. § 202 (2000).

3. 17 U.S.C.A. § 201(d)(2) (2000).

4. 17 U.S.C.A. § 201(d) (2000).

5. *See, e.g.,* Field v. True Comics, 89 F.Supp. 611 (S.D.N.Y.1950); Local Trademarks v. Powers, 56 F.Supp. 751 (E.D.Pa. 1944).

rights, so that the "indivisibility" standard of the old law was something of a myth by the time Congress adopted the 1976 Act. Nonetheless the older provision proved troublesome, and its replacement with the principle of infinite divisibility is a major improvement in the state of the law.

6.4.3   Requirements for Valid Transfers

Notwithstanding its economic virtue the divisibility of copyright discussed above has the potential to lead to considerable confusion. Multiple parties might claim a variety of rights to the same work, and sorting out those claims, particularly if they overlap, could prove quite complex. To reduce some of this potential confusion the 1976 Act requires certain formalities to be observed in connection with copyright transfers. These are in the nature of a statute of frauds requirement, as well as a variety of provisions relating to the recordation of transfers.

6.4.3.1   Writing Required

The first requirement of note is that a "transfer" of copyright must be in writing. According to the statute:

> A transfer of copyright ownership . . . is not valid unless an instrument of conveyance, or a note or memorandum of the transfer is in writing and signed by the owner of the rights conveyed or such owner's duly authorized agent.[6]

This provision, of course, is akin to the Statute of Frauds, familiar from contract law. In interpreting it, however, one must bear in mind that the term "transfer" is specifically defined in the current copyright law and that definition is not entirely intuitive. According to the statute:

> A "transfer of copyright ownership" is an assignment, mortgage, exclusive license, or any other conveyance, alienation or hypothecation of a copyright or of any of the exclusive rights comprised in a copyright, whether or not it is limited in time or place of effect, but not including a nonexclusive license.[7]

Note that under this definition the grant of a non-exclusive licenses is not a "transfer." This means that, unlike an assignment or exclusive license, a *non-exclusive* license need not be in writing in order to be valid.[8]

Although this distinction may seem curious at first glance, it is actually quite logical. After all, in a system where a copyright interest is infinitely divisible it would become very difficult, without a writing requirement, to determine the precise boundaries of the rights of various

---

6. 17 U.S.C.A. § 204(a) (2000).

7. 17 U.S.C.A. § 101 (2000).

8. Effects Associates, Inc. v. Cohen, 908 F.2d 555 (9th Cir.1990), *cert. denied,* 498 U.S. 1103, 111 S.Ct. 1003, 112 L.Ed.2d 1086 (1991). Some states may have laws that require even non-exclusive licenses to be in writing. That raises the question of wheth-er such requirements are pre-empted by the provision in the federal statute. Courts that have considered the issue have held that there is no federal preemption and have refused to enforce the oral licenses under state law. *See, e.g.,* Freedman v. Select Information Sys., Inc., 221 USPQ 848 (N.D.Cal.1983).

exclusive licensees. If two theater companies fell to arguing over which of them had the rights to stage a play in Dallas in February, reliance on alleged oral licenses could become the source of endless controversy at trial. On the other hand, where the purported license is non-exclusive, the only real effect of the license is to immunize the licensee from suit by the copyright owner. The non-exclusive licensee has no rights to sue others and thus the precise boundaries of the rights licensed become less important.

Note also that transfers by will, or bequest are not included within the definition of transfer, and thus not covered by the writing requirement. In this regard, state law will control. Since the vast majority of states require that a valid will be in writing in all but the most unusual circumstances, the practical importance of this observation is small, but if a state did permit an individual to pass property via an oral will, and if such a testator owned copyright interests, the will would be valid and the legatee of the copyright would become the owner despite the absence of a written document.

Where a writing is required, the courts have been fairly liberal in finding the requirement satisfied. For instance, if the assignment or exclusive license is first granted by an oral promise and then subsequently confirmed in a document, the grant is considered effective as of the date of the oral promise.[9] Courts have also been willing to find the necessary memorandum in the contract for sale of a business that did not even mention copyright explicitly[10] and in the endorsement on the back of a check.[11]

The writing requirement under the 1909 Act differed from the current statutory scheme in two interesting respects. First, that law did not require a writing for a license of any sort. Thus an oral exclusive license granted prior to January 1, 1978, is valid and enforceable, if it can be proved. That approach is not entirely surprising, given the assumption of non-divisibility of copyright interests that prevailed under the older law. Second, where a writing was required, only a formal instrument of transfer would suffice—a "note or memorandum" would not be adequate.[12] These differences can be important where a claimant traces his or her rights back to events occurring before 1978.

9. *See, e.g.,* Eden Toys, Inc. v. Florelee Undergarment Co., 697 F.2d 27, 36 (2d Cir.1982). ("The 'note or memorandum of the transfer' need not be made at the time when the license is initiated; the requirement is satisfied by the copyright owner's later execution of a writing which confirms the agreement.").

10. Schiller & Schmidt, Inc. v. Nordisco Corp., 969 F.2d 410, 413 (7th Cir.1992).

11. Franklin Mint Corp. v. National Wildlife Art Exch., Inc., 575 F.2d 62 (3d Cir.), *cert. denied,* 439 U.S. 880, 99 S.Ct. 217, 58 L.Ed.2d 193 (1978). *Cf.* Playboy Enterprises, Inc. v. Dumas, 53 F.3d 549 (2d Cir.1995), *cert. denied,* 516 U.S. 1010, 116 S.Ct. 567, 133 L.Ed.2d 491 (1995) (finding endorsement on check insufficient to meet writing requirement of § 204(a) because it was ambiguous).

12. The relevant provision is section 28 of the 1909 Act, which read "copyright secured under this title or previous copyright laws of the United States may be assigned, granted, or mortgaged by an instrument in writing signed by the proprietor of the copyright, or may be bequeathed by will."

6.4.3.2　Recordation

In addition to the writing requirement specified in the preceding subsection, the current law also has detailed provisions providing for the recordation of transfers of copyright interests, as well as for other documents "pertaining to a copyright."[13] These provisions operate on rough analogy to those governing the recording of deeds and other instruments relating to land. Unlike the system controlling land transfers, however, the recordation system established by the copyright statute is, at the present time, entirely optional. That is to say, an unrecorded assignment or exclusive license will be enforceable *as between the parties* regardless of whether it has been recorded. For transfers prior to 1989, however, recordation was a prerequisite to the filing of an infringement suit. This requirement was dropped from the statute as part of U.S. adherence to the international copyright treaty known as the Berne Convention.[14]

There are, however, numerous advantages that flow from recording. The recording of a document relating to a transfer of copyright, or otherwise pertaining to copyright, gives constructive notice to all other persons of the facts stated in the document, provided that the document specifically identifies the work in question and that registration has been made for the work.[15] The constructive notice principle also means that, as a practical matter, anyone intending to secure an assignment or license of a copyright interest would be well advised to search the records of the copyright office before entering into such a transaction to discover if there are any prior recorded transfers lurking out there that could receive priority.

As the foregoing comments suggest, the most important feature of the recordation system established by the copyright act is the articulation of rules specifying which of several inconsistent grants will prevail in the event of a dispute. Under those rules,

> As between two conflicting transfers, the one executed first prevails if it is recorded ... within one month after its execution in the United States or within two months after its execution outside the United States, or at any time before recordation ... of the later transfer. Otherwise the later transfer prevails if recorded first ... and if taken in good faith, for valuable consideration or on the basis of a binding promise to pay royalties, and without notice of the earlier transfer.[16]

To understand the operation of this provision imagine that Olivia, a copyright owner, assigns the copyright in her novel to Alan on March 1, and then, on March 15th purports to assign the same copyright to Betty.

---

13. Bear in mind that a non-exclusive license in not a "transfer" of copyright. Nonetheless, a document granting such a license in a work would be recordable under this provision, since it "pertains" to copyright.

14. Berne Convention Implementation Act of 1988, § 5, Pub. L. No. 100–568, 102 Stat. 2853 (1988).

15. 17 U.S.C.A. § 205(c) (2000).

16. 17 U.S.C.A. § 205(d) (2000).

If Betty knows of the earlier transaction with Alan, then Betty will have no rights and Alan will prevail—a result that certainly seems both fair and intuitive. Note also that if Betty purportedly received the copyright as a "gift"—that is, she did not pay Olivia any consideration for it—once again Alan will prevail regardless of whether she was aware of Olivia's earlier dealings with Alan.

Assuming, however, that Betty took the assignment for valuable consideration and with no notice of Olivia's prior dealings with Alan, the statute sets up something of a race to record.[17] The first of the two parties to record will prevail, with the qualification that Alan, as the first transferee, has a grace period of either one or two months, depending on where (U.S. or abroad) the transfer was executed. Thus, if Betty records on March 16th (the day after the transfer to her) and Alan does not get around to recording until March 20th, Alan will still prevail, since he recorded within the one month grace period. But if Alan waits until May 3rd to record, Betty will prevail.

The system just described applies to inconsistent or conflicting "transfers," which as noted include assignments, exclusive licenses and a variety of other itemized events. Slightly different rules in the statute govern conflicts between a transfer and a non-exclusive license. Under those provisions a *written* non-exclusive license prevails over a subsequent transfer, even if the license itself was not recorded. It will also prevail over a prior transfer, if the licensee took the license without knowledge of the prior transfer and before that prior transfer was recorded.[18] Of course a non-exclusive license need not be in writing, but if an oral license is granted, it is effectively terminated when the underlying copyright interest is transferred.

Some examples will make this provision a bit more concrete. Assume Paul is a playwright who owns the copyright to a play. In our first case, assume that on April 1st he grants Lucille a non-exclusive license to perform the play in Chicago during the month of September, and further assume that this license is in writing. If, on May 1st, Paul then assigns the copyright in the play to the Shubert organization, that transfer will not affect Lucille's right under the license. She may go ahead and perform the play as agreed. Now, change the situation to assume that on March 1, Paul assigned the rights to Shubert, but then granted the non-exclusive license to Lucille on April 1. In this case, Paul is obviously giving away rights that he no longer owns. If Lucille knows that—if she has notice of the transfer to Shubert—she has no rights. Even if Lucille doesn't actually know about the transfer to Shubert, if that transfer to Shubert was recorded, Lucille would have constructive notice and her purported license would be no good. On the other hand, if Lucille had no notice of the prior transfer, and if the prior transfer was not recorded

17. This approach is often called a "race-notice" statute in the real estate context.

18. 17 U.S.C.A. § 205(e) (2000).

until after April 1st, then the law will protect Lucille by forcing the transferee to honor the license according to its terms.

Prior to 1989, the recordation of a transfer of copyright was also required before the transferee could institute suit for copyright infringement. Congress deleted that provision from the statute as part of U.S. adherence to the Berne Convention, because, as we have repeatedly seen, that international copyright regime forbids the imposition of formalities as a condition of copyright protection.[19]

Although different in a number of particulars, the recordation scheme under the 1909 copyright law closely resembled the one described above. Just as is true today, subsequent transferees would prevail under the older law if they had no notice, actual or constructive, of a prior transfer, if they paid value and if they promptly recorded.[20] Unlike the 1976 Act section, however, the 1909 Act provision does not deal with all copyright "transfers" but rather is limited to "assignments."

6.4.4 Involuntary Transfers

Just like tangible property, copyright interests can be seized involuntarily. An interesting provision of the 1976 copyright act, section 201(e), deals with that situation. It provides that:

> When an individual author's ownership of a copyright ... has not previously been transferred voluntarily by that individual author, no action by any governmental body or other official or organization purporting to seize, expropriate, transfer, or exercise rights of ownership with respect to the copyright ... shall be given effect under this title except as provided under Title 11 [Bankruptcy].[21]

This provision was added to the statute out of a concern that the then Soviet Union might attempt to suppress the writings of dissidents by expropriating the copyrights to those works under Soviet law and then—asserting the status of a lawful copyright owner—suing disseminators of those works in the United States. By its terms, the provision only applies to expropriation from the original individual author. That means that works made for hire are not within the scope of this section. It also means that once an author has parted with title to the work by assignment, the work can be seized from the assignee without violating this provision.

Despite its broad language, section 201(e) will not insulate a copyright holder from a variety of events that might, at first blush look "involuntary." Thus, loss of the copyright through foreclosure on a

---

19. Berne Convention, Art. 5(2).

20. Act of 1909, § 30 ("Every assignment of copyright shall be recorded in the copyright office with three calendar months after its execution in the United States or within six calendar months after its execution without the limits of the United States, in default of which it shall be void as against any subsequent purchaser or mortgagee for a valuable consideration, without notice, whose assignment has been duly recorded.")

21. 17 U.S.C.A. § 201(e) (2000).

mortgage or execution of a lien, are entirely permissible. In these cases, the copyright owner is said to have voluntarily entered into the underlying transaction, making the section inapplicable. Moreover, at least one court construed this provision "as dealing with actions initiated by governmental bodies, not with those where, as in the case of a judgement lienholder, the instruments of government are merely acting in furtherance of private objectives."[22]

While one commentator has suggested that the division or transfer of a copyright interest upon the termination of a marriage under state domestic relations might violate section 201(e),[23] Professor Goldstein, in his treatise, suggests that the provision should be considered inapplicable for several reasons, including the fact that entry into the marriage in question is just as voluntary as entering into a mortgage or other loan.[24]

22. National Peregrine, Inc. v. Capitol Fed. Sav. & Loan Assn. of Denver, 116 B.R. 194, 205–206, n. 16 (C.D.Cal.1990).

23. Francis M. Nevins, *When an Author's Marriage Dies: The Copyright–Divorce Connection,* 37 J. COPYRIGHT SOC'Y 382 (1990).

24. Goldstein, Copyright, 1994 Supplement at p. 92.

Chapter 7

THE EXCLUSIVE RIGHTS OF
A COPYRIGHT HOLDER

Table of Sections

Section 106 of the copyright statute provides copyright holders with six exclusive rights. As originally enacted, the Copyright Act of 1976 included five of these rights: reproduction, adaptation, distribution, public performance and public display. A sixth, the right to perform copyrighted sound recordings publicly by means of a digital audio transmission, was added by the Digital Performance Right in Sound Recordings Act of 1995.[1] The exclusive rights define the protections accorded to a copyright owner. Unauthorized acts that violate an exclusive right are considered a copyright infringement.

Each of the exclusive rights is independent from the others. An infringer need only violate one right to be subject to liability for copyright infringement. Still, the exclusive rights are related, and often one infringing act simultaneously violates multiple exclusive rights granted by the copyright law. If, for example, a publisher prepared a foreign-language translation of a protected novel without authorization from the copyright holder, both the reproduction and adaptation rights would be violated.

The Copyright Act subjects each exclusive right to a number of limitations. A careful reading of § 106 itself reveals several immediate constraints. For example, the rights of display and performance extend only to acts done "publicly." As a result, copyright owners lack control over private performances or displays of their work. As well, only "literary, musical, dramatic, and choreographic works, pantomimes, and motion pictures and other audiovisual works" are granted the right of public performance. Consequentially, the copyright owner of a sound recording cannot prevent the public performance of the work under § 106(4).

Additional limitations on the exclusive rights are set out in sections 107 through 122. The most notable among these is the fair use privilege of § 107. Because of the many issues implicated by this doctrine, we will defer our consideration of it to a subsequent chapter. Generally, the fair use privilege allows a third party to make reasonable use of a protected work without the consent of the copyright owner. Another principal limitation upon the exclusive rights is the first sale doctrine of § 109. This doctrine allows the lawful purchaser of a physical copy of a protected work, such as a book or portrait, to dispose of that copy without regard to the copyright owner. Many of the other provisions limiting the exclusive rights are quite intricate, effectively setting out detailed economic regulatory schemes for various information industries.

In addition, the Copyright Act also authorizes a number of compulsory licenses. A compulsory license allows individuals to use protected works without obtaining the consent of the copyright owner upon payment of fees set by the government. In order to take advantage of a compulsory license, the prospective user must comply with certain statutory procedures. Compulsory licenses exist for secondary transmissions by cable television systems (§ 111), the digital transmission and distribution of sound recordings (§§ 114 and 115), the so-called "mechanical

---

1. Digital Performance Right in Sound Recordings Act of 1995, Pub. L. No. 104–39, 109 Stat. 336 (codified as amended in scat-   tered sections of 17 U.S.C.A.1995) (effective Feb. 1, 1996).

license" for distribution of phonorecords of non-dramatic musical works
(§ 115), public broadcasting by non-commercial entities (§ 118) and
satellite retransmissions (§ 119).

§ 7.1   The Reproduction Right

7.1.1   Basic Principles

The fundamental privilege provided by the copyright laws is the
exclusive right to reproduce a copyrighted work in copies or phonorecords. Section 101 of the Copyright Act defines the term "phonorecords"
as "material objects in which sounds, other than those accompanying a
motion picture or audiovisual work, are fixed by any method now known
or later developed...." "Copies" are defined as "material objects, other
than phonorecords, in which a work is fixed by any method now known
or later developed...." These definitions mean that the reproduction
right is violated whenever an unauthorized party fixes the protected
work in a material object.

For example, suppose that the actor Gerald Garrick lawfully purchases a copy of the play *King John: A One–Man Show*. Without
permission from the copyright owner, Garrick memorizes the script of
King John and performs before paying audiences. Although Garrick may
have infringed the public performance right, he has not violated the
reproduction right. Garrick's mere performance or oral recitation of
King John does not result in the creation of a material object embodying
the protected work.

On the other hand, if Garrick was so struck by the beauty of the
lines of the play that he decided to copy them out in long hand into a
notebook, he would violate the reproduction right, even if he never sold
that notebook, or, for that matter, even showed it to anyone. In fact, as
we shall see, the reproduction right means that making even a single
copy, even as an intermediate step to creating a new work,[1] or even for
personal and private use, is a prima facie infringement, unless it can be
excused under some specific provision of the statute. That is the meaning of the word "exclusive" in the language of § 106 conferring this
right.[2]

Unlike the performance or display rights, the reproduction right is
not limited to copies or phonorecords that are publicly available. Unless
fair use or another limitation upon the reproduction right is available, a
wholly private, undistributed reproduction counts as a copyright infringement. Moreover, although the term "reproduction right" might
suggest otherwise, an individual need not make a slavish copy of a
protected work in order to be judged a copyright infringer. Variations or
departures from the copyrighted work may still constitute an infringe-

---

§ 7.1

1. *See, e.g.,* Walt Disney Productions v.
Filmation Assoc., 628 F.Supp. 871 (C.D.Cal.
1986).

2. *See infra* Chapter 9.

ment if the accused work impermissibly appropriates the expression, rather than the idea of the copyrighted work.[3]

7.1.2 Limitations on the Reproduction Right

The 1976 Act includes a number of provisions that limit the reproduction right. Many of these exemptions are highly technical, complex statutes that reflect hard-fought debates between content providers and the community of users, or between interested constituencies with divergent interests like libraries and patrons. Although a detailed discussion of each of these provisions exceeds the scope of this text, we have endeavored to provide a concise summary of several of these provisions in the paragraphs that follow. As is inevitable with any effort to summarize complex statutory language, these overviews paint with something of a broad brush and cannot substitute for a careful reading of the controlling statutory language.

Section 108—Libraries and Archives. Section 108 exempts certain reproductions produced by qualifying libraries and archives. In order to take advantage of any of the provisions of this section, a library or archive must meet three initial conditions. First, its collections must either be open to the general public, or at least to other researchers besides those affiliated with the institution of which it is a part.[4] Thus a municipal public library would easily satisfy this test, as would a private university library that allowed visiting scholars from other schools to use the collection. On the other hand, a law firm library that did not allow outsiders to use its materials would have no rights under this provision. The second general condition is that any reproductions made under the safe harbor of section 108 must be made without any purpose of direct or indirect commercial advantage.[5] In other words, a library is not permitted to invoke this section to engage in a collateral enterprise of publishing books for profit. Finally, any copies made under the shelter of this provision must contain the same notice of copyright that appears on the version from which the copy is made, or alternatively a statement that work may be protected by copyright.[6]

The statute then goes on to distinguish copies that the library makes for its own purposes, and copies that it makes at the request of a library patron. If the library is copying for its own purposes, the statute provides separate rules depending on whether the work is published or unpublished. In the case of an unpublished work, the library may make up to three copies for either preservation purposes, or in order to deposit the copies in another similar library, provided it already owns a copy of the work.[7] For instance, assume the George Washington University Law Library holds in its collection a brilliant L.L.M. thesis analyzing section 108 of the copyright laws, which has never been published. If that copy is beginning to deteriorate, it could make up to three copies, perhaps even

---

3. *See infra* § 9.1.

4. 17 U.S.C.A. § 108(a)(2) (2000).

5. 17 U.S.C.A. § 108(a)(1) (2000).

6. 17 U.S.C.A. § 108(a)(3) (2000).

7. 17 U.S.C.A. § 108(b) (2000).

in a different medium such as microfilm, for purposes of preservation. Similarly, if Georgetown University were to request a copy of this thesis, George Washington University could make a copy and transfer it to Georgetown. In all these cases there is one further limitation. If the library makes a copy in digital format, it cannot distribute that copy, nor can it be made available to patrons located outside the library premises. Thus, the library could not upload the text of the unpublished thesis onto its computers and make it available generally over the Internet.

Where the work is published, the library's right to copy is a bit more circumscribed. It may make up three copies, but only for the purpose of replacing a copy that is damaged, deteriorating, lost or stolen, or if the existing format of the work becomes obsolete, and even then, only if it determines that it cannot obtain an unused replacement copy on the open market at a fair price.[8] For instance, assume that the Washington, D.C. Public Library discovers that its only copy of an obscure book on the cultural significance of disco music, published in 1973 and now out of print, is missing from its shelves. It must first determine if it can buy a new copy at a fair price. If not, it could borrow the book from another library, make up to three copies, and include those in its collections. Here again, the library must observe the same restrictions regarding copies in a digital format.

In the case of copies made at the request of, and for the use of library patrons, the statute distinguishes between situations where the material can be found on the open market for a fair price and where it is unavailable. In the latter situation, the library can make one copy of the work and give it to the user provided that the copy becomes the private property of the user; the library has no reason to believe that the copy will be used for any purpose other than private study or research, and the library gives the patron due warning of the constraints imposed by the copyright laws.[9] Thus, if a library user wanted a copy of the hypothetical work on disco music described in the previous paragraph, and if neither a new nor a used copy could be found at a fair price, the library would be free to make a copy for that user without running the risk of copyright infringement, provided it had no reason to believe that the user was going to sell the copy or otherwise make commercial use of it. Where the work is generally available, the library is only permitted to copy a "small part" of the work for the patron, or, in case of a magazine or other collective work, to copy only one article from the work.[10]

A separate subsection of the statute makes it clear that the right to copy granted under section 108 only covers isolated and unrelated copying of the same material. Related, concerted or systematic copying of the same material over and over again, even at the behest of different patrons is not protected by this statute and would constitute a violation of the reproduction rights of the relevant copyright owner.[11] Section 108

8. 17 U.S.C.A. § 108(c) (2000).   **10.** 17 U.S.C.A. § 108(d) (2000).

9. 17 U.S.C.A. § 108(e) (2000).   **11.** 17 U.S.C.A. § 108(g) (2000).

also explicitly declares that a library may not make copies of musical, pictorial, graphic, sculptural or audiovisual works, at the request of patron.[12] Thus if one were to saunter into the local public library and ask them to make low cost copies of musical recordings or videotapes in their collections, they would surely refuse, on pain of infringement liability.

Of course, library employees may not be the only ones doing copying inside the library building. Most libraries have coin operated photocopiers on the premises. One could argue that the provision of this equipment in a building filled with copyrighted books is a virtual invitation to patrons to infringe. Indeed, one could argue that the library itself could be held liable for contributory infringement for making the machine available. To avoid that result, section 108(f) deals explicitly with "unsupervised use of reproducing equipment" on the library premises. It insulates the library from any liability, provided the equipment displays a notice informing users of the potential copyright implications of their actions. This explains the rather sternly worded signs titled "Warning Concerning Copyright Restrictions" posted on copy machines in libraries all over the United States. This subsection also specifically declares that the individual using the unsupervised copying equipment remains subject to infringement liability if his or her activities exceed the scope of permissible fair use.

Section 112—Ephemeral Recordings. In copyright parlance, temporary copies or phonorecords produced for purposes of broadcasting a work to the public are termed "ephemeral recordings." A radio or television broadcaster may have obtained the right to perform a work—either through a license or through an exemption under the Copyright Act—but may not have obtained the right to reproduce that work. Yet practical and technological considerations may require the broadcaster to make a copy of the work in order to broadcast it. Section 112 provides a narrow exemption to the reproduction right in such cases, allowing most broadcasters to make a single copy for purposes of transmission to the public.[13] This exemption, however, is not available for motion pictures or other audio-visual works. Any ephemeral copy must ordinarily be destroyed within six months of the first broadcast.[14] Government and non-profit organizations receive broader exemptions under § 112.[15]

For instance, imagine a radio station that has licensed the rights to broadcast the play-by-play coverage of a football game. Such a license gives the radio station the right to perform the work, but no right to make a copy of it. Section 112, however, permits the making of a copy to facilitate its performance rights. Thus, if there is a major Presidential address at the time of the football game, the station might wish to broadcast the President's remarks live, make an "ephemeral recording" of the game, and then use the ephemeral recording subsequently to transmit the play-by-play of the game to its listening audience.

12. 17 U.S.C.A. § 108(i) (2000).

13. 17 U.S.C.A. § 112(a)(1) (2000).

14. 17 U.S.C.A. § 117(a)(1)(C) (2000).

15. 17 U.S.C.A. § 107(b),(c),(d) (2000).

Section 113—Pictorial, Graphic and Sculptural Works. The copyright law has traditionally protected aesthetic rather than utilitarian works. This distinction quickly collapses, however, when a pictorial, graphic or sculptural work has been embodied in a useful article. Section 113(a) helpfully restates the general rule in such cases: the reproduction right "includes the right to reproduce the work in or on any kind of article, whether useful or otherwise."[16] Suppose, for example, that a automobile manufacturer makes copies of a small sculpture and attaches them as hood ornaments on its new line of automobiles, all without obtaining the permission of the copyright owner of the sculpture. Assuming that the sculpture is subject to copyright, this act is a copyright infringement notwithstanding the fact that the sculpture has been placed upon a useful article.

Some works of authorship display a useful article as such. A blueprint may depict the design of an electric circuit, for example, or a model may portray an aircraft engine. For that matter, a pop art painting might depict a toaster or a blender. In such cases § 113(b) specifies that the copyright law provides authors with no "greater or lesser rights with respect to the making, distribution or display of the useful article so portrayed...."[17] Stated more simply, a copyright in a pictorial, graphic or sculptural work depicting a useful object does not extend to embodiments of the useful object itself. If an engineer develops a blueprint depicting a electric circuit, for example, the engineer could use the copyright law to prevent reproductions of the blueprint itself. But others could actually build the circuit without violating the engineer's copyright. If the engineer seeks intellectual property protection for the useful article itself, she must turn to the patent law.

Section 114—Sound Recordings. As compared to other sorts of works, sound recordings receive a diminished form of the reproduction right. Under § 114(b), the reproduction right for sound recordings is limited to recapturing the actual sounds fixed in that recording. The unauthorized use of a "dual deck" tape recorder to duplicate another's sound recording violates the reproduction right. However, even a slavish imitation of a sound recording does not. Suppose, for example, that the popular singing group "The Broadstreet Boys" makes a sound recording of the public domain song "Kitchie." Another band—Outta Synch, perhaps—could permissibly imitate the Broadstreet Boys sound recording down to the last phrasing, so long as they do not use mechanical means to reproduce the actual sounds made by the Broadstreet Boys.

When measuring the impact of § 114, it is important to remember that one phonorecord may embody two copyrights: the copyright in the sound recording, and the copyright in the underlying musical work. Suppose, for example, that in 2003 members of The Broadstreet Boys write the lyrics and compose the music for an original musical work, "Last Night." The Broadstreet Boys then produced a sound recording of

16.   17 U.S.C.A. § 113(a) (2000).   **17.**   17 U.S.C.A. § 113(b) (2000).

"Last Night." If another band slavishly imitated "Last Night," without mechanically reproducing the actual sounds in the Broadstreet Boys recording, they would not infringe the reproduction right in the sound recording. But they would infringe the reproduction right in the underlying musical work.

Section 115—The Mechanical License. Section 115 establishes a compulsory license that significantly limits the reproduction right for musical copyright owners. This compulsory license has traditionally been known as the "mechanical license." It allows individuals to make their own sound recordings of non-dramatic musical works—a so-called "cover" version—provided that a phonorecord of that musical work has previously been distributed to the public. The individual seeking the compulsory license must also follow procedures provided in § 115 and pay a royalty on each phonorecord distributed under the license. The mechanical rate is periodically adjusted by an entity known as a Copyright Arbitration Royalty Panel, or CARP.[18] During 2004 and 2005, for example, the mechanical rate is 8.5¢ per song, or 1.65¢ per minute if the recording exceeds five minutes.

The essential workings of the mechanical license are best illustrated by example. Suppose that composer Bart Backrub composes a song and licenses Checker Records to produce a recording. After procuring the services of a singer and musicians, Checker produces a sound recording. Once the Checker recording has been distributed to the public via phonorecord, a third party, Kay Tell, can invoke the mechanical license of § 115 to make her own cover recording. Tell must serve notice on Checker, or the Copyright Office if Checker's address cannot be determined, at least thirty days prior to making her recording. Tell may then assemble her own band, produce a sound recording and distribute it to the public. Backrub cannot stop her even if he doesn't like the band she will hire or, for that matter, even if he merely harbors a grudge against her. He must content himself with the statutory royalties. Section 115 also provides Kay with "the privilege of making a musical arrangement of the work to the extent necessary to conform it to the style or manner of interpretation involved...."[19] To comply with the mechanical license, however Kay's version must not "change the basic melody or fundamental character of the work."[20]

A few additional details of § 115 are worth noting here. First, the compulsory license can only be obtained if the original sound recording was produced under the authority of the copyright owner.[21] If the Checker Records version of Backrub's song was unauthorized, Tell would not be able to invoke the compulsory license. Second, a compulsory license may only be obtained by a person whose "primary purpose in making phonorecords is to distribute them to the public for private

---

18. That this entity is not known as a Copyright Royalty Arbitration Panel probably reflects some Congressional anxiety that the acronym might reflect negatively on the enterprise.

19. 17 U.S.C.A. § 115(a)(2) (2000).

20. *Ibid.*

21. 17 U.S.C.A. § 115(a) (2000).

use...."[22] Finally, the statute expressly applies only to non-dramatic musical works,[23] leaving such works as operas or musicals exempt from the mechanical license.

In practice, the Copyright Office administers relatively few mechanical licenses. The existence of the statutory compulsory mechanical license usually spurs individuals to make their own, more convenient private arrangements.[24] Entities specializing in the licensing of mechanical rights, such as the Harry Fox Agency, often facilitate these transactions.[25]

Section 117—Computer Programs. This provision provides several limited exemptions to the reproduction right for computer users. Section 117(a)(1) allows owners of a copy of a computer software program to make or authorize the making of a copy of that program if "such a new copy or adaptation is created as an essential step in the utilization of the computer program...." Loading a program from a CD onto a hard drive, in order to improve the performance of the program, would likely fit into this safe harbor.[26] Indeed, the mere act of turning on a computer often "loads" certain software programs into computer memory and some courts have held that this process results in the making of a copy of the program.[27] Thus, without the exemption of section 117(a)(1) it would be virtually impossible to use a computer without violating reproduction rights and committing technical copyright infringement. Section 117(a)(2) also allows an owner to make one backup copy of a computer program for archival purposes.

In addition, § 117(c) allows the owner or lessee of a computer to make, or to authorize the making of, a copy of a computer program for purposes of maintenance or repair of that computer. Congress added this provision in 1998 in order to protect independent computer maintenance enterprises from charges of copyright infringement.[28] Independent maintenance enterprises frequently turn on a client's computer in order to service it, resulting in the automatic loading of the another's software into the computer's memory (RAM). Prior to this amendment, in an attempt to prevent third party providers from engaging in the software maintenance business, copyright holders had successfully asserted that the act of loading the program into a computer's memory infringed their reproduction right.[29] Section 117(c) effectively exempted this practice from the scope of the copyright laws.

22. 17 U.S.C.A. § 115(a) (2000).

23. 17 U.S.C.A. § 115(a) (2000).

24. *See* Ralph Oman, *The Compulsory License Redux: Will It Survive in a Changing Marketplace?*, 5 Cardozo Arts & Ent. L.J. 37, 48 (1986).

25. For more on the Harry Fox Agency, consult its web site at http://www.nmpa.org/hfa.html.

26. Nimmer, Copyright § 8.08[B][1] (2002).

27. *See, e.g.,* Summit Technology, Inc. v. High–Line Medical Instruments Co., Inc., 922 F.Supp. 299, 315 (C.D.Cal. 1996).

28. *See* Title III of the Digital Millennium Copyright Act, Pub. L. No. 105–304, 112 Stat. 2860 § 301 (1998).

29. See MAI Sys. Corp. v. Peak Computer, Inc., 991 F.2d 511 (9th Cir.1993).

Section 120—Architectural Works. Section 120(a) provides that once an architectural work has been constructed such that it is "ordinarily visible from a public place," the copyright owner may not "prevent the making, distributing, or public display of pictures, paintings, photographs, or other pictorial representations of the work."[30] Thus if you choose to photograph striking works of architecture on your next visit to New York or Chicago, you will not violate the architect's reproduction rights. Note that this exception is limited to pictorial representations, and would not exempt the making of three-dimensional replicas of the building, for example.

Section 121—Reproduction for Blind or Other People with Disabilities. This provision provides certain exemptions for governmental and non-profit organizations that have a primary mission of promoting information access for persons with blindness or other disabilities. Under specified conditions, such entities are authorized to make copies or phonorecords of a previously published, nondramatic literary work in specialized formats exclusively for blind or disabled persons.

§ 7.2   The Adaptation Right

7.2.1   Basic Principles

The second paragraph of § 106 invests the copyright holder with the exclusive right "to prepare derivative works based upon the copyrighted work." This entitlement is commonly known as the adaptation right. The adaptation right is violated when a third party makes an unauthorized derivative work that recasts, transforms or adapts the protected work. Exemplary derivative works include dramatizations, translations and musical arrangements.

Often a single infringing work will violate not only the adaptation right, but the reproduction or performance rights as well. For example, suppose that philologist Wilt Coughlan precisely translates a novel entitled "Thus Spoke Jerusalem" from the German into the English language, without the authorization of the copyright holder. The translation may violate the adaptation right, for a translation squarely falls into the definition of "derivative work" set forth in § 101 of the 1976 Act. Coughlan's translation may also violate the reproduction right. A strict English version of "Thus Spoke Jerusalem" would incorporate sufficient expression from the original work to be substantially similar to its German predecessor.

In rare cases courts will find infringement of the adaptation right even though no reproduction of the protected work took place. In *Mirage Editions, Inc. v. Albuquerque A.R.T. Co.,*[1] the defendant purchased commemorative books celebrating the life and artistic works of Patrick Nagel. The defendant then cut photographs of Nagel's works from the books and mounted them on ceramic tiles. The Court of Appeals for the

---

30.   17 U.S.C.A. § 120(a) (2000).

§ 7.2
1.   856 F.2d 1341 (9th Cir.1988).

Ninth Circuit held that this practice resulted in unauthorized derivative works and infringed the adaptation right. According to the Ninth Circuit, the defendant both recast and transformed Nagel's images through its tile preparation process. The Ninth Circuit further rejected the defendant's reliance upon the first sale doctrine, concluding that the mere purchase of a book does not transfer the right to make derivative works to the buyer.

Although the Ninth Circuit subsequently confirmed the holding in *Mirage Editions*,[2] this ruling has attracted great controversy.[3] Notably, under the similar facts presented in *Lee v. A.R.T. Company*,[4] the Court of Appeals for the Seventh Circuit subsequently reached a contrary result. The defendant here purchased notecards and small lithographs that had been produced by artist Annie Lee. These works were then mounted on ceramic tiles. Citing the § 101 definition of "derivative work," Judge Easterbrook concluded that the accused infringer had neither recast, transformed or adapted Lee's works merely by remounting copies of works that it lawfully owned. Lee's works instead remained exactly as they were when they left her studio. Reluctant to turn the humble picture framer into a copyright infringer, or to give artists such an extraordinary degree of control over even slight modifications to their works, the Seventh Circuit declined to find the adaptation right infringed.

As between the two decisions, *Lee* strikes us as the more soundly reasoned case. The *Mirage Editions* approach could seemingly convert trivial acts, such as hanging a painting on a wall such that the painting is slightly crooked, into a copyright infringement. This would make many owners of art objects into inadvertent infringers without advancing any policy goals of copyright or economic interests of artists. The cases can perhaps be distinguished by noting that *Lee* involved a simple mounting of notecards, while in *Mirage Editions* the defendant made more extensive alterations to a book of ordered images. The latter court may have been concerned that the defendant had presented Nagel's works in a sequence and manner the copyright proprietor had not intended, though, if that is the case, the court was less than transparent in explaining its reasoning.

In even more unusual circumstances, the courts have found infringement of the adaptation right even though the protected work does not itself appear in the accused work. One such case was *Micro Star v. Formgen Inc.*[5] The work under copyright was Duke Nukem 3D, a computer game featuring "a beefy commando type named Duke who wanders around post-Apocalypse Los Angeles, shooting Pig Cops with a gun, lobbing hand grenades, searching for medkits and steroids, using a jetpack to leap over obstacles, blowing up gas tanks, [and] avoiding

2. *See* Munoz v. Albuquerque A.R.T. Co., 38 F.3d 1218 (9th Cir.1994).

3. *See* Wendy J. Gordon, *On Owning Information: Intellectual Property and the* *Restitutionary Impulse*, 78 VA. L. REV. 149, 255 n. 401 (1992).

4. 125 F.3d 580 (7th Cir.1997).

5. 154 F.3d 1107 (9th Cir.1998).

radioactive slime." Duke Nukem 3D included 29 levels featuring different combinations of scenery, aliens and other challenges. The computer game further included a "Build Editor," a utility that allowed users to create their own levels. The accused infringer, Micro Star, gathered 300 user-created levels that had been posted on the internet and sold them on a CD titled "Nuke It."

When accused of copyright infringement, Micro Star in part asserted that "Nuke It" did not use any protected expression from the Duke Nukem 3D software. It seems that the Duke Nukem 3D software consisted of three distinct components: (1) a game engine, the program that ran the game using the computer's hardware capabilities and software resources; (2) the source art library, which contained images of scenery, objects and other encounters within the game; and (3) the so-called MAP files, which instructed the game engine about the arrangement of particular levels. The "Nuke It" levels were expressed as MAP files, which the Duke Nuke 3D game engine would consult in order to make the computer hardware to run the game. Micro Star's position was that although "Nuke It" levels referenced the source art library, they did not actually contain any art files themselves. As a result the defendant argued that no violation of the adaptation right could have occurred.

The Court of Appeals for the Ninth Circuit rejected Micro Star's argument and held that "Nuke It" was an infringing derivative work. Judge Kozinski reasoned that the adaptation right included the right to create sequels to the original Duke Nukem game plot, and that the "Nuke It" levels constituted new, if somewhat repetitive stories of the protagonist's post-Holocaust travails regardless of whether they physically incorporated any of the protected images from plaintiff's original work. Rejecting arguments asserting fair use and an implied license, the Ninth Circuit affirmed the trial court's grant of a preliminary injunction against Micro Star.

7.2.2   Limitations on the Adaptation Right

Given the significant overlap between the adaptation right and the reproduction right, that the adaptation right is often subject to the same limitations as the reproduction right is unsurprising.[6] Provisions of the Copyright Act limiting the adaptation right for architectural works, sound recordings and musical works are, however, worthy of particular note here.

Section 120(b) allows the owners of a building embodying an architectural work "without the consent of the owner of the author or copyright owner of the architectural work" to "make or authorize the making of alterations to such building, and destroy or authorize the destruction of such building."[7] Thus adding a multi-level deck onto the

---

6. *See supra* § 7.1.2.   **7.**   17 U.S.C.A. § 120(b) (2000).

back of your designer home will not leave you vulnerable to a claim by the architect that you infringed her exclusive rights.

As discussed earlier, § 114 limits the reproduction right in sound recordings to captures of the actual sounds fixed in the recording. Section 114 similarly restricts the adaptation right, limiting the scope of exclusivity to "the right to prepare a derivative work in which the actual sounds fixed in the sound recording are rearranged, remixed, or otherwise altered in sequence or quality."[8] Finally, under the mechanical license of § 115, a licensee has "the privilege of making a musical arrangement of the work to the extent necessary to conform it to the style or manner of interpretation of the performance involved, but the arrangement shall not change the basic melody or fundamental character of the work...."[9] While such arrangements do not infringe, § 115 declares that they cannot secure separate copyrights as derivative works unless the copyright owner consents.

§ 7.3   The Distribution Right

7.3.1   Basic Principles

The distribution right is provided by § 106(3), which creates the exclusive right "to distribute copies or phonorecords of the copyrighted work to the public by the sale or other transfer of ownership, or by rental, lease, or lending." The distribution right has been described as the "right to vend."[1] It provides the copyright owner with the exclusive right publicly to sell, lease or otherwise dispose of copies or phonorecords of the protected work. The distribution right is significantly restrained by the exhaustion or "first sale" doctrine, which is described in more detail below.

Unlike most of the other § 106 rights, the distribution right is not founded upon the making of an unauthorized copy. The distribution right instead concerns the transfer of copies or phonorecords to members of the public. Sometimes an individual can infringe the distribution right without impinging upon the copyright owner's other exclusive rights. For example, a retailer could purchase pirated movies recorded on DVDs and sell them to members of the public. If the retailer did not itself make the illegal copies, then it has not violated the reproduction right. Yet the retailer could face liability for violation of the distribution right. This would be true even if the retailer did not know that the copies were unlawfully made, and bought them in complete good faith. In this way, the distribution right gives the copyright holder some protection even where the party making illegal reproductions cannot be found and subjected to a lawsuit.

---

8. 17 U.S.C.A. § 114(b) (2000).

9. 17 U.S.C.A. § 115(a)(2) (2000).

§ 7.3

1. NIMMER, COPYRIGHT § 8.11[A] (2002).

7.3.2   Limitations on the Distribution Right

Even though the owner of copyright in a work has the exclusive right to distribute copies or phonorecords of that work, the law has long recognized an important exception to the right. Usually called the "first sale doctrine," this limitation provides that once the copyright owner has parted with ownership of a particular copy of the work, he or she may not restrict further sales. The Supreme Court held as much over ninety years ago in *Bobbs-Merrill Co. v. Straus*[2] and the principle has been codified in the present copyright statute as section 109. That section provides generally that:

> [T]he owner of a particular copy or phonorecord lawfully made under this title, or any person authorized by such owner, is entitled without the authority of the copyright owner, to sell or otherwise dispose of the possession of that copy or phonorecord.[3]

As one court summarized this provision, "[t]he first sale doctrine prevents the copyright owner from controlling the future transfer of a particular copy once its material ownership has been transferred."[4] The justification for the doctrine is that by selling the physical copy initially, the copyright owner has already received the economic reward to which he or she is entitled.

Although the first sale rule of section 109 gives the owner of a particular copy of a work control over the disposition of that copy, at least one state has enacted legislation that, in a sense, limits that control. Under California's Resale Royalties Act[5] when a work of fine art is sold for more than $1000 by an owner other than the original artist, the artist is entitled a royalty equal to 5% of the gross sales price, to be paid by the seller. The goal of the legislation is to permit the artist to share in the economic appreciation of the value of his work. The right to this royalty lasts for 20 years after the artists death. A number of western European countries recognize a similar right under the name *droit de suit*. The California Resale Royalties Act was challenged shortly after its adoption by a litigant who claimed it was pre-empted by section 301 of the Copyright Act, but the Ninth Circuit found no pre-emption and the law remains on the books.[6]

An interesting interpretive problem involving the first sale doctrine occurs when an importer purchases copies of copyrighted works abroad and seeks to bring them into the United States. Under section 602 of the Copyright Act, any such importation without the authority of the copyright owner is declared a violation of the distribution right and an actionable infringement.[7] When the copies involved were made without

---

2.   210 U.S. 339, 28 S.Ct. 722, 52 L.Ed. 1086 (1908).

3.   17 U.S.C.A. § 109 (2000).

4.   Columbia Pictures Industries v. Redd Horne, Inc., 749 F.2d 154, 159 (3d Cir. 1984).

5.   Cal. Civil Code § 986 (West 1983).

6.   Morseburg v. Balyon, 621 F.2d 972 (9th Cir.1980), *cert. denied*, 449 U.S. 983, 101 S.Ct. 399, 66 L.Ed.2d 245 (1980).

7.   17 U.S.C.A. § 602 (2000). The section provides: "Importation into the United States, without the authority of the owner of copyright under this title, of copies or phonorecords of a work that have been acquired outside the Untied States is an in-

the permission of the U.S. copyright owner, the rule seems to make perfect sense and poses no conflict with the first sale doctrine. Such "piratical" copies were never "sold" by the copyright owner, nor did it realize any revenue from them. It seems quite logical that their importation into and subsequent sale in the U.S. should be deemed a violation of the distribution right, and in this particular situation, the statute even provides for seizure of the copies at the border by the U.S. Customs Service.[8]

On the other hand, if the copies in question were originally made in the U.S., exported by the copyright owner, and then sold abroad legally under the authority of the U.S. copyright owner, the first sale doctrine would seem to apply and ought to permit the importer to do whatever it likes with the copies, including reimporting and reselling them in the United States. The Supreme Court so held in *Quality King Distributors, Inc. v. L'anza Research International, Inc.*[9] In that case, L'Anza made hair care products bearing a copyrighted label and sold some of them to a distributor in the United Kingdom. That party then sold the goods to a distributor in Malta. Eventually, some of these products made their way back into the United States. These products were sold in California by unauthorized retailers who purchased them from Quality King. L'Anza sued Quality King for copyright infringement, asserting that the importation and sale of products bearing copyrighted labels violated its exclusive distribution right.

The Supreme Court held that where a copy of a work of authorship is lawfully made and sold in the United States, the first sale doctrine applies under § 109. Thus, even if the manufacturer designated the copy for export, that copy may be reimported without violating the distribution right. The Court rejected L'Anza's argument that § 602(a) compelled a different result. Section 602(a) states that: "Importation into the United States, without the authority of the owner of copyright . . . of copies or phonorecords of a work that has been acquired outside the United States is an infringement of the exclusive right to distribute copies or phonorecords under Section 106. . . ." The Court reasoned that the express language of § 106 provides that the distribution right is "subject to sections 107 through 121"—which included the first sale doctrine of § 109. Stated differently, the Court reasoned that the ban on importation set out in § 602(a) was really a species of the distribution right of § 106, which in turn is subject to the first sale doctrine of § 109.

Reminding us that there are often exceptions to the exception, § 109 includes a significant modification to the first sale doctrine pertaining to the music and software industries. Section 109(b) prohibits the rental for

fringement of the exclusive right to distribute copies or phonorecords under section 106, actionable under section 501." The section then goes on to list three limited exceptions to the prohibition—importations by federal, state and local government, importations for scholarly or educational pur-

poses, and importations of single copies for personal use by tourists returning from abroad.

8.   17 U.S.C.A. § 602(b) (2000).

9.   523 U.S. 135, 118 S.Ct. 1125, 140 L.Ed.2d 254 (1998).

commercial advantage to the public of either (1) phonorecords that contain a protected sound recording or musical work, or (2) storage media, such as disks or CDs, on which computer software has been recorded. Section 109(b) effectively shut down a number of enterprises whose business model encouraged home copying. Such firms would, for example, rent floppy discs containing a popular program to members of the public for a fraction of the cost of that program. Consumers would then purchase blank discs for a fraction of the price of the program and make copies using their personal computers. Concerted lobbying by both the recording and software industry resulted in the targeted response of § 109(b). Lendings by non-profit libraries for non-profit purposes are expressly excluded from § 109(b).

§ 7.4   The Public Performance Right

7.4.1   Basic Principles

Section 106(4) of the Copyright Act provides proprietors with the exclusive right to perform certain copyrighted works publicly. Section 101 reveals that the term "perform" means to recite, render, play, dance, or act [the work], either directly or by means of any device or process. Suppose that a troupe of actors purchases a book including a copyrighted play and, without permission from its author, stages a theatrical performance of that play. This public stage production would constitute a copyright infringement. Even if no unauthorized mechanical copies of the play were made, the troupe has violated the public performance right.

It is important to bear in mind that a single event can give rise to multiple performances by multiple different parties, any one of whom might be an infringer if not licensed or excused. Radio broadcasts constitute performances by the relevant radio stations within the meaning of the § 101 definition, for example. However, individuals who turn on their radios to receive those broadcasts are also "performing" any copyrighted works that they receive. As we shall see shortly, this doctrine has important implications for the structure of various copyright rules.

The public performance right does not apply to all sorts of works. Section 106(4) expressly covers only literary, musical, dramatic, and choreographic works; pantomimes; and motion pictures and other audiovisual works. Consequently, the public performance right does not apply to pictorial, graphic or sculptural works, which instead are entitled to the public display right of § 106(5).

More significantly, sound recordings are not accorded a general public performance right. Thus when a disk jockey plays a CD over the radio, no copyright concerns exist with respect to the singers and instrumentalists that created that sound recording or vis-a-vis the record company that may hold the copyright in that particular sound recording. As always in the field of musical copyrights, however, it is important to distinguish between a copyright in a sound recording and a copyright in the underlying musical work. Although sound recordings are excluded from the reach of § 106(4), musical works do receive the public performance right. As a result, composers and lyricists (or the music publishers to whom they have assigned their rights) are entitled to compensation for the playing of their songs over the radio, and can claim copyright infringement if such performances were unauthorized.

The § 106(4) right is limited to *public* performances. As observed by Justice Stewart: "No license is required by the Copyright Act, for example, to sing a copyrighted lyric in the shower."[1] Such a performance would, presumably, be a private one. A more rigorous analysis of the private-public distinction requires consideration of the Copyright Act's two-part definition of the term "public" in § 101. The first portion of that definition provides that a performance is considered "public" if it occurs "at a place open to the public or at any place where a substantial number of persons outside of a normal circle of family and its social acquaintances are gathered." Stated differently, a performance is public if it occurs in a public setting or before a public audience. Hence the exclusion of one's shower for all but the exhibitionist.

Section 101 further states that to perform a work publicly means "to transmit or otherwise communicate a performance ... of the work to a place specified by clause (1) or to the public, by means of any device or process, whether the members of the public capable of receiving the performance ... receive it in the same place or in separate places and at the same time or at different times." Public performances therefore include, for example, radio and television broadcasts, even though the audience does not gather at the same location or receive the broadcast at the same time or in a public place.

The decision of the Court of Appeals for the Third Circuit in *Columbia Pictures Industries, Inc. v. Aveco, Inc.*[2] provides a helpful discussion of the public performance right. There, Aveco rented rooms to the public that included seating, a video cassette player and a television monitor. Aveco also purchased video cassettes that it made available to members of the public for rent. Customers could rent a room and a video cassette from Aveco, or bring a video cassette from outside the facility in order to play in a rented room. When sued by various motion picture producers for violation of the public performance right, Aveco asserted that its policy was not to allow unrelated groups of customers to share a viewing room. According to Aveco, its practices could not constitute an infringement because the only performance occurred in a private viewing room rather than a public setting. Aveco further asserted that because it had legitimately purchased its videocassettes, its business model was protected by the first sale doctrine of § 109(a).[3]

§ 7.4

1. Twentieth Century Music Corp. v. Aiken, 422 U.S. 151, 155, 95 S.Ct. 2040, 45 L.Ed.2d 84 (1975).

2. 800 F.2d 59 (3d Cir.1986).

3. 800 F.2d at 63.

The Third Circuit disagreed and held that Aveco had infringed the public performance right. Analogizing Aveco's viewing rooms to telephone booths, taxi cabs and pay toilets, the court reasoned that each was "open to the public" even though usually not crowded with people. The key concept was that the viewing rooms were open to any member of the public with the inclination and means to employ Aveco's services. The performances at Aveco's facilities were therefore judged public performances. Nor did the first sale doctrine insulate Aveco, the court reasoned. Section 109(a) applied only to the public distribution right of § 106(3), not the public performance right granted by § 106(4).[4] As a result, Aveco's purchase of videocassettes did not affect the movie producers' exclusive right to authorize public performances.

7.4.2 Limitations on the Public Performance Right

The Copyright Act includes a large number of detailed exceptions to the public performance right. The 1976 Act's specific provisions stand in contrast to the 1909 Act, which generally exempted all non-profit public performances.[5] Experience under the 1909 Act suggested not only considerable difficulties in distinguishing non-profit and for-profit public performances, but also that many non-profit organizations possessed the means to pay copyright royalties.[6] As a result, the 1976 Act rejected the 1909 Act's blanket exemption for non-profit public performances in favor of more particularized exemptions.

Many of these provisions are found in the ten paragraphs of § 110, which concern the following entities and activities:

(1) Classroom Instruction

(2) Transmissions of Instructional Activities, Including Distance Learning over the Internet

(3) Religious Services

(4) Specified Nonprofit Performances

(5) Reception of Certain Transmissions by Commercial Establishments

(6) Agricultural Fairs

(7) Retail Sales of Phonorecords

(8) Performances of Nondramatic Literary Works for the Handicapped

(9) Performances of Dramatic Works for the Handicapped

(10) Veterans and Fraternal Organizations

Under these various provisions, a teacher is permitted to read a poem or show a videotape to her class without infringing any copyright interests,

4. 800 F.2d at 64.

5. *See* 1909 Act, § 1(c).

6. *See* Julien H. Collins III, *When In Doubt, Do Without: Licensing Public Perfor-* *mances by Nonprofit Camping or Volunteer Service Organization Under Federal Copyright Law*, 75 WASHINGTON UNIV. L.Q. 1277 (1997).

even though the act of doing so is technically a public performance. Similarly, a rabbi can quote a magazine article during a sermon, and your local record store can play music over a stereo system.

These exemptions vary in the range of works to which they apply. Thus, the classroom exemption of § 110(1) is very broad, covering all performable works. The phonorecord retailing exemption of § 110(7), in contrast, concerns only non-dramatic musical works. Space limitations preclude a detailed review of all ten exemptions set out in section 110. Two, however, deserve a few words because of their general importance and because of recent legal developments.

Section 110(4), dealing with certain nonprofit public performances, bears the most resemblance to the broader exemption formerly available under the 1909 Act. Under § 110(4), public performances of nondramatic literary and musical works given without any purpose of direct or indirect commercial advantage may be exempted from the public performance right. This exemption applies to such public performances as live musical shows, poetry readings or the playing of phonorecords, but transmissions are expressly not within the § 110(4) exemption. Thus not-for-profit or educational broadcasters must look elsewhere in the statute for provisions that insulate them from infringement liability. To qualify under § 110(4), the public performance must either not be accompanied by a direct or indirect admission charge; or be subject to an admission charge that, after the deduction of reasonable expenses, will be used exclusively for educational, religious or charitable purposes.

Many of us have been members of an unappreciative seaside audience, unwillingly listening to CDs from the blaring boombox of a fellow beach patron. The next time you find yourself in this unfortunate circumstance, one way to pass the time as you hope for a battery failure is to reflect upon the copyright consequences of your neighbor's public performance. Playing CDs from a boombox in front of a sufficient audience of strangers constitutes a public performance within the meaning of § 106. Such a performance is exempted under § 110(4), however, because the boombox devotee is not seeking a commercial advantage and did not impose an admission charge.

Section 110(4) also includes a special "veto" provision available to copyright proprietors. If an admission will be charged for the public performance, § 110(4) allows the copyright proprietor to serve a notice of objection. If the copyright owner provides timely notice in the proper format, then he may assert all rights applicable under the Copyright Act without regard to § 110(4). Congress included this "veto," so that copyright proprietors would not be required to provide fund-raising support towards causes they find objectionable.

The exemption for commercial establishments in § 110(5) has had a controversial history. Congress intended § 110(5) to allow small restaurants, retailers and similar establishments to play ordinary radios and television sets for the benefit of their customers without incurring any financial responsibility to the copyright owner. This exemption applies only to radio and television equipment of the sort commonly used in homes—thus it is often called the "homestyle" exemption—rather than more sophisticated commercial systems. Unlike the other provisions of § 110, the homestyle exception is oriented towards commercial establishments rather than non-profit organizations. Perhaps for that reason, § 110(5) has been the most heavily litigated of the exceptions to the public performance right, and has even been the focus an international trade dispute between the United States and the European Union.[7]

As originally enacted, § 110(5) held that it was not a copyright infringement to communicate "a transmission embodying a performance or display of a work by the public reception of the transmission on a single apparatus of a kind commonly used in private homes, unless (i) a direct charge is made to see or hear the transmission; or (ii) the transmission thus received is further transmitted to the public." This exemption is limited to transmissions as compared to recorded music or video. Thus it does not insulate the merchant who wishes to play CDs or tapes at his place of business. As well, there can be no admission charge to hear or see the performance.

The original version of § 110(5) resulted in two principal difficulties. First, the wording of § 110(5) contributed to uncertainty in judicial application. For example, in an era where sound equipment was increasingly becoming more sophisticated and elaborate every year, the sorts of apparatus that are "of a kind commonly used in private homes" is nebulous.[8] Section 110(5) also seemingly focuses upon the presence of "a single apparatus" at an establishment—a rule that allowed chains with hundreds of stores to claim the exemption so long as they used no more than one apparatus at each one.[9] Given that such stores seem to be able to pay for numerous amenities that add appeal to the shopping experience, such as stylish carpeting and warm lighting, they would seem to be able to pay for the music they use. On the other hand, retailers and restauranteurs have long argued that the demand for payments in connection with radio and television broadcasts is a form of double dipping, because the copyright owners have already been paid by the broadcasters.

Second, the compatibility of § 110(5) with the international copyright commitments of the United States is questionable. Article 11bis of the Berne Convention expressly provides authors with the exclusive right to authorize "the public communication by loudspeaker or any analogous instrument transmitting, by signs, sounds, or images, the broadcast of the work." Although international agreements allow certain narrow exceptions to this exclusive right, some observers believed that the original version of § 110(5) exceeded their permissible scope.

7. *See* Laurence R. Helfer, *World Music on a U.S. Stage: A Berne/TRIPS and Economic Analysis of the Fairness in Music Licensing Act*, 80 Bos. U. L. Rev. 93 (2000).

8. *See* John Wilk, *Seeing the Words and Hearing the Music: Contradictions in the Construction of 17 U.S.C.A. Section 110(5)*, 45 Rutgers L. Rev. 783 (1993).

9. *See* Broadcast Music, Inc. v. Claire's Boutiques, Inc., 949 F.2d 1482 (7th Cir. 1991), *cert. denied*, 504 U.S. 911, 112 S.Ct. 1942, 118 L.Ed.2d 547 (1992).

The Fairness in Music Licensing Act, a 1998 statute that amended § 110(5), ameliorated the first of these concerns but severely aggravated the second. This legislation redesignated the old § 110(5) as § 110(5)(A). Congress then added a new § 110(5)(B) with much more detailed provisions than the original. To enjoy the § 110(5)(B) exception, covered enterprises must not directly charge an admission fee to hear the transmission and must not retransmit the broadcast. If these conditions are met, then § 110(5)(B) provides that commercial establishments of less than 2,000 square feet, and restaurants of less than 3,750 square feet, that provide radio and television broadcasts for the benefit of their customers are exempted from copyright infringement liability. Enterprises of larger size may also enjoy an exemption so long as they have a limited number of speakers (not more than 6, with no more than 4 in one room) and televisions (no more than 4, with a maximum diagonal screen size of 55 inches).

The Fairness in Music Licensing Act was widely perceived as a victory for retailers and restaurant owners. The generous size and equipment specifications of § 110(5)(B) significantly exceed the scope of the original homestyle exception. Unsurprisingly, international attention focused upon § 110(5)(B) and resulted in a legal challenge. Member states of the European Community, after receiving complaints on behalf of the Irish Music Rights Organization, submitted a formal complaint to the World Trade Organization (WTO). This action resulted in a formal decision from the WTO Dispute Settlement Body. The WTO ruling, issued in 2000, resulted in a split judgment. In favor of the United States, the WTO held that the original "homestyle exemption," now codified in§ 110(5)(A), was in accord with Berne Convention requirements. In favor of the European Community, the WTO found that the § 110(5)(B) exemption added by the Fairness in Music Licencing Act did not satisfy the Berne Convention.

Despite the adverse WTO holding, Congress has stubbornly refused to amend § 110(5) to comport with the international copyright commitments of the United States. The WTO Agreement therefore allows the European Community to impose trade sanctions against the United States equal to the amount lost by European artists. Whether the United States will ultimately yield to the WTO interpretation, and what the structure of an acceptable § 110(5) might be, remain open questions.

7.4.3   Performing Rights Societies

Music surrounds us in our everyday lives. Whenever a broadcaster transmits music over the radio or television, a merchant plays "music on hold" or a performer entertains at a live performance, the public performance right of a copyrighted musical work is implicated. The enormous number of musical performances that occur every day in the United States suggests the great potential value of the public performance right. At the same time, the sheer number of times a musical work is played, as well as the ephemeral nature of each performance, make it difficult for copyright owners to police their rights. And even a well-intentioned performer could find it time-consuming and burdensome to obtain licenses from multiple musical copyright holders.

Composers and songwriters, along with their publishers, have attempted to reduce these transaction costs by pooling their copyrights and authorizing a so-called "performing rights society" to license their works as a group and to police unauthorized performances. By definition, a "performing rights society" is "an association, corporation, or other entity that licenses the public performance of nondramatic musical works on behalf of copyright owners of such works, such as the American Society of Composers, Authors and Publishers (ASCAP), Broadcast Music, Inc. (BMI) and SESAC, Inc."[10] Performing rights societies essentially act as middlemen, streamlining the process through which copyright proprietors can offer, and performers can obtain, licenses under the public performance right.

A review of the operations of ASCAP, provides a helpful example of the workings of a performing rights society. ASCAP is the largest U.S. performing rights society, boasting hundreds of thousands of members and a repertory of several million songs. Composers, songwriters and publishers who join ASCAP grant it a non-exclusive right to license nondramatic public performances of their works. Members also grant ASCAP the right to police the performance right and, if necessary, to bring copyright infringement suits in their names.

In turn, persons or enterprises that wish to perform works within this repertory—including radio broadcasters, restaurants, bars, shopping malls, orchestras and concert halls—may contract with ASCAP. ASCAP offers a "blanket license" that allows licensees to perform publicly any song within its repertory an unlimited number of times for a set annual fee. ASCAP license fees are calculated based upon the size and revenues of the licensee, and can range from a modest few hundred dollars a year for a corner bar that has a live garage band one night a week to many millions of dollars for a major television network. ASCAP receives license fees for these public performances and, after deducting operating expenses, distributes these monies to members whose works were performed. ASCAP employs sophisticated sampling methodologies and complex calculations to determine how often a work has been publicly performed as well as the value of each performance. Restaurants, radio stations and other entities that perform music publicly without authorization may be subject to suit by ASCAP. As ASCAP frequently takes advantage of Copyright Act provisions calling for statutory damages, attorney's fees and costs for the prevailing litigant,[11] accused infringers possess significant incentives to pay the relatively modest blanket licensing fee.

Antitrust issues have surrounded ASCAP and the other performing rights societies since their inception. One result has been a consent decree between ASCAP and the Department of Justice that compels

---

10. 17 U.S.C.A. § 101 (2000).   **11.** *See* 17 U.S.C.A. § 505 (2000).

certain ASCAP practices, including the requirement that ASCAP obtain only non-exclusive (rather than exclusive) licenses from its members. As a result, members may operate outside the ASCAP system if they wish. The ASCAP—Department of Justice consent decree has not prevented additional antitrust actions by other parties, particularly broadcasters, however such suits have met with little success.

Performing rights societies restrict their operations to nondramatic, or "small," public performance rights. Dramatic, or "grand" rights, remain for the copyright owner to license and enforce. A performance is considered dramatic when it assists in the development of a larger plot, while nondramatic performances do not advance a separate story line.[12] The rationale for this distinction is that dramatic performances occur less frequently than nondramatic ones and, given the usual publicity and attendance surrounding them, are easier to detect.[13]

7.4.4　Secondary Transmissions

Cable television systems offer certain channels to their subscribers by receiving the signals of broadcast stations and re-transmitting them to those subscribers by wire. The term "secondary transmissions" refers to this—and many similar—practice of making additional, simultaneous transmissions of original transmissions.[14] Section 111 contains a detailed regulatory statute that imposes a complex compulsory license system for secondary transmissions made by cable television providers. Under § 111, a cable television system faces copyright liability for making secondary transmissions unless it complies with specified conditions, including reporting requirements and the payment of a royalty. A similar arrangement is specified in § 119 for satellite television providers.

7.4.5　The Digital Performance Right in Sound Recordings

Section 106(6) contains a limited exception to the unavailability of a public performance right for sound recordings. Introduced by the 1995 Digital Performance Right in Sound Recordings Act (DPRSRA),[15] § 106(6) provides the exclusive right "in the case of sound recordings to perform the copyrighted work publicly by means of a digital audio transmission." DPRSRA also established a compulsory license scheme involving "digital phonorecord" delivery that is codified in certain paragraphs of § 114.

The DPRSRA responded to recent technological innovations that have changed the methods through which consumers listen to and buy music. Unlike the traditional paradigm, where consumers listened to music on the radio and purchased recordings at a record store, music is now available for reception and sale through cable, wireless technologies, the Internet, or direct broadcast satellite. Various subscription and

12. *See* Seltzer v. Sunbrock, 22 F.Supp. 621, 628–29 (S.D.Cal.1938).

13. *See* I. Fred Koenigsberg, *Overview of Basic Principles of Copyright Law*, 238 PLI/Pat. 9, 44 (1987).

14. 17 U.S.C.A. § 111(f) (2000).

15. Pub. L. No. 104–39, 109 Stat. 336.

interactive services allow listeners to pick and choose individual recordings to listen to or to download for permanent retention. These new media provide flawless, digital copies of sound recordings that in turn may be copied onto a personal computer or MP3 player. Congress viewed such services—in particular, subscription and interactive services—as direct competitors with traditional sales avenues for records and CDs. Historically, the sale of such physical objects was the only way copyright owners in sound recordings could secure an economic reward, given the absence of a general performance right for such works. The digital performance right was intended to allow sound recording copyright owners to license sound recordings to digital music subscription and interactive services so that they could recoup the revenue displaced by lost CD sales.[16]

Congress viewed DPRSRA as creating a "carefully crafted and narrow performance right, applicable only to certain digital transmissions of sound recordings."[17] Reflecting this intent, as well as the political tradeoffs that led to the DPRSRA, § 106(6) is subject to a bewilderingly complex set of limitations in § 114(d). Most important is that FCC-licensed terrestrial television and radio stations are exempted from § 106(6). Even if they switch to digital technologies in the future, broadcasters of "free"—that is to say, advertising-supported—radio and television programming may continue to perform sound recordings without paying licensing fees to sound recording copyright owners. (Of course, they remain obligated to pay licensing fees to perform the underlying musical compositions—an obligation they meet by purchasing licenses from ASCAP and BMI.) Similarly, transmission within business establishments are exempted, allowing background music services such as MUZAK to employ digital technologies.

If not expressly exempted by the DPRSRA, most digital music services are subject to the § 106(6) rights of the copyright proprietor. With regard to such services, the copyright holder may ordinarily choose whether or not to license digital performance rights in its sound recording. However, the DPRSRA also identified two narrow classes of non-exempt transmissions that are subject to a compulsory licensing regime.[18] The first of these are non-exempt subscription digital audio transmission services, such as DiSH Network and Music Choice, that transmit in the same medium they used on July 1, 1998. In order to be eligible for the compulsory license, these services must comply with various operating requirements that make it hard for a recipient to record specific transmitted songs. For example, such a service is restricted in the number of songs its can broadcast from the same artist within particular time periods. New subscription services, such as DMX, and certain non-

---

16. *See* David M. Kroeger, *Applicability of the Digital Performance Right in Sound Recordings Act of 1995*, 6 UCLA Ent. L. Rev. 73 (1998).

17. S. Rep. No. 104–128, at 13 (1995).

18. 17 U.S.C.A. § 114(d)(2)(B). *See* David Nimmer, *Appreciating Legislative History: The Sweet and Sour Spots of the DMCA's Commentary*, 23 Cardozo L. Rev. 909, 953–54 (2002).

subscription services, including some promotional web sites and Internet retailers, may also obtain a compulsory license under the DPRSRA.

§ 7.5   The Public Display Right

7.5.1   Basic Principles

Section 106(5) of the Copyright Act grants an exclusive right to display the copyright work publicly. Under § 101, to display a work means to show a copy of it, either directly or indirectly, through the use of a film, slide, television image or any other device or process. The public display right applies to literary, musical, dramatic, and choreographic works, pantomimes, and motion pictures and other audiovisual works.[1] The same definition of "public" applies to the public display right as the public performance right.[2] If, for example, an individual displayed a work of visual art within the privacy of his home, no concerns over the public display right would likely arise.

The distinction between the public performance right and the public display right can sometimes be a fine one. If a theater uses a projector to show a copyrighted motion picture without authorization, would this act constitute a public performance or public display? The answer, it turns out, depends on whether the images of the motion picture are shown in sequence or not. If these images are shown in sequence, then the public performance right is implicated.[3] If the theater instead showed individual images nonsequentially—such as stills from the motion picture—then the public display right would be at stake.[4] This distinction could be important if the theater sought to invoke an exemption that applied only to one right and not the other.

7.5.2   Limitations on the Public Display Right

The Copyright Act includes a significant limitation that severely limits the public display right. Section 109(c) permits the owner of a copy of a "lawfully made" protected work to display that copy publicly, and to authorize others to do so.[5] If, for example, a gallery makes a legitimate purchase of a work of visual art from an artist, then § 109(c) allows that gallery freely to display that work to the public. In a sense § 109(c) acts similarly to the "first sale" doctrine associated with the public distribution right, for as we have seen once members of the public have acquired ownership of a legitimate copy of a protected work, they may further distribute those copies without regard to the copyright proprietor.[6] It only makes sense that if they choose to retain the object, they may display it in ways that make it available to the public. This privilege only applies to the *owner* of a copy, however. One who merely possesses a

§ 7.5

1. 17 U.S.C.A. § 106(5) (2000).
2. *See supra* § 7.4.1.
3. 17 U.S.C.A. § 101 (2000).
4. 17 U.S.C.A. § 101 (2000).
5. 17 U.S.C.A. § 109(c) (2000).
6. *See supra* § 7.3.2.

borrowed copy may not display it publicly without the permission of the copyright owner.

The § 109(c) exception applies whether the copy is displayed directly or by means of projection. In the latter case, however, only one image may be projected at a time, and that image must be visible only to viewers present at the place where the copy is located.[7] If a San Francisco-based art dealer employed videoconferencing technology to display a page of calligraphy to a public audience in New York, then the public display right would be violated even though the dealer owned a legitimate copy of the literary work.

Another source of limitations on the public display right is § 110. Recall that this statute creates numerous limitations on the public performance right. Some, but not all, of the provisions of § 110 also apply to the public display right. In particular, paragraphs 1, 2, and 3 of § 110, pertaining to classroom instruction, transmissions of instructional activities, and religious services, apply to the public display right. Thus an art teacher may show slides of modern works to her students even if she does not own them and has borrowed them from a colleague or a library.

§ 7.6   Moral Rights

7.6.1   Basic Principles

The U.S. copyright law traditionally has had a utilitarian focus. Protection of authors has not been seen as the ultimate purpose of copyright, but rather as a means to achieve the broader social goal of promoting expression.[1] One ramification of this focus is that the U.S. copyright statute provides rights that center upon the economic interest of authors.

Foreign authors' rights laws share this economic grounding, but many additionally recognize "moral rights."[2] Moral rights resemble rights of personality or individual civil rights. Moral rights regimes acknowledge that authored works have significance beyond the marketplace. Works of authorship also reflect their creator's personality in that they are unique extensions of the author herself. Moral rights are said to recognize the dignity and worth of individuals by providing authors with certain controls over their creative processes and their completed works of authorship.

Although details vary in different jurisdictions overseas, moral rights generally call for three basic rights: integrity, attribution and disclosure. The integrity right allows authors to prevent objectionable distortions, mutilations or other modifications of their works. The attribution or paternity right allows authors to claim authorship of their

7.   17 U.S.C.A. § 109(c) (2000).

§ 7.6

1.   *See supra* § 2.4.1.

2.   *See* Henry Hansmann & Marina Santilli, *Authors' and Artists' Moral Rights: A Comparative Legal and Economic Analysis,* 26 J. Legal Studies 95 (1997).

works. Finally, the right of disclosure allows authors to decide when and in what form a work will be distributed to the public.

A few foreign jurisdictions offer additional moral rights. For example, some countries recognize a withdrawal right. This right allows works to be removed from the public eye, even to the extent of requiring current possessors of the works to return them to the author. Although the precise formulations of each of these moral rights differ in various states overseas, moral rights are ordinarily independent of the author's pecuniary interests and remain with the author even after any transfer of ownership.[3]

The U.S. copyright system has had an uneasy relationship with moral rights since the United States joined the Berne Convention for the Protection of Literary and Artistic Works in 1989. Article 6*bis* of the Berne Convention requires signatories to provide the rights of integrity and attribution. Although U.S. adherence to the Berne Convention prompted many changes to the U.S. copyright law, Congress initially declined to establish a full-fledged moral rights regime. The United States instead took the position that various common law causes of action, including the right of privacy, the right of publicity, defamation and unfair competition, provided rights equivalent to the moral rights required in Article 6*bis* of the Berne Convention. In addition, California, New York and other states have enacted "art preservation" and "artist's authorship rights" statutes.[4] These state laws, although limited to works of fine art, create protections resembling the moral rights available abroad.

Perhaps eager to see the United States at last join the world's copyright system, many other Berne signatories did not overly fault the United States on its shortcomings in moral rights protection. Doubts nevertheless persisted over whether the United States had fully met its Berne Convention obligations. Congress responded by enacting the Visual Artists Rights Act of 1990 ("VARA"). Principally codified at § 106A, VARA provides rights of attribution and integrity for certain works of visual art.

7.6.2   The Visual Artists Rights Act of 1990

VARA applies only to works of visual art, a term of art defined in detail in § 101 of the statute. Specifically, qualifying works are limited to paintings, drawings, prints, or sculptures, existing in a single copy, or in a limited edition of 200 copies or fewer that are signed and consecutively numbered by the author. A still photographic image produced for exhibition purposes also qualifies, provided that it exists in a single copy signed by the author, or in a limited edition of 200 copies or fewer that are signed and consecutively numbered by the author. Even though a work

---

3. *See* Adolf Dietz, *The Moral Right of the Author: Moral Rights and the Civil Law Countries*, 19 COLUMBIA-VLA J. L. & ARTS 199 (1995).

4. *See* Nicole B. Wilkes, *Public Responsibilities of Private Owners of Cultural Property: Toward a National Art Preservation Statute*, 24 COLUMBIA-VLA J. L. & ARTS 177 (2001).

meets this definition, VARA further excludes works made for hire and works designed for commercial purposes. This latter category includes advertising, promotions, posters, maps, technical drawings, applied art and other specified works.[5]

VARA confers narrowly defined rights of attribution and integrity on the authors of works of visual art. Parties who violate these rights are subject to the same sanctions as copyright infringers. The attribution right allows visual artists both to claim authorship of their qualifying works and to prevent the use of their names as the authors of qualifying works of visual art that they did not create.[6] In addition, visual artists may prevent the use of their names in the event their qualifying works are distorted, mutilated or otherwise modified in a way that would be prejudicial to their honor or reputation.[7]

The integrity right allows visual artists to prevent any intentional distortion, mutilation, or other modification of their qualifying works that would be prejudicial to their honor or reputation.[8] In the case of qualifying works of "recognized stature," the visual artist may also prevent the destruction of such a work.[9] VARA regrettably does not specify how a work achieves recognized stature. One of the few published opinions discussing VARA, *Martin v. City of Indianapolis*,[10] was forced to grapple with this issue.

Artist Jan Martin constructed a twenty-by-forty-foot metal sculpture titled "Symphony #1." The City of Indianapolis later purchased the property that was home to Symphony #1 as part of an urban renewal project. Martin offered to donate Symphony #1 to the City provided that the City bear the costs of removal to a new site. Although the City told Martin that he would be contacted in the event Symphony #1 was to be removed, it neglected to do so prior to bulldozing and removing the sculpture. Martin then brought suit against the City for a VARA violation. As evidence of the "recognized stature" of his work of visual art, Martin provided the court with letters and newspaper articles extolling Symphony #1, as well as an art show program indicating that the sculpture had won "best of show" honors.

Acknowledging that its jurists "are not art critics, do not pretend to be and do not need to be to decide this case," the Seventh Circuit held that Martin had demonstrated his work was of recognized stature. The Court of Appeals agreed with the district court that respected members of the art community believed that Martin's work was socially valuable and possessed artistic merit. In addition, newspaper articles indicated the newsworthiness of Symphony #1 and Martin's work more generally.

Judge Manion's dissent instead urged that recognized stature should not be shown through old newspaper articles and unverified letters, some of which were not even specifically directed towards Symphony #1.

---

5. 17 U.S.C.A. § 101 (2000).

6. 17 U.S.C.A. § 106A(a)(1) (2000).

7. 17 U.S.C.A. § 106A(a)(2) (2000).

8. 17 U.S.C.A. § 106A(a)(3)(A) (2000).

9. 17 U.S.C.A. § 106A(a)(3)(B) (2000).

10. 192 F.3d 608 (7th Cir.1999).

The dissent viewed the "recognized stature" requirement as an important gatekeeping mechanism, limiting protection to "only those works of art that art experts, the art community of society in general views as possessing stature."[11] Judge Manion expressed concerns that a broad interpretation of VARA could interfere with urban renewal endeavors and cautioned donees of art to obtain at the outset waivers of VARA rights, lest one become "the perpetual curator of a work of art that has lost (or perhaps never had) its luster."[12]

Section 106A provides for some exceptions to the integrity right. Under VARA, a work is not distorted, mutilated or otherwise modified if the modification is the result of the passage of time or the inherent nature of the materials, unless the modification is caused by gross negligence.[13] Modifications for purposes of conservation or public presentation, such as placement or lighting, also do not violate the integrity right unless caused by gross negligence.[14]

Some works of visual arts are incorporated into buildings. During the legislative process that led to VARA, concerns arose that moral rights might conflict with the interests of real estate owners in renovating or destroying their buildings. As a result, Congress amended § 113 to provide for conditions under which a qualifying visual art work may be removed from a building. If the work can be removed without distortion or mutilation, then the work is subject to attribution and integrity rights unless the owner has unsuccessfully attempted to notify the artist through diligence and good faith. If the notice succeeds, the artist has 90 days to remove the work at his expense.[15] If the work cannot be removed without being destroyed or mutilated, the VARA rights do not apply provided the author consented to the installation of the work in the building in a document that specifically recites that fact.[16]

VARA establishes a rather unusual durational scheme. For works created after the effective date of VARA (June 1, 1991), the attribution and integrity rights endure for the life of the artist. For works created before June 1, 1991, the duration of VARA rights depends upon whether the artist transferred title to the qualifying work or not. If the artist has parted with title prior to June 1, 1991, no VARA rights exist at all. However, if the artist created the work before June 1, 1991, but did not transfer title to the work before that date, then the VARA rights will endure for a term of life plus 70 years.[17]

Artists cannot transfer the attribution and integrity rights established by VARA. They can waive these rights, however, provided they do so in a written, signed instrument.[18]

11. *Id.* at 616 (quoting Carter v. Helmsley–Spear, Inc.), 861 F.Supp. 303, 325 (S.D.N.Y.1994), *rev'd in part and aff'd. in part*, 71 F.3d 77 (2d Cir.1995).

12. *Id.* at 616.

13. 17 U.S.C.A. § 106A(c)(1) (2000).

14. 17 U.S.C.A. § 106A(c)(2) (2000).

15. 17 U.S.C.A. § 113(d)(2) (2000).

16. 17 U.S.C.A. § 113(d)(1) (2000).

17. 17 U.S.C.A. § 106A(d) (2000).

18. 17 U.S.C.A. § 106A(e)(1) (2000).

The future of moral rights in U.S. copyright law remains uncertain. At the time the statute was enacted, some commentators believed that VARA would serve as the first step towards a more comprehensive moral rights law in the United States. Yet outside the academic community, few have since stepped forward to support the expansion of moral rights beyond the narrow confines of VARA. Balanced against a desire to fulfill the international commitments of the United States should be concern that moral rights present an uneasy fit with the collaborative nature of many contemporary works of authorship, including broadcasting, film and music. Expansive moral rights would effectively provide one of a number of participants with the ability to hold up sophisticated joint projects. The compatibility of moral rights with the traditional fair use privilege is also questionable. For the near future, at least, U.S. copyright law seems reluctant to further embrace moral rights concepts beyond VARA.

§ 7.7 The Digital Millennium Copyright Act

7.7.1 Basic Principles

With the turn of the century behind us, we have entered the so-called "Digital Millennium." One hallmark of the era is the Internet, a global information system that allows users to deliver perfect copies of digital works to an unlimited number of recipients anywhere in the world. The Internet has created new opportunities for copyright holders to benefit from their works. It has also created challenges. The Internet has been likened to an enormous copying machine. Misappropriation and unauthorized distribution of protected digital works has never been easier.

The Digital Millennium Copyright Act of 1998 ("DMCA")[1] attempts to respond to the opportunities and challenges of the digital information revolution. In enacting DMCA, Congress was also seeking to implement U.S. obligations under two international agreements concluded at the World Intellectual Property Organization ("WIPO"), the WIPO Copyright Treaty and the WIPO Performances and Phonograms Treaty. Title I of the DMCA added a new Chapter 12 to the Copyright Act with two principal provisions, one of which prohibits the circumvention of technological measures that protect copyrighted works and the other of which concerns the integrity of copyright management information. These two provisions are addressed in turn.

7.7.2 Anti–Circumvention Measures

Providers of software and digital information have long used technological measures, such as encryption or copy protection, to protect their works. Prior to the DMCA, however, the law did not prohibit entrepreneurial users from trying to defeat these protection measures. For the

§ **7.7**   (1998).
1. Pub .L. No. 105–304,112 Stat. 2863

first time, the DMCA restricts this previously permissible activity. In addressing anti-circumvention measures, § 1201 divides technological measures into two kinds. Section 1201(a) concerns technological measures that control access to a work. Section 1201(b) concerns technological measures that prevent unauthorized copying of the work.

Under § 1201(a), circumvention of a technological measure that "effectively controls access" to a protected work is prohibited. Additionally, § 1201(a) prohibits the manufacturing or offering to the public of technologies, products or services used to circumvent technological protections measures controlling access. For instance, assume the publisher of a newsletter posts the contents on a password-protected Web Site. It would be a violation of § 1201(a) to "hack" into the site in order to read the newsletter, regardless of whether reading the material violated any other provisions of the copyright laws.

In contrast, § 1201(b) prohibits only the manufacturing or offering to the public of technologies, products or services used to circumvent technological protections used to prevent unauthorized copying. No comparable language within § 1201(b) restricts the actual circumvention of a technological measure restricting unauthorized copying. The DMCA drafters apparently reasoned that because the copying of a copyrighted work may fall within the fair use privilege in certain cases, a *per se* exclusion of copying was inappropriate. Of course, given the prohibition against third party development of technologies to defeat copy protection, it is unclear how individual users will be able to take advantage of their fair use rights.

In response to the concerns of librarians and educational groups, the DMCA provides several exceptions to the prohibitions against circumvention. One of these exceptions allows the Librarian of Congress, on the recommendation of the Register of Copyrights, to engage in rulemaking in favor of "persons who are users of a work which is in a particular class of works, if such persons are or are likely . . . adversely affected by virtue of such prohibition in their ability to make noninfringing uses of that particular class of works. . . ."[2] The Librarian first exercised this authority on October 23, 2000, in a rather circumscribed fashion. Only two rather narrow classes of works were exempted from the prohibition against circumvention: (1) compilations consisting of lists of websites blocked by filtering software applications, and (2) literary works, including computer programs and databases, protected by access control mechanisms that fail to permit access because of malfunction, damage or obsoleteness.[3] It remains to be seen whether the Librarian will be more generous in future rounds of rulemaking under this authority. The DMCA also contains additional exceptions concerning (1) nonprofit libraries, archives and educational institutions; (2) law enforcement and intelligence activities; (3) reverse engineering; (4) encryption research;

---

2. 17 U.S.C.A. § 1201(a)(1)(B) (2000).

3. *See* Library of Congress, Exemption to Prohibition on Circumvention of Copyright Protection Systems for Access Control Technologies, 65 Fed. Reg. 54556 (Oct. 27, 2000).

(5) minors; (6) personally identifying information; (7) security testing; and (8) analog video cassette recorders.[4]

The anti-circumvention provisions of the DMCA have been the source of great contention. Critics have expressed grave concerns that the DMCA's anti-circumvention provisions could obstruct research, limit reverse engineering and chill expressive activity.[5] Moreover, the DMCA is a stunningly complex statute, the precise scope and meaning of which may take years to unravel. One of the first cases involving this new law to reach the courts was *Universal City Studios, Inc. v. Reimerdes*,[6] which on appeal was captioned *Universal City Studios v. Corley*.[7] This litigation was brought by eight U.S. motion picture studios that distributed their copyrighted motion pictures for home use on DVDs. The studios protected the motion pictures from copying by using an encryption system called "Content Scramble System," or "CSS." CSS employs an algorithm configured by a set of "keys" to encrypt a DVD's contents. CSS-protected DVD movies may be viewed only on players and computer drives equipped with licensed technology that decrypts the films but prevents copying.

By late 1999, a 15–year-old Norwegian computer prodigy named Jon Johansen and two other individuals wrote their own software, called "DeCSS," that was able to circumvent the CSS protection system. DeCSS allowed CSS-protected motion pictures to be copied and played on devices lacking the licensed decryption technology. One of the defendants to the litigation, Corley, posted the computer code for DeCSS on his website along with an explanation of how to use the program and an invitation to the public to download it. The movie studios sued under the DMCA to prevent the defendants from posting DeCSS and posting links to other sites that housed DeCSS.

At trial, the defendants offered a number of arguments in response to the plaintiff's contentions. They first asserted that the DMCA did not apply to the present case because the CSS did not "effectively control access" to the plaintiffs' copyrighted movies within the meaning of § 1201(a). The defendants effectively argued that because CSS could be defeated so easily, it didn't meet the test of being an "effective" control. District Judge Kaplan disagreed, however, observing that users could not watch CSS-protected movies without the encryption keys, and as well that users could not obtain the keys without purchasing a DVD player or computer drive under the appropriate license.

The district court also held that DeCSS was developed primarily for the purpose of circumventing CSS. The evidence of record on this point was rather complex. Johansen, the Norwegian teenage programmer, testified that at the time DeCSS was written no Linux-compatible DVD

---

4. 17 U.S.C.A. § 1201(d)-(k) (2000).

5. *See* Michael Landau, *Has the Digital Millennium Copyright Act Really Created a New Exclusive Right of Access?: Attempting to Reach a Balance Between Users' and*

Content Providers' Rights, 49 J. COPYRIGHT SOC'Y USA 277 (2001).

6. 111 F.Supp.2d 294 (S.D.N.Y.2000).

7. 273 F.3d 429 (2d Cir.2001).

players were available on the market.[8] Johansen further explained that
he created DeCSS in order to make a DVD player that would operate on
a computer running the Linux operating system. The seeming difficulty
with Johansen's explanation was that DeCSS was a Windows compatible
file that would operate only on computers running the Windows operating system. The reason the authors constructed a Windows program
rather than a Linux program, Johansen stated, was that at the time
DeCSS was written Linux also did not support the file system used on
DVDs. As a result, DVDs would have to be first decrypted on a Windows
computer before being employed on a Linux machine.

Judge Kaplan did not attribute much significance to this sequence of
events. The court instead stressed that Johansen and his colleagues
created DeCSS with full knowledge that the software could be used on
computers running Windows rather than Linux. The court further
believed that the three programmers were well aware that the movie
files, once decrypted, could be copied like any other computer files. The
district court therefore concluded that the only purpose or use of DeCSS
was to circumvent CSS and that the DMCA had been violated.

The defendants further argued that DeCSS was created for research
purposes: namely to further interoperability between computers using
the Linux system and DVDs. That would have brought the defendants'
conduct within an exception to the DMCA prohibitions. The court
rejected this position by concluding that the defendants were not involved in good faith encryption research, but instead had simply posted
the DeCSS software on their web sites.

Finally, the defendants sought to rely upon the fair use privilege.
Specified in the Copyright Act at § 107, and taken up further in this
Hornbook in Chapter 10, the fair use privilege exempts from liability
certain uses of copyrighted work when those uses will not undermine the
economic interests of the copyright owner. In perhaps the most notable
portion of the *Reimerdes* decision, Judge Kaplan held that fair use did
not apply to acts in violation of § 1201(a)(2) of the DMCA. The court
cited the legislative history of the DMCA for the conclusion that the
congressional "decision not to make fair use a defense to a claim under
Section 1201(a) was quite deliberate." Concluding that none of the
asserted defenses excused their conduct, the district court issued an
injunction against the defendants.

Upholding the district court's judgment on appeal, the Second
Circuit principally addressed the defendants' constitutional challenges to
§ 1201(a). The Court of Appeals initially held that computer programs
qualified as speech protected by the First Amendment and that the
DMCA qualified as a content-neutral restraint on speech. According to
Judge Newman, the DMCA furthered a substantial government interest
unrelated to the suppression of free expression—the protection of digitally encoded works of authorship—and was narrowly tailored, not burdening substantially more speech than necessary to further that interest.

8. Linux is a computer operating system, like Microsoft Windows.

The Court of Appeals also affirmed the district court's conclusion that the defendants could not successfully employ the fair use privilege. Declining to decide the question of whether the fair use privilege was constitutionally required, Judge Newman observed that nothing in the DMCA prevented users from quoting dialogue from movies or even pointing a video camera at a monitor as it displayed a DVD movie if they had a legitimate fair use basis for making use of the plaintiffs' movies. It merely prevented the making of digital copies by circumventing the CSS technology. Fair use, however, does not require access to copyrighted materials by the putative fair user's preferred technique, Judge Newman concluded, and as a result the district court's judgment was affirmed.

The *Reimerdes* and *Corley* decisions can be criticized on several grounds. The courts' classification of CSS as an "access control" under § 1201(a)(2) rather than a "copying control" under § 1201(b)(1) seems questionable. After all, the movie studios principally intended CSS to prevent copying rather than unauthorized access. The court's classification held consequences for both its analysis of the plaintiff's prima facie case and the defendant's fair use claims, for as noted earlier in this section, § 1201(b) is the more narrowly worded provision of the two. As well, arguably neither *Reimerdes* nor *Corley* gives appropriate weight to § 1201(c)(1), which states that: "Nothing in this section shall affect rights, remedies, limitations, or defenses to copyright infringement, including fair use, under this title." Although the movie industry achieved a major victory in this litigation, whether subsequent courts will respect the *Reimerdes* and *Corley* holdings, or ultimately vindicate the efforts of a dedicated group of hackers and electronic activists, remains to be seen.

7.7.3 Copyright Management Information

The term "copyright management information" refers to certain specified categories of information conveyed in connection with a copyrighted work, including the name of the author, the name of the copyright owner, and terms and conditions for use of the work.[9] This information can be embedded in the work or, for works, available on the Internet, be placed only a hyperlink away. The ready availability of copyright management information may facilitate the licensing and dissemination of protected works in the digital environment. To achieve these ends, however, copyright management information must be accurate and reliable and must accompany the work as it moves through cyberspace.

One of the goals of the DMCA was therefore to protect copyright management information against falsification, removal or alteration.[10] Section 1202 prohibits individuals from knowingly providing false copy-

9. 17 U.S.C.A. § 1202(c) (2000). *See* Julie E. Cohen, *Some Reflections on Copyright Management Systems and Laws Designed to Protect Them*, 12 BERKELEY TECHNOLOGY J. 161, 161–62 (1997).

10. *See* Jane C. Ginsburg, *Copyright Legislation for the "Digital Millennium*," 23 COLUMBIA-VLA J. L. & ARTS 137, 157 (1999).

right management information with the intent to facilitate or conceal infringement. The provision also prohibits the intentional alteration or removal of copyright management information, knowing (or having reasonable grounds to know) that the alteration or removal will facilitate or conceal infringement.

Section 1202 allows for several exceptions. The lawfully authorized investigative, protective, information security or intelligence activities of law enforcement, intelligence and other government entities are not affected by the DMCA.[11] Analog broadcasters who do not intend or facilitate copyright infringement need not comply with § 1202 if the mandated activity is not technically feasible or would create an undue financial hardship.[12] Finally, the DMCA encourages digital broadcasters to engage in a voluntary, consensus standard-setting process to place copyright management information in transmitted works. Until such a standard has been established, the DMCA exempts digital broadcasters if the transmission of copyright management information would degrade the digital signal or conflict with a government regulation or industry standard.[13]

The DMCA further specifies that it does not affect other rights, remedies, limitations or defenses to copyright infringement, including fair use, available under the copyright statute.[14] The DMCA also provides for civil and criminal penalties for violations of either § 1201 or § 1202.[15]

Like the anti-circumvention measures, the DMCA's promotion of copyright management information has attracted considerable controversy. Concerned experts are wary over diminishing privacy and the right to read anonymously.[16] Although the exceptions built into the DMCA attempted to address these concerns, commentators note that they are narrowly drawn against the broadly phrased prohibitions of the Act. The jury remains out on whether the DMCA offers new restrictions and unwelcome intrusions upon personal liberties, or simply the natural progression of copyright into the digital era.

---

11. 17 U.S.C.A. § 1202(d) (2000).

12. 17 U.S.C.A. § 1202(e)(1) (2000).

13. 17 U.S.C.A. § 1202(e)(2) (2000).

14. 17 U.S.C.A. § 1201(c)(1) (2000).

15. 17 U.S.C.A. §§ 1203, 1204 (2000).

16. *See* Julie E. Cohen, *A Right to Read Anonymously: A Closer Look at Copyright Management in Cyberspace*, 28 CONN. L. REV. 981 (1996).

Chapter 8

DURATION OF COPYRIGHT INTER-
ESTS AND TERMINATION OF
TRANSFERS

Table of Sections

§ 8.1   Duration Under the 1909 Act

One might think that the rules concerning copyright duration under the 1909 Act would be a matter of purely historical interest. However, many works first created and published prior to 1978 have a great deal of continuing commercial and popular importance today. Movies like *Gone With the Wind* and the *Wizard of Oz*, books like *The Old Man and the Sea* and the songs of composers like Cole Porter and Irving Berlin are just a few of the literally thousands of examples that prove the point. Since the duration of the copyright in these older works cannot be calculated or even understood without reference to the provisions of the 1909 statute, there is considerable practical reason for studying the approach of the 1909 Act.

8.1.1   Basic Principles

In its basic outline, the durational scheme of the 1909 Act was quite simple. It provided for an initial term of copyright protection of 28 years, dating from the time a work was first published with a valid copyright notice. The copyright could then be renewed for an additional 28 years, making for a total possible term of 56 years of protection.[1]

Prior to publication, the work was protected by "common law copyright." This meant that the author had a state common law cause of action against anyone who used or duplicated the work without his or her permission. This common law right was perpetual in duration. Another way to think of this situation is to realize that the act of publishing the work marked the dividing line between the state and federal regimes of protection. It signified that the author had traded state law protection of perpetual duration in favor of the greater protection, but limited term of federal copyright.

Despite the superficial simplicity of these rules, the renewal feature of the 1909 durational scheme led to a number of vexing problems, many of which wound up in the courts. A threshold question is, of course, who owns the right to renew. For four specified types of works, the 1909 Act specified that the renewal interest belonged not to the actual human author, but rather to the "proprietor" of the work. These statutorily itemized categories are (a) posthumous works;[2] (b) periodic, cyclopedic, or other composite works; (c) works copyrighted by corporate bodies; and (d) works made for hire.[3] Thus if an employee of a graphic arts company prepared some illustrations for her employer within the scope of her employment, and those works were first published in 1940, when the initial copyright term expired in 1968, the graphic arts company—not the employee or her heirs—owned the right to renew for the second 28 year term since it was the "proprietor" of a work for hire.

For all other works, the renewal right belongs to an itemized list of parties set out in the 1909 statute. Specifically, the renewal right belongs

---

§ 8.1

1. 1909 Act, § 24. While federal copyright protection for most works under the 1909 act began upon publication with notice, some works that were typically never published, such as motion pictures, would receive federal protection upon registration. In cases of this sort, the initial 28 year term ran from the date of inception of federal protection.

2. The term "posthumous" was construed in Bartok v. Boosey & Hawkes, Inc., 523 F.2d 941 (2d Cir.1975). In that case, the composer Bela Bartok wrote his *Concerto for Orchestra* in 1943, and it was performed publicly in 1944 and 1945. In this time frame, Bartok also assigned his rights to the work to a music publisher who was to prepare and publish printed sheet music for the work. Bartok died in late 1945, and the work was not published and copyrighted until March of 1946. Upon the expiration of the initial copyright term in 1974, both the music publisher and Bartok's son claimed the right to renew. Since the work was not published until after Bartok died, the publisher argued that the work was "posthumous" and that it therefore owned the right to renew as the proprietor. The court disagreed and held that a posthumous work is one as to which no copyright assignment or other contract for exploitation occurred during an author's lifetime. Since there had been exploitations during Bartok's life (the public performances and the assignment), the work was not posthumous and the renewal rights belonged to the surviving son.

3. 1909 Act, § 24.

to "the author of such work if still living, or the widow, widower, or children of the author, if the author be not living, or if such author, widow, widower or children be not living, then the author's executors, or in the absence of a will, his next of kin...."[4] Thus, if the author survives to the start of the renewal term, he or she is entitled to the renewal. If the author dies before the renewal term, the interest goes to the specified statutory heirs.

All this is at least apparent on the face of the statute. Unfortunately, there was also ambiguity concerning whether copyright owners could convey away their interests in the renewal term during the original term of copyright, or only after the commencement of the renewal term. Those who argued that copyright owners should not have the power to convey the renewal interest based their claims on the need to protect the author. They reasoned that an author might convey away a copyright interest in both the original and renewal terms for a meager sum shortly after creating a work because he or she was unaware of the true value of the work or in dire need of funds. Thereafter, the work might prove to be fabulously popular. If the author had an inalienable right to the renewal interest, he or she would be able to capture the economic value of the work during the second 28 year period, regardless of any unremunerative bargain that her or she might have previously entered into.

Despite this argument, the Supreme Court ultimately held, when confronted with the issue, that there was no legal prohibition against the conveyance of the renewal interest of copyright during the initial term. Such a conveyance of the renewal term of copyright would be valid *provided the grantor lived until the commencement of the renewal term.*[5] The court relied primarily on the statutory language and the history of the copyright act in reaching this conclusion, remarking that "[i]t is not for courts to judge whether the interests of authors clearly lie upon one side of this question rather than the other. If an author cannot make an effective assignment of his renewal, it may be worthless to him when he is most in need."[6]

It is crucial to note that this approach treats the renewal interest as a contingent interest, not unlike a contingent remainder interest in real estate. The renewal interest could be conveyed, but the conveyance would only ripen into actual ownership by the grantee if the relevant contingency came to pass—namely the author's survival through the full 28 year first term of copyright. To appreciate the practical consequences of this, assume an author conveys away both the original and renewal terms of copyright under the 1909 act in a conveyance executed shortly after the work is published. Assume further that the author then dies only a few years later, long before the commencement of the renewal

4. 1909 Act, § 24. The case law under the 1909 Act held that the residual category of "next of kin" would be determined as a matter of state law. See Silverman v. Sunrise Pictures Corp., 273 F. 909 (2d Cir. 1921).

5. Fred Fisher Music Co. v. M. Witmark & Sons, 318 U.S. 643, 63 S.Ct. 773, 87 L.Ed. 1055 (1943). *See also* Miller Music v. Daniels, 362 U.S. 373, 80 S.Ct. 792, 4 L.Ed.2d 804 (1960).

6. *Fred Fisher*, 318 U.S. at 657.

term. Who now has the right to renew and who will own the renewal interest? It can't be the author, because he or she is, by hypothesis, dead. Nor will it be the original grantee because that party's interest were only contingent and failed upon the death of the author. In this case the renewal interest will belong to the surviving spouse, children, executor or next of kin depending on which are alive at the end of the 28-year original term of copyright.

Indeed, the rights of the statutory heirs cannot even be defeated by action of the author himself. In other words, under this system, they cannot be "disinherited." For instance, assume a successful novelist who is married prepares a will leaving all his copyright interests to State University. If he dies before the expiration of the first term of copyright, the university inherits the copyrights and would own them for the balance of the initial term of copyright in each book, but as those terms expired, the surviving spouse, not the university would have the right to renew.

Thus a grantee who took an assignment term early in the first term of copyright could only be sure to enjoy the copyright during the renewal term if it obtained assignments of the renewal term interest from all the listed statutory heirs. This follows because there is no way to know in advance which of those parties would be alive 28 years down the road, and thus which one would be considered the actual owner of the renewal term. Moreover, even with assignments from all these parties, divorce, remarriage, and the birth of new children after the original copyright transaction could stymie the plans of even the most cautious grantee. The situation was, to put it mildly, complicated and unsatisfactory save for copyright lawyers who could make a tidy living sorting through the mess.

8.1.2 Renewal and Derivative Works Under the 1909 Scheme

In virtually every case, parties purchase copyright interests in order to exploit them economically. One way a grantee can exploit a copyright is to simply reproduce the work and sell the copies for a profit. Thus a publisher, having obtained assignment of copyright in a novel from an author, can then print copies of the novel and sell them. Another mode of exploitation, however, is for the grantee to prepare derivative works based on the copyrighted work. Thus the publisher could prepare a Spanish translation of the novel for reproduction and sale. Similarly, it could prepare a screenplay and then license a film company to produce a movie. Indeed, sometimes a party will not purchase a copyright outright, but instead take a license solely for the purpose of permitting it to create and exploit derivative works.

As we have seen in the preceding section, under the 1909 Act no assignee or licensee could be absolutely certain that it would continue to own the copyright after the first 28-year term. An assignment of the renewal term from the author might not vest if the author died before the end of the first term. This situation created an interesting ambiguity in the case of the grantee or licensee who prepared derivative works during the first term. Should the grantee or licensee be able to continue to exploit the derivative work during the renewal term without regard to the copyright proprietor? Or, should such exploitation be subject to the consent of whichever party became the owner of the copyright during the renewal term?

The Supreme Court resolved a conflict in the case law on this point in its celebrated *Stewart v. Abend* decision.[7] There, author Cornell Woolrich assigned the film rights to his short story "It Had to Be Murder" to a production company. Woolrich agreed to renew the copyright and assign the rights to the production company for the renewal term. Actor Jimmy Stewart and director Alfred Hitchcock acquired these rights and released the film version, "Rear Window." Woolrich, however, died before he could renew the copyright. Woolrich did not leave either a surviving spouse or any surviving children. At the appropriate time, therefore the executor of Woolrich's estate renewed the copyright and then assigned the renewal term to a man named Abend. Abend sued Stewart and Hitchcock's estate when they allowed "Rear Window" to be broadcast on network television.

The Supreme Court concluded that Abend's renewal term copyright interest in Woolrich's story had been infringed. The Court reasoned that exploitation of a derivative work legitimately created during the initial term of copyright was nonetheless subject to the renewal copyright. The Court could find no language in the Copyright Act upsetting the basic principle that a licensee can exploit only as much copyrighted material as it was authorized to use. The assignment of the renewal term to the film rights in "It Had to Be Murder" was no more than a contingent interest, the Court reasoned, and the predicate of the survival of Woolrich to the renewal term had not occurred. As a result, the Court concluded that continued distribution of "Rear Window" violated the copyright in "It Had to Be Murder."

The merits of the *Stewart v. Abend* holding have been roundly debated. Critics of the decision observe that its holding offers a windfall to authors' heirs at the expense of the creators of derivative works. A comparison of the commercial success of the critically acclaimed "Rear Window" with that of the obscure "It Had to Be Murder" suggests that in many cases, the creators of the derivative work have added more value to the licensed work than the original author himself. *Stewart v. Abend* may also simply discourage the production of derivative works, at least those based on works published prior to the advent of the 1976 Act. And, to the extent that the renewal copyright holder cannot reach a deal with the author of the derivative work, valuable derivative works may actually be removed from the market. For all of these criticisms, *Stewart v. Abend* has been consistently followed by the lower courts.

7. 495 U.S. 207, 110 S.Ct. 1750, 109 L.Ed.2d 184 (1990).

§ 8.2 Duration Under the 1976 Act

Works created after January 1, 1978, are not governed by the two-term approach of the 1909 statute. Instead, the current statute provides for a single unitary term of duration of copyright. As originally enacted, the 1976 Act specified that copyright would last for the life of the author plus 50 years after the authors's death. In 1998, Congress enacted the Sonny Bono Term Extension Act.[1] The Bono Act lengthened the term of works still under copyright in 1998, as well as later authored works, by 20 years. The present term of copyright is therefore the life of the author plus 70 years.[2] In the case of jointly authored works, the copyright lasts for 70 years after the death of the last surviving author.[3]

One advantageous feature of this system is that all the works of an author pass into the public domain at the same time. Under the scheme of the 1909 Act, the works of an author who was productive over a stretch of years would each pass into the public domain on different dates as different 28–or 56–year periods expired.

A slightly different approach is taken for certain works where the identity of a specific human author is either unclear or irrelevant. Thus, works for hire, anonymous works, and pseudonymous works are all governed by a different duration rule. They are each protected for 95 years from publication or 120 years from creation, which ever term expires first.[4]

Obviously, this scheme makes it important to know whether the author of a given work is still living, or if not, when exactly he or she died. The 1976 Act handles this problem by setting up a procedure for registering deaths at the Copyright Office. Under section 302(d)[5] anyone with an interest in a copyright may record at any time a statement either indicating the date of the author's death or the fact that the author is still living. This permits those who want to learn the status of the copyright of a work to check the records at the copyright office to see if the "life plus seventy" term has expired. Of course, in many cases, no one will have bothered to file a section 302(d) document. In these cases, the statute goes on to provide that a presumption that the author has been dead for seventy years will arise if, after 95 years from the publication of a work, or 120 years from its creation (which ever comes first) the Copyright Office certifies that nothing in its records indicates that the author is living or died less than seventy years earlier.[6] Thus, for older works, users have a sure-fire way of ascertaining if the work is still protected by copyright.

§ 8.2

1. Pub. L. No. 105–298, 112 Stat. 2827 (1998).

2. 17 U.S.C.A. § 302(a) (2000).

3. 17 U.S.C.A. § 302(b) (2000).

4. 17 U.S.C.A. § 302(c) (2000). The statute goes on to provide that anyone having an interest in the copyright to an anony-mous or pseudonymous work may file a statement with the Copyright Office identifying the author of the work, in which case the copyright term becomes the life of that identified author plus seventy years.

5. 17 U.S.C.A. § 302(d) (2000).

6. 17 U.S.C.A. § 302(e) (2000).

§ 8.3   Works Created under the 1909 Act and Still Protected Under the 1976 Act

8.3.1   Works Published Before 1950

Simple arithmetic indicates that any work first published[1] before 1950 would have exhausted its first 28 year term of copyright under the 1909 act before the January 1, 1978, effective date of the current law. If the copyright in such a work had not been renewed at the relevant time by the proper person that work would have fallen into the public domain and there is nothing in the 1976 Act that changes that result so as to restore the copyright in such a work. For example, the initial term of copyright for a work first published in 1945 would have expired in 1973, and if no renewal application was filed at that time, the work would thereafter be free for others to use, with no restoration of rights under the 1976 Act.

On the other hand, if a work in this category was renewed on the relevant date then its second, or renewal copyright term would, under the 1909 Act, have lasted for another 28 years. Thus in the preceding example, if the work had been renewed in 1973, the renewal term would have been scheduled to expire in 2001. This durational situation was changed by provisions in the 1976 Act as originally enacted, however. If the renewal term of copyright was subsisting during 1977, the year immediately preceding the effective date of the current law, the statute provides that the total term of copyright shall be calculated as 75 years from the date of first publication.[2] Congress selected this total 75–year term because they felt this term approximated the average length of the life-plus-fifty durational rule that would apply to works first created after January 1, 1978.[3] As a result, this system provided an extra 19 years of protection to copyright owners in comparison to the scheme under the 1909 Act (since 75 is 19 more than 56).

With the passage of the Bono Act in 1998, copyright term in protected works was extended by another 20 years. The renewal term, already lengthened from 28 years to 47 years, was increased again to a total of 67 years. Importantly, the Bono Act did not restore copyright in any works that had previously fallen into the public domain. The 20–

---

§ 8.3

1. For simplicity, the text refers to works "published" on a certain date, since that is the time when most works obtained federal copyright protection under the 1909 Act. It should be noted, however, that for certain unpublished works, federal copyright protection could be obtained by registration. In those cases, all of the durational time periods referred to in the text would be measured from the date that federal protection was originally secured.

2. 17 U.S.C.A. § 304 (b) (2000).

3. In other words, the drafters of the 1976 Act assumed that most creators will die about 25 years after they create the bulk of their works, making a term of 50 years after death equivalent to about 75 total years. Among the arguments in favor of extending copyright term via the Bono Act was that lifespans are increasing. Note also that for a long-lived child prodigy, the actual duration of the current life-plus-seventy-year term can be much more than 95 years. For instance, if a 10–year-old child writes a symphony, and then lives to age 90, the total term of copyright would actually be 150 years—80 remaining years of the composers life, plus 70 years after death.

year term extension only affected works that were still under copyright on its effective date, which was October 29, 1998. To continue the hypothetical from the preceding paragraph, if a work was first published in 1945, and renewed in 1973, its copyright would have been due to expire in 2020 (1945 publication + 75); however since it was still protected in the fall of 1998, it receives the 20–year "Bono bonus" and its copyright will endure until 2040.

A further bit of arithmetic reveals that under this scheme any work first published in 1922 or earlier now lies within the public domain. Assuming effective renewal registration, the copyright on a work published in 1922 expired in 28+47=75 years, or 1997. As a result, such works could not take advantage of the Bono Act, which became effective in 1998. On the other hand, the copyright of a work published in 1923— again assuming effective renewal registration—will not expire until 2018. Thus it follows that one major consequence of the Bono Act was to freeze the public domain for twenty years. No copyrights will expire from 1998 until 2018.

One further complication should be mentioned here. The discussions that led to the ultimate passage of the 1976 copyright act actually started in the early 1960's. In anticipation of an ultimate elongation of copyright terms as part of the new law, Congress periodically extended the terms of copyrights that were already in their renewal periods.[4] Thus, any works that were in their renewal terms on September 19, 1962, or later, had those renewal terms extended until the new act was to become effective, and thereafter were subject to the new term provided by the 1976 Act.

An example will show how this system works. Assume that a work was first published in 1910, and then the copyright was renewed in 1938 at the expiration of the initial 28–year term. Ordinarily, the renewal term would have expired in 1966, 28 years after the 1938 renewal. Because of the legislation described above, however, the renewal term of the work was repeatedly extended until the 1976 act became law, whereupon the work became entitled to the full "75–years-from-publication" term of copyright described in the previous paragraph. Thus, copyright in this work did not expire until 1985. Because the work had already entered the public domain at the time the Bono Act was passed in 1998, the work was not eligible for an additional twenty years of copyright protection.

8.3.2 Works Published Between 1950 and 1963

Any work published in 1950 or later would have been in its first term of copyright when the 1976 Act became effective. That is because 1950 plus the 28 years of the original term takes you past the magic date of January 1, 1978, when the 1976 Act became effective. As part of the

---

4. The statutes in questions are Public Laws 87–668, 89–142, 90–141, 90–416, 91–147, 91–055, 92–170, 92–566, and 93–573.

original 1976 Act Congress decided to retain the requirement of mandatory renewal. It thus provided that works in this category would continue to enjoy a 28–year initial term of protection and then could be renewed for an additional term of 47 years.[5] This would provide a total of 75 years of protection, which as we previously noted is the period Congress used to approximate the life-plus–50 term that applies to works first created after 1978. With the advent of Bono Act in 1998, the renewal term was increased again, from 47 to 67 years, resulting in a 95–year term. *Failure to renew, however, would result in a forfeiture of all further protection.* Thus a work first published in 1960 would have been under its first term of copyright protection until 1988, whereupon it would have been eligible for a renewal that would have conferred further protection through the year 2035, which, in turn, would now be extended to 2055 under the Bono Act. On the other hand, if no steps were taken to secure the renewal, the work would have fallen into the public domain in 1988.

This scheme, of course, retains one of the central defects of the 1909 law—the "trap for the unwary" quality of the renewal requirement. As a result, Congress decided in 1992 to change the renewal requirement by making renewal automatic.[6] However, that provision was written to operate prospectively only. Thus works that were due to be renewed before 1992[7] cannot take advantage of an "automatic renewal" and if they were not renewed by a filing at the Copyright Office, they remain in the public domain. For works published after 1964, the renewal is automatic, as is discussed in the following subsection.

8.3.3 Works Published Between 1964 and 1977

After 1992, works whose first 28–year term under the 1909 statute expire were granted an automatic renewal term of 67 years. Thus a work first published in 1970 would reach the end of its first term in 1998 and thereupon be granted protection through 2065. Although the renewal term is conferred automatically when the first term ends, without the need to register, the statute provides several incentives to encourage parties to register their renewal claims anyway.

First, if a permissive registration is not pursued, then the renewal term vests in which ever person was statutorily entitled to it as of the last day of the original term.[8] However, if a permissive registration is made, then the right to the renewal term is determined as of the date of the permissive renewal application. Thus, permissive registration allows the contingent holder of the renewal copyright term to lock in his rights before the end of the 28th year of the original term.

Suppose, for example, that Michael Malfoy secures copyright in the novel "The Rowling Writ" on March 1, 1975. Malfoy transfers the

5. 17 U.S.C.A. § 304 (1988).

6. Pub. L. No. 102–307, 106 Stat. 264 (1992).

7. This category consists of works published in 1963 or before, as 1963 + 28 is 1991.

8. 17 U.S.C.A. § 204(a)(2).

original and renewal copyright terms in the work to Patricia Potter on January 19, 1978 and also gives Potter a power of attorney allowing her to make copyright filings on his behalf. Malfoy passes away on November 1, 2003, during the 28th year of the original copyright term. The renewal copyright term automatically commences on January 1, 2004. However, in this case, the identity of the proprietor of the renewal term copyright depends upon whether Potter filed a permissive renewal registration. If Potter had filed such a registration prior to Malfoy's death—but no earlier than January 1, 2003, the earliest possible date under the statute—then Potter would be entitled to the renewal term because Malfoy would have been living on the crucial date—the date of the renewal filing. Otherwise, vesting of the renewal term would be judged as of December 31, 2003. Because Malfoy did not survive into the renewal term, his assignment of the renewal term to Potter would fail and it would vest instead in Malfoy's heirs.

A second incentive to register pertains to derivative works legitimately created under license from the copyright proprietor during the original term. If a permissive renewal registration is timely filed, then the rule of *Stewart v. Abend* applies and the grantee may not continue to use the derivative work without the permission of the owner of the renewal term interest.[9] However, if no registration is filed, then a legitimate derivative work prepared during the original term may continue to be used by the grantee under the term of the original grant. However, no new derivative works may be made during the renewal term even in the absence of a registration.[10]

Finally, permissive renewal registration also provides certain evidentiary advantages. If registration is made during the final year of the original term, then the certificate of renewal registration constitutes *prima facie* evidence of the validity of the facts stated in the certificates.[11]

8.3.4 Unpublished Works Created Before 1978

As noted previously, under the 1909 Act an unpublished work was not protected under the federal copyright law at all. Rather, it was protected under state common law copyright. Such state protection effectively endured for an unlimited term, provided the author did not publish the work.

With the adoption of the 1976 Act, as modified by the Bono Act, Congress decided to bring all such unpublished works under the scope of federal copyright. That meant that these pre-existing but unpublished works would now only be protected for a limited time. As a general matter, Congress granted these works the same basic terms as those applying to new works created after the effective date of the 1976 law.[12] In the typical case of a work created by an individual author, that means

9. *See supra* § 8.1.2.

10. 17 U.S.C.A. § 304(a)(4)(A).

11. 17 U.S.C.A. § 304(a)(4)(B).

12. 17 U.S.C.A. § 303 (2000).

life of the author, plus 70 years. For example, assume a work was created in 1970 and never published, and that its author died in 1975. Prior to January 1, 1978 (the effective date of the 1976 act) it was protected by perpetual common law copyright. After that date it was protected under federal law, and the state law protection was preempted. The federal copyright would expire in the year 2045, 70 years after the death of the author.[13]

For older works, however, this system posed a problem. Imagine a work written in 1920 and never published, by an author who died in 1922. Until January 1, 1978 the work was protected by common law copyright. After that date, it is subject to federal protection and the original 1976 Act's term of "life plus fifty." Yet here, this term would have expired in 1972 (1922 + 50), meaning that the work would be immediately injected in the public domain the minute the 1976 Act became effective!

This struck the Congress as both unfair and unwise, so they provided that in the case of previously unpublished works, "[i]n no case, however, shall the term of copyright in such a work expire before December 31, 2002; and if the work is published on or before December 31, 2002, the term of copyright shall not expire before December 31, 2047."[14] Thus, in the preceding hypothetical, if the work remained unpublished, the copyright expired at the end of 2002. If the work was published before the close of 2002, then the copyright will expire in 2047.

At the time this book goes to press, the Sonny Bono Act is facing constitutional challenge in the U.S. Supreme Court. The Court granted certiorari in *Eldred v. Ashcroft* on February 19, 2002,[15] agreeing to hear the petitioners' claims under the First Amendment and Intellectual Property Clause. These constitutional arguments are not centered upon the dubious proposition that a "life plus fifty" term constitutes a limited time within the meaning of the Constitution, while a "life plus seventy" term does not. Instead it is the retroactive nature of the Bono Act that is the focus of petitioner's challenge. An award of an additional two decades of copyright to works already under protection would seem to do little to promote cultural progress, while at the same time presenting significant free speech concerns. Also notable is the fact that the Bono Act effectively imposes a twenty-year moratorium on works entering the public domain: absent the Bono Act, 1998 to 2018 would have seen the entry into the public domain of a large number of works published between 1923 and 1943. The significance of *Eldred v. Ashcroft* upon copyright term, as well as its resolution of the constitutional analysis in

---

13. To be precise, the copyright in this work would have originally been scheduled to expire in 2025 under the life-plus-fifty rule of the original 1976 Act. The term would then have been elongated by the Bono Act for an additional 20 years, taking us to 2045.

14. *Id.*

15. 534 U.S. 1126, 122 S.Ct. 1062, 151 L.Ed.2d 966 (2002), *amended*, 534 U.S. 1160, 122 S.Ct. 1170, 152 L.Ed.2d 115 (2002).

copyright jurisprudence more generally, will probably be known by the time you read these words.

§ 8.4   Termination of Transfers

The 1976 Act introduced two termination of transfer provisions that are found in sections 203 and 304. These provisions work towards the same purpose as the renewal term of the 1909 Act: protecting authors and their families from unremunerative licenses and assignments of works of authorship.[1] Sections 203 and 304 allow authors or their heirs to rescind grants (including both outright assignments and licenses) after a specified period of years has passed if certain formalities are observed. These fairly unique provisions thus allow copyright owners the unilateral and unconditional right to cancel bargains they previously entered into, creating the statutory equivalent of what is known on the grade school playground as a "do over." Thus, even though the 1976 Act eliminated the renewal term in favor of a unitary copyright term, the paternalistic policy of protecting authors from unremunerative transfers remains.

Congress constructed the termination of transfer provisions with the lessons from the 1909 Act and its case law in mind. In particular, the right to terminate may not be assigned in advance.[2] Thus, the termination provisions avoid the problem created by the decisions under the 1909 Act, permitting renewal rights to be assigned away long before their vesting.[3]

The two provisions concerning termination of transfers operate similarly, but they cover distinct circumstances and contain some important differences. Section 203 addresses transfers an author made after 1977. In contrast, § 304 concerns pre–1978 grants of renewal term interests.

Some important limitations on both § 203 and § 304 should be noted at the outset. Terminations of transfer do not occur automatically. Authors and their beneficiaries must observe certain formalities within specified time periods in order to terminate a transfer.[4] In addition, neither termination of transfer provision applies to works made for hire or if the transfer was accomplished via will.[5]

8.4.1   Pre–1978 Transfers

Section 304 allows authors and their families to enjoy the financial rewards resulting from legislative extensions to the copyright term. Recall that the 1976 Act lengthened the renewal term of copyright by 19

§ 8.4

1. H.R. No. 94–1476, 94th Cong., 2d Sess. 124 (1976).

2. 17 U.S.C.A. §§ 203(b)(6), 304(c)(6)(F) (2000).

3. See Fred Fisher Music Co. v. M. Witmark & Sons, 318 U.S. 643, 63 S.Ct. 773, 87 L.Ed. 1055 (1943).

4. 17 U.S.C.A. §§ 203(a)(4), 304(c)(4) (2000).

5. 17 U.S.C.A. §§ 203(a), 304(c) (2000).

years.[6] As a result, the renewal term increased from 28 years to 47 years, for a total of 75 years of copyright protection. The Sonny Bono Act again increased copyright term by another 20 years to 67 years, for a total of 95 total years of protection.[7] Bear in mind that neither party to a pre–1978 contract would have known about these bonus years of copyright protection in advance. They represent an economic windfall. The question is who should enjoy them. Congress decided that these term increases amount to a new property right, and that the associated economic reward should belong to authors and their families rather than their transferees.[8]

In order to implement this policy, section 304 provides two avenues for rescinding transfers that would extend into these additional periods of copyright protection. Section 304(c) allows an author or his successors the right to terminate a transfer in order to recapture the full 39 years of the extended renewal term. In certain circumstances, if an author or successor did not exercise this right with respect to the initial 19–year extension, § 304(d) offers another opportunity to recapture the additional 20 years of extension established by the Sonny Bono Act.

Sections 304(c) and (d) are complex provisions that reward careful reading. However, some of their chief provisions may be quickly summarized. These provisions concern grants that the author, or other statutorily specified owners of renewal terms, executed before January 1, 1978. Works made for hire and disposition by will may not be terminated under this provision.[9] Under § 304(c) termination can occur on any date within a five-year "window" beginning at the end of 56 years from the date copyright was originally secured, or beginning on January 1, 1978, whichever is later.

Of course a copyright owner who conveyed away a renewal term interest need not terminate. He might feel that the financial arrangements he initially made with his grantee are satisfactory, and be content to let the termination window expire without taking any action. However, copyright owners who made such a decision might have regretted it when Congress extended the duration of renewal terms by twenty years in the Sonny Bono Act. The decision that the economic terms of the original grant were acceptable for a 19–year remaining copyright life is one thing; a decision that they are going to be fair for a 39 year period is something else entirely. To deal with this situation, Congress added a second termination provision to the statute when it passed the Sonny Bono Act. Codified in section 304(d)[10] it provides that if the 304(c) window had already expired by October 1998, a second five-year termination window would open at the end of 75 years from the date copyright was secured. For arithmetical reasons that are explained in the

---

6. *See supra* § 8.3.1.

7. Sonny Bono Copyright Term Extension Act, 105–298, 112 Stat. 2827 (1998).

8. H.R. No. 94–1476, 94th Cong., 2d Sess. 140 (1976).

9. 17 U.S.C.A. § 304(c) (2000).

10. 17 U.S.C.A. § 304(d) (2000).

footnote, the termination provisions of section 304(d) will thus only apply to grants involving works first published between 1923 and 1937.[11]

Under either of these two provisions, advance written notice must be sent to the grantee in order to effectuate the termination of transfer. The notice must comply with Copyright Office regulations and be recorded in the Copyright Office.[12] Notice can be served not less than two nor more than ten years before the effective date of the termination.[13]

The statutory provisions detailing the parties that possess the right to terminate are complex. As would be expected, the author of the work may effect a termination of transfer. If more than one co-author executed the grant, any one of them is allowed to terminate to the extent of his particular share. Thus if Al and Bill co-authored a play and then both assigned away their rights to Omega, either Al or Bill or both could terminate. If Al terminates and Bill does not, Al will own half the copyright and Omega will own the other half. If an author is dead, that author's termination interest is owned as follows:

(A) If the author dies without children, leaving only a widow/widower, then the widow or widower owns the entire termination interest.

(B) If the author leaves surviving children, without a widow/widower, then the children take the entire interest *per stirpes*.

(C) If both a widow/widower and children survive, the widow(er) takes a 50% interest and the children take the other 50% *per stirpes*.

(D) If no widow/widower, children or grandchildren are living, then the author's executor, administrator, personal representative, or trustee owns the author's entire termination interest.

If individuals other than the author made the grant that is to be terminated, all surviving grantors are required to terminate.[14]

Termination causes all rights to revert to the those having the power to terminate. The former grantee may continue to use derivative works under the terms of the former grant, however, provided that they were prepared before termination. On the other hand, no new derivative works may be prepared after the effective termination date.[15] The owners are tenants-in-common who can authorize further grants if signed by the same number and proportion as are required to terminate. This further

---

11. The section 304(c) termination window runs from 56 to 61 years after the work is first published. Thus, for that window to have already expired at the time of the Sonny Bono legislation, the work would have had to have been published 61 years before the date of the Bono law. That date was 1998, and 1998 minus 61 yields 1937. Of course, any work published before 1923 would be in the public domain before the Bono law became effective, and thus could not take advantage of the new termination right. Consequently, section 304(d) is only relevant to works published between 1923 and 1937. The owner of a work published after 1937 would be able to make a fully informed decision about the wisdom of terminating during the first termination period. Such a party does not need, and does not get, the benefits of the alternative termination right in § 304(d).

12. 17 U.S.C.A. § 304(c)(4)(B) (2000).

13. 17 U.S.C.A. § 304(c)(4)(A) (2000).

14. 17 U.S.C.A. § 304(c)(1), (2) (2000).

15. 17 U.S.C.A. § 304(c)(6) (2000).

grant is effective for all owners, even those who did not join in signing it.[16]

An example illustrates the workings of § 304. Suppose that author Boggins procured a valid copyright upon her novel, "The Habit," in 1945 by publishing it in that year. Boggins assigns both her initial copyright term, as well as her expectancy interest in the renewal term, to Colossal Movie Studio. Under the split-term regime of the 1909 Act, the renewal term would commence in 1973 (1945 + 28). Assuming that Boggins survived into the renewal term and that the necessary renewal filing was made, the renewal term would vest in Colossal Movie Studio. Under the 1909 Act, the copyright would have expired in 2001 (1945 + 28 + 28). The 1976 Act then extended the copyright term to 2020 (1945 + 28 + 47), with the Sonny Bono Act then delaying the expiration date to 2040 (1945 + 28 + 47 + 20).

Under § 304(c), Boggins and her heirs may terminate the grant to Colossal starting 56 years after publication. This gives Colossal the full term it bargained for when it paid for an assignment of the original and renewal terms under the 1909 Act, since at the time it bought the copyright, it expected to have exclusive rights only for 56 years. This means that Boggins can attempt to effectuate termination as soon as 2002. As a result, she, or her heirs, if she is no longer alive at this point, would own copyright for its remaining 39 years of extended protection under the 1976 Act, as amended by the Sonny Bono Act. (Note that because she has a post–1998 opportunity to terminate under § 304(c) she will not be able to invoke the alternative provisions of § 304(d).).

To effectuate termination Boggins must pick a precise termination date in the five year "window" and also serve a proper notice. To continue the previous example, suppose that Boggins wished to terminate the grant on January 19, 2003. This date is permissible under § 304(c) because January 19, 2003, is within the five year period running from January 1, 2002 through December 31, 2006. However, Boggins would need to send written notice to Colossal Movie Studio no earlier than 1993, but no later than 2001.

Although § 304(c) offers considerable detail on many aspects of notice of termination, that provision stipulates only that "termination shall be effected by serving an advance notice in writing upon the grantee or grantee's successor in title."[17] The statute nowhere defines the term "successor in title." A notable judicial opinion, *Burroughs v. Metro–Goldwyn–Mayer, Inc.*,[18] considers this phrase. There, the famous author Edgar Rice Burroughs had assigned his copyright interests in several of his famous Tarzan stories to a family owned-corporation called ERB, Inc. In turn, ERB, Inc. granted a nonexclusive license to film rights in certain *Tarzan* stories and characters to MGM. The author's heirs served a notice of termination on ERB, Inc., but not MGM, in 1977. When MGM sought to produce the 1981 movie *Tarzan, the Ape Man*, the

16. 17 U.S.C.A. § 304(c)(6)(D) (2000). **18.** 683 F.2d 610 (2d Cir.1982).
17. 17 U.S.C.A. § 304(c)(4) (2000).

author's heirs brought suit, claiming that they had effectively terminated the *Tarzan* license.

The district court held that the heirs' termination notice was defective. The district court reasoned that the notice had been served on ERB, Inc., rather than MGM, the proper "successor in title." Alternatively, explained the district court, the 1977 termination occurred before the effective date of the 1976 Act and was therefore premature.[19] On appeal, the Second Circuit affirmed on different grounds. The Court of Appeals observed that Copyright Office regulation required that notices of termination list the grants covered. Because the heirs' notice had omitted five licensed titles, the rights to the material in those books could not have been terminated. Consequently the un-terminated features of the 1931 grant would still effectively convey sufficient rights to the Tarzan character to permit MGM to go ahead with its planned movie.

Although the Second Circuit majority opinion offered no conclusive statement on the meaning of the term "successor in title," Judge Newman's concurring opinion squarely addressed the issue. The concurrence suggested that the notice was ineffective because it was not served upon MGM. By giving notice only to a closely held family corporation, the heirs were effectively doing nothing more than serving notice upon themselves. Judge Newman concluded that the heirs should have served MGM, the realistic grantee under the circumstances.

8.4.2 Post–1978 Transfers

Section 203 creates a right to terminate transfers, including assignments and licenses, of a copyright or any right under a copyright executed by an author on or after January 1, 1978. This provision covers grants made by the author on or after January 1, 1978. Works made for hire and disposition by will may not be terminated under this provision.[20] Termination can occur during the five-year period starting at the end of 35 years from the date of the execution of the grant. If the grant covers the right of publication, however, the five-year period begins at the earlier of 35 years after publication, or 40 years after the grant was made.[21]

Note three key distinctions between this provision and the termination mechanisms provided under section 304. First, this provision only govern grants that were made by the author himself. If a relative of the author had inherited the copyright interest and then executed a post–1978 assignment or license, that grant would not be terminable under section 203. Second, note that the termination "window" under this section of the statute is measured from the date *of the grant* not from the date *copyright protection began.* Thus if author Boggins wrote a novel in 1985, and then, 15 years later in the year 2000, assigned all rights in that novel to Omega, the grant to Omega could not be terminated until

19. 519 F.Supp. 388 (S.D.N.Y.1981).

20. 17 U.S.C.A. § 203(a) (2000).

21. 17 U.S.C.A. § 203(a)(3) (2000).

2035—35 years after the grant. This insures that the grantee gets a full 35 years to exploit the work under the terms of the original bargain before the author can use the termination provisions to force a renegotiation. Finally, in cases involving a grant executed by two or more authors of a joint work, termination may only be effected by a majority of those who signed the grant. Thus if all 5 members of a band collaborated on a song, and then three of them, John, Paul, and George, co-signed a license with a record company, that license could only be terminated if two of those three acted together. Recall by way of contrast that under section 304, each joint author can terminate independently and recover back fractional shares of the copyright.

The earliest terminations under section 203 will not be effective until 2013, because the earliest grants covered by the provisions are those executed in 1978, and 2013 is 35 years from 1978. However, grantors seeking to use this provision must give advance notice, and, just like the notice required under section 304, that notice must be served no less than two nor more than ten years before the selected termination date.[22] Consequently, the earliest notices relating to terminations under section 203 began being served in January, 2003 (ten years before the earliest termination year of 2013). A section 203 notice must comply with Copyright Office regulations and be recorded in the Copyright Office.[23] If an author is dead, that author's termination interest is owned as follows:

(A) If the author dies without children, leaving only a widow/widower, then the widow or widower owns the entire termination interest.

(B) If the author leaves surviving children, without a widow/widower, then the children take the entire interest *per stirpes*.

(C) If both a widow/widower and children survive, the widow(er) takes a 50% interest and the children take the other 50% *per stirpes*.

(D) If no widow/widower, children or grandchildren are living, then the author's executor, administrator, personal representative, or trustee owns the author's entire termination interest.[24]

Following a termination of transfer, all rights revert to the those having the power to terminate. The former grantee may continue to use derivative works under the terms of the former grant, however, provided that they were prepared before termination. Just as with section 304, no new derivative works may be prepared after the effective termination date.[25] Further grants may be made if signed by the same number and proportion of owners as are required for termination. This further grant is effective for all owners, even those who did not join in signing it.[26]

Thus suppose that a Mr. Rander authors a novel entitled "King of the Rings." Rander assigns copyright in the novel to Magnificent Movie Studios in 1980. Rander would be able to terminate the assignment as

---

22. 17 U.S.C.A. § 203(a)(4)(A) (2000).

23. 17 U.S.C.A. § 203(a)(4) (2000).

24. 17 U.S.C.A. § 203(a)(2) (2000).

25. 17 U.S.C.A. § 203(b) (2000).

26. 17 U.S.C.A. § 203(b)(3) (2000).

early as 35 years later, at the end of 2015. To do so, Rander must serve written notification upon Magnificent Movie Studios no earlier than 2010, and no later than 2013.

§ 8.5   Copyright Restoration

As part of the Uruguay Round Agreements Act,[1] the United States amended § 104A to provide for copyright restoration in certain foreign works of authorship. Through the process of restoration, the Copyright Act achieves the unusual result of recognizing copyright in certain works that had previously fallen into the public domain. The amendments that led to § 104A, effective on January 1, 1996, at last brought the United States into compliance with the Berne Convention. Article 18 of Berne requires new signatories to protect the copyrights of all works from other Berne member states that have not yet entered the public domain in their countries of origin. Due process concerns, and perhaps more than a bit of domestic favoritism, caused the United States initially to avoid the issue when it adhered to the Berne Convention in 1989. With the advent of the World Trade Organization, the United States belatedly fulfilled its Berne obligations by adopting legislation to restore the copyrights of certain foreign works that had fallen into the public domain in the United States because of failures to adhere to formalities under our laws.

A work must fulfill four requirements to be restored. First, the copyright must have been forfeited for a specified reason. The three permissible reasons are: (1) formalities such as notice or registration had not been observed, (2) the work was a sound recording published before February 15, 1972, (3) the U.S. and the nation of the work's origin did not enjoy copyright relations.[2] Second, the work must still be subject to copyright in its nation of origin.[3] Third, at least one of the authors of the work had to have been a national or domiciliary of a so-called "eligible country."[4] An eligible country must either be a World Trade Organization (WTO) member, Berne Convention signatory, or the subject of a Presidential proclamation.[5] Importantly, although the United States is a WTO member and Berne signatory, it is expressly excluded from the list of eligible countries. As a result of this definition, domestic parties whose works were injected into the public domain by publication without notice, or failure to renew, cannot rely upon § 104A for restoration of their copyrights. Fourth, if the work was published, it must have been published in an eligible country and not published in the United States within 30 days following such publication.[6]

If restored, the copyright will subsist for the duration of the statutory term as if the work had never entered the public domain.[7] Ownership

§ 8.5

1. Pub. L. No. 103–465, 108 Stat. 4809 (1994).

2. 17 U.S.C.A. § 104A(h)(6)(c) (2000).

3. 17 U.S.C.A. § 104A(h)(6)(B) (2000).

4. 17 U.S.C.A. § 104A(h)(6)(d) (2000).

5. 17 U.S.C.A. § 104A(h)(3) (2000).

6. 17 U.S.C.A. § 104A(h)(6)(d) (2000).

7. 17 U.S.C.A. § 104A(a)(1) (2000).

of the restored copyright vests initially in the author or other proprietor as determined by the law of the source country of the work.[8] Copyrights in restored works provide their proprietors with the same rights as other sorts of copyrights. However, Congress recognized that third parties may have made substantial investments in the exploitation of a work on the assumption that the work was in the public domain, only to discover that the copyright has been restored.

As a result, § 104A includes provisions that protect the interest of any so-called "reliance party."[9] A qualified "reliance party" may be liable for copyright infringement only if the foreign copyright owner filed a statutorily prescribed notice with the U.S. Copyright Office within 24 months after the adoption of § 104A or if that party served a notice of intent to enforce the restored copyright directly on the reliance party involved.[10] After receiving notice, a reliance party is allowed twelve months to sell copies of the restored work, or to continue to perform, distribute or display the restored work, without liability to the copyright owner.[11] Reliance parties are also allowed to continue to exploit any derivative works they may have made based on a work with a restored copyright, but they are obliged to pay "reasonable compensation" for that privilege.

8.   17 U.S.C.A. § 104A(b) (2000).
9.   17 U.S.C.A. § 104A(h)(4) (2000).
10.   17 U.S.C.A. § 104A(e) (2000).

11.   17 U.S.C.A. § 104A(d)(2) (2000).

Chapter 9

COPYRIGHT INFRINGEMENT

Once one is familiar with the types of works protected by copyright, and the various rights granted copyright owners by the statute, the concept of infringement seems simple enough. Because all of the statutory rights are "exclusive," infringement occurs when anyone other than the copyright owner engages in any of the itemized rights without the copyright owner's permission. Thus it is infringement to copy, adapt, distribute, perform, or display a protected work, or to violate rights of attribution or integrity in a work of visual art, unless the acts in question are expressly exempted from infringement liability by a specific provision in the statute. This principle is codified in section 501(a) of the current copyright act: "Anyone who violates any of the exclusive rights of the copyright owner as provided by section 106 or of the author as provided in section 106A(a), . . . is an infringer of the copyright or the rights of the author, as the case may be."[1] Furthermore, one need not be the owner of the entire copyright interest to bring an infringement suit. The owner of any exclusive right under a copyright may sue for infringement of that particular right.[2]

Despite the straightforward nature of the idea of copyright infringement, complexity in infringement analysis arises for several reasons. First, as noted much earlier in this text, truly independent creation of a work does not constitute infringement even if the result of defendant's efforts is something very similar to plaintiff's work, because such independent creation does not violate any of the copyright owner's exclusive rights.[3] There are other, equally innocent reasons why defendant's work might appear similar to plaintiff's. For instance, they both may have copied from the same public domain source. Thus, merely because the defendant's work resembles the plaintiff's does not by itself mean that the defendant is an infringer. Much of the law of infringement is about distinguishing between cases of permissible resemblance, and cases where the resemblance occurs because the defendant impermissibly copied the plaintiff's work.

Second, infringement does not require verbatim copying. As we shall see, many forms of non-verbatim copying are also actionable. As Judge Learned Hand said in one of his most celebrated copyright decisions, "it is of course essential to any protection of literary property, whether at common-law or under the statute, that the right cannot be limited literally to the text, else a plagiarist would escape by immaterial variation."[4] In other words, changing a few words or notes or colors here or there will not insulate a defendant from liability. Indeed, a defendant can be liable even if there is no literal resemblance at all between his work and the plaintiff's if he has taken the protected non-literal pattern of the work. On the other hand, not all non-literal elements of a work are protected. The basic plot of a novel, the basic tune of a song or the

---

1. 17 U.S.C.A. § 501(a) (2000).

2. 17 U.S.C.A. § 501(b) (2000). This is a function of the divisibility of copyright under the 1976 Act. Thus, an exclusive licensee of a play who was granted the rights to perform that play in Kansas City during the month of April could sue any other party who attempted to perform that play in that city in that month.

3. *See supra* Chapter 3.

4. Nichols v. Universal Pictures Corp., 45 F.2d 119, 121 (2d Cir.1930), *cert. denied*, 282 U.S. 902, 51 S.Ct. 216, 75 L.Ed. 795 (1931)

basic structure of a computer program may be an unprotectable idea.[5] Thus here again, the law of infringement has had to develop various line-drawing principles designed to sort out permissible from impermissible conduct.

§ 9.1   The Elements of Copyright Infringement

There are a surprisingly large number of formulas for infringement floating around in the case law, no doubt due to the difficulties of line drawing alluded to above. Different courts use different terms to express the same concepts, and the concepts are combined or broken up in different ways depending on the nature and complexity of the case. Boiled down, however, all of these different tests and all of the different vocabulary are driving at the same basic concepts. In order to prevail, an infringement plaintiff must prove, first, that the defendant actually did copy plaintiff's work, and second, that this copying was impermissible because it constitutes "improper appropriation."[1] The first issue, copying, is essentially factual in nature. The second, improper appropriation, is a legal conclusion. These concepts are explored in detail in the subsections that follow.

9.1.1   Proof of Copying

Many copyright infringement claims involve alleged violation of the reproduction right—the right to make copies. Even alleged violation of the adaptation and performance rights involve the making of copies as a step in the infringing activities. Consequently, the first thing an infringement plaintiff must do is prove that the defendant actually copied his work. Without such proof, it is possible that any similarity between the two works might be due to coincidence.

Plaintiff's obligation to prove copying does not require the plaintiff to prove that the defendant had an impermissible intent. A defendant will be liable for infringement even if that infringement was innocent. For instance, if a defendant copies portions of plaintiff's work under the mistaken belief that it has fallen into the public domain, that defendant is nonetheless an infringer, despite his good faith. This doctrine has recently become significant in the computer industry. In *Playboy Enterprises, Inc. v. Frena*,[2] the operator of a computer bulletin board was held liable for infringement when a subscriber placed copyrighted pictures from *Playboy* magazine on the bulletin board without his knowledge. The court observed that "it does not matter that [the defendant] may have been unaware of the copyright infringement."[3]

5. *See supra* Chapter 3.

§ 9.1

1. Plaintiff must also prove ownership of a valid copyright in the work. Feist Publications, Inc. v. Rural Tel. Serv. Co., 499 U.S. 340, 111 S.Ct. 1282, 113 L.Ed.2d 358 (1991). The issues that bear on ownership—such as originality, compliance with formalities, etc.—have been covered in previous chapters of this section of the book.

2. 839 F.Supp. 1552 (M.D.Fla.1993).

3. *Id.* at 1559.

Courts have even held that the defendant will still be considered an infringer even if the defendant's copying is merely subconscious. A classic illustration of that situation is the case of *Bright Tunes Music Corp. v. Harrisongs Music, Ltd.*[4] The plaintiff in that case held the copyright on the song *He's So Fine.* The late George Harrison composed a song entitled *My Sweet Lord* which was alleged to infringe on *He's So Fine.* The court concluded that Harrison did not deliberately copy plaintiff's work, but still held him liable as an infringer because it found that he subconsciously had plaintiff's tune in mind when he created his own. The principle was established long before George Harrison got sued. As Learned Hand said in his 1936 decision in *Sheldon v. Metro–Goldwyn Pictures Corp.,* "unconscious plagiarism is actionable quite as much as deliberate."[5]

So how, then, does a plaintiff prove copying? If plaintiff can offer the eyewitness testimony of an observer who saw the defendant engage in copying, the plaintiff will, of course, prevail on this point. As you might guess, however, such testimony is not often available. Plagiarists rarely work with an audience present. Not surprisingly, therefore, infringement plaintiffs usually prove copying through circumstantial evidence.

The usual circumstantial showing has two prongs. The plaintiff must first show that the defendant had access to his copyrighted work. If the defendant never saw or heard plaintiff's work, any similarities between the two could not, by definition, be due to copying. Second, the plaintiff must show some resemblance between the two works. Mere access does not prove copying unless the two works are somewhat alike. It is sometimes said that these two prongs are inversely related to each other. On this view, if there is a high degree of resemblance between the works, then even weak evidence of access will suffice to show that the defendant copied from the plaintiff. Conversely, if access is undisputed, even moderate resemblance might suffice to establish copying. A complete absence of evidence on one of the two prongs, however, should logically preclude a finding of copying, and many courts have said just that.[6]

9.1.1.1   Access

Access can be proved by direct evidence, if such evidence is available. Testimony that the defendant has a copy of plaintiff's book in his office, or a CD recording of plaintiff's song at his home, would be nearly conclusive on the point. Where such direct evidence is lacking, the plaintiff will usually offer a more circumstantial case.

If plaintiff's work has proved popular and has been widely disseminated, that fact by itself may be sufficient to establish access. For example, in the *Bright Tunes* case discussed above, the plaintiff's song

4. 420 F.Supp. 177 (S.D.N.Y.1976), *aff'd sub nom,* ABKCO Music, Inc. v. Harrisongs Music, Ltd., 722 F.2d 988 (2d Cir.1983).

5. 81 F.2d 49, 54 (2d Cir.1936).

6. In Arnstein v. Porter, 154 F.2d 464, 468 (2d Cir.1946), Learned Hand noted that "of course, if there are no similarities, no amount of evidence of access will suffice to prove copying."

He's So Fine had been number one on the Billboard pop music charts in the United States for five weeks and had achieved a comparable degree of success in England. This was sufficient to raise an inference that Harrison had access to the song. On this logic, it is likely that courts would find that everyone has access to a best-selling novel or a blockbuster motion picture.

For less famous or unpublished works, it is usually necessary to offer some evidence that defendant at least had an opportunity to see the plaintiff's work.[7] Proof of this sort is often relied upon in cases where plaintiff has submitted work to one unit of a large organization. For instance, an author might submit a novel or screenplay to a large movie production company in the hope that they will like it enough to want to license the rights to produce a movie. Shortly thereafter, the crestfallen author receives a post-card from a low level employee declaring that the company is not interested. A year later, the company then releases a movie with a plot closely resembling the one in plaintiff's work. If the person who drafted the screenplay for the company's movie was a company employee, the court might infer access in this situation unless the company could prove that it kept plaintiff's submission segregated and its company screenwriter did not look at it.

Another way to show access is to attempt to prove that there are "striking similarities" between plaintiff's and defendant's works. The logic here is that the works resemble each other so closely that the only possible explanation is that defendant must have had access to plaintiff's work. The similarities must be "so striking and of such nature as to preclude the possibility of coincidence, accident or independent creation."[8] Obviously, the more complex the work, the more powerful the inference. If plaintiff has written a computer program with 100,000 lines of code, and if defendant's work is a virtually identical program, the inference of access and copying is very strong. On the other hand, if plaintiff's work is a minimalist abstract painting consisting of only a few spare geometric shapes, the fact that defendant's work is strikingly similar might not be as persuasive. Courts will allow expert testimony on the issue of striking similarity, which can help the plaintiff rule out the possibility of independent creation.

9.1.1.2   Resemblance

It should be obvious that access alone does not prove that defendant copied from plaintiff. For instance, both authors have a copy of the *Lord of the Rings* novels by J.R.R. Tolkien in our homes, but anyone who is familiar with those books and has read portions of this Hornbook can readily see, from the absence of elves and wizards if nothing else, that we did not copy this book from Tolkien's works (which may also explain why no one has contacted us about movie rights thus far). Consequently, in order to establish copying, the plaintiff must show that there are at

---

7. *See, e.g.,* Robert R. Jones Assocs. v. Nino Homes, 858 F.2d 274, 277 (6th Cir. 1988).

8. Scott v. WKJG, Inc., 376 F.2d 467, 469 (7th Cir.1967).

least some resemblances between his work and the one created by defendant.

Before developing this notion any further some discussion of terminology might be helpful. Many cases and law review articles use the term "similarity" rather than resemblance for this second prong of the copying inquiry. That usage has led to confusion because, as we shall see, "similarity" is also used as a term of art in the "improper appropriation" phase of infringement analysis. In an effort to dissipate some of that confusion, the late copyright scholar Alan Latman coined the term "probative similarity."[9] The adjective "probative" reminds us that the similarity in question at this stage of the analysis is probative of the issue of copying. While Professor Latman's phrase adds precision, it is a bit cumbersome. The adjective is sometime forgotten, leaving us back with the initial confusion. To simplify the following discussion we recommend the use of the term "resemblance" instead.

Once plaintiff has proved access, any resemblance of consequence will be enough to show copying. Even if the resemblance relates to unprotected elements of a work, such as public domain material, facts or ideas, the resemblance is evidence that defendant copied from plaintiff. Of course, if the plaintiff relied on a showing of "striking similarity" to prove access, no further proof of resemblance is necessary since by definition there will be a strong resemblance between the two works. The showing of "striking similarity" by itself becomes evidence of copying, merging the two subsidiary inquiries of access and resemblance into a single evidentiary point.

One form of resemblance that has figured prominently in the case law of infringement is the existence of common errors in both defendant's and plaintiff's works. Plaintiff's copyrighted work may contain various factual or artistic errors. Some of these may have crept into plaintiff's work inadvertently, while others might have been intentionally inserted as a trap to detect infringers. For instance, cartographers will sometimes insert fictional towns in their copyrighted maps and directory publishers will sometimes include fictional listings. If a defendant who produces a map or a directory dealing with the same subject matter had access to plaintiff's work, and defendant's work contains the same errors, this will be significant proof of copying. Indeed, one court has observed that "courts have regarded the existence of common errors in two similar works as the strongest evidence of piracy."[10]

In *Feist Publications Inc. v. Rural Telephone Service Co.,*[11] the plaintiff claimed copyright protection in a telephone directory. There was no question that defendant had access to plaintiff's directory as it had been widely distributed in the service area in question. Defendant's work also resembled plaintiff's in that there were more than 1300 entries that

---

9. Alan Latman, *"Probative Similarity" As Proof of Copying: Toward Dispelling Some Myths in Copyright Infringement,* 90 COLUM. L. REV. 1187 (1990).

10. Eckes v. Card Prices Update, 736 F.2d 859, 863 (2d Cir.1984).

11. 499 U.S. 340, 111 S.Ct. 1282, 113 L.Ed.2d 358 (1991).

were identical in the two volumes but, of course, that might be explained by the possibility that the defendant engaged in independent research to compile its listings. Plaintiff was especially aided in showing copying by the fact that defendant's work included four fictitious entries contained in plaintiff's directory. That could only be explained if defendant copied plaintiff's work. Note that plaintiff ultimately lost in *Feist* despite its proof of copying because that copying was not considered to be an improper appropriation, an issue that is addressed in the next section.

9.1.2   Proof of Improper Appropriation

Even though defendant copied from plaintiff's work, defendant might not be an infringer. The copied material might not be protected matter. For instance, it might constitute the unprotected idea at the heart of a work, or it might comprise public domain materials. Thus, plaintiff must do more than show copying to prevail in an infringement suit. Plaintiff must also show that the copying was illicit.

Here again, careful analysis requires dividing the issue into subparts. To demonstrate improper appropriation plaintiff must show first that the copied material was protected expression, and second that an ordinary observer would find the copied protected expression in defendant's work to be substantially similar to plaintiff's work.

9.1.2.1   Copied Material Must Be Protected Expression

Defendant is only an infringer if he has copied protected material from plaintiff's work. In cases involving literal copying, this issue is usually pretty simple. If the copied material meets the tests of originality and the copyright on the material has not yet expired, the material is protected and plaintiff has succeeded on this element of the case. This is true even if defendant copied only bits and pieces of plaintiff's work and scattered the copied material throughout the infringing work—a situation Professor Nimmer has labeled "fragmented literal similarity."[12]

The more controversial cases arise when the alleged copying involves non-literal elements of plaintiff's work—a situation Nimmer calls "comprehensive non-literal similarity."[13] If defendant has copied the general plot of a novel or the overall structure of a computer program, that copying may be either lawful or unlawful depending on whether the plot or structure is considered protectable expression or an unprotectable idea. As Judge Learned Hand noted in one of the most famous passages in all of copyright law:

> Upon any work, and especially upon a play a great number of patterns of increasing generality will fit equally well, as more and more of the incident is left out. The last may perhaps be no more than the most general statement of what the play is about, and at times might consist only of its title; but there is a point in this series of abstractions where they are no longer protected,

---

12. Nimmer, Copyright § 13.03[A][2] (2002).

13. Nimmer, Copyright § 13.03[A][1] (2002).

since otherwise the playwright could prevent the use of his "ideas" to which, apart from their expression, his property is never extended.[14]

While this "abstractions" test is eloquently put, it does not offer any particularly helpful bright line for decisions. The question of whether the copied elements fall on the idea or the expression side of the line is always subjective and decided on a case-by-case basis. Judge Hand said as much in a subsequent decision, *Peter Pan Fabrics, Inc. v. Martin Weiner Corp.,*[15] conceding that "no principle can be stated as to when an imitator has gone beyond the 'idea' and has borrowed its 'expression.' Decisions must therefore inevitably be *ad hoc*."

Some examples from the case law show how courts have attempted to apply this notion to concrete fact patterns. In *Beal v. Paramount Pictures Corp.*[16] the plaintiff alleged that the copyright in her adventure novel *The Arab Heart* had been infringed by defendant's movie *Coming to America,* starring Eddie Murphy. Both works involved stories of "young crown princes from wealthy royal families coming to America where they meet the women they will marry. Both feature a strong ruler who (with varying degrees of intensity) initially prefers that the prince enter into an arranged marriage." There were, however, numerous differences between the plot details in the works. After analyzing the plot, mood, characterization, pace, setting and sequence of events in both works, the court concluded that "although there are a few broad similarities between the works, they involve ideas and other general themes that are not susceptible to copyright protection." In other words, it found that the only copied elements of plaintiff's work were in the realm of the unprotectable, and that therefore the defendant was not an infringer.

In *Sheldon v. Metro–Goldwyn Pictures Corp.*[17] plaintiff alleged that defendant's motion picture, entitled *Letty Lynton*, infringed the copyright in his play, entitled *Dishonored Lady*. Both works were based on a celebrated criminal trial in 19th century Scotland. As Learned Hand explained, that real-world episode began when a young woman named Madeleine Smith had an affair with a man named L'Angelier and then "poured out her feelings in letters of the utmost ardor and indiscretion, and at times of a candor beyond the standards then, and even yet permissible for well-nurtured young women." Ms. Smith eventually broke off this relationship in favor of another man, but L'Angelier threatened to show the rather explicit love letters to her father. Shortly thereafter, L'Angelier died of arsenic poisoning and Smith was accused of the murder. At her trial there was evidence that Smith had purchased arsenic, but she offered evidence of an alibi for the time of the alleged murder and was acquitted by the jury.

---

14. Nichols v. Universal Pictures Corp., 45 F.2d 119, 121 (2d Cir.1930), *cert. denied*, 282 U.S. 902, 51 S.Ct. 216, 75 L.Ed. 795 (1931).

15. 274 F.2d 487, 489 (2d Cir.1960).

16. 20 F.3d 454 (11th Cir.1994), *cert. denied*, 513 U.S. 1062, 115 S.Ct. 675, 130 L.Ed.2d 607 (1994).

17. 81 F.2d 49 (2d Cir.1936).

Plaintiff's play took only the basic outline of this situation—"the acquittal of a wanton young woman, who to extricate herself from an amour that stood in the way of a respectable marriage, poisoned her lover"—and substituted new details for the story, moving the action to New York City and making the lover an Argentinian dancer who is poisoned with strychnine. Defendant's movie was based on a book, which in turn was also based on the real Madeleine Smith case. Many of the details in the movie resembled those in plaintiff's play, however. For instance, the lover in the movie was also South American and he was also poisoned with strychnine. After a detailed review of the similarities of characters and incidents, Judge Hand concluded that the defendant's work had indeed crossed the line and taken not just ideas, but protected expression.

In attempting to determine if defendant has copied protected material, some courts begin by trying to eliminate all unprotected components of plaintiff's work. This technique has been called the "subtractive" approach to infringement analysis.[18] For instance, in a case involving alleged infringement of a computer program, *Computer Associates International, Inc. v. Altai, Inc.,*[19] the Second Circuit indicated that it would "sift out all non-protectable material" in order to arrive at the "kernel, or possible kernels, of creative expression." The approach has also been used in literary copyright cases. In *Alexander v. Haley,*[20] the court reached its conclusion that the book *Roots* did not infringe plaintiff's novel dealing with slavery by first subtracting out unprotected material from plaintiff's work, such as the many historical facts included in that work. Once that process was completed, the court found it obvious that the defendant had not taken any protected material from the plaintiff.

The subtractive approach ensures that a defendant will not be faulted for copying elements of a work that he was legally entitled to copy. Carelessly applied, however, it may not provide plaintiffs with adequate protection. This is because the *organization and arrangement* of otherwise unprotected material can be sufficiently original to warrant protection under copyright law. For instance, many compilations, such as trade directories or almanacs, contain individual nuggets of factual information which are not themselves copyrightable. If the compiler exercises originality in selecting or arranging the data, however, there is little doubt that the compilation as a whole is protectable. An overzealous use of the subtractive approach might lead a court to subtract out each entry in the compilation in order to find the protectable "kernel." Such an approach would leave no protected material at all. This would obviously run counter to the intent of the copyright statute and deny plaintiff protection that he plainly deserves. Thus, like all legal tests, the

---

18. *See* CRAIG JOYCE, WILLIAM PATRY, MARSHALL LEAFFER & PETER JASZI, COPYRIGHT LAW 708–09 (5th ed. 2000).

19. 982 F.2d 693, 706 (2d Cir.1992). This case has been followed by a number of other federal circuits. For further discussion of this case, *see infra* § 9.4.

20. 460 F.Supp. 40 (S.D.N.Y.1978).

subtractive approach must be used cautiously and with an eye towards its underlying purpose.

To avoid the pitfalls of the subtractive approach, other courts have insisted that the works involved in copyright infringement litigation be compared in their entirety. This approach is sometimes labeled either the "totality" or "total concept and feel" approach. The Ninth Circuit opinion in *Sid & Marty Krofft Television Productions, Inc. v. McDonald's Corp.,*[21] illustrates this approach in action. The Kroffts had developed a children's TV program called H.R. Pufnstuf. It featured a variety of fanciful costumed characters who lived in a place called Living Island, which "was inhabited by moving trees and talking books." The mayor of the Island was a cummerbund-wearing dragon with a big head and a wide mouth. McDonald's, the defendant in the case, wanted to develop an advertising campaign targeted at children. When it was unable to license the Pufnstuf characters, it developed its own fantasy land called McDonaldland. It, too, involved an "imaginary world inhabited by anthropomorphic plants and animals and other fanciful creatures." The mayor of McDonaldland, Mayor McCheese, had a big head (which was, not surprisingly, a cheeseburger) and a wide mouth. The court refused to break up or "dissect" plaintiff's work to separate protected from unprotected components, noting that "it is the combination of many different elements which may command copyright protection because of its particular subjective quality." The court found that because the "total concept and feel" of the two works was the same, the defendant had indeed taken protected material and (because the works were substantially similar) was thus liable for infringement.

The totality test avoids undervaluing plaintiff's originality in the selection and arrangement of materials in his or her work. It does, however, run the risk of overextending copyright protection. For instance, plaintiff might prepare a volume containing the complete works of William Shakespeare with critical commentary in a number of footnotes scattered through out the volume. Defendant might prepare his own volume of the works of Shakespeare after consulting plaintiff's book. Obviously, a vast percentage of the two volumes will be the same—namely, the actual text of all the plays. Equally obvious, however, is that plaintiff would have no claim of copyright in the text of the plays. Under a subtractive approach, we would ignore the words of Shakespeare—which are, of course, in the public domain—and compare only the remaining material. Under a totality approach, however, there is a danger that defendant might be found to be an infringer because of the overall similarity of the two books, despite the fact that the similarity relates only to materials that the defendant had a lawful right to copy. Just as with the subtractive approach, therefore, one must use a totality analysis cautiously, with larger principles in mind, in order to ensure that an illogical conclusion is not reached.

21. 562 F.2d 1157 (9th Cir.1977).

9.1.2.2 Substantial Similarity

The final step on plaintiff's road to victory in infringement litigation is to prove that an ordinary observer would view the protected material copied by the defendant to be "substantially similar" to plaintiff's work. As the Seventh Circuit put it, in this phase of the analysis the court must ask "whether the accused work is so similar to the plaintiff's work that an ordinary reasonable person would conclude that the defendant unlawfully appropriated the plaintiff's protectable expression by taking material of substance and value."[22] This test is subjective. We are trying to determine whether the degree of copying of protected material rises to a level of significance warranting legal prohibition. Indeed, some courts and academic writers refer to this step in the analysis as the "audience" test to remind us that the inquiry concerns the reactions of those to whom the work is directed.

The substantial similarity or "audience" test can readily be understood in light of the economic goals of copyright law. If the defendant's work is substantially similar to plaintiff's, users of defendant's work will have no need or desire to subsequently purchase plaintiff's. The fact that the two are substantially similar makes them substitutes for each other, and that means that plaintiff will lose sales unless the defendant's activities are enjoined. As Justice Story put it more than 150 years ago, "[i]f so much is taken that the value of the original is sensibly diminished, or the labors of the original author are substantially to an injurious extent appropriated by another, that is sufficient in point of law to constitute a piracy. . . . "[23] Since the hope of economic reward in the form of sales is what supposedly induced the plaintiff to author his work in the first place, we must forbid defendant's production of substantially similar work, or else incentives for creative activity will be destroyed.

While the ultimate determination of substantial similarity is a subjective question for the jury, there are some principles to guide the decision. For instance, it is irrelevant, in assessing substantial similarity, how much new material a defendant may have added to the portions copied from the plaintiff's work. If a defendant copies one chapter from plaintiff's lengthy book and then adds dozens of new chapters to accompany the copied material that will not, in any way, immunize him from liability. This makes good intuitive sense. If you rob my car and store it in a garage with 50 automobiles you have purchased with your own money, that does not make you any less a car thief than if you had stored my car in an empty garage.

Whether the material copied by defendant must constitute a significant portion of plaintiff's work is somewhat less clear. Professor Nimmer in his treatise says "[t]he question in each case is whether the similarity relates to matter that constitutes a substantial portion of plaintiff's work. . . . The quantitative relation of the similar material to the total

22. Atari, Inc. v. North American Philips Consumer Electronics Corp., 672 F.2d 607, 614 (7th Cir.1982).

23. Folsom v. Marsh, 9 F.Cas. 342 No. 4901 (C.C.D.Mass.1841).

material contained in plaintiff's work is certainly of importance. However even if the similar material is quantitatively small, if it is qualitatively important, the trier of fact may properly find substantial similarity.... If, however, the similarity is only as to nonessential matters, then a finding of no substantial similarity should result."[24] A number of cases support this view. For instance, one case characterized the copying of only 30 characters from a computer program consisting of 50 pages of source code as *de minimis*.[25] There are, of course, cases finding infringement where a defendant has copied only a few lines or notes from plaintiff's work, but those can often be explained on the basis that the copied portion was the "heart" of the work and was thus qualitatively significant, even though quantitatively minimal.

On the other hand, Professor Goldstein takes issue with this view in his treatise. He says "liability should be unaffected by the proportion the elements taken bear to plaintiff's work as a whole.... If the plaintiff had written only the portion appropriated, and if this portion were sufficiently expressive to qualify for copyright, there would be no doubt of plaintiff's success in an infringement action, for defendant in this situation would have copied plaintiff's entire work. It is perverse to excuse a defendant for having taken the very same portion just because plaintiff has published it in conjunction with other expression."[26]

The disagreement between these two noted copyright scholars may not make much of a practical difference. Even if quantitatively small and qualitatively insignificant copying from plaintiff's work is deemed infringing, as Professor Goldstein argues it should be, in many cases it will have little effect on the market for plaintiff's work. That means that it may likely be excused under the fair use defense, as we shall see in the following chapter. Indeed, the disagreement between these two noted treatise writers can be recast as one concerning the assignment of the burden of proof. Under Professor Goldstein's view, since any copying of protected matter, no matter how *de minimis*, is treated as infringing, the defendant will bear the burden of invoking and proving the fair use defense. On the other hand, if *de minimis* copying is held to be non-infringing, as Professor Nimmer suggests, then the plaintiff will have the obligation of proving that the copying is more than *de minimis* and has crossed the line of substantiality.

Given the economic justification for copyright law generally and for the substantial similarity test in particular, it would seem that Professor Nimmer has the better of the argument. A work that bears only a *de minimis* similarity to plaintiff's work is unlikely to be much of a substitute for it, and is thus unlikely to undermine incentives very much. For instance, there is little chance I will forego buying John Grisham's latest novel because another book by another author, which I

---

24. NIMMER, COPYRIGHT § 13.03[A][2] (2002).

25. Vault Corp. v. Quaid Software Ltd., 847 F.2d 255, 267 (5th Cir.1988).

26. PAUL GOLDSTEIN, COPYRIGHT (2d ed. 1996) § 7.3.1 at 7:28–29.

have already read, contains three sentences lifted verbatim from Grisham. Of course, Professor Goldstein could quite properly argue that the question is not whether the works as a whole are substitutes, but whether the pirated portion is a substitute for the corresponding bit of original expression. It is true, at least as an abstract matter, that I would not pay to read Grisham's three sentences if I have already read them in another book. While Professor Goldstein's point has theoretical merit, consumers don't purchase disembodied pieces of a copyrighted works, but rather the work as a whole. There is usually no market for three sentence prose bits. Indeed, the first author's decision to group various bits of expression together into a single work usually reflects a view that it is the full combination of those pieces that will have artistic and commercial appeal. Thus, if defendant has copied only a *de minimis* portion of the plaintiff's work, there seems little reason to afford plaintiff a judicial remedy.

Another important aspect of the substantial similarity or "audience" test is its focus on the "ordinary observer." The essence of the ordinary observer test was summarized, like so many copyright doctrines, in an opinion by Judge Learned Hand. In one of his last decisions on the bench, Hand wrote that works should be deemed substantially similar if "the ordinary observer, unless he set out to detect the disparities, would be disposed to overlook them, and regard their aesthetic appeal as the same."[27] However, courts have sometimes been troubled by the need to use an ordinary observer as the standard of comparison, especially when the works are complex and not directed at the general public. The fear is that for certain specialized works, a hypothetical reasonable person might be inclined to either overestimate or underestimate the degree of similarity.

In *Dawson v. Hinshaw Music, Inc.,*[28] the court confronted allegations of infringement involving two similar arrangements of a traditional spiritual entitled *Ezekiel Saw De Wheel*. The court noted that the reason substantial similarity was usually analyzed from the perspective of an ordinary observer was that most works are intended for an audience composed of just such observers. It went on to observe that "if the intended audience is more narrow in that it possesses specialized expertise, relevant to the purchasing decision, that lay people would lack, the court's inquiry should focus on whether a member of the intended audience would find the two works to be substantially similar."[29] The court concluded that the proper focus in the case before it should be on church choir directors. The court did caution, however, that departures from an ordinary observer standard should only be undertaken when the intended audience for a work possesses specialized expertise. As we shall see, this view has proven particularly influential in cases involving alleged infringement of computer software.

27. Peter Pan Fabrics, Inc. v. Martin Weiner Corp., 274 F.2d 487, 489 (2d Cir. 1960).

28. 905 F.2d 731 (4th Cir.1990), *cert. denied,* 498 U.S. 981, 111 S.Ct. 511, 112 L.Ed.2d 523 (1990).

29. 905 F.2d at 736.

Professor Nimmer argues in his treatise that the "audience" test should be discarded.[30] The treatise suggests that the test has been applied inconsistently, is ill-suited for use in connection with technologically complicated works, and may be inconsistent with the language in the Supreme Court's opinion in *Feist*. Much of Professor Nimmer's criticism seems directed at cases that, under the rhetoric of an audience test, fail to carefully analyze the issue of *copying*. These criticized cases merely ask whether the overall impression of the two works would lead casual observers to a spontaneous impression of copying. As the Nimmer treatise notes, "the Copyright Act is intended to protect writers from the theft of the fruits of their labor, not to protect against the general public's 'spontaneous and immediate' *impression* that the fruits have been stolen."[31]

The problem that prompts Professor Nimmer's criticism is a consequence of the sloppy and inconsistent use of vocabulary that plagues copyright infringement analysis. If the phrase "audience test" leads courts to simply turn both plaintiff's and defendant's work to the jury and ask them if their spontaneous and immediate reaction is one of copying, then Nimmer is surely right that the test is misguided. On the other hand if the phrase "audience test" is properly limited to the final stage of a four step infringement analysis, as detailed in the foregoing sections, most of Nimmer's concerns would vanish. Fortunately, few recent decisions seem to be using the "audience" test in the fashion criticized by Professor Nimmer. Instead, most of these newer cases ask about audience reaction only after unprotected elements of the work have been filtered out.

§ 9.2 Other Ways of Framing the Infringement Analysis

The foregoing discussion sets out a formal infringement analysis that normally requires four steps. Plaintiff must prove (1) access and (2) resemblance (or probative similarity, which is the same thing) in order to show copying, and then must show that the copying was (3) of protected material which (4) an ordinary observer would find substantially similar to plaintiff's work.

Many courts and commentators compress this analysis, however, into two steps. It is often said that proof of infringement requires only a showing of (1) access and (2) substantial similarity. Where, in this foreshortened analytic outline, have the other elements gone? When this type of formula is used, the missing elements are usually either noncontroversial, or implicit in the court's analysis without being stated outright. Thus, courts may dispense with any need to analyze "resemblance" as part of a separate "copying" analysis because they feel such resemblance is inherent in proof of substantial similarity. They may not explicitly discuss "protected expression" as a separate element of the

---

30. NIMMER, COPYRIGHT § 13.03[E][1][b] (2002).   **31.** *Id.* at 13–94.

"improper appropriation" analysis but they may often ask if the works have "substantially similar expression." Professor Leaffer illustrates this compression of concepts in the following passage: "not every taking or use of another's copyrighted work amounts to substantial similarity. A third party may freely copy the ideas embodied in a work but cannot copy the author's expression beyond what the law allows. And even if some of the expression is copied, there must be a substantial, material taking to constitute infringement. Thus, to say that the works are substantially similar is to say that the defendant has copied a substantial and material amount of plaintiff's protected expression."[1]

The Supreme Court seems to have compressed the formal four-step analysis even further. Writing in *Feist,* the Court defined infringement as "copying of constituent elements of the work that are original."[2] This bit of black letter law makes no reference at all to substantial similarity or the ordinary observer, nor is there any reference to protected material, or even to access. It is probable, however, that the Court was merely using a form of shorthand and that all four of the traditional elements lurk within this concise phrase. Copying, of course, can be proved by showing both access and resemblance. The Court in *Feist* had no need to subdivide the copying inquiry and discuss those points, however, because copying was not significantly disputed in the case. The reference to elements of a work that are "original" clearly is synonymous with the "protected expression" prong of the four-part test. While the quoted phrase makes no explicit reference to substantial similarity, that may be because the crucial issue in the case was whether the plaintiff's work possessed sufficient originality to be protected in the first place. Given the Court's conclusion that it did not, there was no reason to worry about how similar plaintiff's and defendant's works might be. Moreover, by using the word "copying," the Court may have meant copying of protected material in an amount that would strike an ordinary observer as more than *de mininis*— the usual test for infringement—but not have spelled the point out because it was unnecessary to the decision in the case before it. This is how some lower courts have interpreted *Feist* in the years since it was decided.[3] Absent further indication from the Supreme Court that it has something special in mind, there is nothing in its phrasing to suggest a substantive—as opposed to a rhetorical— departure from the traditional mode of infringement analysis.

In the Tower of Babel that is infringement analysis, there is still more terminological confusion because of a whole new vocabulary intro-

---

§ 9.2

1. Marshall Leaffer, Understanding Copyright Law 386 (3d Ed. 1999).

2. *Feist Publications, Inc. v. Rural Telephone Service Co.,* 499 U.S. 340, 361, 111 S.Ct. 1282, 113 L.Ed.2d 358 (1991).

3. *See, e.g.,* Lipton v. Nature Co., 71 F.3d 464, 470–71 (2d Cir.1995) ("a successful copyright action requires proof that the defendant copied protected elements of the plaintiff's work . . . copying may be inferred where a plaintiff establishes that the defendant had access to the copyrighted work and that substantial similarities exist as to protectible material in the two works."); Warren Publishing, Inc. v. Microdos Data Corp., 115 F.3d 1509, 1516 n. 19 (11th Cir.1997), *cert. denied,* 522 U.S. 963, 118 S.Ct. 397, 139 L.Ed.2d 311 (1997).

duced by the Ninth Circuit in a line of decisions beginning with *Sid & Marty Krofft Television Productions, Inc. v. McDonald's Corp.*[4] As indicated in section 9.1.2.1 above, that case involved allegations that certain McDonaldland TV commercials infringed plaintiff's copyrighted H.R. Pufnstuf program. In the opinion, the court stated that the first step in infringement analysis was to determine whether the two works have substantially similar ideas, and that the second step was to determine if they use substantially similar expression to express those ideas. This approach can only be described as curious. The fact that two works have similar ideas may indicate that one is copied from the other, although even that may be dubious if the ideas are pedestrian or well-known in the genre. However, similarity of ideas is not at all relevant to a finding of unlawful appropriation, since by definition, defendant is legally entitled to copy plaintiff's ideas.

Krofft then went on to label these two tests. It called the inquiry into identity of ideas an "extrinsic" test, because it was supposedly objective in nature and, the court said, expert testimony and analytic dissection would be appropriate in applying this test. It called the inquiry into identity of expression an "intrinsic" test, because it related to the subjective reactions of the audience for the work, and it declared that this test should be conducted based on the total concept and feel of the work without breaking it up into constituent elements.

Much ink has been spilled by commentators either speculating on just what the *Krofft* court meant or in criticism of its approach. Subsequent Ninth Circuit cases have continued to use the "extrinsic" and "intrinsic" language, but have slowly reshaped the meanings of those words, so that whatever they may have meant originally, they are now practically identical to the concepts of "protected expression" analysis and "substantial similarity" analysis used by most other courts. To the extent that the words extrinsic and intrinsic have become nothing more than alternative ways of saying objective and subjective respectively, they add little to infringement discussions except the potential for confusion.

What emerges from a careful study of judicial language and actual judicial practices is the realization that there is no significant substantive difference implied when some courts and writers analyze copyright infringement in four steps, and some do it in only two or even one. Nor does there appear to be much difference between tests worded in the conventional language and those that are phrased in terms of "intrinsic" and "extrinsic" analysis. Decisions about whether one work infringes another are often excruciatingly difficult. The blizzard of tests, sub-tests, terminological innovations and clarifications reflects nothing more than judicial striving to bring some clarity and predictability to the endeavor. While we can applaud the goals that prompt these efforts, we can only grin and bear it when we encounter the confusing vocabulary.

---

4.   562 F.2d 1157 (9th Cir.1977).

§ 9.3 Infringement Analysis in Computer Related Cases

Verbatim copying of computer code is now clearly understood to be impermissible.[1] On the other hand, one of the more contentious areas of copyright law in recent years has been the degree to which third parties may copy *non-literal* elements of computer software without incurring infringement liability. These non-literal elements might include the organizational structure of the program as a whole, or the "user-interface"—the menus, key commands and other features that govern how the user interacts with the program. The protectability of these elements of computer programs was considered in the chapter on the subject matter of copyright, in section 3.2.3. It is useful to look at the problem again, however, because the same case law also illuminates how infringement analysis is conducted in computer software cases.

One of the first courts to confront the question of non-literal infringement of software was *Whelan Associates, Inc. v. Jaslow Dental Laboratory, Inc.*[2] Both parties in that case had written programs that were designed to be used in managing a dental office. The defendant's program did not incorporate verbatim any of the actual computer code from the plaintiff's work. Nonetheless, there were considerable similarities in the two works. The decision in *Whelan* was notable for at least two reasons. First, although "substantial similarity" analysis in most infringement cases is decided based on the subjective reactions of ordinary observers, *Whelan* departed from the conventional approach and chose instead to rely heavily on the testimony of experts, observing that there were a "growing number of courts which do not apply the ordinary observer test in copyright cases involving exceptionally difficult materials like computer programs." This is the approach embraced by the court in *Dawson*, discussed in section 9.1.2.2 above.

Even more controversially, in trying to identify the non-literal elements of a computer program that were protectable, the *Whelan* court concluded that "copyright protection of computer programs may extend beyond the programs' literal code to their structure, sequence and organization." The court seemed to suggest that each program had only one, single, unprotectable idea, and that all other non-literal aspects of the program were protectable expression. It is, of course, routine to note that copyright protection can extend to non-literal aspects of a copyrighted work. The *Whelan* approach was controversial, however, because, given the unique attributes of computer software, many felt that it extended protection to matters that were not properly within the scope of copyright. For instance, the sequence of a computer program might be dictated by the function the program must perform. It might be impossible for another programmer to write a competing program without following the same sequence. The same might be true for the "structure" or "organization" of the program. In this sense computer pro-

§ 9.3

1. *See supra* Chapter 4.

2. 797 F.2d 1222 (3d Cir.1986).

grams may differ markedly from novels, plays or movies. Affording a plaintiff protection over structure, sequence or organization of a computer program might then expand the plaintiff's monopoly from expression into ideas, methods and processes. Not surprisingly, *Whelan* was criticized by both academic writers and other courts.[3] Its approach struck many as excessively pro-plaintiff and likely to chill software development and competition in the software industry.

Throughout the balance of the 1980's various courts attempted to refine the analysis for copyright infringement in the computer software context. In 1992 the Second Circuit decided *Computer Associates Int'l, Inc. v. Altai, Inc.,*[4] a case that has supplanted *Whelan* as the leading authority on determination of infringement in computer software cases, and has proven influential with other circuits around the country. Computer Associates had authored a job scheduling program for mainframe computers called CA–Scheduler. A sub-program of CA–Scheduler, called Adapter, converted the computer languages of various programs into languages compatible with the mainframe's operating system. In 1982 the defendant, Altai, began marketing its own scheduling program, called Zeke. In the following year, to make Zeke compatible with a wider variety of operating systems, Altai hired a former Computer Associates employee to prepare a sub-program called Oscar. The original version of Oscar was clearly infringing of plaintiff's Adapter sub-program because the former employee had retained copies of the actual computer code for Adapter and incorporated chunks of that code verbatim into Oscar. When that fact was discovered, the Oscar program was rewritten by Altai programmers who had no access to the Adapter code. The question in the case was whether the re-written or second generation version of the Oscar program infringed Adapter. Although there was no literal similarity between the two, there were a number of structural and organizational similarities.

To resolve the question, the *Altai* court developed an approach which is usually labeled the "abstraction-filtration-comparison test." It is profitable to look at the court's language setting out the test:

> In ascertaining substantial similarity under this approach, a court would first break down the alleged infringed program into its constituent structural parts. Then, by examining each of

---

3. See, e.g., Plains Cotton Cooperative Ass'n v. Goodpasture Computer Service, Inc., 807 F.2d 1256 (5th Cir.1987), *cert. denied,* 484 U.S. 821, 108 S.Ct. 80, 98 L.Ed.2d 42 (1987) (declining to "embrace *Whelan*"). "The crucial flaw in [*Whelan's*] reasoning is that it assumes that only one 'idea,' in copyright law terms, underlies any computer program, and that once a separable idea can be identified, everything else must be expression." 3 Nimmer, Copyright § 13.03 [F] (2002). *See also* Steven R. Englund, *Note, Idea, Process, or Protected Expression?: Determining the Scope of Copyright Protection of the Structure of*

Computer Programs, 88 Mich. L. Rev. 866, 881 (1990); Peter S. Menell, *An Analysis of the Scope of Copyright Protection for Application Programs,* 41 Stan. L. Rev. 1045,-1074, 1082 (1989); Mark T. Kretschmer, *Note, Copyright Protection For Software Architecture: Just Say No!,* 1988 Colum. Bus L. Rev. 823, 837–39 (1988); Peter G. Spivack, *Comment, Does Form Follow Function? The Idea/Expression Dichotomy In Copyright Protection of Computer Software,* 35 U.C.L.A. L. Rev. 723, 747–55 (1988).

4. 982 F.2d 693 (2d Cir.1992).

these parts for such things as incorporated ideas, expression
that is necessarily incidental to those ideas, and elements that
are taken from the public domain, a court would be able to sift
out all non-protectable material. Left with a kernel, or possible
kernels, of creative expression after following this process of
elimination, the court's last step would be to compare this
material with the structure of an allegedly infringing program.
The result of this comparison will determine whether the protectable elements of the programs at issue are substantially
similar so as to warrant a finding of infringement.

This, of course, is the basic "improper appropriation" analysis, re-
worded to apply more closely to computer program cases. The abstraction and filtration steps in the *Altai* approach mirror the usual effort to
identify and separate protected material common to both plaintiff's and
defendant's works. The comparison step in *Altai* is analogous to the
substantial similarity analysis that is used more generally in infringement cases.

The abstraction/filtration process helps courts identify aspects of a
program that might be dictated by external factors, such as the need to
make the program compatible with a given operating system or a given
piece of hardware, or standards prevalent in the industry that will be
using the software product. Once identified, these elements or aspects
will be filtered out. A defendant will not be considered an infringer if
these are the only aspects of the program which are copied.

Like *Whelan, Altai* endorses the use of expert witnesses in the final
"comparison" phase of its analysis. Although experts are not usually
used in the substantial similarity phase of infringement litigation because of the traditional focus on the "ordinary observer," computer
software poses unique problems that make an ordinary observer test
awkward. Users of computer programs usually do not even see the
programs themselves, but only the output on a computer screen. Neither
of us have any idea what the code for our word processing programs
looks like, nor could we discern whether the literal code or the non-
literal structure of two competing word processors (such as Microsoft
Word and WordPerfect) were substantially similar. Computer users
might perceive two programs to be similar if they performed the same
functions, even though their expressive elements could be quite different. For example, two spreadsheets might look roughly similar on the
screen and manipulate data the same way, but the expressive elements
of the programs might be completely different. The use of experts in
software infringement cases thus seems both sensible and virtually
inevitable.

The widespread use of computers has also created a rather different
infringement problem, this one involving the internet. Operators of
various internet sites such as bulletin boards (BBS) or companies that
allow subscribers to create personal web pages on their computers often
permit users to post material onto their sites by uploading it. Other

users can then access the material by logging on to the internet through the facilities of an internet service provider (or ISP) and view that material, or if they choose, they may download copies of the material onto their own computers. Not surprisingly, some of the material that winds up at sites such as these is often copyrighted text or images which has been posted without the permission of the copyright owners. While there is little doubt that the subscriber doing the posting is an infringer, pursuing a lawsuit against that individual is not likely to provide much useful relief. Consequently, copyright owners have increasingly focused their legal attention on the BBS operators and the ISPs.

At first blush, the plaintiffs would seem to have a strong case against both the BBS operation and the ISP. After the subscriber posts the copyrighted material both of those internet participants will necessarily have copies of it on the hard drives of their computers at least for temporary periods and often for much longer. Moreover, even if they are not aware of the copyright status of the material in question, copyright infringement does not require knowledge or intent for liability. Thus these entities would appear to be at considerable risk for copyright infringement liability.

This is substantially the view taken in the first case to consider the issue, *Playboy Enterprises, Inc. v. Frena.*[5] Mr. Frena was the operator of a BBS called Techs Warehouse. The material on that BBS included 170 copyrighted photographs from *Playboy* magazine, which had apparently been placed there by subscribers. Frena alleged that he did not know about the subscriber activities and that he removed the material from his BBS as soon as he was notified of Playboy's complaint. The court nonetheless found Frena liable for direct infringement. The court reasoned that Frena had violated both the distribution and display rights of the copyright owner. The opinion did not, however, address whether the activities in question should also be considered violations of the reproduction right.

Two years later, in *Religious Technology Center v. Netcom On–Line Communication Services, Inc.,*[6] another court was confronted with substantially similar facts. In that case, a man named Dennis Erlich was engaged in a dispute with the Church of Scientology. As part of that controversy, he posted on an internet newsgroup called "alt.religion.scientology" lengthy excerpts from various copyrighted works belonging to the Scientology movement. To be more precise, he did this by posting the material on a BBS operated by a Mr. Klemesrud, who in turn, put the material on the internet by using the facilties of Netcom, a large ISP. After failing to convince Erlich to desist, the copyright owner sued him as well as Klemesrud and Netcom for infringement. The court exonerated both the BBS and the ISP. While noting that knowledge and intent are not elements of infringement, the court concluded that one cannot be liable unless he has undertaken the allegedly infringing acts

5. 839 F.Supp. 1552 (M.D.Fla.1993).   **6.** 907 F.Supp. 1361 (N.D.Cal.1995).

volitionally. In other words, the defendant must at least do the copying, even if he does not know that the material is protected. It found that element missing in a situation where the BBS and ISP are passive and the copies of the offending materials are being placed on its computers by subscribers.[7] It used the same reasoning to distinguish *Frena* with regard to the distribution and display rights, observing that "only the subscriber should be liable for causing the distribution of plaintiffs' work, as the contributing actions of the BBS provider are automatic and indiscriminate."[8] The *Netcom* court did clearly indicate, however, that ISPs and BBS operators could be held liable under theories of contributory infringement or vicarious liability, subjects that are taken up in the immediately following section of this chapter.

Legal uncertainties resulting from these and other decisions prompted Congress to act. Title II of the Digital Millennium Copyright Act (DMCA) added a new § 512 to the Copyright Act.[9] This provision was in part intended to clarify the liability of ISPs for infringing acts that occur on their computer systems. Most notable is § 512(c), which immunizes from financial liability ISPs that comply with specified procedures. This protection applies to ISPs that: (1) did not know or have reason to know of infringing material;[10] (2) do not benefit financially from infringing activity, in the event the ISP has the right and ability to control such activity;[11] (3) adopt, implement and notify customers of a policy that allows the ISP to terminate an account holder who repeatedly infringes;[12] and (4) designate on their web site, and submit information to the Copyright Office, identifying an agent to receive notifications from copyright holders of infringing materials.[13]

Pursuant to this provision of DMCA, a copyright holder which feels that someone has posted infringing materials on a site operated by an ISP may serve a written, good faith notice of infringement to that ISP.[14] An ISP that qualifies under the previously noted criteria is then immunized from liability if the ISP complies with a specified procedure for removing the identified material from its computers.[15] This procedure initially calls for the ISP to take reasonable steps to notify the account holder that the ISP has removed or disabled access to the allegedly infringing material. The account holder may then submit a written, signed counter-notification to the ISP stipulating both that the material at issue was removed or disabled due to mistake or misidentification, and that the account holder subjects himself to the personal jurisdiction of a

7. "Although copyright is a strict liability statute, there should still be some elements of volition or causation which is lacking where a defendant's system is merely used to create a copy by a third party." 907 F.Supp. at 1370.

8. *Id.* at 1372. *Netcom* was followed in two later cases from the same district, Sega Enterprises, Ltd. v. MAPHIA, 948 F.Supp. 923 (N.D.Cal.1996) and Sega Enterprises, Ltd. v. Sabella, 1996 WL 780560 (N.D.Cal. 1996).

9. Pub. L. No. 105–304, 112 Stat. 2860 (1998).

10. 17 U.S.C.A. § 512(c)(1)(A) (2000).

11. 17 U.S.C.A. § 512(c)(1)(B) (2000).

12. 17 U.S.C.A. § 512(i)(1)(A) (2000).

13. 17 U.S.C.A. § 512(c)(2) (2000).

14. 17 U.S.C.A. § 512(c)(3) (2000).

15. 17 U.S.C.A. § 512(g) (2000).

federal district court. Upon receipt of a counter-notification, the ISP must then inform the copyright holder that the material will be replaced or reinstated. The ISP must then replace or reinstate the material unless the copyright holder brings suit against the account holder. This elaborate protocol has come to be known as the "notice-and-take-down" procedure. The DMCA also allows copyright holders to obtain from a federal district court, in specified circumstances, a subpoena against the ISP requesting the name of an account holder who is allegedly infringing.[16]

§ 9.4   Indirect Forms of Infringement

As hotels, bar owners and television stations have occasionally discovered to their chagrin, one need not do the actual copying or performing to be held liable for copyright infringement. While the copyright statute itself does not impose liability on anyone other than direct infringers, courts have nonetheless long held that, where appropriate, others can be held liable as well. The principal theories which will lead to the imposition of liability on those only indirectly involved in the infringing conduct are vicarious liability and contributory infringement.

9.4.1   Vicarious Infringement

As one trial court put it, "The purpose of imposing vicarious liability is to punish one who unfairly reaps the benefits of another's infringing behavior."[1] Consequently, vicarious liability for copyright infringement will be imposed on a party who has both (1) the right and ability to supervise a direct infringer plus (2) a financial interest in the infringement.[2] This type of liability can be imposed even in the absence of any knowledge that the infringement is taking place. Moreover, while vicarious copyright liability developed out of the doctrine of respondeat superior, which holds an employer liable for the torts of an employee, it is clear that one can be vicariously liable for copyright infringement based on acts of an independent contractor.[3] Thus theater owners where infringing performances of dramatic or audiovisual works take place can be held as vicarious infringers, as can hotel and restaurant owners, when infringing musical performances occur on their property. In situations like these, the property owner has some degree of control over the activities of the musicians or actors and stands to benefit from ticket sales, drink sales or rentals, as the case may be. At least in the music

16.   17 U.S.C.A. § 512(h) (2000).

§ 9.4

1.   Artists Music, Inc. v. Reed Publishing, Inc., 31 USPQ2d 1623, 1626 (S.D.N.Y. 1994).

2.   Shapiro, Bernstein & Co. v. H.L. Green Co., 316 F.2d 304, 307 (2d Cir.1963) ("When the right and ability to supervise coalesce with an obvious and direct financial interest in the exploitation of copyright materials—even in the absence of actual knowledge that the copyright monopoly is being impaired—the purposes of copyright law may be best effectuated by the imposition of liability upon the beneficiary of that exploitation."); Polygram Int'l Pub. Inc. v. Nevada/TIG, Inc., 855 F.Supp. 1314, 1324 (D.Mass.1994).

3.   Gershwin Publishing Corp. v. Columbia Artists Management, Inc., 443 F.2d 1159, 1162 (2d Cir.1971).

business, premises owners can also easily protect themselves from vicarious liability by obtaining blanket licenses from the major performing rights societies such as ASCAP or BMI.[4]

To satisfy the financial benefit test the benefit realized must in some way relate directly to the infringing activities of the primary infringer. The mere fact that the direct infringer pays rent for the premises where the infringement is conducted will usually not be sufficient. If the infringing activities serve as a magnet, however, attracting patrons to the premises, and if the defendant shares in the income generated by patrons because of commissions, ticket sales, or incidental revenues, there is adequate financial interest to establish vicarious liability. For instance in *Fonovisa, Inc. v. Cherry Auction, Inc.*,[5] the defendant operated a flea market, or "swap meet," at which third-party vendors could rent booths to sell a variety of items to the public. Customers had to pay an admission fee to gain access to the premises. Cherry Auction also charged for parking and sold refreshments to the patrons of its flea market. Some of the vendors at the flea market were engaged in the routine sale of counterfeit musical recordings that infringed plaintiff's copyrights.[6] Plaintiff sued Cherry Auction, in part on a vicarious liability theory. The Ninth Circuit found that "the defendants reap substantial financial benefits from admission fees, concession stand sales and parking fees, all of which flow directly from customers who want to buy the counterfeit recordings at bargain basement prices." That was enough to satisfy the financial benefit requirement because, as the *Fonovisa* court put it, the nub of the matter is whether the infringing activities "enhance the attractiveness of the venue to potential customers."

The control element of the vicarious liability test requires actual, as opposed to mere theoretical or legal, control. In most cases finding vicarious liability, the defendant had a clear right of supervision over the primary infringing party. In *Fonovisa* for instance, the court noted that the defendant swap meet operator "had the right to terminate vendors for any reasons whatsoever and through that right had the ability to control the activities of vendors on the premises."[7] By way of contrast, an ordinary landlord, who turns over possession of premises for a specified term of months or years in return for a flat rental, is unlikely to be found to have the control necessary to trigger vicarious liability even if a tenant uses the property as location to manufacture counterfeit tapes or CD's.

There are other situations where parties may be held vicariously liable. Courts have imposed liability on sponsors of radio or television programs, if they have the requisite power to supervise and control the

---

4. See § 7.4.3., *supra*.

5. 76 F.3d 259, 263 (9th Cir.1996).

6. Note that there might not have been any evidence that the primary infringer—the vendor of the phonorecords—had actually manufactured the infringing items.

Such proof is not required, however, because the mere sale of the infringing recordings violated the copyright owners' distribution rights.

7. 76 F.3d at 262.

program content.[8] A national organization with supervision and control over a local organization was held liable when the latter organized an infringing concert.[9] Parent corporations can be held liable for the acts of their subsidiaries if they have "a direct financial interest in the infringing activity, and...the right and ability to supervise the subsidiary, which is evidenced by some continuing connection between the two in regard to the infringing activity."[10]

9.4.2 Contributory Infringement

Contributory infringement is found when the defendant "with knowledge of the infringing activity, induces, causes or materially contributes to the infringing conduct of another...."[11] Unlike vicarious liability, where knowledge is irrelevant, knowledge of the behavior of the primary infringer is a key aspect of contributory liability. The easiest cases of contributory infringement involve parties who actively encourage or induce the direct or primary infringer to engage in the disputed conduct. For instance, a publisher that suggests the inclusion of a lengthy copyrighted passage in an author's book would plainly be subject to liability as a contributory infringer. Even without encouragement the requisite knowledge and material contribution might also be present when a computer bulletin board operator or internet service provider refuses to remove infringing materials posted by subscribers after receiving complaints from the copyright owner.[12]

The requirement of "material contribution" to the infringement can also be made out by showing the defendant supplied the primary infringer with some item necessary to engage in the infringing activity. Under this principle, it is contributory infringement to lend copyrighted material such as books or tapes to another party with knowledge that the other party is planning to make illegal copies of that material. Similarly, the legislative history notes that "a person who lawfully acquires an authorized copy of a motion picture would be an infringer if he or she engages in the business of renting it to others for purposes of an unauthorized public performance."[13]

In *Columbia Pictures Industries, Inc. v. Aveco, Inc.,*[14] the Third Circuit said that providing the site and facilities for infringing activity is also sufficient to constitute contributory infringement. In that case, defendant operated a videocassette rental store which also provided on-premises viewing rooms for customers. The court found that the playing

---

8. *See e.g.,* Davis v. E.I. DuPont de Nemours & Co., 240 F.Supp. 612 (S.D.N.Y. 1965).

9. Gershwin Publishing Corp. v. Columbia Artists Management, Inc., 443 F.2d 1159 (2d Cir.1971).

10. Banff Ltd. v. Limited, Inc., 869 F.Supp. 1103, 1110 (S.D.N.Y.1994).

11. Gershwin Publish Corp. v. Columbia Artists Management, Inc., 443 F.2d 1159, 1162 (2d Cir.1971).

12. *See, e.g.* Religious Technology Center v. Netcom On–Line Communication Services, 907 F.Supp., 1361, 1374 (N.D.Cal. 1995).

13. H.R.Rep. No. 1476, 94th Cong., 2d Sess. 61, reprinted in 1976 U.S.Code Cong. & Ad.News at 5674; see S.Rep. No. 473, 94th Cong., 1st Sess. 57 (1975).

14. Columbia Pictures Industries, Inc. v. Aveco, Inc., 800 F.2d 59 (3d Cir.1986).

of the cassettes in the viewing rooms was a public performance in violation of the copyright owner's exclusive performance right. It went on to hold that the store operator could be liable as a contributory infringer.

The Supreme Court addressed issues of contributory infringement in *Sony Corp. v. Universal City Studios, Inc.*[15] The plaintiffs in that well-known case alleged that home videotaping of copyrighted television programs constituted infringement. Recognizing that it would be impossible to enforce their copyrights against millions of individuals engaged in home taping they also added claims against Sony, a VCR manufacturer. Plaintiff's theory was that Sony had supplied the machines to consumer with knowledge that they would be used for infringing purposes, thus making Sony a contributory infringer.

The Supreme Court rejected that idea. First, and most famously, it found that the primary copying activity of the VCR users was not itself infringing, because it was protected by the fair use doctrine. That ruling will be considered in detail in the immediately following chapter but for present purposes we can note that absent any primary infringement there cannot be any contributory infringement. Secondly, the Supreme Court found that the sale of VCRs was not contributorily infringing because the VCR was "capable of commercially significant noninfringing uses." In other words, there are many functions for VCRs other than impermissibly taping copyrighted material. They can be used to watch lawfully rented videotapes in private settings. They can be used to both watch and duplicate homemade videos of the family vacation or of grandma kissing the baby. They can be used to tape non-copyrighted materials that might be broadcast, such as old movies on which the copyrights might have lapsed because of non-renewal. With such a wide range of legal uses for the machines it becomes impossible to say that the VCR manufacturer has knowledge that any particular machine will be used to violate the law. The contributory infringement analysis in *Sony* means that those who sell devices such as photocopiers and even printing presses cannot be held liable unless there is some additional proof that the vendor knows the device will be used for infringing purposes.

On the other hand, if a party sells a device which is solely or primarily useful only for conducting infringing acts, that party will be a contributory infringer. A good example is *A & M Records v. Abdallah.*[16] There, defendant was selling "time loaded" audio-cassettes to individuals who used them as blanks to make piratical recordings. A time loaded cassette has only sufficient tape to match a time requirement imposed by a purchaser, rather than an even 30, 60 or 90 minutes of tape. Time loaded cassettes prevent running out of tape at the end of a recording, and avoid waste and silence at the end of one side of the recording before the other side begins to play. Not only did defendant sell such tapes to

---

15. 464 U.S. 417, 104 S.Ct. 774, 78 L.Ed.2d 574 (1984).

16. 948 F.Supp. 1449 (C.D.Cal.1996).

customers with knowledge of the purpose for which they would be used, he even occasionally timed copyrighted sound recordings for his customers so as to inform them of the length of tape to order. The court found defendant liable for contributory infringement, observing "*Sony* requires that the product being sold have a 'substantial' noninfringing use, and although time-loaded cassettes can be used for legitimate purposes, these purposes are insubstantial given the number of Mr. Adballah's customers that were using them for counterfeiting purposes."

§ 9.5   Jurisdiction and Procedure

Under 28 U.S.C.A. § 1338(a), federal courts have subject matter jurisdiction over "any civil action arising under any Act of Congress relating to ... copyrights ..."[1] This statute goes on to provide that this "jurisdiction shall be exclusive of the courts of the states." In other words, claims arising under the copyright laws can only be filed in federal court. While this provision seems simple enough, litigants and courts have had difficulty determining just when a case "arises under" copyright law.

Where the plaintiff makes a straightforward allegation of infringement, there is little question that the claim arises under the statute. Given the limitations of language and the ingenuity of lawyers, however, ambiguous cases can arise. For instance a copyright owner and a licensee may disagree over whether their license permits exploitation of the work in a new medium, such as videotapes or in interactive computer applications. That dispute is, in one sense, a dispute over contract interpretation, a traditional subject of state law. On the other hand, it implicates the policies of the copyright act, and in that sense could be said to "arise" under that act.

In a well-known passage, the Second Circuit attempted to clarify the issue, observing that "an action 'arises under' the Copyright Act if and only if the complaint is for a remedy expressly granted by the Act, ... or asserts a claim requiring construction of the Act ... or at the very least and perhaps more doubtfully, presents a case where a distinctive policy of the Act requires that federal principles control the disposition of the claim. The general interest that copyrights, like all other forms of property, should be enjoyed by their true owner is not enough to meet this last test."[2] The Ninth Circuit, quoting bits of language from a number of different courts, has said that courts should focus on "the 'primary and controlling purpose' of the suit, the 'principle issue,' the 'fundamental controversy,' and the 'gist' or 'essence' of the plaintiff's claim,"[3] to determine if it arises under the copyright statute.

Under this approach exclusive federal jurisdiction has been held appropriate in cases concerning whether a work should be treated as a

§ 9.5

1. 28 U.S.C.A. § 1338(a) (2000).

2. T.B. Harms Co. v. Eliscu, 339 F.2d 823, 828 (2d Cir.1964), *cert. denied*, 381 U.S. 915, 85 S.Ct. 1534, 14 L.Ed.2d 435 (1965).

3. Topolos v. Caldewey, 698 F.2d 991, 993 (9th Cir.1983).

work made for hire,[4] and in disputes over payments owned under the compulsory licensing provisions of the 1976 Act.[5] Another example of this logic at work is the Second Circuit's decision in *Merchant v. Levy*.[6] Plaintiffs in that case had been members of a singing group called "The Teenagers" and claimed that they had written the original version of a song called *Fools* in 1955. However, when the copyright in that song was registered with the Copyright Office in 1956, the documents listed two other individuals as the authors. By the late 80's, having received no royalties, plaintiffs filed suit for a declaration that they were co-owners of the copyright and for an accounting of royalties. Although the defendants argued that there was no basis for federal subject matter jurisdiction, the court rejected those contentions. It noted that unlike a case where an ownership dispute might arise under a contract, the dispute before it concerned the interpretation of the joint authorship concept under the copyright statute itself. This seems logical because Congress presumably wanted the federal courts, and the federal courts alone, to make pronouncement on ambiguous provisions of the copyright laws, and cases such as these require just such pronouncements.

By way of contrast, a suit alleging non-payment of royalties under a copyright licensing agreement does not "arise under" the copyright laws,[7] and must be litigated in state court—unless, of course, there is diversity of citizenship—because the legal issues involved are unlikely to involve consideration of weighty matters of copyright policy. Cases of this type are really nothing more than contract disputes where the subject matter of the contract happens coincidentally to be a copyright. There is little risk that a state court decision on the matter will result in confusion over the meaning of important aspects of the copyright statute.

In those cases where a plaintiff alleges both a claim arising under the copyright laws and additional claims based on state law, the federal courts may have power to decide those additional claims under the doctrine of supplemental jurisdiction. 28 U.S.C.A. § 1338(b) provides that "the district courts shall have original jurisdiction of any civil action asserting a claim of unfair competition when joined with a substantial and related claim under the copyright, patent, plant variety protection or trade-mark laws." This provision gives the federal courts supplemental jurisdiction, but only over state claims that involve "unfair competition" and only when those claims are "related" to a federal intellectual property claim that is "substantial." While the language of this section might suggest that federal jurisdiction is mandatory when the various statutory tests are satisfied, the Federal Circuit has held that trial courts

4. Royalty Control Corp. v. Sanco, Inc., 175 USPQ 641, 643 (N.D.Cal.1972).

5. T.B. Harms Co. v. Eliscu, 339 F.2d 823, 828 (2d Cir.1964), *cert. denied*, 381 U.S. 915, 85 S.Ct. 1534, 14 L.Ed.2d 435 (1965).

6. 92 F.3d 51 (2d Cir.1996), *cert. denied*, 519 U.S. 1108, 117 S.Ct. 943, 136 L.Ed.2d 833 (1997).

7. Bevan v. Columbia Broadcasting System, Inc., 329 F.Supp. 601 (S.D.N.Y.1971).

should still use discretion in determining whether or not to assume jurisdiction over an unfair competition claim.[8]

In administering this supplemental jurisdiction provision the courts have interpreted the concept of "unfair competition" broadly to include such matters as trade secret theft, conversion of intellectual property and various forms of passing off and common law trademark infringement.[9] If plaintiff's non-federal claims are not unfair competition claims, plaintiff can still ask the federal court to take jurisdiction over them under the general doctrine of supplemental jurisdiction, provided those non-federal claims "are so related to claims in the action within such original jurisdiction that they form part of the same case or controversy . . ."[10] In the decided cases, the most difficult issue under section 1338(b) has proven to be whether the state law claim is genuinely "related" to the federal intellectual property claim. While there has been some disagreement among the courts, the emerging consensus seems to require that both the copyright claim and the non-federal claim arise from a common nucleus of operative fact in order for them to be considered related.[11] This standard will, of course, be familiar to aficionados of civil procedure as the general standard for assertion of supplemental jurisdiction.

Most other jurisdictional and procedural aspects of copyright litigation are identical to those governing all civil suits in federal courts. Thus, general principles of personal jurisdiction and venue apply. Not surprisingly, pleading and discovery practice are controlled by the Federal Rules of Civil Procedure. The details of these schemes are, mercifully, beyond the scope of this book.

§ 9.6 Remedies

The copyright statute provides a broad range of remedies to the successful plaintiff. Not all remedies are available in every case, however. Moreover a fairly substantial set of rules has grown up around the various remedies. Obviously, from the point of view of a client considering copyright litigation, the availability of an adequate remedy is a crucial question which counsel should thoroughly consider before going forward with a suit.

8. Verdegaal Bros. v. Union Oil Co., 750 F.2d 947, 950 (Fed Cir.1984).

9. Mars Inc. v. Kabushiki–Kaisha Nippon Conlux, 24 F.3d 1368, 1372–73 (Fed. Cir.1994) ("The common law concept of 'unfair competition' has not been confined to any rigid definition and encompasses a variety of types of commercial or business conduct considered 'contrary to good conscience,' including acts of trademark and trade dress infringement, false advertising, dilution, and trade secret theft . . .")

10. That doctrine is codified in 28 U.S.C.A. § 1367 (2000).

11. See, e.g., J.M. Huber Corp. v. Positive Action Tool Of Ohio Co., Inc., 879 F.Supp. 705, 710 (S.D.Tex.1995); Kupferberg, Goldberg & Niemark, L.L.C., v. Father and Son Pizza, Ltd., 1997 WL 158332, *2 (N.D.Ill.1997).

9.6.1 Injunctions

Copyright plaintiffs may seek two types of injunctions—preliminary and permanent.[1] In determining whether an injunction should be granted, courts in copyright cases are guided by the same principles that generally govern the grant of equitable remedies and injunctive relief in other branches of the law.

Courts grant preliminary injunctions early in the prosecution of a lawsuit to prevent further conduct by the defendant harmful to the plaintiff. A preliminary injunction remains in force until the lawsuit can be fully adjudicated and a final judgment can be rendered. To obtain a preliminary injunction, a plaintiff must show that he will likely prevail on the merits of the case; that he will sustain irreparable harm unless the injunction is granted; and that the balance of hardships tips in his favor.[2] The precise formula used by courts in determining if a preliminary injunction is appropriate varies from circuit to circuit. A strong showing on one of these elements will often balance out a weak showing on another. Indeed, some courts will presume irreparable harm if the plaintiff can make out a strong showing of infringement.[3] The defendant is entitled to notice and a hearing before a preliminary injunction will issue.

If the plaintiff feels that the delay associated with the notice and hearing required for a preliminary injunction will itself cause irreparable harm, the plaintiff can ask for a temporary restraining order (TRO) in an ex parte application to the court.[4] While the copyright statute itself makes no reference to TRO's, the legislative history of section 502 shows that Congress contemplated such relief where appropriate.[5] The procedures for granting TRO's are set out in Rule 65 of the Federal Rules of Civil Procedure. A TRO will usually remain in effect for only a brief period of time—usually until the court can schedule a hearing on the propriety of a preliminary injunction.

At the close of the case, the court may grant a permanent injunction in plaintiff's favor if plaintiff has proven infringement. Such an injunction will forbid further acts of infringement and can be enforced by contempt sanctions. Permanent injunctions are granted routinely to prevailing copyright plaintiffs, largely on the theory that copyright infringement is a continuing harm and that the magnitude of the harm will often be difficult to evaluate in monetary terms. Plaintiff need not show that the infringement was willful in order to obtain an injunction.[6] Issuance of a permanent injunction is not automatic however, and the court can refuse to issue one if it feels that future infringement is

§ 9.6

1. 17 U.S.C.A. § 502 (2000).

2. See, e.g., Hasbro Bradley, Inc. v. Sparkle Toys, Inc., 780 F.2d 189, 192 (2d Cir.1985); Apple Computer, Inc. v. Formula Intl. Inc., 725 F.2d 521, 523 (9th Cir.1984).

3. See, e.g., Video Trip Corp. v. Lightning Video, Inc., 866 F.2d 50, 51–52 (2d Cir.1989) ("existence of irreparable injury is presumed upon a showing of a prima facie case of copyright infringement.").

4. See Fed. R. Civ. P. 65(b).

5. H.R.Rep. No. 1476, 94th Cong., 2d Sess. 160, reprinted in 1976 U.S.Code Cong. & Ad.News at 5674.

6. Williams Elec., Inc. v. Arctic Intl., Inc., 685 F.2d 870, 878 (3d Cir.1982).

unlikely or if other considerations make it unnecessary. The Supreme Court has also suggested that in some cases, such as a parody found to be beyond the scope of the fair use defense,[7] an injunction might not be appropriate, because the defendant's work may have creative elements and there may be a strong public interest in its continued availability.[8] In such a case plaintiff will be limited to a monetary recovery.

9.6.2 Monetary Recoveries

The current copyright statute refers to three types of monetary recovery that may be available to a successful copyright infringement plaintiff—actual damages, defendant's profits and statutory damages. Under section 504(b) of the statute a plaintiff may recover "the actual damages suffered by him or her as a result of the infringement," plus "any profits of the infringer that are attributable to the infringement and ... not taken into account in computing the actual damages." Alternatively, plaintiff may "recover, instead of actual damages and profits, an award of statutory damages for all infringements involved in the action...."[9] The choice of which remedy to pursue lies in the hands of the plaintiff, who may elect either the actual damages/profits measure or the statutory damages measure at any time before final judgement in the case.

The legislative history accompanying the 1976 Act explained why plaintiffs are entitled to *both* their own damages as well as defendant's profits if they chose the first option described above. The two types of awards serve different purposes. "Damages are awarded to compensate the copyright owner for losses from the infringement, and profits are awarded to prevent the infringer from unfairly benefitting from a wrongful act."[10] Of course the two items must be calculated in a way that avoids duplicative recovery. If a defendant has sold infringing copies of a work in direct competition with the plaintiff, plaintiff's damages and defendant's profits may simply be two sides of the same coin. For instance, much of the revenue earned by a defendant who sells bootleg videotapes is revenue that plaintiff would have earned if there had been no infringement. In such a case, awarding the plaintiff its own lost profits as a measure of actual damages and then adding the profits earned by the defendant might be a form of double counting. For all intents and purposes, this plaintiff will have to choose between a recovery based either on its own lost sales or one based on defendant's profits.[11]

---

7. *See infra* § 10.6.

8. Campbell v. Acuff-Rose Music, Inc., 510 U.S. 569, 578 n. 10, 114 S.Ct. 1164, 127 L.Ed.2d 500 (1994) ("the goals of the copyright law .. are not always best served by automatically granting injunctive relief when parodists are found to have gone beyond the bounds of fair use").

9. 17 U.S.C.A. § 504(c) (2000).

10. H.R.Rep. No. 1476, 94th Cong., 2d Sess.1 61, reprinted in 1976 U.S.Code Cong. & Ad.News at 5674.

11. On the other hand, if defendant has low production costs, its profit per copy sold may be greater than plaintiff's profit. In such a case plaintiff is entitled to its own lost profits as a damage remedy plus the difference between its lost profits and de-

9.6.2.1   Actual Damages

A copyright owner's actual damages usually consist of either his own lost profits on sales, or lost royalties. Lost profits on sales is most relevant in cases where the defendant has sold infringing copies of a work in direct competition with the plaintiff or has otherwise competed with the plaintiff in his primary market. Lost royalties are a more logical and typical measure when the defendant has made unauthorized derivative works of a type that do not directly compete with plaintiff or has engaged in unauthorized public performances. For example, if the plaintiff is the owner of the copyright in a novel and the defendant made and sold unauthorized copies of the novel, plaintiffs damages would be based on the lost profit on sales measure, since consumers who purchased from the defendant would, in all likelihood, have bought from plaintiff if no infringing copies were available. On the other hand if the defendant prepares a screenplay based on plaintiff's novel and produces a movie from the screenplay, a lost royalty measure would be more appropriate because plaintiff could have marketed the movie rights to someone else for a reasonable royalty but for the infringing acts of the defendant.

Obviously, there will be much that is uncertain in either measure of actual damages. Where an infringer sells at lower prices or different profit margins than the plaintiff it may be a complex matter to extrapolate from defendant's sales to determine the profits that plaintiff would have made but for those sales. Where the infringer is exploiting a new and different market, there may be no reliable indication of what a reasonable royalty rate might have been. Courts will do the best they can with the evidence offered by the parties, and it is often said that any doubts concerning the amount of damages will be resolved against the defendant.[12] The plaintiff is also entitled to any incidental items of damage over and above the lost profits on sales or the lost royalties if he is able to prove them.

9.6.2.2   Profits

Where the defendant has made and sold multiple copies of plaintiff's copyrighted work or publicly performed the work for a paying audience it is likely that he realized a profit by doing so, and plaintiff may recover that profit as part of the relief in a successful copyright action. The objective of such an award is to deprive the defendant of illicit financial benefit traceable to his infringing conduct. When pursuing an award of defendant's profits, plaintiff need only offer evidence of defendant's gross revenues associated with the infringing activity. It is then up to the defendant to prove "his or her deductible expense and the elements of profit attributable to factors other than the copyrighted work."[13] The award will include not only the direct profits earned from sales of infringing items or of tickets to infringing performances, but also indi-

fendant's actual profits. *See* NIMMER, COPYRIGHT § 14.02[A] (2002).

12. See, e.g., Brewer v. Hustler Magazine, 749 F.2d 527, 529 (9th Cir.1984);

Northwest Airlines v. American Airlines, Inc., 870 F.Supp. 1504, 1513 (D.Minn.1994).

13. 17 U.S.C.A. § 504(b) (2000).

rect profits. In *Frank Music Corp. v. Metro–Goldwyn–Mayer, Inc.,*[14] plaintiffs owned the copyright to various songs from the musical Kismet. The defendant used portions of five of those songs in a revue called Hallelujah Hollywood, staged in the showroom of its lavish Las Vegas hotel and casino. In determining defendant's profits, the Ninth Circuit included a portion of MGM's earnings on hotel and gambling operations attributable to the increased traffic generated by the infringing performance in the showroom.

Deductable expenses include the defendant's costs of producing infringing copies or phonorecords, or of mounting the infringing performance or display, as the case may be, as well as associated overhead costs. They do not include the value of any unsold inventory of infringing materials in defendant's possession at the time of suit, since by definition, defendant has earned no profits in connection with unsold items.

The determination of profits becomes more complex when the defendant has added additional creative material to the portions copied from the plaintiff. Thus, in the *Frank Music* case, MGM coupled the infringing material from Kismet with many other songs and variety acts. The infringing material comprised only 6 minutes of a show that lasted an hour and a half. While MGM was held to be an infringer, not all of its profits were traceable to the use of the copyrighted work. In such a case, courts will attempt to apportion the profits. There is no precise formula used in making such apportionments. The current copyright statute places the burden on the defendant to prove "the elements of profit attributable to factors other than the copyrighted work."[15]

9.6.2.3 Statutory Damages

For certain types of infringement, an award of actual damages plus defendant's profits might not be very satisfactory. The defendant might not have any profits, as would be the case where a defendant posts a copyrighted story on a web page on the internet and thousands of readers then download the story for free. Similarly, the plaintiff might have difficulty proving actual damages, perhaps because the story was only one of many appearing in a magazine, making it hard to show lost sales due to defendant's infringing conduct. Consequently the statute provides an alternative of "statutory damages"—a form of liquidated or "in lieu" monetary compensation which the plaintiff can pursue at its own option. There is one precondition, however. In order to seek statutory damages, the plaintiff must have registered the work prior to the date of the infringing conduct, or, in the case of a published work, within three months thereafter.[16]

14.   772 F.2d 505, 517 (9th Cir.1985).

15.   *Id.* This rule is consistent with that adopted by the Supreme Court under the 1909 Act in Sheldon v. Metro–Goldwyn Pictures Corp., 309 U.S. 390, 396, 60 S.Ct. 681, 84 L.Ed. 825 (1940) ("only that part of the profits found to be attributable to the use of the copyrighted material as distinguished from what the infringer himself has supplied" are recoverable).

16.   17 U.S.C.A. § 412 (2000). *See supra* § 5.3 of this treatise.

The court can fix the amount of the statutory damage award at any amount not less than $750 or more than $30,000. If the plaintiff has proved that the infringement was committed willfully, the court can enhance the amount of the statutory damage award to a sum of not more than $150,000. On the other hand, if the defendant can prove that he "was not aware and had no reason to believe that his or her acts constituted an infringement of copyright" the court can reduce the award to a sum of not less than $200. Statutory damages are not available against nonprofit educational institutions, libraries or public broadcasting entities or their employees if they had reasonable grounds to believe that the challenged activities constituted fair use under section 107 of the statute. Thus a teacher who distributes copies of a work to his students, on the reasonable but mistaken assumption that fair use applies, cannot be held liable for statutory damages. Such a teacher would remain liable for actual damages if the copyright owner could, in fact, document them.

Section 504(c) provides that a statutory damage award is available "for all infringements involved in the action, with respect to any one work, for which any one infringer is liable...." The legislative history elaborates that "a single infringer of a single work is liable for a single amount ... no matter how many acts of infringement are involved in the action and regardless of whether the acts were separate, isolated or occurred in a related series."[17] This means that only one award of statutory damages will be made for each work of the plaintiff's that has been infringed, no matter how many acts of infringement the defendant may have committed. Even if the defendant made tens of thousands of copies of plaintiff's copyrighted videogame or copyrighted movie, or infringed multiple rights of the plaintiff by copying and then performing the work, there can only be a single award.

Of course, if there has been massive copying of a single work, a court is likely to find that the infringement was willful, and also likely to make an award at or near the high end of the permissible range, namely $150,000. Moreover, in such cases, plaintiff may have strong evidence concerning defendant's profit and choose to pursue that remedy instead of asking for statutory damages.

Note, however, that plaintiffs are entitled to multiple awards of statutory damages if the defendant has infringed multiple works. In *Playboy Enterprises, Inc. v. Webbworld, Inc.,*[18] the plaintiff sued the operator of an adult-oriented web site for posting copyrighted pictures from Playboy magazine without permission. The trial judge granted summary judgment for Playboy concerning 62 different photographs.

17. H.R.Rep. No. 1476, 94th Cong., 2d Sess.162, reprinted in 1976 U.S.Code Cong. & Ad.News at 5674. *See also* Walt Disney Co. v. Powell, 897 F.2d 565 (D.C.Cir.1990). For a criticism of this doctrine and an argument in favor of multiple awards of statutory damage for multiple infringements of a single work, see Peter Thea, *Note: Statutory Damages for the Multiple Infringement of a Copyrighted Work: A Doctrine Whose Time Has Come, Again,* 6 Cardozo Arts & Ent. L. J. 463 (1988).

18. 968 F.Supp. 1171 (N.D.Tex.1997).

The judge set the appropriate level of statutory damages at $5,000, but because there were 62 different works involved, multiplied the award times 62 and entered judgment against defendant for $310,000.

The Supreme Court has held that the Seventh Amendment of the U.S. Constitution provides a right to a jury determination of the amount of statutory damages.[19] In the event neither party requests a jury, trial judges consider a variety of factors when fixing the amount of a statutory damage award. They sometimes try to estimate what actual damages and defendant's profits might have been and to use that figure as a basis. The nature of the infringement will also influence the court in setting the amount of a statutory judgement award. If defendant's behavior seems flagrant the court may opt for a higher award to act as a deterrent.[20] Where the plaintiff is unlikely to have been economically harmed by the defendant's activities, and if the defendant did not profit from his infringement, many courts have chosen to award only the minimum statutory amount.[21]

9.6.3 Costs and Attorneys' Fees

Section 505 of the Copyright Act grants the court power to award both costs and attorney's fees to the prevailing party. Such awards are entirely within the discretion of the court. Under the provisions of section 412, however, an award of attorney's fees is not available if the plaintiff did not obtain copyright registration prior to the acts of infringement alleged in the suit or within the statutorily provided grace period thereafter.[22]

Historically, the courts used a different standard depending on whether they were making attorney's fees awards to plaintiffs or defendants. Courts often granted plaintiffs fees routinely, without requiring a showing that the infringement was particularly egregious or willful. On the other hand, these same courts were considerably more reluctant to make such awards to defendants, doing so only when there was an indication that plaintiff sued frivolously or in bad faith.[23] In *Fogerty v. Fantasy Inc.,*[24] the Supreme Court held that such disparate treatment was inconsistent with both the statutory language and the Congressional intent. It also rejected a suggestion by the defendant in the case to interpret the statute to make fee awards to the winner automatic in every case. Consequently, the Court mandated that attorney's fees be

---

19. See Feltner v. Columbia Pictures Television, Inc., 523 U.S. 340, 118 S.Ct. 1279, 140 L.Ed.2d 438 (1998).

20. "Among the factors a court may consider in setting statutory damage amounts are: the expenses saved and profits reaped by the infringer, the deterrent effect of the award on defendant and on third parties, and the infringer's state of mind in committing the infringement." Playboy Enterprises v. Webbworld, Inc., 968 F.Supp. 1171 (N.D.Tex.1997).

21. See e.g. Reader's Digest Assn., Inc. v. Conservative Digest, Inc., 642 F.Supp. 144, 147 (D.D.C.1986); Doehrer v. Caldwell, 207 USPQ 391, 393 (N.D.Ill.1980).

22. *See supra* § 5.3.

23. For a general discussion, see Robert S. La Plante, *Awarding Attorney's Fees in Copyright Infringement Cases: The Sensible Use of a Dual Standard*, 51 ALB. L. REV. 239 (1987).

24. 510 U.S. 517, 114 S.Ct. 1023, 127 L.Ed.2d 455 (1994).

awarded in an "evenhanded" manner in the discretion of the trial judge. Unfortunately, the Supreme Court provided little guidance for lower courts as to the factors that should govern fee awards, conceding that there "is no precise rule or formula for making these determinations."

The adoption of the "evenhanded" approach may reduce the volume of copyright infringement litigation in two ways. First, poorer plaintiffs who might have been guaranteed fees at the conclusion of a successful suit prior to the *Fogerty* case now cannot be sure that such fees will be awarded. It would be a pyrrhic victory for such a plaintiff to recover a piddling sum on the merits but be saddled with a six-figure bill from his lawyer. Rather than take the chance that no fees will be granted, such a plaintiff might not sue at all. Second, plaintiffs with good-faith but uncertain claims would have been relatively sure under the older case law that they would not have to pay for defendant's lawyers if they ultimately lost the case because their case would not be found frivolous. Under the evenhanded approach, they no longer have such an assurance. Plaintiffs in this category might also refrain from commencing suit. It is too soon to tell whether this effect will be significant in degree and whether it will be beneficial or detrimental to society as a whole.

9.6.4 Impounding and Destruction of Infringing Articles

Section 503(a) of the copyright statute empowers the court to order the "impounding," or seizure, of all copies and phonorecords made or used in violation of the copyright owner's rights. The "plates molds, matrices, masters, tapes, film negatives, or other articles by means of which such copies or phonorecords may be reproduced" may also be seized. This provision authorizes the seizure not only of piratical copies held by defendant, but also of items such as printing presses, computers, VCRs, or CD burners in defendant's possession, if they were used in the manufacture of the infringing copies.

The statute provides that the remedy of impoundment may be had "at any time while an action" for copyright infringement is pending. This permits a plaintiff to seek the seizure of infringing articles as a form of preliminary relief to prevent continued violations in the period before the case can be resolved and to insure that infringing materials will be on hand for eventual destruction if plaintiff should win the case. Procedural matters relating to impoundment are governed by a special set of rules promulgated by the Supreme Court and known as the Copyright Rules of Practice.[25] Those rules require that a plaintiff requesting impoundment must post a bond in a sum equal to at least twice the value of the items to be impounded.[26]

Interestingly, the Copyright Rules seem to contemplate that the seizure can be carried out without any advance notice to the defendant, although they do provide that a post-seizure hearing on the impoundment can be granted in the discretion of the court. The Rules also do not

25. These rules can be found immediately following 17 U.S.C.A. § 501.

26. Copyright Rules of Practice, Rules 3, 4.

require the plaintiff to make a showing of likely success as a condition of an impoundment order. At least one court has suggested that the procedure outlined in the Copyright Rules is inconsistent with section 503 of the copyright statute. In *WPOW v. MRLJ Enters.*,[27] the court reasoned that section 503 makes the impoundment remedy discretionary with the court and concluded that discretion could not logically be exercised without a pre-seizure hearing and notice to the defendant in all but the most unusual circumstances.

Some courts have gone even further and opined that these procedures in the Copyright Rules may be unconstitutional because of conflict with the defendant's due process rights. As the court in *Paramount Pictures Corp. v. Doe*[28] explained, "the procedure for impoundment under the Copyright Rules... is constitutionally infirm in multiple respects.... The applicability of the rules is not limited to situations where the defendant likely could conceal or destroy the infringing materials. The rules do not require the plaintiff to demonstrate the merits of the underlying infringement claim and likewise do not even require that the application be made by one with personal knowledge of the pertinent facts."

To avoid these constitutional problems, many courts require copyright plaintiffs seeking impoundment to comply with the provisions of Rule 65 of the Federal Rules of Civil Procedure, which deals with preliminary injunctions and temporary restraining orders. As the *Paramount* court went on to explain, "in addition to requiring plaintiffs to post bond, courts require a showing of the merits of plaintiffs' underlying infringement action and the particular circumstances justifying proceeding ex parte; and they fashion orders of seizure which require the plaintiff and defendant to appear at a post-seizure hearing, thus providing the defendant a prompt opportunity to challenge the propriety of the seizure."[29] In courts following this approach, a plaintiff might still be able to secure pre-trial impoundment on an ex parte application, but only after demonstrating both the urgency of the situation and its own likelihood of success on the merits.

Under the immediately following subsection of the statute, 503(b), the court may order "the destruction or other reasonable disposition of all copies or phonorecords found to have been made or used in violation of the copyright owner's exclusive rights" as part of a final judgement in an infringement case. While the court is empowered to order destruction, it need not do so, and it may instead order the items to be turned over to the plaintiff. This would permit the plaintiff to sell them and realize the profit instead of simply wasting the resources associated with production of the items.

27. 584 F.Supp. 132 (D.D.C.1984).

28. 821 F.Supp. 82, 88 (E.D.N.Y.1993). See generally Paul S. Owens, *Impoundment Procedures Under the Copyright Act: The Constitutional Infirmities*, 14 HOFSTRA L. REV. 211 (1985).

29. 821 F.Supp. at 88, citing district court opinions from Kansas, New York and the District of Columbia.

9.6.5   Criminal Sanctions

As anyone who has ever rented a videotape knows from the accompanying FBI warning, under certain circumstances copyright infringement is a crime. Section 506(a) of the Copyright Act provides that "any person who infringes a copyright willfully and for purposes of commercial advantage or private financial gain," can be punished criminally. The nature of the punishment is set out in § 2319 of Title 18 of the U.S. Code. If defendant reproduces or distributes 10 or more copies or phonorecords of one or more works within a 180–day period and those works have a retail value of more than $2,500, the conduct is classified as a felony and the defendant can be imprisoned for a period of up to five years and fined up to $250,000 for a first offense and imprisoned for up to 10 years and fined up to $250,000 for a second or subsequent offense. In all other cases of criminal conviction for copyright infringement, the conduct is a misdemeanor carrying a maximum term of imprisonment of one year and a maximum potential fine of $25,000.[30] Under section 506(b) of the Copyright Act, upon conviction, all infringing copies or phonorecords and all devices used in the manufactures of such items shall be ordered forfeited to the court and shall be destroyed. This forfeiture and destruction is mandatory in criminal cases.

The more serious, felony-level punishments for infringement were originally limited to offenses involving sound recordings and audiovisual works, but Congress amended those provisions in 1992 so that they now apply to all types of work covered by the copyright statute. The legislative history of the 1992 amendments reflects a particular concern with large-scale software piracy. While the penalties are certainly severe, as a practical matter they have not proved very effective tools against copyright piracy. Even when a defendant is arrested in a warehouse filled with counterfeit videotapes or CDs, the government rarely has direct proof that defendant made the infringing copies. While they may have proof that the defendant sold some of the copies, the government must prove beyond a reasonable doubt that the defendant did not know that the copies had not been subject to a valid first sale by the copyright owner or a licensee.[31] This has proven to be a high hurdle for prosecutors.

As the statutory text indicates, infringement is only criminal if done "willfully." This means that the defendant must know the work in question is protected by copyright, and must also know that his acts constitute copyright infringement. In cases of non-literal copying, therefore, it is unlikely that the defendant can be found criminally liable because he can always argue that he believed he was permissibly copying unprotected ideas rather than protected expression. Where the copying is

---

30. The terms of imprisonment for criminal copyright infringement are set out in section 2319 of title 18. To determine the fines for those same offenses, that provision cross-references to section 3571.

31. United States v. Atherton, 561 F.2d 747 (9th Cir.1977).

large-scale verbatim duplication of computer programs or videotapes, however, the willfulness issue is quite apparent.

The statute also requires that the copying be done for the purposes of "commercial advantage or private financial gain." The reference to private financial gain suggests that even isolated copying of protected works such as computer programs or videotaped movies, done by private users at home, in order to save the cost of a retail copy of the work might be considered a criminal violation, albeit a misdemeanor. Some of the legislative history surrounding the 1992 amendments to the criminal provision imply that this might not be the case. For instance, Senator Hatch, the sponsor of the 1992 legislation, observed in floor debate that "the copying must be undertaken to make money, and even incidental financial benefits that might accrue as a result of the copying should not contravene the law where the achievement of those benefits were not the motivation behind the copying."[32] Of course, this statement is itself ambiguous. When a home user copies software borrowed from a friend, she does not engage in the activity to "make money" but she surely realizes an "incidental financial benefit" because she now need not pay for a copy of the program. Moreover, one might argue that her "motivation" in making that copy was to receive that precise "incidental financial benefit." On the other hand, it is possible her primary motive was actually convenience, not the financial benefit. Fortunately, as a practical matter the issue is probably unimportant because no rational prosecutor is likely to devote resources to prosecuting private users engaged in incidental copying. Indeed, such copying is usually not discoverable by any means short of wholesale violation of the Fourth Amendment though technological innovation may soon make it much easier to detect private copying, especially where computers are involved.

Additional subsections of section 506 deal with the fraudulent use of copyright notices; the fraudulent removal of copyright notices; and false representations made to the Copyright Office in connection with applications for copyright registration. Violation of an author's moral rights under the Visual Artists Rights Act, codified in section 106A of the copyright statute, will subject the offender to civil liability but are specifically exempted from criminal sanction.

§ 9.7 Defenses Other Than Fair Use

Once a plaintiff has made out a prima facie case of copyright infringement the defendant may attempt to interpose an affirmative defense. The most important and perhaps most frequently invoked defense is "fair use," codified in section 107 of the current statute. Because of the significance of that defense and the many issues it raises, we shall defer further consideration of it until the following chapter. The sections that follow take up several other defenses common in copyright litigation.

32. 138 Cong. Rec. S17959 (October 8, 1992).

9.7.1   Copyright Misuse

Parties seeking equitable relief, such as injunctions, have long been subject to a defense known as "unclean hands." Under this principle, a court will not come to the aid of a plaintiff who has himself committed wrongful acts to the prejudice of the defendant. This general principle is the source of the more specific defense known as "copyright misuse." Generally stated, if an alleged infringer can show that the plaintiff-copyright-owner committed some form of misconduct either in obtaining or enforcing the copyright, the court can make a finding of copyright misuse and deny all relief to the copyright owner. Despite the doctrine's roots in the law of equity, a finding of misuse will result in denial not just of injunctive relief, but of monetary relief as well.[1]

Courts were slow to embrace the idea of copyright misuse. While the Supreme Court articulated a concept of *patent* misuse in 1942 in the *Morton Salt* decision,[2] copyright cases in the decades that followed often explicitly declined to entertain the argument of copyright misuse.[3] Only recently have defendants been able to prevail on claims of misuse. One of the first such cases sustaining the defense was the Fourth Circuit's 1990 decision in *Lasercomb America, Inc. v. Reynolds.*[4] Lasercomb owned the copyright in an industrial software program used in box and carton production. Lasercomb licensed various firms to use the software. One of the licensees made copies of the software not permitted by the license and Lasercomb sued for infringement. At trial, the defendant pointed out that Lasercomb's license included a provision forbidding licensees from investigating or developing any competing software products for a period of 99 years. The court found this provision inconsistent with the policies underlying the copyright laws and harmful to the public interest because it tended to inhibit competition and to forbid the free copying of ideas, a central tenet of copyright law. It thus refused to enforce the copyright and denied Lasercomb relief despite the clear evidence of infringement.

The 1997 decision of the Ninth Circuit in *Practice Management Information Corp. v. American Medical Association* also held that a copyright had been misused.[5] There, the AMA licensed a government agency to use a copyrighted system of medical procedure codes in connection with the Medicaid program. Under the license the relevant government agency agreed not to adopt any other competing set of codes. A competitor of the AMA sought a declaratory judgment that it could freely copy the AMA codes. The court held that the restrictive provision

§ 9.7

1. F.E.L. Publications Ltd. v. Catholic Bishop, 506 F.Supp. 1127, 1137 (N.D.Ill. 1981), *rev'd on other grounds*, 214 USPQ 409 (7th Cir.1982).

2. Morton Salt Co. v. G.S. Suppiger, 314 U.S. 488, 62 S.Ct. 402, 86 L.Ed. 363 (1942). See generally the discussion of patent misuse in Chapter 21, *infra*.

3. See e.g., Harms, Inc. v. Sansom House Enterprises, Inc., 162 F.Supp. 129, 135 (E.D.Pa.1958), *aff'd on other grounds sub nom.* Leo Feist, Inc. v. Lew Tendler Tavern, Inc., 267 F.2d 494 (3d Cir.1959); Orth–O–Vision, Inc. v. Home Box Office, 474 F.Supp. 672, 686 (S.D.N.Y.1979).

4. 911 F.2d 970 (4th Cir.1990).

5. 121 F.3d 516 (9th Cir.1997).

in the license agreement constituted misuse of the copyright, and consequently held the copyright to be unenforceable.

The principal type of misconduct that will lead to a finding of misuse is anti-competitive conduct of the sort forbidden by the spirit, if not the letter of the antitrust laws, as illustrated by *Lasercomb* and *PMI*. However, the mere invocation of an antitrust claim will not exonerate the defendant. There must be proof that the antitrust violations or anti-competitive conduct in question are so significant that the policy of enforcing the antitrust laws outweighs the equally important policy of preventing copyright infringement. Though some courts would limit the misuse concept to acts that are outright antitrust violations,[6] other types of behaviors have been held to trigger the doctrine. For instance, if a copyright plaintiff has previously made intentional misrepresentations to the Copyright Office concerning the status of the work, courts may decline to enforce the copyright.[7] Similarly, where the copyright owner has made spurious threats of infringement litigation[8] or has dealt unfairly with the defendant in prior face-to-face transactions,[9] courts have been willing to deny enforcement of the copyright. In all these situations, however, there is a reluctance to exculpate the defendant unless the plaintiff's misconduct is fairly egregious.

9.7.2 Statute of Limitations, Laches and Estoppel

Copyright claims may be stymied by a trio of defenses that all relate to delay, passage of time or the reliance interests of defendants. The first of these, the statute of limitations, is a statutory bright line rule dictating when suit must be brought, while laches and estoppel are more *ad hoc* and equitable in nature. All three are based on the notion that copyright owners who fail to pursue their rights promptly may not deserve the assistance of a court, and that defendants may have developed a reliance interest in the status quo.

Under section 507(b) of the copyright act "no civil action shall be maintained ... unless it is commenced within three years after the claim accrued." The statute of limitations for criminal prosecutions is identical. Where infringing activity involves a series of acts committed over a period of time, the limitations period runs from the last act of infringement.[10] In such a situation, most courts limit recoverable damages to those attributable to the three year period preceding the filing of the

---

6. Saturday Evening Post Company v. Rumbleseat Press, Inc., 816 F.2d 1191 (7th Cir.1987).

7. Masquerade Novelty, Inc. v. Unique Industries, Inc., 912 F.2d 663, 667 (3d Cir. 1990); Russ Berrie & Co. v. Jerry Elsner Co., 482 F.Supp. 980, 988 (S.D.N.Y.1980).

8. Cf. Vogue Ring Creations, Inc. v. Hardman, 410 F.Supp. 609, 616 (D.R.I. 1976). Sham litigation has been held to be a violation of the antitrust laws under certain circumstances, *California Motor Transport*

Co. v. Trucking Unlimited, 404 U.S. 508, 510–11, 92 S.Ct. 609, 30 L.Ed.2d 642 (1972).

9. T.B. Harms & Francis, Day & Hunter v. Stern, 231 F. 645 (2d Cir.1916).

10. Taylor v. Meirick, 712 F.2d 1112, 1117 (7th Cir.1983) (defendant sold copyrighted maps from 1976 through 1979; plaintiff's suit filed in 1980 held not time-barred).

complaint,[11] though there is contrary authority granting plaintiff monetary remedies for all infringements, even those more than three years old.[12]

If the copyright owner can show that he was unaware of the infringing activities, that may operate to "toll" or suspend the statute of limitations. Courts are most inclined to toll the limitations period where the defendant deliberately concealed his infringing activity. The equities in this situation, labeled "fraudulent concealment," strongly favor the plaintiff. To show fraudulent concealment, plaintiff must show that "the defendant used fraudulent means to keep the plaintiff unaware of his cause of action, and also that the plaintiff was, in fact, ignorant of the existence of his cause of action."[13] Even without evidence of affirmative concealment, some courts will toll the statute until a plaintiff exercising reasonable diligence could have learned of his cause of action, although other courts disagree and decline to toll in these circumstances.[14]

The defense of laches is conceptually related to the statute of limitations, but distinct from it in the details of its application. A defendant may invoke laches as a defense if the copyright owner has unnecessarily delayed in bringing suit and defendant both relied on that delay and was prejudiced by it. The most conspicuous difference between the laches defense and the statute of limitations defense is the absence of a specific bright line time period for laches.

For laches the determination of whether plaintiff's delay was excessive is made on a case by case basis. "Factors relevant to the issue include the death or unavailability of important witnesses, the dulling of memories through the passage of time, the loss of relevant records, and continuing investments and outlays by the alleged infringer in connection with the operation of its business."[15] Thus, in *Slifka v. Citation Fabrics Corp.*[16] the plaintiff sent the defendant a telegram in September, 1970, accusing defendant of infringement in connection with a fabric design. The plaintiff took no further action until February, 1971 when it filed its complaint for copyright infringement. In the interim, the defendant had produced 150,000 additional yards of the fabric with the disputed design. The court found that because of plaintiff's failure to pursue the matter more consistently and aggressively, his action was

---

11. See, e.g., Roley v. New World Pictures Ltd., 19 F.3d 479 (9th Cir.1994).

12. Taylor v. Meirick, 712 F.2d 1112, 1119 (7th Cir.1983)

13. Wood v. Santa Barbara Chamber of Commerce, Inc., 705 F.2d 1515, 1521 (9th Cir.1983), *cert. denied*, 465 U.S. 1081, 104 S.Ct. 1446, 79 L.Ed.2d 765 (1984).

14. Compare Taylor v. Meirick, 712 F.2d 1112, 1117 (7th Cir.1983) (tolling) with Wood v. Santa Barbara Chamber of Commerce, Inc., 705 F.2d 1515 (9th Cir. 1983), *cert. denied*, 465 U.S. 1081, 104 S.Ct. 1446, 79 L.Ed.2d 765 (1984) (no tolling).

15. Eisenman Chemical Co. v. NL Industries, 595 F.Supp. 141, 147 (D.Nev. 1984).

16. 329 F.Supp. 1392 (S.D.N.Y.1971).

barred by laches. Generally, if the work is one with a short commercial life, such as a computer program or a pop song, less delay by plaintiff will be tolerated than in more leisurely industries such as book publishing or the live theater.

The third defense in this trilogy is estoppel. Estoppel does not focus on passage of time like laches and statute of limitations claims, but rather on the fact that plaintiff has led defendant to believe that his conduct is unobjectionable, and now ought not be allowed to predicate a lawsuit on that very conduct. In order to make out the defense "(1) the party to be estopped must know the facts; (2) he must intend that his conduct shall be acted on or must so act that the party asserting the estoppel has a right to believe it is so intended; (3) the latter must be ignorant of the true facts; and (4) he must rely on the former's conduct to his injury."[17] Thus, if a screenwriter proposed to prepare a screenplay based loosely on a novel, and explains his concept to the copyright owner in the novel, and if that copyright owner indicates that in his opinion such a screenplay would be non-infringing, and if the screenwriter goes forward and thereafter the novelist sues for infringement, he or she is likely to be estopped from asserting his claim.

9.7.3   Abandonment

The copyright owner of a work is free to dedicate that work to the public domain. Such an owner is said to have abandoned his copyright. Not surprisingly, infringement defendants will occasionally attempt to argue abandonment as a way to avoid liability. Courts find abandonment if the owner has performed "some overt act indicative of an intent to surrender rights in the copyrighted work and to allow the public to copy it."[18] The copyright owner can explicitly abandon his rights by placing a legend on the work indicating that others may freely copy it.

Abandonment can also be found circumstantially based on the conduct of the copyright owner. For example one court found copyright to have been abandoned when the copyright owner, a TV station, destroyed its only copy of broadcast videotapes by erasing or taping over them.[19] Other examples of overt acts that have lead to a finding of abandonment include widespread dissemination of copies of the work without a copyright notice during the period when such notice was legally required, and knowing failure of the copyright owner to take action against widespread infringement.

---

17. Hampton v. Paramount Pictures Corp., 279 F.2d 100, 104 (9th Cir.1960), *cert. denied,* 364 U.S. 882, 81 S.Ct. 170, 5 L.Ed.2d 103 (1960).

18. Rohauer v. Killiam Shows, Inc., 379 F.Supp. 723, 730 (S.D.N.Y.1974), *rev'd on other ground,* 551 F.2d 484 (2d Cir. 1977),

cert. denied, 431 U.S. 949, 97 S.Ct. 2666, 53 L.Ed.2d 266 (1977).

19. Pacific & S. Co. v. Duncan, 572 F.Supp. 1186 (N.D.Ga.1983), *aff'd,* 744 F.2d 1490 (11th Cir.1984), *cert. denied,* 471 U.S. 1004, 105 S.Ct. 1867, 85 L.Ed.2d 161 (1985).

9.7.4   Innocent Intent

Intent is not an element of a copyright infringement cause of action.[20] The defendant can be held liable even if the copying was done innocently and in good faith. Thus, innocent intent is not a defense to copyright infringement. The fact that the defendant acted with an innocent intent can, however, affect the remedies that will be afforded.

A number of factors might cause a court to label defendant's behavior "innocent." Prior to 1989, when copyright notice became optional, the defendant might have copied from a copy lacking notice in the good faith belief that the material was unprotected. Even today the lack of notice may mislead some users not conversant with the subtleties of copyright law. In other situations, common in the music industry, the plaintiff may have reproduced the copyrighted material through subconscious memory of plaintiff's work. In still other cases, a defendant may have honestly believed that he was copying only the unprotected ideas contained with a work and not any of its protected expression only to be subsequently told by a judge that he guessed wrong.

The current statute deals most explicitly with good faith related to lack of notice. Under section 405(b) "any person who innocently infringes a copyright, in reliance upon an authorized copy or phonorecord from which the copyright notice has been omitted and which was publicly distributed by authority of the copyright owner before [March 1, 1989], incurs no liability for actual or statutory damages ... for any infringing acts committed before receiving actual notice that registration for the work has been made ... if such person proves that he or she was misled by the omission of notice." The statute goes on to make it clear, however, that such an innocent infringer can be enjoined from future acts of infringement, can be required to pay over any profits attributable to the infringement, or can be required to pay a reasonable license fee to the copyright owner in order to continue his activities.

There was no comparable provision in the 1909 copyright act, because under that the statute, the public distribution of copies without notice would have injected the work into the public domain, thus completely exonerating the defendant from any infringement liability. Since 1989 copyright notice has been optional. Thus the fact that a defendant copied from a noticeless copy of a recent work should not be automatically treated as evidence that the defendant was acting in good faith, absent further circumstances.

---

20. See, e.g., Fitzgerald Publishing Co. v. Baylor Publishing Co., 807 F.2d 1110, 1113 (2d Cir.1986) ("intent or knowledge is not an element of infringement").

Other forms of good faith can be taken into account by the court in assessing damages. For instance the provision on statutory damages specifically provides for a lowering of the minimum damage award in cases where "the infringer was not aware and had no reason to believe that his or her acts constituted an infringement." In the post–1989 era, however, a copyright owner can foreclose the assertion of innocence in mitigation of damages by the simple device of including a copyright notice on publicly distributed copies of the work. Under section 401(d) "if a notice of copyright . . . appears on the published copy or copies to which a defendant in a copyright infringement suit had access, then no weight shall be given to such a defendant's interposition of a defense based on innocent infringement in mitigation of actual or statutory damages. . . ."[21]

9.7.5 Sovereign Immunity

The federal government has no immunity with respect to alleged copyright infringement. Claims against the United States must, however, be filed in the U.S. Court of Federal Claims.[22] In 1990, Congress sought to clarify the exposure of state governments to copyright infringement liability by adopting the Copyright Remedy Clarification Act of 1990.[23] Section 511 of the Copyright Act now stipulates that "[a]ny State, any instrumentality of a State, and any officer or employee of a State . . . shall be subject to the provisions of this title in the same manner and to the same extent as any nongovernmental entity."[24] Section 511 specifically provides that states will not be immune from suit by virtue of the U.S. Constitution's Eleventh Amendment—a provision that forbids states from being sued by private individuals in federal court—or any other doctrine of sovereign immunity. This legislation overturned the weight of prior authority, which had often held states to be immune from infringement liability, much to the frustration of copyright holders.

Events subsequent to the 1990 legislation have rendered the continued vitality of § 511 extremely suspect, to the say the least. In 1999, the U.S. Supreme Court decided *Florida Prepaid Postsecondary Expense Board v. College Savings Bank*,[25] concerning an analogous provision in the patent statute, as well as *College Savings Bank v. Florida Prepaid Postsecondary Expense Board*,[26] addressing a similar provision in the trademark statute. In these decisions the Court held that Congress had not validly abrogated state immunity to charges of trademark and patent infringement in the federal courts. The virtually inescapable conclusion from these opinions is that the 1990 copyright legislation is similarly invalid.

21. 17 U.S.C.A. § 401(d) (2000). A parallel provision, 17 U.S.C.A. § 402(d) (2000), covers phonorecords.

22. 28 U.S.C.A. § 1498 (2000).

23. Pub. L. No. 101–553, 104 Stat. 2749 (1990).

24. 17 U.S.C.A. § 511(a) (2000).

25. 527 U.S. 627, 119 S.Ct. 2199, 144 L.Ed.2d 575 (1999).

26. 527 U.S. 666, 119 S.Ct. 2219, 144 L.Ed.2d 605 (1999).

It is important to note that, as extended to the copyright law, the two *Florida Prepaid* decisions do not render state governments free from any legal obligations under the federal copyright statutes. These decisions do appear to bar copyright holders from calling state governments before the federal courts, the most effective tribunal for exercising their rights.[27] Copyright holders could, at least in theory, assert applicable common law claims within a state court. A variety of legislative proposals have been forwarded to address the liability of state governments for copyright infringement, but as yet none has been enacted.[28]

27. *See* Peter Bray, *After* College Savings Board v. Florida Prepaid, *Are State Subject to Suit for Copyright Infringement?*, 36 HOUSTON L. REV. 1531 (1999).

28. *See, e.g. Legislation/State Immunity: Draft Leahy/Hatch Amendment Stiffens IP Protection/Immunity Waiver Trade-off*, 64 Patent, Trademark & Copyright J. 32 (May 10, 2002).

Chapter 10

THE FAIR USE DEFENSE

Table of Sections

§ 10.1 History and Rationale of Fair Use

A perfectly airtight system of copyright would probably be intolerable. Many individuals need or desire to use copyrighted works in ways that do not seriously threaten the interests of the copyright owner, but that do tend to promote the social goals of advancement and dissemination of knowledge and learning. One readily thinks of the book reviewer who wishes to quote a portion of a volume being reviewed, or the teacher who wishes to distribute copies of a current news story to her students. Others may merely use copyrighted works in an incidental and casual way, such as the TV or movie producer who prepares a program showing a copyrighted poster in the background of a scene[1] or the VCR owner

---

§ 10.1

1. Sandoval v. New Line Cinema Corp., 973 F.Supp. 409 (S.D.N.Y.1997), *aff'd*, 147 F.3d 215 (2d Cir.1998). In Ringgold v. Black Entertainment TV, Inc., 126 F.3d 70 (2d Cir.1997), however, the user of a copyrighted poster on the set of a TV sitcom where all or part of the poster was visible for 26 seconds was held not entitled to summary judgment on the fair use question.

who tapes a copyrighted broadcast for viewing at a more convenient time. Each of these users might find it impractical to seek permission from the copyright owner because of the expense and nuisance involved. If, as a consequence, such individuals decided to forgo the use of the copyrighted material, our society would be worse off with no corresponding benefit in the form of enhanced incentives to copyright owners.

The fair use defense is the copyright doctrine that provides flexibility in the system. The Supreme Court has noted that it is a "guarantee of breathing space at the heart of copyright,"[2] and the Second Circuit has observed that the fair use doctrine prevents "rigid application of the copyright statute when, on occasion, it would stifle the very creativity which that law is designed to foster."[3] It exempts from liability certain modest uses of copyrighted work when those uses will not undermine the economic interests of the copyright owner. It is unequivocally the most important defense in copyright law, both in terms of how often it is asserted by defendants and in terms of its importance to basic copyright policies.

The fair use doctrine can be traced back to a mid-nineteenth century decision of Justice Story, sitting as a district judge, in *Folsom v. Marsh*.[4] Both parties in that case were biographers of George Washington. Plaintiff had the exclusive rights to publish Washington's papers[5] and did so in the form of a 12 volume work. The defendant prepared a 2 volume pseudo-autobiography, "in which Washington is made mainly to tell the story of his own life, by inserting therein his letters and his messages, and other written documents." Defendant's book contained 388 pages of material copied verbatim from plaintiff's work. Justice Story found this to be infringing, but recognized that sometimes there could be "justifiable use of the original materials such as the law recognizes as no infringement of the copyright of the plaintiff." He went on to indicate that in determining if a defendant's use of plaintiff's materials was "justifiable" we should "look to the nature and objects of the selections made, the quantity and value of the materials used, and the degree in which the use may prejudice the sale, or diminish the profits, or supersede the objects, of the original work."

For the next 135 years, courts relied upon this judicial language as the basis for a common law fair use doctrine. When Congress revised the copyright laws in 1976 it chose to codify the idea of fair use in section

2. Campbell v. Acuff–Rose Music, Inc., 510 U.S. 569, 579, 114 S.Ct. 1164, 127 L.Ed.2d 500 (1994).

3. Iowa State University Research Foundation, Inc. v. American Broadcasting Co., 621 F.2d 57 (2d Cir.1980). Almost 200 years ago the British jurist Lord Ellenborough made the same point when he said "while I shall think myself bound to secure every man in the enjoyment of his copyright, one must not put manacles upon sci-

ence." Carey v. Kearsley, 170 Eng. Rep. 679, 681 (K.B.1802).

4. 9 F.Cas. 342 (C.C.D.Mass.1841).

5. President Washington apparently left his papers to his nephew, Bushrod Washington, a justice of the Supreme Court, who in turn conveyed the interest in these papers to Chief Justice John Marshall and Jared Sparks. Folsom, the plaintiff, was the publisher of Sparks' 12–volume work.

107. The legislative language substantially mirrors the ideas first articulated by Justice Story in *Folsom*. The section provides:

> Notwithstanding the provisions of sections 106 and 106A, the fair use of a copyrighted work, including such use by reproduction in copies or phonorecords or by any other means specified by that section, for purposes such as criticism, comment, news reporting, teaching (including multiple copies for classroom use), scholarship, or research, is not an infringement of copyright. In determining whether the use made of a work in any particular case is a fair use the factors to be considered shall include—
>
> > (1) the purpose and character of the use, including whether such use is of a commercial nature or is for nonprofit education purposes;
> >
> > (2) the nature of the copyrighted work;
> >
> > (3) the amount and substantiality of the portion used in relation to the copyrighted work as a whole; and
> >
> > (4) the effect of the use upon the potential market for or value of the copyrighted work.
>
> The fact that a work is unpublished shall not itself bar a finding of fair use if such a finding is made upon consideration of all the above factors.

There is broad consensus among the courts that the fair use doctrine is a true affirmative defense, meaning that the defendant bears the burden of proof,[6] although some courts have suggested that after a preliminary showing on some of the fair use elements, the burden will shift back to plaintiff to rebut the claim of fair use. Courts also describe the fair use inquiry as a "mixed question of law and fact."[7]

Some scholars have attempted to justify the fair use defense on economic grounds. The argument focuses particularly on the problem of "transaction costs." Economic theory assumes that, since copyright owners want to maximize their revenues, they will license others to use their works when the amount they can obtain for the license exceeds the amount they could earn from other uses of the work that will be precluded if they grant the license. For example, the copyright owner of a novel knows that once he grants movie rights to one party, very few others will want to purchase the same type of rights for the same work. For all practical purposes, any movie producer will want exclusive rights, and thus the grant of a license to movie producer "alpha" will preclude licensing to "beta." In this simple situation, the copyright owner will license the movie to the highest bidder.

---

6. *See, e.g.,* American Geophysical Union v. Texaco, Inc., 60 F.3d 913, 918 (2d Cir.1994), *cert. dismissed,* 516 U.S. 1005, 116 S.Ct. 592, 133 L.Ed.2d 486 (1995).

7. *See, e.g.,* Harper & Row Publishers v. Nation Enterprises, 471 U.S. 539, 560, 105 S.Ct. 2218, 85 L.Ed.2d 588 (1985).

On the other side of the transaction, a prospective licensee will pay a price that reflects his valuation of the copyrighted material. If the copyright owner demands a million dollars for movie rights to his novel, and the producer feels that he cannot pay that much and still make a profit, he will not enter into the license. As a result, licensing will occur when it is to the mutual benefit of both parties, and as the economists see it, society will benefit as well, because the work will be put to its most greatly valued use.

In some cases, however, the parties may never reach this ideal bargain because of "transaction costs." For instance, assume a teacher wishes to duplicate and distribute a magazine article to his class of 25 students. Assume further that the copyright owner of the article would be willing to license that use for a minimum of one dollar a copy. Perhaps the owner feels that $25 is the amount by which demand for the original magazine will be depressed when 25 copies of the article are distributed free in class. Assume still further that the teacher would be willing to pay a maximum of $25 for the privilege of distributing the work. Perhaps this is the value of the license to the teacher because he thinks that by using the article he will be considered a good teacher and get a $25 raise next year, or perhaps he is planning to charge the students and knows that the most they would be willing to pay is $1 per copy. In theory the two ought to be able to strike a deal and such a deal would result in an increase in efficiency and an enhancement of social welfare.

However, in order to obtain a copyright license the teacher may need to spend 30 minutes of his time on the phone procuring the license, which we can value at $5 for the sake of argument, and $5 more on the price of the long distance phone call. Consequently, the cost to the teacher for the license would actually be the $25 license fee plus $10 additional, making a total of $35—more than the maximum he is willing to pay. If the teacher were to ask the magazine to license the use for $15, so that his total cost would drop back to his maximum of $25, the magazine would refuse, because $15 will not compensate it for lost magazine sales, which is to say it is below its minimum license price. In this situation, no license will be granted or even sought and the use will not take place. Yet the use should take place, under economic thinking, because but for the transactions costs, both parties would be better off. The situation is one of "market failure."

Moreover, in this situation, a further benefit would be realized if the teacher were allowed to use the copyrighted materials because, in addition to the private benefits realized by the students and the teacher, the public at large presumably realizes benefits when the use of the article results in a better educated citizenry. Factoring public benefits into the equation means that even if the transaction costs were at or near zero, desirable copyright bargains might not take place. To appreciate the point it might help to change the numbers. Assume that the copyright owner would demand $30 for the license to use the article, while the teacher is still only willing to pay $25. Assume that we can value the public benefit in improved education that flows from the use of this article at $10. In this situation, the total benefits from the use are $35, which can be obtained for a cost of only $30. Again, an economist would reason that use should take place because it is efficient and will enhance total social welfare. Unfortunately, however, the teacher has no way to collect the $10 from the public, and will not pay more than $25 himself. Consequently once again no transaction will take place.

In the economic view of things, the fair use doctrine is responsive to these problems. By permitting the teacher to use the work for free, the teacher (and his students) are benefitted, along with the public to a degree that outweighs the costs to the copyright owner. Thus some scholars have argued that the fair use doctrine should only be available when transaction costs are high and market failure is likely[8] or when public benefits associated with a given use are significant and cannot be captured in the form of private payments.

Other writers have attempted to justify the fair use concept on moral or philosophical grounds.[9] Still others have argued that the fair use doctrine helps implement privacy concerns.[10] These authors have recognized that in recent years, copyright owners have been able to employ new technologies to reduce transaction costs. It now may take only a few seconds and a free Internet connection to pay to use copyrighted materials. If fair use is only available in cases where transaction costs are high, these technological developments would mean that the fair use doctrine will be constantly shrinking without any consideration of the larger public interests the doctrine is designed to serve.

Courts, however, do not often delve into the justification for the fair use doctrine. Not surprisingly, most simply accept it as a given because of its presence in the statutory text. The vast majority of fair use opinions have concerned themselves with elaborating on the itemized statutory factors, applying those factors to the facts of the case and occasionally attempting to lay out rules for how those factors should be balanced. The decisions are highly fact specific and generalizations are hard to come by.

§ 10.2 The Fair Use Factors

Fair use has often been described as an "equitable rule of reason,"[1] an area where judges are expected to balance equities and develop the

---

8. *See, e.g.,* Wendy Gordon, *Fair Use As Market Failure: A Structural and Economic Analysis of the Betamax Case and Its Predecessors,* 82 Colum. L. Rev. 1600 (1982) ("fair use should be awarded ... to the defendant when: 1) market failure is present; 2) transfer of the use to the defendant is socially desirable; and 3) and award of fair use would not cause substantial injury to the incentives of the plaintiff copyright owner."); William M. Landes & Richard Posner, *An Economic Analysis of Copyright Law,* 18 J. Legal Stud. 325 (1989).

9. *See e.g.,* William W. Fisher III, *Reconstructing the Fair Use Doctrine,* 101 Harv. L. Rev. 1659 (1988).

10. Stephen B. Thau, *Copyright, Privacy, and Fair Use,* 24 Hofstra L. Rev. 179 (1995).

§ 10.2

1. Sony Corp. of America v. Universal City Studios, Inc., 464 U.S. 417, 448, 104 S.Ct. 774, 78 L.Ed.2d 574 (1984); H.R. Rep. No. 1476, 94th Cong. 2d Sess. 65 (1976),

law incrementally, in response to the facts of each case. The legislative history of the provision states explicitly that "the courts must be free to adapt the doctrine to particular situations on a case-by-case basis."[2] The rules of fair use are so open-ended that one judge even complained the "doctrine is entirely equitable and is so flexible as virtually to defy definition"[3] and another has called it "the most troublesome in the whole law of copyright."[4] While the Supreme Court has decided three fair use cases to date, those cases did not lay down any clear approach to guide fair use decision making, and there is much in the cases that, at least on the surface, is seemingly contradictory.

In attempting to make sense of this amorphous area, the logical place to begin is with the statutory text. The first portion of section 107 is a preamble that lists several illustrative types of fair use. It then goes on to list four factors that courts are to consider in determining if a use is a fair use. The statute itself does not indicate how the factors are to be weighed.

Fortunately, at least two things seem readily apparent from the statutory list of factors. Section 107 specifies that the analysis "shall include" the itemized criteria. First, the word "include" indicates that other factors may also be considered where the court deems appropriate. Courts have occasionally pointed to factors other than the itemized four. Thus, some courts have considered the bad faith of a defendant as reason to deny the fair use defense,[5] and others have pointed to industry custom as a factor militating in defendant's favor.[6] There are also cases that attempt to weigh the public interest in defendant's activities as a component of the fair use calculus[7] or that consider the privacy implications of defendant's conduct in analyzing the defense.[8] However, it is relatively uncommon for courts to go beyond the statutory list.

Second, the word "shall" indicates that all four of the listed factors must be addressed. This means that fair use opinions tend to have a predictable structure with four separate sections, each one devoted to a

reprinted in 1976 U.S. CODE CONG. & ADMIN. NEWS 5659, 5679.

2. H.R. Rep. No. 1476, 94th Cong. 2d Sess. 66 (1976), reprinted in 1976 U.S. CODE CONG. & ADMIN. NEWS 5659, 5680.

3. Time, Inc. v. Bernard Geis Associates, 293 F.Supp. 130 (S.D.N.Y.1968).

4. Dellar v. Samuel Goldwyn, Inc., 104 F.2d 661, 662 (2d Cir.1939).

5. Roy Export Co. Establishment v. Columbia Broadcasting System, Inc., 503 F.Supp. 1137 (S.D.N.Y.1980), aff'd, 672 F.2d 1095 (2d Cir.1982), cert. denied, 459 U.S. 826, 103 S.Ct. 60, 74 L.Ed.2d 63 (1982); Time Inc. v. Bernard Geis Associates, 293 F.Supp. 130, 146 (S.D.N.Y.1968).

6. See, e.g., Triangle Publications, Inc. v. Knight–Ridder Newspapers, Inc., 626 F.2d 1171 (5th Cir.1980); Williams & Wilkins Co. v. United States, 203 Ct.Cl. 74, 487 F.2d 1345, 1353–56 (Ct.Cl.1973), aff'd by an equally divided court, 420 U.S. 376, 95 S.Ct. 1344, 43 L.Ed.2d 264 (1975).

7. Time, Inc. v. Bernard Geis Assocs., 293 F.Supp. 130 (S.D.N.Y.1968) (noting the "public interest in having the fullest information available on the murder of President Kennedy" in finding magazine's publication of frames of copyrighted movie to be protected by fair use defense).

8. New Era Publications Int'l v. Henry Holt and Co., Inc., 695 F.Supp. 1493, 1505 (S.D.N.Y.1988), aff'd 873 F.2d 576 (2d Cir. 1989) ("in making a fair use analysis balancing the nature of the protected work with the fair use purpose sought to be served, privacy interests may be an appropriate consideration").

member of the statutory quartet. The nuances of these four statutory criteria are considered in the following subsections.

10.2.1 Purpose and Character of the Use

The first fair use factor focuses on the "purpose and character" of the use the defendant is making of the material. This seems to continue the theme of the preamble to section 107, which itemizes several types of uses that the statutory drafters considered illustrative of fair use. The six itemized uses in the preamble are (1) criticism; (2) comment; (3) news reporting; (4) teaching; (5) scholarship; and (6) research. This is neither an exhaustive list, nor is it a list of safe harbors. Because the list is preceded by the words "such as" it seems clear that Congress did not mean to limit the availability of the defense to only these six types of use.[9] The Eleventh Circuit has even held it to be reversible error for a court to decline to engage in fair use analysis simply because the defendant's activities are not on the itemized list.[10]

On the other hand, just because a defendant purports to be engaged in one of the itemized activities does not mean that such a defendant will prevail on a claim of fair use. A teacher should not expect to escape liability under the rubric of "fair use" if he makes two dozen photocopies of a 500 page textbook and distributes one each to every member of his class. An illustration of this principle in action can be found in *Los Angeles News Service v. KCAL–TV Channel 9*.[11] The plaintiff had captured on videotape the beating of Reginald Denny during the rioting in the aftermath of the Rodney King verdict in Los Angeles. The defendant, a TV station, broadcast 30 seconds of the four minute video without obtaining a license from the plaintiff. In the ensuing infringement suit, defendant attempted a fair use defense, pointing out that it was engaged in news reporting, one of the uses mentioned in the preamble to section 107. The district held that the fair use defense applied and granted summary judgment to the defendant. On appeal, the Ninth Circuit reversed, finding that defendant's status as a news reporting entity could be outweighed by other considerations in the case so as to make the fair use defense unavailable.

Many writers have speculated about what the six itemized uses in the preamble have in common. If an underlying theme could be identified, it might be useful in structuring the inquiry under the first fair use factor. Professor Goldstein has noted that all of the itemized uses in the preamble "characteristically involve situations in which the social, political and cultural benefits of the use will outweigh any consequent losses to the copyright proprietor, and in which the time and expense of negotiations ... will often foreclose a negotiated transaction."[12] Profes-

9. Harper & Row Publishers, Inc. v. Nation Enterprises, 471 U.S. 539, 562, 105 S.Ct. 2218, 85 L.Ed.2d 588 (1985).

10. Pacific & Southern Co. v. Duncan, 744 F.2d 1490 (11th Cir.1984).

11. 108 F.3d 1119 (9th Cir.1997), *cert. denied*, 522 U.S. 823, 118 S.Ct. 81, 139 L.Ed.2d 39 (1997).

12. Paul Goldstein, COPYRIGHT § 10.2.1 at 10:19–10:20 (1996).

sor Leaffer points out that all of the listed uses are "productive uses," namely those "that build on the work of others, by adding . . . socially valuable creative elements."[13] The "productive use" idea, sometimes also called "transformative use," seems based on the notion that a defendant who claims the benefit of the fair use defense ought to have contributed in some way to the overall social inventory of literary or artistic products. If the defendant merely engaged in a "reproductive use" by copying plaintiff's work verbatim without adding anything, the argument is that there would be little social benefit to defendant's activities, and thus little reason to excuse the use.

The Supreme Court has vacillated on the importance of "productive use" in the fair use calculus. In *Sony Corp. of America v. Universal City Studios, Inc.*,[14] the Court had to determine whether home videotaping of copyrighted television programming was infringing or protected under the fair use doctrine. In a 5–4 decision, the Court found the practice to be fair use. Home videotaping, of course, is not a productive or transformative use. The home taper does not add material to the tape, manipulate the contents in any way, or create a derivative work. It is a classic "reproductive" use which, on the foregoing logic, ought to be disfavored under the fair use analysis. The *Sony* Court opined, however, that the fair use inquiry is not "rigidly circumscribed" by a productive use requirement, and that while "the distinction between 'productive' and 'unproductive' uses may be helpful in calibrating the balance . . . it cannot be wholly determinative."[15] To fortify the point, the Court cited a number of nonproductive uses that it felt could qualify for the fair use defense, such as "a teacher who copies for the sake of broadening his personal understanding of his specialty . . . a legislator who copies for the sake of broadening her understanding of what her constituents are watching . . . a constituent who copies a news program to help make a decision on how to vote . . . in a hospital setting, using a VTR to enable a patient to see programs he would otherwise miss . . . contributing to the psychological well-being of the patient."[16]

Ten years later, the Supreme Court decided *Campbell v. Acuff–Rose Music, Inc.*[17] The plaintiff in that case owned the copyright to the popular tune *Oh Pretty Woman*. Defendants, the rap group 2 Live Crew, without securing the permission of the plaintiff, prepared an alleged parody version of the song, entitled *Pretty Woman*. Defendant's version, unlike the original, was a rap song, and had substantially different words from the plaintiff's "sweet, not to say syrupy"[18] original, but plainly used much of the original's melody and some of the original's words. When they were sued for infringement, they claimed the protection of the fair use defense for their parody. The issues specific to parody are considered

---

13. Marshall Leaffer, Understanding Copyright Law 430 (3d ed. 1999).

14. 464 U.S. 417, 448, 104 S.Ct. 774, 78 L.Ed.2d 574 (1984).

15. *Id.* at 456, n. 40

16. *Id.*

17. 510 U.S. 569, 114 S.Ct. 1164, 127 L.Ed.2d 500 (1994).

18. Leibovitz v. Paramount Pictures Corp., 948 F.Supp. 1214, 1219 (S.D.N.Y. 1996).

below in section 10.6. For present purposes it is enough to note that the Supreme Court concluded that the fair use defense was valid on these facts and exonerated the defendants.

In contrast to the practice of home taping at issue in Sony, the activities of 2 Live Crew were clearly "transformative." Unlike the passive or purely reproductive conduct of the home video taper, 2 Live Crew added substantially new words to the original tune of plaintiff's work and changed the format from ballad to rap. The *Campbell* Court placed significant reliance on these facts. While it noted that "transformative use is not absolutely necessary for a finding of fair use," it pointed out that "the goal of copyright . . . is generally furthered by the creation of transformative works. . . . [T]he more transformative the new work, the less will be the significance of other factors. . . ."[19] Thus, while the first fair use factor is not "rigidly circumscribed" by a productive use requirement and such a requirement is "not absolutely necessary," *Campbell* suggests that it will be a significant variable in the fair use equation.

Even after *Campbell*, however, the transformative status of a work is not a guarantee that the fair use doctrine is applicable. For instance, in *Castle Rock Entertainment v. Carol Publishing Group*,[20] the defendants had prepared a trivia quiz book called *The Seinfeld Aptitude Test*, based on the popular sitcom *Seinfeld*. Defendant's book included 643 trivia questions about the events and characters depicted in the Seinfeld show, drawing on 84 of the 86 Seinfeld episodes that had been broadcast at the time of publication. Every answer in the book was based on an episode of the show, and dialogue from the program is quoted in 41 of the book's questions. The court found that this was a transformative work, and indeed a work of "comment or criticism" on the Seinfeld show, but nonetheless denied the fair use defense and held the book infringing. The court quite properly reasoned that transformative status alone should not immunize a work from liability because "to hold that the transformative nature of a work automatically shields it from a successful claim would be to reject an unassailable proposition—i.e., that the unauthorized production of a derivative can support a claim for infringement."[21] The court ultimately found defendant's book infringing because of its likely effect on plaintiff's potential market for derivative works, a key issue under the fourth fair use factor.

The "purpose and character of the use" inquiry is not limited to an exploration of the transformative/reproductive dichotomy. The statute itself instructs us to consider "whether such use is of a commercial nature or is for nonprofit education purposes." Consequently, courts have devoted considerable attention to a second dichotomy—the one between commercial and noncommercial uses—as well. The Court in *Sony* placed heavy emphasis on this aspect of the first fair use factor,

---

19. 510 U.S. at 579.

20. 955 F.Supp. 260 (S.D.N.Y.1997), *aff'd*, 150 F.3d 132 (2d Cir.1998).

21. 955 F.Supp. at 268.

relying on the non-commercial nature of home taping as one of the chief reasons for excusing it under the fair use doctrine. By way of contrast, the *Sony* Court suggested that the making of copies for a commercial purpose "would presumptively be unfair." Of course this statement must be considered in light of the purely reproductive, non-transformative type of copying at issue in *Sony*.

Refusing to extend the fair use defense to commercial reproductive copying seems entirely logical. Verbatim copying of a plaintiff's works, combined with commercial motives poses the greatest risk of usurping plaintiff's market and depriving him of an economic reward. That, in turn, poses the threat of undermining incentives for creativity. Moreover, the lack of transformative activity by the defendants tends to reduce the likely social benefit flowing from the activity. With the costs high and the benefits low, there is little reason to label the use "fair." It should therefore be a rare case when a commercial and non-transformative use is excused under the fair use doctrine.

In the years after *Sony* was decided, many lower courts suggested that there was a virtual per se rule against granting the fair use defense to any commercial user, regardless of the other facts and circumstances. Such an interpretation, however, virtually reads the fair use concept right out of the statute. Many uses that seem intuitively within the scope of the fair use concept are nonetheless conducted for profit. News reporting is done primarily by profit-making commercial ventures like magazines, television stations and newspapers. Criticism is often published in similar, commercially oriented publications. Much teaching takes place in commercial trade and vocational schools and much research is conducted at profit making corporations. As one trial judge put it, "publishers of educational textbooks are as profit-motivated as publishers of scandal-mongering tabloid newspapers. And a serious scholar should not be despised and denied the law's protection because he hopes to earn a living through his scholarship. The protection of the statute should not turn on sackcloth and missionary zeal."[22] A blanket rule that denies the fair use defense as soon as a commercial purpose for defendant's conduct is unearthed therefore seems counterintuitive and unworkable.

This concern was addressed and put to rest in the *Campbell* decision. *Campbell* recognized that "if ... commerciality carried presumptive force against a finding of fairness, the presumption would swallow nearly all of the illustrative uses listed in the preamble paragraph of § 107, including news reporting, comment, criticism, teaching, scholarship, and research, since these activities 'are generally conducted for profit in this country.' "[23] Indeed, the defendants' parody in that case was commercial in nature. The Supreme Court nonetheless found them to be fair users, exempt from liability. The *Campbell* Court emphasized

---

22. Salinger v. Random House, Inc., 650 F.Supp. 413, 425 (S.D.N.Y.1986), *rev'd*, 811 F.2d 90 (2d Cir.1987), *cert. denied*, 484 U.S. 890, 108 S.Ct. 213, 98 L.Ed.2d 177 (1987).

23. 510 U.S. at 584. The words in single quotes are from Justice Brennan's dissent in Harper & Row v. The Nation, 471 U.S. 539, 105 S.Ct. 2218, 85 L.Ed.2d 588 (1985).

that *Sony's* discussion of commercial motives was not meant to raise a "hard evidentiary presumption.... *Sony* stands for the proposition that the 'fact that publication was commercial as opposed to nonprofit is a separate factor that tends to weigh against a finding of fair use.' ... But that is all, and the fact that even the force of that tendency will vary with the context is a further reason against elevating commerciality to hard presumptive significance."

Of course, just as *Sony's* views on reproductive use must be considered in the context of the facts before it, so must *Campbell's* views on commercial motives. The *Campbell* Court confronted a transformative use, and one where, because of the parody nature of defendant's activities, it was extremely unlikely that plaintiff would grant permission to use the work at any price. In such a context it is not entirely surprising that the Court did not find the commercial character of defendant's activities controlling.

There is a further problem with both dichotomies considered under the first fair use element. That is the problem of characterization. It is often not at all obvious whether a use should be labeled transformative versus reproductive. The same doubts can arise along the commercial/noncommercial axis. A good illustration of the problem is *Princeton University Press v. Michigan Document Services.*[24] Plaintiffs owned copyrights in a variety of educational and scholarly books. Professors at the University of Michigan selected excerpts from various of these works for inclusion in "coursepacks," and requested a commercial copyshop to mass produce those coursepacks for sale to students. The defendant was one such copyshop, and it produced coursepacks without securing permissions or paying license fees to the plaintiffs. When the plaintiffs sued for copyright infringement, the defendant raised the fair use defense.

Were the activities of the copyshop transformative or reproductive? One could make a case for either categorization. The excepts were copied verbatim, making the use look merely reproductive, but the combination of various works into an anthology format has creative elements that make the activity look arguably transformative. After all, anthologies are a form of compilation which the copyright laws recognize as a species of original authorship. The Sixth Circuit observed that "the inquiry into the transformative aspect of the use assesses the likely benefit to society from the use—the more the original work has been transformed, the more likely it is that a distinct and valuable new product has been created." Here, the benefit to society is not inconsiderable since it enhances education, but the degree of transformation of the work is not overwhelming. The problem is particularly vexing in the context of this case because the preamble of section 107 speaks of "multiple copies for classroom use" when alluding to teaching as an illustration of fair use. The court ultimately resolved this aspect of the first factor against

24. 99 F.3d 1381 (6th Cir.1996) (en banc), *cert. denied*, 520 U.S. 1156, 117 S.Ct. 1336, 137 L.Ed.2d 495 (1997).

defendants, stating "if you make verbatim copies of 95 pages of a 316–page book, you have not transformed the 95 pages very much—even if you juxtapose them to excerpts from other works and package everything conveniently. This kind of mechanical 'transformation' bears little resemblance to the creative metamorphosis accomplished by the parodists in the *Campbell* case."[25] Of course, juxtaposition is a classic form of creative authorship and the court's decision to summarily label it a "mechanical" transformation is frustratingly conclusory.

The same ambiguity surrounds the commercial versus non-commercial categorization of the activities in *Princeton University Press*. The defendant copy shop was a profit making business. That clearly weighs in favor of calling the activities at issue in the case "commercial." Because of the efficiency of its operation, however, it was able to sell the coursepacks for a lower price than if the professor had made the copies at the university and sold them to the students at cost. Moreover, the ultimate use of the material was by students in the purely non-commercial atmosphere of liberal arts courses at the university. In this sense, the ultimate use of the material was "noncommercial." Once again, the court resolved this issue against the defendants, noting that the actual defendant being sued was a for-profit copyshop, and observing that "if the fairness of making copies depends on what the ultimate consumer does with the copies, it is hard to see how the manufacture of pirated editions of any copyrighted work of scholarship could ever be an unfair use."[26]

The facts of *Princeton University Press* illustrate the difficulty of fair use analysis generally and especially of the characterizations required to apply the first fair use factor. The majority[27] may have been persuaded to call the use here commercial and non-transformative because of its concern about the effect the use would have on plaintiff's market for its educational and scholarly books. That concern may be legitimate, but it constitutes a form of double counting, as the effect on the market is supposed to be explicitly considered in the fourth fair use factor.

One final issue that has appeared repeatedly when courts have analyzed the first fair use factor is the relevance of the fact that the defendant requested a license from the plaintiff that was refused. Some courts have reasoned that defendant's request reveals an awareness that the proposed use exceeds the bounds of the permissible. This argument seems to have been put to rest by the Supreme Court in *Campbell*, which stated explicitly that "being denied permission to use a work does not weigh against a finding of fair use."[28] Of course that case involved a parody, and parodists are almost never granted permission. Nonetheless, the statement seems sound as a general rule. No one wants to be sued, even if they are quite confident they can prevail on a fair use defense. It

25. *Id.* at 1389.

26. *Id.* at 1386, n.2.

27. The case was decided by an 8–5 vote of the en banc court, with three of the five dissenters preparing separate opinions.

28. 510 U.S. at 586, n.18.

may be cheaper and less time consuming to secure a license, if plaintiff can be persuaded to grant one at an acceptable price. If permission is denied and defendant nonetheless goes forward, it would be ironic indeed to penalize him "for this modest show of consideration."[29]

10.2.2   Nature of the Work

The second factor instructs us to consider the nature of the copyrighted work. This implies that some works are entitled to a broader scope of protection than others, and that has been the consistent view of the courts. The general rule affords the greatest degree of protection to highly creative works, and the least to works that are factual or practical in nature. The scope of fair use is, of course, reciprocal to the degree of protection. This means that defendants are most likely to succeed on a fair use claim with respect to a factual work, and least likely to succeed where the work is creative. As the Supreme Court recently put it, "[t]his factor calls for recognition that some works are closer to the core of intended copyright protection than others, with the consequence that fair use is more difficult to establish when the former works are copied."[30]

At least one justification for this approach is the general rule that copyright only extends to the original aspects of a work. Works that are primarily factual, like almanacs, statistical tables and the like, contain less original authorship than works of fiction like a novel or stage play. Secondly, the need to reproduce material of a factual nature is often greater than the need to reproduce works of fiction. Consequently, it is appropriate to permit a somewhat broader scope of fair use for works of the former type. Similarly, defendants may be afforded greater latitude to copy from works of an academic or scholarly nature both because it is customary in the academic community to rely heavily on prior academic work and because academic writers may have a strong need to quote extensively from prior work.

Another aspect of the "nature" of plaintiff's work that may bear on fair use analysis is how readily available the work is to the general public. There is language in the legislative history of the 1976 act indicating that fair use should be more liberally applied where copies of the work being copied are difficult or impossible to obtain. As the Committee Report observed "if the work is 'out of print' and unavailable for purchase through normal channels, the user may have more justification for reproducing it than in the ordinary case, but the existence of organizations licensed to provide photocopies of out-of-print works at reasonable cost is a factor to be considered."[31]

29. Fisher v. Dees, 794 F.2d 432, 437 (9th Cir.1986).

30. Campbell v. Acuff–Rose Music, Inc., 510 U.S. 569, 586, 114 S.Ct. 1164, 127 L.Ed.2d 500 (1994). *See also* Harper & Row v. The Nation, 471 U.S. 539, 563, 105 S.Ct. 2218, 85 L.Ed.2d 588 (1985) ("The law generally recognizes a greater need to disseminate factual works than works of fiction or fantasy.").

31. S.Rep. No. 94–473, 94th Cong., 1st Sess. 64 (1965).

Still another aspect of this second factor that has received both judicial and legislative attention is whether plaintiff's work is published or unpublished. Almost by definition, the author of an unpublished work has not yet received any economic reward from the marketing of his work. He may anticipate reaping that reward in the future upon publication of the work and may have chosen to delay so that he can improve the work or wait for a moment when its market value will be at its peak. If another party were to publish the work without permission, that might seriously undermine or totally destroy the author's ability to secure any market reward at all. The effect on incentives for creativity could be considerable. Using a cost-benefit mind set, a defendant should have to make a very strong showing of social benefit in order to overcome the presumed harm to incentives when reproducing unpublished works.

The Supreme Court addressed precisely this point in *Harper & Row, Publishers, Inc. v. Nation Enterprises*.[32] The case involved the memoirs of former President Gerald Ford, prepared after he left office. The most intriguing portions of Ford's book were the sections recounting Ford's decision to pardon his predecessor in office, Richard Nixon, who had resigned under the cloud of the Watergate scandal. Ford had licensed Harper & Row to publish these memoirs, and they, in turn, granted *Time* magazine an exclusive license to publish excerpts of the book one week before the full book was shipped to bookstores. A few weeks before the scheduled publication date, a pirated copy of the manuscript was delivered to a political magazine called *The Nation*. The editors of that publication hastily prepared a story about the book, and arranged to have the manuscript returned to Harper & Row before its absence could be discovered. The *Nation* story quoted only 300 words verbatim from Ford's 200,000–word book. However, one consequence of the *Nation's* actions was that *Time* cancelled its arrangement with Harper & Row, pursuant to its contract. Harper & Row then sued *The Nation* for copyright infringement, and the defendant raised the fair use defense.

The Supreme Court found in favor of Harper & Row and rejected the fair use defense, despite the relatively small amount of material used and the fact that the defendant was purportedly engaged in new reporting. In reaching this result, it put heavy weight on the fact that, at the time of defendant's activities, the plaintiff's work had not yet been published. The Court concluded that "the author's right to control the first public appearance of his expression weighs against such use of the work before its release. The right of first publication encompasses not only the choice whether to publish at all, but also the choices of when, where, and in what form first to publish a work."[33] Quoting from the legislative history of the 1976 Act, the Court stressed that "the unpublished nature of a work is 'a key, though not necessarily determinative, factor' tending to negate a defense of fair use."[34]

32. 471 U.S. 539, 105 S.Ct. 2218, 85 L.Ed.2d 588 (1985).

33. 471 U.S. at 564.

34. Id. at 554.

In the years following the *Harper & Row* decision, however, the lower courts—especially the Second Circuit—tended to afford near conclusive weight to the unpublished status of the work as a basis for denying the fair use defense, despite the "not necessarily determinative" caveat in the Supreme Court's opinion.[35] A per se rule that quoting from unpublished works could never be justified as fair use, however, might significantly hinder the work of historians and biographers who often need to quote from unpublished letters, diaries, and manuscripts of historical or literary figures. One can also imagine the need of news outlets to quote unpublished materials, such as corporate memos, in reporting on instances of public or private corruption. To respond to the growing concern about the direction of the case law, Congress amended the fair use provision of the copyright statute in 1992 to add a new final sentence, reading "the fact that a work is unpublished shall not itself bar a finding of fair use if such finding is made upon consideration of all the above factors."[36] The legislative history of this amendment makes it plain that Congress wanted to ensure that scholars could safely make use of reasonable portions of unpublished materials without being exposed to liability. On the other hand, it is equally clear that the unpublished status of a work will continue to be a significant factor weighing against application of the fair use defense in many situations.

10.2.3   Amount and Substantiality of the Portion Used

The third fair use factor embodies the logical intuition that the more of a work a defendant takes, the more likely the use is to undermine the plaintiff's markets. Consequently extensive takings are less likely to be adjudged fair than more terse borrowings. Courts have often considered the third fair use factor to be closely bound up with the first, which instructs courts to look to the nature and character of the use. As the *Campbell* Court noted "the extent of permissible copying varies with the purpose and character of the use." In the case of parody, fairly extensive copying may be essential to permit the public to recognize the original that the parody is poking fun at. Far less would ordinarily be required for the purposes of a movie review on the evening news.

Moreover, in applying the third factor courts focus not merely on the quantity of material taken, but also on the significance of that material to plaintiff's work as a whole. The inquiry is thus both quantitative and qualitative. An excellent illustration of this is the Supreme Court's decision in *Harper & Row* discussed in the preceding section. In that case, the Nation reproduced only 300 words out of the 200,000 in President Ford's book. The Court nonetheless found that this taking was "substantial" and militated against a finding of fair use, because the

---

35. See e.g., Salinger v. Random House, Inc., 811 F.2d 90 (2d Cir.1987), *cert. denied*, 484 U.S. 890, 108 S.Ct. 213, 98 L.Ed.2d 177 (1987) (no fair use defense available for use of the unpublished letters of author J.D. Salinger in a biography). To the opposite effect, however, is Wright v. Warner Books, 953 F.2d 731 (2d Cir.1991), permitting limited quotations from unpublished letters and journals in a biography.

36. Act of October 24, 1992, Pub.L.No. 102–492, 106 Stat. 3145.

portion taken constituted the very heart of the work, and its appearance in The Nation would quite likely undermine plaintiff's market.

The general principle that animates this factor is that defendants should limit themselves to taking the smallest quantity of plaintiff's work consistent with their own purposes. That will minimize the harm to the copyright owner while still securing the benefits the fair use doctrine was meant to further. If a teacher wants to illustrate the writing style of a contemporary author in a creative writing course, the excerpt should be long enough to provide an adequate illustration, but no longer. If a movie critic wants to show a clip to illustrate his claim that the dialogue of the movie is infantile and unbelievable, the clip should be limited to the length necessary to make the point. When the taking exceeds such limits, it begins to harm the plaintiff without enhancing the social benefit that comes from the defendants activities.

10.2.4 Effect on the Market

The fourth fair use factor directs courts to consider the effect of defendant's use on the potential market for plaintiff's work. The Supreme Court has declared that this factor is "undoubtedly the single most important element of fair use,"[37] and this theme has been echoed repeatedly by the lower courts. This is only logical. If defendant's conduct causes significant numbers of people to refrain from paying for access to the plaintiff's work, that could destroy the very incentives that are at the heart of the copyright system. Such a use should rarely, if ever, be labeled "fair." In applying this factor, a court is supposed to consider not only the market effects of this particular defendant's conduct, but the market implications if the defendant's conduct were to become widely engaged in by others.[38] Moreover, the focus is not merely on the current markets for plaintiff's work, but must consider the consequences in potential markets that the plaintiff-copyright owner may not yet have exploited.

Consideration of potential markets is logically part of the market assessment required by the fair use doctrine because the copyright statute assigns to the copyright owner the exclusive right to make derivative works. The fact that a defendant acts more promptly than the plaintiff in exploiting a particular derivative market should not, by itself, deprive that plaintiff of the statutory adaptation right. To put the point more concretely, it would be odd indeed if a defendant could make a movie based on a copyrighted novel without the permission of the copyright owner, and then invoke the fair use defense on the grounds that the movie will not cut into the sales of the novel, but may even boost them! While that may be true, the activities of such a defendant surely interfere with the copyright owner's rights to profit from deriva-

---

37. Harper & Row v. The Nation, 471 U.S. 539, 566, 105 S.Ct. 2218, 85 L.Ed.2d 588 (1985).

38. To negate fair use one need only show that if the challenged use "should become widespread, it would adversely affect the potential market for the copyrighted work." Sony v. Universal City Studios, 464 U.S. 417, 451, 104 S.Ct. 774, 78 L.Ed.2d 574 (1984).

tive works in the form of motion pictures. The inapplicability of fair use to cases such as these is even more apparent when we remember that copyright owners often delay in producing derivative works for strategic reasons, hoping to bring the derivative work to the market at what they consider to be the optimum moment. Thus, the fact that the copyright owner has not yet licensed movie rights is not necessarily evidence of any lack of interest in doing so in the future.

On the other hand, as many litigants, courts and commentators have noted, this fourth factor, with its focus on potential markets, can degenerate into entirely circular reasoning. In a sense, every use affects a "potential" market for the work. For instance, copyright owners might wish to charge book reviewers a fee for using brief quotations from published books in their book reviews. When the shocked reviewers protest that such use should be protected under the fair use doctrine, the copyright owners could point to the fourth factor and claim that the uncompensated use of quotes adversely affects the "potential" market for "quotation royalties" that they hope to establish, and that it should therefore be held outside the scope of fair use. To put the proposition the other way around, the application of the fair use defense to this practice forecloses any such quotation royalty revenues, and the practice of quoting without getting permission thus has an effect on the "potential market" of licensing such quotes.[39]

This circularity problem is rendered even more complex because the advance of technology makes it possible for copyright owners to develop methods for charging for uses that until recently were impossible to monitor and economically exploit. Twenty years ago it might have been unthinkable to imagine a workable licensing system that could be used to charge for the use of brief quotations in newspaper reviews of newly published books. The advent of virtually instantaneous electronic communication via e-mail, secure methods of on-line payment of fees, comprehensive computer data bases and the availability of the text of many major newspapers on-line might combine to make such a system much more plausible today.

In 1994, a panel of the Second Circuit in *American Geophysical Union v. Texaco Inc.*[40] suggested, over a dissent, that such changes in the ability of copyright owners to collect fees are a significant factor in denying the fair use defense.[41] This seems particularly curious. The fair use defense would mean very little if it only covered those uses that plaintiffs have not yet figured out how to charge for. We want reviewers, teachers, reporters, parodists and scholars to have at least some degree

39. See e.g., Williams & Wilkins Co. v. United States, 487 F.2d 1345 (Ct.Cl.1973), *aff'd by an equally divided Court*, 420 U.S. 376, 95 S.Ct. 1344, 43 L.Ed.2d 264 (1975) ("It is wrong to measure the detriment to plaintiff by loss of presumed royalty income—a standard which necessarily assumed that plaintiff had a right to issue licenses. That would be true, of course, only if it were first decided that the defendant's practices did not constitute 'fair use.' In determining whether the company has been sufficiently hurt to cause these practices to become 'unfair' one cannot assume at the start the merit of plaintiff's position....").

40. 60 F.3d 913 (2d Cir.1994).

41. *Id.* at 929–30.

of free access to copyrighted works not merely as a concession to the practical limits of the copyright owners' abilities to force them to pay. There is a broad consensus that most of these uses promote the common good. Demanding that copyright owners allow such uses without complaint or demand for payment could also be considered a *quid pro quo* for the more general protections afforded by the copyright statute against wholesale copying. Regardless of technical feasibility it is almost unseemly to demand payment for uses of this nature.

To escape from this circularly, the Supreme Court has noted that "the market for potential derivative uses includes only those that creators of original works would in general develop or license others to develop."[42] Similarly, the *American Geophysical* court suggested that inquiry under the fourth factor should be limited to "traditional, reasonable, or likely to be developed markets. ..."[43] For example, it is traditional for movies to be made from novels. If a defendant makes an unauthorized movie version of plaintiff's copyrighted book, that activity will plainly affect a *traditional* potential market, even though the plaintiff may not yet have taken any steps to sell the movie rights to the novel. On the other hand, copyright owners have never attempted to charge reviewers who seek only to quote brief passages from books. Even if a copyright owner claimed an intention to do so in the future, that would not be a traditional market for the work. Of course, one need not be a Holmes or Brandeis to realize that the "traditional, reasonable, or likely to be developed" formula is itself vague and that there is no clear way to discern when a given market is traditional or reasonable. For instance, until recently it would not have been traditional to license a novel for use as the basis of a video game, but that is surely more a function of the novelty of video games than of any lack of interest in such a market by authors.

Professor Nimmer has suggested that the solution lies in what he calls a functional approach.[44] Under this test, "if regardless of medium, the defendant's work, although containing substantially similar material, performs a different function than that of the plaintiff's, the defense of fair use may be invoked."[45] As an illustration of the principle, Nimmer cites a number of cases where the reproduction of song lyrics in magazines was held to be fair use. Nimmer explains the results by noting that "the functions differed in that plaintiff's sheet music was intended to be used for singing or musical performances, while defendant's article was a literary presentation that incidentally included the disputed lyrics. Persons interested in obtaining plaintiff's music for musical purposes would not find that need fulfilled through the purchase of defendant's magazine article." He makes a similar point with respect to the different functions fulfilled by books and book reviews that quote from those

42. Campbell v. Acuff–Rose Music, Inc., 510 U.S. 569, 592, 114 S.Ct. 1164, 127 L.Ed.2d 500 (1994).

43. American Geophysical Union v. Texaco Inc., 60 F.3d 913, 930 (2d Cir.1994), *cert. dismissed,* 516 U.S. 1005, 116 S.Ct. 592, 133 L.Ed.2d 486 (1995).

44. NIMMER, COPYRIGHT, § 13.03[B] (2002).

45. *Id.*

books. While Nimmer's functional test has only been invoked by name in a relatively few cases, it does seem a helpful way to determine which potential markets are properly considered under the fourth fair use factor.

Of course the difficulties that surround application of the "effect on the market" factor vary with the type of situation confronting a court. It is possible to identify three categories of cases. In the first, the defendant's use is directly competitive with the plaintiff's work. Here, the effect on the market can usually be measured in a straightforward way, typically dependant on the amount of the work used and whether the use is commercial in nature. Where the defendant has instead used some or all of plaintiff's work to make a derivative work, the next question should be whether the derivative work in question is a customary or regularly exploited type of derivative for the category of underlying work in question, regardless of whether this particular plaintiff has yet chosen to pursue the market. Examples would include the market for movie versions of novels, and the market for posters depicting one-of-a-kind pictorial and graphic works. In cases such as these, the effect on a potential market can again be assessed based on the quantity of the work used and whether the use is commercial in nature.

It is the final category of cases that poses the real difficulty of circularity. Those are cases where the defendant's derivative work is in a market not customarily or regularly exploited, and one which this particular plaintiff cannot prove he had concrete plans to enter in the foreseeable future. In cases of this sort the fair use dispute is really about whether the plaintiff should be guaranteed the exclusive right to exploit that market in question despite the fact that the market opportunity was not generally recognized or appreciated until the defendant came along.

It seems best to attempt to resolve this difficult case by referring back to the basic trade-offs that animate the fair use defense and copyright law generally. The question in these cases should be recast as whether the defendant's use is likely to undermine incentives to a degree more significant than the social benefits realized from the use in question. If the plaintiff's work has already been highly successful, allowing the defendant who first unearthed the heretofore unexploited derivative use to go forward unmolested is unlikely to undermine either the incentives of this particular plaintiff or those of others similarly situated. Moreover, the suggested approach acts as an incentive to others, encouraging them to invent new ways to use and disseminate works.

For instance, re-consider *Castle Rock Entertainment v. Carol Publishing Group*.[46] In that case defendant prepared a quiz book based on defendant's sitcom. Although the court considered the book to contain creative elements of its own and labeled it a work of criticism, it nonetheless denied the fair use defense. Such books, however, are not customary derivative works associated with even highly popular televi-

46. 955 F.Supp. 260 (S.D.N.Y.1997), aff'd, *150 F.3d 132 (2d Cir.1998).*

sion shows. Moreover the court described plaintiff's production of any such books as a "remote possibility." While allowing the defendant the right to go forward under the fair use defense would deprive plaintiff of potential revenue from the quiz book market, the loss of such revenues seems highly unlikely to undermine incentives for the production of television shows in the future. The desire to create the next *Seinfeld* is surely enough to motivate screenplay writers even if they know, up front, that they will be denied revenue from the hypothetical quiz book market down the road if the show is a blockbuster hit. On the other hand, if one accepts the court's own characterization, the defendant's work was a creative work of criticism, which presumably implicates a non-trivial degree of social benefit. Thus, the "harm to potential market" factor here should have been counted in favor of the defendant. Of course, if the other factors point heavily in the opposite direction, the court may still conclude that fair use is inappropriate.

§ 10.3   Fair Use and Photocopying

The problem of photocopying was very much in the minds of the authors of the 1976 Act. Effective and inexpensive photocopiers had become widely available in the years leading up to the adoption of the new statute and copyright owners lobbied hard for provisions that would ensure their markets would not be destroyed by the use of this new technology. One context where this problem was particularly important was education, given the almost irresistible tendency for teachers to photocopy and distribute materials to their students. The text of section 107 alludes to that problem by including, in the preamble, the phrase "multiple copies for classroom use" in the list of illustrative fair uses. Moreover, even though such uses are reproductive rather than transformative, leading one to assume that they would be disfavored under the first listed factor, the Supreme Court in *Campbell* noted that "[t]he obvious statutory exception to this focus on transformative uses is the straight reproduction of multiple copies for classroom distribution."[1]

Congress did not intend, however, to give carte blanche permission for educational copying. That would make it impossible for the authors and publishers of textbooks to earn any profits for their work, destroying incentives and ultimately impoverishing education. The question was where to draw the lines between permissible and impermissible educational copying. Rather than dealing with the problem directly in the statutory text, the Congress left representatives of copyright owners and the educational community to their own devices to develop a solution. The result was a document entitled *Agreement on Guidelines for Classroom Copying in Not-for-Profit Educational Institutions*. The document was incorporated in the report of the Judiciary Committee of the House of Representatives on the bill that ultimately became the Copyright Act of 1976.[2] It deals only with copying from printed sources such as books

---

§ 10.3

1. *Id.* at 579, n.11

2. H.R. Rep. No. 94–1476, 94th Cong., 2d Sess. 68–70 (1976). Interestingly, both

and periodicals, and does not address at all the copying of musical or audiovisual works for educational purposes. Those matters are dealt with in separate guideline documents.[3] The Classroom Copying Guidelines are meant to provide a safe harbor. Staying within the limits specified by the Guidelines should ensure that a teacher cannot be held liable for infringement by virtue of her classroom copying, although technically the Guidelines are not binding on courts, and even copying within their limits could theoretically be held infringing by an unusually zealous court. Conversely, copying more than the amounts specified, or under conditions different than those specified can still qualify as fair use, based on the traditional analysis of the fair use factors, because the guidelines represent only minimum standards of fair use.[4]

The first section of the Guidelines covers copying by teachers for their own use—such as when a teacher photocopies a newspaper article for later review in connection with the preparation of a lesson plan. The second section addresses the making of multiple copies for classroom use. In order to come within the guidelines, the teacher must meet tests of (1) brevity, (2) spontaneity, and (3) cumulative effect. The Guidelines also require each copy distributed to students to bear a notice of copyright, but the continued force of that requirement is questionable since 1989, when copyright notice was essentially made optional for all purposes.

The brevity test is satisfied when the teacher stays within certain bright line quantitative limits set out in the Guidelines, such as "an excerpt from any prose work of not more than 1,000 words or 10% of the work, whichever is less." The spontaneity test requires that "the copying is at the instance and inspiration of the individual teacher and ... the inspiration and decision to use the work and moment of its use for maximum teaching effectiveness are so close in time that it would be unreasonable to expect a timely reply to a request for permission." Under this test, if, during the summer, a teacher comes across copyrighted material that might be useful in an upcoming class to be taught the following fall, he could not safely rely on the Guidelines since there would be ample time to secure permission before the start of school in September. Also, a teacher who has used a given excerpt once without permission could not use it in subsequent semesters under the Guidelines since, by definition, there would be sufficient time to obtain permission. As Professor Nimmer has wryly observed, the brevity requirements "would seem to place a premium on lack of advance preparation of course materials."[5]

the American Association of University Professors and the Association of American Law Schools (the professional organization of law professors) did not agree to these guidelines because they were, in its view, "too restrictive with respect to classroom situations at the university and graduate level." *Id.* at 72.

3. The music guidelines appear at H.R. Rep. No. 94–1476, 94th Cong., 2d Sess. 70–74 (1976) and Guidelines for Off–Air Taping of copyrighted Works for Educational Use appear at H.R. Rep. No. 97–495, 97th Cong., 2d Sess. (1982).

4. Marcus v. Rowley, 695 F.2d 1171, 1178 (9th Cir.1983).

5. NIMMER, COPYRIGHT § 13.05[E][3][d]

With the advent of e-mail and the Internet, where permission to use copyrighted material can potentially be obtained within a matter of minutes, the spontaneity requirements of the classroom guidelines, read literally, might deny the fair use privilege to virtually all 21st century classroom copying. This is obviously a development that none of the parties who negotiated the Guidelines contemplated, and it suggests that their continued vitality should be a matter of some skepticism. The third test, relating to cumulative effects, limits the number of excerpts that may be copied from the same author; the number of times the same teacher can make classroom copies during each term, and requires that the copies be for only one course in the school.

Anyone who has been even moderately awake in a classroom will appreciate that many teachers engage in photocopying that exceeds the scope of the Guidelines. Excerpts are often much longer than permitted, they are often used over and over again each semester without any effort to secure permission and certain teachers use classroom copies very extensively in violation of the cumulative effects rules in the Guidelines. One might explain this situation in a number of ways. Many teachers may not be aware of the Guidelines. Others may feel that there is little likelihood their activities will come to the attention of the copyright owners, and that any harm suffered by those owners would be virtually zero. Still others might believe that although their activities exceed the Guidelines, they are nonetheless fair use under the general approach of section 107.

It would seem that the case for fair use outside the Guidelines would be stronger for materials that are not designed primarily for a classroom audience, and weaker for those that are. Thus, if a teacher copies a lengthy magazine article from *Newsweek* or *Time* about the exploration of Mars and uses it every semester over a period of three years, the activity probably violates the Guideline tests of brevity and spontaneity. However, the character and purpose of the teacher's use is noncommercial and specifically referenced in the preamble to section 107; the nature of plaintiff's work is at least partially factual in nature; and the effect on the potential market is not likely to be significant (though to be sure, there is obviously an effect on the market for post-publication reprint licensing revenues). On the other hand if the teacher copies and distributes 30 pages of an astronomy text instead, the market effect will likely be much greater because there will be less likelihood that students will be required to buy the book and case for fair use should be correspondingly less.[6] Along these lines two recent cases have held that the photocopying by outside copyshops of significant excerpts from multiple

(2002).

6. Thus in Wihtol v. Crow, 309 F.2d 777 (8th Cir.1962), decided under the 1909 Act and prior to the promulgation of the Classroom Copying Guidelines, the defendant teacher made 48 copies of the entirety of a song and distributed them to the school choir. The court found that the activity was not fair use and held the teacher liable for infringement.

academic works so as to create new anthologies was not protected by fair use and thus infringing.[7]

Another aspect of the photocopying conundrum involves libraries and the degree to which they may make photocopies both for their own purposes or for the use of library patrons. Rather than leave the question of library copying to the relatively vague provisions of the fair use doctrine, Congress addressed it specifically in section 108, which spells out rather precisely the scope of permissible library copying. Because the contours of section 108 do not involve fair use, but rather involve a direct limitation of the reproduction rights of copyright owners, we have discussed the mechanics of that section earlier, in Chapter 7 of this treatise. If a given library engages in photocopying beyond the scope of section 108, it remains free to attempt to justify that copying under the more general provisions of section 107 fair use.

A final context in which the fair use status of photocopying activities should be considered is copying, particularly of copyrighted journal articles, by corporate research departments, hospitals, law firms and other intellectually oriented institutions. When such an enterprise subscribes to only a few copies of a journal and then makes copies of those journals, or selected articles appearing in them, for wider circulation to members of its staff, the copyright owners lose sales to effectively their only real audience for the work. In *Williams & Wilkins Co. v. United States*[8] a publisher of medical journals sued the U.S. government for photocopying taking place at the National Institutes of Health (NIH). The NIH subscribed to only one or two copies of each journal and then routinely made copies of journal articles for researchers who requested them. The total extent of copying was several million pages per year. The Court of Claims found the activity to be fair use, suggesting that a contrary result might be harmful to medical research and indicating that the problem was one which "calls fundamentally for legislative solution." A dissenting judge described the opinion as "the Dred Scott decision of copyright law" and while the Supreme Court agreed to review the case, it deadlocked on a 4–4 vote, Justice Blackmun not participating, leaving the lower court opinion standing. The *Williams & Wilkins* opinion has been sharply criticized by Professor Nimmer and others for failing to adequately safeguard copyright owners against the threats to their economic interests posed by photocopying technology.

By way of contrast, in the more recent case of *American Geophysical Union v. Texaco Inc.*[9] There, the Second Circuit found, that a similar practice of systematic copying of journal articles by the research department of Texaco, a for-profit business, did not constitute fair use. The *American Geophysical* court was heavily influenced by the fact that in

7. Basic Books v. Kinko's Graphics Corp., 758 F.Supp. 1522 (S.D.N.Y.1991); Princeton University Press v. Michigan Document Services, 99 F.3d 1381 (6th Cir. 1996) (en banc), *cert. denied*, 520 U.S. 1156, 117 S.Ct. 1336, 137 L.Ed.2d 495.

8. 487 F.2d 1345 (Ct.Cl.1973), *aff'd by an equally divided court*, 420 U.S. 376, 95 S.Ct. 1344, 43 L.Ed.2d 264 (1975).

9. 60 F.3d 913 (2d Cir.1994), *cert. dismissed*, 516 U.S. 1005, 116 S.Ct. 592, 133 L.Ed.2d 486 (1995).

the years since the decision in *Williams & Wilkins* a system of convenient licensing had been developed. That system, administered by the Copyright Clearance Center (CCC), provides a centralized location to which fees can be paid avoiding the transaction costs associated with contacting the copyright owners of hundreds of different journal articles. Based on a statistical model, the CCC offers users the option of paying a flat annual licensing fee for the privilege of "all you can eat" copying from works registered with the CCC. In the court's view the availability of this system made all the difference. As the *American Geophysical* court observed "it is not unsound to conclude that the right to seek payment for a particular use tends to become legally cognizable under the fourth fair use factor when the means for paying for such a use is made easier. This notion is not inherently troubling: it is sensible that a particular unauthorized use should be considered "more fair" when there is no ready market or means to pay for the use, while such an unauthorized use should be considered "less fair" when there is a ready market or means to pay for the use.[10]

On the other hand, just because copyright owners figure out a way to charge for a particular type of use and can persuade or intimidate some significant portion of users to go along with the system, that should not automatically conclude the fair use inquiry merely on the grounds of lost revenue. If the CCC developed a system of charging for brief excerpts in book reviews, under which entities like the New York Times could pay a flat fee each year for the privilege of quoting from as many books as they liked in such reviews, there would still be strong public policy reasons to allow such quotation free of charge under the fair use defense. It is inconsistent with the free exchange of ideas that copyright law is supposed to promote to suppose that those who wish to comment on the works of others should have to pay those others tribute in order to do so.

§ 10.4　Fair Use and Home Taping

The recent proliferation of devices such as recordable DVD players, MP3 players, broad-band Internet connections and older technologies like dual-deck cassette tape recorders and home video players has made home copying of copyrighted material virtually effortless. These technologies have opened up a veritable Pandora's box of problems in the application of the fair use doctrine. The march of technology has repeatedly forced the courts and Congress to confront the question of just how much private copying should be acceptable under the fair use doctrine.

The facet of the problem involving home videotaping of copyrighted material broadcast for free home viewing via television was resolved by the Supreme Court in *Sony Corp. of America v. Universal City Studios*[1],

---

10.　60 F.3d at 930–31.

1.　464 U.S. 417, 104 S.Ct. 774, 78 L.Ed.2d 574 (1984).

which was discussed above in the connection with the first fair use factor. Universal, the plaintiff in that case, was the owner of copyrights on certain programs broadcast on TV. It sued Sony on a theory of contributory infringement. It alleged that Sony's sale of videocassette recorders was done with the knowledge that home viewers were using the machines to make copies of copyrighted works in violation of the its reproduction rights.[2] Of course, in order for Sony to be liable under this theory, the activities of the home viewers had to be infringing. Sony argued that home taping could not be infringing because it was protected under the fair use defense. The Court sided with Sony, though the result was on a close 5–4 vote with a strong dissent by Justice Blackmun.

The majority concluded that home taping was primarily for "time shifting" purposes, meaning that people did it so that they could watch their favorite programs at hours other than the times that they were broadcast. The court felt that the non-commercial nature of the activity minimized the market effect, and that the plaintiff had failed to make a sufficient evidentiary showing of harm from the activity.

One might wonder what sort of remedy might have been imposed if the case had come out the other way. After all, individual suits against millions of home tapers to secure injunctions that would themselves be virtually impossible to enforce would not be a very practical solution. More plausible would have been an injunction forbidding Sony and other VCR manufacturers from making machines with taping capacity. This would have solved the problem, but at the cost of repressing a valuable new technology. Alternatively, the court might have imposed a royalty on each VCR sold—or for that matter on each blank cassette tape sold—with the money going into a fund to be distributed amongst the affected copyright holders. This resembles the situation in a number of European countries.[3] While this solution has a rough equitable appeal, it calls for a series of complex determinations better suited for legislative than judicial resolution. The majority opinion of Justice Stevens recognizes this point, observing that "it may well be that Congress will take a fresh look at this new technology, just as it so often has examined other innovations in the past. But it is not our job to apply laws that have not yet been written."

Congress declined the invitation to address home videotaping, so *Sony* remains the last word, making it clear that noncommercial home videotaping, at least for "time shifting" purposes, is protected as fair use. The case, however, did not have any occasion to deal with the issue of home *audio* taping, a related and highly significant issue. To understate matters somewhat, it is not unheard of for music fans to borrow a CD from a friend or family member and make a cassette or "burn a CD" for themselves, or to buy a CD and make a second copy on cassette for the car, or to record music as it is broadcast over the radio. Some people

---

2. *See supra* § 9.4.

3. *See* Don E. Tomlinson & Timothy Nielander, *Red Apples and Green Persimmons: A Comparative Analysis of Audio* *Home–Recording Royalty Laws in the United States and Abroad*, 20 Miss. Coll. L. Rev. 5 (1999).

have even been known to download music over the Internet. All these practices raise issues similar to those considered in *Sony*. Unlike the videotaping problem, however, audio-taping has been addressed primarily by Congress, rather than the courts.

Prior to 1972, sound recordings were not protected by copyright in the United States. Thus anyone could copy them without violating the rights of the party who prepared the sound recording. Under this state of the law, record piracy flourished. While duplication of sound recordings did implicate the copyright interests of the holder of copyright in the underlying musical composition, those rights were subject to a compulsory license.[4] Consequently, it was perfectly legal to make unauthorized duplicates of hit albums, provided only that the compulsory license fees were paid for use of the musical composition.

To rectify the situation, Congress amended the copyright act in 1971 to bring sound recordings within the scope of its protection.[5] The issue of home taping was not a primary concern of this legislation, but the legislative history did address the problem, noting "it is not the intention ... to restrain the home recording, from broadcast or from tapes or records, of recorded performances, where home recording is for the private use and with no purpose of reproducing or otherwise capitalizing commercially on it."[6] Of course, only a few years later Congress adopted the 1976 Act, which thoroughly overhauled all of copyright law. Neither the text of the 1976 Act nor its legislative history made any specific reference to the problem of home audio-taping, leading to uncertainty over the continued vitality of the quoted passage from the legislative history of the 1971 statute.

When Congress expressed its views on home audio-taping in 1971, home audio-taping was a relatively minor problem. Audio cassettes and convenient cassette decks were only about 7 or 8 years old, and the sound quality of a homemade tape was nowhere near comparable to that available on commercially produced records. With the march of technology, that situation changed. By the early 1990's the advent of digital recording technology made it possible for homemade tapes to essentially duplicate the quality of commercial CD's. By the late 1990's burnable CD's provide near perfect audio copies.

The recording industry recognized that this posed a serious threat to its financial interests. Once someone bought a CD and lent it to a friend to be digitally copied, that digital copy could be lent to still other friends and so on and so on, ad infinitum. A single CD sale could displace dozens of additional sales down the road. To stave off this situation, the recording industry once again appealed to Congress, and it responded

4. *See supra* § 7.1.2.

5. Pub. L. No. 92–140, 85 Stat. 391 (1971) (codified as amended at 17 U.S.C.A. § 102(7) and other scattered sections).

6. H.R. Rep. No. 487, 92d Cong., 1st Sess. at 7.

with a new piece of legislation called the Audio Home Recording Act (AHRA).[7]

The AHRA, codified as Chapter 10 of Title 17 of the U.S. Code, has two principal features. First, manufacturers of digital audio recording devices were legally obliged to equip them with a "serial copy management system" or SCMS. SCMS prevents making a copy of a copy. Thus home users would be physically able to make a high quality digital copy of an original store-bought CD, including one borrowed from a friend, but would be unable to copy a copy of that CD previously made by a friend. This prevents the problem of each privately made copy becoming a master for still further copying down the line. Second, AHRA imposed a royalty fee on the sale of digital audio devices, the proceeds of which are to be divided among sound recording copyright owners.

In addition, the statute deals specifically with the issue of home audio-taping by providing that: "No action may be brought under this title alleging infringement of copyright based on the manufacture, importation or distribution of a digital audio recording device, a digital audio recording medium, an analog recording device, or an analog recording medium, or based on the noncommercial use by a consumer of such device or medium for making digital musical recordings or analog musical recordings."[8] The provision thus specifically immunizes home taping, whether accomplished with digital equipment or with older devices such as an ordinary cassette deck or even reel-to-reel tape. The legislative history makes this point plain, stating: "In the case of home taping, the exemption protects all noncommercial copying by consumers of digital and analog musical recordings. Manufacturers, importers, and distributors of digital and analog recording devices and media have a complete exemption from copyright infringement claims based on the manufacture, importation, or distribution of such devices and media."[9]

The AHRA is a narrowly worded statute that has not aged well. All of the parties involved in the drafting of the AHRA focused upon digital audio taping—a technology that was quickly superseded by subsequent industrial advances. A principal problem is that AHRA applies only to recording devices that are primarily marketed or designed to copy music.[10] Most home taping of music at the dawn of the 21st century, however, is done on home computers connected to the Internet. Because home computers perform a great number of tasks in addition to copying recordings, they do not fall within the definition of "digital audio recording devices" in AHRA. This means that the most significant disputes involving file swapping and music downloading are simply unaddressed by this legislation. Absent congressional amendment, the AHRA will likely serve as little more than an historical illustration of the continuing challenge the digital revolution has posed for the modern music industry.

7. Pub. L. 102–563, 106 Stat. 4244.

8. 17 U.S.C.A. § 1008.

9. H.R. Rep. No. 102–873(I), at 18 (1992).

10. 17 U.S.C.A. § 1001(3).

§ 10.5   Fair Use and Computers

Just as the widespread use and exploitation of computers has caused problems for copyright law in other areas, it has lead to some troublesome questions under the fair use doctrine as well. One of these concerns the problem of "reverse engineering." Often, in order to develop a software program that can successfully compete with an existing product, a firm must be able to review the specific program code of the existing product. The developer may have the perfectly legitimate goal of learning about the unprotectable ideas that make the program work with no intention of ultimately copying the code that constitutes the protected expression in that program. This, however, poses a problem.

Publicly distributed versions of computer programs are usually in forms that are not humanly readable. First, they are on media such as floppy disks or CD's, and second, they are usually distributed in the form of binary object code—a series of ones and zeros—that are nearly incomprehensible to all but the most extreme computer nerds. A competitor could, of course, run the program through a computer, which can be instructed to convert the program back to a source code form that is comprehensible to human beings (a process known as decompilation) and to display the results on the computer screen. The problem is that courts have repeatedly held that loading a program into memory constitutes making a copy of that program, and the decompilation may even constitute the preparation of a derivative work because it is a translation of sorts. Thus, anyone seeking to study a software program to gain access to its underlying ideas would be in violation of the copyright owner's reproduction rights unless decompilation and loading into memory are held to be within the fair use defense.

When the Ninth Circuit was confronted with just this problem in *Sega Enterprises Ltd. v. Accolade, Inc.*,[1] it held the fair use defense to be applicable. Sega, of course, is a maker of the Genesis game system, which includes a console and game cartridges. Accolade wanted to make its own game cartridges that would run on the Sega console, but this required the software in the Accolade game to be compatible with the Sega system. To do that "Accolade ... 'reverse engineered' Sega's video game programs in order to discover the requirements for compatibility with the Genesis console. As part of the reverse engineering process ... Accolade purchased a Genesis console and three Sega game cartridges, wired a decompiler into the console circuitry, and generated printouts of the resulting source code. Accolade engineers studied and annotated the printouts in order to identify areas of commonality among the three game programs. They then loaded the disassembled code back into a computer, and experimented to discover the interface specifications for the Genesis console by modifying the programs and studying the results."[2]

---

§ **10.5**

1. 977 F.2d 1510 (9th Cir.1992).

2. 977 F.2d at 1515.

The *Accolade* court conducted a conventional fair use analysis, considering each of the four statutory factors. On the first factor, the character of defendant's use, it noted that while Accolade's ultimate purposes were commercial, the immediate purpose of its reverse engineering activity was for study, and no other method for studying Sega programs was available. The court also seemed swayed by the transformative nature of Accolade's activities, noting that it served to increase the number of games available for use with the Sega consol. Insofar as factor two, the nature of the copyrighted work, the court characterized a computer program as a utilitarian work, with many features dictated by functional rather than aesthetic considerations. It noted that unlike other works, where the underlying ideas that animate the work are readily accessible to the human eye, the ideas of a computer program are only accessible after decompilation, and found that this too cut in favor of fair use. Turning to the third factor, the court recognized that Accolade had copied the entirety of Sega's program when it made its decompiled transcripts, but gave that fact little weight because in the ultimate Accolade product, only minimal amounts of plaintiff's work were used. Finally, as to the effect on the market, the court found that while Accolade's games might compete with Sega's in the generic sense, they would not "usurp" the market for any particular game. As they put it, "there is no basis for assuming that Accolade's 'Ishido' has significantly affected the market for Sega's 'Altered Beast,' since a consumer might easily purchase both."

The opinion in *Accolade* seems a sensible accommodation to the realities of computer technology. Without reverse engineering competition in software would undoubtedly be stifled. Reverse engineering, in turn, cannot be accomplished without making at least one copy of the work. It seems entirely appropriate to characterize copying for reverse engineering purposes as a fair use to promote competition, and to ensure that computer programmers have the same access to a fund of common ideas as novelists, poets, architects and choreographers.

10.5.1   Fair Use and File Swapping

The fair use privilege took central stage in one of the most notorious and vigorously contested copyright showdowns in recent years, *A & M Records v. Napster*.[3] The well-known *Napster* litigation involved a "peer-to-peer" system that allow users to swap computer files storing audio recordings. These files were encoded in a digital format known "MP3." The Napster system allowed Internet users to make MP3 files stored on their computer hard drives available to others for download. The Napster software continuously updated links to millions of MP3 files and also facilitated the ready identification, copying and distribution of those files through what amounted to a massive and easily searched index of music files. Because the Napster software was easy to use and attracted

---

3.   239 F.3d 1004 (9th Cir.2001).

so many users, participants could readily access and copy millions of digitally encoded sound recordings.

Members of the music industry brought suit against Napster, claiming that by offering software that allowed users to exchange pirated music, Napster was liable for contributory and vicarious infringement of copyright. Among Napster's defenses was the fair use privilege. Napster urged that its software, like the VCR at issue in *Sony Corp. of America v. Universal City Studios, Inc.*,[4] was capable of substantial non-infringing uses. Napster cited as examples the exchange of both public domain songs as well as authorized samples of protected works. Napster also explained that its users often downloaded songs they already had purchased on audio CD, thereby "space shifting" (from storage on a CD to storage on a computer hard drive) in an effort to create a compelling analogy to the successful "time shifting" argument in *Sony v. Universal.* According to Napster, space shifting was a legitimate use under the fair use principles established in the *Sony v. Universal* case.

The district court rejected Napster's fair use argument, and on appeal the Court of Appeals for the Ninth Circuit affirmed.[5] In applying the first of the four fair use factors, the purpose and character of the use, the Ninth Circuit concluded that the use was not "transformative" and was sufficiently commercial to weigh in favor of infringement. It said the use could not be considered personal in a situation where host users were distributing their music files to anonymous requesters, rather than friends, and that Napster users were receiving for free something they would ordinarily have to buy.

Turning to the second fair use factor, the nature of the plaintiffs' works, the court noted that musical compositions and recordings were clearly creative in nature. This holding cut against a conclusion of fair use. As to the third fair use factor, the portion of the copyrighted work used, the court reasoned that Napster users ordinarily copied the entire work. This conclusion also suggested that the fair use privilege did not apply.

The Ninth Circuit agreed with plaintiffs that the fourth fair use factor, the effect of Napster upon the market for the copyrighted works, also weighed against a finding of fair use. The Ninth Circuit upheld the district court's findings that Napster would have a deleterious effect upon the present and future digital download market. The court sustained the finding that Napster led to reduced purchases of CDs by college students and raised barriers to entry into the market for the digital downloading of music.

The court then turned its attention to two particular sorts of uses, sampling and "space-shifting," that Napster claimed were wrongly excluded as fair uses. Napster first claimed that some of its users downloaded MP3 files in order to sample the music before making a purchase. The Court of Appeals rejected the contention that sampling constituted a

4. 464 U.S. 417, 448, 104 S.Ct. 774, 78 L.Ed.2d 574 (1984).

5. A & M Records, Inc. v. Napster, Inc., 239 F.3d 1004 (9th Cir.2001).

fair use, however. According to the Ninth Circuit, the more music Napster users sampled, the less likely they were to purchase audio CDs. Napster was also judged to have adverse effects on the nascent digital download market.

The Ninth Circuit also held that the *Sony v. Universal* case did not excuse users from "space-shifting" by downloading MP3 files they already own on audio CD. The court reasoned that the majority of the users of the VCRs at issue in *Sony v. Universal* merely enjoyed the broadcasts at home. VCRs ordinarily did not expose the copyrighted material to individuals outside the home of the device's user. In contrast, the Napster software potentially made music available to millions of other users

The court therefore had little trouble concluding that Napster was unlikely to fall within the fair use privilege. The award of an injunction effectively put an end to Napster, which later declared bankruptcy and shut down its site. Yet the battle between the music industry and file-sharing software may have just begun. In the post-*Napster* environment, the music industry has turned its attention to second generation software such as Grokster, KaZaa and Morpheus Music City. A chief distinction between Napster and the second generation software is that the newer systems do not employ a central server with a directory of all the files on users' computers. As a consequence, representatives of the later systems say, they have no way to track or control what their users do. The consequences of this distinction upon judicial reasoning, as well as on the shape of the music industry itself, remains to be seen.

§ 10.6 Fair Use and Parody

Parody has been defined as a "literary or artistic work that imitates the characteristic style of an author or a work for comic effect or ridicule."[1] In other words it might be a spoof of a poem to show how pretentious the author's word choice has been, or a caricature of a painting that mocks the political or aesthetic agenda of the painter. Courts have struggled for decades with the place of parody under the fair use doctrine. At least two aspects of parody have made it especially troubling. First, a parodist must necessarily borrow considerable amounts from the work being mocked. Without such extensive borrowing, the target of the parody will be obscure and the humor will be lost. Of course extensive borrowing has usually resulted in a denial of the fair use defense. Second, because parody is critical of the original work, the author of the underlying work is highly unlikely to grant permission to the parodist, and is likely to litigate with vigor when the parody appears on the market.

Prior to the Supreme Court's decision in *Campbell v. Acuff–Rose Music, Inc.*[2] the lower courts decided a number of parody cases but few consistent themes emerged from those decisions. Some courts manifested

§ 10.6
1. *Campbell*, 510 U.S. at 580.

2. 510 U.S. 569, 114 S.Ct. 1164, 127 L.Ed.2d 500 (1994).

considerable hostility to parody. For instance the Ninth Circuit found an underground comic book mocking Mickey Mouse by depicting him as a sexually promiscuous drug smuggler, did not qualify for the fair use defense.[3] Other courts, however, were more charitable, as when the Second Circuit found that a television parody of the New York advertising jingle "I Love New York" on Saturday Night Live, using the lyrics "I Love Sodom" was fair use.[4]

Campbell was the Supreme Court's first opportunity to clarify the fair use status of parody.[5] At the outset, Justice Souter's opinion makes it clear that parody can qualify for the fair use defense. It is not automatically beyond the pale. On the other hand, just like other forms of comment and criticism, parody is not automatically immunized from infringement liability. The Court explicitly rejected defendant's argument that any parodic use should be considered presumptively fair. Rather, courts must still consider all of the statutory factors and resolve "close questions of judgement" to determine if the fair use defense is appropriate under the facts of the case. The opinion is especially illuminating because each of those factors takes on slightly different characteristics when applied in a parody case.

Under the first fair use factor, the nature and character of the use, parodies pose something of a paradox. On the one hand, they are almost always "transformative" because the parody is a new and different work which builds upon, but alters the original. This normally cuts in favor of the defense. On the other hand, parodies are usually "commercial." 2 Live Crew included its parody song on a publicly marketed CD, inserting it between the tracks *Me So Horny* and *My Seven Bizzos*, presumably with the goal of making money. A commercial purpose of this sort typically cuts against fair use. As noted in section 10.2.1 above, the *Campbell* Court took pains to stress that there is no hard and fast presumption against fair use for commercial works. The opinion seems to suggest that particularly in cases of parody, the more transformative the defendant's work, the less significant will be its commercial nature.

In order to benefit from this somewhat more generous pro-defendant analysis, however, the defendant's work must truly be a parody. A true parody targets and criticizes the original work, not society at large. If one wanted to borrow the words or music of *Oh Pretty Woman* to write a song critical of Hillary Clinton, such a work would not be a parody, because the target of the criticism is not the original musical composition or composer but something external to the work. One can satirize

3. Walt Disney Productions v. Air Pirates, 581 F.2d 751 (9th Cir.1978), *cert. denied*, 439 U.S. 1132, 99 S.Ct. 1054, 59 L.Ed.2d 94 (1979).

4. Elsmere Music, Inc. v. National Broadcasting Co., 623 F.2d 252 (2d Cir. 1980).

5. In the 1950's, the Supreme Court granted certiorari on a parody case involving a television skit by the comedian Jack Benny spoofing the movie *Gaslight*. However, only eight justices participated in the decision of the case, and the Court found itself equally divided, four to four. It issued no opinion. See Benny v. Loew's Inc., 239 F.2d 532 (9th Cir.1956), *aff'd by an equally divided court sub nom* Columbia Broadcasting System, Inc. v. Loew's Inc., 356 U.S. 43, 78 S.Ct. 667, 2 L.Ed.2d 583 (1958).

Senator Clinton by writing new lyrics to virtually any song under the sun. There is no particular reason to borrow *Oh Pretty Woman*.[6] Of course, if one's goal is to criticize *Oh Pretty Woman* itself, the need to use the melody or some of the lyrics of the original work is much more compelling. Moreover, it is in cases of true parody that the original author is least likely to grant a license and thus where the availability of the fair use defense is most important if such works are ever to see the light of day.

Applying this standard to the case before it, the *Campbell* Court held that the 2 Live Crew Song "reasonably could be perceived as commenting on the original or criticizing it to some degree." It found that the words of defendant's song could "be taken as a comment on the naivete of the original of an earlier day, as a rejection of its sentiment that ignores the ugliness of street life and the debasement that it signifies." This is perhaps a generous interpretation of a song whose words included "Big hairy woman you need to shave that stuff/ Big hairy woman, you know I bet it's tough/ Big hairy woman all that hair ain't legit/ Cause you look like Cousin It/ Big hairy woman." Nonetheless, it illustrates the central fact that in order to receive the more favorable consideration under the fair use defense reflected in *Campbell* the work must be a true parody that targets the original.

The importance of this threshold inquiry into whether the work is a true parody is illustrated by two cases decided shortly after the *Campbell* decision. In *Dr. Seuss Enterprises. v. Penguin Books U.S.A., Inc.,*[7] defendant authored a short illustrated book entitled *The Cat NOT In The Hat*. The book recounted the events of the celebrated O.J. Simpson murder trial in the poetry style of Dr. Seuss, the famous author of children's books, and contained illustrations paralleling those that appear in various Seuss books but consisting of such things as a caricature of Mr. Simpson holding a bloody glove. The court refused to analyze defendant's work under the more generous fair use standards set out in *Campbell* because it concluded that the book was not a genuine parody. In its view, the book did not target the works of Dr. Seuss, but was primarily a satire on the various events surrounding the Simpson affair. Viewing the work as a non-parody, the court found its commercial status to weigh heavily against fair use, and ultimately held the work to be infringing.

By way of contrast is *Leibovitz v. Paramount Pictures*.[8] Annie Leibovitz, the celebrated portrait photographer, had taken several pictures of the actress Demi Moore when Moore was eight months pregnant. One of those photographs, of Moore nude but concealing her private parts with her hands, appeared on the cover of Vanity Fair

---

6. "If . . . the commentary has no critical bearing on the substance or style of the original composition, which the alleged infringer merely uses to get attention or to avoid the drudgery in working up something fresh, the claim to fairness in borrowing from another's work diminishes ac- cordingly (if it does not vanish), and other factors, like the extent of its commerciality loom larger." *Campbell*, 510 U.S. at 580.

7. 109 F.3d 1394 (9th Cir.1997).

8. 948 F.Supp. 1214 (S.D.N.Y.1996).

magazine and, not surprisingly, stirred considerable public comment. About two years later, Paramount, as part of its publicity for the movie *Naked Gun 33 1/3,* prepared an advertisement that superimposed the smirking, guilty face of actor Leslie Nielson—the star of the movie—over the body of a very pregnant woman posed identically to Ms. Moore in the Leibovitz photo. This hybrid photo ran over the caption "Due in March," a reference to upcoming movie's release date but, of course, also a pun suggesting that Mr. Nielson would give birth in that month. The court found Paramount's work to be a true parody: "The Nielsen ad clearly takes satiric aim directly at the Moore photograph. From the outset, it was intended to make a mockery of an image that had become 'a cultural icon.' … In fact, without reference to the Moore photograph, the Nielsen ad simply is not very funny. Like all parodies, it relies for its comic effect on the contrast between the original—a serious portrayal of a beautiful woman taking great pride in the majesty of her pregnant body—and the new work—a ridiculous image of a smirking, foolish-looking pregnant man." Having found the work to be a genuine parody, the court went on to exonerate the defendant under the fair use defense.

Turning to the second fair use factor, the "nature of the copyrighted work," *Campbell* reveals that it will usually be of minimal importance in parody cases. Most parodies target creative or fictional works. There are very few parodies of almanacs or statistical tables. While the fact that plaintiff's work is fictional and creative usually cuts against the fair use defense this is not so in parody cases. As Justice Souter explained, the fact that plaintiff's work was creative "is not … ever likely to help much in separating the fair use sheep from the infringing goats in a parody case, since parodies almost invariably copy publicly known, expressive works." The rationale for the diminished importance of this factor seems persuasive. Normally, we allow a broader scope of fair use for factual works because of the need of subsequent authors to use those facts. We are more reluctant to allow borrowing where the work is fictional and expressive because the need to borrow is less pressing. A parodist, however, must borrow from the fictional or expressive works he targets just as surely as a historian must borrow the facts of prior books in his field of research.

The third factor, the "amount and substantiality of the portion used in relation to the copyrighted work as a whole" also takes on a slightly different complexion in parody cases. This is because, as *Campbell* notes, "parody's humor, or in any event its comment, necessarily springs from recognizable allusion to its object through distorted imitation." In other words, the parodist must borrow sufficiently from the underlying work that the public can identify what is being parodied. This often will require not only borrowing a relatively large quantity of material from the original, but may also often require using those portions that are qualitatively most significant—what is sometimes called the "heart" of the work. A music parodist may use the most recognizable few bars of the song being ridiculed, just as a comic spoof of a movie will likely target the most famous or memorable scene. In light of these considerations courts usually permit a parodist to take at least sufficient material so as to be able to "conjure up" the original. The parodist may be entitled to take even more if it builds upon the original and contributes something new for humorous effect or commentary.[9]

Unfortunately, *Campbell* did not attempt to lay down any further guidelines about the scope of permissible borrowing in parody cases. In fact, the Court did not even resolve the issue in the case before it, but remanded for further findings on whether 2 Live Crew's repetitive use of the bass riff in the original song was excessive. Much of the concern about the extent of material taken by the parodist revolves around the scope and nature of the effect of the parody on the market for the original, the fourth factor in fair use analysis.

It is at the level of the final factor that the parodist finds his greatest protection. Parody will, quite often, depress the market for the original work. Those who come into contact with the parody first may conclude that the original work is banal, pretentious or otherwise not worth their time and money. This effect, however, is not the market effect that the statute forbids. As *Campbell* notes, "when a lethal parody, like a scathing theater review, kills demand for the original, it does not produce a harm cognizable under the Copyright Act." The only market harm that is cognizable under fair use analysis is the tendency of defendant's work to substitute for plaintiff's work, or various derivative works that plaintiff might subsequently put on the market. A movie based on a novel will both substitute for the novel in the eyes of some patrons, who now dispense with reading the book because they've seen the movie, and will also make it difficult if not impossible for the copyright owner to prepare an authorized movie version of the book. Parody, as Justice Souter points out in his opinion, rarely has this market substitution effect, because "the parody and the original usually serve different market functions." For instance, a not inconsiderable number of parodies might be considered vulgar or far too sexually explicit by fans of the original work. Consumers who want to enjoy the original version of *Oh Pretty Woman* will not find the 2 Live Crew Version to be much of a proxy.

One might think that there is a market effect flowing from unauthorized parody distinct from the critical disparagement associated with that genre. If parody is protected under the fair use doctrine the owner of the copyright in the original will not be able to obtain any revenue by licensing parodies. That particular derivative market will be foreclosed because no rational parodist will pay to prepare a work the law says that he may prepare for free. The *Campbell* court also refused to recognize this type of lost revenue as a remediable harm under copyright law. "The market for potential derivative uses includes only those that creators of original works would in general develop or license others to develop. Yet the unlikelihood that creators of imaginative works will license critical reviews or lampoons of their own productions removes

9. Tin Pan Apple v. Miller Brewing Co., Inc., 737 F.Supp. 826, 830 (S.D.N.Y.1990).

such uses from the very notion of a potential licensing market." The *Campbell* Court distinguished the derivative market for parodies from the derivative market for a legitimate rap version of *Oh Pretty Woman* and instructed the court of appeals to limit its consideration only to the question of whether the 2 Live Crew version might hurt this latter market on remand.

While *Campbell* did much to clarify the nature of the fair use inquiry in parody cases, the future resolution of such cases will hardly be automatic. Questions of characterization and balancing still abound. Courts must determine whether the defendant's work targets the plaintiff's original or merely uses that original to ridicule society at large. They must determine if the defendant took only as much as was necessary to make an effective parody, but no more. They must sort out the effect the parody may have on legitimate derivative markets from its tendency to depress sales of the original by virtue of its critical message. Where these factors point in opposing directions, courts must attempt a balance. It would seem to be the lesson of *Campbell* that in close cases this balance should be resolved in favor of the parodist. Parodists typically target works that are already famous and well known in popular culture—*Oh Pretty Woman, The Cat in the Hat,* Leibovitz's picture of Demi Moore. These works will already have earned their authors considerable reward. Future authors will hardly hesitate to create new works by reasoning "my work may become fabulously famous, earn me a great deal of money, then become subject to a parody, which will somewhat reduce my ultimate return, so never mind!" Given that parody tends to target only successful works, and tends not to pose any real threat of usurping the market for the original, courts ought to treat parodies generously in the post-*Campbell* world.

§ 10.7   Fair Use and the First Amendment

At first blush one might assume that the copyright laws and the First Amendment guarantee of free speech work at cross-purposes. After all, copyright legally proscribes the use of a wide variety of expression, where those expressions are deemed to be the legal property of another. If we produce a movie, the plot details of which closely resemble the cinematic classic *Legally Blonde*, there is a good chance that we will be enjoined from distributing it. If we want to write a political essay criticizing the president's handling of foreign affairs using substantially the same words as a previous columnist, again, there is a good chance we will be enjoined.

Nonetheless, historically there has been a broad consensus, among both courts and commentators, that enforcement of copyright laws does not conflict with the First Amendment. This is because First Amendment values are considered to be already built in to the structure of the copyright act. Two aspects of copyright doctrine in particular are usually cited as eliminating any risk of interference with free speech concerns. The first of these is the idea/expression distinction, discussed in some depth in Chapter 3 of this treatise. Since copyright only protects the expression of an author—his or her words, notes, lines or images—others are free to use the underlying ideas of the work. It is not a violation of the copyright in *Legally Blonde* for us to make a movie about a blonde sorority member who goes to law school, or even a movie about a blonde woman law student who defies expectations and achieves great academic success despite the initial hostility of her classmates. The idea/expression dichotomy guarantees that any imposition on our ability to express ourselves will be quite minimal, and thus there should be few First Amendment implications from enforcement of the copyright law prohibition against copying protected expression.

The second copyright doctrine that accommodates free speech and copyright is, of course, the fair use defense. Under the fair use doctrine, activities that would otherwise be infringing because they appropriate an impermissible amount of the expression of a copyrighted work can be excused if they advance a socially beneficially purpose. Given the flexibility of fair use, courts can invoke the doctrine whenever there is any danger that copyright enforcement might be inconsistent with free speech principles. Interestingly, the Supreme Court has even cautioned that the fair use defense not be stretched too far in a desire to promote First Amendment values. Because "freedom of thought and expression 'includes both the right to speak freely and the right to refrain from speaking at all,' "[1] carte blanche permission to copy another's expression may actually interfere with the rights of the original author.

In addition to flexibility afforded by the idea/expression and fair use doctrines, courts often point out that rather than stifling expression, copyright actually furthers First Amendment values because of its tendency to encourage the creation of expressive works. As the Fifth Circuit has put it, "the judgment of the Constitution is that free expression is enriched by protecting the creations of authors from exploitation by others, and the Copyright Act is the congressional implementation of that judgment."[2] If the First Amendment is seen not merely as a guarantee to each individual to say whatever he pleases but as a provision designed to advance the goal of robust debate in society, it seems plain that the protections of copyright and the incentives they create for authors fit hand and glove with the First Amendment.

In recent years, however, as Congress and the courts have responded to new digital technologies by giving copyright owners more and more rights and by narrowing the scope of the fair use defense, several academic writers have asserted that explicit First Amendment limitations upon copyright should be established.[3] In a world with little or no fair use prerogatives the courts will have to begin to grapple with more and more claims predicated directly on Constitutional grounds.

§ 10.7

1. Harper & Row Publishers, Inc. v. Nation Enter., 471 U.S. 539, 559, 105 S.Ct. 2218, 85 L.Ed.2d 588 (1985) (quoting Wooley v. Maynard, 430 U.S. 705, 714, 97 S.Ct. 1428, 51 L.Ed.2d 752 (1977)).

2. Dallas Cowboys Cheerleaders, Inc. v. Scoreboard Posters, Inc., 600 F.2d 1184 (5th Cir.1979).

3. *See* Neil Weinstock Natanel, *Locating Copyright Within the First Amendment Skein,* 54 Stan. L. Rev. 1 (2001).

Chapter 11

STATE REMEDIES ANALOGOUS TO COPYRIGHT AND FEDERAL PREEMPTION

Table of Sections

§ 11.1   Compensation for the Use of Ideas

It is a basic premise of copyright law that ideas themselves, as distinguished from the way in which they may be expressed, are not subject to legal protection. We are all free to copy the ideas of others without paying for them and without fear of any legal liability. This is true for both commercial and literary ideas. If someone opens a restaurant with all the servers on roller skates and it proves to be a big smash hit, you too can open a restaurant with all the servers on roller skates. If someone hits on the idea of equipping hotel rooms with business equipment like fax machines and copiers, you too may put fax machines and copiers in the rooms of your hotel. One needs only to scan the prime time offerings of any of the major television networks to see the routine recycling of ideas that is common in that industry, as the proliferation of "reality-based" programming involving contestants consuming live insects amply demonstrates.

There are, however situations where you may incur an obligation to pay for the use of someone else's ideas. If someone approaches you with the representation that they have an idea that will enhance your business, and you agree to pay them to induce them to disclose that idea, it seems morally appropriate to hold you to your bargain and the law will often do just that. Even if you don't explicitly promise to pay for the idea, the circumstances may indicate that you intended for payment to take place, or that your use of the idea without compensation would amount to unjust enrichment. All this is a matter of state law. That of course requires us to note two cautions before getting into details. First, the precise rules concerning who must pay for an idea and what types of ideas are protectable vary from state to state. Second, these rules are subject to possible federal preemption if they conflict with the principles embodied in federal laws such as the copyright act. We will be considering federal preemption in some detail later in this chapter.[1]

As a general rule, an obligation to pay for the use of another party's ideas arises only when (1) the idea is novel; (2) the idea is concrete; and (3) the idea is disclosed in circumstances in which compensation is appropriate.[2] This means that the law will not mandate payment for well-known or trite ideas, vague or nebulous concepts, or ideas lacking in commercial value. It also means that the obligation to pay for the idea requires an advance agreement to do so, or at least circumstances where equitable considerations make payment obligatory.

While disputes over the obligation to pay for ideas can arise in a wide variety of contexts, certain fact patterns recur. Among the more common situations are cases involving plot ideas for entertainment programs, such as television shows or movies, and those involving marketing or product improvement ideas for consumer products. Frequently the plaintiff—the creator of the idea—will have submitted the idea to the defendant without having been asked to do so but with the defendant's knowledge and tacit consent that idea will be received, and sometime later the defendant will make use of the idea or of something fairly close to it. For instance, the plaintiff might contact a consumer goods manufacturer with an idea for changing product packaging to reduce breakage and a few months later, the manufacturer might begin selling the product in a new package resembling the one suggested by the defendant. In some of these cases the plaintiff-idea-submitter may have signed a form contract, often with language absolving the recipient of any duty to pay for the idea at all. Finally, it is typically the case that the plaintiff and defendant have had some face-to-face or one-on-one dealings—the defendant did not merely copy a publicly available idea.

11.1.1 The Novelty Requirement

It is sometimes said that only novel ideas will be protected under state law. Unfortunately, the various idea submission cases have at-

§ 11.1
1. *See infra* § 11.4.

2. Hamilton National Bank v. Belt, 210 F.2d 706 (D.C.Cir.1953).

tached different meanings to the simple term "novel." Some courts have suggested that this requirement means only that the plaintiff came up with the idea herself—a concept reminiscent of the originality requirement of copyright law.[3] Other courts have explained that the meaning of "novelty" depends upon the basis for relief. In cases where the plaintiff claims relief based upon a contract—ranging from a written confidentiality agreement to an implied-in-fact contract—the courts have viewed the novelty requirement to oblige the plaintiff to show only that the idea be new to that particular defendant. On the other hand, where no express contract exists, and the court is unwilling to imply one from the facts, courts characterize the plaintiff's claim as asserting a property right in the disclosed idea. In these property-based cases, courts have stated that the idea must not be within the public domain at the time it was disclosed in order to fulfill the novelty requirement. This more general standard of innovativeness resembles the patent law's novelty requirement.[4]

The decision of the Court of Appeals for the Second Circuit in *Nadel v. Play–By–Play Toys & Novelties, Inc.*,[5] explores this distinction. Nadel was an independent inventor who developed a new table-top monkey toy. Nadel alleged that pursuant to toy industry custom treating the submission of an idea as confidential, he demonstrated his toy to a representative of Play–By–Play. According to Nadel, Play–By–Play later marketed a Tazmanian Devil toy ("Tornado Taz") that incorporated his disclosed idea.

Nadel subsequently brought suit against Play–By–Play for use of his idea. The district court granted summary judgment in favor of Play–By–Play. On appeal, the Second Circuit reversed. The Second Circuit ruled that under New York law, the novelty requirement was not absolute in all cases involving the disclosure of ideas. Only for property-claims did the plaintiff have to show that the submitted idea presented an inventive concept outside the public domain. In contrast, for contract-based claims, the requirement that an idea have novelty mandates only that the plaintiff prove the idea was novel vis-a-vis that particular defendant. The reason for this distinction, the Second Circuit reasoned, is that ideas that are within the public domain are, by definition, free and available to all which precludes the plaintiff from asserting a *property* right in such an idea.[6] The "novelty to the buyer" standard is, however, appropriate for *contract-based* claims, because a particular buyer might promise payment to a plaintiff who is willing to educate him about it and help him exploit it.[7]

The court further specified that, as a matter of law, some ideas are so commonplace that the defendant is deemed to have knowledge of the idea. In such cases, neither a property-based nor a contract-based claim for uncompensated use of an idea would succeed. A wonderful example of

3. 17 U.S.C.A. § 102(a). *See supra* § 3.1.

4. 35 U.S.C.A. § 102. *See infra* § 16.1.

5. 208 F.3d 368 (2d Cir.2000).

6. 208 F.3d at 378.

7. 208 F.3d at 377.

this principle in action is *Soule v. Bon Ami Co.*[8] In that case, the plaintiff approached the defendant company and told them that he had an idea which would increase their profits, and offered to disclose it for one half of any profit increase realized. Plaintiff then disclosed his idea, which was that Bon Ami should raise its prices and this would result in an increase in profits. Shortly thereafter Bon Ami raised its prices. Plaintiff sued to recover, but the court denied relief. Of plaintiff's idea, the court observed "this was not new, it was not original and I am at a loss to understand how it could be deemed valuable.... No person can by contract monopolize an idea that is common and general to the whole world."

11.1.2 The Idea Must Be Concrete

The requirement of concreteness is not often the subject of much controversy in idea cases. The courts that have addressed this requirement seem to contemplate that the idea in question must be ready to use, which is to say capable of commercial application without further intellectual development. Professor Nimmer has pointed out that this requirement is a bit of an anomaly, because when an idea is so concrete that it is ready for immediate use, it ceases to be merely an idea, and may become copyrightable expression.[9] With respect to concreteness, one court has observed in the area of entertainment program ideas that "concreteness may lie between the boundaries of mere generality on the one hand and, on the other, a full script containing the words to be uttered and delineating the action to be portrayed."[10]

11.1.3 Circumstances Evidencing an Obligation to Pay

The easiest case for requiring a defendant to pay for an idea obtained from the plaintiff is when the defendant has agreed to do so in advance in a written contract. While the typical contract will normally make payment contingent on defendant's actual use of the idea, the parties can agree that plaintiff will be paid whether or not defendant chooses to implement the idea in question. Some courts have felt that such contracts should be unenforceable when the idea is not novel, on the theory that because such an idea has no value, there is no consideration for defendant's promise to pay.[11] Professor Nimmer, however, takes the view that consideration can be found in the mere act of plaintiff's disclosure of the idea. As he puts it, "the better view is to find consideration for defendant's promise to pay not in the 'property' to be furnished by plaintiff, but rather in plaintiff's services in disclosing his

---

8. 201 App.Div. 794, 195 N.Y.S. 574 (1922), *aff'd*, 235 N.Y. 609, 139 N.E. 754 (1923).

9. NIMMER, COPYRIGHT § 16.08[A] at 16–53.

10. Hamilton National Bank v. Belt, 210 F.2d 706 (D.C.Cir.1953).

11. See e.g., Masline v. New York, New Haven and Hartford R.R., 95 Conn. 702, 112 A. 639 (1921) (Oral contract for disclosure of plaintiff's idea that defendant railroad should sell advertising space in its stations and cars to make more money held unenforceable because of lack of consideration).

idea regardless of whether or not the idea constitutes 'property.' "[12] Since defendants in idea appropriation cases are usually sophisticated businesses, Professor Nimmer's view seems sound. Such parties are fully capable of conditioning payment on the novelty of the idea to be disclosed if that is their wish. If the contract is silent on that point, then it seems appropriate to require payment regardless of novelty.

Sometimes the contract to pay for the idea will be oral rather than written in nature. The validity of such agreements requires consideration of the Statute of Frauds. Such statutes, which require that certain types of contracts be put in writing, vary from state to state. The typical contract for disclosure and use of an idea should not run afoul of the various prohibitions of the Statute of Frauds, but generalizations can be risky in this murky corner of the contract law landscape, so there are occasional exceptions.

Even when the parties have not explicitly agreed orally or in writing for payment for the use of the idea, the surrounding facts and circumstances of the idea disclosure may lead a court to imply the existence of a contract and a duty to pay. Such factors as the specific conduct of the parties, industry custom and the course of dealing are relevant to determining whether a contract should be implied in fact.[13]

11.1.4   The Defense of Independent Development

To protect themselves from liability, many companies have implemented a practice of segregating unsolicited ideas. In other words, they keep letters and suggestion forms received through the mail from the public in a designated place where product development or marketing personnel cannot have access to them. If the company thereafter comes up with the same idea as one previously submitted by a stranger, by definition, it did not appropriate the idea from that stranger. Thus, if a defendant can document independent development of the idea, that immunizes it from liability for idea appropriation, even if the idea submitted by the outsider is genuinely novel, concrete and useful.

This was the case in *Downey v. General Foods*.[14] Downey, the plaintiff, was an airline pilot by profession. Also a family man, he had the chance to observe the eating habits of his children. He noticed that although they were usually indifferent to the joys of Jello brand gelatin dessert, they became excited about the idea of consuming it when he referred to it as a "wiggling" or "wiggly" substance. Struck by the potential universal appeal of this characterization, he contacted General Foods. They sent him an "Idea Submittal Form," which he used to submit his proposal, namely that General Foods should emphasize the wiggling properties of Jello in future advertising. The form was received by a General Foods employee whose job it was to file these forms away in a locked cabinet. There was evidence in the case that no other General

---

12. Nimmer, Copyright (2002).
13. *Nadel*, 208 F.3d at 377.

14. 31 N.Y.2d 56, 334 N.Y.S.2d 874, 286 N.E.2d 257 (1972).

Foods employee ever saw the form sent in by Mr. Downey. Coincidentally, some time later, General Foods began using the wiggling theme in its advertising for Jello gelatin and Downey sued them seeking payment.

The Second Circuit denied Downey's claim. First, it found that his idea was not novel, based on evidence presented by General Foods that it had used variants on the theme some years prior to receiving Downey's proposal.[15] In an alternative holding, however, the court also noted that General Foods' protocol for handling the idea made it highly unlikely that they had derived the notion from Downey. Because the evidence indicated that they had hit upon the wiggling concept by themselves, they incurred no liability. Of course, while the practice of quarantining ideas that come in unbidden from the general public can prevent liability for idea theft, it can also deprive the company of the benefit of new ideas and fresh perspectives.

§ 11.2   The Misappropriation Doctrine

The cases discussed in the previous section involved parties who produced a creative intangible—an idea—and then disclosed it to a single identifiable party in confidence and with the expectation, or at least hope, of receiving compensation. This is not the only situation where parties have sought legal protection for non-copyrightable intangibles. Many firms regularly engage in the business of producing creative intangible products, such as information, data or entertainment, and selling these intangibles not merely to a single individual, but rather to the public at large. Occasionally others, often competitors, will attempt to reproduce this intangible product and sell it themselves, without the permission of the creator. They are often able to undersell the original creator because they incurred no cost in developing the intangible, merely a cost in reproducing it. One might consider their conduct dubious on both economic and moral grounds.

Over 80 years ago, a creator in just this position turned to the courts for relief, arguing that a competitor had "misappropriated" a valuable asset and should be prevented from continuing to do so under the law of unfair competition. The issue ultimately reached the U.S. Supreme Court, where the cause of action for misappropriation was first articulated in the case of *INS v. Associated Press*.[1] Even when decided the case was controversial, however, and the misappropriation doctrine has remained the subject of criticism down to the present day. While some courts followed *INS* and even expanded the scope of the misappropriation doctrine, many others have expressed skepticism or outright hostility to misappropriation claims. The current status of the claim has been cast into even further doubt by the provisions and commentary of the

---

15. For instance, in a magazine ad published before the receipt of Downey's suggestion, General Foods advised parents to make a "wigglewan" of Jello for their tribe.

§ 11.2

1. 248 U.S. 215, 39 S.Ct. 68, 63 L.Ed. 211 (1918).

new Restatement of Unfair Competition.[2] The story necessarily begins, however, with a look at the details of the *INS* case.

11.2.1 The *INS* Decision

The two parties in the famous *INS* case—the Associated Press and the International News Service—were both news wire services. That means each was a membership organization composed of various newspapers around the country. Each member newspaper promised to share its local stories with other members of the organization by placing them "on the wire." In addition, each member paid dues to the respective organizations. In return, the organization hired correspondents who reported on national and international stories. Those reports were also placed "on the wire." In this way, an AP member paper in Albany, New York or Amarillo, Texas, could get news of a major flood in Sacramento, California (placed on the wire by AP's Sacramento member) as well as news about an assassination in Europe (placed on the wire by an AP correspondent).

During World War I the International News Service had published several war-related reports critical of the British. As a result the British government barred INS from using British cables to transmit news back across the Atlantic. Without the use of those cables, INS was essentially unable to report on the events in Europe, in which the American reading public was keenly interested. Left with no direct source of war news, INS hit upon a scheme. It instructed its employees to purchase copies of AP member newspapers in East Coast cities as soon as those papers hit the streets. INS employees would then rewrite the stories and put them on the INS wire. This enabled INS members in cities further west to publish those stories at the same time as, or sometimes even before the competing AP paper in the same town, because of the time difference between the east and west coasts. The INS papers did not indicate that the stories had been obtained from AP or, for that matter, make any reference to AP whatsoever. Suffice it to say that AP was not pleased.

AP filed suit in federal court against INS for common law unfair competition. The basis of federal jurisdiction was diversity of citizenship. Since the case was decided long before the decision in *Erie RR v. Tompkins,*[3] the substantive basis for the decision was general federal common law. The case was ultimately decided by the U.S. Supreme Court with dissents from both Justice Holmes and Justice Brandeis.

As a preliminary matter, it is useful to note that INS's conduct did not violate the copyright laws because it did not copy the expression contained within the AP stories, only the ideas and facts that they revealed.[4] The case also did not present the usual situation posed by unfair competition allegations. The usual unfair competition claim in-

2. RESTATEMENT (THIRD) OF UNFAIR COMPETITION (1995).

3. 304 U.S. 64, 58 S.Ct. 817, 82 L.Ed. 1188 (1938).

4. *See supra* § 3.3.

volves a defendant who passes off his own goods as those of the plaintiff who has a better or stronger reputation. For the INS case to fit this mold, INS would have had to develop the stories by itself, but then publish them under the AP name (something it might have done if its own name and those of its reporters lacked credibility). In the actual case, just the opposite was involved. INS used not AP's name, but its product, and sold that product under its own name. Thus the cases did not fit easily into any pre-existing legal category and the Supreme Court was sailing on uncharted legal waters when it attempted to resolve the dispute.

Justice Pitney, writing for the majority, found for AP, holding that INS's conduct constituted an actionable variety of unfair competition. He reasoned that AP had a form of property interest in its news reporting, at least while the stories were fresh, and that INS had effectively stolen this intangible property when it "pirated the news stories." Conceding that the news could not be property vis-a-vis the public, he stressed that between competitors it was "stock in trade, to be gathered at the cost of enterprise, organization, skill, labor, and money and to be distributed and sold to those who will pay money for it, as for any other merchandise."[5] In a phrase that has become a pithy summary of the reasoning of the case, he said that INS was "endeavoring to reap where it has not sown, and . . . is appropriating to itself the harvest of those who have sown."[6]

The majority in the INS case seems to have been most concerned with the effect a contrary result might have had on incentives. If INS could freely use AP stories as the basis of its own reportage without permission or payment, INS would not need to hire any of its own reporters (even after the limits on its European activities were lifted). Without the expense of reporters, INS would have lower costs than AP and could charge its members lower dues. That, in turn, might lead to an exodus of members from AP to INS, making it impossible for AP to continue to afford to pay reporters to gather the news. In this view, INS was a typical free rider and its conduct, left unregulated, had the potential to kill the goose that lays the golden eggs.

Justice Brandeis, in dissent, saw things rather differently. His chief concern was with the preservation of vigorous competition. He rejected the idea that the facts and information contained in news stories could be vested with the attributes of property and made the subject of a new tort of misappropriation, pointing out in his usual forceful language that "the general rule of law is, that the noblest of human productions—knowledge, truths ascertained, conceptions and ideas—became, after voluntary communication to others, free as the air to common use."[7] He went on to observe that "the rule for which the plaintiff contends would effect an important extension of property rights and a corresponding curtailment of the free use of knowledge and of ideas." In the end,

5. 248 U.S. at 236.

6. 248 U.S. at 239.

7. 248 U.S. at 250.

Brandeis felt that if a remedy was to be afforded on facts of this sort, it would have to come from the legislature, not the Court.

Justice Holmes agreed with Brandeis that there could be no property interests in the "hot news items" that were at the core of the case. As he put it, "when an uncopyrighted combination of words is published there is no general right to forbid other people repeating them—in other words there is no property in the combination or in the thoughts or facts that the words express." The sole legally cognizable harm he could identify in the conduct of the INS was its failure to give credit to the AP in its stories. Thus, he would have resolved the case by entering a narrow injunction requiring INS to divulge that it had obtained the news from AP, but he would not have enjoined their ongoing practice of using AP materials as the basis for their own stories.

Distilling a black letter holding from *INS* is no mean feat, and the case has provoked considerable academic commentary.[8] Of course the opinion can be read to resolve only the situation directly before the court. On this view, the case would mean nothing more than that the informational content of "hot news" is a protected intangible that cannot be appropriated by a competitor to the detriment of the party who first developed the information. Of course the opinion would be of minimal importance if read in such a stingy fashion. Moreover, such a reading might come perilously close to protecting mere "sweat of the brow"—unoriginal or uncopyrightable material that merely requires labor rather than creative authorship to develop. As more fully developed in earlier chapters, copyright protection for "sweat of the brow" has been, in more recent times, squarely rejected by the Supreme Court in *Feist*,[9] a legal development that might cast considerable doubt on this reading of *INS*.

At a more general level, however, the opinion seems to stand for the proposition that the common law should protect any intangible economic asset not already covered by copyright, at least where the asset is "stock in trade" which will be sold to the public and where the defendant who misappropriates it is a direct competitor. Several courts have read the case at this higher level of generality and tried to distill its essence into a list of elements. One Texas court summarized those elements as "(i) the creation of plaintiff's product through extensive time, labor, skill and money, (ii) the defendant's use of that product in competition with the plaintiff, thereby gaining a special advantage in that competition (i.e., a 'free ride') because defendant is burdened with little or none of the expense incurred by the plaintiff, and (iii) commercial damage to the

---

8. Among the many articles considering the case and the misappropriation doctrine generally are Richard A. Epstein, *International News Service v. Associated Press: Custom and Law as Sources of Property Rights in News*, 78 VA. L. REV. 85 (1992); Leo J. Raskind, *The Misappropriation Doctrine as a Competitive Norm of Intellectual Property Law*, 75 MINN. L. REV. 875 (1991);

and Douglas G. Baird, *Common Law Intellectual Property and the Legacy of International News Service v. Associated Press*, 50 U. CHI. L. REV. 411 (1983).

9. Feist Publications, Inc. v. Rural Telephone Service Co., 506 U.S. 984, 113 S.Ct. 490, 121 L.Ed.2d 429 (1992). See *supra* Chapter 4.

plaintiff."[10] The Wisconsin Supreme Court used a very similar formula, itemizing the elements as "(1) time, labor and money expended in the creation of the thing appropriated; (2) competition; and (3) commercial damage to the plaintiff."[11]

Read this way, the *INS* opinion seeks to advance the same incentive preserving philosophy as the copyright laws themselves, but perhaps at the risk of interfering with robust competition and the free dissemination of ideas. In the years following the *INS* decision lower courts from many jurisdictions were confronted with cases requiring application of the misappropriation concept to a wide variety of fact patterns. It is to their decisions in those cases that we now turn.

11.2.2 From *INS* to the Restatement of Unfair Competition

Although *INS* was a decision of the highest court in the land, its peculiar posture gave the case only limited precedential effect. As a pre-*Erie* non-statutory decision, the Court was expounding on general federal common law, a body of law governing only cases filed in federal court and predicated on diversity of citizenship. After *Erie*, general federal common law ceased to govern even in that category of cases, and the federal courts were required to resort to state law doctrines to resolve cases founded on diversity jurisdiction. Given that *INS* was not binding on the states, it is hardly surprising to discover that some states chose to follow it while others either repudiated it or never had the opportunity to address the issue one way or the other.

The misappropriation doctrine had perhaps its most enthusiastic reception in the courts of New York. In a series of decisions in that state plaintiffs were able to secure legal protection for non-copyrightable intangibles as varied as live opera performances,[12] the live radio broadcast of the World Series,[13] and the appearance of buildings at a world's fair.[14] Other states adopting the *INS* doctrine in the decades shortly after its decision included Missouri,[15] Pennsylvania,[16] and Texas.[17] Interesting-

10. U.S. Sporting Products, Inc. v. Johnny Stewart Game Calls, Inc., 865 S.W.2d 214, 218 (Tex.App.1993).

11. Mercury Record Productions, Inc. v. Economic Consultants, Inc., 64 Wis.2d 163, 218 N.W.2d 705 (1974).

12. Metropolitan Opera Ass'n v. Wagner–Nichols Recorder Corp., 199 Misc. 786, 101 N.Y.S.2d 483 (1950), *aff'd* 279 A.D. 632, 107 N.Y.S.2d 795 (1951).

13. Mutual Broadcasting System v. Muzak Corp., 177 Misc. 489, 30 N.Y.S.2d 419 (1941). Compare the Texas case of Loeb v. Turner, 257 S.W.2d 800 (Tex.Civ.App.1953) where defendant's use of plaintiff's radio broadcast of certain car races as the basis for its own roughly simultaneous broadcast of a "recreation" of the races was held not to be misappropriation.

14. New York World's Fair 1964–1965 Corp. v. Colourpicture Publishers, Inc., 21 A.D.2d 896, 251 N.Y.S.2d 885 (1964).

15. National Tel. Directory Co. v. Dawson Mfg. Co., 214 Mo.App. 683, 263 S.W. 483 (1924).

16. Waring v. WDAS Broadcasting Station, 327 Pa. 433, 194 A. 631 (1937).

17. *Gilmore v. Sammons*, 269 S.W. 861 (Tex.Civ.App.1925). According to one commentator, a total of 14 states have adopted the misappropriation doctrine at one time or another. See Edmund J. Sease, *Misappropriation is Seventy–Five Years Old: Should We Bury It or Revive It?*, 70 No. Dak. L. Rev. 781, 801 (1994) (listing Alaska, California, Colorado, Delaware, Illinois, Maryland, Missouri, New Jersey, New York, North Carolina, Pennsylvania, South Carolina, Texas, and Wisconsin).

ly, the actual outcomes in many of these cases have been rendered moot by the subsequent passage of the 1976 Copyright Act and the numerous amendments to that act which have expanded the scope of copyright protection. Many of the intangibles at the core of those cases are now protected by copyright, such as architecture and live broadcasts that are simultaneously recorded. Even un-fixed musical performances are now protected under federal law by an anti-bootlegging statute, and are also the subject of a recent international agreement. Indeed, the results in these older cases may reflect judicial efforts to use the misappropriation doctrine to fill gaps in a still primitive copyright regime, where moral and equitable considerations seemed to require some form of remedy for the plaintiffs.

Not all judges were equally receptive to the misappropriation concept, however. One of the most skeptical was Learned Hand, who, in his role as a judge on the U.S. Court of Appeals for the Second Circuit was charged with applying New York law in common law diversity cases. He set out his concerns most fully in *Cheney Brothers v. Doris Silk Corp.*[18] Both parties in the case manufactured silks. Every season the plaintiff would, at great effort, develop new designs, only some of which would achieve any measure of popularity and economic success. These designs were not protected by either patent or copyright. The defendant copied one of plaintiff's patterns and the plaintiff filed suit under the misappropriation theory. Judge Hand rejected the claim. He was greatly troubled by the potential for conflict between the federal intellectual property statutes and a broad open-ended version of misappropriation law. He was inclined to limit the *INS* case to its own particular facts because "[t]he difficulties of understanding it otherwise are insuperable. We are to suppose that the court meant to create a sort of common-law patent or copyright for reasons of justice. Either would flagrantly conflict with the scheme which Congress has for more than a century devised to cover the subject-matter."[19] A number of other opinions from the Second Circuit during the 1940's and 1950's followed Judge Hand's approach and read the *INS* case narrowly, even when purportedly applying New York law.[20]

Much of this disagreement, and the state of the pre–1978 misappropriation case law generally, is no longer of much importance. On the one hand, with the modernization and expansion of the scope of copyright coverage, plaintiffs no longer need to invoke misappropriation in nearly so many cases, and state courts no longer have the incentive to expand the cause of action to do justice in what they may previously have seen as troublesome cases. On the other hand, the expansion of copyright has also expanded the range of state law causes of action that are pre-empted

18. 35 F.2d 279 (2d Cir.1929), *cert. denied,* 281 U.S. 728, 50 S.Ct. 245, 74 L.Ed. 1145 (1930).

19. 35 F.2d at 280.

20. See e.g., RCA Mfg. Co. v. Whiteman, 114 F.2d 86 (2d Cir.), *cert. denied,* 311 U.S. 712, 61 S.Ct. 393, 85 L.Ed. 463 (1940); National Comics Publications v. Fawcett Publications, 191 F.2d 594 (2d Cir.1951); G. Ricordi & Co. v. Haendler, 194 F.2d 914 (2d Cir.1952).

by federal law. While preemption is considered in depth at the end of this chapter, it is important to note at this point that many of the older state misappropriation cases would not be decided the same way today because the state claim would be held pre-empted, due to conflict with the letter or spirit of one of the federal intellectual property statutes.

There are relatively few misappropriation cases from the post–1978 era, and many of those have ultimately been resolved on preemption grounds rather than on the state law issue of the scope and applicability of the misappropriation doctrine. Some of these more recent cases have involved a potentially significant variation on the basic fact pattern in *INS*. In that case, and in many of the New York state cases that followed in its wake, the intangible asset created by the plaintiff was one which was created over and over again, and sold anew to the public with each subsequent re-creation. For instance, the AP prepared new stories daily, just as a baseball league plays new games daily and an opera company stages new performances daily. The public would not pay for old news, nor does it want to see the same baseball game or opera over and over. In this sense, Justice Pitney used a very apt phrase when, in *INS* he characterized the intangible there at issue as "stock in trade." To enlarge on this metaphor, these assets are almost a form of intangible inventory.

By contrast, a few of the more recent cases have involved an intangible asset that can best be characterized as a capital asset, such as a formula. These formulas are not re-created periodically, but rather developed only once, usually early in the plaintiff's business activities, nor are they sold to the public in any real sense. For instance, in both *Standard & Poor's Corp. v. Commodity Exchange, Inc.*,[21] and *Board of Trade of the City of Chicago v. Dow Jones & Co.*[22] the intangible in question was a securities index. Such indices, including the well known Standard and Poor's 500 and Dow Jones Industrial Index involved in the cases, are arrived at by an algebraic manipulation of the prices of several securities that the index-creator chooses to include in the index. Once created, the index can then provide a record of market performance that is comparable from day to day and year to year. In both of these cases, after the plaintiffs had created its index, and after it had achieved credibility in the financial markets, defendants wanted to use that index as the basis for the sale of futures contracts. Both courts enjoined the use of the index, invoking the misappropriation doctrine to do so.

United States Golf Assoc. v. St. Andrews Systems[23] also involved a formula. Plaintiffs here had developed the methodology for calculating a golf handicap. This is a number that adjusts golfing scores so that players of differing abilities can compete against each other. Like a stock index it requires a relatively simple algebraic manipulation of data, in this case the scores achieved by a given golfer over the past several

---

21. 683 F.2d 704 (2d Cir.1982).

22. 98 Ill.2d 109, 74 Ill.Dec. 582, 456 N.E.2d 84 (1983).

23. 749 F.2d 1028 (3d Cir.1984).

rounds he has played. The defendant began marketing a handheld computer which would enable golfers to calculate and update their handicaps automatically. The computer was programmed with plaintiff's formula. Plaintiff alleged misappropriation, and brought a diversity case in federal court. The Third Circuit, applying New Jersey law, concluded that no misappropriation claim was set out because the parties were not in direct competition, and direct competition was a necessary element of the tort under the law of New Jersey. Presumably, the court would have granted relief if the defendant had been a competing golf association attempting to use the USGA's handicap formula as its own.

Whatever one makes of the misappropriation doctrine generally, its extension to the "formula" cases seems curious. The defendants in these cases are typically not using plaintiff's formula to save effort or engage in direct free-riding. Rather, they do so because the formula in question has become an industry standard. There is nothing inherently superior about the USGA formula for calculating handicaps, but given its dominance in the golfing world, it has become the standard way in which golfers measure their performance against each other. There are many ways to design a stock index, but the Dow has become, by its long usage if nothing else, the yardstick by which stock market performance is measured. Anyone, whether a newspaper, a computer vendor, or even a direct competitor, could not really enter the market or any collateral markets without access to these types of formula. Also, almost by definition, when a formula has achieved "industry standard" status, it has already earned its developer a significant reward. Thus, even if the balancing act between preservation of incentives and promotion of competition is difficult in the usual misappropriation case, the formula cases seem easy. Third party access to them is a competitive necessity that poses little risk of undermining incentives, so the conduct ought to be held permissible.

11.2.3   The Restatement and Misappropriation

Competitive injury and theft of intellectual property have always been considered a branch of the law of Torts. Although both the first and second Restatement of Torts addressed some matters of unfair competition law, such as trade secrets, neither considered the status of the misappropriation doctrine at all. In the early 1990's the America Law Institute began the preparation of a new restatement dealing directly and exclusively with law regulating competitive practices. The result of this effort was the publication, in 1995, of the Restatement (Third) of Unfair Competition, so named because of its roots in the two earlier Torts Restatements. We will encounter this new Restatement repeatedly and in some depth in the materials dealing with trademark issues a bit further on in this Hornbook.

Section 38 of the Restatement provides:

> One who causes harm to the commercial relations of another by appropriating the other's intangible trade values is subject to liability to the other for such harm only if:

(a) the actor is subject to liability for an appropriation of the other's trade secret under the rules sated in §§ 39–45; or

(b) the actor is subject to liability for an appropriation of the commercial value of the other's identity under the rules states in §§ 46–49; or

(c) the appropriation is actionable by the other under federal or state statutes or international agreements, or is actionable as a breach of contract, or as an infringement of common law copyright as preserved under federal copyright law.

This provision declares that there can be no common law remedies for theft of intangible assets other than trade secret law and the right of publicity. Under this approach, the misappropriation doctrine of *INS* no longer exists. If a defendant uses someone else's information or formula or other intangible but is not guilty of transgressing a federal intellectual property statute such as the copyright laws, and if his conduct does not logically fit within the categories of trade secret theft or the right of publicity, the Restatement authors take the view that the conduct is a permissible form of competition. If there is any doubt about that interpretation from the text of the Restatement, the accompanying commentary makes the point explicit. That commentary points out

> Although courts have occasionally invoked the *INS* decision on an ad hoc basis ... they have not articulated coherent principles for its application. It is clear that no general rule of law prohibits the appropriation of a competitor's ideas, innovations, or other intangible assets once they become publicly known. In addition, the federal patent and copyright statutes now preempt a considerable portion of the domain in which the common law tort might otherwise apply. The better approach, and the one most likely to achieve an appropriate balance between the competing interests, does not recognize a residual common law tort of misappropriation.[24]

In the time since the promulgation of this new Restatement, the quoted passages have not been widely embraced by the courts. Nonetheless, the future does not look bright for the misappropriation concept as a separate cause of action in intellectual property law. Much of the need for the claim has vanished with the expansion of federal statutory intellectual property law. Many of the situations where those federal laws do not provide a remedy are exactly the ones where any state effort to do so would be pre-empted. The Restatement has weighed in against the misappropriation concept and its commentary on the subject is both

24. RESTATEMENT (THIRD) UNFAIR COMPETItion § 38, COMMENT B (1995).

thoughtful and persuasive. Moreover, the concept had only been explicitly adopted in a minority of states in the first place.

This is all probably for the best. Because of the amorphous nature of the elements of misappropriation, courts were often asked to apply it to squelch pro-competitive activities or to shrink the public domain. Plaintiffs sought to use it to prevent the copying of books or comic strips[25] on which the copyright had expired, and to restrain the use of words that did not otherwise qualify for trademark protection because they lacked sufficient distinctiveness.[26] While claims like these should fail on grounds of federal preemption, that issue is not always raised by defendants or understood by courts. It seems best to quietly dispose of the misappropriation doctrine to avoid the mischief it can cause, recognizing that there may be a rare case in which a deserving plaintiff is left without a remedy, but that this is a tolerable price to pay for robust competition and a rich public domain.

§ 11.3   The Right of Publicity

As anyone living in the early twenty-first century United States is aware, the exploitation of the images of celebrities is a big business. Items sporting the picture or name of a well-known and charismatic athlete or entertainer can sell for a significant premium over generic versions of the same item. Even objects that have no value other than as icons of the celebrity, such as dolls, posters or masks, can command a lucrative market. Not surprisingly celebrities have attempted to capture the economic benefit associated with this market for themselves. For ease of discussion, we can call the intangible asset that is the basis of this market "persona."

By its very nature, persona is not fixed in a tangible medium of expression, and is thus not protected by federal copyright law, although manifestations of persona can be, such as when an actor appears in a movie. Over the last three decades, however, state courts have extended greater and greater protection to persona. The resulting legal right to control exploitation of one's name and likeness is usually called the "right of publicity."

The right of publicity is sometimes said to have its roots in the misappropriation doctrine, and sometimes in the law of privacy. The outgrowth and relationship of the right of publicity to the misappropriation concept seems clear. The economic value of one's persona is an intangible asset developed by the expenditure of effort on the part of the person in question, just as the news was an asset belonging to the Associated Press and developed by it after considerable effort. Where the party seeking protection is a celebrity, persona is also his or her stock in trade. When others attempt to capitalize on the value of a celebrity's

---

25. National Comics Publications v. Fawcett Publications, 191 F.2d 594 (2d Cir. 1951).

26. See Flexitized, Inc. v. National Flexitized Corp., 335 F.2d 774 (2d Cir.1964), *cert. denied*, 380 U.S. 913, 85 S.Ct. 899, 13 L.Ed.2d 799 (1965).

persona—perhaps by marketing posters bearing his or her likeness—without having paid for it, they are reaping where they have not sown, just as the INS did when it misappropriated news stories from the Associated Press.

The connections between the right of publicity and the law of privacy are a bit more complicated. Although often referred to as a single concept in the law, Dean Prosser demonstrated in a famous law review article[1] that "privacy" is actually an umbrella term that includes four quite different causes of action. Three of these are not particularly relevant to the right of publicity—namely (1) the tort of "intrusion," which protects us from invasions of our physical privacy such as wiretapping; (2) the tort of "disclosure," which forbids the revelation of private matter that would prove embarrassing or disturbing, such as the unauthorized release of medical records; and (3) the tort of "false light," which addresses the circulation of material that would place the plaintiff in an inaccurate context, such as adding the name of an individual to a political petition despite his disagreement with its contents. It is the fourth branch of the law of privacy that has been said to form the basis for the right of publicity. That branch grants a cause of action against anyone who appropriates the name or likeness of another for a commercial advantage. In other words, the definition of the fourth privacy tort identified by Dean Prosser is essentially equivalent to the right of publicity.[2]

Given this history, some courts have referred to the right of publicity as a privacy-based tort, while others have considered it property based. At first, the distinction seems odd and of purely formal or semantic interest. The fourth privacy tort seems identical to misappropriation, or at least to a special or specific case of misappropriation. Moreover, the historical roots of the right of publicity and its similarity to other doctrines seems of little consequences in resolving concrete cases. However, whether a court conceives the right of publicity as rooted in the law of intangible property or in the law of personal privacy can have significant consequences for how that court chooses to structure various details of the rules of the right of publicity. For instance a privacy based conception of the publicity claim might focus on compensating for psychological or emotional harms while a misappropriation theory would emphasize economic injuries such as lost profit opportunities. Most recent decisions appear to embrace the misappropriation/economic vision of the publicity claim.

Regardless of its theoretical underpinnings, the right of publicity generally forbids the unauthorized use of the name or likeness of another individual for commercial purposes without that person's consent. Thus one cannot sell dolls that look like sitcom star Jerry Seinfeld

---

§ 11.3

1. William L. Prosser, *Privacy*, 48 CAL. L. REV. 383 (1960).

2. For a discussion of the privacy roots of the publicity doctrine see Hirsch v. S.C. Johnson & Son, Inc., 90 Wis.2d 379, 280 N.W.2d 129 (1979).

without his permission, nor could one sell basketball trading cards bearing a picture of Michael Jordan without his. In this spirit, a court invoked the doctrine to provide relief against a video rental store that used a celebrity look-alike for Woody Allen in one of its commercials.[3] The doctrine has been codified by statute in some jurisdictions[4] and is a matter of judge-made law in others. Several jurisdictions have expanded the attributes of persona covered by the doctrine to matters beyond name and likeness, and controversy over the range of included attributes has been a source of disagreement in right of publicity cases.

For instance, by both statute and common law, California's right of publicity also protects voice. In *Midler v. Ford*[5] the Ford Motor Company wanted to hire the performer Bette Midler to sing the song *Do You Want To Dance* as background music for an upcoming commercial. Ms. Midler declined to participate, so Ford hired another singer who had previously worked with Midler and could do a convincing imitation of her voice. They recorded this other individual singing the song in question and used it in the commercial. The upshot was, of course, a suit by Midler, alleging violation of her rights under California law.

The court held that Midler could not state a claim under the California statute because it only protects the voice of the plaintiff, and Ford did not use Midler's actual voice but rather the voice of a sound alike. Interestingly however, it did find that Ford had violated Midler's common law publicity rights. The court reached this result by asking itself a series of rhetorical questions: "Why did the defendants ask Midler to sing if her voice was not of value to them? Why did they studiously acquire the services of a sound-alike and instruct her to imitate Midler if Midler's voice was not of value to them? What they sought was an attribute of Midler's identity.... The human voice is one of the most palpable ways identity is manifested.... To impersonate her voice is to pirate her identity." The court cautioned that not every vocal imitation in an advertisement would amount to a violation of the right of publicity, but suggested no bright line to distinguish the permissible from impermissible uses.

In other cases, the defendant has not used the actual likeness of the plaintiff, but some approximation of the likeness or some physical object associated with the plaintiff, a situation which raises tricky questions. In *Motschenbacher v. R.J. Reynolds Tobacco Co.,*[6] plaintiff Motsenbacher was a famous race car driver. The defendant prepared a television commercial that included a picture of his highly recognizable car. It was not possible to make out the features of the driver himself in the ad. Nonetheless, the Ninth Circuit found a violation of California's common law right of publicity because the "markings were not only peculiar to the plaintiff's cars but they caused some persons to think the car in

3. Allen v. National Video, Inc., 610 F.Supp. 612 (S.D.N.Y.1985).

4. *See, e.g.,* California Civil Code § 3334.1; Virginia Code § 8.01–40.

5. 849 F.2d 460 (9th Cir.1988).

6. 498 F.2d 821 (9th Cir.1974).

question was plaintiff's and to infer that the person driving the car was the plaintiff."

Both *Motschenbacher* and *Midler* seem to have reached plausible results, but perhaps for the wrong reasons. In both cases, the use of the sound-alike singer and the picture of the car were highly evocative of the celebrity plaintiff. That evocation, however, was not being sold to the public by the defendants, who were tobacco and automobile merchants respectively. It was not as if a poster of the car or a CD with the voice of the sound-alike was put on sale. Rather, the vocal imitation and the photo of the car were being used to bolster the credibility of an advertisement. Consumers were left to conclude that Motschenbacher supported Reynolds' products and that Midler supported Ford's. In other words, the defendants were communicating a message of celebrity endorsement which was entirely inaccurate. False representations of this sort in advertising are, as we shall see later on in this volume, actionable under section 43(a) of the Lanham Act.[7] There is no need to expand the right of publicity to reach such cases, and such an expansion can only lead to a muddling of publicity law, but it seems equally clear that the celebrity should have a right to enjoin such activities when they take place.

That the essence of the wrongs in these cases was primarily the false claim of endorsement rather than the "theft" of "intangible persona" can be illustrated by a variation on the facts of *Midler*. If the defendants had decided to have the sound-alike singer appear in front of the camera during the commercial, rather than using the voice over, they would still have been using a vocal imitation of Ms. Midler. In such a case, however, consumers could see for themselves that it was someone other than Midler in the ad, and would be much less likely to infer any endorsement by her of the Ford products. Consequently, it seems much less likely that a court would afford relief, even though the disputed aspect of her persona, her distinctive vocal style, would still be used without her permission. The error can be avoided if publicity's roots in the misappropriation doctrine are kept in mind. A defendant should only liable for misappropriation when he takes the saleable intangible of the plaintiff, and sells it as his own. That was not the situation in either *Motschenbacher* or *Midler*.

A further layer of complexity is added by the fact pattern in *White v. Samsung Electronics America, Inc.*[8] Samsung had developed a series of advertisements designed to emphasize the longevity of its products. Each ad depicted a Samsung product in the early 21st century along with some fictional and humorous counter-intuitive information. One ad, for instance, depicted a raw steak along side the text "revealed to be health food, 2010 A.D." The ad that was the subject of the litigation "depicted a robot, dressed in a wig, gown, and jewelry ... consciously selected to

---

7. *See infra* § 28.8.

8. 971 F.2d 1395 (9th Cir.1992), *cert. denied*, 508 U.S. 951, 113 S.Ct. 2443, 124 L.Ed.2d 660 (1993).

resemble (Vanna) White's hair and dress. The robot was posed next to a game board which is instantly recognizable as the Wheel of Fortune game show set, in a stance for which White is famous. The caption of the ad read 'Longest-running game show, 2012 A.D.' '' Of course Samsung had not obtained permission from Vanna White before running these ads, and when she learned of them, she sued. The court found in Ms. White's favor, holding that the defendants had "appropriated her identity" and rejected Samsung's argument that the advertisement should escape liability as a parody.

Judge Alarcon dissented. He observed that "the majority's position seems to allow any famous person or entity to bring suit based on any commercial advertisement that depicts a character or role performed by the plaintiff. Under the majority's view of the law, Gene Autry could have brought an action for damages against all other singing cowboys. Clint Eastwood would be able to sue anyone who plays a tall, soft-spoken cowboy, unless, of course, Jimmy Stewart had not previously enjoined Clint Eastwood. Johnny Weismuller would have been able to sue each actor who played the role of Tarzan. Sylvester Stallone could sue actors who play blue-collar boxers. . . . ''

Although Samsung petitioned for rehearing en banc, its request was denied. Judge Kozinski, however, filed a blistering dissent from the denial of rehearing,[9] arguing passionately about the dangers of an overbroad interpretation of the right of publicity. He wrote "consider how sweeping this new right is. What is it about the ad that makes people think of White? It's not the robot's wig, clothes or jewelry; there must be ten million blond women (many of them quasi-famous) who wear dresses and jewelry like White's. It's that the robot is posed near the 'Wheel of Fortune' game board. Remove the game board from the ad, and no one would think of Vanna White. But once you include the game board, anybody standing beside it—a brunette woman, a man wearing women's clothes, a monkey in a wig and gown—would evoke White's image, precisely the way the robot did. It's the 'Wheel of Fortune' set, not the robot's face or dress or jewelry that evokes White's image. The panel is giving White an exclusive right not in what she looks like or who she is, but in what she does for a living."

As in *Midler* and *Motschenbacher*, the defendants clearly did evoke an association with the plaintiff. Unlike those cases, however, it is unlikely that the consuming public assumed that there was any endorsement. The humorous or parody nature of the ad dispelled any such notions. Thus, using the right of publicity as an alternative route to squelch an unauthorized implicit endorsement was hardly necessary in this case. Moreover, there was no attempt here by the defendant to sell an item who's value was enhanced by its association with Vanna White. There was no picture of White on the actual Samsung VCR's which would make them more coveted to owners, nor was Samsung planning to sell videotapes of its own advertisement to Vanna fans. Finally, there is

9. White v. Samsung Electronics America, Inc., 989 F.2d 1512 (9th Cir.1993).

little chance that Samsung's conduct undermined the incentives of either Ms. White or other aspiring game show hostesses. Given the cumulative weight of these factors the case seems to stretch the right of publicity to the breaking point and, in our view, judge Kozinski's criticisms seem well founded.

An issue related to the questions of what attributes of persona are protected by the right of publicity is the question of who may claim the right. There is no question that public figures, such as well-known actors, athletes and musicians, may claim the right of publicity. The courts have split, however, on whether noncelebrities may claim the right of publicity as well.[10] The majority of courts, supported by the Restatement, hold that the right of publicity potentially extends to everyone.[11] Under this view, the extent of the plaintiff's fame determines only the amount of damages, not the existence of a cause of action in tort.[12] In contrast, the minority position is that the right of publicity is enjoyed only by those who can prove that their identities enjoy a significant commercial value.[13]

The merits of these competing views have been subject to some debate. Some commentators believe that extending the right of publicity beyond a "celebrity right" provokes litigation and places overly expansive restrictions upon commercial speech. On the other hand, determining whether a particular individual enjoys "public figure" status has been likened to "trying to nail a jellyfish to the wall."[14] Because noncelebrity plaintiffs can be expected to turn to the right of publicity only rarely, given the limited damages available even in jurisdictions following the majority view, this issue may be somewhat more of theoretical than practical importance.

The states also vary upon whether the right survives the death of the plaintiff. Although New York and a few other jurisdictions terminate the right of publicity with the death of the individual,[15] the majority provide for a descendible right of publicity if a survivor or transferee exists.[16] The Virginia statute calls for a right of publicity extending 20 years beyond the death of the personality,[17] for example, while Indiana and Oklahoma legislation call for a duration of 100 years after death;[18] most of the other state statutes provide a term somewhere in between

---

10. *See* Alicia M. Hunt, *Everyone Wants to Be a Star: Extensive Publicity Rights for Noncelebrities Unduly Restrict Commercial Speech*, 95 Nw. L. Rev. 1605 (2001).

11. *See* Restatement (Third) Unfair Competition § 46, comment d (1995).

12. See Canessa v. J.I. Kislak, 97 N.J.Super. 327, 235 A.2d 62, 75 (Law Div. 1967) (stating that the degree of celebrity is "relevant only to the question of damages.").

13. *See, e.g.,* Cox v. Hatch, 761 P.2d 556, 557 (Utah 1988).

14. Rosanova v. Playboy Enters., Inc., 411 F.Supp. 440, 443 (S.D.Ga.1976).

15. See Pirone v. MacMillan, Inc., 894 F.2d 579, 585–86 (2d Cir.1990).

16. *See, e.g.,* California Civil Code § 3334.1.

17. Virginia Code § 8.01–40.

18. Indiana § 32–36–1–8; Oklahoma Title 12, § 1448(G).

these extremes. The general rule is that the existence of a *post mortem* right of publicity is determined by the law of the domicile of the estate.[19]

§ 11.4   Federal Preemption Under the Copyright Laws

In our federal system, federal law takes precedence over state law. To be more precise, state statutes and common law doctrines are void if they conflict outright with federal statutes or undermine their basic purposes. The three state remedies discussed in this chapter all seem to nibble around the edges of copyright law. When states forbid the use of data or information generated by others under the rubric of the misappropriation doctrine, there is the potential of conflict with the copyright rule that denies protection to facts and historical data.[1] Requiring those who receive ideas from outsiders to pay for them might conflict with the general rule of copyright law that there is no protection for ideas.[2] Protection of a celebrity's persona under the heading of the right of publicity poses many of the same problems. As a result, each of these three regimes, along with other doctrines of state law, may raise issues of federal preemption.

With the passage of the Copyright Act of 1976, Congress divested the states of the authority to provide for common law copyright in favor of a unified federal copyright system for both published and unpublished works.[3] To further clarify the boundary between permissible state protections and federal law the 1976 Act also expressly addresses federal preemption of state laws in § 301. Section 301 calls for the preemption of state law claims that provide rights "equivalent to any of the exclusive rights within the general scope of copyright as specified by section 106 in works of authorship that are fixed in a tangible medium of expression and come within the subject matter of copyright as specified by sections 102 and 103...." As restated by the Court of Appeals for the Second Circuit, § 301 preempts a state law claim if:

> (i) the state law claim seeks to vindicate "legal or equitable rights that are equivalent" to one of the bundle of exclusive rights already protected by copyright law under 17 U.S.C.A. § 106—styled the "general scope requirement"; and (ii) the particular work to which the state law claim is being applied falls within the type of works protected by the Copyright Act under Sections 102 and 103—styled the "subject matter requirement."[4]

The "general scope requirement" compels an inquiry into whether the state law provides a right that may be violated by an act which, in

19.   See Cairns v. Franklin Mint Co., 24 F.Supp.2d 1013 (C.D.Cal.1998).

§ 11.4

1.   *See supra* § 3.3.

2.   *Id.*

3.   *See supra* § 2.2.5.

4.   National Basketball Ass'n v. Motorola, Inc., 105 F.3d 841, 848 (2d Cir.1997).

and of itself, would infringe one of the § 106 exclusive rights, namely those of reproduction, adaptation, distribution, public display or public performance.[5] In performing this prong of the preemption analysis, courts often employ what has been termed the "extra element" test.[6] This test asks whether violation of the state law requires an additional element instead of, or in addition to, the acts of reproduction, adaptation, distribution, public display or public performance. If so, then the state law is judged qualitatively different from a charge of copyright infringement and therefore withstands federal preemption because it is outside the "general scope" of copyright.

The second prong of the federal preemption analysis, the "subject matter requirement," determines whether the state law protects a work of authorship within the subject matter of copyright as provided in sections 102 and 103. Thus, to be pre-empted the state law must relate to an original work of authorship fixed in a tangible medium of expression. The subject matter of copyright also encompasses those things that are specifically left *unprotected* by § 102(b), such as ideas, methods of operation and discoveries.

A simple example illustrates the workings of § 301. Suppose that the state of West Carolina enacted the Marcel Marceau Act, a statute that prohibits the public performance of pantomimes without the permission of the author, if those pantomimes had been appropriately fixed in a tangible medium of expression. This legislation fulfills the general scope requirement because a public performance right is provided by § 106(4). The subject matter requirement is also met because pantomimes are copyrightable subject matter under § 102(4). As a result, § 301 applies and this hypothetical legislation would be preempted. In contrast, suppose that a state statute protected *unfixed* pantomimes against appropriation against video camera-wielding pirates. Because unfixed pantomimes are not within the subject matter copyright laws, such a statute would survive preemption.

Actual preemption cases are seldom so straightforward as the foregoing example, however. Perhaps the most persistent source of perplexing preemption issues are cases involving issues of state contract law. Contracting parties may agree on terms that regulate the reproduction, adaptation, distribution, public display or public performance of works of authorship. Consider, for example, an agreement through which one contracting party agrees to disclose an idea to another. Such idea submission agreements often stipulate that the disclosed subject matter may not be used by the recipient without compensation to the disclosing party. This stipulation may be equivalent to the reproduction, adaptation or other right provided by § 106 of the 1976 Act, and as a result litigants have frequently argued that § 301 preempts the state cause of action. Although the courts have generally agreed that most state contract

---

5. *See supra* Chapter 7.

6. See Worth v. Universal Pictures, Inc., 5 F.Supp.2d 816, 821 (C.D.Cal.1997).

claims survive federal preemption, two lines of authority have arisen concerning this issue.

In *ProCD, Inc. v. Zeidenberg*,[7] the Court of Appeals for the Seventh Circuit announced the more extreme position that virtually no contractual provision would ever be preempted under § 301. There the plaintiff distributed a national directory of telephone listing on compact discs. The discs included a "shrinkwrap license"—a form contract intended to bind the purchaser when she opens the software packaging. The plaintiff's shrinkwrap license limited consumer access to the directory for personal use only. The defendants ignored the license, downloaded the telephone directory and made it available over the Internet for commercial purposes. The plaintiffs then brought, *inter alia*, a claim for breach of contract. The defendants in part asserted that the contract cause of action had been preempted under § 301.

On appeal, the Seventh Circuit held that § 301 did not preempt the contact claim. Judge Easterbrook reasoned that the exclusive rights granted by the federal Copyright Act apply to all persons, even strangers to the copyright proprietor. To be judged equivalent to copyright, the state law rights under consideration must also be ubiquitous. Contract claims did not fulfill this standard according to the *ProCD* court because they generally affect only the parties that have assented to the agreement. Although the Seventh Circuit stated that it did not intend to announce a categorical rule that all state claims identified as "contract" would survive preemption, it is difficult to imagine a contract claim that would not survive Judge Easterbrook's test.

Other courts, however, have concluded that "the rule safeguarding contract causes of action against copyright pre-emption is less than categorical."[8] The decision of the U.S. District Court for the Central District of California in *Endemol Entertainment B.V. v. Twentieth Television Inc.*[9] illustrates this approach. Endemol had developed a television show produced in Europe under the title "Forgive Me." With the intention of licensing rights to the show in the United States, Endemol presented Mr. Goodson with the "Forgive Me" show concept. The parties understood that this disclosure was made in confidence and that Endemol would be compensated for any use of the disclosed ideas. Goodson and the co-defendants later developed a U.S. show titled "Forgive and Forget" that, according to Endemol, improperly appropriated the substance of "Forgive Me." Endemol brought suit, in part claiming that the defendants had breached an implied-in-fact contract. The defendants moved to dismiss this claim on preemption grounds.

The trial court agreed with the defendants and held that § 301 preempted Endemol's implied-in-fact contract claim. Judge Collins disagreed with Endemol that contracts differed from copyright because

---

7. 86 F.3d 1447 (7th Cir.1996).

8. Wrench LLC v. Taco Bell Corp., 51 F.Supp.2d 840, 852–53 (W.D. Mich.1999), *rev'd* 256 F.3d 446 (6th Cir.2001), *cert. denied*, 534 U.S. 1114, 122 S.Ct. 921, 151 L.Ed.2d 885 (2002) (relying, in part, on Nimmer, Copyright § 1.01[B][1][a]).

9. 48 USPQ2d 1524 (C.D.Cal.1998).

contract rights were generally not enforceable against strangers to the transaction. The court instead reasoned that the claim asserted "no violation of rights separate from those copyright law was designed to protect" and would create "no additional rights other than promising not to benefit from the copyrighted work."[10] The *ProCD* decision was distinguished on the grounds that the contract at issue there included additional promises that provided an "extra element" beyond the rights afforded by the Copyright Act.[11]

As these two opinions suggest, the "general scope requirement" at times compels a perplexing inquiry. Although § 301 calls upon the courts to determine whether a state law provides rights "equivalent to any of the exclusive rights within the general scope of copyright," the statute does not define the term "equivalent." The result has been a great deal of confusion and varying judicial interpretations. Judicial focus upon the "extra element" standard has arguably encouraged courts to focus upon the technicalities of a particular state law, rather than its policies and effects, and may merely invite the states to incorporate a trivial additional requirement into an intrusive cause of action. Copyright law would benefit if courts focused their attention upon whether a challenged state law poses an obstacle to the policy aspirations of the Copyright Act, an inquiry which is, after all, the central question raised by traditional preemption analysis under the Constitution's Supremacy Clause.

10. *Id.* at 1528.   **11.** *Id.*

Chapter 12

COPYRIGHT IN THE INTERNATIONAL PERSPECTIVE

Table of Sections

The international dimension of copyright has never been so important. Movies, music, software and other works authored by U.S. citizens enjoy popularity around the world. In the era of the Internet, these works may be copied and distributed globally in a matter of moments. Yet, although copyrighted works observe few boundaries, copyright law itself remains strictly territorial. Each nation's copyright laws extend only as far as its own borders.

Although no true global copyright system exists, the copyright regimes of the United States and its trading partners are linked through a handful of international agreements. These agreements do not create a universal copyright law, in that they do not provide for a single source of rights effective worldwide. Yet they allow authors to claim a national copyright almost anywhere in the world. This Chapter discusses the most significant of the agreements that, together, comprise the international copyright system.

§ 12.1 The Berne Convention

The International Union for the Protection of Literary and Artistic Works, known more simply as the Berne Union or Berne Convention, is the premier multilateral copyright agreement. The Berne Convention was formed in 1886 and was subsequently revised on seven occasions.[1] The latest of these provisions, concluded in Paris in 1971, forms the current Berne Convention text.

The Berne Convention was not fashioned as a model copyright code. Berne is instead based upon the principle of "national treatment."[2] National treatment requires that Berne signatory states accord to foreign works eligible under Berne the same protection granted to their own nationals. It is essentially a simple principle of non-discrimination. In addition, it specifies minimum standards of protection that Berne signatories agree to offer domestically. As these standards provide the floor, not the ceiling of required copyright protection, member states may choose to provide more robust copyright laws than mandated by Berne and, historically, many have done so.

Among the core substantive provisions of the Berne Convention, Article 2, mandates a capacious scope of copyright protection. Copyright extends to "every production in the literary, scientific and artistic domain, whatever may be the mode or form of expression."[3] Article 2 offers an illustrative list of works eligible for copyright, including writings, choreographic works, works of drawing, architecture, photographic works and applied art.[4]

The Berne Convention further specifies the individuals eligible for protection in Article 3. Berne requires that protection be afforded to works, whether published or not, of an author who is a national or habitual resident of a Berne signatory state. In addition, authors who are not nationals or residents of a Berne signatory state may obtain protection if their works are either (1) first published in a Berne signatory state or (2) published simultaneously in a Berne signatory state and a state that has not acceded to the Berne Convention.[5] Under Berne, a work is considered to have been simultaneously published in a Berne signatory state so long as the work was published there within 30 days of the first publication in a non-member state.[6]

Article 5(2) of the Berne Convention requires that, for works outside their country of origin, copyright protection be afforded without formalities. The term "formalities" includes several traditional features of U.S. copyright law, including Copyright Office registration and the placement of notice on copies of the work. Article 5(2) abolishes these requirements for works outside of their country of origin. Although formalities can be imposed in the country in which the work originated, if a work originates from a Berne signatory state, that work must be protected automatically in all other Berne countries.

§ 12.1

1. Convention concerning the creation of an International Union for the Protection of Literary and Artistic Works (Sept. 9, 1886, revised in 1896, 1908, 1928, 1948, 1967, 1971).

2. Peter Berger, *The Berne Convention: Its History and Its Key Role in the Future*, 3 J. L. & Tech. 1, 16–17 (1988).

3. Berne Convention, Article 2(1).

4. Berne Convention, Article 2(1).

5. Berne Convention, Article 3(1).

6. Berne Convention, Article 3(4).

The Berne Convention also requires that member states afford authors certain economic and moral rights. Among the economic rights are the reproduction, adaptation, translation and public performance rights.[7] Article 6*bis* additionally recognizes two moral rights—those of attribution and integrity. Berne also recognizes certain limitations on these rights, including a right to make quotations and to use protected works for teaching purposes.[8]

The minimum copyright term under Berne is the life of the author plus 50 years or, in the case of anonymous or pseduonymous works, 50 years from the date of publication. Article 7 of the Berne Convention specifies that signatories may grant terms in excess of this minimum.[9] In cases where Berne Convention signatories offer different terms of protection, "the term shall not exceed the term fixed in the country of the origin of the work."[10] If, for example, Country A offers the Berne minimum term of life plus fifty years, while Country B offers a term of life plus seventy years, then Country B need offer only a term of protection of life plus fifty years to works originating from Country A. This "rule of the shorter term" forms a significant exception to the usual national treatment principle central to the Berne Convention. Congress kept this principle in mind when it recently extended copyright term by twenty years through the 1998 Sonny Bono Act. Although some other Berne signatory states offered a term of protection of life plus seventy years to their own nationals, these jurisdictions would have accorded U.S. works the shorter term of life plus fifty years, because that was the term under the 1976 Act as originally enacted. The proposition that U.S. authors would be disadvantaged in "Berne plus" jurisdictions was among the arguments offered for passing the Bono Act.

§ 12.2   U.S. Accession to Berne

The United States did not accede to the Berne Convention until March 1, 1989, more than a century after Berne's formation.[1] Among the factors motivating this delay was the distinct U.S. copyright tradition. Features such as notice, registration, deposit, and a set term based upon the date of publication simply did not comport with Berne Convention requirements. Domestic publishers, who took economic advantage of these distinctions, further encouraged the United States to go its own way.

Although the United States long remained aloof from the Berne Union, it did rely upon other agreements to protect its copyright interests abroad. The very first multilateral copyright treaty signed by the United States was the Buenos Aires Convention in 1911, which provided protection in 16 other nations of the Western Hemisphere. The most

7. Berne Convention, Articles 8, 9, 11, 12.

8. Berne Convention, Articles 10, 10*bis*.

9. Berne Convention, Article 7(6).

10. Berne Convention, Article 7(8).

§ 12.2

1. *See* William Belanger, *U.S. Compliance with the Berne Convention*, 3 GEORGE MASON INDEPENDENT L. REV. 373 (1995).

interesting feature of that treaty was that it required the use of the words "All Rights Reserved" in order to guarantee that protection would be afforded by all member states. All members of the Buenos Aires Convention are now bound by the TRIPS Agreement and must dispense with formalities as a condition for copyright protection. Use of "All Rights Reserved" is now completely unnecessary, but the phrase lingers on in some kind of odd legal inertia by book publishers.

Through the first half of the twentieth century, the United States entered into a number of additional bilateral agreements calling for mutual recognition in copyright. In 1955, the United States encouraged the formation of the Universal Copyright Convention ("UCC").[2] The UCC was effectively a more tolerant version of the Berne Convention. Formalities were assessed more leniently, and the compulsory copyright term was shorter, resulting in compatibility with U.S. copyright law. With the subsequent U.S. accession to the Berne Convention, as well as the rise of the TRIPS Agreement, the UCC has become nearly irrelevant to the world copyright order.

The 1976 Act moved the United States in the direction of compliance with the Berne Convention. For example, the 1976 Act eliminated a copyright term based upon the date of publication, instead moving to the term required by the Berne Convention, the life of the author plus 50 years. There was much work to be done, however, before the U.S. could join Berne. As originally enacted, the 1976 Act maintained formalities such as notice, deposit and registration, and it did not recognize moral rights.

As U.S. popular culture and information goods became increasingly valuable export commodities, the value of U.S. membership in the Berne Union became apparent. At last moved to accede to Berne, Congress in 1988 enacted the Berne Convention Implementation Act ("BCIA").[3] Congress adopted a minimalist approach with the BCIA. Only changes deemed absolutely necessary to ensure Berne compliance were introduced into U.S. law. The most significant of these changes, discussed earlier in this book, in Chapter 3, concerned statutory formalities. Once an obligatory feature of U.S. copyright law, the formalities of notice, deposit and registration have been reduced to recommended but ultimately voluntary options.

The BCIA also declares the Berne Convention to be executory, rather than self-executing, under U.S. law.[4] As a result, the Berne Convention is effective in the United States only to the extent that Congress passes domestic legislation implementing its obligations. It is not possible in the United States, as is the case in some other countries, for private parties to claim legal rights directly under the Berne Convention.

2. Universal Copyright Convention, Sept. 8 1952, 216 U.N.T.S. 132, revised July 24, 1971, 943 U.N.T.S. 178.

3. Pub. L. No. 100–568, 102 Stat. 2853.

4. *Id.* at § 2(1).

Upon further consideration of the BCIA's minimalist approach, Congress later judged some of its changes to be overly modest. Additional implementing legislation was deemed prudent. The Visual Artist's Rights Act of 1990 (VARA),[5] which establishes the rights of attribution and integrity for certain visual artwork, furthered U.S. compliance with the moral rights standards of Article 6*bis* of Berne. VARA is discussed further in this text at § 7.6.2. As well, the "useful article" doctrine, discussed above at § 4.5, had rendered uncertain the availability of copyright protection for architectural works. In view of the Berne Article 2 requirement that architectural works enjoy copyright, Congress amended § 102(a) of the Copyright Act to recognize expressly copyright in architectural works.[6]

§ 12.3   The TRIPS Agreement

Although the venerable Berne Convention remains the world's prominent copyright treaty, it suffers from two notable defects. First, consensus must be achieved among its signatory states for revision to occur.[1] As Berne's numerous signatory states possess widely varying copyright interests, unanimity has become virtually impossible to achieve. Consequently the Berne Convention no longer serves as a viable platform for copyright reform.

Second, the obligations of the Berne Convention cannot be practically enforced. The Berne Convention stipulates that compliance disputes are to be adjudicated before the International Court of Justice. As this tribunal effectively lacks the authority to enforce its judgments, no such suit has ever been brought.[2] Each signatory's sense of honor, along with diplomatic efforts from other member states, are effectively the only compliance measures that exist under Berne.

A recognition of these failings, along with a growing perception of the strong connection between intellectual property and international trade, resulted in the shift of copyright treaty-making efforts into new fora. In 1993, the United States joined with Canada and Mexico in the North American Free Trade Agreement (NAFTA). NAFTA includes a number of provisions harmonizing its signatories' intellectual property laws, including copyright.

Shortly after acceding to NAFTA, the United States became a member of the newly formed World Trade Organization (WTO). Negotiations leading to the WTO resulted in an Agreement on Trade–Related Aspects of Intellectual Property Rights, the so-called TRIPS Agreement.[3]

5. Pub. L. No. 101–650, 104 Stat. 5089, 5128–33 (1990).

6. Pub. L. No. 101–650, §§ 704, 705 (1990).

§ 12.3

1. Berne Convention, Art. 27(3).

2. Ralph Oman, *The United States the Berne Union: An Extended Courtship*, 3 J. L. & Tech. 71, 115 (1988).

3. Agreement on Trade–Related Aspects of Intellectual Property Rights, Apr. 15, 1994, Marrekesh Agreement Establishing the World Trade Organization [hereinafter the WTO Agreement], Annex 1C, in Results of the Uruguay Round of Multilateral Trade

The TRIPS Agreement is the most advanced multinational agreement on intellectual property yet completed. Because every WTO member has agreed to comply with the TRIPS Agreement, its core provisions merit review here.

The TRIPS Agreement expounds both national treatment and "most favored nation" principles.[4] The national treatment principle provides that each WTO member must accord to nationals of another member treatment no less favorable than it accords to its own nationals. Under the "most favored nation" provisions, with limited exceptions, any privilege granted to nationals of one WTO member state must be afforded to nationals of all WTO member states.

The TRIPS Agreement also sets forth minimum standards of intellectual property protection. With respect to copyright, the TRIPS Agreement incorporates Berne's substantive obligations. All WTO members must comply with Articles 1 through 21 of the Berne Convention, with the exception of Article 6*bis* (pertaining to moral rights).[5] The TRIPS Agreement additionally requires WTO member states to protect computer programs as literary works, as well as data compilations that, by virtue of their selection or arrangement, constitute "intellectual creations."[6] The TRIPS Agreement also calls for rental rights for computer programs and cinematographic works.[7]

Perhaps the most significant aspect of the TRIPS Agreement is that its obligations are more readily enforced than those of predecessor agreements. Disagreements between WTO member states over TRIPS Agreement compliance are subject to the WTO Dispute Settlement Understanding.[8] These provisions call for initial consultations between WTO member states in order to resolve a dispute. If the consultations fail, one of the parties may request the Dispute Settlement Body to establish a panel. This process leads to briefings, meetings before the panel, and ultimately a final panel report. The right to appeal the case to an Appellate Body is automatic. Failure to abide by WTO Dispute Settlement Body rulings may result in compensation to the injured party. The injured party may suspend concessions or other obligations under the TRIPS Agreement, or possibly another WTO agreement, at a level equivalent to the damages suffered.

§ 12.4 Additional International Copyright Agreements

The Rome Convention. The International Convention for the Protection of Performers, Producers of Phonograms and Broadcasting Organizations was signed in Rome in 1961.[1] By focusing upon perform-

Negotiations 1 (1994) [hereinafter Uruguay Round Results] 365 (1994), 33 I.L.M. 1197.

4. TRIPS Agreement, Art. 3 (national treatment) and Art. 4 (most favored nation).

5. TRIPS Agreement, Art. 9(1).

6. TRIPS Agreement, Art. 10(2).

7. TRIPS Agreement, Art. 11.

8. TRIPS Agreement, Art. 64.

§ 12.4

1. International Convention for the Protection of Performers, Producers of Phonograms and Broadcasting Organizations, art. 15(2), 496 U.N.T.S. 43 (Oct. 26, 1961).

ers, record producers and broadcasters, the Rome Convention is said to concern "neighboring rights"—rights akin to copyright but concerning nontraditional subject matter. Rome Convention signatories agree to provide minimum protection standards by restricting the broadcasting of live performances, the recording of unfixed performances, and in certain circumstances the reproduction of a fixation of the performance. The United States, which does not confer public performance rights in sound recordings, has not joined the Rome Convention.

The Geneva Phonograms Convention. The Convention for the Protection of Producers of Phonograms Against Unauthorized Duplication of Their Phonograms was formed in Geneva in 1971.[2] Signatories agree to protect nationals of other member states against the unauthorized manufacture, importation and distribution of copies of sound recordings. The United States became a party to the Geneva Phonogram Convention in 1974.

Brussels Satellite Convention. The Convention Relating to the Distribution of Programme–Carrying Signals Transmitted by Satellite was formed in Brussels in 1974.[3] Signatories to the Brussels Convention pledge to take adequate measures to prevent the misappropriation of satellite signals. The United States became a party to the Brussels Satellite Convention in 1985.

The WIPO Treaties. Two treaties were completed under the auspices of the World Intellectual Property Organization (WIPO) in 1996. The WIPO Copyright Treaty includes a number of different provisions that build upon the Berne Convention.[4] Article 2 of the WIPO Copyright Treaty calls for the protection of computer programs as literary works, while Article 5 provides for the copyright protection of data compilations that, by virtue of their selection or arrangement, constitute "intellectual creations." Signatories to the WIPO Copyright Treaty also agree to confer distribution and rental rights to computer works, movies and works embodied in phonograms. The WIPO Copyright Treaty further obliged signatories to provide legal protection for technological protection measures and rights management information. The Digital Millennium Copyright Act of 1998, discussed previously at § 7.7 of this text, implemented these latter obligations domestically.

The second WIPO treaty, the WIPO Performances and Phonograms Treaty, calls for the grant of additional rights beyond those mandated by the Geneva Phonograms Convention.[5] This treaty confirms that the

2. Convention for the Protection of Producers of Phonograms Against Unauthorized Duplication of Their Phonograms, Oct. 29, 1971, 25 U.S.T. 309, 866 U.N.T.S. 67.

3. Convention Relating to the Distribution of Programme–Carrying Signals Transmitted by Satellite, May 21, 1974, 13 I.L.M. 1444.

4. World Intellectual Property Organization Copyright Treaty, adopted Dec. 20, 1996, art. 11, 36 I.L.M. 65, 71.

5. World Intellectual Property Organization, Performances and Phonograms Treaty, adopted Dec. 20, 1996, art. 18, 36 I.L.M. 76, 86.

reproduction right accorded to phonogram producers extends to "any manner or form," including digital media. The treaty also builds upon the TRIPS Agreement by articulating a right to prevent the fixation, reproduction, broadcasting and communication to the public of live performances. The United States became a signatory to both WIPO treaties in 1998.

Chapter 13

INTRODUCTION TO THE LAW OF PATENTS

Table of Sections

The patent law often seems the most daunting and elusive of the intellectual property regimes. The patent statute has become an increasingly intricate work of legislation. As well, the proprietary rights extended by individual patents often concern complex subject matter. As a result, many students are drawn to the field less out of intellectual curiosity than from a desire to obtain a return on investment in earlier technical training. Others come to the patent law out of the recognition that it is important. Of all of the intellectual property systems, the patent law provides the most robust rights; has been most subject to sweeping domestic and international reforms; and, perhaps of most immediate significance, generates far more work for practitioners than copyright, trademark and related disciplines put together.

Although paths to the patent system vary, students quickly discover that this discipline is as engaging as any they will encounter in their legal careers. The patent law is a venerable regime with a rich history. But in many ways it remains a work in progress. The most important problems seemingly resist solution, and there are always many more questions than answers. Diverse factors contribute to this state of affairs, but at bottom the unsettled state of the patent regime results from a course of technological progress that is both relentless and unpredictable. The patent law must balance its past with the mandate to remain as current as the latest developments in biotechnology, computer science, finance and other diverse endeavors. In succeeding chapters of this treatise, the authors hope not only to explain the technical workings of this discipline, but to convey the fascination and enthusiasm that has resulted from their own studies of the patent law.

§ 13.1   Brief Overview of the Patent Law

Since the first Congress enacted the Patent Act of 1790, the patent law has been a wholly federal, statutory subject. Today the patent law is governed by the Patent Act of 1952, found in Title 35 of the United States Code. This statute allows inventors to obtain patents on processes, machines, manufactures and compositions of matter that are useful, new and nonobviousness.[1] An invention is judged as useful if it is minimally operable towards some practical purpose.[2] The invention must also not be wholly anticipated by the so-called "prior art," or public domain materials such as publications and other patents.[3] The nonobviousness requirement is met if the invention is beyond the ordinary abilities of a skilled artisan knowledgeable in the appropriate field.[4]

In order to receive a patent, an inventor must file a patent application with a specialized government agency known as the United States Patent and Trademark Office, or PTO.[5] Patent applications must include a specification that so completely describes the invention that skilled artisans are enabled to practice it without undue experimentation.[6] The patent application must also contain distinct, definite claims that set out the proprietary interest asserted by the inventor.[7]

The PTO examines applications to ensure that the invention described and claimed in the application fulfills the pertinent requirements of the patent law. Acquisition proceedings at the PTO are commonly known as "prosecutions." If the PTO believes that the application fulfills the statutory requirements, it will allow the application to issue as a

§ 13.1

1. 35 U.S.C.A. §§ 101, 102, 103 (2000).

2. *See* Brenner v. Manson, 383 U.S. 519, 86 S.Ct. 1033, 16 L.Ed.2d 69 (1966).

3. 35 U.S.C.A. § 102 (2000).

4. 35 U.S.C.A. § 103(a) (2000).

5. 35 U.S.C.A. § 111 (2000).

6. 35 U.S.C.A. § 112 (2000).

7. 35 U.S.C.A. § 112 (2000).

granted patent.[8] At this time the PTO will assemble and publish the corresponding patent instrument, which includes the complete specification, claims, and prior art references considered during prosecution.[9] Issued patents provide interested parties with notice of the patentee's proprietary rights and are also a valued source of technical information.

Granted patents confer the right to exclude others from making, using, selling, offering to sell, or importing into the United States the patented invention.[10] Each patent ordinarily enjoys a term of twenty years commencing from the date the patent application was filed.[11] The patentee may file a civil suit in federal court in order to enjoin infringers and obtain monetary remedies.[12] Although issued patents enjoy a presumption of validity, accused infringers may assert that the patent is invalid or unenforceable on a number of grounds.[13] Patents have the attributes of personal property and may be assigned or licensed to others.[14]

§ 13.2   History

13.2.1   Origins

Legal historians have been quick to seize upon venerable antecedents to our contemporary patent law regime. An ancient Greek system of rewarding cooks for excellent recipes,[1] exclusive privileges granted for innovations relating to Tyrolean mines in the Fourteenth Century,[2] and a Florentine patent granted in 1421 have been variously cited as predecessors to the modern patent law.[3] However, most observers consider legislation enacted on March 19, 1474, by the Venetian Republic as the first true patent statute.[4] With its requirements that the invention be new, useful, and reduced to practice; provision for a ten-year term; and registration and remedial scheme, the Venetian statute bears a remarkable resemblance to the modern law. By the Seventeenth Century, numerous European states had enacted similar legislation.[5] For purposes of the common law world, the most significant of these successors was the English Statute of Monopolies, an important commercial statute of the Jacobean era.

8. 35 U.S.C.A. § 151 (2000).

9. 35 U.S.C.A. § 154 (2000).

10. 35 U.S.C.A. § 271(a) (2000).

11. 35 U.S.C.A. § 154 (2000).

12. 35 U.S.C.A. § 281 (2000).

13. 35 U.S.C.A. § 282 (2000).

14. 35 U.S.C.A. § 261 (2000).

§ 13.2

1. *See* BRUCE BUGBEE, GENESIS OF AMERICAN PATENT AND COPYRIGHT LAW 166 n.5 (1967).

2. ERICH KAUFER, THE ECONOMICS OF THE PATENT SYSTEM (1989).

3. M. Frumkin, *The Origin of Patents*, 27 J. PAT. OFF. SOC'Y 143, 144 (1943).

4. *See* Giulio Mandich, *Venentian Patents (1450–1550)*, 30 J. PAT. OFF. SOC'Y 166 (1948).

5. F.D. Prager, *A History of Intellectual Property From 1545 to 1787*, 26 J. PAT. OFF. SOC'Y 711 (1944).

13.2.2 The Statute of Monopolies

By the start of the seventeenth century, the English Crown had a long history of awarding importation franchises and other exclusive rights. But this practice had become subject to abuse during the reigns of Elizabeth I and James I, as favored subjects obtained grants of supervision or control over long-established industries. Parliament responded in 1624 by enacting the Statute of Monopolies.[6] Although the Statute was principally designed to proscribe monopolistic grants by the Crown, it did authorize the issuance of "letters patent" directed towards the "working or making of any manner of new manufacture" to "the true and first inventor or inventors." Such patents possessed terms of fourteen years and could not be "contrary to law" or "mischievous to the State."

13.2.3 Colonial Patents and the Constitution

The patent tradition established by the Statute of Monopolies continued in many of the New World colonies. For example, a Connecticut statute of 1672 outlawed the award of monopolies except for "such new inventions as shall be judged profitable for the country and for such time as the general court shall judge meet." As well, many colonial governments granted individuals privileges or rewards for their inventions very early in their histories.[7] By 1787, state grants of patents were at their zenith, and the delegates to the Constitutional Convention apparently realized the possibility of interstate conflicts among competing inventors. As a result, Convention delegates unanimously agreed that the U.S. Congress should possess the power to "promote the Progress of ... useful Arts by securing for limited Times to ... Inventors the exclusive Right to their ... Discoveries." Article I, section 8, clause 8 of the Constitution houses this grant of authority.

13.2.4 The 1790 and 1793 Acts

The first Congress quickly acted upon this constitutional grant, when President George Washington signed the first U.S. patent statute into law on April 10, 1790.[8] The Act created a board, known as the "Commissioners for the Promotion of the Useful Arts," authorized to determine whether "the invention or discovery [was] sufficiently useful and important" to deserve a patent. The board consisted of the Secretary of State (Thomas Jefferson), the Secretary of War (Henry Knox) and the Attorney General (Edmund Randolph).[9]

This Heroic Age of the patent law proved short lived, as examination duties proved too onerous for the three-member board. Congress re-

6. Chris R. Kyle, *"But a New Button to an Old Coat": The Enactment of the Statute of Monopolies*, 19 J. LEGAL HISTORY 203 (1998).

7. *See* Edward C. Walterscheid, *The Early Evolution of United States Patent Law: Antecedents (Part I)*, 78 J. PAT. & TRADEMARK OFF. SOC'Y 615 (1996).

8. Act of April 10, 1790, Ch. 7, 1 Stat. 109.

9. *See* KENNETH W. DOBYNS, THE PATENT OFFICE PONY: A HISTORY OF THE EARLY PATENT OFFICE (1994).

sponded by enacting the Patent Act of 1793,[10] which abandoned patent examination in favor of a registration scheme. Under the 1793 Act, the State Department was assigned the wholly administrative task of maintaining a registry of patents. Whether a registered patent was valid and enforceable was left solely to the courts.

13.2.5   The 1836 and 1870 Acts

Observing that the registration system of the 1793 Act had sometimes encouraged duplicative and fraudulent patents, Congress restored an examination system with the Patent Act of 1836.[11] The 1836 Act created a Patent Office within the Department of State and provided for the filing and formal examination of patent applications. The 1870 Act largely maintained the provisions of its predecessor,[12] but at several points stressed that patentees define their proprietary interest in a distinctly drafted claim. Litigation under these two statutes frequently culminated at the Supreme Court, resulting in opinions that established nonobviousness, enablement, experimental use and other fundamental doctrines of contemporary patent law.

13.2.6   The 1952 Act

Although judicial postures towards patents varied with the U.S. economic climate throughout the nineteenth and early twentieth Centuries, the Depression Era amounted to a Dark Age for the patent system. The vigorous anti-monopoly sentiments of that period were accompanied by an active dislike of patents. Although the U.S. patent system predated the Sherman Act by more than a century, the courts were quick to find ordinary patent licensing and enforcement efforts as violative of the antitrust laws and the related doctrine of patent misuse. In particular, the Supreme Court's propensity to strike down patents in this era reached such proportions that Justice Jackson was compelled to lament in dissent that "the only patent that is valid is one which this Court has not been able to get its hands on."[13]

The drafters of the Patent Act of 1952 sought to reverse this anti-patent trend; as events have borne out, it has become apparent that they dramatically succeeded. Among the innovations of the 1952 Act were the codification of the nonobviousness standard and the curtailing of patent misuse.[14] The 1952 Act is wholly codified into Title 35 of the United States Code and, as subjected to frequent amendments, remains the dominant U.S. patent statute.

10. Act of Feb. 21, 1793, Ch. 11, 2 Stat. 318.

11. Act of July 4, 1836, Ch. 357, 5 Stat. 117.

12. Act of July 8, 1870, Ch. 230, 16 Stat. 198.

13. *See* Jungersen v. Ostby & Barton Co., 335 U.S. 560, 572, 69 S.Ct. 269, 93 L.Ed. 235 (1949).

14. Act of July 19, 1952, Ch. 950, 66 Stat. 797.

13.2.7 The Federal Courts Improvement Act of 1982

Another significant patent law reform was procedural in nature. The Evarts Act of 1891 established the familiar circuit courts of appeal, numbered and organized on a geographic basis.[15] Experience demonstrated that the different regional courts of appeal held widely varying views of the patent system. While some circuits were not inhospitable to patents, others would only rarely find a patent valid and enforceable. These disparities undermined the uniformity of the federal patent system and led to an unseemly amount of forum shopping.

Law reform efforts ultimately led to the creation of a new intermediate appellate court, the United States Court of Appeals for the Federal Circuit, via the Federal Courts Improvement Act of 1982.[16] The Federal Circuit hears, among other matters, appeals from the PTO and from the federal district courts in patent matters. These dual routes of appeal indicate that most patent issues quickly darken the door of the Federal Circuit. As a result, any study of U.S. patent law largely concerns the work product of the Federal Circuit. Federal Circuit decisions are subject to review at the Supreme Court.

Proponents of the Federal Circuit believe that the court has brought stability and predictability to the patent law.[17] Detractors have questioned whether the patent law has prospered under the stewardship of a tribunal that considers a limited variety of cases and arguably has a vested interest in a robust patent system.[18] All observers agree that the Federal Circuit has dramatically expanded the range of patentable subject matter, liberally upheld large damages awards and preliminary injunctions, and strengthened the patent grant in comparison to many predecessor courts.

The Federal Circuit is housed in the Howard T. Markey Building, which sits just across Pennsylvania Avenue from the White House in Washington, D.C. The Federal Circuit consists of twelve active circuit judges and a number of senior circuit judges. Ordinarily a panel of three judges resolves appeals placed before the court. Occasionally, in order to resolve important issues, all of the active judges of the Federal Circuit convene in special *en banc* proceedings.[19]

13.2.8 The American Inventors Protection Act of 1999

Following several years of discussion, Congress lent final approval to the American Inventors Protection Act of 1999 (AIPA).[20] The AIPA worked numerous reforms to the U.S. patent law, including the creation of an infringement defense to first inventors of business methods later

15. Act of March 3, 1891, Ch. 517, 26 Stat. 826.

16. Pub. L. No. 97–164, 96 Stat. 25 (April 2, 1982).

17. *See* Joan E. Schaffner, *Federal Circuit Choice of Law:* Erie *Through the Looking Glass,* 81 Iowa L. Rev. 1173 (1996) (noting these aspirations for the Federal Circuit).

18. *See* Steven Anderson, *Federal Circuit Gets Passing Marks to Date But There's A Lot of Room for Improvement,* 10 Corporate Legal Times no. 10 at 86 (March 2000).

19. *See* South Corp. v. United States, 690 F.2d 1368 (Fed.Cir.1982).

20. Pub. L. No. 106–113, 113 Stat. 1501 (Nov. 29, 1999).

patented by another; the extension of the patent term in the event of processing delays at the PTO; the mandate for publication of certain pending patent applications; and the provision of optional *inter partes* reexamination procedures.

§ 13.3   International Patent Harmonization

Despite increasing international trade and the longstanding recognition that technology knows no borders, the nations of the earth have yet to agree to a global patent system. Patent prosecution and litigation therefore occurs on a piecemeal, jurisdiction-by-jurisdiction basis. Still, the desire to facilitate multinational patent acquisition and harmonize national laws has been keenly felt, and has led to several international agreements concerning patents. The United States has joined three such agreements that are worthy of note here.

13.3.1   The Paris Convention

The 1883 Paris Convention for the Protection of Industrial Property is the foundational international agreement concerning patents (and trademarks).[1] The Paris Convention contains few provisions mandating particular legal requirements for the patent law, but it does provide for national treatment. As a result, signatory states must treat domiciles of Paris Convention signatory states in the same manner as their own domiciles.

Article 4 of the Paris Convention also allows an applicant to obtain a so-called "priority date" by filing an patent application in any signatory state. This applicant may then file a subsequent patent application in any other signatory state within twelve months and claim the benefit of the original application. Each Paris Convention signatory has agreed to treat the subsequent application as if it were filed on the date of the original application. Among other benefits, this twelve-month grace period prevents unscrupulous individuals from copying the original patent application and becoming the first to claim the invention as their own in other countries, before the true inventor has the opportunity to file foreign applications.

13.3.2   The Patent Cooperation Treaty

The Patent Cooperation Treaty, or PCT,[2] was formed in 1970 and is open to any country that has joined the Paris Convention. This agreement provides an optional application procedure in order to simplify multinational patent acquisition. Over one hundred signatory nations have adopted the PCT filing mechanisms and standardized application format.

§ 13.3

1. Paris Convention for the Protection of Industrial Property, Mar. 20, 1883, 13 U.S.T. 1.

2. Patent Cooperation Treaty, June 19, 1970, 28 U.S.T. 7645.

13.3.3 The TRIPS Agreement

The Agreement on Trade–Related Aspects of Intellectual Property Rights, a component of the international agreement establishing the World Trade Organization (WTO),[3] has been joined by virtually every member of the world trading community. As the first treaty that extensively required signatory nations to maintain specified standards of substantive patent law, the so-called "TRIPS Agreement" was an impressive accomplishment. The TRIPS Agreement specifies that member states must observe certain requirements pertaining to patent-eligible subject matter, patent term, and standards of patentability such as novelty and nonobviousness. In order to comply with the TRIPS Agreement, the United States enacted the Uruguay Round Agreements Act in 1995. Among the changes worked by this legislation were the introduction of provisional patent applications, the change of patent term to twenty years measured from the date the patent application was filed, and the acceptance of evidence of dates of inventive activity performed in WTO member countries.

§ 13.4 Rationales for the Patent Law

The patent system has been justified by appeals to instrumental rationales and, to a lesser extent, the natural rights of individuals to enjoy a proprietary interest in their inventions. These rationales are tempered by the recognition that inventors have sometimes abused the patent system, as well as the observation that no conclusive demonstration proves the patent system achieves its laudable goals.

13.4.1 Instrumental Rationales

The patent system is motivated by a number of public policies that are instrumental in character. These theories view the patent system as providing incentives for individuals to engage in desirable behavior. For example, many commentators have observed that the patent system encourages individuals to invent. Proponents of this theory reason that absent a patent system, inventions can easily be duplicated or exploited by free riders. The resulting inability of inventors to capitalize on their inventions would lead to an environment where too few inventions are made.[1] The courts have also suggested that absent a patent law, individuals would favor maintaining their inventions as trade secrets so that competitors could not exploit them. Trade secrets do not enrich the collective knowledge of society, however, nor do they discourage others from engaging in duplicative research. The patent system avoids these

---

3. Agreement on Trade–Related Aspects of Intellectual Property Rights, General Agreement on Tariffs and Trade, Final Act Embodying the Results of the Uruguay Round of Multilateral Trade Negotiations, Apr. 15, 1994, Annex 1C, 33 I.L.M. 1197.

§ 13.4

1. *See* Rebecca S. Eisenberg, *Patents and the Progress of Science: Exclusive Rights and Experimental Use*, 56 U. CHI. L. REV. 1017 (1989).

inefficiencies by requiring inventors to consent to the disclosure of their inventions in issued patent instruments.[2]

The Patent Act is also thought to stimulate technological advancement by inducing individuals to "invent around" patented technology. Issued patent instruments may point the way for others to develop improvements, exploit new markets or discover new applications for the patented technology. Moreover, the patent system may encourage patentees to exploit their proprietary technologies during the term of the patent. The protection provided by a patent's proprietary rights increases the likelihood a firm will continue to refine, produce and market the patented technology.[3] Finally, the patent law has been identified as a facilitator of markets. Absent patent rights, an inventor may have scant tangible assets to sell or license, and even less ability to police the conduct of a contracting party. By reducing a licensee's opportunistic possibilities, the patent system lowers transaction costs and makes technology-based transactions more feasible.[4]

13.4.2 Natural Rights

Although patent laws are most often considered in terms of their economic consequences, some commentators have stressed the grant of patents as a mechanism for recognizing the dignity and worth of individual inventors. Under this view, the patent system provides a legal mechanism recognizing that inventors enjoy inherent rights in the fruits of their labors. These themes tend to resonate far less deeply here than in the copyright law, perhaps due to our different sense of individual expression in works of authorship than in patentable inventions.[5]

13.4.3 Criticisms of the Patent System

In its long history, the patent system has inspired a great number of detractors. Some critics have asserted that the patent system is unnecessary due to market forces that already suffice to create an optimal level of invention. The desire to gain a lead time advantage over competitors, as well as the recognition that technologically backwards firms lose out to their rivals, may well provide sufficient inducement to invent without the need for further incentives.[6] Commentators have also observed that successful inventors all too often are transformed into complacent, established enterprises that use patents to suppress the innovations of others.[7] In many differing eras and industries, speculators have been accused of building vast patent portfolios that contribute little to technological advancement, but reportedly have been used merely to threaten

2. *See, e.g.,* Grant v. Raymond, 31 U.S. 218, 247, 6 Pet. 218, 8 L.Ed. 376 (1832).

3. F. Scott Kieff, *Property Rights and Property Rules for Commercializing Inventions*, 85 MINN. L. REV. 697 (2000).

4. *See* Robert P. Merges, *Intellectual Property and the Costs of Commercial Exchange: A Review Essay*, 93 MICH. L. REV. 1570 (1995).

5. *See generally* PETER DRAHOS, A PHILOSOPHY OF INTELLECTUAL PROPERTY (1996).

6. *See* FREDERIC M. SCHERER, INDUSTRIAL MARKET STRUCTURE AND ECONOMIC PERFORMANCE 384–87 (1970).

7. *See* Robert P. Merges and Richard R. Nelson, *On the Complex Economics of Patent Scope*, 90 COLUM. L. REV. 839 (1990).

legitimate manufacturers and service providers.[8] It is also undeniably true that the inventions that fueled our most dynamic industries, such as early biotechnologies and computer software, arose at a time when patent rights were unavailable or uncertain.[9]

Many of these criticisms are well taken, but they too suffer from the lack of a sound empirical foundation. Supporters and critics of the patent system alike agree that the nature of technological progress is at best poorly understood. The question of whether the patent system advances the interests of society is not yet within our abilities to answer precisely, and is perhaps unknowable. Most are content to recognize the realities that industry has become increasingly enthusiastic in its pursuit of patents, the number of patent professionals is at historically high levels, and the public interest in the patent system is virtually without precedent. The patent law has plainly risen from its obscure station to the status of mainstream legal discipline, and careful students of its often complex provisions should discover a rich source of both intellectual and material rewards.

8. *See, e.g.*, Nicholas Varchaver, *The Patent King*, 143 Fortune no. 10 at 202 (May 14, 2001).

9. *See, e.g.*, Pamela Samuelson, Benson *Revisited: The Case Against Patent Protec-* *tion for Algorithms and Other Computer Program–Related Inventions*, 39 Emory L.J. 1025, 1135–36 (1990).

Chapter 14

PATENT ELIGIBILITY

§ 14.1   Basic Concepts

Section 101 defines the subject matter that may be patented. According to the statute, a person who "invents or discovers any new and useful process, machine, manufacture, or any composition of matter, or any new and useful improvement thereof, may obtain a patent therefore, subject to the conditions and requirements of this title." An invention that falls within one of the four statutory categories—processes, machines, manufactures, and compositions of matter—may be subject to a so-called "utility patent." Two other sorts of patents, pertaining to designs and plants, are discussed at the close of this Chapter.

The four categories set forth in section 101 refine the term "useful arts," the constitutional expression of the subject matter appropriate for patenting. Historically, the useful arts were contrasted with the liberal and fine arts. This approach confined the patent system to inventions in the field of applied technology. Inventions that employed the natural sciences to manipulate physical forces fell within the useful arts. Those that relied upon such things as the social sciences, commercial strategy or personal skill were judged unpatentable.[1]

In recent years, however, the patent system has demonstrated an increasing permissiveness towards patentable subject matter. In particular, the Federal Circuit has steadily dismantled earlier prohibitions upon patent eligibility, ranging from computer software, to printed matter, to methods of doing business. In response to this trend, the PTO has issued patents involving inventions from a broad range of disciplines, including a golf putt,[2] teaching methods[3] and techniques of psychological analysis.[4]

The present state of affairs suggests that few, if any, restrictions limit the range of patentable subject matter. Once limited to natural scientists and engineers, the patent system now appears poised to embrace the broadest reaches of human experience. It is hardly an exaggeration to say that under current law, if you can name it, you can claim it. Much of this chapter will appear of historical significance, with the removal of earlier limitations upon patent eligibility by an increasingly lenient judiciary becoming a familiar pattern. Still, patent eligibility continually proves itself to be an unsettled field. To understand our current state of affairs it is helpful to know how we got here.

Before proceeding further, the reader should note that section 101 twice employs the phrase "new and useful." Despite this wording, the courts have traditionally distinguished the requirement of patent eligibility from those of novelty and utility.[5] Thus, the inquiry of whether a particular invention is of the kind the patent laws were intended to protect has traditionally been considered a different matter from whether the invention possess novelty, and is useful, within the meaning of the patent law. Utility and novelty are addressed in Chapters Fifteen and Sixteen of this text respectively.

§ 14.2 Product and Process Claims

Patent attorneys typically speak of inventions in terms of either a product or process.[1] Product claims concern tangible things, including

§ 14.1

1. *See* John R. Thomas, *The Patenting of the Liberal Professions*, 40 Boston College L. Rev. 1139 (1999).

2. U.S. Patent No. 5,616,089 (Apr. 1, 1997) ("Method of putting").

3. U.S. Patent No. 5,558,519 (Sept. 24, 1996) ("Method for instruction of golf and the like").

4. U.S. Patent No. 5,190,458 (Mar. 2, 1993) ("Character assessment method").

5. Brian P. Biddinger, *Limiting the Business Method Patent: A Comparison and Proposed Alignment of European, Japanese and United States Patent Law*, 69 Fordham L. Rev. 2523 (2001).

§ 14.2

1. John R. Thomas, *Of Text, Technique and the Tangible: Drafting Patent Claims Around Patent Rules*, 17 John Marshall J. of Computer & Information L. 219 (1998).

objects and artifacts. In terms of § 101, product inventions consist either of machines, manufactures or compositions of matter. A machine includes an apparatus or mechanical device.[2] Compositions of matter include such things as chemical compounds, mechanical or physical mixtures and alloys.[3] Finally, a manufacture is a broadly oriented, residual category of manmade items.[4]

When the product invention is presented in the fashion of a patent claim, it is defined in terms of its structural elements. Consider the following invention, patented by the IBM Corporation, that allows an individual to submit a reservation request for restroom use.[5] A reservation system determines when the request can be accommodated and notifies the individual when a restroom becomes available. The system could be used on an airplane, for example, to improve safety by minimizing the time passengers spent standing while an airplane is in flight. A product claim towards this invention might read:

> An apparatus for providing reservations for restroom use, comprising:
>
>> means for receiving a reservation request from a user; and
>>
>> means for notifying the user when the restroom is available for use.

Note that the claim is drafted broadly, using general language. More limited claims could define this invention by detailing the specific devices that achieve the claimed functions. The "means for notifying the user when the restroom is available for use" might consist of a video screen in an airplane's cabin or an indicator display in the arm of the passenger's seat.

Process inventions involve a series of acts performed in order to produce a given result. Processes concern methods, techniques and behavioral engagements. When a process invention is drafted as a patent claim, the claim consists of a list of steps. The following claim, directed to the same restroom use reservation system previously recited, is illustrative:

> A method of providing reservations for restroom use, comprising the steps of:
>
>> receiving a reservation request from a user; and
>>
>> notifying the user when the restroom is available for his or her use.

Process inventions are commonly divided into two types, although this distinction is largely a matter of characterization rather than of substantive effect. These are termed "method of using" and "method of

---

2. *See* Nestle–Le Mur Co. v. Eugene, Ltd., 55 F.2d 854 (6th Cir.1932).

3. Diamond v. Chakrabarty, 447 U.S. 303, 100 S.Ct. 2204, 65 L.Ed.2d 144 (1980).

4. *Id.*

5. U.S. Patent No. 6,329,919 (Dec. 11, 2001).

making" claims.[6] Suppose that an inventor manufactures a new chemical compound and also discovers that the compound may be employed in a certain technical context. The manner in which the compound may be employed to achieve a particular result may be drafted in the form of a claim towards a method of using. In addition, the inventor may obtain claims for a method of making the compound, stating the techniques he employed to synthesize the compound.

Processes were traditionally required to work a physical transformation in order to be patentable. In its 1877 opinion in *Cochrane v. Deener*,[7] the Supreme Court explained that a process "is a mode of treatment of certain materials to produce a given result. It is an act, or a series of acts, performed upon the subject-matter to be transformed and reduced to a different state or thing." As the technological community has moved from the industrial to the information age, the courts viewed this requirement with increasing leniency. For example, in *In re Schrader*,[8] the Federal Circuit noted that the "transformation or conversion" could occur with respect to subject matter that was merely "representative of" physical things. The *Schrader* holding allows many inventions from the field of data processing to be eligible for patenting.

A later case, *AT&T Corp. v. Excel Communications*,[9] completely laid to rest the notion that a process must achieve a physical transformation to be patentable. This appeal arose from AT&T's efforts to enforce a patent directed towards the composition of billing records used in telephone networks. The AT&T patent claimed a method for a phone company to determine whether both the caller and the recipient of a long-distance telephone subscribed to the company's network. If so, the phone company could provide a different billing treatment to such calls, most likely discounting the fee in order to encourage both individuals to subscribe to the same phone company.

The invention relied upon the fact that when a customer makes a long-distance telephone call, the telephone network contemporaneously maintains billing records. These records included such information as the originating and terminating telephone numbers, as well as the length of the call. Also associated with the call was data indicating an individual's chosen "primary interexchange carrier," or long-distance service provider.

The claimed invention called for the addition of a discrete item of data, termed the "PIC indicator," to the billing record. The value of the PIC indicator was determined by applying the logical "AND" function to the data identifying the primary interexchange carriers of the originator and recipient of the long-distance call. If both customers have subscribed to the same phone company, the PIC indicator was set to a logical "one." Otherwise the PIC indicator remained at the value of "zero." The phone

6. *See* In re Pleuddemann, 910 F.2d 823 (Fed.Cir.1990).

7. 94 U.S. 780, 24 L.Ed. 139 (1876).

8. 22 F.3d 290, 294–96 (Fed.Cir.1994).

9. 172 F.3d 1352 (Fed.Cir.1999), *cert. denied*, 528 U.S. 946, 120 S.Ct. 368, 145 L.Ed.2d 284 (1999).

company could then apply its discounted rate to any call where the PIC indicator is set to one, without more extensive data processing at the time of billing.

The district court held that the AT&T patent was improvidently granted because the invention it claimed was not within § 101.[10] According to the district court, the patented invention merely retrieved and reorganized data known to the telephone company. Because the invention's only physical step involved data gathering for use in an algorithm, the district court concluded that it was not patentable subject matter.

Following an appeal, the Federal Circuit reversed. The Federal Circuit quickly disposed of Excel's argument that because AT&T's claims did not recite a physical transformation, they were not patentable subject matter. Upon its review of the precedents, the court concluded that physical transformation was not an absolute requisite for patentability. Instead, observing a tangible outcome was merely one way of determining whether the patented invention achieved a useful, concrete and tangible result. Because AT&T's claimed process produced "a number which had a specific meaning," it could be employed in a discrete setting and was therefore patentable.

The case law thus reveals that, as the patent system enters the twenty-first century, it is no longer appropriate to judge the patentability of processes solely by whether they work a physical transformation or not. The ultimate question is whether these processes achieve a useful, concrete and tangible result. As the PTO and the courts apply this lenient standard, the patent system should continue to open its doors to inventions from the information sciences.

14.2.1 New Uses

Section 100(b) notes that a process "includes a new use of a known process, machine, manufacture, composition of matter, or method." This definition allows inventors to obtain a proprietary interest in a newly discovered property of a known product. Suppose that inventor Gina Gardner discovers that a well-known chemical compound, understood to act as a skin softening lotion, also serves as an excellent lawn fertilizer. Gardner could not obtain patent protection on a compound already known to the art. But she could seek a patent claiming a process of using the compound as a fertilizer.

Although inventors are allowed to obtain process patents on newly discovered uses, the patent law limits the scope of protection to the particular method claimed. To continue the above example, suppose that another inventor, Aaron Avon, previously obtained a patent claiming the chemical compound itself. Avon's product patent is termed the "dominant" patent. In these circumstances, Gardner cannot practice her process without employing Avon's patented product. Nor could Avon employ the patented composition as a lawn fertilizer without infringing

---

10. 1998 WL 175878 (D.Del.1998).

Gardner's patent. In these circumstances the holders of the dominant and subservient patents often possess incentives to cross-license one another.[11]

14.2.2   The Function of a Machine Doctrine

Contemporary patent law takes a liberal view towards the format in which a claim is drafted. In particular, the patent law often allows a particular invention to be claimed as both a product and process. For example, suppose that the inventor of a new shovel files an application at the PTO. He might draft the following set of claims: (1) a product claim towards the shovel itself; (2) a method of making the shovel; and (3) a method of using the shovel to excavate items from the earth.

The reasons an inventor may wish to obtain such a variety of claims may at first seem elusive. The format of a patent claim is pivotal, however, because substantive rights hinge upon whether the claimed invention comprises product or process. Sometimes product claims offer a more robust set of rights than process claims. For example, infringement of a product claim occurs due to the unauthorized making, using, selling, offering for sale or importing into the United States the claimed physical technology.[12] In contrast, courts have traditionally held that one infringes a process claim only by performing the steps of the claimed process.[13] Suppose, for example, that an inventor wished to obtain patent protection against a distributor, retailer or other entity that did not itself practice the claimed technology. Only a product claim would allow the patentee to bring a charge of direct infringement against such an entity.

At other times, inventors would prefer to obtain process claims. As an example, the patent statute limits the remedies available to patentees that do not label their products with the number of the appropriate patent.[14] This requirement is known as "marking." Recognizing that it would be quite difficult to mark the intangible steps of a process, the courts have held that patentees of process claims may obtain all of the remedies available under the Patent Act even where they have not marked.[15] For these and other reasons, technologists have recognized that claims directed towards processes offer a different bundle of rights than that provided by product claims. Where possible, then, inventors obtain patents with both sorts of claims from the PTO, often within the same patent instrument.

The courts were originally hostile to efforts to claim the same invention in both product and process formats. Exemplary is the 1853 decision of the Supreme Court in *Corning v. Burden*, where the Court concluded that "it is well settled that a man cannot have a patent for the

---

11. *See* Steven C. Carlson, *Patent Pools and the Antitrust Dilemma*, 16 Yale J. Reg. 359, 362–65 (1999).

12. 35 U.S.C.A. § 271(a) (2000).

13. *See* Joy Technologies v. Flakt, Inc., 6 F.3d 770, 773 (Fed.Cir.1993).

14. 35 U.S.C.A. § 287(a) (2000).

15. *See* Bandag, Inc. v. Gerrard Tire Co., 704 F.2d 1578, 1581 (Fed.Cir.1983) (It is "settled in the case law that the notice requirement of the statute does not apply where the patent is directed to a process or method.").

function or abstract effect of a machine, but only for the machine that produces it."[16] The effect of this so-called "function of a machine" doctrine was that inventors of tangible artifacts were limited to product claims.

Over time, the courts wearied of the function of a machine doctrine, and in its *In re Tarczy–Hornoch* decision the CCPA overturned it.[17] There, the applicant appealed an adverse opinion from the Patent Office Board of Appeals. The Board had affirmed the examiner's rejection of certain claims of an application directed towards a "Pulse Sorting Apparatus and Method." While the examiner had allowed the applicant's apparatus claims, those claims directed towards a method of using were rejected for merely defining the function of the apparatus.

On appeal, the CCPA reversed, taking the opportunity to reverse earlier decisions relying upon the function of a machine doctrine. According to Judge Rich, sometimes inventors know of only one apparatus that is capable of carrying out the process at the time they file patent applications. However, other devices may become known later that are fairly grounded in the patented invention. By limiting patent claims to the specific structure of a particular product, Judge Rich reasoned, the function of a machine doctrine unnecessarily limited the protection accorded to inventors. As a result of *Tarczy-Harnoch* and related decisions, many patent applicants define their inventions in terms of the product, method of making of the product and a method of using the product.

§ 14.3   Biotechnology

14.3.1   Products of Nature

Patent eligibility principles pose few obstacles to the patenting of biotechnologies in the United States. The most significant restriction is that a "product of nature"—a naturally occurring substance discovered in the wild—may not be patented *per se*. Suppose, for example, that noted metallurgist and explorer Danny Steele travels to an uncharted region of the Himalayas. Steele then unearths a new mineral deposit on one of the highest peaks of Nepal. Even if this mineral had not been previously known to exist, longstanding case law establishes that Steele may not obtain a utility patent claiming the mineral itself.[1]

The same case law does provide that significant artificial changes to a product of nature may render it patentable.[2] To continue this hypothetical, suppose that Steele discovers that certain compounds within the mineral have valuable heat-resistant properties. He then develops a

16. Corning v. Burden, 56 U.S. (15 How.) 252, 14 L.Ed. 683 (1853).

17. 397 F.2d 856 (1968).

§ 14.3

1. *See, e.g.*, Ex parte Latimer, 1889 Comm'r Dec. 13 (1889).

2. *See, e.g.*, Amgen, Inc. v. Chugai Pharmaceutical Co., 927 F.2d 1200, 18 USPQ2d 1016 (Fed.Cir.1991) (claiming a purified and isolated DNA sequence encoding erythropoietin).

purified form of these compounds. Steele may obtain a product patent on the isolated compounds. He may also obtain process claims towards any heat-resistant uses of the mineral that he discovers.

The most notorious and confusing episode concerning the "product of nature" rule was the Supreme Court's 1948 opinion in *Funk Brothers Seed Co. v. Kalo Inoculant Co.*[3] The patented invention related to an innoculant for leguminous plants, such as soybeans or peanuts. The Court opens its opinion by explaining that these innoculants comprise bacteria that are introduced into seeds, assisting the growth of plants. The inventor, Bond, recognized a problem in the art: that only a specific strain of bacteria works with a particular plant. Indeed, if a farmer used the wrong strain, even in combination with the right strain, she might inhibit the growth of a particular crop. Bond claimed a combination of bacteria that were mutually non-inhibitive and sought to enforce his patent against a competitor.

Writing for the majority, Justice Douglas struck down the patent as merely claiming "the discovery of some of the handiwork of nature." Because "the ancient secrets of nature now disclosed" were to be reserved for all, Bond could not obtain a patent on his invention. This reasoning is curious because Justice Douglas himself noted that the combination of bacteria that Bond brought together did not exist in natural form. Therefore, the view that Bond's invention went towards a true product of nature seems difficult to accept at face value. Perhaps more sense can be made of the Court's remark that "however ingenious the discovery of that natural principle may have been, the application of it is hardly more than an advance in the packaging of the innoculants." Here Justice Douglas seems more concerned with the question of technical advance. Of course, this inquiry concerns the so-called "nonobviousness" requirement of § 103, rather than patent eligibility concerns under § 101.

Justice Frankfurter wrote a concurring opinion that has better withstood the passage of years. He recognized that exceptions to patentability based upon such terms of "laws of nature" are, outside of the obvious cases of discoveries from the wild, extremely dubious. Everything that happens does so in accordance with the "laws of nature," even if they are imperfectly understood. Justice Frankfurter would have struck down the claimed invention on an alternative ground. He noted that Bond's claims did not recite the specific combination of bacterial strains that he employed, but rather attempted to secure exclusive rights to any combination of bacteria that possessed non-inhibitive properties. According to the concurrence, Bond's patent presented overly broad claims in comparison with his narrow technical disclosure. In modern terms, these issues would be addressed in terms of enablement under § 112.

3. 333 U.S. 127, 68 S.Ct. 440, 92 L.Ed. 588 (1948).

14.3.2 Genetically Engineered Organisms

The issue of whether living organisms are merely unpatentable products of nature, or whether ethical or policy concerns should bar their patenting, continues to attract considerable commentary. The 1980 Supreme Court opinion in *Diamond v. Chakrabarty* made short work of the matter, however, readily concluding that a genetically engineered microorganism was patentable.[4] *Diamond v. Chakrabarty* involved the PTO rejection of Dr. Ananda Chakrabarty's claims towards an artificially generated bacterium with the ability to degrade crude oil. The CCPA reversed the PTO rejection on appeal, and following a grant of certiorari the Supreme Court addressed whether a microorganism constituted a composition of matter or manufacture within the meaning of § 101.

At the Supreme Court, the PTO Solicitor's chief argument was that because genetic technology could not have been foreseen at the time the patent statute was drafted, the resolution of the patentability of such inventions should be left to Congress. On its way to reversing the PTO decision, the Court disagreed: "A rule that unanticipated inventions are without protection would conflict with the core concept of the patent law that anticipation undermines patentability." The Court also quickly dismissed concerns over the possible perils of genetic research. Researchers would assuredly pursue work in biotechnology whether their results were patentable or not, the court reasoned, and the regulation of genetic research was a task that also fell to the legislature.

Following the lead of the Supreme Court, the PTO Board has held that an artificial animal life form also constitutes patentable subject matter. In *Ex parte Allen*,[5] the Board reasoned that certain claimed polyploid Pacific oysters constituted a non-naturally occurring manufacture or composition of matter. Contemporaneously, PTO Commissioner Donald Quigg issued a formal notice, stating that non-naturally occurring, non-human multicellular living organisms are patentable subject matter.[6] Among the notable patents the PTO issued in keeping with this notice was the Harvard mouse, which was genetically engineered such that half the females developed cancer.

The PTO Notice did advise that "the grant of a limited, but exclusive property right in a human being is prohibited by the Constitution." Presumably Commissioner Quigg referred to the Thirteenth Amendment, which provides that "[n]either slavery nor involuntary servitude, except as a punishment for crime whereof the party shall have been duly convicted, shall exist within the United States." The Commissioner further advised that claims directed to a non-plant multicellular organism which would include a human being within its scope should include the limitation "non-human" to avoid a § 101 rejection.

4. 447 U.S. 303, 100 S.Ct. 2204, 65 L.Ed.2d 144 (1980).

5. 2 USPQ2d 1425 (BPAI 1987), *aff'd*, 846 F.2d 77 (Fed.Cir.1988) (nonprecedential).

6. *See* 1077 PTO Off. Gazette 24 (April 21, 1987).

Observers have continued to question the morality of the patenting of living inventions. In the late 1990's, a team of inventors decided to place the issue of biotechnology patenting squarely before the PTO and the courts. In conjunction with biotechnology activist Jeremy Rifkin, cellular biologist Dr. Stuart Newman recently filed a patent application claiming a method for combining human and animal embryo cells to produce a single embryo. This embryo could then be implanted in a human or animal surrogate mother, resulting in the birth of a "chimera," or mixture of the two species. The Newman–Rifkin application specifically mentions chimeras made in part from mice, chimpanzees, baboons, and pigs. At the time this book goes to press, the PTO has rejected the application on several grounds, among them ineligible subject matter under § 101. No matter what the ultimate disposition of their application, Newman and Rifkin have renewed the debate on the extent of patentability of living inventions.[7]

§ 14.4 Methods of Medical Treatment

The U.S. patent system has never questioned that inventors may patent medical devices. Patents have issued on such devices as surgical instruments, catheters and artificial hearts. The propriety of patenting methods of medical treatment has proven more controversial, however. Although some have urged that such patents offered individuals incentives to invent and disclose new medical methods, others pointed to the possibility that patents might restrict access to life-saving techniques, lead to invasions of patient privacy, and override the culture of disclosure and peer review that pervades the medical community.[1]

One of the earliest judicial manifestations of these concerns, *Morton v. New York Eye Infirmary*,[2] involved the use of ether. That ether had an intoxicating effect when inhaled was known to the art. Co-inventors Jackson and Morton had discovered that, when breathed in sufficient quantities, ether was also useful as an anaesthetic. Their invention allowed surgery to proceed with a great reduction in human suffering. Jackson and Morton obtained a patent claiming the use of ether in surgical operations.

While acknowledging that this invention was among the "great discoveries of modern times," the New York Circuit Court nonetheless struck down the patent. The court's dated and rather enigmatic language leaves the modern reader in doubt over the precise basis for invalidity. For example, the court suggests both that the invention was merely a product of nature, and that the invention lacked novelty—both rather dubious grounds for invalidity under the facts. In other language,

---

7. *See* Barry S. Edwards, *". . . And On His Farm He Had a Geep": Patenting Transgenic Animals*, 2 MINN. INTELL. PROP. REV. 89 (2001).

§ 14.4

1. *See* Scott D. Anderson, *A Right Without A Remedy: The Unenforceable Medical*

Procedure Patent, 3 MARQ. INTELL. PROP. L. REV. 117 (1999).

2. 17 F.Cas. 879 (No. 9865) (S.D.N.Y. 1862).

however, the *Morton* opinion suggested that inventions manipulating the "natural functions of an animal" were unpatentable. Subsequent nineteenth century decisions relied upon *Morton* to hold that methods of medical treatment were inappropriate for patenting.[3]

Later opinions evidenced a more liberal posture towards patents on medical procedures. For example, the 1954 opinion of the PTO Board in *Ex parte Scherer*[4] allowed a claimed "method of injecting medicaments by pressure jet." The Board distinguished *Morton* on a rather suspect ground, stating that the invention there involved known methods and materials. Following the *Scherer* decision, medical practitioners obtained numerous U.S. patents on methods of medical treatment, ranging from administering insulin to treating cancer.

Traditionally, few patentees had attempted to enforce such patents. But in the early 1990's a Dr. Samuel Pallin alleged that another physician infringed his patented cataract surgery procedure.[5] The lawsuit led to a raging debate that questioned the impact of patents upon medical ethics, patient care and professional autonomy. Following the condemnation of patents on medical procedures by the American Medical Association House of Delegates, Congress chose to limit the interaction between the patent system and the performance of medical methods.

Of course, the most obvious possibility for Congress was to enact legislation declaring methods of medical treatment ineligible for patent protection. Many foreign patent statutes contain such a provision. But Congress instead opted to cabin the scope of patent rights associated with medical methods. As codified in § 287(c), the legislation deprives patentees of all remedies, both monetary and injunctive, against medical practitioners engaged in infringing "medical activity."[6] Thus, as the law currently stands, methods of medical treatment remain eligible subject matter under § 101, but the scope of such patents has been significantly constrained.

§ 14.5 Computer–Related Inventions

The patentability of computer-related inventions proved extremely controversial. Dozens of reported cases, and hundreds of law review articles and other commentary, discussed and disputed the merits of extending patent protection to software and other computer technologies. Events at the PTO and Federal Circuit have now outstripped this debate. There is now no doubt that patent protection is broadly available for computer-related inventions. Still, a review of the high points of this long saga is a familiar waystation in the patent law. The past debate over the patent eligibility of computer-related inventions may provide clues as to the scope of protection accorded such patents in the future,

3. *See* Ex parte Brinkerhoff, 27 J. Pat. Off. Soc'y 797 (1883).

4. 103 USPQ 107 (PTO Bd.1954).

5. *See* Pallin v. Singer, 36 USPQ2d 1050 (D.Vt.1995).

6. 35 U.S.C.A. § 287(c) (2000). *See* Gerald J. Mossinghoff, *Remdies Under Patents on Medical and Surgical Procedures*, 78 J. PAT. & TRADEMARK OFF. SOC'Y 789 (1996).

and its teachings provide general guidance as to the responses of the patent system to new technologies.

14.5.1 The Mental Steps Doctrine

Although the venerable doctrine of mental steps was developed long before the advent of the solid state transistor or semiconductor chip, it serves as an appropriate starting point in considering computer-related inventions. Under the mental steps doctrine, an invention that was principally a matter of human selection, interpretation or decision-making was not patentable. For example, in *In re Heritage*,[1] the CCPA considered a claimed method of coating a porous, sound-reducing fiber board. The method called for the progressive coating of individual boards. Heritage's application explained that a technician should periodically test the board in order to ensure that it maintained desirable acoustic properties.

The CCPA affirmed the PTO's rejection of the application, explaining that the "mental process of making a selection of the amount of coating material to be used in accordance with a predetermined system" was not patentable. According to the CCPA, the claim called solely for human calculation and judgment, which as purely mental acts were not patentable subject matter. The CCPA and other courts that applied the mental steps doctrine concluded that such inventions were no more than abstract ideas or mathematical algorithms. Because the claims of these patents were not tied to discrete physical apparatus, courts made the armchair judgment that technological progress would be better served by preserving these broad principles within the public domain. They also sensed that such abstractions did not present completed inventions, and that granting and enforcing such rarefied objects of property would present practical difficulties.

The advent of computer technology resulted in electronic execution of the process steps that had previously been performed by the human mind. When computer scientists inevitably turned to the patent system, they urged that their inventions comprised applied technology, not abstract mental steps. The PTO and courts were initially unpersuaded. Simply because the claimed process steps could also be performed by a machine did not render them patentable. Therefore, the policy concerns that animated the doctrines prohibiting patents on mental steps, abstract ideas or mathematical algorithms were at first applied to computer technology.

14.5.2 Computer–Related Inventions at the Supreme Court

Representative of this early posture is the 1972 Supreme Court opinion in *Gottschalk v. Benson*.[2] There the applicant claimed a method of converting numerals from binary-coded decimal to pure binary format. The steps of the method comprised mathematical operations that shuf-

§ 14.5
1. 150 F.2d 554 (CCPA 1945).

2. 409 U.S. 63, 93 S.Ct. 253, 34 L.Ed.2d 273 (1972).

fled a sequence of bits in order to express appropriately a particular number. The application contained claims both reciting the method as performed by a computer, and the abstract performance of the method without regard to any particular physical means. The method had broad application in data processing tasks, ranging from "the operation of a train to verification of drivers' licenses to researching the law books" in the words of the Court.[3]

In a cryptic opinion, the Court upheld the Patent Office's rejection of the application. The Court first recited the traditional requirement that patentability hinged upon the "[t]ransformation and reduction of an article 'to a different state or thing.' "[4] Arguably, at least those claims reciting computer implementation of the numerical conversion method did involve some sort of physical conversion. Operation of the computer would not only manipulate those electrical signals representing the data, but generate electrical signals in order to instruct the computer to perform certain tasks. Yet the Court found this hardware insufficient, drawing its analysis to a close with a self-styled "nutshell":

> It is conceded that one may not patent an idea. But in practical effect that would be the result if the formula for converting BCD numerals to pure binary numerals in this case. The mathematical formula involved here has no substantial practical application except in connection with a digital computer, which means that if the judgment below is affirmed, the patent would wholly pre-empt the mathematical formula and in practical effect would be a patent on the algorithm itself.[5]

Thus the Court held that computerization of mathematical equations could not shift them from the realm of ideas to that of industry. Internal circuitry operations were not enough to uphold even those claims reciting computer hardware, for barring the presence of an idiot savant or enormous mechanical device to perform the claimed conversions rapidly, a digital computer presented the only context in which the equations had meaning. The computer amounted only to nominal apparatus that placed no meaningful limitations upon the scope of the claims.

This early resistance to patents on computer-related inventions faded over time, however. By the early 1980's, PTO examiners found more favor in computer-related inventions, and the courts seemed more willing to uphold the issued patents.[6] While the omnipresence of computer technology and its significance to the United States economy may have carried the day, one suspects that both the PTO and the courts grew weary of the relentless argumentation of a bar that has scant motivation to favor restraints upon the scope of patenting.

3. 409 U.S. at 68.
4. 409 U.S. at 70.
5. 409 U.S. at 71–72.

6. *See, e.g.,* In re Deutsch, 553 F.2d 689 (CCPA 1977); In re Chatfield, 545 F.2d 152 (CCPA 1976).

The first sense of this change of tack at the Supreme Court was its 1981 opinion in *Diamond v. Diehr*.[7] The *Diehr* applicants claimed a process for operating a rubber-molding press with the aid of a digital computer. Their computer continuously monitored the temperature within a press and employed the well-known Arrhenius equation to calculate the amount of time required to cure rubber placed within the press. When the computer calculated that the elapsed time equaled the actual molding time, it signaled a device to open the press.[8]

At the Patent Office, the examiner considered that the process steps that were implemented in computer software were not statutory subject matter for patents. The examiner further reasoned that the "remaining steps—installing rubber in the press and the subsequent closing of the process—were 'conventional and necessary to the process and cannot be the basis of patentability.' "[9] The CCPA reversed the rejection, however. Following a grant of *certiorari*, the Supreme Court affirmed, explaining that the applicants were not seeking to patent a mathematical formula, but instead an industrial process that involved a number of discrete steps, including installing rubber in a press, closing the mold, constantly determining the temperature of the mold, constantly recalculating the appropriate cure time through the use of a formula and a digital computer, and automatically opening the press at the proper time.[10]

Many observers have noted that the advancement offered by the *Diehr* applicants consisted not so much of rubber-making, but of mathematical computations. The physical steps on which so much depended— reading a thermometer and signaling a press door to open—appear trite. Allowing patentability to hinge upon the minimal recitation of these steps within the claims seems unfounded, for they merely stated the only valid technical context in which the mathematics would operate. They did not present meaningful limitations upon the scope of the claimed formula.[11] Still, *Diehr* signaled the PTO and the lower courts that, in appropriate circumstances, computer-related inventions were appropriate for patenting.

14.5.3 Computer–Related Inventions at the Federal Circuit

In response to these pronouncements by the Supreme Court, the predecessor to the Federal Circuit, the Court of Customs and Patent Appeals, formed the two-part *Freeman–Walter–Abele* test. Initiated in 1978 by the *In re Freeman*[12] decision, the court refined the test in the 1980 opinion *In re Walter*.[13] Following the Supreme Court's issuance of its *Diehr* decision, the court once again modified the standard in its 1982 decision *In re Abele*.[14] As later described by the Federal Circuit:

7. 450 U.S. 175, 101 S.Ct. 1048, 67 L.Ed.2d 155 (1981).

8. 450 U.S. at 177–78.

9. 450 U.S. at 181.

10. 450 U.S. at 187.

11. Richard H. Stern, *Tales from the Algorithm War: Benson to Iwahashi, It's*

Deja Vu All Over Again, 18 AIPLA Q.J. 371(1991).

12. 573 F.2d 1237 (CCPA 1978).

13. 618 F.2d 758 (CCPA 1980).

14. 684 F.2d 902 (CCPA 1982).

It is first determined whether a mathematical algorithm is recited directly or indirectly in the claim. If so, it is next determined whether the claimed invention as a whole is no more than the algorithm itself; that is, whether the claim is directed to a mathematical algorithm that is not applied to or limited by physical elements or process steps. Such claims are nonstautory. However, when the mathematical algorithm is applied in one or more steps of an otherwise statutory process claim, or one or more elements of an otherwise statutory apparatus claim, the requirements of section 101 are met.[15]

The Federal Circuit employed the *Freeman–Walter–Abele* test both to reject[16] and allow[17] various applications as patentable subject matter. But its decisions demonstrated an increasingly permissive tenor, and a glance through the PTO Gazette showed a growing number of issued patents directed towards computer-related inventions.

The Federal Circuit's increasing permissiveness towards patent eligibility ultimately led to its turning away from the *Freeman–Walter–Abele* test. The *en banc* decision in *In re Alappat*,[18] which failed to follow the usual *Freeman–Walter–Abele* formulation, suggested that changes were in store in the court's § 101 subject matter jurisprudence. There, the court considered a claimed apparatus useful for generating smooth and continuous lines for display on an oscilloscope. Alappat's invention completed various mathematical computations in order to convert so-called "vector list data" into "pixel illumination intensity data;" that is, it translated one set of numbers into another set of numbers.[19] The majority held that the claimed invention comprised statutory subject matter:

> Although many, or arguably even all, of the means elements recited in claim 15 represent circuitry elements that perform mathematical calculations, which is essentially true of all digital electrical circuits, the claimed invention as a whole is directed to a combination of interrelated elements which combine to form a machine for converting discrete waveform data samples into anti-aliased pixel illumination intensity data to be displayed on a display means. This is not a disembodied mathematical concept which may be characterized as an "abstract idea," but

15. Arrhythmia Research Technology, Inc. v. Corazonix Corp., 958 F.2d 1053 (Fed. Cir.1992).

16. In re Grams, 888 F.2d 835 (Fed.Cir. 1989).

17. In re Iwahashi, 888 F.2d 1370 (Fed. Cir.1989).

18. 33 F.3d 1526 (Fed.Cir.1994). *See* John A. Burtis, Note, *Towards a Rational Jurisprudence of Computer–Related Patent-*

ability in Light of In re Alappat, 79 Minn. L. Rev. 1129 (1995); Sang Hui Michael Kim, *In re Alappat: A Strict Statutory Interpretation Determining Patentable Subject Matter Relating to Computer Software?*, 13 John Marshall J. Computer & Info. L. 635 (1995); W. Wayt King, Jr., *The Soul of the Virtual Machine: In re Alappat*, 2 J. Intell. Prop. L. 575 (1995).

19. 33 F.3d at 1537–39.

rather a specific machine to produce a useful, concrete, and tangible result.[20]

In its later decision in *AT&T Corp. v. Excel Communications, Inc.*,[21] the Federal Circuit confirmed that the *Freeman–Walter–Abele* test was all but dead. According to the Federal Circuit, a § 101 analysis should not focus upon whether the claim recited physical limitations or not. Instead, it should be determined whether the claimed invention achieves a "useful, concrete and tangible result." Under the latest thinking of the Federal Circuit, then, virtually any invention that can be used to obtain a practical result is patentable.

Apparent to any reader of the *AT&T v. Excel* opinion is that the "useful, concrete and tangible result" standard is very lenient. Only a few computer-related inventions for which a patent is sought will not minimally achieve a functional or serviceable result. As a result, computer scientists and engineers should rarely encounter statutory subject matter rejections at the PTO.

Computer technology has taken the patent system a long way from the mental steps doctrine. As we shall see, computer-related inventions also triggered the movement towards the patentability of two other subjects traditionally excluded from the patent system, printed matter and methods of doing business. This text addresses these largely outdated exclusionary doctrines in turn.

§ 14.6   Presentations of Information

Presentations of information traditionally did not comprise patentable subject matter. Under the printed matter doctrine, information inscribed upon a substrate for purposes of presentation was held outside the scope of § 101. Courts viewed such inventions as no more than memorialized versions of abstract ideas and reasoned that the mere act of recording information should not impart patentability. This rule also performed a channeling function, diverting works of authorship from the patent law to the copyright law.

One significant exception to the printed matter arose in the case law. An invention was patentable if it included a physical structure that resulted in a functional relationship between the substrate and written material. The line between the printed matter rule and its exception did not sparkle with clarity, and the case law reflects some rather subtle distinctions between printed matter and patentable invention. For example, a system of blank checks and stubs useful in a combined checking/savings account was considered unpatentable printed matter.[1] But a railway ticket consisting of a base and separable attachment was judged a unique physical structure and therefore appropriate for patenting.[2]

---

20.   33 F.3d at 1544.

21.   172 F.3d 1352 (Fed.Cir.1999), *cert. denied*, 528 U.S. 946, 120 S.Ct. 368, 145 L.Ed.2d 284 (1999).

§ 14.6

1.   In re Sterling, 70 F.2d 910 (CCPA 1934).

2.   Cincinnati Traction Co. v. Pope, 210 F. 443 (6th Cir.1913).

Although the Federal Circuit has not expressly overturned the printed matter doctrine, its early decision in *In re Gulack* offered the view that the rule "stands on questionable legal and logical footing."[3] Later, in *In re Lowry*,[4] the Federal Circuit reversed a PTO rejection based upon the printed matter rule. Lowry's patent application claimed a computer memory for storing data for access by a computer program. According to the Federal Circuit, Lowry's invention was not analogous to printed matter because it included "electronic structural elements which impart a physical organization on the information stored in memory."

PTO allowance of patents claiming encoded machine instruction further suggests the decline of the printed matter rule. Traditionally, software was claimed in method format, as a series of instructions to be performed by a computer. But applicants also have claimed computer programs as an article of manufacture, in terms of the computer-readable media on which the software has been stored. Consider the following example of such claims:

> 1. A method for enabling maintenance communication by a line element interconnected to a digital transmission line, said digital transmission line carrying a stream of coded data, comprising the steps of:
>
> > detecting a maintenance code; and
> >
> > introducing a responsive communication signal into said stream of coded data.
>
> 2. A program storage device readable by a machine, tangibly embodying a program of instructions executable by the machine to perform the method steps of claim 1.

Possible program storage devices of the sort recited in claim 2 include floppy disks, compact disks, hard drives, or even electrical signals onto which the appropriate software program has been recorded.

The only formal treatment of claims of this sort, *In re Beauregard*,[5] consists of an unpublished decision from the PTO Board of Appeals. There, the PTO rejected a claim towards encoded computer instruction based upon the printed matter rule. Beauregard brought an appeal to the Federal Circuit, but the court never heard oral argument. The position of the Solicitor of the Patent Office changed hands during the pendency of Beauregard's appeal, with the new incumbent quickly filing a motion to dismiss. According to the Solicitor, the Patent Office now accepted "that computer programs embodied in a tangible medium, such as floppy diskettes, are patentable subject matter." Following *Beauregard*, inventors of computer software commonly obtain claims directed towards encoded machine instruction alongside traditional method claims.

3. In re Gulack, 703 F.2d 1381, 217 USPQ 401 (Fed.Cir.1983).

4. 32 F.3d 1579, 32 USPQ2d 1031 (Fed. Cir.1994).

5. 53 F.3d 1583, 35 USPQ2d 1383 (Fed. Cir.1995).

§ 14.7 Methods of Doing Business

Until recent years, whether business methods could be patented was not entirely certain. A number of decisions suggested that methods of doing business were not patentable *per se*. As early as 1868, the Patent Commissioner explained that "[i]t is contrary to the spirit of the law ... to grant patents for methods of book-keeping."[1] Nineteenth century courts also opined that "a method of transacting common business"[2] or "a mere contract"[3] were unpatentable. The best-known of these decisions was probably *Hotel Security Checking Co. v. Lorraine Co.*,[4] which concerned a "method and means for cash-registering and account-checking" designed to prevent fraud by waiters and cashiers. The system employed certain forms that tracked sales and ensured that waiters submitted appropriate funds at the close of business. The Second Circuit invalidated the patent on the basis of prior knowledge, finding that the patented technology "would occur to anyone conversant with the business." However, the court further observed that a "system of transacting business disconnected from the means of carrying out the system is not, within the most liberal interpretation of the term, an art" amenable to patenting.

Still, over the years the PTO allowed a number of patents to issue on inventions that could arguably be described as business methods.[5] At least one judicial opinion, *Paine, Webber, Jackson & Curtis v. Merrill, Lynch*,[6] also appeared to approve of patents on business methods. There the district court upheld a patent on a data processing methodology for a combined securities brokerage/cash management account. The court stressed that the patent taught a method of operation on a computer.

Consistent with its ambitious view of patentable subject matter, the Federal Circuit ultimately rejected the methods of doing business exception. The occasion was the celebrated opinion in *State Street Bank v. Signature Financial Group*.[7] Signature Financial Group held the patent at suit. Directed to a "Data Processing System for Hub and Spoke Financial Services Configuration," it described a data processing system for implementing an investment structure known as a "Hub and Spoke" system. This system allowed individual mutual funds (Spokes) to pool their assets in an investment portfolio (Hub) organized as a partnership. According to the patent, this investment regime provided the advantageous combination of economies of scale in administering investments coupled with the tax advantages of a partnership.

§ 14.7

1. Ex parte Abraham, 1868 Comm'r Dec. 59, 59 (Comm'r Pat. 1868).

2. United States Credit Sys. Co. v. American Credit Indemnity Co., 53 F. 818, 819 (S.D.N.Y.1893).

3. In re Moeser, 27 App.D.C. 307, 310 (1906).

4. 160 F. 467 (2d Cir.1908).

5. *See* William D. Wiese, *Death of a Myth: The Patenting of Internet Business Models After* State Street Bank, 4 MARQUETTE INTELL. PROP. L. REV. 17, 30–33 (2000).

6. 564 F.Supp. 1358 (D.Del.1983).

7. State Street Bank and Trust Co. v. Signature Financial Group, Inc., 149 F.3d 1368 (Fed.Cir.1998), *cert. denied*, 525 U.S. 1093, 119 S.Ct. 881, 142 L.Ed.2d 704 (1999).

Maintaining a proper accounting of this sophisticated financial structure proved difficult. Indeed, due to "the complexity of the calculations, a computer or equivalent device is a virtual necessity to perform the task." Signature's patented system purported to allow administrators to "monitor and record the financial information flow and make all calculations necessary for maintaining a partner fund financial services configuration." In addition, it tracked "all the relevant data determined on a daily basis for the Hub and each Spoke, so that aggregate year end income, expenses, and capital gain or loss can be determined for accounting and for tax purposes for the Hub and, as a result, for each publicly traded Spoke." Crucially, Signature's invention marked no advance in computer technology or mathematical calculations. The basis for patentability was the uniqueness of the investment package Signature claimed in its patent.

Following issuance of the patent, Signature entered into licensing negotiations with a competitor, State Street Bank, that ultimately proved unsuccessful. State Street then brought a declaratory judgment action against Signature, seeking the invalidity of the patent. The district court granted summary judgment in favor of State Street under two alternative grounds.[8] First, the court applied the *Freeman–Walter–Abele* test, concluding that:

> At bottom, the invention is an accounting system for a certain type of financial investment vehicle claimed as means for performing a series of mathematical functions. Quite simply, it involves no further physical transformation or reduction than inputting numbers, calculating numbers, outputting numbers, and storing numbers. The same functions could be performed, albeit less efficiently, by an accountant armed with pencil, paper, calculator, and a filing system.

The court then buttressed its holding by turning to "the long-established principle that business 'plans' and 'systems' are not patentable." The court judged that "patenting an accounting system necessary to carry on a certain type of business is tantamount to a patent on the business itself. Because such abstract ideas are not patentable, either as methods of doing business or as mathematical algorithms," the patent was held invalid.

On appeal, the Federal Circuit reversed in a magisterial opinion. Writing for a three-judge panel, Judge Rich found the patent claimed not an abstract idea but a programmed machine that produced a "useful, concrete, and tangible result." "This renders it statutory subject matter, even if the useful result is expressed in numbers, such as price, profit, percentage, cost, or loss." According to the court, "[t]he question of whether a claim encompasses statutory subject matter should not focus on which of the four categories of subject matter a claim is directed to—

8. State Street Bank and Trust Co. v. Signature Financial Group, Inc., 927 F.Supp. 502 (D.Mass.1996).

process, machine, manufacture, or composition of matter—but rather on the essential characteristics of the subject matter, in particular, its practical utility." The court further trumpeted that:

> Today, we hold that the transformation of data, representing discrete dollar amounts, by a machine through a series of mathematical calculations into a final share price, constitutes a practical application of a mathematical algorithm, formula, or calculation, because it produces "a useful, concrete and tangible result"—a final share price momentarily fixed for recording and reporting purposes and even accepted and relied upon by regulatory authorities and in subsequent trades.

The Federal Circuit then turned to the district court's business methods rejection, opting to "take the opportunity to lay this ill-conceived exception to rest." According to Judge Rich, restrictions upon patents for methods of doing business were inappropriate from the start and no longer the law under the 1952 Patent Act. Following issuance of the *State Street* opinion, methods of doing business were to be subject only to the same patentability analysis as any other sort of process.

The *State Street Bank* decision has prompted many industries to enter the patent system. Internet-based business models have been most quickly subject to appropriation via the patent system, given their close affinity to computer-related inventions. But few believe that computer hardware is an invariable requirement under the lenient patentability standard established in *State Street*. The financial, insurance and service industries are also turning to the patent system. As the proprietors of these patents begin to commence litigation against their competitors, we should learn more about their enforceability and scope.

§ 14.8 Designs

Title 35 of the United States Code provides for design patents in a short series of provisions codified at §§ 171–173. Design patents may be awarded for "any new, original and ornamental design for an article of manufacture."[1] The surface ornamentation, configuration or shape of an object form the most typical subjects of design patents. The design may be patented only if it is embodied in an article of manufacture, such as furniture, tools or athletic footwear. The chief limitation on the patentability of designs is that they must be primarily ornamental in character. If the design is dictated by the performance of the article, then it is judged "primarily functional" and ineligible for design patent protection.[2]

Suppose, for example, that inventor Tori Irons invents a new golf club. The club features an sleek shaft and a broad, angular head. Suppose further that Irons seeks design patent protection on the club. In judging whether design patent protection is appropriate, a PTO examin-

§ 14.8
1. 35 U.S.C.A. § 171 (2000).

2. *See* Best Lock Corp. v. Ilco Unican Corp., 94 F.3d 1563 (Fed.Cir.1996).

er would consider whether the club's configuration is dictated by Irons' desire to lower the golf handicap of club users. If so, then the design is not principally directed towards ornamentation, and the award of a design patent would not promote the decorative arts. Irons should seek a utility patent in these circumstances. But if her design is principally directed towards giving the club a graceful and pleasing appearance, with the function of the club a secondary consideration, then a design patent is appropriate.

Because subsequent discussion within this text is limited to utility patents, some additional comments on design patents are appropriate here. An inventor must file an application at the PTO in order to obtain design patent protection. Design patents are generally subject to all provisions applicable to utility patents, including originality and novelty. The design must also fulfill the requirement of nonobviousness, which is judged from the perspective of "the designer of ordinary capability who designs articles of the type presented in the application."[3] If the application matures into an issued design patent, the resulting design patent instrument is relatively straightforward. It principally consists of one or more drawings illustrating the proprietary design. The term of a design patent is fourteen years.[4]

Whether an accused design infringes the patented design is judged from the perspective of the ordinary observer. As explained by the Supreme Court in its 1871 opinion in *Gorham v. White*:

> if, in the eye of an ordinary observer, giving such attention as a purchaser usually gives, two designs are substantially the same, if the resemblance is such as to deceive such an observer, inducing him to purchase one supposing it to be the other, the first one patented is infringed by the other.[5]

The lower courts have added one important refinement to this standard. In the words of the Federal Circuit, "the accused design must appropriate the novelty in the patented device which distinguishes it from the prior art."[6] Under this qualification, the accused design must include the novel features of the patented design to constitute an infringement.

The Federal Circuit opinion in *Avia Group International, Inc. v. L.A. Gear California, Inc.* illustrates the workings of these standards.[7] The patented design related to an athletic shoe sole. As compared to prior art sole designs, the patented design was notable for its use of a pivot point surrounded by a swirl effect. In approving the district court's finding of infringement, the Federal Circuit held both that (1) the patented and accused designs bore an overall similarity from the perspective of the ordinary observer, and (2) the accused design incorporated both novel features of the patented design, namely the pivot point and swirl effect.

---

3. In re Nalbandian, 661 F.2d 1214, 211 USPQ 782 (CCPA 1981).

4. 35 U.S.C.A. § 173 (2000).

5. 81 U.S. 511, 528, 20 L.Ed. 731 (1871).

6. L.A. Gear, Inc. v. Thom McAn Shoe Co., 988 F.2d 1117, 1125 (Fed.Cir.1993).

7. 853 F.2d 1557 (Fed.Cir.1988).

§ 14.9 Plants

Plant breeders have long borne an uneasy relationship with the utility patent statute. First, even where bred under artificial conditions, plants seem readily classified as unpatentable products of nature. Second, unlike other sorts of inventions, plants are not especially amenable to description in a written patent instrument. Diagrams or textual illustrations may fully convey the workings of a mechanical, chemical or electrical technology, but plant breeders usually require a sample of the plant in order to practice it.[1] Although many inventors have managed to overcome these hurdles and obtain utility patents for plant-related inventions, Congress has nonetheless enacted two specialized statutes to level the patent playing field for agriculture and industry.

The first of these, the Plant Patent Act, is codified in sections 161 through 164 of Title 35. A plant patent may be issued for a distinct and new variety of plant that has been asexually reproduced, through grafting, budding or similar techniques. Expressly excluded from the Plant Patent Act are tuberpropagated plants or plants found in an uncultivated state.[2] The other possibility is the Plant Variety Protection Act, or PVPA. This statute may be found in 7 U.S.C.A. § 2321 and subsequent sections. The PVPA provides for the issuance of plant variety protection certificates pertaining to sexually reproduced plants, including most seed-bearing plants. Fungi and bacteria are ineligible for certification. The plant must be clearly distinguishable from known varieties and stable, in that its distinctive characteristics must breed true with a reasonable degree of reliability.[3]

The key distinction between the two regimes is the manner in which the inventor has reproduced the protected plant. Asexual reproduction, which results in a plant genetically identical to its parent, forms the basis of plant patent protection. Certification under the PVPA instead depends upon sexual reproduction, which results in a distinct plant that combines the characteristics of its parents.

An example illustrates this distinction. Suppose that inventor Johnny Peachpit cultivates a unique orange tree growing in his orchard. The tree bears seedless oranges of excellent color and taste. Peachpit's nurturing of the tree is by itself insufficient to support a plant patent, and because the tree does not reproduce sexually it is ineligible for a PVPA certificate. But if Peachpit is able to reproduce the tree asexually, through the use of budwood or other techniques, then he would be able to pursue plant patent protection.

Suppose further that Peachpit experiments with soybeans, eventually arriving at a variety that grows well in cooler climates. Because soybeans reproduce sexually, Peachpit may be able to obtain a plant variety certificate under the PVPA. He would have to demonstrate that

§ 14.9

1. *See* Nicholas J. Seay, *Protecting the Seeds of Innovation: Patenting Plants*, 16 AIPLA Q.J. 418 (1989).

2. 35 U.S.C.A. § 161 (2000).

3. 7 U.S.C.A. § 2402(a) (2000).

his soybean variety demonstrated at least one distinct, uniform and stable trait.

A plant protected under the Plant Patent Act or PVPA may also be claimed in a utility patent. In *J.E.M. AG Supply, Inc. v. Pioneer Hi–Bred International, Inc.*,[4] the Supreme Court rejected arguments that congressional enactment of this more specialized legislation evidenced the congressional intent that living plants could not be the subject of utility patents. Justice Thomas observed that the PTO had a long history of granting utility patents towards plants and that the Court's own precedent had interpreted § 101 quite broadly. The Court also observed that a particular legal or property interest is often the subject of multiple statutes. For example, computer software may qualify for protection under both the copyright and patent laws. The Supreme Court concluded that merely because these laws may be of different scope does not suggest that they are invalid.

The key features of the Plant Patent Act and PVPA are worth noting here. Plant patents are issued by the PTO provided that the novelty and nonobviousness requirements are met. Applicants must submit an application featuring color drawings that disclose all the distinctive characteristics of the plant capable of visual representation. Importantly, the Plant Patent Act provides that these applications need only include a written description that "is as complete as is reasonably possible."[5] A plant patent enjoys a term of twenty years from the date of filing,[6] and is infringed if any other party asexually reproduces the plant, or uses or sells the plant so reproduced.

In contrast, the PVPA is administered by the Department of Agriculture. The holder of a plant variety certificate obtains the right to "exclude others from selling the variety, or offering it for sale, or reproducing it, importing, or exporting it, or using it in producing (as distinguished from developing) a hybrid or different variety therefrom."[7] The statute exempts research activities from infringement and also grants farmers a limited right to save and sell seeds. The term of a PVPA certificate is twenty years (twenty-five years for trees and vines).[8]

§ 14.10   Closing Thoughts on Patent Eligibility

If our experience with the patent law has taught us one thing, it is that the scope of patentable subject matter will inevitably broaden. This trend has accelerated to the point that few cognizable restraints appear to limit the scope of patenting. With the patent system poised to impact a range of activities as broad as human experience itself, we may justly question why the law of patent eligibility has become a one-way ratchet. A review of structural aspects of the U.S. patent system goes a long way to offering an explanation for this historical trend.

4. 534 U.S. 124, 122 S.Ct. 593, 151 L.Ed.2d 508 (2001), *reh'g denied,* ___ U.S. ___, 122 S.Ct. 1600, 152 L.Ed.2d 515 (2002).

5. 35 U.S.C.A. § 162 (2000).

6. 35 U.S.C.A. §§ 161, 154(a)(2) (2000).

7. 7 U.S.C.A. § 2483(a) (2000).

8. 7 U.S.C.A. § 2483(b) (2000).

First, most accused infringers are patentees themselves. Although the defendant in a patent infringement suit ordinarily encourages the court to strike down the asserted patent, the preferred grounds for invalidity are ones that do not endanger the defendant's own patent portfolio. With these incentives understood, it is easy to see that the adversary system often provides only a lackluster exchange of views on patent eligibility.

Second, the structure of the patent bar encourages attorneys to urge a robust sense of patent eligibility. The organization of the patent bar differs starkly from that of attorneys in other disciplines, such as the labor bar. There, attorneys tend to represent exclusively either management or employees. This organization tends to generate healthy discussion on issues of moment in labor law. But patent attorneys most often establish long-term relationships with particular clients, whether they are asserting a patent against a competitor or themselves stand accused of infringement. As a result, the structure of the bar fails to create an entity opposed to patents on methods of doing business or other inventions previously thought to be without the patent system.

Finally, broad notions of patent eligibility appear to be in the best interest of the patent bar, the PTO and the Federal Circuit. Workloads increase and regulatory authority expands when new industries become subject to the appropriations authorized by the patent law. Noticeably absent from this private, administrative and judicial structure is a high regard for the public interest.

Determining the appropriate subject matter for patenting is important because a paucity of constraining doctrines allay the proprietary rights associated with granted patents. As discussed in subsequent chapters of this book, the adjudicated infringer need not have derived the patented invention from the patentee, as liability rests solely upon a comparison of the text of the patent instrument with an accused infringement.[1] The patent law as well lacks a robust experimental use exemption in the nature of copyright law's fair use privilege.[2] The decision to subject particular areas of endeavor to the patent system is therefore of great moment, in effect subjecting entire industries to a private regulatory environment with constantly shifting contours. As you make your way through this material, you might pause to think about the impact of the patent system upon traditionally patent-free industries such as services or finance, and to ponder whether every aspect of human endeavor is appropriately subjected to, in the words of Thomas Jefferson, the "embarrassment" of exclusive patent rights.[3]

---

§ 14.10

1. *See* J.H. Reichman, *Legal Hybrids Between the Patent and Copyright Paradigms*, 94 COLUM. L. REV. 2432 (1994).

2. *See* Maureen O'Rourke, *Towards a Doctrine of Fair Use in Patent Law*, 100 COLUM. L. REV. 1177 (2000).

3. Quoted in Graham v. John Deere Co., 383 U.S. 1, 10–11, 86 S.Ct. 684, 15 L.Ed.2d 545 (1966).

Chapter 15

UTILITY

§ 15.1   Basic Concepts

Section 101 of the Patent Act mandates that patents issue only to "useful" inventions. Utility ordinarily presents a minimal requirement that the invention be capable of achieving a pragmatic result.[1] Patent applicants need only supply a single, operable use of the invention that is credible to persons of ordinary skill in the art. Although the utility requirement is readily met in most fields, it presents a more significant obstacle to patentability in the disciplines of chemistry and biotechnology. In these fields, inventors sometimes synthesize compounds without a precise knowledge of how they may be used to achieve a practical working result. When patent applications are filed claiming such compounds, they may be rejected as lacking utility within the meaning of the patent law.

As demonstrated by Justice Story's 1817 instructions to the jury in *Lowell v. Lewis*[2] and *Bedford v. Hunt*,[3] the notion of utility is a longstanding feature of United States patent law. In *Lowell*, Justice Story remarked:

> All that the law requires is, that the invention should not be frivolous or injurious to the well-being, good policy, or sound morals of society. The word "useful", therefore, is incorporated

---

§ 15.1

1. Mitchell v. Tilghman, 86 U.S. (19 Wall.) 287, 396, 22 L.Ed. 125 (1873).

2. 15 F.Cas. 1018, 1019 (No. 8568) (C.C.D.Mass.1817).

3. 3 F.Cas. 37 (No. 1217) (C.C.D.Mass. 1817).

into the act in contradistinction to mischievous or immoral. . . . But if the invention steers wide of these objections, whether it be more or less useful is a circumstance very material to the interest of the patentee, but of no importance to the public. If it be not extensively useful, it will silently sink into contempt and disregard.

Under Justice Story's view, the utility requirement does not provide a significant place for technology assessment. Outside of the most narrow limits, valuation of the invention is left to the market rather than to the mechanisms of the patent law.

Justice Story's jury instructions also explain that the utility require- ment does not mandate that the invention be superior to existing products and processes in order to qualify for a patent. The utility standard reflects the judgment that society is better served by access to a library of issued patents describing as many inventions as possible, even if many of them do not achieve better results than public domain technology. This liberal view of utility allows subsequent inventors access to a greater variety of previous technologies, some of which may yet be judged the superior solution when employed within a different context.[4]

§ 15.2 Immoral, Fraudulent and Incredible Inventions

Historically, courts employed the utility requirement to strike down patents concerning inventions that were judged to be immoral or fraudu- lent. A handful of early decisions invalidated patents on inventions intended for use in gambling or other disfavored activities. Most of these dour opinions originated in the nineteenth century or the early part of the twentieth. A patented toy automatic race course,[1] lottery devices[2] and a slot machine[3] were among those held to lack utility because their functions were judged unwholesome. Inventions that were designed to mislead consumers were similarly invalidated. Among this latter class of inventions was a patented process for causing lower quality tobacco to simulate high-quality tobacco by artificially causing spots to form on the leaf. In stern, scolding language, the Court of Appeals for the Second Circuit believed the sole purpose of the invention was to practice deception and fraud upon the public.[4]

The modern view is that so long as the invention may be put to a single lawful use, it possesses utility within the patent statute. That the invention might also be put to an illegal purpose does not make it

4. Vornado Air Circulation Systems Inc. v. Duracraft Corp., 58 F.3d 1498, 1508 (10th Cir.1995).

§ 15.2

1. National Automatic Device Co. v. Lloyd, 40 F. 89 (N.D.Ill.1889).

2. Brewer v. Lichtenstein, 278 F. 512 (7th Cir.1922).

3. Schultze v. Holtz, 82 F. 448 (N.D.Cal. 1897).

4. Richard v. Du Bon, 103 F. 868, 873 (2d Cir.1900).

unpatentable. This position recognizes that public mores are susceptible to change, and that once reviled race tracks, lotteries and birth control devices have moved from a position of illegality to one of widespread adoption by the state and members of the public. It also avoids subjective judicial judgments as to the moral worth of a particular technology.[5]

Similarly, inventions that allow manufacturers to make cheaper substitutes for more expensive products are now judged to possess utility. Representative of the contemporary position is the Federal Circuit opinion in *Juicy Whip, Inc. v. Orange Bang, Inc.*[6] The reader of this opinion learns much about beverage displays in shopping mall food courts. It seems that so-called "post-mix" dispensers maintain beverage syrup concentrate and water in separate locations, only combining the two ingredients immediately before the beverage is dispensed. While post-mix dispensers have a large capacity and are quite sanitary, they do not allow vendors to promote impulse purchases by displaying a frothing, succulent beverage for all to see. In contrast, "pre-mix" dispensers hold a combination of syrup concentrate and water at the ready, but suffer from limited storage capacity and are prone to bacterial contamination.

The plaintiff, Juicy Whip, held a patent concerning a post-mix dispenser that included a transparent bowl. According to the patent, the bowl was filled with a liquid that appeared to be the beverage available for purchase. While the bowl was arranged in such a way that it seemed to be the source of the beverage, in fact no fluid connection existed between the bowl and the beverage dispenser at all. Instead, the beverage was mixed on the fly, immediately prior to each beverage sale. The district court struck Juicy Whip's patent on the ground of lack of utility, reasoning that the patented invention acted only to deceive consumers. The court stated that the purpose of the invention "was to create an illusion, whereby customers believe that the fluid contained in the bowl is the actual beverage they are receiving, when of course it is not."

The Federal Circuit reversed on appeal, concluding that the fact that one product can be altered to make it look like another is, in itself, a specific benefit sufficient to satisfy the statutory requirement of utility. The appeals court noted that many valued products, ranging from cubic zirconium to synthetic fabrics, are designed to appear as something that they are not. Because the claimed post-mix dispenser possessed the features of a post-mix dispenser while imitating the visual appearance of a pre-mix dispenser, the utility requirement was met. The Federal Circuit also noted that simply because some customers might believe they are receiving fluid directly from the display tank did not defeat utility. The utility requirement did not direct the PTO or the courts to resolve issues of deceptive trade practices, which were left to such agencies as the Federal Trade Commission or the Food and Drug Administration.

5. *See* ROBERT A. CHOATE ET AL., CASES AND MATERIALS ON PATENT LAW 375–76 (3d ed. 1987).

6. 185 F.3d 1364 (Fed.Cir.1999).

As a result, in most technical fields the utility requirement is employed merely to sift out utterly incredible inventions from the domain of patentability. Citing the utility requirement, the PTO has disallowed patents on such wonders as a perpetual motion machine[7] or a method of slowing the aging process.[8] The PTO has also issued Utility Guidelines for use by its examiners. The guidelines explain that an invention fulfills the utility requirement if it has a well-established use in the art or the applicant has disclosed a specific utility that is credible to a person of ordinary skill in the art.[9]

§ 15.3   Utility in Chemistry and Biotechnology

In modern practice, the utility requirement most often comes into play in the fields of chemistry and biotechnology. In these disciplines, inventors often synthesize a new compound, or a method of making a new compound, without a preexisting knowledge of a particular use for that compound. They may generate the compounds based on their knowledge of the behavior of related compounds, or may wish to explore a class of compounds for which some application may develop in the future. However, at the time the inventor generates the compound, no precise knowledge of the compound's utility is known.

The utility requirement should be viewed in light of the considerable incentives chemists and biotechnicians possess to obtain patent protection on compounds of interest as soon as possible. For example, in the case of pharmaceutical compounds, food and drug authorities require considerable product testing before the pharmaceutical can be broadly marketed. Before investing further time and effort on laboratory testing and clinical trials, actors in the pharmaceutical field desire to obtain patent rights on promising compounds even where their particular properties are, as yet, not well understood. But when patent applications are filed too close to the laboratory bench, chemists and biotechnicians have discovered that the ordinarily dormant utility requirement has posed considerable obstacles.

The Supreme Court opinion in *Brenner v. Manson* addressed such a situation.[1] The inventor Manson filed a patent application claiming a method of making a known steroid compound. Although the particular compound Manson was concerned with was already known to the art, chemists had yet to identify any setting in which it could be gainfully employed. However, as skilled artisans knew that another steroid with a very similar structure had tumor-inhibiting effects in mice, Manson's new method of making the compound was a research tool of interest to the scientific community.

---

7. Newman v. Quigg, 877 F.2d 1575, 11 USPQ2d 1340 (Fed.Cir.1989).

8. Ex parte Heicklen, 16 USPQ2d 1463 (BPAI 1990).

9. 64 Fed. Reg. 71440 (Dec. 21, 1999).

§ 15.3

1. 383 U.S. 519, 86 S.Ct. 1033, 16 L.Ed.2d 69 (1966).

The PTO Board of Appeals affirmed the examiner's rejection of the application. The Board reasoned that because Manson could not identify a single use for the steroid he produced, the utility requirement was not satisfied. The Board was unimpressed that a similar compound did have beneficial effects, noting that in the unpredictable art of steroid chemistry, even minor changes in chemical structure often lead to significant and unforeseeable changes in the performance of the compound. Manson then appealed to the CCPA, which reversed. Key to the CCPA's reasoning was that the sequence of process steps claimed by Manson would produce the steroid of interest. According to the CCPA, because the claimed process worked to produce a compound, the utility requirement was satisfied.

The Supreme Court granted certiorari and once more reversed. The Court took issue with Justice Story's understanding that the utility requirement is fulfilled so long as the claimed invention is not socially undesirable. At least within the context of scientific research tools, the Court imposed a requirement that an invention may not be patentable until it has been developed to a point where "specific benefit exists in currently available form." Chief among the Court's concerns was the breadth of the proprietary interest that could result from claims such as those in Manson's application. "Until the process claim has been reduced to production of a product shown to be useful, the metes and bounds of that monopoly are not capable of precise delineation.... Such a patent may confer power to block whole areas of scientific development, without compensating benefit to the public." The Court closed by noting that "a patent is not a hunting license. It is not a reward for the search, but compensation for its successful conclusion. 'A patent system must be related to the world of commerce rather than to the realm of philosophy.'"

The merits of *Brenner v. Manson* have been roundly debated. As noted by Justice Harlan in dissent, patented products and processes often are later found to possess additional, more valuable uses. In such cases advance knowledge of one particular use does not somehow restrain the patentee's proprietary interest in those additional applications. For example, the chemical compound nitroglycerine, originally developed as an explosive, was later found to be useful as a heart medication. If an inventor had obtained a patent on the nitroglycerine compound itself, then he would continue to possess a proprietary interest in that compound no matter what applications were discovered for it. Indeed, whether characterized as a basic research tool or an applied technology, any invention potentially serves as the basis for later developments.

That the influence of *Brenner v. Manson* may be waning is suggested by the leading Federal Circuit opinion on utility, *In re Brana*.[2] Like Manson, Brana claimed chemical compounds and stated they were useful as antitumor substances. The scientific community knew that structural-

---

2. 51 F.3d 1560, 34 USPQ2d 1436 (Fed. Cir.1995).

ly similar compounds had shown antitumor activity during both *in vitro* testing, done in the laboratory using tissue samples, and *in vivo* testing using mice as test subjects. The latter tests had been conducted using cell lines known to cause lymphocytic tumors in mice.

The PTO Board rejected the application for lack of utility, and on appeal the Federal Circuit reversed. Among the objections of the PTO was that the tests cited by Brana were conducted upon lymphomas induced in laboratory animals, rather than real diseases. The Federal Circuit responded that an inventor need not wait until an animal or human develops a disease naturally before finding a cure. The PTO further protested that Brana cited no clinical testing, and therefore had no proof of actual treatment of the disease in live animals. The Federal Circuit countered that proof of utility did not demand tests for the full safety and effectiveness of the compound, but only acceptable evidence of medical effects in a standard experimental animal.

Incredibly, the *Brana* opinion fails to discuss or even cite *Brenner v. Manson*. This lapse certainly suggests that the Federal Circuit will adopt a more liberal approach to the utility requirement than the Supreme Court did in *Brenner v. Manson*. The Federal Circuit did indicate that, in cases where the invention lacks a well-established use in the art, the applicant must disclose a specific, credible use within the patent's specification. Beyond this minimal statement, however, neither tribunal has set forth a statement of the utility standard notable for its clarity. The extent to which a particular chemical or pharmaceutical inventions will suffice to fulfill the utility requirement remains a matter to be decided on a case-by-case basis.

While *Brenner v. Manson* and *Brana* continue to generate heated discussion, the PTO has struggled to apply the utility requirement in the context of applications claiming genetic materials. Inventors often seek patent protection on biological compounds soon after they have been synthesized. Such compounds include complementary DNA ("cDNA"), which corresponds to proteins used by human cells, and expressed sequence tags ("ESTs"), DNA sequences that correspond to a small portion of each cDNA. Because this nascent field is highly unpredictable, the functions of cDNA fragments and ESTs are usually unknown at the time they are discovered. Yet they remain extraordinarily valuable for their potential uses, and scientists from private industry, government facilities and university laboratories alike have marketed these research tools for commercial sale.

The patentability of these genetic materials has proven controversial. While *Brenner v. Manson* holds that serious scientific interest alone does not fulfill the utility requirement, *Brana* and other Federal Circuit opinions suggest a more lenient posture. Some legal and scientific commentators have expressed concern that proprietary interests in scientific knowledge will impede research efforts overall. They have also suggested that inventors of cDNA sequences and ESTs seek an overly broad scope of patent protection, out of proportion with their relatively modest technical achievements. Others have urged that originators of cDNA sequences, like other inventors, also require a return on investment, and that allowing patents only on final products would merely further industry concentration.[3] Both the patent bar and the scientific community await judicial resolution of the legal protectability of these crucial technologies, a decision that will undoubtedly compel a further unpacking of the precise scope of the patent law's utility requirement.

3. *See generally* Rebecca S. Eisenberg, *Intellectual Property at the Public–Private Divide: The Case of Large–Scale cDNA Se-* *quencing*, 3 U. Chi. L. Sch. Roundtable 557, 560 (1996).

Chapter 16

NOVELTY

§ 16.1 Introduction

Novelty presents the core value of the patent system. To obtain the proprietary rights granted by the patent system, an inventor must create something new. There are at least two important policy bases for demanding novelty as a prerequisite for a patent. First, the novelty standard preserves the public domain by de____ ___ patents to already existing technology. Patentees may not app___ ____ ~hat others have justly regarded to be free of proprietary ____ ___ the novelty standard promotes efficiency, by discour__ _____ ~m engaging in duplicative development efforts. ____ _____ ~btain patent rights only when they advanc_ ____ _____ ~s will be motivated to turn first to li__ ____ gain needed technology.[2]

A determination of novelty ____ current state of technology m_ ____ This step requires a determi___ ____ of available knowledge are pe__ ____ . Act defines the materials—us___ ____ ~sed to judge the novelty of th_ ____ ~erences under § 102 include s_ ____ ~d publications, as well as evi___ ____ ~logy within the United State_ ____ ~minated the "prior art."

Making or____ ____ ~K. The authors of this complex ____ ~ng the often dated language of ____ ~mmaries of consider- ably nuar____ ____ ~d difficult even for the leading ____ ~atute cannot be read in isolati____ ____ ~nat has interpreted nearly each ____ ~n § 102 will be appreciably as____ ____ ~ctions of the provision in two g____ ____ ~eal directly with novelty, while para____ ____ ~a related, but distinct problem known ___ ____ ~ty provisions deal with events that occurred pr____ ____ ~plicant claims to have *invented* the alleged patenta____ ____ ~e statutory bar provisions, by contrast, deal with events th___ ____ ~prior to the date an applicant *filed* her patent application. A c____ ____ ~ook will help make this distinction more vivid.

The reason for the distinctions is that inventors do not always file for patents immediately upon conceptualizing their invention. They may delay for a wide variety of reasons. Thus an inventor may invent

[handwritten notes: Week 1 / Chapter 1 / Chapter 24.1–24.4 / Week 2 / Chapter 13.1, 13.4 / 17.1, 17.3.2.1, 16.1–16.2, 17.3.5]

---

§ 16.1

1. Pfaff v. Wells Electronics, 525 U.S. 55, 119 S.Ct. 304, 310, 142 L.Ed.2d 261 (1998), *reh'g denied*, 525 U.S. 1094, 119 S.Ct. 854, 142 L.Ed.2d 707 (1999).

2. *See* Brett Frischmann, *Innovation and Institutions: Rethinking the Economics of U.S. Science and Technology Policy*, 24 VERMONT L. REV. 347 (2000).

something in May, 2000, but not file for a patent until October, 2002. Events that occur prior to May 2000 are those that can defeat novelty—they predate the invention. Those events that occur before October, 2002 are those that can give rise to a statutory bar. Either type of problem will result in a denial of the patent application, but the logic differs.

As noted, the statutory bars are tied to the date the inventor filed an application at the PTO. In practice, § 102(b) is the primary source of a statutory bar. Under § 102(b), the point in time one year prior to the filing date is termed the "critical date," and statutorily specified activities, such as publications or sales, act to bar, or prevent, the acquisition of a patent if they occur before that time. The one-year period generated by § 102(b) is commonly termed the "grace period." Section 102(d) also creates a statutory bar if the U.S. application has not been filed within one year of a foreign application on the same invention where the foreign application ultimately matured into a granted patent. Lastly, § 102(c) offers a broadly stated, if little used, provision denying patentability when the invention has been abandoned to the public. Each of these provisions is treated in more detail in § 16.2 of this Chapter.

The novelty provisions mandate that one who is not the first inventor of a technology cannot obtain a patent, regardless of when or even whether another application has been filed. Crucial to this set of provisions is the invention date. Sections 102(a) and (g) implement the first-to-invent rule by declaring public knowledge of an earlier invention to be a form of prior art. Section 102(g) also serves as the basis for the PTO priority contests known as interferences, which determine who among several competing inventors should be entitled to a patent. Section 102(e) deals with a special category of secret knowledge of an earlier inventor's work: a patent application, filed by another prior to the invention date, which has actually matured into a granted patent, and discloses but does not claim the invention. Section 102(f) prevents a patent from issuing to an applicant who did not himself invent the claimed invention. The novelty provisions of § 102 are discussed in § 16.3 of this Chapter.

Once we have identified all possible references that might give rise to novelty or statutory bar issues, the second determination is whether any of those references actually anticipates a claim. The standard of anticipation is a strict one. Each and every element of the claimed invention must be disclosed in a single, enabling reference. These issues are considered in § 16.4 of this Chapter.

It should be noted here that the novelty standard is not the only one based upon the prior art. Novelty is complemented by the requisite of nonobviousness. Not only must a patentable invention not be strictly anticipated by a single reference, it must not have been obvious to persons of ordinary skill in the art at the time it was made. In practice, novelty presents the first stage of a prior art-based analysis, with nonobviousness conducted next. Nonobviousness will be taken up in Chapter Seventeen of this book.

Regrettably, the world's patent laws do not exhibit a great deal of uniformity in their definitions of the prior art. The United States in particular has gone its own way by maintaining a unique "first-to-invent" system. In the United States, when more than one patent application is filed claiming the same invention, the patent will be awarded to the applicant who establishes the earliest acts of invention. Other countries have opted for a "first-to-file" rule under which entitlement to a patent is established by the earliest effective filing date of a patent application. Although inventors around the world have long maligned the interface problems created by the first-to-invent system, the United States has yet to muster the political will to harmonize its patent law with global norms.[3]

§ 16.2   Prior Art for Novelty: The Statutory Bars

16.2.1   Introduction to § 102(b)

Because they are fundamental to all patent systems, the statutory bar provisions of the Patent Act are an appropriate starting point. Of the three statutory bars, § 102(b) is by far the most frequently employed. Section 102(b) denies a patent where "the invention was patented or described in a printed publication in this or a foreign country or in public use or on sale in this country, more than one year prior to the date of the application for patent in the United States." The statute focuses attention on the so-called "critical date," set to one year before the date the patent application was filed. Section 102(b) bars patentability where, before the critical date, the invention was in public use or on sale in the United States; or either patented or described in a printed publication anywhere.

Section 102(b) acts in the nature of a statute of limitation. Once inventors publish an article describing the invention, or otherwise engage in activity specified by § 102(b), they must file a patent application at the PTO within one year or forfeit their United States patent rights. Of course, inventors must be concerned with the activities of others as well. Should another individual have also arrived at the same invention, and performed acts specified by § 102(b) prior to the critical date, then the statutory bar is triggered.

The Federal Circuit has identified § 102(b) as serving the following purposes:

> First, there is a policy against removing inventions from the public which the public has justifiably come to believe are freely available to all as a consequence of prolonged sales activity. Next, there is a policy favoring prompt and widespread disclosure of new inventions to the public. The inventor is forced to file promptly or risk possible forfeiture of his [patent] rights due

3. *See* Charles L. Gholz, *First-to-File or First-to-Invent*, 82 J. Pat. & Trademark Off. Soc'y 891 (2000).

to prior sales. A third policy is to prevent the inventor from commercially exploiting the exclusivity of his invention substantially beyond the statutorily authorized [20–year] period. The on-sale bar forces the inventor to choose between seeking patent protection promptly following sales activity or taking his chances with his competitors without the benefit of patent protection. The fourth and final identifiable policy is to give the inventor a reasonable amount of time following sales activity (set by statute as 1 year) to determine whether a patent is a worthwhile investment. This benefits the public because it tends to minimize the filing of [patent applications concerning inventions] of only marginal public interest.[1]

Unhappily, the great patent statutes of the world diverge with regard to the grace period. With its one-year grace period, the United States patent laws stand in juxtaposition to the "absolute novelty" provisions of the European Patent Convention. Under the European regime, disclosure of an invention even one day before the filing date bars patentability.[2] The Japanese system lies in between, providing for a six-month period that applies only to inventor activities.[3] Under the Japanese patent law, then, disclosure by a third party prior to the filing date acts as a bar. Thus, while pre-filing date activities may not prejudice U.S. patent rights under § 102(b), they may seriously compromise the possibility of obtaining patents abroad.

Opinion differs as to the wisdom of a grace period. Proponents of the grace period urge that because inventors often labor under the "publish or perish" principle, they face pressure to publish their results promptly—often long before a patent application can be drafted and filed. Thus, a grace period comports with the norms of the scientific community and promotes a more prompt disclosure of inventions. It further avoids the prospect of forfeiture, where inventors have inadvertently published descriptions of their inventions shortly before a patent application was filed. Finally, a grace period is said to benefit inventions that require testing in a "real world" environment. In contrast, supporters of the European absolute novelty regime have advocated that a grace period increases legal uncertainties. They suggest that an inventor's ability to delay the filing of a patent application until after a full year of commercial activity has transpired is unjustified, for it slows the inventor's entry into the patent system. According to the supporters of an "absolute novelty" regime, education on the existing requirements to obtain a patent presents the most effective way of avoiding forfeitures.[4]

§ 16.2

1. General Electric v. United States, 654 F.2d 55, 61–64 (Ct.Cl.1981) (en banc).

2. Convention on the Grant of European Patents, Oct. 5, 1973, Art. 54 (2), 13 I.L.M. 286 (1974).

3. *See* William LaMarca, *Reevaluating the Geographical Limitation of 35 U.S.C.A.* § *102(b)*, 22 Univ. Dayton L. Rev. 25, 43–44 (1996).

4. *Compare* Jan E.M. Galama, *Expert Opinion on the Case For and Against the Introduction of a Grace Period in the European Patent Law* (April 30, 2000), *with* Joseph Straus, *Expert Opinion on the Introduction of a Grace Period in the European Patent Law* (May 8, 2000).

Although views vary on the propriety of a grace period, most would admit that the choice of a one-year period within § 102(b) is an arbitrary one. There is nothing inviolate about one year: prior to 1939, the grace period consisted of two years within the United States. And as noted, the Japanese patent statute, which provides a grace period solely of use by inventors, is currently set at six months. At least we can be grateful for the ease of calculation that the statute presently provides.

16.2.2 "Public Use" Under § 102(b)

One event that will raise a statutory bar is "public use" of the technology in question by either the patent applicant or anyone else, within the United States more than one year prior to the date of the application. The concept of "public use" owes its origins to the Supreme Court's early opinion in *Pennock v. Dialogue*.[5] The plaintiff's patent went towards a method for manufacturing a type of rubber hose useful for conveying air and fluids. The invention had been built by 1811, but the inventor did not file a patent application until seven years later. In the meantime, the inventor had licensed a third party to market the hose and enjoyed considerable sales. The inventor later asserted his patent against a competitor. The defendant urged that the patent should be struck down based upon section 1 of the Patent Act of 1793, which provided that an invention must be one that was "not known or used before the application" to be patentable.

Writing for the Supreme Court, Justice Story affirmed a judgment for the defendant. Story reasoned that the words "not known or used before the application" did not refer to knowledge or use by inventors themselves. Because inventors must know of their own work product, a literal interpretation of section 1 would lead to a rejection of every patent application. In addition, Story reasoned, Congress could not have meant to deny patents where the inventor merely employed others to assist in the construction or use of the invention, or in cases where the invention had been used without the inventor's consent. Instead, the Court held that the "true meaning" of the statute was to deny patents to inventions "known or used by the public before the application."

Subsequent patent statutes codified the concept of "public use" pioneered in *Pennock v. Dialogue*. The courts have interpreted the term broadly, holding that even a limited use that results in negligible public exposure will trigger the "public use" bar. *Egbert v. Lippmann*,[6] long the target of feeble classroom wit, well illustrates this point. There, a Samuel H. Barnes invented an improved corset spring (or "steel") after hearing complaints from a young lady friend, Frances Lee, as well as a Miss Cugier. Samuel gave one set to Frances in 1855 and another to her in 1858. Frances wore the springs within some of her corsets for a "long time," even inserting them into different corsets when the original garment wore out. Samuel and Frances later "intermarried." Sometime

5. 27 U.S. 1, 7 L.Ed. 327 (1829).
6. 104 U.S. 333, 26 L.Ed. 755 (1881).

in 1863, a Mr. Sturgis visited the couple and received an explanation of the working of the corset springs from Frances. A patent application was filed in 1866 and in due course a patent issued. After Samuel passed away and Frances remarried, she brought a patent infringement suit. Among the defenses was that the corset spring was in public use before the critical date.

The Supreme Court held that Frances' employment of the corset springs was a "public use" in the sense of the patent law. The Court judged that the "public use" standard could be satisfied by the inventor's gift of a single patented article to one person. Noting that "some inventions are by their very character only capable of being used where they cannot be seen or observed by the public eye," the Court further concluded that "if its inventor sells a machine of which his invention forms a part, and allows it to be used without restriction of any kind, the use is a public one." Accordingly, the patent-at-suit was held invalid.

The dissenting opinion by Justice Miller observed that the majority's holding seemed to remove the term "public" from the statute: "If the little steep spring inserted in a single pair of corsets, and used by only one woman, covered by her outer-clothing, and in a position always withheld from public observation, is a public use of that piece of steel, I am at a loss to know the line between a public and a private use." Although the dissent's reading of the statute initially seems persuasive, modern technologies increasingly justify the holding of the majority. Like the corset springs of *Egbert v. Lippmann*, inventions in disciplines ranging from biotechnology to electronics exhibit a noninforming character. For example, members of the public remain unable to discern the inner workings of new electronic circuitry even after listening to the radio of which those circuits form a part. A contrary holding would have loosened the impact of § 102(b) upon inventors within such technical fields. A better ground for dissent may have been the unwillingness of the seemingly scandalized Court, which took pains to note that Samuel "slept on his rights for seven years," to imply a relationship of confidentiality between Samuel and Frances.

The treatment of prior, secret uses of an invention has also lead to some strained interpretations of the term "public use." Although the text of § 102(b) does not differentiate between patent applicants and third parties, the courts have nonetheless drawn distinctions between these two categories of actors when determining the prior art effect of secret uses. In particular, the courts have held that secret activity comprises a "public use" within the meaning of § 102(b) when performed by the patent applicant. However, the identical use, when performed by a third party, will not serve as prior art against an unrelated applicant. In so doing, the courts have sought to balance two of the chief policies undergirding § 102, preservation of the public domain and maintenance of the statutory patent term.

The Federal Circuit's early opinion in *Gore v. Garlock*[7] exemplifies third party secret use cases. Gore obtained a patent including process claims for quickly stretching crystalline, unsintered polytetrafluroethylene (commonly known under the trademark "Teflon"). During later enforcement litigation, a competitor learned that a John Cropper, living in New Zealand, had earlier invented the same technology. Prior to the critical date, Cropper both sent a letter describing the invention to a Massachusetts company, and sold his machine to Budd. Budd employees were told to maintain the Cropper machine in confidence, and at some later point Budd practiced the process.

On appeal from a patent enforcement proceeding, the Federal Circuit described the Budd and Cropper commercializations as secret and not a "public use" under § 102(b). Chief Judge Markey noted that if Budd had sold anything, it was stretched Teflon, and not the process used in producing it. Further, Budd's use of the machine did not enrich the public domain, because an observer of the machine could not determine such parameters as the stretching speed or traits of the stretched material. The court concluded that "[a]s between a prior inventor who benefits from a process by selling its product but suppresses, conceals, or otherwise keeps the process from the public, and a later inventor who promptly files a patent application from which the public will gain a disclosure of the process, the law favors the latter."[8]

Judge Learned Hand's decision in *Metallizing Engineering Co. v. Kenyon Bearing & Auto Parts*,[9] demonstrates that a court will reach a different holding where the secret use is made by the applicant himself. The technology there concerned a process for reconstructing machine parts known as "metallizing." The inventor, Meduna, maintained the process as a trade secret. Only the reconditioned parts could be viewed by the public, for Meduna kept the process under lock and key. He filed a patent application on August 6, 1942, but had been practicing the process before the critical date. During patent infringement litigation, the district court held that Meduna's concealed process did not comprise a "public use" within the statute.

Following an appeal, the Second Circuit panel reversed the trial court. Judge Hand identified a distinction in secret use cases between "(1) [t]he effect upon his right to a patent of the inventor's competitive exploitation of his machine or of his process" and "(2) the contribution which a prior use by another person makes to the art."[10] Judge Hand agreed that in the second set of circumstances, the third party had not made a "public use" under the predecessor statute to § 102(b). Citing his earlier opinion in *Gillman v. Stern*, Judge Hand concluded that the issue in third party cases "was whether a prior use which did not

---

7. W.L. Gore & Associates v. Garlock, Inc., 721 F.2d 1540 (Fed.Cir.1983), *cert. denied*, 469 U.S. 851, 105 S.Ct. 172, 83 L.Ed.2d 107 (1984).

8. 721 F.2d at 1550.

9. 153 F.2d 516 (2d Cir.), *cert. denied*, 328 U.S. 840, 66 S.Ct. 1016, 90 L.Ed. 1615 (1946).

10. 153 F.2d at 520.

disclose the invention to the art was within the statute, and it is well settled that it is not."[11]

Judge Hand went on to explain, however, that a different policy concern arose in the event of secret uses by the inventor. He noted that secret uses allow inventors to delay filing a patent application beyond the grace period and thus "extend the period of monopoly."[12] Concerning an inventor who secretly exploited his technology for a time longer than the grace period, Hand concluded that if "he goes beyond that period of probation, he forfeits his right regardless of how little the public may have learned about the invention."[13]

Hand's observations bear further discussion. The statute currently limits the patent term to twenty years from the date a patent application is filed at the PTO. Section 102(b) also offers inventors the privilege of a one-year grace period in which to put the invention to public use before filing that application. The maximum period from the initial commercialization to expiration of an associated patent, then, is ordinarily twenty-one years. An inventor who practiced a technology as a trade secret for many years before filing an application could disrupt this scheme, in effect delaying the patent expiration date. Declaring the inventor's secret use to be a "public use" within § 102(b) prevents this abuse. In effect this scheme forces the inventor to choose between patent law and trade secret law as the desired legal regime to protect the commercially operable invention.[14] Yet because this policy concern is not present when the secret commercial use was not made by the inventor, the more natural reading of the term "public use" should prevail in third party cases like *Gore v. Garlock*.

Both *Gore v. Garlock* and *Metallizing Engineering* involved process claims. Similar logic would seem to apply to product patents, provided that the product had been kept in secrecy and used commercially. For example, suppose that Warhol, a taxi driver, invents an improved fuel injector for use in an internal combustion engine. Warhol installs the fuel injector in her taxi and, beginning on January 19, 2003, uses the fuel injector on a daily basis. Further suppose that Warhol never shows the fuel injector to others and never opens the hood of her automobile outside of her locked, personal garage. Provided that Warhol files a patent application at the PTO directed towards her fuel injector by January 19, 2004, she will fall within the statutory grace period. However, should she file the application after that date, § 102(b) would prohibit the issuance of a patent due to a "public use" of the fuel injector. In that case a third party inventor would be able to obtain a patent on the same fuel injector, unhindered by Warhol's secret use.

---

11. *Id.* at 519.
12. *Id.* at 520.
13. *Id.*

14. For more on trade secrets, *see infra* Chapter 24.

16.2.3 "On Sale" Under § 102(b)

Another patent-defeating event specified by § 102(b) is that the invention was placed "on sale" in the United States by anyone, more than one year before the filing of the patent application. This event is distinct from "public use," although judicial opinions sometimes do not carefully distinguish between the two events. The statutory language calls for the invention merely to be "on sale," not necessarily sold. Even a single offer to sell may suffice to bar patentability.[15] The on-sale bar may be triggered by anyone,[16] so long as the sales activities occur in the United States.

Although § 102(b) speaks of the invention being on sale in the United States, the courts have interpreted the statute to require sales activity with respect to a physical embodiment of the invention, as compared to more abstract patent rights in the invention.[17] Thus, an offer to license patent rights or the transfer of patent rights from an employee to an employer does not trigger the bar. The on-sale bar would apply to sales activity involving commercial embodiments of the invention, however.

The Federal Circuit has recognized a notable exception to the on-sale bar. The on-sale bar must involve separate and unrelated parties. Where the parties are related, the courts may disregard the sale provided that "the seller so controls the purchaser that the invention remains out of the public's hands."[18] Pertinent factors to see whether the on-sale bar applies to transactions between related parties include whether there was a need for testing by other than the patentee; the amount of control exercised; the stage of development of the invention; whether payments were made and the basis thereof; whether confidentiality was required; and whether technological changes were made.[19]

A recurring issue under § 102(b) was whether sales activity may trigger the on-sale bar where the invention has not yet been physically constructed. Some opinions, such as *Timely Products Corp. v. Arron*,[20] held or assumed that the on-sale bar was inapplicable where the invention was not ready "on hand" at the time of sale. Others, most notably the controversial opinion in *UMC Electronics Co. v. United States*,[21] concluded that there was no strict requirement that the invention be "reduced to practice" for the on-sale bar to apply. A choice between these competing positions depended upon a weighing of the common sense view that something cannot be sold if it has not yet been constructed; an awareness of everyday commercial practices, such as the

15. Intel Corp. v. United States Int'l Trade Comm'n, 946 F.2d 821 (Fed.Cir. 1991).

16. J.A. LaPorte, Inc. v. Norfolk Dredging Co., 787 F.2d 1577 (Fed.Cir.1986).

17. Moleculon Research Corp. v. CBS, Inc., 793 F.2d 1261 (Fed.Cir.1986).

18. Ferag AG v. Quipp Inc., 45 F.3d 1562 (Fed.Cir.), *cert. denied*, 516 U.S. 816, 116 S.Ct. 71, 133 L.Ed.2d 31 (1995).

19. Continental Can Co. v. Monsanto Co., 948 F.2d 1264 (Fed.Cir.1991).

20. 523 F.2d 288 (2d Cir.1975).

21. 816 F.2d 647 (Fed.Cir.1987), *cert. denied*, 484 U.S. 1025, 108 S.Ct. 748, 98 L.Ed.2d 761 (1988).

"vaporware" phenomenon in the software industry; and the desire to provide inventors with a definite standard for determining when they must file a patent application.

The Supreme Court opinion in *Pfaff v. Wells Electronics*[22] resolved the "reduction to practice" issue. Pfaff was the named inventor on a patent directed towards a computer chip socket. Prior to the critical date, Pfaff presented his inventive concept to representatives of Texas Instruments. Although Pfaff had not yet constructed even a single prototype, the Texas Instruments representatives nonetheless placed a large purchase order for the sockets. A third party manufacturer ultimately produced a working embodiment of the invention after the critical date. Following the issuance of the chip socket patent, Pfaff brought suit against a competitor, which argued that the claims were invalid due to the on sale bar.

The Court agreed with the defendant that the on-sale bar applied under the facts. Justice Stevens set forth a two-part test to determine whether an invention was "on sale" within the meaning of § 102(b). "First, the product must be the subject of a commercial offer for sale." The Court believed that this test satisfied the inventive community's desire for certainty, because inventors could "both understand and control the timing of the first commercial marketing of the invention." Here, Pfaff had accepted the Texas Instruments purchase order before the critical date.

The second part of the test was that "the invention must be ready for patenting." The Court recognized at least two ways to satisfy this condition. The invention may have been physically constructed: an "actual reduction to practice" in the language of the patent law. Alternatively, "drawings or other descriptions of the invention sufficiently detailed to enable a person skilled in the art to practice the invention" would also suffice. Pfaff's delivery of detailed engineering specifications and diagrams to the manufacturer prior to the critical date demonstrated that he had fulfilled this second prong.

16.2.4 Experimental Use

The concept of experimental use further refines the meaning of the statutory term "public use" in § 102(b). If the use is judged as experimental, then it is not a "public use" within the meaning of § 102(b). The experimental use doctrine also appears to apply to inventions placed "on sale" prior to the critical date, although far less precedent addresses this situation.

The doctrine of experimental use essentially provides inventors with additional "tinker time" beyond the one-year grace period. In deciding experimental use cases, courts must balance two competing policies. The first, a principal focus of § 102(b), is to allow inventors sufficient time to determine whether an invention is suitable for its intended purposes.

22. 525 U.S. 55, 119 S.Ct. 304, 142 L.Ed.2d 261 (1998), *reh'g denied*, 525 U.S. 1094, 119 S.Ct. 854, 142 L.Ed.2d 707 (1999).

The second is a concern for the integrity of the statutory patent term. Overbroad application of the experimental use doctrine would allow an inventor to delay filing a patent application and, consequentially, delay the date of patent expiration.

The 1877 Supreme Court opinion in *City of Elizabeth v. American Nicholson Pavement Co.*[23] remains the most significant experimental use case. There, Nicholson invented an improved wooden pavement. In 1848, Nicholson installed the pavement on a portion of a toll road owned by his company. The road was open to the public and subject to continuous use through 1854, when Nicholson filed a patent application. During this time, Nicholson regularly inspected the pavement to determine its durability under various traffic and weather conditions. Nicholson later brought suit against the city of Elizabeth, New Jersey, which had laid allegedly infringing pavement.

The Court decided that because Nicholson's use was experimental in nature, it was not a "public use" within the meaning of the predecessor statute to § 102(b). The Court reasoned that the public interest supported the filing of application on "perfect and properly tested" inventions, as compared to less refined technologies. Where an inventor has made "a bona fide effort to bring his invention to perfection, or to ascertain whether it will answer the purpose intended," the Court held that the public use bar should not apply.

City of Elizabeth may be subjected to ready criticism. One wonders why the statutory grace period did not suffice for Nicholson's testing purposes, particularly since he did not appear to make a single change to the pavement during a seven-year period. And surely testing in a laboratory or otherwise more secluded environment—say, a factory grounds where the employees could have been subjected to a confidentiality agreement—would have fulfilled Nicholson's purposes. If the Court was so moved by Nicholson's desire to build a long-lasting pavement, then seemingly every patent applicant would do well to stress that durability was among the aims of the invention. Perhaps the weakness of the concept of a procrustean grace period of varying length for each patent applicant has lead to only infrequent findings of experimental use in modern patent cases.

More recently, the precedent of the Federal Circuit has called for an analysis of the totality of the circumstances to determine whether the inventor has engaged in an experimental use. Among the numerous indicia of experimentation identified by the court are:

(1) the number of prototypes and duration of testing;

(2) the attention to records or reports during the testing;

(3) the existence of a confidentiality arrangement;

(4) the receipt of any commercial advantage by the patentee;

(5) the inventor's control over the testing;

23. 97 U.S. 126, 24 L.Ed. 1000 (1877).

(6) the tailoring of the sort of testing with respect to the specific features of the invention; and

(7) whether the invention allowed the testing to be conducted without public access, through concealment of the technology or other means.[24]

The Federal Circuit has also stressed that the putative experimentation must go towards the technical features of the invention.[25] Testing to predict whether the invention will enjoy marketplace success does not constitute experimental use within the meaning of § 102(b).

16.2.5 Patented, Printed Publications and "In This Country"

Under § 102(b), the fact that an invention has been subject to public use or been placed on sale is germane only if those events occurred "in this country." Section 102(b) also denies patentability to inventions that have been "patented" or described in a "printed publication" before the critical date anywhere in the world. As with the terms "public use" and "on sale," each of these terms has been subjected to a detailed construction by the courts and PTO. An overview of this interpretative project is necessary to achieve a proper understanding of § 102(b).

Review of these terms is appropriate for a second reason. Several of these terms also appear in other parts of § 102, in particular paragraphs (a), (d) and (g). Because the courts have generally interpreted these terms consistently within § 102, their introduction here will be of appreciable assistance in future reading.

16.2.5.1 "Patented"

An invention that has been "patented" one year before the date of filing under § 102(b) will bar a later U.S. application. Issues over the term "patented" ordinarily arise with respect to patents granted abroad. Global legal regimes yield an exotic array of intellectual property rights that can differ significantly from familiar domestic patents. The courts have been left to determine which of these rights constitutes a patent within the terms of § 102.

The Federal Circuit opinion in *In re Carlson* is illustrative.[26] The PTO became aware of several pieces of prior art pertinent to Carlson's claimed dual compartment bottle. One of them was a so-called Geschmacksmuster (GM), a German design registration. Registration of the GM was effective at the time it was deposited at a local government office in Germany. Lists of registered designs were published shortly thereafter in the German Federal Gazette. The Gazette provided a general description of the general design, the class of articles deposited, identifying numbers of the deposited designs, the name and location of

24. Lough v. Brunswick, 86 F.3d 1113 (Fed.Cir.1996), *reh'g denied*, 103 F.3d 1517 (Fed.Cir.1997).

25. *See* In re Smith, 714 F.2d 1127 (Fed.Cir.1983).

26. 983 F.2d 1032 (Fed.Cir.1992).

the registrant, the date and time of registration, and the city location of the registered design.

Following PTO rejection of the claim of his design patent based in part upon the GM, Carlson appealed to the Federal Circuit. Carlson proposed that under § 102 "the embodiment of foreign protection must take a form that fully discloses the nature of the protected design in a medium of communication capable of being widely disseminated." Arguing that the Gazette entry did not fulfill this standard, Carlson urged that the GM could not be considered "patented" within the meaning of § 102(a).

Writing for a three-judge panel, Judge Clevenger upheld the PTO rejection. The court reasoned that the Gazette entry sufficed to alert readers that a multiple bottle design had been registered. An interested reader could then proceed to the appropriate German office to obtain the actual design, either in person or through an agent. Although cognizant of the difficulties entailed for a U.S. applicant to scrutinize a particular GM, the court noted that this burden was imposed by statute.

As suggested by *Carlson*, a second complexity with regard to foreign rights is the determination of the precise date an invention has been "patented." In the United States this analysis is straightforward. U.S. patents are granted on the same day that notice of their issuance is published in the PTO Official Gazette. This single date also marks the time when the exclusive rights associated with the patent become effective, and also the point at which interested members of the public may obtain a complete copy of the patent instrument and the prosecution history. Foreign patent systems may cause these events to occur on different dates. Where some occur more than one year before the applicant filed in the United States and some less than a year, the choice of the key date becomes crucial to patentability.

The moment at which an invention becomes "patented" within the meaning of § 102 is subject to a case-by-case determination. The prevailing view, however, is that an invention is patented at the time the sovereign bestows a formal grant of legal rights to the applicant.[27] In addition, courts have required that the patent be publicly available, typically through public notice, publication, or the possibility of inspection at a government office.

16.2.5.2   Printed Publications

The term "printed publication" has been afforded a liberal construction. A document need neither be formally typeset nor published to serve as a source of prior art under § 102. Instead, the courts have accounted for "ongoing advances in the technologies of data storage, retrieval and dissemination."[28] Any document available to the public, no matter where located, constitutes a "printed publication" within § 102. Thus, such documents as handwritten notes, papers distributed at a conference, or

27. In re Monks, 588 F.2d 308 (CCPA 1978).

28. In re Hall, 781 F.2d 897 (Fed.Cir. 1986).

advertising circulars may all constitute printed publications.[29] Documents distributed to a small group under circumstances of confidentiality would not.[30]

The effective date of a publication is the date it becomes accessible to the public. The document comprises prior art under § 102 whether or not anyone has actually reviewed its contents. The text of the printed publication need not be written in the English language to be effective prior art.

The Federal Circuit opinion in *In re Hall*, a § 102(b) case, offers an instructive application of these principles. There, the PTO cited a doctoral thesis available at the library of the University of Freiburg, Germany, which had been written more than one year before the applicant applied for a patent, as a bar to granting the patent. Although the applicant argued that the reference was invalid because the exact date of cataloging and shelving was unknown, the court recognized that ordinary business practices do not always call for the memorialization of such information. Judge Baldwin was satisfied that general practices of the Freiburg library would have rendered the doctoral thesis publicly accessible well before the critical date.

The applicant next urged that even if catalogued, a single thesis in one university library should not constitute prior art. According to the applicant, the Freiburg thesis was not sufficiently accessible so as to inform interested practitioners about the technology. The Federal Circuit agreed that a printed publication must be publicly accessible, but held that the Freiburg thesis was sufficiently attainable to diligent individuals interested in the art. That a distant, foreign language thesis should serve as prior art against a domestic applicant may trouble some readers. Yet Congress fashioned § 102 out of the apparent belief that U.S. inventors should be held accountable for knowledge that had been reduced to a tangible form, even where that knowledge has been memorialized abroad. In an era of increasing technical harmonization and access to information, this judgment seems sound.

The Federal Circuit went the other way in *In re Cronyn*.[31] The reference at issue there was a senior thesis deposited in the library of Reed College, a solely undergraduate institution located in Portland, Oregon. Although the library was open to the public, the thesis was neither generally catalogued nor indexed. Instead, all student theses were listed on a special index of cards available for public examination, both at the main college library and in a shoebox stored in the chemistry department. Identifying "dissemination and public accessibility" as the pertinent indicia of whether a prior art reference was "published" or not, the court held that the latter standard was not fulfilled here. The fact that the theses were distinctly filed, as well as the sorting of

---

29. *See* In re Wyer, 655 F.2d 221 (CCPA 1981).

30. *See* Northern Telecom, Inc. v. Datapoint Corp., 908 F.2d 931 (Fed.Cir.1990).

31. 890 F.2d 1158 (Fed.Cir.1989).

individual cards only via the name of the author, led to the conclusion that the theses "had not been catalogued or indexed in a meaningful way." Comparison of *Cronyn* with *Hall* suggests that the decision whether a particular reference rises to the level of a "printed publication" is an intensely factual one.

16.2.5.3 "In this Country"

Under § 102(b), the fact that an invention is in "public use" or "on sale" is significant only if those events occur "in this country." An instructive opinion on the "in this country" limitation of § 102(b) is *Robbins Co. v. Lawrence Manufacturing Co.*[32] *Robbins* considered whether an embodiment of a patented tunnel boring machine was on sale "in this country" before the critical date of February 18, 1962. The U.S.-based patentee had submitted a detailed written offer in response to the Hydro–Electric Commission of Tasmania, Australia. The parties entered into a contract in 1960, resulting in patentee delivery of a set of machine components to Seattle in 1961. The components were then shipped to Australia, assembled under the supervision of the patentee, and extensively employed prior to the critical date.

The Ninth Circuit judged that a "product is 'on sale' in the United States, within the proscription of the statute, if substantial activity prefatory to a sale occurs in the United States. An offer for sale, made in this country, is sufficient prefatory activity occurring here, to bring the matter within the statute."[33] According to Judge Carter, that standard was met because Sugden, a representative of the Hydro–Electric Commission, negotiated the contract with the patentee in Seattle. Sugden also traveled to Seattle to observe the shop testing, disassembly and packing of the machine. Interestingly, the court's holding suggests that domestic manufacture of a patented invention would not fulfill the "in this country" limitation of § 102 if the entirety of sales activity occurred abroad.[34]

Commentators have questioned the wisdom of maintaining a geographical distinction in § 102.[35] Although the likely motivation for this statutory language was the perceived difficulty of obtaining evidence of foreign activity, modern conveniences of communication and transportation mitigate against this concern. More recently drafted patent statutes, most notably the European Patent Convention, do not restrict the prior art territorially. Additionally, the "in this country" limitation of § 102 also appears as a rare instance of discrimination against those members of the technological community based in the United States. Activity that would not prejudice foreign actors acting in their home markets may deleteriously impact U.S. inventors, a seemingly unsound result as a matter of U.S. patent policy.

32. 482 F.2d 426 (9th Cir.1973).

33. 482 F.2d at 434.

34. DONALD S. CHISUM, PATENTS: A TREATISE ON THE LAW OF PATENTABILITY, VALIDITY AND INFRINGEMENT § 6.02[6] (2002).

35. PRESIDENT'S COMMISSION ON THE PATENT SYSTEM, TO PROMOTE THE PROGRESS OF . . . USEFUL ARTS IN AN AGE OF EXPLODING TECHNOLOGY 2, 3 (1966).

16.2.6   Abandonment Under § 102(c)

Section 102(c) bars a patent where the applicant "has abandoned the invention." This statute does not refer to disposal of the invention itself, however, but instead to the intentional surrender of an invention *to the public*. Once an inventor has donated the technology to the public, she will be barred from seeking a patent. Older Supreme Court opinions instruct that abandonment may occur where an inventor expressly dedicates it to the public, through a deliberate relinquishment or conduct evidencing an intent not to pursue patent protection.[36] The circumstances must be such that others could reasonably rely upon the inventor's renunciation.[37]

The course of human affairs is such that few individuals expressly cede their patentable inventions to the public without seeking compensation. As a result, a paucity of more recent precedent considers § 102(c) in any meaningful way. Perhaps the only circumstance implicating this statute would involve an express public statement by an inventor dedicating a technology to the public. If a subsequent call from the inventor's creditors led to second thoughts and the filing of a patent application, § 102(c) might then come into play.

It is important not to confuse the use of the term "abandonment" in § 102(c) with other uses of the term in the patent law. In particular, § 102(g) refers to individuals who have "abandoned, suppressed or concealed" the invention itself, for example, by suspending work on a project before developing a working model. Section 102(c) instead concerns abandonment of the right to obtain a patent. This statute also does not prevent inventors from withdrawing applications from the PTO, an action that is also termed an "abandonment." The Patent Act allows inventors to retract patent applications from the PTO without necessarily prejudicing their right ultimately to obtain a patent. Inventors who earlier abandoned applications are always free to file again. Although these applicants will lose the benefit of their earlier filing date, and thus may expose themselves to bars under §§ 102(b) or (d), they will not be impacted by § 102(c) if all the circumstances do not indicate abandonment of the invention to the public.

16.2.7   Delayed United States Filing Under § 102(d)

Section 102(d) bars a U.S. patent when (1) an inventor files a foreign patent application more than twelve months before filing the U.S. application, and (2) a foreign patent results from that application prior to the U.S. filing date. The requirements are conjunctive: both requirements must be met in order to trigger § 102(d) and bar the issuance of a patent. By encouraging prompt filing in the United States,

36. *See* Beedle v. Bennett, 122 U.S. 71, 7 S.Ct. 1090, 30 L.Ed. 1074 (1887); Agawam Woolen Co. v. Jordan, 74 U.S. (7 Wall.) 583, 19 L.Ed. 177 (1868); Kendall v. Winsor, 62 U.S. (21 How.) 322, 16 L.Ed. 165 (1858).

37. *See* Mendenhall v. Astec Indus., Inc., 13 USPQ2d 1913, 1937 (E.D.Tenn. 1988), *aff'd*, 887 F.2d 1094 (Fed.Cir.1989).

§ 102(d) ensures that the term of U.S. patents will not appreciably extend past the expiration date of parallel foreign patents.[38]

An example illustrates the application of § 102(d). Suppose that Orlanth, the inventor of an electric trolling motor, files an application at the Swedish Patent Office on May 25, 2002. The Swedish application matures into a granted Swedish patent on August 1, 2003. If Orlanth has not filed his U.S. patent application at the PTO as of August 1, 2003, the date of the Swedish patent grant, the § 102(d) bar would be triggered.

Commentators have often approached § 102(d) with some distaste.[39] Because inventors may choose to file a patent application only in the United States, the policy goal of assuring that the U.S. market will become patent-free contemporaneously with foreign markets seems poorly served via the § 102(d) bar. More telling is that § 102(d) almost exclusively works against foreign inventors. Individuals based in the United States seldom encounter problems with § 102(d), for inventors the world over tend to file applications in their home patent offices first. And while this statute comports with the letter of Article 27 of the TRIPS Agreement, which requires that "patents shall be available ... without discrimination as to the place of the invention," § 102(d) in practice derogates from the principle of national treatment of foreign inventors.

Until recently, the best that could be said about § 102(d) is that it was seldom employed. Because patent prosecution almost always requires more than one year to complete, and because most foreign patent applications are published more than twelve months before their grant, the published application itself might be available as "printed publication" under § 102(b). However, a 1993 Federal Circuit opinion interpreting § 102(d), *In re Kathawala*,[40] appears to have breathed new life into the statute.

Kathawala, inventor of cholesterol-inhibiting compounds, filed patent applications in the United States, Greece and Spain. The three applications included substantially the same specifications but contained differing claims. The Greek patent claimed compounds, pharmaceutical compositions, methods of use and methods of making. The U.S. patent contained all but the method claims. The Spanish patent claimed only the method of making the compound. Not only was the U.S. application filed more than one year after the Greek and Spanish applications were filed, each of these foreign applications actually led to granted patents before the U.S. filing date.

Appealing the PTO's imposition of a § 102(d) bar before the Federal Circuit, Kathawala offered two arguments worthy of note here. First, Kathawala asserted that because the Spanish patent contained only method of making claims, which were not claimed in the U.S. applica-

---

38. *See* Ex parte Mushet, 1870 Comm'r Dec. 106.

39. *See* Donald S. Chisum, *Foreign Activity: Its Effect on Patentability under Unit-* *ed States Law*, 11 INT'L REV. INDUS. PROP. & COPYRIGHT L. 26 (1980).

40. 9 F.3d 942 (Fed.Cir.1993).

tion, the invention claimed in the United States had not been previously "patented" in a foreign country within the meaning of § 102(d). Kathawala also urged that the claims of the Greek patent were invalid because, at the time the patent issued, the Greek patent law actually disallowed patents directed to pharmaceuticals.

The Federal Circuit had little trouble dispensing with these arguments. According to Judge Lourie, § 102(d) should not be given a constrained reading. It was enough that Kathawala's Spanish application disclosed and provided the opportunity to claim all aspects of his invention, including the compounds themselves. Allowing dilatory inventors to obtain U.S. patents on others aspect of the same "invention" patented too long ago abroad would frustrate the policy of the statute, according to the court. The court also dismissed Kathawala's arguments regarding the Greek patent, declining to speculate on the patent eligibility law of Greece. Both Greek and U.S. patents included claims towards the same subject matter because Kathawala had put them there, and their validity was irrelevant to whether the subject matter was "patented" in accordance with § 102(d).

Not only was the *Kathawala* court's unwillingness to consider Greek patent law surprising, its generous view of patented subject matter seems questionable. Few members of the patent community would say that disclosed but unclaimed subject matter is patented, for the claims are the measure of patentee rights. Perhaps *Kathawala* should have been an obviousness case. But given the robust holding in *Kathawala*, applicants should be particularly wary of foreign patent registration regimes. Under these systems, foreign patent offices do not fully examine applications for compliance with the patent law, leading to short processing times and prompt issuances of foreign patents.

§ 16.3   Prior Art for Novelty: Prior Invention

The remaining provisions of § 102, paragraphs (a), (e), (f) and (g), do not concern the date an inventor filed a patent application at the PTO. They instead pertain to a real world event: the date on which the subject matter sought to be patented was actually invented. These provisions indicate that the first individual to invent a particular technology should be awarded the patent. At the time this treatise goes to press, the United States faces mounting pressure to switch to the world norm of a first-to-file patent system, where novelty is assessed solely on the filing date. But at least for the near future, the first-to-invent system appears firmly fixed within the U.S. patent regime.

16.3.1   Prior Invention Under § 102(a)

Section 102(a) states the essential first-to-invent rule unique to the U.S. patent system. An invention "known or used by others in this country, or patented or described in a printed publication in this or a foreign country, before the invention thereof by the applicant for a patent" may not be patented. Under this rule, in order to obtain a patent, an applicant must prove that he actually invented a claimed invention prior to the date of an anticipatory reference. For example, suppose that Professor Cool files a patent application on December 1, 2003, claiming a new refrigeration technology. During prosecution of the application, a PTO examiner discovers that another person, Otto, had used the same technology claimed by Cool as of October 12, 2003. Because Otto used the invention less than one year before Cool's filing date, the § 102(b) bar does not apply. Nonetheless, to obtain a patent, Cool must demonstrate that she invented the subject matter of her patent application prior to Otto's use. Two concepts are critical here: the meaning of the term "known or used" within § 102(a), and the precise activity sufficient to demonstrate a date of invention.

The literal language of § 102(a) requires only that the prior invention be "known or used:" unlike § 102(b), § 102(a) does not include the word "public." The courts have nonetheless interpreted § 102(a) to require some form of public knowledge of the first inventor's invention before the second inventor's patent application will be rejected. Judge Learned Hand's opinion in *Gillman v. Stern* remains a leading case on this point.

In *Gillman*, one Wenczel obtained a patent on a pneumatic machine for quilting fabric. The patent was later asserted during infringement litigation. The accused infringer learned of a third party, Haas, who had employed a substantially similar machine. Because Wenczel had filed his application in 1931, uses by Haas in 1929 and 1930 did not trigger a statutory bar under the two-year grace period of the day. In contemporary terms, the issue before the court was whether the prior use by Haas rendered the quilting machine "known or used by others" as provided in § 102(a). The controlling fact was that Haas maintained the machine as a trade secret. Haas sold quilted fabric, not the pneumatic machine, and the fabric he produced appeared the same as any other.

After canvassing the precedents, Judge Hand concluded that an inventor who kept his technology as a trade secret could not be judged the first inventor in terms of the patent law. Inventors like Haas had chosen not to augment the store of public knowledge, and therefore their efforts should not prejudice later patent applicants. In contrast to Haas, Wenczel had brought about the publication of a patent instrument and the enrichment of the art. In dicta, Judge Hand also noted that the patent law distinguished between secret and noninforming uses. According to Judge Hand, the precedent had afforded noninforming uses the status of prior art. Judge Hand observed that this scheme might potentially lead to anomalous results where the public was unable to profit from the noninforming use.

The holding in *Gillman* has the merit of placing §§ 102(a) and (b) in accord with regard to the prior art status of secret and noninforming uses. For example, opinions like *Gore v. Garlock* have lent consistent interpretations to the term "public use" in cases of third party secret uses. This happy harmony may have actually originated from an oversight: in the later case of *Metallizing Engineering*, Judge Hand candidly admitted to confusing §§ 102(a) and (b), as demonstrated by his frequent reference to the term "public use" in *Gillman*. Subsequent opinions have nonetheless been persuaded by the reasoning of *Gillman* and upheld its result.

National Tractor Pullers Association v. Watkins,[1] presents one of the more unusual factual circumstances in which a court applied the *Gillman* rule. There, the declaratory judgment plaintiff asserted that a patented device useful in tractor pulling contests was invalid under § 102(a). The plaintiff pointed to earlier drawings made by a third party on the underside of a tablecloth in his mother's kitchen. The drawings had never been publicized, nor had the depicted device been commercialized. The court concluded that these drawings did not comprise prior art, declaring: "Prior knowledge as set forth in 35 U.S.C. § 102(a) must be prior public knowledge, that is knowledge which is reasonably accessible to the public."

The other key aspect of § 102(a) is determining an applicant's date of invention. The nature of the activity that comprises the applicant's invention date is also not elaborated in § 102(a). The statute merely states the phrase "the invention thereof by the applicant for a patent" without further definition. However, the drafters of the 1952 Act relied upon extensive case law concerning predecessor statutes to § 102(a). This precedent set forth an elaborate definition of the level of activity that amounted to an "invention date" in the patent law. This definition involves three terms of art: conception, reduction to practice and diligence.

For present purposes, a working definition of each of these terms suffices. Conception concerns the mental act of invention. It occurs when the inventor has formed "a definite and permanent idea of the complete and operative invention, as it is hereafter to be applied in practice."[2] Reduction to practice ordinarily follows conception. An actual reduction to practice consists of a demonstration that the invention is suitable for its intended purpose.[3] Actual reduction to practice involves the construction of a working model of the invention and often some minimal testing. Constructive reduction to practice consists of the filing of a patent application at the PTO. Last, diligence involves the showing of continuous and reasonable efforts towards the reduction to practice of an invention.

These concepts interface with the time of "invention" noted in § 102(a) in the following way. An actual reduction to practice presents the most straightforward way to demonstrate that an inventor was possessed of the invention prior to the date of a reference. That is, if an inventor can show that he constructed an operable, proven prototype of

§ 16.3

1. 205 USPQ 892 (N.D.Ill.1980).

2. Burroughs Wellcome Co. v. Barr Labs., Inc., 40 F.3d 1223, 1228 (Fed.Cir. 1994), *cert. denied,* 516 U.S. 1070, 116 S.Ct. 771, 133 L.Ed.2d 724 (1996).

3. Coffin v. Ogden, 85 U.S. (18 Wall.) 120, 21 L.Ed. 821 (1873).

the invention prior to the effective date of a reference, then that reference is disregarded under the terms of § 102(a).

Even if the applicant has not reduced the invention to practice prior to the reference date, however, he still has the opportunity to remove the reference. First, he must demonstrate that he conceived of the invention prior to the date of the reference. Second, he must show that he acted diligently from the reference date until a subsequent reduction to practice. Such a reduction to practice may be actual or constructive.

That an actual reduction to practice, achieved before the effective date of a reference, demonstrates possession of an invention to the satisfaction of the patent law should be unsurprising. But that the combination of conception and diligence should allow an inventor to avoid a § 102(a) reference may at first appear elusive. In this regard the patent law recognizes that anyone can have a good idea without requiring considerable funding. In contrast, a reduction to practice usually demands that an inventor marshal significant resources, whether he attempts to construct a working prototype or chooses to file a patent application. So long as he remains diligent in working towards either sort of reduction to practice, § 102(a) will allow him to obtain a patent. The statute may thus be seen as promoting an equality of opportunity between actors in the technological community with different levels of financial means.

It is important to note that in the 1952 Act, Congress expressly articulated the concepts of conception, reduction to practice and diligence within § 102(g). The use of these concepts to specify an invention date still governs under § 102(a). This text more thoroughly discusses the concepts of conception, reduction to practice and diligence in § 16.3.2 below.

Another point worth mentioning is that § 102(a) applies only to activities by persons other than the inventor herself. Obviously, you can't out-invent yourself, so the first-to-invent principle of § 102(a) makes prior art only out of knowledge, use, patents, or publications originating from someone other than the patent applicant (in cases of acquisition proceedings at the PTO) or patentee (in cases of infringement litigation). For example, suppose that Dr. Barleybean uses a method of canning shrimp in the United States on March 1, 2004. Barleybean then files a patent application at the PTO on June 1, 2004. The Barleybean use does not count as prior art under § 102(a) because it was not "by others," as § 102(a) compels. Of course, if Barleybean made a public use of her invention more than one year before her filing date, then the statutory bar of § 102(b) would apply.

An important procedural aspect of § 102(a) involves the use of Rule 131 at the PTO. This rule allows patent applicants to declare an invention date prior to the date of a prior art reference. This declaration is typically accompanied by a detailed factual showing, such as diagrams or laboratory notebooks, that demonstrate sufficient inventive activity to pre-date the reference. The need for Rule 131 arises because inventors need not attest to their date of inventive activity when they file patent applications. Instead, they reveal their invention date on an *ad hoc* basis when the examiner produces a pertinent prior art reference. Use of Rule 131 is informally known as "swearing behind" or "antedating" a reference.

A brief example best illustrates the workings of § 102(a) and Rule 131. Suppose that a patent examiner discovers a technical journal article published one month before a particular application's filing date. That article fully discloses the claimed invention and would anticipate the application if it serves as prior art under § 102. Because the article was published within the one-year grace period established under § 102(b), the application is not subject to a statutory bar.

The examiner may issue a rejection under § 102(a), however. Without any knowledge of the true invention date, the examiner must assume that the applicant invented the claimed technology on the same date the application was filed. The examiner's § 102(a) rejection is in the nature of an invitation, however. The applicant may file a Rule 131 affidavit showing sufficient inventive activity prior to the effective date of the reference. In particular, the applicant must show either (1) an actual reduction to practice prior to the publication date of the journal article, or (2) conception of the invention prior to the publication date, coupled with diligence from the publication date until a subsequent reduction to practice. This reduction to practice may be either actual, which would involve the construction and testing of a prototype, or constructive, which would rely upon the filing date of the patent application. If the examiner is satisfied with the applicant's showing, she will withdraw the rejection.

By its own terms, Rule 131 applies only to §§ 102(a) and (e). Rule 131 does not apply to statutory bars such as § 102(b), which are keyed to the filing date of the patent application. Further, the use of Rule 131 should not be confused with a true interference proceeding under § 102(g). If two patents or patent applications claim the same subject matter, then the rival inventors must engage in a priority contest to determine which is entitled to a patent.

The following hypothetical sums up our understanding of § 102(a) and Rule 131. Suppose, for example, that Dr. Quark conceived of a new machine for making shatterproof glass on March 1, 2003. He then diligently works on building a working model of his device, at last building a working prototype on May 15, 2003. Quark then files a patent application at the PTO on December 12, 2003. During the prosecution of the application, the PTO examiner discovers a Finnish patent application, published on April 20, 2003, that fully anticipates the invention claimed in Quark's application. The § 102(b) bar does not apply because the patent application was published less than one year before the date Quark filed his application. However, the PTO examiner may reject Quark's application based upon the published Finnish application and § 102(a). In such cases, the examiner's rejection is essentially in the nature of an invitation. Quark has the opportunity to overcome the rejection by showing that, within the technical meaning of the patent law, he invented his glass-making machine prior to the date the Finnish application was published.

In this case, assuming that all of his dates of inventive activity are properly corroborated, Quark will be able to overcome the examiner's § 102(a) rejection. Because Quark did not reduce his invention to practice until May 15, 2003, almost one month after the publication date of the Finnish application, Quark cannot rely upon his reduction to practice date alone. However, Quark may submit evidence that (1) he conceived of the invention on March 1, 2003, prior to the April 20, 2003, publication date of the Finnish patent application; and (2) he was diligent until his own actual reduction to practice on May 15, 2003. Upon receipt of this evidence via a Rule 131 affidavit, the PTO examiner will withdraw this rejection and, absent any other objections, allow Quark to obtain his patent.

Curious readers may wonder why the PTO examiner does not further pursue the dates of invention concerning the Finnish patent application. After all, someone–presumably someone in Finland–invented the same glass-making machine as Quark, and almost certainly did so prior to the date the Finnish application was published. Given that administrative processing must have delayed the publication of the Finnish application, why doesn't the PTO examiner telephone Helsinki in order to determine when that application was filed at the Finnish Patent Office or, better yet, learn when the Finnish applicant actually invented the glass-making machine? The short answer is that activities such as merely inventing a machine, or filing a patent application, do not necessarily result in public disclosure of that machine. Besides, while such activity might mean that the glass-making technology was "known or used," no evidence suggests that this knowledge or use occurred in the United States, as § 102(a) requires. Patents and printed publications are the only foreign references that count under § 102(a). As a result, the day the Finnish application was published is the first permissible date that the examiner may employ under § 102(a).

16.3.2 Priority and Prior Art Under § 102(g)

Section 102(g) consists of two sub-paragraphs. The second of these, § 102(g)(2), expressly states the general rule of priority: "A person shall be entitled to a patent unless . . . before the applicant's invention thereof the invention was made in this country by another. . . ." Section 102(g)(2) then states an important exception to this rule. If the first inventor has "abandoned, suppressed or concealed" the technology at issue, then he has essentially forfeited his special status in accordance with § 102(g)(2). Section 102(g)(2) goes on to instruct that "[i]n determining priority of invention there shall be considered not only the respective dates of conception and reduction to practice of the invention, but also the reasonable diligence of one who was first to conceive and last to reduce to practice, from a time prior to conception by the other."

As suggested by its division into sub-paragraphs, § 102(g) serves two principal purposes in the patent law. Like § 102(a), § 102(g)(2) provides a source of prior art that may be used as the basis of a rejection for anticipation or nonobviousness. In these circumstances, the party asserting a § 102(g) reference is not claiming the invention for itself, but arguing that the issued patent is invalid. This effort usually involves the identification of a third party that allegedly invented first. In this sense, § 102(g) functions similarly to § 102(a).

At least two important distinctions exist between § 102(a) and (g), however. First, § 102(g) applies only to inventions "made in this country." Under § 102(a), patents and printed publications may originate "in this or a foreign country."

Second, we have seen that the courts have interpreted § 102(a) to require knowledge or use that was publicly accessible at the time the patented invention was made.[4] Section 102(g) has not been similarly construed, however. Instead, as explained by the Court of Claims in *International Glass Co. v. United States*, "prior invention under 102(g) requires only that the invention be complete, i.e., conceived and reduced to practice, and not abandoned, suppressed or concealed."[5] Thus, under § 102(g) a completely private invention may serve as prior art against a later inventor. It is important to note that such private inventors may well be judged to have "abandoned, suppressed or concealed" the invention at issue, typically by maintaining the technology as a trade secret. In such cases these earlier, private inventions will not be considered within the prior art. The sorts of conduct that cause an invention to be judged "abandoned, suppressed or concealed" are discussed in § 16.3.2.7 below.

Section 102(g) serves a second function, provided in § 102(g)(1). This provision also provides a mechanism for resolving disputes relating to so-called "priority of invention." In this class of cases, one party seeks more than merely the denial of another's entitlement to patent rights on a particular technology. She also seeks to obtain patent rights for herself.

The need to determine priority of invention should be clear. As rivals across the globe compete to develop valuable technologies, they will often develop similar or identical inventions at approximately the same time. In such circumstances, the U.S. patent system has adopted a winner-take-all policy. Only the person or persons that first developed a particular technology will be awarded a patent. This policy is implemented through the rules set forth in § 102(g), which determine which actor will be judged the first inventor in terms of the patent law.

Section 102(g)'s function both as a rule of priority and as a source of novelty-destroying prior art can be confusing at first blush. Professor Merges has suggested a helpful framework for coming to grips with these

---

4. *See supra* § 16.3.1.

5. International Glass Co. v. United States, 408 F.2d 395 (Ct.Cl.1969).

distinct roles. He suggests that students consider patent priority contests as cases in which each competing inventor attempts to defeat the other's claim of novelty. The first inventor at law is awarded the patent once she removes the last obstacle to patentability, her rival's claim to an earlier invention date under § 102(g).[6]

It should be noted that until 1999, § 102(g) consisted of only a single paragraph that was nearly identical to present-day § 102(g)(2). The American Inventors Protection Act of 1999 recast existing § 102(g) as § 102(g)(2) and added a new § 102(g)(1). This legislation was intended only to clarify the rules for determining priority of invention during interference proceedings. The new, expanded version of § 102(g) more clearly demonstrates that the statute serves both as a source of prior art and a mechanism for resolving interferences.

16.3.2.1 Patent Interference Practice

Most § 102(g) priority contests are resolved at the PTO via so-called "interference" practice. A patent interference is a complex administrative proceeding that ordinarily results in the award of priority to one of its participants. These proceedings are not especially common. One estimate is that less than one-quarter of one percent of patents are subject to an interference.[7] This statistic may mislead, however, because the expense of interference cases may lead to their use only for the most commercially significant applications.[8] In any event, because many § 102(g) cases involve interferences, a word on their special procedures and terminology is appropriate at the start.

Interferences may occur between two pending applications, or between a pending application and an issued, unexpired patent. Section 135 requires the PTO to call for an interference when "an application is made for a patent which ... would interfere with any pending application, or with any unexpired patent." An examiner may declare an interference when she learns of two conflicting applications without any activity by the applicants. Alternatively, an applicant may initiate an interference upon discovering an issued patent, or an application published prior to its formal issuance, that claims the same invention.

Patent interference procedures typically involve some particular terminology. Many cases will refer to so-called "senior" and "junior" parties: "A senior party is the party with the earliest effective filing date.... A junior party is any other party."[9] Interferences also make use of a concept called a "count," which corresponds to a claim which the interfering parties share. The counts of an interference define what the

6. ROBERT PATRICK MERGES, PATENT LAW AND POLICY 395 (2d ed. 1997).

7. Clifford A. Ulrich, *The Patent Systems Harmonization Act of 1992: Conformity at What Price?*, N.Y.L. SCH. J. INT'L & COMP. L. 405, 415 (1996).

8. *See* Gerald D. Malpass, Jr., *Life After the GATT TRIPS Agreement—Has the Competitive Position of U.S. Inventors Changed?*, 19 HOUSTON J. INT'L L. 207 (1996).

9. 37 C.F.R. § 1.601(m).

dispute is about; this is the subject matter which each of the parties asserts that it invented first.

When an application for an interference is filed, a primary examiner makes a preliminary determination "whether a basis upon which the applicant would be entitled to a judgment relative to the patentee is alleged and, if a basis is alleged, an interference may be declared."[10] If the primary examiner preliminarily determines that the application meets that requirement, the application is referred to an examiner-in-chief to determine whether an interference should go forward.[11] If the examiner-in-chief determines that a prima facie case for priority has been established, the interference proceeds.[12] If however, the examiner-in-chief concludes that a prima facie case has not been shown, the examiner-in-chief declares an interference but "enter[s] an order stating the reasons for the opinion and directing the applicant, within a time set in the order, to show cause why summary judgment should not be entered against the applicant."[13] If such an order to show cause issues, the applicant "may file a response to the order and state any reasons why summary judgment should not be entered."[14]

If the interference continues, next comes the filing of the applicant's preliminary statements. These statements contain allegations of the dates of various inventive activities the parties believe they can establish during an interference. After preliminary statements have been filed, the parties may submit various motions to the Board of Patent Appeals and Interferences, raising issues that will be contested during the interference.[15] The trial phase of the interference follows. The parties are given the opportunity to present affidavits, declarations and exhibits such as laboratory notebooks and publications. After the trial comes a final hearing before a three-member panel of the Board of Patent Appeals and Interferences, consisting solely of oral argument by the parties. The Board then issues its decision, typically awarding priority of invention to one of the interfering parties. The unsuccessful party may then appeal to the Federal Circuit.

Interferences may be resolved in other ways, however. One party may assert ordinary grounds for patent invalidity; for example, that the patent claims subject matter ineligible for patenting. This effort tends to be rather uncommon, as often a defense which invalidates one application or patent will be effective for them all; but sometimes the result that no one obtains a patent is a satisfactory conclusion for one of the parties to the interference. Settlement between the parties is another option, although Congress has recognized the possibility of collusive arrangements with anticompetitive effects. The result is 35 U.S.C.A. § 135(c), which requires that the parties file copies of agreements

10. 37 C.F.R. § 1.608(b).

11. 37 C.F.R. §§ 1.609 & 1.610(a).

12. 37 C.F.R. § 1.617(a).

13. Id.

14. 37 C.F.R. § 1.617(b).

15. 37 C.F.R. § 1.633.

reached in contemplation of termination of an interference. The filed agreements are available for public inspection.

Occasionally the Patent Office and applicants remain unaware of interfering applications, with the result that two patents directed towards the same inventive concept issue. Section 291 of the Patent Act, entitled "Interfering Patents," addresses these hopefully rare circumstances. Owners of interfering patents may have their respective rights determined by a federal district court following the filing of a civil suit.

16.3.2.2   Inventive Activity in Foreign Countries

Before considering the statutory language of § 102(g) in greater detail, a review of the special rules regarding inventive activity performed abroad is necessary. Historically, § 104 provided that an inventor could not rely upon activity in a foreign country to establish dates of conception, reduction to practice or diligence. The only exception, which the statute continues to provide, is for persons "serving in any other country in connection with operations by or on behalf of the United States." Although § 104 was arguably motivated by concerns over the quality of evidence of inventive activity that might be obtained from overseas, its effect was to shut foreign inventors out of the first-to-invent system. Inventors based overseas were typically left to rely upon the priority date of a foreign patent application as provided by the Paris Convention and § 119(a).[16]

In the face of stern international opposition to § 104, Congress twice amended the statute. In 1993, in connection with the North American Free Trade Agreement Act (NAFTA), § 104 was amended to allow proof of inventive activity in a NAFTA country. The effective date of the NAFTA amendment to § 104 is December 8, 1993. In 1994, in connection with the Uruguay Round Agreements Act (URAA), § 104 was amended to allow proof of inventive activity in WTO member countries. Although the URAA legislation appears confused as to the effective date of the § 104 amendment, observers generally agree that it is January 1, 1996.[17]

The final episode in this saga concerns the enactment of the American Inventors Protection Act of 1999. That statute designated the existing § 102(g) as § 102(g)(2) and added § 102(g)(1). New § 102(g)(1) specifies that "during the course of an interference" inventors may establish dates of inventive activity "to the extent permitted in section 104." This express reference to § 104 allows parties to an interference to introduce dates of inventive activity performed in the United States as well as in NAFTA and WTO member countries.

So much for interferences. Section 102(g) also serves as a source of prior art, however, as specified in § 102(g)(2). The discerning reader of

16. *See* Fujikawa v. Wattanasin, 93 F.3d 1559, 1561 (Fed.Cir.1996).

17. *See* Thomas L. Irving & Stacey D. Lewis, *Proving a Date of Invention and* *Infringement After GATT/TRIPS,* 22 AIPLA Q.J. 309, 313 (1994).

§ 102(g) will note that § 102(g)(2) continues to require that the "invention was made in this country." Although § 102(g)(1) recognizes NAFTA- and WTO-based amendments to § 104, § 102(g)(2) appears to suffer from a disconnect. Of what use could the newfound ability to prove dates of inventive activity under § 104 be to foreign inventors if, when they seek to apply these dates to the substantive law of § 102(g)(2), these dates have no prior art effect? Until this issue is the subject of judicial resolution or further legislative reform efforts, the prior art status of dates of foreign inventive activity remains clouded.[18]

Having offered the context of interference proceedings and foreign inventive activity, we can now turn to a more detailed consideration of those acts that rise to invention within § 102(g).

16.3.2.3 Conception

Conception is the formation in the mind of the inventor of a definite and permanent idea of the complete and operative invention, as it is to be applied in practice. The conception must include every feature of the claimed invention.[19] The conception is complete when a person of ordinary skill in the art could practice the invention without undue experimentation.[20] Although conception is a purely mental act, the courts have held that inventors may not demonstrate their date of conception solely through their own, uncorroborated testimony. Inventors must instead provide evidence of a conception date with such proofs as models, documentation and the testimony of others. In this text, this requirement of corroboration is more extensively discussed below at § 16.3.2.6.

Oka v. Youssefyeh,[21] decided on appeal by the Federal Circuit following an interference, illustrates the requirement of conception. The senior party, Oka, had invented the enzyme inhibitor compounds of the count in Japan. Because § 104 at that time prohibited the entry of evidence relating to inventive acts performed abroad, Oka was left to rely upon the filing date of his Japanese application, October 31, 1980, under § 119(a).

The junior party, Youssefyeh, worked in the United States. Youssefyeh sought to rely upon § 102(g) to displace Oka as the first inventor. He wished to show that he conceived of the invention prior to October 31, 1980. If Youssefyeh could make this preliminary showing, and also demonstrate diligence at the appropriate times, he could become the first inventor in terms of § 102(g).

The Federal Circuit held that Youssefyeh had conceived of the invention during the last week of October 1980. At that point, work had begun on actually synthesizing compounds within the scope of the count.

---

18. *See* Harold C. Wegner, *TRIPS Boomerang: Obligations for Domestic Reform*, 29 VAND. J. TRANSNAT'L L. 535, 549 (1996).

19. Kridl v. McCormick, 105 F.3d 1446 (Fed.Cir.1997).

20. Sewall v. Walters, 21 F.3d 411 (Fed. Cir.1994).

21. 849 F.2d 581 (Fed.Cir.1988).

The court dismissed the earlier date selected by the PTO Board, October 10, 1980, at which point Youssefyeh was in possession of a method of making a compound outside the scope of the count. Chief Judge Markey recognized the general rule that, within the chemical arts, conception of a species within a genus may constitute conception of the genus. But even Youssefyeh acknowledged that the compound he had invented as of October 10th was in fact a different species, not a genus.

Having decided that Youssefyeh had conceived during the last week of October, the court was faced with an interesting priority problem. Precedent established that the actual date associated with the "last week of October" was the final date of the period, October 31, 1980. In essence, then, the parties had tied, for Youssefyeh's conception date was the same as Oka's filing date. Chief Judge Markey decided the case on procedural grounds. Because Oka was the senior party, he was presumptively entitled to the patent. As Youssefyeh could not show an *earlier* conception date, Oka was entitled to priority. Although this result appears questionable in light of PTO interference rules, which only place the burden on the junior party to demonstrate entitlement to an interference in the first instance, it appears eminently fair. Oka had undoubtedly conceived of the invention prior to filing a Japanese application and, had § 104 not barred him from demonstrating his inventive activity in Japan, could have shown he was the first inventor in fact.

16.3.2.4 Reduction to Practice

An inventor may reduce an invention to practice in two ways: (1) constructively, by filing a patent application, and (2) actually, at a minimum by constructing a working physical embodiment of the invention. If the reduction to practice is constructive, the filed application "must be for the same invention as that defined in the count in an interference, and it must contain a disclosure of the invention sufficiently adequate to enable one skilled in the art to practice the invention defined by the count, with all the limitations contained in the count, without the exercise of inventive facilities."[22]

The doctrine of constructive reduction to practice strikes many observers as an odd policy choice. The very term "reduction to practice" suggests real world engineering, not the filing of papers at the PTO. Yet the patent law does not require that applicants build working models in order to participate in the first-to-invent system. A constructive reduction to practice theory also comports with the requirement that the patent instrument fully instruct skilled artisans to practice the claimed invention. The enabling disclosure required at the time the application is filed ensures that the technology is ripe for implementation.

An actual reduction to practice involves the construction of a physical embodiment that includes all the elements of the claimed invention. The prototype need not be entirely perfected and ready for commercial development. Slight deficiencies that can be readily solved by skilled

22. Travis v. Baker, 137 F.2d 109, 58 USPQ 558 (CCPA 1943).

artisans will not prevent a showing of an actual reduction to practice, so long as the prototype manifests the invention in an operative form.[23] The courts have also required the inventor to show that the invention successfully performs its intended function. Typically this demonstration involves some sort of testing or actual use. *Scott v. Finney*,[24] a newfound source of risqué humor for patent law instructors and treatise authors alike, presents the Federal Circuit's mature views on the amount of testing required to achieve an actual reduction to practice.

Scott, the junior party, filed a patent application relating to a penile implant exactly one year after Finney did. The implant employed two reservoirs connected through a manipulable valve. In order to show that he actually reduced the invention to practice prior to Finney's invention date, Scott submitted a video tape. The tape showed Scott at the operating table simulating the operation of a prototype that had been implanted into an anesthetized patient. An expert testified that the video demonstrated sufficient rigidity for intercourse. The PTO Board disagreed, however, asserting that Scott must show testing "under actual use conditions or testing under conditions that closely simulate actual use conditions for an appropriate period of time."[25]

Scott appealed to the Federal Circuit, which reversed. The court held that the Board had applied an overly rigid standard of reduction to practice. According to the court, "[t]esting need not show utility beyond a possibility of failure, but only utility beyond a probability of failure."[26] Further, the nature of testing required depended upon "the character of the invention and the problems it solves."[27] While complex inventions might require laboratory testing that accurately duplicate actual working conditions, the mere construction of simpler inventions may be sufficient to demonstrate successful operation. The invention of the *Scott v. Finney* count, a relatively uncomplicated mechanical device, fell in this latter class. In light of the videotape and expert testimony, Scott had made "a reasonable showing that the invention will work to overcome the problem it addresses."[28]

16.3.2.5 Diligence

An inventor who is first to conceive, but last to reduce to practice, will be entitled to priority by showing "reasonable diligence" toward reduction to practice. The required period of diligence for the inventor who was first to conceive, but last to reduce to practice, begins at the time "prior to the conception by the other" and ends when the inventor who was first to conceive reduces the invention to practice. Diligence which begins after the other's conception date, or occurs after reduction to practice has taken place, does not bear upon the priority contest. The diligence standard balances the interest in rewarding the first inventor

23. Hildreth v. Mastoras, 257 U.S. 27, 34, 42 S.Ct. 20, 66 L.Ed. 112 (1921).

24. 34 F.3d 1058 (Fed.Cir.1994).

25. 34 F.3d at 1060–61.

26. 34 F.3d at 1062.

27. *Id.*

28. 34 F.3d at 1063.

with the public's interest in obtaining prompt disclosure of the invention.[29]

It is important to remember that the patent law never sponsors a diligence race.[30] Only one party's diligence is ever relevant in a priority contest between two inventors. That party is the inventor who was first to conceive, but second to reduce to practice. The inventor who is both first to conceive and first to reduce an invention to practice wins the priority contest without having to show diligence at all. If the first inventor to reduce the invention to practice overly delays in employing the invention commercially or filing a patent application, however, she may well have been considered to have "abandoned, suppressed, or concealed" the invention, a topic discussed here at § 16.3.2.7.

The level of inventor activity that constitutes diligence must necessarily be judged on a case-by-case basis. In general, the courts have judged inventors quite strictly. Inventors must show "a continuous course of activity, carried on without significant interruption and accomplished in reasonably prompt manner, considered in light of all the attendant circumstances."[31] The inventor must account for the entire period mandated by § 102(g), specifically demonstrating either diligent efforts or excused activities. Although older precedent recognizes several justifications for lapses in inventive activity, including poverty, illness and employment demands,[32] more contemporary decisions have seldom excused activities unrelated to the invention.

Gould v. Schawlow[33] reflects this exacting posture. Gould, the junior party in an interference, was the first to conceive but the second to reduce to practice. To obtain an award of priority, Gould needed to show diligence from his conception date of July 30, 1958, until the date of his constructive reduction to practice, April 6, 1959. Gould provided ample evidence of significant inventive efforts, including his departure from Columbia University for the private sector, authorship of a grant proposal, discussions with colleagues, and maintenance of a "laser notebook." The court nonetheless held that Gould had not demonstrated sufficient diligence. According to the court, Gould had not correlated his efforts with particular times, and much of his testimony consisted of general assertions. *Gould v. Schawlow* demonstrates that inventors may show diligence only with difficulty, and only if particularized evidence of inventive activities at definite times can be produced.

Sometimes an inventor wishes to show a constructive, rather than an actual, reduction to practice. Because only the filing of a patent application constitutes a constructive reduction to practice, often the diligence of a patent attorney is called into question. Perhaps due to the

29. Griffith v. Kanamaru, 816 F.2d 624 (Fed.Cir.1987).

30. Steinberg v. Seitz, 517 F.2d 1359, 1364 (CCPA 1975).

31. Diasonics, Inc. v. Acuson Corp., 1993 WL 248654, *16 (N.D.Cal.1993).

32. *See* Courson v. O'Connor, 227 F. 890 (7th Cir.1915); Christie v. Seybold, 55 F. 69, 77 (6th Cir.1893).

33. 363 F.2d 908 (CCPA 1966).

federal judiciary's fuller appreciation of the demands of legal practice, the courts have been decidedly more lenient towards patent attorneys than to inventors in diligence cases. Patent attorneys need not drop all other cases when they receive an inventor's disclosure. The attorney need only show reasonable diligence in taking up the cases on her docket. Ordinarily, if the attorney takes up the cases in the order they are received, the courts will consider the diligence standard to have been met.[34]

16.3.2.6 Corroboration

An inventor may make use of the various inventive activities—conception, reduction to practice, and diligence—only if they have been corroborated. The corroboration requirement serves to prevent fraud.[35] Particularly in the case of conception, a purely mental act, the acceptance of the inventor's unsupported testimony would offer great temptation to perjury and provide the adverse party scant opportunity to rebut such evidence.[36]

The Federal Circuit applies a so-called "rule of reason" analysis to determine whether an inventor has corroborated his testimony. This analysis calls for review of all pertinent evidence in order to reach a sound determination of the credibility of the inventor.[37] Factors bearing on whether an inventor's testimony has been adequately corroborated include: (1) delay between the event and the trial, (2) interest of corroborating witnesses, (3) contradiction or impeachment, (4) corroboration, (5) the corroborating witnesses' familiarity with details of alleged prior structure, (6) improbability of prior use considering state of the art, (7) impact of the invention on the industry, and (8) relationship between witness and alleged prior user.[38] Corroborating evidence typically consists of laboratory notebooks and statements of witnesses. Only the inventor's testimony need be corroborated. If the inventor submits physical exhibits to demonstrate inventive activity, the trier of fact can conclude for itself what those exhibits show.[39]

In *Hahn v. Wong*,[40] an appeal to the Federal Circuit following an interference, the count related to an organic chemical compound. Wong filed on December 23, 1985; Hahn and his co-inventors on June 9, 1986. As the junior party, Hahn and his co-inventors opted to demonstrate an actual reduction to practice prior to Wong's filing date. They attempted to do so by submitting three affidavits. The affidavits were submitted by Hahn, one of the inventors; and by two co-employees, Hughes and Harris. The latter two individuals stated that they had read and under-

34. *See* Bey v. Kollonitsch, 806 F.2d 1024, 231 USPQ 967 (Fed. Cir. 1986).

35. Berry v. Webb, 412 F.2d 261, 267 (CCPA 1969).

36. Price v. Symsek, 988 F.2d 1187 (Fed.Cir.1993).

37. Holmwood v. Sugavanam, 948 F.2d 1236, 1239 (Fed.Cir.1991).

38. Price v. Symsek, 988 F.2d 1187, 1195 n. 3 (Fed.Cir.1993).

39. Mahurkar v. C.R. Bard, 79 F.3d 1572 (Fed.Cir.1996).

40. 892 F.2d 1028 (Fed.Cir.1989).

stood the relevant pages of Hahn's laboratory notebook. After the PTO Board of Interferences held that this evidence did not fulfill the corroboration requirement, Hahn appealed to the Federal Circuit.

The court agreed that Hahn had failed to submit sufficient corroborating evidence of his reduction to practice. The Hahn affidavit was accompanied by photocopies of pages from his laboratory notebook, but it did not explain the significance of the graphs that appeared on those pages. Further, the Hughes and Harris affidavits established only that the pages of Hahn's laboratory notebook existed on a certain date. Their affidavits did not independently corroborate the statements made on those pages—namely, that Hahn had actually performed the noted experiments and therefore actually reduced the compound to practice.

16.3.2.7   Patent Award to the Second Inventor

Section 102(g) provides that a first inventor may forfeit priority where she "abandoned, suppressed, or concealed" the invention. Congress intended this language, which appeared for the first time in the 1952 Patent Act, to codify the existing case law concerning priority. These early cases typically involved a first inventor who opted to withhold a technology, either by maintaining it as a trade secret or simply neglecting it. At some later point, a second individual independently invented the same technology. Still later, the first inventor learned of this second invention, often through the grant of a patent to the second inventor. "Spurred" into action by the second inventor, the first inventor filed a patent application and claimed priority of invention as being the first inventor in fact.

In such cases the courts declined to award priority to the first inventor. The second inventor, who had made efforts to disclose the technology, had acted consistently with sound patent policy. Had the second inventor not acted, the first inventor may never have disclosed the invention at all. Although expressed in three words, the term "abandoned, suppressed, or concealed" captures this single concept.

Dunlop Holdings, Ltd. v. Ram Golf Corp.[41] presented the Seventh Circuit with an interesting question as to the sorts of activity that amount to an abandonment, suppression or concealment. This opinion resulted from Dunlop's assertion of its patent on a material useful as a golf ball cover. The alleged infringer, Ram Golf Corporation, knew of the use of the same material by a third party, Butch Wagner. Prior to Dunlop's date of invention, Wagner had not only made the identical invention, but distributed numerous golf balls embodying the invention to friends and potential customers. However, Wagner arguably took efforts to conceal the precise material he used as a golf ball cover, and at least one expert in the field was unable to determine the content of the cover following a thorough examination.

41.   524 F.2d 33 (7th Cir.1975).

Although Dunlop was not the first inventor in fact, it argued that it should be considered the first inventor at law. According to Dunlop, Wagner had "abandoned, suppressed or concealed" the use of Surlyn as a golf ball cover because he did not disclose to the public the reason his golf ball cover was so durable. The trial court rejected the argument and struck down Dunlop's patent under § 102(g).

Following an appeal, the Seventh Circuit affirmed. Judge Stevens, as he was then, offered three reasons why Wagner's public, noninforming use demonstrated that he had not "abandoned, suppressed or concealed" the invention. First, the public still had the benefit of the invention because the golf balls had entered the stream of commerce. Similarly, potential competitors would likely be able to discern the nature of the invention through reverse engineering. Finally, Judge Stevens viewed inventors such as Wagner as public benefactors, who should not themselves be impeded from marketing their inventions by a later inventor's patent.

Commentators have criticized *Dunlop Holdings*, for the evidence suggested that competitors were not so able to determine the composition of the cover as the court assumed. Many competitors take their chances on maintaining their innovations as a secret for as long as they can, and one wonders why their efforts should bar a later patent applicant.[42] Still, *Dunlop Holdings* stands for the proposition that if one commercially exploits an invention, there is no abandonment, suppression or concealment even if the underlying technology cannot be deduced by examination or reverse engineering.

The Federal Circuit had occasion to interpret the same statutory language in *Paulik v. Rizkalla*.[43] Rizkalla was the senior party in an interference, having filed a patent application on March 10, 1975. Paulik had actually reduced the invention to practice as early as November 1970 and filed an invention disclosure form with his employer's patent department at that time. The patent department initially opted not to pursue patent protection on the invention, but began to draft an application in January or February 1975. Paulik's application was filed on June 30, 1975. The PTO Board awarded priority of invention to Rizkalla. According to the Board, Paulik's conduct fell within the language of § 102(g) denying priority of inventorship to those who have "abandoned, suppressed or concealed" the invention.

Following Paulik's appeal to the Federal Circuit, the *en banc* court reversed. The majority of the court held that an inventor, after taking no action for years, could renew inventive activities and recover from a charge of abandonment. Paulik could obtain priority if, on remand, he could "demonstrate that he had renewed activity on the invention and that he proceeded diligently to file his patent application, starting before the earliest date to which Rizkalla is entitled." Writing for the majority,

42. 1 Martin J. Adelman, Patent Law Perspectives § 2.3[8–4] at 2–270.2 to 2–270.3 (2d ed. 1992).

43. 760 F.2d 1270 (Fed.Cir.1985).

Judge Newman reasoned that a contrary result would discourage inventors "from working on projects that had been 'too long' set aside, because of the impossibility of relying, in a priority contest, on either their original work or their renewed work."[44]

A vigorous dissent authored by Judge Friedman urged that the majority's view could not be squared with the plain language of § 102(g). According to the dissent, the statute provided only that one who has abandoned, suppressed or concealed an invention has forfeited priority, with no opportunity for redemption. The dissent also questioned whether Paulik, whose deliberate suppression of the invention caused it to be the junior party, was truly deserving of priority over Rizkalla. Finally, the dissent charged the majority with adding an additional complexity to interference proceedings.

As a technical matter, the terms "diligence" and "abandoned, suppressed or concealed" present distinct legal concepts under § 102(g). Diligence is limited to instances when an inventor is second to reduce to practice, but first to conceive of the invention. The concept of inventor abandonment, suppression and concealment instead concerns the conduct of the first individual to reduce the invention to practice. In practice, however, both notions involve similar acts and intentions on behalf of an inventor.

16.3.2.8 First Inventor Defense

The First Inventor Defense Act of 1999 created an infringement defense for an earlier inventor of a method of doing business that was later patented by another. The defendant must have reduced the infringing subject matter to practice one year before the effective filing date of the patent and made commercial use of that subject matter in the United States before the effective filing date.

The impetus for this provision lies in the rather complex relationship between the law of trade secrets and the patent system. Trade secrecy protects individuals from misappropriation of valuable information that is useful in commerce. One reason an inventor might maintain the invention as a trade secret rather than seek patent protection is that the subject matter of the invention may not be regarded as patentable. Such inventions as customer lists or data compilations have traditionally been regarded as amenable to trade secret protection but not to patenting. Inventors might also maintain trade secret protection due to ignorance of the patent system or because they believe they can keep their invention secret longer than the period of exclusivity granted through the patent system.[45]

It is important to note from the outset that the patent system has not favored trade secret holders. Well-established patent law establishes that an inventor who makes a secret, commercial use of an invention for

---

44. 760 F.2d at 1276.

45. *See* David D. Friedman, et al., *Some Economics of Trade Secret Law*, 5 J. Econ. Persps. 61, 64 (1991).

more than one year prior to filing a patent application at the PTO forfeits his own right to a patent.[46] This policy is principally based upon the desire to maintain the integrity of the patent term. The Patent Act grants patents a term of twenty years commencing from the date a patent application is filed.[47] If the trade secret holder could make commercial use of an invention for many years before choosing to file a patent application, he could disrupt this regime by delaying the expiration date of his patent.

On the other hand, settled patent law principles established that prior secret uses would not defeat the patents of later inventors.[48] If an earlier inventor made secret commercial use of an invention, and another person independently invented the same technology later and obtained patent protection, then the trade secret holder could face liability for patent infringement. This policy was based upon the reasoning that issued, published patent instruments fully inform the public about the invention, while trade secrets do not. As between a subsequent inventor who patented the invention, and had disclosed the invention to the public, and an earlier trade secret holder who did not, the law favored the patent holder.

Legal developments in the late 1990's concerning methods of doing business focused attention upon the relationship between patents and trade secrets. Inventors of methods of doing business traditionally relied upon trade secret protection because such inventions had long been regarded as unpatentable subject matter. As a result, inventors of innovative business methods obtained legal advice not to file applications at the PTO. This advice was sound under the patent law as it then stood.

The 1998 Federal Circuit opinion in *State Street Bank and Trust Co. v. Signature Financial Group*[49] altered this traditional principle. In the *State Street Bank* opinion, the Federal Circuit overturned the historical bar denying patents on methods of doing business. As a consequence, inventors in such sectors as finance, insurance and services have sought proprietary interests in their inventions through the patent system.

The change in this background principle was perceived as dealing a harsh blow to individuals who invented business methods prior to the issuance of the *State Street Bank* opinion. Many of these inventors had maintained their innovative business methods as trade secrets for many years. As a result, they were unable belatedly to obtain patent protection on their business methods. Moreover, because trade secrets did not constitute prior art against the patent applications of others, a subsequent inventor would be able to obtain patent protection. Under these

46. *See* Metallizing Eng'g Co. v. Kenyon Bearing & Auto Parts, 153 F.2d 516 (2d Cir.), *cert. denied*, 328 U.S. 840, 66 S.Ct. 1016, 90 L.Ed. 1615 (1946).

47. 35 U.S.C.A. § 154 (2000).

48. *See* W.L. Gore & Assocs. v. Garlock, Inc., 721 F.2d 1540 (Fed.Cir.), *cert. denied*, 469 U.S. 851, 105 S.Ct. 172, 83 L.Ed.2d 107 (1984).

49. 149 F.3d 1368 (Fed.Cir.1998), *cert. denied*, 525 U.S. 1093, 119 S.Ct. 851, 142 L.Ed.2d 704 (1999).

circumstances, a trade secret holder could find himself an adjudicated infringer of a patented business method that he actually invented first.

The First Inventor Defense Act reconciles these principles by providing an infringement defense for an earlier inventor of a method of doing business that was later patented by another. This infringement defense is subject to several qualifications. First, the defendant must have reduced the infringing subject matter to practice at least one year before the effective filing date of the patent application. Second, the defendant must have commercially used the infringing subject matter prior to the effective filing date of the patent. Finally, any reduction to practice or use must have been made in good faith, without derivation from the patentee or persons in privity with the patentee.

Looking forward, it would seem a rather straightforward matter to alter the first inventor defense to embrace a more expansive range of patentable subject matter. In this regard the first inventor defense could prove quite similar to those prevailing in other countries.[50] These statutes are commonly referred to as creating "prior user rights." Unlike the more limited regime created by the First Inventor Defense Act of 1999, prior user rights abroad are not limited to methods of doing business. They instead apply to any sort of invention. Experience with the First Inventor Defense Act of 1999 might suggest whether the Congress should consider a more full-fledged prior user rights regime, or maintain the current system as a limited cure of a specific problem.

16.3.3 Disclosure in U.S. Patent Applications Under § 102(e)

Section 102(e) presents a complex rule that governs the prior art status of a special category of secret knowledge of a first inventor's work. As amended by the American Inventors Protection Act of 1999 and the Intellectual Property and High Technology Technical Amendments Act of 2002, § 102(e) consists of two sub-paragraphs. Section 102(e)(1) provides that a published patent application that discloses, but does not claim the invention constitutes prior art as of its filing date. Section 102(e)(2) works similarly: an issued patent that discloses, but does not claim the invention, constitutes prior art as of its filing date.

Section 102(e) differs from § 102(g) in that the invention must be described in the patent's specification, but not claimed. In cases where two patents or applications claim the same invention, the inventors are subject to a priority contest, either through an interference proceeding or in the courts. By its own terms, § 102(e) speaks to patents or applications "by another." Therefore § 102(e) does not apply to patents or applications belonging to the same inventor.

In approaching § 102(e) for the first time, one should remember procedures followed at the PTO. The PTO's current practice is to

---

50. *See* THE ADVISORY COMMISSION ON PATENT LAW REFORM, A REPORT TO THE SECRETARY of Commerce 48 (1992).

publish some of the pending patent applications eighteen months after the filing date. Not all applications are published, however. Specifically, where an applicant certifies that he will not seek foreign patent rights pertaining to that invention, the PTO will not publish the U.S. application. As a result, some patent applications are published eighteen months after they are filed. Other patent applications are never published at all, and their contents become publicly accessible only if the PTO allows them to issue as granted patents.

The purpose of § 102(e) is to define the point at which these published applications and issued patents serve as prior art against others. Our discussion of § 102(a) and (b) has shown that the patent law usually does not allow references that are not available to the public, such as trade secrets, to have patent-defeating effect. The most appropriate date for a published application or issued patent to have prior art effect might seem to be the date it actually issues from the PTO.

In the famous opinion in *Alexander Milburn Co. v. Davis–Bournonville Co.*,[51] however, Justice Holmes reached a different conclusion. He determined that the disclosures of the patent instrument should have the status of prior art as of their filing date. As Congress subsequently codified the *Alexander Milburn* rule in § 102(e)(2), a review of the opinion of Justice Holmes will help explain how the patent law came to this seemingly discordant result.

The *Alexander Milburn* case involved the following facts. Clifford filed a patent application on January 31, 1911, that disclosed, but did not claim, a welding and cutting apparatus. On March 4, 1911, Whitford filed a patent application claiming the apparatus that Clifford had not claimed. Apparently Whitford lacked sufficient evidence to demonstrate an earlier invention date. The Patent Office granted Clifford's patent on February 6, 1912, while Whitford's patent issued on June 4, 1912. An accused infringer of Whitford's patent urged that Clifford's disclosure of the apparatus served as anticipatory prior art against Whitford. Note that because Clifford had not claimed the same apparatus as Whitford, priority of invention was not an issue in the case.

During arguments before the Supreme Court, Whitford asserted that Clifford's patent could not be considered prior art until the date of its issuance. According to Whitford, Clifford's application disclosed nothing to the public at the time of filing, for the Patent Office maintained it in secrecy until the date of issuance. Although Whitford's characterizations were undoubtedly correct, Justice Holmes nonetheless disagreed in a pithy opinion. According to Holmes, "Clifford had done all that he could do to make his description public" by filing a patent application.[52] Clifford merely waited for the Patent Office to approve his application. In such circumstances, Patent Office delays in processing applications should not control the content of the prior art.

51. 270 U.S. 390, 46 S.Ct. 324, 70 L.Ed. 651 (1926).   **52.** 270 U.S. at 400.

Justice Holmes' reasoning has some apparent flaws. At the time he was writing, the grace period provided by the predecessor statute to § 102(b) was two years.[53] If indeed the Patent Office was a model of rapidity, granting patents on the day they were filed, then Whitford would seemingly be able to avoid the Clifford reference by filing before January 31, 1913. Nor could Clifford's application be available as prior art under the earlier version of § 102(a), for his prior knowledge or use was of a totally private character.[54]

Yet the *Alexander Milburn* holding, and its codification in § 102(e), present a sensible compromise. Inventors file hundreds of applications at the PTO on a daily basis. These patent applications paint a telling portrait of the state of the art. It would seem anomalous for the PTO to disregard earlier filed applications when making patentability decisions, particularly since PTO officials are adept at cataloguing and retrieving patent-related documents

Justice Holmes authored *Alexander Milburn* at a time when the PTO maintained patent applications in secrecy. The American Inventors Protection Act of 1999 caused the PTO to publish pending patent applications eighteen months following the filing date, unless the applicant certifies that he will not file a parallel application abroad. When Congress provided for the publication of patent applications, it opted to apply the reasoning of *Alexander Milburn* in this new context. As a result, under § 102(e)(1), published patent applications count as prior art as of the date they are filed. Section 102(e)(1) therefore creates an eighteen-month period in which the pending application has prior art effect, but is not available to the public.

The PTO applies § 102(e) in the following manner. If an examiner becomes aware of a granted patent that discloses, but does not claim, the invention claimed in a pending application, she may issue a § 102(e) rejection. The applicant may elect to respond with a Rule 131 affidavit.[55] That affidavit must demonstrate sufficient inventive activity prior to the filing date associated with the granted patent. The applicant must show either (1) an actual reduction to practice prior to the patent's filing date, or (2) conception of the invention prior to the patent's filing date, coupled with diligence from the filing date until a subsequent reduction to practice.

Alternatively, suppose that an examiner encounters two copending applications filed by different inventors. Further assume that the earlier application discloses subject matter that would anticipate the later filed application. The PTO allows examiners to issue provisional rejections of applications where they share common inventors or ownership. Otherwise, the examiner must wait until one of two events occurs before dispensing a rejection under § 102(e): Either the application is published, under § 102(e)(1); or, for those applications the PTO will not

53. Rev. Stat. § 4486, as amended March 3, 1897, ch. 391, 29 Stat. 692.

54. *See supra* § 16.3.1.

55. *See supra* § 16.3.1.

publish, the issuance of the application as a granted patent under § 102(e)(2).[56]

Section 102(e) expressly applies only to U.S. patents. For foreign patents, their date of effectiveness as prior art is the first date they are publicly disclosed. Although different patent systems overseas include varying provisions, generally speaking the first date foreign patent offices publish a patent document is either (1) the date on which the foreign patent actually issues, or (2) an earlier date, mandated by foreign patent statutes, on which pending patent applications are published (in most countries this date is approximately 18 months after the application is filed). For example, suppose that Dr. Nanuck files a Canadian patent application on May 1, 2004. The Canadian Patent Office publishes that application on November 1, 2005, and grants Nanuck an issued Canadian patent on September 12, 2006. Because § 102(e) does not apply, the first date that the Canadian patent can serve as prior art under U.S. law is November 1, 2005, the date the Canadian Patent Office published Nanuck's application.

The courts have read the requirement that § 102(e) applies to applications "filed in the United States" quite literally. Even though a patent application may have obtained foreign priority through § 119(a) and the Paris Convention, the issued patent that results has prior art effect only at the time of the actual U.S. filing date.[57]

In alluding to § 351(a) of the Patent Act, § 102(e) obliquely refers to the provisions of the Patent Cooperation Treaty (PCT). The PCT is discussed further in §§ 19.8.4 and 23.2 of this volume. In short, the PCT allows applicants to file an "international application" at one qualified patent office that designates all signatory countries in which patent protection is sought. By operation of the treaty, that single application is deemed to have the same legal effect as the filing of multiple applications in all signatory countries designated by the applicant. Because over 100 states have joined the PCT, the filing of one international application can do the work of many regular national filings. All international applications are published 18 months after they are filed.

When acceding to the PCT, the United States had to adopt the *Alexander Milburn* rule to international applications. Following 2002 amendments to § 102(e), the basic prior art rules are as follows. Publications of international applications that designate the United States and are published in the English language fall within § 102(e)(1), and are accorded prior art effectiveness as of the date of their filings. Similarly, § 102(e)(2) states that a U.S. patent shall enjoy prior art effect as of the filing date of the international application if that application designated the United States and was published in the English language. Neither of these provisions changes the basic *Alexander Milburn* rule with respect to non-PCT applications filed in the United States.

---

56. *See* MANUAL OF PATENT EXAMINING PROCEDURE § 706.02(f).

57. *See* In re Hilmer, 359 F.2d 859. *See infra* § 19.8.2.

An example demonstrates the basic workings of § 102(e). Suppose that Professor Gizmo conceives of a new X-ray machine on July 7, 2004, actually reduces the machine to practice on October 13, 2004, and files an application directed towards the machine at the PTO on February 28, 2005. During prosecution, the PTO examiner discovers an issued U.S. patent to Gizmo's rival, Dr. Nefarious. The Nefarious patent discloses, but does not claim, the same X-ray machine that Gizmo claims. The Nefarious patent issued on March 17, 2007, based upon an application filed on November 1, 2004. Assume further that the PTO did not publish the pending application of Nefarious eighteen months after its filing date because Nefarious sought patent rights only in the United States.

Under these facts, the PTO examiner may issue a § 102(e) rejection to Gizmo based upon the Nefarious patent. Assuming that Gizmo has sufficient corroboration of her dates of inventive activity, Gizmo may file a Rule 131 affidavit demonstrating that prior to the filing date of the Nefarious patent (Nefarious filed on November 1, 2004), Gizmo reduced her invention to practice (Gizmo did so on October 13, 2004). If the PTO examiner harbors no further objections, then Gizmo will be awarded a patent.

Concerned readers may be troubled about the status of Dr. Nefarious in this situation. After all, the PTO did not contact Nefarious concerning the Gizmo application, and Gizmo will obtain a patent that may be quite similar to that of Nefarious. The answer is that because Nefarious did not expressly claim the X-ray machine, but instead merely disclosed it in his patent, he is not deemed to possess a sufficient interest in that invention. That Gizmo later claimed that X-ray machine is of no moment to Nefarious. Of course, if Nefarious had expressly claimed the X-ray machine that Gizmo later claimed, then the PTO would have declared an interference and awarded a patent only to the party that was the first inventor. If Gizmo does procure a patent, and Nefarious belatedly wishes to appropriate the X-ray machine invention, Nefarious may be able to file a so-called "reissue application" at the PTO in order to claim the X-ray machine expressly. Nefarious must meet certain requirements to invoke the mechanism of reissue, however, the details of which are discussed in § 19.6.3 of this volume.

16.3.4　Derivation Under § 102(f)

Section 102(f) prevents a patent from issuing to an applicant who "did not himself invent the subject matter sought to be patented." If an individual derived the invention from another, then no patent should result from his application. Section 102(f) thus presents something of a standing requirement, reinforced by § 101 and the Constitution itself, mandating that only the true inventor apply for the patent. A prima facie case of derivation entails a showing of another's prior conception of the claimed subject matter along with an awareness of that conception to the applicant or patentee.[58]

58. *See* Price v. Symsek, 988 F.2d 1187 (Fed.Cir.1993).

The courts have not employed § 102(f) with great frequency. Because a predicate to derivation is that another first invented the subject matter sought to be patented, § 102(a) ordinarily will also apply to such cases. Parties adverse to the patent generally will find proofs of patent invalidity more straightforward under § 102(a), which does not entail the nettlesome issues of communication and copying. Section 102(f) is most often employed in those factual circumstances where § 102(a) does not apply. In particular, § 102(f) is not limited to inventions conceived "in this country," nor have courts imposed a requirement of public knowledge as they have in § 102(a).[59]

For example, suppose that on May 27, 2004, Dr. Nefarious is enjoying a poolside drink in an Ensenada, Mexico resort. Nefarious overhears Professor Gizmo's oral description of her latest invention to an academic colleague. Nefarious rushes back to the United States and files a patent application at the PTO on May 29, 2004, claiming Gizmo's invention. Under these circumstances, the § 102(b) statutory bar does not apply because Gizmo's invention has neither been "on sale" nor in "public use" in the United States. Section 102(a) also does not apply because Gizmo's invention was not "known or used" in the United States either. Under these facts, assuming Gizmo can prove that Nefarious derived his claimed invention from her, then § 102(f) would apply and serve as the basis for rejection of the Nefarious patent application.

§ 16.4 The Novelty Standard

Once the pertinent prior art has been identified, each reference should be evaluated to determine whether it anticipates the claimed invention. As will be seen, an invention is judged novel unless a single reference discloses every element of the challenged claim and enables one skilled in the art to make the anticipating subject matter.

16.4.1 The Strict Identity Requirement

Anticipation requires the presence in a single prior art disclosure of each and every element of a claimed invention.[1] Although older cases suggest a looser standard, allowing courts to find anticipation where a single reference includes the equivalents of all of the claimed elements,[2] the Federal Circuit has rigidly upheld a standard of total identity.[3] Even the presence of minor or insubstantial differences between the claimed invention and the reference will result in a conclusion of novelty. It is important to note that in such circumstances, a nonobviousness analysis might well prove fatal to the patentability of the claimed invention.[4] In

59. *See generally* OddzOn Products, Inc. v. Just Toys, Inc., 122 F.3d 1396 (Fed.Cir. 1997).

§ 16.4

1. *E.g.,* Glaverbel Societe Anonyme v. Northlake Marketing & Supply, Inc., 45 F.3d 1550, 1554 (Fed.Cir.1995).

2. *See* RCA Corp. v. Applied Digital Data Sys., Inc., 730 F.2d 1440 (Fed.Cir. 1984) (Kashiwa, J., dissenting).

3. *E.g.,* PPG Indus., Inc. v. Guardian Indus. Corp., 75 F.3d 1558, 1566 (Fed.Cir. 1996).

4. *See* Continental Can Co. USA v. Monsanto Co., 948 F.2d 1264, 1267 (Fed.Cir. 1991).

order to demonstrate that a claimed invention is anticipated, attorneys often construct so-called "claim charts" that contrast claim language with the properties of the prior art reference.

This anticipation inquiry is similar to the analysis undertaken by courts when considering literal infringement. The difference between the two queries is largely a matter of timing. "That which would literally infringe if later in time anticipates if earlier than the date of invention."[5] Suppose, for example, that the manufacturer of a chemical compound learns that a competitor has obtained a patent on that compound. If the manufacturer's earlier activities serve as prior art against the patent, then the patent is invalid for anticipation. Otherwise, continued production by the manufacturer will infringe the patent.

In contrast to pertinent prior art for nonobviousness, an anticipating reference need not originate from an analogous art.[6] While nonobviousness is conducted from the perspective of the skilled artisan, the novelty inquiry is far more open-ended. A reference might originate from a technical discipline far removed from the field of interest to the inventor yet still constitute an anticipation.

Sometimes a patent discloses a set or group of technological things, such as an entire class of chemical compounds. The PTO will then learn of a prior art reference that describes the use of a subordinate member of that group, such as a discrete compound within the claimed class. In the patent law, these sorts of problems are referred to as those of "genus" and "species." Genus-species relationships create logical difficulties for the anticipation analysis of the patent law, but they have been resolved as follows.

When a species disclosed by the prior art literally falls within a claimed genus, the claimed genus will be considered anticipated. The Federal Circuit opinion in *Titanium Metals Corp. v. Banner* illustrates this concept.[7] The application at issue, which had been assigned to Titanium Metals, claimed a "titanium base alloy consisting essentially by weight of about 0.6% to 0.9% nickel, 0.2% to 0.4% molybdenum, up to 0.2% maximum iron, balance titanium, said alloy being characterized by good corrosion resistance in hot brine environments." Cited against the claim was an article written in the Russian language. The Russian article included a chart that showed a compound consisting of 0.75% nickel, 0.25% molybdenum, and 99% titanium. The court recited "an elementary principle of patent law that when, as by a recitation of ranges or otherwise, a claim covers several compositions, the claim is 'anticipated' if one of them is in the prior art."

Whether a genus within the prior art should anticipate a later claimed species presents more difficult concepts. In a sense, an earlier disclosed genus encompasses all of the species within that genus. But the

5. Lewmar Marine Inc. v. Barient Inc., 827 F.2d 744 (Fed.Cir.1987), *cert. denied*, 484 U.S. 1007, 108 S.Ct. 702, 98 L.Ed.2d 653 (1988).

6. Ex parte Lee, 31 USPQ2d 1105, 1110 n. 1 (Bd.Pat.App. & Int'f 1993).

7. 778 F.2d 775 (Fed.Cir.1985).

courts and the PTO have reasoned that a reference that describes a genus does not necessarily anticipate later claims to a species. Particularly in biotechnology and the chemical arts, a genus can sometimes encompass millions of species, and a particular reference may not suggest that any particular species should be employed.[8] In cases where the prior art discloses a genus, the usual mechanism for evaluation is nonobviousness. The selection of an optimum value within a range of parameters is normally within the realm of ordinary skill.[9] But where the number of possibilities is vast, or the results unexpectedly good, the discovery of the optimal species might not have been obvious to a skilled artisan.

16.4.2 The Enablement Requirement

The Supreme Court has long recognized that anticipation cannot occur unless a prior art reference is "enabling"—that is, it contains "a substantial representation of the patented improvement in such full, clear, and exact terms as to enable any person skilled in the art or science to which it appertains to make, construct, and practice the invention to the same practical extent as they would be enabled to do so if the information was derived from a prior patent."[10] This so-called "enablement" requirement denies patentability only where earlier efforts have truly enriched the technological arts. Consequently, such references as technological forecasts or works of speculative fiction cannot ordinarily serve as anticipations. Although the phrase "Beam me up, Scotty" has inspired millions of devoted Trekies, the *Star Trek* television series would be of little moment to the inventor of an operative personal teleportation device. Because Captain Kirk, Spock and the other members of the *Enterprise* crew neglected to explain how their transporter actually worked in between their struggles with the Romulans, Gorn and the dreaded Horta, the enablement requirement of anticipation has not been met.

The *Titanium Metals* case also serves as a useful illustration of the enablement requirement. There, the prior art Russian article offered no instruction on how to synthesize the claimed titanium alloy. Nor did it disclose that the compound had special corrosion resistance properties. The court readily dismissed the argument of Titanium Metals that the Russian article was nonenabling, however. Expert testimony established that skilled metallurgists could readily generate the compound. Further, the application at issue also presumed that skilled artisans could prepare the claimed alloy. That the Russian article did not mention the corrosion resistance properties of the compound was also besides the point. According to the court, Congress had not authorized the patenting of an old alloy by one who had merely discovered some of its useful properties.

8. *See* In re Deuel, 51 F.3d 1552, 1558–59 (Fed.Cir.1995).

9. *See* L'Esperance v. Nishimoto, 18 USPQ2d 1534, 1539–40 (Bd.Pat.App. & Int'f 1991).

10. Seymour v. Osborne, 78 U.S. (11 Wall.) 516, 20 L.Ed. 33 (1870).

The holding of *Titanium Metals* may initially seem troubling. That a point on a graph in a foreign language publication could deny patentability may seem poor patent policy. The applicant was not left without any patent position, however. Titanium Metals could freely seek process protection by claiming its invention as a "new use of a known . . . composition of matter."[11] And had the field of titanium metallurgy been less well understood, then the Russian article would assuredly have had to contain further teachings in order for it to anticipate the Titanium Metals application.

16.4.3   Inherency and Accidental Anticipation

Difficult policy questions and some fine distinctions arise in cases of accidental anticipations. Suppose the proprietor of a patented chemical compound brings an infringement suit against a competitor. A painstaking search by the accused infringer reveals that a third party had unknowingly synthesized the patented chemical compound years before. Should the third party's unintended, unappreciated technology serve as an anticipation? Plainly the compound had been earlier invented. Yet this prior effort cannot be said to have informed the public domain, for others were unable to profit from the original inventor's effort.

The Supreme Court addressed this situation in *Tilghman v. Proctor*.[12] That case involved Tilghman's patented process for manufacturing fat acids and glycerine from fatty bodies by the action of water at a high temperature and pressure. The accused infringers alleged several different anticipations, ranging from a steam cylinder to a water barometer. During the operation of each of these earlier devices, fat acids had likely been decomposed as later claimed by Tilghman. But this technical effect was incidental to another purpose and had not been understood by the earlier inventors. The Court held that these prior uses did not destroy the novelty of Tilghman's patent. "If the acids were accidentally and unwittingly produced, whilst the operators were in pursuit of other and different results, without exciting attention and without it even being known what was done or how it had been done, it would be absurd to say that this was an anticipation of Tilghman's discovery."

Yet where the relevant technical effect necessarily follows from a deliberate act, even though all of its aspects have not been understood, courts have nonetheless held that the reference anticipates. They have done so under the doctrine of inherency, which brings some modest flexibility to the strict standard of anticipation. Under inherency principles, an anticipating reference need not expressly state each of the elements of the subject matter it describes. Where the missing feature undeniably forms a part of the reference as a matter of scientific fact, and skilled artisans would so understand, then that reference will nonetheless serve as an anticipating reference. The inherency doctrine in part arises out of the recognition that writers often assume certain knowledge on behalf of readers. It also forms part of the policy judgment

---

11. 35 U.S.C.A. § 101 (2000).   **12.** 102 U.S. 707, 26 L.Ed. 279 (1880).

that the mere perception of technological qualities that others had not seen does not rise to patentable invention.[13]

The Federal Circuit opinion in *Continental Can Co. v. Monsanto Co.*[14] is illustrative. The asserted patent claimed a plastic bottle with a sturdy, ribbed bottom structure. The claims of the patent required that the ribs of the bottom structure be hollow. The basis for the defendant's invalidity argument was the prior art Marcus patent, which also described a sturdy plastic bottle. On its face, the Marcus reference did not expressly state whether ribs on the bottom of the bottle were hollow or not. The defendant argued that because the ribs of the Marcus reference were formed by injection blow molding, they necessarily would have been hollow. The trial court granted summary judgment in favor of the defendant, holding the patent invalid as anticipated by the Marcus reference.

On appeal, the Federal Circuit vacated the summary judgment and remanded the matter for trial. Because a genuine dispute existed over whether the Marcus reference inherently disclosed hollow ribs or not, it was inappropriate for the trial court to declare summarily that the patent was anticipated. The Federal Circuit offered some guidance for the trial court to follow, explaining that inherency must not be a matter of possibility or probability. Conjecture or the possibility of making slight modifications to known technology would not do. Instead, the subject matter asserted to be present via inherency must necessarily form part of the reference's technical disclosure. The court further instructed that inherency is to be judged from the perspective of a person of ordinary skill in the art.

This line of cases suggests that accidental technical effects will not defeat the novelty of a later patent where they are sporadic and unappreciated. Paradigmatic of such circumstances are technologies momentarily formed through mistake or unusual conditions, for "[c]hance hits in the dark will not anticipate an invention."[15] However, where a technical effect was consistently obtained, detectable and reproducible, even though incidental to what was deliberately intended and not fully understood by the inventor, then it will be accorded anticipatory effect through the inherency doctrine.

---

13. General Electric Co. v. Jewel Incandescent Lamp Co., 326 U.S. 242, 66 S.Ct. 81, 90 L.Ed. 43 (1945).

14. 948 F.2d 1264 (Fed.Cir.1991).

15. United Chromium, Inc. v. International Silver Co., 60 F.2d 913, 917 (2d Cir. 1932).

Chapter 17

NONOBVIOUSNESS

§ 17.1 Introduction

Section 103(a) denies patentability "if the differences between the subject matter sought to be patented and the prior art are such that the subject matter as a whole would have been obvious at the time the invention was made to a person having ordinary skill in the art to which said subject matter pertains." The patent community employs the awkward term "nonobviousness" to express this requirement. As we shall see, nonobviousness descends from the historical and more ephemeral standard of "invention." In practice, nonobviousness is the most significant hurdle to patentability. Much of the dialogue between an applicant and a PTO examiner typically concerns nonobviousness, and it is the favored validity defense raised by accused infringers in court.

Section 103(a) requires jurists and PTO examiners to decide whether an inventor's work product differs from the state of the art enough to be patent-worthy. In resolving this issue, the nonobviousness analysis proceeds in the same fashion as the novelty inquiry. First, the class of technology relevant to the assessment of obviousness must be identified. The relevant prior art for nonobviousness generally is the same as that for novelty, with one additional requirement. Not only must the reference fall into a § 102 category recognized as a source of prior art for § 103(a), the reference must also be considered analogous to what is claimed in the patent or patent application. Prior art for nonobviousness is addressed here in § 17.2 below.

Once the apposite prior art has been determined, then the claimed invention must be found to be nonobvious with respect to those references. This Chapter considers this issue in § 17.3. Section 103(a) requires that the knowledge possessed by a typical scientist or engineer working within the relevant technical area must form the yardstick for the nonobviousness decision. In contrast to the novelty requirement, multiple references may be employed when considering nonobviousness. As will be seen, however, the references must suggest to the skilled artisan that they can be combined and that this combination would have a reasonable probability of success.

Closely akin, if not identical to nonobviousness is the standard of "inventive step" employed overseas. For example, Article 56 of the European Patent Convention provides that "[a]n invention shall be considered as involving an inventive step if, having regard to the state of the art, it is not obvious to a person skilled in the art."[1] Still, as we shall see, the U.S. patent bar possesses such a collective bad memory over the historical standard of "invention" that use of the term "inventive step" should be avoided domestically. Further, to reflect the fact that the nonobviousness analysis is based upon the prior art, rather than employing today's hindsight, the U.S. patent community frowns upon the use of the present tense when describing nonobviousness. It is good practice to employ the language "*would have been* obvious" when articulating § 103(a) problems.[2]

Those new to the patent system should not lose sight of the impact of the nonobviousness requirement. It allows the PTO and the courts to deny or invalidate a patent even where it claims a product or process that has never itself been realized. The nonobviousness requirement has received many rationalizations. Most readily apparent is that nonobvi-

§ 17.1

1. Convention on the Grant of European Patents, Oct. 5, 1973, 13 I.L.M. 268 (1974).

2. Panduit v. Dennison, 774 F.2d 1082, 1088 n. 7 (Fed.Cir.1985), *judgment vacated on other grounds*, 475 U.S. 809, 106 S.Ct. 1578, 89 L.Ed.2d 817 (1986), *on remand* 810 F.2d 1561 (Fed.Cir.1987).

ousness creates a "patent-free" zone around the state of the art, allowing skilled technicians to complete routine work such as the straightforward substitution of materials, the ordinary streamlining of parts and technical processes, and the usual marginal improvements that occur as a technology matures.[3]

Economic studies have advanced a more theoretical justification. Legal economists have urged that an optimal patent system would only grant patents to inventions that have been induced by the patent system itself. If ordinary market forces provided sufficient incentives to invent and disclose new technologies, then the award of a patent would be unnecessary to promote innovation. In such cases, the public should not be made to suffer the inconvenience of having a patent issue. Although the patent system does not attempt to discern the motivation of individual inventors, it does employ the proxy of nonobviousness. Under this view, the nonobviousness requirement encourages individuals to pursue projects that, because they require expansion of the state of the art, are of uncertain success.[4]

§ 17.2   Prior Art for Nonobviousness

Section 103(a) requires the patent community to determine "the differences between the subject matter sought to be patented and the prior art." But the statute nowhere defines the term "prior art." The courts have filled in this gap by declaring that § 102 prior art is generally available for nonobviousness as well.[1] Thus, the question courts have posed is whether technology described within, say, § 102(b), applies not only to a novelty analysis but also towards nonobviousness under § 103(a).

The availability of a technology under § 102 is a necessary, but insufficient condition for it to apply to an analysis under § 103(a). The technology must also originate within an "analogous art," a technical discipline relevant to the claimed invention or concern a problem pertinent to the claimed subject matter. The Patent Act also exempts from consideration certain prior art that arose due to joint research efforts. Under § 103(c), when the prior art and the claimed invention are, at the time of invention, owned by a single entity, then they may not be

---

3.   Martin J. Adelman et al., Patent Law: Cases and Materials 310 (2d ed. 2003).

4.   *See generally* Rebecca Eisenberg, *Patents and the Exclusive Progress of Science: Exclusive Rights and Experimental Use*, 56 U. Chi. L. Rev. 1017 (1989).

§ 17.2

1.   Whether subject matter available under §§ 102(c) or 102(d) applies as well to § 103(a) has yet to be conclusively determined. This circumstance is likely due to the relatively infrequent use of either provision. Both the CCPA, in In re Bass, 474 F.2d 1276, 1290 (CCPA 1973), and the Federal Circuit, in OddzOn Products, Inc. v. Just Toys, Inc., 122 F.3d 1396, 1403 (Fed. Cir.1997), have stated in dicta that neither provision serves as a source or prior art to § 103(a). This result is questionable with regard to § 102(c). If an inventor has truly abandoned an invention to the public, sound patent policy would suggest that his dedication should not apply to obvious variations of that technology as well. And given the breadth accorded to the § 102(d) bar by the Federal Circuit in In re Kathawala, 9 F.3d 942 (Fed.Cir.1993), the fact that foreign patents within § 102(d) do not input into § 103(a) may be of little moment.

considered in a nonobviousness analysis. These topics are taken up in turn below.

17.2.1 Analogous Arts

Simply because a technology is available under § 102 is not enough to render it applicable to the nonobviousness determination. The technology must also issue from a technical area judged sufficiently germane to that of the claimed invention. Such areas are known as "analogous arts." This doctrine, which does not apply to novelty determinations, follows from the requirement of § 103(a) that nonobviousness be judged from the perspective of "a person having ordinary skill in the art." Thus, although a person of skill in a given technical area is presumed to have access to all of the technical knowledge comprising the state of the art, this knowledge can only be employed within the constraints of the abilities and expertise of practitioners within that field.

In re Clay[2] presented a thorough explanation of the Federal Circuit's view of analogous arts. Clay's application concerned a process for storing refined liquid hydrocarbon product in a storage tank having a dead volume between the tank bottom and its outlet port. The process involved the placement of a gelation solution into a tank's dead volume and later allowing the solution to gel. According to Clay, the addition of a gel-degrading agent would allow the gel to be readily removed from the tank. The PTO had rejected Clay's application under § 103(a) in part due to the Syndansk reference. Syndansk called for the introduction of a similar gel into an underground, natural, oil-bearing formation in order to better channel oil flow during extraction. The Marathon Oil Company owned both Syndansk's patent and Clay's application.

Judge Lourie first noted that a two-part standard governed whether prior art is analogous. The first determination was "whether the art is from the same field of endeavor, regardless of the problem addressed."[3] If so, then the art should be considered analogous and within the § 103(a) inquiry. Even if this first step was not met, however, the reference could still be deemed analogous if "reasonably pertinent to the particular problem with which the inventor is involved."[4] Such a reference "logically would have commended itself to the inventor's attention in considering his problem."[5]

According to Judge Lourie, the Syndansk reference fulfilled neither test. With regard to the field of endeavor, Syndansk addressed the use of gel in unconfined, irregular volumes of natural subterranean formations, in extreme operating conditions. Clay instead manipulated the confined, dead volume of an artificial storage tank under ordinary atmospheric conditions. And concerning the pertinence of the problem, the court reasoned that Syndansk dealt with the removal of oil from rock, while Clay with oil from a storage tank. As the problem concerning Clay

2. 966 F.2d 656 (Fed.Cir.1992).   4. *Id.*
3. 966 F.2d at 659.   5. *Id.*

involved dissimilar structures and working conditions, a person of ordinary skill would not have been led to Syndansk.

Although the second aspect of the inquiry seems correctly decided, the *Clay* court appeared to give lip service to the first part of its analogy test. That both the Clay and Syndansk inventions dealt with the use of gel in oil extraction, and were owned by the same company, suggests that both fell within the same field of endeavor. The Federal Circuit also seemingly collapsed the first part of its analogy standard into the second, for the same facts guided its reasoning for each.

Despite *Clay*, the trend is towards a broadening of the prior art that courts consider pertinent.[6] The Federal Circuit opinion in *In re Paulsen*[7] is representative. Prior art "directed to hinges and latches as used in a desktop telephone directory, a piano lid, a kitchen cabinet, a washing machine cabinet, a wooden furniture cabinet, or a two-part housing for storing stereo cassettes" were held to be analogous to a claimed portable computer. According to the court, the problems addressed in the patent application were not unique to the computing field. They instead concerned how to connect and secure the two parts of a clamshell-style portable computer, a problem well known to the simple mechanical arts.

Although prior art for § 103(a) must come from an analogous art to the claimed invention, such a reference need not be enabling. That is to say, while a reference must enable a skilled artisan to practice the invention in order to anticipate under § 102, a non-enabling reference will be considered within a nonobviousness analysis.[8] Even if a reference discloses an inoperative technology, it may be employed for all that it teaches in the context of nonobviousness.

17.2.2 Section 103(c)

Congress amended § 103 in 1984 by adding a new provision now codified at § 103(c).[9] As amended in 1999, § 103(c) exempts prior art arising from "one or more of subsections (e), (f), and (g)" from consideration in the § 103(a) inquiry if certain conditions are met. Specifically, the putative prior art under § 102(e), (f) or (g), as well as the claimed invention, must either be owned by, or subject to an obligation of assignment to, a single entity at the time the invention was made.

A knowledge of the history of § 103(c) may aid understanding of this rather technical provision. Congress enacted § 103(c) in response to the CCPA's decision in *In re Bass*.[10] There, co-inventors Bass, Jenkins and Horvat had applied for a patent on an air control system for carding machines. Their effective filing date was October 11, 1965. The PTO rejected their claims on the ground of nonobviousness, and following an appeal the CCPA affirmed. Among the references cited were two patents:

6. *See* Twin Disc, Inc. v. United States, 231 USPQ 417, 427 (Cl.Ct.1986).

7. 30 F.3d 1475 (Fed.Cir.1994).

8. Symbol Technologies, Inc. v. Opticon, Inc., 935 F.2d 1569 (Fed.Cir.1991).

9. Patent Law Amendments of 1984, Pub. L. No. 98–622, § 104, 98 Stat. 3385.

10. 474 F.2d 1276 (CCPA 1973).

a patent granted to Bass and Horvat, which had matured from an application filed on August 23, 1965; and a patent issued to Jenkins, based upon an October 13, 1964, application.

The correspondence of inventor surnames between the application and the prior art patents was not a coincidence. In fact, the PTO and CCPA cited the earlier work of Bass, Jenkins and Horvat against them. They did so by following the traditional patent law principle that each new combination of joint inventors constitutes a distinct inventive entity. This principle holds even where these combinations share individual inventors. For example, the joint inventors Bass, Jenkins and Horvat were considered a different inventive entity than the team of Bass and Horvat. Each group of natural persons essentially acquires its own legal identity; they, as a whole, constitute "the inventor" of that technology.

In re Bass demonstrated that the setting of contemporary technology development may lead to harsh results when corporations file patent applications. Where one corporation employs numerous technologists to engage in collaborative research and development efforts, the shifting composition of inventive teams can result in rather strained holdings of nonobviousness. Ordinarily, the patent statute establishes that an inventor's own prior inventive efforts may not anticipate a subsequent patent application. For example, in § 102(g), the invention must be made by "another" to serve as prior art. But since legally distinct inventors result from different inventive entities, an anticipation rejection is possible even if only a slight change in personnel occurs. In a particularly fertile and interactive corporate research department, inventors could find themselves unable to obtain patents due to "in-house" rejections for obviousness based upon efforts by their peers, and even in part by themselves!

Congress intended § 103(c) to solve the problem highlighted in *In re Bass* by exempting § 102 (e), (f) and (g) prior art from the obviousness analysis in joint research and development settings. The workings of § 103(c) can prove elusive, but an example should lend some clarity to its provisions. Suppose that two inventors, Roger and Joy, each work for the Coif Corporation. As part of their employment contracts, Roger and Joy have agreed to assign inventions that they develop to the Coif Corporation. Roger conceives of a new electromagnetic generator on November 1, 2002. He immediately informs Joy about his idea. Working diligently in his laboratory, Roger reduces the invention to practice on December 22, 2002. The Coif Corporation files a patent application on Roger's behalf on February 12, 2003. The Roger patent issues on January 19, 2004.

On April 10, 2003, Joy realizes that she can improve upon Roger's generator. Because of her workload, she does not start on the project until May 3, 2003. Without further consulting Roger, she ultimately completes her generator on June 1, 2003. Although Joy's invention represents an improvement over Roger's work, it would have been obvious in light of the Roger generator. The Coif Corporation files a patent application on behalf of Joy on October 1, 2003.

Under these facts, the Roger patent cannot serve as prior art against Joy. The statutory bars of § 102(b) and (d) are not triggered here. There is also no indication that Roger's invention was "known or used by others" within the meaning of § 102(a), given the judicial requirement of a public knowledge or use.[11] If § 103(c) were not available, the Roger patent would constitute prior art under § 102(e) because Joy's invention date occurred after the Roger application was filed. Absent § 103(c), the Roger patent would also serve as prior art under § 102(f) because Joy derived a obvious variation of her invention from Roger. Further, without § 103(c) Roger's work would be available under § 102(g), because Roger both conceived and reduced his invention to practice prior to Joy's conception date. However, because § 103(c) exempts § 102(e), (f) and (g) art from the nonobviousness inquiry where the inventions were subject to an common obligation of assignment, the Roger patent may not be employed as a prior art reference against the Joy application.

Section 103(c) is a narrowly worded provision. If a reference is otherwise available as prior art, such as under § 102(a) or (b), then it remains pertinent to § 103(a). Also recall that § 103(c) solely concerns nonobviousness. It does not affect the availability of prior art for purposes of anticipation.

§ 17.3   The Nonobviousness Inquiry

Having identified the set of permissible prior art that applies to a claimed invention, a decision maker may next determine whether that invention would have been obvious to a person of skill in the art. Our present framework for addressing nonobviousness issues is accompanied by a considerable heritage. Without a sense of that history, a full grasp of the nonobviousness standard will prove difficult. This Chapter therefore addresses the leading Supreme Court precedents addressing nonobviousness and its historical predecessor, the standard of invention, at the start. It then turns to more recent refinements of the nonobviousness standard announced by the Federal Circuit.

17.3.1   The Historical Standard of Invention

The Supreme Court opinion in *Hotchkiss v. Greenwood*[1] proved to be the seminal decision regarding a prior art-based patentability requirement that exceeded novelty. The patent there concerned a door knob constructed of potter's clay or porcelain. Others had constructed similar knobs out of metal or wood, but the patented door knobs could be produced "better and cheaper."[2] Having lost at trial following a jury

---

11.   *See supra* § 16.3.1.   **2.**   *Id.* at 264.

1.   52 U.S. 248, 11 How. 248, 13 L.Ed. 683 (1850).

verdict, the patentee appealed to the Supreme Court. The chief argument on appeal was the propriety of a jury instruction that the patent was void if it called for "the mere substitution of one material for another" such that "no other ingenuity or skill being necessary to construct the knob than that of an ordinary mechanic acquainted with the business."[3] The Court upheld the instruction, stating that unless the knowledge required to construct the knob exceeded that "possessed by an ordinary mechanic acquainted with the business, there was an absence of that degree of skill and ingenuity which constitute essential elements of every invention. In other words, the improvement is the work of the skillful mechanic, not that of the inventor."[4]

Although the *Hotchkiss* standard took the abilities of the "skillful mechanic" as its point of reference, it also employed the rhetoric of "invention" and "ingenuity." The latter language seemed to many courts to suggest a more subjective standard, in particular one which favored the Romantic inventor who conceived of the invention in a "flash of creative genius."[5] Over time this latter vision seemed to prevail. Courts demanded that inventors demonstrate "a substantial discovery and a substantial invention,"[6] "something new, unexpected and exciting,"[7] and even "that impalpable something."[8] Judge Learned Hand was led to comment that the so-called "invention" standard was "as fugitive, impalpable, wayward and vague a phantom as exists in the whole paraphernalia of legal concepts."[9]

The anti-monopoly sentiments that arose during the Depression era did not bode well for the patent system. Courts began to apply an increasingly stringent "invention" standard that found most patents wanting. At the Supreme Court, Justice Jackson remarked in 1949 that "the only patent that is valid is one which this Court has not been able to get its hands on."[10] The apex of this movement was to occur one year later, in the Court's 1950 decision in *Great A&P Tea Co. v. Supermarket Equipment Corp.*[11]

The patent in *Great A&P* concerned a cashier's counter for use in grocery and other stores. The two lower courts had upheld the patent, but the Court granted certiorari and struck the patent down. According to Justice Jackson himself, the disputed invention claimed a combination of known elements and, as such, must be judged under the so-called "synergy" test. "The conjunction or concert of known elements must contribute something; only when the whole in some way exceeds the sum of its parts is the accumulation of old devices patentable." This demand

3. *Id.* at 265.

4. *Id.* at 267.

5. *See* Cuno Eng'g Corp. v. Automatic Devices Corp., 314 U.S. 84, 91, 62 S.Ct. 37, 86 L.Ed. 58 (1941).

6. *See* Bradley v. Eccles, 122 F. 867, 870 (C.C.N.D.N.Y.1903).

7. *See* Thurber Corp. v. Fairchild Motor Corp., 269 F.2d 841, 849 (5th Cir.1959).

8. *See* McClain v. Ortmayer, 141 U.S. 419, 427, 12 S.Ct. 76, 35 L.Ed. 800 (1891).

9. Harries v. Air King Products Co., 183 F.2d 158, 162 (2d Cir.1950).

10. Jungersen v. Ostby & Barton Co., 335 U.S. 560, 572, 69 S.Ct. 269, 93 L.Ed. 235 (1949).

11. 340 U.S. 147, 71 S.Ct. 127, 95 L.Ed. 162 (1950).

for "unusual or surprising consequences" seemed to call for the downfall of nearly every patent claim, for nearly every invention may be cast as a combination of old elements. The patent community sought relief from this unfavorable precedent, ultimately prevailing with the enactment of the nonobviousness standard in § 103 in the 1952 Patent Act.

17.3.2   The Modern Standard of Nonobviousness

Dissatisfaction with such arduous standards as "synergy" and the "flash of genius" led Congress to include a statutory basis for invention within the 1952 Patent Act. Section 103(a) does not refer to the historical "invention" standard, but instead to an objective nonobviousness standard founded upon the knowledge of a person of ordinary skill in the art. The Supreme Court first interpreted this new statutory language in three 1966 opinions of such importance that the patent bar commonly refers to them simply as "The Trilogy."

17.3.2.1   The Trilogy

In *Graham v. John Deere Co.*,[12] the Court presented a lengthy exposition of the constitutional framework for the nonobviousness requirement, judicial development of the invention standard, as well as the impact of § 103 and the requirement of nonobviousness. In the most frequently cited passage of the opinion, the Court then set forth the well-heeded "Graham test," a technique for determining nonobviousness:

> While the ultimate question of patent validity is one of law, . . . [§ 103] lends itself to several basic factual inquiries. Under § 103, the scope and content of the prior art are to be determined; differences between the prior art and the claims at issue are to be ascertained; and the level of ordinary skill in the pertinent art resolved. . . . Such secondary considerations as commercial success, long felt but unresolved needs, failure of others, etc., might be utilized to give light to the circumstances surrounding the origin of the subject matter sought to be patented. As indicia of obviousness or nonobviousness, these inquiries may have relevancy.[13]

The Court then applied this standard to the facts at hand. Graham was concerned with the construction of a plow that would not break upon striking soil obstructions such as rocks. In 1950, he obtained the '811 patent, directed towards a plow with a spring clamp. The device featured an upper plate secured to the lower flange of the H-beam of a plow frame. A hinge plate was pivoted to the upper plate, with one end of the plow shank resiliently and frictionally held between the upper and hinge plates. An opening in the shank allowed a rod to extend through it. A coil spring was placed around the rod and seated on the upper plate. When the plow hit an obstruction, the shank moved downward against the tension of the coil spring and pivoted the hinge plate. This pivoting

---

12.   383 U.S. 1, 86 S.Ct. 684, 15 L.Ed.2d 545 (1966).   **13.**   *Id.* at 17–18.

action allowed the plow to pass over obstructions and increased the resiliency of the shank.

In 1953, Graham obtained the patent-at-suit, the '798, which improved upon his earlier effort. The two inventions differed in that (1) the '798 invention featured a stirrup and bolted connection of the shank to the hinge plate and (2) the '798 invention placed the shank below the hinge plate. This distinction shifted the point of wear from the bottom of the upper plate to the top of the stirrup of the hinge plate, a more easily replaced part. The patentee also argued that the reversal allowed the shank to flex away from the hinge plate when the plow encountered an obstruction.

Two lower courts had held the '798 patent invalid in light of § 103, a result which was affirmed by the Supreme Court. Justice Clark concluded that the '798 patent would have been obvious due to the teachings of two references: the '811 patent and a reference not before the examiner, a device marketed by the Glencoe Manufacturing Company. The Glencoe device included a stirrup, and the Court judged that any skilled artisan would have immediately sought to reverse the shank and the plate in order to improve the flex. Interestingly, the Court seemed scarcely concerned with the three-part test it had just pronounced. The Court did not consider the level of skill in the art, nor did it explicitly address any of the so-called "secondary considerations" such as commercial success or long-felt need.

The opinion in *Graham* involved a second case, *Calmar, Inc. v. Cook Chemical Co.* This litigation arose from a falling out between two former contracting parties, Calmar and Cook Chemical. The technical problem here was how to keep a spray insecticide bottle from leaking during shipment. To prevent leaking during shipment, the prior art often detached the pumping unit from the bottle of insecticide itself. The consumer needed to remove the cap from the bottle and then attach the pumping unit in order to spray the insecticide. Apparently this arrangement was difficult to package, and in addition thieves were making off with the pumping units. So Cook, which made the insecticide, asked its pump maker, Calmar, to develop a leak-proof pump.

After several failures by Calmar, Cook decided to enter the pump-making market itself. Cook ultimately developed the invention described in the patent at suit, the so-called "Scroggin patent," by adding a tiny lip to help seal the insecticide during shipment. In essence, Scroggin invented a finger-operated, leak-proof sprayer top. This arrangement allowed the consumer simply to remove the overcap and start killing insects immediately. Conveniently enough, Calmar later marketed a pump similar to that of Cook. Cook then sued its former supplier for patent infringement.

The trial court held the Scroggin patent not invalid and infringed, and the Eighth Circuit affirmed. The Supreme Court reversed, finding that the Scroggin patent would have been obvious in light of three prior art patents to Lohse, Mellon and Livingstone. Lohse and Mellon both taught the use of shipper-sprayers similar to that of Scroggin. The Livingstone patent, which was not before the examiner, concerned a seal designed to cover and protect pouring spots that functioned without the use of a gasket or washer. The Court rejected the argument that the Livingstone patent comprised nonanalogous art: "Closure devices in such a closely related art as pouring spouts for liquid containers are at the very least pertinent references."[14]

The Court then considered the proper scope of the Scroggin patent claims. Turning to the patent's prosecution history, or record of the dialogue between the examiner and applicant, the Court found that the examiner had imposed rejections based upon Lohse and Mellon. In response, Scroggin accepted claim limitations that confined the scope of his invention to two features. In the view of the Court, the first feature, "the space between the skirt of the overcap and the container cap," was taught by Mellon. Livingstone taught the second feature, "the substitution of a rib built into the collar to achieve a seal for a washer or gasket." Finally, the Court was unpersuaded that secondary considerations supported the patentability of the Scroggin patent. The patent rested on a narrow advance, already disclosed by Livingstone and available to anyone who had conducted a patent search. The Court concluded that the Scoggin patent would have been obvious under § 103.

The final case of the Trilogy, *United States v. Adams*,[15] appeared under a separate caption. Adams invented a battery employing cuprous chloride and magnesium, a combination of electrodes never previously placed in a single battery. The prior art did teach the use of zinc and silver chloride as electrode material in batteries, however, and that prior art further disclosed that cuprous chloride and silver chloride, as well as magnesium and zinc, were equivalent electrode materials. The Adams battery nonetheless possessed quite desirable characteristics over the prior art, to the extent that experts in the field initially expressed skepticism over its claimed abilities.

As part of the wartime effort, Adams notified the U.S. government about his battery. The Government ultimately employed Adams' battery design without notifying him. Years later, Adams learned of the use of his battery and brought suit in the predecessor to the Court of Federal Claims. The Court of Claims held the patent not invalid and infringed.

Following a grant of certiorari, the Government primarily relied upon six references before the Supreme Court. The Niadudet treatise and Hayes patent taught a battery with a zinc anode and a silver chloride cathode that could work in an electrolyte of pure water. The Wood patent described the possibility of substituting magnesium for zinc on the anode, while the Codd treatise indicated that magnesium was a theoretically desirable electrode. The Wensky patent taught a battery with zinc and copper electrodes, with cuprous chloride added as a salt in an electrolyte solution. Finally, the Skrivanoff patent described the use

---

14. *Id.* at 35.

15. 383 U.S. 39, 86 S.Ct. 708, 15 L.Ed.2d 572 (1966).

of a magnesium anode; a cathode pasted with, among other compounds, cuprous chloride; and an electrolyte of alcoline, chloro-chromate, or a permanganate strengthened with sulphuric acid. An expert for Adams testified that he met with first a fire, and then an explosion, when he attempted to assemble the Skrivanoff battery.

After reaching several preliminary issues, the Court concluded that the invention claimed by Adams would not have been obvious in light of the six Government references. Although it noted the extreme structural similarities between the claimed invention and the prior art, the Court was moved by the many advantages of the Adams battery. The Adams battery could be stored while dry and activated with ordinary water or salt water. It also operated well at extreme temperatures and delivered a constant voltage regardless of the rate at which current was withdrawn. Secondary considerations, such as the initial disbelief and ultimate acknowledgment of experts, as well as the inability of the PTO to find a single pertinent reference within the crowded battery art, also supported the nonobviousness of the Adams patent.

As we leave the Trilogy, it should be noted again that they comprise central opinions within the modern patent law. At least, the Federal Circuit has lent them great significance. Arguably the Supreme Court did not comprehend the importance of the Trilogy because, in subsequent cases such as and *Anderson's–Black Rock v. Pavement Salvage Co.*[16] and *Sakraida v. Ag Pro, Inc.,*[17] the Court seemed to apply its earlier "invention" standard. Upon the consolidation of patent appeals to the Federal Circuit, however, the court opted to follow the *Graham* test for nonobviousness. The Federal Circuit simply ignored without comment these intervening opinions, holding fast to the *Graham* test.

17.3.2.2 Nonobviousness at the Federal Circuit

Federal Circuit application of the nonobviousness standard has suggested various refinements worthy of note here. Although a conclusion of nonobviousness may be founded upon a single prior art reference, most nonobviousness analyses concern multiple references. The Federal Circuit has spoken in length about the circumstances in which teachings from multiple references may be combined in order to produce the claimed invention.

The most significant requirement is that some reason, suggestion, or motivation must have provided a person of ordinary skill in the art cause to combine the references to produce the claimed invention. The "reason, suggestion, or motivation" can come from the references themselves, knowledge known to the art, or "the nature of the problem to be solved, leading inventors to look to references relating to possible solutions to that problem."[18]

16. 396 U.S. 57, 90 S.Ct. 305, 24 L.Ed.2d 258 (1969).

17. 425 U.S. 273, 96 S.Ct. 1532, 47 L.Ed.2d 784 (1976).

18. Pro–Mold & Tool Co. v. Great Lakes Plastics, Inc., 75 F.3d 1568 (Fed.Cir.1996).

In imposing this requirement, the court seeks to guard against the use of hindsight. The inventor's specification should not be used as a blueprint in deciding nonobviousness.[19] "Care must be taken to avoid hindsight reconstruction by using 'the patent in suit as a guide through a maze of prior art references, combining the right references in the right way so as to achieve the result of the claims at suit.' "[20] To similar, but rather more abstract effect, the Federal Circuit counsels that in nonobviousness analyses, "the invention must be considered as a whole."[21] A proper nonobviousness analysis judges the claimed invention holistically, not by cobbling together the teachings of different references to match different claim limitations in a piecemeal fashion.

For example, suppose that Professor Gadget invents a combination lawn mower-metal detector device. Gadget reasons that homeowners will want to hunt for "buried treasure" as they periodically mow their lawns. On January 1, 2005, Professor Gadget files a patent application claiming that combination. During prosecution, the PTO examiner discovers a March 21, 2003, article in the *Journal of Beachcombing* that provides a full disclosure of the metal detector employed by Gadget. The PTO examiner also discovers a German patent, issued on December 13, 2002, that provides a detailed disclosure of a lawn mower of the type claimed by Gadget. Because both references were publicly available more than one year before the filing date of Gadget's application, they both quality as prior art under § 102(b) and may be considered for purposes of § 103. Without more, however, the PTO examiner cannot issue a proper rejection for obviousness. There must be some suggestion or motivation to combine the disclosures of the journal article and German patent. If the examiner found a third reference, say a textbook that generally suggested the possibility of installing metal detectors on lawn mowers, then the examiner could appropriately reject Gadget's application for obviousness.

Sometimes prior art references "teach away" from the solution realized by the inventor. Such references would discourage a person of ordinary skill in the art from pursuing the path taken by the inventor. The presence of prior art that "teaches away" supports the nonobviousness of the claimed invention.[22] For example, suppose that an article published by a respected scientist in a leading scholarly journal confidently predicts that "no one will ever be able to construct a gadget out of Compound X." If Professor Gizmo later accomplishes just that feat, then she may submit the journal article as evidence of the nonobviousness of her invention.

The final sentence of § 103(a) provides that "[p]atentability shall not be negatived by the manner in which the invention was made." This language was meant to overturn precedent requiring that the invention be realized in a "flash of genius." Methodological, persistent investiga-

19. Interconnect Planning Corp. v. Feil, 774 F.2d 1132, 1138 (Fed.Cir.1985).

20. Grain Processing Corp. v. American Maize–Products Co., 840 F.2d 902, 907 (Fed.Cir.1988).

21. Rockwell Int'l Corp. v. United States, 147 F.3d 1358 (Fed.Cir.1998).

22. Arkie Lures, Inc. v. Gene Larew Tackle, Inc., 119 F.3d 953 (Fed.Cir.1997).

tion may also yield a patentable invention.[23] Indeed, the Federal Circuit has held that lengthy periods of research preceding a claimed invention support a conclusion of nonobviousness.[24]

Section 103(a) mandates the assessment of nonobviousness from the perspective of "a person having ordinary skill in the art." The Federal Circuit has provided the following list of factors to be considered in determining the level of ordinary skill in the art:

(1) the educational level of the inventor;

(2) type of problems encountered in the art;

(3) prior art solutions to those problems;

(4) rapidity with which inventions are made;

(5) sophistication of the technology; and

(6) educational level of active workers in the field.[25]

Surprisingly few judicial opinions actually reach a specific determination of the level of ordinary skill in the art, however. For example, neither *Graham v. John Deere*, nor any of the other opinions comprising the Trilogy, actually tell us whether the level of skill in the art was that of a high school graduate or Ph.D. with post-doctoral studies and ten years of industry experience. In practice, the concept of "a person of ordinary skill in the art" seems more to remind judges to put themselves in the shoes of a skilled artisan, rather than compel a specific factual finding.

All things being equal, however, accused infringers typically seek to prove a high level of skill in the art. In developed arts with expert practitioners, many inventions would be routine. In contrast, patentees prefer that the level of ordinary skill in the art be that of a neophyte, to whom very little would be obvious.

The Federal Circuit often speaks of a "prima facie" case of obviousness. The prima facie case is a procedural tool of patent examination at the PTO.[26] During prosecution, the PTO examiner bears the burden of producing a prima facie case of obviousness, or some other ground denying patentability. If the examiner makes that showing, then the burden of going forward shifts to the applicant. Once the applicant produces rebuttal evidence, the examiner must determine the patentability of the invention on the totality of the record.[27] A prima facie case of obviousness ordinarily involves a showing that the teachings of the prior art would have suggested the claimed invention to a person of ordinary skill in the art.[28]

23. In re Dow Chemical Co., 837 F.2d 469 (Fed.Cir.1988).

24. Id.

25. Environmental Designs, Ltd. v. Union Oil Co., 713 F.2d 693, 696, 218 USPQ 865, 868 (Fed.Cir.1983), *cert. denied*, 464 U.S. 1043, 104 S.Ct. 709, 79 L.Ed.2d 173 (1984).

26. In re Piasecki, 745 F.2d 1468 (Fed. Cir.1984).

27. In re Oetiker, 977 F.2d 1443 (Fed. Cir.1992).

28. In re Rijckaert, 9 F.3d 1531 (Fed. Cir.1993).

17.3.2.3 Disfavored Frameworks for Nonobviousness

The Federal Circuit has cautioned against the use of two different frameworks when conducting a nonobviousness inquiry. The first is the so-called "*Winslow* Tableau." This standard, first depicted by the CCPA in *In re Winslow*,[29] called for the decision-maker to picture "the inventor as working in his shop with the prior art references—which he is presumed to know—hanging on the walls around him." The decision-maker would then determine whether the inventor would have readily achieved the combination that comprised the claimed subject matter.

The difficulty with this image is that it visualized the inventor in physical possession of only the most pertinent prior art, making a conclusion of nonobviousness of the claimed invention all too readily reached. Judge Rich recognized this difficulty in *In re Antle*,[30] where he noted that the *Winslow* tableau could not convey that helpful references would be interspersed alongside numerous unhelpful sources, and perhaps even references that taught away from the solution. It should also be stressed that the nonobviousness inquiry should be conducted from the perspective of a person of ordinary skill in the art, not of the actual inventor herself.

A second disapproved framework is the standard of "obvious to try," sometimes called "obvious to experiment."[31] An "obvious to try" situation exists when prior art references may be of interest to a skilled artisan who is attempting to achieve a desired result, but rather than sufficiently teaching how to obtain that result, the references simply invite further experimentation.[32] Where no suggestion indicates which of many possibilities was likely to be successful, it is inappropriate to conclude that a claimed invention would have been obvious simply because the inventor could have tried each of numerous possible choices until he eventually arrived at a successful result.[33]

For example, suppose that a reference suggests that a broad class of chemical compounds might prove useful for achieving a particular technical effect. However, the class of compounds has millions of individual members, and the reference offers no suggestion about which compound will prove successful. Such a reference is not germane to § 103(a), for it merely made each of the particular compounds "obvious to try" rather than obvious to the skilled artisan.

17.3.3 The Secondary Considerations

In *Graham*, the Court noted that "secondary considerations as commercial success, long felt but unresolved needs, failure of others, etc., might be utilized to give light to the circumstances surrounding the

29.   365 F.2d 1017 (CCPA 1966).

30.   444 F.2d 1168 (CCPA 1971).

31.   In re Dow Chemical Co., 837 F.2d 469 (Fed.Cir.1988).

32.   In re Eli Lilly & Co., 902 F.2d 943 (Fed.Cir.1990).

33.   In re O'Farrell, 853 F.2d 894 (Fed. Cir.1988).

origin of the subject matter sought to be patented."[34] The Court recognized that the secondary considerations "focus attention on economic and motivational rather than technical issues and are, therefore more susceptible of judicial treatment than are the highly technical facts often present in patent litigation."[35] The secondary considerations are believed to provide objective evidence of how interested industry actors perceived the claimed invention.[36]

The *Graham* Court noted that the secondary considerations were "indicia of obviousness or nonobviousness" that "may have relevancy" in particular cases.[37] Arguably the Federal Circuit has more eagerly employed them than this Supreme Court language would suggest.[38] According to the Federal Circuit, which appears to prefer the label "objective evidence of nonobviousness,"[39] the term "secondary" does not refer to the importance of the considerations. The term instead indicates that these considerations necessarily arise second in time, after the invention has been introduced in the market, in contrast to the other *Graham* factors which focus upon the "time the invention was made."[40] Accordingly, the Federal Circuit has instructed that secondary considerations must be considered in every case, both by the courts and PTO.[41]

For a secondary consideration to be accorded probative value, its proponent must establish a "nexus" between the evidence and the merits of the claimed invention.[42] The nexus requirement compels a showing of a legally and factually sufficient connection between the commercial success and the claimed invention.[43] The sorts of showings that will fulfill the nexus requirement accompany the following review of the usual secondary considerations.

17.3.3.1 Commercial Success

The Federal Circuit views an invention's commercial success as presenting strong evidence of nonobviousness. In such circumstances the marketplace is presumed to have provided others with ample incentive to perfect the invention, and their failure to do so suggests nonobviousness. The commercial success may occur abroad[44] and may have been enjoyed

---

34. 383 U.S. at 17–18.

35. *Id.* at 36.

36. Heidelberger Druckmaschinen AG v. Hantscho Commercial Products, Inc., 21 F.3d 1068 (Fed.Cir.1994).

37. 383 U.S. at 18.

38. *See* Robert P. Merges, *Commercial Success and Patent Standards: Economic Perspectives on Innovation*, 76 Cal. L. Rev. 805 (1988).

39. *See* Minnesota Mining & Mfg. Co. v. Johnson & Johnson Orthopaedics, Inc., 976 F.2d 1559 (Fed.Cir.1992).

40. Truswal Sys. Corp. v. Hydro–Air Eng'g, 813 F.2d 1207, 1212 (Fed.Cir.1987).

41. Custom Accessories, Inc. v. Jeffrey–Allan Industries, Inc., 807 F.2d 955 (Fed. Cir.1986).

42. Ashland Oil, Inc. v. Delta Resins & Refractories, Inc., 776 F.2d 281 (Fed.Cir. 1985), *cert. denied*, 475 U.S. 1017, 106 S.Ct. 1201, 89 L.Ed.2d 315 (1986).

43. Demaco Corp. v. F. Von Langsdorff Licensing Ltd., 851 F.2d 1387 (Fed.Cir. 1988).

44. Lindemann Maschinenfabrik GmbH v. American Hoist & Derrick Co., 730 F.2d 1452 (Fed. Cir. 1984).

by an infringer.[45] Evidence merely showing that the patentee sold a large number of goods supposedly embodying the claimed invention does not sufficiently demonstrate that the invention enjoyed commercial success.[46] The success must be due to the claimed features of the invention, rather than advertising, superior workmanship or other features within the commercialized technology, in order to fulfill the nexus requirement.

For example, suppose that Macrosoft, a software company with a huge share of the market for personal computer operating systems, begins selling data compression software. Macrosoft files a patent application and, in response to an examiner's rejection for obviousness, argues that it has sold several million copies of the software. It may be that many consumers simply bought the data compression software along with their operating system due to Macrosoft's general reputation, the assurance that the program would function with the Macrosoft operating system, or an irresistible Macrosoft advertising campaign. On the other hand, if Macrosoft presents expert testimony or purchaser affidavits explaining that the software was purchased due to the merits of the claimed invention, then its large sales will suggest a conclusion of nonobviousness.

17.3.3.2 Copying

If others copy the patented invention, then the courts have inferred that the invention would not have been obvious.[47] Otherwise the copyists would have copied a noninfringing prior art technology, or could have developed their own, noninfringing technology. Although copying may be a high form of flattery, other motivations may have inspired a copyist. For example, the copyist may have reasonably believed that the invention was unpatentable because it lacked novelty or would have been obvious. In such cases, this secondary consideration will not be accorded weight during the analysis.

Suppose, for example, that an inventor is awarded a patent on a new fuel filter. A large automobile manufacturer with ample resources precisely copies the patented filter. If the patentee can show that many different fuel filters were available within the public domain and that a noninfringing substitute could have readily been developed, a court would likely find that copying supports a conclusion of nonobviousness.

17.3.3.3 Licenses

The existence of licenses under the patented invention suggests that other industry actors believed the invention to be nonobvious.[48] Otherwise, they would have challenged the validity of the patent in the courts or at the PTO. In enforcing the nexus requirement, the courts will ensure that the competitors did not take a relatively inexpensive license

---

45. Syntex (U.S.A.) Inc. v. Paragon Optical Inc., 7 USPQ2d 1001 (D. Ariz. 1987).

46. In re Baxter Travenol Labs., 952 F.2d 388 (Fed. Cir. 1991).

47. Diamond Rubber Co. v. Consolidated Rubber Tire Co., 220 U.S. 428 (1991).

48. Eibel Process Co. v. Minnesota & Ontario Paper Co., 261 U.S. 45 (1923).

simply to avoid costly litigation, as part of a larger cross-licensing arrangement, or for other reasons that do not support the nonobviousness of the claimed invention.

Consider the hypothetical Pervasive Polymers, Inc., a company that enjoys a 70% market share in the polymer market. No other company in that market has more than a 2% market share. During infringement litigation, Pervasive Polymers argues that it has licensed the asserted patent to 20 different competitors. Twenty is an impressive number of patent licenses, but suppose the facts further indicate that these licenses involved the entire Pervasive Polymers portfolio of over 1200 patents. In addition, the terms of the licenses called for extremely reasonable royalty rates. In such a case, the aggressive licensing activities of Pervasive Polymers are not likely to be given weight during the nonobviousness analysis. Without further evidence, the court cannot assume that the licensees sought permission to use the asserted patent, as compared to another patent within the vast Pervasive Polymers portfolio. Perhaps the licensees simply wanted their much larger rival to leave them alone. On the other hand, if a number of competitors paid higher royalties in order to practice the subject matter of a particular patent, then such evidence is pertinent to nonobviousness.

17.3.3.4 Long–Felt Need

Sometimes an industry faces a technical problem that remains unresolved despite efforts to improve the situation. That the claimed invention solved this problem suggests that the invention was nonobvious.[49] The expressed need must correlate with the problem solved by the claimed invention in order to satisfy the nexus requirement.

For example, suppose that for several decades the semiconductor industry sought a way to mass produce inexpensive transistors. The concept of packaging the transistors in plastic held great promise, but for many years was hindered by various technical problems. If a patented invention solved these problems by providing an inexpensive method of packaging transistors in plastic, then the secondary consideration of long-felt need suggests the invention would not have been obvious.[50]

17.3.3.5 Praise and Skepticism

The skepticism of skilled artisans that the claimed invention could ever be achieved bolsters the case for nonobviousness.[51] Evidence that others initially doubted that the invention would produce the asserted results, or that the solution achieved by the invention was illogical or impossible, would support the patentability of the claimed invention. Similarly, recognition of the merits of the claimed invention by skilled artisans, varying from product evaluations to industry awards, also

49. Graham v. John Deere, 383 U.S. at 17–18.

50. *See* Texas Instruments, Inc. v. U.S. Int'l Trade Comm'n, 988 F.2d 1165, 26 USPQ2d 1018 (Fed. Cir. 1993).

51. Environmental Designs, Ltd. v. Union Oil Co., 713 F.2d 693 (Fed. Cir. 1983).

suggests the invention is patentable.[52] For example, in one case various representatives of multinational corporations referred to the patented product as "magical," "bewitching" and "remarkable"–high accolades indeed, suggesting that the claimed invention would not have been obvious.[53] Both the praise and doubt must relate to the technical features of the claimed invention for the nexus requirement to be satisfied.

17.3.3.6   Prior Failures of Others

Prior failures by skilled artisans who attempted to achieve the claimed invention also suggests nonobviousness.[54] For example, suppose that several teams of accomplished scientists had previously tried to invent a method of achieving room-temperature superconductivity, but failed. Ultimately an inventor discovers a way to achieve this effect. Demonstration that others had unsuccessfully tried where the inventor succeeded will bolster the case for nonobviousness. Because industrial demands often provoke individuals to research and experiment, the prior failures of others often enters into the obviousness analysis along with another secondary consideration, long-felt need.

This secondary consideration would seem to present potent proof of nonobviousness. Rather than hypothesizing about what skilled persons might have done years in the past, evidence of the prior failure of others seems to provide an actual glimpse into real-world capabilities. By demonstrating the prior failures of others, the proponent of the patent offers direct proof of facts that some of the other secondary considerations, such as commercial success and long-felt need, merely assume.

The relevance of the prior failures of others to the nonobviousness inquiry can be misleading, however. The standard of nonobviousness is judged from the perspective of the hypothetical person of ordinary skill in the art, not an actual individual. One especially salient difference between a person of ordinary skill and an actual individual is that the former is judged to know of the full contents of the prior art. Such knowledge is not likely attributable to any living person, or even a interdisciplinary team of inventors. As a consequence, evidence of the prior failures of others should be carefully scrutinized to ensure that it does not unfairly tip the obviousness analysis towards patentability.

17.3.3.7   Unexpected Results

The law does not require that an invention exhibit unexpected results to be patentable. But a finding that the invention does demonstrate superior and unexpected properties suggests nonobviousness.[55] For example, suppose that manufacturers produce "safety glass" by coating ordinary glass with a protective layer of chemicals. The field has long

52. Akzo N.V. v. U.S. Int'l Trade Comm'n, 808 F.2d 1471, 1481 (Fed. Cir. 1986).

53. W.L. Gore & Associates, Inc. v. Garlock, Inc., 721 F.2d 1540, 220 USPQ 303 (Fed. Cir. 1983).

54. Graham v. John Deere, 383 U.S. at 17–18.

55. *American Hoist & Derrick Co. v. Sowa & Sons*, 725 F.2d 1350 (Fed. Cir. 1984).

operated under the assumption that the thicker the coating of protective layer applied to the glass, the stronger the resulting glass. By demonstrating that the use of thinner coatings led to dramatically stronger automobile glass, an inventor has bolstered her case for patentability by showing unexpected results.

The policy rationale for use of this secondary consideration is straightforward: Something that would have been surprising to a person of ordinary skill in a particular art would probably not have been obvious. Whether a result is unexpected or not is judged from the perspective of the person of ordinary skill in the art.

17.3.4 Nonobviousness in Chemistry and Biotechnology

The law of nonobviousness applies with equal force to inventions from the chemical and biotechnological arts as it does to inventions from other disciplines.[56] However, the unpredictable nature of these arts often lends complexity to nonobviousness analyses. A recurring problem is that a newly-synthesized chemical compound may possess a very similar structure to compounds well known to the art. In other words, the claimed and prior art compounds may have nearly identical chemical formulae. Yet the two compounds may display widely varying behaviors, technical effects or properties. Whether the newly synthesized compounds should be judged nonobvious in the sense of § 103(a) is an issue that has long plagued the courts. This issue has also arisen in terms of PTO practice. The extent to which a prima facie case must consider the chemical properties of the prior art and claimed compounds, in addition to their structure, has been of great procedural importance.

The Federal Circuit took up these issues *en banc* in *In re Dillon.*[57] Dillon had claimed compositions containing tetra-orthoesthers useful as fuel additives to reduce fuel emissions. The PTO had rejected her application based upon prior art that disclosed structurally similar tetra-orthoestheters. The prior art taught that these compounds should be added to fuels, but in order to obtain the benefit of dewatering. The majority held that a prima facie case of nonobviousness was created when there was "structural similarity between claimed and prior art subject matter, proved by combining references or otherwise, where the prior art gives reason or motivation to make the claimed compositions." The applicant or patentee then possessed the burden of rebutting the prima facie case, and would be able to submit evidence that the claimed compound possessed new properties or improved properties that were unexpected. The ultimate question of nonobviousness depended upon consideration of the structure and all of the properties of the claimed composition.

Method claims have also raised perplexing issues with regard to chemistry and biotechnology. It is often the case that skilled artisans

---

56. *See* In re Johnson, 747 F.2d 1456, 1460 (Fed.Cir.1984).

57. 919 F.2d 688 (Fed.Cir.1990), *cert. denied*, 500 U.S. 904, 111 S.Ct. 1682, 114 L.Ed.2d 77 (1991).

would have been readily able to generate a new chemical compound or biotechnological product, using well-known, conventional processes, once they were told the precise composition of a given end product. However, they would have lacked motivation to perform this process without knowledge of the special properties of the new product. In terms of the patent law, the question then becomes whether claims directed towards such a method of making would have been obvious. In one sense, since the method is being used to produce a novel and nonobvious product, the method too must be novel and nonobvious. But on the other hand, if the process is used in a conventional way to generate a product, perhaps we should view the process as novel but not necessarily nonobvious. In appropriate cases, the same reasoning applies not just to end products, but also to starting materials.

A simple analogy may focus attention on the nub of this problem.[58] Consider a team of botanists which jointly invents a new sort of fruit hybrid, such as a fanciful "appleberry." They file an application at the PTO claiming the appleberry and a method of making an appleberry pie. Plainly the applicants' appleberry pie recipe is novel. Indeed, it could not have possibly existed prior to the invention of the appleberry. But should the mere substitution of a new filling entitle the botanists to a patent on a method of making a fruit pie? The rejection of the botanists' method claims on the ground of nonobviousness amounts to the policy judgment that they should not.

The Federal Circuit addressed these issues in *In re Durden.*[59] There, the applicants had filed applications claiming oxime compounds, insecticidal carbamate compounds, and a process for producing the carbamate compounds using the oxime compounds as starting materials. Patents had issued on the oxime and carbamate compounds, but the PTO had rejected the process claims over a prior art patent.

On appeal, the applicants conceded that "the claimed process, apart from the fact of employing a novel and unobvious starting material and apart from the fact of producing a new and unobvious product, is obvious." The Federal Circuit stated the issue to be resolved as "whether a chemical process, otherwise obvious, is patentable *because* either or both the specific starting material employed and the product obtained, are novel and unobvious." The court affirmed the rejection, concluding that:

> Of course, an otherwise old process becomes a *new* process when a previously unknown starting material, for example, is used in it which is then subjected to a conventional manipulation or reaction to produce a product which may also be *new*, albeit the *expected* result of what is done. But it does not necessarily mean that the whole process has become *unobvious* in the sense of § 103. In short, a *new* process may still be obvious, even when considered "as a whole," notwithstanding the specific starting

58. *See* ROBERT P. MERGES, PATENT LAW AND POLICY 606 (2d. ed. 1997).

59. 763 F.2d 1406 (Fed.Cir.1985).

material or resulting product, or both, is not to be found in the prior art.[60]

Durden proved burdensome precedent for actors in the recombinant biotechnology industry. Broadly speaking, recombinant technologies involve the alteration of a host cell so that it produces a desirable protein. The resulting products, including erythropoietin, interferon, and tissue plasminogen activator (tPA), are identical or similar to naturally occurring products. As such, the valuable protein product is often not patent eligible in and of itself.[61] Biotechnologists do claim the transformed host cells as a sort of "machine" capable of producing a desirable protein. They also seek to claim the method of making the end product. Biotechnologists discovered significant opposition to such method claims within the PTO, however. Based upon *Durden*, many examiners rejected such claims because the process of obtaining desirable protein products from transformed host cells is ordinarily well understood by skilled artisans. This set of skills applies even to host cells that are themselves patentable starting materials.[62]

Congress responded by enacting the Biotechnological Process Patents Act of 1995.[63] This legislation created § 103(b), a complex statute that applicants may elect to employ. Section 103(b) provides that a "biotechnological process" that uses or results in a novel, nonobvious composition of matter will be considered nonobvious if (1) the inventor files an application or applications claiming the process and the composition of matter at the same time; and (2) the process and composition of matter were owned by the same person at the time they were invented. The term "biotechnological process" is elaborately defined to tie the statute to contemporary biotechnology research, including such processes as "cell fusion procedures yielding a cell line that expresses a specific protein, such as a monoclonal antibody."

The Federal Circuit opinion in *In re Ochiai*,[64] issued just a few weeks after Congress enacted § 103(b), suggests that this legislative effort may have been unnecessary. Claim 6 of Ochiai's application recited a process for preparing a cephem compound. Although the cephem compound generated by this process was novel and nonobvious, the PTO reasoned that the process recited in claim 6 would have been obvious. Several prior art references taught the use of an extremely similar process to create a slightly different final product than claimed by Ochiai. The PTO concluded that the holding of *Durden* mandated the rejection of claim 6.

On appeal, the Federal Circuit reversed the PTO rejection. The court reasoned that the claimed starting material was unknown to skilled artisans prior to the filing of Ochiai's application. The court then concluded that although the claimed method was extremely similar to

60. 763 F.2d at 1410.

61. *See supra* § 14.3.1.

62. *See* Jeremy (Je) Zhe Zhang, In re Ochiai, In re Brouwer *and the Biotechnology Process Patent Act of 1995: The End of*

the Durden *Legacy?*, 37 IDEA: J.L. & Tech. 405, 415 (1997).

63. Pub. L. 104–41, 109 Stat. 351.

64. 71 F.3d 1565 (Fed.Cir.1995).

teachings of the prior art, the prior art nonetheless offered no suggestion or motivation to perform the claimed process. According to the *Ochiai* panel, "[s]imilarity is . . . not necessarily obviousness." The court distinguished *Durden*, stating that it presented no more than an application of the general rule "that section 103 requires a fact-intensive comparison of the claimed process with the prior art rather than the mechanical application of another *per se* rule." Because nonobviousness cases involve complex factual issues and "applications of a unitary legal regime to different claims and fields of art to yield particularized results," reasonable persons could well disagree about the outcome of a particular nonobviousness determination.

The PTO Commissioner responded to *Ochiai* with a Notice that resembled a sigh of relief. Recognizing the holding of *Ochiai*, the Commissioner discouraged use of § 103(b) and additionally announced that the PTO would not issue regulations to implement that statute. Instead, applicants wishing to employ the statute were invited to petition the Commissioner. The Notice further instructed examiners that "language in a process claim which recites making or using a unobvious product must be treated as a material limitation."

Although difficult to reconcile with *Durden*, *Ochiai* has been favorably received by most commentators. Nonetheless, its consistency with the congressional intent underlying § 103(b) may be questioned. Congress enacted § 103(b) as a narrow provision that solved a specific problem for a single industry. More broadly worded proposals that would have applied to all technologies had been considered and rejected. For example, because Ochiai's application involved a chemical technology, it would not be considered a "biotechnological process" under the statute ultimately enacted. Plainly *Ochiai*'s holding considerably opens up what Congress had crafted as a narrow exception to the prevailing case law.

17.3.5 Synopsis

The following example summarizes important nonobviousness concepts. Assume that an inventor, Bramer, files a patent application claiming an electrical circuit on July 1, 2003. The circuit is used as a digital signal processor in home stereo systems. It consists of two sub-circuits: an amplifier, followed by a filter.

The PTO examiner first considers Bramer's application on February 15, 2004. The examiner immediately locates two pertinent references. The first, a magazine article authored by Haas and published on March 21, 2001, describes the identical amplifier claimed by Bramer. Haas states that this amplifier is useful in high-voltage electrical power systems. The second is a U.S. patent that issued to Cline on February 1, 2004. The Cline patent matured from an application filed on April 1, 2003, and describes, but does not claim, the identical filter claimed by Bramer. Cline's patent also concerns home stereo systems.

Although the Haas and Cline references describe the components of Bramer's claimed invention, the examiner determines that neither reference suggests the desirability of combining the two elements. The examiner therefore cites a third reference, an engineering textbook authored by Jones and published on September 1, 1995. Jones concerns the design of signal processing circuits and generally discusses the desirability of combining amplifiers with filters to process digital signals. With these references available under § 102, the examiner has generated a prima facie case of obviousness under § 103(a).

Although Bramer may offer a number of responses to the examiner's rejection, two options suggest themselves in particular.[65] First, Bramer may attempt to demonstrate that at least one of the references cited by the examiner is not pertinent prior art for nonobviousness. If Bramer can remove any of the references as prior art, then the examiner must withdraw the entire nonobviousness rejection. Both Haas and Jones are prior art under § 102(b), as they were both published before Bramer's critical date of July 1, 2002. However, the Cline patent is available as prior art only under § 102(e). Bramer may be able to antedate Cline by filing a Rule 131 affidavit. He would have to prove that he invented the claimed subject matter prior to Cline's filing date of April 1, 2003.[66]

Bramer may also argue that the Haas reference comprises nonanalogous art. Bramer could urge that high-voltage electrical power systems do not arise from the same field of endeavor as home stereo systems, nor was Haas reasonably pertinent to the particular problem faced by Bramer. The success of this argument depends upon additional facts beyond the scope of this example.

If Bramer cannot remove any of the references as prior art, his second option is to offer a substantive argument of nonobviousness. In the language of the patent community, such arguments on the merits are termed a "traverse." These arguments typically invoke an expert's opinion that skilled artisans would not have found the claimed invention obvious in light of the prior art. Bramer may also submit evidence of any secondary considerations that support the nonobviousness of his invention. Given the close correspondence between the prior art and the claimed invention here, Bramer's attempt to traverse the examiner's rejection seems unlikely to prevail, but his arguments must be judged in light of a full consideration of the *Graham* test and § 103(a).

---

65. Bramer could also amend the claims of the application, narrowing them so as to avoid the combined teachings of the prior art references. As well, Bramer could abandon the application.

66. *See supra* § 16.3.1.

Chapter 18

THE PATENT INSTRUMENT

Table of Sections

Patents may be distinguished from other intellectual property rights in that they necessarily arise from a formal application process. Individuals must present written applications to the PTO in order to secure proprietary interests in their inventions. These applications may ultimately mature into issued patent instruments, the documents that form the basis of individual patent rights. The Patent Code mandates the contents of each patent instrument in § 112, a statute comprised of six unnumbered paragraphs. The first two of these paragraphs are of central significance to the patent project.

The first paragraph of § 112 requires that the patent instrument disclose the invention. The patent community commonly refers to that portion of the patent instrument describing the invention as the "specification" or "description." Section 112 ¶ 1 subjects the specification to three requirements. First, the specification must enable skilled artisans to make and use the invention. Second, the specification must contain a "written description" of the invention, sufficient to show that the inventor had accomplished the invention at the time he filed the application. Finally, the specification must detail the "best mode" contemplated by the inventor. This text reviews these three requirements in § 18.1 below.

The second paragraph of § 112 requires that the specification "conclude with one or more claims particularly pointing out and distinctly claiming the subject matter which the applicant regards as his invention." Although the claims technically form part of the specification, patent practitioners commonly refer to the specification and claims as distinct portions of the patent instrument. This is so because the claims are the most important part of the patent instrument, setting forth the proprietary rights possessed by the patentee. Section 112 ¶ 2 sets forth the requirement of definiteness, a mandate that claims be sufficiently precise so that others may have notice of the scope of the patentee's proprietary interest.

The remaining paragraphs of § 112 also concern the claims. The third through fifth paragraphs of § 112 set interpretational standards for the construction of so-called "dependent claims." Dependent claims recite the contents of an earlier, independent claim, but then continue to provide further limitations. In addition, § 112 ¶ 6 concerns a particular sort of claim format, so-called "means-plus-function" claims. Claims are reviewed in § 18.2 below.

§ 18.1   The Specification

Each patent instrument must include a specification that explains the invention in detail. Although the patent statute does not mandate a particular format for the specification, the PTO has promulgated regulations setting forth a standard ordering, including such components as a title, abstract, and a detailed textual description of the invention.[1] Drawings should be included "where necessary to the understanding of the subject matter sought to be patented."[2] The statute does require that the specification fulfill three essential requirements, however: enablement, written description, and best mode, each of which is discussed at length below.

18.1.1   Enablement

Section 112 ¶ 1 provides that the specification must "enable any person skilled in the art to which it pertains, or with which it is most nearly connected, to make and use" the claimed invention. Some commentators have viewed the enablement requirement as presenting a contract between the inventor and the public.[3] In exchange for the

§ 18.1

1. 37 C.F.R. § 1.77.

2. 35 U.S.C. § 113 (2000).

3. *See* Orin S. Kerr, *Rethinking Patent Law in the Administrative State*, 42 WM. & MARY L. REV. 127 (2000).

exclusive rights granted by a patent, an inventor must enrich the art such that other persons may practice his invention. A detailed example of a specific embodiment of the invention, along with a more general description of its mode of operation or technical principles, typically suffices to fulfill the enablement requirement.

The courts have traditionally read the enablement requirement to mandate that a skilled artisan be able to practice the claimed invention without undue experimentation.[4] Whether the amount of required experimentation will be considered undue depends upon such factors as the complexity of the invention, the predictability of the art, the amount of guidance provided in the specification and the knowledge of practitioners in the field. Courts base the enablement requirement upon the exercise of ordinary skill and the reasonableness of the efforts needed to practice the claimed invention.

For example, suppose that noted software tycoons Gil Bates and Steve Hobbes obtain a patent relating to a computerized inventory control system. Among the elements of the claimed invention is a computer program that coordinates suppliers, warehousers and retailers. Suppose further that the patent does not disclose a detailed, line-by-line listing of software code written in a particular programming language. Bates and Hobbes instead set forth high-level flow charts and a more abstract description of the program expressed in English.

So long as the Bates and Hobbes disclosure would allow a skilled computer programmer to develop functional software through ordinary efforts in a reasonable amount of time, their patent will be judged enabling. Although a program listing within the Bates and Hobbes specification would render the matter more certain, it is not required provided that the description sufficiently allows persons of ordinary skill to practice the invention. That different programmers might work out the details of the disclosed software in different ways is irrelevant to whether Bates and Hobbes met the enablement requirement. Similarly, that a highly skilled computer scientist might be able to generate software superior to that described in the specification has no bearing on the enablement inquiry.[5]

The Bates and Hobbes example illustrates that patents need not disclose information well understood by knowledgeable artisans. As patent specifications are directed towards persons of skill in the art, they need not, and for purposes of brevity preferably do not, start from the most elementary principles and work their way to the claimed technology.[6] The Federal Circuit has also held that patent specifications need not constitute detailed production documents. Exacting manufacturing data

4. In re Vaeck, 947 F.2d 488 (Fed.Cir. 1991).

5. *See* Northern Telecom, Inc. v. Datapoint Corp., 908 F.2d 931 (Fed.Cir.1990); White Consolidated Indus., Inc. v. Vega Servo–Control, Inc., 713 F.2d 788 (Fed.Cir. 1983).

6. Hybritech Inc. v. Monoclonal Antibodies, Inc., 802 F.2d 1367 (Fed.Cir.1986), *cert. denied*, 480 U.S. 947, 107 S.Ct. 1606, 94 L.Ed.2d 792 (1987).

concerning the dimensions, tolerances and other parameters of mass production need not be disclosed.[7]

The specification must be enabling at the time the inventor filed his application. Subsequent progress in the state of the art should not be considered in determining whether an earlier filed application or patent fulfills the enablement requirement.[8] The unusual facts in *Gould v. Hellwarth*,[9] which involves one of the famous series of applications on laser technology filed by Gordon Gould, illustrate this principle. This appeal resulted from an interference declared between Gould and a Dr. Hellwarth. The count of the interference related to a so-called "Q-switch," a device for controlling laser emissions.

Interestingly, neither party submitted the usual evidence of inventive activity common to interferences. With both sides relying solely upon their filing dates, one would suspect that Gould, the senior party, would prevail. But Hellwarth offered another argument: that although the Q-switch disclosure was adequate in and of itself, as of Gould's 1959 filing date neither Gould nor anyone else could build an operable laser. As a result, Hellwarth urged that Gould's application did not meet the enablement requirement. This contention was a clever one for Hellwarth, who had filed his application in 1961 after Hughes Aircraft, Bell Laboratories and other entities had constructed operating lasers.

The Board of Interferences agreed with Hellwarth, and on appeal the CCPA affirmed. Writing for the court, Judge Lane agreed that Gould's application did not contain a set of parameters sufficient to construct a laser. Although Gould did list ruby as a possible laser medium, a forecast that proved accurate, necessary data such as the type, size and orientation of the ruby crystal were absent. The fact that numerous actors, including leading members of the U.S. technological community, failed to produce a laser until 1960 further supported the conclusion that the Gould application offered insufficient guidance. This result may seem harsh, particularly since we know that Gould's Q-switch actually worked quite well once the industry finally generated a functioning laser. But Gould's broad claims did plainly recite laser activity, which in 1959 fell more in the realm of speculative fiction than scientific reality.

Whether a particular specification is enabling must always be understood in relationship to what has been claimed. Patented subject matter must be enabled to the full breadth of a particular claim.[10] This rule does not often present problems for inventors operating in predictable fields like mechanics or electronics. Using well-known physical laws and the knowledge of these disciplines, skilled artisans may not only construct alternative embodiments, but foresee their performance without difficulty.

7. Christianson v. Colt Industries Operating Corp., 822 F.2d 1544 (Fed.Cir.1987).

8. *See* In re Goodman, 11 F.3d 1046 (Fed.Cir.1993).

9. 472 F.2d 1383 (CCPA 1973).

10. In re Wright, 999 F.2d 1557 (Fed. Cir.1993).

In unpredictable arts such as biotechnology and some branches of chemistry, however, the courts have been more strict in judging whether a particular disclosure supports a broadly drafted claim. In these less certain fields, small changes to the structure of the invention may lead to vastly different behaviors. For example, a very minor alteration to a functional chemical compound may render it inert or useless for a particular purpose. As such, patent specifications within unpredictable arts must provide more than a few illustrations in order to support a broadly drafted, generic claim. Instead, the specification must show with reasonable specificity how to practice the invention across the entire scope of the claim.[11]

The balance between enablement and claim breadth is well illustrated by *In re Wright*,[12] a biotechnology case. Wright filed an application describing processes for producing live, non-pathogenic vaccines against RNA viruses, as well as methods for their use. The description within Wright's specification was much more narrow, however, detailing only the use of a recombinant vaccine that conferred immunity in chickens against the Prague Avian Sarcoma Virus. The Federal Circuit affirmed the allowance of claims directed towards the specifically disclosed process, but disallowed much broader claims reciting methods of protecting living organisms against RNA viruses. Based upon the level of skill in the art as of the February 1983 filing date, Judge Rich reasoned that Wright's application offered skilled artisans no more than an invitation to engage in lengthy experimentation. According to the court, Wright's success against a particular strain of an avian RNA virus could not be extrapolated with a reasonable expectation of success to the subject matter of the rejected claims.

Although previous patent practice required applicants to prepare models or exhibits to accompany the specification, the PTO today strongly discourages these submissions. While the PTO retains the authority to require applicants to submit specimens for purposes of exhibit or inspection, it exercises that power only in rare cases.[13]

An exception to the rule disfavoring the submission of samples exists with regard to biological inventions. When an invention depends upon the use of living materials such as microorganisms or cultured cells, a mere written account within a patent specification may not suffice to enable others conveniently to make and use the invention. A sample of the biological material itself is needed. In such cases the patent applicant must submit these materials to one of a number of recognized biological depositories. Upon request, the depositories distribute samples to interested members of the public.[14]

Patent specifications typically describe so-called "working examples" that correspond to results actually achieved by the inventor.

11. PPG Industries, Inc. v. Guardian Industries Corp., 75 F.3d 1558 (Fed.Cir.1996).

12. 999 F.2d 1557, 27 USPQ2d 1510 (Fed.Cir.1993).

13. 35 U.S.C. § 114.

14. *See* In re Lundak, 773 F.2d 1216 (Fed.Cir.1985).

However, specifications may also contain simulated or predicted illustrations. Known in the patent law as "prophetic examples," such "paper experiments" may contribute to enablement so long as they actually aid those of ordinary skill in the art to achieve the invention.

One of the more explosive opinions in patent law, *Atlas Powder Co. v. E.I. du Pont De Nemours & Co.*,[15] exemplifies the effect of prophetic examples and the workings of the enablement requirement more generally. Atlas obtained a patent claiming water-resistant blasting agents and sought to enforce it against DuPont. The claim called for the mixture of such ingredients as salts, fuels and emulsifiers to form an emulsion. The patent's specification then offered numerous particular examples of each sort of ingredient.

Among DuPont's defenses was that the patent was invalid for lack of enablement. It seems that if a particular salt, fuel and emulsifier were chosen indiscriminately, the resulting mixture wouldn't necessarily achieve an explosive with the desired properties. Further, although Atlas scientists had performed approximately 300 experiments while perfecting the emulsion, Atlas described additional experiments that it had actually not conducted.

Initially, the combination of numerous failures and prophetic examples would suggest a finding of undue experimentation. The Federal Circuit nonetheless affirmed the finding of the district court that the Atlas patent contained an enabling disclosure. Both courts agreed that the prophetic examples were closely tied to actual experiments, with slight modifications introduced with the expectation of achieving better outcomes. Judge Baldwin further noted that patents need not teach optimal results in order to fulfill the enablement requirement, but instead must provide enough description to enable the invention to work for its intended purpose. Because the combination of compounds that were described worked most of the time, the Atlas patent met this requirement. Additionally, the Federal Circuit found that a skilled chemist would know how to modify unsatisfactory compounds in order to form a superior emulsion. In sum, skill in the art in this predictable field readily bridged any gaps in the Atlas patent disclosure.

18.1.2 Written Description

A U.S. patent must include a "written description" of the invention claimed therein under § 112 ¶ 1. The written description requirement has been recognized as distinct from enablement, which considers whether the patent instrument allows persons of skill in the art to practice the claimed invention without undue experimentation. The written description requirement instead concerns whether the inventor had possession, as of the filing date of the application, of the subject matter that he claims.

15.   750 F.2d 1569 (Fed.Cir.1984).

The great majority of written description cases involve amendments to claims made during the course of prosecution at the PTO. When claims are amended after the original filing date—either in their entirety or through alterations to earlier claims—the "written description" test seeks to determine if the additional material was disclosed somewhere in the original application. The written description requirement ensures that inventors do not improperly augment their patents by including subsequent technical advances in a previously filed application.

The written description requirement is best understood in the context of other conditions that an applicant must fulfill to obtain patent protection. Most prominent of these is 35 U.S.C. § 102(b), which bars a patent if the invention was in public use, on sale or subject to other specified events more than one year prior to the filing date.[16] Under § 102(b), the filing date of a particular application is crucial. But if applications could be freely amended after filing, then inventors might be sorely tempted to tack late developments onto earlier filed applications. This subterfuge would allow inventors to take unfair advantage of an early filing date, avoiding the impact of § 102(b). Similarly, because an application's filing date is considered a constructive reduction to practice, this tactic would allow inventors to unfairly avoid prior art references and obtain priority of invention under § 102(a), (e) and (g).[17]

The written description requirement guards against these abuses by ensuring that later amendments find support in earlier filings. If the amendments in fact contain information that was not previously disclosed, the amendment will be judged for prior art and other purposes as of the date it was actually filed. Most importantly, the benefit of the filing date of an earlier patent application will not be awarded.

Application of Barker,[18] a 1977 CCPA case, demonstrates the impact of the written description requirement. Barker filed an application directed towards a method of making prefabricated panels of shingles. Barker's invention concerned the construction of shingle panels with a length of 48 inches. As industry standards called for 16–inch gaps between roofing studs, prefabricated panels could then be easily used to cover three successive gaps during housing construction. The specification called for the construction of panels comprised of either eight or sixteen shingles. At some point following his initial filing, Barker filed an amendment with the PTO adding claim 18 to his application. Claim 18 recited a method of making prefabricated shingle panels with "at least six shingles." The PTO Board rejected claim 18 as not within the written description of the original application.

The CCPA affirmed the decision of the Board. According to the majority opinion of Judge Miller, the specification and drawings showed only panels consisting of eight or sixteen shingles. The use of a different

16. *See supra* § 16.2.
17. *See supra* § 16.3.

18. 559 F.2d 588, 194 USPQ 470 (CCPA 1977).

number of shingles simply was not articulated until the filing of claim 18, and as such the written description requirement was not fulfilled.

Barker keenly illustrates the differences between enablement and written description. As urged by Judge Markey in his vigorous dissent, this invention was clearly enabled by the disclosure. A person with expertise in the construction trade, and indeed even one of little skill, could have readily prefabricated a panel using any number of shingles upon reviewing Barker's patent application. The only practical restraint was that the combined shingles needed to reach a total length of 48 inches. Yet because Barker disclosed only the use of eight or sixteen shingles, he could not later claim a panel comprised of at least six shingles. Note that Barker was not left entirely without recourse with respect to claim 18. If he opted to follow the appropriate procedural steps at the PTO, claim 18 could be judged as of the date Barker entered his amendment for novelty and other purposes.

Written description cases such as *Barker* often refer to the concept of "new matter." This phrase appears in § 132 of the patent statute, which provides that "[n]o amendment shall introduce new matter into the disclosure of the invention."[19] Although new matter and written description present closely related concepts, they are not interchangeable. Section 132 prohibits the introduction of new matter into the disclosure of an application. Section 112 ¶ 1 requires that claim language be supported by a written description in the specification. The proper basis for rejection of a claim amended to recite elements thought to be without support in the original disclosure is § 112 ¶ 1, not § 132.[20]

Although most written description cases concern amendments to claims during prosecution at the PTO, a handful of Federal Circuit opinions have found written description violations even where the claims were originally filed with an application. At the time this treatise goes to press, most of these opinions have involved biotechnological inventions.[21] Representative of this line of cases is *Regents of the University of California v. Eli Lilly and Co.*,[22] which concerned a pioneering patent directed to the recombinant production of insulin.

The University of California filed the application that led to the patent-in-suit in 1977. The University based the application upon its cloning of the rat insulin gene. At this point, the University had determined and isolated the appropriate complementary DNA sequences found in rats, but not in humans. Although the University patent included a prophetic example describing a method that could be used to isolate human insulin-encoding complementary DNA, University researchers did not actually accomplish this feat until nearly two years after the 1977 filing date. As originally filed, the patent included both

19. 35 U.S.C. § 132 (2000).

20. In re Rasmussen, 650 F.2d 1212 (CCPA 1981).

21. *See* Fiers v. Revel, 984 F.2d 1164 (Fed.Cir.1993); Amgen, Inc. v. Chugai Phar-maceutical Co., 927 F.2d 1200 (Fed.Cir. 1991).

22. 119 F.3d 1559 (Fed.Cir.1997), *cert. denied*, 523 U.S. 1089, 118 S.Ct. 1548, 140 L.Ed.2d 695 (1998).

broad claims directed towards complementary DNA encoding vertebrate or mammalian insulin, as well as a narrower claim specifically reciting complementary DNA encoding human insulin. When the University brought suit against Eli Lilly for patent infringement in 1990, among Eli Lilly's defenses was that the patent did not contain a written description of the claimed invention.

The Federal Circuit agreed that the University patent did not comply with the written description requirement. According to Judge Lourie, the patent's failure to describe the claimed complementary DNA through its relevant structural or physical characteristics amounted to a fatal defect. The fact that the patent defined the claimed complementary DNA functionally, by the insulin it could be used to produce, was more a statement of result rather than a description of what the patented invention was. The court noted that many possible gene sequences might achieve this outcome. The court suggested that in order to fulfill the written description requirement, the University should have disclosed the complete and correct nucleotide sequence comprising the complementary DNA.

The applicability of the written description requirement to cases such as *Regents v. Eli Lilly* has proven controversial. Commentators have urged that the written description requirement should not concern originally-filed claims, which under § 112 ¶ 2 form part of the specification. In addition, the requirement that patents must expressly specify the nucleotide sequence of any claimed DNA arguably places a higher standard of disclosure for the protection of genetic materials than exists for other sorts of inventions.[23] The Federal Circuit might have achieved the same result in this case by concluding that the University had not constructively reduced the claimed invention to practice by the 1977 filing date, or perhaps by finding that the patent did not fulfill the enablement requirement. In any event, this new interpretation of the written description requirement appears entrenched in the patent law, as evidenced by PTO attempts to develop guidelines so that examiners may follow *Regents v. Eli Lilly* and related precedent.[24]

18.1.3 Best Mode

The final requirement of § 112 ¶ 1 is that the specification "set forth the best mode contemplated by the inventor of carrying out his invention." The best mode requirement ensures that the public receives the most advantageous implementation of the technology known to the inventor, allowing competitors to compete with the patentee on equal footing after the patent expires. Typically the best mode requirement

---

23. *See* Janice M. Mueller, *The Evolving Application of the Written Description Requirement to Biotechnological Inventions,* 13 BERKELEY TECH. L.J. 615, 633 (1998).

24. *See* Department of Commerce, Patent and Trademark Office, *Request for*

Comments on Interim Guidelines for Patent Applications Under the 35 U.S.C. 112–1 "Written Description" Requirement, 63 FED. REG. 32639 (June 15, 1998).

compels inventors to disclose information that might otherwise be maintained as a trade secret.

The leading case on the best mode requirement is *Chemcast Corp. v. Arco Industries Corp.*[25] The inventor, Rubright, formerly worked for the accused infringer, Arco. He later left to start his own company, the plaintiff Chemcast. While at Chemcast, Rubright invented and obtained a patent on a grommet designed to seal an opening in a sheet metal panel. When Chemcast asserted that Arco infringed the Rubright patent, Arco contended that the patent failed to disclose the best mode known to Rubright. Specifically, Arco urged that the absence of the type, hardness, supplier and trade name of material used to make the locking portion of the grommet was fatal to the patent.

The Federal Circuit agreed with Arco that Chemcast's patent rubbed it the wrong way. The court initially set forth an influential two-part test for determining whether a patent specification fulfills the best mode requirement. The first inquiry was whether the inventor knew of a mode of practicing the claimed invention that he considered superior to any other. If this first, subjective standard was met, then a court should enter into a second, objective inquiry: does the specification identify, and disclose sufficient information to enable persons of skill in the art to practice, the best mode?

Considering the first, subjective inquiry, the *Chemcast* court affirmed the finding that Rubright preferred a rigid PVC composition, available under the trade name R–4467, for use in the locking portion of the grommet. Indeed, as this material had been developed specifically for Chemcast at some expense, Rubright likely found his knowledge of a best mode difficult to deny. Proceeding to the second prong of the best mode inquiry, the court also found Rubright's specification wanting. His patent failed to disclose R–4467, its supplier in the marketplace, or even the preferred material hardness. Although the inventor did discuss the use of PVC at a 70 or higher on the Shore A scale, this material was three hardness scales away from his preferred material hardness and was manifestly inferior. The reader of the opinion is left with the impression that R–4667 was a very valuable trade secret and that the inventor's specification almost misled those who wished to practice the invention.

The two-part test articulated in *Chemcast* demonstrates that the best mode requirement is distinct from enablement. Enablement forms an objective standard that focuses upon knowledge of persons of ordinary skill in the art, while the best mode requirement includes a subjective component that stresses the knowledge of the inventor. As can be readily appreciated, a patent may contain an enabling disclosure yet not provide the best mode.

For example, suppose that the noted food chemist Rhonda Ramon obtains a patent claiming a method of making fried instant noodles. The

25. 913 F.2d 923 (Fed.Cir.1990).

application discloses sufficient information to allow skilled artisans to make the noodles without undue experimentation. However, Ramon fails to explain that numerous experiments have shown that her process achieves unexpectedly superior results when performed at a temperature of 137.5° C. Ramon's patent would fulfill the enablement requirement. However, by failing to disclose the optimal temperature, Ramon has concealed the best mode of her invention, and as a result her patent should be held invalid.

The inventor must disclose the best mode known to him at the time he files a patent application. Technical understandings gained subsequent to the filing date need not be disclosed, even if the application is still pending at the PTO. This rule holds even if the inventor files a so-called "continuing application," a technique of extending PTO prosecution discussed in the following chapter of this text.[26]

Additionally, the best mode requirement applies only to the inventors named in the patent application. The controversial Federal Circuit opinion in *Glaxo Inc. v. Novopharm Ltd.*[27] illustrates this point. That case concerned an anti-ulcer medication invented by a Dr. Crookes during his employment with Glaxo. Consistent with an employment contract, Glaxo filed a patent application on behalf of Crookes. The application ultimately matured into a patent claiming the compound and disclosing a method of making it. While Glaxo management was aware that other employees had invented a better technique for making the medication originally discovered by Crookes, they never informed Crookes prior to the filing of the application.

Under these circumstances, the Federal Circuit held that no best mode violation occurred. Concluding that the wording of the statute expressly limited the best mode requirement to knowledge held by the inventor, the court saw no evidence that suggested Crookes himself knew of a better way to manufacture the medication. A vigorous dissent by Judge Mayer urged that the best mode requirement should not be given such a pinched reading. Judge Mayer concluded that because Glaxo both directed the prosecution and enjoyed the proprietary rights afforded by the issued patent, the district court should have further inquired into whether Glaxo had deliberately concealed a superior mode of practicing the invention from Crookes.

The best mode requirement has encountered severe criticism in recent years. A 1992 Presidential Commission urged that Congress eliminate the best mode requirement, reasoning that the enablement requirement already compels sufficient technical disclosures and that the best mode at the time of filing is unlikely to remain the best mode when the patent expires.[28] Because many foreign patent laws include no analog

26. *See* Transco Products, Inc. v. Performance Contracting, Inc., 38 F.3d 551 (Fed.Cir.1994), *cert. denied*, 513 U.S. 1151, 115 S.Ct. 1102, 130 L.Ed.2d 1069 (1995).

27. *See* Glaxo Inc. v. Novopharm Ltd., 52 F.3d 1043 (Fed.Cir.1995), *cert. denied*, 516 U.S. 988, 116 S.Ct. 516, 133 L.Ed.2d 424 (1995).

28. *See* THE ADVISORY COMMISSION ON PATENT LAW REFORM, A REPORT TO THE SECRETARY OF COMMERCE 102–03 (1992).

to the best mode requirement in U.S. law, inventors based overseas have also disfavored disclosing their best mode. At the time this book goes to press, however, scant effort has been directed towards legislative reform of the best mode requirement.

§ 18.2   The Claims

The claims form the most significant part of the entire patent instrument, for it is the claims themselves that set forth the proprietary technological rights possessed by the patentee. When considering patentability and infringement issues, courts and PTO examiners turn to the particular wording of the invention as claimed.[1] Because the claims define the invention for purposes of the patent law, it is inappropriate to rely upon another portion of the specification, such as a drawing or the abstract of the invention, for this purpose.

The U.S. patent system employs a peripheral claiming system. Under this regime the claims mark out the outer boundaries of the technology considered proprietary to the patentee.[2] Like a real property deed, a claim in a patent sets the "metes and bounds" of the rights associated with that instrument.[3] Patentability and infringement issues should also focus upon a careful reading of a claim, rather than some more conceptual sense of the "heart," "gist" or "essence" of the invention.

Although claims hold a central place in the patent system, they are difficult texts to draft properly.[4] Claim drafting requires considerable analytic, research and writing skills, as well as scientific and technical competence. Claims submitted to the PTO must reduce sophisticated technical concepts to a single sentence, and yet present an accurate description of the invention. They must also be written with a keen awareness of the technical field in which the invention lies. Often only a few carefully chosen words of limitation mark a patentable distinction between the claimed invention and prior technical knowledge.

Claims drafters must also bear in mind the legal standards for properly drafted claims. The most significant statutory provision governing claiming is the second paragraph of § 112. That provision calls for the patent specification to close with "one or more claims," and in practice most U.S. patents contain multiple claims. Under this regime each claim presents a separate statement of the patented invention. It is quite possible for some claims of a patent to be invalid on prior art grounds, while others are valid. Similarly, a competitor may infringe

§ 18.2

1. *See* In re Van Geuns, 988 F.2d 1181, 1184 (Fed.Cir.1993).

2. Ex parte Fressola, 27 USPQ2d 1608 (PTO Bd.1993), *aff'd*, 17 F.3d 1442 (Fed. Cir.1993).

3. *See* Corning Glass Works v. Sumitomo Elec. U.S.A., Inc., 868 F.2d 1251, 1257 (Fed.Cir.1989).

4. *See* Advanced Cardiovascular Sys., Inc. v. C.R. Bard Inc., 144 F.R.D. 372, 25 USPQ2d 1354, 1357 (N.D.Cal.1992).

some claims of a patent but not others, depending upon the precise formulation of each claim. Individual claims effectively afford distinct proprietary interests that must be judged on their own merits.[5]

Section 112 ¶ 2 also requires that the claims particularly point out and distinctly claim the subject matter which the applicant regards as his invention. Before turning to this requirement of definiteness in claim language, this treatise addresses the basic mechanics of claim drafting and formatting in U.S. patent practice.

18.2.1   Basic Claim Drafting

Although patent applicants enjoy a great deal of discretion in setting forth the substance of a claim,[6] years of PTO interpretation and judicial precedent have resulted in a standardized drafting protocol. Among the most notable practices is that each claim must be expressed in a single sentence. Often this rule results in a lengthy sentence with stilted language, but has been upheld as contributing to the efficient processing of patent applications.[7] The PTO further directs that claims be stated in three parts: a preamble, transition phrase, and body.

18.2.1.1   The Preamble

The preamble, or introductory words of a claim, provides the general nature of the invention. Sometimes the preamble simply recites an apparatus, article of manufacture, composition of matter, or method, tracking the categories of statutory subject matter of § 101. Most preambles are more specific, stating such things as "a packaged semiconductor," "a steering wheel unit for mounting on a steering column of a motor vehicle," or "a method of preparing Factor VIII pro-coagulant activity protein."

A recurring issue concerning the preamble is whether the subject matter it recites should act as a limitation upon the scope of the claim. Unlike the elements of the invention listed in the body of the claim, which define the invention and therefore limit the scope of claim coverage, the preamble often does no more than name the invention's intended purpose. As a result, the courts ordinarily do not consider the preamble as a claim limitation. Therefore, a prior art reference could anticipate the claimed invention under § 102 even though the subject matter of the preamble was not disclosed by the reference. Similarly, during enforcement litigation, an accused technology need not embody the language of the preamble in order to be judged a literal infringement.

Sometimes a preamble will be held to rise to the level of a claim limitation, however. The Federal Circuit has stated that if a preamble

---

5. *See* Continental Can Co. USA, Inc. v. Monsanto Co., 948 F.2d 1264 (Fed.Cir. 1991).

6. *See* Ex parte Tanksley, 37 USPQ2d 1382, 1386 (PTO Bd. 1994).

7. *See* Fressola v. Manbeck, 36 USPQ2d 1211 (D.D.C.1995).

breathes "life and meaning" to the claim, it should be considered a claim limitation.[8] More concretely, if the preamble is necessary to define the claimed invention, then it will usually be held to limit the scope of the claim.

An illustration may lend some clarity to this distinction. Consider the following hypothetical patent claims:

1.   A diagnostic medical imaging system comprising:

an ultrasound image generator; and

a flat panel display capable of displaying an ultrasound image generated by said ultrasound generator.

2.   A diagnostic medical imaging ultrasound system capable of being housed on a portable support, comprising:

an ultrasound image generator integrated with said support; and

a flat panel display integrated with said support, capable of displaying an ultrasound image generated by said ultrasound generator.

In claim 1, the body of the claim completely defines the invention without reference to the preamble. The preamble simply notes that the intended field of use of the invention is medical diagnostics. This intended use would not limit the scope of the claims. In claim 2, however, both elements recited in the body of the claim expressly refer to subject matter introduced in the preamble. A court would likely consider not merely a support, but a portable support as a necessary limitation of claim 2.

18.2.1.2   The Transition Phrase

The transition phrase connects the preamble to the body of the claim. In practice, the drafter must choose from one of three transition phrases: "comprising," "consisting of," or "essentially consisting of." This humble choice of words actually has significant substantive effect upon the scope of the claim. The transition phrase determines whether the claim is limited to structures with only those elements (closed terminology) or is open to structures containing at least those elements, and possibly others (open or hybrid terminology).

The use of the term "comprising" encompasses technologies with all the elements described in the body of the claim. Whether the technology incorporates additional elements is irrelevant.[9] Consider, for example, a claim reciting "a composition of matter *comprising* element A; element B; and element C." The term "comprising" renders the claim open to additional ingredients. This open claim covers any composition with at

8. Corning Glass Works v. Sumitomo Electric U.S.A., Inc., 868 F.2d 1251 (Fed. Cir.1989).

9. Mannesmann Demag Corp. v. Engineered Metal Products Co., Inc., 793 F.2d 1279 (Fed.Cir.1986).

least the elements A + B + C. Thus, both the combination of A + B + C and A + B + C + D are encompassed by the claim.

In contrast, a claim which employs the term "consisting of" is closed to additional ingredients. Infringement can occur only when the accused technology has exactly the same elements recited in the claim—no more or no less. Thus, a competitor's sale of a composition with ingredients A + B + C + D is outside the literal scope of a claim towards "a composition of matter *consisting of* element A; element B; and element C."

Why would anyone want to employ such a limiting transitional phrase? Often the nature of an invention lies in the elimination of certain components or process steps known to the prior art. "Closed" claim language allows an inventor to avoid an anticipation rejection. As one can imagine, however, claims drafters do not favor this extremely restrictive transition phrase. They are well aware that their competitors may easily avoid the claim by adding a superfluous element to an otherwise infringing technology.

In such circumstances, drafters prefer to use the phrase "consisting essentially of," a hybrid transition. This terminology renders the claim open to additional elements, so long as they do not materially affect the basic and novel characteristics of the claimed combination. Suppose that a claim recited "a composition of matter *consisting essentially of* element A; element B; and element C." If element D would not materially change the composition, then A + B + C + D lies within the literal scope of this hybrid claim. In appropriate situations, most often in the chemical arts, this form of transition can be very powerful.

Note that the words "the steps of" are ordinarily added to the transition phrase when the claim is directed towards a process or method.

18.2.1.3   The Body

The body of the claim provides the elements of the invention, as well as how these elements cooperate either structurally or functionally. Claims ordinarily devote one clause to each of the primary elements of the invention, often separating them with a semicolon. These clauses may be given a reference label, such as "(a)," "(b)," "(c)," and so on, to allow readers to refer to its language more readily. The drafter should also indicate how one element interacts with the others to form an operative technology, employing such language as "attached to," "operated by," or "positioned above."

Elements of an invention are ordinarily introduced with an indefinite article, such as "a" or "an," as well as terms such as "one," "several," or "a plurality of." When that element is noted later in the claim, claims-drafters ordinarily employ the definite article "the" or the term "said." If an element appearing for the first time is accompanied by "the" or "said," then it will ordinarily be rejected by an examiner as lacking so-called "antecedent basis." The following claim employs these articles correctly:

An ion source comprising:

a housing which defines a discharge chamber;

a wave guide transmitting a microwave to generate plasma within said discharge chamber; and

a matching tube having a cross-sectional form that gradually varies in a direction of propagation of the microwave.[10]

This claim also illustrates a peculiarity of the patent law: the reluctance to claim an empty space, such as a chamber, hollow, hole, or gap, directly. Instead, drafters usually define such spaces in terms of the structures that form them. This rule may seem vacuous, but it is commonly observed in modern patent practice. Apparently patent drafters believe that claims should recite structure—not the absence of structure![11]

Courts routinely state that the patent applicants are allowed to coin their own terms for use in claims. As expressed in the vernacular of the patent law, "a patentee is free to be his or her own lexicographer."[12] However, newly minted terms may not be misdescriptive, nor should the applicant employ such banal terms as "gadget" or "widget." The courts and PTO have been more hostile to the use of trademarks or trade names within patent claims however. Typical of such cases is *Ex parte Bolton*,[13] which rejected a claim reciting the trademark "FORMICA." The PTO Board of Appeals reasoned that the manufacturer was free to change the composition of FORMICA as it pleased, rendering Bolton's claim of indefinite scope.

18.2.2   Claim Formats

Beyond these basic tenets of claim drafting lie a great number of refining principles. In particular, a number of claim formats are either described in the Patent Act or have been the subject of extensive judicial treatment. Each of these formats provides an understood protocol that may be advantageous for the drafter, perhaps providing the optimal way to claim a particular invention. The most important claim formats are reviewed next.

18.2.2.1   Dependent Claims

Section 112, paragraphs 3–5 allow the use of so-called "dependent" patent claims. The statute mandates that dependent claims must recite an earlier claim and provide additional limitations. For example, following independent claim 1, dependent claim 2 might provide: "A tape cassette handling system as recited in claim 1, further comprising...." Such claims are interpreted to include all of the previous limitations as

---

10. This claim is based upon U.S. Patent No. 5,925,886 (July 20, 1999).

11. ROBERT C. FABER, LANDIS ON MECHANICS OF PATENT CLAIM DRAFTING § 26 (4th ed. 1996).

12. Hormone Research Foundation, Inc. v. Genentech, Inc., 904 F.2d 1558, 1563 (Fed.Cir.1990), *cert. denied*, 499 U.S. 955, 111 S.Ct. 1434, 113 L.Ed.2d 485 (1991).

13. 42 USPQ 40 (Pat.Off.Bd.App.1938).

well as those which are newly recited. Claims may also be multiple dependent format, as in a claim which recites "a tape cassette handling system as recited in claims 1 or 2, further comprising. . . . " The statute instructs readers to "incorporate by reference all the limitations of the particular claim in relation to which it is being considered."[14]

The possibility of dependent claims presents a drafting convenience for patent applicants. They enable drafters to express claims of increasingly diminished scope in a succinct fashion. The result of this system is that claims drafters typically craft a series of claims in each application, forming a "reverse pyramid" of successively narrower claims. The first, independent claim of the patent is the most broad and abstractly written. The most narrow, dependent claim usually describes a product the inventor would actually consider putting into commercial practice. Intermediate claims are set to varying levels of abstraction, each taking a place on the spectrum of technologies surrounding the narrowly focused commercial embodiment of the invention.

Skilled drafters employ this technique because they recognize the patentee may wish to enforce the narrowest possible claim against an accused infringer. After all, the narrower the claim, the higher the likelihood that such a claim will withstand a defense of invalidity. The greater the number of limitations in a claim, the more unlikely it is that prior art will render that claim anticipated under § 102 or obvious under § 103. Importantly, not all the pertinent prior art may be known to the applicant, and the claims-drafter must speculate as to the sorts of references that may bear upon the claimed invention. Also, the narrower the claim, the greater the difficulty an accused infringer will have in attacking it based upon lack of enablement.

On the other hand, the patentee also wants the broadest claim possible in order to have the possibility of reaching as many competitors as possible. Other industry actors will find efforts to design competing technologies that do not fall within the scope of the claims more difficult, and thus avoid literal infringement less easily. So a claims-drafter will attempt to write the broadest claim the PTO will allow, allowing a range of potential technological protection in each patent instrument.

The following hypothetical illuminates the workings of dependent claims. Suppose that Moe Jackson is the proprietor of a patent with the following claims:

1. A method of forming a porous surface for use with an orthopaedic implant, said method comprising the steps of:

    providing a plurality of metallic particles; and

    mixing a water-soluble protein compound with said metallic particles.

2. The method of claim 1, wherein said protein compound comprises gelatin.

14. 35 U.S.C. § 112 ¶ 4 (2000).

3. The method of claim 2, where said metallic particles comprise titanium.

4. The method of claim 3, where said mixing is performed at a temperature of 421.6° C.[15]

Jackson brings an enforcement action against Leon Sanders, alleging infringement of claims 1–4. During trial, Sanders introduces into evidence an article from a medical journal article. That article, a § 102(b) reference not discovered by the PTO examiner, explained that a mixture of chromium particles and gelatin formed a superior coating for use with artificial hip implants. The court concludes that, in view of the reference, claims 1 and 2 were anticipated and claim 3 would have been obvious. However, the court holds that the invention defined in claim 4 would not have been obvious to one of skill in the art because performing the method with titanium at 421.6° C produced unexpectedly good results.

In this case, the more narrowly drafted claim 4 is not invalid even though it formally depends from an invalid claim. For the sake of convenience, claim 4 could be viewed in independent form as follows:

4. A method of forming a porous surface for use with an orthopaedic implant, said method comprising the steps of:

> providing a plurality of titanium particles; and
>
> mixing gelatin with said titanium particles;
>
> whereby said mixing is performed at a temperature of 421.6° C.

To the extent that Sanders practices the method recited in claim 4, he has committed patent infringement. Jackson would be able to obtain remedies for patent infringement as provided by the statute.

18.2.2.2 Functional Claims

Functional claims define an invention in terms of what it does rather than in terms of its structure. Patent practitioners generally term such claims as "means-plus-function" claims, a reference to the final paragraph of § 112. Section 112 ¶ 6 provides that an element in a combination claim may be expressed as a means or step for performing a specified function. It further directs that such a claim shall be construed to cover the corresponding structure, material or acts described in the specification and equivalents thereof.

In the following simplified claim, elements (a) and (b) are expressed structurally, while element (c) is drafted in means-plus-function form.

1. A hammer, comprising:

(a) a head;

(b) a handle; and

(c) means for attaching said head and said handle.

---

15. This hypothetical is loosely based on U.S. Pat. No. 5,926,685 (July 20, 1999).

To determine the literal scope of element (b), § 112 ¶ 6 directs that the reader turn to the patent's specification. Assume that the patent's specification explained that the "handle and head may be attached through the use of a nail or bolt." In this case claim 1 should be literally read to cover the following combination:

1. A hammer, comprising:

(a) a head;

(b) a handle; and

(c) [a nail, bolt and equivalents thereof] for attaching said head and said handle.

Because § 112 ¶ 6 refers to "a claim for a combination," a claim that consists of a single means for accomplishing a particular task is improper.[16]

Section 112 ¶ 6 owes its origin to increasing judicial hostility to functional claiming in the first half of the Twentieth Century. This trend culminated in the 1946 Supreme Court decision *Halliburton Oil Well Cementing Co. v. Walker*.[17] Walker's patent claims, directed towards an apparatus for measuring the depth of oil wells, included a number of limitations cast in means-plus-function format. These included "means communicating with said well for creating a pressure impulse in said well" and "echo receiving means." The Court struck down Walker's claims, reasoning that because they were not tied to the specific structures Walker had invented they were overbroad and indefinite. According to the Court, "unless frightened from the course of experimentation by broad functional claims like these, inventive genius may evolve many more devices to accomplish the same purpose."[18]

The patent bar protested mightily against *Halliburton Oil*, which cast great doubt upon a large number of issued patents that had employed a functional claiming style. In response Congress amended the patent statute by adding the provision now codified at § 112 ¶ 6.[19] The intent of Congress was to establish clear parameters within which functional claims could be written and interpreted.[20]

For present purposes, three principal issues concern the operation of § 112 ¶ 6. The first is the applicability of the statute towards PTO determination of patentability issues during prosecution. A second issue concerns which claims should be read as invoking § 112 ¶ 6 and its interpretational protocol. Finally, the precise parameters of the closing phrase of § 112 ¶ 6, "and equivalents thereof," is of paramount concern during the interpretation of means plus function claims. This treatise address these subjects in turn.

16. *See* In re Hyatt, 708 F.2d 712 (Fed. Cir.1983).

17. 329 U.S. 1, 67 S.Ct. 6, 91 L.Ed. 3 (1946).

18. 329 U.S. at 12.

19. Warner–Jenkinson Co. v. Hilton Davis Chem. Co., 520 U.S. 17, 117 S.Ct. 1040, 137 L.Ed.2d 146 (1997).

20. Dawn Equip. Co. v. Kentucky Farms, Inc., 140 F.3d 1009 (Fed.Cir.1998) (Plager, J., additional views).

The Federal Circuit addressed the first of these issues in its *en banc* opinion in *In re Donaldson*.[21] Although § 112 ¶ 6 does not by its own terms distinguish between prosecution and litigation, PTO policy prior to 1994 was not to employ this interpretational protocol when it considered functional claims. The PTO took the position that it was to give claims their broadest reasonable meaning. Therefore, claims in means-plus-function were read literally, covering all possible means for performing the stated function. Because broader claims read upon a greater range of prior art references, this policy resulted in the rejection of claims that would have been approved had § 112 ¶ 6 been applied.

This disharmony between PTO practice and the statute came to a head in *In re Donaldson*. Donaldson's claims concerned an industrial dust collector. The dust collector's filter featured flexible, diaphragm-like walls. When the filter required cleaning, an operator needed only to reverse the air pressure, causing the walls to flex in the opposite direction and dislodging caked dust into a bin below. Claim 1 of Donaldson's application claimed this element of the invention in the following terms: "means, responsive to pressure increases in said chamber caused by said cleaning means, for moving particulate matter in a downward direction." The PTO rejected the application over the Swift prior art reference. Swift, which also performed a cleaning function with reverse air pulses, had sloped rather than flexible walls. Donaldson appealed to the Federal Circuit, arguing that had the PTO interpreted his claims in accordance with § 112 ¶ 6, the Swift reference would not have rendered the claimed invention obvious.

The Federal Circuit heard Donaldson's appeal *en banc*. Writing for the unanimous court, Judge Rich reasoned that nothing in the statute exempted the PTO from following § 112 ¶ 6. No statutory language or legislative history supported this conclusion, and Judge Rich was quick to point out that § 112 is found in Chapter 11 of Title 35, titled "Application for Patent." The court further found no harm to the PTO's policy of giving claims their broadest reasonable interpretation. The PTO could continue to give claims their broadest fair reading so long as it followed § 112 ¶ 6 when construing functional claims. The Federal Circuit also rejected the PTO's argument that § 112 ¶ 6 raised issues of indefiniteness because that statute required limitations to be exported from the specification into the claims. If an inventor opted to employ means-plus-function language in a claim, then he must set forth in the specification an adequate disclosure showing what was meant by that language. Failure to do so would constitute a violation of § 112 ¶ 2. Concluding that Donaldson's claims were patentable over Swift when properly interpreted, the court reversed the PTO rejection.

With the statutory procedures of § 112 ¶ 6 now applying to both prosecution and litigation, both examiners and courts now require mechanisms for determining which claims should be considered to be written in means-plus-function format. The Federal Circuit has held that the use

21. 16 F.3d 1189, 29 USPQ2d 1845 (Fed.Cir.1994).

of the word "means" triggers a presumption that the inventor used this term to invoke the statutory mandates for means-plus-function clauses.[22] However, not every use of the term "means" indicates that the claim is a means-plus-function claim. The presumption of invoking § 112 ¶ 6 can be rebutted if the claim language does not link the term "means" to a recited function.

Cole v. Kimberly–Clark Corp.[23] demonstrates how courts determine whether a particular claims is drafted in means-plus-function format. There the Federal Circuit construed a claim involving disposable diapers with sides that easily tear open to facilitate removal of a soiled brief. Among the claim elements was "perforation means extending from the leg band means to the waist band means through the outer impermeable layer means for tearing the outer impermeable layer means for removing the training brief in the case of an accident by the user." The district court determined on summary judgment that a "perforation means" is merely a "perforation" and that the bonded tearable side seams on the accused briefs were not perforations.

The Federal Circuit affirmed on appeal, also declining to apply § 112 ¶ 6. According to the court, the "perforation means ... for tearing" element of Cole's claim failed to satisfy that statute because it recited not only perforations, the structure supporting the tearing function, but also their location (extending from the leg band to the waist band) and range (extending through the impermeable layer). The court reasoned that a claim that cited such detailed structure should not qualify as functional.

The term "means" is not the only one which will invoke § 112 ¶ 6. In *Mas–Hamilton Group v. LaGard, Inc.*,[24] the Federal Circuit considered a claim that recited a "lever moving element." The court held that § 112 ¶ 6 applied to this claim element as well, despite its failure to use the usual catch word "means." The court recognized that many devices take their name from the functions they perform, such as a screwdriver, brake or lock, and that the use of these terms in a claim would count as a structural, rather than functional definition. However, the phrase "lever moving element" lacked a well-understood structural meaning in the art. As a result, the court held that the claim defined this element functionally rather than structurally. Its literal scope was therefore restricted to structures disclosed in the specification and equivalents thereof that performed the identical function, rather than to any conceivable device for moving a lever. Similarly, a PTO Board decision has found claim language reciting "a jet driving device" to invoke § 112 ¶ 6.[25]

22. York Products Inc. v. Central Tractor Farm & Family Center, 99 F.3d 1568 (Fed.Cir.1996); Greenberg v. Ethicon Endo-Surgery, Inc., 91 F.3d 1580, 1584 (Fed.Cir. 1996).

23. 102 F.3d 524, 531 (Fed.Cir.1996).

24. 156 F.3d 1206 (Fed.Cir.1998).

25. Ex parte Stanley, 121 USPQ 621 (PTO Bd.1959).

Section 112 ¶ 6 also refers to process or method claims, providing that "an element in a claim for a combination may be expressed as a . . . step for performing a specified function without the recital of . . . acts in support thereof." The Federal Circuit has acknowledged the propriety of step-plus-function claims,[26] but scant case law has thus far been devoted towards interpreting them. That court has been quick to point out that not every claimed process step invokes the interpretational method of § 112 ¶ 6. Step-plus-function claim elements provide a step, or generic description of a portion of a process, without the recital of more specific acts to perform that abstract function. Such claims should be construed as covering the corresponding "acts described in the specification and equivalents thereof." For example, suppose that one of the elements of a process claim was "the step of raising the temperature to 300 degrees." If the patent's specification described the use of an oven to raise the temperature to 300 degrees, the literal coverage of the claim would extend to the use of an oven and equivalent acts.

A final issue concerning § 112 ¶ 6 is the operation of its equivalency provision. The statute calls for functional claim language "to cover the corresponding structure, material, or acts described in the specification and equivalents thereof." The Federal Circuit has interpreted this provision to hold that for a means-plus-function limitation to read on an accused device, the accused device must employ means identical or equivalent to the structures, material, or acts described in the patent specification. The accused device must also perform the identical function as specified in the claims.[27]

The Federal Circuit has provided that, for purposes of § 112 ¶ 6, an equivalent results from an insubstantial change which adds nothing of significance to the structure, material, or acts disclosed in the patent specification.[28] The court often expresses this concept through the succinct phrase "structural equivalency."[29] For example, recall that in the hammer example above, the specification explained that "the handle and head may be attached through the use of a nail or bolt." A screw would likely be considered a structural equivalent to a nail or bolt, but the use of glue to secure the head and the handle would probably not be judged structurally equivalent.

The court has often stressed that structural equivalency under § 112 ¶ 6 differs from equivalency under the doctrine of equivalents.[30] The doctrine of equivalents will be further discussed in Chapter 20 of this text. For present purposes, it is enough to recognize that despite their demands for clear claiming, the courts have been willing to find

---

26. *See* O.I. Corp. v. Tekmar Co., 115 F.3d 1576 (Fed.Cir.1997).

27. King Instruments Corp. v. Perego, 65 F.3d 941 (Fed.Cir.1995), *cert. denied,* 517 U.S. 1188, 116 S.Ct. 1675, 134 L.Ed.2d 778 (1996).

28. Valmont Indus., Inc. v. Reinke Mfg. Co., 983 F.2d 1039 (Fed.Cir.1993).

29. Laitram Corp. v. Rexnord, Inc., 939 F.2d 1533 (Fed.Cir.1991).

30. *See* Endress + Hauser, Inc. v. Hawk Measurement Sys.Pty. Ltd., 122 F.3d 1040 (Fed.Cir.1997).

liability even where an accused infringer diverges slightly from a strict reading of the claims. An equivalent under the doctrine results from an insubstantial change which, from the perspective of persons of ordinary skill in the art, adds nothing of significance to the claimed invention. An equivalent under the doctrine, though not literally meeting the claims, still infringes the patent.[31] As can be imagined, the contrast between structural equivalency and equivalency under the doctrine has proven a rather subtle affair. These distinctions may largely be academic given that claims written in means-plus-function format are as subject to the doctrine of equivalents as any other sort of claim.[32]

18.2.2.3 Product-by-Process Claims

Sometimes an inventor realizes that she has arrived at a new composition, but cannot specify that composition either by name or structure. In these cases the inventor cannot define the composition directly. But she is able to describe the composition as the product of the process she used to make the composition. So-called "product-by-process" claims reflect these circumstances. The following claim is representative:

A diamond-bearing material prepared by a process comprising the steps of

detonating a charge consisting essentially of a carbon-containing explosive having a negative oxygen balance to form a detonation product; and

cooling the detonation product at a rate of about 200 to 6,000 degrees/minute.

For example, suppose that amateur inventor Steven Serendip is working in his makeshift basement laboratory one evening. Serendip accidentally mixes together some chemical compounds with which he has been experimenting. Serendip realizes that the resulting compound, which he immediately names "flabber," possesses incredible strength and elasticity. Serendip's formal chemistry education is modest and he only possesses a vague notion of the chemical reactions that must have occurred to produce flabber. Nor does he own a spectroscope or other expensive equipment to find out the precise composition of flabber. These circumstances will not prevent him from filing a patent application claiming flabber, however, if he defines his invention via the process he used to produce it.

Product-by-process claims are not mentioned in the patent statute, but have been the subject of a modest number of judicial and PTO decisions.[33] These claims are most common in chemical practice but sometimes arise in other fields. Some inventors employ this claim format

31. *See* Warner–Jenkinson Co. v. Hilton Davis Chem. Co., 520 U.S. 17, 117 S.Ct. 1040, 137 L.Ed.2d 146 (1997).

32. *See* Kahn v. General Motors Corp., 135 F.3d 1472 (Fed.Cir.1998), *cert. denied*, 525 U.S. 875, 119 S.Ct. 177, 142 L.Ed.2d 144 (1998).

33. *See* In re Thorpe, 777 F.2d 695, 697 (Fed.Cir.1985).

even when they are able to claim the product directly, usually as a supplementary claim.[34]

A recurring issue regarding product-by-process claims concerns the extent of their claim coverage. One school of thought is that these claims cover the resulting product no matter how it is made. To further the above example, suppose that Serendip were issued a patent containing a single product-by-process claim towards flabber. Under this line of reasoning, Serendip's claim would cover competitor sales of flabber even though that others employed different manufacturing techniques. In the 1991 opinion *Scripps Clinic & Research Foundation v. Genentech, Inc.*,[35] a three-judge panel of the Federal Circuit adopted this view.

Another possibility is that product-by-process claims are restricted to the method of making recited in the claims. Under this outlook, Serendip's competitors would be able to avoid his product-by-process claim by using another method to make flabber. Just one year after *Scripps Clinic*, a different three-judge panel of the Federal Circuit issued its opinion in *Atlantic Thermoplastics Co. v. Faytex Corp.*,[36] adopting this reasoning. According to the *Atlantic Thermoplastics* panel, both binding Supreme Court precedent and sound claiming practice indicated that product-by-process should be given a more restrictive interpretation. *Scripps Clinic* was distinguished because that panel had "ruled without reference to the Supreme Court's previous cases involving product claims with process limitations."[37]

Atlantic Thermoplastics proved a controversial opinion, particularly given the Federal Circuit's self-described "obligation of promoting uniformity in the field of patent law."[38] Judge Rich went so far to describe *Atlantic Thermoplastics* as "mutiny," "heresy," and "illegal."[39] But the *Atlantic Thermoplastics* panel did seem to have the better reading of the earlier cases, and subsequent district court opinions have limited product-by-process claims to the actual process recited therein.[40]

18.2.2.4 Jepson Claims

A "Jepson claim" defines an invention in two parts: a preamble which recites the admitted prior art, followed by an "improvement" clause which recites what the applicant regards as his invention. Jepson claims may be identified by the transition phrase "where the improvement comprises," or words to that effect. The following claim was drafted in Jepson format:

34. *See* Ex parte Edwards, 231 USPQ 981 (PTO Bd.1986).

35. 927 F.2d 1565 (Fed.Cir.1991).

36. 970 F.2d 834 (Fed.Cir.1992).

37. *Id.* at 839 n.2.

38. Midwest Industries, Inc. v. Karavan Trailers, Inc., 175 F.3d 1356, 1360 (Fed.Cir.

1999), *cert. denied*, 528 U.S. 1019, 120 S.Ct. 527, 145 L.Ed.2d 409 (1999).

39. Atlantic Thermoplastics Co. v. Faytex Corp., 974 F.2d 1279 (Fed.Cir.1992) (Rich, J., dissenting from the denial of rehearing en banc).

40. *See* Tropix, Inc. v. Lumigen, 825 F.Supp. 7, 10 (D.Mass.1993).

An improved polarized sunglass lens laminate comprising a first lens portion, a second lens portion, a polarizing film disposed between the first and second lens portions, and an adhesive binding the two lens portions and the polarizing film together,

the improvement of which comprises incorporating sufficient ultraviolet absorber into the adhesive to block substantially all of the UVA radiation in sunlight.[41]

Jepson claims take their name from an early opinion from the Patent Office Board, *In re Jepson*,[42] which approved this format. Although Jepson was not the first inventor to employ this style of claim, the fact that his application was associated with this seminal opinion has provided him a measure of fame in the patent community.

The use of the Jepson format has two primary effects. First, the preamble unquestionably acts as a limitation upon the scope of the claims in a Jepson claim.[43] The second, and more important effect is that any subject matter recited in the preamble presumptively constitutes prior art even if not available under a § 102 category.[44] This presumption may be rebutted by a showing that the preamble recites the inventor's own work product and is not otherwise prior art under § 102.[45]

PTO examiners highly favor the use of Jepson claims. In the event that no anticipatory reference is available, the task of generating nonobviousness rejections is greatly simplified when an applicant opts to admit that everything in the claim but the "improvement" clause constitutes prior art. With regard to the previous example, the PTO examiner would take as a given that the combination of a sunglass lens, polarizing film and adhesive binding is known to the art. The examiner need only show that it would have been obvious to incorporate ultraviolet absorber into the adhesive binding in order to reject the claim under § 103. However, suppose alternatively that this claim had been drafted in the usual style, as a combination of elements. In this case the examiner would have to demonstrate that a skilled artisan would have been motivated to combine references to produce each of the elements of the claimed invention, a task likely more difficult than had a Jepson format been employed.

Given that Jepson claims tend not to portray inventions in a favorable light, the fact that applicants continue to use them may appear puzzling. One reason Jepson claims remain popular is that foreign patent offices, and in particular the European Patent Office, strongly encourage the use of this claim format.[46] Many applicants based abroad

41. U.S. Patent No. 5,926,248 (July 20, 1999).

42. 1917 Comm. Dec. 62, 243 O.G. 525 (Ass't Comm'r Pat. 1917).

43. Pentec, Inc. v. Graphic Controls Corp., 776 F.2d 309 (Fed.Cir.1985).

44. In re Fout, 675 F.2d 297 (CCPA 1982).

45. Reading & Bates Construction Co. v. Baker Energy Resources Corp., 748 F.2d 645 (Fed.Cir.1984).

46. *See* Arthur L. Plevy, *Some Important Differences Between Patent Practice in Europe and the United States*, 209 N.J. LAW. 40, 41–42 (June 2001).

simply file the same set of claims at the PTO that they did abroad. Foreign applicants are ordinarily well advised to avoid the Jepson format in the United States, however, simply by reformatting their claims. Absent special circumstances, domestic inventors would be wise to avoid Jepson claims entirely.

18.2.2.5 Markush Claims

So-called "Markush" claims are common only in chemical practice. Like Jepson, Eugene Markush was not the first inventor to employ this style of claim. But because his application was concerned with the seminal Patent Office opinion approving this claiming protocol, his name has become associated with it both in the United States and abroad.[47] Drafters employ the Markush format when no commonly accepted generic term is commensurate in scope with the invention the applicant wishes to claim.[48]

Markush groups usually claim a family of compounds by defining the structure common to all members of that family, along with one or more alternatives selected from the set consisting of named chemical compounds. A letter, most often "R," typically represents this latter set of alternatives. A sample Markush claim appears as follows:

> A compound of the formula OH—CH—R, where R is selected from the group consisting of chlorine, bromine and iodine.

Although this simple example neatly illustrates the Markush format, it may not fully convey the desirability of this type of claim. In this case, if the Markush format were unavailable an inventor could simply draft three claims individually reciting chlorine, bromine and iodine. But it should be appreciated that the alternatives often constitute chemical radicals that may themselves consist of hundreds of closely related compounds. Inventors in such fields as pharmacology, ceramics and metallurgy would be sorely pressed if required to draft numerous claims to define each and every member of the alternative group.

A proper Markush group claims a set of substances that share at least one common trait.[49] For example, the chemical compounds claimed above must have the same use, perhaps as a dye or detergent, in order to be arranged in a Markush format.

Unlike Jepson claims, Markush claims are not construed as including an admission concerning the prior art. In particular, use of the Markush format does not amount to an admission that the claimed alternatives comprise obvious variations of one another. To continue the above example, suppose that an examiner discovers a scientific journal article available under § 102(a). That article describes the nucleus of the claimed compound along with chlorine. Unless the examiner can additionally demonstrate that the other claimed alternatives were anticipat-

47. *See* Ex parte Markush, 1925 C.D. 126, 340 O.G. 839 (Comm'r Pat. 1924).

48. U.S. Department of Commerce, Patent and Trademark Office, Manual of Patent Examining Procedure § 803.02 (7th ed. July 1998).

49. *See* In re Harnisch, 631 F.2d 716 (CCPA 1980).

ed or would have been obvious within the terms of § 103, the applicant would be allowed to narrow the claim to bromine and iodine, unprejudiced by the fact that a Markush grouping was employed.[50]

18.2.3   Definiteness

Section 112 ¶ 2 requires that the claims particularly point out and distinctly claim the subject matter which the applicant regards as his invention. Patent attorneys more succinctly refer to this requirement as one of definiteness.[51] The Federal Circuit has interpreted the statute as calling for such precision in claim language that the subject matter they encompass is clearly articulated.[52] Definite claims allow examiners to determine whether the invention fulfills the strictures of patentability or not. Once the patent issues, interested parties may also obtain clear warning of which technologies will infringe the claim.[53]

A claim meets the standard of § 112 ¶ 2 if it has a clear and specific meaning to persons of skill in the art. Claims are not to be read in the abstract, but in view of the disclosure of the entire patent instrument. If a claim, when read in view of the remainder of the specification, reasonably apprises skilled artisans of the scope of the patented invention, then the definiteness requirement is satisfied.[54]

The definiteness standard is distinct from the requirements governing a patent's disclosure in § 112 ¶ 1. In particular, a claim need not teach others how to practice the patented invention. The enablement standard applies to the patent specification as a whole, not to the claims in particular.[55]

A leading opinion on definiteness in claim language is *Orthokinetics, Inc. v. Safety Travel Chairs, Inc.*[56] The patent-at-suit concerned a collapsible wheelchair that facilitated the placement of wheelchair-bound persons in and out of an automobile. Each of its claims required the front part of the wheelchair to be "so dimensioned as to be insertable through the space between the doorframe of an automobile and one of the seats thereof." The accused infringer argued that this claim language was fatally indefinite, an argument accepted by the trial court.

On appeal, the Federal Circuit reversed. Chief Judge Markey reasoned that because automobiles come in various sizes, calling for a portion of the wheelchair to be "so dimensioned" was "as accurate as the subject matter permits." Expert testimony demonstrated that, upon reviewing the patent's specification, persons of ordinary skill could have easily measured the interior dimensions of a particular automobile in

---

50. Application of Ruff, 256 F.2d 590 (CCPA 1958).

51. *See* Miles Labs., Inc. v. Shandon Inc., 997 F.2d 870, 874–75 (Fed.Cir.1993).

52. *See* In re Borkowski, 422 F.2d 904, 909 (CCPA 1970).

53. *See* Leeds v. Commissioner of Patents and Trademarks, 955 F.2d 757, 759 (D.C.Cir.1992).

54. Morton Int'l, Inc. v. Cardinal Chem. Co., 5 F.3d 1464, 1470 (Fed.Cir.1993).

55. *See* Miles Labs., Inc. v. Shandon Inc., 997 F.2d 870, 874 (Fed.Cir.1993).

56. 806 F.2d 1565 (Fed.Cir.1986).

order to build a functioning wheelchair. In such circumstances, the patent law did not require the applicant to claim all possible lengths corresponding to the dimensions of hundreds of different automobiles. Because Orthokinetic's claims were sufficiently distinct such that skilled artisans could understand their meaning, they fulfilled the definiteness requirement.

Patent claims often employ words of degree, such as "about," "approximately," "close to," "substantially equal," or "closely approximate." Such terms can raise perplexing issues of definiteness. The courts have usually assumed a lenient posture towards their use in claims, provided that the claims reasonably define the invention under § 112 ¶ 2 standards.[57] The Federal Circuit will turn to other portions of the specification, the prior art, prosecution history and understandings of persons of skill in the art to identify some standard for measuring the precise limits of a word of degree.[58]

57. *See* Andrew Corp. v. Gabriel Electronics, 847 F.2d 819 (Fed.Cir.1988).

58. *See* Amgen, Inc. v. Chugai Pharmaceutical Co., 927 F.2d 1200 (Fed.Cir.1991).

Chapter 19

PATENT PROSECUTION

Table of Sections

Unlike other sorts of intellectual property, patents come into existence only through the intervention of the government. The entity assigned the task of approving patent applications is an agency entitled the United States Patent and Trademark Office, or PTO. The administrative process through which an inventor acquires a patent from the PTO is known as prosecution. The most frequent professional duty of patent practitioners, prosecution is also the task assigned to most entry-level patent lawyers. Even those engaged exclusively in patent litigation need to be thoroughly apprized of the events at the PTO that lead to the grant of any patent to be sued upon or defended against. Attorneys who do not routinely practice in the patent law may also find themselves more frequently approached by inventors wishing to obtain a patent than by patent proprietors who wish to enforce their intellectual property rights. For all these reasons, a basic grasp of prosecution mechanisms is elemental to an understanding of the patent law.

§ 19.1   Introduction to the Patent and Trademark Office

The Patent and Trademark Office, or PTO, is an administrative agency of the federal government.[1] The PTO is organized within the Department of Commerce and is under the policy direction of the Secretary of Commerce. A Director, who is appointed by the President by and with the consent of the Senate, heads the PTO. The Secretary of Commerce also appoints a Commissioner of Patents with the specific responsibility of managing the PTO's patent operations.[2] The PTO is currently housed in several office buildings in northern Virginia, near Washington, DC.

The examining corps itself is organized into various Examining Groups, which are further divided into Group and Individual Art Units. A Group Director heads each of the Examining Groups, while the various Group Units are directed by a senior official entitled the Supervisory Primary Examiner, or SPE. Front-line examiners are classified as either primary or assistant. Primary examiners possess considerable experience and are authorized to make decisions pertinent to patentability on an independent basis. Each primary examiner acts, in a sense, like a one-person patent office. Assistant examiners tend to be more recent

§ 19.1
1. 35 U.S.C.A. § 1 (2000).

2. 35 U.S.C.A. § 3 (2000).

hires who work under the supervision of primary examiners. At the time this book went to press, the PTO employed over 3000 patent examiners.

Several additional entities within the PTO are worthy of note here. The PTO maintains a Board of Patent Appeals and Interferences.[3] The Board consists of approximately sixty administrative patent judges. The Board hears appeals in panels of three, although sometimes the PTO convenes expanded panels to hear important cases. The PTO also maintains an Office of the Solicitor. The PTO Solicitor and his or her staff of attorneys represent the PTO in judicial proceedings, in particular appeals to the Federal Circuit by aggrieved applicants. Finally, the American Inventors Protection Act of 1999 established a Patent Public Advisory Committee.[4] The Committee has nine voting members appointed by the Secretary of Commerce for three-year terms. The Committee meets to discuss policies, goals, performance, budget and user fees that bear upon the PTO's patent operations, and prepares an annual report.

The PTO is virtually unique among federal agencies in its licensing of practitioners. Before someone may prepare and prosecute patent applications on behalf of others, he must pass a difficult test administered by the PTO. The PTO waives the testing requirement for former patent examiners with sufficient experience. PTO registration and practice is open to lawyers and nonlawyers alike. Registered nonlawyers are termed patent agents.[5]

§ 19.2   The Mechanics of Prosecution

19.2.1   Preparation of Applications

An inventor who wishes to obtain patent protection must first prepare an application. Although inventors may represent themselves before the PTO, the vast majority engage the services of a patent attorney or agent for this purpose. Applicants may chose to prepare either a provisional or nonprovisional application. Most inventors opt for nonprovisional, or regular applications. In this text, as in patent practice, a reference to a patent application should be taken as referring to a nonprovisional application.

An application must include a specification, at least one claim, and the proper filing fee. The filing fee as of January 1, 2003, was $750.[1] The Patent Act also requires that the applicant submit an oath or declaration stating that he believes himself to be the original and first inventor of the invention for which he seeks a patent.[2] Drawings should be included when necessary.[3] PTO regulations further provide that the elements of a patent application should appear in the following order:

3. 35 U.S.C.A. § 6 (2000).

4. 35 U.S.C.A. § 5 (2000).

5. *See* Michelle J. Burke & Thomas G. Field, Jr., *Promulgating Requirements for Admission to Prosecute Patent Applications*, 36 IDEA: J. L. & TECH. 145 (1995).

§ 19.2

1. 37 C.F.R. § 1.16 (2000).

2. 35 U.S.C.A. § 115 (2000).

3. 35 U.S.C.A. § 113 (2000).

(1) the title of the invention;

(2) a cross-reference to any related applications;

(3) a reference to a microfiche appendix containing a computer program;

(4) a brief summary of the invention;

(5) a brief description of any drawings;

(6) a detailed description;

(7) at least one claim;

(8) an abstract;

(9) a signed oath or declaration; and

(10) any drawings.[4]

Inventors possess no duty to perform a prior art search prior to filing a patent application. However, if an applicant does know of a prior art reference that is material to the patentability of the claimed invention, he must disclose it to the PTO.[5] Any prior art that the applicant wishes the PTO to consider should be listed in a so-called Information Disclosure Statement, or IDS.[6] An IDS includes a copy of all patents, publications or other information submitted for consideration. References not available in the English language must be accompanied by a concise English explanation.

19.2.2 Provisional Applications

Commencing on June 8, 1995, the PTO began to accept provisional patent applications. The fee associated with a provisional application is only $160,[7] considerably less than that required to file a nonprovisional application. Provisional applications also need not include claims, nor must they be accompanied by an inventor oath or declaration.[8] Although provisional applications are less expensive and simpler to prepare than nonprovisional applications, they also provide fewer benefits. The PTO does not examine provisional applications. In addition, the PTO will consider the applicant to have abandoned a provisional application twelve months after it is filed.

The value of filing a provisional application is that the applicant may gain the benefit of its filing date. If an applicant files a nonprovisional application within twelve months of the provisional application, he may claim the benefit of the earlier filing date. Importantly, the pendency of a provisional application does not subtract from the term of any subsequent nonprovisional application that matures into an issued patent.

An example may illustrate the workings of the provisional application scheme. Suppose that inventor Wyatt Wingfoot files a provisional

4. 37 C.F.R. § 1.77 (2000).

5. 37 C.F.R. § 1.56 (2000).

6. 37 C.F.R. §§ 1.97, 1.98 (2000).

7. 35 U.S.C.A. § 41(a)(1)(C) (2000).

8. 35 U.S.C.A. § 111(b) (2000).

application on December 1, 2000. Unless Wingfoot files a nonprovisional patent application by December 1, 2001, claiming the benefit of the earlier filing, the PTO will consider the provisional application to have been abandoned. If the PTO issues a patent to Wingfoot, that patent will expire on December 1, 2021—twenty years from the filing date of the nonprovisional application.

Provisional applications may not claim priority from any other application. An inventor could not, for example, file a series of provisional applications and claim the benefit of earlier provisional application filing dates. Amendments to the patent statute in 1999 clarified that if the twelve-month pendency period of a provisional application ends on a holiday, the applicant may file a corresponding nonprovisional application on the next working day.

19.2.3   Examination of Applications

Once an inventor has completed a patent application, he should forward it to the PTO for further consideration. It is important to note from the outset that the prosecution of a patent at the PTO is an *ex parte* procedure. Members of the public, and in particular the patent applicant's competitors, do not participate in patent acquisition procedures. Moreover, PTO examiners do not possess a competing interest relative to the applicant. Instead, they assist the applicant in fulfilling the statutory requirements for obtaining a patent grant.[9]

Once the PTO receives a patent application, PTO staff will forward it to the examining group bearing responsibility for that sort of invention. A supervisory primary examiner then assigns the application to an individual examiner. The examiner will review the application and conduct a search of the prior art. The examiner then judges whether the application properly discloses and claims a patentable invention.

The examiner must notify the applicant of her response to the application.[10] Termed an Office Action, this response may either allow the application to issue or reject it in whole or in part. The Office Action must identify each claim, indicate whether it has been rejected or allowed, and offer the examiner's reason for her actions. If the claim is to be rejected, the examiner ordinarily must establish a prima facie case of unpatentability by a preponderance of the evidence.

If a rejection has resulted, the attorney will usually respond by either amending the claims or by asserting that the rejection was improper. Under the first option, the attorney introduces changes to the claims, typically augmenting the claim language in order to overcome a rejection founded on the prior art or lack of claim definiteness. Alternatively, the attorney may argue on the merits that the rejection was

---

9. *See* Russell E. Levine *et al.*, *Ex Parte Patent Practice and the Rights of Third Parties*, 45 AMERICAN UNIV. L. REV. 1987 (1996).

10. 35 U.S.C.A. § 132 (2000).

improper. The patent bar refers to this sort of substantive argument as a "traverse."

Applicant attempts to traverse an examiner's rejection often involve the use of affidavits. Two PTO rules describe the kinds of affidavits an applicant is most likely to file. Rule 131 affidavits, which declare dates of inventive activity such as conception or reduction to practice, are employed to circumvent rejections based upon 35 U.S.C.A. §§ 102(a) or (e). This treatise considers Rule 131 affidavits in § 16.3.1. Most of the other affidavits an applicant might wish to file at the PTO fall under Rule 132. This rule provides applicants with the broad ability to offer affidavits for consideration by the examiner. Rule 132 affidavits are typically prepared by technical experts, who express opinions or report laboratory tests that support the patentability of the claimed invention.

If the examiner remains unconvinced by the applicant's response, she will issue a second Office Action titled a "Final Rejection." The applicant ordinarily has three options: abandon the application,[11] file a so-called "continuing application,"[12] or seek review of the examiner's actions by filing a petition to the Commissioner or appeal to the Board of Patent Appeals and Interferences.[13] The latter two options are discussed below. Alternatively, if the examiner agrees that the application should mature into a granted patent, she will issue a Notice of Allowance.[14] The payment of an issuance fee will then result in a granted patent, along with the publication of its abstract, a selected drawing and its broadest claim in the PTO's Official Gazette. Along with the patent itself, the "prosecution history" or "file wrapper," comprising the application and all subsequently generated documents, is then made available to the public.

19.2.4 Continuing Applications

Continuation application practice exists out of the recognition that the path to a Final Rejection can be a short one. The filing of an ordinary application usually purchases the applicant a scant two Official Actions by the examiner. Agreement often cannot be reached by this point, however, leaving the applicant with only the alternatives of abandonment of patent protection or the filing of an appeal. Under the so-called "file wrapper continuing" procedure, an applicant essentially purchases an additional period of prosecution.[15] This time allows additional further dialogue between the applicant and examiner, with the goal of more accurate and proper claiming of a previously disclosed invention without the necessity of an appeal.

PTO practice also allows for so-called "continuation-in-part," or CIP applications. A CIP application repeats a substantial portion of an earlier application, but adds new matter not disclosed in the original applica-

---

11. 35 U.S.C.A. § 133 (2000).

12. 35 U.S.C.A. § 120 (2000).

13. 35 U.S.C.A. § 134 (2000).

14. 35 U.S.C.A. § 151 (2000).

15. 35 U.S.C.A. § 120 (2000); 37 C.F.R. § 1.60 (2000).

tion. Inventors sometimes file CIP applications in order to add improvements they have made to the invention after they originally filed a patent application. Claims that are dependent upon the latter-added new matter are entitled only to the filing date of the CIP.[16]

19.2.5　The Restriction Requirement and Divisional Applications

If one application concerns multiple independent and distinct inventions, the PTO may require the applicant to select one invention for further prosecution in that application.[17] This procedure is known as a restriction. Although the applicant must elect only a single invention for further prosecution in the original application, he may opt to file so-called divisional applications relating to the remaining inventions. If the applicant pays the noted fees and follows the appropriate procedures, all applications will continue to benefit from the filing date of the original application.

For example, suppose that inventor Kenneth Cline files a patent application on August 1, 2003. Cline's application discloses and claims both a novel type of dental floss and a heat-seeking missile. The PTO will likely impose a restriction requirement, forcing Cline to elect either the floss or the missile for further prosecution with regard to that application. Suppose Cline elects to continue prosecuting the missile. PTO procedures would then allow Cline to file a divisional application directed towards the dental floss. If both applications resulted in issued patents, they would each be accorded a filing date of August 1, 2003, and would ordinarily expire on August 1, 2023.

The restriction requirements serves several purposes. Easily the most important is the maintenance of the PTO fee structure. Otherwise, applicants would be sorely tempted to cut their prosecution costs by claiming several distinct inventions in one application. The restriction requirement also better enables the PTO to classify applications and to assign a qualified examiner to consider the application.[18]

Restriction is not an absolute requirement. Section 121 of the Patent Act merely authorizes the PTO to compel applicants to elect a single disclosed invention.[19] If the PTO opts not to do so, the resulting patent is valid even though it concerns more than one invention.

19.2.6　Publication of Applications

The Domestic Publication of Foreign Filed Patent Applications Act of 1999 requires the PTO to publish pending patent applications eigh-

---

16. *See* Cecil D. Quillen, Jr. & Ogden H. Webster, *Continuing Patent Applications and Performance of the U.S. Patent and Trademark Office*, 11 Fed. Cir. B.J. 1 (2001).

17. 35 U.S.C.A. § 122 (2000).

18. *See* Applied Materials, Inc. v. Advanced Semiconductor Materials America,

Inc., 98 F.3d 1563, 40 USPQ2d 1481 (Fed. Cir.1996) (Archer, C.J., dissenting), *cert. denied*, 520 U.S. 1230, 117 S.Ct. 1822, 137 L.Ed.2d 1030 (1997).

19. 35 U.S.C.A. § 121 (2000).

teen months from the earliest filing date to which they are entitled.[20] Significantly, if an applicant certifies that the invention disclosed in the application will not be the subject of a patent application in another country that requires publication of applications 18 months after filing, then the application shall not be published. This Act also creates provisional rights, equivalent to a reasonable royalty, owed from persons who employ the invention as claimed in the published patent application.[21]

Some background into international and comparative patent law will assist understanding of this provision. First, there is no global patent system. Patent rights must be applied for and secured in each jurisdiction. In a world where technology knows no borders and international trade increasingly dominates, patent protection in a single country is often insufficient to protect inventors.

In recognition of these realities, the United States has long been a signatory of the Paris Convention for the Protection of Industrial Property.[22] This treaty attempts to ease the burdens of maintaining patent rights in many jurisdictions. Among the chief provisions of the Paris Convention is the so-called priority right. The priority right allows patent applicants to benefit from an earlier filing date in a foreign country. So long as an inventor files abroad within one year of his first filing and complies with certain formalities, his subsequent foreign filings will be treated as if they were made as of the date of his initial filing.

A second important background principle is that foreign patent offices ordinarily publish patent applications eighteen months after their first effective filing date. As an example, suppose that an inventor filed an application at the U.S. PTO on June 1, 2003. Suppose further that the inventor sought patent rights in Germany, which is also a signatory to the Paris Convention. If the inventor files a German patent application by June 1, 2004, his application will be treated as having been filed on the U.S. filing date of June 1, 2003. The German Patent Office will publish the German application on December 1, 2004, eighteen months after the first effective filing date to which the inventor is entitled.

In contrast to overseas regimes, the U.S. patent system traditionally maintained filed applications in secrecy. This regime advantaged patent applicants because it allowed them to understand exactly what the scope of any allowed claims might be prior to disclosing an invention. Thus, if the applicant was wise enough to maintain the invention that was subject to a patent application as a trade secret, then he could choose between procuring the allowed patent claims or retaining trade secret status.

---

20. 35 U.S.C.A. § 122(b) (2000).

21. 35 U.S.C.A. § 154(d) (2000).

22. Paris Convention for the Protection of Industrial Property, Mar. 20, 1883, art. 6

bis, 21 U.S.T. 1629, 828 U.N.T.S. 305 (revised July 14, 1967).

However, this secrecy regime has been perceived as imposing costs as well. Others might well engage in repetitive research efforts during the pendency of patent applications, unaware that an earlier inventor had already staked a claim to that technology. This arrangement also allows inventors to commence infringement litigation on the very day a patent issues, without any degree of notice to other members of the technological community.

The Domestic Publication of Foreign Filed Patent Applications Act of 1999 attempts to strike a middle ground between these competing concerns. U.S. patent applications will be published eighteen months from the date of filing, except where the inventor represents that he will not seek patent protection abroad. To discourage applicants from delaying their claims of foreign priority under the Paris Convention, the Act allows the PTO Director to consider the failure of the applicant to file a timely claim for priority as a waiver of such claim.

Sometimes inventors seek more robust patent protection in some countries than in others. This step may be taken for business reasons or due to differences in the patent or competition laws in varying jurisdictions. The Act therefore contains a provision allowing applicants to "submit a redacted copy of the application filed in the Patent and Trademark Office eliminating any part or description of the invention in such application that is not also contained in any of the corresponding application filed in a foreign country."[23] As a result, if an applicant seeks broader patent protection in the United States than in other countries, only the more limited version of the application will be published here.

Proponents of the legislation have asserted that this change will allow foreign competitors to view proprietary technologies earlier than they previously did.[24] Detractors have observed that the Domestic Publication of Foreign Filed Patent Applications Act of 1999 essentially does nothing. Because the legislation only makes available applications that were already published by foreign patent offices, no more or less information is made available at particular times than was before. The only advantage of this legislation would lie in convenience. Inventors may find the U.S. PTO more accessible than foreign counterparts, and the published applications would be available in the English language.

Detractors also note that this legislation might antagonize our trading partners. Inventors ordinarily file patent applications in their home jurisdictions first. Foreign filings are taken up later. As a practical matter, then, the only applications that will not be published under this statute are those filed by U.S. inventors. This domestic favoritism strikes against the principle of national treatment, a pledge the United States made when it signed the Paris Convention to treat domestic and foreign inventors equally. The Act's piecemeal publication regime hopefully

23. 35 U.S.C.A. § 122(b)(2)(B)(v) (2000).

24. *See* Christopher R. Balzan, Comment, 18 Loyola Los. Ang. Int'l & Comp. L.J. 143 (1995).

marks a transition period in U.S. patent law, providing a first step towards an ecumenical publication system.

19.2.7 Petition and Appeal

If an applicant reaches an impasse with the examiner, he may either appeal to the Board of Patent Appeals and Interferences,[25] or file a petition with the PTO Director. The forum of review depends upon the nature of the issue in dispute. It is often said that substantive issues may be resolved through appeal, while procedural matters may be petitioned.[26] Although this expression is more of a rule of thumb than a wholly accurate precept, as a general matter decisions of the examiner directly relating to the rejection of claims are appealable. The Board therefore considers such issues as statutory subject matter, utility, novelty, nonobviousness, enablement and claim definiteness.

In contrast, petitions involve such issues as expediting examination, requesting an extension of time, reviving an abandoned application or reviewing a restriction requirement. Petitions are usually resolved by Group Directors within the PTO. As compared with appeals practice, the pursuit of a petition within the PTO is much more informal and summary in character.

Dissatisfied applicants may ordinarily seek judicial review of appeals or petitions. If the applicant receives an adverse decision from the Board, he may opt to bring a civil action against the Director. This action must be filed in either the United States District Court for the District of Columbia[27] or the Court of Appeals for the Federal Circuit.[28] The primary advantage of the former route is that the applicant may submit new evidence into the record, an option unavailable at the Federal Circuit. Appeals from suits lodged in the D.C. District Court go to the Federal Circuit as well. In contrast, an unsuccessful petitioner may seek judicial review through a number of mechanisms, including the Administrative Procedure Act,[29] the All Writs Act,[30] or a civil action against the Commissioner.[31] Such actions may be brought in any United States district court, with the Federal Circuit as the court of second instance.

§ 19.3 Inventorship

A topic conveniently taken up alongside prosecution is that of inventorship. A patent application ordinarily must be made, or authorized to be made, by the inventor.[1] Even if the inventor has assigned his invention to his employer or other entity, the inventor himself must ordinarily sign a declaration or oath stating that he believes he is the first inventor.

25. *See* 35 U.S.C.A. § 134 (2000).

26. *See* In re Searles, 422 F.2d 431, 435, 164 USPQ 623, 626 (CCPA 1970).

27. 35 U.S.C.A. § 145 (2000).

28. 35 U.S.C.A. § 141 (2000).

29. 5 U.S.C.A. §§ 701–706 (2000).

30. 28 U.S.C.A. § 1651 (2000).

31. 28 U.S.C.A. § 1338(a) (2000).

§ 19.3

1. *See* 35 U.S.C.A. § 115 (2000).

Inventorship determinations have many other consequences in the patent law. Inventors are presumptively the owners of a patent, so a defendant's successful assertion of joint inventorship serves as a fine infringement defense. In addition, inventorship determinations influence the definition of many of the categories of prior art under § 102. For example, paragraph (a) refers to prior knowledge or use "by others," while paragraph (e) makes prior art out of patent applications filed "by another" in appropriate circumstances.[2] Without knowledge of the inventors appropriately associated with the patent or application under consideration, these prior art categories cannot be properly defined.

Many patented inventions were conceived and reduced to practice by a single individual. But in addition to individual inventors, joint inventors are also recognized by the patent statute. Amendments introduced in 1984 to § 116 specified that individuals may be joint inventors "even though (1) they did not physically work together or at the same time, (2) each did not make the same type or amount of contribution, or (3) each did not make a contribution to the subject matter of every claim of the patent." Although this negative definition is of some use in inventorship determinations, the statute does not specify affirmative technical contributions that cause an individual to rise to the level of an inventor. Courts agree that to qualify as an inventor, an individual must have contributed to the conception of the invention, and that the conceiver's status as inventor is not defeated if he employs the services of others to perfect the invention. But beyond these simple defining principles, inventorship cases tend to be highly fact specific and seldom provide firm guidance on resolving future disputes.

An exemplary decision is *Hess v. Advanced Cardiovascular Systems, Inc.*[3] There, two surgeons named Simpson and Robert received a patent on a balloon angioplasty catheter. When their assignee brought an infringement suit, the defendant produced declarations by Hess asserting that he should have been named a co-inventor. It seems that while working for a tubing supply company, Hess had discussed the catheter project with Simpson and Robert. Some of the contributions of Hess made their way into the patented product following further development by Simpson and Robert.

Following the rejection of his assertion of co-inventorship, Hess appealed to the Federal Circuit. The appeals court agreed that the contributions of Hess did not rise to the level of an inventor. According to the Federal Circuit, the contributions of Hess were known to the art and available on the marketplace. Hess was seen as no more than a skilled salesman who explained how his employer's products could be used to meet the technical requirements of Simpson and Robert.

The Federal Circuit does not provide an exhaustive explanation of the technical contributions of Hess towards the catheter project. Still, the outcome of the opinion appears subject to doubt given that Simpson

2. *See* 35 U.S.C.A. § 102(a), (e) (2000).

3. 106 F.3d 976, 41 USPQ2d 1782 (Fed. Cir.1997), *cert. denied*, 520 U.S. 1277, 117 S.Ct. 2459, 138 L.Ed.2d 216 (1997).

and Robert had themselves stated that Hess was responsible for significant portions of the patented catheter. One supposes that although Simpson and Robert were superlative surgeons, their skills in the art of plastics manufacturing were less developed. It seems unlikely that the catheter project could have gotten off the ground without Hess, who should have been valued as more than merely a walking, talking catalogue of the prior art. The reader of the *Hess* opinion senses that the Federal Circuit distrusted Hess's tardy claims of inventorship and questioned the standing of a rather humble sales engineer against the qualifications of two highly skilled surgeons.

Some hypotheticals further illustrate the implications of *Hess*. Suppose that Professor Gizmo asks her laboratory technician, Steve Schlep, to combine certain chemicals in such a way as to form Compound X. Gizmo further asks Schlep to determine, using standard testing methodologies well known in the field, whether or not Compound X functions as an adhesive at high temperatures. If Schlep merely follows Gizmo's instructions, making no inventive contribution to the project, then Schlep will not qualify as an inventor even though Schelp was literally the first person to synthesize Compound X. The courts have long held that inventors may employ others to help them achieve a reduction to practice without making co-inventors out of their assistants.

In contrast, suppose that Gizmo had the idea of Compound X but did not possess an operative way of synthesizing it. Upon explaining her idea to Schelp, Schlep discovers a new, nonobvious way to formulate Compound X. Or, alternatively, suppose that Gizmo tells Schlep precisely how to fabricate Compound X, but she has no idea to what uses the new compound can be put. After trial and error at the laboratory bench, Schlep identifies an unexpected application for Compound X–say, as a depilatory. In either of these alternative hypotheticals, Schlep would likely qualify as a co-inventor. He has made an inventive contribution to the development of Compound X and should be named on any patent instrument that claims that invention.

As inventors named in a patent often receive benefits ranging from financial rewards from their employers to recognition from the technical community, intracorporate disputes over inventorship are not uncommon. Patent attorneys must often demonstrate persistence and tact in order to ensure that the appropriate individuals are named in a given patent. They should also be aware of corporate technical disclosure forms and other documents that label a person as the "inventor," for such determinations are often made without awareness of the strictures of the Patent Act.[4]

§ 19.4 Abuses of the Patent Acquisition Process

Experience has taught us that the patent prosecution system is susceptible to abuse by applicants. The judiciary has responded by

4. *See generally* W. Fritz Fasse, *The Muddy Metaphysics of Joint Inventorship*, 5 Harv. J. L. & Tech. 153 (1992).

developing various doctrines to curb the worst of these misuses. The most significant of these doctrines, which concern inequitable conduct and double patenting, are considered in turn below.

19.4.1 Inequitable Conduct

Because the usual advantages of an adversarial system do not attach to the *ex parte* prosecution process, the patent system relies to a great extent upon applicant observance of a duty of candor and truthfulness towards the PTO. However, the applicant's obligation to proceed in good faith may be tempered by the great incentive applicants possess not to disclose prior art or to misrepresent facts that might deleteriously impact their prospective patent rights. The patent law therefore imposes a draconian penalty for those who stray from honest and forthright dealings with the PTO. Under the doctrine of inequitable conduct, if an applicant intentionally misrepresents a material fact or fails to disclose material information, then the resulting patent will be declared unenforceable.[1]

Most inequitable conduct cases involve an applicant's knowing failure to disclose material prior art to the PTO. But numerous other circumstances have also caused courts to find inequitable conduct and judge the asserted patent unenforceable. These include deceitful statements in affidavits, the submission of misleading test results, and dishonest inventor's oaths. Although this doctrine applies to a number of factual circumstances, the case law unfailingly requires two elements to exist before a court will decide that the applicant has engaged in inequitable conduct. First, the patentee must have misrepresented or failed to disclose material information to the PTO in the prosecution of the patent. Second, such misrepresentation must have been intentional.[2]

19.4.1.1 Materiality

A misrepresented or undisclosed fact must be "material" to serve as the basis for inequitable conduct. When deciding whether particular information is material or not, the courts have most often relied upon the definition that occurs in PTO Rule 56. Entitled "Duty to Disclose Information Material to Patentability," Rule 56 is a basic provision governing ethical representation of inventors at the PTO. From 1977 to 1992, Rule 56 provided that "information is material where there is a substantial likelihood that a reasonable examiner would consider it important in deciding whether to allow the application to issue as a patent." Under the new Rule 56 promulgated by the PTO in 1992, a reference is judged material if it either (1) establishes, by itself or in combination with other information, a prima facie case of unpatentability of a claim; or (2) is inconsistent with a position taken by the applicant.

§ 19.4

1. *See* Robert J. Goldman, *Evolution of the Inequitable Conduct Defense in Patent Litigation*, 7 HARV. J. L. & TECH. 37 (1993).

2. *Id.*

The Federal Circuit's opinion in *Molins PLC v. Textron, Inc.*[3] considers the materiality standard under the earlier version of Rule 56. There, the U.K. enterprise Molins filed patent applications relating to a batch machining process in many countries, including the United States. During prosecution overseas, several foreign patent examiners discovered the Wagenseil prior art reference. A member of the Molins patent department, Whitson, concluded that Wagenseil anticipated the batch process claims. However, Whitson never informed Molins's U.S. patent representative about the Wagenseil reference. As a result, the PTO examiner did not know of Wagenseil during the original prosecution. Although Molins eventually abandoned all of its foreign applications, it obtained two U.S. patents pertaining to the batch process.

Following Whitson's retirement, his successor, Hirsch, reviewed the U.S. patent files and realized that the PTO had not been informed of Wagenseil. Hirsch quickly filed a prior art statement that listed the Wagenseil reference. Later, based in part on Wagenseil, a competitor filed a reexamination request directed towards one of Molins's patents. Although the PTO granted the request, none of the claims were rejected based upon Wagenseil during the reexamination. Seemingly emboldened by this successful outcome, Molins then filed an infringement suit against several competing corporations.

The trial court easily found that Molins had violated its duty of candor with the PTO. The court concluded that Whitson had engaged in inequitable conduct by failing to disclose Wagenseil to the PTO even though he knew it was highly material. As a result, both of Molins's patents were unenforceable. Following an appeal, the Federal Circuit affirmed. The court agreed that the Wagenseil reference was material under the "reasonable examiner" standard. According to Judge Lourie, extensive evidence demonstrated that many foreign patent examiners considered Wagneseil significant; that Whitson had amended many claims in light of rejections based upon Wagenseil overseas; and that Whitson had indicated during several foreign patent examinations that Wagenseil was the most pertinent reference of which he was aware.

The court did recognize a significant problem with the application of the "reasonable examiner" standard to these facts. One PTO examiner had actually considered the Wagnseil reference during reexamination. The result of that viewing was that the examiner did not call for a single change to any of Molins's patent claims. However, Judge Lourie noted that the materiality standard is not concerned with whether the particular examiner assigned to the application at issue believed the reference to be important. According to the court, materiality instead rested upon the view of a hypothetical, reasonable examiner. More persuasive was the court's point that a reference is not immaterial simply because the claims are eventually deemed to be allowable over that reference.

Molins strongly suggests that patent applicants should err on the side of disclosure when considering whether or not to submit a reference

3. 48 F.3d 1172, 33 USPQ2d 1823 (Fed. Cir.1995).

to the PTO. An important point mentioned, but not further discussed in *Molins*, is that applicants have no duty to disclose an otherwise material prior art reference if the reference is cumulative to, or less material than, references already before the examiner. Applying this concept in *Halliburton Co. v. Schlumberger Technology Corp.*,[4] the Federal Circuit overturned the district court's holding of inequitable conduct by reasoning that references discovered by the examiner were more pertinent to the claimed invention than those that were not cited. Although this opinion appears to allow examiner competence to excuse an unscrupulous applicant, the courts have reasoned that cumulative prior art adds nothing to what is already of record and therefore need not be disclosed.

19.4.1.2 Intent

An applicant's misrepresentation or nondisclosure of a material fact is a necessary, but not sufficient, component of a finding of inequitable conduct. The applicant must also have affirmatively sought to mislead the PTO. In *Kingsdown Medical Consultants, Ltd. v. Hollister, Inc.*,[5] the Federal Circuit overturned earlier decisions that had found inequitable conduct based upon grossly negligent behavior by the applicant. According to the *en banc* court, the involved conduct, viewed in light of all of the evidence, must indicate sufficient culpability to require a finding of an intent to deceive.

In the *Kingsdown* case, Kingsdown was in the midst of prosecuting an application directed towards a two-piece ostomy appliance when Hollister introduced a similar product to the marketplace. Kingsdown opted to file a continuation application in order to obtain claims that tracked Hollister's device. Unfortunately, when Kingsdown took the ministerial step of copying its lengthy claims from the original to the continuation application, it accidentally transferred an earlier, unamended version of one of the claims into the continuation. Once the patent issued, Kingsdown sued Hollister for infringement. The district court found inequitable conduct on two grounds. First, the court concluded that Kingsdown's miscopying evidenced gross negligence, sufficient to support a finding of inequitable conduct. Second, the district court held that Kingsdown's tactics in seeking tight claim coverage against the Hollister device evidenced an intent to deceive.

The Federal Circuit reversed on appeal. The court noted that even if Kingsdown's conduct could be characterized as gross negligence, that level of scienter was insufficient to support a conclusion of inequitable conduct. Nor does an applicant's effort to obtain claims that read upon a competitor's product constitute deceit, whether the applicant first learned of that product during or prior to prosecution. The court instead held that challenged conduct would be judged inequitable only where all the circumstances indicate that the applicant affirmatively maintained a fraudulent intent towards the PTO.

4. 925 F.2d 1435, 17 USPQ2d 1834 (Fed.Cir.1991).

5. 863 F.2d 867, 9 USPQ2d 1384 (Fed. Cir.1988).

Courts seldom encounter direct evidence of an applicant's intent to deceive. They must instead infer the applicant's mental state based on circumstantial evidence. A pattern of deliberately withholding or mischaracterizing information would be most probative of fraudulent intent, particularly if the patentee cannot provide a believable, good faith explanation for its repeated conduct. Some judicial opinions also speak towards a balancing of materiality and intent. In cases where an applicant knowingly withheld prior art references, for example, courts have reasoned that the more material the references to the patentability of the claimed invention, the more likely the applicant intended to deceive the PTO.

Suppose, for example, that Dr. Nefarious files an application at the PTO directed towards a new machine for making dental floss. Nefarious does not disclose an article published two years earlier in the well-known journal *Fiendish Fluoridators Fortnightly*. Because that article includes many of the elements claimed in the patent application of Nefarious, it is highly material. Although no direct evidence of the intent of Nefarious may exist, a court would put great weight on the fact that Nefarious had cited the article in earlier writings, had mentioned the article in a speech, and had even written a letter to the editor of *Fiendish Fluoridators Fortnightly* discussing the article in question. In such an extreme case, a court could readily assume that Nefarious was very much aware of the importance of the journal article and harbored an intent to deceive the PTO.

19.4.1.3 Reconsidering Inequitable Conduct

The doctrine of inequitable conduct has suffered its fair share of criticism over the years. One perceptive commentator has questioned whether the patent system benefits from striking down otherwise valid patents that happen to have been inequitably procured. If, for example, the applicant knowingly withheld a pertinent prior art reference, then the resulting patent is likely invalid due to the requisites of novelty and nonobviousness. But if that patent would stand over the reference, we do well to question whether the applicant has engaged in conduct worthy of condemnation. In such circumstances even the inequitable inventor has obtained a patent that objectively functions as well as any other.[6]

The Federal Circuit has also described inequitable conduct as "an absolute plague" upon patent litigation.[7] In recent years accused infringers seem to bring charges of inequitable conduct in every case. The strategic advantages of doing so are almost too good to resist: Not only does inequitable conduct effectively place the inventor and her patent attorney on trial, it also provides a mechanism for discovery of documents otherwise protected by the attorney-client privilege and work product doctrine. Despite these telling criticisms, the Federal Circuit has

---

6. *See* John F. Lynch, *An Argument for Eliminating the Defense of Patent Unenforceability Based on Inequitable Conduct*, 16 AM. INTELL. PROP. L. ASS'N Q.J. 7 (1988).

7. *See* Burlington Indus. v. Dayco Corp., 849 F.2d 1418, 1422, 7 USPQ2d 1158 (Fed. Cir.1988).

remained a vigorous enforcer of the patent applicant's duty of candor during prosecution.

19.4.2   Double Patenting

The patent system envisions the issuance of only a single patent per invention. Allowing inventors to obtain multiple patents on a single invention could disturb the integrity of the twenty-year patent term and present accused infringers with the possibility of paying multiple damages for a single infringing act.[8] The following example illustrates these difficulties.

Suppose that inventor Carla Complement files a patent application claiming a photocopier on March 21, 2000. That patent issues as U.S. Patent No. 6,789,123 on August 1, 2002. On July 31, 2003, Complement files a second patent application. Complement's 2003 application contains a disclosure and claims identical to that of the '123 patent. The harms that might result from the issuance of Complement's 2003 application as a separate patent are apparent. The '123 patent will expire on March 21, 2020, but the patent resulting from the 2003 application would provide Complement with over three years of additional patent protection. Further, if Complement brought suit against another, that individual would face the possibility of twofold infringement liability.

Despite the conspicuous drawbacks of double patenting, the prior art definition provided by § 102 contains no express statutory mechanism for addressing this abuse of the patent acquisition process. Many activities must be performed by another to be patent-defeating under § 102, including the secret prior art established by § 102(e). Only the statutory bars of § 102(b) and (d) generate prior art from the applicant's own work.[9] Thus, in the absence of other activities that disclose the invention to the public, an inventor could extend the statutory protection period through a simple policy: file an application no later than one year after an earlier, related application has matured into a patent.

As a result, the courts have been left to develop the law of double patenting on their own. They have identified two sorts of double patenting. The first kind, which occurs when both patents have claims of identical scope, is known as "same-invention double patenting." If the claims of the later patent could not be literally infringed without literally infringing the claims of the earlier patent, then a court will strike down the later patent for double patenting. Courts have sometimes based same invention doubling patenting on § 101, which allows an applicant to "obtain *a* patent" on an invention. As a result, this doctrine is sometimes referred to as statutory double patenting.

When two patents do not claim the identical invention, but instead obvious variations of each other, the later patent will also be invalidated

---

8. *See* Applied Materials Inc. v. Advanced Semiconductor Materials America, Inc., 98 F.3d 1563, 1568, 40 USPQ2d 1481, 1484 (Fed.Cir.1996), *cert. denied*, 520 U.S. 1230, 117 S.Ct. 1822, 137 L.Ed.2d 1030 (1997).

9.   35 U.S.C.A. § 102 (b), (d) (2000).

due to so-called "obviousness-type double patenting." In contrast to same invention double patenting, judges may employ prior art references in combination with the claims of the earlier patent to determine whether the later patent claims an invention that would have been obvious to those of skill in the art. Because no provision of the Patent Act concerns obviousness-style double patenting, courts sometimes refer to this doctrine as nonstatutory double patenting.

Double patenting may occur when the same inventor obtains two issued patents directed towards the same inventive concept. However, the PTO also considers the double patenting doctrine during prosecution. As a result, an applicant may face a double patenting rejection based upon either an granted patent or another pending application. *In re Vogel*,[10] one of the meatier decisions in the patent law, was such a case. There the PTO imposed a double patenting rejection based upon a granted patent that claimed a method of preparing pork products for long term storage. Claims 7 and 10 of Vogel's pending application performed an analogous process applied to meat, while claim 11 was directed towards a similar process on beef products.

Vogel appealed to the CCPA, contending that the double patenting rejection was improper. The court first considered whether this was a case of same invention double patenting. The court thought not: the patent claims concerned pork, while the claims of Vogel's application recited beef and meat. Beef is not the same as pork, and many processes that would infringe claims 7 and 10 of the application would not infringe the patented claims, which were limited to pork.

The CCPA then turned to obviousness-style double patenting. Turning first to claim 11 of Vogel's application, the court found no evidence of record that beef and pork exhibited similar characteristics for purposes of long term storage. With nothing to suggest that beef and pork were obvious variants of one another, the court overturned the PTO's double patenting rejection. The CCPA next considered whether claims 7 and 10 were appropriately rejected for double patenting. The court observed that the term "pork" was literally covered by the term "meat." As a result, allowance of Vogel's pending application would effectively extend the term of the already patented pork preparation process. The court therefore affirmed the PTO's double patenting rejection with respect to those claims.

The reader of *Vogel* obtains the fortunately rare privilege of simultaneously learning about the making of both law and sausages. But beyond being tempted into vegetarianism by the rather graphic claim language in that case, most readers of *Vogel* find it easy to scoff at the court's reasoning regarding the relationship of beef and pork. Most cooks would freely substitute beef for pork in the majority of recipes if no pork was on hand.[11] As well, the meat packing industry likely knew the spoilage characteristics of both beef and pork quite well. Still, the PTO always

---

10. 422 F.2d 438, 164 USPQ 619 (CCPA 1970).

11. *See* Johnston, *On the Validity of Double Patents*, 54 J. Pat. Off. Soc'y 291, 303 (1972).

possesses the burden of presenting evidence that opposes patentability, and its failure to present proof may well have allowed Vogel to avoid a double patenting rejection at the CCPA.

Vogel also reminds us that double patenting focuses upon the claims. The double patenting doctrine rejects attempts of an inventor to claim the same inventive concept twice. If a later patent discloses but does not claim the same or similar invention as an earlier patent, then double patenting issues do not arise. Section 121 of the Patent Act also provides that "[t]he validity of a patent shall not be questioned for failure of the Director to require the application to be restricted to one invention."[12] The practical effect of this language is that the double patenting doctrine does not apply when the two patents at issue resulted from a PTO restriction requirement.

Courts have authorized the use of a "terminal disclaimer" to overcome obviousness-style double patenting rejections.[13] A terminal disclaimer causes patent granted to a given inventor to expire on the same date as an earlier patent. By arranging for all related patents to elapse at the same time, the patentee overcomes the concerns of extended patent protection for the same inventive concept. The terminal disclaimer technique allows inventors to file applications claiming obvious variants on a single inventive idea, in order to create prior art against other applicants and to obtain a tight fit for potential infringements.

Patents that issue due to terminal disclaimers may be subject to abuse. Suppose that the owner of several closely related patents—all but one valid due to the filing of terminal disclaimers—sells one patent each to different, unrelated entities. This scenario would potentially subject an accused infringer to multiple infringement suits based on patents to the same invention. Such concerns led the PTO to mandate that terminal disclaimers include a provision that any subsequent patent shall be enforceable only while it is commonly owned with the application or patent which formed the basis for the double patenting rejection.

Terminal disclaimers may not be used to overcome same invention double patenting rejections. The courts have reasoned that the use of terminal disclaimers in overcoming an obviousness-style double patenting is in the public interest because it encourages the disclosure of additional developments, the earlier filing of applications and the earlier expiration of patents.[14] Because none of these benefits appears to flow when two patents claim the identical subject matter, neither the courts nor the PTO will allow the use of terminal disclaimers in such cases.

§ 19.5 Duration of Rights

Once the PTO issues a patent, that patent enjoys an effective term established by the statute. As this book goes to press U.S. patent law is

---

12. 35 U.S.C.A. § 121 (2000).

13. *See* In re Robeson, 331 F.2d 610, 141 USPQ 485 (CCPA 1964).

14. *See* In re Berg, 140 F.3d 1428, 1436, 46 USPQ2d 1226, 1233 (Fed.Cir.1998).

in a transition period regarding patent term. For patents resulting from applications filed after June 8, 1995, the patent term is ordinarily twenty years from the date the patent application was filed. For patents issued prior to June 8, 1995, as well as for patents resulting from applications pending at the PTO as of that date, the patent endures for the greater of twenty years from filing or seventeen years from grant.[1]

Although the life of the patent is measured from the filing date, the patentee gains no enforceable rights merely by filing a patent application. These rights accrue only at such time that the patent issues, and include the power to enjoin infringers and obtain an award of damages. If the application was published in accordance with the Domestic Publication of Patent Applications Abroad Act of 1999, then the patentee also obtains provisional rights equivalent to a reasonable royalty. Although provisional rights extend from the time the application was published, the patentee may not assert them until the patent issues.

The term of U.S. patents was traditionally measured from the date the PTO issued the application. The Act of 1790 allowed the issuance of patents "for any term not exceeding fourteen years." The Act of 1861 increased this term to "seventeen years from the date of issue." On June 8, 1995, the U.S. patent system shifted to a term based upon the filing date. Transitional provisions ensured that patents in force on June 8, 1995, as well as patents that issued from applications filed prior to that date, enjoyed the longer of the two terms: seventeen years from issuance or twenty years from filing.

Although the distinction between the two regimes may not appear to loom particularly large, significant consequences flow from United States adoption of a twenty-year patent term measured from the filing date. Prior to June 8, 1995, the filing of continuing applications did not affect the length of the effective patent term. Once the patent issued, it obtained a seventeen-year term. Currently, the term of a patent is measured as twenty years from the earliest filing date. The new term scheme puts an end to so-called "submarine" patents which plagued particular industries in the United States. Submarine patents emerged from a series of concealed continuation applications, sometimes filed thirty or more years earlier, to "torpedo" industries that had developed in ignorance of the pending applications.[2]

Three significant qualifications may alter the basic twenty-year term. First, the term of a patent may be extended under § 156, a provision of the Hatch–Waxman Act. This complex statute authorizes increased patent terms on inventions that have been subject to a lengthy premarket approval process under the Federal Food, Drug and Cosmetic Act.

§ 19.5

1. *See* Mark A. Lemley, *An Empirical Study of the Twenty–Year Patent Term*, 22 AM. INTELL. PROP. L. Q.J. 369 (1994).

2. *See* Steve Blount & Louis S. Zarfas, *The Use of Delaying Tactics to Obtain Sub-* *marine Patents and Amend Around A Patent That A Competitor Has Designed Around*, 81 J. PAT. & TRADEMARK OFF. SOC'Y 11 (1999).

Second, enjoyment of the full patent term is subject to the payment of maintenance fees. Currently, a patent expires after four, eight, or twelve years if maintenance fees are not timely paid on each occasion. As of January 1, 2003, the amounts due are $890 by the fourth year, $2,050 by the eighth year, and $3,150 by the twelfth year. As only about thirty-three percent of the patents issued in the United States are maintained beyond their eleventh year,[3] maintenance fees effectively dedicate a great deal of patented technology into the public domain.

Finally, the Patent Term Guarantee Act of 1999 provides certain deadlines that, if not met by the PTO, result in an automatic extension of the term of individual patents.[4] The most significant of these deadlines appear to be fourteen months for a First Office Action and four months for a subsequent Office Action. In addition, the prosecution of an original patent application must be complete within three years of the actual U.S. filing date, with exceptions granted for continuing applications and appeals. As might be expected, each day of PTO delay beyond these limits results in one additional day of patent term. The Director is charged with calculating any patent term extensions that might result from missed PTO deadlines.

§ 19.6   Post–Grant Proceedings

The Patent and Trademark Office's involvement in the United States patent system does not necessarily end when it formally grants a patent. The law has long recognized the numerous possibilities for mistakes, ranging from minor typesetting errors to significant substantive flaws, to make their way into the patent instrument. The patent statute thus provides the PTO with several different mechanisms for correcting the inevitable. The magnitude of the mistake largely determines which procedure will be employed.

19.6.1   Certificates of Correction

The least onerous and most frequently used of these procedures is a certificate of correction.[1] Patentees employ a certificate of correction to address minor typographical errors. Such errors typically include misspelled words, omission of the name of an assignee or the printing of a claim in original rather than amended form. Mistakes incurred through the fault of the PTO may be corrected free of charge. Most of these mistakes occur during the formatting and typesetting of the formal copy of the patent instrument. Otherwise, the petitioner must submit a fee along with proof that the error occurred in good faith.

The PTO may also issue a certificate correcting the inventors named on a particular patent instrument.[2] When the correct inventors are not

3. *See* Charles E. Van Horn, *Practicalities and Potential Pitfalls When Using Provisional Patent Applications*, 22 AIPLA Q.J. 259, 296 (1994).

4. 35 U.S.C.A. § 154(b) (2000).

§ 19.6

1. 35 U.S.C.A. §§ 254, 255 (2000).

2. 35 U.S.C.A. § 256 (2000).

named in an issued patent, through error and without deceptive intent, the parties and assignees may petition the PTO to amend the patent. Provided that a sufficient factual showing is made, the PTO will issue a certificate correcting the error in inventorship.

19.6.2 Disclaimers

The Patent Act provides for two sorts of disclaimers.[3] Applicants employ the first kind, terminal disclaimers, in order to avoid double patenting rejections. Terminal disclaimers are discussed in section 19.4.2 of this Chapter. Patentees file the second kind, statutory disclaimers, in order to eliminate invalid claims from otherwise sound patents. A statutory disclaimer effectively cancels the claim from the patent. Failure to file a statutory disclaimer does not render the remaining claims of a patent invalid or unenforceable. The Patent Act merely provides that a patentee may not recover costs for a litigation unless he filed a disclaimer of any invalid claims with the PTO prior to commencing litigation.[4]

Suppose, for example, that Carol Kinkead is the proprietor of U.S. Patent No. 6,797,617. As issued, the '617 patent contained ten claims. Suppose that Kinkead brought suit against a competitor. During this litigation, the court held that claim 1 of the '617 patent was invalid due to obviousness. If Kinkead wished to commence a second litigation, she should file a statutory disclaimer of claim 1 at the PTO. Taking this step prior to filing the second suit would allow her to recover costs from the defendant should she prevail.

19.6.3 Reissue

A patentee may employ the reissue proceeding to correct a patent that he believes to be inoperative or invalid. In contrast to certificates of correction or disclaimers, which are quite limited in scope, reissues allow for a comprehensive dialogue between the patentee and examiner. The reissue proceeding thus provides a powerful mechanism for preparing a patent for litigation or licensing negotiations.

19.6.3.1 The Error Requirement

In order to be reissued, a patent must be defective due to an "error without any deceptive intention."[5] Towards this end, the PTO requires that the reissue applicant file a reissue oath or declaration stating at least one error that forms the basis for reissue. Although the term "error" appears straightforward, it has developed into a term of art in the patent law. Not every sort of mistake constitutes an error within the meaning of the reissue statute.

The Patent Act explains that reissues may be obtained where the patent contains "a defective specification or drawing," or if the patentee claimed "more or less than he had a right to claim."[6] In practice, most

3. 35 U.S.C.A. § 253 (2000).   5. 35 U.S.C.A. § 251 (2000).

4. 35 U.S.C.A. § 288 (2000).   6. 35 U.S.C.A. § 251 (2000).

reissue proceedings amend the patent claims. For example, the patentee might recognize that the claims contain an ambiguity that might render them invalid under the definiteness requirement of § 112, ¶ 1. Alternatively, subsequent to the issuance of a patent, the patentee may learn of prior art that would invalidate the claimed invention due to anticipation or obviousness. By incorporating additional limitations into the claim through reissue, the patentee may yet be able to define a patentable advance over the prior art.

Suppose, for example, that Dr. Tinker obtains a patent claiming a new radiator cap on December 1, 2003, based upon an application filed on August 12, 2000. While Dr. Tinker is reviewing some back issues of the *Radiator Review* monthly magazine, she discovers an article in the May 1996 issue that describes a radiator cap almost identical to her claimed invention. Tinker realizes that the magazine article counts as prior art under § 102(b)—it was published more than one year before her filing date—and that it might render her invention obvious within the meaning of § 103. Because her patent already issued and administrative proceedings with the PTO have closed, Tinker cannot simply telephone the PTO and ask an examiner to narrow the scope of her claims. Tinker may wish to file a reissue application, however, in order to add further language of restriction to her patent's claims. Tinker may be able to distinguish successfully her patented radiator cap from the prior art and turn an invalid patent into a valid, albeit more circumscribed one.

A third possibility is that the patentee claimed less than he had a right to claim. In such cases, although the written description of the patent may cover particular commercial embodiments of the disclosed invention, the patent claims were not drafted to read upon these embodiments. Consider the example of Herr Knies, who hypothetically obtains a patent concerning a method of brewing beer. Assume that the specification of the Knies patent includes two "working examples" discussing the brewing of lager-and pilsner-style beers. However, the claims of the Knies patent are specifically restricted to the use of lager-style beer. If Goldmann, a competitor of Knies, began brewing pilsner-style beer, then the Knies patent would not literally cover his competitor's activities. Nor would Knies be able to employ the doctrine of equivalents against Goldman, because under the "public dedication doctrine" subject matter that is disclosed, but not claimed in a patent is disclaimed.[7] Knies may be able to pursue a so-called broadening reissue, however, in order to broaden the scope of his claims. Broadening reissues are subject to special restrictions described in § 19.6.3.3 below.

Although the grounds listed in the statute appear broad, the Federal Circuit has stated on numerous occasions that reissue is not a universal curative for all patent prosecution problems. Some flaws are simply too grave to be corrected through the use of a reissue proceeding. These include a specification that does not fulfill the requirements of § 112;

---

7. *See infra* § 20.2.2.3.4.

when the applicant has engaged in inequitable conduct during the original prosecution; and when the invention has been entirely anticipated under § 102. None of these sorts of mistakes constitutes an error cognizable by the reissue statute.

The courts have also specified that other sorts of mistakes are uncorrectable simply because they are not the sort the reissue statute was designed to remedy. Jurists have uniformly reasoned that if the error requirement did not serve as a gatekeeper, unlimited access to reissue would diminish incentives for applicants to get things right in the initial prosecution. But beyond this fundamental principle of administrative efficiency, the courts have lacked mechanisms for determining what sort of conduct amounts to an error within the reissue statute. The result has been some varying case law and fine reasoning about the precise scope of the error requirement.

Exemplary of this uncertainty is the 1989 opinion of the Federal Circuit in *Hewlett–Packard Co. v. Bausch & Lomb Inc.*[8] Bausch & Lomb (B&L) had purchased the '950 patent, which was directed towards a plotter. The '950 patent contained nine claims. Prior to commencing enforcement litigation against Hewlett–Packard (H–P), B&L realized that only the broadest '950 patent claim, claim 1, read on a H–P plotter. But this same broad claim was likely invalid over the prior art. While claims 2–9 of the '950 patent were likely not invalid, they also were too narrow to cover H–P's product.

B&L opted to file a reissue application at the PTO. Its affidavits provided that the drafter of the '950 patent application had limited contact with the inventor and did not realize which limitations were significant in light of the prior art. After some wrangling with PTO officials, B&L ultimately obtained a reissue of the '950 patent that included three additional claims. These three claims were of intermediate scope and specifically covered the H–P plotter. When B&L commenced infringement litigation, H–P argued that a failure to include multiple dependent claims of varying scope was insufficient in itself to establish error warranting reissue. Following an appeal, the Federal Circuit agreed. Because B&L neither disclaimed claim 1 nor added claims narrower than those originally in the '950 patent, B&L could not assert that the '950 patent was ineffective to protect the patented invention.

The reasoning of the *Hewlett–Packard* opinion may be justly criticized. The patent law employs dependent claims to ameliorate the principle that limitations may not be read from the specification into the claims in order to preserve their validity. The failure to include appropriate dependent claims in the '950 patent appears to have been a simple lack of foresight, rather than some sort of strategic calculation. Perhaps the Federal Circuit was influenced by the affidavits filed by B&L at the PTO, some of which appeared inaccurate and even bordered on the fraudulent. In any event, B&L would have been better advised simply to

8. 882 F.2d 1556, 11 USPQ2d 1750 (Fed.Cir.1989).

confess to the PTO its actual suspicions and disclaim claim 1 when filing the reissue application.

19.6.3.2　Reissue Procedures at the PTO

A patentee commences reissue proceedings by filing a reissue application. The PTO requests that reissue applicants include the originally issued patent instrument, usually known as the "ribboned copy," along with the other paperwork. This requirement is in keeping with the statute's mandate that the patentee surrender the original patent in order to obtain a reissued patent. Although a patentee may ultimately abandon a reissue proceeding and arrange for the return of her patent, she should be reluctant to do so: the cloud this abandoned application would cast upon the patent will be duly noted by courts and competitors.

Once the PTO accepts a reissue application, it oversees the customary procedures of patent prosecution. The standard sequence of Office Actions and responses occurs, and applicants may also file continuation and divisional applications as necessary. Note that continuation-in-part applications are not allowed during reissue proceedings: this step would involve the introduction of new matter, which is prohibited by the first paragraph of § 251. The second paragraph of § 251 also allows several patents to issue from a single reissue application.

In high relief to the usual prosecution process, reissue proceedings are open to the public. To this end, the PTO Official Gazette announces the filing of reissue applications each week. PTO regulations then mandate that the reissue proceeding not commence for at least two months, in order to allow third parties to submit evidence and arguments relating to the patentability of the reissue application.

Reissue proceedings therefore expose the patentee to some risk. Although he may have carefully calculated the steps he needs to take to move through the reissue proceeding, these plans may be thrown off by interested parties. Competitors and licensors in particular may vigorously contest the reissue of the patent by submitting additional prior art or arguments against patentability. If the patent reissues, however, the patentee has likely strengthened his patent for use in licensing negotiations or during litigation.

Reissued patents receive a new number, but their term is set to the remaining term of the original patent. Suppose, for example, that a patent application was filed on January 19, 1997, resulting in an issued patent on March 15, 1999. The patentee then filed a reissue application on December 1, 1999, which led to a reissued patent on August 1, 2000. The expiration date of the reissued patent would ordinarily be January 19, 2017, twenty years from the filing date of the original patent.

19.6.3.3　Broadening Reissues

A patentee may employ a reissue to expand the scope of its claims. The fourth paragraph of § 251 sets forth a two-year statute of limitations for seeking a broadening reissue.[9] Suppose, for example, that Ed Alva obtains a patent directed towards a method of grating cheese. The PTO issues the Alva patent on July 4, 2004. Although the specification of the Alva patent discloses the use of the method with regard to American, Swiss and Gouda cheese, the patent's claims recite only the grating of American cheese. If Alva wishes to obtain additional claims that specifically recite the grating of Swiss or Gouda cheese, then he must file a reissue application no later than July 4, 2006. Otherwise the claims can never be broadened through the use of the reissue proceeding.

Meeting this deadline has proved a somewhat subtle affair, as suggested by two cases, *In re Doll*[10] and *In re Graff*.[11] In *Doll*, the patentee filed a reissue application containing broadened claims within the two-year statutory period. The claims were further broadened during the course of prosecution after the two-year period had expired, prompting a rejection by the examiner under the fourth paragraph of § 251. The Court of Customs and Patent Appeals reversed in a terse opinion, holding that the reissue oath was proper.

Graff involved an applicant who filed a reissue application approximately twenty-two months after the issuance date. The initial reissue application was solely directed towards an erroneous drawing and contained no changes to the claims whatsoever. During the course of prosecution and following the expiration of the two-year period, however, Graff introduced broadened claims. The examiner rejected these claims as untimely under the fourth paragraph of § 251. On appeal, the Federal Circuit affirmed. The court characterized the holding in *Doll* as recognizing that "the public was placed on notice of the patentee's intention to enlarge the claims by the filing of a broadening reissue application within the two year statutory period." According to the Federal Circuit, because the public lacked notice that Graff sought a broadening reissue within the statutory period, any enlarged claims were properly rejected.

19.6.3.4 The Recapture Rule

Along with the two-year statute of limitations, the courts have developed another significant restriction on broadening reissues. The recapture rule prevents a patentee from acquiring, through reissue, claims of the same or broader scope than those canceled from the original application.[12] This doctrine typically arises when an examiner rejected the original application based upon the prior art. If the patentee opted to narrow its claims to avoid a prior art reference, then he cannot use the reissue proceeding to recapture the abandoned subject matter.

The Federal Circuit opinion in *Mentor Corp. v. Coloplast, Inc.*[13] demonstrates the recapture rule. Mentor had obtained a patent claiming

9. 35 U.S.C.A. § 251 (2000).

10. 419 F.2d 925, 164 USPQ 218 (CCPA 1970).

11. 111 F.3d 874, 42 USPQ2d 1471 (Fed.Cir.1997).

12. *See* Ball Corp. v. United States, 729 F.2d 1429, 221 USPQ 289 (Fed.Cir.1984).

13. 998 F.2d 992 (Fed.Cir.1993).

a condom catheter that transferred an adhesive from its outer to its inner surfaces upon unrolling. A review of the prosecution history indicated that Mentor had inserted this limitation into the claims following the examiner's prior art rejection. Mentor later learned of Coloplast's competing product, a catheter with adhesive applied directly to its inner surface. Aware that its patent claims did not read directly on the Coloplast product, Mentor initiated a reissue proceeding at the PTO. After Mentor submitted detailed evidence of commercial success, the examiner reissued the patent. Notably absent from the reissued claims were limitations calling for adhesive transfer.

Mentor then sued Coloplast for infringement of both the original and reissue patents. Coloplast denied infringement of the original patent claims because its catheters did not transfer adhesive from the outer to the inner surface. Coloplast admitted infringement of the reissue patent but asserted that Mentor had improperly invoked the reissue statute by recapturing what it had deliberately surrendered during the original prosecution in response to a prior art rejection. The jury disagreed, and the trial judge denied Coloplast's motion for judgment as a matter of law after the adverse verdict.

On appeal, the Federal Circuit reversed. The court concluded that Mentor could not use the reissue proceeding to modify its deliberate actions during the original prosecution. Because Mentor had deliberately added claim language requiring adhesive transfer following the examiner's prior art rejection, the court reasoned, Mentor should not be allowed to recapture that subject matter by deleting these claim limitations during reissue. In so doing, the court justified the recapture rule both upon the requirement of error as well as concerns for the reliance interests of third parties. The Federal Circuit did not consider Mentor's deliberate decision to narrow its claims, instead of filing a continuation application or appealing to the Board, to be the sort of error comprehended by the reissue statute. Additionally, the court sympathized with a hypothetical third party that might have reviewed the prosecution history and made commercial decisions based upon Mentor's express surrender of subject matter that had originally been claimed.

Neither of these grounds provides an entirely satisfactory explanation for the recapture rule. Reissue is a broad-reaching curative mechanism that corrects many sorts of mistakes that patentees made deliberately, albeit ill advisedly. For example, patentees commonly use reissue to rectify claims of inappropriate scope, even though each word of those claims was purposefully written. The court's notice rationale is entirely circular: if there was no recapture rule, third parties would not so rely upon the prosecution history. In addition, the reissue statute's provisions for intervening rights, which are discussed immediately below, provide an adequate mechanism for addressing the reliance interests of others.[14]

14. *See* John R. Thomas, *On Preparatory Texts and Proprietary Technologies: The Place of Prosecution Histories in Patent* *Claim Intepretation*, 47 UCLA L. Rev. 183. 237–40 (1999).

In any event, the venerable recapture rule remains a fixed part of the law of reissue at the Federal Circuit.

19.6.3.5 Intervening Rights

Congress recognized that third parties may have made commercial decisions based upon the precise wording of the claims of an issued patent. If that patent is later reissued with different claims, this reliance interest could be frustrated. In order to protect individuals who may have relied upon the scope of the claims of the original patent, the second paragraph of § 251 provides for so-called intervening rights.[15] There are two sorts of intervening rights: absolute and equitable.

Absolute intervening rights are set forth in the first sentence of the second paragraph of § 251. According to that provision, no reissued patent shall prevent one from employing a "specific thing" covered by the reissue patent, so long as that individual made use of that thing prior to the grant of the reissue. Absolute intervening rights are limited to the sale or continued use of individual machines, manufactures or products covered by the reissue patent. There is one significant exception: if the infringed claim of the reissue patent was also within the original patent, then no absolute intervening right arises.

The second sentence of the second paragraph of § 251 provides for equitable intervening rights. This statute allows a court to authorize the continued practice of an invention claimed in a reissue patent "to the extent and under such terms as the court deems equitable for the protection of investments made or business commenced before the grant of the reissue." To qualify for equitable intervening rights, an infringer must have made at least substantial preparations to practice the patented invention. As with the absolute intervening right, equitable intervening rights apply only when a valid, infringed claim appears solely in the reissue patent.

That intervening rights may apply to broadening reissues should be apparent. Less intuitive is that intervening rights may also arise when the claims are narrowed during reissue. However, even prior to a narrowing reissue, a defendant may have believed the original, broader claims to be invalid. Such grounds as anticipation, nonobviousness, indefiniteness or lack of an enabling disclosure may apply to the claims of the original patents but not to those that were reissued. The better view is that intervening rights may apply during any reissue, not just a broadening one.

A paucity of case law considers either sort of intervening right. This absence is likely due to artful reissue practice on behalf of patentees. Wise to the wording of the reissue statute, most patentees transfer as many claims from the original patent to the reissued patent as possible without amendment. Of course, if the defendant infringes a claim that

---

15. 35 U.S.C.A. § 252 (2000).

appears in both the original and reissued patents, then no intervening rights are possible.

19.6.4　Reexamination

Reexamination proceedings were introduced into the U.S. patent law in 1980.[16] The Reexamination Act of 1999 renamed the traditional sort of reexamination as an *"ex parte* reexamination*"* and also introduced the possibility of an *"inter partes* reexamination.*"* The principal purpose of either sort of reexamination is to provide third parties with an avenue for resolving validity disputes more quickly and less expensively than litigation. Indeed, prior to the adoption of the reexamination statute, third parties were ordinarily unable to challenge the validity of an issued patent at all unless they had been accused of infringement.

The chief limitation upon reexamination is that the cited grounds for invalidity must constitute a patent or printed publication.[17] Other grounds for patent invalidity, such as the public use or on sale bars of § 102(b), may not be considered during reexamination. The reason for this restriction is that the PTO is much more able to assess patents or printed publications than other sorts of prior art. Full consideration of such issues as public use, offers to sell, inventorship and fraud ordinarily entails examination of witnesses and other techniques of litigation, procedures which the PTO is not well equipped to oversee.

19.6.4.1　*Ex parte* Reexamination

Under the *ex parte* reexamination regime, any individual, including the patentee, a licensee, and even the PTO Director himself, may cite a patent or printed publication to the PTO and request that a reexamination occur.[18] The reexamination request must be in writing and explain the relevance of the cited reference to every claim for which reexamination is requested. The request must also be accompanied by the appropriate fee, which as of January 1, 2003, was $2,520. Although the PTO does not maintain the identify of the requester in confidence, individuals desiring anonymity may authorize a patent agent or attorney to file the request in the agent's own name.

A PTO examiner then must determine whether the patents or printed publications cited in the request raise "a substantial new question of patentability."[19] This standard is met when there is a significant likelihood that a reasonable examiner would consider the reference important in deciding whether the claim is patentable. If the PTO determines that the cited reference does not raise "a substantial new question of patentability," then it will refund a large portion of the requestor's fee. The PTO's denial of a reexamination request may not be appealed.[20] But if the PTO does present a substantial new patentability

---

16.　35 U.S.C.A. §§ 301, 302 (2000).

17.　*See* 35 U.S.C.A. § 302 (2000).

18.　*See* 35 U.S.C.A. § 302 (2000).

19.　35 U.S.C.A. § 303(a) (2000).

20.　35 U.S.C.A. § 303(c) (2000).

question, then it will issue an order for reexamination.[21] Under § 304, the patentee is given the opportunity to file a preliminary statement for consideration in the reexamination. If the patentee does so, then the requestor may then file a reply to the patentee's statements. As a practical matter, because most patentees do not wish to encourage further participation by the requestor, few preliminary statements are filed.

Following this preliminary period, the PTO will essentially reinitiate examination of the patent. Because the PTO has determined that a substantial new question of patentability exists, ordinarily the First Office Action includes a rejection of at least one of the claims. Prosecution then continues following the usual rules for examination of applications.[22] However, several special rules apply to reexaminations. First, the PTO does not accord patents under reexamination the usual presumption of validity under § 282. Second, the PTO conducts reexaminations with special dispatch.[23] Examiners must give priority to patents under reexamination, and will set aside their work on other patent applications in favor of the reexamination proceeding. To further ensure their timely resolution, patentees may not file a continuation application in connection with a reexamination.[24] Finally, no new matter may be introduced into the patent during reexamination.[25]

If the reexamined claims are upheld in original or amended form, the PTO will issue a certificate of conformation. Once this certificate has issued, the reexamined patent once more enjoys the statutory presumption of validity.[26] The doctrine of intervening rights, discussed at section 19.6.3.5 in connection with reissue, also applies to claims that survive reexamination.[27] If the PTO judges the claims to be unpatentable over the cited reference, then it will issue a certificate of cancellation.[28] Patentees adversely affected by a reexamination may appeal to the Board or to the courts as necessary.[29]

Frequently a defendant accused of infringement before a court files a reexamination request at the PTO. If the PTO accepts the request, the PTO and a court will find themselves in the awkward situation of simultaneously considering the validity of the same patent. In *Ethicon, Inc. v. Quigg*,[30] the Federal Circuit concluded that because the Patent Act required reexaminations to be conducted with "special dispatch," the PTO may not stay reexamination proceedings due to ongoing litigation. Whether a court will stay litigation in favor of the reexamination lies within the discretion of the judge. Such factors as the technical complexity of the invention, the overall workload of the court, and

21. 35 U.S.C.A. § 304 (2000).

22. 35 U.S.C.A. § 305 (2000).

23. 35 U.S.C.A. § 305 (2000).

24. *Id.*

25. *Id.*

26. 35 U.S.C.A. § 307(a) (2000).

27. *See* 35 U.S.C.A. § 307(b)(2000).

28. *See* 35 U.S.C.A. § 307(a) (2000).

29. *See* 35 U.S.C.A. § 306 (2000).

30. 849 F.2d 1422, 7 USPQ2d 1152 (Fed.Cir.1988).

whether the reexamination request was filed early or late in the litigation typically influence this determination.

19.6.4.2   *Inter partes* Reexamination

As traditionally structured, the *ex parte* reexamination statute encountered criticism. As the title "*ex parte* reexamination" suggests, the role of the reexamination requestor is very limited in these proceedings. Only the patentee may participate in the dialogue with the examiner, and only the patentee may appeal the matter to the Board or to the courts if the PTO reaches an unsatisfactory conclusion. Many third parties did not believe the limited role provided for them offered a viable alternative to validity challenges in court. As a result, the ability of *ex parte* reexamination to provide an expert forum as a faster, less expensive alternative to litigation of patent validity was compromised. Data supported these observations, for far fewer *ex parte* reexaminations were requested than had been originally anticipated.[31]

The Optional Inter Partes Reexamination Procedure Act of 1999 responded to these concerns by providing third party requesters with an additional option.[32] They may employ the traditional reexamination system, which has been renamed an *ex parte* reexamination. Or, they may opt for a considerable degree of participation in the newly minted *inter partes* reexamination. Under this legislation, third party requesters may opt to submit written comments to accompany patentee responses to the PTO. The requester may also appeal PTO determinations that a reexamined patent is not invalid to the Board and the courts. To discourage abuse of *inter partes* reexamination proceedings, the statute provides that third party participants are estopped from raising issues that they raised or could have raised during reexamination during subsequent litigation. The filing fee for *inter partes* reexaminations is also quite steep; it was $8,800 as of January 1, 2003.

We have little experience with these procedures at the time this book goes to press. It will be interesting to observe the willingness of the patent bar to engage in these proceedings and the ability of the PTO to step out of its ordinarily *ex parte* mindset.[33] This expansion of the scope of reexamination also suggests that the restrictions upon patents and printed publications may also be deserving of reconsideration in the near future.

19.6.4.3   Reexamination vs. Reissue Review

The difference between a reexamination and a reissue may appear elusive to newcomers to the patent system. The following points may help illuminate the distinctions between the two post-grant proceedings:

---

31. *See* Mark D. Janis, *Rethinking Reexamination: Toward a Viable Administrative Revocation System for U.S. Patent Law*, 11 HARV. J. L. & TECH. 1 (1997).

32. 35 U.S.C.A. §§ 311–318 (2000).

33. *See* Mark D. Janis, *Inter Partes Reexamination*, 10 FORDHAM INTELL. PROP. MEDIA & ENT. L.J. 481 (2000).

· A request for reexamination may be filed by "any person," while a reissue must be filed with the approval of the patentee.

· A request for reexamination need not assert an "error" without deceptive intent, while a reissue application must do so.

· A reexamination is directed towards prior art patents and printed publications, while a reissue is directed towards any issue that is pertinent to the original application. Where the patentee amends matter in the patent, however, ancillary issues concerning compliance with § 112 and other statutes may arise in a reexamination as well.

· A reexamination cannot be employed to broaden the patent's claims, nor may it be abandoned by the patentee. An applicant may employ a reissue to provide broadened claims if the reissue application is filed within two years from the date of the patent grant, and may also choose to abandon the reissue and have the PTO return its original patent.

· Claims may be copied from a reissue application in order to place the application into an interference. Reexaminations do not give rise to interferences.

§ 19.7   Other PTO Proceedings

19.7.1   Interferences

Sometimes two or more inventors seeks to obtain patent rights for the same invention. In such circumstances, the PTO may conduct an interference proceeding in order to determine which claimant was the first inventor within the meaning of the patent law. These contests over priority of inventorship are termed interferences. They are discussed in this text at § 16.3.2.1.

19.7.2   Protests

Members of the public are allowed to enter a protest against a patent application.[1] The protest must specifically identify the application and be served upon the applicant. The protest must also include a copy and, if necessary, an English translation, of any patent, publication or other information relied upon. The protester also must explain the relevance of each item.

The rights of the protester are extremely limited. The only PTO acknowledgment of the protest will occur if the protestor opts to include a self-addressed stamped postcard along with the protest papers. In that case the PTO will simply mail the postcard upon receipt of the protest papers. The PTO possesses complete discretion in deciding whether the patent applicant must respond to the protester's contentions. The pro-

§ 19.7
1. 37 C.F.R. § 1.291 (2000).

tester will learn of the disposition of the protest only upon the issuance of the patent and the opening of the prosecution history to the public.

Protest proceedings have traditionally played a small role in PTO practice. Until Congress enacted the Domestic Publication of Foreign Filed Patent Applications Act of 1999, the PTO maintained applications in secrecy. Therefore, the circumstances in which members of the public would learn of a patent application were relatively limited. With the PTO commencing publication of some pending patent applications as of November 30, 2000, protests would seem far more likely. Seemingly aware of this possibility, the Domestic Publication of Foreign Filed Patent Applications Act of 1999 provides that the PTO shall "ensure that no protest or other form of pre-issuance opposition ... may be initiated after publication of the application without the express written consent of the applicant."[2] It remains to be seen both whether this restriction can be meaningfully enforced and whether the patent bar will make more active use of protests in the future.

19.7.3   Citation of Prior Art

In lieu of filing a protest or provoking a reexamination, individuals may simply cite patents or printed publications to the Patent and Trademark Office.[3] If accompanied by a written explanation of the relevance of the cited prior art to the patent, this submission will be included in the patent's official record. Section 301 allows competitors to place prior art on the record, ensuring that it will be considered if a reexamination is declared. Of course, particularly pertinent prior art will undoubtedly hamper the patentee's enforcement or licensing efforts, and may even encourage another party to file a reexamination or protest itself.

19.7.4   Public Use Proceedings

Individuals may also file a petition with the PTO showing that an invention described in a pending patent application had been in public use or on sale more than one year prior to the filing of the patent application or before the date of invention.[4] If the examiner determines that this petition makes a prima facie case, she may order a preliminary hearing to determine whether a public use proceeding is appropriate. Any resulting public use proceeding may be conducted as an *inter partes* hearing, including the taking of testing and cross-examination as appropriate. If the examiner concludes that a public use bar exists, then she will reject the claims. Although the examiner's decision in a public use proceeding may not be appealed, the application will be returned to *ex parte* prosecution at the close of the proceeding. The applicant may then appeal an adverse examiner decision to the Board.

As with protests, public use proceedings have traditionally not been of great moment in patent practice. The PTO's former practice of

---

2. 35 U.S.C.A. § 122(c) (2000).

3. 35 U.S.C.A. § 301 (2000).

4. *See* 37 C.F.R. § 1.292 (2000).

maintaining applications in secrecy suggested that few persons, other than the patent applicant, would know of the pending application. With a partial publication regime now in place following the Domestic Publication of Foreign Filed Patent Applications Act of 1999, public use proceedings may play a greater role in the future.

§ 19.8   International Prosecution

The world's patent-granting states have yet to agree to a true global patent system. Yet in a world where international trade consistently increases and technology knows few borders, patent protection in a single jurisdiction seldom suffices to remunerate an inventor. Inventors must instead seek patent protection in each jurisdiction where they hope to obtain proprietary rights. The result is that U.S. patent attorneys are frequently called upon to coordinate patent acquisition efforts before many different administrative agencies overseas.

Multinational patent acquisition is among the most difficult professional tasks faced by patent attorneys. The responsible attorney must operate in an environment marked by multiple substantive patent laws, granting procedures and languages. He must also ensure that prosecution efforts in one country must also not negatively impact patentability elsewhere, by triggering the § 102(d) statutory bar or otherwise limiting patent rights. Fortunately, the foundational patent law treaty, the Paris Convention, eases some of the burdens of obtaining patents in many countries. Its most significant provision, Article 4, creates a right of international priority that is discussed at length below.

19.8.1   Obtaining Paris Convention Priority

Article 4 of the Paris Convention allows an applicant to obtain a priority date by filing an initial application for a patent in any signatory state. The applicant may then file a patent application in any other signatory state within twelve months and obtain the benefit of the earlier filing date. As implemented in § 119 of the Patent Act, the applicant must fulfill certain additional requirements in order to gain the benefit of the Paris Convention priority date.

First, both the foreign and domestic applications must be filed by the same "applicant, legal representatives or assigns." Second, the applicant must formally declare his entitlement to priority at the PTO. Failure to claim priority promptly may result in a waiver of the priority right.[1] Third, the foreign application must have been for a "patent." Inventor's certificates, utility model registrations and other foreign intellectual property rights may qualify as a patent within the meaning of § 119.[2]

§ 19.8
1. 35 U.S.C.A. § 119(b)(2) (2000).
2. *See* 35 U.S.C.A. § 119(d) (2000); American Infra–Red Radiant Co. v. Lam-bert Indus. Inc., 360 F.2d 977, 149 USPQ 722 (8th Cir.), *cert. denied*, 385 U.S. 920, 87 S.Ct. 233, 17 L.Ed.2d 144 (1966).

Finally, in order to serve as an effective priority document, the foreign application must fulfill the disclosure requirements of § 112 of the Patent Act, including enablement, written description and best mode. One decision in which a foreign applicant ran afoul of this requirement is *In re Gosteli*.[3] On May 4, 1978, Gosteli filed a U.S. patent application that included claims directed towards a generic class of antibiotic compounds. Gosteli's priority application had been filed in Luxembourg on May 9, 1977. Notably, Gosteli's Luxembourg application did not disclose the generic class that was later claimed in the United States. The examiner rejected the claims due to the disclosure of the Menard patent, which was filed in the United States on December 14, 1977. Menard disclosed two antibiotics that were members of the class of compounds recited in Gosteli's generic claims.

On appeal to the Federal Circuit, Gosteli attempted to rely upon the filing date of his Luxembourg application in order to antedate Menard. The Federal Circuit determined that a number of differences existed between what was disclosed in the Luxembourg application and what was claimed in the United States. Alternatively, Gosteli argued that because the Luxembourg application did disclose the two compounds taught by Menard, then the Luxembourg application should at least be enough to remove Menard as a reference. The Federal Circuit disagreed: § 119(a) compelled a comparison between the priority application and the U.S. application, not between the priority application and the reference.

Note that § 119(a) does not limit the right of priority to Paris Convention signatories. Patent applications that were filed in a country that affords "similar privileges" to applications first filed in the United States may also be awarded priority. Because Article 2 of the TRIPS Agreement requires signatories to respect Article 4 of the Paris Convention, as a practical matter any application originating in a WTO member country will be accorded priority.

19.8.2 Benefits of Paris Convention Priority

Under § 119(a), a priority application has the same effect as if it had been filed in the United States. As a result, a foreign priority date allows applicants to avoid prior art rejections under § 102(a) or (g). For example, suppose that an inventor files an application in Japan on January 19, 2003, and then in the United States on January 4, 2004. The PTO examiner then cites an anticipatory article published on August 1, 2003. The applicant may point to her Japanese priority date in order to antedate the reference. A foreign priority date may also be used to demonstrate a date of constructive reduction to practice in an interference under § 102(g).

Section 119(a) further specifies that if the invention had been in public use or on sale in the United States, or patented or described in a printed publication anywhere more than one year before the actual U.S.

---

3. 872 F.2d 1008, 10 USPQ2d 1614 (Fed.Cir.1989).

filing date, then no patent shall issue. The practical effect of this provision is that the one-year grace period provided by § 102(b) is measured from the U.S. filing date, not the foreign priority date. For example, suppose that an invention is described in a published magazine article on March 21, 2002. A German patent application directed towards that invention is filed on April 1, 2002, followed by a corresponding U.S. patent application on March 31, 2001. In this case the March 21, 2002, publication bars the issuance of a U.S. patent even though the applicant is otherwise entitled to a priority date of April 1, 2002.

Recall that under § 102(e), a granted patent has prior art effect as of its U.S. filing date, rather than its issue date, for subject matter it discloses but does not claim. When a U.S. application enjoys a foreign priority date under § 119, the question has arisen whether the appropriate § 102(e) date is the foreign priority date or the actual U.S. filing date. In its infamous *Hilmer* opinions,[4] the CCPA decided that § 102(e) concerned the date the application was filed in the United States, even where the application enjoys a foreign priority date. The following timeline displays the pertinent facts at issue in the *Hilmer* cases:

```
                    Files            Files           U.S. Patent
Habicht——Switzerland————United States————Issues————>
         Jan. 24, 1957    Jan. 23, 1958    Nov. 29, 1960


                            Files            Files
Hilmer————————Germany————————United States————————>
              July 31, 1957    July 25, 1958
```

The PTO initially conducted an interference between Habicht and Hilmer. Because the U.S. patent law does not consider inventive activity performed overseas prior to January 1, 1996, Habicht readily prevailed. The PTO then dissolved the interference and returned the Hilmer application to the examiner. The rather clever Hilmer then drafted a new set of claims that were distinct from the count of the interference he had just lost. However, Hilmer's new claims would have been obvious in view of the disclosure of the Habicht patent. The examiner quickly imposed an obviousness rejection, relying upon Habicht as prior art under § 102(e). Hilmer disagreed, asserting that priority applications under § 119 cannot be accorded prior art status under § 102(e). Hilmer lost before the Board, but then appealed the matter to the CCPA.

The CCPA was then left to decide the point at which the disclosure of the Habicht patent served as prior art against Hilmer. Although Habicht was entitled to his Swiss filing date under § 119, the court held that the Habicht patent was effective as a prior art reference only as of its U.S. filing date. Section 102(e) expressly refers to patent applications "filed in the United States," the court reasoned, and priority applications under § 119 should not be read into this language. According to

4. *See* In re Hilmer, 359 F.2d 859 (CCPA 1966) ("Hilmer I"); In re Hilmer, 424 F.2d 1108 (CCPA 1970) ("Hilmer II").

the court, Paris Convention priority under § 119 served only as a shield to fend off prior art references, not as a sword to defeat the applications of others. The result was that Hilmer was entitled to employ his German filing date to antedate Habicht's U.S. filing date, even though Habicht's first filing predated Hilmer.

The so-called *Hilmer* rule has two uncontestable effects on U.S. patent practice. First, more patents proceed to grant as a result of *Hilmer*. The opinion in *Hilmer* demonstrates some of the resulting mischief, for the immediate result of that opinion was two patents claiming the same inventive concept. Second, the *Hilmer* rule favors patent applicants based in the United States. Those who file their priority application elsewhere learn that their application is not accorded prior art effect until such time as they file in the United States. As a result, up to one year's worth of patent-defeating effect is lost, an eternity in many fast-moving and competitive industries.[5]

The foreign patent community continues to voice its outrage at the holdings in *Hilmer*. Most patent systems provide both priority and patent-defeating effect to the Paris Convention priority application. As a result, the winner of the race to the first patent office potentially wins exclusive rights in the disclosed invention almost everywhere in the world. In the United States, however, a subsequent applicant can obtain a patent claiming subject matter disclosed in the earlier application. Most observers believe that the *Hilmer* rule violates at least the spirit of the priority mechanism of Paris Convention Article 4.[6]

19.8.3   Foreign Filing Licenses

The Invention Secrecy Act prohibits an inventor from filing a patent application in another country on an invention made in the United States unless he obtains a license from the PTO.[7] Inventors may obtain the license through one of two routes. One option is to file a petition with the PTO expressly requesting a foreign filing license. Alternatively, and far more typically, the inventor simply files a U.S. patent application, which is deemed an application for a license to pursue patent protection in other countries. In either case, officials from the PTO and other government agencies will review the application to determine whether disclosure of the invention would be detrimental to the national security.[8] Following this review, the PTO sends a filing receipt to the applicant that indicates whether the license has been granted or not.

If the PTO grants the foreign filing license, the inventor is free to seek patent protection abroad. However, if the government concludes that disclosure of the invention would implicate national security interests, then it will deny the license and issue a secrecy order. The order compels the inventor to neither disclose the subject matter of the

---

5. *See* Richard A. Neifeld, *Viability of the Hilmer Doctrine*, 81 J. Pat. & Trademark Off. Soc'y 544 (1999).

6. *See* Kevin L. Leffel, Comment, 26 Akron L. Rev. 355 (1992).

7. 35 U.S.C.A. § 184 (2000).

8. 35 U.S.C.A. § 181 (2000).

application nor file a patent application in another country. The PTO will also withhold the issuance of a U.S. patent on that invention. The inventor may seek compensation for damages caused by the secrecy order.[9] Government officials periodically review the secrecy order and may rescind it when disclosure of the invention is no longer deemed detrimental to national security.

Sometimes inventors fail to obtain a license before filing patent applications overseas. As a penalty, the Patent Act declares any U.S. patent on that subject matter invalid.[10] The statute does provide a liberal mechanism for curing a violation of the foreign filing license requirement. Following the 1988 Patent Law Foreign Filing Amendments Act, a license may be granted retroactively where the application was filed abroad "through error and without deceptive intent" and the application does not disclose an invention that implicated national security concerns.[11]

19.8.4 The Patent Cooperation Treaty

The Patent Cooperation Treaty, or PCT, is an international agreement open to any signatory of the Paris Convention.[12] Its purpose is to simplify multinational patent acquisition by providing an optional application procedure. Over one hundred signatory nations, including the United States, have adopted the PCT filing mechanisms and standardized application format. Although a detailed review of the PCT exceeds the scope of this treatise, some fundamentals of this increasingly popular patent acquisition technique are worthy of note here.

The PCT allows an inventor to file an "international application" at a so-called Receiving Office, typically the patent office of the PCT member country. The applicant may designate those nations where patent protection is desired on the international application. The application is automatically published eighteen months from the priority date. It is also sent to an International Searching Authority, which conducts a prior art search and forwards the results to the applicant. The purpose of this search is to allow the applicant to learn of relevant prior art and decide whether to take further steps towards perfecting the patent right. After receiving the international search report, the applicant may amend the claims of the international application by filing the appropriate papers at the so-called International Bureau, which is housed in the World Intellectual Property Office in Geneva, Switzerland.

The PCT provides applicants with two options at this point. One possibility is the immediate commencement of prosecution at the patent offices designated in the international application. This option is termed the National Stage. If the applicant opts to move to the National Stage immediately, he must undertake local prosecution upon the expiration of 20 months from the filing date of the international application.

9. 35 U.S.C.A. § 183 (2000).
10. 35 U.S.C.A. § 185 (2000).
11. 35 U.S.C.A. § 184 (2000).

12. Patent Cooperation Treaty, June 19, 1970, 28 U.S.T. 7645.

Alternatively, the applicant may delay entering the National Stage in favor of an intermediate step. This step consists of an "international preliminary examination" in accordance with Chapter II of the PCT. A demand for an international preliminary examination must be filed by the expiration of the nineteenth month from the priority date of the international application. The objective of this examination is to formulate a tentative, non-binding opinion on the patentability of the claimed invention. Applicants who opt for the international preliminary examination also gain a significant practical benefit: the applicant may postpone entering the National Stage, with its expensive translations, individual patent office fees and costs of local patent counsel, until the expiration of 30 months from the filing date of the international application.

Two relatively technical points concerning the PCT process are worthy of note here. First, the PCT provides that priority may be claimed based on earlier applications filed in any Paris Convention signatory state. In terms of U.S. practice, priority may be claimed under § 119 or § 120 in connection with the PCT.[13] Either a national application or an international application designating the United States may obtain priority under § 119 based upon an earlier foreign application or international application designating a foreign country. In accordance with § 120, either a national application or international application designating the United States will be entitled to the benefit of the filing date of a prior international application that designated, but did not originate in, the United States.

Second, the prior art effect of a PCT application is specifically noted in § 102(e). According to that statute, U.S. patents issuing from international applications are effective as prior art only at such time as the applicant paid the appropriate fee and filed at the PTO; a copy of the international application; a verified English translation of the international application, if necessary; and a proper oath or declaration. These requirements correspond to items (1), (2) and (4) of § 371(c). The filing of these items normally coincides with the start of the National Stage at the PTO. Because § 102(e) provides that an international application filed outside the United States does not by itself have prior art effect until the application is actually perfected at the PTO, the effect of this statute is to preserve the *Hilmer* rule in the context of the PCT.

13. 35 U.S.C.A. § 365 (2000).

Chapter 20

PATENT INFRINGEMENT

Table of Sections

The patent statute addresses infringement at section 271. Its opening paragraph, § 271(a), provides:

> Except as otherwise provided in this title, whoever without authority makes, uses, offers to sell, or sells any patented

invention, within the United States or imports into the United States any patented invention during the term of the patent therefor, infringes the patent.

Surprisingly for many, beyond providing a list of infringing acts and offering a fleeting reference to the "patented invention," the statute does not further define how one should determine whether a patent has been infringed or not. This challenging task has fallen to the courts, who have faced a number of perplexing issues along the way.

§ 20.1   Scope of Rights

Broadly speaking, an individual may face liability for patent infringement in two ways. He may himself engage in one of the acts that are exclusive to the patentee, a practice termed direct infringement. Alternatively, a person may have engaged in indirect or dependent infringement. In such cases liability rests not upon the direct practice of the patented invention, but the successful encouragement of others to do so.

20.1.1   Direct Infringement

A patent confers the right to exclude others from making, using, selling, offering for sale, or importing into the United States the patented invention.[1] An individual need only perform one of these acts to be liable as an infringer. One who manufactures a patented product, but never sells or personally uses it, is nonetheless guilty of patent infringement.

This definition reveals that patent infringement concerns behavior. Patent rights become relevant when an individual engages in one of the five noted activities. However, the patent community commonly employs such phrases as the "accused device" or the "infringing method." This terminology is a concise way of expressing the concept that an individual has engaged in acts forbidden by the patent statute with respect to that product or process.

A defendant's intent is irrelevant to the outcome of an infringement inquiry. Even an individual who has never previously known of the asserted patent or even of the entire patent system may be found to be an infringer. Infringement analyses thus have a *quasi in rem* flavor, as they focus upon a comparison of the patent claims to the accused technology.[2]

Importantly, the exclusive patent rights do not provide an affirmative right for the patentee to employ the invention himself.[3] For example, the fact that an individual obtained a patent on a pharmaceutical

§ 20.1

1. 35 U.S.C.A. § 271(a) (2000).

2. *See* Jurgens v. CBK, Ltd., 80 F.3d 1566, 1570 n. 2, 38 USPQ2d 1397, 1400 n. 2 (Fed.Cir.1996).

3. Leatherman Tool Group Inc. v. Cooper Industries, Inc., 131 F.3d 1011, 1015, 44 USPQ2d 1837, 1841 (Fed.Cir.1997).

compound does not allow him to market this medication to others. Approval of the appropriate food and drug authorities must first be obtained.

The patents of others might also interfere with a patentee's ability to practice his own patented invention.[4] For example, suppose that Admiral Motors obtains a patent on an internal combustion engine for use in automobiles. Later, Betty Beta purchases an automobile marketed by Admiral Motors that embodies the patented invention. Beta experiments with her new car and develops a dramatically improved fuel injector usable only in the patented Admiral Motors engine. Even if Beta patents her improved fuel injector, she cannot practice that technology without infringing Alpha's basic patent. In this case, the Admiral Motors patent is said to be a blocking, or dominant patent over Beta's improvement or subservient patent. Unless one of the parties licenses the other, Beta must wait until Admiral Motors' patent expires before practicing her own patented improvement invention.

The rights provided by U.S. patents are effective only in the United States.[5] They provide no protection against acts occurring in foreign countries. Individuals must obtain patent protection in each nation where they wish to guard against unauthorized uses of their inventions.

As has been discussed here previously,[6] patent rights ordinarily extend for a period of twenty years from the date the patent application was filed. This term may be modified based upon events at the PTO or at other regulatory agencies. Further, the patentee may not exercise his exclusive rights until such time as the patent has been granted by the PTO.

20.1.1.1 Process Patents

When a patent claim is expressed as a series of steps, it is known as a method or process claim.[7] Traditionally the patent law held that a process claim could be directly infringed only by the performance of those steps.[8] Suppose, for example, that a manufacturer sold a device capable of performing a patented process. Such a manufacturer could not be liable for directly infringing the process unless it also performs the steps of this process. The manufacturer could face infringement liability for contributing to or inducing the infringing of others, however.

This general principle was altered to some degree in the Process Patent Amendments Act of 1988. As codified in § 271(g), Congress provided process patent owners with the right to exclude others from

---

4. *See* Bio–Technology General Corp. v. Genentech, Inc., 80 F.3d 1553, 1559, 38 USPQ2d 1321, 1325 (Fed.Cir.), *cert. denied*, 519 U.S. 911, 117 S.Ct. 274, 136 L.Ed.2d 197 (1996).

5. *See* Dowagiac Mfg. Co. v. Minnesota Moline Plow Co., 235 U.S. 641, 650, 35 S.Ct. 221, 59 L.Ed. 398 (1915).

6. *See supra* § 19.5.

7. John R. Thomas, *Of Text, Technique and the Tangible: Drafting Patent Claims Around Patent Rules*, 17 John Marshall J. Computer & Info. L. 219 (1998).

8. United States v. Studiengesellschaft Kohle, m.b.H., 670 F.2d 1122, 212 USPQ 889 (D.C.Cir.1981).

using or selling in the United States, or importing into the United States, products made by a patented process. For example, suppose that an enterprise based in Italy manufactures chocolate employing a process patented in the United States. If the Italian company exports chocolate into the United States, it may face liability even though it performed every step of the patented process abroad.

A number of exceptions limit liability under the Process Patent Amendments Act. In particular, § 271(g) provides that if the product is materially changed by subsequent processes, or becomes a trivial or nonessential component of another product, then there is no infringement.[9] The Process Patents Amendment Act also created a new § 287(b), a complex statute that modifies the usual scheme of remedies available for patent infringement. Among other provisions, § 287(b) provides a grace period for individuals unaware of the patent implication of a particular process. Such persons may, upon receiving notice of infringement, dispose of products that would infringe under § 271(g) and avoid liability.

The Process Patents Amendment Act also introduced § 295 into the Patent Act. Congress enacted this provision out of the recognition that patentees may face great difficulties in proving that a particular product resulted from the performance of the patented process. Section 295 creates a presumption as to when a product is made by the patented process if two conditions are met. First, there must be a substantial likelihood that the product was made by the patented process. Second, the plaintiff must have made a reasonable effort to determine the process actually used in the production of the product and was unable to so determine. The effect of the presumption is that the accused infringer bears the burden of showing that the accused product was not made by the patented process.

20.1.1.2 The First Sale Doctrine

Under the "first sale" or "exhaustion" doctrine, an authorized, unrestricted sale of a patented product depletes the patent right with respect to that product.[10] As a result of this doctrine, the purchaser of a patented good ordinarily may use, charge others to use, or resell the good without further regard to the patentee. The courts have reasoned that when a patentee sells a product without restriction, it impliedly promises its customer that it will not interfere with the full enjoyment of that product.[11] The result of the first sale doctrine is that the lawful purchasers of patented goods may use or resell these goods free of the patent.[12]

---

9. *See* Eli Lilly & Co. v. American Cyanamid Co., 82 F.3d 1568, 38 USPQ2d 1705 (Fed.Cir.1996).

10. *See* Intel Corp. v. ULSI System Technology, 995 F.2d 1566, 1568, 27 USPQ2d 1136, 1138 (Fed.Cir.1993), *cert. denied*, 510 U.S. 1092, 114 S.Ct. 923, 127 L.Ed.2d 216 (1994).

11. *See* B. Braun Medical, Inc. v. Abbott Laboratories, 124 F.3d 1419, 1426, 43 USPQ2d 1896, 1901 (Fed.Cir.1997).

12. *See* Intel Corp. v. ULSI System Technology, 995 F.2d 1566, 27 USPQ2d 1136 (Fed.Cir.1993), *cert. denied*, 510 U.S. 1092, 114 S.Ct. 923, 127 L.Ed.2d 216 (1994).

Often a patentee will restrict a sale or license of the patented invention upon certain conditions. For example, a sales contract might stipulate that the purchaser only use the patented goods in a named geographical location; resell the goods at specified prices; or purchase replacement parts from the patentee. It is in the nature of things for purchasers to violate these restrictions, and patentees have sometimes pursued charges of patent infringement against them. The reasoning of the patentee is typically that the purchaser's use of the patented invention is unauthorized and therefore an infringement.

Although early Supreme Court opinions were reluctant to employ the patent law to police these infractions,[13] Federal Circuit case law has strongly upheld a cause of action for patent infringement where the sale was conditional, despite the first sale doctrine.[14] According to the Federal Circuit, restricted sales by the patentee do not allow the inference that the patentee intended customers to enjoy unrestricted use of the invention. As a result, contractual conditions will generally be enforced through the patent law unless the court determines they violate some other law or policy, such as the antitrust law or the doctrine of patent misuse.

The Federal Circuit decision in *Monsanto Co. v. McFarling* is exemplary.[15] Monsanto had obtained patents claiming seeds and plants that were resistant to glyphosate herbicides such as ROUNDUP brand. Farmers that used the patented plants could broadly spray these herbicides in their fields, killing the weeds but not harming the resistant crops. Monsanto required that purchasers of its patented seed submit to a "Technology Agreement" that Monsanto styled as a license under the patents. The agreement in part stipulated that the patented seeds were to be used "for planting a commercial crop only in a single season" and further directed purchasers not to "save any crop produced from the seed for replanting."

McFarling, a soybean farmer, purchased Monsanto seeds in 1997 and 1998, both times submitting to the license. McFarling disregarded the agreement's terms, however. He saved seed from earlier harvests and planted them in subsequent years instead of purchasing further Monsanto seed. Monsanto sued McFarling for patent infringement and breach of contract. The trial court awarded Monsanto a preliminary injunction and, following an appeal, the Federal Circuit affirmed. Judge Newman reasoned that the Technology Agreement required purchasers to use the seed only for the purpose of growing crops and not for the purpose of growing new seed. Absent a countervailing principle from antitrust, contract or other law, these provisions were enforceable. Judge Newman further reasoned that the exhaustion doctrine did not apply to

13. *See, e.g.,* United States v. Univis Lens Co., 316 U.S. 241, 62 S.Ct. 1088, 86 L.Ed. 1408 (1942); Keeler v. Standard Folding–Bed Co., 157 U.S. 659, 15 S.Ct. 738, 39 L.Ed. 848 (1895); Adams v. Burke, 84 U.S. (17 Wall.) 453, 21 L.Ed. 700 (1873).

14. *See* Mallinckrodt, Inc. v. Medipart, Inc., 976 F.2d 700, 24 USPQ2d 1173 (Fed. Cir.1992).

15. 302 F.3d 1291, 64 USPQ2d 1161 (Fed. Cir. 2002).

the case: "The original sale of the seeds did not confer a license to construct new seeds, and since the new seeds were not sold by the patentee they entailed no principle of patent exhaustion."

The Federal Circuit's effective characterization of plants as self-replicating machines may cause readers to raise an eyebrow. Cases such as *Monsanto Co. v. McFarling* nonetheless epitomize the Federal Circuit viewpoint that starts with the proposition that patentees can ordinarily refuse to sell or license their intellectual properties altogether. As a result, the reasoning continues, patentees can freely impose conditions upon these transactions that, absent special circumstances such as an antitrust violation, will generally be enforced.

20.1.1.3 Repair and Reconstruction

A corollary of the right to use a patented product under the first sale doctrine is the right to repair the product as necessary for continued use. The patent law provides customers of the patentee with an implied license to repair or even replace parts of a patented product without paying further compensation. However, the customer may not reconstruct the patented product without violating the patentee's exclusive right to make the patented invention.[16] The courts have learned that the line between a repair and a reconstruction is often not a clear one, although most opinions lean towards finding a permissible repair rather than an infringing reconstruction.

Exemplary of repair and reconstruction cases is the 1995 opinion of the Federal Circuit in *Sage Products, Inc. v. Devon Industries, Inc.*[17] As is often true in this line of cases, the defendant, Devon, was a replacement parts manufacturer accused of contributory infringement. Sage held a patent claiming a medical waste disposal system consisting of the combination of an outer enclosure, which may be mounted on a wall, and a removable inner container. Sage sold embodiments of the patented invention and instructed customers to dispose filled inner containers. Of course, Sage also sold replacement inner containers. When Devon began to sell inner containers as well, Sage brought an infringement suit.

The issue before the Federal Circuit was whether hospitals that replaced the removable inner containers with Devon's containers impermissibly reconstructed the combination claimed in Sage's patents. The Federal Circuit answered in the negative. The court clarified that permissible repairs were not limited to temporary or minor repairs. Instead, where the spent part was but an unpatented element of a patented combination, the user could perform repairs as necessary to maintain the use of the invention. According to the court, the inner enclosure was a depletable, unpatented component that Sage intended users to replace. As a result, the court concluded that the hospitals did not infringe the Sage patent.

16. *See* Mark D. Janis, *A Tale of the Apocryphal Axe: Repair, Reconstruction, and the Implied License in Intellectual Property Law*, 58 MD. L. REV. 423 (1999).

17. 45 F.3d 1575, 33 USPQ2d 1765 (Fed.Cir.1995).

Sage Products presents a relatively easy case. The inner containers had a shorter useful life than the whole system; the patentee's technical design encouraged their replacement; and a secondary market had developed to manufacture them.[18] A stronger argument can be made for an impermissible reconstruction when the accused infringer replaces a durable component by engaging in more elaborate technical efforts than were involved in *Sage Products*.

The right of repair does not arise if the owner of the combination patent also obtains patents separately claiming the individual component at issue. For example, suppose that Sage had also obtained patent claims towards the inner containers themselves. In this case, Devon would have directly infringed these narrow components claims. Devon would also have been judged a contributory infringer of Sage's system claims. In reaching this conclusion, the courts have recalled that the right of repair is founded upon the existence of an implied license between the patentee and its customers. No such license should be presumed where the patentee also obtains a proprietary interest in the replaced component itself.[19]

20.1.1.4 Experimental Use

A handful of older cases recognize a limited "experimental use" defense to patent infringement. In his 1813 opinion in *Whittemore v. Cutter*,[20] Justice Story explained that "it could never have been the intention of the legislature to punish a man, who constructed such a machine merely for philosophical experiments, or for the purpose of ascertaining the sufficiency of the machine to produce its described effects." To similar effect was the 1861 decision in *Poppenhusen v. Falke*, which explained "that an experiment with a patented article for the sole purpose of gratifying a philosophical taste, or curiosity, or for mere amusement is not an infringement of the rights of the patentee."[21]

Subsequent decisions interpreted this defense extremely narrowly. Where a commercial purpose animated the accused infringer even in part, courts have universally refused to apply the experimental use defense. Perhaps because of the limited applicability of this doctrine, or simply because patentees have only rarely sued pure philosophers, the number of cases in which an accused infringer has successfully pled an experimental use defense are few indeed.[22] The fact that a general experimental use defense has never achieved a codification in the Patent Act betrays its quite limited nature.

18. *See* Sandvik Aktiebolag v. E.J. Co., 121 F.3d 669, 673, 43 USPQ2d 1620 (Fed. Cir.1997), *cert. denied*, 523 U.S. 1040, 118 S.Ct. 1337, 140 L.Ed.2d 499 (1998).

19. *See* R2 Medical Sys., Inc. v. Katecho, Inc., 931 F.Supp. 1397, 1444–45 (N.D.Ill. 1996).

20. 29 F.Cas. 1120, 1121 (C.C.D.Mass. 1813) (No. 17,600).

21. *Poppenhusen v. Falke*, 19 F.Cas. 1048, 1049 (C.C.S.D.N.Y.1861) (No. 11,279).

22. *See* Note, *Experimental Use as Patent Infringement: The Impropriety of a Broad Exception*, 100 Yale L.J. 2169 (1991); Richard E. Bee, *Experimental Use as An Act of Patent Infringement*, 39 J. Pat. Off. Soc'y 357 (1957).

Madey v. Duke University presents the Federal Circuit's latest thinking on the experimental use exception.[23] Duke University employed Mabley as a research professor and director of a laser laboratory. After Mabley resigned, he brought suit for infringement of two patents relating to the operation of specialized equipment used in the Duke laser laboratory. In turn, Duke sought to take advantage of the experimental use defense to patent infringement. Duke explained that it was a non-profit institution that served educational objectives. The district court agreed and granted summary judgment in favor of Duke. On appeal, the Federal Circuit reversed and remanded, explaining that:

> major research universities, such as Duke, often sanction and fund research projects with arguably no commercial application whatsoever. However, these projects unmistakably further the institution's legitimate business objectives, including educating and enlightening students and faculty participating in these projects. The projects also serve, for example, to increase the status of the institution and lure lucrative research grants, students and faculty.
>
> In short, regardless of whether a particular institution or entity is engaged in an endeavor for commercial gain, so long as the act is in furtherance of the alleged infringer's legitimate business and is not solely for amusement, to satisfy idle curiosity, or for strictly philosophical inquiry, the act does not qualify for the very narrow and strictly limited experimental use defense. Moreover, the profit or non-profit status of the user is not determinative.[24]

From one perspective, *Madey* merely extends a line of judicial opinions taking an ever more cabined view of the experimental use defense. On the other hand, few patent proprietors have been so bold to sue universities for their fundamental research activities. After *Madey*, perhaps patentees will be less circumspect. We suppose this is a price that universities must pay in an era where these institutions have become increasingly sophisticated in developing and marketing sophisticated patent portfolios. The broader implications of *Madey* are nonetheless troubling. Even philosophers must eat, and to the extent they form organized centers of research and education, they now possess the duty to account for the patent system. As our copyright and patent regimes increasingly overlap, most notably with regard to the protection of computer software, the patent law threatens to detract from freedoms long recognized within the copyright system. With society becoming increasingly embedded in technology, and the swift rate of technological advance increasingly at odds with the 20–year patent term, perhaps it is time to recognize that a broader right to tinker might better serve the policy goals that animate the patent law.

23. 307 F.3d 1351, 64 USPQ2d 1737 (Fed. Cir. 2002).   **24.** 307 F.3d at 1362.

The experimental use defense to patent infringement should be contrasted with the experimental use principles relating to the statutory bars. Recall that courts and PTO examiners will toll the one-year grace period under § 102(b) if they are satisfied that the inventor engaged in legitimate experimentation beyond the statutory period.[25] Although this concept is also termed "experimental use," it is a patent validity principle that does relate to the infringement analysis.

A very limited form of the experimental use exception, relating to patents on pharmaceuticals and medical devices, is found in the Patent Act. Congress added this provision because of the time-consuming Food & Drug Administration (FDA) approval process these products must undergo prior to marketing. When generic drug manufacturers and other competitors grow interested in marketing a medical product patented by another, they often wish to complete product testing and obtain regulatory approval during the term of the patent, so that on the day the patent expires, the generic manufacturer could begin to sell its own version of the product. Of course, the patentee will ordinarily commence an infringement suit when it becomes aware of competitor testing. The patentee hopes to prevent the generic manufacturer from commencing the regulatory approval process until the close of the patent term.

In its 1984 opinion in *Roche Products, Inc. v. Bolar Pharmaceutical Co.*,[26] the Federal Circuit resolved these competing positions in a manner consistent with the limited nature of the experimental use defense. The court held that even restricted uses of a patented drug, made solely for testing pursuant to regulatory approval, were infringements. The court reasoned that because such tests were pursued for business purposes, rather than to amuse or satisfy curiosity, the experimental use defense was inapplicable. The practical effect of *Roche v. Bolar* was to extend the term of patents on drugs by the length of the FDA approval process.

Congress responded to *Roche v. Bolar* by enacting Title II of the Drug Price Competition and Patent Term Restoration Act of 1984, commonly known as the Hatch–Waxman Act.[27] This statute was intended to eliminate the *de facto* extension of patent term resulting from regulatory approval delays. This statute worked a compromise between innovative developers of so-called "pioneer drugs" and generic manufacturers. In favor of the generic manufacturers, Congress enacted § 271(e)(1), which exempts from infringement "uses reasonably related to the development and submission of information under a Federal law which regulates the manufacture, use, or sale of drugs." Cases such as *Intermedics, Inc. v. Ventritex, Inc.* have interpreted this exemption generously.[28] According to Magistrate Judge Brazil, "[w]here it would have been reasonable, objectively, for an accused infringer to believe that there was a decent prospect that the use in question would contribute

25. *See supra* § 16.2.5.1.

26. 733 F.2d 858, 221 USPQ 937 (Fed. Cir.), *cert. denied*, 469 U.S. 856, 105 S.Ct. 183, 83 L.Ed.2d 117 (1984).

27. Pub. Law. No. 98–417, Title II, 98 Stat. 1585 (Sept. 28, 1984).

28. 775 F.Supp. 1269, 20 USPQ2d 1422 (N.D.Cal.1991), *aff'd*, 991 F.2d 808, 26 USPQ2d 1524 (Fed.Cir.1993).

(relatively directly) to the generation of information that was likely to be relevant in the processes by which the FDA would decide to approve the product,'' then the court should apply the § 271(e)(1) infringement exemption.

Congress also provided for two sorts of expedited FDA applications for generic drug manufacturers who seek regulatory approval to market generic equivalents of previously approved pioneer drugs. Rather than submit extensive data concerning the safety and effectiveness of the drug, the generic drug manufacturers may employ more easily garnered information. So-called abbreviated new drug applications (ANDAs) may employ data demonstrating that the pioneer and generic drugs are bioequivalents, while "paper new drug applications" (paper NDAs) may rely upon published literature to show the safety and effectiveness of the generic drug.

Two provisions of the Hatch–Waxman Act favor patentees of pioneer drugs. First, as provided in § 156, the patent terms of products subject to regulatory approval by the FDA were extended. Second, Congress established a specialized patent registration and infringement regime. Under the Hatch–Waxman Act, pioneer drug manufacturers must file with the FDA the number and expiration date of any patent concerning the pioneer drug. When a generic manufacturer files an ANDA or paper NDA, it must include one of four certifications with respect to each pertinent patent: (1) that the manufacturer of the pioneer drug has not filed this information; (2) that the patent has expired; (3) the date on which such patent will expire; or (4) that such patent is invalid or will not be infringed by the generic drug. If the generic manufacturer opts for the fourth sort of certification, § 271(e) allows a patentee to launch infringement litigation against the would-be generic manufacturer immediately.

A charge of infringement under § 271(e) is technical in nature. The generic manufacturer has done nothing more than request FDA approval to market a drug. If the patentee's charge of infringement is successful, however, he may prevent the marketing of that generic equivalent until the date the patent expires. Further, if the patentee brings such an infringement suit, the FDA may not finally approve the application until a court rules that the patent is not infringed or the expiration of a set period of time, usually 30 months, whichever comes first.

20.1.1.5   Exports and Imports

Under U.S. patent law, the unauthorized exportation of patented goods does not by itself constitute an infringing act.[29] However, it is often the case that the exporter has manufactured or sold the exported goods as well. In such cases the exporter has violated the patentee's exclusive right to make or sell the patented invention in the United

---

29. *See* Johns Hopkins University v. CellPro Inc., 152 F.3d 1342, 47 USPQ2d 1705 (Fed.Cir.1998).

States.[30] Unauthorized importations are addressed more straightforward-ly: § 271(a) expressly declares that a patentee possesses the exclusive right to import the patented invention into the United States.

Although both the copyright[31] and trademark law[32] have extensively considered parallel importation, this issue has arisen only infrequently in the patent law. The Federal Circuit has yet to speak definitively on this point, while the only relevant Supreme Court opinions are over a century old.[33] Therefore, the question of whether the authorized sale of a patented product abroad exhausts the patent right covering the product in the United States, such that the importation of the product into the United States is not an infringement, is not entirely settled. However, recent district court opinions suggest that the first sale doctrine general-ly applies if the owner of both the U.S. and foreign patent makes an unrestricted sale abroad. But where the sale is restricted, or if the holders of the U.S. and foreign patent rights are distinct entities, the U.S. patent will likely not be exhausted by an overseas sale.[34]

20.1.1.6 Government Infringers

Sometimes a patentee learns of the unauthorized use or manufac-ture of the patented invention by an agency of the federal or state government. Where the federal government commits the infringing acts, 28 U.S.C.A. § 1498 authorizes the patentee to file suit in the United States Court of Federal Claims in order to obtain "reasonable and entire compensation." The patentee ordinarily may recover the equivalent of a reasonable royalty from the federal government. Injunctive relief is not available. Although § 1498 litigation is based upon the government's eminent domain taking of a patent license, these suits are otherwise quite similar to ordinary infringement actions against private parties.

If the infringing entity is a state government or agency of a state, then the patentee's ability to obtain relief is entirely less clear. Most observers believe that the states are, or should be, subject to the patent rights of private parties. However, the U.S. Constitution places a signifi-cant jurisdictional hurdle before the patentee. The Eleventh Amendment provides that a federal court is without power to entertain a suit by a private person against a state. As a result, aggrieved inventors must seek redress for patent infringement in that state's own courts. Because the federal courts otherwise possess exclusive jurisdiction over patent in-fringement litigation, this state of affairs is an unusual one. Individuals will likely be left to charge the state government with a taking, or assert

30. *See* Amgen, Inc. v. Elanex Pharma-ceuticals, Inc., 1996 WL 84590, *4 (W.D.Wash.1996).

31. Quality King Distributors, Inc. v. L'anza Research Int'l, Inc., 523 U.S. 135, 118 S.Ct. 1125, 140 L.Ed.2d 254 (1998).

32. K Mart Corp. v. Cartier, Inc., 486 U.S. 281, 108 S.Ct. 1811, 100 L.Ed.2d 313 (1988).

33. *See* Boesch v. Graff, 133 U.S. 697, 10 S.Ct. 378, 33 L.Ed. 787 (1890); Adams v. Burke, 84 U.S. (17 Wall.) 453, 21 L.Ed. 700 (1873).

34. *See* PCI Parfums Et Cosmetiques International v. Perfumania, Inc., 35 USPQ2d 1159 (S.D.N.Y.1995).

general unfair competition principles, in order to vindicate their patent rights.

Cognizant of this state of affairs, Congress attempted to abrogate the Eleventh Amendment immunity of states to patent infringement suits in 1992. The Patent and Plant Variety Protection Remedy Clarification Act introduced § 271(h) into the statute.[35] That provision specified not only that the states were subject to patent infringement suits in the federal courts, but that they were liable for any remedies that could be had against a private party.[36] However, the 1999 opinion of the Supreme Court in *Florida Prepaid Postsecondary Education Expense Board v. College Savings Bank* found that Congress lacked the authority to abrogate state immunity to patent infringement litigation in the federal courts under the Eleventh Amendment.[37]

At the time this book goes to press, Congress appears poised to try again. Whether the Supreme Court will sanction a different mechanism for providing private actors with redress against the states for patent infringement remains of extreme importance for enterprises which compete against universities, laboratories, highway administrations and other entities associated with state governments.

20.1.2   Indirect Infringement

The patent law has long considered persons who encourage the unauthorized practice of another's patented invention to have engaged in culpable conduct. Such individuals face liability for patent infringement even if they never directly employ the patented invention themselves.[38] The patent law terms this sort of conduct as "indirect" or "dependent" infringement.

The 1952 Act was the first U.S. patent statute to codify the indirect infringement doctrines that had been developed by the courts. Sections 271(b) and (c) are complementary provisions that Congress intended to lend clarity to the law of active inducement and contributory infringement. Section 271(b) addresses so-called "active inducement" by reciting in broad terms that one who aids and abets an infringement is likewise an infringer. Section 271(c) is a more specific provision that concerns a common circumstance in which indirect infringement occurs: the sale of a nonstaple component that is specially adapted for use in the patented invention. This sort of indirect infringement is termed "contributory infringement."

A direct infringement must occur for a party to face liability as an indirect infringer.[39] However, most courts do not require the patentee to prove another's actual act of direct infringement during litigation. It is

---

35. Pub. L. No. 102–560, 106 Stat. 4230 (Oct. 28, 1992).

36. 35 U.S.C.A. § 271(h) (2000).

37. 527 U.S. 627, 119 S.Ct. 2199, 144 L.Ed.2d 575 (1999).

38. *See* American Cotton–Tie Co. v. Simmons, 106 U.S. (16 Otto) 89, 1 S.Ct. 52, 27 L.Ed. 79 (1882).

39. Aro Mfg. Co. v. Convertible Top Replacement Co., 365 U.S. 336, 341–42, 81 S.Ct. 599, 5 L.Ed.2d 592 (1961).

enough that the patentee demonstrates that a customer of the accused indirect infringer would infringe if she used her purchase in its intended way.[40]

20.1.2.1   Active Inducement

Section 271(b) provides that "[w]hoever actively induces infringement of a patent shall be liable as an infringer." This broadly worded statute was intended to codify existing case law that extended infringement liability to persons who encouraged and assisted the infringement of others. It is important to note that the common law required, as one element of an inducement claim, evidence that the indirect infringer knew that it was encouraging infringing activity. Although § 271(b) does not expressly refer to the inducer's knowledge or purposes, the courts have continued to require that the defendant intended to cause the acts which it had reason to know were patented and infringing.[41]

Subject to this requirement of intent, courts have found active inducement of infringement in varying circumstances. A typical case of active inducement occurs when a supplier sells a product that is capable of both infringing and noninfringing uses. If the supplier provides instructions, distributes advertising or offers training that promotes the infringing use, then it may be found to have violated § 271(b).[42] The courts have also found an active inducement of infringement when a defendant designed an infringing apparatus that another subsequently manufactured.[43] Finally, the courts have sometimes found active inducement where one party repairs or maintains another's infringing good, on the theory that such activities perpetuate the infringing use.[44]

20.1.2.2   Contributory Infringement

In contrast to § 271(b), § 271(c) is a narrowly focused provision. It concerns the specific situation where one party sells a specially manufactured component that the customer intends to employ in the practice of a patented invention. Section 271(c) renders such a seller liable for contributory infringement subject to three important qualifications. First, the component must constitute a material part of the patented invention that is especially made or adapted for use in the infringement. Second, the component must not constitute a staple article of commerce suitable for noninfringing uses. Finally, the alleged contributory infringer must have known of the patent and that the use of the component would constitute an infringement.

40. *See* Standard Oil Co. v. Nippon Shokubai Kagaku Kogyo Co., 754 F.2d 345, 224 USPQ 863 (Fed.Cir.1985).

41. Hewlett–Packard Co. v. Bausch & Lomb Inc., 909 F.2d 1464, 1469, 15 USPQ2d 1525, 1529 (Fed.Cir.1990).

42. *See* Chiuminatta Concrete Concepts, Inc. v. Cardinal Industries Inc., 145 F.3d 1303, 46 USPQ2d 1752 (Fed.Cir.1998).

43. *See* Preemption Devices, Inc. v. Minnesota Mining & Mfg. Co., 803 F.2d 1170, 231 USPQ 297 (Fed.Cir.1986).

44. *See* National Tractor Pullers Ass'n, Inc. v. Watkins, 205 USPQ 892 (N.D.Ill. 1980).

For example, suppose that one Rod Cohen manufactures and sells button-shaped pieces of a particular sort of plastic.[45] The plastic buttons are purchased by independent cutting laboratories and made into contact lenses. Cohen is well aware that a competitor, Terri Tarsal, holds a patent claiming contact lenses made of the same plastic composition. Under these circumstances, it is likely that the cutting laboratories directly infringe the Tarsal patent and that Cohen is a contributory infringer. In addition, because the cutting laboratories may be present or potential customers of Tarsal, Tarsal will likely prefer to sue Cohen. Cohen may be able to argue that the plastic buttons constitute staple articles of commerce that are capable of noninfringing uses, such as on shirts or blouses. In so doing, Cohen should be aware that courts are wary of the farfetched, illusory or theoretical alternative uses often proposed by accused contributory infringers.[46]

The Patent Act nowhere explains the relationship between § 271(b) and (c). However, it is apparent that all conduct that falls under § 271(c) would also be actionable under § 271(b). Courts typically apply § 271(b) to situations where the technology has multiple uses, only one of which infringes. Section 271(c) concerns situations where the only legitimate use of a sold component is an infringing one. But even where a technology has only a single infringing use, its seller could still actively induce patent infringement through advertising, instructions or similar activities. The principal reason that Congress legislated § 271(c) is established in § 271(d). Section 271(d) specifies that a patentee may obtain relief for direct or contributory infringement even though it engaged in specified activities, such as refusal to market an embodiment of the patented invention, that many observers had previously believed to constitute patent misuse. Section 271(d) and the doctrine of patent misuse are further addressed in § 21.3 of this volume.

20.1.2.3   *Deepsouth* and § 271(f)

Prior to the 1984 amendments to the Patent Act, the manufacture and exportation of the unassembled components of a patented article was not considered an infringing act. Exemplifying this rule was the 1972 decision of the Supreme Court in *Deepsouth Packing Co. v. Laitram Corp.*[47] There, the defendant manufactured all the components of a patented shrimp peeler and shipped them in an unassembled state to clients abroad. The defendant's customers could assemble the machine parts in less than one hour. The Supreme Court held that no infringement occurred in the United States because the defendant had not made or sold the combination of elements as claimed.

Congress responded to *Deepsouth* by adding paragraph (f) to § 271 of the Patent Act. The two subparagraphs of § 271(f) specify that the export of unassembled components of a patented invention may consti-

45. *See* Syntex (U.S.A.) Inc. v. Paragon Optical Inc., 7 USPQ2d 1001 (D.Ariz.1987).

46. *See* D.O.C.C. Inc. v. Spintech Inc., 36 USPQ2d 1145, 1155 (S.D.N.Y.1994).

47. 406 U.S. 518, 92 S.Ct. 1700, 32 L.Ed.2d 273, 173 USPQ 769 (1972).

tute an infringing act. Section 271(f)(1) parallels § 271(b) by stating that the supply of all or a substantial portion of the components of a patented invention for combination abroad is an active inducement. Section 271(f)(2) corresponds to § 271(c) by specifying conduct that is considered a contributory infringement. Under § 271(f)(2), the exported component must constitute a material part of the patented invention that is especially made or adapted for use in the infringement and must not be a staple article of commerce suitable for noninfringing uses. The accused infringer must also have known that the component would be combined outside the United States in a manner that would infringe a U.S. patent if such combination took place in the United States.

§ 20.2   Claim Interpretation

The Patent Act consistently bases the patentee's exclusive rights upon the "patented invention."[1] Modern courts have consistently judged this phrase to refer to the invention as recited in the claims. Interpretation of the text of the claims is thus a central issue of contemporary patent law. When construing claims, courts consider their express language along with the specification, drawings and prosecution history associated with the patent.

Once the claims have been construed, they are compared to the product or process that the accused infringer has made, used, sold, placed on sale, or imported into the United States.[2] If the defendant has performed one of the activities reserved to the patentee, then the court will find infringement. The burden falls to the patentee to prove infringement by a preponderance of the evidence. The defendant may assert a number of defenses to the charge of infringement, including invalidity, unenforceability and various equitable defenses.[3]

If the accused infringement embodies every limitation of the claim, the claim is said to "read on" that product or process. In such cases the defendant has literally infringed the patent. The patentee's exclusive rights are not necessarily limited to the express language of the claims, however. Under the doctrine of equivalents, if the accused technology presents insubstantial differences from the claimed invention, then the court may find infringement even though the claim language is not literally met.

Before we take up the topics of literal and equivalent infringement, a preliminary word on claim interpretation is in order. Those new to the patent law may be pleased to learn that, unlike other intellectual property disciplines, individuals must define their patent interests expressly in a government-approved instrument before filing an infringement suit. Further, although patent claims employ notoriously stilted language, they are at bottom quite humble texts. Each claim is but a

---

§ 20.2

1. *E.g.,* 35 U.S.C.A. § 271(a) (2000).

2. *See* Cybor Corp. v. FAS Techs., Inc., 138 F.3d 1448, 1454 (Fed.Cir.1998) (*en banc*).

3. 35 U.S.C.A. § 282 (2000).

single sentence that verbally portrays a product or process. As compared to the ambiguous substantial similarity analysis found in copyrights, or vague likelihood of confusion standard of the trademark law, patent infringement analyses might appear at first blush to be entirely straightforward.

Experience has unfortunately taught us that infringement analyses in the patent law are as nettlesome as in any intellectual property discipline. Few claims prove so clear as to withstand the withering gaze of high stakes litigation without the exposure of an ambiguity or uncertainty. Claim interpretation issues recur so frequently because these texts are exceptionally difficult to draft. Patent practitioners must marshal considerable legal and technological skills to write claims that capture the inventor's contribution, avoid subject matter known to the prior art, and anticipate future embodiments that others might employ. Yet financial limitations and marketplace demands for timely issuance weigh against comprehensive preparatory efforts. With each patent claim tied to a unique specification and prosecution history, the search for meaning becomes contextual and resort to the precedents unavailing. Claim drafters and interpreters have found certainty an elusive goal, but they have also encountered a set of intriguing issues that form the core of the patent project.

20.2.1 Literal Infringement

A patent is literally infringed if the accused product or process includes every element exactly as recited in at least one of its claims. Courts often compare literal infringement to the standard of anticipation. If the claimed subject matter existed within the public domain as defined in § 102, then the claim is anticipated; but if the claimed subject matter is employed after the date the patent is granted, then the claim is literally infringed.[4] To ensure that the claim precisely reads upon the accused technology, patent practitioners commonly prepare a claim chart comparing the claimed and accused subject matter.

Under this standard of absolute identity, if an accused product or process includes fewer elements or steps than were recited in the claims, there can be no literal infringement. Whether the accused technology can include more than the listed elements depends upon which transition phrase appears in the claims. Most claims employ the "comprising" transition phrase, which is open to additional elements beyond those recited in the claims. Other claims employ a closed or hybrid transition phrase, which may deny a finding of infringement if the accused technology includes elements beyond those included in the claim.[5]

---

4. *See* Lewmar Marine, Inc. v. Barient, Inc., 827 F.2d 744, 3 USPQ2d 1766 (Fed. Cir.1987), *cert. denied*, 484 U.S. 1007, 108 S.Ct. 702, 98 L.Ed.2d 653 (1988).

5. *See supra* § 18.2.1.2.

20.2.1.1 *Markman v. Westview Instruments*

Although the standards for literal infringement analysis are straightforward, they provide scant assistance in determining the meaning of particular claim terms. For example, suppose that a composition of matter claim calls for "approximately 20% vegetable paste." The accused compound consists of 18.86% tomato paste. Whether a content of 18.86% amounts to "approximately 20%" within the meaning of this claim will be subject to interpretation in the courts. A second issue is whether tomato paste qualifies as vegetable paste. Botanists have long classified tomatoes as fruits, but even today most lay persons would look for tomatoes in their grocer's vegetable section.[6]

In answering questions such as these, the courts traditionally faced two basic questions. The first is the determination of the materials that may be appropriately considered during claim interpretation. Beyond the asserted patent claim itself, litigants have offered such evidence as the prosecution history, prior art documents, learned treatises, dictionary definitions and the testimony of inventors, technical experts and legal experts. As these sources often provide conflicting evidence of meaning, the courts have required an essential interpretational protocol for construing patent claims. Second, whether the issue of claim interpretation is one of fact or law determined whether juries or judges decided the meaning of the claims, as well as the standard of review on appeal.

The *en banc* opinion of the Federal Circuit in *Markman v. Westview Instruments, Inc.* provided answers to these fundamental questions. As such, it has become the governing precedent on both the substance and procedure of contemporary claim interpretation. The patented invention at issue there was a rather humble one, an inventory tracking system for a dry cleaning shop. Markman combined computer and bar code technology to minimize lost garments and employee theft during the dry cleaning process. His claimed "inventory control and reporting system" allowed the detection of "spurious additions to inventory as well as spurious deletions therefrom."

Markman's assertion of the patent against a competitor led to a jury trial. Although the jury had found for Markman, the trial judge instead directed a verdict of noninfringement. Asserting that claim interpretation was a matter of law for the court, the trial judge determined that the term "inventory" referred exclusively to articles of clothing. Because the accused device merely maintained a listing of invoices, it could not track the location of individual garments as they moved about the shop and therefore could not infringe.

On appeal, the Federal Circuit affirmed. In so doing, the court established two categories of evidentiary inputs for use in claim interpretation. The first, so-called "intrinsic evidence," consisted of the claims, the specification, and the prosecution history. Courts were required to consider all of the intrinsic evidence of record to determine the meaning

6. This example is drawn from the well-known Supreme Court opinion in Nix v. Hedden, 149 U.S. 304, 13 S.Ct. 881, 37 L.Ed. 745 (1893), a statutory interpretation case.

of the claims. All other sources, ranging from dictionary definitions to expert testimony, was classified as "extrinsic evidence." The trial court judge possessed discretion to consider extrinsic evidence, but need not do so if the intrinsic evidence established the proper interpretation of the claim.

The Federal Circuit also held that claim interpretation was a matter of law solely for the judge to decide. The majority reasoned that patents, like other written instruments, had traditionally been subject to interpretation by the courts. Further, participants in the patent system were best served by an articulated, reasoned analysis of the claim scope by a trained jurist. As a result, in a jury trial, it is the responsibility of the judge to resolve the meaning of the claims and to so instruct the jury. On appeal, the Federal Circuit would review claim interpretation holdings *de novo*, without discretion to the trial court.

Applying these principles to the case at hand, the court concluded that the claim term "inventory" consisted of "articles of clothing" rather than money or receipts. The claims, specification and prosecution history all referred to movement of inventory throughout a dry cleaning establishment, an event that does not occur to dollars or slips of paper. The Federal Circuit also discounted the testimony of a patent attorney and Markman himself during the trial. According to the court, this testimony amounted to a legal opinion, a matter that lies solely within the province of the trial court. The court also reasoned that extrinsic evidence should not control the interpretation of the claims in the face of consistent intrinsic evidence as to claim meaning.

The Supreme Court affirmed the Federal Circuit in a short opinion principally devoted towards Seventh Amendment concerns.[7] Justice Souter's review of early patent precedents revealed that judges, not juries, had interpretative responsibilities at the time the Seventh Amendment was enacted. The Court further reasoned that, as compared to juries, judges were the more able claims-interpreters due to their training and experience. Finally, the Court concluded that assigning claim interpretation tasks to judges would encourage uniformity through the application of stare decisis and the publicity of articulated judgments.

The outcome of the *Markman* opinions appears sensible. Unless Markman was running a money laundering establishment, his patent instrument simply could not cause cash to be embraced by the term "inventory." Yet the courts' conclusion that a patent claim should be subjected solely to judicial construction seems questionable. Patent claims are replete with technical terms ranging from electrodes to polypeptides to moments of inertia, words which lawyers are not well trained to construe. One also wonders how the decision that claim interpretation is a matter of law squares with the venerable patent law principle that claims are directed towards persons of ordinary skill in the art. If the trial judge hears one skilled artisan testifying in favor of the

---

7. 517 U.S. 370, 116 S.Ct. 1384, 134 L.Ed.2d 577 (1996).

plaintiff's proposed interpretation, and another testifying in favor of the defendant's construction, surely the resolution of this dispute amounts to a question of fact.

Although neither *Markman* opinion devotes much thought to trial procedures, these decisions have considerably impacted the conduct of patent litigation. Viewing claim interpretation as a pure issue of law promotes a sort of summary judgment procedure in which the trial judge resolves the meaning of the claims. The district courts have differed on the timing of these so-called "*Markman* hearings." Some courts conduct *Markman* hearings early in the litigation. These courts hope to narrow issues and promote settlement, but often must make decisions with scant evidence before them. Other courts hear evidence of claim meaning at the same time as the infringement trial and instruct the jury on the appropriate construction just before it retires. Although this technique allows the court to receive evidence after discovery has been completed and litigation positions have been fully formed, it may prevent parties from offering testimony and argument concerning the judge's claim interpretation at the trial level.

The Federal Circuit's *de novo* standard of review on claim interpretation issues has also been keenly felt. If district court claim interpretations are reviewed without deference, then trial court proceedings become a mere waystation to appeal. Predictably, the Federal Circuit has demonstrated a high reversal rate following *Markman*. Indeed, in some celebrated cases, the Federal Circuit reached a claim interpretation that neither the district court, nor the accused infringer, nor the patentee had adopted. The jurists of the Federal Circuit have been admirably receptive of the views of the patent community, however, and their opinions will continue to refine the ubiquitous question of claim interpretation in the post-*Markman* era.

20.2.1.2   Canons of Claim Construction

Beyond the basic principles of claim interpretation delineated in *Markman*, Federal Circuit cases have intoned that "a number of canons . . . guide our construction of all patent claims."[8] A review of the Federal Circuit's jurisprudence reveals a modest set of these interpretational protocols. Although commentators have doubted whether these universal rules of interpretation are of much use in deciding actual cases, Federal Circuit decisions persist in relying upon them to interpret claims. The more significant canons are described below.

Numerous decisions explain that patentees are free to be their own lexicographers.[9] By this the courts mean that patentees are allowed to coin their own words for use in claims. In such cases the patent's specification or prosecution history should clearly state that word's meaning. The lexocographic privilege arises because patent claims neces-

8. Athletic Alternatives, Inc. v. Prince Mfg., Inc., 73 F.3d 1573, 1578, 37 USPQ2d 1365, 1370 (Fed.Cir.1996).

9. *E.g.*, Vitronics Corp. v. Conceptronic, 90 F.3d 1576, 1582 (Fed.Cir.1996).

sarily concern novel technologies for which established descriptive terms may not yet exist. However, any newly minted words should not be misleading, nor should the patentee employ such banal terms as "gadget" or "widget."

Another fundamental canon of construction is that a claim term should be accorded a consistent meaning.[10] A particular term should be accorded the same meaning even though it has been used in different claims. Similarly, a claim cannot be interpreted narrowly in order to distinguish a claimed invention from the prior art, but then be accorded a broad construction in order to achieve a finding of infringement.

The canon of claim differentiation has also been frequently invoked. Under this doctrine, the reader should presume that each claim of a patent conveys a different meaning. In an exemplary decision applying the claim differentiation doctrine, *Transmatic, Inc. v. Gulton Industries, Inc.*,[11] the Federal Circuit considered a patented light fixture for buses and other public transit vehicles. Claim 1 of the asserted patent called for a "light housing" but recited no other structural limitations on that claim element. In contrast, claim 3 of the patent-in-suit, which depended from claim 1, required that the light housing have "a horizontal wall with an inward securement formation" for securing the light fixture to a vehicle. The Federal Circuit applied the doctrine of claim differentiation to hold that claim 1 did not require the specific structure recited in claim 3.

The seminal *Markman* decision explained that claims are to be interpreted in light of the specification. The courts have also stressed, however, that limitations from the specification should not be imported into the claims. The Federal Circuit opinion in *Unique Concepts, Inc. v. Brown* illustrates the tension between these two competing canons.[12] Unique Concepts held an exclusive license on a patented assembly of border pieces used to fasten fabric wall coverings to walls. The patent's claims included a limitation calling for "linear border pieces and right angle corner border pieces." Unique Concepts brought a patent infringement suit against Brown, but lost the trial after the district court held that Brown's assembly did meet this limitation. The trial court noted that Brown's assembly provided only mitered[13] linear pieces. Brown apparently formed border pieces simply by joining the linear pieces together on the fly during the installation of the wall coverings. Unique appealed to the Federal Circuit, which affirmed over a dissent by Judge Rich.

The majority opinion of the Federal Circuit agreed with the trial court that Brown did not infringe. According to Judges Lourie and Mayer, the claim limitation referred to two distinct parts of the assem-

10. Fonar Corp. v. Johnson & Johnson, 821 F.2d 627, 632, 3 USPQ2d 1109, 1113 (Fed.Cir.1987).

11. 53 F.3d 1270, 35 USPQ2d 1035 (Fed.Cir.1995).

12. 939 F.2d 1558, 19 USPQ2d 1500 (Fed.Cir.1991).

13. Mitered pieces are cut at an angle other than ninety degrees, so that they are beveled, and those pieces are then joined together.

bly: "linear border pieces" and "right angle corner border pieces." The majority viewed the specification as demonstrating that the claim language "right angle corner border pieces" referred to a single preformed piece. The fact that linear border pieces could be arranged to form a right angle corner did not convert them into "right angle corner border pieces."

The dissenting opinion of Judge Rich viewed the patent's written description differently. Judge Rich pointed to language in the patent's written description that provided: "Instead of using preformed right-angle corner pieces of the type previously disclosed, one may improvise corner pieces by miter-cutting the ends of a pair of short linear border pieces placed at right angles to each other...." According to Judge Rich, the specification demonstrated that mitered, linear pieces could be placed at right angles and joined to form borders.

In sum, the majority contended that it interpreted the claim term "right angle corner border pieces" in light of the specification. The dissent instead charged the majority with importing limitations from the specification into the claims. At the end of the day, *Unique Concepts* demonstrates that the difference between using the specification to alter the scope of a claim term and importing claim scope from the specification is a subtle one.

20.2.2 Doctrine of Equivalents

The exclusive rights provided by a patent are founded upon, but not exclusively limited to, the text of its claims. Although the courts have long recognized the value of clear and certain claims, they have refused to confine the infringement inquiry to their precise choice of words. Instead, the scope of protection associated with a patent may be expanded beyond the literal wording of the claims under the doctrine of equivalents. Under the current formulation of the doctrine, an accused product or process that presents insubstantial differences from the claimed invention will be judged an equivalent and therefore an infringement.[14]

The doctrine of equivalents arose from judicial efforts to stop competitors who would introduce insignificant modifications into the claimed invention in order to avoid literal infringement.[15] However, courts have not limited use of the doctrine to cases of bad faith, copying or piracy. Every patent infringement case potentially involves the doctrine of equivalents. When courts apply the doctrine of equivalents, they attempt to balance fair protection for the patentee with appropriate notice to competitors of the scope of the patentee's exclusive rights.

Four principal limitations restrict the scope of the doctrine of equivalents. The first, prosecution history estoppel, prevents patentees

---

14. *See* Toro Corp. v. White Consol. Industries, 266 F.3d 1367, 1370 (Fed.Cir. 2001).

15. Martin J. Adelman & Gary L. Francione, *The Doctrine of Equivalents in Patent Law: Questions that* Pennwalt *Did Not Answer*, 137 U. PA. L. REV. 673 (1989).

from receiving a scope of protection that they have surrendered at the PTO in order to persuade the examiner to allow the claim. Second, patentees are also restricted by the prior art, and may not obtain a claim construction that would embrace technologies known to the art or their obvious variants. Third, the doctrine of equivalents may not extend to subject matter that is disclosed within a patent but not expressly claimed—a principle known as the public dedication doctrine. Finally, under the All Elements Rule, each element recited in the claim is considered material to defining the invention. As such, the doctrine of equivalents is applied not to the invention as a whole, but to the individual elements recited within the claim.

20.2.2.1 *Graver Tank* and the Function–Way–Result Test

The 1950 decision of the Supreme Court in *Graver Tank v. Linde Air Products Co.*[16] stood as the most important doctrine of equivalents decision for most of the latter half of the Twentieth Century. Although the Supreme Court would revisit the doctrine in its 1997 *Warner–Jenkinson* decision,[17] the dialogue between the majority and dissenting justices in *Graver Tank* continues to inform legal and policy discussions concerning patent infringement. *Graver Tank* thus remains an appropriate starting point for consideration of the doctrine of equivalents.

The patent at issue in *Graver Tank* concerned an electric welding composition termed a "flux." When applied to the surfaces to be joined through welding, a flux assists in the fusing of the two metals. The claimed flux consisted of calcium fluoride and alkaline earth metal silicate. The accused flux was known under the trademark Lincolnweld 660. It consisted of silicates of calcium and manganese. Manganese is not an alkaline earth metal. However, the patentee also marketed a flux composition known as Unionmelt Grade 20 consisting of silicates of calcium and magnesium. Also, prior art patents employed manganese as a welding composition.

The Court began its opinion by reviewing basic policies underlying the doctrine of equivalents. The Court observed that confining patent rights to cases of literal infringement would merely encourage competitors to make unimportant substitutions to the invention as claimed. Such a hollow grant of rights would discourage inventors from seeking patents and thwart a principal purpose of the patent system, the disclosure of new inventions. In sum, the "essence" of the doctrine of equivalents was to prevent "fraud on a patent."[18]

Quoting from its earlier opinion in *Sanitary Refrigerator Co. v. Winters*,[19] the Court next confirmed the famous tripartite test of the

16. 339 U.S. 605, 70 S.Ct. 854, 94 L.Ed. 1097 (1950).

17. Warner–Jenkinson Co., Inc. v. Hilton Davis Chemical Co., 520 U.S. 17, 117 S.Ct. 1040, 137 L.Ed.2d 146 (1997).

18. 339 U.S. at 608.

19. 280 U.S. 30, 42, 50 S.Ct. 9, 74 L.Ed. 147 (1929).

doctrine of equivalents. When an accused product or process performed "substantially the same function in substantially the same way to obtain the same result," an infringement occurred under the doctrine. The known interchangeability of the claimed and substituted ingredients was an important factor in an equivalency determination, according to the Court. The Court also stated that a finding of equivalence was a question of fact, provable through the use of experts, learned texts and the disclosures of the prior art.[20]

Applying these principles to the facts at hand, the Court affirmed the finding of infringement under the doctrine of equivalents. According to the Court, chemists had testified that magnesium and manganese were equivalents in the welding art, and the trial court had properly found that the Lincolnweld and Unionmelt fluxes were in all respects equivalent. The Court also saw no evidence that the defendant had engaged in independent development of the Lincolnweld flux. The Court found it "difficult to conceive of a case more appropriate for application of the doctrine of equivalents."[21]

Justices Black and Douglas each dissented. Justice Black principally urged that the Court should have pointed the plaintiff to the reissue statute rather than freely apply the doctrine of equivalents.[22] He reminded the majority that Congress had expressly provided procedures for obtaining broader claims through a reissue proceeding. To balance the interest of patentees and their competitors, the Patent Act subjects broadening reissues to a two-year statute of limitations and intervening rights. According to Justice Black, judicial readiness to find infringement through equivalency would ignore these sound safeguards and ultimately emasculate the reissue statute. Fifty years later, Justice Black's criticisms remain substantially unanswered.

The pithy dissent of Justice Douglas observed that the Jones patent had originally included broad, generic claims that would have read upon the Lincolnweld flux.[23] These claims had been struck down during infringement litigation due to lack of enablement. Justice Douglas urged that the doctrine of equivalents should not be used to resurrect claims that had been invalidated.

Although the premises of Justice Douglas are sound, most observers have reached exactly the opposite conclusion from them.[24] By obtaining generic claims from the PTO, Jones had expressly declared a proprietary interest in the combination later embodied in the Lincolnweld flux. PTO policies of the day also prevented Jones from separately claiming more than three species of the distinctly claimed genus. Because technical reasons limited Jones' opportunity to obtain a valid claim covering the Lincolnweld flux, the case for the equivalent infringement was strong.

20. 339 U.S. at 608–10.
21. 339 U.S. at 612.
22. 339 U.S. at 612–18.
23. 339 U.S. at 618.

24. *See, e.g.,* Hilton Davis Chem. Co. v. Warner–Jenkinson Co., 62 F.3d 1512, 1535 (Fed.Cir.1995) (*in banc*) (Newman, J., concurring).

The patent community took from *Graver Tank* the function-way-result test for equivalency. Hundreds of subsequent equivalency opinions proceeded to apply it. Experience did not assist the courts in refining this standard, however, but instead demonstrated that its extraordinary vagueness was of scant use in resolving most infringement cases. Litigants placed vastly different meanings upon the terms "function," "way," and "result," with patentees reading these terms broadly and accused infringers narrowly. And often this standard simply collapsed into a test of "way": if the accused technology did not perform the same function to achieve the same result, it ordinarily would not be the subject of a patent infringement suit at all. As stated more succinctly by Judge Learned Hand in *Claude Neon Lights, Inc. v. E. Machlett & Son*:

> Each case is inevitably a matter of degree, as so often happens, and other decisions have little or no value. The usual ritual, which is so often repeated and which has so little meaning ... does not help much in application; it is no more than a way of stating the problem.[25]

This experience led to considerable unrest in the lower courts, culminating 45 years later in a revisiting of the doctrine of equivalents by the Supreme Court.

20.2.2.2 *Warner–Jenkinson* and the Insubstantial Differences Test

The Supreme Court's 1997 opinion in *Warner–Jenkinson Co. v. Hilton Davis Chemical Co.* provides a full-featured discussion of contemporary doctrine of equivalents issues.[26] Both the plaintiff-patentee, Hilton Davis, and the accused infringer, Warner–Jenkinson, manufactured dyes. The patent-in-suit claimed a method of removing impurities by filtering the dye through a porous membrane. As originally presented to the PTO, the claims did not speak towards the pH level at which this ultrafiltration process should be performed. Later during prosecution, in order to distinguish a prior art patent that operated at a pH above 9.0, Hilton Davis added the limitation "at a pH from approximately 6.0 to 9.0." The accused process operated at a pH of 5.0. A jury trial resulted in a finding of infringement under the doctrine of equivalents. The jurists of the Federal Circuit agreed to hear the case *en banc* and affirmed in a set of lengthy, deeply divided opinions. The Supreme Court then granted *certiorari* and offered a sweeping review of the doctrine of equivalents.

Warner–Jenkinson's first series of arguments contended that the doctrine of equivalents did not survive the enactment of the 1952 Patent Act. Its position was that the doctrine of equivalents was inconsistent with the statutory requirements for definite claims and broadening reissue proceedings, as well as the role of the PTO in determining claim scope. The Court tersely responded that each of these points had been

25. 36 F.2d 574, 3 USPQ 220 (2d Cir. 1929), *cert. denied*, 281 U.S. 741, 50 S.Ct. 347, 74 L.Ed. 1155 (1930).

26. 520 U.S. 17, 117 S.Ct. 1040, 137 L.Ed.2d 146 (1997).

raised and rejected in *Graver Tank*, and there was no basis for overturning that decision today.[27]

Another, more interesting argument was that Congress had wholly codified the doctrine of equivalents when it authorized functional claiming in the sixth paragraph of § 112. This statute allows applicants to draft so-called "means plus function" claims that are "construed to cover the corresponding structure, material, or acts described in the specification and equivalents thereof." According to Warner–Jenkinson, congressional authorization of an equivalency provision for functional claims amounted to the rejection of a general doctrine of equivalents for other sorts of claims. Justice Thomas rejected this position as well, reasoning that Congress specifically intended § 112 ¶ 6 to overturn the Supreme Court's 1946 opinion in *Halliburton Oil Well Cementing Co. v. Walker*, which had cast grave doubts on the validity of functional claiming. Such limited congressional action could not be seen to have such sweeping consequences for the venerable doctrine of equivalents.[28]

Warner–Jenkinson also urged that equivalents should be limited to variants described in the patent's specification or, alternatively, to those variants known at the time the patent issued. Justice Thomas quickly dismissed both of these positions, reasoning that the perspective of the person of ordinary skill in the art placed sufficient limits on the doctrine. The Court also upheld the ample precedent proclaiming equivalency to be a factual determination, to be decided by the jury in a jury trial.[29]

The Court went on to address a position that had been gaining increasing currency in the patent community: that the doctrine of equivalents should apply only to cases where the accused infringer engaged in bad faith, copying or intent. It readily rejected this proposal as well. Although the *Graver Tank* opinion had reasoned that the doctrine of equivalents discourages piracy and the "unscrupulous copyist," the Court did not read *Graver Tank* as limiting the doctrine to cases where those benefits were obtained. Ample precedent had described the doctrine in more neutral terms and had not limited equivalency to actors in bad faith. Following *Warner–Jenkinson*, then, intent is not an element of a doctrine of equivalents analysis.[30]

The final portion of the Supreme Court's *Warner–Jenkinson* opinion addressed the appropriate standard for the doctrine of equivalents. Concerned that the function-way-result test usually associated with *Graver Tank* did not easily apply to sophisticated, nonmechanical technologies, the *en banc* Federal Circuit had engaged in a thorough rereading of the *Graver Tank* opinion. Observing that *Graver Tank* had several times described cases of "insubstantial differences" as appropriate for a finding of equivalency, the Federal Circuit explicitly held that "the application of the doctrine of equivalents rests on the substantiality of

27. 520 U.S. at 25–27.   **29.** 520 U.S. at 37.

28. 520 U.S. at 27–28.   **30.** 520 U.S. at 34–36.

the differences between the claimed and accused product or processes, assessed according to an objective standard."[31]

The Supreme Court was surprisingly nonchalant towards the Federal Circuit's reinterpretation of *Graver Tank*. Declining to select the appropriate standard of equivalency, the Court observed that "[d]ifferent linguistic frameworks may be more suitable to different cases, depending on their particular facts." According to Justice Thomas, the essential inquiry was whether the accused product or process contained elements identical or equivalent to each element recited in the patent claim. The Court left for the Federal Circuit the further refinement of appropriate equivalency standards on a case-by-case basis.[32]

Given the Court's detached view of the appropriate standard of equivalency, Justice Thomas did not elaborate upon the newly approved insubstantial differences standard. However, the *Warner–Jenkinson* opinion and subsequent Federal Circuit opinions have suggested several mechanisms for determining whether insubstantial differences exist between the claimed invention and accused technology. As in *Graver Tank*, known interchangeability of substitutes for an element of the patented invention and independent experimentation by the accused infringer might be probative.[33] The familiar nonobviousness analysis may also be pertinent to the equivalency inquiry.[34] That a skilled artisan would have found the substitution of one ingredient of the claimed invention for the ingredient appearing in the accused product is probative of insubstantial differences. Finally, the function-way-result test is not dead after *Warner–Jenkinson*, but has evolved into one way of articulating whether the differences between the claimed and accused technologies are insubstantial.

20.2.2.3   Limitations on the Doctrine of Equivalents

The insubstantial differences test is the starting point for the doctrine of equivalents, but the fulfillment of this standard does not necessarily compel a conclusion of infringement. Four significant constraints place limits upon the application of the doctrine of equivalents. These are the All Elements Rule, the prior art, prosecution history estoppel and the public dedication doctrine. These limiting principles are frequently tested in patent infringement litigation and are worthy of further discussion here.

20.2.2.3.1   The All Elements Rule

In *Warner–Jenkinson*, the Supreme Court confirmed the principle that "[e]ach element contained in a patent claim is deemed material to defining the scope of the patented invention, and thus the doctrine of equivalents must be applied to individual elements of the claim, not the

31. 62 F.3d 1512, 1518 (Fed.Cir.1995).

32. 520 U.S. at 39–40.

33. 520 U.S. at 36.

34. *Roton Barrier, Inc. v. Stanley Works*, 79 F.3d 1112, 1128, 37 USPQ2d 1816, 1828 (Fed.Cir.1996) (Nies, J., concurring).

invention as a whole."[35] This principle is known as the All Elements Rule. In applying it, a finding of infringement may arise only if each element of a claim is expressed in the accused infringement, either literally or equivalently. The doctrine of equivalents is thus not oriented to the patented invention as a whole, but instead is more strictly employed with respect to each element of a patent claim.

Although the All Elements Rule arguably has ancient origins in U.S. law, the Federal Circuit's *en banc* decision in *Pennwalt Corp. v. Durand–Wayland, Inc.*[36] provides its fullest articulation. Pennwalt's '628 patent bore the title "Sorter for Fruit and the Like." The '628 patent disclosed a mechanism that rapidly sorted fruit or other items based upon color, weight or a combination of these traits. A hard-wired network, including hardware registers, followed each piece of fruit as it moved down a track. Among the claimed elements were first and second "position indicating means" that shifted the data corresponding to the fruit as it was conveyed along the sorting mechanism.

Pennwalt brought an infringement suit against Durand–Wayland, asserting that its '628 patent claims read on the accused Microsizer product. The district court held for the defendants. According to the trial judge, the Microsizer lacked the claimed "position indicating means" because it never shifted data. The Microsizer instead employed random access memory that stored the color and weight data in a discrete location. Thus, rather than shuffling data down a queue to match the progression of a piece of fruit, the Microsizer managed queue pointers. According to the trial court, because the accused device wholly lacked a claimed element of the '628 patent, it could not infringe either literally or under the doctrine of equivalents.

The majority of the Federal Circuit agreed with the trial court that the Microsizer's lack of a "position indicating means" was fatal to Pennwalt's contention of infringement. According to the majority, an accused technology must embody every element of a claimed invention, either literally or equivalently, to be judged an infringement. To hold otherwise would divest the infringement inquiry from the language of the claims themselves. A lengthy opinion offering the "additional views" of Judge Nies dubbed this canon the All Elements Rule.

A dissenting opinion from Judge Bennett and supplementary "commentary" from Judge Newman stridently disagreed with the All Elements Rule. According to the dissenters, the majority had devised an analytical framework for the doctrine of equivalents that was little more than a redundant literal infringement inquiry. The dissenters viewed the doctrine of equivalents as an equitable creation designed to work justice in individual cases, a goal that would be undone by such a restrictive and inflexible canon of construction.

---

35. 520 U.S. at 29.

36. 833 F.2d 931, 4 USPQ2d 1737 (Fed. Cir.1987).

The All Elements Rule is of great practical significance to claims-drafters. Consider the example of the following, simplified claims:

1. A fork comprising:

    a cylindrical handle; and

    four tines attached to said handle.

2. A fork comprising:

    a cylindrical handle;

    a first tine attached to said handle;

    a second tine attached to said handle;

    a third tine attached to said handle; and

    a fourth tine attached to said handle.[37]

These claims appear to provide the same scope of protection in terms of literal infringement. Yet suppose a competitor markets a fork with three tines. The holding of *Pennwalt* would not bar a finding of equivalent infringement with regard to claim 1. But with respect to claim 2, the absence of the final recited element—"a fourth tine attached to said handle"—would violate the All Elements Rule and prove fatal to the case of equivalency.

Although this example is straightforward enough, application of the All Elements Rule has proven rather more difficult in the litigated cases. The most notorious episode concerning this canon arose in the Federal Circuit's later opinion in *Corning Glass Works v. Sumitomo Electric USA, Inc.*[38] That appeal concerned a patented fiber optic cable with a low signal attenuation rate. The claim at issue recited a fiber with a cladding and a core, the former comprising a glass coating to help prevent scratching. The core was "positively" doped to create the appropriate refraction index differential. The claim read in part as follows:

An optical waveguide comprising

(a) a cladding layer . . . , and

(b) a core formed of fused silica to which a dopant material on at least an elemental basis has been added to a degree in excess of that of the cladding layer so that the index of refraction thereof is of a value greater than the index of refraction of said cladding layer. . . . [39]

In what proved to be a fascinating set of circumstances, the defendants obtained the appropriate index of refraction differential by negatively doping the cladding. The district court found the defendants liable for infringement. The defendants appealed, citing the *Pennwalt* rule, and with a rather surprising opinion the Federal Circuit affirmed. According

37. *See* MARTIN J. ADELMAN ET AL., PATENT LAW: CASES AND MATERIALS 947 (1998).

38. 868 F.2d 1251, 9 USPQ2d 1962 (Fed.Cir.1989).

39. 868 F.2d at 1256.

to Judge Nies, the defendants misunderstood the sense of the term "element" in the All Elements Rule:

> "Element" may be used to mean a single limitation, but it has also been used to mean a series of limitations which, taken together, make up a component of the claimed invention. In the All Elements Rule, "element" is used in the sense of a limitation of a claim ..... [T]he determination of equivalency is not subject to a rigid formula. An equivalent must be found for every limitation of the claim somewhere in the accused device, but not necessarily in a corresponding component, although that is generally the case.[40]

Many commentators have doubted whether *Pennwalt* and *Corning Glass* can be reconciled.[41] *Pennwalt* pronounces an elemental equivalency standard, while *Corning Glass* seemingly reverts to a holistic view of the doctrine of equivalents. And while these cases reach differing results, each concerned claims that were written too restrictively. The claims in *Pennwalt* included too many elements. A watchful drafter likely would have been able to define a patentable advance with a less comprehensive depiction of the invention. In *Corning Glass*, the claims were too narrow in a different sense. Rather than expressly call for the addition of dopant to the core, the claims-drafter could have more abstractly provided for the "addition of dopant to change the refraction index" or simply the "alteration of the refraction index differential."

Some observers have attempted to distinguish *Corning Glass* as involving unusual facts. For example, Judge Lourie's subsequent opinion in *Ethicon Endo–Surgery, Inc. v. United States Surgical Corp.*[42] speaks of *Corning Glass* as involving a special case: the "simultaneous substitution of two reciprocal limitations (cladding for core and negative dopant for positive).''[43] As well, the *Corning Glass* court was plainly impressed with Corning's landmark invention. Perhaps *Corning Glass* suggests that the doctrine of equivalents can be used to correct claim scope in the case of pioneering advances.

Whatever the merits of the All Elements Rule, the Supreme Court opinion in *Warner–Jenkinson* broadly upheld it.[44] Interestingly, the facts of *Warner–Jenkinson* did not provide an apt vehicle for the approving statement of Justice Thomas. Recall that the crucial claim limitation there identified the pH at which a dye purification process should be performed. No one doubted that the accused process occurred at some acidity—it could hardly be otherwise. *Warner–Jenkinson* simply wasn't a case of a missing claim limitation. Nor did the Court see fit to discuss or even cite the crucial *Pennwalt* and *Corning Glass* opinions. The lower courts have always found the dicta of the Supreme Court extremely

40. 868 F.2d at 1259.

41. *E.g.*, Toshiko Takenaka, Interpreting Patent Claims: The United States, Germany and Japan 124–25 (1995).

42. 149 F.3d 1309, 47 USPQ2d 1272 (Fed.Cir.1998).

43. 149 F.3d at 1319.

44. 520 U.S. at 28–30.

persuasive, however, and the All Elements Rule remains with us as a significant constraint upon the doctrine of equivalents.

20.2.2.3.2   Prior Art Limitations

The prior art also restrains the application of the doctrine of equivalents. Sound patent policy dictates that patentees should not be able to obtain a construction of their claims that would reach technologies that have entered the public domain. Those who practice a technology known to the prior art, or its obvious variant, are immune from a finding of infringement under the Doctrine of Equivalents.

Suppose, for example, that Lance Lumen files a patent application on July 4, 2003, directed towards a light bulb. The Lumen patent specifically claims a light bulb with a tungsten filament. That application matures into a U.S. patent granted on November 12, 2005. Lumen brings an infringement lawsuit against Arthur Aurelius. Because Aurelius manufactures light bulbs using a carbon filament, there is no literal infringement. Lumen's infringement case is based upon the doctrine of equivalents and the argument that a carbon filament is equivalent to a tungsten filament. At trial, Aurelius produces an article published in the January 1, 2000, issue of *Bright Ideas*, extensively discussing the use of carbon filaments in light bulbs. That article, published more than one year before Lumen's filing date, is prior art against the Lumen patent under § 102(b). Because Aurelius is merely practicing a technology that is disclosed by the prior art, Lumen cannot successfully assert a claim of equivalent infringement against him.

All of this makes good sense as a policy matter. Had Lumen's patent literally claimed the use of carbon filaments in light bulbs, those claims would have been anticipated by the *Bright Ideas* article and therefore invalid. Lumen should not, through the doctrine of equivalents, obtain a proprietary interest to which he is not entitled. Of course, where the accused infringer practices a technology that is not precisely identical to a prior art reference, but is said to be an obvious variant of it, the analysis becomes rather more treacherous.

The leading case limiting the doctrine of equivalents on the basis of prior art is *Wilson Sporting Goods Co. v. David Geoffrey & Associates.*[45] That litigation concerned Wilson's assertion of a patent involving a golf ball cover dimple arrangement. The dimples were placed in such a manner as to allow the ball to fly higher and farther. In particular, the claims required that no dimples intersect with six "great circles," or arcs of circles that passed completely around the widest part of the ball.

The defendant, Dunlop, marketed golf balls with a dimple configuration similar to that of the patent. The great circles of Dunlop's balls were not dimple-free as the claims literally required, however. Approximately 14% of the dimples intersected a great circle. At trial, the jury found that the accused golf balls infringed under the doctrine of equivalents.

---

45. 904 F.2d 677 (Fed.Cir.1990).

On appeal, Dunlop pointed to evidence of record regarding a prior art golf ball marketed by Uniroyal. According to Dunlop, the range of equivalency accorded to the Wilson patent should have been constrained by the Uniroyal ball, which featured a 12% dimple intersection rate. With such a slight distinction between the Dunlop and Uniroyal balls, Dunlop urged that a finding of infringement was improper.

The Federal Circuit agreed with Dunlop and reversed in a much-discussed opinion. Judge Rich set forward a new methodology for considering prior art restraints upon the doctrine of equivalents:

> Whether prior art restricts the range of equivalents of what is literally claimed can be a difficult question to answer. To simplify analysis and bring the issue onto familiar turf, it may be helpful to conceptualize the limitation on the scope of equivalents by visualizing a *hypothetical* patent claim, sufficient in scope to *literally* cover the accused product. The pertinent question then becomes whether that hypothetical claim could have been allowed by the PTO over the prior art. If not, then it would be improper to permit the patentee to obtain that coverage in an infringement suit under the doctrine of equivalents. If the hypothetical claim could have been allowed, then *prior art* is not a bar to infringement under the doctrine of equivalents.[46]

The court then held that a hypothetical claim broad enough to capture the accused Dunlop balls would also have been obvious in light of the prior art Uniroyal ball. Because the distinction between a 12% and 14% dimple intersection rate did not constitute to a principled difference, Wilson's claim could not be accorded a range of equivalents broad enough to capture the accused golf balls.

Notable about the *Wilson Sporting Goods* decision is the seeming discomfort the Federal Circuit experienced about the analytical technique it had just announced. The court did not provide the hypothetical claim it presumably drafted when reaching its decision. As well, the court's analysis of the obviousness of the differences between the prior art and this unrevealed hypothetical claim was not an especially rigorous one. Not only did the court not remand for an analysis of the *Graham* factors under the law of obviousness—the prior art, the differences between the claimed invention and the prior art, the level of ordinary skill in the art, and the pertinent secondary considerations—the court did not even discuss them in a systematic way.

Although practitioners have criticized the hypothetical claim methodology as burdensome and confusing, particularly in jury trials, the Federal Circuit has emphasized that *Wilson Sporting Goods* did not establish rules of patent trial procedure.[47] *Wilson Sporting Goods* instead offered substantive guidance on the extent to which the prior art restrains the scope of equivalency. With or without hypothetical claims,

46. 904 F.2d at 684–85.

47. *See* Conroy v. Reebok Int'l, Inc., 14 F.3d 1570, 1576–77 (Fed.Cir.1994); Key Mfg. v. Microdot, Inc., 925 F.2d 1444, 1449 (Fed.Cir.1991).

numerous Federal Circuit cases have recognized that the prior art influences the permissible range of equivalents.[48] Where the circumstances allow, most accused infringers simply argue that they are practicing a technology that is available as prior art against the asserted patent, without the cumbersome apparatus of the hypothetical claim.

Wilson Sporting Goods also has the merit of putting some analytical rigor upon the enduring maxim of the patent law that claims towards pioneering inventions are entitled to a broader range of equivalents than patents claiming a narrow improvement in a crowded art.[49] This often recited canon of claim construction recognizes that the prior art is unlikely to restrain the scope of equivalents on patents that claim revolutionary advances. However, where the patented invention presents a more humble advance, then the prior art may restrain the range of equivalency to those claims.

20.2.2.3.3 Prosecution History Estoppel

The principle of prosecution history estoppel precludes a patentee from obtaining a claim construction before a court that would include subject matter surrendered at the PTO during prosecution. It is named for the "prosecution history" or "file wrapper," the publicly available papers that document the dialogue between the inventor and examiner during the patent acquisition. If the court concludes that an applicant relinquished certain subject matter in order to secure the allowance of her claims then, as a patentee, she may not employ the doctrine of equivalents to recapture the renounced subject matter.[50]

For example, suppose that Professor Gadget filed a patent application claiming a vaccine.[51] As filed, Gadget's claims contain no limitations concerning the number of times the vaccine should be administered in order to provide an effective immunization. During prosecution, the examiner cites a prior art reference that discloses a vaccine similar to Gadget's invention. In order to distinguish his vaccine from the prior art, Gadget inserts a limitation into his claims. As amended, Gadget's claims recite a "single administration vaccine" such that "said patient may be effectively immunized with one dose." Satisfied that Gadget's vaccine presents a patentable advance over the prior art, the examiner allows the claims to issue.

Suppose further that Gadget later sues a competitor, Rue Bella, for patent infringement. Bella manufactures a vaccine very similar to that of Gadget, but the accused vaccine must be administered in two separate doses at least one month apart. Bella may order a copy of the prosecu-

48. *See*, e.g., Baxter Healthcare Corp. v. Spectramed, Inc., 49 F.3d 1575 (Fed.Cir. 1995), *cert. denied*, 516 U.S. 906, 116 S.Ct. 272, 133 L.Ed.2d 194 (1995); We Care, Inc. v. Ultra–Mark Int'l Corp., 930 F.2d 1567 (Fed.Cir.1991).

49. *See* Westinghouse v. Boyden Power-Brake Co., 170 U.S. 537, 561–62, 18 S.Ct. 707, 42 L.Ed. 1136 (1898).

50. *E.g.*, Loral Fairchild Corp. v. Sony Corp., 181 F.3d 1313 (Fed.Cir.1999), *cert. denied*, 528 U.S. 1075, 120 S.Ct. 789, 145 L.Ed.2d 666 (2000).

51. This example is loosely based upon Intervet America, Inc. v. Kee–Vet Laboratories, Inc., 887 F.2d 1050 (Fed.Cir.1989).

tion history of the Gadget patent from the PTO and place it into evidence before the trial court. The court would then realize that Gadget expressly limited his claims to a single administration vaccine in order to avoid the prior art. Bella would further assert that as a result, the "one dose" limitation should not be expanded to "two doses" via the doctrine of equivalents. Because there is no literal infringement and prosecution history estoppel bars the application of the doctrine of equivalents, the court should dismiss Gadget's infringement suit.

In addition to estoppel through claim amendment, courts have also recognized estoppel by argument.[52] If an applicant makes an argument to the examiner characterizing the claimed invention or distinguishing it from the prior art, then prosecution history estoppel may apply as well. No claim need be amended in these circumstances. Courts consider whether a competitor reading the administrative record would reasonably believe the applicant surrendered subject matter. Absent a strong indication from the prosecution history, PTO examiners are assumed to rely upon applicants' arguments when deciding whether to allow patents to issue.

The doctrine of prosecution history estoppel formally differs from the use of prosecution histories as intrinsic evidence of the meaning of a claim. As described in the *Markman* opinion, prosecution histories complement the patent instrument as an essential input towards resolving the meaning of claim terms.[53] Prosecution history estoppel is a more rigid doctrine that comes into play only when the patentee resorts to the doctrine of equivalents. In practice, however, these two uses of the prosecution history are complementary. Whether employed in the context of the initial task of interpretation, or in a subsequent infringement inquiry under the doctrine of equivalents, resort to the prosecution history ensures that claims may not be construed one way in order to obtain their allowance and in another way against accused infringers.

The Supreme Court's opinion in *Warner–Jenkinson* explained the procedural aspects of prosecution history estoppel. According to Justice Thomas, when the prosecution history shows that the patentee amended the claims during prosecution, the burden fell to the patentee to explain the reason for the amendment. The court must then "decide whether that reason is sufficient to overcome prosecution history estoppel as a bar to application of the doctrine of equivalents to the element added by that amendment."[54] If the patentee failed to offer a suitable explanation, "the court should presume that the PTO had a substantial reason related to patentability for including the limited element added by amendment" and that prosecution history estoppel should apply.[55]

52. *See* Cybor Corp. v. FAS Technologies, Inc., 138 F.3d 1448 (Fed.Cir.1998) (*in banc*).

53. *See* Markman v. Westview Instruments, Inc., 52 F.3d 967 (Fed.Cir.1995) (*in banc*), *aff'd,* 517 U.S. 370, 116 S.Ct. 1384, 134 L.Ed.2d 577 (1996).

54. *Warner–Jenkinson*, 520 U.S. at 33.

55. *Id.*

Courts have struggled over the extent to which prosecution history estoppel impacts the doctrine of equivalents. The following example, using dated technology, illustrates these difficulties. Suppose that, prior to the invention of the transistor, an inventor presents a claim reciting a computer that in part uses an "electric switch." The PTO examiner rejects the claim based upon prior art. The inventor then narrows the claim by deleting the term "electric switch" and replacing it with the term "vacuum tube." The PTO examiner then approves the claim. Subsequently, near the end of the patent's term, the inventor brings suit against a competitor that manufactures computers using a new, state-of-the-art device—the transistor.

The case law provides two alternative approaches, the strict bar and the flexible bar, to address the scope of equivalents left to an amended claim limitation. Under the strict bar approach, if a claim limitation has been amended during prosecution, then no range of equivalents exists for that amended limitation. In the above example, because transistors can act as electric switches, the patentee is deemed to have confined his invention to vacuum tubes and purposefully disclaimed transistors. Prosecution history estoppel would therefore completely defeat the patentee's charge of infringement. The strict bar approach has the advantage of providing a "bright line" rule, but may hold harsh consequences for patentees.

In contrast, applying the flexible bar, a court would assess the reason for the claim amendment to determine the remaining scope of the doctrine of equivalents. Prosecution history estoppel would apply only where the court concluded that a person skilled in the art would reasonably believe that the patentee had surrendered subject matter during prosecution. To continue the previous example, no reasonable competitor would believe that the patentee had surrendered subject matter by amending the claims. At the time the patentee made the amendment, the transistor had yet to be invented! As a result, the court would likely hold that prosecution history estoppel did not apply, and proceed to the doctrine of equivalents analysis.

The Federal Circuit has traditionally employed a flexible bar approach. In its *Festo Corp. v. Shoketsu Kinzoku Kogyo Kabushiki Co.* decision,[56] however, the Federal Circuit abruptly announced its shift to a strict bar approach, only to be reversed by the Supreme Court. Here the plaintiff, Festo, owned the Stoll and Carroll patents. Each patent concerned magnetic rodless cylinders. During prosecution, the claims of both patents were amended to require a pair of sealing rings. The Carroll patent was additionally amended to require a sleeve made of magnetizable material. The accused infringer, SMC, produced a device employing a single, two-way sealing ring and a sleeve made of nonmagnetizable material.

Although the Stoll and Carroll patents were not literally infringed, Festo argued that infringement existed under the doctrine of equiva-

56. 234 F.3d 558 (Fed.Cir.2000) (*en banc*).

lents. SMC in turn contended that prosecution history estoppel barred Festo from resorting to the doctrine. Festo's position was that, following *Warner–Jenkinson*, an explanation existed for the two claim amendments. Festo characterized the sealing ring amendment as relating to the examiner's rejection based on § 112, pertaining to claim definiteness. Festo further described the sleeve material amendment as wholly voluntary.

SMC appealed an unfavorable judgment from the trial court, and on appeal the Federal Circuit reversed. The Federal Circuit applied the strict bar rule and held that prosecution history estoppel creates a complete bar to the doctrine of equivalents. "When a claim amendment creates prosecution history estoppel with regard to a claim element, there is no range of equivalents available for the amended claim element," the court explained.[57] The Federal Circuit reasoned that the need for certainty as to the scope of patent protection was paramount. According to the Court of Appeals, amendments should be treated as disclaimers and construed against the inventor, and in favor of the public.

A unanimous Supreme Court vacated and remanded the case, effectively restoring the flexible bar approach to the law of prosecution history estoppel.[58] Justice Kennedy explained that prosecution history does not bar the inventor from asserting infringement against every equivalent to the narrowed element. The Court instead mandated a specific determination of the range of subject matter surrendered by a narrowing amendment. The Court followed the approach established in *Warner–Jenkinson* by confirming the presumption that any territory surrendered through claim amendment is an equivalent of the territory claimed. Patentees can rebut this presumption, however, by showing that at the time of the amendment one skilled in the art could not reasonably be expected to have drafted a claim that would literally encompass the alleged equivalent.

In *Festo*, the Supreme Court did agree with the Federal Circuit that amendments to satisfy § 112 also could trigger prosecution history estoppel.[59] Most prosecution history estoppel cases concern amendments made to distinguish prior art, and therefore involve §§ 102 or 103 of the Patent Act. But sometimes applicants change claims in order to make them more definite, a requirement under § 112. An examiner might ask the patentee to clarify an ambiguous word, for example, or provide more detail on how the different parts of the invention interact with each other. The Court reasoned that inventors made such amendments in order to procure a patent, and that as a result prosecution history could apply in the context of § 112 as well.

57. 234 F.3d at 569.
58. 535 U.S. 722, 122 S.Ct. 1831, 152 L.Ed.2d 944 (2002).
59. 122 S.Ct. at 1839–40.

The use of prosecution histories in the task of claim interpretation has suffered criticism.[60] Like legislative histories or parol evidence, prosecution histories consist of preparatory documents of uncertain relation to the text ultimately approved. Unlike succinct, integrated patent instruments, these episodic and often lengthy compilations of correspondence can be time-consuming and costly to understand. Commentary has called for the abandonment of the principle of prosecution history estoppel in favor of an objective analysis of prior art and patentability constraints upon the scope of equivalents. However, as Federal Circuit cases have increasingly relied upon the prosecution history despite such critiques, the patent bar would do well to heed the consequences of the prosecution history both during enforcement proceedings and while corresponding with examiners during prosecution.

20.2.2.3.4   The Public Dedication Doctrine

In its 2002 decision in *Johnson & Johnston Associates, Inc. v. R.E. Service Co., Inc.*,[61] the *en banc* Federal Circuit recognized an additional restraint upon the doctrine of equivalents. Under the *Johnson & Johnston* "public dedication doctrine," subject matter that is disclosed in a patent, but not claimed, may not be appropriated through the doctrine of equivalents. Such unclaimed subject matter is considered to have been deliberately disclaimed and therefore dedicated to the public.

The *Johnson & Johnston* case involved a recurring situation: sometimes the claims of a patent are not as broad as the technical disclosure contained in that patent's written description. The patent at issue in that case, owned by Johnson & Johnston, concerned a printed circuit board. A printed circuit board is a thin plate on which computer chips or other electronic components are placed. The patent's specification explained that the substrate of the circuit board could be manufactured of a number of materials, including aluminum, steel and nickel. However, the patent's claims were limited to a substrate made of aluminum. Accused infringer R.E. Service manufactured printed circuit boards with a steel substrate.

Prior to *Johnson & Johnston*, competing views arose as to the impact of described, yet unclaimed subject matter upon the doctrine of equivalents. One possibility is that disclosure within the patent instrument acts in favor of a finding of equivalency. Under this perspective, the patent as a whole provides notice to interested competitors what the patentee regarded as an equivalent at the time the patent was granted.

At the other extreme, as represented by the 1996 Federal Circuit decision in *Maxwell v. J. Baker, Inc.*,[62] is the position that subject matter disclosed but not claimed in a patent application is, as a matter of law, dedicated to the public. Under this view, by failing to claim the full

---

60. *See* John R. Thomas, *On Preparatory Texts and Proprietary Technologies: The Place of Prosecution Histories in Patent Claim Interpretation*, 47 UCLA L. Rev. 183 (1999).

61. 285 F.3d 1046 (Fed.Cir.2002).

62. 86 F.3d 1098 (Fed.Cir.1996), *cert. denied*, 520 U.S. 1115, 117 S.Ct. 1244, 137 L.Ed.2d 327 (1997).

extent of the disclosed subject matter, an applicant deprives the PTO of the opportunity to consider whether this subject matter is patentable. Allowing an applicant to obtain narrow claims from the PTO, and then assert broader protection for unclaimed alternatives described in the specification, would defeat the fundamental principle that a patent's claims define its scope of proprietary rights.

A third position, adopted by the 1998 Federal Circuit opinion in *YBM Magnex, Inc. v. International Trade Commission,*[63] was that no *per se* rule should dictate whether subject matter included in the written description but not claimed is equivalent to the claimed invention. Proponents of this view emphasized that the doctrine of equivalents seeks to establish a just balance between providing competitors with notice of what is patented, and the judicial responsibility to avoid a "fraud on the patent" based on insubstantial changes from the patented invention. Whether the accused infringement was disclosed, but not claimed in the asserted patent simply formed one of many factors to consider in the equivalency determination.

The *en banc* Federal Circuit resolved its inconsistent precedent in *Johnson & Johnston* by adopting *Maxwell* and expressly overruling *YBM Magnex.* The Federal Circuit reasoned that allowing the doctrine of equivalents to extend to disclosed, but unclaimed subject matter would conflict with the primacy of the claims in defining the scope of the patentee's exclusive right. Otherwise patent applicants would be encouraged to present a broad disclosure in the specification of the application and file narrow claims, avoiding examination of broader claims that the applicant could have filed consistent with the specification. Applying this principle to the facts of the case, the Federal Circuit concluded that R.E. Service did not infringe the Johnson & Johnston patent under the doctrine of equivalents.

In the wake of the *Johnson & Johnston* decision, patent applicants have been encouraged to draft claims with increasing care. Commentators have suggested that applicants draft a broad generic claim as well as more specific claims to each embodiment that can be envisioned. If a patent issued prior to the *Johnson & Johnston* case, and failed to claim disclosed subject matter, the Federal Circuit further suggested that the patentee pursue a reissue or continuation application as the circumstances allow.[64] Most apparent is the Federal Circuit has introduced a significant restraint upon the doctrine of equivalents that will require patent applicants to craft claims with increasing precision.

20.2.2.4   The Reverse Doctrine of Equivalents

In its *Graver Tank* opinion, the Supreme Court recognized that the doctrine of equivalents may also act against the interest of the paten-

63.   145 F.3d 1317 (Fed.Cir.1998), *overruled by*, Johnson & Johnston Associates, Inc. v. R.E. Service Co., 285 F.3d 1046 (Fed.Cir.2002).

64.   285 F.3d at 1055. Reissue applications are discussed *supra* at § 19.6.3, while continuation applications are taken up *supra* at § 19.2.4.

tee.[65] When an accused product or process is literally covered by the words of a patent claim, but is "so far changed in principle" that it performs in a "substantially different way," the court may reach a finding of noninfringement. The so-called "reverse doctrine of equivalents" amounts to a defense to literal infringement. Although the reverse doctrine is equitable in nature, whether an accused technology goes sufficiently outside the principles of the patented invention is a question of fact.[66]

The reverse doctrine of equivalents has been of greater interest to scholars than to the courts.[67] The Federal Circuit has termed the reverse doctrine of equivalents an "anachronistic exception, long mentioned but rarely applied,"[68] and has yet to apply this principle squarely in any of its cases. Given this paucity of precedent, it is more important to recognize situations where the reverse doctrine does not apply. One such case is where a defendant merely puts a claimed invention towards a new use.

For example, suppose that the Major Drug Company holds a patent claiming a chemical composition and a method of using the composition to cure hypertension. An independent researcher named Harry Hirsute discovers that the compound also prevents male pattern baldness, a previously unknown use. If Hirsute manufactures the compound, then he has undoubtedly infringed the Major Drug Company patent. The reverse doctrine of equivalents would not apply even if Hirsute intends to sell the compound only to balding men with normal blood pressure, and even if his invention is separately patentable as a process.

The reverse doctrine of equivalents was instead intended to apply to extraordinary cases. It provides courts with something of an escape hatch, useful when a finding of literal infringement would work an unwarranted extension of the claims. The reverse doctrine might pertain to rapidly progressing fields of high technology, where radical subsequent advances allow predecessor patents to appropriate subject matter entirely beyond the scope of their technical contribution. Such circumstances appear so uncommon that, in its two decades of existence, the Federal Circuit has yet to encounter them.

20.2.2.5 Equivalents Under § 112 ¶ 6

Recall that the sixth paragraph of § 112 provides a mandatory procedure for interpreting functional claims.[69] Under that provision, if a claim element is drafted as a means for performing a specified function, readers must construe that claim element as covering "the corresponding structure, material, or acts described in the specification and equivalents thereof." Expressed differently, the reader must review the patent

65. 339 U.S. at 608–09.

66. *See* SRI Int'l v. Matsushita Elec. Corp., 775 F.2d 1107, 227 USPQ 577 (Fed. Cir.1985).

67. *See* Robert P. Merges & Richard R. Nelson, *On the Complex Economics of Patent Scope*, 90 Colum. L. Rev. 839 (1990).

68. Tate Access Floors, Inc. v. Interface Architectural Resources, Inc., 279 F.3d 1357, 1368, 61 USPQ2d 1647 (Fed.Cir. 2002).

69. *See supra* § 18.2.2.2.

specification to find the specific structure that performs to the claimed function. The claim element should be understood to provide literal coverage of the expressly described structure along with "equivalents thereof."

The extent of the "equivalents thereof" under § 112 ¶ 6 continues to confound all who confront this issue. Not only have decades of experience failed to provide a sharp definition of the doctrine of equivalents, the patent law does not readily yield alternative conceptions of equivalency. Like the doctrine of equivalents, § 112 ¶ 6 equivalence must focus upon the substantiality of the differences between the claimed element and a component of the accused product. Still, the Supreme Court's treatment of § 112 ¶ 6 in *Warner–Jenkinson* requires that some distinction exist between these two notions of equivalency.[70]

A Federal Circuit opinion subsequent to *Warner–Jenkinson*, *Al–Site Corp. v. VSI International, Inc.*,[71] presents the most thoughtful attempt to demarcate the scope of § 112 ¶ 6 equivalents. Judge Rader identified three differences between the doctrine of equivalents and § 112 ¶ 6 equivalents. The first is a matter of timing. Under *Warner–Jenkinson*, the proper time for evaluating insubstantial differences under the doctrine of equivalents is at the time of infringement. However, an equivalent under § 112 ¶ 6 cannot embrace technology developed after the time the patent issues because the PTO fixes the literal meaning of the claims at that time. Therefore, an "after-arising" technology could infringe under the doctrine of equivalents without being considered a § 112 ¶ 6 equivalent.

Second, under the literal language of § 112 ¶ 6, the equivalent must perform the identical function recited in the claim element. Under the function-way-result test, the doctrine of equivalents may be satisfied when the function performed by the accused device is only substantially the same as that of the claimed invention.

Finally, the *Al–Site* court employed the term "structural equivalents" in connection with § 112 ¶ 6. This wording appears to demand an equivalency comparison that exclusively concerns physical structure. Under this view, § 112 ¶ 6 provides a scope of equivalents far more narrow than that of the doctrine of equivalents. Suppose, for example, that a patent claimed a "means for securing said engine to said frame." The corresponding portion of the specification describes the use of bolts to attach the frame to the engine. Although nails and screws have the same structure as bolts, such well-known securing mechanisms as adhesives or magnets do not. Professor Mark Janis has observed that such a cramped claim coverage is little more than a subterfuge for no equivalen-

70. *See* 520 U.S. at 27.

71. 174 F.3d 1308, 50 USPQ2d 1161 (Fed.Cir.1999).

cy.[72] As the term "structural equivalents" does not appear in § 112 ¶ 6, the legitimacy of this interpretation is also suspect as a textual matter.

72. *See* Mark Janis, *Who's Afraid of Functional Claims? Reforming the Patent Law's § 112 ¶ 6 Jurisprudence*, 15 Santa Clara Computer & High Tech. L.J. 231 (1999).

Chapter 21

EQUITABLE DEFENSES TO
PATENT INFRINGEMENT

Table of Sections

In addition to the doctrine of inequitable conduct, reviewed previously in Chapter 19,[1] the U.S. patent law includes a number of other defenses that may ultimately bar the patentee from relief in an infringement action. Chief among them are laches, estoppel, shop rights and misuse. These doctrines relate not to the validity of a patent but to its enforceability against another. If successfully invoked, they essentially provide the defendant with license to practice the patented technology.

A successful laches defense requires a showing that a patentee unreasonably and inexcusably delayed in bringing an infringement suit such that the infringer suffered material prejudice. Related to laches is estoppel, which applies if a patentee leads the infringer to believe that the patentee does not intend to enforce its patent against the infringer, and the infringer relies on that representation to its detriment. Shop rights entitle an employer, in appropriate circumstances, to use an invention patented by an employee without liability for infringement. Finally, a patent owner may commit misuse by improperly extending a patent's exclusive rights. Such extensions frequently are, but need not be, violations of the antitrust laws. Practices previously held to be misuse include tying the purchase of unpatented goods along with a patented technology, conditioning the licensing of a patent upon an agreement not to sell competing products and price fixing.

1.   *See* § 19.4.1, *supra.*

§ 21.1 Laches and Estoppel

Although hardly unique to the patent law, the equitable defenses of laches and estoppel have recently been of considerable importance in this discipline. In an era where patent litigation has become an increasingly lucrative endeavor, patentees have demonstrated a renewed willingness to review their portfolios in order to consider whether any claims are being infringed. Sometimes this effort results in the "dusting off" of patents that are near expiration or have in fact expired, with litigation commenced regarding infringements that began years before. A review of laches and estoppel cases in the patent context therefore seems well worthwhile.

The chief Federal Circuit opinion concerning laches and estoppel is *A.C. Aukerman Co. v. R. L. Chaides Construction Co.*[1] Aukerman owned two patents relating to a "slip-form" and a method of using that product to construct concrete highway barriers. Chaides used a slip-form product purchased from a third party, Gomaco, to manufacture concrete highway barriers. Between February and April 1979, Aukerman sent letters to Chaides accusing Chaides of infringing the patents, but offering Chaides a license under the patents. In April 1979, Chaides provided a written response stating that any responsibility was Gomaco's, and that "if Aukerman wished to sue Chaides 'for $200—$300 a year,' Aukerman should do so." The parties had no further contact for over eight years, during which time Chaides markedly increased its slip-form business.

In October 1987, prompted by a licensee's complaint about the competition provided by Chaides, Aukerman sent a letter to Chaides advising Chaides "that litigation against another company had been resolved, and threatening litigation unless Chaides executed [a] license...." Chaides refused to enter into a license, and on October 26, 1988, Aukerman sued Chaides for infringement. The district court granted summary judgment, holding that Aukerman was barred under principles of laches and estoppel from maintaining its cause of action. On appeal, the *en banc* Federal Circuit reversed, holding that the district court inappropriately granted summary judgment.

Turning first to laches, Chief Judge Nies listed the two elements of this defense. First, the infringer must prove that the patentee delayed filing suit for an unreasonable and inexcusable period of time, starting from the time the patentee should have known of its claim against the infringer. The court listed several possible factors that might excuse a dilatory patentee, including: other litigation, negotiations with the accused, possibly poverty and illness under limited circumstances, wartime conditions, extent of infringement and dispute over ownership of the patent. The court also noted the possibility that laches may not apply where the infringer was guilty of particularly egregious conduct. Such

§ 21.1

1. 960 F.2d 1020, 22 USPQ2d 1321 (Fed.Cir.1992) (in banc).

conduct, that would tip the equities sharply in favor of the patentee, could include conscious copying or misrepresentations.

The second element is that the delay must have operated to the prejudice of the infringer. The court identified two sorts of prejudice, economic and evidentiary. Economic prejudice might arise where a defendant would suffer the loss of investment and business expansion due to the delay in filing suit. Evidentiary prejudice might arise through the death of a witness, destruction of records or the unreliability of memories of distant events.

The court adhered to settled law that the effect of a laches defense is to bar relief on a patentee's claim only with respect to damages accumulated prior to the filing of suit. Equitable relief and claims for future damages may still be awarded in favor of the patentee even in cases where laches was successfully proven.

The Federal Circuit also instructed the lower courts how to allocate the burden of proof in laches cases. The infringer ordinarily maintains both the burden of production and the burden of persuasion regarding laches. However, the court upheld the judicially created presumption that a delay of six years from the time the patentee knew of an infringement, until the time suit was filed, acted to shift the burden of production. Thus, in cases where the patentee's delay exceeded six years, the patent owner then bore the burden of production to provide an adequate excuse for putting off the filing of suit. This six-year period was borrowed from 35 U.S.C.A. § 286, a statute that denies patentees the ability to obtain damages beyond six years from the time suit is filed. The court was quick to note that the presumption of laches only shifts the burden of producing evidence, not the ultimate burden of persuasion, which is always maintained by the accused infringer. Because the district court did not apply this framework, the Federal Circuit remanded the case for further consideration.

The *Aukerman* decision was generally seen as weakening the effectiveness of the laches defense in patent litigation, particularly when raised in a summary judgment motion. Some observers believe that, in practice, patentees are readily able to present reasons excusing their delay in filing suit. Further, the infringer always maintains the burden of persuasion under the *Auckerman* framework, even though many issues in laches cases may be more readily demonstrated or disproved by evidence in the control of the patentee. That the infringer bears the burden of persuasion also means that where the trier of fact cannot decide whether the patentee's delay was reasonable or unreasonable, the patentee should prevail.[2]

The *Auckerman* court also considered the defense of estoppel, breaking its elements into three parts. First, the patentee, through misleading conduct, must lead the accused infringer to believe that the patentee does not intend to enforce its patent against the alleged infringer. Such

---

2. *See* Evan Finkel, *What Remains of the Laches and Estoppel Defenses After*   Auckerman?, 9 Santa Clara Computer & High Tech. L.J. 1 (1993).

conduct could include an affirmative statement, action, inaction or even silence where there was an obligation to speak. Second, the infringer must have relied upon that conduct. Finally, the infringer must show that it has suffered material prejudice as a result of the patentee's conduct. As with laches, material prejudice would ordinarily comprise either a change in economic position or the loss of evidence.

Applying this law to the facts before it, the court again reversed and remanded. Chief Judge Nies particularly relied upon Chaides' 1979 statement that its infringing constructions of slip-forms were extremely minimal. As one could well infer that Auckerman merely waived an infringement claim worth at most $300 per year, the grant of summary judgment of estoppel was improper. This observation proved a telling one on remand, for the district court held that Chaides could invoke neither the laches nor estoppel defense. Because Chaides had substantially increased its infringing activities after advising Auckerman that its use of the patented slip-forms was minimal, the trial court held that Chaides was marred by unclean hands and unable to use these equitable defenses.[3]

§ 21.2　Shop Rights

The great majority of contemporary inventors create new technologies while serving as employees. In many of the world's patent systems, legislation provides employed inventors with rights to their inventions. The U.S. patent law tends to favor employers over employees, however.[1] Express assignments to rights pertaining to inventions, among the provisions of a typical scientist's or engineer's employment contract, vest title in patents in employers. A license in favor of the employer may also be implied where the employee was hired to perform a specific function that would include inventing. Even where no express agreement exists between the employee and the employer and where the employee was not hired to invent, however, an employer may still obtain the legal authorization to use a patented invention. This authorization goes by the curious name "shop right."

A "shop right" is not a machinist's tool, but an employer's entitlement to employ an invention patented by its employee without liability for infringement. This entitlement most clearly arises where an employee conceived of the invention during working hours, reduced the invention to practice using the employer's resources and allowed the invention to be incorporated into the employer's facilities.[2] Shop right cases often involve inventors who implemented improvements upon an employer's manufacturing equipment. Subsequently, the inventor leaves the service of the employer and obtains a patent upon the invention. When the

3.　29 USPQ2d 1054, 1057–59 (N.D.Cal. 1993).

§ 21.2

1. *See* Jay Dratler, Jr., *Incentives for People: The Forgotten Purpose of the United*

States Patent System, 16 Harv. J. Legis. 129 (1979).

2.　*See* United States v. Dubilier Condenser Corp., 289 U.S. 178, 188–89, 53 S.Ct. 554, 77 L.Ed. 1114, 17 USPQ 154 (1933).

inventor sues his former employer for patent infringement, the shop right defense comes into play.

The leading Federal Circuit case on shop rights remains Judge Rich's instructive opinion in *McElmurry v. Arkansas Power & Light Co.*[3] The plaintiffs brought suit against Arkansas Power & Light (AP&L) for infringement of the '714 patent, which named Bowman as the inventor. Bowman had developed the patented level detector while serving as a consultant to AP&L. AP&L successfully moved for summary judgment based on its possession of shop rights in the claimed level detector, and on appeal the Federal Circuit affirmed.

The Federal Circuit began by identifying the varying doctrinal bases for shop rights. Judge Rich noted that the courts tended to rely upon two underlying foundations for judging the existence and extent of a shop right. The first is under the theory of an implied license. This basis focuses attention upon whether the employee engaged in activities, such as using the employer's time and tools, that demand a finding the employer was impliedly licensed to use the resulting invention. The second is based upon an estoppel theory. The estoppel rationale suggests that shop rights should be based upon whether the employee consented or acquiesced to an employer's use of the invention.

Declining to pick whether the implied license or estoppel theory provided the superior basis for shop rights, the court held that the proper methodology in shop right cases was "to look to the totality of the circumstances on a case by case basis and determine whether the facts of a particular case demand, under principles of equity and fairness, a finding that a 'shop right' exists." Applying this general principle to the facts of the case, Judge Rich noted that Bowman had developed the patented level detector while working at AP&L; had consented to the installation of numerous level detectors onto AP&L's equipment; and had never asserted, at least prior to this litigation, that AP&L was required to compensate him for use of the level detector. Each of these factors supported the conclusion that AP&L enjoyed a shop right in Bowman's patented invention.

Defining the exact scope of the shop right proves a perplexing task. Although the very name "shop right" suggests that it is limited to the specific site to which the employer was assigned, the courts have tended to allow employers greater flexibility. Speaking generally, the shop right has been liberally construed with an eye towards the business requirements of the employer. However, as befits an equitable doctrine, the precise extent to which the employer may expand its use of the patented invention over the life of the shop right has been subject to a case by case determination.[4]

3. 995 F.2d 1576, 27 USPQ2d 1129 (Fed.Cir.1993).

4. *See* Kierulff v. Metropolitan Stevedore Co., 315 F.2d 839 (9th Cir.1963); Thompson v. American Tobacco Co., 174 F.2d 773, 81 USPQ 323 (4th Cir.1949); Pure Oil Co. v. Hyman, 95 F.2d 22, 25, 36 USPQ 306, 310 (7th Cir.1938).

The case law more clearly explains that a shop right endures through the duration of the patent.[5] A shop right remains personal to the employer and cannot be transferred,[6] except if the employer sells its entire business.[7] Title to the patent remains vested in the patentee, who is free to license or assign the patent to others.[8]

§ 21.3   Misuse

A patent owner commits misuse when he exploits a patent in such a manner as to exceed its lawful scope. The key inquiry in patent misuse cases is whether the patentee has impermissibly broadened the scope of his patent with anticompetitive effect.[1] A successful showing of patent misuse renders the patent unenforceable. Misuse is an elusive doctrine, since there is scant statutory language explaining which activities constitute misuse and which do not. As such, patent misuse is very much a creature of the case law. However, because the patent misuse doctrine arose in the era of anti-monopoly sentiment following the Great Depression, most of these cases are of questionable vitality today. Still, the Supreme Court has yet to overturn its misuse precedent, and perhaps some of its dated holdings may continue to have some force in the future.

Morton Salt Co. v. G.S. Suppiger Co.[2] presents the Supreme Court's most thorough review of the misuse doctrine. Morton was the proprietor of the '645 patent, relating to a machine for depositing salt tablets. The machine was useful for adding predetermined amounts of salt to the contents of cans. Morton brought an infringement suit against Suppiger for making and leasing allegedly infringing machines. Suppiger defended on the ground that Morton had "exceeded its monopoly" by leasing its patented machines on the condition that the licensors make exclusive use of Morton's unpatented salt tablets. The district court accepted this defense, but on appeal the Seventh Circuit reversed after concluding that Morton's tying arrangement did not violate the Clayton Act.

After granting *certiorari*, the Supreme Court again reversed, concluding that Morton had misused its patent. The Court started from the proposition that the use of a patent to secure an exclusive right not granted by the Patent Office violated the constitutional goal of promoting the useful arts. Because such a "maintenance and enlargement" of the patentee's rights depended in part upon successful results in infringement litigation, the courts should withhold relief where a patent was used as a means of restraining competition in the sale of unpatented

5. *See* Wiegand v. Dover Mfg. Co., 292 F. 255 (N.D.Ohio 1923).

6. *See* Tripp v. United States, 406 F.2d 1066, 1070, 157 USPQ 90, 161 USPQ 115 (Ct.Cl.1969).

7. Pursche v. Atlas Scraper & Eng'g Co., 300 F.2d 467, 485, 132 USPQ 104 (9th Cir.1961).

8. *See* United States v. Dubilier Condenser Corp., 289 U.S. 178, 53 S.Ct. 554, 77 L.Ed. 1114, 17 USPQ 154 (1933).

§ 21.3

1. Windsurfing Int'l, Inc. v. AMF, Inc., 782 F.2d 995, 1001–02, 228 USPQ 562, 566 (Fed.Cir.1986).

2. 314 U.S. 488, 62 S.Ct. 402, 86 L.Ed. 363, 52 USPQ 30 (1942).

products. As a holder of an exclusive privilege granted to further a public policy, an individual who used his patent to subvert that policy could not expect to gain protection from the courts.

In keeping with *Morton Salt*, the courts identified a number of other acts that could constitute patent misuse. Among them were fixing prices;[3] prohibiting the manufacture of competing products;[4] conditioning the grant of one license upon the acceptance of another license;[5] and basing royalty payments on total sales, regardless of the extent to which the patented invention was used.[6] Judicial opinions from the *Morton Salt* era of patent misuse cases also established several core precepts concerning this doctrine. Misuse serves as an effective defense even though the accused infringer itself is not harmed by the improper practice.[7] An effective assertion of the misuse defense renders the patent unenforceable.[8] However, a patentee may purge his misuse by abandoning the improper practice. When the effects of the misuse has dissipated, then the patent may once again be enforced.[9] Activities that amounted to misuse need not rise to the level of antitrust violations, although they frequently did.

Two later Supreme Court opinions, *Mercoid Corp. v. Mid–Continent Investment Co,*[10] and *Mercoid v. Minneapolis–Honeywell Regulator Co.,*[11] went even further than *Morton Salt*. The patent at issue in *Mercoid* concerned a domestic heating system. Among the elements of the claimed invention was a stoker switch. Unlike the salt tablets in *Morton Salt*, which were a staple article of commerce with many uses outside the claimed invention, the stoker switch was useful only in connection with the practice of the patented heating system. When the Mercoid Corporation manufactured stoker switches without a license, the patentee brought charges of contributory infringement.

When the *Mercoid* cases at last reached the Supreme Court, the Court again concluded that the patentee was guilty of misuse. Calling the case "a graphic illustration of the evils of an expansion of the patent monopoly by private engagements," Justice Douglas relied upon the principle that the patent covered only the claimed combination, not its individual components. Under this reasoning, the attempt to suppress the sale of stoker switches also amounted to an anticompetitive restraint upon unpatented goods. The Court was unimpressed both with the fact

3. *See* Bauer & Cie. v. O'Donnell, 229 U.S. 1, 33 S.Ct. 616, 57 L.Ed. 1041 (1913).

4. National Lockwasher Co. v. George K. Garrett Co., 137 F.2d 255, 58 USPQ 460 (3d Cir.1943).

5. American Securit Co. v. Shatterproof Glass Corp., 268 F.2d 769, 122 USPQ 167 (3d Cir.1959), *cert. denied,* 361 U.S. 902, 80 S.Ct. 210, 4 L.Ed.2d 157 (1959).

6. Zenith Radio Corp. v. Hazeltine Research, Inc., 401 U.S. 321, 91 S.Ct. 795, 28 L.Ed.2d 77 (1971).

7. Morton Salt Co. v. G.S. Suppiger Co., 314 U.S. 488, 62 S.Ct. 402, 86 L.Ed. 363, 52 USPQ 30 (1942).

8. *See* B.B. Chem. Co. v. Ellis, 314 U.S. 495, 62 S.Ct. 406, 86 L.Ed. 367, 52 USPQ 33 (1942).

9. *See* B.B. Chem. Co. v. Ellis, 314 U.S. 495, 62 S.Ct. 406, 86 L.Ed. 367, 52 USPQ 33 (1942).

10. 320 U.S. 661, 64 S.Ct. 268, 88 L.Ed. 376 (1944).

11. 320 U.S. 680, 64 S.Ct. 278, 88 L.Ed. 396 (1944).

that the patentee measured royalty rates through the sale of heating system's components and that the patentee's stoker switch formed an advance in the art that had no use outside the patented invention.

Had the *Mercoid* cases remained good law, little would have been left of the doctrine of contributory infringement. However, Congress acted to curb the misuse doctrine by incorporating § 271(d) into the 1952 Act. As originally enacted, the statute declared that no misuse occurred where the patentee: (1) gained revenue from acts that would constitute contributory (as compared to direct) infringement if performed by another, (2) licensed others to perform acts that would constitute contributory (as compared to direct) infringement if performed by another, or (3) sought to enforce his patent.

The Supreme Court first interpreted § 271(d) in its 1980 opinion in *Dawson Chemical Co. v. Rohm and Haas Co.*[12] Rohm & Haas owned the '092 patent claiming a method of using the herbicide propanil. Rohm & Haas brought suit against Dawson, asserting that Dawson sold propanil to farmers along with instructions on how to apply propanil to crops. Dawson had earlier sought a license from Rohm & Haas. Rohm & Haas refused to license Dawson, however, unless Dawson agreed to purchase its propanil from Rohm & Haas. Dawson subsequently argued that Rohm & Haas had misused the '092 patent.

Under the facts of the case, propanil was not itself subject to patent protection. However, the only known use of propanil would infringe the Rohm & Haas process patent. So the essential question in this case was whether Rohm & Haas, which had identified the only valuable application for propanil, should be able to control its use. The District Court granted summary judgment on the misuse issue in favor of Dawson, but on appeal the Fifth Circuit reversed on the basis of § 271(d). The Supreme Court granted *certiorari* and affirmed the opinion of the Court of Appeals. Agreeing that Congress meant to overrule the *Mercoid* cases, the Court concluded that a patentee may "control nonstaple goods that are capable only of infringing use in a patented invention, and that are essential to that invention's advance over the prior art."

Congress augmented § 271(d) in 1988 by adding paragraphs (4) and (5), which further limited the misuse defense. Paragraph (4) states that a refusal to license or use patent rights does not constitute misuse, while paragraph (5) exempts tying practices from the patent misuse doctrine unless the patentee enjoys market power. Following the 1988 amendments to § 271(d), tying practices only constitute misuse if the patentee enjoys market power and the tied goods are staple articles of commerce.

The amendments to § 271(d) suggest the waning influence of patent misuse law, a trend reflected in Federal Circuit opinions. That court's thinking regarding misuse is demonstrated by its 1992 decision in *Mallinckrodt Inc. v. Medipart Inc.*[13] Mallinckrodt held a patent on an apparatus for delivery of radioactive or therapeutic material in aerosol

---

12. 448 U.S. 176, 100 S.Ct. 2601, 65 L.Ed.2d 696 (1980).

13. 976 F.2d 700, 24 USPQ2d 1173 (Fed.Cir.1992).

mist form. It sold a commercial embodiment of the claimed technology for approximately $50. Mallinckrodt marked its products with a "single use only" notice. Mallinckrodt filed a patent infringement suit against Medipart, which had disregarded the notice, refilled emptied devices and sold them for approximately $20. The district court held that violation of the notice was not a matter within the purview of the Patent Act. Mallinckrodt appealed and obtained a reversal from the Federal Circuit.

Judge Newman began by considering whether any Supreme Court case had held that a patentee engaged in misuse by using any form of a limited license in selling patented products. Finding none, and rejecting analogies from price-fixing and tying cases, the Federal Circuit overturned the trial court. The *Mallinckrodt* opinion offers two principal lessons. The first is that a patentee may limit the use of patented articles and may obtain a remedy through the patent laws if others disobey that restriction. Restraints on the repair or modification of patented equipment will be struck down only if they violate some other positive law, in particular the antitrust laws. The second is that the Federal Circuit will find misuse only when the Supreme Court has specifically declared a commercial arrangement as such, or when the conduct is demonstrably anticompetitive.[14]

A more direct attack on the misuse doctrine can be found in many law review articles, as well as in Judge Posner's thoughtful opinion in *USM Corp. v. SPS Technologies, Inc.*[15] Following a 1969 infringement suit brought by SPS against USM, the parties settled and obtained a consent judgment. Under the terms of the consent judgment, USM acknowledged the validity of the SPS patent and agreed to pay royalties. In 1974, it was USM's turn to file suit. USM urged this time that the license agreement the parties had entered into following the consent judgment constituted a patent misuse due to a differential royalty scheme. The District Court held in part that the arrangement did not constitute misuse.[16] On appeal, the Seventh Circuit affirmed.

Judge Posner's opinion attacked the foundations of patent misuse doctrine. He reasoned that misuse does not extend the patent beyond the scope of the claims because, as a matter of economics, patentees are only able to charge what others will pay for use of the patent. That charge can take the form of license restrictions, such as grant-back clauses, differential royalties, measurement of the royalty by the sale of a non-patented product, or simply a higher monetary price. On the facts of the case, Judge Posner concluded that competition policies did not prohibit the patentee's maximization of its income from the patent. Because the SPS royalty arrangement was not shown to have anticompetitive effects in the market of the patentee's customers, the defense of patent misuse could not stand.

---

14. *See* Windsurfing Int'l, Inc. v. AMF Inc., 782 F.2d 995, 228 USPQ 562 (Fed.Cir. 1986).

15. 694 F.2d 505, 216 USPQ 959 (Fed. Cir.1982).

16. 453 F.Supp. at 743, 200 USPQ at 788.

Chapter 22

REMEDIES FOR PATENT INFRINGEMENT

Table of Sections

The Patent Act sets forth the remedies a patentee may obtain upon a finding of infringement. These remedies include injunctions, monetary damages and attorney fees. The statute also allows for damages to be increased by up to three times in exceptional cases of willful infringement. The Patent Act does not provide for criminal sanctions for violation of patent rights, nor does it allow the patentee to obtain statutory damages in the manner of the copyright law.

§ 22.1   Injunctions

Section 283 allows courts to "grant injunctions in accordance with the principles of equity to prevent the violation of any right secured by patent, or such terms as the court deems reasonable."[1] In practice courts routinely grant permanent injunctions to patentees that prevail in infringement litigation.[2] Any injunction awarded under the Patent Act

---

§ 22.1

1. 35 U.S.C.A. § 283 (2000).

2. *See* Richardson v. Suzuki Motor Co., 868 F.2d 1226, 9 USPQ2d 1913 (Fed.Cir. 1989).

must end on the same date that the patent expires.[3]

A patentee may also obtain a preliminary injunction against an accused infringer. Courts assess the traditional four factors when considering whether to grant such an injunction. The factors are typically stated as: (1) the probability of success on the merits; (2) the possibility of irreparable harm to the patentee if the injunction is not granted; (3) the balance of hardships between the parties; and (4) the public interest.[4]

Prior to the creation of the Federal Circuit, the trial courts were disinclined to award preliminary injunctions in patent cases. Concern over the reliability of PTO procedures was the usual reason given for their reluctance.[5] Since its creation, the Federal Circuit has eased this restrictive posture. Observing that patent terms are finite and patent litigation notoriously prolonged, the court has stated that when the patentee makes a clear showing of validity and infringement, the court should presume irreparable harm will result from denial of the injunction.[6] Contemporary district courts have also increasingly identified a strong public interest in the protection of patent rights.[7]

Courts are more likely to deny preliminary injunctions, and in extreme cases may even limit or refuse to grant a permanent injunction, if the accused or adjudicated infringement pertains to public health, safety or the environment.[8] For example, in *Schneider (Europe) AG v. SciMed Life Systems, Inc.*,[9] the adjudicated infringer marketed a rapid-exchange catheter used by surgeons. Although the court concluded that no evidence of record supported a finding that the infringing product was more safe or objectively superior to other catheters on the market, the court recognized that some physicians did strongly prefer the infringing product.[10] The court opted to grant a permanent injunction with a delay of one year from the entry of judgment. This year-long transition period would allow surgeons to switch from the infringing product with a minimum of disruption. The court provided that the patentee would receive a 15% royalty rate during the transition period.

§ 22.2 Damages

The Patent Act succinctly provides for the award of damages "adequate to compensate for the infringement, but in no event less than a

---

3. *See* Kearns v. Chrysler Corp., 32 F.3d 1541, 31 USPQ2d 1746 (Fed.Cir.1994), *cert. denied*, 514 U.S. 1032, 115 S.Ct. 1392, 131 L.Ed.2d 244 (1995).

4. *See* Mentor Graphics Corp. v. Quickturn Design Systems, Inc., 150 F.3d 1374, 1377, 47 USPQ2d 1683, 1685 (Fed.Cir. 1998).

5. *See* Chemical Engineering Corp. v. Marlo, Inc., 754 F.2d 331, 222 USPQ 738 (Fed.Cir.1984).

6. *See* Smith International, Inc. v. Hughes Tool Corp., 718 F.2d 1573, 219 USPQ 686 (Fed.Cir.), *cert. denied*, 464 U.S. 996, 104 S.Ct. 493, 78 L.Ed.2d 687 (1983).

7. *See, e.g.,* California Medical Prods. Inc. v. Emergency Medical Prods., Inc., 796 F.Supp. 640, 648, 24 USPQ2d 1205, 1211 (D.R.I.1992).

8. *See, e.g.,* Ethicon Endo–Surgery v. United States Surgical Corp., 855 F.Supp. 1500 (S.D.Ohio 1994).

9. 852 F.Supp. 813 (D.Minn.1994).

10. *Id.* at 850–51.

reasonable royalty for the use made of the invention by the infringer."[1] In practice, patentees seek lost profits as damages when they are able to make the required showing. Otherwise a reasonable royalty serves as the default measure of damages.

The Patent Act limits recovery to six years prior to the filing of the complaint or counterclaim for patent infringement.[2] For example, suppose that Professor Gizmo procured a patent on a method of refurbishing metal tools on April 1, 1994. Suppose further that Dr. Nefarious began using Gizmo's patented invention on March 15, 1995. Gizmo files suit for infringement on March 15, 2005. Although Nefarious has practiced the patented invention for a full decade, the period for which Gizmo may recover infringement damages commences on March 15, 1999. Courts ordinarily award prejudgment interest in order to afford the patentee full compensation for the infringement during that six-year period, however.[3]

22.2.1 Reasonable Royalties

The patent statute provides that the award of damages to a prevailing patentee shall be no less than a reasonable royalty.[4] To determine this amount, the courts indulge in the legal fiction of a hypothetical licensing negotiation.[5] The reasonable royalty is set to the rate a willing patent owner and willing licensee would have decided upon had they negotiated the license on the date the infringement began.[6]

To determine the outcome of this fictional negotiation, the courts consider many elements. The often cited opinion in *Georgia-Pacific Corp. v. United States Plywood Corp.* provides an extensive list.[7] If the patentee has actually licensed the patent in suit to others, the actual royalty rate charged is the prominent factor.[8] Other factors include the rate paid by the infringer to license a comparable patent; the effect of selling the patented invention in promoting other sales; the advantages of the patented invention; the availability of noninfringing substitutes; the infringer's expected profits; and industry licensing practices.

Even this brief description should indicate that the calculation of reasonable royalties is not an exact science. District courts necessarily engage in a good deal of approximation when determining a reasonable royalty rate, and the Federal Circuit affords them considerable discretion

§ 22.2

1. 35 U.S.C.A. § 284 (2000).

2. 35 U.S.C.A. § 286 (2000).

3. *See* General Motors Corp. v. Devex Corp., 461 U.S. 648, 103 S.Ct. 2058, 76 L.Ed.2d 211 (1983).

4. 35 U.S.C.A. § 284 (2000).

5. *See* Minco, Inc. v. Combustion Engineering, Inc., 95 F.3d 1109, 1119, 40 USPQ2d 1001, 1008–09 (Fed.Cir.1996).

6. *See* Unisplay, S.A. v. American Elec. Sign Co., 69 F.3d 512, 518, 36 USPQ2d 1540, 1545 (Fed.Cir.1995).

7. 318 F.Supp. 1116, 166 USPQ 235 (S.D.N.Y.1970), *modified and aff'd,* 446 F.2d 295, 170 USPQ 369 (2d Cir.), *cert. denied,* 404 U.S. 870, 92 S.Ct. 105, 30 L.Ed.2d 114 (1971).

8. *See* Unisplay, S.A. v. American Elec. Sign Co., 69 F.3d 512, 519, 36 USPQ2d 1540, 1545 (Fed.Cir.1995).

in so doing.[9] However, the rate that is ultimately chosen must be supported by evidence of record rather than amount to mere speculation.[10]

22.2.2 Lost Profits

Courts will award lost profits for patent infringement if two conditions are met. First, the patentee must reasonably demonstrate that, "but for" the infringement, it would have made the sales consummated by the infringer.[11] When the patentee and the infringer are the only actors in the relevant market, the courts will ordinarily infer "but for" causation.[12] Another mechanism for demonstrating causation is the well-known standard set forth in *Panduit Corp. v. Stahlin Brothers Fibre Works, Inc.*[13] Under *Panduit*, the patentee must show that (1) the patented product was in demand; (2) no acceptable noninfringing substitute was available; (3) the patentee or its licensees possessed the manufacturing and marketing capability to exploit the demand; and (4) the amount of profit the patentee would have made.

Second, the asserted harm must have been reasonably foreseeable, rather than indirect, removed or remote. This requirement follows from the traditional tort law concept of proximate cause. In *Rite-Hite Corp. v. Kelley Co.*,[14] the Federal Circuit explained that not every injury of which the patentee complains may be the type the patent laws were designed to remedy. For example, if the patentee is so shocked to learn of the infringement that he suffers a heart attack, he is not entitled to claim damages under the Patent Act. The court explained that although this sort of harm is traceable to the infringement, it is too remote to justify compensation under the patent laws.

While these two showings ordinarily entitle the patent owner to an award of lost profits, the courts have faced two recurring situations where they will demand additional proof. Sometimes unpatented goods are sold alongside the patented product or process. Suppose that the owner of a photocopier patent sells not just photocopiers, but the paper used in the photocopier as well. The lost paper sales may actually be more financially harmful to the patentee than the lost sales of the patented photocopier. Yet since the prior art has long since prevented anyone from patenting ordinary paper, the propriety of awarding damages for these so-called "derivative sales" is questionable.[15]

---

9. *See* Endress + Hauser, Inc. v. Hawk Measurement Sys. Pty. Ltd., 122 F.3d 1040, 1043, 43 USPQ2d 1849, 1852 (Fed.Cir. 1997).

10. *See* King Instruments Corp. v. Perego, 65 F.3d 941, 952, 36 USPQ2d 1129, 1137 (Fed.Cir.1995), *reh'g denied*, 72 F.3d 855 (Fed.Cir.1995).

11. *See* Kearns v. Chrysler Corp., 32 F.3d 1541, 1551, 31 USPQ2d 1746, 1754 (Fed.Cir.1994), *cert. denied*, 514 U.S. 1032, 115 S.Ct. 1393, 131 L.Ed.2d 244 (1995).

12. *See* Lam, Inc. v. Johns–Manville Corp., 718 F.2d 1056, 1068, 219 USPQ 670, 678 (Fed.Cir.1983).

13. 575 F.2d 1152, 197 USPQ 726 (6th Cir.1978).

14. 56 F.3d 1538, 1545, 35 USPQ2d 1065, 1069 (Fed.Cir.1995) (*en banc*).

15. *See* Carborundum Co. v. Molten Metal Equip. Innovations, Inc., 72 F.3d 872, 882 n. 8, 37 USPQ2d 1169, 1175 n. 8 (Fed. Cir.1995).

A related problem occurs when the infringing technology forms but one component of a larger commercial product or process. For example, suppose that an automobile manufacturer holds a patent on a rear view mirror. If that manufacturer obtains an infringement judgment against a competitor, the court will be hard-pressed to assess damages based on the purchase price of the entire automobile. Sales made simultaneously with the patented invention are termed "convoyed sales."[16]

The courts crafted the "entire market value rule" to address such circumstances. The entire market value rule allows patentees to claim damages for unpatented products sold alongside the patented invention if three relatively strict standards are met. First, the patented feature must form the basis for customer demand for the entire product or products sold.[17] Second, the patentee must reasonably anticipate the sale of the unpatented parts along with the patented component.[18] Finally, the Federal Circuit has imposed a requirement of functional relatedness. Unless the unpatented component operates together with the patented invention in the manner of a single machine, the patentee cannot obtain a damages award based upon that unpatented component.[19]

Note that the 1952 Patent Act does not authorize the equitable accounting remedy for utility patents.[20] The award of damages for infringement of utility patents is compensatory in nature. Utility patentees may obtain their own lost profits, not the profits the infringer made. However, in what can only be described as an unusual exception to this rule, the Patent Act does allow proprietors of design patents to opt for an "additional remedy" consisting of the infringer's profits.[21]

22.2.3   Provisional Rights

The Domestic Publication of Foreign Filed Patent Applications Act of 1999 created so-called "provisional rights." Provisional rights apply only to patent applications that were published during their pendency at the PTO. They are equivalent to a reasonable royalty and may be obtained from anyone who makes, uses, sells, offers to sell, or imports into the United States the invention as claimed in a published patent application. Although provisional rights extend from the time the application was published until the date the PTO granted the patent, they may be invoked only when the patent issues.

---

16. *See* Carborundum Co. v. Molten Metal Equip. Innovations, Inc., 72 F.3d 872, 882 n. 8, 37 USPQ2d 1169, 1175 n. 8 (Fed. Cir.1995).

17. *See* TWM Mfg. Co. v. Dura Corp., 789 F.2d 895, 901, 229 USPQ 525, 528 (Fed.Cir.), *cert. denied*, 479 U.S. 852, 107 S.Ct. 183, 93 L.Ed.2d 117 (1986).

18. *See* King Instrument Corp. v. Otari Corp., 767 F.2d 853, 226 USPQ 402 (Fed. Cir.1985), *cert. denied*, 475 U.S. 1016, 106 S.Ct. 1197, 89 L.Ed.2d 312 (1986).

19. Rite-Hite Corp.v Kelley Co., 56 F.3d 1538, 35 USPQ2d 1065 (Fed.Cir.), *cert. denied*, 516 U.S. 867, 116 S.Ct. 184, 133 L.Ed.2d 122 (1995).

20. *See* Kori Corp. v. Wilco Marsh Buggies and Draglines, Inc., 761 F.2d 649, 654, 225 USPQ 985, 988 (Fed.Cir.), *cert. denied*, 474 U.S. 902, 106 S.Ct. 230, 88 L.Ed.2d 229 (1985).

21. 35 U.S.C.A. § 289 (2000).

As codified in § 154(d), provisional rights are subject to two other important qualifications. First, the claims of the published application must be substantially identical to the claims of the issued patent for provisional rights to arise. Second, the infringer must have had actual notice of the published application in order to face liability under the provisional rights scheme.[22]

22.2.4 Enhanced Damages

Section 284 provides that the court "may increase the damages up to three times the amount found or assessed."[23] An award of enhanced damages, as well as the amount by which the damages will be increased, is committed to the discretion of the trial court.[24] Although the statute does not specify the circumstances in which enhanced damages are appropriate, the courts most commonly award them when the infringer acted in blatant disregard of the patentee's rights. This circumstance is termed "willful infringement."[25]

The Federal Circuit will not ordinarily enhance damages due to willful infringement if the adjudicated infringer did not know of the patent until charged with infringement in court, or if the infringer acted with the reasonable belief that the patent was not infringed or that it was invalid. Federal Circuit decisions emphasize the duty of someone with actual notice of a competitor's patent to exercise due care in determining if his acts will infringe that patent. This duty may be fulfilled by obtaining and observing competent legal advice before commencing, or continuing, activity that may infringe another's patent. The best practice appears to be the commissioning of an infringement and validity opinion from a member of the patent bar who is fully conversant with the patent law; has familiarized herself with the patent, its prosecution history, and the pertinent prior art; and is knowledgeable of the products or processes that might be accused of infringement.

In *Read Corp. v. Portec, Inc,*[26] the Federal Circuit explained that the most important consideration in willful infringement cases is the egregiousness of the defendant's conduct based on all the facts and circumstances. In judging whether to award enhanced damages or not, the courts consider whether the infringer investigated the scope of the patent and formed a good faith belief that it was invalid or not infringed. Prompt, competent advice from a qualified patent attorney significantly decreases the likelihood an infringement will be declared willful.[27] Other pertinent factors include whether the infringer deliberately copied from another, the infringer's behavior as a party to the litigation, the size and financial condition of the defendant, the closeness of the case and the

22. 35 U.S.C.A. § 154(d) (2000).

23. 35 U.S.C.A. § 284 (2000).

24. *See* Read Corp. v. Portec, Inc., 970 F.2d 816, 23 USPQ2d 1426 (Fed.Cir.1992).

25. *See* Beatrice Foods Co. v. New England Printing & Lithographing Co., 923 F.2d 1576, 17 USPQ2d 1553 (Fed.Cir.1991).

26. 970 F.2d 816, 23 USPQ2d 1426 (Fed.Cir.1992).

27. *See* Underwater Devices Inc. v. Morrison–Knudsen Co., 717 F.2d 1380, 219 USPQ 569 (Fed.Cir.1983).

duration of the defendant's misconduct. Where willful infringement is found, the Federal Circuit explained, damages need not always be tripled. The trial court can increase them by a lesser amount, or not at all, depending upon the totality of the circumstances.

The wisdom of awarding enhanced damages in cases of patent infringement has been roundly debated. Critics of the policy believe that the possibility of trebled damages discourages individuals from reviewing issued patents. Out of fear that their inquisitiveness will result in multiple damages, innovators may simply avoid looking at patents until they are sued for infringement. To the extent this observation is correct, the law of willful infringement discourages the dissemination of technical knowledge, thereby thwarting one of the principal goals of the patent system. With willful infringement principles encouraging industry to seek out opinion letters of patent counsel, these developments have been likened to a "full employment act" for the patent bar. Fear of increased liability for willful infringement may also discourage firms from performing the public service of challenging patents of dubious validity. Perhaps it is time for the patent system to shift to a "no-fault" regime of strictly compensatory damages, without regard to the state of mind of the adjudicated infringer.

22.2.5 Attorney Fees

Section 285 provides that the "court in exceptional cases may award reasonable attorney fees to the prevailing party."[28] As this language suggests, attorney fees are not routinely awarded to the victor of a patent infringement case. The patentee may obtain an award of fees in cases of willful infringement, following the identical standard to that of enhanced damages.[29] Courts have also awarded attorney fees in cases where the patentee committed inequitable conduct or either party engaged in bad faith litigation.[30]

22.2.6 Marking

The Patent Act encourages patentees who make or sell embodiments of their patented invention to give notice to the public of their patent rights. Section 287(a) provides that patentees and their licensees should fix the word "patent" or the abbreviation "pat.", along with the number of the patent, on patented articles.[31] If the nature of the article does not allow this notice to be placed directly upon it, a label may be placed on the article or its packaging.

There is no absolute duty to mark. If the patentee or its licensees fail to mark in the specified manner, however, then damages are available only for acts occurring after the infringer receives actual notice of the infringement. The Federal Circuit has strictly construed the require-

---

28. 35 U.S.C.A. § 285 (2000).

29. *See* Avia Group Int'l, Inc. v. L.A. Gear California, Inc., 853 F.2d 1557, 1567, 7 USPQ2d 1548, 1556 (Fed.Cir.1988).

30. Mahurkar v. C.R. Bard, Inc., 79 F.3d 1572, 1580, 38 USPQ2d 1288, 1292 (Fed.Cir.1996).

31. 35 U.S.C.A. § 287(c) (2000).

ment of actual notice. Even if the infringer is already fully aware of the patent, the patentee must affirmatively communicate a specific charge of infringement to trigger entitlement to damages.[32] The marking statute does provide that the filing of an infringement suit suffices to provide actual notice.[33]

Patentees who do not make or sell their invention have no duty to mark.[34] The marking requirement also does not apply to process claims, which by their very nature concern intangible behavior.[35] Other patentees, concerned with the expense and inconvenience of marking or desirous of surprising competitors, make the affirmative choice not to mark.

Many readers have doubtlessly observed the legend "patent pending" on a variety of products and packaging. The phrase may mean that the manufacturer has filed a patent application pertaining to that product. The mere filing of a patent application ordinarily lacks legal significance for anyone except the applicant and the PTO, however. Until the patent issues, the applicant obtains no legally enforceable rights, and there is some chance that the PTO will refuse to issue a patent at all. Use of "patent pending" is essentially a form of "self help" through which applicants warn others that a patent may be in the works. The phrase "patent pending" bears no relationship to the patent marking statute and, absent special circumstances, generally has no legal ramifications at all.

---

32. *See* Amsted Industries Inc. v. Buckeye Steel Castings Co., 24 F.3d 178, 30 USPQ2d 1462 (Fed.Cir.1994).

33. 35 U.S.C.A. § 287(a) (2000).

34. *See* Wine Railway Appliance Co. v. Enterprise Railway Equip. Co., 297 U.S. 387, 56 S.Ct. 528, 80 L.Ed. 736 (1936).

35. *See* American Medical Sys., Inc. v. Medical Eng'g Corp., 6 F.3d 1523, 1538, 28 USPQ2d 1321, 1332 (Fed.Cir.1993), *cert. denied*, 511 U.S. 1070, 114 S.Ct. 1647, 128 L.Ed.2d 366 (1994).

Chapter 23

PATENT LAW IN INTERNATIONAL PERSPECTIVE

Table of Sections

Globalization trends have resulted in growing international trade, increasing flows of information and more distributed manufacturing capabilities. One consequence is that more than ever before, patent protection in a single country is insufficient for competitive enterprise. Patent rights must instead be secured in multiple jurisdictions.

A principal difficulty of multinational patent acquisition is that no true global patent system exists. Inventors who seek intellectual property protection must file individual applications in each country or region where patent rights are sought. Fortunately, the patent regimes of the United States and its trading partners are linked through a handful of international agreements that, together, comprise the international patent system. These international agreements do not create a true global patent system, in that they do not provide for a single patent application and grant procedure that can lead to rights effective worldwide. However, they do provide inventors with mechanisms for expediting the acquisition of patent rights in many countries. This text discusses the most significant of these international agreements in the order that they were enacted.

§ 23.1   The Paris Convention

The foundational patent harmonization treaty, the Paris Convention, was formed in 1884.[1] As of April 15, 2002, 163 nations had signed the Paris Convention. The World Intellectual Property Organization (WIPO), a specialized agency located in Geneva, Switzerland, administers this international agreement (and a number of subsequent instruments addressing intellectual property). The Paris Convention commits its signatories to the principle of national treatment, the principle of patent independence, and a system of international priority. Through the national treatment principle, Paris Convention signatories agree to treat foreign inventors no worse than domestic inventors in their patent laws, so long as these foreign inventors are nationals of a Paris Convention signatory state.[2]

The Paris Convention also calls for the independence of different national patents.[3] Prior to the Paris Convention, many national laws applied a principle of patent dependence against foreign inventors. As a result, domestic patents would expire at the same time any foreign patent covering the same invention lapsed, regardless of the term the patentee was ordinarily due. These provisions sometimes worked a hardship against inventors who had obtained patent protection in many countries, only to discover that marketing the invention was feasible only in some subset of them. Such an inventor would prefer to let some patent rights lapse rather than incur expensive maintenance fees. In a world where patent rights depended on one another, however, allowing one patent to lapse would amount to a global forfeiture of patent rights.

The independence principle established by the Paris Convention put an end to this situation. One significant consequence of the independence of national patents is that they must be enforced individually. Even different national patent instruments with identically drafted descriptions, drawings and claims do not stand or fall together. A competitor who succeeds in invalidating one national patent may face the prospect of repeating the effort within another set of national borders. Similarly, the successful enforcement of a patent in one forum may simply signal the start of patent litigation elsewhere.

The international priority system allows an inventor to file a patent application in one Paris Convention signatory state, which is usually the inventor's home country.[4] If the inventor subsequently files patent applications in any other Paris Convention signatory state within the next 12 months, overseas patent-granting authorities will treat the application as if it were filed on the first filing date. Critically, information that enters the public domain between the priority date and subsequent filing dates does not prejudice the later applications. Paris

---

§ 23.1

1. Convention of Paris for the Protection of Industrial Property, 13 U.S.T. 25 (1962).

2. Paris Convention, Art. 2.

3. Paris Convention, Art. 4bis.

4. For further discussion of the Paris Convention priority system, see § 19.8.

Convention priority allows inventors to preserve their original filing dates as they make arrangements to file patent applications overseas.[5]

Suppose, for example, that an inventor files a patent application at the USPTO on October 1, 2001. The inventor then files a patent application claiming the same invention in the Japanese Patent Office on September 1, 2002. As part of his Japanese application, the inventor informs the Japanese Patent Office of the earlier U.S. application. Because Japan has acceded to the Paris Convention, the Japanese Patent Office will treat that inventor's application as if it had been filed on October 1, 2001. As a result, information that entered the public domain after the U.S. filing date would not prejudice the inventor's Japanese application. A journal article published on January 1, 2002, for example, would not limit the opportunity of the inventor to obtain a Japanese patent.

The Paris Convention was an advanced treaty at the time of its formation in the late nineteenth century. However, many observers believed that its shortcomings became more pronounced with the passage of time. Other than the minimal standard of national treatment, the Paris Convention does not provide substantive patent law standards for its signatories to adopt within their domestic patent systems.[6] The Paris Convention further lacks an effective enforcement mechanism. Although one nation could commence an action against another for Paris Convention violations in the International Court of Justice, that tribunal's lack of enforcement powers made this possibility more theoretical than practical. In the long history of the Paris Convention, no such suit has ever been brought.[7]

Finally, the Paris Convention requires unanimous consent to amend. As the number of signatory states grew, such consensus became difficult to obtain. The opportunity to advance the international patent system shifted to other vehicles, including the Patent Cooperation Treaty, NAFTA and the TRIPS Agreement.

§ 23.2   The Patent Cooperation Treaty

The Patent Cooperation Treaty, or PCT, was formed in Washington, DC in 1970.[1] Recognizing the needless repetition of duplicative patent examinations around the world, representatives of different patent offices agreed to a procedural framework to facilitate the often burdensome task of multinational patent acquisition. The PCT is open to any nation that has acceded to the Paris Convention, and in fact over 100

5. *See* G.H.C. Bodenhausen, GUIDE TO THE PARIS CONVENTION FOR THE PROTECTION OF INDUSTRIAL PROPERTY (United International Bureau for the Protection of Intellectual Property, Geneva, Switzerland 1968).

6. Frederick Abbott et al., THE INTERNATIONAL INTELLECTUAL PROPERTY SYSTEM: COM-

MENTARY AND MATERIALS (Kluwer Law International, The Hague 1999), 646.

7. *Id.* at 661–62.

§ 23.2

1. Patent Cooperation Treaty, June 19, 1970, 28 U.S.T. 7645, T.I.A.S. No. 8733.

nations have currently signed the PCT. It provides for the filing of one patent application that can lead to issued patents in many countries.[2]

An inventor may use the PCT if he is a national or domicile of a PCT contracting state. Most often, an inventor commences the PCT process by filing a so-called "international application" at his local patent office. The international application designates all PCT member states in which the inventor wishes to obtain patent protection. An international application has the effect of a national application in all of the countries that the applicant designates.

This application will then be sent to one of several entities designated as an International Searching Authority. In addition to the USPTO, the national patent offices of Australia, Austria, China, Japan, the Republic of Korea, the Russian Federation, Spain, and Sweden, as well as the European Patent Office, have been designated as International Searching Authorities. These entities research existing patent documents and other technical literature in order to determine public domain knowledge pertinent to the invention claimed in the patent application. The applicant then receives an international search report, which lists citations of prior art relevant to the claims of the international patent application and gives an indication of the possible relevance of the citations to the questions of novelty and nonobviousness.

If the international search report does not reveal any public domain knowledge that would defeat the patentability of the claimed invention, the applicant may wish to enter the second part of the PCT process, the so-called "national stage." Here the applicant submits the PCT application to various national offices. At this time, patent examiners in each country examine the application based upon their own national laws, either allowing or rejecting the patent application.

The PCT also allows for an optional intermediate step between the time an applicant receives an international search report and enters the national stage. The applicant must also request an international preliminary examination of his application. This preliminary examination is made, on the basis of the international search report, according to internationally accepted criteria of patentability, including novelty and nonobviousness. It is carried out by an International Preliminary Examining Authority, which consists of one of the International Searching Authorities mentioned above, with the exception of the national patent office of Spain. An international preliminary examination provides inventors with an even stronger basis on which to evaluate their chances of obtaining patents in the national stage. However, the ultimate decision on the granting of a patent remains the task of individual national or regional patent offices; the international preliminary examination report is authoritative but not binding upon those agencies.

The PCT has attracted a large number of applicants, with a disproportionate share of users based in the United States. Still, the PCT has

---

2. *Id.* at 1430–41.

been subject to some criticism. Upon entering the national stage, many patent offices do not appear to respect fully the work product of the International Search Authority. In fact, most patent offices normally repeat the search and examination at the national phase in the same manner as for an ordinary national application. Under the view of some observers, these redundant efforts appear to undermine much of the logic behind PCT.[3]

§ 23.3   Regional Agreements

A number of regional agreements provide for some sort of centralized examination procedure, through which an inventor obtains patents effective in member nations designated by the applicant. Although the United States is not a party to any of these treaties, domestic inventors frequently take advantage of these regional examination techniques when seeking patents abroad.

The European Patent Convention (EPC) is the most prominent example of a regional patent harmonization agreement.[1] Among other measures, the EPC creates a European Patent Office based principally in Munich, Germany and the Hague, the Netherlands. An inventor may file a single patent application at the European Patent Office, which, if accepted, matures into a number of individual national patents in the European states the applicant has designated. Significantly, the EPC does not create a unitary European patent. A European Patent Office application amounts to a group of national patent applications that are processed together but then are given individual legal effect within the appropriate jurisdictions. Once issued by the European Patent Office, these patents enjoy independent legal lives, and must be enforced and maintained separately. A draft treaty known as the Community Patent Convention would take this system one step further, creating a true unified European patent, but its ratification has been delayed for many years.[2]

Other regional agreements include:

• the African Intellectual Property Organization (more properly known as the Organization Africaine de la Propriete Intellectuelle or OAPI), for portions of French-speaking Africa.

• the African Regional Intellectual Property Organization (ARIPO), for portions of English-speaking Africa.

• the Eurasian Patent Convention, joined by certain former members of the Soviet Union.

3. *See* Markus Nolff, *TRIPS, PCT and Global Patent Procurement*, 83 JOURNAL OF THE PATENT AND TRADEMARK OFFICE SOCIETY 479 (2001).

§ 23.3

1. *See* Gerald Paterson, THE EUROPEAN PATENT SYSTEM: THE LAW AND PRACTICE OF THE EUROPEAN PATENT CONVENTION (Sweet & Maxwell, London 2000).

2. Christian Hilti, *The Future European Community Patent System and Its Effects on Non–EEC–Member–States*, 18 AIPLA Q.J. 289, 293 (1990).

§ 23.4 NAFTA

The North American Free Trade Agreement (NAFTA), currently joined by the United States, Canada and Mexico, includes a number of intellectual property provisions.[1] More rigorous than the Paris Convention or the PCT, NAFTA requires its signatories to commit to substantive patent law measures, including term of protection, scope of rights accorded to patentees, and standards of patentability such as novelty and nonobviousness. At the time of its effective date of January 1, 1994, NAFTA was a premier intellectual property treaty. However, in terms of the extent of its obligations and the scope of signatories, NAFTA was quickly eclipsed by the World Trade Organization's TRIPS Agreement. Rather than focus on the particulars of NAFTA, this report next discusses the TRIPS Agreement.

§ 23.5 The TRIPS Agreement

One component of the international agreement forming the World Trade Organization (WTO) is the so-called TRIPS Agreement, or Agreement on Trade–Related Aspects of Intellectual Property Rights.[1] The TRIPS Agreement is the most detailed and comprehensive multilateral agreement on intellectual property yet achieved. That every WTO member state has accepted the TRIPS Agreement standards makes this accomplishment even more impressive. As the most significant advances of the TRIPS Agreement occurred with respect to the patent law, a review of that agreement is especially apt here.

23.5.1 Minimum Standards of Protection

Under Part III of the TRIPS Agreement, all WTO member countries agreed to enact patent statutes that include certain substantive provisions. In particular, each signatory agreed to allow patents to issue on inventions "in all fields of technology, provided that they are new, involve an inventive step and are capable of industrial application."[2] The TRIPS Agreement includes some exceptions to this broad principle, however. Certain methods of medical treatment, plants and animals other than microorganisms, and inventions that violate the *ordre public* or morality may be excluded from patentability at the option of the member state.[3]

WTO members also agreed that patentees shall have the right to exclude others from making, using, offering for sale, selling, or importing

§ 23.4

1. North American Free Trade Agreement, Dec. 17, 1992, 32 I.L.M. 289; *see also* North American Free Trade Agreement Implementation Act, P. L. 103–182, 107 Stat. 2057 (1993).

§ 23.5

1. *See* Agreement on Trade–Related Aspects of Intellectual Property Rights, Apr.

15, 1994, Annex 1C, 33 I.L.M. 1197 (1994) [hereinafter "TRIPS Agreement"].

2. TRIPS Agreement, Article 27(1).

3. TRIPS Agreement, Article 27(2).

the patented invention.[4] The TRIPS Agreement again creates an exception to this broad principle, however, allowing member states to limit patent rights under certain circumstances. Article 30 of the TRIPS Agreement states:

> Members may provide limited exceptions to the exclusive rights conferred by a patent, provided that such exceptions do not unreasonably conflict with a normal exploitation of the patent and do not unreasonably prejudice the legitimate interests of the patent owner, taking account of the legitimate interests of third parties.

WTO members further agreed that the term of patent protection available shall not end before the expiration of a period of 20 years counted from the filing date.[5] In addition, the TRIPS Agreement requires that member states must provide patent owners with the opportunity for judicial review of any decision to revoke or forfeit a patent.[6]

The TRIPS Agreement also speaks at some length towards compulsory licenses. A compulsory license allows a competitor of the patent owner to use the patented invention without the patent owner's permission.[7] Although compulsory licenses have played only a minor role in the U.S. patent system,[8] many foreign patent statutes include such provisions.[9] These statutes typically require an interested party formally to request the compulsory license from the foreign government. Competent authorities then decide whether to grant the license as well as the terms of any granted license. Grounds for granting a compulsory license include the abusive exercise of patent rights, lack of domestic manufacture of the patented product, commercialization of the patented good that does not satisfy the needs of the local market and national emergencies. While some accounts suggest that formal compulsory licensing proceedings are commenced only infrequently, the mere existence of a compulsory licensing statute may do much to encourage bargaining between a foreign patentee and domestic industry, on terms favorable to local manufacturers.[10]

The TRIPS Agreement places some limits upon the ability of WTO member states to award compulsory licenses for the use of another's patented invention. Among the most detailed provisions of the TRIPS Agreement, Article 31 imposes in part the following restrictions upon the issuance of compulsory licenses:

4. TRIPS Agreement, Article 28.

5. TRIPS Agreement, Article 33.

6. TRIPS Agreement, Article 32.

7. Robert Sherwood, *Intellectual Property and Investment Stimulation: The Ratings of Systems in Eighteen Developing Countries*, 37 IDEA (1997), 261.

8. Dawson Chemical Co. v. Rohm and Haas Co., 448 U.S. 176 n. 21, 100 S.Ct. 2601, 65 L.Ed.2d 696 (1980).

9. Gianna Julian–Arnold, *International Compulsory Licensing: The Rationales and the Reality*, 33 IDEA (1993), 349.

10. Boseley, Sarah, *Opinion: Pharmaceuticals Move Their Battleground to Brazil to Stem the Tide of Cheaper Drugs,* IRISH TIMES (April 20, 2001), at 14.

- Each application for a compulsory license must be considered on its individual merits.

- The proposed user must have made efforts to obtain authorization from the patent owner on reasonable commercial terms and conditions and must demonstrate that such efforts have not been successful within a reasonable period of time. However, this requirement may be waived in the case of a national emergency or other circumstances of extreme urgency.

- Any such use shall be authorized predominantly for the supply of the domestic market of the member authorizing such use.

- The compulsory license must be revocable if and when its motivating circumstances cease to exist and are unlikely to recur.

- The patent owner must be paid adequate remuneration in the circumstances of each case, taking into account the economic value of the authorization.

- The legal validity of any decision relating to the authorization of such use shall be subject to judicial or other independent review.

WTO members agreed that patentees should be subject to certain conditions. In particular, the TRIPS Agreement requires that WTO member states "shall require that an applicant for a patent shall disclose the invention in a manner sufficiently clear and complete for the invention to be carried out by a person skilled in the art."[11]

The TRIPS Agreement also requires its signatories to comply with certain provisions of the Paris Convention, including its foreign priority system.[12] This requirement has led to a dramatic increase in the number of Paris Convention signatories.[13] Apparently realizing that they were already obliged to respect the Paris Convention, many WTO member states that were not previously Paris Convention signatories acceded to that treaty.

23.5.2 Dispute Settlement

As with other obligations imposed by the WTO, TRIPS Agreement obligations are subject to enforcement through the WTO Dispute Settlement Body (DSB).[14] If one WTO member state believes that another member state is in violation of the TRIPS Agreement, the member states may enter into consultation through the DSB. If the member states

11. TRIPS Agreement, Article 29.

12. TRIPS Agreement, Article 2.

13. KEITH E. MASKUS, INTELLECTUAL PROPERTY RIGHTS IN THE GLOBAL ECONOMY (Washington, D.C., Institute for International Economics, 2000).

14. Understanding on Rules and Procedures Governing the Settlement of Disputes, Apr. 15, 1994, WTO Agreement, Annex 2, Legal Instruments—Results of the Uruguay Round vol. 31, 33 I.L.M. 1226 (1994).

cannot resolve their dispute, the DSB will convene a panel to hear and resolve the dispute. Panel decisions are subject to review by the DSB Appellate Body. The WTO Agreement calls for compensatory trade measures in circumstances where the DSB finds a WTO member state to be in violation of the TRIPS Agreement, yet that member state does not amend its laws.[15]

23.5.3 Effective Dates

The various patent portions of the TRIPS Agreement feature a variety of effective dates. These dates depend upon whether the WTO member state designates itself a developed, developing or least developed country. For WTO members other than developing and least developed countries, the compliance date for all requirements of the TRIPS Agreement was set to January 1, 1996.[16]

For signatory states designated as developing countries, the TRIPS Agreement set the general compliance date as January 1, 2000. However, there is one exception to this general date. If on January 1, 2000, a developing country did not extend patent protection to all areas of technology within the meaning of Article 27, that developing country may delay implementation of these provisions for an additional five years. Prior to the TRIPS Agreement, for example, many developing countries did not allow patents to issue on pharmaceuticals. The practical effect of this additional transition period was that developing countries need not allow patents on pharmaceuticals until January 1, 2005.[17]

The TRIPS Agreement also allows a signatory state designated as a least-developed country to delay implementing the TRIPS Agreement until January 1, 2010. A showing of hardship may qualify least-developed countries for further delays and other concessions.[18]

The TRIPS Agreement does not oblige its signatories to protect subject matter that fell into the public domain prior to the time its obligations became effective.[19] For example, suppose that a particular developed country traditionally did not allow patents to issue on pharmaceuticals. If that developed country joins the WTO, it must amend its patent law to authorize pharmaceutical patents. The TRIPS Agreement requires only that patents be allowed on new products as of January 1, 1996, however, and does not mandate that patents be granted retroactively. As a result, patent protection need not be afforded to pharmaceuticals that were known to the public prior to January 1, 1996, even if those pharmaceuticals were patented elsewhere.

The TRIPS Agreement includes two other transitional measures known as pipeline protection and exclusive marketing rights. Although the TRIPS Agreement allows developing countries to delay implementing

---

15. Mark Clough, *The WTO Dispute Settlement System—A Practitioner's Perspective,* 24 FORDHAM INT'L L. J. (2000), 252.

16. TRIPS Agreement, Article 65.

17. *Id.*

18. TRIPS Agreement, Article 66.

19. TRIPS Agreement, Article 70.

their patent law obligations, it requires that they immediately establish so-called pipeline protection for pharmaceuticals. Some sources refer to pipeline protection as the "mailbox rule."[20] Under this requirement, countries that do not allow pharmaceutical patents to issue must nonetheless accept patent applications. These patent applications will essentially be held at the national patent office until it comes time for the patent application to be considered.

Pipeline protection is valuable because it allows inventors to establish a date of priority of invention. Although many years might pass between the application's filing date and the date on which it would be examined, the inventiveness of the claimed invention must be judged as of its filing date. Pipeline protection allows inventors to obtain patents even though many years have passed between the date of filing and the date of compliance with the TRIPS agreement.

The TRIPS Agreement also mandates that WTO member states award an Exclusive Marketing Right ("EMR") to inventors in specified circumstances. The holder of an EMR concerning a particular product is designated as the only entity authorized to distribute that product within the member state. The award of EMRs provides innovators with transitional, patent-like market exclusivity in member states that do not yet offer patent protection for pharmaceuticals.

In order for an enterprise to obtain an EMR in one WTO member state, that enterprise must obtain both a patent and marketing approval on that pharmaceutical in another WTO member state. That enterprise must also take two additional steps within the jurisdiction in which an EMR is sought. First, the enterprise must obtain marketing approval for the pharmaceutical. Second, that enterprise must file a patent application claiming that pharmaceutical. Upon completing these two steps, the enterprise may obtain an EMR with a maximum duration of five years. The EMR will expire prior to the expiration of five years if either the marketed product is patented, or the local patent office rejects the enterprise's patent application.

23.5.4 Debate on the TRIPS Agreement

The patent portions of the TRIPS Agreement have generated considerable controversy. Some commentators predict that the TRIPS Agreement will lead to large transfers of wealth from poor countries to the developed world, and in particular to the United States. Others believe that deleterious public health consequences will result from the TRIPS Agreement requirement that patents issue on pharmaceuticals. Still others have contended that the introduction of patents into the developing world restricts sustainable development and perpetuates their dependence upon developed nations.[21]

20. John E. Guist, *Noncompliance with TRIPS by Developed and Developing Countries: Is TRIPS Working?*, 8 INDIANA INTERNA-TIONAL AND COMPARATIVE LAW REVIEW 69 (1997).

21. *See* A. Samuel Oddi, *TRIPS—Natural Rights and a "Polite Form of Economic*

Proponents of the TRIPS Agreement instead believe that the introduction of full-fledged patent systems around the globe will provide needed incentives for investment and innovation.[22] Such efforts could promote solutions to problems that are particular to the developing world, including the provision of nutritional needs and cures for diseases not common in the developed world. Supporters also observe that the TRIPS Agreement was one component of a multi-faceted WTO agreement, and believe that the developing world obtained trade benefits in exchange for assuming obligations to protect intellectual property.

Discussion regarding the TRIPS Agreement and pharmaceutical patents most recently climaxed in a World Trade Organization ministerial conference held in Doha, Qatar. The result was a "Declaration on the TRIPS Agreement and Public Health" issued on November 15, 2001. That declaration called for both the liberalization of the compulsory license provisions of the TRIPS Agreement and significant delay in TRIPS Agreement implementation deadlines for least-developed countries. At the time this book goes to press, the exchange of views about implementation of the Doha Declaration, as well as further reforms to the TRIPS Agreement, continues at a brisk pace.

Imperialism," 29 Vanderbilt Journal of Transnational Law 415 (1996).

22. *See* Evelyn Su, *The Winners and the Losers: The Agreement on Trade—Related* *Aspects of Intellectual Property Rights and Its Effects on Developing Countries,* 23 Houston Journal of International Law 169 (2000).

Chapter 24

TRADE SECRET LAW

Table of Sections

Trade secret law protects secret, valuable business information from misappropriation by others. Subject matter ranging from marketing data to manufacturing know-how may be protected under the trade secret laws. Trade secret status is not limited to a fixed number of years, but endures so long as the information is valuable and maintained as a secret.[1] A trade secret is misappropriated when it has been obtained through the abuse of a confidential relationship or improper means of acquisition.[2] Unlike the Patent Act, trade secret law does not provide a cause of action against an individual who independently developed or reverse engineered the subject matter of the trade secret.[3]

Trade secrecy serves as the chief alternative to the patent system.[4] An inventor must either maintain a technology as a trade secret, seek

---

1. *See* United States v. Dubilier Condenser Corp., 289 U.S. 178, 186, 53 S.Ct. 554, 77 L.Ed. 1114 (1933).

2. RESTATEMENT THIRD, UNFAIR COMPETITION § 43 (1995).

3. RESTATEMENT THIRD, UNFAIR COMPETITION § 39 cmt. c (1995).

4. *See* David D. Friedman, et al., *Some Economics of Trade Secret Law*, 5 J. ECON. PERSPS. 61, 64 (1991).

patent protection from the PTO, or allow the technology to enter the public domain.[5] The regime of trade secrets is broader than this, however, for trade secret law may also be used to protect subject matter that is unpatentable. For example, although a list of valued customers does not constitute patent eligible subject matter, it is amenable to protection as a trade secret.[6]

Judicial opinions evince two distinct conceptions of the trade secret law.[7] Some courts focus on trade secrecy as an intellectual property discipline. Under this view, trade secret law creates a proprietary interest just like a copyright, patent or mark. In deciding whether to grant relief for misappropriation of trade secrets, these courts stress the value and secrecy of the subject matter for which trade secret status is claimed. Other courts have viewed trade secret law as less concerned with creating property than in ensuring proper conduct. In resolving trade secret cases, these courts stress whether the accused misappropriator acquired the information at issue in a fair and ethical manner.

As Judge Posner noted in the leading opinion of *Rockwell Graphic Systems, Inc. v. DEV Industries, Inc.*,[8] these conceptions are entirely complementary. Trade secret law encourages industry actors to develop valuable informational resources by protecting them from improper acquisition by others. In addition, potential liability for trade secret misappropriation discourages individuals from engaging in activities that do not create wealth, but merely redistribute wealth from one individual to another.

§ 24.1 Sources of Law

The modern U.S. law of trade secrets arises from the common law tradition. The English equity courts of the early Nineteenth Century considered the misappropriation of such secret subject matter as the composition of medical compounds and dyes. Many of these cases involved breaches of confidence between partners, family members or a master and apprentice.[1] The U.S. courts turned to this early precedent while considering the increasingly complex commercial relationships of an industrial society.[2] Trade secret law continues as an adaptive discipline that has responded to changing technology, increasing employee mobility and heightened entrepreneurial activity.

The American Law Institute's 1939 Restatement of Torts included two sections that defined the subject matter of trade secrets and the misappropriation cause of action. Although this treatment was succinct,

5. *See* Metallizing Eng'g Co. v. Kenyon Bearing & Auto Parts, 153 F.2d 516, 68 USPQ 54 (2d Cir.), *cert. denied*, 328 U.S. 840, 66 S.Ct. 1016, 90 L.Ed. 1615 (1946).

6. *See* Courtesy Temporary Serv., Inc. v. Camacho, 222 Cal.App.3d 1278, 1287–88, 272 Cal.Rptr. 352 (1990).

7. RESTATEMENT THIRD, UNFAIR COMPETITION § 39 cmt. a (1995).

8. 925 F.2d 174, 17 USPQ2d 1780 (Fed. Cir.1991).

§ 24.1

1. I MELVIN F. JAGER, TRADE SECRET LAW § 2.01 (1998).

2. *Id.* at § 2.02.

these definitions proved influential in the courts. However, trade secrets were not addressed in the 1978 Second Restatement of Torts.[3] The American Law Institute concluded that trade secret law had grown "no more dependent on Tort law than it is on many other general fields of law and upon broad statutory developments," and opted not to house trade secrets there.

The Uniform Trade Secrets Act filled this breach in 1979.[4] Published by the National Conference of Commissioners on Uniform State Law, the Uniform Act has been enacted in the majority of states. The Uniform Act generally follows the Restatement of Torts, but also relies upon subsequent case law to provide more useful and definitive legal standards.

The American Law Institute was not content to rest, however. A distinct Restatement (Third) of Unfair Competition was promulgated in 1993 with a thorough treatment of trade secrets in sections 39–45. The remainder of the work is devoted to trademarks, misappropriation, deceptive marking, the right of publicity and related doctrines. Like the Restatement of Torts and the Uniform Act, the Restatement of Unfair Competition remains faithful to the case law and does not presume to be an instrument of radical legal reform.

Trade secrets have traditionally been the subject of state law. However, the federal government firmly engaged the law of trade secrets in the Economic Espionage Act of 1996.[5] That statute renders the misappropriation of trade secrets a federal crime. Housed in Title 18 of the United States Code, the Economic Espionage Act provides for substantial fines and imprisonment penalties, as well as criminal forfeiture of property and court orders preserving confidentiality of trade secrets. Stiffer penalties are available when trade secrets are misappropriated for the benefit of a foreign government, instrumentality or agent.[6]

That the common law has been supplemented by these four accounts of trade secrets law may seem to hold tremendous possibility for confusion. However, the substantive law of trade secrets provided in the Restatements, Uniform Act and Economic Espionage Act is largely consistent.[7] The later sources are marked by more familiar language and a greater level of detail than their predecessors. Although judicial opinions may cite to different authorities, the core precepts of trade secret law remain intact.

3. *Id.* at § 3.01[1].

4. 14 U.L.A. 438 (1990).

5. Pub. L. No. 104–294, §§ 1831–1839, 110 Stat. 3488 (codified at 18 U.S.C.A. §§ 1831–39).

6. *See* James H.A. Pooley, *Understanding the Economic Espionage Act of 1996*, 5 Tex. Intell. Prop. L.J. 177 (1997).

7. The chief exception to this broad statement concerns the requirement of the Restatement of Torts that the trade secret be capable of "continuous use in the operation of a business." Reflecting subsequent developments in the case law, both the Restatement of Unfair Competition and Uniform Act have rejected this earlier requirement. Restatement Third, Unfair Competition § 39 cmt. d (1995).

§ 24.2   Eligible Subject Matter

Perhaps due to its origins in the courts of equity, the trade secret law has never overly concerned itself with achieving an exact definition of the sorts of information that may be subjected to trade secret protection.[1] The authorities do agree that there are two principle requirements for maintaining information as a trade secret. First and foremost, the information must have been the subject of reasonable efforts to maintain secrecy. Second, the information must derive commercial value from not being generally known or readily ascertainable by others.[2]

Subject to these overriding requirements of secrecy and value, the Restatements provide that formulae, patterns, devices or compilations of information may be protected as trade secrets.[3] The case law reveals an enormous variety of information subject to the trade secret laws. This subject matter includes lists of customers, marketing data, bid price information, technical designs, manufacturing know-how, computer programs and chemical formulae. In sum, any distinct, clearly identifiable information may become a trade secret provided that it has value and has been kept secret.[4]

24.2.1   Secrecy

The principal gatekeeper to trade secret status is that the information must have been subjected to reasonable efforts to maintain its secrecy.[5] The case law provides no precise standard as to the efforts necessary to qualify the protected subject matter as a trade secret. A would-be trade secret holder need not erect an utterly impenetrable fortress around the information. On the other hand, the owner must make satisfactory efforts to identify the secret subject matter, notify others that it regards the subject matter as proprietary, and protect against reasonably foreseeable intrusions.

In deciding whether reasonable efforts have been made to maintain secrecy, courts will balance the costs of the efforts made against the benefits obtained.[6] The courts do not require costly, burdensome safeguards that would overly disrupt the owner's usual commercial practices. However, if the owner did not engage in prudent precautions that would have yielded security benefits greater than their costs, the case for reasonable secrecy efforts is diminished.

The precautions the holder of commercially valuable information might take to maintain secrecy are legion. For example, employees, visitors and joint venturers could be required to sign confidentiality

§ 24.2

1. Restatement Third, Unfair Competition § 39 cmt. d (1995).

2. Restatement Third, Unfair Competition § 39 (1995).

3. Restatement Third, Unfair Competition § 39 cmt. d (1995).

4. Restatement Third, Unfair Competition § 39 cmt. d (1995).

5. Uniform Trade Secrets Act § 2, 14 U.L.A. 438 (1990).

6. See Rockwell Graphic Sys., Inc. v. DEV Industries, Inc., 925 F.2d 174 (7th Cir.1991).

agreements. Signs, stamps and legends may declare that certain subject matter is proprietary. Locked doors, alarms and guards might deny access to individuals who do not need to know the information. Exit interviews may remind departing employees of their obligations to maintain the protected subject matter in confidence. Pertinent documents and laboratory samples could be destroyed on the premises. Although numerous other measures should be apparent, no absolute rule governs the degree of vigilance that the putative trade secret holder must maintain. Whether a court will find the existence of a trade secret depends upon an overall balancing of the equities of particular cases.

A number of circumstances may negate secrecy. Knowledge that may be readily gained from an inspection of a commercially available product is not secret. Similarly, information that may be found in publicly available journals, texts or other published materials may not be kept as a trade secret. Issuance of a U.S. patent or publication of a pending patent application also destroys the secrecy of any information claimed within. This result holds even if the published application does not mature into a granted patent, or if the patent is later held invalid.[7]

Litigation also holds the potential of destroying a claimed trade secret. Without further precautions, enforcement of the trade secret would ordinarily require its disclosure in open court. However, Rule 26(c)(7) of the Federal Rules of Civil Procedure allows courts to mandate "that a trade secret or other confidential research, development, or commercial information not be revealed or be revealed only in a designated way." Rule 45 of the Federal Rules of Civil Procedure also allows a court to quash or modify a subpoena if it requires disclosure of a trade secret or other confidential information. Experience demonstrates that of these two options, courts strongly favor disclosure of trade secrets during discovery. The Supreme Court has recognized that "[o]rders forbidding any disclosure of trade secrets are rare. More commonly, the trial court will enter a protective order restricting disclosure to counsel or to the parties."[8]

24.2.2 Commercial Value

Information must be sufficiently valuable to provide an actual or potential economic advantage over others to qualify for trade secret protection.[9] Ordinarily the putative trade secret holder demonstrates value through direct evidence of the significance of the subject matter to its business, or its superiority as compared to public domain alternatives. Courts have also accepted evidence of the cost of developing the information and the extent of the pains taken to protect its secrecy as evidence of value.

7. RESTATEMENT THIRD, UNFAIR COMPETITION § 39 cmt. c (1995).

8. Federal Open Market Committee v. Merrill, 443 U.S. 340, 362 n. 24, 99 S.Ct. 2800, 61 L.Ed.2d 587 (1979).

9. RESTATEMENT THIRD, UNFAIR COMPETITION § 39 cmt. e (1995).

Value is seldom a practical issue in trade secret cases. The high cost of enforcing intellectual property rights suggests that plaintiffs will only commence litigation concerning information of considerable value. One decision that did deny a claim for trade secret misappropriation based upon the value requirement was *Religious Technology Center v. Wollersheim*.[10] There, the Church of Scientology accused a former practitioner of misappropriating scriptural materials that addressed a person's spiritual well-being. The Court of Appeals for the Ninth Circuit denied the Church's trade secret claim, concluding that the value of the confidential materials were religious rather than commercial in character.

The continued vitality of this precedent is questionable in light of subsequent opinions from the Ninth Circuit, however.[11] One district court concluded that the ''Advanced Technology'' scriptures of the Church of Scientology possessed commercial value as a matter of law.[12] The court noted that the accused misappropriator used the materials to teach a course for which she was paid. It also reasoned that, like other entities, religious organizations required funds to exist. This logic suggests that the value requirement will exclude few churches, charitable organizations and non-profit groups from employing trade secret alongside commercial entities.

§ 24.3 Misappropriation

An enterprise possessing trade secrets will be protected against misappropriation of those trade secrets by others. Sometimes trade secrets are acquired by individuals with no relationship to the trade secret holder. In those cases, the dispositive legal issue is whether the trade secret was acquired by improper means. Other trade secret cases involve parties who initially learn of the trade secret through voluntary disclosure by the trade secret holder, and thereafter either use the secret for their commercial advantage or disclose it to others. Courts will grant relief in this latter class of cases where the defendant violated either an express or implied obligation of confidentiality.

24.3.1 Improper Acquisition

A trade secret owner may claim misappropriation if the defendant acquired the trade secret by performing illegal acts. Wiretapping, bribery, fraud, and theft of personal property are exemplary of the industrial espionage condemned under the trade secret law. However, trade secret protection is not limited to acts that are themselves violations of other laws. The courts have also condemned activities that amount to calculated attempts to overcome reasonable efforts to maintain secrecy.

E.I. duPont deNemours v. Christopher[1] is the leading opinion on trade secret misappropriation through improper, as compared to illegal

---

10. 796 F.2d 1076 (9th Cir.1986).

11. *See* Religious Technology Center v. Scott, 869 F.2d 1306, 10 USPQ2d 1379 (9th Cir.1989).

12. *See* Bridge Publications, Inc. v. Vien, 827 F.Supp. 629 (S.D.Cal.1993).

§ 24.3

1. 431 F.2d 1012 (5th Cir.1970).

means. The litigation involved DuPont's claims to trade secrets on methanol production methods. DuPont began construction on a new chemical plant that would make use of these trade secrets, taking various precautions to restrict access to, and views of, the plant. For a brief period in the midst of construction, however, the plant's unfinished roof allowed an overhead view of the plant's workings. This view would reveal DuPont's method of making methanol to a trained eye. At that time, an unnamed competitor of DuPont hired the Christophers to fly an airplane over the DuPont facility and take photographs. DuPont sued the Christophers for misappropriation of trade secrets. The Christophers argued that taking aerial photographs of DuPont's plant was not in violation of any criminal law nor did it constitute trespassing.

The Court of Appeals for the Fifth Circuit agreed that the precedents before it found a trade secret misappropriation only when the defendant committed a trespass or illegal act. The court nonetheless condemned the Christophers for engaging in improper means of acquisition and affirmed the trial court's finding of misappropriation. Judge Goldberg's opinion stressed the momentary advantage the Christophers obtained over DuPont despite extensive efforts to maintain secrecy, as well as the great expenses that would be incurred in protecting the plant from aerial views. In extending the misappropriation cause of action beyond illegal activities, the court hoped to encourage efficient self-protection and investment in research and development, yet discourage extravagant security expenditures and disreputable commercial practices. Under the influential holding in *duPont v. Christopher*, if an individual takes reasonable precautions to protect a trade secret, industrial espionage that circumvents those precautions will be condemned as improper.

24.3.2 Breach of Confidential Relationship

An individual may owe another a duty of confidence through an express promise of confidentiality. Such promises are most typically made by employees, prospective buyers, visitors to a facility or joint venturers. A duty of confidence may also be implied from the relationship of the parties, even where no express contractual provision exists. If the trade secret holder was reasonable in inferring that the other person consented to an obligation of confidentiality, and the other knew or should have known the disclosure was made in confidence, the court will infer that an obligation of confidentiality existed.

A representative case implying a duty of confidentiality is *Smith v. Dravo Corp.*[2] Smith was in the cargo and freight container business. Dravo expressed an interest in buying Smith's business, and the two entered into negotiations. As part of these discussions Smith showed Dravo secret blueprints and patent applications concerning its innovative cargo containers. The deal fell through and shortly thereafter Dravo began to market freight containers similar to Smith's. Smith sued Dravo

2.   203 F.2d 369 (7th Cir.1953).

for trade secret misappropriation. Although the Court of Appeals for the Seventh Circuit observed that "no express promise of trust was exacted from the defendant," it held that a relationship of trust should be implied from the facts and granted relief.

§ 24.4 Remedies

An adjudicated trade secret misappropriator may be enjoined and found liable for damages. The modern rule is that injunctions are appropriate only for the period of time that the subject matter of the trade secret would have remained unavailable to the defendant but for the misappropriation. This principle offers a compromise between two more extreme positions established in the case law. Some courts have followed the holding in *Shellmar Products Co. v. Allen–Qualley Co.*[1] and concluded that permanent injunctions were an appropriate remedy for trade secret misappropriation on the ground that trade secrets have no set duration. Other opinions found more favor in Judge Learned Hand's opinion in *Conmar Products Corp. v. Universal Slide Fastener Co.*,[2] to the effect that once a trade secret entered into the public domain, the plaintiff could obtain no injunctive relief whatsoever.

Each of these extreme positions is now in disfavor. Contemporary courts have reasoned that the draconian *Shellmar* rule is punitive in character and undermines the public interest in legitimate competition. On the other hand, the *Conmar* rule leads to hard results in cases where the defendant engaged in egregious conduct, particularly where he exposed the trade secret to the public himself. The compromise position of the Uniform Trade Secrets Act states that "an injunction shall be terminated when the trade secret has ceased to exist, but the injunction may be continued for an additional reasonable period of time in order to eliminate commercial advantage that otherwise would be derived from the misappropriation."[3]

As a result, successful plaintiffs in trade secret proceedings may obtain injunctions limited to the lead time advantage inappropriately gained by the misappropriator. In determining the length of this "head start," courts will weigh evidence as to the amount of time a person of ordinary skill would have required to discover independently or reverse engineer the subject matter of the trade secret. If the misappropriator can demonstrate that the trade secret holder's competitors have legitimately acquired the protected knowledge, then the court will likely decline to award an injunction at all.

Courts have demonstrated flexibility in fashioning monetary remedies for trade secret misappropriation. They will typically award an amount equal to either the loss suffered by the trade secret holder, or the gain realized by misappropriator, whichever is greater. Monetary

§ 24.4

1. 87 F.2d 104, 32 USPQ 24 (7th Cir.), *cert. denied*, 301 U.S. 695, 57 S.Ct. 923, 81 L.Ed. 1350 (1937).

2. 172 F.2d 150, 80 USPQ 108 (2d Cir. 1949).

3. Uniform Trade Secrets Act § 2(a), 14 U.L.A. 438 (1990).

damages are ordinarily limited to the time that the misappropriated information would not have been available otherwise to the defendant.[4]

An example demonstrates the remedial structure of trade secret law. Suppose that Jufi and Lojak compete in the field of photographic film. Jufi spends one million dollars to develop an improved method of making film. Lojak misappropriates the trade secret on May 1, 2000, and begins to produce film in competition with Jufi on September 1, 2000. Lojak earns $575,000 in net profits on film sales from September 1, 2000 through January 1, 2001. In the meantime, another market entrant, Solanoid, purchases samples of the Jufi film and engages in extensive reverse engineering efforts. Following six weeks of work and reasonable expenditures of $200,000, Solanoid determines the steps of the Jufi process and publishes them in an industry newsletter on January 1, 2001.

Assuming a trial is held in early 2001, and Jufi produces no evidence indicating losses exceeding $575,000, Jufi may recover that amount from Lojak. Jufi may also obtain damages of $200,000, equal to the amount of reverse engineering expenses that Lojak saved. Jufi's total damages award would amount to $775,000. A court would decline to issue an injunction because the short period of time needed to reverse engineer the trade secret has already elapsed.

§ 24.5   Trade Secrets and Patents

Trade secrets and patents coexist in what can be described as an uneasy relationship. A principal purpose of the patent law is the dissemination of knowledge.[1] This goal is realized through the publication of patent instruments that fully disclose the patented invention such that skilled artisans could practice it without undue experimentation.[2] A law of trade secrets that encourages the withholding of patentable inventions appears fundamentally at odds with this precept.[3]

This tension results in a patent law that does not favor trade secret holders. One patent law principle that deleteriously impacts trade secret holders is that a later, independent inventor may patent the subject matter of an earlier inventor's trade secret. A first inventor may quickly transition from the status of a trade secret holder to an adjudicated patent infringer.[4] The First Inventor Defense Act of 1999 did soften this traditional principle somewhat, allowing earlier inventors an infringement defense against subsequent patentees of methods of doing business.[5]

4.   *See, e.g.,* Engelhard Industries, Inc. v. Research Instrumental Corp., 324 F.2d 347 (9th Cir.1963), *cert. denied,* 377 U.S. 923, 84 S.Ct. 1220, 12 L.Ed.2d 215 (1964).

§ 24.5

1.   *See supra* § 13.4.1.

2.   35 U.S.C.A. § 112 (2000).

3.   Joan E. Schaffner, *Patent Preemption Unlocked,* 1995 Wis. L. Rev. 1081.

4.   *See* Albert C. Smith & Jared A. Stosberg, *Beware! Trade Secret Software May Be Patented By A Later Inventor,* 7 Computer Lawyer no. 11 at 15 (Nov. 1990).

5.   35 U.S.C.A. § 273 (2000). *See supra* § 16.3.2.8.

Trade secrets perform a valuable role in the U.S. intellectual property scheme, however. Although the patent law is an increasingly capacious regime, its subject matter does not extend to the full array of valuable information that may be the subject of a trade secret.[6] Patent rights too must be affirmatively sought, and their acquisition usually entails significant costs and delays.[7] Some inventors are not well schooled in the rather rarefied patent law regime and may wait overly long before filing a patent application. Even sophisticated enterprises may not recognize the value of an invention until they too have performed acts that defeat its patentability. The trade secret law fills these gaps by providing a modicum of protection for those who take prudent measures to protect valuable information.

Inventors who do not wish to dedicate their technologies to the public domain must choose between maintaining the technology as a trade secret or pursuing patent protection. A number of factors inform this decision. Whether the inventor can keep the technology secret is the most obvious. Many mechanical inventions betray their design upon inspection, while the composition of a chemical compound may be much easier to conceal. The costs associated with acquiring and maintaining patents are another element. A U.S. patent provides rights only within the United States,[8] but discloses its subject matter for anyone in the world to see. Inventors should therefore also consider the expenses of obtaining a patent in each jurisdiction in which he does or wishes to do business.

The product cycle associated with the invention is also of importance. Products with a very short lifespan may be unmarketable by the time a patent issues. Inventors should also consider whether the industry in which they act is patent-intensive. If industry actors tend to invest heavily in maintaining their patent portfolios, then the inventor may well wish to patent for defensive purposes or to have a bargaining chip available if he is accused of infringement himself. Legislative enactment of the First Inventor Defense Act of 1999 introduced another element into this calculation. If the invention concerns a "method of doing business" within the meaning of the Act, then the inventor may gain an infringement defense effective against the patents of others that claim that method.[9]

The publication of a patent application or issuance of a patent will destroy trade secret status for the subject matter that it properly discloses. Nothing prevents a patentee from maintaining an invention as a trade secret until such time, however. This strategy requires the applicant to preserve secrecy until the first of two events: (1) the publication of the application eighteen months following its filing date;

6. 35 U.S.C.A. § 101 (2000); *see supra* Chapter 14 for more on patent eligibility requirements.

7. 35 U.S.C.A. § 131 (2000); *see supra* Chapter 19 for more on patent acquisition procedures.

8. Dowagiac Mfg. Co. v. Minnesota Moline Plow Co., 235 U.S. 641, 650, 35 S.Ct. 221, 59 L.Ed. 398 (1915).

9. 35 U.S.C.A. § 273 (2000).

or (2) when the PTO issues the patent, for those applications exempted from the publication requirement.

§ 24.6 Federal Preemption

The tensions between the patent and trade secret laws have sometimes erupted into arguments that the patent statute preempts state trade secret laws. In addition to asserting that trade secrecy discourages disclosure of new inventions,[1] commentators have also observed that the patent law reflects the policy that only new and nonobvious inventions merit proprietary patent rights. Although the requirement that a trade secret not be public knowledge has been equated to the patent law's novelty requirement,[2] the trade secret laws do not demand that the secret subject matter be nonobvious.

Despite these apparent conflicts, the courts have ruled that trade secret protection may co-exist alongside the patent and other intellectual property laws. In *Kewanee Oil Co. v Bicron Corp.*,[3] the Supreme Court observed that trade secret laws also serve a principal purpose of the patent laws, the promotion of innovation. The Court also considered the patent law a far more attractive option for inventors of patentable subject matter and reasoned that most inventors would opt for the patent system. The Court also noted that, historically, the two bodies of law had been in place since the earliest days of the Republic.

§ 24.6

1. James R. Barney, *The Prior User Defense: A Reprieve for Trade Secret Owners or a Disaster for the Patent Law?*, 82 J. Pat. & Trademark Off. Soc'y 261 (2000).

2. Gale R. Peterson, *Trade Secrets in an Information Age*, 32 Houston L. Rev. 385, 416 (1995).

3. 416 U.S. 470, 94 S.Ct. 1879, 40 L.Ed.2d 315 (1974).

Chapter 25

INTRODUCTION TO THE LAW OF TRADEMARKS

Table of Sections

§ 25.1 Brief Overview of Trademark Law

Almost everyone has an intuitive understanding of what a trademark is. It is a brand name—the designation for a particular type or style of goods or services that come from a particular producer and have consistent attributes each time you buy them. This intuition is basically sound. A trademark can be more formally defined as a device used by a merchant to identify its goods or services and to distinguish them from those of others. Just as you use your friend Jennifer's name to distinguish her from your friend Jessica, you use the name COCA–COLA to distinguish one type of carbonated cola flavored beverage from another that you call PEPSI–COLA.[1]

Almost any identifying symbol that can be conjured by the human imagination can be used as a trademark. Most trademarks, however, consist of one or more words. Those words may be written in a particular

---

§ 25.1

1. By convention, trademarks are often written in all upper case letters in legal materials dealing with trademark issues.

This helps them stand out from surrounding text and eliminates ambiguity about the exact words included in any given trademark. We follow that tradition in this book.

format using special fonts or in a particular color scheme, but usually, a merchant is entitled to claim exclusive protection for the words regardless of the format in which they are written. A trademark can also be a picture, symbol or logo. Many of the strongest American trademarks are pictorial in nature, and one can imagine a bizarre cocktail party populated by the many anthropomorphic trademarks that have become universally familiar to consumers around the world—the PILLSBURY DOUGHBOY, MR. PEANUT, MRS. BUTTERWORTH, TONY THE TIGER, ELSIE THE COW and ALFRED E. NEWMAN—to name just a few. In recent years firms have also sought, and obtained, trademark protection for the overall shape and design of the packaging in which their product is sold, and often for the shape and design of the product itself, or for the architecture and decor of the building where their services are provided. A few companies have even been able to protect sounds or smells as trademarks.

The law generally grants trademark protection to words and symbols only for a particular category of goods and services, not to the word or symbol in the abstract. Thus, while trademark protection resembles copyright and patent protection because it involves a government grant of exclusivity, the exclusivity is limited. Firms in unrelated lines of commerce can usually employ similar or even identical trademarks without infringing on each other's rights. That is why we can have a DELTA airlines, a DELTA faucets, and a DELTA dental insurance at the same time. That is also why we can write books and articles referring to the Mississippi River delta, and use the Greek letter delta as part of the name of a fraternity or sorority.

Trademarks are omnipresent. In our highly commercialized society they so thoroughly saturate our lives that we often don't even notice them. We are exposed to dozens of marks every time we go to the supermarket, drug store or shopping mall, and to dozens more whenever we turn on our radios, televisions and personal computers. Moreover, we often use trademarks in casual speech to make a political point, spice up a joke, or enliven a metaphor without paying particular attention to their trademark status.[2] This diversity of uses, along with the incredible proliferation of competing brands in our economy, produces inevitable tensions between those who wish to monopolize a designating symbol and others who feel that they have a right or need to use it for their own purposes. The rules of trademark law aspire to resolve those tensions in ways that are both fair to the competing parties and consistent with the public interest.

In broad outline, those legal rules are quite straightforward. Unlike patents and copyrights, trademarks are protected by both state and federal law. State law protection is almost always based on the common law, though, to be precise, quite a few states also have trademark

2. For more on this type of use of trademarks *see* Rochelle Cooper Dreyfuss, *Expressive Genericity: Trademarks as Language in the Pepsi Generation*, 65 Notre Dame L. Rev. 397 (1990).

statutes. For common law purposes the first party to adopt a mark and use it in connection with a particular category of goods or services is deemed to be the owner of that mark. No further formalities or governmental applications are required. Once a party has used a mark, it may also apply to the United States Patent and Trademark Office to federally register the mark. The relevant federal statute also provides a way for a firm to begin the application process even before it has used the desired mark, however no federal registration will be granted until after such use takes place. Federal registration confers a variety of additional legal protections and privileges, but it is not mandatory and many smaller businesses rely strictly on state common law protection for their trademarks.

Any person who uses a trademark belonging to another in a way that is likely to confuse the consuming public about the source or sponsorship of the goods or services will be liable for trademark infringement. In addition, if a trademark is in that small subset of marks that are considered "famous" the owner of the mark may be able to prevent even non-confusing uses by third parties. Like other forms of intellectual property, trademarks can be licensed, or sold outright to other parties, but there are certain technical requirements associated with such transactions that can be traps for the unwary.

If a party desires trademark protection outside the United States it must apply for that protection in each nation where it plans to do business. At this time, there is no way to secure global protection in a single step. Certain treaties, most notably one known as the Madrid Protocol, do exist to facilitate the process of obtaining trademarks abroad, and they will be considered in some detail in a subsequent chapter.

§ 25.2   Historical Background

25.2.1 Ancient Roots

It is not certain when marks were first put on goods, though the practice surely goes back to ancient times. In many cases, these marks were probably just ways to identify ownership in the event of loss or theft, analogous to writing your name inside a book's cover. Perhaps one of the oldest examples of this form of "marking" is the branding of cattle, which has been dated as far back as ancient Egypt.[1] It is no coincidence that the word "branding" today has the dual meaning of a rancher marking cattle and an MBA developing a catchy trademark and memorable advertising campaign for a new consumer product.

Other ancient marks may have been simply appended to goods as an act of pride by the artisan or craftsman who fabricated them, just as it is

---

§ 25.2

1. For a reproduction of an ancient Egyptian wall painting showing cattle branding activity, see the Web site at <http://www.barbwiremuseum.com/cattle-brandhistory.htm>. Similar activities are also depicted in ancient European cave paintings, though the animals in these cases appear to be bison rather than domesticated cattle.

customary for modern day painters and sculptors to sign their work. Archaeologists have identified marks of this sort on a variety of artifacts, most notably pottery, coming from a wide range of cultures around the globe.[2]

It is unlikely that ancient peoples used these markings as we use trademarks today. Commerce was primitive, most goods were made within the family unit, and the number of producers of any particular category of goods was probably quite small. In such a world, it would not be likely that one would rely on pottery markings when shopping for a new crock. On the other hand, some historians have speculated that even in ancient days, markings on products enabled users to relocate the maker of the item if it proved unsatisfactory, so that a complaint could be registered or a replacement obtained—a function that trademarks still serve down to the present day.

25.2.2 Medieval Trademarks

In the middle ages, merchants producing various categories of goods often were located in close proximity to each other. In larger towns and cities various neighborhoods might contain concentrations of leather tanners, cloth dyers, sword makers, goldsmiths, or butchers. This made it very easy for consumers to shop for low prices, which in turn often led to intense price competition making it difficult for many merchants to survive. As a response, medieval producers organized themselves into "guilds." These were essentially primitive cartels in which the members agreed to refrain from price competition with each other. In addition, however, the guilds usually imposed quality requirements on their members. To make it easier to identify any guild member violating those quality requirements, the guilds also often required merchants to mark their goods with identifying symbols. Thus, as one source explains:

> In 1202 A.D., England adopted laws to regulate the price of bread and limit bakers' profits. Many bakers were prosecuted for selling loaves that did not conform to the weights required by local laws. As a result of the "bread trials" in England in 1266, bakers were ordered to mark each loaf of bread so if a non-conforming loaf turned up, the baker could be found. The bakers' marks were among the first trademarks.[3]

As the leading work on trademark history has summarized, these medieval guild marks were used primarily "to facilitate the tracing of 'false'

---

2. For a general discussion, *see* Gerald Ruston, *On the Origin of Trademarks,* 54 TRADEMARK REP. 127 (1955).

3. <http://www.cyberspaceag.com/bread history.html>. The law provided that a "baker must set his owne proper marke upon every loafe of bread that hee maketh and selleth, to the end that if any bread be faultie in weight, it may be then known in whom the fault is." *See* Frank I. Schechter, THE HISTORICAL FOUNDATIONS OF THE LAW RELATING TO TRADEMARKS 51 (1925). The concept of the "baker's dozen," in which 13 items are provided for the price of 12, has been traced to the 1266 statute mentioned in text, because medieval bakers would often provide a 13th loaf for free to be sure that the total amount of bread being delivered was not "faultie in weight."

or defective wares and the punishment of the offending craftsman."[4]

By the late middle ages, these mandatory markings were beginning to take on some of the features and functions of contemporary trademarks. Perhaps the earliest case of what we might consider modern trademark infringement is the decision in *J.G. v. Samford*.[5] The plaintiff in this 1584 litigation was a maker of woolen cloth. When the defendant, a competitor who made lower grade cloth, marked his goods with the plaintiff's trademark, the plaintiff sued for deceit and the court held that these facts stated a cause of action.

25.2.3 Early Common Law Developments

From the colonial era through the civil war, most economic activity in the United States was conducted on a local level. It was expensive to transport goods over long distances, and consumers rarely traveled far from home. Consequently, unlike the situation in copyright and patent law, where there was a perceived need for national uniformity from the earliest days of the republic, trademark law remained strictly a matter of local concern until after the Civil War.

It was also apparently not a source of much controversy. The first reported trademark decision after American independence was not handed down until 1837.[6] In the following three decades only a few dozen additional cases were decided, barely averaging two cases per year.[7] Substantively, trademark law in this era remained essentially an offshoot of the law of fraud. To recover plaintiffs effectively had to demonstrate that the defendant was using a virtually exact replica of a trade symbol, and doing so with an intent to defraud the consuming public.

For instance in *Partridge v. Menck*,[8] an 1847 decision from New York, the plaintiff was the successor to a merchant who sold matches in boxes marked with a beehive logo. When the defendant began using a somewhat similar logo on its matches, the plaintiff sought an injunction. The court of chancery began with an explanation of the basis of trademark law that sounds entirely contemporary, noting that:

> [C]omplainant has a valuable interest in the good will of his trade or business; and that having appropriated to himself a particular label, or sign or trade-mark, indicating to those who wish to give him their patronage that the article is manufac-

4. Frank I. Schechter, THE HISTORICAL FOUNDATIONS OF THE LAW RELATING TO TRADEMARKS 47 (1925).

5. An abstract of the case is reprinted in J.H. Baker & S.F.C. Milsom, SOURCES OF ENGLISH LEGAL HISTORY—PRIVATE LAW TO 1750, pp.615–18 (1986). The case, referenced as *Sandforth's Case* is discussed in Keith M. Stolte, *How Early Did Anglo–American Trademark Law Begin? An Answer To Schechter's Conundrum*, 8 FORDHAM INTELL. PROP. MEDIA & ENT. L.J. 505, 541–43 (1988).

6. Thomson v. Winchester, 36 Mass. (19 Pick.) 214, 1837 WL 2452, 31 Am. Dec. 135 (1837). In 1845, New York became the first state to adopt a trademark statute.

7. *See* Jerome Gilson, TRADEMARK PROTECTION AND PRACTICE § 1.01[2].

8. 5 N.Y.Leg.Obs. 94, 2 Barb.Ch. 101, 1847 WL 4112, 47 Am. Dec. 281, 5 N.Y.Ch. Ann. 572 (N.Y.Ch.1847).

tured or sold by him, or by his authority, or that he carries on his business at a particular place, he is entitled to protection against any other person who attempts to pirate upon the good will of the complainant's friends or customers, or of the patrons of his trade or business, by sailing under his flag without his authority or consent.... [I]f the court sees that the complainant's trade-marks are simulated, in such a manner as probably to deceive his customers, or the patrons of his trade or business, the piracy should be checked at once, by injunction.

However, after closely examining the labels of the competing products, the court denied relief because it found a number of subtle differences between them, differences which a modern court would likely view as insignificant.

After the civil war, social, technological, and economic changes accelerated. Professor Merges has explained how these developments created pressure for trademark laws that were both national in reach and more comprehensive in scope:

[M]odern trademark law emerged with the expanding consumer economy of the late-nineteenth-century. According to business historian Alfred Chandler, new manufacturing and processing technologies, coupled with expanded transportation networks, fueled the growth of late nineteenth-century consumer-products firms. In industries as diverse as cigarettes, grains, canned goods, and soap, innovations in processing and packaging made feasible large-scale production and thus national distribution. Sharp-eyed "first-movers" quickly seized the opportunity to transform what had been regional, commodity goods into the first true national brands. According to Chandler, "[a]ll the new enterprises reinforced their first-mover advantages by spending much of the income resulting from the cost advantages of scale on massive national advertising campaigns." And so were born many of the brands still recognized by consumers today: Quaker Oats, Campbell Soup, Heinz Ketchup, Libby canned vegetables, Proctor & Gamble soap products, Colgate products, Swift meats, and Pabst, Schlitz, and Anheuser Brewing beers. With these developments in mind, it is no surprise that agitation for the first national trademark legislation appeared in the 1870s.[9]

25.2.4 The Federal Trademark Laws of 1870, 1881 and 1905

In 1870, the United States Congress passed the first federal trademark act, establishing for the first time a national scheme for the registration of trademarks.[10] Unfortunately, Congress adopted this act as an exercise of its authority under the Copyright and Patent Clause of the

---

9. Robert P. Merges, *One Hundred Years of Solicitude: Intellectual Property Law, 1900–2000*, 88 CALIF. L. REV. 2187 (2000).

10. Act of July 8, 1870, 16 Stat. at L. 198 §§ 77–84, Ch. 2 Tit. 60 Rev. Stat. §§ 4937–47 The same legislation also significantly revised the patent and copyright laws.

Constitution.[11] This proved to be a fatal flaw. Only nine years later, the Supreme Court held the statute to be unconstitutional.[12] The Court found that this clause of the Constitution simply did not provide a basis for federal trademark legislation, observing that "any attempt ... to identify the essential characteristics of a trade-mark with inventions and discoveries in the arts and sciences, or with the writings of authors will show that the effort is surrounded with insurmountable difficulties." Although the government argued that the 1870 statute should be upheld on the alternative ground that it was a valid exercise of Congress's power to regulate interstate commerce, the Court rejected that argument as well, because nothing in the law of 1870 limited its provisions to marks that were used in connection with interstate transactions.

Two years later Congress responded by adopting another trademark statute.[13] Perhaps unduly chastened by the Supreme Court, the law of 1881 provided for federal registration only of those marks used in connection with foreign commerce or in commerce with the Indian nations. It made no provision for registration of marks used domestically, interstate or otherwise. As Professor McCarthy has observed in his definitive treatise on trademark law, "for twenty-four years American business chafed under the totally inadequate provisions of the 1881 Act."[14]

Finally, in 1905, Congress passed the first modern trademark registration act. Though far more sophisticated than any previous law, the 1905 statute suffered from a number of shortcomings. Most significantly, it sharply limited the types of trade-identifying symbols that could be registered. Many types of trademarks that are well-accepted and commonly used today were simply ineligible for registration under the 1905 law.

25.2.5 The Lanham Act

As early as 1920, only 15 years after the passage of the 1905 Act, there were already calls for a revision of federal trademark law.[15] The process of enacting a new law ultimately took a quarter of a century. The end result was the 1946 Trademark Act, conventionally known as the Lanham Act, after Congressman Fritz Lanham who chaired the Patent Committee in the U.S. House of Representatives.[16] The law became effective on July 5, 1947.

11. Article I, Section 8, Clause 8.

12. Trade-Mark Cases, 100 U.S. 82, 25 L.Ed. 550 (1879). The defendants in these cases, Steffens, Witteman and Johnson were being criminally prosecuted for counterfeiting, using, and selling marks that had been registered by other parties under the 1870 Act.

13. Act of March 3, 1881, 21 Stat. 502.

14. J. Thomas McCarthy, TRADEMARKS AND UNFAIR COMPETITION § 5:3.

15. *See generally*, J. Thomas McCarthy, TRADEMARKS & UNFAIR COMPETITION § 5:4 ("The Lanham Act had its genesis at a meeting of the Patent Section of the American Bar Association in St. Louis in 1920." citing, Edward S. Rogers, *The Lanham Act and the Social Function of Trademarks,* 14 LAW & CONTEMP. PROBS. 173 (1949)).

16. Law of July 5, 1946, c. 540, P.L. 489, 60 Stat. 427. The Lanham Act is codified as 15 U.S.C.A. §§ 1051–1126.

The Lanham Act greatly expanded the types of marks eligible for federal protection, while simultaneously expanding the nature of that protection from essentially procedural matters to a grant of substantive rights. Not long after its adoption, Judge Learned Hand observed that it "did indeed put federal trademark law on a new footing."[17]

In the fifty-five years since the effective date of the Lanham Act, it has been amended nearly thirty times. Some of these amendments have been designed to conform U.S. practices more closely to those that prevail in the rest of the world. Others have been reactions to new technological developments such as the rise of the Internet. Still others were responses to lobbying by trademark owners seeking ever greater protection for assets that have become increasingly valuable in our brand-conscious, media driven society. Although it is the oldest of the three principal federal intellectual property statutes, these frequent amendments have kept the Lanham Act a reasonably modern and effective statute. If nothing else, the system it established is heavily used. In fiscal year 2000 there were just under 300,000 applications filed for federal trademark registrations.[18]

§ 25.3   The Function of Trademarks and Rationales for Protection

The rationale for protecting trademarks differs somewhat from those which animate the other two major branches of intellectual property. A major justification for the protection of both technological innovation through patents, and artistic creativity through copyright, is the need to create an incentive for people to engage in such activities in the first place. The notion is that we would have too few inventors and artists if free riders could simply duplicate their work without fear of legal sanction, because there would be no way to make a living as an artist or an inventor.

The incentive rationale, however, is not really at the root of trademark law. Our legal system does not protect trademarks to encourage firms to come up with wittier brand names or more attractive logos. The goal is not to induce another make-over of Betty Crocker or an even better name for athletic shoes than NIKE.

To be more precise, trademark law does seek to provide incentives, but those incentives are designed to encourage firms to produce high quality, or at least consistent quality, *good and services*, rather than to produce high quality *trademarks*. The theory is that when the legal system grants exclusive rights to trademarks, consumers are able to use those marks to easily relocate those firm whose products have pleased them in the past, and to reward those firms with continued patronage. As the Supreme Court has put it, "trademarks foster competition and

17. S.C. Johnson & Son v. Johnson, 175 F.2d 176 (2d Cir.1949).

18. <http://www.uspto.gov/web/offices/com/annual/2000/00trademarks.pdf>.

the maintenance of quality by securing to the producer the benefits of good reputation."[1]

More recently, the Court expanded on this observation, explaining the justification for trademark protection in greater detail:

> Trademark law, by preventing others from copying a source-identifying mark, 'reduce[s] the customer's costs of shopping and making purchasing decisions' ... for it quickly and easily assures a potential customer that this item—the item with this mark—is made by the same producer as other similarly marked items that he or she liked (or disliked) in the past. At the same time, the law helps assure a producer that it (and not an imitating competitor) will reap the financial reputation-related rewards associated with a desirable product. The law thereby 'encourages[s] the production of quality products' and simultaneously discourages those who hope to sell inferior products by capitalizing on a consumer's inability quickly to evaluate the quality of an item offered for sale.[2]

These same ideas can be put in slightly more formal, economic terms. Professor Landes and Judge Posner have argued that "trademark law ... can best be explained on the hypothesis that the law is trying to promote economic efficiency."[3] One of the principal ways that it does this is by reducing "search costs," the time energy, and money spent by consumers in identifying products that will suit their needs.[4] It also serves a "quality encouragement function," giving manufacturers incentives to improve products by guaranteeing that consumers will be able to distinguish the higher quality products from the inferior ones.[5]

Others have suggested that trademark protection might also be justified in some cases by moral considerations.[6] On this view, a party, having developed positive associations with a given trade symbol, is entitled to reap the economic rewards triggered by that symbol as a matter of fairness and justice. Unauthorized parties who use the mark to sell goods in competition with the trademark originator are simply behaving unscrupulously. The same type of reasoning suggests that a trademark owner should also be allowed to prevent others from using the symbol in ways which may be inconsistent with the image it is trying to cultivate for its products. As the Pennsylvania Supreme Court put it several decades ago, courts enforce trademarks "to promote honesty and

§ 25.3

1. Park 'N Fly, Inc. v. Dollar Park and Fly, Inc., 469 U.S. 189, 105 S.Ct. 658, 83 L.Ed.2d 582 (1985).

2. Qualitex Co. v. Jacobson Products Co., Inc., 514 U.S. 159, 115 S.Ct. 1300, 131 L.Ed.2d 248 (1995) (quoting, in part, J. Thomas McCarthy, TRADEMARKS AND UNFAIR COMPETITION § 2.01[2]).

3. *See,* William M. Landes & Richard A. Posner, *Trademark Law: An Economic Perspective,* 30 J.L. & ECON. 265, 275 (1987).

4. The case law has recognized this role of trademarks. *See, e.g.,* New Kids on the Block v. New America Pub., Inc., 971 F.2d 302, 305 n. 2 (9th Cir.1992)

5. J. Thomas McCarthy, TRADEMARKS AND UNFAIR COMPETITION § 2:4.

6. *See, e.g.,* Alex Kozinski, *Trademarks Unplugged,* 68 N.Y.U. L. REV. 960, 966 (1993).

fair dealing, and because no one has a right to sell his goods as the goods of another."[7]

As you might predict, those who advocate more limited versions of trademark protection have advanced counter-arguments. For instance, periodically some have voiced the concern that trademarks foster monopolies and actually harm consumers. As long ago as 1742, Lord Harwicke, in denying an injunction for alleged trademark infringement in a case involving playing cards, observed that the plaintiff was trying to enforce "one of those monopolies which were so frequent" in earlier British history.[8]

In the 1930's the economist Edward Chamberlain formulated a more sophisticated version of the trademarks-foster-monopoly argument. He developed the theory that trademarks facilitated "brand differentiation." Brand differentiation leads consumers to view essentially identical products as poor substitutes for one another, and thus can give trademark owners an unhealthy degree of control over price.[9] Thus the consumer who views BENADRYL brand antihistamine and CHLOR–TRIMETON brand antihistamine as strikingly different from each other may tolerate significant price increases in one brand before shifting to the other, even though the two brands may be chemically identical. Another thread in the "monopoly" attack on trademarks is the claim that they can constitute barriers to entry. This means that in industries where there are a few strong national brands, any new firm will have to spend enormous sums on advertising to lure consumers away from purchasing habits that have been ingrained through the use of trademarks if there is to be any hope of persuading them to try a new product.

Many thoughtful experts bristle at the characterization of trademark rights as "monopolies,"[10] and the monopoly-based criticism of trademark law abated significantly during most of the latter half of the twentieth century. Recent expansions of trademark protection, however, have once again raised the anxiety of some observers who fear significant anti-competitive consequences from an over-broad conception of trademark law.[11]

Others critics have suggested that trademark rights must be limited so that they do not hamper free communication or conflict with First Amendment values. Judge Kozinski observes that "words and images do

7. B.V.D. Co. v. Kaufmann & Baer Co., 272 Pa. 240, 116 A. 508 (1922). *See also* People ex rel. Mosk v. National Research Co., 201 Cal.App.2d 765, 20 Cal.Rptr. 516, 520 (1962) ("The tendency of the law, both legislative and common, has been in the direction of enforcing increasingly higher standards of fairness or commercial morality in trade.").

8. *See* Blanchard v. Hill, 26 Eng.Rep. 692, 693 (Ch.1742).

9. Edward Chamberlin, The Theory of Monopolistic Competition 56, 204 (1933).

10. *See, e.g.,* J. Thomas McCarthy, Trademarks and Unfair Competition § 2:10–11

11. *See, e.g.,* Mark A. Lemley, *The Modern Lanham Act and the Death of Common Sense,* 108 Yale L.J. 1687 (1999); Glynn S. Lunney, Jr., *Trademark Monopolies,* 48 Emory L.J. 367 (1999); Robert N. Klieger, *Trademark Dilution: The Whittling Away of the Rational Basis for Trademark Protection,* 58 U. Pitt. L. Rev. 789 (1997).

not worm their way into our discourse by accident; they're generally thrust there by well-orchestrated campaigns intended to burn them into our collective consciousness. Having embarked on that endeavor, the originator of the symbol necessarily—and justly—must give up some measure of control. The originator must understand that the mark or symbol or image is no longer entirely its own, and that in some sense it also belongs to all these other minds who have received and integrated it."[12]

12. Kozinski, *supra* note 5, at 975.

Chapter 26

ACQUIRING TRADEMARK RIGHTS

The United States has a "dual" system of trademark law. A firm can secure trademark protection under state law, usually under state common law, or it can seek federal rights, under the federal trademark statute known as the Lanham Act, or both. The two are independent of each other. A mark can be valid and protectable under state common law even though the owner has not taken any steps to secure federal rights. Conversely, a mark can be protected under federal law even though state common law rights have not accrued, though this would be somewhat less likely.

This chapter considers the various requirements necessary to obtain trademark rights under both of these systems. As we shall see, under both systems, the essential requirement is for the merchant to actually *use* the mark in making sales to the public here in the United States. The only exception to that overarching principle is one that permits certain foreign firms to secure Lanham Act protection if they first take certain steps in their home countries.

§ 26.1   Obtaining Rights at Common Law Through Use

At common law, a firm cannot receive legal protection for a mark until it begins to associate the desired mark with its own particular brand of goods or services—in other words it must begin the process of building goodwill and educating the public about what the mark is going to represent. In the usual case, this means that the mark must "travel with the goods" into the marketplace so as to begin the process of familiarizing the public about what the mark stands for. The Supreme Court laid down the rule almost 100 years ago, commenting: "There is no such thing as property in a trade-mark except as a right appurtenant to an established business or trade in connection with which the mark is employed.... [T]he right to a particular mark grows out of its use, not its mere adoption; its function is simply to designate the goods as the product of a particular trader and to protect his good will against the sale of another's product as his; and it is not the subject of property except in connection with an existing business."[1] As the Seventh Circuit put it more recently, in *Zazu Designs v. L'Oreal, S.A.*, "[o]nly active use allows consumers to associate a mark with particular goods and notifies other firms that the mark is so associated."

This principle is often summarized by saying that the merchant must first affix the mark to the goods or their containers and then must use the mark by making sales to actual customers in order to obtain common law trademark rights. However, this summary rule statement is both somewhat cryptic and even somewhat inaccurate under contemporary case law, as a closer look at these requirements reveals.

In taking this closer look it is helpful bear in mind that the question of whether a firm has done enough to "own" a particular trademark under state common law does not usually arise until there is a dispute between two firms. This typically happens when two firms have both adopted the same, or closely similar marks, for the same, or closely similar goods. In this kind of case—often referred to as a priority dispute—the rights to the mark will be awarded to which ever firm was the first to use it, and that firm will be able to enjoin the other from continued use.[2] It thus becomes important to determine which of the competitors was the senior user of the mark. Not every type of use will suffice to establish priority in a common law dispute, however. It must be the right kind of use, and the amount or degree of use much be sufficient.

26.1.1   Affixation Under Common Law and its Substitutes

Older cases were fairly strict in requiring the merchant to actually attach or affix the mark to the goods or their containers prior to sales in

§ 26.1

1. United Drug Co. v. Theodore Recta- nus Co., 248 U.S. 90, 97, 39 S.Ct. 48, 50, 63 L.Ed. 141 (1918).

2. *See, e.g.,* Blisscraft of Hollywood v. United Plastics Co., 294 F.2d 694 (2d Cir. 1961).

order to obtain common law rights in the mark. Use of the mark in any other way was not considered adequate and would not be the basis for a finding of trademark rights. Thus, older common law opinions held advertisement of the mark on the radio[3] or display of the mark on a sign over a store[4] insufficient bases upon which to ground trademark rights. One case even found the use of a name for a food product on a menu to be inadequate use to confer trademark rights because the mark was not actually "affixed" to the goods,[5] implying, perhaps, that the merchant should have spelled out the trademark in melted cheese right on the plate! Under this strict approach, in a contest between two firms seeking to use the same mark, the common law rule was to grant rights in the mark to the party who first sold goods *with the mark affixed,* not to the party who first thought of the mark or even first advertised it. Only use of the mark in sales counted—use in pre-sale advertising and promotion was irrelevant.

More recently, it has become obvious to common law courts around the country that contemporary marketing techniques permit a firm to begin building the necessary goods/mark association without actually selling items with the mark physically attached to them. Advertising in a variety of media can vividly imprint the mark on the mind of the public long before actual goods make their first appearance on the shelves. Section 18 of the Restatement (Third) of Unfair Competition recognizes this change in commercial reality by specifying that:

> A designation is "used" as a trademark, ... when the designation is displayed or otherwise made known to prospective purchasers in the ordinary course of business in a manner that associates the designation with the goods, services or business or the user....[6]

Comment d to this provision goes on to observe: "Use of a designation in the various advertising media can now establish its significance as an identifying symbol as surely as its appearance on packaging or labels. Although physical affixation remains a common form of trademark use, the rule stated in this section recognizes any manner of use sufficient to create an association between the designation and the user's goods or services." Thus, the Restatement view does not require that a mark be physically attached to the goods or their containers before the user of the mark can claim a protectable common law right in the designation.

Under this liberalized approach, advertising uses that predate any actual sales have been held to establish a protectable common law right to the mark. A good illustration of this principle is *New West Corp. v. NYM Co.*[7] That case involved a dispute between two parties each of

3. Western Stove Co. v. Geo. D. Roper Corp., 82 F.Supp. 206 (S.D.Cal.1949).

4. Covert v. Bernat, 156 Mo.App. 687, 138 S.W. 103 (1911).

5. Persha v. Armour & Co. 239 F.2d 628 (5th Cir.1957).

6. Restatement (Third) of Unfair Competition § 18 (1995).

7. 595 F.2d 1194 (9th Cir.1979).

whom wanted to use the name NEW WEST as the mark for a new magazine. As usual, resolution of the controversy turned on which party had "used" the mark first. The court found for the defendants based on their use of the mark on over 400,000 solicitations mailed to prospective subscribers, despite the fact that no issues of the magazine had been published at the time of the mailing in question, and that the mark was thus not technically "affixed" to the goods which hadn't even been produced yet. Similar cases are *Marvel Comics Ltd. v. Defiant*,[8] holding that a pre-sales announcement of a new comic series was sufficient trademark use to establish a common law right of priority, and *Cascades of Levitt Homes, Inc. v. Cascades of Sabatello Dev. Corp.*,[9] where the court found a billboard announcing an upcoming real estate development project to be adequate as a form of trademark use.

Note, however, that the advertising or pre-sale promotion must be significant in scope or visibility in order to suffice. The Federal Circuit has declared that for pre-sales advertising to demonstrate a right of priority, the advertising must be "of sufficient clarity and repetition to create the required identification [and] must have reached a substantial portion of the public that might be expected to purchase the service."[10]

Of course, literal affixation is impossible in situations involving services. For instance there is no obvious place for a hotel chain or a firm specializing in income tax preparation services to "affix" its marks. It is, however, clear that use of the mark on signs and displays at the place where the services are provided, as well as on letterhead or in promotional literature would be sufficient to establish the requisite connection.[11]

Perhaps most importantly, even non-affixed symbols of trade identity are almost always protected under general principles of unfair competition law even if they do not qualify as technical trademarks. For instance, one who exactly copies the inventive and unique name of a sandwich being sold by a store across the street is guilty of generic unfair competition regardless of whether the sandwich name was considered "affixed" so as to rise to the level of a formal trademark.[12] Consequently, as the leading commentator on trademark law has ob-

---

8. 837 F.Supp. 546, 548–9 (S.D.N.Y. 1993).

9. 43 USPQ2d 1920 (S.D.Fla.1997).

10. T.A.B. Systems v. Pactel Teletrac, 77 F.3d 1372, 1377 (Fed.Cir.1996). In this regard, *see* Lucent Information Management, Inc. v. Lucent Technologies, 986 F.Supp. 253 (D.Del.1997), holding that an announcement letter and a few product presentations made before any actual sales took place were insufficient to establish a right of priority.

11. "Both the common law and the Lanham Act recognize that rights can be acquired in a service mark through use of the designation in rendering the service, such as its appearance on vehicles, equipment, or documents connected with the service, and also through use in advertising the service, whether at the point of sale or otherwise." Restatement (Third) of Unfair Competition § 18, Comment d (1995).

12. As the Supreme Court has noted, "The law of unfair competition has its roots in the common-law tort of deceit; its general concern is with protecting consumers from confusion as to source." Bonito Boats, Inc. v. Thunder Craft Boats, Inc., 489 U.S. 141, 157, 109 S.Ct. 971, 103 L.Ed.2d 118 (1989).

served, "the common law requirement of affixation is of little significance today."[13]

26.1.2 Type and Scope of Use Required Under Common Law

Since the point of trademarks is to enable consumers to relocate goods that they approve of, affixation of the mark to the goods by itself is not enough to create protectable trademark rights. After all, consumers are not likely to begin associating the mark with a particular producer if there are thousands of units of the merchandise with the mark affixed all sitting in a warehouse behind locked doors and none available for actual purchase in retail stores. Thus, at common law, a merchant must actually "use" the trademark, by selling or leasing goods or services bearing the mark to the public in bona fide transactions in order to earn protectable trademark rights. As one court has put it, "[t]he gist of trademark rights is actual use in trade."[14] Moreover, the use "must have substantial impact on the purchasing public."[15] Trivial or virtually invisible use of a mark will not be enough to establish common law trademark rights.

Many disputes have arisen about the details of what kind of use is necessary to achieve a protectable trademark right. A good illustration is *Blue Bell v. Farah Mfg. Co., Inc.*[16] There both parties hit upon the same trademark for men's clothing—TIME OUT. On July 3rd, Farah shipped 12 pairs of its new TIME OUT brand men's slacks to its own regional sales managers. Two days later Blue Bell took several pairs of another line of its own slacks, with a different cut and style from those that it eventually intended to market under the TIME OUT trademark, added new TIME OUT labels to them and shipped some of these double-labeled slacks to retail stores. The court held that neither of these actions created protectable trademark rights under Texas state law. Rather it found that Farah was the first user based on sales it subsequently made in the month of September.

The court disregarded Farah's July 3rd shipment because internal sales or transfers are not a type of use that can form the basis for a valid claim of trademark rights. Transfers of this type do not begin the process of acquainting the purchasing public with the mark.[17] It thus follows from *Blue Bell,* that the use in question must be in connection with genuine sales to the relevant consumers in order to secure trademark priority. Of course, for many goods, the relevant consumers may not be end users, but instead, retailers of various sorts. Thus if the maker of a

13. J Thomas McCarthy, Trademarks and Unfair Competition Law § 16:26 at 16–34.

14. Blue Bell v. Farah Mfg. Co., Inc., 508 F.2d 1260 (5th Cir.1975). When the merchant in question is a manufacturer who ordinarily distributes goods by selling them to retailers, rather than directly to end-users, the sales to the retailers are sufficient to create trademark rights. Indeed, that was the situation in the *Blue Bell* case itself.

15. T.A.B. Systems v. Pactel Teletrac, 77 F.3d 1372, 1376 (Fed.Cir.1996).

16. *Id.*

17. *See* Blue Bell, 508 F.2d at 1264–65 ("secret, undisclosed internal shipments are generally inadequate to support the denomination 'use.' ").

new branded men's electric razor sold several units to department stores or consumer electronics stores, those sales would be a legitimate basis for a claim of priority and ownership of the mark.

The *Blue Bell* court held that Blue Bell's July 5th shipment did not confer any trademark rights because "elementary tenets of trademark law require that labels or designs be affixed to the merchandise actually intended to bear the mark in commercial transactions."[18] This seems only logical. For instance, imagine that the Coca–Cola corporation came up with a great idea for a new mark for a new non-carbonated lemonade product—lets say LEMONTASTIC. If they began marking cans of their carbonated lemon-lime soda, now known as SPRITE, by adding the additional mark LEMONTASTIC and selling such dual-labeled cans to the public, this could not begin associating the word LEMONTASTIC with non-carbonated lemonade in the minds of the consuming public. If anything, such a course would only baffle consumers who would have no idea about the attributes of the product ultimately destined to bear the new mark. Similarly, courts have also found shipments of a prototype product bearing the proposed mark to a prospective manufacturer to be legally insufficient.[19]

What all this means is that courts usually look for genuine sales to actual end users of the actual goods destined to bear the mark when they determine who will prevail in a priority dispute.[20] Moreover, not only must a merchant make the right kind of use in order to acquire rights in the mark, but the amount of use must be adequate as well. A number of courts have indicated that if a merchant makes only a sporadic or inconsequential use of the mark, or if the sole purpose of the sales in question is to reserve rights in the mark, the use may be disregarded for priority purposes. In one opinion, the Third Circuit went so far as to characterize anything less than sales to 50 customers as "de minimis," and hence inadequate to establish rights to a mark,[21] though it is doubtful if other courts would, or should follow such a purported bright line test. Along the same lines, if a firm suspends sales shortly after making its first few sales, it may forfeit whatever ownership rights would normally accrue. In other words, use must normally be both non-trivial and continuous in order to sustain a claim of ownership of the trademark.

A good example of this sort of situation came up in *Zazu Designs v. L'Oreal, S.A.*[22] That cases concerned competing claims to the mark ZAZU for hair care products. The plaintiff, ZHD, was was a small hair salon in the Chicago suburb of Hinsdale, Illinois. While ZHD was technically the

---

18. *See* Blue Bell, 508 F.2d at 1267.

19. Walt Disney Productions v. Kusan, Inc., 204 USPQ 284 (C.D.Cal.1979).

20. Sometimes, however, other types of use will suffice. Thus, in G.D. Searle & Co. v. Nutrapharm, Inc., 1999 WL 988533 (S.D.N.Y.1999), the court found that the plaintiff's shipments of pharmaceutical drugs to an independent laboratory for purposes of clinical testing was sufficient to establish common law trademark rights.

21. Natural Footwear, Ltd. v. Hart, Schaffner & Marx, 760 F.2d 1383, 1400 (3d Cir.1985).

22. 979 F.2d 499 (7th Cir.1992).

first to use the mark, the court discounted its earliest efforts, commenting "ZHD's sales of its product are insufficient to establish priority over L'Oreal. A few bottles sold over the counter in Hinsdale, and a few more mailed to friends in Texas and Florida, neither link the ZAZU mark with ZHD's product in the minds of consumers nor put other producers on notice." The Seventh Circuit gave little weight to ZHD's de minimis use because it was unlikely to have come to the attention of competitors contemplating adoption of the mark. The *Zazu* court feared that any other approach would be unfair to subsequent users who might invest heavily in developing a mark, only to have their claim of ownership thwarted by a minimal user whose use would have been nearly impossible to discover.

To recapitulate, under state common law, the first party to "properly" use the mark will usually be deemed the owner. Courts will consider both the type and the amount of the use. The use in question may be advertisements that precede actual sales. It may be use on displays. Earlier sporadic uses by others may be disregarded, as well as uses that were merely designed to reserve rights. In essence, the courts try to resolve the question of ownership and priority on an equitable basis because "the concept of priority in the law of trademarks is applied 'not in the calendar sense' but on the basis of 'the equities involved.' "[23]

§ 26.2 Obtaining Federal Trademark Rights Through Federal Registration

Federal protection for trademarks is based on a "registration" system. This system is established by the federal trademark statute known as the Lanham Act.[1] Federal trademark registration is entirely optional. Once a firm has commenced use of a mark in bona fide sales to the public, it will be protected under the common law of its home state regardless of whether it has obtained a federal registration. Federal registration, however, confers numerous advantages. For instance, it guarantees the registrant trademark rights in all parts of the United States, even those regions where it might not have made any sales or done any advertising. As we shall see, the common law is not so generous. Second, only a federal registrant may use the ® symbol, which not only serves to put potential infringers on notice that the mark is protected, but may subliminally suggest some degree of quality to the consuming public. Third, federal registrants may invoke the assistance of the U.S. Customs service to prevent infringing imports from entering the country. In addition, registration provides constructive notice to other parties of the registrant's claim of ownership and the registration can be used in litigation as prima facie evidence of the registrant's ownership of the trademark. After five years, the registration can be declared incon-

23. Manhattan Industries, Inc. v. Sweater Bee by Banff, Ltd., 627 F.2d 628, 630 (2d Cir.1980), quoting Chandon Champagne Corp. v. San Marino Wine Corp., 335 F.2d 531, 534 (2d Cir.1964).

§ 26.2

1. 15 U.S.C.A. §§ 1051–1127 (1994).

testible, and can then be used in litigation as conclusive evidence of registrant's right to use the mark, subject only to itemized defenses. There are additional advantages of somewhat lesser importance as well, all of which serve as a strong incentive for many merchants to pursue federal registration.[2]

The Lanham Act allows registration of four different categories of trade identifying symbols. The first, obviously enough, is a trademark, which the statute defines as "any word, name, symbol, or device, or any combination thereof" that serves "to identify and distinguish his or her goods, including a unique product, from those manufactured or sold by others and to indicate the source of the goods, even if that source is unknown."[3] While there are some aspects of this definition that warrant exploration later, for present purposes this is simply a broad definition of any mark for goods. The statute refers separately to a "service mark" as the second type of registrable material. There are no surprises here— this is simply a mark for services.[4] The third potentially registrable mark is a "certification mark," defined as "any word, name, symbol, or device, or any combination thereof" that serves "to certify regional or other origin, material, mode of manufacture, quality, accuracy, or other characteristics" of goods or services.[5] Examples of certification marks include the Good Housekeeping Seal of Approval and the "UL" symbol of Underwriters Laboratories. Certification marks are not used by the entity that owns them. Rather, the owner permits others to use them when those others live up to certain standards. Finally, the statute refers to "collective marks" which are used "by the members of a cooperative, an association, or other collective group or organization."[6] Examples here might include the marks of organizations such as the Rotary Club, the Lions, the Elks, and the always popular International Order of Odd Fellows.

All four types of symbols can be referred to as "marks," and in most judicial and administrative opinions, any reference to trademarks is meant to encompass the other three varieties of marks as well. That is also true for the discussion that follows in this text. The Restatement (Third) of Unfair Competition tracks the Lanham Act by separately defining trademarks, service marks, certification marks, and collective marks[7] but earlier state law opinions rarely used any terminology other than "trademark" regardless of the type of identifying symbol at issue.[8]

---

2. *See* Peter B. Maggs and Roger E. Schechter, TRADEMARK AND UNFAIR COMPETITION LAW: CASES AND COMMENTS (6th ed. 2002) 42–43.

3. 15 U.S.C.A. § 1127 (2000).

4. Id.

5. Id.

6. Id.

7. *See* Restatement (Third) of Unfair Competition §§ 9–11.

8. The term "service mark" does appear in some older common law decisions. *See, e.g.,* Younker v. Nationwide Mutual Ins. Co., 175 Ohio St. 1, 191 N.E.2d 145, 149 (1963) ("A service mark, which is comparatively new in the law, is in effect a trademark which relates to a service rather than a product. It is a mark used in the advertising and sale of services of one person or firm to distinguish them from the services of another.").

There are two different bases upon which one may apply for federal registration of a mark. The first of these is a "use-based" application, which was the sole method provided until the Lanham Act was amended in 1988. That procedure is now set out in section 1(a) of the statute.[9] The alternative basis for registration created in 1988 is an application based on a "bona fide intent to use" the mark, described in section 1(b).[10] In addition, foreign applicants have a third potential basis of application—namely that they have obtained a previous registration in their country of origin. Each of these is discussed in turn in the subsections that follow.

26.2.1 Federal Registration Applications Based on Use

26.2.1.1 Type and Scope of Use Required

As we have seen, if a firm has made a valid first use of mark before seeking federal registration, that firm already has common law rights in that mark under the rules discussed in the previous section. One might conceive of federal trademark law as essentially nothing more than a system for registering these state law rights. The obvious analogy is to the procedure for automobile registration that exists in most jurisdictions—first one establishes ownership of the car by paying the seller and getting a certificate of title; then one registers that claim of ownership at the Department of Motor Vehicles by filling out some forms and paying a fee. This view of federal trademark law is only roughly accurate however.

First, federal trademark registration does not merely confirm state law rights, but actually affords new and additional rights, many of which are explored in the chapters to follow.[11] The Lanham Act, in other words, while a registration scheme in form, is much more than that in substance. Second, the "use" required as a predicate for a federal registration is not the same in nature and degree as that necessary to secure state common law rights. A firm may have used a mark in a way and to a degree that would give it a right to federally register even though it had not yet done enough to earn state common law rights. Alternatively, it might have earned the state right but still be unable to obtain registration because the use was inadequate for federal law purposes.

The Lanham Act says that a mark is used on goods when "it is placed in any manner on the goods or their containers or the displays associated therewith or on the tags or labels affixed thereto, or if the nature of the goods makes such placement impracticable, then on documents associated with the goods or their sale . . . ."[12] This definition is a bit narrower than the modern approach to "affixation" and "use" recognized under the common law and discussed in the preceding sec-

---

9. 15 U.S.C.A. § 1051(a) (2000).

10. 15 U.S.C.A. § 1051(b) (2000).

11. For instance, a federal registration provides constructive notice of the registrant's claim of ownership, and hence gives a registrant essentially nationwide rights even if it has only used the mark in a few states. *See* 15 U.S.C.A. § 1072 (2000). This provision is discussed in further depth in the section on geographically remote users in the chapter on Trademark Infringement further on in this text. *See* § 29.4, *infra*.

12. 15 U.S.C.A. § 1127 (2000).

tion. For instance it does not include pre-sales advertising within its scope. Nonetheless, the courts and the agency that actually registers trademarks—the United States Patent and Trademark Office or PTO—tend to interpret the language broadly, thus minimizing the differences. For instance, use of the mark on an instruction manual accompanying a hang glider was found a sufficient basis for federal registration in *In re Ultraflight*.[13] Usage in catalogs[14] and on trade show exhibit booths[15] has also been found to be a sufficient basis for federal registration. In the case of services, the Lanham Act is a bit more flexible, declaring that the mark is used "when it is used or displayed in the sale or advertising of services."[16]

Regarding the scope or amount of use necessary to support a registration, the story is a bit complicated. Prior to 1989, a less extensive quantity of use was required to qualify for a federal trademark registration than was necessary to prevail in a common law priority dispute.[17] In this era, sometimes the PTO and courts found even a single occasion of use to be sufficient for federal registration, under what was called the "token use" doctrine. As the Trademark Trials and Appeals Board of the PTO observed in 1974, "[i]t has been recognized and especially so in the last few years that, in view of the expenditures involved in introducing a new product on the market generally and the attendant risk involved therein prior to the screening process involved in resorting to the federal registration system . . . , a token sale or a single shipment in commerce may be sufficient to support an application to register a trademark in the Patent Office. . . ."[18]

The logic of the "token use" rule is hinted at in that last quotation. It can often take a firm many months to conceive of an appropriate and desirable mark for a new product. The firm then must design relevant packaging and develop an advertising campaign. Before making any use of the new mark in actual sales to real customers it may have spent hundreds of thousands of dollars and several months may have elapsed. Yet prior to 1989, the Lanham Act did not allow the firm to "reserve" the mark in question. Consequently, the firm might go to all this effort only to discover at the end of the process that its mark was ineligible for federal registration. Even more worrisome, in the interim, another firm

13. 221 USPQ 903 (T.T.A.B.1984).

14. Lands' End, Inc. v. Manback, 797 F.Supp. 511 (E.D.Va.1992).

15. In re Shipley Co., 230 USPQ 691 (T.T.A.B.1986).

16. 15 U.S.C.A. § 1127 (2000) (definition of "use in commerce").

17. "The 'use' required to establish trademark ownership under the common law is much stricter than the 'use' necessary to obtain trademark registration." Anthony L. Fletcher & David J. Kera, *Annual Review: The Fifty–First Year of Administration of the Lanham Trademark Act of 1946*, 89 T.M. REP. 1, 71 (1999). *See, e.g.*, Smith International, Inc. v. Olin Corp., 209 USPQ 1033, 1046 n. 4 (T.T.A.B.1981). Professor McCarthy has observed that "the distinction made between 'registration use' and 'priority use' does not and should not dictate that different legal standards apply, merely that the evidence should be more closely scrutinized in the latter situation." McCarthy § 19:116 at 19–208–09. It is unclear, however, that courts follow McCarthy's subtle suggestion in this regard.

18. Standard Pressed Steel Co. v. Midwest Chrome Process Co., 183 USPQ 758, 764 (T.T.A.B.1974).

might use the exact same mark on a very modest scale and then promptly register it, depriving the first firm of its right to federally register, once again resulting in the loss of its entire investment in developing the mark.

The courts and the PTO attempted to help firms mitigate these risks by accepting relatively minimal use as a sufficient predicate for a federal trademark registration application. Under this liberal view, the firm might be able to ship a single prototype unit bearing a mock-up label fairly early in the development process, and then apply for federal registration on the basis of that single sale, preventing it from losing its priority to a second party who coincidentally adopted the same mark a short time later. While some commentators have criticized the "token use" doctrine as unfair and harmful to consumers,[19] it was well-established in the pre–1989 period.

However, there were two key limitations on the idea that a mere token use could suffice as a predicate for federal registration prior to 1989. First, there had to be some evidence of an intent to continue making sales using the alleged trademark after the initial token use. As one court put it, "token transactions [are] accepted only where there is an accompanying intent to engage in continuing commercial use in the future."[20] If a token transaction was followed by a long period of non-use of the mark, courts essentially concluded that the firm in question abandoned any claim of rights in that particular trademark. Rather than use the rhetoric of abandonment of a vested right, however, courts often simply pointed to subsequent non-use to conclude that the earlier token use was not sufficient because it was evidence that the firm lacked the required intent when it made the "token use." Regardless of the language, however, the result was the same—without continuing use after the initial "token use," federal registration would be denied.

The second limit on the token use concept was that a sale could not be the basis for federal registration if it was a mere "sham." The PTO did not consider a sale to be a sham because it was made solely to establish the right to register, and as we have seen, it accepted quite minimal use of the mark as an adequate predicate for registration. However the PTO consistently held purely internal transfers, or alleged sales to friends and relatives to be in the sham category and thus not adequate for federal registration.[21] Of course the line between token and sham uses was never one that shimmered with great clarity. In the pre–

19. *See, e.g.,* Michael H. Davis, *Death of a Salesman's Doctrine: A Critical Look at Trademark Use,* 19 Ga. L. Rev. 233 (1985).

20. Blue Bell v. Jaymar–Ruby, Inc., 497 F.2d 433, 436 (2d Cir.1974).

21. *See, e.g.,* Management Publishing Group, Inc. v. Bill Brothers Publications, Inc., 154 USPQ 445 (T.T.A.B.1967) (copies of a company newsletter shipped to its own employees held insufficient to create any rights); Car Subx Service Systems, Inc. v. Exxon Corp., 215 USPQ 345 (T.T.A.B.1982) (shipment of car parts across state lines to spouse held not sufficient to create rights); Signature Guardian Systems, Inc. v. Lee, 209 USPQ 81 (T.T.A.B.1980) (shipment of check verification seals to friend for use "as he saw fit" held not a bona fide use of the mark in commerce).

1989 period the courts and the PTO attempted to draw that line as best they could based on the totality of all the circumstances.

Fortunately the "token use" doctrine and its various limitations and complexities came to an end in 1989 when amendments to the Lanham Act known as the Trademark Law Reform Act (TLRA) took effect. Those amendments created, for the first time in U.S. history, an intent-to-use basis for federal trademark registration. They also redefined the concept of use, for federal registration purposes, as "the bona fide use of a mark in the ordinary course of trade, and not made merely to reserve a right in a mark."[22] This effectively brings the federal statutory and state common law approaches to the problem of trademark use into rough harmony. Consequently today, the scope of use necessary to qualify for federal registration is much closer to that needed to demonstrate rights under state law. Nonetheless, some subtle differences may remain, as the Seventh Circuit suggested in 1992, when it observed that "use sufficient to register a mark that soon is widely distributed is not necessarily enough to acquire rights in the absence of registration."[23]

At all events, Congress did not mean to set the bar too high under the new standard of "bona fide use." The legislative history of the TLRA reveals that such activities as sales in a test market, or infrequent sales of large or expensive items qualify as "bona fide."[24] What will not qualify, however, is a single isolated sale that bears no relationship to a genuine plan for commercially exploiting the mark—something that would have been adequate under the repudiated token use doctrine. The logic of this new, more demanding standard regarding scope of use is that the need to resort to "token use" is now superfluous given the new "intent-to-use" provisions of the Lanham Act. As we shall see in the following sections, under those provisions, any firm desiring to lock in rights to a mark at an early stage in product development may now do so long before making even token sales, by simply declaring an intention to use the mark in the future.

The Lanham Act tests of use differ from those used under state common law in one other way. Regardless of whether one sought registration before or after 1989, the use relied on as a basis for federal registration must be a use "in commerce." This follows because Congress adopted the Lanham Act as an exercise of its commerce clause powers.[25] The Lanham Act appears to reach to the outer limits of

---

22.   15 U.S.C.A. § 1127 (2000).

23.   Zazu Designs v. L'Oreal, S.A., 979 F.2d 499, 503 (7th Cir.1992). *See also* Lucent Information Management, Inc. v. Lucent Technologies, 986 F.Supp. 253, 259 (D.Del.1997), *aff'd*, 186 F.3d 311 (3d Cir. 1999) ("the standard for determining which activities will establish ownership of a trademark without registration is much stricter than the standard for determining whether a mark is registrable").

24.   S. Rep. No. 100–525, 100th Cong. 2d Sess. 45 (1988).

25.   The Supreme Court held in the Trade–Mark Cases, 100 U.S. 82, 25 L.Ed. 550 (1879), that Congress could not regulate trademarks under the intellectual property clause of the Constitution, but only under the commerce clause.

Congress's constitutional authority, by defining use in commerce to include "all commerce which may lawfully be regulated by Congress."[26]

In cases involving services, courts agree that the rendering of services in a single state to persons traveling in interstate commerce is sufficient "use in commerce" to allow the merchant to secure a federal registration. Thus, in the *Gastown* case,[27] the Court of Customs and Patent Appeals found that automobile repair and maintenance services performed exclusively within the state of Ohio "affected" interstate commerce because the services were provided near an interstate highway to interstate travelers. Similarly, the Federal Circuit found that a single-location restaurant in a small town in Tennessee was using its mark in interstate commerce because approximately 15% of its customers came from out of state.[28] This approach, of course, is consistent with interpretations of the Commerce Clause that prevail in other areas of the law, such as those dealing with civil rights and anti-discrimination statutes.[29]

In cases involving the sale of goods, however, the PTO has traditionally been a bit more strict. Until recently, the agency demanded proof that goods bearing the trademark in question had actually crossed a state line. This seems to be both a somewhat mechanical interpretation of the commerce requirement and a stingy view of the extent of Congress's commerce power. In recent years, the agency has relaxed its practice a bit in response to criticism. Under current practice, an intrastate sale may be an adequate basis for registration, provide the applicant can demonstrate how the sale directly affects interstate commerce.[30] This approach certainly seems more consistent with recent Supreme Court commerce clause jurisprudence, even though it may occasionally impose some administrative burden on the PTO.

26.2.1.2 Registration Procedure at the Patent & Trademark Office

The first step in securing registration is filling out an application with the U.S. Patent and Trademark Office, or PTO. The federal trademark application form is a relatively short and simple one, as government forms go. The application must disclose the mark[31] and the categories of goods on which the mark has been used. These categories are grouped in various "international classes" that have been established by the World Intellectual Property Organization (WIPO) in Gene-

26. 15 U.S.C.A. § 1127 (2000).

27. 326 F.2d 780 (CCPA 1964).

28. Larry Harmon Pictures Corp. v. Williams Restaurant Corp., 929 F.2d 662 (Fed.Cir.1991), *cert. denied*, 502 U.S. 823, 112 S.Ct. 85, 116 L.Ed.2d 58 (1991).

29. *See, e.g.,* Heart of Atlanta Motel, Inc. v. United States, 379 U.S. 241, 85 S.Ct. 348, 13 L.Ed.2d 258 (1964) (motel that served interstate travelers held subject to federal civil rights statute); Katzenbach v. McClung, 379 U.S. 294, 85 S.Ct. 377, 13 L.Ed.2d 290 (1964) (restaurant that pur-

chased food from out of state held subject to federal civil rights statute).

30. *See* T.M.E.P. § 904.03 (1993).

31. In the parlance of the PTO, the applicant must submit a "drawing" of the mark. Where the mark consists of a logo of some kind, the PTO requires an ink drawing of the mark in the form in which it is being used. For marks that consist solely of words or phrases, the "drawing" is a single page with the mark typed in capital letters. See 37 C.F.R. § 2.51–52 (1998).

va. For example, an applicant might seek registration for a mark in International Class 5—Pharmaceuticals, and then list specific types of goods on which the mark had been used, such as "pain relief cream for arthritis" or "anti-depressant medication." The application must also include samples, such as labels, illustrating how the mark has been used and a declaration of when the mark was used for the first time. The applicant must swear that it knows of no one with a superior right to use the mark in question, and, naturally, the applicant must also pay the requisite fees as set out in regulations promulgated by the Patent and Trademark Office. At this writing the basic application fee is $325 per "class" of goods for which registration is being sought.[32] Registration applicants need not be represented by a lawyer, though it is often useful to have legal advice in navigating the registration process.

The application will then be assigned to an examining attorney. These examining attorneys are lawyers employed by the PTO who are charged with reviewing the application to determine if registration is proper. The attorney will first attempt to ascertain if the proposed mark is of a type which the statute forbids to be registered. We will review these various types of forbidden marks in detail in subsequent chapters, but just to take a concrete example for the purposes of this discussion, a mark cannot be registered if it "consists of or comprises the flag or coat of arms or any other insignia of the United States, or of any State or municipality, or of any foreign nation, or any simulation thereof."[33] If the examining attorney felt that the mark proposed in the application violated this prohibition—for instance because a proposed mark for spaghetti sauce appeared to resemble the flag of Italy—then that would be a reason for denial of registration.

One of the most important categories of forbidden marks are those which conflict with marks that have been previously used or registered by others for goods of the same or similar type. For obvious reasons it would make no sense to permit two different firms to register the same or closely similar marks for the same goods, since the whole point of a trademark is to identify a unique brand. As a result, examining attorneys must often make subjective judgments as to whether the proposed mark in an application is so similar to a previously registered or used mark as to be likely to cause confusion.[34]

During the course of this examination process the examining attorney usually communicates with the applicant in writing to discuss any perceived problems with the application. For instance, the examining attorney might feel that the description of the goods in the application is too broad, or that the submitted specimens are not adequate. These communications are called "office actions" and the applicant has six months to respond. An applicant can often persuade the examining

32. 37 C.F.R. § 2.6 (2000).

33. 15 U.S.C.A. § 1052(b) (2000).

34. They are guided in this exercise, and in most other administrative determi-nations, by a volume known as the "Trade-mark Manual of Examining Procedure" or TMEP.

attorney that a problem with the proposed mark is really not so serious as to warrant denial of registration, or alternatively, amend the application to eliminate the problem. In some cases, where the mark consists of multiple words, some of which are basic generic or descriptive terms, the examining attorney may request the applicant to "disclaim" those terms. This simply means that the applicant agrees to forego any claim of exclusive use of the terms in question, except as part of the larger composite mark. For instance, the applicant for the mark MONEY STORE for a lending business was required to disclaim the word "money" as part of the registration process.[35]

If, after this correspondence, the examining attorney ultimately concludes that the mark deserves to be registered, the proposed mark will then be published in a periodical called the Official Gazette of the Patent and Trademark Office. The Official Gazette is not what the average reader would consider to be a riveting magazine. It consists of page after page of proposed trademarks along with information about the party who has applied for the registration. The purpose of this publication is to allow members of the general public who have objections to registration to learn of the pending registration and to raise those objections with the PTO.

This procedure of raising an objection to registration after the mark is published is known as an "opposition." Oppositions must be filed within 30 days of publication in the Gazette.[36] If no opposition is filed within the 30 day period, the registration process is considered complete and the registration certificate will be issued. This registration will last for 10 years, but it may be renewed an unlimited number of times, provided the mark is still being used.[37] Moreover, even after registration, anyone damaged by the registration may petition to have it cancelled, though some grounds for cancellation cannot be asserted more than five years after registration.[38]

On the other hand, if an opposition is filed, the matter will be referred to an agency within the PTO known as the Trademark Trial and Appeals Board, or T.T.A.B. The opposing party will be given an opportunity to explain why it believes the mark should not be registered and the applicant will, of course, have a chance to respond.[39] Opposition proceedings are sometimes referred to as *inter partes* (Latin for "between parties") proceedings to indicate that there are two private litigants involved—the applicant and the opposer. After the T.T.A.B. renders its decision, the unsuccessful party may appeal the ruling to the Court of Appeals for the Federal Circuit.[40]

---

35. *See,* Federal Trademark Registration 0981752 (Registered April 2, 1974, Renewed April 2, 1994).

36. 15 U.S.C.A. § 1063 (2000).

37. 15 U.S.C.A. § 1059(a) (2000). The applicant must also file an affidavit between the fifth and sixth year after registration attesting that mark is still in use in interstate commerce. Failure to do so will result in cancellation of the registration. 15 U.S.C.A. § 1058 (a) (2000).

38. 15 U.S.C.A. § 1064 (2000).

39. 15 U.S.C.A. § 1067 (2000).

40. 15 U.S.C.A. § 1071(a) (2000).

If the examining attorney concludes that the mark is not eligible for registration, it will not be published at all. Instead, the examining attorney will send the applicant a notice of final denial. At that point, the unsuccessful applicant may appeal the decision to the T.T.A.B.[41] A proceeding of this sort is sometimes called an *ex parte* proceeding, because there is only one interested party before the tribunal—the unsuccessful trademark applicant. In an *ex parte* proceeding, the examining attorney will explain the reasons for denial, while the applicant will make the case for registration. After the T.T.A.B. decides, the matter is, as before, appealable to the Federal Circuit.

26.2.2 Federal Registration Applications Based on Intent–To–Use

One significant problem with the federal registration scheme described in the last subsection is that it requires the applicant to have already made use of the mark in question before beginning the trademark application process. As noted above, a firm might invest heavily in conceptualizing a mark and designing appropriate advertising and packaging materials to promote it, yet discover that before it actually begins use of the mark that another firm has beat it to the punch. It is for this reason that many other nations of the world do not require the use of a trademark as a prerequisite to legal protection.[42]

The United States did not get around to responding to this difficulty until the late 1980's, and even then, the solution did not dispense with the focus on actual use entirely. Amendments to the Lanham Act effective in 1989 created a new basis for filing a registration application. Codified in section 1(b) of the statute, this procedure is usually referred to as an "intent-to-use," or ITU, application.

Under this provision an applicant may file for federal registration before having used the mark, provided it has a *bona fide* intention to make such use in the future. Congress did not define the concept of "bona fide intent" to use, but the legislative history does observe that "[i]n connection with this bill, 'bona fide' should be read to mean a fair, objective determination of the applicant's intent based on all the circumstances," and that "applicant's bona fide intention must reflect the good-faith circumstances surrounding the intended use."[43] Elsewhere, the legislative history implies that multiple applications seeking to reserve a large number of proposed marks for the same new product might be an indication of lack of good faith.[44]

---

41. 15 U.S.C.A. § 1070 (2000).

42. Historically, the civil law countries—those in continental Europe, South America and much of Asia—have granted trademark rights to the first party to register a given mark, regardless of actual use. In most nations, the failure to use the mark within some specified period after registration—usually from 3 to 5 years—will result in a cancellation of the registration. For a good nation-by-nation summary of the basic rules governing trademark registration, *see* Robert Weston, John Hornick & Mario Arrigucci, COUNTRY GUIDES: BASIC INFORMATION ON TRADEMARK REGISTRATION WORLDWIDE (INTA 2d ed. 1998).

43. S. Rep. 100–515, 100th Cong., 2d Sess. 24 (1988).

44. Id. at 23–24.

If an applicant really does intend to begin use of a new trademark relatively soon, one would expect it to be able to produce a variety of written materials evidencing its plans. The lack of such material can suggest that the applicant does not have the statutorily required intent. Thus, in one of the few rulings on the issue, the T.T.A.B. has held "that absent other facts which adequately explain or outweigh the failure of an applicant to have any documents supportive of or bearing upon its claimed intent to use its mark in commerce, the absence of any documentary evidence on the part of an applicant regarding such intent is sufficient to prove that the applicant lacks a bona fide intention to use its mark in commerce as required by Section 1(b)."[45] On the other hand, the T.T.A.B. has recently cautioned that if the applicant is engaged in litigation over the right to use the mark, it might not undertake planning activities in connection with it until the legal controversy has been resolved. In such a situation, the absence of documents would be less significant.[46]

The ITU application materials are substantially the same as those filed with an application predicated on actual use, except of course that the ITU applicant need not provide specimens illustrating how the mark is being used. The ITU examination procedure is also basically the same as the one used for a use-based application. If the mark is found acceptable it will be published in the Official Gazette, and other parties will have the same 30 days to file an opposition as in the case of use-based applications. If the applicant begins using the mark in actual sales to the public before the PTO finishes reviewing the application, that applicant can file an "Amendment to Allege Use" essentially converting the application to one under section 1(a).[47]

If no oppositions are filed, or if one is filed but found meritless, the ITU applicant will then receive not a finalized registration, but rather something called a "notice of allowance."[48] Within six months of receiving this notice, the applicant must begin actually using the mark and file a statement to that effect at the PTO, known, amazingly enough, as a "Statement of Use" or SOU. Only after the applicant submits the SOU will an actual federal trademark registration be issued. The six month period can be extended for another six months if the applicant so requests. It can be extended still further if the applicant can show good cause, but any such further extensions cannot be for more than 24 months.[49]

Of course it is possible that after an ITU applicant files for federal registration, but before the process is completed, someone else may begin using the same or a highly similar mark on the same or closely related goods. For instance, assume that Alpha filed an ITU to register the mark

45. Commodore Electronics Ltd. v. Cbm Kabushiki Kaisha, 26 USPQ2d 1503 (T.T.A.B.1993).

46. Nautica Apparel, Inc. v. Crain, 2001 WL 1182881 (T.T.A.B.2001).

47. 15 U.S.C.A. § 1051(c) (2000).

48. 15 U.S.C.A. § 1063(b)(2) (2000).

49. 15 U.S.C.A. § 1051(d)(2) (2000). PTO regulations specify what constitutes a showing of good cause. *See* 37 C.F.R. § 2.89 (d) (2000).

BARIMBO for guitars on April 1, 2003. The examination process might take as much as 18 months, until October of 2004. Let us say that Beta corporation begins actually using the mark BARIMBA on ukeleles in September of 2003. Beta might argue that since it is the first user of the mark, Alpha should not be allowed to register its confusingly similar mark for such closely related goods. Yet, if Beta is allowed to prevail on an argument of this sort, the advantages of ITU registration would be substantially destroyed. The statute deals with this problem is section 7(c), which provides:

> Contingent on the registration of a mark on the principal register provided by this chapter, the filing of the application to register such mark shall constitute constructive use of the mark, conferring a right of priority, nationwide in effect, on or in connection with the goods or services specified in the registration against any other person except for a person whose mark has not been abandoned and who, prior to such filing—(1) has used the mark; (2) has filed an application to register the mark which is pending or has resulted in registration of the mark; or (3) has filed a foreign application to register the mark on the basis of which she or she has acquired a right of priority....[50]

Applying this section to the example discussed above, Alpha would be able to assert constructive use, and thus priority for the BARIMBO mark as of April 1, 2003—the date of its application—even though it had not actually made any sales until many months later. Its application of that date would—contingent on ultimate registration—be sufficient to permit it to defeat any argument by Beta of superior rights to the mark.[51] This is not only a necessary result to preserve the benefits of the ITU registration system, but it isn't really all that unfair to Beta. After all, before commencing its use in September, 2003, Beta could have done a trademark search.[52] Had it done so, it would have learned of Alpha's pending ITU application for a virtually identical mark on closely related goods. It could have then chosen an alternative mark. Having failed to do so, its not entirely unreasonable that its claims must yield to those of Alpha.

As you might expect, there are a number of additional technical issues surrounding the ITU application procedure and these are necessarily beyond the scope of this text. Indeed, demonstrating that no legal topic is so narrow that it cannot be the basis for searching examination, there is a 500–plus page book devoted solely to the intricacies of ITU applications under the Lanham Act.[53]

50. 15 U.S.C.A. § 1057(c) (2000).

51. Zirco Corp. v. American Telephone and Telegraph Co., 21 USPQ2d 1542 (T.T.A.B.1991).

52. One can hire a private firm to conduct a trademark search for a relatively modest fee. Increasingly, data about trade-

mark registrations and pending applications at the PTO are available on a variety of databases which can be searched directly by a lawyer at his or her desk.

53. See Phillip H. Smith, INTENT-TO-USE TRADEMARK PRACTICE (1992).

The key point to bear in mind about the ITU registration procedure is that ultimately, federal trademark registration in the U.S. still requires use. If, after receiving a Notice of Allowance, the ITU applicant never actually begins making sales of products or services bearing the mark in question, no final registration will issue.

26.2.3 Federal Registration Applications Based on Foreign Registrations

Firms based in the United States are not the only ones that seek federal trademark registrations under U.S. law. Many foreign firms wish to protect their marks in the U.S. as part of their efforts to market goods here. Their ability to do so follows not only from the provisions of the federal trademark statute, but also from U.S. obligations under various treaties, most notably a venerable one called the Paris Convention.[54] Where a foreign applicant for federal registration has already obtained a trademark registration from its home country,[55] it can use that foreign registration as a basis for an application under the Lanham Act.[56]

The procedure is basically the same as outlined in the sections above but with one significant distinction—registration will issue even if the applicant has NOT used the mark anywhere in the world. This is the only case where one can obtain a final, valid federal trademark registration under U.S. law without having made actual commercial use of the proposed mark. In this case however, the applicant holding the foreign trademark must allege a bona fide intention to use the mark in the future as part of its application in order to obtain the registration. Moreover, it must begin use of the mark in the United States within a reasonable time after the registration is granted.[57] Failure to do so will be considered abandonment of the mark and will result in cancellation of the registration.[58]

The foregoing discussion assumed that the foreign applicant for Lanham Act registration already had obtained a registration in its country of origin. However, even before a foreign firm obtains its foreign registration it may wish to pursue a U.S. registration. If it has previously filed a foreign trademark *application* in its country of origin, and it then files a U.S. application within six months, that U.S. application will be treated as if it was filed back on the earlier date of the foreign

---

54. The formal name of this treaty is the International Convention for the Protection of Industrial Property of 1883. It was most recently revised at Stockholm in 1967.

55. The Lanham Act refers to the "country of origin" which is the country where the applicant "has a bona fide and effective industrial or commercial establishment." 15 U.S.C.A. § 1126 (c) (2000).

56. 15 U.S.C.A. § 1126(e) (2000).

57. Sinclair v. Deb Chemical Proprietaries Ltd., 137 USPQ 161 (T.T.A.B.1963).

58. Imperial Tobacco, Ltd. v. Philip Morris, Inc., 899 F.2d 1575, 1582 (Fed.Cir. 1990) ("A section 44(e) registrant is merely granted a dispensation from actual use prior to registration, but after registration there is no dispensation of use requirements. If the registrant fails to make us of the registered mark for two years, the presumption of abandonment may be invoked against that registrant, as against any other.").

application.[59] This "priority" may allow the foreign applicant to obtain rights superior to a U.S. firm who is the actual first user of the mark in the U.S. Note that this is only a rule used to determine priority and not an independent basis for registration. The foreign application must ripen into a foreign registration (or the applicant must use the mark in domestic U.S. commerce) before any U.S. registration will be granted.[60]

While all this may sound convoluted, an example can help clarify the situation. Assume that MegaMuesli, a German firm, filed for a German trademark registration for the mark GUTTEN–TAG for breakfast cereal on March 10, under a German law that does not require any allegations of use. On May 5, Ellog, an American firm, by coincidence, began making sales of its own GUTTEN–TAG brand cereal here in the U.S. On June 25, Ellog then files an application for Lanham Act registration, under section 1(a) of the statute, alleging prior use of the mark in interstate commerce. Finally on August 20, MegaMuesli gets around to filing its own application for Lanham Act registration. Assume that at this point MegaMuesli still has not yet made any use of the mark either in the U.S. or elsewhere in the world.

In this situation, the American firm is both the first to use—indeed the only one to use—the mark in question, and the first to seek registration, since its June application pre-dates the German firm's August application. Nonetheless, MegaMuesli's application will be treated as if it was filed on March 10, because its U.S. filing is within six months of its original home country filing. The consequence is that MegaMuesli will be deemed to have priority[61] and, assuming that it eventually obtains a German trademark registration, it will be successful in getting the Lanham Act registration as well. Despite its investment in developing the name and actually marketing goods, Ellog, the U.S. firm, will now be forced to come up with a new trademark.

Of course, firms in the position of the U.S. cereal maker in the previous paragraph could attempt to avoid this "ambush" by searching foreign data bases for pending applications before beginning use of a mark. If the U.S. firm had done so in early May, before its first sales of GUTTEN–TAG, it would have found the pending March 10th German application filed by MegaMuesli. Nonetheless, searching numerous foreign registers to locate such applications, and then attempting to predict whether the applicant is planning to file a U.S. application, is time consuming, expensive and speculative business. It is not surprising, therefore, that the system for allowing foreign firms to use foreign application dates for priority purposes has been criticized.[62] It is, howev-

---

59. 15 U.S.C.A. § 1126(d) (2000).

60. The foreign applicant can also base the application on intent-to-use, just like any U.S. based applicant. Of course, in that case, no final registration will issue until proof of use is submitted to the trademark office.

61. Section 7(c), the constructive use provision of the Lanham Act, means that the foreign applicant will be treated as if it made first use of the mark on its priority date, namely the date of its *foreign* application. 15 U.S.C.A. § 1057(c) (1994).

62. *See, e.g.,* John B. Pegram, *Section 44 Revisions: After the 1988 Act,* 79 TRADE-MARK REP 220 (1989).

er, the price the U.S. pays for participation in otherwise beneficial international trademark treaty regimes—regimes that are discussed in greater detail in subsequent chapters of this book.

Chapter 27

THE DISTINCTIVENESS REQUIRE-
MENT AND ISSUES OF TRADE-
MARK VALIDITY

Table of Sections

While a firm might want to adopt and use a particular symbol to identify its goods or services, the proposed mark might not be eligible for trademark protection. The law does not recognize every possible symbol as a valid trademark. Some proposed marks may mislead the public through inaccurate representations. Others may already be viewed by the public as representing a competing merchant. Still others may violate some extrinsic social policy, such as the desire to keep the marketplace free from obscene words and pictures, or the desire to give individuals control over their personality. Finally giving a firm exclusive rights to some potential symbols may interfere with the rights of competing merchants to freely describe their goods and communicate with the public.

In thinking about trademark validity it is useful to bear in mind that the issue can come up in at least two contexts. First, when a firm seeks federal protection by applying for a Lanham Act registration, there will be an administrative determination of validity. If the mark is found unsuitable, registration will be refused. Second, if one firm accuses another of trademark infringement, the defendant will often argue that the plaintiff's mark is invalid. This argument can be raised whether the mark is federally registered, or whether it is allegedly protected under state common law. In either case, if the defendant can persuade a court that the term in question is not a valid mark, the plaintiff will be denied relief. Thus the rules governing trademark validity pervade a large number of trademark disputes.

Many prospective trademarks are nothing more than ordinary words or phrases drawn from regular language. Those words or phrases may—to a greater or lesser degree—describe the goods being sold. The more descriptive the words are, however, the more likely it is that other merchants will also need them, suggesting that no one firm should be allowed to monopolize them as a trademark. For instance, if the first firm in an area to sell baked loaves of yeast, flour and water was permitted.to sell them under the trademark BREAD, subsequent bakers might have a rather awkward time telling the public what they had available for sale. Protecting a mark consisting of the words FRESHLY BAKED might also lead to the same difficulties. To avoid such problems, the law requires that a trademark be "distinctive." No word, symbol or device can be protected as a trademark unless it satisfies this requirement of distinctiveness.

The distinctiveness of word-based trademarks is usually said to fall along a continuum or spectrum, explained perhaps most concisely in Judge Friendly's famous opinion in *Abercrombie & Fitch Co. v. Hunting World, Inc*.[1] Highly distinctive marks are those that have little or no capacity to describe the goods or services to which they are attached and, correspondingly, a high degree of uniqueness. Less distinctive marks are those that do little more than describe attributes of the goods or services in question. The less distinctive the mark, the less likely it is to be valid. Placing a mark precisely along this continuum is, of course, a subjective and tricky business. As one court put it, "these categories, like the tones in a spectrum, tend to blur at the edges and merge together. The labels are more advisory than definitional, more like guidelines than pigeon-holes."[2] The details of this principle are discussed in the several subsections that follow.

§ 27.1 Inherently Distinctive Terms

The distinctiveness of a mark depends on the relationship between the mark and the goods that are labeled with it. One cannot assess the

---

1. 537 F.2d 4, 9 (2d Cir.1976) ("The cases, and in some instances the Lanham Act, identify four different categories of terms with respect to trademark protection. Arrayed in an ascending order which roughly reflects their eligibility to trademark status and the degree of protection accorded, these classes are (1) generic, (2) descriptive, (3) suggestive, and (4) arbitrary or fanciful. The lines of demarcation, however, are not always bright.").

2. Zatarains, Inc. v. Oak Grove Smokehouse, Inc., 698 F.2d 786, 790 (5th Cir. 1983).

distinctiveness of a mark in a vacuum. Certain marks are considered to be inherently distinctive for certain types of goods. This is because they provide little if any direct information about the underlying product or service. As a consequence, their sole function in the eyes of the public is to designate a brand name. Consumers immediately assume that these terms are trademarks because they communicate no other information. Moreover, because words of this type convey little information it is unlikely that protecting them as trademarks will burden the ability of competitors to communicate with the public. As a consequence, the common law protects inherently distinctive marks from the time of first use in the market, and the Lanham Act permits their registration as soon as they have been used in interstate commerce.

There are three categories of word-marks that are usually considered inherently distinctive. The first of these are "fanciful" marks. There are marks consisting of wholly made up or "coined" words. Such marks have no other meaning besides their implication as the identifying symbol for a particular brand of goods or services. Classic examples of marks in this category include KODAK for films and cameras and KOTEX for sanitary napkins. A more modern example is the mark INTERMATIC for electronic products.[1] Since these words have no prior existence in the English language, giving the originator exclusive rights to use them does not impose any burden on competing firms.

Second are the "arbitrary" marks. Marks of this type are ordinary English words, but they have no particular connection to the goods or services being sold by the purported trademark owner. For instance the mark FOUR ROSES for whiskey or STORK CLUB[2] for a night club are arbitrary because the whiskey is not made out of flowers, nor do long-legged birds frequent the night club. Here again, note that competitors are not burdened by the legal decision to protect these marks. While a florist might need to use the phrase "four roses" and an exotic pet shop the words "stork club," competing distillers or night club owners have no real need for these terms in the ordinary conduct of their business. Another, more modern example of an arbitrary mark is APPLE for computers.

Both arbitrary and fanciful marks are usually considered highly distinctive and they conceptually belong at one extreme end of the distinctiveness continuum. Moving further down that continuum we come to "suggestive" trademarks. These marks hint at some of the properties of the goods or services they label, but do not provide an outright description of them. For example, COPPERTONE for suntan oil[3] suggests that the user of the product might achieve a coppery skin

§ 27.1

1. Intermatic, Inc. v. Toeppen, 40 USPQ2d 12 (N.D.Ill.1996), *adopted*, 947 F.Supp. 1227 (N.D.Ill.1996).

2. *See* Stork Restaurant v. Sahati, 166 F.2d 348, 355 (9th Cir.1948) (" 'The Stork Club' ... is in no way descriptive of the appellant's night club, for in its primary significance it would denote a club for storks. Nor is it likely that the sophisticates who are its most publicized customers are particularly interested in storks.").

3. Douglas Laboratories Corp. v. Copper Tan, Inc., 210 F.2d 453 (2d Cir.), *cert. de-*

tone—a look once considered highly desirable—but it requires some significant degree of imagination for the consumer to connect the brand name with suntan oil. Here, some competitors might wish to advertise that their product also gives the skin a copper-like tone, and trademark protection for the first user might prevent them from doing so. Nonetheless, their need to use that phrase seems slight at best. There are many other more direct ways to describe the properties of a tanning product. Based on this analysis, suggestive marks are treated exactly the same as arbitrary and fanciful marks—they are considered inherently distinctive; protected from the moment of first use; and registrable under the Lanham Act as soon as they are used in interstate commerce.

Inherently distinctive marks—whether arbitrary, fanciful, or suggestive—used to be known as "technical trademarks." In the first half of the 20th century, only technical trademarks could be protected via the common law cause of action for trademark infringement. Owners of all other types of trademarks had to resort to the more general claim for "unfair competition" in order to protect their marks. Moreover, only technical trademarks were eligible for protection under the Federal Trademark Law of 1905—the predecessor of the Lanham Act. This terminology is now no longer used, and the Reporter's Notes to the Restatement (Third) of Unfair Competition refers to it as "obsolete."[4] Nonetheless, familiarity with the vocabulary can help decode some language in older cases.

§ 27.2 Terms That May Become Distinctive Over Time

Some possible trademarks may not be considered legally "distinctive" when they are first used, because they provide relatively straightforward information about the attributes of the product or service being sold, where it comes from, or who is selling it. In other words, unlike fanciful, arbitrary or suggestive marks, they fall further down the continuum mentioned above, towards the non-distinctive side of the scales. Because these terms provide a relatively high degree of product information in a straightforward manner, competitor need for them is likely to be high. Moreover, consumers are likely to view them as mere explanations when they see them on packages, rather than as brand names. Consequently the law hesitates before assigning rights in such words exclusively to one merchant.

On the other hand, if a firm *is the only one* to use a term of this sort *for an extended period of time,* our reluctance to grant that firm trademark rights is likely to be diminished for two reasons. First, the fact that no one else is using the words in question for the type of product at issue tends to suggest that the competitors' need to use those words is somewhat less than we might have initially predicted—after all, if no one else is using them, than it would appear they don't need them.

nied, 347 U.S. 968, 74 S.Ct. 779, 98 L.Ed. 1109 (1954).

4. *See* Restatement (Third) of Unfair Competition, § 13 (Reporter's Note) (1995).

Second, the protracted exclusive use of the terms by one firm is likely to have caused consumers to now think of them as a true brand name. In circumstances such as this, it is said that the word or phrase has achieved "secondary meaning" and, as a result, is protectable as a trademark.

In the following subsections we will consider several different types of marks that are not inherently distinctive, but can become distinctive when they acquire secondary meaning. In the final subsection, the nature of secondary meaning is explored in greater detail.

27.2.1 Descriptive, Misdescriptive and Deceptive Terms

A mark is considered descriptive if it provides direct information about some aspect of the goods or services being sold. A descriptive mark might reveal something about the ingredients of the product, or its properties, or about the kind of people who are the likely users of the product. For example, courts have held the marks HOUR AFTER HOUR[1] for spray deodorant and STEAK AND BREW[2] for a restaurant to be descriptive terms. These are phrases that a competitor might very well need in communicating with the public. It is quite plausible that a rival deodorant maker might want to tell consumers that its product also lasts for hour after hour, not merely for ten or fifteen minutes, and a rival restauranteur might want prospective customers to know that both steak and brew are available at its establishment. Minor alterations or misspellings of descriptive terms do not alter their status as descriptive

As a general rule, self-congratulatory marks are treated in the same way. Thus terms such as DELUXE and GOLD MEDAL also fall in the "descriptive" category. There are, after all, dozens of merchants who would be happy to award themselves a gold medal of some kind or another. If a mark consists of foreign words, its descriptiveness is tested after translating the mark into English, unless it is from a dead or obscure language unlikely to be familiar to the American public. This is know as the doctrine of foreign equivalents. Thus, the mark SAPORITO for a brand of sausages was held descriptive because the word is Spanish for tasty.[3] On the other hand, a mark consisting of the ancient Babylonian word for tasty is unlikely to be classified as descriptive given the minuscule portion of the population literate in Babylonian.

If a mark consists of a composite of several words, its descriptiveness is determined based on a consideration of the mark as a whole—it is not "dissected." Thus, the U.S. Court of Appeals for the Ninth Circuit observed that the validity of "a composite term ... is not judged by an examination of its parts. Rather, the validity of a trademark is to be determined by viewing the trademark as a whole.... Thus the composite may become a distinguishing mark even though its component parts

§ 27.2

1. Johnson & Johnson v. Colgate–Palmolive Co., 345 F.Supp. 1216 (D.N.J.1972).

2. Longchamps, Inc. v. Eig, 315 F.Supp. 456 (S.D.N.Y.1970).

3. In re George A. Hormel & Co., 227 USPQ 813 (T.T.A.B.1985).

individually cannot.''[4] In a classic application of this rule, the mark
SUGAR & SPICE for bakery products was held to be a valid trademark
even though the individual terms in the mark were surely descriptive of
the products.[5]

Slogans can also pose problems of descriptiveness. Some slogans, of
course, are sufficiently clever to warrant classification as inherently
distinctive marks deserving of instantaneous trademark protection. For
instance, one court held the phrase UNDERNEATH IT ALL for wom-
en's undergarments to be suggestive because "the phrase 'requires
imagination, thought and perception to reach a conclusion as to the
nature of the goods.' "[6] Many other slogans, however, because they are
long explanatory phrases, are more likely to be categorized as descriptive. That was the case with the slogans USE ARRID TO BE SURE for
underarm deodorant,[7] and HAIRCOLOR SO NATURAL ONLY HER
HAIRDRESSER KNOWS FOR SURE for a hair coloring product.[8]

Descriptive marks are treated the same under both the common law
and the Lanham Act. They will not be given trademark protection until
the user has shown that secondary meaning has developed in the minds
of the consuming public.[9] As the U.S. Supreme Court summarized:

> Marks which are merely descriptive of a product are not inher-
> ently distinctive. When used to describe a product, they do not
> inherently identify a particular source, and hence cannot be
> protected. However, descriptive marks may acquire the distinc-
> tiveness which will allow them to be protected .... This ac-
> quired distinctiveness is generally called secondary meaning.[10]

Oddly, Congress did not actually use the term "secondary meaning" in
the Lanham Act. The statute declares that merely descriptive marks are
not eligible for immediate registration,[11] but goes on to provide that they
will be registered if they have "become distinctive of the applicant's
goods in commerce."[12] Substantively, this Lanham Act concept of "acquired distinctiveness" is identical to that of secondary meaning—the
difference is only one of terminology. Many judicial opinions refer to
secondary meaning even when discussing registrability under the Lanham Act,[13] and we use the term "secondary meaning" in this text to

4. California Cooler, Inc. v. Loretto Winery, Ltd., 774 F.2d 1451, 1455 (9th Cir. 1985).

5. In re Colonial Stores, 394 F.2d 549 (CCPA 1968).

6. Maidenform, Inc. v. Munsingwear, Inc., 195 USPQ 297 (S.D.N.Y.1977), quoting Stix Products, Inc. v. United Merchants & Mfrs. Inc., 295 F.Supp. 479, 488 (S.D.N.Y. 1968).

7. Carter–Wallace, Inc. v. Procter & Gamble Co., 434 F.2d 794 (9th Cir.1970).

8. Roux Laboratories, Inc. v. Clairol, Inc., 427 F.2d 823 (CCPA 1970).

9. Restatement (Third) of Unfair Competition § 14 (1995). Under the Lanham Act, this result is reached by the combined effect of subsections 2(e) and 2(f) of the statute.

10. Two Pesos, Inc. v. Taco Cabana, Inc., 505 U.S. 763, 769, 112 S.Ct. 2753, 120 L.Ed.2d 615 (1992).

11. 15 U.S.C.A. § 1052(e)(1) (2000).

12. 15 U.S.C.A. § 1052(f) (2000).

13. *See* J. Thomas McCarthy, TRADE-MARKS AND UNFAIR COMPETITION § 15:60 ("The phrase 'has become distinctive' in the Lanham Act is synonymous with the

cover both the common law concept and the parallel Lanham Act idea of acquired distinctiveness.

Since a suggestive mark will be protected—and registrable—from the moment of first use, while a descriptive mark requires proof of secondary meaning before protection and registration, categorizing a mark as either suggestive or descriptive is of great legal significance.[14] Unfortunately, deciding which side of this line a given term falls on is an extremely imprecise process. No less a figure than Learned Hand effectively threw up his hands and conceded that the whole matter is subjective when he commented that "it is quite impossible to get any rule out of the cases beyond this: That the validity of the mark ends when suggestion ends and description begins."[15] With all respect to the great jurist, this is less than entirely helpful.

Courts and commentators have suggested a number of tests for determining if a mark is descriptive. As a first step, courts often consider the degree of consumer imagination that is required to derive useful information from the mark. If significant imagination is required, the mark will be treated as suggestive. If little or no imagination is required, than the descriptive designation is more appropriate. As one judge summarized, "a term is suggestive if it requires imagination, thought and perception to reach a conclusion as to the nature of the goods. A term is descriptive if it forthwith conveys an immediate idea of the ingredients, qualities or characteristics of the goods"[16]. Applying this test, the U.S. District Court for New Jersey found that the mark JEWS FOR JESUS was descriptive because it would not take much imagination to deduce that it was an organization of Jewish persons who had embraced the teachings of Jesus.[17] This is essentially the same thing as asking how much creativity inheres in the mark.[18] Naturally, the more creative the mark, the more imagination consumers will require to extract product related data from it.

Trademark examining attorneys at the PTO often consider usage in popular newspapers and magazines to shed light on how consumers understand a given term.[19] The Fifth Circuit has observed that "a

---

term 'secondary meaning.' "); In re Dial–A–Mattress Operating Corp., 240 F.3d 1341, 1347 (Fed.Cir.2001).

14. The assignment of a mark to one side or the other of the descriptive/suggestive line is considered a question of fact. Thus, it is normally not disturbed on appellate review unless the appellant can demonstrate that the trial court's conclusion was clearly erroneous. *See, e.g.,* Mil–Mar Shoe Co. v. Shonac Corp., 75 F.3d 1153 (7th Cir.1996); Bristol–Myers Squibb Co. v. McNeil–P.P.C., Inc., 973 F.2d 1033 (2d Cir.1992); Towers v. Advent Software, Inc., 913 F.2d 942 (Fed.Cir.1990).

15. Franklin Knitting Mills v. Fashionit Sweater Mills, 297 F. 247, 248 (S.D.N.Y.1923), *aff'd,* 4 F.2d 1018 (2d Cir.1925).

16. Stix Products, Inc. v. United Merchants & Mfrs. Inc., 295 F.Supp. 479 (S.D.N.Y.1968).

17. Jews for Jesus v. Brodsky, 993 F.Supp. 282 (D.N.J.1998).

18. *See* Security Center Ltd. v. First National Security Centers, 750 F.2d 1295, 1299 (5th Cir.1985).

19. In one recent case the Board declared: "The use of a term in a descriptive or generic manner in a variety of general circulation newspapers is a strong indication that the general public views the term as a descriptive or generic term for the particular goods." In re Ralph S. Gray, 2002 WL 550241 (T.T.A.B.2002). In making descriptiveness determinations, the focus is

suitable starting place is the dictionary, for the dictionary definition of the word is an appropriate and relevant indication of 'the ordinary significance and meaning of words' to the public."[20]

Another approach to categorizing marks as suggestive or descriptive is to consider the likely degree of competitor need for the terms in question. The higher the perceived need, the more appropriate the "descriptive" designation will be. Of course, this is merely the reciprocal of the imagination test. "As the amount of imagination needed increases, the need of [competitors to use] the mark to describe the product decreases."[21] Closely related to this competitor need inquiry is an examination of how often, if at all, the term is actually being used by competitors. "If it has been frequently so used, the inference is warranted that it is not purely arbitrary; that it would be likely to be understood by purchasers as identifying or describing the merchandise itself, rather than the source thereof and hence as having little or no trademark significance."[22]

While these various tests can help guide decisions, the suggestive/descriptive determination still remains subjective. That hardly makes it unique in the law. The questions of reasonableness in the law of negligence and of unconscionability in the law of contracts suffer from the same difficulty. The best that can be done is to make the decision in light of its purposes. The key question is whether granting immediate legal protection to the prospective mark would be fair to consumers and competitors, or whether it would be preferable to demand something more from the proponent of the mark, namely proof of secondary meaning, before the protection is granted.

A further complexity can be introduced when a merchant seeks trademark protection for descriptive terms that are factually inaccurate when applied to its own products. For instance, a firm might apply the purported trademark GLASS WAX to a glass polish that contains no wax.[23] This has the same problem as the use of any descriptive term because competitors who market a wax based polish may need the phrase to describe their own products, and consumers might not perceive the phrase to be a brand name, but rather a mere description of contents. It also has a further vice. It can potentially mislead consumers. Obviously, the law should hesitate considerably before granting terms likes these the status of a trademark.

supposed to be on prospective customers of the goods in question, not on the general public. Educational Dev. Corp., v. Economy Co., 562 F.2d 26 (10th Cir.1977). Thus reliance on general circulation magazines and newspapers is appropriate only when the product is one that will be marketed to the general public.

20. Zatarains, Inc. v. Oak Grove Smokehouse, Inc., 698 F.2d 786, 792 (5th Cir. 1983).

21. Miss World (UK) Ltd. v. Mrs. America Pageants, 856 F.2d 1445, 1449 (9th Cir. 1988).

22. Shoe Corp. of America v. Juvenile Shoe Corp., 266 F.2d 793, 796 (CCPA 1959).

23. This example is based on Gold Seal v. Weeks, 129 F.Supp. 928 (D.D.C.1955), aff'd, 230 F.2d 832 (D.C.Cir.1956), cert. denied, 352 U.S. 829, 77 S.Ct. 41, 1 L.Ed.2d 50 (1956).

The Lanham Act does exactly that by declaring, in section 2(e) that a mark that is "merely ... deceptively misdescriptive" of the goods or services in questions cannot be registered without proof of secondary meaning.[24] The Restatement (Third) of Unfair Competition takes the same approach for cases involving common law trademark rights. It observes:

> The issue in determining descriptiveness is whether the designation is likely to be perceived as merely descriptive, not whether the perceived description is factually correct. Thus, a person claiming rights in a descriptive designation cannot avoid the requirement of establishing secondary meaning by arguing that the description is inaccurate. "Misdescriptive" designations are therefore subject to the same rules applicable to other descriptive terms. [The mark] G.I. used on gun-cleaning equipment, for example, is descriptive if the equipment is in fact government issue and misdescriptive if it is not; in neither case is the designation inherently distinctive.[25]

In order to be classified as "deceptively misdescriptive" a mark must first "misdescribe." In other words, it must be inaccurate. But that alone is not enough. Mere falsity will not render the mark problematic. For instance, BLACK & WHITE for scotch whiskey is arguably inaccurate, because the whiskey is not, one hopes, colored black and white. Nonetheless, this mark is not *deceptively* misdescriptive because only a tiny number of rather peculiar consumers would be duped. A mark such as this is actually arbitrary, and protectable without any showing of secondary meaning.[26] Thus, only marks that are *believably* false will be put into the "deceptively misdescriptive" pigeonhole.

Deceptively misdescriptive marks should be distinguished from marks that are flat out "deceptive." Unlike deceptively misdescriptive terms, deceptive terms are absolutely ineligible for trademark protection and proof of secondary meaning cannot save them.[27] The difference between "deceptively misdescriptive" marks and those that are "deceptive" turns on the question of materiality.[28] For instance, the mark GLASS WAX, for a window cleaner with no wax content, is both inaccurate, and believable—the product lacks an ingredient that is promised by the brand name, and the average consumer would assume that a product with such a name would contain some wax. It is thus "deceptively misdescriptive" and not protectable as a trademark without

24. 15 U.S.C.A. § 1052(e) (2002).

25. Restatement (Third) of Unfair Competition, § 14, comment c (1995).

26. Fleischmann Distilling Corp. v. Maier Brewing Co., 314 F.2d 149 (9th Cir.), *cert. denied*, 374 U.S. 830, 83 S.Ct. 1870, 10 L.Ed.2d 1053 (1963).

27. *See* 15 U.S.C.A. § 1052(a) (1996) (Lanham Act provision barring registration of deceptive marks); Restatement (Third) of Unfair Competition § 32 ("If a designation used as a [mark]... is deceptive ... the owner may be barred in whole or in part from [common law] relief that would otherwise be available."). *See also* Worden v. California Fig Syrup Co., 187 U.S. 516, 23 S.Ct. 161, 47 L.Ed. 282 (1903) (Mark SYRUP OF FIGS denied protection where fig syrup was not a product ingredient).

28. In re Shapely, Inc. 231 USPQ 72 (T.T.A.B.1986).

proof of secondary meaning. Nonetheless, the consumer ultimately does not care whether the product has wax or not, so long as it works well. Upon being told the truth the consumer is not likely to fly into a rage. The misrepresented characteristic is simply not material to the purchaser.

On the other hand, the mark SILKEASE for polyester blouses is not only believably false, but goes to a product attribute that consumers undoubtedly consider material. The purchaser of this blouse will almost certainly feel duped upon learning it was made from petroleum derivatives rather than from elegant silk fibers. Hence this mark, because it does, in fact, make a material misrepresentation, will be deemed "deceptive."[29]

27.2.2 Geographic Terms

Many merchants quite naturally attempt to use the name of the place where their activities are located as a brand name for their goods or services. There is a pretty good chance that the owner of a bagel factory located in Brooklyn might choose to call the products BROOKLYN bagels, just as the owner of a Los Angeles plastic surgery clinic might opt to use that city's name as the service mark for the business. Consumers, however, may regard such terms not as signaling a particular source for the goods or services, but rather merely as information that describes where they come from or where the vendor is located. Moreover, other firms in the same area may wish to use the relevant geographic term in connection with their own competing marketing activities. Surely there is more than one plastic surgeon in L.A., and they all may wish to boast of their strategic location in Hollywood's back yard. In other words, a geographic term is like virtually any other descriptive word or phrase, and consequently trademark law treats it just that way.

Under both the common law and Lanham Act, a geographically descriptive term is not protected as a valid trademark until it has achieved secondary meaning. As the comments to the Restatement (Third) of Unfair Competition explain, "the rationale for the requirement of secondary meaning for geographically descriptive terms is analogous to that applicable to other descriptive designations. Consumers may perceive the designation only in its geographically descriptive sense rather than as a symbol of source or other association with a particular person.... That a watch is Swiss, that wine is from California, that maple syrup is from Vermont, or that a dress has been designed in New York or Paris are facts in which consumers are interested and which sellers therefore wish to disclose in a prominent manner.... [M]erchants should remain free to indicate their place of business or the origin of their goods without unnecessary risk of infringement."[30]

29. Gold Seal Co. v. Weeks, 129 F.Supp. 928 (D.D.C.1955), *aff'd per curiam*, 230 F.2d 832 (D.C.Cir.1956), *cert. denied* 352 U.S. 829, 77 S.Ct. 41, 1 L.Ed.2d 50 (1956).

30. Restatement (Third) of Unfair Competition § 14, comment d (1995).

Application of this principle has required courts and the Patent and Trademark Office to develop some rules about what terms should be considered "geographic" and when geographic terms will be considered "descriptive" of goods. As to the first question, courts have taken a broad approach, holding that the use of almost any recognizable place name on earth should be treated as geographic in nature. Thus the names of countries, states and cities, and their subdivisions such as counties or neighborhoods are "geographic" term. So are the names of geographic features like mountains, and rivers. Even the map of Canada that appears as a logo on the label of CANADA DRY brand soft drinks was held, logically enough, to be geographic in nature.[31]

On the other hand, remote and obscure place names may not convey any specific geographic impression to the public, and are usually granted trademark protection without any requirement of secondary meaning. Thus, the Trademark Trial & Appeals Board found that the mark JEVER for beer made in the small German village of Jever did not primarily denote a geographic place.[32] Similarly, terms like WORLD or GLOBE are not considered "geographic" since they communicate only the unremarkable fact that the product was made on planet Earth.[33] By the same logic, terms that imply extraterrestrial origin for a product, such as SATURN for automobiles, are similarly outside the orbit of the geographically descriptiveness concept, and can be protected without proof of secondary meaning.

The more challenging question is to determine when a geographic term is being used in a descriptive way. If the goods are actually made in the geographic place designated by the mark a finding of geographic descriptiveness is appropriate, if there is a "good-place association." This will arise when consumers would assume that goods of this type come from the geographic place designated by the mark. For example, on seeing the mark WALTHAM used on watches made in Waltham, Massachusetts, consumers are likely to think that the watches do indeed come from that town as that town used to have something of a reputation as a watch-making center. As a result, such a mark is classified as geographically descriptive. It requires secondary meaning both in order to be protected at common law and in order to be federally registered under the Lanham Act.

On the other hand, if the products do not come from the indicated locale things can get a bit more puzzling. If no reasonable consumer would conclude that the goods come from the indicated place, the mark is considered arbitrary. A classic example is the mark DUTCH BOY for paint. As the Ninth Circuit pointed out:

> [T]here is no likelihood that the use of the name "Dutch" or "Dutch Boy" in connection with the appellant's goods would be

31. In re Canada Dry Ginger Ale, Inc., 86 F.2d 830 (CCPA 1936).

32. In re Bavaria St. Pauli Brauerei ag, 222 USPQ 926 (T.T.A.B.1984).

33. *See* World Carpets, Inc. v. Dick Littrell's New World Carpets, 438 F.2d 482 (5th Cir.1971).

understood by purchasers as representing that the goods or their constituent materials were produced or processed in Holland or that they are of the same distinctive kind or quality as those produced, processed or used in that place.[34]

A mark of this sort is entitled to trademark protection at common law from the time of first use, and will be eligible for immediate federal registration under the Lanham Act. Other examples of arbitrary usage of geographic terms include ATLANTIC for magazines and books, and PHILADELPHIA for cream cheese.

Of course, there can be situations where the geographic designator used as a purported mark is inaccurate but plausible. If consumers are likely to assume that the goods do, in fact, come from the place indicated, an inaccurate geographic mark has the potential both of deceiving consumers, and of handicapping merchants who are truly located at the designated place. Under the Lanham Act, such marks are considered "primarily geographically deceptively misdescriptive."

Originally, a primarily geographically deceptively misdescriptive term was registrable upon a showing of secondary meaning. However, in order to comply with provisions of the NAFTA agreement, Congress changed this provision in 1993. Under the amended provisions, primarily geographically deceptively misdescriptive terms are now absolutely ineligible for federal trademark protection and cannot be saved by secondary meaning. This absolute prohibition is also required by the even more recent TRIPS Agreement, which declares that: "Members shall provide the legal means for interested parties to prevent: (a) the use of any means in the designation or presentation of a good that indicates or suggests that the good in question originates in a geographical area other than the true place of origin in a manner which misleads the public as to the geographical origin of the good."[35]

The Federal Circuit recently restated the test for a mark to be considered primarily geographically deceptively misdescriptive. Such a "mark must (1) have as its primary significance a generally known geographical place; and (2) identify products that purchasers are likely to believe mistakenly are connected with that location."[36]

Another provision, recently added to section 2(a) of the Lanham Act, absolutely bars the registration of "a geographical indication which, when used on or in connection with wines or spirits, identifies a place other than the origin of the goods and is first used on or in connection with wines or spirits by the applicant" after January 1, 1996. As with the new rules on primarily geographically deceptively misdescriptive marks, Congress also added this provision to bring U.S. law into compliance with international agreements. It is obviously designed to ban the

34. *See* National Lead Co. v. Wolfe, 223 F.2d 195, 199 (9th Cir.1955).

35. Article 22, TRIPS Agreement.

36. In re Wada, 194 F.3d 1297 (Fed.Cir. 1999) (NEW YORK WAYS GALLERY for luggage and other leather items held primarily geographically deceptively misdescriptive).

federal registration of such place names as Bordeaux or Champagne as trademarks for wine, but grandfathers certain parties who began their use before the effective date of the amendments. This resolves a long simmering grievance between the United States and certain other countries who resented the geographic presumptuousness of various U.S. wineries and distillers.

27.2.3 Personal Names

One of the most natural and obvious brand names for a new product or service is the surname of the person operating the business. From KRAFT cheese and MCDONALD'S restaurants to the BATES Motel, marks based on personal names pervade the commercial landscape. These marks, however, have much in common with descriptive phrases and geographic place names, or at least this has been traditionally thought to be the case. The argument is that all competitors who share the same name have a significant interest in informing the public who is behind the business, and that this will be true whether they enter the trade early or late. Thus, granting trademark status to the first party who happens to use the common name would work a hardship on all the others. Moreover, because many people have the same names, consumers will not necessary assume that all products bearing the same personal name designation come from the same source. To take an obvious example, few souls think that all diners named JOE's are owned by the same Joe. While the validity of these arguments in the impersonal world of 21st century marketing is open to question, they have been influential in shaping the state of the law.

Consequently, the law does not provide immediate protection to a personal name used as a trademark, protecting it only upon a showing of secondary meaning. The rule applies under both the common law and the Lanham Act. As the Restatement (Third) of Unfair Competition summarizes, "[p]ersonal names, including both first names and surnames, are not considered to be inherently distinctive and therefore are protectable as trademarks or trade names only if they have acquired secondary meaning."[37] The governing Lanham Act provisions are found in section 2(e)(3), which permits the PTO to deny registration to a mark that "is primarily merely a surname," and in section 2(f) which then provides that a surname mark may be registered if it has "become distinctive" of the goods.

In order to implement this principle, the case law has developed guidelines for identifying surnames. The key principle is straightforward and no surprise—a word is a surname if that is its primary significance to the public. As the PTO has put it: "When [a word] is used in trade it must have some impact upon the purchasing public, and it is that impact or impression which should be evaluated in determining whether or not the primary significance of a word when applied to a product is a surname significance. If it is, and it is only that, then it is primarily

---

37. Restatement (Third) of Unfair Competition § 14, comment e (1995).

merely a surname.''[38] Under this rule, when a word is both a normal term in the English language and a surname, it will not be considered *primarily merely* a surname. For instance King happens to be the surname of a considerable number of people in this country, but it is also a common noun meaning a male monarch. If a firm chooses to market KING brand razors or KING brand ironing boards, the term will not be considered a surname because the public is not like to perceive it as such. Consequently those marks are likely to be considered arbitrary and protected from first use without a need for the user to show secondary meaning. On the other hand, words like Goldstein, McCarthy, Gonzalez, Gandhi, Habib and Armstrong are widely recognized as surnames, and have no other possible meaning. Thus they require secondary meaning for trademark protection.

Under federal law, it does not matter if the proposed trademark is the name of anyone actually affiliated with the business in question. Thus, McCarthy is primarily merely a surname whether a person named McCarthy runs the business or not. However, according to the PTO, ''the fact that a term is the surname of an individual associated with the applicant ... is evidence of the surname significance of the term.''[39] Consider a case where a firm wishes to use the word REBO as a mark. The word Rebo could be a somewhat unusual surname, of course, or it simply could be a coined, arbitrary word. In making the judgment, the PTO will tip towards the surname categorization if someone named Rebo is the chief operating officer of the company.[40] The Restatement, requires secondary meaning when the term ''is likely to be perceived by prospective purchasers .. as the personal name of a person connected with the goods, services or business....'' This does not, of course, require that any such person actually be connected with the business, merely that the public might believe that to be the case, as the language clearly directs our attention to public perception, not the underlying factual reality. The Restatement standard is substantially equivalent to the primary significance test that prevails under federal law.

Other factors the Office considers in determining if a mark is primarily merely a surname include telephone directory listings, information obtained from computerized data bases, and specimens showing how the mark is actually being used. The addition of an initial or a title to a surname does not eliminate the primary surname significance of the term, and indeed may make a finding of surname significance more likely. Thus S. SEIDENBERG & CO'S and MLLE. REVILLON were both held to be primarily merely surnames.[41] The same approach is used where the surname is in plural or possessive form.

The surname of a famous historical personage that is immediately recognizable as such is treated differently. When consumers encounter

---

38. Ex parte Rivera Watch Corp., 106 USPQ 145 (Comm'r Pat.1955).

39. Trademark Manual of Examining Procedures, § 1211.02(b)(iii) (3d Ed. 2002).

40. In re Rebo High Definition Studio, Inc., 15 USPQ2d 1314 (T.T.A.B.1990).

41. In re I. Lewis Cigar Mfg. Co., 205 F.2d 204 (CCPA 1953); In re Revillon, 154 USPQ 494 (T.T.A.B.1967).

names such as WASHINGTON, LINCOLN and JEFFERSON in connection with sober and patriotic businesses such as banking or insurance, they are not likely to think that anyone with those names is running the business. Rather their minds are likely to evoke an image of the three presidents who bore those names. In the words of the Lanham Act, these names are not "merely" surnames. As one court explained in considering the mark DA VINCI for jewelry: "The contention that the mark is primarily a surname and hence barred from registration on the principal register by § 1052(e) is met by the fact that names of historical characters or noted persons are registrable, provided the primary connotation of the mark is of the historical character.... [T]he name Da Vinci, even without the given name Leonardo, comes very near having as its exclusive connotation the world-renowned 15th century artist, sculptor, architect, musician, engineer and philosopher ... and hardly suggest that he personally had something to do with the designing of plaintiff's luggage."[42] The common law view on this point is the same, and this is reflected in a comment to section 14 of the Restatement.[43]

Where a surname is combined with the generic term for the type of goods being marketed, it will still be considered "primarily" merely a surname. Thus marks such as O'CONNER COMPUTERS or LEVINE SHIRTS are no different than simple, unadorned surnames in the eyes of the law. However, when a surname is combined with other, non-generic, words, the compound mark is also no longer "merely" a surname and is likely to be registrable at the PTO and protectable under common law from the time of first use. This is because of the general legal principle that marks should not be "dissected" when their validity is analyzed, and because of the policy observation that competitors have a much weaker case of need where the mark is compound.

An example of a protectable compound mark involving a surname is the mark HUTCHINSON TECHNOLOGY for disk drives and other electronic products, which the Federal Circuit held registrable regardless of secondary meaning.[44] Certainly, in a mechanical sense, this mark is not "merely" a surname, because it includes a second word, and not even "primarily merely" a surname, because the second word is non-generic. Nonetheless, cases of this sort may be a bit more problematic than the Federal Circuit implied. If a second Hutchinson were to market its own disk drives under the unadorned mark HUTCHINSON, the owners of the HUTCHINSON TECHNOLOGY mark would no doubt bring trademark infringement claims, alleging a likelihood of confusion, and they might very well prevail. Thus the second Mr. Hutchinson is hindered in the use of his name just as much as if the first firm had secured a registration on the single word HUTCHINSON prior to achieving secondary meaning. That being so, perhaps HUTCHINSON

42. Lucien Piccard Watch Corp. v. 1868 Crescent Corporation, 314 F.Supp. 329 (S.D.N.Y.1970).

43. Restatement (Third) of Unfair Competition § 14, comment 3 (1995).

44. In re Hutchinson Technology Inc., 852 F.2d 552 (Fed.Cir.1988).

TECHNOLOGY should not have been protected until secondary meaning had been shown.

The concern for second users with similar names has been the source of much of the litigation involving personal names marks. Defendants in such cases usually argue that everyone should have a right to use his own name is business, even if a senior party has been making long use of the name in question. Courts have often been moved by this plea. Historically there has been significant judicial reluctance to prohibit entirely a merchant's right to use his own name in commerce. Some older cases even refer to the right to use one own name as "sacred" and "absolute" and deny the senior user any relief at all.

The contemporary view, however, is that the junior user's supposed right is, at most, only a qualified one. Thus, a plaintiff who has secondary meaning in a surname mark will usually be granted some relief against a similarly named junior user, but he or she may not be able to secure an absolute injunction forbidding a competitor from all uses of the common name in his or her business. Rather the courts will often opt for a "qualified injunction" that might permit some subordinate use of the surname provided that it is done in such a way as to minimize confusion. For instance, the junior user of the surname might be permitted to continue use of the name so long as it is always accompanied by both a first name and a disclaimer. Or the injunction might limit the defendant to using the name only in a non-trademark fashion—for instance, only as part of an address that might appear on the back of a label. The Lanham Act provides, in fact, that the non-trademark use of a "party's individual name in his own business" is not considered infringement.[45]

An interesting illustration of how courts try to balance interests in this area is the litigation that arose over the use of the name "Taylor" for wine. The Taylor Wine Company had sold wines since 1880 under the TAYLOR mark, had developed a strong reputation and owned several federal trademark registrations for the mark. Walter S. Taylor was a grandson of one of the original participants in the Taylor Wine Company, and a serious vintner in his own right. As owner and operator of the Bully Hilly Vineyards, he began selling a line of wines under the brand WALTER S. TAYLOR and litigation ensued. The trial court entered an absolute injunction, but on appeal, the Second Circuit modified the order.[46] It observed:

> We do not doubt the necessity for an injunction in this case, but we think that its provisions were too broad. Walter S. Taylor is apparently a scholar of enology and a commentator on wines. He runs a wine museum in the Finger Lakes District, and seems to be a person sincerely concerned with the art of wine-growing. Yet, in granting him the right to let people know that he is personally a grower and distributor of regional wines,

45. 15 U.S.C.A. § 1115(b)(4) (2000).　　**46.** Taylor Wine Co. v. Bully Hill Vineyards, Inc., 569 F.2d 731 (2d Cir.1978).

the public must be assured that he does not by his "estate bottled" nomenclature and his claims to being the "original" Taylor, confuse the public into believing that his product originates from the Taylor Wine Company.

> We have concluded that neither Bully Hill nor Walter S. Taylor should use the "Taylor" name as a trademark, but that the defendant may show Walter's personal connection with Bully Hill. He may use his signature on a Bully Hill label or advertisement if he chooses, but only with appropriate disclaimer that he is not connected with, or a successor to, the Taylor Wine Company....

The Second Circuit remanded to allow the trial judge to fashion an appropriate order. Walter, however, was not content to let well enough alone. He circulated labels, advertisements and other materials in violation of the order, and which mocked the court. Eventually, he was found in contempt and the court amended the order to forbid any use of his name whatsoever.

As the subsequent history of the *Taylor* case suggests, where there is any indication of bad faith in the adoption and use of the name by the junior party the courts usually dispense with qualified injunctions filled with subtly tailored provisions and enter an absolute order instead. Examples of bad faith might include evidence that the defendant changed his name to make it conform more closely to a famous surname-trademark, or the fact that the junior party entered a business in which he had no training or experience merely to capitalize on the coincidence of a famous name.

The special rules associated with surnames in trademark law may be a vestige of older ways of doing business. In a localized economy, the reputation of the flesh and blood individual who made or sold a particular brand of goods was often the most important piece of information available to the consumer. As intimated at the beginning of this section, this may no longer to be the case in the twenty-first century world of multinational corporations and e-commerce. When contemporary entrepreneurs launch a new business they are likely unknown to their customers and have little to gain by placing their surname front and center in their marketing efforts. It thus may be that eventually the law will grant automatic protection to the first user of a surname because there will be so little demand by others for such an old-fashioned way of branding merchandise. That day, however, is still probably a long way off.

27.2.4 Secondary Meaning

Descriptive, geographic, and personal name marks, though lacking inherent distinctiveness, are not necessarily doomed. As noted at several points above, they can still secure legal protection if the merchant using them can demonstrate that they have achieved the blessed status known as "secondary meaning." This means, quite simply, that a substantial segment of the public has come to view the words in question as denoting a single and unique source of goods, rather than as merely providing information about the product. It is not necessary that all consumers, or even a majority, have come to view the words as a trademark. It is enough that the view is held by an "appreciable number" or a "significant number" of the relevant purchasers.[47]

Judicial and scholarly definitions of secondary meaning abound. The Supreme Court has said that "to establish secondary meaning, a manufacturer must show that, in the minds of the public, the primary significance of a product feature or term is to identify the source of the product rather than the product itself."[48] The Restatement is to the same effect, declaring that when a "designation, although not 'inherently distinctive,' has become distinctive, in that, as a result of its use, prospective purchasers have come to perceive it as a designation that identifies goods, services, businesses, or members ..." the designation has "secondary meaning."[49] Thus "secondary meaning exists only if a significant number of prospective purchasers understand the term, when used in connection with particular goods, services, or businesses, not merely in its lexicographic sense, but also as indicative of an association with a specific person."[50]

The adjective "secondary" can be slightly confusing when one initially thinks about the concept of secondary meaning. It does not mean subordinate, inferior, or of secondary importance. The brand signifying meaning must actually be the primary or dominant meaning to yield a finding of secondary meaning. The word "secondary" refers instead to the fact that the brand signifying meaning came chronologically "second," because the words initially carried only a descriptive or geographic or personal name implication. For instance, when consumers first encounter the words STEAK & BREW on a sign outside a restaurant they may think only that the sign is descriptive of certain menu items, just like a sign that might say "Home Cooking" or "Coffee and Donuts." After some period of time, however, and repeated exposures to the name, consumers may come to appreciate that the words designate a particular branded restaurant. At this point, the term will have a new, second, meaning which has become paramount in the consumer mind. This new, second meaning is the one which entitles it to trademark protection.

As you might expect, there is no bright line test indicating when non-inherently distinctive marks have achieved secondary meaning. It is

47. President and Trustees of Colby College v. Colby College–New Hampshire, 508 F.2d 804 (1st Cir.1975) ("appreciable number"); Carling Brewing Co. v. Philip Morris, Inc., 277 F.Supp. 326 (N.D.Ga.1967) ("Significant part of the public").

48. Inwood Laboratories, Inc. v. Ives Laboratories, Inc., 456 U.S. 844, 851 n. 11, 102 S.Ct. 2182, 72 L.Ed.2d 606 (1982). *See also* Two Pesos, Inc. v. Taco Cabana, Inc.,

505 U.S. 763, 766 n. 4, 112 S.Ct. 2753, 120 L.Ed.2d 615 (1992) (A mark has secondary meaning when it "has come through use to be uniquely associated with a specific source").

49. Restatement (Third) of Unfair Competition § 13 (1995).

50. Id. at comment e.

a question of fact, requiring case-by-case determination and the party claiming validity of the trademark bears the burden of proof on the issue. "No hard and fast line can be drawn and no general rule can be enunciated by which one can determine precisely where a word such as JOY acquires such distinctiveness that it can function as a mark indicating a particular producer as the source or origin of such goods. Each case must stand on its own record."[51] As a general rule, the more straightforwardly descriptive the words in question, the stronger the proof a court or the PTO will require before finding secondary meaning because of the correspondingly greater risk of hindering competitors.

Many courts have articulated lists of factors to be used to demonstrate secondary meaning.[52] While these various lists differ in some respects, they are substantially similar to each other. In virtually all courts, the most straightforward proof of secondary meaning is direct evidence of consumer understanding of the words in question. An obvious form of such evidence is a consumer survey, demonstrating consumer understanding of the alleged mark. While various courts have characterized survey evidence as the "most persuasive" proof of secondary meaning,[53] the would-be owner of the mark is not obliged to offer survey evidence, which is actually fortunate, because the development of a methodologically acceptable survey can be quite expensive.

Quite often, then, secondary meaning will be proven by circumstantial evidence. There are several types of proof that fall in this category. First, the mark owner can offer evidence of lengthy exclusive use of the designation in question. The longer the words have been used by this merchant and no one else, the more likely it is that public has come to associate them with that merchant alone. In fact, for registration purposes, the Lanham Act treats proof that the mark has been used exclusively and continuously for a period of five year as prima facie evidence of secondary meaning.[54] As the Restatement cautions, however, "in some cases distinctiveness is not acquired even after an extended period of time; in others it may be acquired soon after adoption."[55] Given the rapidity with which information can be spread in the current digital media age, it is quite easy to imagine that a company could acquire secondary meaning in short order. It might take as little as one ad on the Super Bowl to imprint the brand name significance of the word or

51. Clinton Detergent Co. v. Procter & Gamble Co., 302 F.2d 745, 748 (CCPA 1962).

52. See, e.g., Genesee Brewing Co. v. Stroh Brewing Co., 124 F.3d 137, 143 n. 4 (2d Cir.1997); Sunbeam Products Inc. v. West Bend Co., 123 F.3d 246, 254 (5th Cir.1997), cert. denied, 523 U.S. 1118, 118 S.Ct. 1795, 140 L.Ed.2d 936 (1998); Tools USA and Equipment Co. v. Champ Frame Straightening Equipment, Inc., 87 F.3d 654 (4th Cir.1996); Madison Reprographics, Inc. v. Cook's Reprographics Inc., 203 Wis.2d 226, 552 N.W.2d 440 (App.1996).

53. See, e.g., Vision Sports, Inc. v. Melville Corp., 888 F.2d 609 (9th Cir.1989); Security Center, Ltd. v. First National Security Centers, 750 F.2d 1295, 1300 (5th Cir.1985). The Restatement speaks of survey evidence as "particularly persuasive." Restatement (Third) of Unfair Competition § 13, comment e (1995).

54. 15 U.S.C.A. § 1052 (f) (2000).

55. Restatement (Third) of Unfair Competition § 13, comment e (1995).

phrase onto the minds of tens of millions of consumers, though it is doubtful that any court would, or even should, make so generous a finding.

Closely related to evidence concerning the length of time the mark has been used is evidence dealing with sales volume. Once again, the logical connection is straightforward—the more goods which have been sold bearing the disputed phrase, the more likely it is that the public has come to view that phrase as a trademark. Here too, however, caution is necessary because a high sales volume may merely indicate that the product is a high quality item which is desired for its underlying attributes, rather than that the trademark has developed cachet as a brand name.

Still another type of evidence bearing circumstantially on secondary meaning is evidence showing the amount of advertising and related promotional activities that the mark owner has undertaken, along with references to the term in a trademark sense by the media. Thus, in *Jews For Jesus v. Brodsky*[56] the court—in finding secondary meaning for the descriptive phrase JEWS FOR JESUS—noted that the plaintiff had spent nearly half a million dollars annually on advertising, had distributed over 35 million pamphlets bearing its purported trademark, and that its mark had been mentioned in over 850 news stories over a period of five years. On the other hand, the descriptive phrase ENVIRONMENTAL TECHNOLOGY for a magazine was found to lack secondary meaning despite promotional expenses of $100,000 a year and the annual distribution of several thousand copies of the magazine.[57] Of course the magnitude of advertising expenditures is not conclusive on the issue of secondary meaning. As one court noted, "it must be remembered that the question is not the extent of the promotional efforts, but their effectiveness in altering the meaning of [the descriptive phrase] to the consuming public."[58]

Finally, many courts view evidence that a defendant knowingly copied the plaintiff's mark as additional proof of secondary meaning. The logic here is that deliberate copying must be a calculated attempt to confuse the public, and that it would only be logical to copy the plaintiff's mark if it already had achieved secondary meaning. As the Ninth Circuit once put it: "There is no logical reason for the precise copying save an attempt to realize upon a secondary meaning that is in existence."[59] This argument seems dubious, however. As other courts have noted, the defendant might be copying the phrase in question for the simple reason that it is descriptive in nature and because it needs

56. 993 F.Supp. 282, 298 (D.N.J.1998).

57. Adams/Green Industry Publishing, Inc. v. International Labmate Ltd., 45 USPQ2d 1046 (N.D.Ill.1997).

58. Aloe Creme Laboratories Inc. v. Milsan, Inc., 423 F.2d 845, 850 (5th Cir.1970), *cert. denied,* 398 U.S. 928, 90 S.Ct. 1818, 26 L.Ed.2d 90 (1970). *See also* Premier–Pabst Corp. v. Elm City Brewing Co., 9 F.Supp. 754 (D.Conn.1935) ("the issue is the achievement of an identity and not the effort expended in the attempted achievement").

59. Audio Fidelity, Inc. v. High Fidelity Recordings, Inc., 283 F.2d 551, 558 (9th Cir.1960).

that phrase to communicate with the public.[60] For this reason, at least one commentator has argued that evidence of copying should be entirely ignored in secondary meaning determinations.[61] Despite the shaky logic, many courts continue to give evidence of deliberate copying at least some weight in most cases. Provided that this type of evidence is interpreted in light of the other circumstances of the case, it seems appropriate to at least consider it for whatever it may be worth.

For a brief period of time from the mid 1970's to the early 1990's some of the district courts in the Second Circuit began to speak of a doctrine which they labeled "secondary meaning in the making." In these case, the plaintiff would be using a descriptive term or symbol to designate its goods and services, and would be expending money and effort to build consumer recognition and establish secondary meaning. Before secondary meaning could actually be proved, however, the defendant would enter the market and deliberately begin using the same descriptive designation or one closely similar to it. Troubled by the supposedly unsavory nature of these defendants' conduct, the court would afford relief to the plaintiff despite the absence of secondary meaning.[62] In the 1992 case of *Laureyssens v. Idea Group, Inc.,*[63] the Second Circuit clearly rejected the doctrine, observing that "the so-called doctrine of secondary meaning in the making, by affording protection before prospective purchasers are likely to associate the [mark] with a particular sponsor, constrains unnecessarily the freedom to copy and compete." The result in *Laureyssens* is consistent with the approach taken by other federal appellate courts around the country,[64] as well as with the views of commentators on the subject.[65] The doctrine of "secondary meaning the making" has not been much heard from since the mid-nineties and is best viewed now as a historical curiosity.

§ 27.3 Generic Words: Terms Incapable of Distinctiveness

Some words are considered legally incapable of ever achieving the distinctiveness required of a trademark, and thus may never be appropri-

60. *See, e.g.,* Blau Plumbing, Inc. v. S.O.S. Fix–It, Inc., 781 F.2d 604 (7th Cir. 1986) (copying is "ambiguous" evidence of secondary meaning because it "is consistent with an inference that the copier merely wanted to inform customers about the properties of his own product or service.").

61. Timothy Bryant, Comment, *Trademark Infringement: The Irrelevance of Evidence of Copying to Secondary Meaning,* 83 Nw. L. Rev. 473 (1989). Some courts appear to have been persuaded by the argument. *See* Continental Laboratory Products, Inc. v. Medax Intern., Inc., 114 F.Supp.2d 992, 1009 (S.D.Cal.2000).

62. Cases invoking the doctrine include Metro Kane Imports, Ltd. v. Federated Dep't Stores, Inc., 625 F.Supp. 313 (S.D.N.Y.1985) and Jolly Good Industries, Inc. v. Elegra, Inc., 690 F.Supp. 227 (S.D.N.Y.1988).

63. 964 F.2d 131 (2d Cir.1992).

64. *See, e.g.,* Black & Decker Mfg. Co. v. Ever–Ready Appliance Mfg. Co., 684 F.2d 546 (8th Cir.1982); Cicena, Ltd. v. Columbia Telecommunications Group, 900 F.2d 1546 (Fed.Cir.1990).

65. *See, e.g.,* J Thomas McCarthy, McCarthy on Trademarks & Unfair Competition § 15:58; Scagnelli, *Dawn of a New Doctrine? Trademark Protection for Incipient Secondary Meaning,* 71 T.M. Rep. 527 (1981).

ated by a merchant for its own exclusive use. These words, known as "generic" names, are the basic names by which categories of products are known. For example, "milk," "bread," "toaster," and "gun" are all generic names. Quite clearly, it would impose an unhealthy obstacle to competition if the first in the market to sell a machine for browning bread could prevent everyone else selling similar machines from calling them toasters.[1] It follows that no amount of use will convert generic terms into protectable marks—in other words they cannot be transformed into valid marks through a showing of secondary meaning. Indeed, the phrase "generic mark," which sometimes appears in judicial opinions, is an oxymoron.

The refusal to protect generic terms as trademarks is a feature of both the common law and the Lanham Act. The Lanham Act implements that rule somewhat obliquely however. Section 2 of the statute, which itemizes types of symbols which are ineligible for trademark protection, does not mention generic terms at all. However, the introductory paragraph of that provision provides that "no trademark by which the goods of the applicant may be distinguished from the goods of others shall be refused registration...."[2] By definition a generic term is *incapable* of distinguishing one brand of goods from another, thus at least implying that generic terms should not be registered. Moreover, a generic term can also be considered "descriptive" but incapable of ever achieving secondary meaning. Under that view it would also be barred from registration under section 2(e) of the statute, and unsalvageable by section 2(f). Even if a generic term were to slip through the registration process, under section 14 of the Lanham Act, a registered mark may be cancelled at any time if it can be shown to be generic. Thus, what ever the theory, the Federal Circuit has made it clear that generic terms are not registrable at the PTO.[3]

Not very many firms try to claim trademark rights in a previously used and well-established generic name for an established category of goods. Even the boldest executives at General Motors do not think of CAR as a plausible trademark. (Those at Harley–Davidson were, however, predictably bolder, and attempted to assert trademark rights in the term HOG for large motorcycles, until the Second Circuit ruled that the words was generic.[4]) Merchants do, however, sometimes attempt to seek trademark protection for a well recognized generic term by coupling it with a foreign article and calling the result a trademark—a technique

§ 27.3

1. As Judge Posner put it, "To allow a firm to use as a trademark a generic word ... would make it difficult for competitors to market their own brands of the same product. Imagine being forbidden to describe a Chevrolet as a 'car' or an 'automobile' because Ford or Chrysler or Volvo had trademarked their generic words." Blau Plumbing, Inc. v. S.O.S. Fix–It, Inc., 781 F.2d 604, 609 (7th Cir.1986).

2. 15 U.S.C.A. § 1052 (1996).

3. In re Northland Aluminum Products, Inc., 777 F.2d 1556 (Fed.Cir.1985). *See also* J. Thomas McCarthy, TRADEMARKS AND UNFAIR COMPETITION § 12.57.

4. Harley–Davidson, Inc. v. Grottanelli, 164 F.3d 806 (2d Cir.1999).

that they must think gives the term an exotic cachet. Examples might be LE BREAD for bread or DER GUN for pistols.

The Trademark Trials & Appeals Board addressed this practice in a case involving an applicant's attempt to register the mark LA YOGURT for yogurt.[5] Although initially of the view that such a mark was not registrable as the generic name for the product, the Board ultimately concluded that the addition of a foreign article created a sufficiently different commercial impression than the generic word alone so as to make the composite phrase a valid and protectable trademark. Note, however, that where the purported mark is simply a foreign generic term, such as LA CRAVAT for neckties, the term is considered generic under the doctrine of foreign equivalents. Consequently the Second Circuit recently found the term OTOKOYAMA generic for a type of Japanese Sake, because that is what the word means in Japanese.[6] Moreover, even where trademark status is appropriate, like in the LA YOGURT decision, the protection for any such mark will be rather "thin." This means that the mark receives protection only from competing marks that are virtually identical to it, and, of course, the owner of this mark would not be entitled to prevent others from using the generic word "yogurt" on their competing brands.

Other firms have occasionally incorporated a generic term into a heavily promoted, and often toll-free, phone number, such as 1–800– LAWYER or 1–800–MATTRESS. Courts confronting these situations have held that such phone numbers may be entitled to trademark protection,[7] though again, the protection afforded will be rather thin.

More typically, disputes over genericness have involved two recurring types of situations. In one, the vendor of a brand new, and previously unknown, product or service, sells it under a newly coined, but relatively straightforward name. When others begin to compete, they often try to use the same name for the new product. This leads inevitably to infringement litigation and a need to assess the genericness of the newly coined terminology. In the second situation, a once perfectly valid mark has become so popular that it has become essentially a synonym for an entire class of products—such as CELLOPHANE for plastic wrap. Other firms may claim that, while the term may have once been protectable as a mark, it has now lost its distinctiveness and lapsed into the generic category, entitling them to use it.

In both types of cases, classifying a word or phrase as the generic term for a product has proven vexing for the courts. It is clear that the public understanding of the term is supposed to control, and that the matter is a question of fact rather than an issue of law. Thus, in one of the earliest opinions on the subject, Judge Learned Hand observed that

5. In re Johanna Farms Inc., 8 USPQ2d 1408 (T.T.A.B.1988).

6. Otokoyama Co., Ltd. v. Wine of Japan Import Inc., 175 F.3d 266 (2d Cir. 1999).

7. *See, e.g.,* Dial–A–Mattress Franchise Corp. v. Page, 880 F.2d 675 (2d Cir.1989).

"the single question ... in all these cases, is merely one of fact: What do buyers understand by the word for whose use the parties are contend-ing."[8] Almost two decades later the Supreme Court declared in the celebrated *Kellogg* case that to avoid generic categorization, a firm must show that "the primary significance of the term in the minds of the consuming public is not the product but the producer."[9] Language inserted in the Lanham Act in 1984 is to the same effect, providing that the "primary significance of the registered mark to the relevant public ... shall be the test for determining whether a registered mark has become the generic name of goods or services on or in connection with which it has been used."[10] All this has come to be called the "primary significance" test.

Another rhetorical formulation that is supposed to guide courts in determining genericness is the "genus/species" distinction. According to the Supreme court a "generic term is one that refers to the genus of which the particular product is a species."[11] In biology, of course, a genus is a somewhat general category such as all "hominoids." A species is a subcategory within the genus consisting of organisms so sufficiently similar that they are capable of breeding with each other—for example "homo sapiens." If this strikes you as a bit far afield from trademark law, you are not alone. The general idea is, however, easy enough to grasp. A genus is a broad product class and a species is a single brand within the class.

As is true so often of legal tests, the primary significance and genus/species tests are much easier to propound than they are to apply. At first blush the tests seem straightforward enough. Since they revolve around the public understanding of the challenged term, a litigant attempting to prove that the term is generic could simply survey the public. This should work well enough when there is a clear understand-ing of just what the product category—the genus—consists of, and when there are multiple brands within that category. For instance, there is probably a consensus that facial tissues constitute a discrete product category, not fully interchangeable with paper towels or toilet tissue. Moreover, lots of companies sell facial tissues. If the question is whether the word KLEENEX is a brand name or a generic term, we can ask people what they think, and their answers should be helpful in resolving the issue. If a majority realize that the word is a brand name then its primary significance would be exactly that and it would not be generic. Other evidence of the primary significance of a term might be found in how that term is used by various participants in the relevant industry including the party who claims trademark status for the word; how it is used by the media; and how it is listed in various reputable dictionaries.

---

8. Bayer Co. v. United Drug Co., 272 F. 505 (D.N.Y.1921).

9. Kellogg Co. v. National Biscuit Co., 305 U.S. 111, 59 S.Ct. 109, 83 L.Ed. 73 (1938).

10. 15 U.S.C.A. § 1064(3) (2000).

11. Park 'N Fly v. Dollar Park and Fly, Inc., 469 U.S. 189, 194, 105 S.Ct. 658, 83 L.Ed.2d 582 (1985).

In reality, however, the boundary between a generic term and one that is legally descriptive is just as blurry as the line that separates the descriptive term from the suggestive one. This can be especially so where the disputed term is an adjective rather than a noun. Adjectives can be generic terms, like the word LITE for low alcohol beer. However CUSTOM BLENDED for gasoline and TASTY for salad dressing were found to fall on the descriptive side of the line. No amount of survey evidence or dictionary research will relieve courts from the burden of making close judgment calls regarding phrases such as these.

When there is no consensus as to the boundaries of the product category, however, and only one firm sells a version with a specific combination of attributes, things become even more difficult. For instance, assume a firm develops a facial tissue impregnated with aloe lotion, and sells it under the name SOOTHING TISSUES. The phrase SOOTHING TISSUES could be a brand name within the larger category of facial tissues, or it could be the new generic name for the new, narrower product category of aloe impregnated tissues. Consumers, however, are not likely to have a helpful opinion on which it is, because only one firm sells the product with that precise configuration of attributes. When they ask for "soothing tissues," the same phrase simultaneously signifies the type of product and the brand of product. The Third Circuit identified the precise problem in its thoughtful opinion in *A.J. Canfield Co. v. Honickman*.[12] As it observed:

> [W]e do not believe that a direct survey of public views can truly measure consumer understanding if a term identifies a product that arguably constitutes its own genus.... [G]eneric marks signifying goods produced by only one manufacturer may function both as generic terms, signifying the product genus, and as brand names, indicating continuity of source. Faced with a mark like shredded wheat, the consumer has no reason to define it either as the name of a brand or as the name of a genus because the term functions most efficiently as both. Accordingly, a survey inquiring whether a designation like shredded wheat is a brand name or a product name forces respondents to make a false dichotomy.

Fortunately, the *Canfield* court offered a solution to the conundrum. It propounded the following rule: "If a producer introduces a product that differs from an established product class in a particular characteristic, and uses a common descriptive term of that characteristic as the name of the product, then the product should be considered its own genus. Whether the term that identifies the product is generic then depends on the competitors' need to use it." In that case, the issue was whether phrase CHOCOLATE FUDGE was generic for Canfield's especially rich tasting diet chocolate soda. Applying its test, the court first determined that Canfield's soda differed from ordinary chocolate sodas because of its different, more fudge-like taste. It then determined that

---

12. 808 F.2d 291 (3d Cir.1986).

the term "chocolate fudge" was a common descriptive way to communicate that specific product difference. Finally, it found that there would be a general need for competitors to use the term because "we can imagine no term other than 'chocolate fudge' that communicates the same functional information, namely, that this soda has the taste of chocolate fudge, a particular, full, rich chocolate taste."

While the *Canfield* decision is an admirable attempt to grapple with a difficult problem, the court's application of its own test to the facts before it seems somewhat arbitrary. Did the plaintiff's soda really differ significantly from other chocolate sodas, or even other diet chocolate, sodas in "a particular characteristic" or did it just taste somewhat richer or better? After all, some consumers may think the PEPSI COLA brand of cola has a slightly sweeter taste than COCA–COLA brand. Does that mean that if the makers of PEPSI COLA were to label it as "The Sweeter Cola" it would suddenly become a new product genus? Was "fudge" really the common descriptive way of referring to this allegedly superior taste? Our dictionary defines fudge as "a kind of candy composed of sugar, butter, milk, chocolate, or the like." Were competitors really unable to describe a comparably rich soda without the use of the word fudge? What about Ultra–Rich, or Chocolate Mousse, or Super–Chocolate?

All is this is not to say that the court reached a wrong-headed or indefensible result. Rather, it illustrates that despite the best efforts of a thoughtful bench, resolving questions of genericness still remains a subjective and elusive business, that cannot be reduced to formula. The underlying policy question always remains the pragmatic one whether the term is important enough and convenient enough that it should be declared public property—off limits to all merchants who might seek to appropriate it.

Canfield and cases like it involve words or phrases that are alleged to have been generic *ab initio*—that is, from its first use. A somewhat different situation arises when a defendant alleges that a previously recognized brand name has, because of changed patterns of consumer usage, lost its distinctiveness and lapsed into genericness. Often, though not always, the terms involved in such cases were highly arbitrary or fanciful when they were first adopted, and were initially indisputably deserving of trademark protection. By the time of litigation, however, the public understanding of the term may have changed, and consequently, the term may now properly be considered generic—a fate that some writers have called "genericide."

The test in genericide, or loss of distinctiveness, cases remains the primary significance test. The classic case of *Kellogg Co. v. National Biscuit Co.,*[13] is illustrative. There, National Biscuit, the predecessor of Nabisco, had been making and selling a breakfast cereal of pillow shaped wheat biscuits for several decades under the name SHREDDED WHEAT. It had no competition during much of that period because the

---

13. 305 U.S. 111, 59 S.Ct. 109, 83 L.Ed. 73 (1938).

relevant manufacturing processes had been covered by patents. When those patents expired, Kellogg entered the business and began making a comparable biscuit cereal. It also began using the "shredded wheat" terminology to describe its product. The U.S. Supreme Court held that whatever the status of the term might have been in earlier times, it had become generic by the time of the lawsuit. Justice Brandeis, writing for the Court, observed that:

> The evidence shows only that due to the long period in which the plaintiff ... was the only manufacturer of the product, many people have come to associate the product, and as a consequence, the name by which the product is generally known, with the plaintiff's factory at Niagara Falls. But to establish a trade name in the term "shredded wheat" the plaintiff must show more than a subordinate meaning which applies to it. It must show that the primary significance of the term in the minds of the consuming public is not the product but the producer. This it has not done.

One might think that the outcome in the *Kellogg* case followed from the plaintiff's rather unimaginative choice of a trademark. The term SHREDDED WHEAT is at best descriptive for the cereal in question, and might even have been found generic if the question had been litigated immediately after National Biscuit adopted it under the logic of the *Canfield* decision. However, many highly arbitrary, coined terms have also been held generic long after their adoption because of changes in public understanding and usage. Examples of words that have suffered this fate include "THERMOS" to designate a vacuum bottle that can keep beverages warm or cold, "ASPIRIN" to designate an analgesic medicine made from acetyl salicylic acid, "ESCALATOR" for a moving staircase, and even the word "HEROIN" for a particular form of morphine. Despite the fact that none of those words even existed until they were coined by the first vendor of the goods in question, because the public began to use them as synonyms for an entire product category regardless of manufacturer identity, they fell into the public domain.

Of course, consumers often use a strong brand name as shorthand for a product even though they fully recognize that it is in fact a brand name. Thus one might ask for JELLO for dessert rather than using the more cumbersome "fruit flavored gelatin," not least of all to avoid peculiar looks from one's waitress. The would be true when asking for a KLEENEX in lieu of a tissue or for a BAND–AID instead of an adhesive bandage. In cases like these, Prof. McCarthy notes that "the fact that buyers often call for or order a product by a term does not necessarily evidence that the term is a 'generic name.' ... Quite the contrary. It shows that these terms are such strong well-known trademarks that they need no generic name to convey the message. The generic name is understood by all and dropped off."[14] He emphasizes that the important question is what do consumers think the word designates when they are

14. J Thomas McCarthy, Trademarks and Unfair Competition § 12:8.

involved in making actual purchasing decisions, rather than engaging in casual conversation.

It is possible, however that many shoppers who run into the store to get a box of BAND–AIDS may be using the word to mean any brand of adhesive bandage, not just the BAND–AID brand, and only a carefully designed survey would be able to tell us if they still recognize the word BAND–AID as having brand significance. In other words, casual generic usage in everyday speech may be some evidence that at least a few of the most popular marks in America actually teeter on the brink of genericness and survive mostly because no competitor is willing to incur the likely litigation costs necessary to establish the right to use the word.

Legal commentators and practicing lawyers have developed a number of recommendations designed to help trademark owners avoid the fate that befell the marks alluded to above. For instance, in order to avoid genericide, it is helpful if the vendor uses two terms to designate the product, one which will treated as generic and the other which will be preserved as a trademark. It is even more effective if the two terms are separated by the word "brand." Thus, the first seller of aspirin would have had a much stronger case for retaining trademark status for the word if it had labeled its bottles "ASPIRIN brand Pain Reliever" and used that terminology in its advertising. Another recommendation is that a manufacturer should be vigilant in policing the market place. When generic usage of its trademarks is called to its attention, it should send letters or otherwise make its displeasure known. This is no doubt why the Coca–Cola company has become legendary for warning restaurants to avoid serving other cola products when a patron asks for a COKE. Still another traditional bit of advice is to use the mark on a wide variety of different products so that it cannot become a synonym for any one of them. Thus, XEROX might be used as a trademark for not just photocopiers, but also for scanners, fax machines, computer laser printers and the like.

While most issues of trademark validity revolve around the distinctiveness problems considered in this and the previous sections, there are several other types of problems that may prevent a given symbol from being accorded trademark status. Even if a mark is highly distinctive, it may already have been appropriated by another merchant, it may tend to confuse the public or it may transgress social and moral sensibilities. We consider those issues in the few sections that follow.

§ 27.4 Previously Used Marks

As discussed in the previous chapter, the first party properly to adopt and use a mark at common law is considered the owner of that mark. Subsequent users of the same or closely similar mark on the same goods can be enjoined by the senior user. The same notion is carried into the Lanham Act through the provisions of section 2(d). It bars the registration of a mark which so resembles a mark registered in the Patent and Trademark Office, or a mark or trade name previously used in the United States by another and not abandoned, as to be likely, when used on or in connection with the goods of the applicant, to cause confusion, or to cause mistake, or to deceive. . . .

A careful look at this language reveals a number of interesting points.

First, the statutory ban on registrability does not require exact identity between the proposed mark and the one that has been previously used. Rather, registration will be denied whenever there is sufficient resemblance to cause a "likelihood of confusion." Registration can also be denied even though the applicant proposes to use the mark on different goods than the prior user, if the goods are related. For example, an applicant was not permitted to register the mark LUBA–DERMAL for shaving cream because of a likelihood of confusion with the previously registered mark LUBRIDERM for a medicinal skin lotion,[1] and another was not permitted to register BEN'S BREAD for bread mixes, because of a likelihood of confusion with the previously registered mark UNCLE BEN'S for rice and other foods products.[2]

The notion of likelihood of confusion is central to much of trademark law and constitutes the key test for determining questions of infringement. It is explored in some depth in the chapter on trademark infringement later in this volume. At this point, it will suffice to note that there is much subjective judgment involved in determining when a proposed mark is so confusingly similar to one previously used as to warrant a denial of registration. In its 1973 *DuPont* decision, the Court of Customs and Patent Appeals, which at the time had jurisdiction to review the decisions of the U.S. Patent and Trademark Office, identified thirteen factors to guide the PTO in making "likelihood of confusion" determinations.[3] The Court of Appeals for the Federal Circuit, the successor to the Court of Customs and Patent Appeals, has declared that "any doubts about likelihood of confusion under § 2(d) must be resolved against applicant as the newcomer."[4]

A second interesting aspect of section 2(d) is that it bars registration of a proposed mark if it will engender a likelihood of confusion with any one of three different types of trade symbols. The first is a previously registered mark. The second is a previously used mark, which would mean a mark protected under state common law but not registered under the Lanham Act. Third, and finally is a previously used "trade name." The statute defines a trade name as "any name used by a person to identify his or her business or vocation." While many companies use their business name as a trademark for one or more products that they sell, many others do not. Thus, the Procter & Gamble Company, makers

§ 27.4

1. Warner–Lambert Co. v. Sports Solutions Inc., 39 USPQ2d 1686 (T.T.A.B.1996).

2. Uncle Ben's Inc. v. Stubenberg Int'l, Inc., 47 USPQ2d 1310 (T.T.A.B.1998).

3. In re E.I. DuPont DeNemours & Co., 476 F.2d 1357 (CCPA 1973).

4. In re Hyper Shoppes (Ohio), Inc., 837 F.2d 463 (Fed.Cir.1988).

of many extremely well-known products such as TIDE laundry detergent, CREST toothpaste, and PRINGLES potato chips, does not use the name Procter & Gamble as a trademark. Nonetheless, if someone attempted to register the mark PRACTER & GUMBLE for laundry detergent, there is a good chance that the registration would be denied because of potential confusion with a "trade name previously used."

Like all the statutorily itemized bars to registration, the section 2(d) bar can be raised "ex parte" by the examining attorney at the PTO. In other words, the examining attorney considering the application may discover one or more prior conflicting trademarks though his or her own research, conclude that confusion would be likely, and deny registration based on that analysis. Not surprisingly, however, many controversies under this provision of the Lanham Act arise after the examiner has approved the mark, and published it. At that point, the owner of the other mark usually will file an opposition, which will lead to a contested administrative hearing before the Trademark Trial and Appeals Board to resolve the question of likely confusion.

§ 27.5 Immoral, Scandalous, and Disparaging Marks

Most merchants try to select appealing trademarks with positive associations for the obvious reason that such marks are most likely to interest and retain customers. Sometimes, however, a firm will choose an arguably offensive or shocking word or logo to serve as a mark. The logic may be that such a mark will attract attention in a crowded marketplace or perhaps make the product attractive to consumers who fancy themselves rebels or non-conformists.

When merchants in this latter group attempt to register their marks, however, the PTO may deny the registration on the grounds that mark is "immoral or scandalous." Unlike most of the other bars to registration which appear in section 2 of the Lanham Act, this provision is neither grounded on the need of competitors to communicate with the public nor on the policy of avoiding deception of the public. Rather it appears to be based on a Congressional desire to avoid any implication that the government endorses trademarks that are offensive to significant segments of society.

The Court of Appeals for the Federal Circuit has held that the determination of whether a mark is scandalous should be made from "the standpoint of not necessarily a majority, but a substantial composite of the general public," and "in the context of contemporary attitudes."[1] It has also held that "officials of the PTO may not readily assume, without more, that they know the view of a substantial composite of the public" and it has "commended the practice of resolving the issue of whether a mark comprises scandalous matter by first permitting the mark to pass for publication, and then allowing interested members

§ 27.5

1. In re Mavety Media Group Ltd., 33 F.3d 1367 (Fed.Cir.1994).

of a composite of the general public who consider the mark to be scandalous to bring opposition proceedings."[2]

Many of the cases involving this provision have involved trademarks with sexual or other vulgar connotations, or those that refer to drugs. The trend has been towards an ever more narrow construction of this provision, presumably reflecting the increasingly relaxation of "contemporary attitudes" in recent decades Where the mark is susceptible to multiple interpretations, the PTO will often ignore the more scandalous of those and allow the mark to be registered. Thus in one case, the mark BIG PECKER BRAND was held to be registrable for T-shirts, in part because the word pecker could mean a bird as well as a part of the male anatomy.[3] In another, the Trademark Trial and Appeals Board allowed registration of a logo of a frog arguably making an obscene gesture with his middle finger, reasoning in part that:

> In viewing the right front leg of applicant's frog (the only portion of the frog of concern to the Examining Attorney), the digits of the leg are positioned such that they bear, at most, only a very remote similarity to the gesture of flipping the bird or giving the finger. The Examining Attorney has made of record literally dozens of pictures of humans flipping the bird. In each of these pictures, there are no gaps whatsoever between the middle or "flicker finger" and the fingers on either side of the middle finger. In striking' contrast, the right front leg of applicant's frog is depicted with wide gaps between the highest digit (which the Examining Attorney contends is the flicker finger) and the digits on either side of it.[4]

Of course some marks go too far. In *Greyhound Corp. v. Both Worlds, Inc.*[5] the Trademark Trial and Appeals Board refused to register a logo of a defecating greyhound as a mark for shirts, and in *In re Wilcher Corp.*,[6] it refused to register a logo of man with a penis for a nose as a trademark for a bar called "Dick Head's."

In *Ritchie v. Simpson,*[7] the Federal Circuit considered the question of who has standing to oppose a registration on the grounds that the mark is allegedly scandalous. In that case O.J. Simpson sought to register the marks O.J. and THE JUICE for a variety of goods including sportswear, trading cards and figurines. The opposer, Mr. Ritchie, was a member of the general public who claimed that he was outraged by the marks in question, which he alleged were "synonymous with wife-beater and wife-murderer" and which he felt attempted to "justify physical violence against women." In a 2–1 decision, the court held that Mr. Ritchie had standing to raise these contentions. It reasoned that an

---

2. Ritchie v. Simpson, 170 F.3d 1092 (Fed.Cir.1999).

3. In re Hershey, 6 USPQ2d 1470 (T.T.A.B.1988).

4. In re Bad Frog Brewery, Inc., 1999 WL 149819 (T.T.A.B.1999).

5. 6 USPQ2d 1635 (T.T.A.B.1988).

6. 40 USPQ2d 1929, 1996 WL 725479 (T.T.A.B.1996).

7. 170 F.3d 1092 (Fed.Cir.1999).

opposer need not have a specifically commercial interest in order to go forward with a trademark opposition, and that he had demonstrated that he was "more than a mere intermeddler."

The same provision of the Lanham Act which forbids the registration of immoral and scandalous marks also bars the registration of marks which "may disparage ... persons, living or dead, institutions, beliefs or national symbols, or bring them into contempt or disrepute." The leading case interpreting this aspect of the statute is the administrative decision in *Harjo v. Pro–Football, Inc.*[8] In that proceeding, a group of Native American Indians petitioned to cancel various federal registrations of the mark REDSKINS for the Washington, D.C. National Football League franchise. They argued, in part, that the mark disparaged Native Americans. The Trademark Trial & Appeals Board agreed and cancelled the mark.

The Board pointed out that while the statute refers to marks that "comprise" immoral or scandalous matter, the language dealing with disparagement refers to marks that "may disparage." Emphasizing the word "may," it held that this phrasing dispensed with any requirement that a cancellation petitioner alleging disparagement must prove a disparaging intent on the part of the registrant. Thus the fact that the team allegedly adopted the REDSKINS trademark to honor or compliment Native Americans rather than to insult them would be irrelevant. It also noted that the test for disparagement under the statute is whether a substantial composite of members *of the referenced group* would find the term dishonorable, offensive or degrading, and that the reactions of the general public are irrelevant in such cases. By way of examples, it declared that "if the alleged disparagement is of a religious group or its iconography, the relevant group may be the members and clergy of that religion; if the alleged disparagement is of an academic institution, the relevant group may be the students, faculty, administration, and alumni; if the alleged disparagement is of a national symbol, the relevant group may be citizens of that country." Because survey evidence offered by the petitioners showed that 37% of Native Americans found the term "Redskins" offensive, the Board concluded that the mark was ineligible for continued registration.

At this writing, the owners of the REDSKINS mark have a suit pending in U.S. District Court seeking de novo review of the T.T.A.B. determination. Among the arguments they have raised in that litigation is the contention that section 2(a) of the Lanham Act is unconstitutional because it is inconsistent with the First Amendment. The cancellation petitioners filed a motion to dismiss the constitutional defense, but the court denied that motion as premature.[9]

Although immoral, scandalous and disparaging marks cannot be registered under the Lanham Act, that does not mean that they cannot be used. Denial of registration means only that the trademark owner

8. 50 USPQ2d 1705, 1999 WL 375907 (T.T.A.B.1999).

9. *See* Pro–Football, Inc. v. Harjo, 2000 WL 1923326 (D.D.C.2000).

cannot take advantage of the various federal statutory benefits. More-over, when such marks are used, they are likely to receive common law protection except in the very rare cases where a court would find that such protection violated some strong public policy. Nonetheless, the symbolic stakes are often high in cases arising under this provision and the opinions certainly make entertaining reading.

§ 27.6   Other Bars to Federal Registrability

Section 2 of the Lanham Act contains a number of other bars to registration. These tend to be relatively narrow in scope, or duplicative of some of the more important provisions we have already considered. Section 2(a) of the statute bars registration of any mark that "may ... falsely suggest a connection with persons, living or dead, institutions, beliefs, or national symbols...." This provision is analogous to the prohibition in section 2(d), which forbids the registration of marks that are likely to cause confusion with previously registered or used marks or trade names. Of course, the wording of this prong of section 2(a) permits it to be used by non-commercial entities and private individuals.

The Trademark Trial and Appeals Board has held that a mark will be denied registration on this basis if: (1) it is the same as, or a close approximation of, the name or identity previously used by the other person; (2) it would be recognized as such, because it points uniquely and unmistakably to that person; (3) the person named by the marks is not connected with the activities performed by applicant under the marks; and (4) the prior user's name or identity is of sufficient fame or reputation that a connection with such person would be presumed when applicant's marks are used on applicant's goods.[1] An interesting illustration is *Buffett v. Chi–Chi's, Inc.,*[2] where the applicant attempted to register the mark MARGARITAVILLE for restaurant services. Singer and songwriter Jimmy Buffett, who wrote a song by that name and was widely associated with that song title, filed an opposition. The applicant moved for summary judgment before the T.T.A.B., but the Board denied the motion, holding that Buffett had raised material questions of fact under the "falsely suggests a connection" language of section 2(a).

Section 2(a) will usually not prevent registration of a mark consist-ing of the name of a long-deceased historical personage. The mark REMBRANDT for a restaurant or JOHN HANCOCK for an insurance company is not likely to cause the public to presume that there is a connection between those applicants' businesses and the Renaissance Dutch painter or the American founding father respectively. Such marks are merely arbitrary.

To a large degree, this provision in section 2(a) protects interests similar to those which lie at the heart of the "right of publicity," a concept discussed at some length earlier this volume. Thus in most cases,

§ 27.6

1. In re Wielinski, 49 USPQ2d 1754, 1998 WL 998961 (T.T.A.B.1998).

2. 226 USPQ 428 (T.T.A.B.1985).

not only will marks that "falsely suggest a connection" with living persons be denied registration under the Lanham Act, but their use can be forbidden under a variety of state common law or statutory provisions as well.

Under Section 2(b) of the statute, it is impermissible to register a mark that "consists of or comprises the flag or coat of arms or other insignia of the United States, or of any State or municipality, or of any foreign nation or any simulation thereof." Thus a seller of pasta could not secure a federal registration for a mark consisting of the red, white and green Italian national flag. Presumably this provision is designed, at least in part, to avoid offending foreign governments and provoking them into allowing the use of the U.S. flag on shoddy or inappropriate goods in their countries. It also serves to prevent public confusion about whether a brand of goods is authorized by a foreign nation—preventing any chance that consumers might think a given brand of pasta is the "official pasta of Italy."

A few cases that have arisen under section 2(b) have addressed whether such symbols as the Statue of Liberty or the Capitol building should be considered "insignia" of the U.S., and they have generally held that they are not.[3] While such icons might also be alleged to "falsely suggest a connection" with the federal government, which might render them unregistrable under section 2(a), this contention has generally been rejected as well. The T.T.A.B. has suggested in dicta that the reference in section 2(b) to "municipalities" might be limited to U.S. municipalities only, and not those in foreign nations.[4] The use of marks that consist of a flag or other insignia are not necessarily forbidden under state law. Thus, although they may not be registered, they can still be used and even protected against infringement under the common law.

Finally, section 2(c) forbids the registration of mark that "consists of or comprises a name, portrait, or signature identifying a particular living individual except by his written consent, or the name, signature, or portrait of a deceased President of the United States during the life of his widow, if any, except by the written consent of the widow." This provision is only applicable if the particular living individual in question is either generally known to the public or, at a minimum, publicly

3. Liberty Mutual Insurance Co. v. Liberty Insurance Co., 185 F.Supp. 895 (E.D.Ark.1960); Heroes, Inc. v. Boomer Esiason Hero's Foundation, Inc., 43 USPQ2d 1193 (D.D.C.1997).

4. Ceccato v. Manifattura Lane Gaetano Marzotto & Figli, S.P.A., 32 USPQ2d 1192 (T.T.A.B.1994) ("it is not clear from the wording of Section 2(b) that the prohibition against the registration of the coat of arms of a municipality applies to that of a foreign municipality. The Statute refers to the flag or coat of arms or other insignia of the United States, or any State or municipality, or of any foreign nation. By the manner in which the clauses are arranged, it would appear that the reference to 'municipality' in the Statute is to a municipality in the United States, and that prohibition of registration with respect to foreign coats of arms, etc., is to those of the countries themselves, rather than to those of the states or municipalities of the foreign countries. However, in view of applicant's failure to prove that the design in opposer's registration is the coat of arms of the municipality of Aosta, Italy, or a simulation thereof, we need not decide this issue.").

connected with the business in question.[5] It is not meant to bar the registration of fictitious or obscure names that happen, coincidentally, to also be the names of real people. Thus, even though a quick Internet search will reveal hundreds of married women with the surname "Butterworth," that is not an obstacle to the registration of the mark MRS. BUTTERWORTH'S for pancake syrup because that mark plainly does not refer to any "particular" individual.

5. Ross v. Analytical Technology, Inc., 51 USPQ2d 1269, 1999 WL 517200 (T.T.A.B.1999).

Chapter 28

PROTECTION FOR TRADE DRESS AND OTHER UNCONVENTIONAL TRADEMARKS

Table of Sections

It is most common to think of legally protectable brand identifying symbols as the various words, phrases or pictorial logos we know as trademarks. Many merchants, however, especially in recent years, have also attempted to secure comparable protection for the shape and design of their product's labeling or packaging, or even for the shape and configuration of the product itself. In other instances, they have sought to have the overall color of the product declared protectable. In still others they have claimed a protectable interest in such exotic attributes as a sound or a smell.

Collectively, product or packaging attributes which serve to identify goods or services are known as "trade dress." As a general rule, the law protects trade dress, provided that it does, in fact, function to identify the goods or services in question, and provided that protection would not unduly burden competition. However, it took the courts some time to arrive at this straightforward result, and older cases sometimes denied protection where the brand identifying material was unconventional in format. Moreover, for most of these more esoteric categories of identifying symbols the law imposes special or additional requirements before granting protection.

§ 28.1   Definition of Trade Dress and Requirements for Protection

The trade dress of a product is the overall visual image that it presents to consumers. It can consist of the shape and color of the packaging or container either in isolation or combined with the shape, placement and color scheme of any labels, and the various visual design aspects of those labels. Moreover, as the Supreme Court has recently noted, although "trade dress ... originally included only the packaging, or 'dressing,' of a product, ... in recent years [it] has been expanded by many courts of appeals to encompass the design of a product."[1] In other words the shape or configuration or coloring of the product itself may also function as trade dress. In the case of a service business such as a restaurant or a golf course, trade dress can even consist of such elements as the interior decor or exterior design features of the building or land where the business is conducted.

While a few courts have even considered various procedural aspects of how a service is provided—such as the registration process for a trade show[2]—to be trade dress, the decisions clearly indicate that general business themes are not within the definition of trade dress. For instance, a firm cannot secure exclusive rights in the marketing device of promoting domestic ice cream as having a Scandinavian flair under trademark or unfair competition principles.[3] A concept such as this can be protected only under the patent laws, and only then if it meets the rigorous requirements for patents canvassed elsewhere in this volume.

Thus, as one court summarized, "[t]rade dress involves the total image of a product and may include features such as size, shape, color or color combinations, texture, graphics or even particular sales techniques."[4] The comments to the Restatement (Third) of Unfair Competition are largely parallel, noting that:

> The term "trade dress" often is used to describe the general image or appearance of goods or services as offered for sale in the marketplace. "Trade dress" traditionally includes the appearance of labels, wrappers, and containers used in packaging the product, and displays and other materials used in presenting the goods or services to prospective purchasers.[5]

---

§ 28.1

1. *See* Wal–Mart Stores, Inc. v. Samara Brothers, Inc., 529 U.S. 205, 209, 120 S.Ct. 1339, 146 L.Ed.2d 182 (2000).

2. Toy Mfrs. of America, Inc. v. Helmsley–Spear, Inc., 960 F.Supp. 673 (S.D.N.Y. 1997).

3. Haagen–Dazs, Inc. v. Frusen Gladje, Ltd., 493 F.Supp. 73 (S.D.N.Y.1980).

4. John H. Harland Co. v. Clarke Checks, Inc., 711 F.2d 966, 980 (11th Cir. 1983), *quoted with approval* in Two Pesos, Inc. v. Taco Cabana, Inc., 505 U.S. 763, 764 n. 1, 112 S.Ct. 2753, 120 L.Ed.2d 615 (1992).

5. Restatement (Third) of Unfair Competition § 16, comment a (1995).

In British legal parlance, trade dress is sometimes referred to as the "get up" of the product, a nice phrase which captures the essence of the concept. Invoking still other useful foreign metaphors, courts have referred to trade dress as both the "tout ensemble"[6] of the product and as its "gestalt."[7]

Although trade dress protection is frequently sought for the totality of all the product or packaging features, it is entirely permissible for a merchant to seek such protection for a subset of features. Consequently, a firm might endeavor to protect only the shape of its container, independent of colors, labels and the like. The classically shaped glass COCA–COLA bottle is an apt illustration of a product container that serves to identify the source of the beverage inside for many consumers, even when the bottle is stripped of all labeling.

Initially the law was reluctant to provide a grant of exclusive protection to product containers. Indeed, courts in the nineteenth century denied all protection in this situation, fearing that a limited number of packaging forms would soon be appropriated, unduly burdening competitors, and that eventually "some one, bolder than the others, might go to the very root of things, and claim for his goods the primitive brown paper and tow string, as a peculiar property."[8] It is now well settled, however, that container shapes—and trade dress generally—may be protected when they meet the necessary requirements discussed elsewhere in this chapter. The balance of the discussion in this chapter will use the phrase "trade dress" to refer either to the totality of all product or container features or to any subset of those features, such as container shape, that a merchant is attempting to protect in a given situation.

Not every aspect of a visual appearance, shape, design and color will be treated as protectable trade dress, however. If a product is adorned with features which strike the consumer as primarily decorative or ornamental rather than as source designating, those features do not constitute trade dress, because they do not serve a source-designating function. For instance in *Knitwaves, Inc. v. Lollytogs, Ltd*,[9] the plaintiffs sought to protect two different designs for girls' sweaters as trade dress. One involved a striped design with puffy autumn leaf appliques and the other consisted of a cartoonish buck-toothed squirrel along with more autumn leaves on a multi-panel background. The Second Circuit concluded that the sweater designs did not constitute protectable trade dress observing that "[a]s Knitwaves' objective in the two sweater designs was primarily aesthetic, the designs were not primarily intended as source identification." This seems entirely sound. On encountering these sweaters consumers' presumably responded to the design by thinking "oh how lovely" (or "oh how awful") rather than by thinking, "aha,

6. Chun King Sales, Inc. v. Oriental Foods, 136 F.Supp. 659 (S.D.Cal.1955), *aff'd in part and rev'd in part,* 244 F.2d 909 (9th Cir.1957).

7. Faberge, Inc. v. Saxony Products, Inc., 605 F.2d 426 (9th Cir.1979).

8. Harrington v. Libby, 11 F.Cas. 605, 606 (C.C.S.D.N.Y.1877) (no. 6,107).

9. 71 F.3d 996 (2d Cir.1995).

the design of these sweaters tells me they come from a single source," because long experience has taught consumers to view most external design elements on items of clothing as merely decorative.[10]

This does not mean that a firm such as Knitwaves is without protection for its designs. Copyright law is often a viable and more appropriate legal alternative. Indeed, Knitwaves was able to prevail on its copyright claim involving these very sweaters. It also does not mean that all appliques on clothing are merely decorative. As any alert consumer will have noticed, clothing vendors routinely use alligator, polo pony, warthog and kangaroo patches as source-designating emblems on the breast of their respective lines of knit shirts. Given that consumers surely view these types of embellishments as brand-signifying, competing shirt manufacturers would not be permitted to duplicate these zoological designators.

Both the common law and the Lanham Act protect trade dress. The common law originally protected it under the rubric of "unfair competition" rather than "trademark infringement," but as the distinction between those causes of action has faded, common law courts generally now treat both types of claims identically. Lanham Act protection has long been available under the terms of section 43(a) of the statute—the general federal unfair competition remedy—even though the section did not, until a few years ago, address trade dress explicitly.[11] Recent amendments to section 43(a), dealing with the allocation of burdens of proof in trade dress infringement cases, have now removed any doubt about its applicability to these types of claims.

For the first ten years after the adoption of the Lanham Action, the Patent and Trademark Office refused to register trade dress on the principal register. However, since a reversal of course in the late 1950's, the PTO has consistently allowed federal registration of trade dress.[12] Although at least one academic commentator has challenged the statutory basis for this practice,[13] it is very well settled and has been approved by several federal circuit courts of appeal.[14] Over the years, the PTO has registered forms of trade dress as varied as the shape of LIFESAVERS

---

10. To the same effect are I.P. Lund Trading ApS v. Kohler Co., 118 F.Supp.2d 92 (D.Mass.2000), holding that promotion of the alleged trade dress of a faucet did not create secondary meaning where consumers viewed the shape of the faucet as primarily aesthetically pleasing, and In re Sandberg & Sikorski Diamond Corp., 42 USPQ2d 1544 (T.T.A.B.1996), where the arrangement of gemstones on a ring was held not to constitute registrable trade dress because there was no evidence that consumers would view it as anything other than ornamentation.

11. *See, e.g.,* Two Pesos, Inc. v. Taco Cabana Inc., 505 U.S. 763, 776, 112 S.Ct. 2753, 120 L.Ed.2d 615 (1992) (Section 43(a) has "created a federal cause of action for

infringement of unregistered trademark or trade dress and ... such ... trade dress should receive essentially the same protection as those that are registered") (Stevens, J. Concurring).

12. *See* Ex parte Haig & Haig Ltd., 118 USPQ 229 (Comm'r Pat.1958).

13. Glynn S. Lunney, Jr., *The Trade Dress Emperor's New Clothes: Why Trade Dress Does not Belong on the Principal Register,* 51 HASTINGS L.J. 1131 (2000).

14. *See, e.g.,* Application of Kotzin, 276 F.2d 411 (CCPA 1960); Kohler Co. v. Moen Inc., 12 F.3d 632 (7th Cir.1993); Aromatique, Inc. v. Gold Seal, 28 F.3d 863 (8th Cir.1994).

brand candy,[15] to the inverted Y design of the fly on the front of JOCKEY brand men's underwear.[16]

To be protectable under either common law or in a section 43(a) action, and to be federally registrable, trade dress must satisfy two independent tests. First, it must be "non-functional." The requirement of non-functionality has long been a feature of the common law doctrine concerning trade dress, and the federal courts judicially incorporated it into most decisions under the Lanham Act from the very start, even though the statute was silent on the subject. Congress finally got around to adding explicit functionality provisions to the Lanham Act in 1998. Under section 2(e)(5) it is now unequivocal that functionality is an absolute bar to Lanham Act registration. In addition, section 14(3) expressly provides that a federal trademark registration may be cancelled at any time if the mark covers material that is functional and section 33(b)(8) makes proof of functionality a defense to a claim of infringement. These amendments now leave no doubt that the Lanham Act and the common law on the subject of functionality are congruous.

The second requirement for protectable trade dress is that the features in question be "distinctive." While we have encountered the distinctiveness concept earlier, in connection with words and slogans used as trademarks, it takes on a new complexion in the context of trade dress, and the courts have especially struggled over whether the same rules for distinctiveness can be sensibly applied to trade dress that consists of product packaging and to trade dress that consists of the actual design of the product itself. As we shall see, the Supreme Court has weighed in twice in the last decade on the issue of trade dress distinctiveness.

§ 28.2   The Non–Functionality Requirement

Manufacturers often incorporate elements into product or packaging design in order to make the product work better, to make it easier to use, display or ship, or to make it cheaper to manufacture. Examples might include an improved and more comfortable handle on a gallon jug of bleach, or a new shape of lampshade for a desk lamp that reduces glare and better focuses the beam of light. Such features are considered "functional." Trade dress rights cannot be claimed in functional features and, to put the same idea the other way around, non-functionality is thus a prerequisite for trade dress rights.

Functional features are not protectable for at least two intertwined reasons. First, protecting them would hamper competition. Courts and scholars often note that imitation is the lifeblood of competition,[1] and as the Supreme Court has observed, "[w]here an item in general circulation

15. Nabisco Brands, Inc. v. Conusa Corp., 722 F.Supp. 1287 (M.D.N.C.1989), *aff'd,* 892 F.2d 74 (4th Cir.1989).

16. In re Jockey International, Inc., 192 USPQ 579 (T.T.A.B.1976).

§ 28.2

1. *See, e.g.,* American Safety Table Co. v. Schreiber, 269 F.2d 255, 272 (2d Cir. 1959).

is unprotected by patent, 'reproduction of a functional attribute is legitimate competitive activity.'"[2] If a firm comes up with a cheaper or better way to design a lamp or a cereal box, consumers benefit if other firms are permitted to duplicate the new design, especially because the other firms may offer it at a lower price. To quote the Supreme Court yet again, "[t]he functionality doctrine prevents trademark law ... from ... inhibiting legitimate competition by allowing a producer to control a useful product feature."[3]

Second, protecting functional package or product features under trademark law would undermine the policies of the patent system. Under patent law, one is only entitled to exclusivity for a new technological development if the development meets the fairly exacting standards of novelty and non-obviousness.[4] More pedestrian innovations are not considered worthy of an exclusive right. If such features could nonetheless be protected as trade dress, firms would be able to make an end run around the standards of patentability,[5] and they would be able to claim this protection for an indefinite period, rather than for the limited term of years provided under patent law.

Thus there are ample reasons to insist that a proponent of trade dress protection show that the alleged trade dress is "non-functional" before the law will grant exclusive rights. Viewed casually, however, this notion of "functionality" could lead to absurdities. For instance, one might reason that all product containers—no matter what they look like—are "functional" because they serve the function of keeping the product from running all over the place. It is undeniable, after all, that even the most elaborate bottle or the most intricate box performs the purpose of containing the product, preventing it from being spoiled or damaged, and making it convenient to transport. Similarly, no costume or uniform could ever be deemed non-functional since costumes and uniforms serve the function of preventing the user from appearing naked in public—undeniably useful for all but a few of us. Such a view of functionality would, however, deny protection to virtually all trade dress, a result that is both counter-intuitive and not required by any sound policy relating to competitor need and the integrity of the patent system.

To avoid this result, when determining whether trade dress is functional, courts focus on the *specific design* of the package or the

---

2. Bonito Boats, Inc. v. Thunder Craft Boats, Inc., 489 U.S. 141, 164, 109 S.Ct. 971, 103 L.Ed.2d 118 (1989).

3. Qualitex Co. v. Jacobson Prods. Co., 514 U.S. 159, 164–65, 115 S.Ct. 1300, 131 L.Ed.2d 248 (1995).

4. *See* Chapters 16 and 17 of this text.

5. *See, e.g.,* Qualitex Co. v. Jacobson Prods. Co., 514 U.S. 159, 164, 115 S.Ct. 1300, 131 L.Ed.2d 248 (1995) ("It is the province of patent law, not trademark law, to encourage invention by granting inventors a monopoly over new product designs or functions for a limited time ... after which competitors are free to use the innovation."); Elmer v. ICC Fabricating, 67 F.3d 1571, 1580 (Fed.Cir.1995) ("Patent law, not trade dress law, is the principal means for providing exclusive rights in useful product features."); Stormy Clime, Ltd. v. Pro-Group, Inc., 809 F.2d 971, 977–78 (2d Cir. 1987) ("Courts must proceed with caution in assessing claims to unregistered trademark protection in the design of products so as not to undermine the objectives of the patent laws.").

product. According to *In re Morton–Norwich Products, Inc.,*[6] a leading case on the issue, the trade dress design is functional—and thus not eligible for trademark protection—if the *design* of the features in question is superior in operation or economy in light of competitive necessity to copy. In other words, courts ask whether the design under analysis is "the best or one of a few superior *designs* available."[7] The Second Circuit made the same point in slightly different words when it noted that "the true test of functionality is not whether the feature in question performs a function, but whether the feature 'is dictated by the functions to be performed.'"[8] An essentially similar emphasis on *design* can be found in the Restatement (Third) of Unfair Competition's definition of functionality.[9]

In attempting to identify what types of design features should be deemed functional, legions of courts and commentators have weighed in with their own, specific definitions of functionality. Judge Posner, of the Seventh Circuit, put a predictably economic spin on his version of a definition of functionality, declaring that "a functional feature is one which competitors would have to spend money not to copy but to design around, ... It is something costly to do without . . . rather than costly to have . . . . "[10] Other courts have been more colloquial, and declared that a feature should be deemed functional when it helps the product to "work better."[11] The Restatement declares that:

> A design is "functional" . . . if the design affords benefits in the manufacturing, marketing, or use of the goods or services with which the design is used, apart from any benefits attributable to the design's significance as an indication of source, that are important to effective competition by others and that are not practically available through the use of alternative designs.[12]

Key aspects of these definitions may have been called into serious question by recent Supreme Court authority. In its *Inwood* decision, the Supreme Court said that "a product feature is functional if it is essential

---

6. 671 F.2d 1332 (CCPA 1982).

7. 671 F.2d at 1341(emphasis added).

8. Brandir Int'l, Inc. v. Cascade Pacific Lumber Co., 834 F.2d 1142 (2d Cir.1987).

9. Restatement (Third) of Unfair Competition § 17 (1995). The Restatement illustrates the proposition with a number of examples. For instance, Illustration 4 to § 17 says "A manufactures chocolate candy in the form of a six-sided bar with sloping ends. The bars are wrapped with an inner layer of silver foil covered by an outer white paper wrapper that leaves a significant portion of the foil visible at both ends of the bar. The packaging retains the shape of the enclosed chocolate bar. The evidence establishes that chocolate bars can be shaped and wrapped in a variety of forms and styles. In the absence of evidence indicating

that A's overall design affords benefits not available through other designs, the design is not functional under the rule stated in the Section, and it is protectable as a trademark upon proof of distinctiveness." This illustration is apparently drawn from In re World's Finest Chocolate, Inc., 474 F.2d 1012 (CCPA 1973).

10. W.T. Rogers Co., Inc. v. Keene, 778 F.2d 334, 339 (7th Cir.1985). *See also* Schwinn Bicycle Co. v. Ross Bicycles, Inc., 870 F.2d 1176 (7th Cir.1989).

11. "[F]unctionality . . . means that the product is in its particular shape because it works better in this shape." In re R.M. Smith, Inc., 734 F.2d 1482, 1484 (Fed.Cir. 1984).

12. Restatement (Third) of Unfair Competition § 17 (1995).

to the use or purpose of the article or if it affects the cost or quality of the article."[13] This formula makes no reference to the availability of alternatives or the competitive need for the features in question. More recently, in *TrafFix Devices, Inc. v. Marketing Displays, Inc.*[14] the Supreme Court was even more explicit in declaring that competitive necessity should not be part of the functionality analysis at all. Speaking for a unanimous Court, Justice Kennedy held that "[w]here the design is functional under the *Inwood* formulation there is no need to proceed further to consider if there is a competitive necessity for the feature." On this view, if the design provides advantages that make the product easier to use, the design is functional even if there are hundreds of other designs available that might yield the same advantages at a comparable cost. A similar result would obtain if the design helps lower the cost of the product or makes it easier to ship, display, or market. *TrafFix* holds that economical designs and useful designs cannot ever become protectable features of trade dress.

Because trade dress consists of the total assemblage of a number of features, it is entirely possible that some of the features comprising the trade dress may be functional, while others may not be. In fact, it is possible that trade dress might consist of a number of elements, every one of which is functional when considered independently. Thus, the question arises as to whether the various component features of a trade dress should be analyzed for functionality individually, or whether the court should focus on all of them as a whole. While a few courts have taken the feature-by-feature approach,[15] most have embraced the rule that it is the functionality of all of the features combined that is to be considered.[16] As the Ninth Circuit pointed out, "functional elements that are separately unprotectable can be protected together as part of a trade dress.... In other words, our inquiry is not addressed to whether individual elements of the trade dress fall within the definition of functional, but to whether the whole collection of elements taken together are functional."[17] This is the position of the Restatement (Third) of Unfair Competition, which observes that "[t]he fact that the overall design or combination contains individual features that are themselves functional does not preclude protection for the composite."[18]

Of course this does not mean that "composite" trade dress is always non-functional. It is entirely possible that a merchant will aggregate

13. Inwood Labs., Inc. v. Ives Labs., Inc., 456 U.S. 844, 851 n. 10, 102 S.Ct. 2182, 72 L.Ed.2d 606 (1982).

14. 532 U.S. 23, 121 S.Ct. 1255, 149 L.Ed.2d 164 (2001).

15. *See, e.g.,* Warner Lambert Co. v. McCrory's Corp., 718 F.Supp. 389 (D.N.J. 1989).

16. *See, e.g.,* Hartford House, Ltd. v. Hallmark Cards, Inc., 846 F.2d 1268, 1272 (10th Cir.1988) ("A combination of features may be nonfunctional and thus protectable,

even though the combination includes functional features"); SK&F, Co. v. Premo Pharmaceutical Laboratories, Inc., 481 F.Supp. 1184, 1187 (D.N.J.1979) ("The law of unfair competition in respect to trade dress requires that all of the features be considered together, not separately.").

17. Fuddruckers, Inc. v. Doc's B.R. Others, Inc., 826 F.2d 837, 842 (9th Cir.1987).

18. Restatement (Third) of Unfair Competition § 17, comment b (1995).

functional features in the only way possible, or in a way that is itself one of only a few superior combinations. For instance in *Atlantis Silverworks, Inc. v. 7th Sense, Inc.*,[19] the plaintiff claimed trade dress protection for its rings. The court found that each of the individual features of the rings was functional, but plaintiff argued that the combination was nonetheless protectable. The court rejected the argument, observing that "the functional elements of plaintiff's rings are not combined in a non-functional way. Indeed, the head, the strand and the beads are combined in the only functional way they can be combined." In cases such as these, the overall design should not receive trade dress protection.

In litigation, the functionality issue is treated as a question of fact.[20] Under the Lanham Act, a plaintiff alleging infringement of unregistered trade dress bears the burden of proving that the trade dress is non-functional.[21] On the other hand, if the trade dress has been registered, that will create a presumption of validity of the trade dress, and thus a presumption of non-functionality. In this situation, it would be up to the defendant to raise functionality as a challenge to the trade dress and such a defendant would bear the burden of proof on the issue. Thus, for registered trade dress, functionality effectively becomes something akin to an affirmative defense.

Courts have identified several different types of evidence that may be probative on the question of functionality. Clearly, direct evidence on the cost of the disputed design feature and testimony about how it does or does not improve product performance will always be relevant. Often, however, courts will look to additional circumstantial facts to shed light on the issue.

Prior to the recent Supreme Court decision in *Traffix*, information about the number and cost of available design alternatives was one such fact held relevant by the vast majority of courts. Thus, a plaintiff claiming that its trade dress is non-functional was allowed to offer evidence of both actual and theoretical alternative designs for the product or container that would work equally well, and that would be comparably economical, to show that competitors have ample options. As the Federal Circuit noted, "[s]ince the effect upon competition 'is really the crux of the matter,' it is ... significant that there are other alternatives available." The importance of evidence of this sort is also reflected in the commentary to the Restatement (Third) of Unfair Competition, which notes that "[t]he availability of alternative designs that satisfy the utilitarian requirements or that otherwise afford similar advantages is ... decisive in determining functionality."[22]

19. 42 USPQ2d 1904, 1911 (S.D.N.Y. 1997).

20. Vuitton et Fils, S.A. v. J. Young Enterprises, Inc., 644 F.2d 769, 775 (9th Cir.1981).

21. 15 U.S.C.A. § 1125(a)(3) (1999) ("In a civil action for trade dress infringement under this Act for trade dress not registered on the principal register, the person who asserts trade dress protection has the burden of proving that the matter sought to be protected in not functional.").

22. Restatement (Third) of Unfair Competition § 17, comment b (1995).

After the *Traffix* opinion, however, evidence of this sort now appears irrelevant. In that case the plaintiff MDI sold temporary road signs emblazoned with warnings such as "Road Work Ahead." To enable the signs to resist sudden strong gusts of wind, MDI used a patented dual spring mechanism to connect the sign to its frame. After the patent expired a competitor called TrafFix began making signs with a visible spring mechanism that resembled the one used by MDI. Claiming that the appearance of the spring design was a protectable feature of trade dress, MDI brought suit under the Lanham Act. The Sixth Circuit found in favor of plaintiff MDI, in large measure because it felt that the defendant had other available options for designing such mechanisms, and that trade dress protection for MDI would not put competitors at a disadvantage. The Supreme Court reversed. In doing so, the Court observed that:

> [T]he functionality of the spring design means that competitors need not explore whether other spring juxtapositions might be used. The dual-spring design is not an arbitrary flourish in the configuration of MDI's product; it is the reason the device works. Other designs need not be attempted. Because the dual-spring design is functional, it is unnecessary for competitors to explore designs to hide the springs, say by using a box or framework to cover them.... The dual-spring design assures the user the device will work. If buyers are assured the product serves its purpose by seeing the operative mechanism that in itself serves an important market need.[23]

A rather different type of evidence pertinent to the functionality question is whether or not the seller has touted the utilitarian advantages of the alleged trade dress in its advertising. A firm that has promoted its new container in television commercials as "easier to carry and easier to use" will be hard pressed to argue that the container design is non-functional in a subsequent trade dress law suit. On the other hand, advertising that merely instructs consumers to "look for the bright green box" or to "pick the one in the orange jug shaped like a monkey" does not imply functionality, because it is does not make a claim of superiority of performance or economy. If anything, advertising of this latter sort is evidence of an effort to build secondary meaning—an issue that we will consider in the section on trade dress distinctiveness that follows.

Finally, courts also rely on whether the alleged trade dress was previously protected by a now-expired utility patent as indicative of functionality. Of course, if the configuration is protected by a still valid patent, the patentee would be able to sue imitators under the patent laws with a high likelihood of success. Once the patent has expired, that option is foreclosed. More importantly for the present discussion, the representations in the patent claims about the superiority of the design may also preclude an effort to protect it under the law of trade dress by

---

23.　532 U.S. at 33–34.

evidencing its functionality. As the Ninth Circuit noted, "the existence of an expired utility patent is weighty evidence of functionality, although that fact alone is not dispositive."[24] This is not a "per se" rule. As the quoted language plainly states, the expired utility patent is not conclusive on the question of functionality, but only strong evidence of it.[25] In this regard, Professor McCarthy has cautioned, that a "utility patent must be examined in detail to determine whether the disclosed configuration is really primarily functional or just incidentally appears in the disclosure of a patent."[26]

This approach, moreover, was approved in the Supreme Court's most recent declaration on the subject. In the *Traffix* opinion, the court said:

> A prior patent ... has vital significance in resolving the trade dress claim. A utility patent is strong evidence that the features therein claimed are functional. If trade dress protection is sought for those features the strong evidence of functionality based on the previous patent adds great weigh to the statutory presumption that features are deemed functional until proved otherwise by the party seeking trade dress protection. Where the expired patent claimed the features in question, one who seeks to establish trade dress protection must carry the heavy burden of showing that the feature is not functional, for instance by showing that it is merely an ornamental, incidental, or arbitrary aspect of the device.[27]

§ 28.3 Aesthetic Functionality

While many goods are purchased because of how they will work, others are purchased because of how they look. Items such as home furnishings, china, flatware, jewelry and clothing sell, in a large measure, because they are attractive and compatible with the purchaser's decor or sense of style. Items such as Halloween or Christmas decorations sell because they visually evoke the spirit of the holiday. Items such as dolls and toys are purchased because they look adorable, or in some cases, frightening. Some merchants selling items of this sort who have hit upon a successful "look" have attempted to protect it against duplication by claiming that it is trade dress. If, however, the "look" is one of only a few superior designs plausible for making the product acceptable to consumers, some courts refuse protection, and label the look "aesthetically functional."

Perhaps the classic example of "aesthetically functional" packaging would be a red, heart-shaped box for chocolates sold during February.

---

24. Disc Golf Ass'n, Inc. v. Champion Discs, Inc., 158 F.3d 1002, 1006 (9th Cir. 1998).

25. *See, e.g.,* Clamp Mfg. Co. v. Enco Mfg. Co., 870 F.2d 512 (9th Cir.1989); Best Lock Corp. v. Schlage Lock Co., 413 F.2d 1195 (CCPA 1969); In re Shenango Ceram-

ics, Inc., 362 F.2d 287 (CCPA 1966); In re Deister Concentrator Co., 289 F.2d 496 (CCPA 1961).

26. J. Thomas McCarthy, McCARTHY ON TRADEMARKS § 7:89.

27. 532 U.S. at 29–30.

Such a box does not provide utilitarian advantages to either consumers or retailers—it is not easier to carry or stack on store shelves—nor does it provide an advantage in economy of manufacture, as it is probably more, rather than less, expensive to make a box in this shape. Thus, it is not functional in the sense discussed in the previous section—it does not have "utilitarian" functionality. Nonetheless, it satisfies a unique consumer demand for signaling love and affection at Valentine's Day, and other shaped boxes—for instance in the form of a kidney or spleen— simply will not do the trick. Thus the first vendor of candy in boxes of this type should not be granted exclusive rights to the shape lest competitors be unduly hindered. The concept of aesthetic functionality is one way to deny protection in a case such as this.

In its *Qualitex* opinion, the Supreme Court provided a formal definition, and seeming approval, of the doctrine when it favorably cited the Restatement of Unfair Competition's commentary on aesthetic functionality. According to the Court,

> if a design's "aesthetic value" lies in its ability to "confe[r] a significant benefit that cannot practically be duplicated by the use of alternative designs," then the design is "functional." Restatement (Third) of Unfair Competition § 17, Comment c, pp. 175–76 (1995). The "ultimate test of aesthetic functionality," it explains, "is whether the recognition of trademark rights would significantly hinder competition."[1]

On this view, three elements must exist for trade dress to be labeled aesthetically functional. First, the item must be one which is purchased, in significant part, for aesthetic reasons. Thus, spark plugs or even cans of tuna fish would not be the types of products where it is necessary to undertake an aesthetic functionality analysis. Second, the specific product or package design used by the plaintiff must have significant aesthetic appeal to customers. In other words, there must some reason to believe that plaintiff has hit upon an especially pleasing look for the item in question. Third, and finally, there must be a paucity of viable design alternatives that would have similar aesthetic appeal to customers.

This final condition is crucial if the concept of aesthetic functionality is to avoid swallowing all of trade dress law. For instance, some might consider the sleek look of the PALM PILOT brand of personal digital assistant to have considerable aesthetic appeal. Some, no doubt, find it more elegant than many other hand held computing devices on the market, and the manufacturer quite probably designed it with aesthetic considerations in mind. Nonetheless, it would serve no purpose to declare it functional and allow others to copy it—indeed, such copying might work a considerable fraud on consumers. This illogical result is avoided by noting that there are abundant alternative designs available

§ 28.3

1. Qualitex Co. v. Jacobson Prods. Co., 514 U.S. 159, 170, 115 S.Ct. 1300, 131 L.Ed.2d 248 (1995).

to make personal digital computing devices aesthetically appealing to consumers. Thus, whatever the appeal of the PALM PILOT design, other firms are not burdened in any way when they are forced to design their own devices in different shapes.

While this much may seem clear, the concept of aesthetic functionality had a controversial origin and tortured history in the courts. The seeds of the difficulty were sown with the Ninth Circuit's 1952 decision in *Pagliero v. Wallace China Co.*[2] The plaintiff there sold plates adorned with a floral design. The defendant copied the same design onto its own plates, which it sold to hotels and restaurants who desired replacements for broken dishes. In denying relief to the plaintiff, who sued on a trade dress theory, the court held that the design was "functional" because the china sold due to "the attractiveness and eye-appeal of the design." There was no discussion of the viability of alternative designs. This seems to mean that any attractive or aesthetically pleasing packaging or product design should always be considered functional and unprotectable under the law of trade dress, regardless of available alternatives. Such a rule could work a great deal of mischief, as noted above.

Even more troublesome was a passage in *Pagliero* where the court remarked that the china design in question was functional because it was "an important ingredient in the commercial success of the product." This unfortunate bit of language plainly paints with too broad a brush. After all, well known logos such as the NIKE "swoosh" and the RALPH LAUREN polo player are undoubtedly "key ingredients" in the success of the products they adorn, but this is overwhelmingly because of the goodwill that those vendors have developed and because of the reliability of the logos as accurate source designators. If *Pagliero* meant to suggest that such logos were "functional" and consequently not worthy of protection, it was plainly misguided, yet that is what it seems to say.

Ironically, the actual result in *Pagliero* seems defensible based on the more straightforward rationale that consumers probably perceived the floral design on plaintiff's plates as mere ornamentation, rather than as a designation of source. As noted earlier in this chapter, this was the logic adopted by the Second Circuit in *Knitwaves, Inc. v. Lollytogs, Ltd.*[3] where the court declined to provide protection for children's sweaters decorated in fall fashion patterns. In *Knitwaves* the court refused to find that the patterns in question were functional, because it recognized that competitors had abundant alternative designs to choose from. Nonetheless, it declined protection on a trade dress theory because it concluded that the patterns did not serve as marks that identified and distinguished the source of the goods.

Subsequent cases have struggled with the *Pagliero* language. Several courts have repudiated the "important ingredient in the commercial success" language of *Pagliero* explicitly.[4] Moreover, the Second Circuit

2. 198 F.2d 339 (9th Cir.1952).

3. 71 F.3d 996 (2d Cir.1995).

4. *See, e.g.*, Keene Corp. v. Paraflex Industries, Inc., 653 F.2d 822 (3d Cir.1981);

Sicilia Di R. Biebow & Co. v. Cox, 732 F.2d 417 (5th Cir.1984).

has refused to follow *Pagliero* on essentially identical facts, finding that a VILLEROY & BOCH china pattern was not functional as a matter of law—though it did remand for a factual determination of whether the defendant would suffer competitive disadvantage if it was unable to copy the design as well as for a determination of the distinctiveness of the design.[5]

In grappling with *Pagliero* some courts have gone even further, declaring that they reject entirely the theory of "aesthetic functionality." Thus, one district court observed that "[a]esthetic functionality is a discredited theory which has been used only sparingly since its 1952 introduction in the Ninth Circuit."[6] To the same effect is the manual used by Trademark Examiners at the PTO which declares:

> For many years, the concept of "aesthetic functionality" was applied to aesthetic design elements which were considered important features in the success of the product. This concept was finally rejected as a legal issue in functionality cases in *In re DC Comics, Inc.*[7] See also *In re Deere & Co.*[8] (green color of machine body considered ornamentation for which a secondary meaning had been achieved, the Board expressing "little doubt that aesthetic functionality, per se, (sometimes referred to as ornamentation functionality) is a doctrine which has been rejected by the Court of Customs and Patent Appeals (now the Court of Appeals for the Federal Circuit)"). The ornamentation refusal is now used in situations where the "aesthetic functionality" refusal once was made.... Applicants and courts may still use this terminology on occasion. When they do, the examining attorney should determine whether the design element in question is functional or ornamental and clarify the terminology for appropriate treatment of the issue.[9]

Of course the Supreme Court's apparent endorsement of the aesthetic functionality concept in its *Qualitex* opinion might give the PTO and these lower courts some incentive to rethink their hostile positions on the issue. Moreover, when read closely most of the opinions with this sort of rhetoric seem to mean only that they reject the version of the doctrine embodied in *Pagliero*, rather than the more carefully drawn version which focuses on competitive burden. It is this latter formulation that is found in the Restatement and was endorsed by the Supreme Court in *Qualitex*.

That the doctrine is not entirely dead or repudiated everywhere is evidenced by, among other decisions, the Seventh Circuit's recent deci-

5. Villeroy & Boch Keramische Werke K.G. v. THC Sys., Inc., 999 F.2d 619 (2d Cir.1993). See also Libbey Glass, Inc. v. Oneida Ltd., 61 F.Supp.2d 700, 710 (N.D.Ohio 1999).

6. Gucci Timepieces America Inc. v. Yidah Watch Co., 47 USPQ2d 1938, 1941 (C.D.Cal.1998).

7. 689 F.2d 1042 (CCPA 1982).

8. 7 USPQ2d 1401, 1403 (T.T.A.B. 1988).

9. Trademark Manual of Examining Procedures § 1202.03(e) (2000).

sion in *Publications International Ltd. v. Landoll, Inc.*[10] Plaintiffs were
vendors of a line of cookbooks, and sought to protect, as trade dress,
"the size of the pages (8 ½ inches by 11 inches), the gilded edges of the
pages, and the covers, which are oil cloth or the equivalent." In concluding that the gold gilding was not protectable, the court observed:

> [G]ilded pages are necessary to prevent the unsightly appear-
> ance that printers call 'bleeding.'... What is true is that the
> problem of bleeding could be solved by giving the ends of the
> pages any uniform color; it needn't be gold. But the color gold
> on a product or its package is a prime example of aesthetic
> functionality.... Gold connotes opulence, and so is a standard
> element of the decor of food products, such as chocolate, that
> are valued for their rich taste rather than for their nutritional
> value. It also has a long history of use in bookbinding; the spine
> of the book in which this opinion is printed is decorated with
> gilt. Gold is a natural color to use on a fancy cookbook.[11]

Academic opinions on aesthetic functionality are also divided. Professor McCarthy has expressed skepticism about the idea of aesthetic
functionality in his treatise, commenting that it "is an unwarranted and
illogical expansion of the functionality policy, carrying it far outside the
utilitarian rationale that created the policy.... 'Aesthetic functionality'
is an oxymoron. Ornamental aesthetic designs are the antithesis of
utilitarian designs."[12] Essentially he argues first, that there will always
be other aesthetically pleasing design alternatives, and hence never be
the necessary burden on competition required to trigger the functionality concept and second, that the "merely ornamental" rule can dispose of
fact patterns like the one at issue in *Pagliero* itself.

Other commentators are more receptive to the doctrine, however, at
least to the version of the doctrine that includes a focus on competitive
alternatives. For instance, Professor Dinwoodie has observed that
"[o]nce a general competitive role is assigned to the doctrine of functionality, there is little reason to confine its remit to utilitarian design
features. Protecting features that are primarily aesthetic or a combination of various influences might also cause anti-competitive consequences."[13]

Adding to this confusing state of affairs is the fact that some courts
have used the phrase "aesthetic functionality" in an entirely different
sense—referring not to a doctrine that precludes trade dress protection
ab initio, but rather to something that resembles an affirmative defense.
The most vivid example of this phenomenon is *International Order of
Job's Daughters v. Lindeburg & Co.*[14] Plaintiff in that case was an

10. 164 F.3d 337 (7th Cir.1998), *cert. denied*, 526 U.S. 1088, 119 S.Ct. 1498, 143 L.Ed.2d 652 (1999).

11. 164 F.3d at 342.

12. J. Thomas McCarthy, McCarthy on Trademarks § 7:81 at 7–193 (2000).

13. Graham Dinwoodie, *The Death of Ontology: A Teleological Approach to Trademark Law*, 84 Iowa L. Rev. 611, 696 (1999).

14. 633 F.2d 912 (9th Cir.1980), *cert. denied*, 452 U.S. 941, 101 S.Ct. 3086, 69 L.Ed.2d 956 (1981).

organization for young women aged 11 through 20. It had adopted a logo trademark consisting of a double triangle enclosing three women dressed in robes and crowns and holding, respectively, a dove, an urn, and a cornucopia. The defendant, a jeweler, began selling items displaying that mark without authorization from the plaintiff.

The Ninth Circuit found no infringement. It reasoned that the defendant was not using the symbol to indicate the source of the jewelry, but was rather selling the jewelry to people who desired only to display the symbol. In other words, people bought the items not because they *came from* Job's Daughters, but rather because they signified *loyalty to* Job's Daughters. The result may be defensible on a number of grounds. Because plaintiff had never use the mark in question on jewelry, its rights in the mark arguably did not extend to this product category. Moreover, given plaintiff's failure to expand into the jewelry market, there may have been little likelihood of confusion in the minds of consumers about the source of the jewelry.[15] Indeed, there was no evidence in the case suggesting that consumers thought they were getting "official" Job's Daughters rings or pendants. Essentially, then, the court could have disposed of the case with a simple ruling that the plaintiff had failed to demonstrate any likelihood of confusion—the key requirement for relief in a trademark infringement case. Instead, however, the court relied on the idea of an "aesthetic functionality" defense to infringement. Specifically, it said:

> Trademark law does not prevent a person from copying so-called 'functional' features of a product which constitute the actual benefit that the consumer wishes to purchase.... [I]n the context of this case, the name and emblem are functional aesthetic components of the jewelry, in that they are being merchandised on the basis of their intrinsic value, not as a designation or origin or sponsorship.

This use of the word "functional" in this context is unfortunate and confusing. The term "functionality" is best reserved for cases considering whether trade dress should be granted protection in the first instance. In *Job's Daughter*, there was no claim that the mark itself was invalid because of functionality concerns. After all, competing fraternal organizations could hardly claim that they needed a logo identical to the one designed by Job's Daughters in order to compete. There were ample alternatives—two girls in a trapezoid holding a lamb and a flute, for

15. This is the approach of the Restatement in cases such as these. *See* Restatement (Third) of Unfair Competition § 20, comment e (1995) ("Several decisions allow the unauthorized sale of goods such as jewelry and clothing bearing another's collective membership mark by finding that in such contexts the mark is functional and thus unprotectable. *See* § 17. The proper inquiry, however, is what the unauthorized use of the mark signified to prospective purchasers. If purchasers believe that the organization has authorized or approved the sale of the merchandise bearing the mark, the mark serves a trademark function and the unauthorized use is an infringement. On the other hand, if the appearance of the mark on the merchandise is perceived by prospective purchasers merely as a means for them to use the goods to indicate membership or support for the organization, the use of the mark creates no likelihood of confusion and is not an infringement.").

instance. Moreover, most purchasers of items bearing this logo did not buy them because they were intrinsically attractive or aesthetically pleasing—rather they bought them to display their loyalty to and affiliation with the plaintiff's organization.

Should specific cases warrant the creation of an affirmative defense allowing firms to use otherwise protected trade dress in limited ways for limited purposes, it would be best to coin entirely new vocabulary to designate that doctrine. For instance, if the Ninth Circuit had not wanted to rest merely on the absence of confusion in the fact pattern before it, it might have attempted to fashion an affirmative defense for "affiliative use" of a mark—allowing defendants under limited circumstances to sell replicas of the mark itself to organization members to enable those members to display or demonstrate their affiliation. By conjuring up a separate label, the court would have been forced to justify the creation of a new defense and also forced to set out the various elements necessary to invoke it. By not doing this, it further muddled the already murky rules surrounding aesthetic functionality.[16] While a few cases have followed *Job's Daughter*'s diction, the use of the phrase "aesthetic functionality" to refer to a defense to infringement seems, fortunately, to be dwindling in the more recent decisions.

While the aesthetic functionality doctrine has engendered more than its share of confusion, properly construed it would seem to have some merit, notwithstanding the many criticisms and ambiguities. There may be cases where one firm—the first in a market—develops a uniquely attractive product shape or package design. If it is the sole vendor for a considerable period, consumers may begin to associate the design with it. When competitors desire to enter the market, they should be free to show that there are few viable design alternatives, and if they can do so, they should be allowed to duplicate the design. Any free riding or imposition on the originator of the design is more than offset by the benefits to consumers in having a choice of suppliers.

§ 28.4 Distinctiveness of Trade Dress

Non-functionality of trade dress is not enough, by itself, to warrant legal protection. The combination of features identified by the merchant must also be distinctive—they must serve to identify the brand of goods and distinguish it from competitive brands. This is hardly surprising, since distinctiveness is the core attribute of all trade-identifying symbols and lies at the heart of the various rules governing word-marks examined in the preceding chapters. The Supreme Court has noted that "courts have universally imposed" a distinctiveness requirement for trade dress, "since without distinctiveness the use of similar trade dress

---

16. *See, e.g.,* Anthony Fletcher, *The Defense of "Functional" Trademark Use,* 75 TRADEMARK REP. 249, 268 (1985) (An aesthetic functionality defense "confuses an already complicated subject (functionality). Its tests are meaningless (and wrong). It is a doctrine, whatever its parameters, of uncertain applicability. It appears to serve no useful or necessary purpose. It should be buried.").

by multiple firms would not 'cause confusion ... as to the origin, sponsorship, or approval of [the] goods' " as trademark law requires.[1]

We have previously seen that with respect to word-marks, some words and phrases are deemed inherently distinctive, which entitles them to instantaneous legal protection against confusing imitations. Other words and phrases are only protected after they have achieved secondary meaning because their source identifying capacities are weaker and competitor need to use them are correspondingly greater. Historically, however, many courts took the view that there could be no such thing as inherently distinctive *trade dress* and that therefore a trade dress plaintiff would always have to show secondary meaning in order to prevail.[2]

This judicial caution was in all probability a function of marketing realities during the first half of the twentieth century. Since most firms did not attempt to use the overall look of their package or the configuration of their product as an identifying symbol, most consumers were not primed to think of the features of trade dress as denoting a brand. Thus, when the occasional manufacturer wanted to claim a trade dress as an identifying symbol, it took some time to educate consumers about this association.

By the early 1980's however, most courts had begun to abandon this categorical rule. A key turning point was the Fifth Circuit's influential opinion in *Chevron Chemical Co. v. Voluntary Purchasing Groups, Inc.*[3] The trade dress at issue in *Chevron* was plaintiff's packaging for various lawn and garden products that it sold under the ORTHO brand name. The package

> shows a background composed of three horizontal bands of color; the top 20% is white, the next 30% is yellow, and the bottom 50% is red. Ortho's registered trademark, "ORTHO" is printed on the white band in bold black letters, along with the distinctive chevron mark of the Chevron companies. The yellow band contains the name of the particular product.... The red band contains the required warning regarding toxicity, general information about the product and its ingredients, and a drawing suggestive of the uses of the product, e.g., the insects which a particular pesticide will eradicate.[4]

The court concluded that there was no legal or conceptual obstacle to finding a trade dress inherently distinctive. As it explained, "if the features of the trade dress sought to be protected are arbitrary and serve no function either to describe the product or assist in its effective

§ 28.4

1. Wal–Mart Stores, Inc. v. Samara Brothers, Inc., 529 U.S. 205, 210, 120 S.Ct. 1339, 146 L.Ed.2d 182 (2000).

2. *See, e.g.*, Vibrant Sales Inc. v. New Body Boutique Inc., 652 F.2d 299, 303 (2d Cir.1981).

3. 659 F.2d 695 (5th Cir.1981), *cert. denied*, 457 U.S. 1126, 102 S.Ct. 2947, 73 L.Ed.2d 1342 (1982).

4. 659 F.2d at 697.

packaging, there is no reason to require a plaintiff to show consumer connotations associated with such arbitrarily selected features."

The reference in *Chevron* to "arbitrary" trade dress recalls, of course, the continuum of categories usually used in analyzing the distinctiveness of word-marks, which is often referred to as the *Abercrombie* test.[5] As we have seen in previous chapters, under that scheme marks are classified as either fanciful, arbitrary, suggestive, or descriptive. Because the packaging of the Ortho products did not in any way "describe" the goods, but rather was arbitrarily selected, the Fifth Circuit found it to be inherently distinctive, just like the mark CAMEL for cigarettes is arbitrary and inherently distinctive.

While *Chevron* marked a turning point, not all of the federal circuits chose to follow its lead. Cases from the Second Circuit, in particular, continued to insist that there could be no such thing as inherently distinctive trade dress. For instance in *Stormy Clime, Ltd v. ProGroup, Inc.*, the Second Circuit noted that in order to recover under section 43(a) in a claim of trade dress infringement "the plaintiff must show that the trade dress of its product has acquired secondary meaning in the marketplace."[6] A few years later in *Murphy v. Provident Mutual Life Ins. Co.*,[7] the court was still adhering to this view, noting that "nonverbal marks that are unregistered always require proof of secondary meaning." Cases from the Third and Eighth Circuits also followed this rule.[8]

In 1992 the Supreme Court waded into the dispute and settled the split among the circuits when it decided *Two Pesos, Inc. v. Taco Cabana, Inc.*[9] The plaintiff in that case—Taco Cabana—operated a chain of Mexican restaurants, each of which was decorated similarly. Taco Cabana claimed its decor as its trade dress, and described it as consisting of "a festive eating atmosphere having interior dining and patio areas decorated with artifacts, bright colors, paintings and murals. The patio includes interior and exterior areas with the interior patio capable of being sealed off from the outside patio by overhead garage doors. The stepped exterior of the building is a festive and vivid color scheme using top border paint and neon stripes. Bright awnings and umbrellas continue the theme." The defendant, Two Pesos, adopted a very similar decor for its competing chain of restaurants, and Taco Cabana sued Two Pesos for trade dress infringement under section 43(a) of the Lanham Act.

5. The reference is to Abercrombie & Fitch, Co. v. Hunting World, Inc., 537 F.2d 4 (2d Cir.1976). *See generally* §§ 27.1–27.2, *supra.*

6. 809 F.2d 971, 974 (2d Cir.1987). *See also* LeSportsac, Inc. v. K Mart Corp., 754 F.2d 71, 75 (2d Cir.1985).

7. 923 F.2d 923, 927 (2d Cir.1990), *cert. denied*, 502 U.S. 814, 112 S.Ct. 65, 116 L.Ed.2d 40 (1991).

8. *See, e.g.,* Truck Equip. Serv. Co. v. Fruehauf Corp., 536 F.2d 1210 (8th Cir.), *cert. denied*, 429 U.S. 861, 97 S.Ct. 164, 50 L.Ed.2d 139 (1976); Woodsmith Publishing Co. v. Meredith Corp., 11 USPQ2d 1651 (S.D.Iowa 1989), *aff'd*, 904 F.2d 1244 (8th Cir.1990).

9. 505 U.S. 763, 112 S.Ct. 2753, 120 L.Ed.2d 615 (1992).

After a jury trial, the jury was instructed to answer five questions framed by the trial judge. In response to the two questions most relevant to the distinctiveness inquiry the jury found that Taco Cabana's trade dress had not acquired a secondary meaning, but that the trade dress was inherently distinctive. On the basis of those findings the trial court held that the plaintiff was entitled to relief. Both the Fifth Circuit and the Supreme Court upheld that decision. In doing so, the Supreme Court explicitly endorsed the approach of *Chevron* and concluded that "[t]here is no persuasive reason to apply to trade dress a general requirement of secondary meaning which is at odds with the principles generally applicable to infringement suits under § 43(a)." Elsewhere in its opinion the Supreme Court also noted that "[t]he Fifth Circuit was quite right in *Chevron,* and in this case, to follow the *Abercrombie* classifications consistently and to inquire whether trade dress for which protection is claimed under § 43(a) is inherently distinctive."

Although it referred in passing to the *Abercrombie* classifications, the *Taco Cabana* opinion did not provide any further guidance on what test should be applied to determine when trade dress should be deemed inherently distinctive. In the years immediately following the decision, several cases posing just this question arose in the lower courts, and once again, there was considerable diversity of opinion between the various federal circuits. As one trio of commentators put it, "the case law following *Two Pesos* has been a morass, with the various circuits taking widely varying approaches to the inherent distinctiveness question...."[10]

Some cases focused on likely consumer reaction to the trade dress, rather than on the relationship between the trade dress and the attributes of the underlying product, an inquiry which is the basis of the *Abercrombie* classifications. In one such case, the Third Circuit held that trade dress could be "inherently distinctive" only if it was "unusual or memorable" and "likely to serve primarily as a designator of origin of the product."[11] Other courts, however, tried to apply the *Abercrombie* spectrum quite literally. Thus, the Eight Circuit observed that "the classification of trade dress as arbitrary or fanciful or suggestive, and thus inherently distinctive, requires no showing that the trade dress is memorable or striking.... The question ... is whether, and how much, the trade dress is dictated by the nature of the product, not whether consumers remember or are struck by the design...."[12]

Of course very few package designs or shapes are "dictated" by the nature of the product, and consequently the Eighth Circuit's approach to inherent distinctiveness resulted in a very expansive view of when trade

10. Steven F. Mohr, Glenn Mitchell & Steven J. Wadyka, Jr., U.S. TRADE DRESS LAW: EXPLORING THE BOUNDARIES 71 (Int'l Trademark Asso. 1997).

11. Duraco Products, Inc. v. Joy Plastic Enterprises, Ltd., 40 F.3d 1431, 1434 (3d Cir.1994).

12. Stuart Hall, Co., Inc. v. Ampad Corp., 51 F.3d 780, 785–86 (8th Cir.1995). *See also* Paddington Corp. v. Attiki Importers & Distribs., Inc., 996 F.2d 577 (2d Cir. 1993).

dress was protectable. Especially because many of these post-*Two Pesos* cases involved claims of trade dress in *product* design rather than in *packaging*, a sweeping view of inherent distinctiveness in these types of cases could pose especially heavy burdens on competition. Protection in cases of this sort effectively prevents competitors from selling products that are identical to the plaintiff's, and thus grants a potential monopoly to every firm that comes up with a new product design.

Against this backdrop, the Supreme Court returned to the issue of trade dress distinctiveness in *Wal-Mart Stores, Inc. v. Samara Brothers, Inc.*[13] The trade dress at issue in this case was the design of children's seersucker outfits decorated with appliques of hearts, flowers, fruits and the like. When Wal–Mart began selling virtually identical garments for a lower price, Samara Brothers sued for trade dress infringement. The lower courts found the product design to be an inherently distinctive trade dress and had awarded Samara $1.6 million plus injunctive relief. The Supreme Court reversed, however, holding that when the trade dress involved product design, it could *never* be inherently distinctive. As Justice Scalia explained:

> The attribution of inherent distinctiveness to certain categories of word marks and product packaging derives from the fact that the very purpose of attaching a particular word to a product, or encasing it in a distinctive packaging, is most often to identify the source of the product. Although the words and packaging can serve subsidiary functions—a suggestive word mark (such as ''Tide'' for laundry detergent), for instance, may invoke positive connotations in the consumer's mind, and a garish form of packaging (such as Tide's squat, brightly decorated plastic bottles for its liquid laundry detergent) may attract an otherwise indifferent consumer's attention on a crowded store shelf— their predominant function remains source identification.... In the case of product design, ... we think consumer predisposition to equate the feature with the source does not exist. Consumers are aware of the reality that, almost invariably, even the most unusual of product designs—such as a cocktail shaker shaped like a penguin—is intend not to identify the source, but to render the product itself more useful or more appealing.[14]

The Court distinguished its prior decision in *Two Pesos* by noting that ''the decor of a restaurant seems to us not to constitute product design. It was either product packaging ... or else some tertium quid[15] that is akin to product packaging....'' The Court recognized that it might not always be clear whether a given trade dress consisted of product packaging or product design, and it declared that in close cases,

13. 529 U.S. 205, 120 S.Ct. 1339, 146 L.Ed.2d 182 (2000).

14. 529 U.S. at 212–13.

15. This is Latin for ''third thing''— presumably meaning in the context of the discussion that restaurant decor is neither product design nor product packaging but rather a special category unto itself.

the trade dress should be treated as if it were product design, thereby requiring secondary meaning.

In reaching this result, the Court was heavily influenced by its desire to avoid burdening competition, and by its perception that any test of inherent distinctiveness for product design cases would encourage meritless suits designed to intimidate competitors. Again, to quote from the opinion:

> Consumers should not be deprived of the benefits of competition with regard to the utilitarian and aesthetic purposes that product design ordinarily serves by a rule of law that facilitates plausible threats of suit against new entrants based upon alleged inherent distinctiveness.... Competition is deterred ... not merely by successful suit but by the plausible threat of successful suit, and given the unlikelihood of inherently source-identifying design, the game of allowing suit based upon alleged inherent distinctiveness seems to us not worth the candle.[16]

Thus, after *Wal-Mart,* the first step in analyzing the distinctiveness of trade dress will be to categorize the trade dress as either "packaging" or "product design" with close or ambiguous types of trade dress being placed in the latter category. As an aid to this categorization process it is worth noting that product design will often be the issue when the product is big, bulky, and sold or displayed without a package. Examples include furniture, cars and boats, many clothing items and large appliances like vacuum cleaners. Where the trade dress consists of product design, the merchant seeking protection *must* show secondary meaning in order to prevail. Where the trade dress consists of packaging, however, the merchant can attempt to persuade the court that the trade dress is "inherently distinctive."

This still leaves unresolved, however, what test should be used to determine when product packaging is inherently distinctive. While some courts will, no doubt, continue to try to apply the *Abercrombie* continuum—reasoning that the Supreme Court endorsed this approach in *Two Pesos*—that effort could lead to an overly generous stance on the inherent distinctiveness inquiry, for as the Second Circuit recently noted, "the varieties of labels and packaging available to wholesalers and manufacturers are virtually unlimited. As a consequence, a product's trade dress *typically* will be arbitrary or fanciful and meet the inherently distinctive requirement for § 43(a) protection."[17] In other words, on this view virtually all packaging is inherently distinctive.

More importantly, trying to use the *Abercrombie* analysis for product packaging seems to be very much like trying to put a square peg into a round hole. The *Abercrombie* approach compares the informational con-

16.   529 U.S. at 213–214.

17.   *See, e.g.,* Fun-Damental Too, Ltd. v. Gemmy Industries Corp., 111 F.3d 993, 1000 (2d Cir.1997), (emphasis added), citing Mana Prods., Inc. v. Columbia Cosmetics Mfg., Inc., 65 F.3d 1063, 1069 (2d Cir.1995) and Chevron Chem. Co. v. Voluntary Purchasing Groups, Inc., 659 F.2d 695, 703 (5th Cir.1981).

tent of word marks to the underlying attributes of the product in question—MOP 'N' GLOW might be descriptive of a floor polish because it tells us about the product, while FOUR ROSES would be arbitrary for whisky because it provides no meaningful data. While some packaging attributes can provide information about the product inside—such as a picture of a toilet bowl on a bottle of toilet bowl cleanser—most packaging will not. For instance a white rectangular box with gold script lettering containing an assortment of chocolates does not really provide any information about the contents of the box. It could just as well contain men's neckties or dried beef jerky. Such a box, however, seems sufficiently pedestrian that it ought not be the exclusive property of a single vendor unless that vendor can demonstrate secondary meaning.

In search of an alternative test, some courts and commentators have embraced the rule first articulated by the Court of Customs and Patent Appeals in *Seabrook Foods, Inc. v. Bar–Well Foods, Ltd.*[18] That court suggested that to determine if product packaging is inherently distinctive, courts should consider "whether it was a 'common' basic shape or design, whether it was unique or unusual in a particular field, [and] whether it was a mere refinement of a commonly-adopted and well-known form of ornamentation for a particular class of goods viewed by the public as a dress or ornamentation for the goods."[19] *Seabrook* essentially looks to common practice in the industry to determine if packaging is inherently distinctive. If it is customary to package tuna fish in squat cylindrical tins bearing labels with colors evocative of the ocean, such as blue or green, that package is not inherently distinctive under the *Seabrook* test—which certainly seems logical enough. Conversely, under this rule it is possible that a plastic squeeze bottle for maple syrup in the shape of a maple tree might be found inherently distinctive even though it arguably "describes" the contents of the container, because such a package is quite unusual and not at all commonly used by other syrup sellers.

The Court of Appeals for the Federal Circuit has intimated that the *Seabrook* and *Abercrombie* tests are not mutually exclusive, and can be used to complement each other.[20] Similarly, the Trademark Trials and Appeals Board has rejected a "contention that, because of *Two Pesos, Abercrombie* alone is the test for inherent distinctiveness of trade dress. On the other hand, we do not reject any application of *Abercrombie* nor rely solely on *Seabrook*."[21] Other courts have attempted to follow this same middle path. It is likely, however, that the Supreme Court will have to plunge into the swamp once again and provide a definitive definition of inherent distinctiveness in order to bring coherence and uniformity to the subject.

18. 568 F.2d 1342, 1344 (CCPA 1977).

19. A bill introduced in the 105th Congress attempted to essentially codify the *Seabrook* test. *See* H.R. 3162 (105th Cong. 2d Sess.) (1998).

20. Tone Brothers, Inc. v. Sysco Corp., 28 F.3d 1192, 1205 (Fed.Cir.1994), *cert. de-* *nied,* 514 U.S. 1015, 115 S.Ct. 1356, 131 L.Ed.2d 214 (1995).

21. In re Creative Beauty Innovations, 56 USPQ2d 1203, 2000 WL 1160455, *1160455 (T.T.A.B.2000).

§ 28.5   Federal Pre-emption of State Trade Dress Infringement Claims

In 1964, in two cases decided on the same day, and known collectively as *Sears-Compco,* the U.S. Supreme Court held that states could not preclude competitors from copying objects that were unprotected by the patent laws.[1] In each case, the plaintiff claimed trade dress protection for a product configuration—in one instance for a pole lamp and in the other for a ceiling light fixture. In each case a defendant began selling a copycat product that duplicated the appearance of the plaintiff's merchandise. The plaintiffs asserted claims under Illinois state law for unfair competition. Although the Supreme Court acknowledged that both plaintiffs' trade dresses were non-functional and had secondary meaning, it held that "a State ... cannot, under [a] ... law ... forbidding unfair competition, give protection of a kind that clashes with the objectives of the federal patent laws." Because the plaintiffs' goods were not protected by patents, the Court declared that the defendants had an absolute right to copy them, and that Illinois law to the contrary was preempted.

Because the cases deal with conflicts between state and federal law, they have no relevance to claims asserted under section 43(a) of the Lanham Act alleging infringement of unregistered trade dress, nor do they apply in cases alleging infringement of federally registered trade dress, which implicate section 32 of the Lanham Act, because these are federal claims. The implications for state law, however seem sweeping. Read broadly, the decisions seem to suggest that the states were precluded from providing any state level common law protection for trade dress in cases where the trade dress had not been patented.

The Court did leave the door slightly open for states to regulate imitation of competitors' trade dress if the copying could have the effect of deceiving the public. As Justice Black explained:

> [A] state may, in appropriate circumstances, require that goods, whether patented or unpatented, be labeled, or that other precautionary steps be taken to prevent customers from being misled as to the source, just as it may protect businesses in the use of their trademarks, labels, or distinctive dress in the packaging of goods, so as to prevent others, by imitating such markings from misleading purchasers as to the source of the goods.

The opinions seem clear that the copying itself, however, could not be forbidden.

In the years that followed, lower courts struggled mightily to distinguish *Sears-Compco,* and largely succeeded in doing so.[2] Moreover, the

§ 28.5

1. Sears, Roebuck & Co. v. Stiffel Co., 376 U.S. 225, 84 S.Ct. 784, 11 L.Ed.2d 661 (1964); Compco Corp. v. Day–Brite Lighting, Inc., 376 U.S. 234, 84 S.Ct. 779, 11 L.Ed.2d 669 (1964).

2. *See, e.g.,* Truck Equipment Service Co. v. Fruehauf Corp., 536 F.2d 1210, 1214 (8th Cir.1976), *cert. denied,* 429 U.S. 861, 97 S.Ct. 164, 50 L.Ed.2d 139 (1976); Dallas Cowboys Cheerleaders, Inc. v. Pussycat Cinema, Ltd., 604 F.2d 200, 204 (2d Cir.1979);

Supreme Court itself, in a line of cases beginning in the early 1970's, began to signal that the preemptive force of the patent laws was narrower than *Sears-Compco* had implied.[3]

Any ambiguity on this subject was eliminated 25 years later when the court returned to essentially the same issue in *Bonito Boats, Inc. v. Thunder Craft Boats, Inc.*[4] In that case, a Florida statute prevented anyone from duplicating the design of a boat hull through a method known as "plug molding"—the most efficient and inexpensive way to duplicate a design. The statute was not predicated on trademark or trade dress notions of public confusion, but rather on more general concerns about the unfairness—and negative effects on incentives—of allowing unrestricted copying of another firm's design. The Supreme Court held that the statute in question was pre-empted under the federal patent laws. Noting that the boat hulls covered by its provisions were not protected by federal patents, it held that Congress wanted everyone to be free to copy them. In reaching that conclusion, however, Justice O'Connor took the opportunity to narrow the scope of *Sears* and *Compco*. She observed that

> the extrapolation of ... a broad pre-emptive principle from *Sears* is inappropriate. [This] is clear from the balance struck in *Sears* itself.... [O]ur decision in *Sears* clearly indicates that the States may place limited regulations on the circumstances in which [product] designs are used in order to prevent consumer confusion as to source.

After *Bonito Boats* it thus seems clear that if state common law insists on both non-functionality and distinctiveness for trade dress—as it does in all jurisdictions—and if relief is predicated on a showing of likelihood of confusion—as it is—then state common law trade dress protection can peacefully co-exist with the federal patent regime. Moreover, the availability of a federal remedy for infringement of even unregistered trade dress under section 43(a) of the Lanham Act means that few litigants will want or need to assert claims under state law in any event.

§ 28.6 Special Considerations Concerning Protection for Product Color

Color is a central attribute of many trademarks. One need only think of the red and white of the COCA–COLA logo, or the brown and gold combination associated with West Publications casebooks to appreciate this fact. Nonetheless, one of the more troublesome questions in trademark law has been whether a single overall color can, by itself and

SK&F, Co. v. Premo Pharmaceutical Laboratories, Inc., 625 F.2d 1055, 1064 (3d Cir. 1980).

3. *See, e.g.*, Kewanee Oil Co. v. Bicron Corp., 416 U.S. 470, 94 S.Ct. 1879, 40 L.Ed.2d 315 (1974); Aronson v. Quick Point Pencil Co., 440 U.S. 257, 99 S.Ct. 1096, 59 L.Ed.2d 296 (1979).

4. 489 U.S. 141, 109 S.Ct. 971, 103 L.Ed.2d 118 (1989).

independent of any design or color scheme, function as a trademark. Those with an affinity for Latin refer to this issue as one involving the protectability of color "simpliciter."

Historically, the courts denied trademark protection to overall color because of two major concerns. The first of these was their fear of the problem of "shade confusion." In other words, the courts were concerned that they would be sucked into endless subjective controversies over whether two colors differed sufficiently to be distinguishable or were sufficiently close to each other to engender confusion. Secondly, courts also fretted over "color depletion." This fear was based on the idea that there are only a limited number of colors available and after a few firms snapped up the basic colors, other competitors in the same field would be handicapped in their efforts to adopt appealing trademarks or trade dress. These two concerns influenced the court of appeals in *Nutra–Sweet Co. v. Stadt Corp.,*[1] to deny protection to the overall blue coloring of the packets in which EQUAL brand sugar substitute is marketed. On the other hand, the Court of Appeals for the Federal Circuit found the very same arguments unpersuasive and granted protection to the overall pink color of insulation in *In re Owens–Corning Fiberglas Corp.*[2]

Not long after these cases were decided, the Supreme Court resolved the dispute between the circuits. In *Qualitex Co. v. Jacobson Prods. Co.,*[3] the plaintiff was a marketer of "press pads"—cushiony covers for the steam irons used in professional dry cleaning establishments. For many years it had colored these press pads a distinctive green-gold color. In the late 1980's a competitor named Jacobson began marketing pads in a similar color. Qualitex sued, alleging infringement based on the duplication of the color of its product.

The Court found that there was no legal obstacle to the use of color alone as a trademark, provided that the color had achieved secondary meaning and was not functional. The Court could not "find in the basic objectives of trademark law any obvious theoretical objection to the use of color alone as a trademark ..." and observed that "[i]t is the source-distinguishing ability of a mark—not its ontological status as color, shape, fragrance, word or sign—that permits it to" function as a mark.

In reaching this conclusion, the Court rejected the shade confusion argument, observing that "we do not believe ... that color, in this respect, is special. Courts traditionally decide quite difficult questions about whether two words or phrases or symbols are sufficiently similar in context to confuse buyers." It also found the color depletion argument unpersuasive because "it relies on an occasional problem to justify a blanket prohibition," and because "if a 'color depletion' or 'color scarcity' problem does arise—the trademark doctrine of 'functionality' normal-

§ 28.6
1. 917 F.2d 1024 (7th Cir.1990).
2. 774 F.2d 1116 (Fed.Cir.1985).

3. 514 U.S. 159, 164–65, 115 S.Ct. 1300, 131 L.Ed.2d 248 (1995).

ly would seem available to prevent the anticompetitive consequences...."

Like trade dress generally, a party claiming legal protection for the
single overall color of its product must show that the color is both
distinctive and non-functional. The Court in *Qualitex* made it clear that
distinctiveness of color always requires a showing of secondary meaning—in other words color can never be inherently distinctive. The Court
reiterated this point just a few year later when it decided *Wal-Mart*.
Thus for distinctiveness analysis product color is treated the same way
as product design or configuration.

Overall product color might be functional in either the utilitarian or
in the aesthetic sense. For instance clothing marketed to hunters is often
colored a bright orange sometimes referred to as "blaze orange." The
same fetching shade is used on traffic cones. This color obviously has
utilitarian advantages because of its visibility, a virtue of especial value
in a dense forest filled with over-zealous deer hunters. Any merchant
attempting to claim exclusivity in orange hunting vests would fail on the
grounds of functionality.[4] Similarly, much Halloween paraphernalia is
also colored orange—not for reasons of visibility, but rather to conform
to consumer's aesthetic desires to decorate their homes in shades reminiscent of pumpkins. It is a fair guess that other colors, such as pink or
turquoise would not sell very well for trick-or-treat buckets. Consequently, a merchant attempting to claim exclusivity in orange Halloween
buckets would be turned out of court on grounds of aesthetic functionality.

§ 28.7 Unconventional Trademarks Including Sound and Smell

Because the Lanham Act defines a trademark as "any word, name,
symbol or *device*" that can identify and distinguish goods, ingenious
merchants have occasionally sought protection for exotic types of trademark formats. Provided that these items do in fact serve as source
designators, that they are distinctive, and that they are non-functional,
there is no obstacle to protection.

Take sound. The three-chime melody associated with the NBC
television network has been in use for decades. It is widely, if not
universally recognized as a designator for NBC and its programming. It
serves no particular utilitarian or aesthetic function, and competitors
have a host of other sounds to choose from. Thus it is well-suited for
trademark protection.[1] Sound marks that have been registered by the

---

4. *See also* In re Ferris Corporation, 59
U.S.P.Q.2d 1587 (T.T.A.B.2000) (pink color
for surgical dressing denied registration on
ground of functionality because of its ability
to blend with the color of many patients'
skin).

§ 28.7

1. *See generally*, In re General Electric
Broadcasting Co., 199 USPQ 560 (T.T.A.B.

1978) ("sounds may, under certain conditions, at least as far as services are concerned ... function as source indicators in
those situations where they assume a definitive shape or arrangement and are used in
such a manner so as to create in the hear-
er's mind an association of the sound with a
service.").

PTO include the sound of a cat meowing for entertainment services[2] and the sound of Tarzan's inimitable yell.[3] On the other hand, one might imagine that if a railroad company wanted to claim the sound of a locomotive whistle as a trademark, it would be imprudent to grant the request. Other railroads might find it awkward to warn pedestrians and motorists crossing the tracks if trademark law made it impossible for them to use a whistle.

Scent or fragrance can also function as a trademark, but here the situation is a bit trickier, since some products are sold primarily, or at least partially, for their scent—such as perfume or soap. On the other hand, many products normally have no particular fragrance at all—such as pens or eyeglasses.[4] The case for trademark protection of a fragrance is strongest with products in the latter category. Imparting the smell of bubble gum to a pen would certainly be highly distinctive, and entirely non-functional since it is hard to see how other pen makers would suffer if they were legally barred from copying that smell. The leading case on federal registration for fragrance as a trademark is a case of this sort. In *In re Clarke*,[5] the Patent Office allowed the applicant to register "a high impact, fresh, floral fragrance reminiscent of Plumeria blossoms" for "sewing thread and embroidery yarn." In granting the registration in *Clarke*, the Trademark Board distinguished the case of perfumes and other scented household products.

Where perfumes and other scented products, such as air fresheners, are concerned, the case for trademark protection seems considerably weaker. First, there may only be a limited number of acceptable scents available for competitors. Second, since the product is, itself, "a smell," the smell is necessarily descriptive of the product. Perhaps most importantly, however, is the fact that absent patent protection, competitors should be free to duplicate scented products if they can, provided that they do not confuse the public as to who they are.[6] There is no reason cab drivers should be limited to only one brand of pine scented air freshener to hang from their rear view mirrors.

Other somewhat unconventional types of marks that have secured protection include building exteriors, distinctively designed vehicles such as taxicabs or delivery vans, and clothing, such as cheerleaders' uniforms. At least one commentator has explored the possibility of trademark protection for flavors—at least for prescription drugs—and has expressed opposition to the idea, noting that "the flavors of most

2. *See* U.S. Trademark Registration No. 1,158,156 issued to MTM Enter., Inc. (May 19, 1998).

3. *See* U.S. Trademark Registration No. 2,210,506 issued to Edgar Rice Burroughs, Inc. (Dec. 15, 1998).

4. *See* Faye M. Hammersley, *The Smell of Success: Trade Dress Protection for Scent Marks*, 2 MARQ. INTELL. PROP. L. REV. 105, 124 (1998); Bettina Elias, *Do Scents Signify Source? An Argument Against Trademark Protection for Fragrances*, 82 TRADEMARK REP. 475, 509 (1992).

5. 17 USPQ2d 1238 (T.T.A.B.1990).

6. *See* Smith v. Chanel, Inc., 402 F.2d 562 (9th Cir.1968).

prescription pharmaceutical products function as masks, placebos or suspension media,'' which would make them functional.[7] Comparable objections can be imagined if one sought to register a flavor as a trademark for a food or beverage. On the other hand, if one sought to register flavor for objects occasionally put in the mouth, but not normally consumed, such as pens or spoons, concerns seems greatly diminished. If a pencil vendor chooses to impart a lemon flavor to erasers that top its pencils so that those chewing on them while preparing their taxes can develop brand loyalty, there seems little risk of imposition on either consumers or competitors.

7. Nancy L. Clarke, *Note, Issues in the Federal Registration of Flavors as Trade-* *marks for Pharmaceutical Products*, 1993 U. Ill. L. Rev. 105.

Chapter 29

TRADEMARK INFRINGEMENT, COUNTERFEITING AND FALSE ADVERTISING

Table of Sections

As we have seen in previous chapters, a merchant who selects the right kind of trade-identifying symbol and appropriates it in the right kind of way is given trademark rights in that symbol. Those rights are essentially a form of legally enforced exclusivity—a limited property right if you prefer[1]—forbidding others to use the trademark in certain ways. It follows that the unauthorized use of another party's trademark will *sometimes* be actionable as trademark infringement. There is, however, a lot of law hiding behind that word "sometimes."

We can begin with the procedural formalities. There are several different causes of action that may be invoked to secure relief against trademark infringement. If the complaining party holds a federal trademark registration, it can assert a claim under section 32 of the Lanham Act for infringement of a registered mark.[2] Owners of unregistered marks may not use this section. Instead, they can, of course, bring infringement claims under state common law.[3] In addition, owners of both registered *and* unregistered marks also have a federal cause of action for infringement under the provisions of section 43 of the Lanham Act, which forbids false designations or origin or sponsorship.[4] In many suits, multiple counts of the complaint will plead several of these claims side-by-side.

Substantively there are virtually no differences between these various claims,[5] and in the discussion that follows you can safely assume that the same principles and policies govern regardless of the exact infringement cause of action being asserted unless the text specifically indicates to the contrary. These principles also will apply whether plaintiff is suing for infringement of a conventional trademark or for infringement of trade dress.

1. *See, e.g.,* New Kids on the Block v. New America Pub., Inc., 971 F.2d 302, 305 n. 2 (9th Cir.1992) ("A trademark is a limited property right in a particular word, phrase or symbol.").

2. Section 32 provides that "any person who shall, without the consent of the registrant—(a) use in commerce any reproduction, counterfeit, copy, or colorable imitation of a registered mark in connection with the sale, offering for sale, distribution, or advertising of any goods or services on or in connection with which such use is likely to cause confusion, or to cause mistake, or to deceive . . . shall be liable in a civil action by the registrant. . . ." 15 U.S.C.A. § 1114(1) (2000).

3. *See, e.g.,* Restatement (Third) of Unfair Competition § 20, which provides: "One is subject to liability for infringement of another's trademark, trade name, collective mark, or certification mark if . . . that actor uses a designation that causes a likelihood of confusion."

4. Section 43 provides that "any person who, on or in connection with any goods or services, or any container for goods, uses in commerce any word, term, name, symbol, or device, or any combination thereof, or any false designation of origin, false or misleading description of fact, or false or misleading representation of fact, which—(A) is likely to cause confusion, or to cause mistake, or to deceive as to the affiliation, connection, or association of such person with another person as to the origin, sponsorship, or approval of his or her goods, services, or commercial activities by another person . . . shall be liable in a civil action by any person who believe that he or she is or is likely to be damaged by such act." 15 U.S.C.A. § 1125(a)(1) (2000).

5. *See, e.g.,* International Order of Job's Daughters v. Lindeburg & Co., 633 F.2d 912 (9th Cir.1980) ("federal and state laws regarding trademarks and related claims of unfair competition are substantially congruent."); TMT North America, Inc. v. Magic Touch GmbH, 124 F.3d 876 (7th Cir.1997).

§ 29.1　Likelihood of Confusion as The General Test of Infringement

As the previous chapters have explained, one of the primary functions of trademarks is aiding consumers in relocating goods that have pleased them in the past. The chief vice of trademark infringement is that it misleads consumers into purchasing the "wrong" product. This is unfair to the consumer who does not get what he or she was expecting, and it is unfair to the merchant who owns the trademark because it deprives that merchant of an expected sale. For either of these harms to result, however, there must be some risk that the consumer will be confused into thinking that the defendant's product has some connection with the owner of the mark. It is for this reason that the central concept in all trademark infringement litigation is the concept of "likelihood of confusion."

The Patent and Trademark Office also uses the same standard of likelihood of confusion in ruling on the registrability of marks which are challenged as being too similar to marks previous used by others.[1] However, the Second Circuit had held that a PTO finding of likely confusion in an administrative opposition proceeding may not always have collateral estoppel effect in a subsequent suit for infringement.[2] The court reasoned that in some cases, the PTO is only able to compare the marks in a vacuum, while the issue in infringement litigation is always likely confusion in the real marketplace. Collateral estoppel on the issue of likelihood of confusion will only be applied if the administrative record demonstrates that the PTO took "into account, in a meaningful way, the context of the marketplace."

Confusion is most likely to result when an unauthorized party uses a mark identical to that of the plaintiff on the exact same type of goods or services as are sold by the plaintiff and sells those in the exact same geographic area. For instance, if an unauthorized party began selling potato chips in the Washington, D.C. area with the word UTZ marked on the packages, it is almost inevitable that consumers would be confused into thinking that these chips came from the company that owns the UTZ trademark and sells potato chips in Washington, D.C. Since the chips in question are actually made by someone else, the consumer is being duped. Moreover, since such a consumer presumably wanted and would have purchased genuine UTZ brand chips but for being tricked, the trademark owner has lost a sale. This would be a slam dunk case of infringement.

Of course most litigated cases of trademark infringement are not this easy. It is quite common to encounter legal controversies where the defendant is using a similar, but not identical version of the plaintiff's trademark—for instance OOTS brand potato chips—or where the defendant is using the same mark on different types of goods—for instance

§ 29.1

1. 15 U.S.C.A. § 1052(d) (2000). *See generally,* § 27.4, *supra.*

2. Levy v. Kosher Overseers Ass'n of America, Inc., 104 F.3d 38 (2d Cir.1997).

UTZ brand chocolate chip cookies—or where the defendant is doing business in a region of the country remote from the plaintiff's area of operations—for instance a defendant selling UTZ brand potato chips in Arizona. Moreover, these permutations can be combined, suggesting a case where the owner of the UTZ mark for potato chips sold in Washington D.C. might want to assert a claim of infringement against the user of the mark OOTS for chocolate chip cookies sold in Arizona. In all these variations the central legal questions continues to be whether the defendant's conduct generates a likelihood of consumer confusion, but the resolution of that question can become quite vexing. Indeed, no less an authority than Learned Hand admitted that "no two cases are alike. One must trust one's own sense of the likelihood of confusion..."[3]—an observation more than a little daunting to those of us who may trust our judgment somewhat less than Learned Hand trusted his.

Fortunately, there are some base line principles that guide decisions in this area. As is suggested by the word "likelihood," the test does not require a trademark infringement plaintiff to show that actual confusion has already occurred in the marketplace. On the other hand, demonstration of only a possibility of confusion will not suffice. The formula contemplates the middle ground—the confusion must be "probable."[4] The Seventh Circuit, in reversing a injunction against alleged trademark infringement based on the trial court's find of only a "possibility" of confusion, concisely explained why a test predicated on mere possibility would be inappropriate: "Many consumers are ignorant or inattentive so some are bound to misunderstand no matter how careful a producer is."[5] In other words, there might be some consumers who think that COCA–COLA and PEPSI–COLA are made by the same company because they both have the word "cola" in their trademarks. While that makes confusion a possibility, it would overprotect the first of those two marks to prohibit the second, to protect such a small and naive segment of the public.

A second basic principle of trademark infringement law is that the plaintiff is entitled to relief if it can show likely confusion either as to the source of the goods, or as to their sponsorship.[6] Source confusion exists if consumers think that the plaintiff actually manufactured the defendant's goods. Sponsorship confusion can exist if defendant's actions will induce consumers to think that the plaintiff in some way endorsed the defendant's goods, perhaps through a licensing arrangement, some form of corporate or contractual affiliation or otherwise. As the commentary to the Restatement explains, the likelihood of confusion rule

3. Lambert Pharmacal Co. v. Bolton Chemical Corp., 219 F. 325 (S.D.N.Y.1915).

4. *See, e.g.,* Rodeo Collection, Ltd. v. West Seventh, 812 F.2d 1215 (9th Cir.1987) ("Likelihood of confusion requires that confusion be probable, not simply a possibility."); A & H Sportswear, Inc. v. Victoria's Secret Stores, Inc., 166 F.3d 197 (3d Cir. 1999).

5. August Storck K.G. v. Nabisco, Inc., 59 F.3d 616 (7th Cir.1995).

6. *See, e.g.,* New York Stock Exchange v. New York, New York Hotel LLC, 293 F.3d 550, 554–55 (2d Cir.2002).

applies to all forms of confusion of sponsorship, including the false belief that the prior user of the mark has formally certified the goods as meeting particular standards, as in the case of certification marks, the false belief that the producer or distributor of the goods is affiliated with the prior user as a franchisee, agent, or distributor, or the false belief that the producer or distributor has obtained the approval of the prior user in manufacturing or marketing the goods.[7]

One common situation raising likelihood of confusion as to sponsorship arises when a former franchisee continues using the trademarks of the franchisor after the expiration or termination of the franchise agreement. If a service station owner formerly associated with EXXON continues to use EXXON signs after the relationship with the owner of the mark has ended, that almost certainly will lead consumers to think that there is still an affiliation, and therefore it will constitute a clear case of infringement.[8] Ditto for the former MCDONALD'S franchisee. Issues concerning confusion as to sponsorship are also particularly relevant in cases involving non-competing goods, a topic considered below in section 29.3 of this chapter.

A third reliable generalization about the likelihood of confusion rule is that in applying it, courts require the plaintiff to show that an appreciable or substantial number of consumers are likely to be confused.[9] Thus, if the defendant's behavior risks confusing only a handful of buyers, there will be no finding of infringement. Unfortunately, there is no bright line test as to what constitutes the required "substantial number of consumers." Some courts have focused on the percentage of applicable consumers confused, and others have emphasized the absolute numbers. Several cases have found a 15% level of confusion to be sufficient for infringement,[10] and it seems quite clear that numbers well short of a majority of relevant consumers will be held to satisfy the test. Other courts frame the requirement in terms of the confusion of a "reasonably prudent consumer."[11] This amounts to the same thing

---

7. Restatement (Third) of Unfair Competition § 20, comment d (1995).

8. Burger King Corp. v. Mason, 710 F.2d 1480 (11th Cir.1983), *cert. denied*, 465 U.S. 1102, 104 S.Ct. 1599, 80 L.Ed.2d 130 (1984). ("Common sense compels the conclusion that a strong risk of consumer confusion arises when a terminated franchisee continues to use the former franchisor's trademarks."). Often, the key issue in cases of this sort is whether the franchisor had valid grounds to terminate the franchise agreement. Once that issue is resolved, the trademark rights are easily determined.

9. Mushroom Makers, Inc. v. R. G. Barry Corp., 580 F.2d 44 (2d Cir.1978) ("the crucial issue in an action for trademark infringement or unfair competition is whether there is any likelihood that an appreciable number of ordinarily prudent purchasers are likely to be misled, or indeed simply confused, as to the source of the goods in question").

10. *See, e.g.*, James Burrough, Ltd. v. Sign of Beefeater, Inc., 540 F.2d 266 (7th Cir.1976); Exxon Corp. v. Texas Motor Exchange, Inc., 628 F.2d 500 (5th Cir.1980).

11. Dreamwerks Production Group, Inc. v. SKG Studio, 142 F.3d 1127, 1129 (9th Cir.1998) ("The test for likelihood of confusion is whether a 'reasonably prudent consumer' in the marketplace is likely to be confused as to the origin of the good or service bearing one of the marks.").

because it disregards conduct that will only confuse the (hopefully small number of) inattentive or foolish consumers.

Beyond these generalities, most courts consider a broad range of factors in determining if a likelihood of confusion exists. Indeed, each of the federal circuits has a identified a formal list of factors that it deems relevant to the confusion analysis. These lists can be found in specific opinions that have evolved into each circuit's authoritative catalogue for this purpose. Thus, in the Second Circuit, courts make frequent reference to the *Polaroid*[12] factors, while in the Third Circuit the key precedent is *Interpace Corp. v. Lapp.*[13] Further examples are the Fourth Circuit's reliance on *Pizzeria Uno Corp. v. Temple,*[14] and the Sixth's use of the factors identified in *Frisch's Restaurants v. Elby's Big Boy.*[15] The Restatement of Unfair Competition has its own, comparable, list of factors, available to guide state courts adjudicating common law trademark disputes.[16]

While these lists of factors vary somewhat in their details, most of the factors are rather similar from circuit to circuit. Moreover, the various circuit-specific factor lists are meant more as guidelines than as an ironclad litmus test. The Seventh Circuit has observed that the "likelihood of confusion test is an equitable balancing test... no single factor is dispositive ... and courts may assign varying weights to each of the factors in different cases."[17] The Third Circuit has commented that the confusion "factors are not to be mechanically tallied but rather they are tools to guide a qualitative decision,"[18] and the Fourth echoed this sentiment, observing that "[t]he 'factors' ... are not meant to be a 'rigid formula' for infringement. Rather, the ... factors are only a guide—a catalog of various considerations that may be relevant in determining the ultimate statutory question of likelihood of confusion."[19] Indeed, while trial courts often march through each and every factor in their discussion of the confusion issue, this is often a formalistic exercise in cases where the confusion seems quite likely given the factual posture of the case. The sections below consider several of the most important factors bearing on the confusion inquiry that are common to all or virtually all courts confronting the issue.

29.1.1   Similarity of Marks

The first factor invariably considered by the courts is the similarity between the plaintiff's and the defendant's marks. Indeed, some courts

12. Polaroid Corp. v. Polarad Electronics Corp., 287 F.2d 492 (2d Cir.), *cert. denied*, 368 U.S. 820, 82 S.Ct. 36, 7 L.Ed.2d 25 (1961).

13. 721 F.2d 460 (3d Cir.1983).

14. 747 F.2d 1522 (4th Cir.1984).

15. 670 F.2d 642 (6th Cir.1982), *cert. denied*, 459 U.S. 916, 103 S.Ct. 231, 74 L.Ed.2d 182 (1982).

16. Restatement (Third) of Unfair Competition §§ 21–23 (1995).

17. Barbecue Marx, Inc. v. 551 Ogden, Inc., 235 F.3d 1041 (7th Cir.2000).

18. A & H Sportswear, Inc. v. Victoria's Secret Stores, Inc., 237 F.3d 198, 216 (3d Cir.2000).

19. Anheuser–Busch, Inc. v. L & L Wings, Inc., 962 F.2d 316, 320 (4th Cir. 1992), *cert. denied*, 506 U.S. 872, 113 S.Ct. 206, 121 L.Ed.2d 147 (1992).

have suggested that this is the only factor that matters where the goods of the two parties compete directly.[20] It should be clear in any case that the closer the defendant's symbol, slogan, design or packaging is to the plaintiff's, the more likely it is that confusion will be found. It should be equally clear, however, that exact identity between defendant's and plaintiff's marks is not necessary in order to find infringement. A rule insisting on exact identity would be an open invitation to unscrupulous parties to confuse the public by simply changing a single letter in a well-known brand name.

In comparing marks that consist of multiple words, or words combined with design elements, the marks are considered in their entirety under what is sometimes called a rule against "dissecting" the mark.[21] Some courts also warn that a "side-by-side" comparison is not the test because "a prospective purchaser does not ordinarily carry a sample or specimen of the article he knows ... he necessarily depends upon [a] mental picture ...."[22] Given the variety of trademark formats that are protected by the law, courts and treatise writers apply what is usually termed a "sound, sight or meaning" test for determining the similarity of the marks.[23] By this, they mean that the marks can be found confusingly close to each other if they either look closely alike, sound alike, or mean roughly the same thing. Examples abound.

Thus, in one early case, the mark "Cup–A–Cola" was held confusingly similar to COCA–COLA, a predictable result given the near identical sound of the two marks when spoken out loud.[24] In another case two tear drop shaped cartoon figures were held to be confusingly similar to each other given their similar visual appearance,[25] and of course visual similarity will be particularly significant in cases involving alleged infringement of trade dress. Findings of similarity based on the meaning of

---

20. *See, e.g.,* Homeowners Group, Inc. v. Home Marketing Specialists, Inc., 931 F.2d 1100, 1107 n. 4 (6th Cir.1991) ("In some cases it may be unnecessary to undertake an extended analysis to infer confusion, e.g., where there is no difference between the marks of directly competitive goods/services." *citing* AMF Inc. v. Sleekcraft Boats, 599 F.2d 341, 348 (9th Cir.1979)); Interpace Corp. v. Lapp, Inc., 721 F.2d 460, 462 (3d Cir.1983) (in a case involving competing goods "the court need rarely look beyond the mark itself").

21. *See, e.g,* Massey Junior College, Inc. v. Fashion Institute of Technology, 492 F.2d 1399, 1402 (CCPA 1974) ("It is axiomatic that a mark should not be dissected and considered piecemeal; rather it must be considered as a whole in determining likelihood of confusion."); Sun–Fun Products, Inc. v. Suntan Research & Development, Inc., 656 F.2d 186 (5th Cir.1981); Official Airline Guides, Inc. v. Goss, 6 F.3d 1385 (9th Cir.1993).

22. Beer Nuts, Inc. v. Clover Club Foods Co., 711 F.2d 934 (10th Cir.1983).

23. The current Restatement endorses these rules, instructing courts to consider "the degree of similarity between the respective designations, including a comparison of (i) the overall impression created by the designations as they are used in marketing the respective goods or services or in identifying the respective businesses; (ii) the pronunciation of the designations; (iii) the translation of any foreign words contained in the designations; (iv) the verbal translation of any pictures, illustrations, or designs contained in the designations; [and] (v) the suggestions, connotations, or meanings of the designations...." Restatement (Third) of Unfair Competition § 21(a) (1995).

24. Coca–Cola Co. v. Clay, 324 F.2d 198 (CCPA 1963).

25. In re Triple R Mfg. Corp., 168 USPQ 447 (T.T.A.B.1970).

the marks involved are illustrated by one decision holding that the designation "tornado" infringed the mark CYCLONE for chain link fences because the two marks are virtual synonyms,[26] and by another finding the word PEGASUS to be confusingly similar to MOBIL's trademark logo of a flying horse.[27] In determining whether two marks are confusingly similar in meaning, courts will usually translate foreign terms back into English, at least where an appreciable segment of the American consuming public is likely to be familiar with the language in question. Thus the mark CHAT NOIR would likely infringe the mark BLACK CAT if the parties sold competing or related goods.

Sometimes a large company will use a several trademarks for different products that all have a root element in common. When consumers identify all such marks as emanating from a common source, the clusters of similar marks is often called a "family of marks." Examples are the many marks used by the McDonald's restaurant chain that begin with the "MC" letter combination, (such as MCDLT, CHICKEN MCNUGGETS and EGG MCMUFFIN), and the variety of marks used by the Kodak company for its film related product all beginning with "KODA" (such as KODACOLOR and KODACHROME). If another firm adopts a mark using the common root element, it is quite likely that such a mark will be found infringing. This is why McDonald's prevailed against both a bagel bakery that adopted the mark MCBAGEL[28] and a discount motel chain that adopted the mark MCSLEEP,[29] among others.

The cases bristle with a variety of "micro-rules" that attempt to lend precision to the task of determining the similarity of marks, dealing with everything from how to weigh differences in the spelling of the marks to a rule that the "salient" feature of a mark should be given greater weight than surrounding elements in assessing similarity. Close examination usually reveals that these so-called rules are riddled with exceptions. Sadly, there is no objective yardstick available to tell us when marks are "too similar" to each other. If a firm wanted to use the designation "wind storm" for chain link fence, it would be difficult to predict whether such a designation inches too close to the CYCLONE mark to be acceptable.[30] Fortunately, courts do not decide the likelihood of confusion issue based solely on the similarity of the marks. Instead, the remaining factors of the likelihood of confusion analysis are designed to ground the determination in the market realities of the particular case at hand.

26. Hancock v. American Steel & Wire Co., 203 F.2d 737 (CCPA 1953).

27. Mobil Oil Corp. v. Pegasus Petroleum Corp., 818 F.2d 254 (2d Cir.1987).

28. McDonald's Corp. v. McBagel's, Inc., 649 F.Supp. 1268 (S.D.N.Y.1986).

29. Quality Inns Int'l, Inc. v. McDonald's Corp., 695 F.Supp. 198 (D.Md.1988).

30. A New York State court, for instance, found that the marks TORNADO and TYPHOON for fencing were not confusingly similar. Tornado Industries, Inc. v. Typhoon Industries, Inc., 20 Misc.2d 43, 187 N.Y.S.2d 83 (1959).

29.1.2   Sophistication of Consumers

A second inter-connected group of factors courts often consider in assessing likelihood of confusion are the cost of the goods or services in question, the degree of care purchasers of these goods usually exercise and the level of sophistication of the consumers who buy those goods.[31] The theory here is that consumers pay more attention when buying expensive items, so that more similarity in the marks can be tolerated without engendering any serious risk of confusion. Conversely, when the items are cheap and purchased on the spur of the moment, consumers might be inattentive and even minimal similarity in the marks might lead to significant confusion.[32] As the Federal Circuit observed in a recent case involving dog food, "[w]hen the products are relatively low-priced and subject to impulse buying, the risk of likelihood of confusion is increased because purchasers of such products are held to a lesser standard of purchasing care."[33] Thus, one might expect that the mark "JACKANAR" would be less likely to be found to infringe JAGUAR for luxury automobiles, than the mark "BAZOOMA" would be to infringe BAZOOKA for bubble gum. All other things being equal people pay a bit more attention when buying a $75,000 car than when buying a five cent piece of gum.[34]

The same logic leads courts to consider the sophistication of consumers. It is assumed that well-educated, mature consumers, and those who are merchants who make frequent purchases of a given type of item, will be more attentive to subtle differences in trademarks than the less well educated, less mature or more casual purchaser. To cite just one of a multitude of examples, Judge Wollin refused to find that the mark BARR for powdered pharmaceutical products would infringe the mark BARRE for liquid pharmaceuticals because of "the care and sophistication exercised by the professional purchasers of pharmaceuticals."[35] Of course there are always the curious cases. In 1959, a federal district court in Alabama confronted a case in which plaintiff alleged that its THUNDER-BIRD mark for fortified wine was infringed by the defendant's use of THUNDERBOLT on a competing product. The court declined to find infringement, noting, in part that: "The evidence in this case makes it

---

31. The Restatement encompasses this factor by instructing courts to consider "the characteristics of the prospective purchasers of the goods or services and the degree of care they are likely to exercise in making purchasing decisions." Restatement (Third) of Unfair Competition § 21(c).

32. *See id.* at comment h ("If the goods or services are normally purchased only after considerable attention and inspection, greater similarity between the designations may be permitted than when the goods or services are purchased casually or impulsively.").

33. Recot Inc. v. Becton, 214 F.3d 1322 (Fed.Cir.2000); *See also* Beer Nuts v. Clover Club Foods Co., 805 F.2d 920 (10th Cir. 1986) (peanuts are impulse items purchased

with little care and thus similar marks are likely to engender confusion).

34. Of course, courts are not always inclined to favor defendants just because the goods are expensive. For instance, the designation "Pineapple" used on computer kits was held to infringe APPLE for desktop computers and software, despite the expense of the product and the presumed sophistication of most computer buyers. Apple Computer, Inc. v. Formula Intern. Inc., 725 F.2d 521 (9th Cir.1984).

35. Barre–National, Inc. v. Barr Laboratories, Inc., 773 F.Supp. 735 (D.N.J.1991) (court also influenced by absence of actual confusion over a 16-year period that marks were used concurrently).

clear that the wine-buying public—insofar as their selection and purchase of wine is concerned—is a highly discriminating group."[36] The characterization of consumers of this particular product as "highly discriminating" is one that readers familiar with plaintiff's product might find amusing.

The issue of consumer sophistication can take on particular importance when the goods are targeted at children. Several cases have suggested that where children are either the actual purchasers, or the ones who drive the purchasing decision by hounding their parents into buying the item in question, the court should focus on the sophistication of those children, rather than on that of the adults who supply the funds or who make the actual purchase. Moreover, courts generally assume that children are less sophisticated and less careful consumers, and thus incline to find confusion more readily where the goods are targeted at a child market.[37] Whether this latter judicial assumption reflects reality is unclear. Children are often deeply attached to brands and will often notice even very minute distinctions between products that are being offered as alternatives—distinctions that can sometimes escape the weary eye of an adult shopping for a gift. The idea that a little girl would be confused into thinking that a doll labeled BARVÉ is the same as one labeled BARBIE, or that a boy would be as happy with a GI JACK as a GI JOE may underestimate children considerably.

29.1.3 Strength of Plaintiff's Mark

Trademarks differ in strength. Some have enormous public recognition, and some are barely known. Some signal their trademark status immediately because they consist of fanciful words or non-functional design attributes, where others (such as descriptive words or surnames) only achieve trademark status after developing secondary meaning. The stronger the mark, the more likely courts are to find a likelihood of confusion. As one appellate court recently put it: "The strength of a mark is a determination of the mark's distinctiveness and degree of recognition in the marketplace. A mark is strong if it is highly distinctive, i.e., if the public readily accepts it as the hallmark of a particular source; it can become so because it is unique, because it has been the subject of wide and intensive advertisement, or because of a combination of both. The stronger the mark, all else equal, the greater the likelihood of confusion."[38]

Where other firms have made extensive use of a key term in plaintiff's mark, the mark is generally considered to be rather weak, and only entitled to "thin" protection. In one recent case, the Tenth Circuit

36. E. & J. Gallo Winery v. Ben R. Goltsman & Co., 172 F.Supp. 826, (M.D.Ala.1959).

37. *See, e.g.,* Toys R Us, Inc. v. Canarsie Kiddie Shop, Inc., 559 F.Supp. 1189 (E.D.N.Y.1983).

38. Gray v. Meijer, Inc., 295 F.3d 641 (6th Cir.2002). *See also* Daddy's Junky Music Stores Inc. v. Big Daddy's Family Music Center, 109 F.3d 275 (6th Cir.1997) ("The more distinct a mark, the more likely is the confusion resulting from its infringement, and, therefore, the more protection it is due.").

was asked to decide whether the marks FIRSTBANK and FIRST BANK SYSTEM were confusingly similar.[39] Not surprisingly, given the rather pedestrian nature of the marks at issue, the record contained considerable evidence of third party usage of the same or similar mark. As the court observed, "These registrations and applications provide compelling evidence of what most consumers would recognize from experience; namely, that banks are wont to refer to themselves as the 'First.' " The court characterized the marks as weak and held that a jury could not reasonably find a likelihood of confusion between them.[40]

Here again, however, care and common sense are important. Not every "strong" mark is automatically entitled to an advantage in the likelihood of confusion inquiry. For instance, in *New York Stock Exchange, Inc. v. New York, New York Hotel LLC*,[41] the plaintiff was the indisputably famous New York Stock Exchange. It had obtained federal trademark registrations for a variety of marks including NEW YORK STOCK EXCHANGE, NYSE, and a mark incorporating a picture of the facade of the New York Stock Exchange building as a logo. The defendant operates a casino on the Las Vegas Strip, called New York, New York. As part of its New York based theme, it replicated the facade of the New York Stock Exchange inside its hotel, and promoted a gambling club called the New York New York $lot Exchange.

After the trial court dismissed the Stock Exchange's claims of infringement, the Exchange argued on appeal that the judge had given insufficient weight to the fame of its mark. The Second Circuit, noting that the defendant's usage was an "attempt at a humorous theme" and an "obvious pun" was unmoved by this argument. It tersely observed that "the strength of NYSE's marks does not necessarily increase the likelihood of confusion under these circumstances." This seems quite sound. In order for the defendant's pun to work, consumers would have to be familiar with the plaintiff's mark, but it is the very fame of that mark that makes it an obvious target for ribbing, and dispels any risk that gamblers will think that the defendant's casino is a branch office of the famous Wall Street stock market.

29.1.4 Defendant's Intent

Intent is not an element of trademark infringement. A defendant can be found liable and enjoined even if it is pure of heart and adopted its trademark wholly ignorant of the plaintiff's prior use and superior rights. This was not always the case. Early nineteenth century trademark law conceived of trademark infringement as a form of fraud or deceit, and thus required a showing of illicit intent. However, as courts began to focus on the reaction of the consuming public instead of on the

---

39. First Sav. Bank, F.S.B. v. First Bank System, Inc., 101 F.3d 645 (10th Cir. 1996).

40. *See also* Sun Banks of Fla., Inc. v. Sun Fed. Sav. & Loan Ass'n, 651 F.2d 311 (5th Cir.1981) ("[W]e find the extensive third-party use of the word 'Sun' impressive evidence that there would be *no* likelihood of confusion between Sun Banks and Sun Federal.").

41. 293 F.3d 550 (2d Cir.2002).

motivations of the alleged infringer, they began to dispense with any insistence that the plaintiff show intent. As the Fifth Circuit has explained, "good faith is not a defense to trademark infringement.... The reason for this is clear: if potential purchasers are confused, no amount of good faith can make them less so."[42] An intermediate appellate court in Arizona made the same point with a zoological metaphor when it said "both the first user and the public may be as readily wounded by the ostrich as the fox."[43]

While a plaintiff thus need not prove bad intent on the part of the defendant, evidence of bad intent is universally considered probative of likelihood of confusion. To be precise, the intent which counts against the defendant is an intent to confuse the public, not an intent to copy some elements of the plaintiff's mark. Thus, a firm that copies portions of a mark in order to sell a parody product engages in the copying intentionally, but almost certainly lacks an intent to confuse consumers about the source or sponsorship of the goods.

This distinction is especially important in cases of trade dress infringement, where there may be legitimate reasons to copy elements of plaintiff's packaging or product configuration, without any underlying purpose of misleading the public about the source of the product. For instance, the copier may believe that the copied elements are functional product features that it is entitled to copy. Mindful of this concern, the Third Circuit has cautioned that "in the product configuration context, a defendant's intent weighs in favor of a finding of likelihood of confusion only if intent to confuse or deceive is demonstrated by clear and convincing evidence, and only where the product's labeling and marketing are also affirmatively misleading."[44]

The federal circuits are split on the precise evidentiary effect to afford to proof of intent to deceive. Some circuits have held that such evidence creates a presumption of likelihood of confusion. This in effect shifts the burden of proof to the defendant to show that consumers will not be deceived by its conduct. Other circuits, however, have refused to go this far, and say that evidence of bad intent merely creates an inference of likelihood of confusion.[45] As a practical matter there may be little difference between the two approaches in all but the closest of cases.

42. Fuji Photo Film Co. v. Shinohara Shoji Kabushiki Kaisha, 754 F.2d 591 (5th Cir.1985).

43. V.J. Doyle Plumbing Co. v. Doyle, 120 Ariz. 130, 584 P.2d 594 (App.1978).

44. Versa Prods. Co. v. Bifold Co., 50 F.3d 189 (3d Cir.1995), *cert. denied,* 516 U.S. 808, 116 S.Ct. 54, 133 L.Ed.2d 19 (1995). *See also* Restatement (Third) of Unfair Competition § 22, comment c ("proof that the actor adopted a similar designation with knowledge of the other's prior use, or even that the actor intentionally copied all or part of the other's designation, is not in itself sufficient to establish an intent to confuse").

45. The line up at this point in time seems to have the First, Second, Fourth, Sixth and Ninth Circuits following the presumption approach, and the Third, Fifth and Seventh following the inference approach. There are different decisions from the Eleventh Circuit that can be read in support of each approach. *See generally* J. Thomas McCarthy, TRADEMARKS AND UNFAIR COMPETITION, § 23:111 (collecting case citations).

Professor McCarthy has concisely explained the logic of inferring a likelihood of confusion from an intent to deceive by noting that "it is not often that a firm intentionally sets out to divert sales or ride on another's reputation, yet is so inept at doing so that it fails."[46] The Restatement also endorses this idea that a firm with an evil heart is likely to accomplish what it sets out to do, noting in a comment that "it may be appropriate to assume that an actor who intends to cause confusion will be successful in doing so."[47] The Sixth Circuit has justified the inference not so much based on the defendant's skill in making its wishes come true, but rather based on its superior knowledge about market conditions, saying that "intent is relevant because purposeful copying indicates that the alleged infringer, who has a least as much knowledge as the trier of fact regarding the likelihood of confusion, believes that his copying may divert some business from the senior user."[48]

Proving that a defendant has an intent to deceive the public is no easier than proving any other state of mind. Absent a memorandum turned over in discovery that says "let's adopt this trademark because its close resemblance to the mark of our national competitor will surely deceive the public," the plaintiff is left to fall back on circumstantial evidence. In this regard there is some risk of "double counting" because the plaintiff will often ask the court to infer an intent to deceive from nothing more than the fact that the defendant has adopted a mark or a trade dress that closely resembles plaintiff's. Why, the plaintiff will ask, would they have come up with a mark that differs from ours in only small details, if they did not have a wrongful intent?

Many courts have found this argument persuasive. For instance, in *Beer Nuts, Inc. v. Clover Club Foods Co.,*[49] plaintiff owned the mark BEER NUTS for peanuts, and sued a defendant which adopted the mark BREW NUTS for its own brand. The court there commented that "deliberate adoption of a similar mark may lead to an inference of intent to pass off goods as those of another which in turn supports a finding of likelihood of confusion." A blanket rule of this sort would seem to cut too deep. Certainly where the plaintiff's mark is arbitrary, and where there were a range of other viable marks from which the defendant could have selected, the choice of a highly similar mark would seem difficult to explain on any basis other than a desire to confuse the public. On the other hand, however, where the plaintiff is using a mark with descriptive elements, or where the mark is not especially well-known, or where the nature of the product limits the range of feasible marks, the inference of bad intent merely from adoption of a similar mark would seem inappropriate.

46. J. Thomas McCarthy, Trademarks and Unfair Competition § 23:124.

47. Restatement (Third) of Unfair Competition § 22, comment c (1995).

48. Daddy's Junky Music Stores, Inc. v. Big Daddy's Family Music Ctr., 109 F.3d 275 (6th Cir.1997).

49. 805 F.2d 920 (10th Cir.1986).

Defendants are often successful in refuting a claim of bad faith by showing that they conducted a trademark search before adopting the mark in question, or that they relied on the advice of counsel. On the other hand, if counsel advises against the use of a mark, or indicates that a more thorough trademark search would be in order, the defendant who ignores that advice may be found in bad faith.

29.1.5 Other Relevant Factors

There are a number of other factors that courts have found relevant in assessing likelihood of confusion. Some of these are essentially rules about the admissibility and weight of various types of evidence. For instance, courts view evidence of episodes of *actual* confusion experienced by *specific* consumers to be strongly indicative of a more general *likelihood* of confusion among *consumers as a whole*. Even a relatively small number of instances may carry the day for the plaintiff. On the other hand, where the defendant has engaged in widespread commercial activities and there is little or no evidence of actual confusion, the opposite inference can be drawn—namely that the marks can peacefully co-exist in the marketplace.

The Restatement codifies these ideas, declaring that: "(1) A likelihood of confusion may be inferred from proof of actual confusion; (2) An absence of likelihood of confusion may be inferred from the absence of proof of actual confusion if the actor and the other have made significant use of their respective designations in the same geographic market for a substantial period of time, and any resulting confusion would ordinarily be manifested by probable facts."[50] It goes on to say, in comments, that "evidence of substantial actual confusion is ordinarily decisive,"[51] a view that is echoed in the case law.[52]

Actual confusion evidence might consist of testimony about misdirected phone calls or e-mails from consumers inquiring about, or complaining about products, or testimony by consumers that they bought the defendant's product thinking it to be the plaintiff's, only discovering the error after they had arrived home. Thus, if several partially used tubes of the hypothetical CULLGAY toothpaste had been mailed to the owner of the COLGATE mark, with letters complaining of its "new bitter taste," evidence of that fact would be highly suggestive of a likelihood of confusion between the two marks. Where an instance of actual confusion is traceable to outright consumer careless or ignorance, however, courts understandably give the evidence less weight or ignore it entirely. Moreover, as the First Circuit has cautioned: "Just as one tree does not constitute a forest, an isolated instance of confusion does not prove probable confusion."[53]

50. Restatement (Third) of Unfair Competition § 23 (1995).

51. *Id.* at comment b.

52. *See, e.g.,* Lyons Partnership, L.P. v. Morris Costumes, Inc., 243 F.3d 789, 804 (4th Cir.2001) (actual confusion evidence is "often dispositive to a trademark infringement analysis.").

53. International Ass'n of Machinists and Aerospace Workers, AFL–CIO v. Winship Green Nursing Center, 103 F.3d 196, 200–01 (1st Cir.1996).

Another type of evidence probative of likelihood of confusion is a consumer survey indicating that such confusion is likely. When litigants first began offering survey evidence several decades ago, some courts hesitated to receive it, fearing that such surveys constituted inadmissible hearsay because they consisted of out-of-court responses of consumers, offered to prove the truth of the matters asserted. Those qualms have long since vanished and survey evidence has now become commonplace in much trademark litigation, especially when the trademark owner is a large company that can afford the not inconsiderable cost of paying to have a survey conducted. The usual issues surrounding survey evidence relate to the design and methodology of the survey. Naturally, where the questions are biased or where the sample of consumers is non-random, courts have given surveys less weight or even excluded them from evidence entirely. The Second Circuit has noted that methodological errors in trademark surveys generally go only to the weight of the evidence unless the survey is so flawed that its probative value is outweighed by the risk of prejudice.[54]

Still another factor considered by many courts is the similarity of trade dress between the two products. All other things being equal, a defendant who uses a trademark somewhat similar to plaintiff's but adopts entirely different forms of packaging, color schemes, label designs and lettering, is less likely to cause confusion than one who couples the similar trademark with a container adorned with graphics that closely simulate those of the plaintiff. Thus, even if the plaintiff has not asserted a separate cause of action for infringement of trade dress, defendant's copying of key elements of the trade dress fortifies the conclusion that the similar marks will mislead the public.

In some cases, the defendant may attempt to dispel any possible confusion by including a "disclaimer" on its packaging or labels, declaring that it is not affiliated with the plaintiff-trademark-owner. Courts naturally will consider any such disclaimer in analyzing the likelihood of confusion, but the use of a disclaimer does not provide a "safe harbor," and likelihood of confusion has been found in many cases despite disclaimers, especially where the disclaimer was small or inconspicuous or ambiguously worded.[55] Because empirical research suggests that many disclaimers are ineffective,[56] this judicial skepticism seems warranted, but where the other evidence of likelihood of confusion is weak, a disclaimer may tip the balance in favor of the defendant.

Finally, the Second Circuit also includes "the quality of defendant's goods" on its list of likelihood of confusion factors. Different courts in that circuit have treated this factor differently. Some have taken the view that the key question is whether the defendant's goods are of the

---

54. Schering Corp. v. Pfizer Inc., 189 F.3d 218 (2d Cir.1999).

55. *See, e.g.,* Cartier v. Deziner Wholesale, L.L.C., 55 USPQ2d 1131, 2000 WL 347171 (S.D.N.Y.2000); Weight Watchers

Int'l, Inc. v. Stouffer Corp., 744 F.Supp. 1259 (S.D.N.Y.1990).

56. *See, e.g.,* Jacob Jacoby & George J. Szybillo, *Why Disclaimers Fail,* 84 TRADE-MARK REP. 224 (1994).

same quality level as the plaintiff's on the theory that comparable quality will reinforce a public perception that the two items come from a common source or have common sponsorship. On this view the sale of expensive, well-made bejeweled wrist watches under the trademark RALLIX would be more likely to infringe the ROLEX mark than would the use of that mark to sell inexpensive, digital watches bearing a flimsy plastic strap. On the other hand some courts take the view that infringement should be more readily found when the defendant is selling low quality goods because that scenario poses the greatest threat to plaintiff's reputation. While this second view is certainly correct on the question of harm, it does not really seem to bear on the issue of likely confusion. Harm from defendant's sale of shoddy goods can only result if there is confusion in the first place, and the shoddy quality of the goods seems not to shed much light on that fact.

While the plaintiff bears the burden of proving likelihood of confusion, many courts have indicated that in close cases, any uncertainty should be resolved in favor of the plaintiff. As the Ninth Circuit put it, "in a close case amounting to a tie, doubts are resolved in favor of the senior user."[57] The logic of this doctrine is that courts should err on the side of protecting consumers from confusion, and established merchants from harm to their investment in building up goodwill. The newcomer is perceived to have less at stake.

We conclude where we began. All the judicially itemized confusion factors are merely means to an end—deducing the probable public reaction to the defendant's behavior. There is nothing magical about any list of factors, and no list of factors can be complete. Courts are always free to consider the unique facts of the case before them regardless of whether those facts fit neatly into any previously promulgated factor list.

§ 29.2   Special Likelihood of Confusion Situations

29.2.1   Initial Interest Confusion

Imagine a moderately brand loyal consumer of COCA–COLA brand soft drinks, walking down the street on a hot summer day. Passing by a convenience store, she sees a large sign that says: "Frosty cold COCA–COLA brand soda inside." Already thirsty, and tempted by the sign, she enters the store and requests a COCA–COLA. The clerk informs her, "sorry, we don't carry any COCA–COLA products. We do, however, have our own store brand cola if you would like." If this consumer decides to make a purchase at this point, it would be very difficult to say that she is confused about either the source or the sponsorship of the soda she purchases. She knows that it is not COCA–COLA, not made by the same people who make COCA–COLA, and not licensed or otherwise sponsored by them. The clerk in the store told her as much. If she buys the product, she does so with full knowledge of its pedigree.

---

57. Dr. Seuss Enterprises, L.P. v. Penguin Books USA, Inc., 109 F.3d 1394 (9th Cir.1997).

But she is very thirsty. And she's already entered the store, lured in by that sign mentioning COCA–COLA. So she might be particularly tempted to depart from her usual brand preference and buy the alternative brand. If there had been no false sign outside, she would have kept on walking, perhaps until she found a retailer who really did sell COCA–COLA.

If owner of the COCA–COLA mark were to claim trademark infringement in a case like this, most courts would grant relief by invoking a theory that has come to be known as "initial interest confusion." The logic is that although the consumer was not confused at the moment the purchase was consummated, the consumer was led to consider the competing product by the use of the plaintiff's trademark, and might not have considered it otherwise. As the Seventh Circuit explained,

> the Lanham Act forbids a competitor from luring potential customers away from a producer by initially passing off its goods as those of the producer's, even if confusion as to the source of the goods is dispelled by the time any sales are consummated. This 'bait and switch' of producers, also known as 'initial interest' confusion, will affect the buying decision of consumers in the market for the goods, effectively allowing the competitor to get its foot in the door by confusing consumers.[1]

In *Elvis Presley Enterprises, Inc. v. Capece*,[2] the Fifth Circuit applied the initial interest confusion doctrine to find infringement in a case where the defendant operated a 1960's themed nightclub under the name VELVET ELVIS. The court recognized that consumers might deduce that the nightclub was not affiliated with Elvis Presley's estate before spending any money there, but said "once in the door, the confusion has succeeded because some patrons may stay, despite realizing that the bar has no relationship with" plaintiff.

One of the most interesting recent applications of the doctrine is *Brookfield Communications, Inc. v. West Coast Entertainment Corp.*[3] The defendant there used the plaintiff's trademark in hidden code on its Web Site. This led search engines to give a high relevancy ranking to the defendant's site when web searchers typed in the plaintiff's mark. The Ninth Circuit admitted that most consumers who clicked on the defendant's Web address would immediately realize that they were not on the plaintiff's site. Nonetheless, it found the conduct actionable because it gave rise to initial interest confusion. (We will return to this case in greater detail in Chapter 33, which deals in detail with trademark issues on the Internet).

The rules condemning initial interest confusion should be contrasted with those that permit comparative advertising. It is entirely permissible for a store to post a sign that says: "Try our store brand cola—Tastes

§ 29.2

1. Dorr–Oliver, Inc. v. Fluid-Quip, Inc., 94 F.3d 376, 382 (7th Cir.1996).

2. 141 F.3d 188 (5th Cir.1998).

3. 174 F.3d 1036 (9th Cir.1999).

just like COCA–COLA, but only half the price!" The difference between this, and the infringing sign may be subtle, but it is nothing more than the difference between telling the truth and lying.

29.2.2 Reverse Confusion

In the typical infringement situation the plaintiff is a relatively large firm with a relatively well-known trademark. The alleged infringer is usually a smaller firm which may be motivated to adopt a confusingly similar symbol in order to free ride on the plaintiff's goodwill. In such cases consumers seeing defendant's goods will think they come from or are authorized by the plaintiff. This is the conventional type of consumer confusion which we have been considering throughout this chapter, and which for present purposes we can also call "forward confusion."

In other cases, however, the senior user of the mark may be a small company and the mark may not have achieved much prominence in the minds of consumers. Thereafter, a very large company may adopt that same mark, or one very similar to it, and begin using it widely and advertising it extensively throughout the country. This latter situation creates the possibility for a somewhat different type of confusion. When consumers encounter the junior user's products in this case, they will not necessarily think they come from the senior user or have been authorized by it, because they have never even heard of the senior user or its trademark. On the other hand, if they eventually encounter the senior user's products, they may think either that the senior user's products come from, or are endorsed by, the junior user or perhaps alternatively, that the senior user is guilty of infringement because they believe it to have copied its mark from the junior user. This is what is usually referred to as "reverse confusion." The Seventh Circuit explained it this way:

> A reverse confusion claim differs from the stereotypical confusion of source or sponsorship claim. Rather than seeking to profit from the goodwill captured in the senior user's trademark, the junior user saturates the market with a similar trademark and overwhelms the senior user. The public comes to assume the senior user's products are really the junior user's or that the former has become somehow connected to the latter. The result is that the senior user loses the value of the trademark—its product identity, corporate identity, control over its goodwill and reputation, and ability to move into new markets.[4]

Reverse confusion is actionable, and a senior user who establishes it makes out a valid case of trademark infringement. The case usually credited with establishing the theory of reverse confusion is *Big O Tire Dealers, Inc. v. Goodyear Tire & Rubber, Co.*[5] Big O, the plaintiff in this case, was a relatively small firm that had adopted the mark BIGFOOT

---

4. Ameritech, Inc. v. American Information Technologies Corp., 811 F.2d 960 (6th Cir.1987).

5. 561 F.2d 1365 (10th Cir.1977).

for a line of automobile tires. Goodyear subsequently adopted the same mark and launched a major advertising campaign to promote its BIG-FOOT brand tires. The court recognized that "Big O does not claim nor was any evidence presented showing Goodyear intended to trade on the goodwill of Big O or to palm off Goodyear products as being those of Big O. Instead, Big O contends Goodyear's use of Big O's trademark created a likelihood of confusion concerning the source of Big O's 'Big Foot' tires." The *Big O* court candidly noted that it could only find one previously reported case involving reverse confusion—a Seventh Circuit opinion denying relief under Indiana law.[6]

It concluded, however, applying Colorado law, that the courts of that state would recognize the new theory. It agreed with the trial court that the failure to recognize the theory would result in

> the immunization from unfair competition liability of a company with a well established trade name and with the economic power to advertise extensively for a product name taken from a competitor. If the law is to limit recovery to passing off, anyone with adequate size and resources can adopt any trademark and develop a new meaning for that trademark as identification of the second user's products. The activities of Goodyear in this case are unquestionably unfair competition through an improper use of a trademark and that must be actionable.

The subsequent case law follows *Big O* in treating reverse confusion as a viable theory of recovery and the Restatement (Third) of Unfair Competition has endorsed the theory as well.[7]

Of course, not every party claiming reverse confusion will be able to establish it. In the mid–1990's the Washington, D.C. National Basketball Association franchise decided that its name, the WASHINGTON BULLETS, was unnecessarily evocative of the gun violence that had plagued our nation's capital. After due deliberation, they announced in 1996 that they would be adopting the name WASHINGTON WIZARDS effective with the 1997–1998 NBA season. Not long thereafter, they were sued by the HARLEM WIZARDS, a "theatrical basketball organization that performs 'show basketball' in the tradition established by the world famous Harlem Globetrotters." The court characterized the plaintiff's complaint as alleging a "classic case" of reverse confusion. It nonetheless declined to find confusion, primarily because it felt that the parties services were non-competing and that the "show basketball performed by plaintiff is markedly distinct from NBA competitive basketball in myriad ways," and that "when every aspect of the two teams is compared, there is glaring dissimilarity."[8]

6. The reference is to Westward Coach Mfg. Co. v. Ford Motor Co., 388 F.2d 627 (7th Cir.1968), *cert. denied,* 392 U.S. 927, 88 S.Ct. 2286, 20 L.Ed.2d 1386 (1968).

7. Restatement (Third) of Unfair Competition § 20, comment f ("the creation of reverse confusion falls within the tradition-

al rules governing the infringement of trademarks").

8. Harlem Wizards Entertainment v. NBA Properties, 952 F.Supp. 1084 (D.N.J. 1997).

Although the court in the *Harlem Wizards* case applied the conventional likelihood of confusion factors in analyzing the case, the Third Circuit has subsequently suggested that several of those factors should be modified when the issue is reverse, rather than "forward," confusion. In *A & H Sportswear, Inc. v. Victoria's Secret Stores, Inc.*,[9] the relatively small plaintiff had been using the mark MIRACLESUIT for swimwear. Thereafter, Victoria's Secret, a well known national retailer of female clothing began selling its own line of bathing suits and bikinis under its THE MIRACLE BRA trademark. The court recognized that mechanical application of the traditional factors might lead to odd results in a reverse confusion case. Consequently, it formulated a slightly revised list of factors to govern in reverse confusion situations.[10]

For instance, it noted that "in a direct confusion claim, a plaintiff with a commercially strong mark is more likely to prevail than a plaintiff with a commercially weak mark. Conversely, in a reverse confusion claim, a plaintiff with a commercially weak mark is more likely to prevail than a plaintiff with a stronger mark, and this is particularly true when the plaintiff's weaker mark is pitted against a defendant with a far stronger mark." It also noted that disclaimers on the junior user's goods about lack of affiliation with the senior user should be given little or no weight in reverse confusion cases, because the focus is on consumers' reactions when they encounter the *senior user's* goods and mistakenly attribute them to the junior user, not vice versa.

Some courts and some commentators have criticized the reverse confusion theory. The Third Circuit itself, in *A & H*, cautioned that:

> The chief danger inherent in recognizing reverse confusion claims is that innovative junior users, who have invested heavily in promoting a particular mark, will suddenly find their use of the mark blocked by plaintiffs who have not invested in, or promoted, their own marks. Further, an overly-vigorous use of the doctrine of reverse confusion could potentially inhibit larger companies with established marks from expanding their product lines—for instance, had Victoria's Secret thought, at the outset, that it would not be permitted [to] carry over its popular THE MIRACLE BRA mark from lingerie to swimwear, it might have chosen not to enter the swimsuit market at all.

This anxiety presupposes that a large company like Victoria's Secret would not be able to find out about the prior use of a mark that it is contemplating using on its own products. Given the resources available to large companies to engage in comprehensive trademark searching, and given the tendency of the courts to limit the reverse confusion doctrine to directly competing goods, this seems a bit oversolicitous.[11]

9. 237 F.3d 198 (3d Cir.2000).

10. *See* 237 F.3d at 234. *See also* Cohn v. Petsmart, Inc., 281 F.3d 837, 841 n. 5 (9th Cir.2002) ("analysis of some [likelihood of confusion] factors ... is affected by the context of a reverse confusion case").

11. According to the *A & H* court, Victoria's Secret "had previously conducted a search for THE MIRACLE BRA as applied to lingerie, which had led it to the conclusion that THE MIRACLE BRA did not threaten to infringe on other trademarks.

Justice Stephen Breyer, when he was serving as a judge on the First Circuit Court of Appeals, expressed a slightly different concern about the reverse confusion doctrine. He noted that "dicta in the Second Circuit suggest that a plaintiff, claiming reverse confusion, can recover for harm suffered, not because the buying public may wrongly believe that the defendant makes or sponsors the plaintiff's product, but simply because the public wrongly believes that the plaintiff copied the defendant's name." He found this worrisome and noted that "[i]f 'falsely being thought a pirate' were an actionable harm, no one could safely use a mark ever previously used by another, no matter how different the product, place of sale, or class of buyer." As he put it, the essence of a trademark suit should confusion over "the source of the product, not the source of the name."[12]

Notwithstanding these concerns, the reverse confusion doctrine seems fairly solidly entrenched in the law. Some cases will involve big firms that are simply trying to use their size to "push around" a small firm with a legitimate interest in the mark. On the other hand, others may involve small firms with little serious commercial investment in the trademark that are merely trying to "hold up" the large firm that adopted a similar mark in good faith in the hope of extorting a large cash settlement. Putting the cases into the proper categories may therefore sometimes require courts to walk a conceptual tightrope but, of course, that's why we have courts.

29.2.3   Post–Sale Confusion

In certain cases of blatant trademark infringement the customer will be well aware that he is getting a fake. No one paying $5 for a tissue-paper-thin knit shirt with a badly stitched polo pony on it thinks that it is made or sponsored by the owner of the POLO trademark, nor does one buying a $20 watch off of a card table at a flea market think it is a genuine ROLEX even if the ROLEX name is printed prominently on the dial. In addition, most purchasers of such cheap knock-offs would not have bought the real item, because it is usually priced at a level that they cannot afford or do not want to pay for such an item. Consequently, such cases seem to be ones where there is no confusion of the purchasers, and no harm, in the form of lost sales, to the trademark owner.

Nonetheless, courts generally grant relief in cases such as this, because of the risk of what they have come to call "post-sale" confusion. While the purchasers themselves may not be confused, others who see the goods at a subsequent time very well may be. Moreover, the confu-

Victoria's Secret had not conduct a separate trademark search of THE MIRACLE BRA trademark as it applied to swimwear." The court also noted that the PTO denied Victoria's Secret's application to register the disputed mark for swimwear because it found that it conflicted with A & H's previous registration for THE MIRACLESUIT.

12. DeCosta v. Viacom Int'l, Inc., 981 F.2d 602 (1st Cir.1992), *cert. denied*, 509 U.S. 923, 113 S.Ct. 3039, 125 L.Ed.2d 725 (1993). *See generally* Thad G. Long & Alfred M. Marks, *Reverse Confusion: Fundamentals and Limits*, 84 TRADEMARK REP. 1 (1994).

sion of those non-purchasers may eventually result in harm to the trademark owners. First, individuals seeing the shabby knock-off shirt, or the rusted and non-functioning ersatz watch might conclude, erroneously, that genuine POLO and ROLEX brand products are of poor quality. Those confused third parties might subsequently shun the genuine trademarked goods because of concerns about product quality. Second, the existence of the infringing merchandise may flood the market, thus destroying the exclusivity and scarcity of the trademarked brand, making it less desirable. With that loss of cachet will also come a loss of sales of the genuine item.

Of course, for post-sale confusion to be a viable theory for the trademark owner, the product must be one on which the trademark is normally visible after purchase. For products where the trademark is only on packaging that is normally removed after purchase or is inconspicuous, such as an all-white men's button down shirt with a label inside the collar, post-purchase confusion would be unlikely. Thus many of the post-sale confusion cases have involved prestige or designer goods.[13]

One of the first cases to recognize post-sale confusion is the 1955 decision in *Mastercrafters Clock & Radio Co. v. Vacheron & Constantin–LeCoultre Watches, Inc.*,[14] Vacheron made an "atmospheric clock" with a distinctive appearance, which it sold under the ATMOS trademark. Mastercrafters began selling a look-alike clock, and then sought a declaratory judgment that it was not guilty of any infringement. Vacheron counterclaimed alleging common law unfair competition for what we would now characterize as trade dress infringement. Judge Frank, writing for the Second Circuit admitted that Mastercrafters' customers themselves were unlikely to be confused because "a customer examining plaintiff's clock would see from the electric cord, that it was not an 'atmospheric' clock." He went on to note, however, that

> plaintiff copied the design of the Atmos clock because plaintiff intended to, and did, attract purchasers who wanted a 'luxury design' clock. This goes to show at least that some customers would buy plaintiff's cheaper clock for the purpose of acquiring the prestige gained by displaying what many visitors at the customers' homes would regard as a prestigious article. Plaintiff's wrong thus consisted of the fact that such a visitor would be likely to assume that the clock was an Atmos clock. Neither the electric cord attached to, nor the plaintiff's name on, its clock would be likely to come to the attention of such a visitor; the likelihood of such confusion suffices to render plaintiff's conduct actionable.

13. *See, e.g.,* Rolex Watch U.S.A., Inc. v. Canner, 645 F.Supp. 484 (S.D.Fla.1986); Polo Fashions, Inc. v. Craftex, Inc., 816 F.2d 145 (4th Cir.1987).

14. 221 F.2d 464 (2d Cir.1955), *cert. denied,* 350 U.S. 832, 76 S.Ct. 67, 100 L.Ed. 743 (1955).

The innovation in Judge Frank's analysis was his focus on the confusion of the purchasers' house guests rather than on the confusion of the purchasers themselves.

The *Mastercrafters* opinion, decided as a matter of state unfair competition law, was not immediately influential in Lanham Act litigation, because the Lanham Act, as originally adopted, required a plaintiff to demonstrate confusion of "purchasers as to the source of origin of [the] goods or services." The explicit reference to purchasers precluded reliance on post-sale confusion. In 1962, however, Congress amended the statute and deleted that language. Many courts interpreted that amendment as a legislative endorsement of the post-sale confusion theory. Although initially there were few cases, by the early 1990's the doctrine had become well established and is now routinely invoked.[15]

§ 29.3　Non-competing Goods

When the defendant is a direct competitor of the plaintiff, the use of a confusingly similar mark poses the greatest risk of injury to both the consuming public and the trademark owner. When the two parties do not compete, the harm may not be readily apparent. For instance, assume a firm were to begin selling STAR–KIST brand olives. A consumer looking for the well-known STAR–KIST brand of tuna would not be likely to buy defendant's product as a substitute. Olives and tuna are not the same, and our hypothetical consumer would pass by the olives, and purchase the desired tuna without any problem. Moreover, the owner of the trademark cannot lose a sale in this scenario, because all the consumers looking for STAR–KIST tuna still encounter only one product with that designation—the genuine product made by plaintiff.

This analysis led courts initially to the view that there could not be any actionable trademark infringement in cases involving non-competing goods. For instance, in one famous example dating from 1912, a federal court held that the mark BORDEN for milk was not infringed when a competitor began selling BORDEN brand ice cream.[1] Eventually, however, the courts began to realize that the non-competing goods situation did pose a risk of harm to both the trademark owner and the public.

The harm to the merchant was, in the first instance, the risk that its reputation could be damaged if the infringer's goods were of poor quality. If a consumer purchases STAR–KIST olives on a whim and finds them unappealing—mealy, perhaps, or too salty—that consumer may think "those STAR–KIST people have really let their quality slip." As a result she may refrain from buying the genuine STAR–KIST tuna fish and the trademark owner will lose subsequent sales. A merchant might also suffer harm in a non-competing goods situation if it was contemplating expanding into new product lines under its established mark. If

---

15. *See generally* David M. Tichane, *The Maturing Trademark Doctrine of Post-sales Confusion,* 85 TRADEMARK REP. 399 (1995).

§ 29.3

1. Borden Ice Cream Co. v. Borden's Condensed Milk Co., 201 F. 510 (7th Cir. 1912).

STAR–KIST were thinking about moving into the olive business the appropriation of its well-known trademark by a third party would prevent it from doing so or force it to develop and promote an entirely new name for its olive business at great expense.

Consumers can also suffer in this kind of situation. A past purchaser of STAR–KIST tuna might have formed the opinion that it is a superior product. In reliance on that judgment he might buy a jar of olives bearing the same mark. If the olives turn out to be mediocre, he has been manipulated into an undesired purchase. Perhaps not a tragedy when we think about olives (although the spoiled martinis may be tragedy enough), but a potentially serious economic harm if the products are more expensive. Not surprisingly, therefore, the case law eventually evolved, to treat certain non-competing goods cases as actionable trademark infringement.

29.3.1 The Related Goods Rule

Once one embraces the idea that the use of similar trademarks on non-competing goods can sometimes be infringing, there is still the question of how closely the different goods should be associated with each other in order for a court to find a likelihood of confusion. Initially, the scope of protection given trademark owners in non-competing goods cases was very stingy. The 1905 Trademark Act specified that infringement of a registered mark required a showing that the defendant was using the challenged symbol on goods of "substantially the same descriptive properties as those set forth in the registration." The result was rulings such as *American Tobacco Co. v. Gordon*,[2] which affirmed a Patent Office decision that an existing registration for PALL MALL for cigarettes did not bar another party's application to register PALL MALL for cigars and pipes because the goods were not of the "same descriptive properties."

This miserly approach did not last long. Two early twentieth century cases were influential in expanding the scope of protection for trademarks in non-competing goods cases. In *Aunt Jemima Mills Co. v. Rigney & Co.*,[3] the plaintiff used the mark AUNT JEMIMA for pancake batter. The defendant adopted the same mark for pancake syrup, and was able to secure a federal registration for it under the 1905 statute. Plaintiff ultimately sued both for infringement of the registered mark, and for common law unfair competition. The trial court denied relief, reasoning that "no one wanting syrup could possibly be made to take flour." The Second Circuit disagreed, however, saying that the "goods, though different, may be so related as to fall within the mischief which equity should prevent. Syrup and flour are both food products, and food products commonly used together. Obviously, the public, or a large part of it, seeing this trademark on a syrup, would conclude that it was made by the complainant. Perhaps they might not do so, if it were used for

2. 10 F.2d 646, 647 (D.C.Cir.1925).

3. 247 F. 407 (2d Cir.1917), *cert. denied*, 245 U.S. 672, 38 S.Ct. 222, 62 L.Ed. 540 (1918).

flatirons.''[4] Interestingly, in reaching this decision the court made no reference to the 1905 Act or its "same descriptive properties" language.

A decade later, the Second Circuit decided another celebrated non-competing goods case, *Yale Electric Corp. v. Robertson.*[5] This case involved a dispute over the registrability of the trademark YALE for flashlights and batteries. An opposition was filed by the firm that owned the mark YALE for locks and keys. That opposition was sustained and the Patent Office denied the application. The flashlight company then sued the Commissioner of Patents to compel registration of the mark, and joined the lock maker as a party to the suit. The lock maker counterclaimed seeking an injunction. The trial court affirmed the administrative decision on the registration question and granted the injunction. Writing for the appellate court, Learned Hand affirmed. He summed up the problem and explained his solution with his usually literary panache:

> [I]t was at first a debatable point whether a merchant's good will, indicated by his mark, could extend beyond such goods as he sold. How could he lose bargains which he had no means to fill? What harm did it do a chewing gum maker to have an ironmonger use his trade-mark? The law often ignores the nicer sensibilities. However, it has of recent years been recognized that a merchant may have a sufficient economic interest in the use of his mark outside the field of his own exploitation to justify interposition by a court. His mark is his authentic seal; by it he vouches for the goods which bear it; it carries his name for good or ill. If another uses it, he borrows the owner's reputation, whose quality no longer lies within has own control. This is an injury, even though the borrower does not tarnish it, or divert any sales by its use; for a reputation, like a face, is the symbol of its possessor and creator, and another can use it only as a mask. And so it has come to be recognized that, unless the borrower's use is so foreign to the owner's as to insure against any identification of the two, it is unlawful.[6]

He candidly admitted that his approach did some "violence" to the "same descriptive properties" language of the 1905 statute, but he argued that those words had to be interpreted expansively if the law was to make any sense. As he put it, "the fact that flash-lights and locks are made of metal does not appear to us to give them the same descriptive properties, except as the trade has so classed them. But we regard what the trade thinks as the critical consideration, and we think the statute meant to make it the test, despite the language used."

While some decisions after *Yale Electric* continued to take a very limited view of when confusion might arise in non-competing goods cases, the opinion proved highly influential. With the adoption of the

---

4. A "flatiron" is a heavy metal iron used for pressing or ironing clothes.

5. 26 F.2d 972 (2d Cir.1928).

6. 26 F.2d at 974.

Lanham Act in 1946, the "same descriptive properties" straightjacket dropped out of the law. What emerged was the idea that the use of similar marks could cause confusion if the marks were used on "related goods."

Goods can be related in any number of ways. The real question is whether consumers will assume that they come from a common source, or have common sponsorship—nothing more. Thus, goods may be deemed related because they are customarily used together, like pancake batter and pancake syrup, or because they are sold in the same kind of stores, made of the same kind of materials, and implicate the same kind of manufacturing technology, like padlocks and flashlights. Alternatively, the defendant's goods may fall into a category that would likely be endorsed, licensed or sponsored by someone in plaintiff's line of commerce. For instance the use of the mark MISS SEVENTEEN on girl's clothing was held to infringe the mark SEVENTEEN on a magazine targeted at teenage girls because the court felt that consumers would assume that the magazine had sponsored the clothing, and its reputation would be at risk if the clothing proved inferior.[7] Indeed, as licensing arrangements have become commonplace in our economy, the range of products that may be deemed "related" because of confusion as to sponsorship has grown accordingly. However, as Learned Hand (again) noted, "[t]here is indeed a limit; the goods on which the supposed infringer puts the mark may be too remote from any that the owner would be likely to make or sell. It would be hard, for example, for the seller of a steam shovel to find ground for complaint in the use of his trademark on a lipstick."[8]

The "related goods" rule finds its way into the likelihood of confusion analysis through the confusion factors that virtually all courts have promulgated. Those lists invariably include "similarity of the goods" as one of the factors relevant in assessing confusion.[9] The Restatement does the same, saying that "when the goods, services, or business of the actor differ in kind from those of the other, the likelihood that the actor's prospective purchasers would expect a party in the position of the other to expand its marketing or sponsorship into the product, service, or business market of the actor . . ." is a relevant consideration.[10]

Some courts—especially in the Second Circuit—list a second, separate factor also bearing on the connection between the parties' products. These courts speak of the probability that the trademark owner will "bridge the gap" between its current product lines and the goods being

7. Triangle Publications v. Rohrlich, 167 F.2d 969 (2d Cir.1948).

8. L. E. Waterman Co. v. Gordon, 72 F.2d 272 (2d Cir.1934).

9. The precise wording varies circuit by circuit. For instance, the Second Circuit speaks of "the proximity of the products," Polaroid Corp. v. Polarad Electronics Corp., 287 F.2d 492 (2d Cir.1961), *cert. denied*, 368 U.S. 820, 82 S.Ct. 36, 7 L.Ed.2d 25 (1961).

The Third Circuit asks "whether the goods, though not competing, are marketed through the same channels of trade and advertised through the same media," and considers "the relationship of the goods in the minds of the public because of similarity of function." Scott Paper Co. v. Scott's Liquid Gold, 589 F.2d 1225 (3d Cir.1978).

10. Restatement (Third) of Unfair Competition § 21(e) (1995).

sold by the defendant. The Second Circuit has explained "the term 'bridging the gap' is used to describe the senior user's interest in preserving avenues of expansion and entering into related fields."[11] In applying this factor consideration should be given both to the actual expansion plans of the trademark owner, and to the likely consumer perception of those plans. Indeed, consumer perceptions are far more significant than actual expansion plans in assessing likelihood of confusion. As the Restatement explains:

> Some cases purport to protect the prior user of a mark with respect to use on goods or services falling within its "natural expansion" by finding that the prior user is likely to "bridge the gap" between its current product market and that of the subsequent user. If consumers believe, even though falsely, that the natural tendency of producers of the type of goods marketed by the prior user is to expand into the market for the type of goods marketed by the subsequent user, confusion may be likely. On the other hand, the actual intentions of the prior user with respect to future expansion will not ordinarily affect the likelihood that prospective purchasers are confused.[12]

In our view the inclusion of a separate "bridging the gap" factor in the confusion analysis seems both unnecessary and potentially distracting. The related goods rule, which instructs courts to consider the similarity or proximity of the products, would seem more than flexible enough to capture cases where there is a consumer perception of expansion by the mark owner into a new product line. To the extent that the "bridging the gap" rhetoric focuses the court's attention on the mark owner's future plans rather than on the public's current perceptions, it may even distract from the key issue under consideration.

Like virtually all other trademark concepts, the related goods notion is not a bright line test. Rather than being a "yes/no" inquiry, it is more of a sliding scale, and it must always be evaluated in conjunction with the other relevant likelihood of confusion factors. Thus, the relatedness of the goods and the similarity of the marks usually stand in a reciprocal relationship. If the marks are virtually identical, infringement may be found even if the goods are quite dissimilar. If the goods are very close, infringement may be found despite some non-trivial differences in the marks. Intent, customer sophistication, the fame of the mark, instances of actual confusion, and survey evidence all continue to be relevant. As we have previously observed, there are no mechanical formulas.

29.3.2 Promotional Goods

It has become routine to see shirts, caps, jackets, coffee mugs, mouse pads, key rings and a host of other similar and relatively inexpensive items, often called "promotional goods," emblazoned with well-known trademarks. Usually those trademarks belong to firms that are not in

11. C.L.A.S.S. Promotions, Inc. v. D. S. Magazines, Inc., 753 F.2d 14 (2d Cir.1985).

12. Restatement (Third) of Unfair Competition § 21, comment j (1995).

the clothing or coffee mug business. You can buy a HARLEY–DAVID-SON tee shirt even though the company that owns that mark makes motorcycles, not shirts. You can buy a NEW YORK YANKEES coffee mug even though the company that owns that mark provides entertainment services, not ceramic products.

If a third party were to begin making HARLEY–DAVIDSON tee-shirts or NEW YORK YANKEES mugs without authorization, those two trademark owners would likely assert claims of infringement. Should such goods be considered "related" and should such situations be considered likely to cause confusion, so as to grant those plaintiff's relief? A pair of circuit court decisions decided over twenty years ago came to opposite conclusions on that question, and set out the competing arguments for the alternative results.

The first of these two interesting cases is the Fifth Circuit's decision in *Boston Professional Hockey Ass'n, Inc. v. Dallas Cap & Emblem Mfg., Inc.*[13] Dallas Cap, the defendant in that case, sold embroidered cloth patches depicting the trademarks of several professional hockey teams. The National Hockey League and thirteen of its teams filed suit alleging trademark infringement. The trial court found that there was no likelihood of confusion because "the usual purchaser, a sports fan in his local sporting goods store, would not be likely to think that defendant's emblems were manufactured by or had some connection with plaintiffs." Lest that conclusion strike you as odd, it should be noted that back in the early seventies, most professional sports teams had not yet embarked upon the sale of licensed promotional merchandise, and much merchandise that was available was manufactured by unauthorized third parties.

When the case arrived at the Fifth Circuit, it reversed. It said that the district court had overlooked the fact that the Lanham Act reaches confusion as to sponsorship as well as to source. Whether that is a fair characterization of the district court's analysis is unclear, given that it had specifically ruled that consumers would not think there was "some connection" with the teams—a phrase that seems broad enough to capture the idea of sponsorship. At all events, the appellate court went on to declare that "the confusion or deceit requirement is met by the fact that the defendant duplicated the protected trademarks and sold them to the public knowing that the public would identify them as being the teams' trademarks. The certain knowledge of the buyer that the source and origin of the trademark symbols were in plaintiffs satisfies the requirement of the act." The court confessed that its decision "may slightly tilt the trademark laws from the purpose of protecting the public to the protection of the business interests of plaintiffs" but concluded that this result was more desirable than the alternative of allowing the defendant to escape liability.

Five years later, the Ninth Circuit criticized the *Dallas Cap* opinion in *International Order of Job's Daughters v. Lindeburg & Co.*[14] The

---

13. 510 F.2d 1004 (5th Cir.1975).   **14.** 633 F.2d 912 (9th Cir.1980).

plaintiff in that suit was a fraternal organization for women. The defendant, a jeweler, sold various items decorated with the plaintiff's trademark. Despite the fact that the plaintiff had licensed at least one jeweler to produce items bearing its insignia, which it sold directly to its members, the court refused to find the defendant liable for infringement. It reasoned that consumers would not think that the emblem displayed as the principal design element on a piece of jewelry signified either source or sponsorship. Moreover, it felt that consumers would buy such an item not because of who they thought made or sponsored it, but rather because it permitted the consumer to make a statement about her allegiances and loyalties. The *Job's Daughter* court refused to follow *Dallas Cap*, expressing the fear that it granted trademark owners a "complete monopoly" over the use of their marks regardless of likelihood of confusion. It characterized the earlier opinion as an "extraordinary extension of the protection heretofore afforded trademark owners."

Despite the fears expressed in *Job's Daughter*, it is clear two decades down the road that the philosophy of *Dallas Cap* has carried the day. In the years since these cases were decided, innumerable firms with strong trademarks have embarked on ambitious programs of trademark licensing of promotional goods. Consequently, contemporary consumers assume that such products cannot be sold without permission of the mark owner, and when they see the products, they assume them to be authorized. This widespread public assumption of authorization means that if a defendant sells such goods without authorization, it has created confusion as to sponsorship. To put the same point slightly differently, commercial practices have evolved to the point where promotional goods are almost always "related" for purposes of infringement analysis regardless of the trademark owner's primary line of commerce.

If this sounds a bit circular, that's because it is. In all probability, consumers assume sponsorship when they encounter promotional goods because they presume the law requires permission before one can make and sell such goods. If the law changed, consumers would soon be confronted with an abundance of unauthorized promotional items bearing prominent trademarks; they would consequently quickly come to assume that not all such goods are authorized; they would therefore no longer assume sponsorship; and the sale of those goods would therefore not create a likelihood of confusion.[15] It is a problem of which came first, the chicken, or the egg, with the law being the chicken and the consumer perception being the egg.

Presumably, having realized the circularity, it would make sense to base legal outcomes on something other than consumer perceptions in cases involving promotional goods. For instance, courts might focus on an analysis of what kinds of incentives would be fostered by alternative rules. One might predict more abundant, cheaper, but lower quality promotional goods if protection were denied the trademark owner, and scarcer, more expensive, but higher quality promotional goods if protec-

---

15. *See,* Robert Denicola, *Freedom to Copy, 108* YALE *L. J. 1661, 1668 (1999).*

tion were granted. Thus far, however, the courts have not gone that route.

It is now quite common for firms with strong marks to seek federal registration for those marks in connection with promotional goods. Thus, many professional sports teams, consumer packaged goods companies, food and beverage makers, automobile companies and others have obtained numerous multiple registrations on all manner of miscellaneous goods, which are manufactured by their licensees. To cite just one example, the Coca–Cola company has secured several registrations for the mark COCA–COLA in connection with clothing. The description of the diverse and extensive covered goods in one such registration is set out in the footnote.[16]

29.3.3 Parody Goods

Another type of non-competing goods that have required special judicial attention are those that poke fun at or ridicule the trademark owner or its mark. One of the most common examples is the sarcastic T-shirt, but parody merchandise can include a variety of other expressive products such as bumper stickers, buttons, books, movies magazines, web sites, musical recordings or live performances, as well as more conventional commercial goods, like blue jeans[17] or condoms.[18] It should be noted, by way of cross-reference, that in recent years many challenges to goods purporting to constitute trademark parodies have been predicated on the dilution doctrine, rather than on charges of conventional trademark infringement. We will consider the dilution doctrine in some depth in the following chapter. The discussion which follows is limited to parody in the context of conventional infringement litigation only.

Obviously, where parody products express messages that fall within the core of the First Amendment, the defendant's constitutional rights will trump any efforts by the trademark owner to enjoin the activities as infringement. Space limitations do not permit exploration of those First Amendment principles here. Even short of the constitutional line, however, the parody status of a product can affect the likelihood of confusion analysis and alter the outcome of an infringement case. This is because many consumers automatically understand that trademark owners rarely will make fun of themselves or license others to do so. Therefore, if

---

16. Federal Trademark Registration 1508297 for the mark COCA–COLA covers "clothing, namely blouses, coats, dresses, jackets, jeans, jumpsuits, pants, shirts, shorts, skirts, sweaters, swimwear, t-shirts, tops, vests, aerobicwear, namely bodysuits, leotards, leg warmers, exercise pants, jogging pants and sweatshirts; sleepwear, namely pajamas, robes, sleepshirts, and nightgowns; belts, bow ties, gloves, hats, neckties, scarves, shoulder pads, socks, suspenders, underwear, bibs, sleepers and diaper covers for infants."

17. Jordache Enterprises, Inc. v. Hogg Wyld, Ltd., 828 F.2d 1482 (10th Cir.1987) (JORDACHE mark for jeans not infringed by jeans for larger women sold under LAR-DASHE mark).

18. American Exp. Co. v. Vibra Approved Laboratories Corp., 10 USPQ2d 2006, 1989 WL 39679 (S.D.N.Y.1989) (plaintiff's trademark slogan DON'T LEAVE HOME WITHOUT IT held infringed by condoms marketed as AMERICA EXPRESS, with slogan NEVER LEAVE HOME WITHOUT IT).

the parody is a good one, consumers will get the joke, not draw any inference of sponsorship, and there will be no infringement.

A good example is *Anheuser-Busch, Inc. v. L & L Wings, Inc.*[19] As the court explained the genesis of the dispute, "in 1987, Michael Berard was a student at the University of North Carolina at Chapel Hill. In order to supplement his income, Berard decided to go into the business of designing and selling T-shirts." Specifically, Mr. Berard made tee-shirts bearing an illustration closely modeled on the label of BUDWEIS-ER brand beer, but celebrating the virtues of Myrtle Beach, South Carolina. His shirts did not use the word BUDWEISER, but did use the phrase "King of Beaches," an obvious pun on Anheuser–Busch's slogan KING OF BEERS. His shirts were also printed in the same color scheme with the same layout and graphic elements as the BUDWEISER labels. Anheuser–Busch brought suit for infringement. After a three-day trial, the jury returned a verdict for the defendant.

The Fourth Circuit affirmed. It held that the jury could rationally have found no likelihood of confusion because the differences in the wording of the defendant's shirt could negate any confusion engendered by the similar design elements. Of more immediate relevance, however, it went on to hold that a reasonable jury could find that Berard's tee-shirt was "readily recognizable as a parody," and that this further supported the jury verdict. It reasoned that "successful trademark takeoffs dispel consumer confusion by conveying just enough of the original design to allow the consumer to appreciate the point of the parody. Here the T-shirt necessarily adopts the basic format of the Budweiser label, but we think the similarities merely convey the message that the T-shirt is a parody of the original, and are not indicative of consumer confusion."

Associate Justice Lewis Powell, sitting by designation on the *L & L Wings* case, dissented. He argued that the alleged parody "does little to prevent consumer confusion as to the sponsor of defendant's T-shirt. It does not ridicule Budweiser or offer social commentary on the evils of alcohol. Nor could it be deemed 'so obvious and heavy handed that a clear distinction was preserved in the viewer's mind between the source of the actual product and the source of the parody.' "[20]

In copyright law, courts assessing claims under the fair use doctrine have held that a work is not entitled to special consideration as a "parody" unless it targets or pokes fun at the plaintiff's work.[21] This seems to have been Justice Powell's concern in *L & L Wings*, though it should be noted that even under that standard, Berard's tee-shirt could

---

19. 962 F.2d 316 (4th Cir.1992), *cert. denied*, 506 U.S. 872, 113 S.Ct. 206, 121 L.Ed.2d 147 (1992).

20. Id. at 327 (quoting Mutual of Omaha Ins. Co. v. Novak, 648 F.Supp. 905, 910 (D.Neb.1986)), *aff'd*, 836 F.2d 397 (8th Cir. 1987), *cert. denied,* 488 U.S. 933, 109 S.Ct. 326, 102 L.Ed.2d 344 (1988).

21. *See* Campbell v. Acuff–Rose Music, 510 U.S. 569, 114 S.Ct. 1164, 127 L.Ed.2d 500 (1994). The fair use defense for parody in the copyright context is discussed fully in this text in Chapter 10.

be seen as ridiculing Budweiser's self-congratulatory tone and the purple prose on Budweiser's label. Professor McCarthy shares Justice Powell's view of the matter, stating outright that "if defendant appropriates a trademarked symbol . . . not to parody the product or company symbolized by the trademark, but only as a prominent means to satirize and poke fun at something else in society, this is not 'parody' of a trademark."[22]

While this may be correct as a matter of precise linguistic usage, it may underestimate consumer insights and perceptions and ignore some basic differences between copyright and trademark cases. A tee-shirt depicting an altered label for BUSH's brand baked beans showing an illustration of President George W. Bush drowning in a bowl of beans might not be making much social commentary on the role of beans in modern American life or on the corporate practices of Bush Brothers & Company, the makers of BUSH brand beans, but most consumers would nonetheless instantly suspect that it was not prepared or sponsored by the owner of the BUSH trademark for beans.[23] If linguistic precision is crucial here, it might be more accurate to call this hypothetical tee-shirt a satire, rather than a parody, but the fact remains that satire may go just as far as parody towards dispelling likely confusion in the trademark context.

Of course, not all parodists and satirists have escaped trademark infringement liability, nor should they. As Professor McCarthy summarizes, "the cry of 'parody!' does not magically fend off otherwise legitimate claims of trademark infringement. . . . There are confusing parodies and non-confusing parodies. All they have in common is an attempt at humor through the use of someone else's trademark. A non-infringing parody is merely amusing, not confusing."[24] Indeed, in a number of older cases involving crude sexual or drug-related humor, courts showed little patience for the purported parodist and found likelihood of confusion without much discussion.

One of the best known cases of this type is *Coca-Cola Co. v. Gemini Rising, Inc.*,[25] where the defendant sold a poster which consisted of an exact blown-up reproduction of plaintiff's "familiar 'Coca–Cola' trademark and distinctive format except for the substitution of the script letters 'ine' for '-Cola', so that the poster reads 'Enjoy Cocaine.'" Coca–Cola offered evidence that it had received consumer complaints, and even threats of a boycott from irate consumers who thought that it had sponsored these posters and was thus endorsing a dangerous drug. Judge

---

22. J. Thomas McCarthy, TRADEMARKS & UNFAIR COMPETITION § 31:153.

23. *But see* Mutual of Omaha Ins. Co. v. Novak, 836 F.2d 397 (8th Cir.1987), *cert. denied,* 488 U.S. 933, 109 S.Ct. 326, 102 L.Ed.2d 344 (1988), where the defendant sold tee-shirts bearing an altered form of plaintiff's "Indian Head" logo, and the words MUTANT OF OMAHA as a protest against nuclear weapons. Plaintiff offered

survey evidence that 10 per cent of respondents thought that it had "gone along" with the tee-shirt, and the court, in a 2–1 decision, affirmed an injunction for plaintiff.

24. J. Thomas McCarthy, TRADEMARKS & UNFAIR COMPETITION § 31:153.

25. 346 F.Supp. 1183 (E.D.N.Y.1972).

Neaher preliminarily enjoined the defendant finding that "a strong probability exists that some patrons of Coca-Cola will be 'turned off' rather than 'turned on' by defendant's so-called 'spoof', with resulting immeasurable loss to plaintiff."

A similar case is *Dallas Cowboys Cheerleaders, Inc. v. Pussycat Cinema, Ltd.*[26] There, the defendant produced a pornographic film featuring performers wearing the uniform of the Dallas Cowboys Cheerleading squad engaging in a variety of explicit sexual acts. One could easily characterize this use of the plaintiff's trade symbol as a somewhat vulgar effort to parody the sexually provocative nature of their half-time performances during NFL football games. The Second Circuit, however, showed no tolerance for the defendant on these facts. It declared: "The public's belief that the mark's owner sponsored or otherwise approved the use of the trademark satisfies the confusion requirement. In the instant case, the uniform depicted in 'Debbie Does Dallas' unquestionably brings to mind the Dallas Cowboys Cheerleaders. Indeed, it is hard to believe that anyone who had seen defendants' sexually depraved film could ever thereafter disassociate it from plaintiff's cheerleaders. This association results in confusion which has 'a tendency to impugn (plaintiff's services) and injure plaintiff's business reputation.'"

The *Dallas Cowboys* court's willingness to equate conduct that brings the plaintiff to mind, with conduct that confuses the public into believing that the defendant has the sponsorship or blessing of the plaintiff seems more than a little strange. An editorial about the manufacturing practices of the NIKE corporation, or the environmental policies of those who refine EXXON brand gasoline surely brings those companies to mind, but hardly suggests sponsorship, especially if the editorial is critical.

It seems reasonable to speculate that the courts in these two cases were willing to indulge every inference against the defendants because of what they felt was a grave risk of commercial harm to the trademark owners flowing from an association with drugs or pornography. That having been said, it is unclear whether these cases would be decided the same way today. As consumers have been exposed to more parody in a variety of formats it is arguable that their antenna have been sensitized and that plaintiffs would have a more difficult time persuading a judge that there is the requisite confusion as to sponsorship. In addition, the items at issue in *Gemini Rising* and *Dallas Cowboys* were, respectively, a poster and a movie, classic types of expressive material. Modern trends in First Amendment jurisprudence might lead a court to hesitate before allowing a trademark owner to suppress these kinds of materials.[27]

26. 604 F.2d 200 (2d Cir.1979).

27. As the Second Circuit has said, "in deciding the reach of the Lanham Act in any case where an expressive work is alleged to infringe a trademark, it is appropriate to weigh the public interest in free expression against the public interest in avoiding consumer confusion.... [T]he expressive element of parodies requires more protection than the labeling of ordinary commercial products." Cliffs Notes, Inc. v. Bantam Doubleday Dell Pub. Group, Inc., 886 F.2d 490 (2d Cir.1989).

Where the goods are non-expressive, routine commercial products or services, and where the defendant uses plaintiff's trademark merely to make a cute play on words, rather than to communicate any form of social commentary, courts tend to find confusion notwithstanding defendant's attempts at humor. Thus, when a condom manufacturer purported to spoof the American Express trademark slogan DON'T LEAVE HOME WITHOUT IT, by printing NEVER LEAVE HOME WITHOUT IT on its packages, the court found infringement.[28] Similarly, when an insect exterminating company played off of an old BUDWEISER trademark slogan WHERE THERE'S LIFE ... THERE'S BUD by advertising its services using the phrase WHERE THERE'S LIFE THERE'S BUGS, the court also found infringement.[29] On the other hand, the mark BAGZILLA for garbage bags described by the vendor as "monstrously strong" was held not to infringe the GODZILLA mark for an oversize cinematic reptilian monster, the court saying that the defendant's mark was "merely a pun."[30] The bottom line, frustrating as it may be, is that every parody is different, and every case will turn on its own facts with likelihood of confusion, as always, the touchstone.

§ 29.4 Geographically Remote Use

At common law, a merchant owns its trademark only in its actual area of trade. One consequence of this rule is that multiple firms can have common law rights to the same mark for the same category of goods or services provided that they do not do business in overlapping geographic regions. To put the same proposition another way, concurrent use of the same mark is permissible provided the users are geographically remote from each other. The first, or senior, user nationally can not prevent the distant second, or junior, user from using the mark in its own remote region. Moreover, if the senior user were to eventually try to use the mark in the junior user's territory, that junior user, being the owner of the mark in that territory, is the party that would prevail in any litigation.

This principle was established in a pair of early twentieth century Supreme Court decisions—*Hanover Star Milling Co. v. Metcalf,*[1] known as the *Tea Rose* decision, and *United Drug Co. v. Theodore Rectanus Co.*[2] As the *Tea Rose* case declared:

> [W]here two parties independently are employing the same mark upon goods of the same class, but in separate markets wholly remote the one from the other, the question of prior appropriation is legally insignificant, unless at least it appear

28. American Exp. Co. v. Vibra Approved Laboratories Corp., 10 USPQ2d 2006, 1989 WL 39679 (S.D.N.Y.1989).

29. Chemical Corp. of America v. Anheuser–Busch, Inc., 306 F.2d 433 (5th Cir. 1962).

30. Toho Co. v. Sears, Roebuck & Co., 645 F.2d 788 (9th Cir.1981).

§ 29.4

1. 240 U.S. 403, 36 S.Ct. 357, 60 L.Ed. 713 (1916).

2. 248 U.S. 90, 39 S.Ct. 48, 63 L.Ed. 141 (1918).

that the second adopter has selected the mark with some design inimical to the interests of the first user.

Under this rule, which ever firm is the first to expand into new territory where neither has yet done business becomes the owner of the mark in that territory. The courts have consistently followed this rule over the last nine decades, and it is now codified in the Restatement (Third) of Unfair Competition.[3]

This basic common law rule is embellished by a number of further details. First, a firm's "area of trade" includes any region to which its reputation and goodwill have spread. The *Tea Rose* case itself noted that "into whatever markets the use of a trademark has extended, or *its meaning has become known*, there will the manufacturer or trader whose trade is pirated by an infringing use be entitled to protection and redress." The comments to the Restatement make the same point in more modern language, observing that "territorial priority extends beyond the area in which the prior user actually markets its goods or services if its association with the mark is known to prospective purchasers in other areas. Advertising may carry the reputation of the mark beyond the geographic market in which the trademark owner conducts its business."[4] In a nation with a highly mobile and affluent public, and with methods such as Internet selling that permit the distribution of goods nationwide from only a single location, many firms have a reputation, and thus an "area of trade" that is far broader than the places where they have constructed "bricks and mortar" stores or factories.

A famous example of this phenomenon is *Stork Restaurant v. Sahati*.[5] The plaintiff in that case operated a night club in New York City, starting in the 1920's, under the mark STORK CLUB. It became a popular watering hole for the celebrities of the day, and was thus frequently mentioned in newspapers, magazines, and on the radio. It also engaged in extensive national advertising, and had even been the subject of nationally distributed motion picture. In 1945, the defendant opened a bar in a less than elegant neighborhood of San Francisco, and called it the STORK CLUB. Although the trial court denied relief, reasoning that the parties were in distinct geographic markets, the Ninth Circuit reversed. Given the national reputation of the plaintiff's business, the appellate court concluded that its "area of trade" was truly nationwide. Consequently, the defendant in this case was thus not really doing business in a "remote" area at all.

A second gloss on the common law rules dealing with geographical remoteness is that a firm is considered to own trademark rights not merely in its actual area of trade, but also in a "zone of reasonable expansion."[6] The notion here is that many merchants plan to expand eventually, but proceed slowly as they build a business, and that their

3. Restatement (Third) of Unfair Competition § 19 (1995).

4. *Id.* at comment b.

5. 166 F.2d 348 (9th Cir.1948).

6. *See, e.g.,* Tally–Ho, Inc. v. Coast Community College Dist., 889 F.2d 1018 (11th Cir.1989).

plans should not be thwarted by a junior user who could box them in. Under this doctrine, they are given a little extra geographic "breathing space." The problem is that the courts were never able to articulate a clear theory by which the boundaries of the "zone of expansion" could be established. As a practical matter, most cases defined the zone quite narrowly. In 1980, the First Circuit rejected the zone of expansion doctrine entirely, characterizing it as "unworkable, unfair and ... unnecessary," because an expansion minded senior user could simply file for Lanham Act registration.[7] The Restatement has followed suit and it too rejects the "zone of expansion" concept.[8] The doctrine may thus be on its last legs, headed for the dustbin of history.

A third and crucial feature of these geographic remoteness rules is that the junior user in the remote geographic region is allowed to use the trademark in question in that region only if it had initially adopted that trademark "in good faith." There is some ambiguity about what constitutes good faith. The junior user is unequivocally in good faith if it had absolutely no prior knowledge of the senior user's use of the mark, and hit upon the mark entirely coincidentally. There is a question, however, about cases where the junior user knew of the senior user's prior use, but consumers in the junior user's territory have never heard of the senior user. For instance, a junior user in Florida may travel to Seattle, Washington, to visit friends, and while there see a clever trademark for a small local business, like a bakery, or a coffee shop. Upon returning home to Florida, that junior user might adopt that mark for a similar business. He plainly has knowledge of the senior user's prior use, but just as plainly is not trying to capitalize on the senior user's goodwill, because no customers in Florida have ever heard of the Seattle business.

The bulk of the cases take the view that any knowledge of the senior user's prior use on the part of the junior user destroys good faith, so that the hypothetical Florida merchant could not claim valid rights to the mark in the example just posed. There is however, a trend in the cases, to a more flexible interpretation of good faith. Typifying this emerging view is the Tenth Circuit's opinion in *GTE v. Williams*,[9] where the court said that "while a subsequent user's adoption of a mark with knowledge of another's use can certainly support an inference of bad faith ... mere knowledge should not foreclose further inquiry. The ultimate focus is on whether the second user had the intent to benefit from the reputation or goodwill of the first user." The Restatement appears to cautiously endorse this more lenient view, stating in comments that its rule "does not accord conclusive significance to the subsequent user's knowledge of the prior user."[10] One of the Restatement's examples deals specifically with the above hypothetical and declares that the Florida merchant

7. Raxton Corp. v. Anania Asso., Inc., 635 F.2d 924 (1st Cir.1980).

8. Restatement (Third) of Unfair Competition § 19, comment c (1995).

9. 904 F.2d 536, 541 (10th Cir.1990), *cert. denied,* 498 U.S. 998, 111 S.Ct. 557, 112 L.Ed.2d 564 (1990).

10. Restatement (Third) of Unfair Competition § 19, comment d (1995).

should be found in good faith, and be deemed the owner of the mark in Florida.[11]

Because the Lanham Act is designed to confer nationwide rights in trademarks one might think that the problems of "geographically remote" trademark rights does not come up where one party has obtained a federal trademark registration. However, there are a number of ways in which the statute has had to accommodate itself to the common law principles discussed thus far. The treatment of remote junior users under the Lanham Act is illustrated in a trilogy of cases, all involving fast food businesses.

In the *Dawn Donut* case,[12] the plaintiff had been making and selling donut mix under the DAWN trademark since 1922. It also franchised retailers who purchased its mix, granting them rights to become exclusive DAWN DONUT shops. In 1927 it obtained a federal registration for its mark under the then controlling federal trademark statute. In 1947, it renewed that registration under the Lanham Act. Although it conducted its business over a relatively wide geographic area, it had not franchised any retailers in Rochester, New York. The defendant, a local baker in Rochester, began doing business under the DAWN trademark in 1951, without any actual knowledge of the plaintiff's prior use or registration of that trademark. Some time thereafter, plaintiff filed suit for infringement.

Under the common law, since the defendant had no prior knowledge of the plaintiff's use of the mark, and since the plaintiff had not done business in Rochester, the defendant would have the status of "good faith remote junior user" and be entitled to the rights to the DAWN mark in Rochester. However, section 22 of the Lanham provides that "registration of a mark on the principal register provided by this chapter or under [prior acts] shall be constructive notice of the registrant's claim of ownership thereof."[13] Thus, when the defendant in this case adopted and began using the mark in 1951, it was, as a matter of law, charged with knowledge of the plaintiff's prior use and claim of ownership flowing from plaintiff's 1927 federal trademark registration. That constructive knowledge destroyed its good faith status, and gave the plaintiff superior rights to the mark, even in Rochester. As the court summarized, the Lanham Act, through its constructive notice device "affords nationwide protection to registered marks, regardless of the areas in which the registrant actually uses the mark."

Although the *Dawn Donut* court found that plaintiff had superior rights to the mark, it declined to grant an injunction. It reasoned that "as long as plaintiff and defendant confine their use of the mark DAWN in connection with the retail sale of baked goods to their present separate trading areas it is clear that no public confusion is likely." Because it found that "there is no present prospect that plaintiff will

11. *Id.*, Illustration 3.

12. Dawn Donut Co. v. Hart's Food Stores, Inc., 267 F.2d 358 (2d Cir.1959).

13. 15 U.S.C.A. § 1072 (2002).

expand its use of the mark at the retail level into defendant's trading area," it allowed the defendant to continue using the mark, subject to the future plans of the plaintiff. As soon as the plaintiff formed a concrete plan to enter the Rochester, New York market, confusion would become likely, and the plaintiff, as the party with superior rights to the mark, would then be able to secure the injunction.

Two comments about *Dawn Donut* are in order before we consider the next case in our trilogy. First, the court's approach to the issue of injunctive relief seems a bit quaint 40 years down the road. It may be that people in Rochester did not travel much in the 1950's and thus had never come into contact with the plaintiff's trademark in other markets, though that seems unlikely. In any event, if the same issue was presented today, some courts might take the view that significant numbers of Rochesterites might be familiar with plaintiff's mark from out-of-town travel, and might experience some confusion when they encountered defendant's DAWN donut shop back home in Rochester. Students at the University of Rochester presumably hail from other cities where plaintiff's DAWN Donut shops may exist. Moreover, national advertising media, not to mention the Internet, might have exposed even the agoraphobic Rochester citizen to the plaintiff's mark. That having been said, however, it should be noted that modern courts continue to follow this aspect of the *Dawn Donut* analysis in appropriate cases.

The other point to note about *Dawn Donut* is a pragmatic one. The virtue of the Lanham Act is that it creates a searchable database of registered trademarks. The defendant in the case—the smaller, Rochester-based baker—could have avoided the entire mess if only it had conducted a trademark search in 1951, when it was contemplating using the DAWN trademark. It would have quickly found the plaintiff's prior registration for the same mark on identical goods, and it would have been able to select another mark. The moral of the story is that even small firms should check for trademark registrations before adopting a mark.

The next case in this area moves us from dessert to the main course. In the *Burger King*[14] case, the plaintiff began using the mark BURGER KING for hamburger restaurants in Florida in 1953. It began opening additional outlets in nearby states, and within four years was running a total of thirty-eight restaurants under this name. In 1957, the defendant, Mr. Hoots, opened a hamburger restaurant in the town of Matoon, Illinois, and dubbed it BURGER KING as well. At that time, Hoots had no knowledge of the plaintiff's prior use of the mark. In 1961, the plaintiff obtained a federal trademark registration under the Lanham Act. In that same year, it opened its first restaurant in Illinois, and shortly thereafter the parties became aware of their overlapping use of the same mark. Naturally, litigation ensued.

The case poses an interesting variation on the facts of *Dawn Donut*. In that case, the junior user began its use *after* the senior user had

---

14. Burger King of Florida, Inc. v. Hoots, 403 F.2d 904 (7th Cir.1968).

obtained Lanham Act registration. In *Burger King*, however, the junior user—Hoots—began using the mark *before* the senior user registered. Fortunately, the Lanham Act explicitly contemplates this situation, and deals with it in section 33. That section provides that it is a defense to a charge of infringement "that the mark whose use by a party is charged as an infringement was adopted without knowledge of the registrant's prior use and has been continuously used by such party ... from a date" prior to the filing of the registration application. The statute goes on to specify, however, that "this defense or defect shall apply only for the area in which such continuous prior use is proved."[15]

Effectively, this provision guarantees a junior user the perpetual right to use the mark in its own "enclave" or actual trading area, if it adopted the mark prior to the senior user's Lanham Act application and in good faith. This largely replicates the common law situation, with this one variation. The senior user, having obtained Lanham Act registration, is the owner of the mark not just in its own area of trade, but in all of the rest of the United States except for the junior user's market. This solution seems equitable at a number of levels. If Hoots had done a trademark search in 1957 he would have had no way to discover the plaintiff's use of the mark, because they hadn't registered yet. It seems only fair not to penalize him under these circumstances by taking away his trademark. In addition, the plaintiff failed to seek federal trademark registration promptly, and thus it seems appropriate to force it to forfeit geographic trading areas where someone else made prior use of the mark. Indeed, one can read the *Burger King* case as creating strong incentives for prompt registration to avoid exactly this kind of scenario.

There was one further complicating factor in the *Burger King* case. Mr. Hoots had obtained an Illinois state trademark registration in 1959, prior to plaintiff's Lanham Act registration, and prior to plaintiff's expansion into Illinois. Relying on that registration, Hoots argued that he should be entitled to exclusive use of the BURGER KING name not just in Matoon, Illinois and its environs, but throughout the entire state of Illinois. The court rejected this argument. It held that to the extent that the Illinois registration might purport to give a junior user broader rights than the Lanham Act it "must yield to the superior federal law." Since the federal law provided for protection of the junior user only in "the area in which such continuous prior use is proved," Hoots' efforts to claim the entire state as his domain could not succeed.

A dozen years after *Burger King* the federal courts confronted a case posing yet another chronological variation of the remote geographic user problem. In the *Weiner King*[16] case the senior user began using the WEINER KING trademark for a hot dog stand at the Jersey shore in the mid–1960's. In 1970, the junior user adopted virtually the same mark

15. 15 U.S.C.A. 1115(b)(5) (2000). Although this defense is itemized in a provision listing defenses to *incontestable* trademark registrations, § 33(a) makes all such itemized defenses equally applicable to registrations that have not yet become incontestable.

16. Weiner King, Inc. v. Wiener King Corp., 615 F.2d 512 (CCPA 1980).

(reversing only the "e" and the "i" in the impossible-to-spell-correctly word "weiner") for its own hot dog emporium in North Carolina. At that time, it had no knowledge of the senior user's prior use. In 1972, having expanded to 11 restaurants, the junior user obtained a federal registration for the WIENER KING trademark. It continued to expand its operations geographically, even after learning of the senior user's existence, and by 1975 it had grown to 100 restaurants. In that year the senior user filed its own application for federal registration, along with a petition to cancel the registration that had been previously obtained by the North Carolina based company.

The twist in this fact pattern is that it is the *junior* user who obtained the federal registration. In theory, such a registration should not have issued at all. After all, § 2(d) of the Lanham Act provides that one may not register a mark that "consists of or comprises a mark which so resembles a mark . . . previously used in the United States by another and not abandoned, as to be likely, when used on or in connection with the goods of the applicant, to cause confusion . . . ." Of course, the examining attorney at the PTO who approved the junior user's application to register WEINER KING had no way of knowing that there was a previous user out there, given that the previous user had not itself registered the trademark and only operated a few hot dog stands at the beach.

So how should the controversy be resolved? Now that the senior user has appeared on the scene and demanded cancellation, one might think that it would prevail, because the registration should never have issued in the first place. However, things are not that simple. Section 2(d) goes on to provide that if the Patent and Trademark Office "determines that confusion . . . is not likely to result from the continued use by more than one person of the same or similar marks under conditions and limitations as to the mode or place of use of the marks or the goods on or in connection with which such marks are used, concurrent registrations may be issued to such persons . . . ." In the *Weiner King* case, the PTO decided to invoke this provision, and declared a "concurrent use" proceeding. That required it to carve up the geographic territory of the United States and declare which firm could use the mark where. Clearly, each firm would get to keep the rights to the mark in the areas where it was already doing business. That is both consistent with the common law, and necessary to avoid confusing the public. The challenge was deciding which firm would get rights in the significant areas to which neither had yet expanded.

The PTO held that the senior user would be entitled to the mark only in its current trading area in New Jersey, and that the junior user would be granted a registration covering the entire balance of the United States. This result was affirmed by the Court of Customs and Patent Appeals. At least two reasons support this approach. First, it most closely reflects commercial realities. Given that the junior user had been engaged in consistent growth and expansion, and that the senior user had been dormant throughout the relevant time frame, it was highly likely that if consumers around the country associated the mark with either firm, they would associate it with the junior user. Second, giving the junior user the lion's share of the territory on these facts was consistent with "a policy of encouraging prompt registration of marks by rewarding those who first seek registration under the Lanham Act."

Even in this day and age it is still possible for multiple firms to use the same marks in remote areas without being aware of each other. There are, of course, any number of JOE'S diners and DEW DROP inns, each owning their trademarks in their respective enclaves. Nonetheless, one might predict that the problems resolved by the Donut–Hamburger– Hot Dog line of cases will crop up with less and less frequency in the future. Problems of geographically remote trademark users presuppose geographic markets that are relatively discrete and consumers who are relatively stationary. They also presuppose that it is difficult for firms to search for prior trademark uses and that few firms take advantage of federal registration.

All these suppositions seems less and less likely to hold true in coming years. Markets overlap more than ever because of the vast changes in marketing and advertising that have been wrought by our new "information" economy. Consumers are more mobile than ever. Extraordinarily comprehensive databases now exist that will reveal prior use of a trademark by even very small firms operating a single shop in a remote town. Even businesses of modest size routinely take advantage of federal registration, and the availability of the intent-to-use mechanism under the Lanham Act now often allows firms to resolve trademark controversies before investing heavily in promoting their marks. Thus, while the "fast food" cases remain an accurate exposition of governing legal principles, their future legal significance may be increasingly minor in our ever-shrinking national and international marketplace.

§ 29.5 Infringement, Passing Off and Unfair Competition

Many cases involving unauthorized use of symbols of trade identity characterize the defendant's conduct as "passing off" or "palming off." Still others refer to the behavior in question as "unfair competition," and many of the leading texts and treatises in the field speak generally of "trademark and unfair competition law." It is useful, now that the basic scope of trademark infringement has been canvassed, to consider just what all these terms mean and how they relate to each other.

"Passing off" and "palming off" are synonyms. The words connote a degree of deliberate fraud or trickery. To pass yourself off as a partner when you are a mere associate, or to pass yourself off as a golf pro when you have a 15 handicap, is deliberately to misrepresent yourself. In early common law trademark decisions courts viewed the claim as essentially a type of fraud and required the plaintiff to prove that the defendant had engaged in a pattern of deliberate deception of the public. When the defendant was found liable, they would say that it had "passed off" its goods as those of the plaintiff. Used in this fashion, the term denotes that subset of trademark infringement cases that are marked by an intent to deceive or bad faith.

Courts also use the "passing off" language to cover another type of situation. In some cases when consumers would ask for one particular brand of goods, the vendor might substitute another without making any disclosure. Think of ordering COCA–COLA in a restaurant. If the restaurant does not stock genuine COCA–COLA brand beverages, but the server says nothing in response to the order and brings a glass of carbonated cola, the patron will suppose that she has gotten the brand she asked for. In fact, a different brand has been "passed off" as genuine COKE.[1]

Professor McCarthy has suggested in his treatise that the "passing off" terminology should be limited to these two situations, both cases "where there is real proof that defendant subjectively and knowingly intended to confuse buyers."[2] As he points out, however, many courts have used the phrase to encompass any fact pattern where the evidence indicates a likelihood of confusion, regardless of whether the defendant had a deceptive intent. He refers to this usage as "rhetorical hyperbole for likelihood of confusion."[3] Consequently, the actual meaning of the phrase "passing off" can only be ascertained by considering the context in which it is being used. In our opinion, the phrase adds little to the law except confusion, and it would be best if its use were phased out entirely.

The term "unfair competition" is an umbrella designation for any inappropriate, overzealous or inequitable commercial conduct. It is one of the more elastic terms in the law, with no precise boundaries.[4] It can be conceived of as conduct which offends prevailing standards of commercial morality, or conduct which is unlikely to yield the usual competitive benefits of lower prices, higher output and better quality goods. Trademark infringement, because it misleads consumers and deprives trademark owners of sales that would have otherwise come their way, has long been considered one type of unfair competition.[5] The label has also been applied to a wide range of other behaviors running the gamut from trade secret theft to bait and switch advertising.

In a confusing bit of legal history, there was time when only parties with inherently distinctive trademarks could bring suit for trademark infringement. Firms using symbols that were not initially distinctive, but which had acquired secondary meaning, were required to plead and

§ 29.5

1. *See, e.g.,* Coca–Cola Co. v. Overland, Inc., 692 F.2d 1250 (9th Cir.1982).

2. J. Thomas McCarthy, TRADEMARKS AND UNFAIR COMPETITION § 25:3.

3. *Id.* at § 25:2.

4. For instance, one state court noted that the "law of unfair competition is an amorphous area of jurisprudence. It knows of no clear boundaries.... The concept is as flexible and elastic as the evolving standards of commercial morality demand." New Jersey Optometric Ass'n v. Hillman–Kohan Eyeglasses, Inc., 144 N.J.Super. 411, 427, 365 A.2d 956 (Ch.Div.1976).

5. Hanover Star Milling Co. v. Metcalf, 240 U.S. 403, 413, 36 S.Ct. 357, 60 L.Ed. 713 (1916) ("the common law of trademarks is but a part of the broader law of unfair competition").

prove "unfair competition" instead. Moreover, some very old case law indicated that while an intent to deceive would not be required in trademark infringement cases, it would be required in cases of unfair competition. All of this is now strictly a matter of legal history. The modern rule is quite clear that all trademark owners—regardless of where their marks might fall on the continuum of distinctiveness—are now entitled to sue for trademark infringement, and that intent is not a required element of plaintiff's case. Of course, as we have seen earlier in this chapter, proof of intent to confuse the public remains relevant as a factor bearing on the issue of likelihood of confusion.

To recap: From a purely linguistic point of view unfair competition today is the broadest of the terms under consideration, encompassing all forms of illegitimate business practices. Trademark infringement is but one type of unfair competition. Passing off, in turn, is a subset of trademark infringement, occurring when the defendant acts intentionally to dupe the public.

§ 29.6   Trademark Counterfeiting

As noted at the very outset of this chapter, the absolute core case of trademark infringement arises when a defendant uses the identical mark owned by plaintiff on the same type of goods and sells those goods in direct competition in the exact same geographic area. Such cases are often designated as instances of trademark counterfeiting. According to the Lanham Act, a counterfeit trademark is "a spurious mark which is identical with, or substantially indistinguishable from, a registered mark."[1]

Trademark counterfeiting is a serious problem, not just in terms of its economic impact on trademark owners and consumers, but in terms of the risks it poses to the health and safety of large numbers of people. Counterfeit goods are often shoddy. Congressional testimony and academic scholarship have established that counterfeit parts for cars, airplanes, and military hardware have endangered lives and caused fatalities. Counterfeit medications have caused illness and death. Counterfeit baby formula has made infants sick. Counterfeit agricultural products have destroyed crops. Professor McCarthy has detailed many of these incidents in his treatise.[2] Other researchers have documented links between trademark counterfeiting and organized crime.

While the problem is thus a serious one, from a substantive law point of view, there is little to say about trademark counterfeiting. It is illegal. Likelihood of confusion is self-evident, and infringement liability is clear. Trademark counterfeiting does, however, pose unique practical difficulties that have prompted the Congress to adopt certain special

---

§ 29.6

1. The definition excludes goods on which the manufacturer was authorized to use the mark. This means that "gray goods" or parallel imports, which are dis-

cussed further on in this text, in § 31.1.4, are not considered counterfeit. 15 U.S.C.A. § 1116(d) (2000).

2. J. Thomas McCarthy, Trademarks and Unfair Competition § 25:10.

procedural mechanisms to deal with it. These difficulties arise because counterfeiters, almost by definition, are not reputable business people. When sued, they will often disappear, taking their inventory with them, only to crop up again in another locale. They often distribute their goods through itinerant resellers with no fixed place of business. They are elusive, slippery targets. In addition, much counterfeit merchandise is manufactured abroad.

The first line of defense against foreign counterfeit goods is to prevent them from ever entering the country. The 1978 Customs Act endeavors to accomplish exactly that. Under its provisions goods bearing counterfeit trademarks will be automatically seized by the Customs Service at the border, and must be destroyed, unless the trademark owner consents to an alternative disposition.[3] Of course, despite this provision some imported counterfeit goods still slip in to the United States. Moreover, other counterfeit items are manufactured here, and thus not subject to the Customs Act.

To provide more effective procedures for combating domestic counterfeiting, Congress passed the Trademark Counterfeiting Act in 1984, and strengthened it still further with significant amendments in 1996. This statute, for the first time, criminalized trademark counterfeiting.[4] Under its provisions, individuals can be imprisoned up to 10 years and fined up to $2,000,000 for a first offense, and up to 20 years with a $5,000,000 fine for second offenses. According to the Report of the Department of Justice for Fiscal Year 2000, 64 cases of criminal trademark infringement were filed in that year against a total of 103 defendants.[5]

The government must prove four elements to establish criminal liability for counterfeiting: (1) that the defendant trafficked, or attempted to traffic, in goods or services; (2) that such trafficking, or attempt to traffic, was intentional; (3) that the defendant used a "counterfeit mark" on or in connection with such goods or services; and (4) that the defendant knew that the mark so used was counterfeit. In 1996, Congress also made trafficking in counterfeit goods a "predicate act" under RICO, a complex and far-reaching statute designed to combat organized crime.[6] A number of states also have criminal provisions dealing with trademark counterfeiting.

On the civil side, the 1984 legislation created a special procedure permitting judges to grant ex parte seizure orders against trademark counterfeiters.[7] An ex parte order, of course, is one granted without any advance notification to the opposing party. The goal of such orders is to prevent the counterfeiter from either destroying the evidence of its

3. *See* 19 U.S.C.A. § 1526(e) (2000) and 19 C.F.R. § 133.23a (2002).

4. 18 U.S.C.A. § 2320 (2000).

5. *See* <http://www.usdoj.gov/ag/annual reports/pr2000/AppFIntellProperty.htm>.

6. 18 U.S.C.A. §§ 1961–1968 (2000).

7. 15 U.S.C.A. § 1116(d) (2000).

wrongdoing, or merely transporting the counterfeits and their means of production to another locale. It strives to enlist the element of surprise on the side of those battling counterfeiters.

To be entitled to such an order, the applicant must post financial security, which will insure that if the seizure is wrongful, the victim can recover damages.[8] In addition, the applicant must convince the court of seven pre-requisite facts. Some of these are conventional showings required of all applicants for equitable relief. Thus, the applicant must show that: (1) no remedy other than an ex parte seizure will be adequate to protect its interests; (2) it will suffer immediate and irreparable harm without the seizure; (3) it is likely to succeed on the merits in proving counterfeiting; and (4) harm to the applicant outweighs the harm to the defendant. In addition, the applicant must also demonstrate that: (1) it has not publicized the seizure request; (2) the items to be seized are located in the place specified in the application; and (3) the defendant would likely destroy, move, or hide the merchandise if it were given notice of the application. The legislative history refers to this last item as the "key to obtaining an ex parte seizure." The statute also requires the applicant for the ex parte seizure order to notify the local U.S. Attorney. The court must hold a hearing no sooner than 10 and no later than 15 days after any such order is issued.

Along with the potent weapon of ex parte seizure, the 1984 statute also provides for enhanced monetary remedies against trademark counterfeiters. Unless the court finds extenuating circumstances, the plaintiff is entitled have any award of damages or profits trebled, and to recover its attorney fees.[9] To recover these treble damages, plaintiff must prove that the defendant intentionally used the mark in question with knowledge that it was a counterfeit. The courts have held, however, that this knowledge can be inferred from the surrounding circumstances. As the Seventh Circuit explained, it is enough to show that the defendant "failed to inquire further because he was afraid of what the inquiry would yield. Willful blindness is knowledge enough."[10]

In lieu of the treble damage remedy, the plaintiff may elect to recover statutory damages in the amount of "not less than $500 or more than $100,000 per counterfeit mark per type of goods or services sold . . . or . . . if the court finds that the use of the counterfeit mark was willful, not more than $1,000,000 per counterfeit mark per type of goods or services sold . . . as the court considers just."[11] This remedy, analogous to one existing under the copyright laws, guarantees that the counterfeiter

---

8. A claim for wrongful ex parte counterfeit seizures is provided in section 34(d)(11) of the Lanham Act, 15 U.S.C.A. § 1116(d)(11) (2000). It requires the claimant to show either that the plaintiff sought the seizure in bad faith, or that the goods in question were predominantly non-infringing.

9. 15 U.S.C.A. § 1117(b) (2000).

10. Louis Vuitton S.A. v. Lee, 875 F.2d 584 (7th Cir.1989). See also Chanel , Inc. v. Italian Activewear of Florida, Inc., 931 F.2d 1472 (11th Cir.1991); Hard Rock Café Licensing Corp. v. Concession Services, Inc., 955 F.2d 1143, 1151 (7th Cir.1992).

11. 15 U.S.C.A. § 1117(c) (2000).

will not benefit from its conduct even if the plaintiff cannot prove any concrete amount of damages or profits flowing from the illegal activities.

§ 29.7   Contributory and Vicarious Infringement

In almost every branch of the law, parties can be held responsible for the conduct of others. In criminal law, those who drive the getaway car can be convicted just as surely as the triggerman who holds the gun on the bank teller. In personal injury situations, the employer is often liable for the clumsiness of the employee. The same general rule obtains in trademark law. Those who encourage, or benefit from, acts of infringement can be held liable just as readily as those who actually sell the infringing goods.

There are two principal forms of secondary trademark infringement. The first of these is contributory infringement. The Supreme Court has explained that "if a manufacturer or distributor intentionally induces another to infringe a trademark, or if it continues to supply its product to one whom it knows or has reason to know is engaging in trademark infringement, the manufacturer or distributor is contributorially responsible for any harm done as a result of the deceit."[1] This test means that to be liable as a contributory infringer one must either encourage the direct infringer to violate the law, or at a minimum, know of the violations and continue to do business with that direct infringer. The Restatement rule is similar, but not identical, advocating the imposition of contributory infringement liability when the supplier of goods either "intentionally induces the third person to engage in the infringing conduct" or when the supplier "fails to take reasonable precautions against the third person's infringing conduct in circumstances in which the infringement can be reasonably anticipated."[2]

The inducing or encouraging cases of contributory infringement often involve products that are either sold with no packaging or labeling or ones which are packaged and labeled by the retailer. Examples might include bulk hardware items, such as pipes or nails, certain food products such as meat or produce, or commodities such as gasoline or home heating fuel. In such cases a manufacturer can make it easier for its retailers to infringe though a variety of words and deeds.

In one example from the case law, a wholesaler of SEALY brand mattresses also sold non-SEALY foundations (such as box springs) that it covered in identically patterned fabric. The foundations lacked any identifying labels, and because of the matching fabrics, gave the appearance of a being part of a matched set. Indeed, the wholesaler suggested to retailers that they advertise the combination as "SEALY Back–Saver and matching foundation." The wholesaler was not a direct infringer of the SEALY mark, because it did not itself apply the SEALY mark to any

§ 29.7

1. Inwood Laboratories, Inc. v. Ives Laboratories, Inc., 456 U.S. 844, 102 S.Ct. 2182, 72 L.Ed.2d 606 (1982).

2. Restatement (Third) of Unfair Competition § 27 (1995).

non-SEALY goods. Nonetheless, the trial court found its behavior sufficient to establish contributory infringement because its practices induced the retailers to pass off the foundation as a SEALY product—a conclusion affirmed on appeal by the Ninth Circuit.[3] The defendant on these facts was goading or encouraging the retailers into infringing by supplying a foundation so similar in appearance to the SEALY mattress, and advocating a form of advertising that was so ambiguously worded.

While the usual contributory infringement situation involves a manufacturer or distributor, the doctrine has been extended to other situations as well. In *Fonovisa, Inc. v. Cherry Auction, Inc.*,[4] the plaintiff Fonovisa held both copyrights and trademarks for several Latin music recordings. The defendant, Cherry Auction, operated a "swap meet," renting booths in its facilities to independent vendors who sold merchandise directly to the public. Those vendors paid Cherry a daily fee for the space, and Cherry retained the right to exclude any vendor at any time for any reason. Cherry also charged an entrance fee to customers who wanted to attend the swap meet. By the time of the litigation, it was undisputed that certain of the vendors at Cherry's swap meet were selling counterfeit recordings in violation of Fonovisa's copyrights and trademarks, and that Cherry knew of these activities. Plaintiff offered evidence that the local sheriff's department had even informed Cherry of the infringing activities.

The Ninth Circuit observed that "while Cherry Auction is not alleged to be supplying the recordings themselves, it is supplying the necessary marketplace for their sale in substantial quantities." That being so, it reversed a finding for the defendant, reasoning that "a swap meet can not disregard its vendors' blatant trademark infringements with impunity. Thus, Fonovisa has also stated a claim for contributory trademark infringement."

Other cases have suggested that liability will attach even without proof that the defendant had actual knowledge of the direct infringements, if it suspects wrongdoing, and fails to investigate. As the courts often put it, one cannot insulate oneself from contributory infringement liability by remaining "willfully blind" and then arguing lack of knowledge. On the other hand, the Supreme Court has cautioned that a party should not be held liable for contributory infringement just because it "could reasonably anticipate" that its retail outlets might engage in direct infringement.[5]

The other sort of secondary responsibility for infringement recognized by the cases is vicarious liability. One of the few cases to address this theory is *American Tel. & Tel. Co. v. Winback & Conserve Program.*[6]

3. Sealy, Inc. v. Easy Living, Inc., 743 F.2d 1378 (9th Cir.1984).

4. 76 F.3d 259 (9th Cir.1996).

5. Inwood Laboratories, Inc. v. Ives Laboratories, Inc., 456 U.S. 844, 102 S.Ct. 2182, 72 L.Ed.2d 606 (1982).

6. 42 F.3d 1421 (3d Cir.1994), *cert. denied*, 514 U.S. 1103, 115 S.Ct. 1838, 131 L.Ed.2d 757 (1995).

The defendant in this case was a reseller of in-bound toll-free telecommunications services. It bought large blocks of telephone time from plaintiff A T & T and resold that time to small businesses. It conducted this resale business through independent sales representatives. In many instances those sales representatives falsely claimed that they were affiliated with A T & T. The defendant itself, however, did not make any such false claims. A T & T brought a claim under section 43(a) of the Lanham Act arguing that the defendant should be held liable under common law agency principles for the false claims of the sales representatives. The Third Circuit held that ordinary agency law principles were indeed applicable in Lanham Act litigation. On the actual facts before it, it concluded that the sales representatives were independent contractors not servants, but remanded for a determination of whether those representatives could nonetheless be classified as agents, so as to charge defendant with responsibility for their actions.

§ 29.8   False Advertising

False advertising is a large subject, which could easily warrant its own book-length treatment. At first blush, it may also seem far afield from issues of trademark protection or intellectual property generally. Further reflection reveals, however, that misrepresentation of the source or sponsorship of goods through the unauthorized use of another's trademark is merely one way falsely to represent those goods. Lying about a product's ingredients, place of manufacture, warranty terms, expected performance, or any other product attribute can be seen as a close cousin to lying about source or sponsorship. As a result, there has been much historical connection between false advertising issues and trademark law. In addition, the most important federal statutory provision granting private rights against false advertisers is contained in the Lanham Act. Space limitations prevent an in-depth treatment of false advertising, but the sections that follow provide a simplified map of the legal terrain.

29.8.1   Common Law Remedies for False Advertising

False advertising was essentially not actionable under traditional common law principles. While the behavior might have substantively fit within the expansive notion of unfair competition, courts confronting such cases found it impossible to determine if the complaining plaintiff had been harmed. Those courts viewed the essence of commercial harm to be lost sales. When a defendant firm engages in trademark infringement it is pretty clear that, but for the infringement, consumers would have purchased from the plaintiff, which was the true owner of the mark and hence the only vendor of the desired goods. On the other hand, when a firm lies about some other aspect of its goods—perhaps by describing a polyester shirt as being made of all cotton—one cannot make the same assumption. If the duped consumer had known the truth he might have bought from any number of other firms that sold genuine all-cotton shirts, not necessarily from the plaintiff.

As Learned Hand put it, "in an open market, it is generally impossible to prove that a customer, whom the defendant has secured by falsely describing his goods, would have bought of the plaintiff, if the defendant had been truthful. Without that, the plaintiff, though aggrieved in company with other honest traders, cannot show any ascertainable loss.... The law does not allow him to sue as a vicarious avenger of the defendant's customers."[1] On this view, the only plausible case for relief would be one where the plaintiff alleging false advertising had a monopoly on goods possessing the falsely advertised trait. If there is only one firm in the market selling all cotton shirts, that is the firm that would get the sale if only the false advertiser was restrained from saying that its shirts were also made of cotton. This principle came to be known as the "sole source" rule.

Conceptually, the narrow "sole source" view of the old common law cases is hardly inevitable. It would be perfectly reasonable, for instance, to allow any competitor to sue a false advertiser, but to limit the relief to an injunction unless the plaintiff could show with specific evidence that it would have been the beneficiary of any diverted sales. That would also have the salutary effect of ridding the market of the deception to the benefit of consumers which, notwithstanding Learned Hand's dismissal of vicarious avengers, seems all to the good. Alternatively, the plaintiff could be allowed to recover that percentage of the false advertiser's profits equal to its market share—a firm that sells 10% of all the cotton shirts could recover 10% of the profits of the lying polyester shirt vendor. One could posit any number of other creative alternatives.

By the end of the 20th century the sparse common law cases dealing with false advertising had abandoned a strict insistence that the plaintiff be the "sole source" in order to recover. The Restatement (Third) of Unfair Competition, reflecting this metamorphosis provides that "one who makes a representation relating to the goods or services that it markets, which is likely to deceive or mislead prospective purchasers to the likely commercial detriment of another ... is subject to liability to the other ...."[2] It then goes on to specify that "a representation is to the likely commercial detriment of another if ... there is a reasonable basis for believing that the representation has caused or is likely to cause a diversion of trade from the other ...."[3] The comments explain that "proof that such harm has in fact occurred is not required; nor is it necessary to establish that injury is certain to result if the actor continues in its course of conduct. The actor is subject to liability if the evidence indicates that there is a reasonable probability that the party seeking relief has incurred or will incur injury as a result of the misrepresentation."[4]

§ 29.8

1. Ely–Norris Safe Co. v. Mosler Safe Co., 7 F.2d 603 (2d Cir.1925), *reversed,* 273 U.S. 132, 47 S.Ct. 314, 71 L.Ed. 578 (1927).

2. Restatement (Third) of Unfair Competition § 2 (1995).

3. *Id.,* § 3.

4. *Id.,* comment e.

While a few recent cases have followed this approach, and granted common law relief for false advertising even when the plaintiff is not a "sole source,"[5] the common law rules for false advertising have proved to be of minimal legal importance. This is because, long before the relaxation of the common law sole source rule, aggrieved firms discovered that they had a far superior weapon against false advertising in section 43(a) of the Lanham Act.

29.8.2   False Advertising Under the Lanham Act

Initially, the federal courts vacillated when confronted with false advertising claims under the Lanham Act. Although the original language in section 43(a) of the statute could have been read broadly enough to encompass such claims, that reading was not free from doubt. Consequently, while some courts gave the section an expansive construction, others opted for a much more narrow interpretation, going so far as to hold that it did not alter the common law "sole source" requirement at all.[6] By the 1970's however, the more generous interpretation had begun to carry the day and the Lanham Act had become the weapon of choice for competitors alleging false advertising.

Congress decided to remove any ambiguity on the issue of the statute's scope in 1988 by amending section 43(a) of the Lanham to provide an explicit false advertising remedy.[7] It now provides a cause of action against:

> Any person who, on or in connection with any goods or services, or any container for goods, uses in commerce any word, term, name, symbol, or device, or any combination thereof, or any false designation of origin, false or misleading description of fact, or false or misleading representation of fact, which ... (2) in commercial advertising or promotion, misrepresents the nature, characteristics, qualities, or geographic origin of his or her or another person's goods, services, or commercial activities....[8]

In the years since the adoption of this explicit language, the statute has only continued to grow in importance.

29.8.2.1   Standing

One of the chief advantages of the Lanham Act over the traditional common law false advertising rules is that it removed the "sole source" hurdle. Firms are permitted to assert a cause of action under the statute even if they do not have a monopoly on goods possessing the falsely claimed attribute. The statutory language confers a cause of action on "any person who believes that he or she is or is likely to be damaged by

---

5. *See, e.g.,* Pacamor Bearings, Inc. v. Minebea Co., Ltd., 918 F.Supp. 491, 501 (D.N.H.1996).

6. *See, e.g.,* Chamberlain v. Columbia Pictures Corp., 186 F.2d 923 (9th Cir.1951).

7. *See* Trademark Law Revision Act of 1988, Pub. L. 100–667, 102 Stat. 3935 (effective November 16, 1989).

8. 15 U.S.C.A. § 1125 (2000).

such act." While this might suggest a purely subjective rule, allowing any firm to sue based on its own perception of potential harm, the courts have not dispensed with all standing requirements. There must be some factual basis suggesting that the plaintiff is at least a potential victim of the false advertising in question before it will be allowed to go forward.

If the plaintiff is seeking injunctive relief and nothing more, it need only demonstrate that it is "likely to be harmed" by the defendant's false advertising, and that the harm is "likely to have been caused" by that false advertising. The leading case establishing this rule is *Johnson & Johnson v. Carter–Wallace, Inc.*[9] The plaintiff, the makers of a leading brand of baby oil and baby lotion, complained that the defendant had falsely advertised a new version of its hair removal product NAIR. Specifically, Johnson & Johnson alleged that Carter–Wallace falsely implied that its NAIR WITH BABY OIL made it possible for users to dispense with the separate use of baby oil for moisturization purposes. The initial question in the case, however, was not the truth or falsity of the advertising, but whether Johnson & Johnson had demonstrated a sufficient likelihood of harm to establish standing to seek an injunction under the Lanham Act.

Johnson & Johnson argued that a likelihood of harm, should be presumed from the fact that the two firms were engaged in competition. The Second Circuit purported to reject that rule, saying: "The correct standard is whether it is *likely* that Carter's advertising has caused or will cause a loss of Johnson sales.... Contrary to Johnson's argument, however, the likelihood of injury and causation will not be presumed, but must be demonstrated. If such a showing is made, the plaintiff will have established a reasonable belief that he is likely to be damaged within the meaning of § 43(a) and will be entitled to injunctive relief." In other words, while the court adopted a rule much more lenient than the common law sole source doctrine, it refused to simply assume that every complaining competitor will be injured by a rival's false advertisement. There must be some proof.

The actual demonstration demanded by the Second Circuit, however, was quite slight. On the record before it, it held that the plaintiff had made an adequate showing of harm because (1) it was engaged in at least indirect competition with the defendant, and even indirect competitors may suffer potential harm from false advertising; (2) the defendant's advertising, by referring to baby oil, had "linked" the depilation and moisturizer markets; and (3) plaintiff had offered evidence to show a logical causal connection between the alleged false advertising and its own sales position. On this last point, the court pointed to plaintiff's proof that many consumers used its baby oil as an after-shave and after-depiliation moisturizer, that its own sales of baby oil did, in fact, decline, after the defendant began the challenged advertising, and its survey evidence that some people, after viewing defendant's advertising, thought they would not have to use baby oil if they used defendant's new

---

9.   631 F.2d 186 (2d Cir.1980).

product. Almost any competitor should be able to marshal similar evidence, and Professor McCarthy concludes that while the *Johnson & Johnson* case "purported to reject the theory that damage and standing is presumed if the plaintiff and defendant are competitors, this appears to be the net result" of the case.[10] We concur in his assessment.

When a Lanham Act false advertising plaintiff seeks damages in addition to injunctive relief, the requirement for standing become more rigorous, because the plaintiff will now be required to make a more specific and particularized showing of harm. Elements of recoverable damages in a false advertising case might include both the profits lost by plaintiff on sales actually diverted to the false advertiser and additional profits lost on any sales made at reduced prices necessary to counter the false advertising In addition, plaintiff is entitled to recover the cost of any advertising that it undertakes in response to defendant's false advertising and any quantifiable harm to its good will, to the extent that corrective advertising has not remedied that harm.

In this regard, the D.C. Circuit has cautioned that the trial judge must ensure that "the record adequately supports all items of damages claimed and establishes a causal link between the damages and the defendant's conduct, lest the award become speculative . . . ."[11] This does not mean that the plaintiff must be the "sole source" in order to recover damages, but it plainly requires more than the evidence of a mere likelihood of harm which suffices for an injunction. There must be specific evidence that at least some consumers were actually deceived by the advertising, which usually will require customer testimony or consumer surveys. However, the Ninth Circuit has held that where the defendant acted with an intent to deceive the public, resulting deception can be presumed.[12]

If the plaintiff seeks the additional monetary remedy of a recovery of the profits earned by the false advertiser, it must offer evidence that the defendant acted willfully or in bad faith in promulgating the advertising. This is the general rule in all Lanham Act cases, including trademark infringement, and is discussed in greater detail in the chapter on trademark remedies further on in the book.[13]

While Congress and the courts have thus allowed a broad range of competitors to use the Lanham Act to seek relief against false advertising, they have not been so generous to consumers. On virtually every occasion when consumers have attempted to invoke the provisions of section 43(a) to seek relief for financial loss in connection with false advertising the courts have held that they lack standing under the statute.[14] This conclusion is usually based on the language in section 45

---

10. J. Thomas McCarthy, Trademarks and Unfair Competition § 27:29.

11. ALPO Petfoods v. Ralston Purina Co., 913 F.2d 958 (D.C.Cir.1990).

12. U–Haul International, Inc. v. Jartran, Inc., 793 F.2d 1034 (9th Cir.1986).

13. *See,* § 31.5.2, *infra.*

14. *See, e.g.,* Stanfield v. Osborne Indus. Inc., 52 F.3d 867, 873 (10th Cir.1995), *cert. denied,* 516 U.S. 920, 116 S.Ct. 314, 133 L.Ed.2d 217 (1995) ("to have standing for a false advertising claim, the plaintiff must be

of the Lanham Act, declaring that the purpose of the statute is "to protect persons engaged in ... commerce against unfair competition." Consumers, the courts reason, are not engaged in commerce. As a consequence, aggrieved consumers have had to look elsewhere—usually to state law—when they wish to litigate over false advertisements. In our view, the cases denying consumers standing are probably more concerned about preventing a flood of small stakes claims in federal court than about faithful statutory interpretation. After all, speaking literally, buyers are just as much engaged in "commerce" as sellers.

Several circuits have allowed commercial parties who are not competitors to sue under the section 43(a). Thus in one case a trade association of firms selling garments made of genuine camel hair and cashmere fibers was allowed to assert false advertising claims against retailers selling allegedly mislabeled clothes[15] and in another, a stockholder of a competitor of the alleged false advertiser was allowed to go forward.[16] The Ninth Circuit, however, has held that only direct commercial competitors possess standing.[17]

29.8.2.2 Substantive Elements

As most courts have summarized them, the elements required to recover on a false advertising claim under the Lanham Act are: (1) a false statement of fact by a defendant in a commercial advertisement about its own or another's product; (2) the statement actually deceived or has the tendency to deceive a substantial segment of its audience; (3) the deception is material, in that it is likely to influence the purchasing decision; (4) the defendant caused its false statement to enter interstate commerce; and (5) the plaintiff has been or is likely to be injured as a result of the false statement, either by direct diversion of sales from itself to defendant or by a lessening of the goodwill associated with its products.[18]

The fifth itemized element—dealing with likely injury—relates to the standing issues that were considered in the immediately preceding section. The fourth listed element is jurisdictional, since the Lanham Act is an exercise of Congress's commerce clause powers. It has not proved especially controversial in most cases, and is largely self-explanatory.

Some caution, however, may be in order in thinking about the first three items on this list. As two commentators recently observed:

a competitor of the defendant and allege competitive injury"); Serbin v. Ziebart Int'l Corp., 11 F.3d 1163, 1177 (3d Cir.1993); Colligan v. Activities Club of New York, Ltd., 442 F.2d 686 (2d Cir.1971).

15. Camel Hair and Cashmere Institute of America, Inc. v. Associated Dry Goods Corp., 799 F.2d 6 (1st Cir.1986).

16. Thorn v. Reliance Van Co., 736 F.2d 929 (3d Cir.1984).

17. Halicki v. United Artists Communications, Inc., 812 F.2d 1213 (9th Cir.1987)

(film producer lacks standing to challenge movie theaters for falsely advertising his PG-rated movie as being R-rated).

18. *See, e.g.,* Cook, Perkiss and Liehe, Inc. v. Northern California Collection Service Inc., 911 F.2d 242, 244 (9th Cir.1990); Federal Express Corp. v. United States Postal Serv., 40 F.Supp.2d 943, 950 (W.D.Tenn.1999); Skil Corp. v. Rockwell Int'l Corp., 375 F.Supp. 777, 783 (N.D.Ill. 1974).

This list of elements appears to be an historical accident. It originated in a 1974 district court decision, which did not analyze the elements and cited as its only authority a 1956 law review article that had formulated the elements based solely on pre-Lanham Act case law. Courts have widely repeated these elements without analysis, but have rarely (if ever) applied them as stated.[19]

As those commentators point out, several of the elements tend to get combined or to collapse into each other in actual litigation.

Semantically, the second element, requiring "deception" of the public, means that the falsehood in the advertising must be plausible, or believable, so that significant numbers of consumers are misled into accepting it as true. When the plaintiff satisfies the first element, requiring a "false statement," by proof that the advertisement is literally or expressly false, courts do not require any further proof of deception of the public. Effectively, the courts assume that consumers will always believe an express falsehood, and the second element drops out of the case. As the Second Circuit explained, "When a merchandising statement or representation is literally or explicitly false, the court may grant relief without reference to the advertisement's impact on the buying public. . . ."[20] This seems logical. If an advertisement states that goods were made "at our factory in Wisconsin" or that the product will "cut your energy usage in half" or that it "contains no artificial coloring," the vast majority of consumers will take the claim at face value. They will believe it and if it is false, they are "deceived" plain and simple.

There is one exception to this conclusion. If an advertising claim is extremely general, inherently preposterous, or worded in the superlative, consumers are likely to ignore it, rather than believe it, or so the courts have reasoned. Examples might include claims that a product is "the best" or "amazing," that it will "change your life forever" or that it is "delicious" or "beautiful." Such claims are usually called "puffing." Because courts assume that customers will be either indifferent to, or cynical about, puffing, it is not actionable, either under the Lanham Act or under any other set of legal prohibitions against false advertising.

Of course, an advertisement need not be literally false to communicate a false message. A falsehood can be communicated by implication or innuendo. Clever use of words, or subtle juxtaposition of words and pictures can dupe all but the most attentive. The text of section 43(a) recognizes this possibility because it condemns not merely "false" descriptions or representations, but "misleading" ones as well. For instance, the maker of a non-aspirin pain-relieving-rub might advertise that it "puts the powerful relief of aspirin right where you need it most." Although read carefully, the wording does not claim that the product

19. Courtland L. Reichman & M. Melissa Cannady, *False Advertising Under the Lanham Act,* 21 Franchise Law J. 197 (2002).

20. Coca–Cola Co. v. Tropicana Products, Inc., 690 F.2d 312 (2d Cir.1982).

actually contains any aspirin, it implies as much, and many consumers might assume exactly that.

Where the plaintiff alleges falsity of this sort, it must offer actual proof that the public has received the message in question and accepted it as true. To quote again from the Second Circuit, "[w]hen the challenged advertisement is implicitly rather than explicitly false, its tendency to violate the Lanham Act by misleading, confusing or deceiving should be tested by public reaction."[21] This normally will require consumer survey evidence. The survey need not demonstrate that all consumers will receive and believe the false claim, but courts usually require a demonstration that a substantial proportion of the intended audience will be misled. Some cases have suggested that this means at least 20 per cent,[22] though, of course, there is no universally applicable bright-line mathematical rule.

The third substantive element in a false advertising case under the Lanham Act is "materiality." Conceptually, this means that consumers not only believe the falsehood in question, but that it influences their purchasing decisions—it relates to something they care about or consider important. In theory one could imagine an advertiser promulgating a believable lie about which consumers are largely indifferent. For instance, the seller of pencils might advertise that they are manufactured from oak, when in actuality they are made from maple. The representation would be explicitly false and would "deceive" consumers, who would naturally assume based on the advertisement that the products were made from oak. However, one might predict that most consumers would be fairly indifferent to the wood used to make their pencils and would merely shrug and mutter "whatever" when told that the pencils were not oak at all. If that prediction about consumer reaction is correct, this particular falsehood would not be material.

Courts rarely discuss materiality separately in Lanham Act false advertising opinions. Essentially, they assume that if plaintiff can show either a literal falsehood, or corroborate an implied falsehood with survey evidence showing that the public has been deceived, that is enough to show materiality as well. Put simply, this element also tends to drop out of the analysis in the vast majority of decisions. This is not entirely surprising. Most advertising messages are terse, and most advertisers are trying to break through the "clutter" of a world where consumers are being bombarded with dozens of advertisements each hour. Few advertisers will spend time or money on representations that they do not feel have the potential to trigger a sale. If it is in the advertisement, the advertiser must have thought it was material, and if the advertiser thought that, the court will usually assume it as well.

The materiality prong of the cause of action is not entirely without significance however. The Second Circuit has held that misrepresenta-

21. *Id.*

22. Johnson & Johnson–Merck Consumer Pharmaceuticals Co. v. Rhone–Poulenc Rorer Pharmaceuticals, 19 F.3d 125 (3d Cir.1994).

tion must relate to the "inherent quality or characteristics" of the goods in order to be actionable under the Lanham Act and has characterized this as essentially a test of materiality.[23] Thus it refused to find fault with an advertising claim that updated NBA basketball game scores came "direct from each arena" when, in actuality, the defendant obtained them from broadcasts of the game, not from its own employees stationed in each arena. The court concluded that this is the kind of factual inaccuracy about which consumers would be indifferent—"[w]hether the data is taken from broadcasts instead of being observed first-hand is, therefore, simply irrelevant."[24]

While this result seems sound enough on the facts, the introduction of the fuzzy phrase "inherent quality or characteristics" seems only likely to add further confusion rather than clarity to false advertising law. For instance, the type of wood used in a pencil is almost certainly an "inherent quality or characteristic" of that pencil, yet as we speculated above, few consumers would care on way or the other. It would seem preferable, therefore, to define materiality directly in terms of importance or significance to consumers.

The false advertising features of section 43(a) have their detractors. Some academic observers have criticized the case law interpreting the provision as confused, and insufficiently focused on consumer welfare,[25] or as providing nothing more than a weapon for competitors to use to harass their more innovative rivals.[26] No doubt, as courts gain more experience with suits under this statute, they will be able to fine tune it to reduce the potential for abuse. It seems to us, however, even in advance of that fine-tuning, that a relatively expansive private competitor remedy against false advertising serves as a useful check on the tendency of some firms to manipulate the public to their own financial advantage, and that it has been a useful legal development to liberate firms to serve as "vicarious avengers" of consumers' rights.

29.8.3 Governmental Sanctions For False Advertising

At the Federal level, public enforcement against false advertising is chiefly the responsibility of the Federal Trade Commission, or FTC. Its principal substantive tool is section 5 of the Federal Trade Commission Act, which forbids "unfair or deceptive acts and practices."[27] This broad and extremely flexible language has been interpreted to reach a wide variety of anti-consumer practices, including, but not limited to, false advertising.

Unfair practices are those which injure consumers substantially, which have no offsetting benefits, and which consumers cannot reason-

23. National Basketball Ass'n v. Motorola, Inc., 105 F.3d 841 (2d Cir.1997).

24. *Id.*

25. Jean Wegman Burns, *Confused Jurisprudence: False Advertising Under the Lanham Act*, 79 B.U.L. Rev. 807 (1999).

26. Lillian R. BeVier, *Competitor Suits for False Advertising Under Section 43(a) of the Lanham Act: A Puzzle in the Law of Deception*, 78 Va. L. Rev. 1 (1992).

27. 15 U.S.C.A. § 45(a) (2002).

able avoid by themselves.[28] Although the FTC sometimes challenges advertising as "unfair," that is relatively uncommon. Instead, the FTC has typically used its "unfairness" authority to challenge a variety of non-advertising abuses. Thus in one case it brought a claim against a mail order company that routinely sued defaulting customers in Illinois regardless of where they lived,[29] and in another, it sued a home exterminating company that breached contractual promises to numerous consumers that annual fees would not be raised for as long as they owned their homes.[30]

One of the few instances of an FTC effort to challenge advertising under the unfairness theory was the administrative complaint the agency filed against the R.J. Reynolds tobacco company in 1997, alleging that its use of the cartoon character Joe Camel in advertising was unfair. The gravamen of the complaint was that the advertising was targeted at children, who would be harmed by taking up smoking and who were incapable of understanding the risks of smoking. Before the case concluded, however, the tobacco companies reached a comprehensive settlement in a lawsuit that had been filed against them by 46 states. Under that settlement, Reynolds agreed to abandon its Joe Camel advertising, and, in 1999, the administrative law judge hearing the FTC case dismissed the complaint as essentially moot.

Far more commonly, the FTC attacks false advertising under its authority to combat deception. Under its decisional law, the FTC will find a practice deceptive if "first, there is a representation, omission, or practice that, second, is likely to mislead consumers acting reasonably under the circumstances, and third, the representation, omission, or practice is material."[31] This standard permits the FTC to challenge not just explicit falsehoods, but implied misrepresentations as well. Where there is some ambiguity about the message conveyed by an advertisement, the FTC will consider consumer survey evidence, but the courts have held that it has the discretion to dispense with such evidence where it feels that it can interpret the advertisement without it.

Using this deception rubric, the FTC has successfully challenged an extremely broad range of problematic advertisements. Many of the cases involve falsehoods about product performance, sometimes also referred to as product "efficacy." A few of the very many such cases include challenges to falsehoods about the ability of a device to improve gas mileage, the ability of a medicinal preparation to prevent baldness, the ability of vitamin supplements to improve energy or health, the ability of an electronic mosquito repeller to repel mosquitos, or the ability of a

---

28. 15 U.S.C.A. § 45(n) (2000). *See also* Orkin Exterminating Co., Inc. v. Federal Trade Commission, 849 F.2d 1354 (11th Cir.1988), *cert. denied,* 488 U.S. 1041, 109 S.Ct. 865, 102 L.Ed.2d 989 (1989); International Harvester Co., 104 F.T.C. 949 (1984).

29. Spiegel, Inc. v. Federal Trade Commission, 540 F.2d 287 (7th Cir.1976).

30. Orkin Exterminating Co., Inc. v. Federal Trade Commission, 849 F.2d 1354 (11th Cir.1988).

31. Cliffdale Associates, Inc., 103 F.T.C. 110 (1984).

special patch to stop harmful cell phone radiation. In addition to its product efficacy cases, the FTC has attacked misrepresentations about where goods have been manufactured, misrepresentations of the privacy policies of firms, the use of undisclosed mock-ups in television advertising and misleading pricing practice, among many other practices.

The case law interpreting the FTC Act has also established that it is both unfair and deceptive for a firm to promulgate an "unsubstantiated" advertisement.[32] This means that an advertiser must have a reasonable basis for all the claims it makes in its advertising prior to running the ad. It cannot just guess about how its product will perform. If a firm runs an unsubstantiated advertisement, it can be found liable for a violation of the FTC Act even though the underlying claims themselves fortuitously turn out to be true.

Procedurally, the FTC may pursue claims both administratively and judicially. If it chooses the administrative route, the case will be heard before an administrative law judge within the FTC, with the FTC staff (known as "complaint counsel") arguing for liability and the advertiser (or "respondent") arguing against. The unsuccessful party may appeal to the 5–member Commission for review of the decision. If the respondent prevails before the Commission that is the end of the matter. If complaint counsel prevails, the respondent is entitled to seek judicial review in the U.S. Court of Appeals.

In an administrative proceeding, the sole remedy available to the FTC is a "cease and desist order," which is essentially a type of injunction forbidding the respondent from engaging in the challenged practices in the future. A cease and desist order may include provisions requiring the respondent to undertake corrective advertising.[33] Alternatively, the FTC may file a complaint in U.S. District Court. It can ask for preliminary and permanent injunctive relief in such a case, and it also may secure certain monetary remedies.

In cases of egregious fraud, other federal agencies, such as the U.S. Department of Justice or the Securities and Exchange Commission, can seek civil and criminal sanctions under several different statutory schemes, including provisions against wire and mail fraud, and more specific laws such as the securities statutes.

At the state level, virtually all of the states have general statutes prohibiting deceptive and/or unfair consumer practices. Some of these laws are based on the Uniform Deceptive Trade Practices Act (UDTPA), which was promulgated in the mid–1960's; others are based on the Uniform Consumer Sales Practices Act (UCSPA), promulgated in 1971; while still others are based on a Model Law for State Government proposed by the FTC in that same year. This last type of law is often referred to as a "baby" or "little" FTC Act. Of course some states (especially California) also have additional laws that deal with specific

32. *See* Pfizer, Inc., 81 F.T.C. 23 (1972); Novartis Corp., 1999 WL 353248 (FTC).

33. Warner–Lambert Co. v. Federal Trade Commission, 562 F.2d 749 (D.C.Cir. 1977).

consumer problems such as odometer tampering, health club membership disputes or abusive debt collection practices and those statutes often
have public enforcement provisions as well. Public enforcement actions
under these laws are usually brought by the state attorney-general.

29.8.4 Consumer Remedies For False Advertising

It is rarely logical for consumers to challenge false advertising in
court. Where the falsely advertised product is a relatively inexpensive
mass produced consumer item, like an article of clothing, a small kitchen
appliance, or an over-the-counter medicine, the cost of litigation would
dwarf the economic loss associated with being tricked into buying a
product under false pretenses. When consumers do litigate, it is usually
in connection with big ticket purchases like cars, boats and houses, and
many such suits involve disputes over individualized representations,
rather than over the content of advertisements that the seller promulgated to the public as a whole.

If a consumer does wish to challenge a false advertisement in court,
he or she cannot do so under the Lanham Act. As noted above, the
courts have repeatedly held that consumers lack standing under that
statute. The vast majority of the states, however, do permit such suits
under their "little FTC" or Uniform Deceptive Trade Practices Acts. The
substantive requirements in such cases are usually much easier for
consumers to establish than those required to make out a common law
case of fraud. Thus it is often not necessary to prove an intent to deceive
on the part of the advertiser, nor any reliance on the advertising claim
on the part of the buyer. On the other hand, some of these statutes have
procedural hurdles than can diminish their utility. One of the most
crucial issues from the perspective of consumers is the ease with which a
case can be brought as a class action, something which varies considerably from state to state.

29.8.5 Disparagement

Disparagement is the mirror image of false advertising. In false
advertising, a merchant tells flattering lies about its own goods or
services. In disparagement situations, a merchant tells insulting lies
about its competitor's goods or services. Disparagement is sometimes
also referred to as trade libel, slander of goods, or injurious falsehood,
but all the labels designate the same kind of conduct and the same legal
cause of action.

Disparagement is actionable under both the common law and section 43(a) of the Lanham Act. At common law, a disparagement plaintiff
had to show that the defendant disseminated a false statement about
plaintiff's goods or services, and that defendant either knew of the falsity
of the statement at the time it was disseminated, or acted with reckless
disregard of whether it was true or false. In addition, plaintiff had to
show "special damages," or specific economic harm caused by the
disparaging statements. Defendants in such cases often argue that their
statements are actually expressions of opinion shielded by the First

Amendment. This is especially true when the defendant is not a competitor, but a consumer rating organization, or members of the media.

A plaintiff can attempt to show that the defendant's critical statements went beyond disparagement of products, and called into question the plaintiff's character for honesty or some other relevant trait. When that is so, the plaintiff can frame the case as a suit for defamation rather than one for product disparagement. In such cases, the plaintiff may be able to take advantage of certain more lenient substantive rules, such as those allowing it to dispense with proof of actual damages or of fault. However, where the plaintiff is a "public figure," such as a major corporation, and where the subject of the controversy can be characterized as a matter of "public concern," there will be little difference in the elements of defamation and disparagement.

Prior to 1988, courts uniformly held that there was no disparagement cause of action under the Lanham Act. In that year, when Congress amended section 43(a) of the act, it included language condemning falsehoods about "another person's goods, services, or commercial activities," thus creating, for the first time, a federal remedy for product disparagement. The Lanham Act provision only applies to "commercial advertising or promotion" and only to false or misleading "facts." The legislative history reflects that Congress included these limitation to make sure that the statute could not be used to challenge non-commercial speech or opinions about the merits of products.

Chapter 30

TRADEMARK DILUTION

Table of Sections

§ 30.1   Historical Development and Definition of Dilution

In 1927 an influential law review article, by an academically accomplished, prominent New York lawyer named Frank Schechter, suggested that the main purpose of trademark law ought not to be the prevention of consumer confusion, but rather the preservation of the uniqueness of merchants' trademarks. He expressed the concern that even non-confusing uses of a firm's trademark might cause "the gradual whittling away or dispersion of the identity and hold upon the public mind of the mark." Effectively Schechter was arguing that strong trademarks were entitled to a property-like protection that should prevent any other party from using the mark, even if the use was on non-competing and utterly unrelated goods.[1] While he did not use the term, his idea became the stimulus for a new cause of action to protect trademarks known as

---

§ 30.1

1. Frank Schechter, *The Rational Basis of Trademark Protection*, 40 HARV. L. REV.

813 (1927). Mr. Schechter is not related to Roger E. Schechter, a co-author of this text.

"dilution." As the name suggests, the doctrine is designed to provide relief when the acts of an unauthorized third party water down, erode or weaken the cachet and magnetism of a strong trademark.

As early as 1932 Congress considered legislation that would have enacted the dilution doctrine as federal trademark law.[2] Frank Schechter helped draft that legislation, and testified in its behalf, but the bill was not adopted. The dilution concept, however, did not fade away. Rather, proponents turned their attention to the state legislatures. In 1947, Massachusetts became the first state to enact a state trademark dilution statute. The dilution concept received further impetus in 1964 when the then United States Trademark Association (now the International Trademark Association or INTA) promulgated a model state trademark bill which included a dilution provision. By the early 1990's dilution statutes had been adopted by about half of all American jurisdictions, including such populous and commercially important states as New York, California, Illinois, Florida and Texas. Nonetheless many courts gave these state dilution laws a narrow construction, for instance often requiring the plaintiff to prove likelihood of confusion despite clear statutory text dispensing with that requirement.[3]

When Congress undertook a major revision of the Lanham Act in 1988, the Trademark Review Commission recommended that the time was ripe to adopt a federal dilution law. Although the Senate agreed, the dilution component of the bill failed to secure passage in the House of Representatives and consequently, when the President signed the Trademark Law Revision Act of 1988, it did not include any dilution provisions. Nonetheless, the International Trademark Association continued to push for a federal dilution law, and in 1995, Congress finally passed the Federal Trademark Dilution Act (or FTDA), codified as new section 43(c) of the Lanham Act.[4]

This new federal law does not displace state dilution statutes. The legislative history of the FTDA indicates that Congress did not mean to "occupy the field" by pre-empting state law in this area.[5] The Restatement (Third) of Unfair Competition also recognizes the continued relevance and potential applicability of state antidilution statutes.[6]

2. *See* H.R. 11592, 72d Cong., 1st Sess. (1932).

3. "Despite the seeming intention of [the New York dilution] statute to confer protection where the federal Lanham Act might not, viz., even where there is no confusion as to the origin of the goods, the courts have denied relief where confusion is absent." Girl Scouts of United States v. Personality Posters Mfg. Co., 304 F.Supp. 1228 (S.D.N.Y.1969).

4. 15 U.S.C.A. § 1125(c) (2000).

5. *See* H.R. Rep. 104–374 (Nov. 30. 1995) ("[T]he proposed federal dilution statute would not preempt state dilution

laws. Unlike patent and copyright laws, federal trademark law coexists with state trademark law, and it is to be expected that the federal dilution statute should similarly coexist with state dilution statutes.").

6. Restatement (Third) of Unfair Competition, § 25. ("One may be subject to liability under the law of trademarks for the use of a designation that resembles the trademark, trade name, collective mark, or certification mark of another without proof of a likelihood of confusion only under an applicable antidilution statute.").

Since the enactment of the FTDA there have been a number of contradictory opinions on several key aspects of the new statute. Despite the unsettled quality of the law, there are some clear points of departure. First, in order to be eligible for protection against dilution, a mark must be strong. Just as a cup of weak tea cannot be meaningfully diluted because it is already weak, a weak mark cannot complain of dilution. Unfortunately, as we shall see shortly, how strong is strong enough, and how to define "strength" in the context of dilution have become matters of considerable complexity. Second, it is fairly widely agreed that a defendant can dilute a strong mark in either of two ways—through either "blurring" or "tarnishment"—although courts have occasionally suggested that there might be other species of dilution that should be added to the list. Third, neither likelihood of confusion nor competition need be shown in order to prevail on a dilution claim. Beyond these basics, however, courts are still trying to work out the resolution of several contentious issues that surround the concept of dilution.

§ 30.2　Marks Eligible for Protection Against Dilution—The Fame Requirement

Under both state and federal law, only strong marks are protected against dilution. The vast majority of trademarks and service marks are not strong enough. Such marks are used by small or local businesses or on goods that circulate to only limited groups of consumers. Relatively few consumers are familiar with marks such as these, and they have little magnetism or selling power in the economy as a whole. The dilution doctrine is not designed to protect marks of this sort. The LUCKY SHAMROCK pub on the corner, the ARGYLE dry cleaners down the block, the regionally distributed POMPEII brand macaroni or the locally available BUZZ brand potato chips simply lack the renown that is a threshold requirement for invoking a claim of dilution.

While some state statutes explicitly require that plaintiff's mark be strong or famous before a dilution claim can proceed,[1] many say nothing on the subject. Even when the statutes are silent, courts have frequently imposed such a requirement as a matter of judicial interpretation.[2] There are, however, exceptions. A few courts have extended the dilution statute to marks that are not especially prominent. Thus, one Oregon appellate court commented: "The words 'distinctive quality' [in the Oregon dilution statute] do not connote to us only the high degree of strength or renown that defendant contends a name must have to be protected...."[3]

§ 30.2

1. *See, e.g.,* Rev. Code Wash. § 19.77.160.

2. *See, e.g.* Avery Dennison Corp. v. Sumpton, 189 F.3d 868 (9th Cir.1999) (California dilution statute is meant "to protect only famous marks."); Kern v. WKQX Radio, 175 Ill.App.3d 624, 125 Ill.Dec. 73, 529 N.E.2d 1149 (1st Dist. 1988) ("The [Illinois] Anti–Dilution Act is designed to protect a strong trade name or mark from use by another ..."); Sally Gee, Inc. v. Myra Hogan, Inc., 699 F.2d 621 (2d Cir.1983)(New York "anti-dilution statute protects only extremely strong marks").

3. Wedgwood Homes, Inc. v. Lund, 58 Or.App. 240, 248, 648 P.2d 393, 398 (1982), *aff'd,* 294 Or. 493, 659 P.2d 377 (1983). In affirming, the Oregon Supreme Court stat-

More recently, the Fifth Circuit, in interpreting the Texas and Louisiana dilution statutes, held that they required only a showing of "distinctiveness" and not of fame.[4] These cases, however, appear to be a clear minority. Moreover, by throwing open the door of dilution to the owners of virtually all marks in the economy, they run the risk of turning the dilution doctrine into an anti-competitive and anti-consumer weapon rather than a tool for the protection of a legitimate trademark interest.

The Restatement (Third) of Unfair Competition specifically requires that a mark be "highly distinctive" in order to merit protection against dilution.[5] The comments to the Restatement helpfully provide some further information about how the authors define this concept:

> As a general matter, a trademark is sufficiently distinctive to be diluted by a nonconfusing use if the mark retains its source significance when encountered outside the context of the goods or services with which it is used by the trademark owner. For example, the trademark KODAK evokes an association with the cameras sold under that mark whether the word is displayed with the cameras or used in the abstract. On the other hand, the designation ALPHA could become sufficiently distinctive to be protected as a trademark for cameras, but a use of the term by itself might still evoke a variety of different associations, including nothing more than the first letter of the Greek alphabet. A mark that evokes an association with a specific source only when used in connection with the particular goods or services that it identifies is not ordinarily sufficiently distinctive to be protected against dilution.[6]

Similarly, the federal dilution law, the FTDA, removes any ambiguity by explicitly specifying that a mark must be "famous" in order to be entitled to a remedy against alleged dilution.

Both courts and commentators have repeatedly cautioned that the fame requirement should be interpreted stringently. As one federal trial court summarized, "under the FTDA marks qualify as 'famous' only if they carry a 'substantial degree of fame,' approaching the level of fame enjoyed by 'household' names such as 'Dupont, Buick, or Kodak.'"[7] Another court has noted that "courts should be discriminating and selective in categorizing a mark as famous," and cited with approval a treatise indicating that the dilution doctrine is only available for "Super-

---

ed: "If the mark has come to signify plaintiff's product in the minds of a significant portion of consumers and if the mark evokes favorable images of plaintiff or its product it possesses the distinctive quality of advertising value—consumer recognition, association and acceptance,—and will be entitled to protection from dilution."

4. Advantage Rent–A–Car, Inc. v. Enterprise Rent–A Car, Co., 238 F.3d 378 (5th Cir.2001) (Rental car company's slogan trademark "We'll Pick You Up" held insufficiently famous for protection under federal dilution action, but capable of protection under Texas and Louisiana state dilution laws).

5. Restatement (Third) of Unfair Competition § 25.

6. *Id.*, comment e.

7. A.B.C. Carpet Co., Inc. v. Naeini, 2002 WL 100604, *5 (E.D.N.Y.2002) (citing TCPIP Holding Co., Inc. v. Haar Communications, Inc., 244 F.3d 88 (2d Cir.2001)).

marks."[8] Professor McCarthy has written that "Congress intended that the courts should be discerning and selective in dubbing a mark 'famous' so as to qualify for protection against dilution. The Trademark Review Commission referred to the dilution remedy as an 'extraordinary' one that required a significant showing of fame. Thus to be protected a mark must be truly prominent and renowned.'"[9] The standard is meant to be a high hurdle. Just as only a small number of people in the United States could justifiably be called "famous," only a small minority of trademarks are likely to meet that test as well.

In some cases, the fame of a mark may be so obvious as to warrant judicial notice. There could be little dispute that marks like COCA–COLA or ROLLS ROYCE are famous under any standard. Unfortunately, most cases are not this easy. Moreover, there is no "registry" of famous marks and no easy mechanism by which one can determine, in advance of litigation, if one's mark has achieved the glorified status of fame. Instead, the FTDA itemizes eight factors that a court is to consider in making that determination once a dilution claim is filed.[10] The statute specifically declares that the list is non-exclusive and that other factors may be considered as well. The listed factors are:

> (A) the degree of inherent or acquired distinctiveness of the mark; (B) the duration and extent of use of the mark in connection with the goods or services with which the mark is used; (C) the duration and extent of advertising and publicity of the mark: (D) the geographical extent of the trading area in which the mark is used; (E) the channels of trade for the goods or services with which the mark is used; (F) the degree of recognition of the mark in the trading areas and channels of trade used by the marks' owner and the person against whom the injunction is sought; (G) the nature and extent of the use of the same or similar marks by third parties; and (H) whether the mark was registered under the Act of March 3, 1881, or the Act of February 20, 1905, or on the principal register.[11]

Like most lists of factors, several of those above are interrelated or even duplicative. While most courts making a determination of "fame" for purposes of a federal dilution claim will likely march through all of the factors in turn, such a formulaic exercise seems pointless where a conclusion one way or the other is not in doubt. Thus, at least one federal appellate court has already taken the pragmatic position that it was not an abuse of discretion for the trial court to focus on only five of the eight factors.[12]

8. I.P. Lund Trading v. Kohler Co., 163 F.3d 27 (1st Cir.1998) (citing Gilson trademark treatise).

9. J. Thomas McCarthy, Trademarks and Unfair Competition, (4th ed.), § 24:109.

10. This same approach is used in the 1992 revision of the Model State Trademark Act promulgated by the International Trademark Association. The list of factors appears in section 13 of that proposed law.

11. 15 U.S.C.A. § 1125 (c)(1) (2000).

12. Times Mirror Magazines, Inc. v. Las Vegas Sports News, L.L.C., 212 F.3d 157 (3d Cir.2000), *cert. denied,* 531 U.S. 1071, 121 S.Ct. 760, 148 L.Ed.2d 662 (2001).

The first factor suggests that, all other things being equal, a mark that falls in the "fanciful" pigeonhole on the spectrum of distinctiveness may be more likely to be famous than one that is merely suggestive or descriptive, and that a mark with significant secondary meaning is similarly more likely to be famous than one with just barely enough secondary meaning to qualify as a trademark. This first factor does not suggest, however, that all fanciful marks are by that fact alone "famous" and entitled to protection against dilution. Fame is not an intrinsic attribute of a trademark—it is a marketplace reality that only arises when consumers, in vast numbers, become familiar with the mark. Presumably survey evidence reflecting strong public recognition would be highly persuasive under this factor.

The second and third factors focus on the actual commercial activities of the plaintiff asserting the dilution claim. Common sense suggests that the longer and more widely the mark has been used, advertised, or referenced in the media, the more likely it is to be famous. Such facts are, in effect, a form of circumstantial evidence. Consumers are unlikely to remain unaware of a trademark that has been heavily advertised or highly successful in the marketplace. Thus, these factors quite rationally permit an inference of widespread public recognition, which is the essence of "fame."

The fourth factor, dealing with geographic extent of use indicates that marks used all over the United States are more likely to be famous than those used only in a single city, state or region. As with all the fame factors, however, this factor does not establish an absolute rule. For example, one can think of various restaurants, or night clubs that, although located in only one city, have achieved an extraordinary degree of national fame—for instance, in their day both THE STORK CLUB and STUDIO 54 were nationally known, and the sale of STUDIO 54 pencils or STORK CLUB diapers might very well have been actionable dilution.

By focusing on "channels of trade," the fifth factor suggests that fame may be more readily found if the trademark is used on goods that are sold in contexts where the trademark is likely to come to the attention of many consumers, such as chain stores, or if it is used on a family of related goods rather than on only a single product. For example, the KODAK trademark is used for cameras, film, photographic papers and chemicals, and even for photocopying machines. Its use in these multiple channels of trade, which brings the mark to the attention of a wide variety of consumers, would naturally tend to fortify the conclusion that it is a famous mark.

Factor six alludes to the degree of recognition among both plaintiff's and defendant's customers. Of course, if those who buy from the defendant have never heard of the plaintiff or its mark, then defendant's conduct cannot dilute the mark in the minds of those consumers. More generally, if there exists populations of consumers, such as defendant's customers, who have never heard of the mark, that indicates that plaintiff's mark is not really very "famous" across the entire economy. In a sense "degree of recognition" is just a synonym for fame, and thus this factor may not add much to a general inquiry about how many people have heard of the mark and associate it with the plaintiff.

The degree of third party usage, which is referenced in the seventh factor, indicates that a mark cannot be famous for dilution purposes unless it is relatively unique. A mark such as UNITED might be well known, when coupled with the generic word "airlines," as the mark of a major U.S. airline company, but the UNITED mark itself is used by so many different firms on so many different types of goods and services that it should not be considered "famous" for purposes of a claim under the FTDA.

Federal registration is not a requirement for bringing a claim under the FTDA. However, the last fame factor indicates that the existence of such a registration will further a finding of the necessary fame and that its absence at least raises a doubt. Indeed, in most cases, it is hard to imagine a situation where the owner of a truly famous mark would not take the relatively simple step of securing federal trademark registration, and the failure to register should raise at least a yellow flag with a court attempting to determine if the mark is truly famous.

Like many categorization problems in trademark law, there will inevitably be subjectivity in applying these factors. Under this multi-factor approach marks such as BARBIE for dolls,[13] BUDWEISER for beer,[14] PORSCHE for automobiles,[15] and WAWA for convenience stores[16] have all been found famous. While the first three are "household names," you may not be familiar with the fourth unless you live in Philadelphia or the surrounding areas. On the other hand marks such as CHILDREN'S PLACE for children's clothing stores,[17] BONGO for clothing[18] and CLUE for board games[19] have been held not to be famous. While the first two seem, intuitively, to lack the stature required for "fame," almost everyone has heard of the CLUE game and the movie based upon it, though to be fair, there are numerous third-party users of this mark, which lessens its fame. As courts gain more experience with the FTDA and as more cases are decided, the accumulated decisions may provide a somewhat greater degree of predictability, but it is unlikely that the process will ever evolve from art into pure science.

13. Mattel Inc. v. Jcom Inc., 48 USPQ2d 1467 (S.D.N.Y.1998).

14. Anheuser–Busch Inc. v. Andy's Sportswear Inc., 40 USPQ2d 1542 (N.D.Cal. 1996).

15. Porsche Cars North America, Inc. v. Manny's Porshop, Inc., 972 F.Supp. 1128 (N.D.Ill.1997).

16. WAWA Dairy Farms v. Haaf, 40 USPQ2d 1629 (E.D.Pa.1996), *aff'd,* 116 F.3d 471 (3d Cir.1997).

17. TCPIP Holding Co. v. Haar Communications, Inc., 244 F.3d 88 (2d Cir. 2001).

18. Michael Caruso & Co. v. Estefan Enterprises, Inc., 994 F.Supp. 1454 (S.D.Fla.1998).

19. Hasbro, Inc. v. Clue Computing, Inc., 66 F.Supp.2d 117 (D.Mass.1999), *aff'd,* 232 F.3d 1 (1st Cir.2000).

30.2.1 Requiring Both "Distinctiveness" and Fame

While the FTDA begins by saying that "the owner of a famous mark shall be entitled" to relief from dilution, the second sentence of the provision—the one that introduces the list of the eight factors considered above—provides that, "[i]n determining whether a mark is distinctive and famous a court may consider factors such as...." Because this phrase contains a separate reference to both distinctiveness and fame, one could read this language to mean that "distinctiveness" and "fame" are two discrete concepts, and that in order to qualify for anti-dilution protection a mark must be *both* distinctive *and* famous. On the other hand, the words could just be synonyms and the three-word phrase "distinctive and famous" might be nothing more than a forceful way to communicate a single unitary concept, like the phrases "rough and ready" or "hot and bothered."

The Second Circuit has taken the former view and held that a mark must be both distinctive and famous before its owner can pursue a dilution claim. In *Nabisco, Inc. v. PF Brands, Inc.*[20] the court explained:

> It is quite clear that the statute intends distinctiveness in addition to fame, as an essential element ... both qualities are required.... A mark that, notwithstanding its fame, has no distinctiveness is lacking the very attribute that the antidilution statute seeks to protect.... Many famous marks are of the common or quality-claiming or prominence-claiming type—such as American, National, Federal, Federated, First, United, Acme, Merit or Ace. It seems most unlikely that the statute contemplates allowing the holders of such common, albeit famous marks to exclude all new entrants.[21]

There is no small amount of terminological confusion lurking in this analysis. In conventional trademark vocabulary all marks are distinctive! Indeed, distinctiveness is the very essence of a protectable mark. Some marks—such as those classified as fanciful, arbitrary and suggestive—are inherently distinctive while others—such as descriptive words—only acquire their distinctiveness over time under the doctrine of secondary meaning.[22] They are all, however, "distinctive." The examples given by the *Nabisco* court of "common" or "quality claiming" marks are all marks that would be considered descriptive, but there is little question that the marks ACE for retail hardware stores or UNITED for airline services have acquired secondary meaning and are thus distinctive in the trademark sense when used in connection with the specified goods or services.

Thus what the *Nabisco* court must have been saying is that only marks that fall into the "inherently distinctive" categories could assert claims of dilution. The court reiterated and expanded upon this analysis in *TCPIP Holding Co., Inc. v. Haar Communications, Inc.*,[23] where the

20. 191 F.3d 208 (1999).

21. 191 F.3d at 216.

22. *See* § 27.2.4 *supra*.

23. 244 F.3d 88 (2d Cir.2001).

mark at issue was CHILDREN'S PLACE for children's clothing stores. Its discussion is worth quoting at some length:

> The argument might be made that the Dilution Act's requirement of *distinctiveness* may be satisfied by either inherent distinctiveness or acquired distinctiveness. There is ambiguous language in the statute that could be read to support that argument. The statute states: "In determining whether a mark is distinctive and famous a court may consider ... (A) the degree of inherent or acquired distinctiveness of the mark,"
>
> . . . .
>
> On the basis of this language, two arguments might be advanced: (1) Clause (A) treats "inherent" and "acquired" distinctiveness as equivalents; and (2) if acquired distinctiveness does not satisfy the statute's requirement of distinctiveness, then the reference to acquired distinctiveness is meaningless and superfluous; and such an interpretation of a statute—one that renders a portion of the statute superfluous—should be avoided.
>
> Both arguments are ill-conceived. As to the first argument, the fact that the statute invites courts to consider both inherent and acquired distinctiveness in no way implies that they are to be deemed equivalent to one another. In fact, they refer to quite different phenomena. Inherent distinctiveness refers to a mark's theoretical *capacity* to serve forcefully as an identifier of its owner's goods, regardless whether the mark has fulfilled those expectations. Acquired distinctiveness refers to a different phenomenon, one measured solely by the extent of recognition that the mark in fact has earned in the marketplace as a designator of its owner's goods or services, regardless of the mark's innate suitability to serve as a mark. . . .
>
> As to the second argument, it is incorrect that the concept of acquired distinctiveness has no discernable function in the statute, unless as a substitute for inherent distinctiveness. The list of factors set forth in § 1125(c)(1)(A)-(H) is relevant to two separate questions. The factors are listed as pertinent to the court's "determin[ation] whether a mark is *distinctive and famous*." 15 U.S.C.A. § 1125(c)(1) (emphasis added). The "degree of ... acquired distinctiveness of the [plaintiff's] mark" is directly relevant to the determination whether the mark is "famous," as the Act requires. Acquired distinctiveness is the essential ingredient in the determination of fame, within the meaning of the statute. The statute's requirement of fame is not satisfied by any kind of fame. The mark must have become famous *as the designator of the plaintiff's goods or services*. A merchant's taking a famous name—Shakespeare or Zeus—as the mark for its product would not thereby satisfy the statute's requirement of fame. It is true, such a mark would be famous in

the sense that universal recognition would attach to the name Shakespeare or Zeus. To satisfy the statute, however, the mark must be famous in its capacity as a mark designating the plaintiff's goods. In other words, to be famous within the meaning of the statute, the mark must have achieved a high "degree of ... acquired distinctiveness," meaning that it must have become very widely recognized by the U.S. consumer public as the designator of the plaintiff's goods.

Because a high "degree of ... acquired distinctiveness" is crucial to a finding of fame, there is no merit to the proposition that the statute's reference to acquired distinctiveness would be meaningless unless the element of distinctiveness could be satisfied by acquired distinctiveness. Indeed, it is just the other way around. If the statute's requirement of distinctiveness could be satisfied by "acquired distinctiveness," as opposed to "inherent distinctiveness," the reference to inherent distinctiveness would become superfluous. Why is this so? In order to qualify for the Act's protection, the mark must be famous. By definition, every mark that is famous, in the sense intended by the Act, has a high degree of acquired distinctiveness. Thus, no mark can qualify for the Act's protection without acquired distinctiveness. If that acquired distinctiveness satisfies not only the fame requirement, but also the distinctiveness requirement, then there will never be a case when a court needs to consider whether the mark has inherent distinctiveness. The statute's invitation to courts to consider the mark's degree of inherent distinctiveness would serve no function.

We therefore understand Clause (A) of § 1125(c)(1) to invite two inquiries: (1) Has the plaintiff's mark achieved a sufficient degree of consumer recognition ("acquired distinctiveness") to satisfy the Act's requirement of fame? (2) Does the mark possess a sufficient degree of "inherent distinctiveness" to satisfy the Act's requirement of "distinctive quality." The latter requirement cannot be satisfied by the mere fact that the public has come to associate the mark with the source. Thus, weak, non-distinctive, descriptive marks do not qualify for the Act's protection, even if famous.[24]

Under this analysis, a brand new made-up mark such as RIBOVA for shoes cannot be diluted because though it is inherently distinctive, it is not yet famous. That much seems uncontroversial. The analysis also suggests, however, that a mark such as MCDONALD'S cannot be diluted because, as a surname, it lacks "a sufficient degree of 'inherent distinctiveness' to satisfy the Act's requirement of 'distinctive quality.'" This seems more than a little curious, given that the MCDONALD'S mark is surely one of the strongest in the world.

24. 244 F.3d at 97-98.

The Third Circuit has explicitly declined to follow the Second in imposing a separate requirement of "distinctiveness" under the FTDA. Relying heavily on the analysis in Professor McCarthy's treatise, that court, in *Times Mirror Magazines, Inc. v. Las Vegas Sports News, L.L.C.*,[25] held that the terms "distinctive" and "famous" in the FTDA are essentially synonyms and that their dual appearance in the statutory text was merely an artifact of the legislative drafting process. The court concluded that Congress simply did not intend to set up two separate requirements as a prerequisite for invoking the FTDA. As of this writing, the Supreme Court has yet to resolve the resulting circuit split.

The Second Circuit's desire to limit the dilution doctrine to only a narrow category of marks is understandable, given the potential mischief of an overbroad dilution concept. Its decision to articulate a separate requirement of "distinctiveness" seems, however, a cumbersome way to get to that result. Its terminology has the potential of confusing other courts in applying the idea of "distinctiveness" outside the law of dilution. In addition, the requirement seems an unnecessary embellishment, and one that does not comfortably fit into the textual structure of the FTDA. A strict reading of the fame requirement ought to screen out all but the small minority of marks that truly deserve protection.

30.2.2 Niche Fame

In a highly specialized economy, some trademarks may be very well known to narrow groups of consumers, but largely unknown to everyone else. This might be the case with respect to highly technical categories of goods and services, such as replacement parts for nuclear reactors, surgical implements, sophisticated computer consulting services, or even law books. It might also be the case with a mark that has great local or regional cachet, but is not known outside its own trading area. For instance, though virtually everyone who lives in or visits Indianapolis might be familiar with a restaurant known as ST. ELMO STEAK HOUSE, consumers in New York or Los Angeles may be completely oblivious of this business and its service mark. One might say that all such marks are famous only within a given product or territorial "niche."

The courts have struggled with whether niche fame is sufficient to allow a plaintiff to pursue a claim of trademark dilution. The emerging judicial consensus is that it is not. As one court put it, "much of the relevant case law indicates that marks famous only in a specialized market, rather than well known to the general public, should not be considered 'famous' under the federal dilution statute."[26] This analysis was a significant factor in the court's refusal to grant relief under the New York dilution statute in *Mead Data Cent., Inc. v. Toyota Motor*

---

25. 212 F.3d 157 (3d Cir.2000), *cert. denied*, 531 U.S. 1071, 121 S.Ct. 760, 148 L.Ed.2d 662(2001)

26. Washington Speakers Bureau, Inc. v. Leading Authorities, Inc., 33 F.Supp.2d 488 (E.D.Va.1999) (citing cases), *aff'd*, 217 F.3d 843 (4th Cir.2000).

Sales, Inc.[27] The plaintiff in the case was the then owner of the LEXIS trademark for a computerized legal research data base. When the defendant announced plans to market a luxury automobile under the trademark LEXUS, the plaintiff filed suit under the New York dilution statute. The court concluded that while the LEXIS mark was very well known among lawyers and accountants, it was only known by 1% of the population as a whole, and thus not deserving of protection against dilution, saying "for the general public, LEXIS has no distinctive quality that LEXUS will dilute."

There is, however, a line of cases, holding that a mark with only limited or niche fame is entitled to protection against dilution where the defendant is using the mark in sales to the same narrow market segment. For instance, in *Times Mirror Magazines, Inc. v. Las Vegas Sports News, L.L.C.,*[28] the plaintiff owned the mark THE SPORTING NEWS for a sports oriented newspaper. When defendant began using the mark LAS VEGAS SPORTING NEWS for a paper targeted at sports fans interested in betting on the outcomes of sporting events, the plaintiff sued for dilution. The Third Circuit was "persuaded that a mark not famous to the general public is nevertheless entitled to protection from dilution where both the plaintiff and defendant are operating in the same or related markets, so long as the plaintiff's mark possesses a high degree of fame in its niche market."

Under the rule of *Time Mirror*, niche fame will suffice to allow a dilution plaintiff to go forward where the two parties market to overlapping populations of consumers, but presumably not otherwise. Thus, the owners of a hypothetical mark EXACTA for surgical scalpels, which was famous to doctors, could stop another party from using the mark EXACTA on syringes or bedpans, even in the absence of likelihood of confusion, by pursuing a dilution claim. If the mark did not have fame in the general population, however, they would be unable to assert a dilution claim against a party using the mark EXACTA on pencils or on clocks.

The comments to the Restatement (Third) of Unfair Competition are consistent with this view. According to those authors:

> A mark that is highly distinctive only to a particular class or group of purchasers may be protected from diluting uses directed at that particular class or group. For example, a mark may be highly distinctive among purchasers of a specific type of product. In such circumstances, protection against a dilution of the mark's distinctiveness is ordinarily appropriate only against uses specifically directed at that particular class of purchasers; uses of the mark in broader markets, although they may pro-

27. 875 F.3d 1026 (2d Cir.1989).

28. 212 F.3d 157 (3rd Cir.2000), *cert. denied*, 531 U.S. 1071, 121 S.Ct. 760, 148 L.Ed.2d 662 (2001).

duce an incidental diluting effect in the protected market, are not normally actionable.[29]

Courts have also found support for this niche fame approach in factor (F) of the FTDA itemized list of fame factors—because it refers to "the degree of recognition of the mark in the trading areas and channels of trade used by the marks' owner and the person against whom the injunction is sought."

On the other hand, any recognition of niche fame seems at odds with portions of the legislative history of the FTDA. For instance, the Senate Judiciary Committee Report on the 1988 version of the dilution legislation, which ultimately became law in 1996, observed that the dilution remedy "is to be applied selectively and is intended to provide protection only to those marks which are both truly distinctive and famous.... [T]he new dilution provisions should apply only to those very unique marks which qualify for dilution protection in light of all the factors which are weighed by the court."[30] Moreover, even when a mark has the high degree of niche recognition referenced by factor (F), the text of the FTDA seems to contemplate that the determination of "fame" should be made based on a consideration of all relevant factors. Factors (D) and (E), which mention "the geographical extent of the trading area in which the mark is used" and "the channels of trade for the goods or services with which the mark is used" seem especially significant in suggesting that marks well known only in a single product or territorial "niche" should not be considered "famous."

Some judges have also criticized the acceptance of the niche fame concept, and argued that it is inconsistent with the rationale of dilution law, which is to provide protection against the use of a mark on completely distinct goods sold to entirely different populations of consumers. Judge Barry, in dissenting from the result in the SPORTING NEWS case, also pointed out that almost any mark might be able to show "niche" fame if the "niche" were defined narrowly enough.

In most cases, allowing dilution claims for marks famous only in one market niche when the defendant does business in that same niche should be superfluous. That is because in such cases, the mark owner should have little difficulty showing a likelihood of confusion, at least as to sponsorship. In the hypothetical involving EXACTA scalpels, most doctors and surgeons would assume that EXACTA syringes came from the same company or were being made under a license from the company that makes the scalpels. As one court put it recently, "it seems an odd act of statutory interpretation that permits the owner of a famous mark to prevent dilution only by competitors in the owner's niche market, particularly since in such an instance, relief would likely already be available to the mark's owner under a § 43(a) infringement theory."[31]

---

29. Restatement (Third) of Unfair Competition § 25, comment e (1995).

30. S.Rep. No. 100–515, at 41–42 (1988).

31. Washington Speakers Bureau, Inc. v. Leading Authorities, Inc., 33 F.Supp.2d 488 (E.D.Va.1999), aff'd, 217 F.3d 843 (4th Cir.2000).

The real risk is that by making a dilution remedy available in such cases, the courts will increasingly be persuaded to dispense with the requirement of likelihood of confusion. Yet it is the likelihood of confusion standard that keeps trademark law focused on the consumer interest in using trademarks as devices that minimize search costs and permit efficiencies in relocating goods that have been enjoyed in the past. The result may be a shift to greater treatment of trademarks as a "pure property" right, divorced from their information function in the market. To once again quote Judge Barry's dissent in the SPORTING NEWS case, the result will be to have the dilution doctrine "devour" infringement law.

30.2.3   Fame of Trade Dress

There is nothing in the FTDA limiting its provisions to any particular types of marks. The courts have held, therefore, that the owner of a protected trade dress may use the dilution statute in those cases where it can demonstrate that the trade dress is famous. Where the trade dress consists of a highly recognizable package, this seems both sound as a matter of policy and feasible as a matter of judicial administration. For instance, if a firm were to begin selling insect repellent or furniture polish in a bottle that was substantially identical to the famous COCA–COLA bottle, consumers might not be confused as to source or sponsorship of the products. However the uniqueness of that bottle as a trade dress that signifies only one company would be eventually eroded, making it a legitimate situation for a remedy against dilution.

The situation becomes both more complicated and more dubious as a matter of policy, however, where the trade dress is product shape, rather than product packaging. In the vast majority of cases, a defendant mimicking product shape will be a defendant marketing a directly competing product. In such situations, the invocation of the dilution doctrine has the potential to be extremely anti-competitive, because it could result in an outright prohibition against the sale of a competing product, even in the absence of consumer confusion.

As noted elsewhere in this text, the Supreme Court has held that product shape can never be found "inherently distinctive" and thus always requires proof of secondary meaning before it can be protected as trade dress.[32] One might therefore expect the courts to be especially rigorous in demanding proof of "fame" where the trade dress is a product shape. That seems to have been the philosophy of the First Circuit in *I.P. Lund Trading v. Kohler Co.*[33] In that case, the plaintiff, a Danish firm, sold an attractive faucet under the brand name VOLA. The defendant, a major producer of plumbing equipment in the United States, began selling a "look alike" faucet. The court noted that the two products were not identical, but there were numerous similarities and it seems clear that the defendant was consciously trying to emulate the look of plaintiff's product. The court indicated that secondary meaning

---

32. *See* § 28.4 *supra*.   **33.** 163 F.3d 27 (1st Cir.1998).

by itself would not suffice to establish that the plaintiff's trade dress was famous. Without laying down a specific test, the court intimated that consumer surveys might be necessary to establish fame in a case like this one and found evidence of the faucet's renown in "the world of interior design" to be inadequate. The court also pointed to the availability of design patent protection for a product's shape as still another reason to hesitate before declaring such shape "famous" for purposes of the dilution laws.

Not all of the cases have been so strict regarding the fame of product shapes, however. In *Nabisco, Inc. v. PF Brands, Inc.*,[34] both parties were engaged in the sale of cheddar cheese flavored snack crackers. The plaintiff's snacks were marketed under the well known GOLDFISH trademark and were shaped, predictably enough, like little fish. The defendant sold an assortment of three different shaped crackers, designed to resemble characters from a children's television show called CATDOG. One of its three cracker shapes was also a fish. Strictly speaking, the court in the *Nabisco* case never addressed the fame of plaintiff's fish shaped product configuration, because, in the words of the opinion, "it is not disputed ... that Pepperidge Farm's Goldfish constitutes a famous mark...." The court instead focused its attention on whether the fish shape should be considered "distinctive," because, as discussed earlier in this chapter, the *Nabisco* court had announced a rule requiring that a dilution plaintiff must show *both* fame and distinctiveness in order to prevail. On the question of distinctiveness, it held that the "shape of Pepperidge Farm's Goldfish crackers exhibits a moderate degree of distinctiveness. The fish shape has no logical relationship to a cheese cracker. However, we recognize it is not in the highest category of distinctiveness that belongs to a purely fanciful made-up pattern or design, or made-up word like Kodak."

It should be noted, however, that *Nabisco* was decided before the Supreme Court's decision in Wal-Mart, which held that a product shape can never be deemed inherently distinctive. Since the Second Circuit subsequently held, in its TCPIP decision, that inherent distinctiveness is a pre-requisite for dilution protection, it would seem to follow that there now can be no claims for dilution of a product shape in the Second Circuit and that *Nabisco* would not be decided the same way if the issue came up again today.

Moreover, despite the defendant's concession on the fame issue in the *Nabisco* case, it is difficult to see how a fish-shape trade dress for a product could be considered "famous" given the large number of different products that are sold in such a shape—pillows, pet toys, kites, fishing lures, wall plaques, and soaps are just a few of the examples that come to mind. Such a shape seems almost the opposite of the famous COCA–COLA bottle, which evokes the products of the Coca–Cola company even when stripped of all its labeling and seen entirely out of its ordinary commercial context. The most that could be said is that a fish

---

34. 191 F.3d 208 (2d Cir.1999).

shape might have "niche" fame in the snack cracker market, as the trade dress of Pepperidge Farm's crackers.

In *Syndicate Sales, Inc. v. Hampshire Paper Corp.*,[35] a case involving alleged dilution of the trade dress of floral baskets, the Seventh Circuit specifically endorsed the applicability of the niche fame concept to trade dress, and in a sense *Nabisco* agrees by necessary implication. However, there is little in the legislative history of the FTDA to suggest that Congress meant to allow the owners of product-shape trade dress with only niche fame to pursue dilution claims, and the expansion of the doctrine to such unusual types of marks with such relatively small recognition is highly unlikely to have been what Congress had in mind when it enacted the statute.

Moreover, non-rigorous application of the fame requirement to trade dress runs the risk of exposing the dilution statute to constitutional challenge. Product design is arguably within the scope of the patent laws, and the Patent clause of the Constitution specifically grants Congress the power to protect such material only "for limited times." Protection against dilution, however, is perpetual, lasting as long as the plaintiff continues to make use of the protected trademark (or trade dress). Moreover, because protection against dilution is available without any evidence of consumer confusion, it cannot be justified as a device to protect against "unfair competition." Instead, it is simply the grant of a property-like protection to a trademark or trade dress. While Congress enacted the dilution statute in the exercise of its powers under the Commerce clause, its grant of perpetual protection to subject matter so close to the core of the patent laws might thus be held inappropriate by the Supreme Court. Indeed, the defendant in the *Lund* (faucet) case made this exact argument to the First Circuit, but that court declined to reach the issue because it found the faucet non-famous and ineligible for protection against dilution.

At this early date in the life of the dilution statute, there is a paucity of cases specifically addressing the issue of fame in the context of trade dress, and no authority purporting to resolve the constitutional issue mentioned above. Consequently, generalities are difficult and premature. It seems obvious, however, that courts ought to be especially wary in this area, because of the unusually high risk that broad rulings may deprive consumers of the benefits of robust competition, and because of the potential constitutional problems that expansive rulings may generate.

§ 30.3   Dilution By Blurring

The vast majority of dilution claims allege the form of dilution known as "blurring." Blurring is a lessening of the fame possessed by a famous mark. One might begin to think about blurring by recalling "free association" exercises or games, in which one player says a word and the other player must respond instantly with the first word that pops into

---

35.   192 F.3d 633 (7th Cir.1999).

his or her head. By definition, a strong or famous mark is likely to produce both a prompt and a uniform "free association" response when mentioned to most consumers. Thus, when I say ROLEX, you—and almost everyone else—will likely say "watches." When I say NIKE, you—and almost everyone else—will likely say "athletic shoes." On the other hand, a weak mark will either produce no response at all, or a variety of responses from different consumers. If I say RIGDON (a made-up trademark) you might say "huh." If I say UNITED, you might say "airlines" but someone else might say "van lines" and still another response might be "states."

Blurring of a famous mark occurs when the activities of a defendant cause plaintiff's mark to move from the first category of "free associations" to the second. If the owners of the ROLEX mark had no way to prevent the use of that mark on pencils, or pianos, or pistachio nuts, because those products are so remote from watches that they could not prove any likelihood of confusion, eventually, the automatic free association of the ROLEX mark with watches, and watches alone would be destroyed. The mark would be less famous than before. It would be blurred.

Judicial definitions of the blurring concept are plentiful. The Sixth Circuit has called it a use that "corrodes the senior user's interest in the trademark by blurring its product identification."[1] The Seventh Circuit has said on one occasion that it is a doctrine designed to prevent a "proliferation of borrowings" that will "deprive the mark of its distinctiveness and hence impact,"[2] and on another that it is a use that creates "dissonance."[3] One district court has said that the doctrine is designed to prevent erosion of the "magic" of a trademark,[4] and the New York Court of Appeals has said that dilution seeks to prevent a "cancer-like growth" of uses on unrelated products that will destroy the distinctiveness of the mark.[5]

The FTDA definition of dilution, which appears in section 45 of the Lanham Act, provides that "the term 'dilution' means the lessening of the capacity of a famous mark to identify and distinguish goods or services, regardless of the presence or absence of (1) competition between the owner of the famous mark and other parties, or (2) likelihood of confusion, mistake, or deception."

Blurring is not a variant on "likelihood of confusion." Rather, it is an entirely different phenomenon. Indeed, blurring and likelihood of confusion are mutually exclusive and inconsistent states of mind. The

§ 30.3

1. Ameritech, Inc. v. American Information Technologies Corp., 811 F.2d 960 (6th Cir.1987).

2. Illinois High School Ass'n v. GTE Vantage, Inc., 99 F.3d 244 (7th Cir.1996), *cert. denied*, 519 U.S. 1150, 117 S.Ct. 1083, 137 L.Ed.2d 218 (1997).

3. Exxon Corp. v. Exxene Corp., 696 F.2d 544 (7th Cir.1982).

4. Augusta Nat'l Inc. v. Northwestern Mut. Life Ins. Co., 193 U.S.P.Q. 210 (S.D.Ga.1976).

5. Allied Maintenance Corp. v. Allied Mechanical Trades, Inc., 42 N.Y.2d 538, 399 N.Y.S.2d 628 (1977).

confused consumer thinks that defendant's products come from or are "blessed by" the plaintiff. Thus, the confused consumer thinks that there is one, and only one party using or controlling the trademark in question (something which is incorrect, given the defendant's infringing activities). The "blurry eyed" consumer perceives, correctly, that there are multiple firms using or controlling the trademark in question, and as a result, can no longer come up with the prompt and consistent "free association" that may have existed before the defendant began its sales. This consumer is, quite accurately, "seeing double" because there are multiple users of the mark in question. It follows that no one consumer can be confused and "blurry eyed" at the same time.

There is fairly widespread agreement that to show blurring, plaintiff must demonstrate that defendant is using either a precise replication of the protected trademark or a virtually identical variation. Courts have invoked formulas such as "essentially the same,"[6] and "sufficient similarity ... to evoke an 'instinctive mental association' of the two by a relevant universe of consumers."[7] The opinion in *Mead Data Central, Inc. v. Toyota Motor Sales, Inc.*,[8] is illustrative. In that dispute between the owners of the LEXIS mark for a legal research data base, and the LEXUS mark for luxury automobiles, the Second Circuit found the marks insufficiently similar to warrant relief under the New York State dilution law. The court ruled that pronounced carefully, as they would be by radio and television announcers, the two marks were not "very" or "substantially" similar.

Once the analysis moves beyond the question of the degree of similarity of the marks, the legal doctrine on blurring is in a state of considerable disarray. Some courts have been willing to find the requisite whittling away based on the mere fact that the defendant is using a mark that is virtually identical to plaintiff's famous mark. Cases of this sort effectively hold that once a mark achieves the status of "fame," no other merchant may use that mark on any goods or services anywhere else in the economy. The mark is given a property-like right that is analogous to a copyright.

Other courts have felt that such broad protection under the dilution doctrine goes too far, and have attempted to articulate multi-factor tests that can be brought to bear in resolving the question of blurring. One of the early efforts to articulate a multi-factor test for blurring was made by Judge Sweet in his concurring opinion in the *Mead Data* case mentioned above. Judge Sweet identified six factors which he thought relevant—namely (1) similarity of the marks; (2) similarity of the products covered by the marks; (3) sophistication of consumers; (4) predatory intent; (5) renown of the senior mark and (6) renown of the junior mark.

6. Luigino's, Inc. v. Stouffer Corp., 170 F.3d 827 (8th Cir.1999) (quoting McCarthy Treatise); Planet Hollywood (Region IV), Inc. v. Hollywood Casino Corp., 80 F.Supp.2d 815 (N.D.Ill.,1999).

7. Ringling Brothers–Barnum & Bailey Combined Shows v. Utah Div. Of Travel Dev., 170 F.3d 449 (4th Cir.1999), *cert. denied*, 528 U.S. 923, 120 S.Ct. 286, 145 L.Ed.2d 239 (1999).

8. 875 F.2d 1026 (2d Cir.1989).

Most, if not all, of Judge Sweet's factors are borrowed from the traditional likelihood of confusion analysis required in cases of trademark infringement. Several—perhaps all but the first—seem awkward or ill-adapted to resolving the question of blurring. For instance, there is no reason to think that the sophistication of consumers will in any way mitigate the "blurring" effect of a defendant's non-confusing use of a famous mark. Sophisticated consumers may be precisely those who will deduce that the divergent products come from two unrelated sources, and thus whose prior association of the mark with a singular source will more likely be blurred into the accurate "double vision" discussed above. Judge Sweet's reference to similarity of products is even more baffling, because where the products are highly similar, most consumers are likely to have the mistaken impression of common source or sponsorship. It is only when the products are highly dissimilar that consumers are likely to remain unconfused, and instead to have the accurate perception that the mark now symbolizes multiple independent sources—the state of mind that is the essence of blurring.

Both recent cases[9] and academic commentary[10] have largely come to reject the "Sweet Six" factors. In 1999, Judge Sweet's own circuit, the Second, declared in its *Nabisco* decision that it would not "adopt the *Mead Data* [Sweet] factors as a fixed test for dilution under the FTDA." Instead, the *Nabisco* court advocated a "cautious and gradual approach." It announced a new 10–factor test for blurring cases, but declared that this list of ten factors did not "exhaust the test of what is pertinent. New fact patterns will inevitably suggest additional pertinent factors." Thus, in the Second Circuit, the test for blurring remains a somewhat murky evaluation of all of the facts and circumstances that the parties wish to call to the attention of the court with no bottom-line guidance on what those factors must show.

The specific factors mentioned in the *Nabisco* opinion are: (1) the degree of distinctiveness of the senior user's mark; (2) the similarity of the marks; (3) the proximity of the products and the likelihood of bridging the gap; (4) the interrelationship among distinctiveness of the senior mark, similarity of the junior mark and proximity of the products; (5) shared consumers and geographic limitations; (6) sophistication of consumers; (7) actual confusion; (8) adjectival or referential quality of the junior use; (9) harm to the junior user and delay by the senior user; and (10) effect of the senior user's prior laxity in protecting the mark.

This list does not seem to improve greatly on the one propounded by Judge Sweet. It continues to borrow heavily from likelihood of confusion analysis, and continues to focus on several issues that are not really at stake in a true blurring case. For example, the inclusion of "actual confusion" as the seventh factor suggests that the court may have lost

9. I.P. Lund Trading v. Kohler Co., 163 F.3d 27 (1st Cir.1998) (Judge Sweet's factors inappropriate and unhelpful).

10. J. Thomas McCarthy, Trademarks and Unfair Competition, (4th ed.), § 24:94.2

(Judge Sweet's six factor test "not particularly relevant or helpful" and "likely to lead to erroneous results").

sight of the key fact that dilution and infringement are distinct and mutually inconsistent states of mind. Fortunately, because the *Nabisco* court made it clear that it was not announcing a firm test to govern all future cases, subsequent cases may find it easy to clarify this list of factors—and to delete those that are inappropriate—in order to more precisely focus on blurring.

Yet another comprehensive effort to define the idea of blurring was made by the Fourth Circuit in *Ringling Bros.-Barnum & Bailey Combined Shows, Inc. v. Utah Division of Travel Development.*[11] The plaintiff in that case owned the indisputably famous mark THE GREATEST SHOW ON EARTH for circus shows. The defendant, a state agency charged with promoting tourism in Utah, began using the mark THE GREATEST SNOW ON EARTH to advertise Utah's virtues as a winter sports destination. After a careful review of the authorities, the Fourth Circuit defined blurring as the whittling away or lessening of the "selling power" of the plaintiff's mark. It then went on to hold that under the FTDA, plaintiff must factually demonstrate an actual reduction in selling power, not merely a likelihood of such reduced selling power in the future. In reaching that conclusion it stressed that the text of the FTDA provides a remedy only where the defendant's use "causes dilution of the distinctive quality of the mark," a present tense phrasing that, in its view, requires actual rather than prospective injury.

The *Ringling Bros.* court posited three specific ways a dilution plaintiff could prove this actual harm to selling power. First, it suggested that plaintiff could show actual loss of revenue and could link that loss to defendant's use of the mark by "disproving other possible causes." Second, it proposed the use of consumer surveys showing "consumer impressions from which actual harm and cause might rationally be inferred." Finally, it noted that plaintiff could make out its case of blurring through "relevant contextual factors such as the extent of the junior mark's exposure, the similarity of the marks, [and] the firmness of the senior mark's hold."

The insistence of the *Ringling Bros.* court on evidence of actual dilution proved to be a controversial aspect of the decision. The Second Circuit refused to follow that rule in its *Nabisco* decision, observing that "if the famous senior mark were being exploited with continually growing success, the senior user might never be able to show diminished revenues, no matter how obvious it was that the junior use diluted the distinctiveness of the senior." It recognized the textual basis for the *Ringling Bros.* holding, but characterized the Fourth Circuit's reading of the language in question as "excessive literalism." It also noted that it made little sense to force a plaintiff to suffer harm before securing injunctive relief.

11. 170 F.3d 449 (4th Cir.1999), *cert. denied*, 528 U.S. 923, 120 S.Ct. 286, 145 L.Ed.2d 239 (1999).

At this writing, the Sixth and Seventh Circuits have joined with the Second, in holding that blurring can be shown without evidence of actual consummated harm.[12] The Fifth Circuit has opted to follow the Fourth in requiring proof of actual harm.[13] In early 2002, some members of Congress indicated an intention to introduce legislation that would resolve the circuit split and clarify the statute by indicating that plaintiffs need only prove a likelihood of dilution. However, no such bill has yet been introduced and it is too soon to venture a guess about its likely chances of passage. In the meantime, in April, 2002 the Supreme Court granted certiorari to review the Sixth Circuit case mentioned above, presumably with the intention of resolving the Circuit split. That case was argued in the fall of 2002 and a decision is pending as this book goes to press, with a decision expected in mid-2003. It would be perilous to predict the outcome given that most readers of these words will be able to compare our prediction with the actual opinion. We are, however, brave, and so offer the hunch that the Court will come down somewhere in the middle—not requiring dilution plaintiffs to prove actual lost sales, but insisting on a concrete showing of harm that goes beyond demonstrating that someone else is using its mark. What precisely the Court may demand as part of that concrete showing we are neither brave nor wise enough to know.

It is hard to deny that the current state of the law on blurring is unsatisfactory. Many courts either have failed entirely to articulate a definition of the concept, or have confused the concept with principles that properly relate to conventional trademark infringement. Where the courts have ventured somewhat more definite opinions, they have more often than not disagreed with each other. If courts settle on a rigorous definition of fame and only consider blurring claims where the defendant is using a virtually identical mark to the plaintiff's, perhaps the precise definition of blurring does not really matter. To be more precise, in such a climate, the definition of blurring could be quite broad without posing a grave risk to competition or undermining general principles of trademark law. If more and more marks are made eligible to be protected against dilution, however, and if only modest similarity between defendants' and plaintiffs' marks is held sufficient to trigger the dilution statute, a more coherent and predictable definition of blurring will become crucially important in keeping the dilution doctrine within coherent bounds. For that, we await word from the Supreme Court.

§ 30.4   Dilution By Tarnishment

The owners of famous trademarks are not merely interested in strong and consistent "free associations" of their mark with their products. They are also interested in positive associations. Marks such as

---

12. *See* Eli Lilly & Co. v. Natural Answers, Inc., 233 F.3d 456 (7th Cir.2000); V Secret Catalogue Inc. v. Moseley, 259 F.3d 464 (6th Cir.2001), *cert. granted*, ___ U.S. ___, 122 S.Ct. 1536, 152 L.Ed.2d 463 (2002).

13. Westchester Media v. PRL, USA Holdings, Inc., 214 F.3d 658 (5th Cir.2000).

KODAK for cameras, PILLSBURY DOUGH BOY for baked goods, COCA–COLA for beverages or MR. PEANUT for salted nuts and snack foods are meant to invoke specific images of wholesome, high quality products, along with generalized "warm and fuzzy feelings" about the products and the companies that make them. If an unauthorized party were to make a non-confusing use of such marks on products that evoke inconsistent images, the favorable aspects of the mark might be lessened. On hearing KODAK, some consumers might think "ugh" or "gross" instead of "nice" and "reputable." This is the form of dilution known as tarnishment. As the Second Circuit put it, "the *sine qua non* of tarnishment is a finding that plaintiff's mark will suffer negative associations through defendant's use."[1]

There is some authority that tarnishment can be established when a defendant uses plaintiff's mark on shoddy, low quality, or perhaps even dangerous goods. More commonly, however, courts tend to find tarnishment when the defendant uses plaintiff's famous mark in some unwholesome or unsavory context. Many of the cases have involved use of the mark in a sexually explicit fashion, or occasionally in connection with references to illegal drugs. For instance, in *Pillsbury Co. v. Milky Way Productions, Inc.*,[2] the defendant published a pornographic newspaper, one issue of which contained a cartoon showing plaintiff's PILLSBURY DOUGH BOY engaged in sexual intercourse.[3] Observing that "[a]ll the plaintiff need show to prevail is that the contested use is likely to injure its commercial reputation or dilute the distinctive quality of its marks," the court granted relief under Georgia's dilution statute. One of the most well known tarnishment cases is *Coca-Cola Co. v. Gemini Rising, Inc.*,[4] where the defendant sold posters bearing the legend "Enjoy Cocaine" in the same stylized script and color scheme as the famous COCA–COLA trademark. The court granted the plaintiff relief on claims of both infringement and dilution. The analysis in the opinion seems, however, to rely primarily on the finding that consumers will think that the plaintiff is "responsible for defendant's poster," a finding that is more consistent with an infringement theory than the tarnishment form of dilution.

The harm to a mark owner from a KODAK topless bar or a BUICK brand bong[5] seems evident enough. The cases reviewed in the preceding paragraph, are, however, fundamentally different because they involve parodies. The treatment of parodies under the dilution doctrine is considered in a following section of this text, but we should note at this juncture that it is questionable whether either the *Pillsbury* or *Coca-Cola* cases would be decided the same way today.

§ 30.4

1. Hormel Foods Corp. v. Jim Henson Prods., 73 F.3d 497 (2d Cir.1996).

2. 215 U.S.P.Q. 124 (N.D.Ga.1981).

3. His partner was a female dough-person, not an actual human.

4. 346 F.Supp. 1183 (E.D.N.Y.1972).

5. A bong is a pipe used for smoking marijuana.

In any event, the tarnishment doctrine is "not limited to seamy conduct" involving drugs or sex.[6] In *New York Stock Exchange v. New York, New York Hotel, LLC*,[7] the Second Circuit confronted a state law claim of tarnishment where the defendant used the mark NEW YORK NEW YORK $LOT EXCHANGE, and a replica of the facade of the New York Stock Exchange building as part of its Las Vegas Casino. The court assumed that the New York Stock Exchange "wants to preserve a reputation for listing companies that adhere to its rules for accounting, disclosure, and management . . ." and concluded that associating its trademarks with activities "deemed by many to involve odds stacked heavily in favor of the house" could injure its reputation. It therefore held that the Exchange had made out a jury question on the issue of tarnishment and remanded for further proceedings. Ironically, the court was writing just weeks before the spate of corporate and accounting scandals in mid–2002—events which may have led many investors to conclude that they could have done better investing their money with defendant's casino's than on plaintiff's stock exchange.

In thinking about tarnishment, it is crucial to bear in mind that the "negative associations" that the tarnishment doctrine is meant to combat are the negative associations that flow from *commercial* conduct, not from expressive conduct. It may hurt the image of the KODAK mark for someone to say bad things about KODAK brand products in a consumer magazine, or to depict KODAK brand products being used in connection with drug culture or sexual activity in a movie, but that kind of "hurt" ought not to be the focus of dilution law, lest that law run headlong into conflict with core First Amendment values. The tarnishment concept should be reserved for the infrequent case where the defendant is using the mark on non-expressive commercial products that have clear unsavory or disreputable connections.

§ 30.5 Dilution Claims Against Direct Competitors

Increasingly, dilution claims are being asserted against direct competitors. For instance, the *Nabisco* case, you may recall, involved litigation between two parties which both made cheddar cheese flavored snack crackers. One might question whether the dilution doctrine has any applicability to cases of this sort at all. Historically, the dilution doctrine was developed to combat junior uses of famous marks on products entirely different from those sold by the senior user. The legislative histories of both the state and federal dilution laws recite the same list of hypothetical examples—DUPONT shoes, BUICK aspirin, SCHLITZ varnish, KODAK pianos and BULOVA gowns[1]—examples which involve

---

6. The quoted language is from Hormel Foods Corp. v. Jim Henson Prod., Inc., 73 F.3d 497, 507 (2d Cir.1996).

7. 293 F.3d 550 (2d Cir.2002).

§ 30.5

1. This list appears in the legislative history of the New York Dilution Statute,

see, 1954 N.Y.Legis.Annual 49, and in the legislative history of the FTDA, *see* H.R. Rep. 104–374 (1995).

entirely non-competitive goods from those sold by the owners of those famous marks. Moreover, where the plaintiff and defendant sell directly competing goods, the probability of consumer confusion will be significant and plaintiff should be able to prevail on a garden variety infringement claim without invoking the dilution doctrine.

Some courts have specifically held that state dilution statutes cannot be used in cases involving competing goods. The most significant example is Illinois, where there is authority coming from both the state and federal courts to this effect. On the other hand, courts have held the New York dilution statute applicable in cases involving direct competitors.[2] The FTDA definition of dilution provides that dilution can exist "regardless of the presence or absence of—(1) competition between the owner of the famous mark and other parties." Courts have relied on this language in allowing direct competitors to use the FTDA.

From a theoretical point of view, it is possible that the harms of dilution—particularly blurring—could occur in a head-to-head competitive situation. For instance, assume a defendant, called Gamma Corporation, without authorization from the Eastman Kodak company, begins marketing film under the KODAK trademark, but because of the color scheme of Gamma's packaging, the lettering used by Gamma for the trademark, the prominent appearance of the Gamma name on Gamma's boxes, and perhaps even because of a disclaimer on the defendant's boxes, consumers know that defendant's film does not come from, nor is it sponsored by, Eastman Kodak. In such a case, these alert consumers would not be confused about source or sponsorship. However, after Gamma's film had been on the market for some time, they would think, on hearing the word "KODAK" that it could mean either the products of Eastman Kodak, or the products of Gamma. A mark that once strongly designated a single source would have come to designate two sources. It would have been blurred and diluted.

Indeed, in a situation like this, it is possible that one group of consumers would be confused, thinking inaccurately that both films come from the same source, while another, distinct and non-overlapping group will merely have their perception of the mark diluted, because they correctly understand that there are now two film makers using the identical mark. If plaintiff can prove that a significant number of consumers fall into each category, it would logically be entitled to recover for both infringement and dilution.

As a practical matter, however, this seems both unnecessary and unlikely. In a situation like the one posited above, the plaintiff will almost always be able to prove confusion given that the defendant is selling the very products for which the plaintiff is famous. That will be enough to secure an injunction. Thus a dilution cause of action on these facts adds little to plaintiff's tool kit for preventing injuries to its

2. *See, e.g.,* E.P. Lehmann Co. v. Polk's Modelcraft Hobbies, Inc., 770 F.Supp. 202 (S.D.N.Y.1991).

business or trademark. Its availability may, however, prompt courts to focus on dilution as a watered-down version of infringement instead of as a distinct theory with its own unique elements. The consequence is that plaintiff may be allowed to prevail without demonstrating clearly *either* the requisite likelihood of confusion *or* the requisite blurring, to the ultimate detriment of robust competition.

§ 30.6 Parody and Dilution

In the context of conventional trademark infringement, when a defendant engages in parody of a plaintiff's mark, many courts are inclined to find that the ridicule actually dispels any likelihood of confusion.[1] The logic is that merchants are not very likely to make fun of their own symbols, that consumers know that, and that consumers therefore will conclude that the parody neither comes from nor is sponsored by the trademark owner. However, that logic would not suffice to protect a parodist accused of dilution. As we have seen, the harm in dilution is lessening the "commercial magnetism" or "magic" of the mark by either associating it with a multiplicity of diverse sources, or by associating it with something distasteful or off-putting. The latter consequence is often precisely the objective of a parody. Thus, the question arises whether trademark parodies can be challenged as actionable dilution, particularly of the "tarnishment" variety.

The Restatement (Third) of Unfair Competition provides in § 25(2) that

> one who uses a designation that resembles the trademark ... of another, not in a manner that is likely to associate the other's mark with the goods, services, or business of the actor, but rather to comment on, criticize, ridicule, parody or disparage the other or the other's goods, services, business or mark, is subject to liability without proof of a likelihood of confusion only if the actor's conduct meets the requirements of a cause of action for defamation, invasion of privacy or injurious falsehood.

In other words, if the very thing being sold is the parody itself, in the form of a book, magazine, poster, greeting card, bumper sticker, or the like, the Restatement takes the view that the mark is not being "associated" with goods, but rather is "being commented on" and there can be no dilution as a matter of substantive dilution law.

Even if a court rejects the Restatement position, and interprets a given dilution statute to reach parodies, the parodist may be able to prevail by invoking a First Amendment defense. The leading case on point is *L.L. Bean, Inc. v. Drake Publishers, Inc.*[2] The plaintiff in *L.L. Bean* was the well-known vendor of camping equipment and rugged outdoor clothing. Its mail order catalogue is widely distributed and has a distinct format. The defendant in the case was the publisher of a

§ 30.6

1. *See* § 29.3.3 *supra*.

2. 811 F.2d 26 (1st Cir.1987).

pornographic magazine called *High Society*. In one of its issues it ran a two page parody entitled "L.L. Beam's Back–To–School–Sex–Catalogue" which, as the court explained, "displayed a facsimile of Bean's trademark and featured pictures of nude models in sexually explicit positions using 'products' that were described in a crudely humorous fashion." Plaintiff sought relief, in part, under the Maine dilution statute, and the district court granted summary judgement in its favor on that claim.

On appeal, the First Circuit reversed, holding that "[n]either the strictures of the First Amendment nor the history and theory of anti-dilution law permit a finding of tarnishment based solely on the presence of an unwholesome or negative context in which a trademark is used without authorization." It emphasized that the context involved in the case before it was non-commercial, and noted that:

> If the anti-dilution statute were construed as permitting a trademark owner to enjoin the use of his mark in a noncommercial context found to be negative or offensive, then a corporation could shield itself from criticism by forbidding the use of its name in commentaries critical of its conduct. The legitimate aim of the anti-dilution statute is to prohibit the unauthorized use of another's trademark in order to market incompatible products or services. The Constitution does not, however, permit the range of the anti-dilution statute to encompass the unauthorized use of a trademark in a noncommercial setting such as an editorial or artistic context.

On the other hand, where a trademark parody is being used for more explicitly commercial purposes, the First Amendment concerns will recede and the defendant may be held liable. That was the case in *Deere & Co. v. MTD Products, Inc.*[3] In that case, the parties were competitors in the lawn tractor business. The defendant produced a television commercial which, in part, featured an altered version of plaintiff's trademarked "leaping deer" logo. As the court described, in the commercial, the plaintiff's logo "is animated and assumes various poses. Specifically ... [it] looks over its shoulder, jumps through the logo frame (which breaks into pieces and tumbles to the ground), hops to a pinging noise, and, as a two-dimensional cartoon, runs in apparent fear, as it is pursued by the Yard Man lawn tractor and a barking dog." Plaintiff, the Deere Company, filed a lawsuit alleging, in part, violations of the New York State dilution statute. (The plaintiff was unable to pursue a claim under the FTDA because the case arose prior to its enactment).

As the Second Circuit framed it, the issue in the *Deere* case was "whether [an] advertiser may depict an altered form of a competitor's trademark to identify the competitor's product in a comparative advertisement." The court answered that question in the negative and found that the use of plaintiff's mark in the television commercial in question constituted an actionable form of dilution. Conceptually, the court had some difficulty in fitting this activity into the usual categories of trade-

---

3. 41 F.3d 39 (2d Cir.1994).

mark dilution. It noted candidly that "the MTD commercial is not really a typical instance of blurring ... because it poses slight if any risk of impairing the identification of Deere's mark with its products. Nor is there tarnishment, which is usually found where a distinctive mark is depicted in a context of sexual activity, obscenity or illegal activity." However, it went on to note that "the blurring/tarnishment dichotomy does not necessarily represent the full range of uses that can dilute a mark under New York law."

The court declared that the use of an *unaltered* form of a competitor's trademark in a comparative advertisement would not cause dilution, and that the use of *altered* trademarks in parodies by "satirists" who sell "no product other than the publication that contains their expression" would not constitute dilution either. What crossed the line here was the parody of the plaintiff's trademark in an advertisement, the sole purpose of which was to sell a directly competing product. The court felt that where the alteration of a trademark took place in an advertisement for a directly competing product, there was too much risk that the advertiser would have an incentive to "diminish the favorable attributes of the mark." Moreover, it noted that such an advertiser has many other alternative ways to promote its products in humorous or attention getting advertisements without depicting altered versions of a rival's trademarks.

The limited scope of the *Deere* holding is further illustrated by the Second Circuit's subsequent decision in *Hormel Foods Corp. v. Jim Henson Productions, Inc.*[4] In that case, the defendant was the creator of the celebrated puppet troupe known as the Muppets, and planned to release a new Muppet movie featuring a character named Spa'am. As the court explained, "Spa'am is the high priest of a tribe of wild boars that worships Miss Piggy as its Queen Sha Ka La Ka La." As has become customary with movies of this sort, the defendant was also planning to use the likeness of the Spa'am character on a variety of movie-related licensed merchandise items, such as candy, clothing, books and computer games. Plaintiff, the owner of the famous trademark SPAM, for processed meat products, claimed that this character was unsavory and that the association of its name with a beast that they characterized as "evil in porcine form" would tarnish the fine reputation of its mark.

In a whimsical opinion, the court gently turned aside the claim. It pointed to the long history of jokes that have been made at SPAM's expense and wryly remarked that: "In view of the more or less humorous takeoffs such as these, one might think Hormel would welcome the association with a genuine source of pork." It found that there would not be any blurring, because the defendant's parody would actually tend to increase public identification of the SPAM mark with Hormel. Similarly, it held that there would not be any tarnishment because Spa'am was actually a likeable and positive character—"not the boarish Beelzebub that Hormel seems to fear"—when viewed in the context of the full plot

4.   73 F.3d 497 (2d Cir.1996).

of the defendant's movie. Thus, despite the fact that the defendant was making a clearly commercial use of a parody of the mark to sell goods other than the parody itself, the court found that the relatively gentle nature and good taste of the parody precluded a claim for dilution.

§ 30.7 Dilution and Federal Trademark Registration

The Lanham Act does not permit the PTO, on its own initiative, to deny registration to a mark because the mark may dilute another previously used famous mark. If someone wished to register KODAK for pianos, the PTO could only deny registration if it found, under section 2(d), that the use of that mark on those goods would create a likelihood of confusion, or if it found under section 2(a) that the use of the mark "falsely suggested a connection" with the Eastman Kodak company. If the goods specified in the application were so far removed from those sold by the senior user of the mark as to preclude a reasonable chance of confusion or connection, the mark will be approved by the examiner, and published in the Official Gazette of the PTO.

In 1999, however, Congress amended the Lanham Act to provide that once the mark has been published, any party who believes that the applicant's proposed mark will dilute its trademark is permitted to file an opposition.[1] Similarly, even once a mark is registered, a prior user of the mark may file to cancel the registration on the grounds that its previously used mark will be diluted by the newly registered mark, provided that it files that cancellation petition within five years after the registration issues.[2]

Thus dilution is not a basis for an *ex parte* denial of registration, but it can result in denial after an *inter partes* proceeding. In deciding any such *inter partes* administrative cases, such as an opposition or cancellation, the PTO will apply all of the various substantive provisions of the FTDA. Consequently its first task will be to determine if the opposer's (or cancellation petitioner's) mark is famous. If it resolves that question in the negative, there could be no dilution and the mark in question should be (or remain) registered. For instance, in *The Toro Co. v. ToroHead, Inc.*,[3] the Trademark Trial and Appeals Board dismissed an opposition, in part, because the opposer failed to submit sufficient evidence to support a finding that its TORO marks were famous.

§ 30.8 Defenses and Remedies

The FTDA specifically itemizes three defenses to a claim of dilution.[1] The first defense is "fair use of a famous mark by another person in comparative commercial advertising or promotion to identify the competing goods or services of the owner of the famous mark." Without such a

§ 30.7
1. 15 U.S.C.A. § 1063(a) (2000).
2. 15 U.S.C.A. § 1064 (2000).
3. 61 USPQ2d 1164, 2001 WL 1734485 (T.T.A.B.2001).

§ 30.8
1. These are found in section 43(c)(4) of the Lanham Act. 15 U.S.C.A. § 1125(c)(4) (2000).

defense, if the seller of an obscure brand of carbonated cola wanted to compare its own product to the COCA–COLA brand by explicitly mentioning the COCA–COLA trademarks in print or broadcast advertising, the owners of the COCA–COLA mark might be able to threaten a suit for violation of the federal dilution statute. The quoted statutory language prevents this counter-intuitive and counter-productive result.

It should be noted, however, that even without this particular statutory language, it is unlikely that most comparative advertising should be found to dilute the other party's trademark. It certainly doesn't "blur" because the advertisement does not associate the COCA–COLA mark with a multiplicity of diverse products or sources. Rather, it reinforces the association of the mark with the owner of the mark, by using the mark to refer to the owner's products. It almost certainly doesn't tarnish, because while the reference in the comparative ad may be critical ("Why spend top dollar on COCA–COLA when you can get the same refreshment for less with SCHEC–THOM COLA instead?"), it is highly unlikely to involve the unsavory connotations usually involved in a tarnishment fact pattern. If, however, the comparative advertiser alters or parodies the famous mark, that would seem to negate the availability of this defense and expose the advertiser to liability for dilution, as we saw above in the *Deere* case.

The second statutory defense is for "noncommercial use of a mark." On first reading this seems to be simply the mirror image of the substantive requirement for liability that the defendant make a "commercial use" of the mark, and as a technical matter might very well be superfluous. Further reflection and recent case law, however, reveal that this defense is quite significant. The scope of the defense was recently explored by Judge Alex Kozinski, writing for the Ninth Circuit in *Mattel, Inc. v. MCA Records, Inc.*[2] Mattel, the plaintiff in that case, is the manufacturer of the world-famous BARBIE doll. The defendants released a song, by a Danish band called Aqua, which was titled "Barbie Girl." The song was not entirely flattering to the Barbie character, suggesting that she was, in the words of the court, a "bimbo." Mattel sued for both infringement and dilution.

Judge Kozinski noted that infringement claims, by requiring evidence of consumer confusion, have a built in mechanism to avoid conflict with First Amendment values. This is because the confusing use of another's party's trademarks is essentially a fraud on the public, and there is generally no First Amendment protection for false speech or fraud. On the other hand, the dilution statute, by dispensing with the confusion requirement, poses a greater risk of conflict with free expression. He then went on to note that "the legislative history of the FTDA suggests an interpretation of the 'noncommercial use' exemption that ... diminishes ... First Amendment concerns: 'Noncommercial use' refers to a use that consists entirely of noncommercial, or fully constitutionally protected speech." He then went on to conclude that if the

---

2. 296 F.3d 894 (9th Cir.2002).

defendant's speech in a dilution case is not "purely commercial—that is, if it does more than propose a commercial transaction," it should be classified as falling within the noncommercial use exception of the statute.

Applying this test to the facts before the court, Judge Kozinski had no problem in concluding that the use of the BARBIE trademark in both the song title and the song lyrics did more than merely propose a commercial transaction, and that it was thus immune from attack under the dilution doctrine because of the noncommercial use exception. Note that the court was willing to reach this result even though the production and distribution of pop music is plainly a "commercial" or profit-making activity. This holding will make the noncommercial use defense applicable to a wide range of uses, including references to trademarks in books, magazines, and product reviews. This defense should be especially helpful to parties who have posted web sites critical of specific companies, often referring to the company by name or using parodies of the company's marks on the site, and sometimes even using the company's trademark as part of a domain name. Thus, a web site with the domain name of "microsoftsucks.com" should be immune from dilution liability so long as the web site is not purely commercial.[3]

The final statutory defense permits the use of a famous mark in "all forms of news reporting and news commentary." This defense overlaps with the "noncommercial use" category discussed in the preceding paragraph, and is probably compelled as a matter of First Amendment jurisprudence. Critical references to companies and their trademarks in editorials or investigative reporting are obviously highly valuable forms of speech in an open and democratic society, and Congress wanted to be clear that such speech would not run any risk of liability for dilution. Non-commercial parodies of famous marks in the form of political cartoons, bumper stickers, posters or greeting cards also come within the protection of this defense. As the commentary to the Restatement (Third) of Unfair Competition points out, "the expression of an idea by means of the use of another's trademark in a parody, for example, will often lie within the substantial constitutional protection accorded non-commercial speech and may thus be the subject of liability only in the most narrow circumstances. Although such non-trademark uses of another's mark may undermine the reputation and value of the mark they should not be actionable under the law of trademarks."[4]

In addition to the trilogy of statutorily itemized defenses, courts are likely to recognize certain additional defenses borrowed from other branches of trademark law or from principles of equitable remedies. Thus, the use of a famous trademark to describe truthfully one's background or achievements is not actionable as dilution. If a business

---

3. *See* § 33.2, *infra.* As we shall see in the cited section of this text, certain uses of other parties' trademarks in domain names may be actionable under other statutes besides the FTDA.

4. Restatement (Third) of Unfair Competition, § 25, comment i (1995).

person is described in a magazine as "a former senior executive of XEROX," or if an actor is described on a web page as "the winner of two EMMY awards," such uses are immune from challenge as dilution.[5] While many such references will be non-commercial and thus fall within the second statutory defense, even commercial uses of marks in this fashion, such as on a web site offering consulting services, are not actionable so long as they are truthful. Yet another non-statutory defense that might bar a dilution claim would be laches—an undue delay by the plaintiff prior to filing suit. If the owner of a famous mark waits years before challenging a junior user, the plaintiff is not entitled to equitable relief and the case ought to be dismissed.[6]

Although not technically a defense, some dilution defendants may also be able to avoid liability by arguing that their conduct began before the effective date of the FTDA and that the statute should not be given retroactive effect. There seems general agreement that a party cannot be held liable for money damages for violating the FTDA if it adopted the challenged mark prior to January 16, 1996, when that statute became law. The courts have divided, however, on whether an injunction is available in this sort of situation. Thus, in *Circuit City Stores v. Office-Max, Inc.*,[7] the court refused to grant an injunction because it felt that the dilution statute attached new legal consequences to events completed before its enactment, and as such, could not be retroactively applied absent clear Congressional intent. "Whether forced to pay money damages or to suffer an injunction barring future use of the CarMax marks, the effect on CarMax of applying the Dilution Act is effectively the same—CarMax would lose its very identity, achieved as the result of conduct and commercial investment, which was perfectly lawful at the time.... [E]nforcement of the Dilution Act here would violate [fundamental] 'considerations of fairness'...."

On the other hand, in *Viacom Inc. v. Ingram Enterprises, Inc.*,[8] the court granted an injunction even though defendant began the challenged use of the trademark in question before the effective date of the FTDA, noting that "the conduct sought to be enjoined ... is [defendant's] continuing use of its ... marks, not its pre-enactment conduct." Other courts have lined up on both sides of the issue, but the weight of judicial opinion, particularly at the appellate level, appears to be moving in favor of the *Viacom* rule.

The ordinary remedy for trademark dilution is an injunction. When the claim is based on the FTDA, the injunction will likely be nationwide in scope. If the claim is based on a state dilution statute, the court also has power to order a nationwide injunction—assuming that it has personal jurisdiction over the defendant—but pragmatic concerns may convince it to limit the scope of the order to only one state, in order to

---

5. *See, e.g.,* Playboy Enterprises, Inc. v. Welles, 47 U.S.P.Q.2d 1186 (S.D.Cal.1998), *aff'd without opinion*, 162 F.3d 1169 (9th Cir.1998).

6. The laches defense is discussed in detail in the following chapter at § 31.4.2.

7. 949 F.Supp. 409 (E.D.Va.1996).

8. 141 F.3d 886 (8th Cir.1998).

avoid prohibiting activity that would be considered legal in other jurisdictions and to avoid potential conflict with the Commerce Clause of the U.S. Constitution.[9] Appellate courts have held that the decision over the scope of the order in a case arising under a state dilution law is committed to the discretion of the trial judge. If, as is usual, the plaintiff requests a preliminary injunction prior to a full trial on the merits, at least one case has indicated that such a request should be denied, if the likely pace of dilution pending trial will be slow and if the defendant is not making widespread use of the allegedly diluting mark.[10] On the other hand, if the defendant is making large-scale use of the mark and there is a genuine risk of irreparable injury, a preliminary injunction is appropriate.

The FTDA provides for monetary relief, but specifies that it is only available where the defendant "willfully intended to trade on the owner's reputation or to cause dilution of the famous mark."[11] At this early point in the interpretation of the FTDA the courts have not defined "willful intent," but at least one court has indicated that it may require more than the bad faith registration of a confusingly similar domain name. Even where such willful intent is proved, an award of monetary relief is subject to the discretion of the court.

9. *See, e.g.,* Hyatt Corp. v. Hyatt Legal Services, 610 F.Supp. 381 (N.D.Ill.1985); Deere Co. v. MTD Prods., 34 U.S.P.Q.2d 1706 (S.D.N.Y.1995).

10. Federal Express Corp. v. Federal Espresso, Inc., 201 F.3d 168 (2d Cir.2000).

11. 15 U.S.C.A. § 1125(c)(2) (2000). *See also* Pub. L. 107-273 § 13207 (November 2, 2002) (making technical corrections to § 35 of the Lanham Act to conform it to § 43(c)).

Chapter 31

FAIR USE, OTHER AFFIRMATIVE DEFENSES AND REMEDIES

Table of Sections

Not every use of another firm's trademark is considered impermissible. There are many situations where it is both legally acceptable and practically necessary to use trademarks belonging to others. Factually, these situations can be viewed as falling into three broad categories.

In the first group, the unauthorized user of the trademark might be engaged in selling or leasing goods that trace their origin ultimately back to the owner of the trademark in question. For instance, the user might sell second hand KODAK brand cameras with the KODAK trademark still plainly visible or rent FORD automobiles bearing Ford's hood ornaments. As we shall see, this is legally permissible provided that certain logical limitations are observed. Terminologically, these fact patterns are usually said to involve the use of the mark on "genuine goods" and much of the controversy in such cases turns on whether the goods in question are, in fact, "genuine" for the purposes of trademark law.

In the second category are cases where the user of the mark may be selling goods, or in this case services as well, of its own creation, but may wish to make some kind of cross-reference to another company, and may choose to do so by invoking that other company's trademarks. This invocation of another's party's marks might be made in advertisements, or on packaging, or it might be made in a variety of communicative contexts such as newspapers, magazines or books. These cases are usually said to involve "referential" or "nominative" uses of the trademark in question, and this, too, is generally permissible.

Finally, a firm may wish to use another firm's trademarks not in their trademark sense at all, but rather in their everyday dictionary sense, merely to communicate information to the public. Here again, the law has been tolerant, allowing the use of the words under a concept usually labeled the "descriptive fair use" doctrine.

In all three situations, the broad principles are the same. The non-owner of the trademark will be permitted to use it for any of the purposes mentioned, provided that it does so truthfully, and in a way that avoids confusing the public. While the precise determination of whether a given usage is truthful or confusing will vary depending on the kind of situation involved, the general notion is both simple and unchanging across all these categories of permissible third-party use.

Of course, even in cases where there is something less than a truthful use by a defendant or something more than a trivial risk of consumer confusion, the defendant may be able to escape liability for trademark infringement by invoking a number of other affirmative defenses, such as the delay or wrongdoing of the plaintiff-trademark-owner. We will encounter some of these defenses towards the end of this chapter, along with a discussion of the remedies available to the trademark owner who succeeds in establishing liability.

§ 31.1 Uses on Genuine Goods

31.1.1 Resale, First Sale Exhaustion and Quality Control

After a trademark owner sells trademarked goods the buyer may wish to resell those goods to others. Sometimes, of course, the trademark owner anticipates that such reselling will take place and may even expressly or impliedly authorize it. For instance, when a manufacturer such as Procter & Gamble (P & G) sells CREST brand toothpaste to a retailer, such as the CVS or Rite–Aid pharmacy chains, P & G expects that the drug store will resell those branded tubes of toothpaste to the public. It would be absurd to treat the resale of the goods by CVS as trademark infringement, even though CVS does not own the CREST trademark. The drug store is reselling the goods with the implied permission of the manufacturer, the goods are "genuine" CREST products, and there is no risk of either consumer confusion or injury to the trademark owner by such sales. Not surprisingly, therefore, such resale is immune from attack as trademark infringement. This doctrine is conventionally known as the "first sale exhaustion" principle. Under this rule, once a trademark owner sells trademarked goods, the buyer is free to resell those goods to others without having to remove the trademarks. As the Ninth Circuit summarized, "the right of a producer to control distribution of its trademarked product does not extend beyond the first sale of the product. Resale by the first purchaser of the original article under the producer's trademark is neither trademark infringement nor unfair competition."[1]

This first sale exhaustion rule is not limited to authorized resales. It applies even when no subsequent resales are anticipated or even contemplated by the trademark owner. This is why it is not trademark infringement for you to sell your old MERCEDES automobile with the trademark hood ornament still visible, even though you are neither an authorized Mercedes dealer nor the owner of the MERCEDES mark. Even when trademarked goods are diverted by wholesalers to unauthorized retail outlets, such as discounters, it is not trademark infringement for those discounters to sell those goods, despite the displeasure or objections of the trademark owner.[2]

The first sale principle even applies in cases involving damaged or surplus goods. For instance, in one case, a shipment of DUNHILL brand tobacco, which had been exposed to water damage in transit, was sold at salvage by the owner of the DUNHILL trademark. When the buyer resold the tobacco as DUNHILL brand and refused to label the goods as "subjected to possible water damage," Dunhill sued for trademark infringement, but the court denied relief, noting that "if Dunhill had wished to distinguish the salvaged tobacco from that sold through its normal channels of distribution it should have done so while the allegedly damaged tobacco was still under its control...."[3]

There is an important limit on the first sale principle, however. Generally, trademarked goods are only "genuine" if the distributor or reseller observes any relevant quality control requirements imposed by the trademark owner. Several courts have held that the resale of goods without the requisite quality control constitutes infringement. In *Shell Oil Co. v. Commercial Petroleum, Inc.*[4] the defendant was a reseller of

§ 31.1

1. Sebastian Int'l v. Longs Drug Stores Corp., 53 F.3d 1073 (9th Cir.1995), *cert. denied,* 516 U.S. 914, 116 S.Ct. 302, 133 L.Ed.2d 207 (1995).

2. *See, e.g.,* Adobe Systems Inc. v. One Stop Micro Inc., 84 F.Supp.2d 1086 (N.D.Cal.2000) (unauthorized sale of edu-cational version of trademarked software to non-students not trademark infringement where products were not changed or altered prior to sale).

3. Alfred Dunhill Ltd. v. Interstate Cigar Co., Inc., 499 F.2d 232 (2d Cir.1974).

4. 928 F.2d 104 (4th Cir.1991).

bulk oil products, including SHELL brand products. Shell imposed various quality control procedures concerning the handling, storage and transportation practices of such products on its authorized dealers. The defendant, however, was not an authorized SHELL dealer. Consequently, the Fourth Circuit held that since Shell was unable to enforce its quality control program with respect to this defendant, the oil sold by it could not be considered "genuine" SHELL oil, and the defendant would be enjoined from selling it under the SHELL trademark.

In a similar case, the Second Circuit held that the owner of the HALLS trademark for cough drops could enjoin a wholesaler from selling any cough drops past their freshness expiration date, declaring "[d]istribution of a product that does not meet the trademark holder's quality control standards may result in the devaluation of the mark by tarnishing its image. If so, the non-conforming product is deemed for Lanham Act purposes not to be the genuine product of the holder, and its distribution constitutes trademark infringement."[5] However, as the Third Circuit has cautioned, " 'quality control' is not a talisman the mere utterance of which entitles the trademark owner to judgment.... Rather, the test is whether the quality control procedures established by the trademark owner are likely to result in differences between the products such that consumer confusion regarding the sponsorship of the products could injure the trademark owner's goodwill."[6]

The logic of these quality control cases is that the consumer could be misled if the reseller who ignores the quality control requirements is allowed to use the original trademark, because the consumer would assume that the product conformed to the usual quality standards maintained by the trademark owner. In cases where the consumer can deduce for herself that quality control requirements may not have been followed, however, the result may be different.

For instance, in *Matrix Essentials, Inc. v. Emporium Drug Mart, Inc.*,[7] the plaintiff manufactured MATRIX brand shampoo. It attempted to limit distribution of the shampoo to hair salons, but defendant, a discount store, obtained some of the trademarked shampoo and began selling it to the public. Plaintiff argued that the shampoo was meant to be sold only after a "consultation" from a trained hair care professional, and that the sale of the product in the discount store without that consultation meant that the defendant was not selling "genuine" MATRIX products. The Fifth Circuit rejected that argument. It noted that unlike the issues of storage and handling in the *Shell Oil* case, any consumer buying shampoo at a discount store would be well aware of the fact that she had not received a hair consultation while standing in the shampoo aisle of defendant's establishment. Since the situation did not pose the risk of deception or confusion of the public, the sale of the

5. Warner–Lambert Co. v. Northside Development Corp., 86 F.3d 3 (2d Cir.1996).

6. Iberia Foods Corp. v. Romeo, 150 F.3d 298, 304 (3d Cir.1998).

7. 988 F.2d 587 (5th Cir.1993).

products was non-infringing and within defendant's rights under the first sale doctrine.

31.1.2 Repackaged or Rebottled Goods

Sometimes a purchaser of trademarked goods may wish to rebottle or repackage them before reselling them to the public under the original trademark. The trademark owner may object, and argue that the change in packaging means that the goods are no longer "genuine." This was the situation the Supreme Court confronted in *Prestonettes v. Coty*.[8] In that case, Prestonettes was an American firm that obtained quantities of genuine imported COTY brand perfume and face powder on the open market. It then transferred the perfume to smaller bottles and combined the face powder with a binding agent to sell it in the form of "compacts." Presumably this enabled it to sell the items for lower per-unit prices which would be more attractive to consumers of modest means. In each case, Prestonettes labeled the product with the COTY trademarks. Coty brought suit alleging trademark infringement. The lower court entered an order requiring Prestonettes to include on its packages a disclaimer, specifying how it had altered the products and revealing that it was not affiliated with Coty. Coty appealed, seeking an absolute prohibition against any use of its name. The court of appeals entered an absolute injunction prohibiting any reference to the COTY trademarks on plaintiff's labels, reasoning that the delicate nature of the products and the possibility of adulteration required such drastic relief.

The Supreme Court reversed, and reinstated the qualified injunction. It a typically terse opinion by Justice Holmes, the Court held that "[w]hen the mark is used in such a way that does not deceive the public we see no such sanctity in the word as to prevent its being used to tell the truth. It is not taboo." Since the rebottled or repackaged products were, indeed, genuine COTY brand items, and since the defendant would be obliged under the trial court's order to make full disclosure of the limited changes to the products that it had made, the opinion concluded that there could be no confusion of the public and no harm to the business reputation of the plaintiff. This kind of use of another's mark is sometimes labeled a legitimate "collateral use."

To come within the doctrine of the *Prestonettes* case courts usually require repackagers to observe four requirements if they wish to use the original merchant's trademark. First, they must disclose the fact that product has been repackaged. Second, they must reveal their own name. Third, they must declare that they are not in any way affiliated with the trademark owner. Finally, they must not give "undue prominence" to the trademark. Moreover, if the rebottling or repackaging significantly lessens the quality of the goods and the rebottler or repackager retains the original trademark, there is some authority suggesting that the

8. 264 U.S. 359, 44 S.Ct. 350, 68 L.Ed. 731 (1924).

trademark owner might have a valid claim for trademark dilution of the tarnishment variety.[9]

31.1.3   Used, Repaired or Reconditioned Goods

Much the same rule obtains in the case of used goods as with repackaged goods, even when the used goods have been repaired, restored, or reconditioned in some way before resale. They may be sold under the original manufacturer's trademark, provided that the reseller discloses the fact that the goods are used, and any other pertinent information about repairs. The leading case, once again, is a Supreme Court opinion from several decades ago.

In *Champion Spark Plug Co. v. Sanders,*[10] the defendant reconditioned CHAMPION brand spark plugs and sold them with the trademark still visible on the plugs, in boxes also bearing the CHAMPION mark. The boxes also contained the legends "Perfect Process Spark Plugs Guaranteed Dependable" and "Perfect Process Renewed Spark Plugs." When Champion brought suit, the trial court entered an order requiring that the original trademarks on the plugs be obliterated, however the court of appeals reversed that aspect of the decree, requiring only that the defendant stamp the word "repaired" or "used" on each plug, and that he print a legend on the cartons disclosing that the plugs were reconditioned, along with his name.

On review, Justice Douglas affirmed the court of appeals and held that it was permissible to sell the reconditioned spark plugs with the CHAMPION trademark still visible on them. He reasoned that the extent of the repairs in question was not so great that continued use of the original trademark could be considered inaccurate or misleading. Relying on *Prestonettes,* the Court took the view that so long as the public received truthful information about both the original pedigree of the products, and their subsequent history, there could be no complaint. Reasoning by analogy, the Court commented that "we would not suppose that one could be enjoined from selling a car whose valves had been reground and whose piston rings had been replaced unless he removed the name Ford or Chevrolet." As the Court put it, "full disclosure gives the manufacturer all the protection to which he is entitled."

There can be cases where the extent of repair or reconditioning is so great that the product cannot properly be considered the same any longer. In cases of this sort, the rule of the *Champion* case does not apply, and the continued use of the original trademark would be considered infringement. The *Champion* opinion itself recognized this possibility, when it observed that "cases may be imagined where the reconditioning or repair would be so extensive or so basic that it would be a misnomer to call the article by its original name, even though the words 'used' or 'repaired' were added." Thus, in *Rolex Watch, U.S.A., Inc. v.*

---

9. *See, e.g.,* Clairol, Inc. v. Cody's Cosmetics, Inc., 353 Mass. 385, 231 N.E.2d 912 (1967). *See generally* § 30.4, *supra.*

10. 331 U.S. 125, 67 S.Ct. 1136, 91 L.Ed. 1386 (1947).

Michel Co.,[11] where the defendant reconditioned used ROLEX brand watches using non-Rolex parts, it was permanently enjoined from making any use of the ROLEX trademark on the altered watches and was forbidden to sell them to jewelers with the original ROLEX marks still on the dials.[12]

Decisions such as *Rolex* serve to protect consumers from buying a watch on the mistaken impression that it contains genuine ROLEX parts because it bears the ROLEX mark on the dial. It is not, however, meant to grant Rolex a monopoly on replacement parts for its own watches. If a consumer already owned a ROLEX watch, and knowingly decided to have it reconditioned with non-Rolex parts, the result would presumably be different, and the reconditioner ought not be obligated to remove the trademark. As the Fourth Circuit observed, in a case involving the repair of trademarked medical instruments at the behest of the hospital that owned them, "the Lanham Act does not apply in the narrow category of cases where a trademarked product is repaired, rebuilt or modified at the request of the product's owner ... [assuming] that there is no misrepresentation of the repairer's authority to the owner and that the owner is not, to the repairer's knowledge, merely obtaining modifications or repairs for purposes of resale."[13]

31.1.4 Imported Goods

It is quite possible that different and completely unrelated firms may own the identical trademark for the same category of goods in different nations of the world. This is because trademarks are "territorial" in nature, and there is no way for any one firm to automatically secure global rights.[14] The use of the identical mark by firms in different countries could be a function of pure coincidence. For instance, both a U.S. and an Australian firm might hit upon the idea of using the mark CONFIDENT for underarm deodorant without even being aware of each other's activities. Alternatively, it could be that one firm originally owned the mark in multiple countries, and then subsequently sold or licensed the rights in each of them to a different party. Thus, the Australian firm might have secured the U.S. registration for the mark CONFIDENT, and then assigned it with accompanying goodwill to an unrelated American firm in an arm's length transaction. Still another possibility would be a case where legally distinct corporate entities each do business under the same trademark in a different country because they have a common corporate parent. For instance, a British firm might

11.   179 F.3d 704 (9th Cir.1999).

12.   Other cases to the same effect include Rolex Watch U.S.A., Inc. v. Meece, 158 F.3d 816 (5th Cir.1998), *cert. denied,* 526 U.S. 1133, 119 S.Ct. 1808, 143 L.Ed.2d 1011 (1999) (similar injunction as to modified new and used Rolex watches); and Bulova Watch Co. v. Allerton Co., 328 F.2d 20 (7th Cir.1964) (company that placed Bulova watch movements into non-Bulova dia-mond-decorated cases and resold the watches through catalog houses was enjoined under the Lanham Act from retaining the Bulova trademark on the watches).

13.   Karl Storz Endoscopy–America, Inc. v. Fiber Tech Medical, Inc., 4 Fed.Appx. 128 (4th Cir.2001).

14.   For a detailed discussion *see* § 34.1, *infra.*

have an Australian subsidiary which owns the Australian registration for the mark CONFIDENT for deodorant and a U.S. subsidiary which owns the U.S. registration for that same mark for the same goods.

In any of these cases, the foreign goods may be cheaper than the U.S. goods bearing the same marks. This might be because of differences in wage rates or other costs of production in different nations of the world, because of deliberate pricing policies of a common parent company, or perhaps because of currency fluctuations. Whatever the cause, it means that the Australian CONFIDENT brand deodorant could be several dollars cheaper than the U.S. product bearing the same brand name. When this situation exists unauthorized parties will sometimes buy large quantities of the trademarked goods abroad and attempt to import them into the United States, with the plan of selling them at prices lower than those offered by the U.S. trademark owner. Goods of this sort are usually called "gray market" goods or imports, and the commercial activity of bringing such goods into the U.S. is sometimes called "parallel importation." As the U.S. Supreme Court has concisely explained, "a gray-market good is a foreign-manufactured good, bearing a valid United States trademark, that is imported without the consent of the U.S. trademark holder."[15]

The U.S. trademark owner is likely to protest when an importer seeks to bring gray market goods into the country. It may fear that the poor quality of the foreign goods will damage its reputation, and in any event, it will not appreciate losing sales to the importer that otherwise would likely have gone to enhance its own bottom line. Thus, it may try to invoke various statutes to prevent the goods from entering the U.S. in the first place. Alternatively, if the goods do make it into the country, it might sue the importer or retailers of the gray market products and allege trademark infringement. When that happens the gray market importer will usually argue that it cannot be an infringer because the goods are "genuine." After all, the importer will say, "I didn't apply the trademark to them, it was already on them when I bought them, and it was applied by the lawful owner of the mark in the countries where the goods were made." Much judicial energy has been devoted to deciding whether such goods are, in fact, genuine, whether they should be excluded from the U.S. market, and whether their sale here constitutes infringement.

As a general rule, gray market goods are not "genuine" and their sale constitutes trademark infringement. This follows because in the United States, the mark means "the goods of the U.S. trademark owner" and the gray market goods are, by definition, the goods of some foreign party instead. One of the earliest cases to articulate this principle is the Supreme Court decision in *A Bourjois & Co. v. Katzel*.[16]

---

15. K–Mart Corp. v. Cartier, Inc., 486 U.S. 281, 108 S.Ct. 1811, 100 L.Ed.2d 313 (1988).

16. 260 U.S. 689, 43 S.Ct. 244, 67 L.Ed. 464 (1923).

In that case, a French company, called A. Bourjois & Cie., E. Wertheimer & Cie., Successeurs (more conveniently called "the French firm"), began selling face powder in the United States in the late 1870's under the trademark JAVA. It secured a U.S. trademark registration for that mark in 1888, and subsequently obtained additional trademark registrations on related marks. In 1913, the French firm sold its entire U.S. business, along with the JAVA trademarks and associated goodwill to a New York corporation, called A. Bourjois & Co. (a name so similar to the French firm's that it will be helpful to call this American firm ABC). After that transaction, ABC imported face powder in bulk that had been manufactured by the French firm in France, repackaged it in the United States, and sold it under the JAVA mark. ABC's packaging identified the powder as imported, and identified itself as the American successor of the French firm. Meanwhile, the French firm continued to sell the face powder directly to consumers in France under the JAVA marks.

In the early 1920's, Anna Katzel, who owned a retail pharmacy business, began to import packages of the French firm's face powder, and resold those to consumers in their original boxes bearing the JAVA trademarks. When ABC sued Katzel for trademark infringement, the trial court granted ABC a preliminary injunction. On appeal, the Second Circuit reversed, holding that Katzel could not be guilty of any trademark violation because the face powder being sold by her was "genuine" JAVA face powder. Relying on a trilogy of earlier cases, the Second Circuit concluded that the relevant statute only prohibited importation of merchandise which "copied" or "simulated" a registered U.S. mark. Where the imported goods were the "genuine article identified by the trademark," the Second Circuit reasoned that there could be no violation of this provision.

The Supreme Court disagreed and held the conduct of defendant Katzel to be infringement. In a very brief opinion, Justice Holmes began by noting that the JAVA and other trademarks and associated labels "have come to be understood by the public here as meaning goods coming from the plaintiff." He then noted that "there is no question that the defendant infringes the plaintiff's rights unless the fact that her boxes and powder are the genuine product of the French concern gives her a right to sell them in the present form." Reasoning that the French firm was contractually barred from selling powder bearing the relevant trademarks in the United States by its own contract with ABC, Holmes essentially concluded that, therefore, all goods sold by the French firm, and bearing the relevant marks, carried an implied restriction preventing their subsequent resale in the United States. He concluded by noting that the JAVA mark "is the trade-mark of the plaintiff only in the United States and indicates in law, and, it is found, by public understanding, that the goods come from the plaintiff although not made by it."

There are two quirks in the facts of *Katzel* that sometimes make it difficult to interpret. First, ABC was importing and repackaging powder from the French firm rather than manufacturing its own powder. Thus, any consumer deception or disappointment is likely to have been minimal on the precise facts of the case because the powder available in Ms. Katzel's store is likely to have been identical to the powder sold elsewhere by ABC. The facts would have presented a greater risk of unfairness to consumers if ABC had been manufacturing the face powder itself, and especially so if it had given that powder properties different from the French powder (for instance it might have had a different fragrance). In such a situation, consumers buying JAVA powder at Ms. Katzel's store would have been highly likely to be disappointed when they got the powder home and began to use it. Of course, given that the Supreme Court condemned the importation on the less compelling facts of the actual case, it presumably follows that it would have done so even more readily had ABC been making its own power.

Secondly, however, and on the other hand, the past dealings between the French firm and ABC made it quite clear that the French firm would have been engaging in a breach of its 1913 contract if it had directly entered the U.S. market to compete with ABC. After all, it had assigned all its U.S. rights to ABC in a binding contract. As noted above, the Court relied on the notion that the goods of the French firm carried an "implied restriction" against their subsequent resale in the U.S. It was presumably concerned that any other result might have created a back-door mechanism for the French firm to evade its contractual promise to abandon the U.S. market. Obviously, if the French firm and ABC had been complete strangers who had never dealt with each other previously, and who were simply both using the JAVA trademark by coincidence, the Court could not have relied on this "implied restriction" reasoning.

At all events, the usual interpretation of the *Katzel* opinion is that gray market goods are not "genuine" goods, because the trademark they bear communicates false information to the public, and that their sale is thus trademark infringement. This follows from the Court's observation in *Katzel* that any given trademark means to American consumers that the goods come from the American owner of that trademark and have been subject to its quality control and other processes. By definition, this is not true with respect to grey market goods because, in reality, they come from a foreign trademark owner instead. Simply put, the powder labeled JAVA in Ms. Katzel's stores was not the product of ABC.

As noted, *Katzel* itself was a trademark infringement case. U.S. trademark owners would presumably prefer that grey market goods never even enter the United States, rather than waiting for them to appear on retail shelves and then having to bring suit for infringement. There are two statutory provisions that permit the U.S. trademark owner to attempt such pre-emptive action. Section 42 of the Lanham Act, specifically declares that "no article of imported merchandise ... which shall copy or simulate a trademark registered in accordance with the provisions of this chapter ... shall be admitted to entry at any customhouse of the United States...." Interestingly, this provision is quite similar to section 27 of the 1905 Trademark Act, which was on the books at the time of the *Katzel* decision, but which was not cited or discussed by Justice Holmes. Because of that silence, in 1922 Congress adopted section 526 of the Tariff Act, which provides that "it shall be unlawful to import into the United States any merchandise of foreign manufacture if such merchandise ... bears a trademark owned by a citizen of, or by a corporation or association created or organized within the United States, and registered in the Patent and Trademark Office ...."[17] A close reading reveals some subtle differences between these two provisions. For instance the Tariff Act limits its protection to U.S. citizens or domestic corporations, while the Lanham Act provision does not. The Lanham Act provision refers to imports that "simulate" a registered mark, while the Tariff Act does not. At a general level, however, the two laws are to the same effect, both making it illegal to import gray market goods.

This ought to be the end of the story. Statutory law makes it illegal to import gray market goods and commands the Customs Service to turn them away at the border. If they somehow slip into the country, *Katzel* makes their subsequent sale in domestic commerce actionable as trademark infringement. Unfortunately, the tale gets somewhat more complicated as a result of regulations promulgated by the U.S. Customs Service in the mid–1930's to implement the two statutory provisions quoted in the previous paragraph.

Those regulations contained two exceptions to the general ban on importation, which reflected the Custom Services' interpretation of certain ambiguities in the statutory text and its conclusions regarding the underlying Congressional intent. Under the first regulatory exception if "both the foreign and the U.S. trademark ... are owned by the same person or business entity ... [or if] the foreign and domestic trademark ... owners are parent and subsidiary companies or are otherwise subject to common ownership and control,"[18] the gray market goods would be admitted to the United States despite the exclusionary language of both section 526 of the Tariff Act and that of section 42 of the Lanham Act. This provision is usually denominated the "common control" exception.

Under the second exception, gray market goods would be allowed into the U.S. when "the articles of foreign manufacture bear a recorded trademark or trade name applied under the authorization of the U.S. owner." Known as the "authorized use" exception, this situation can arise when a U.S. trademark owner contracts to have goods produced abroad, rather than manufacturing them domestically, perhaps to take advantage of lower wage rates. It can also come up when a U.S.

17. This provision is now codified as 19 U.S.C.A. § 1526 (2000).

18. 19 C.F.R. § 133.21(c) (2001). Structurally, subsection (a) of this regulation implements the prohibition against importation contained in Lanham Act § 42, sub-section (b) implements the prohibition against importation contained in Tariff Act § 526, and subsection (c) contains the "common control" exceptions cited in the text.

trademark owner licenses a foreign producer to sell products under its well-known trademark in the home country of the licensee.

As you might imagine, U.S. trademark owners have never been happy with this regulatory gloss on the anti-importation statutes, and eventually a coalition of trademark owners brought a declaratory judgment action challenging these provisions of the regulations. That case, the aptly named *K–Mart Corp v. Cartier, Inc.*[19] eventually wound up in the U.S. Supreme Court. The *K–Mart* case does not make for pleasant reading because of the different groups of justices who joined in different portions of the multiple opinions. In essence, however, one majority of Justices upheld the "common control" exception contained in the regulations as a valid interpretation of certain statutory ambiguities, while a different majority struck down the "authorized use" exception as being inconsistent with the statutory text. Shortly after the decision, the Customs Service deleted the authorized use exception from the regulation.

This is *still* not the end of the story, however, because the *K Mart* case only addressed the question of whether the regulations were a valid interpretation *of the Tariff Act.* This left domestic trademark owners free to argue that they were entitled to exclude all gray market goods *under the Lanham Act,* regardless of affiliation between the U.S. trademark owner and the foreign manufacturer, and that the Customs Service regulations to the contrary were inconsistent with the language of the Lanham Act. It also left them free to argue that the sale of any gray market goods that were allowed to enter the country, even in a "common control" fact pattern, constituted trademark infringement.

In *Lever Brothers v. United States,*[20] the plaintiffs sold a deodorant soap in the U.S. under the SHIELD trademark and a dishwashing liquid using the trademark SUNLIGHT. A corporate sibling owned by the same parent as the U.S. firm, sold similar products under the same trademarks in Great Britain. The British products, however, differed from the American versions in several key attributes. For instance, as the court explained, "US SHIELD contains a higher concentration of coconut soap and fatty acids, and thus more readily generates lather. The manufacturing choice evidently arises in part out of the British preference for baths, which permit time for lather to develop, as opposed to a US preference for showers.... Further US SHIELD contains an agent that inhibits growth of bacteria." There were even more pronounced differences between the American and British dishwashing products. When third parties began importing the British versions of the two products to the United States and selling them to U.S. consumers, the U.S. trademark owner began to receive complaints. It then contacted the Customs Service and, invoking section 42 of the Lanham Act, asked it to exclude the imported goods. The Customs Service declined to do so based on the

---

19. 486 U.S. 281, 108 S.Ct. 1811, 100 L.Ed.2d 313 (1988).

20. 877 F.2d 101 (D.C.Cir.1989).

"common control" exception in its implementing regulations, and Lever Brothers sued to have the regulation declared invalid.

The D.C. Circuit concluded that the common control exception in the regulations was inconsistent with the Lanham Act in any case where the imported goods were physically different from those sold domestically in a material way. As the court put it, the "virtually inevitable reading of § 42 is that it bars foreign goods bearing a trademark identical to a valid US trademark but physically different, regardless of the trademarks' genuine character abroad or affiliation between the producing firms. On its surface the section appears to aim at deceit and consumer confusion; when identical trademarks have acquired different meanings in different countries, one who imports the foreign version to sell it under the trademark will ... cause the confusion Congress sought to avoid." The court was careful to declare that its conclusion was merely "provisional" and it remanded to the district court for further development of the record. Not surprisingly, however, the district court took the hint and found the regulation inconsistent with the Lanham Act in any situation where the imported goods were materially physically different from the domestic ones. In a subsequent appeal, the D.C. Circuit predictably affirmed that result.[21]

One possible criticism of the result in *Lever Brothers* is that the problem was one of the plaintiff's own making. If the ultimate corporate parent knew that it was going to be using different formulations for the products to be sold in the US and British markets, it could have avoided any risk of grey market sales by adopting different trademarks for the products in those two different national markets. The D.C. Circuit addressed this point in its opinion, commenting that:

> [T]he 'boardroom' that evidently controls both Lever US and Lever UK could solve the problem by abandoning use of the SHIELD and SUNLIGHT trademarks in the United Kingdom, or at least by abandoning their use for physically distinct products. But this solution is obviously costly. The Lever affiliates have succeeded in attaching to products designed for their respective markets ordinary words that have both a favorable 'spin' and a natural link to those products. Customs has offered us no shadow of a reason why it would serve any public interest implicit in § 42 to compel Lever to abandon the resulting goodwill, or (looking ahead) to refrain in the first place from establish such goodwill by use of identical words. The resources of English are finite and the quest for an apt word costly.

In our view this analysis somewhat begs the question. Even without gray market imports, consumers presumably travel between the U.S. and the U.K. all the time, and will encounter both the British and the American versions of the products sold under the same trademark. If the corporate parent of the two firms felt that the use of the identical trademarks in the two countries was important enough to put up with

---

21. *See* Lever Brothers v. United States, 981 F.2d 1330 (D.C.Cir.1993).

what ever consumer disappointment or frustration might result from encountering different product formulations in the two countries, it is unclear why the law should assist them in preventing those products from moving across international borders.

At all events, the Customs Service ultimately relented, and amended its regulations to conform to the result in the *Lever Brothers* case. Under the amended regulations "restricted gray market goods" are now defined to include goods bearing a genuine trademark "applied by the U.S. owner, a parent or subsidiary of the U.S. owner, or a party otherwise subject to common ownership or control with the U.S. owner ... to goods that the Customs Service has determined to be physically and materially different from the articles authorized by the U.S. trademark owner for importation or sale in the U.S." If goods of this type bear "a conspicuous and legible label ... stating that: 'This product is not a product authorized by the United States trademark owner for importation and is physically and materially different from the authorized product,'" they will be allowed into the United States. If the goods lack that label, however, they will be turned away at the border.[22]

While neither *K–Mart* nor *Lever Brothers* were infringement suits, courts confronting claims of infringement in gray goods fact patterns have tended to use the same approach as those opinions. For instance, in *Original Appalachian Artworks, Inc. v. Granada Electronics, Inc.,*[23] a case that pre-dates those two decisions, plaintiff OAA was the U.S. seller of the once fabulously popular (though somewhat disturbing looking) CABBAGE PATCH brand hand-sewn soft-sculpture dolls. Those dolls were sold with "adoption papers" which, as the Second Circuit explained, were "to be filled out by the 'parent' or owner of the doll, who takes an 'oath of adoption.' The adoption papers are returned to OAA, and the information is entered into the OAA computer so that on the first anniversary of the adoption the adopting parent receives a 'birthday card' from OAA. [The trial court] found that this adoption process is an 'important element of the mystique of the [Cabbage Patch Kids] dolls, which has substantially contributed to their enormous popularity and commercial success....'"

OAA had licensed a firm named Jesmar to manufacture similar dolls in Spain, and to sell them in Spain using the CABBAGE PATCH trademarks. Jesmar specifically agreed in this licensing agreement not to sell or distribute those dolls outside of its assigned territory. Not surprisingly, the Jesmar dolls came with adoption papers printed in Spanish rather than English. The defendant Granada purchased dolls in Spain made by Jesmar and imported them into the United States. The Customs Service admitted those dolls under the "authorized use" exception in its regulations, (which at the time had not yet been struck down

22. *See* 19 C.F.R. § 133.23 (2002).

23. 816 F.2d 68 (2d Cir.1987), *cert. denied*, 484 U.S. 847, 108 S.Ct. 143, 98 L.Ed.2d 99 (1987).

by the Supreme Court), because Jesmar was a licensee of OAA, using the trademark with its permission.

Once the dolls appeared in U.S. stores, OAA sued Granada for trademark infringement. The trial court found infringement and the Second Circuit affirmed. The court of appeals reasoned that: "There is a very real difference in the product itself—the foreign language adoption papers and birth certificate, coupled with the United States fulfillment houses' inability or unwillingness to process Jesmar's adoption papers or mail adoption certificates and birthday cards to Jesmar doll owners, and the concomitant inability of consumers to 'adopt' the dolls. It is this difference that creates the confusion over the source of the product and results in a loss of OAA's . . . good will. Thus, even though the goods do bear OAA's trademark and were manufactured under license with OAA, they are not 'genuine' goods because they differ from the [OAA] dolls and were not authorized for sale in the United States."

The more recent case law has continued to follow the approach of the *Original Appalachian Artworks* decision. Thus, in *Ferrero U.S.A., Inc. v. Ozak Trading, Inc.,*[24] the sale of gray goods TIC TAC brand breath mints was found infringing because the imported mints were found to be materially different in caloric content and size from the authorized product distributed in the United States, and in *Fender Musical Instruments Corp. v. Unlimited Music Ctr.,*[25] the sale of gray goods FENDER brand guitars was found infringing because the imported guitars differed from the domestic products with regard to different shape of neck, replacement parts, available colors and manufacturer's warranty terms.

Where does this complex history leave us? Essentially, domestic trademark owners have won a near total battle against gray market imports, with only a small keyhole remaining for the would-be parallel importer. All gray goods will be excluded by Customs unless there is "common control" between the foreign and domestic trademark owners. Even if there is common control, the imported goods will still be excluded by Customs if they are not physically identical to the domestic goods unless they bear labels calling the physical differences to the attention of the consumer. Moreover, the subsequent sale of such physically different products may expose the seller to liability for trademark infringement, although where the physical differences have been clearly called to the consumer's attention prior to sale, some courts might decline to find confusion or infringement. With courts willing to find "physical differences" based on details of warranty programs, based on the language of instruction manuals, or even based on the caloric content of a breath mint, it is likely to be a rare case when the parallel importer can establish the physical identity necessary to allow it to continue to sell the goods.

24. 753 F.Supp. 1240 (D.N.J.1991), *aff'd without op.*, 935 F.2d 1281 (3d Cir.1991).   **25.** 35 USPQ2d 1053 (D.Conn.1995).

Whether this state of affairs is good for American consumers is unclear. It certainly prevents the mistaken purchase of goods that bear a familiar trademark but that fail to perform in ways that consumers have come to expect. On the other hand, however, it denies consumers the ability to knowingly purchase goods that are likely to be reasonably similar to those sold by the domestic trademark owner, that trace their origin to a corporate affiliate of that trademark owner, and most importantly, that are likely to be cheaper. It does this even when consumers are aware of the ways in which the imported goods differ from the domestic goods and are willing to put up with those differences in order to buy at lower prices.

§ 31.2   Referential Uses

31.2.1   Repair Services or Replacement Goods

Things break. And even in our disposable society, it is sometimes more efficient to repair the broken object, or get a spare part for it, rather than to buy a brand new object. Absent a patent, however, the original manufacturer will not necessarily have a monopoly on repair services or spare parts. There will be an "after market." In other words, you can get your TOYOTA brand automobile fixed at a TOYOTA dealership, but you could also take it to BOB'S GARAGE. You could get a new motor for your MAYTAG dryer from MAYTAG, but an ACME brand motor might do the trick for only half the price.

The question is whether unaffiliated and unauthorized repair service providers and repair part vendors may specifically mention other parties' trademarks in describing their own goods and services. So long as they speak the truth, the answer is yes. The maker of the ACME motor may state in advertising, or on signs at its store, that its motor "will work in any MAYTAG brand dryer." BOB'S GARAGE may advertise, "we repair TOYOTA brand cars." This is nothing more than straightforward communication with the public in natural language, and as we have repeatedly seen in this chapter, trademark law does not prevent merchants from speaking the truth.

One of the commonly cited cases for this point is *Volkswagenwerk Aktiengesellschaft v. Church.*[1] In that case, the court concluded that

> [i]t is not disputed that Church may specialize in the repair of Volkswagen vehicles. He may also advertise to the effect that he does so, and in such advertising it would be difficult, if not impossible, for him to avoid altogether the use of the word 'Volkswagen' or its abbreviation 'VW' which are the normal terms which, to the public at large signify appellant's cars.... Although he may advertise to the public that he repairs appellant's cars, Church must not do so in a manner which is likely

1.   411 F.2d 350 (9th Cir.1969), *supplemented*, 413 F.2d 1126 (1969).

to suggest to his prospective customers that he is part of Volkswagen's organization of franchised dealers and repairmen.

The line that cannot be crossed in these situations is for the third party user of the mark to in any way falsely suggest that it is authorized by or affiliated with the trademark owner. If a firm gives undue prominence to a trademark in its advertising or on its signs in such a way as to imply a connection between itself and the trademark owner, the law will no longer tolerate the behavior because of the risk of consumer confusion.

31.2.2 Comparative Advertising

There was a time when it was quite rare for firms to explicitly refer to their competitors in print and broadcast advertising. As recently as the 1960's, some firms felt that it was a poor strategy to give a rival any publicity by mentioning it by name. Other firms thought that such aggressive tactics might alienate consumers and backfire on the party making the comparative reference. Whatever the logic, there was a time when the furthest a company might go would be to compare its own wonderful product with a hypothetical alternative mentioned in the advertisement only as "Brand X."

Such compunctions have largely vanished. Explicit reference to competitors is now such a common aspect of mass market advertising that most consumers hardly notice that it is going on. Of course, in order to engage in this type of advertising, the advertiser usually has to invoke the trademarks of its rival. It is well settled that the use of a trademark in a truthful comparative advertisement to refer to another company is entirely permissible.

Perhaps the leading case on the use of another firm's trademark in comparative advertising is the Ninth Circuit decision in *Smith v. Chanel, Inc.*[2] The defendant in that case claimed to have duplicated precisely the scent of plaintiff's famous CHANEL NO. 5 brand perfume, and specifically advertised its product as a duplicate, mentioning plaintiff's product and trademark by name. The court assumed for the purposes of the appeal that the claim of product equivalence was truthful, and went on to hold that "one who has copied an unpatented product sold under a trademark may use the trademark in his advertising to identify the product he has copied." The court noted that if the defendant's perfume was not an exact duplicate, the plaintiff could have a remedy for false advertising, which, in fact, is what happened on remand.[3]

Of course the principle of *Smith* extends beyond cases where the comparative advertiser is claiming precise equivalence. It is also permissible to use a rival's mark in a comparative advertisement that touts product superiority or makes price comparisons. The key point to remember is that when the advertising is truthful, the use of another's mark is allowed.

---

2. 402 F.2d 562 (9th Cir.1968).

3. *See* Chanel, Inc. v. Smith, 178 USPQ 630 (N.D.Cal.1973).

A variant on the comparative advertising problem comes up when firms seek to include comparative statements directly on product packaging that refer to a rival's trademarks. In cases of this sort there is, perhaps, a greater risk of customer confusion, because most customers expect any trademarks appearing on labels or boxes to refer only to the actual manufacturer or distributor of the product, and not to a competitor. Whether that risk of confusion warrants forbidding the reference, however, will turn on the precise facts before the court. In *Charles of the Ritz Group, Ltd. v. Quality King Distributors, Inc.*[4] the court had to consider whether the seller of a supposed "smell-alike" perfume could use a slogan on a box top tab that made explicit reference to the famous trademark of a nationally known rival. The precise wording at issue on appeal was "If you like OPIUM, a fragrance by Yves Saint Laurent, you'll love OMNI, a fragrance by Deborah Int'l Beauty. Yves Saint Laurent and Opium are not related in any manner to Deborah Int'l Beauty and Omni." Despite the comparative phrasing and the disclaimer the Second Circuit found that there would still be a likelihood of confusion, and enjoined the use of the plaintiff's trademark on defendant's boxes. In reaching this result, the court was particularly influenced by evidence of actual confusion in the record and by the fact that the defendant's trade dress closely resembled that of the plaintiff.

By way of contrast, however, is *August Storck, K.G. v. Nabisco, Inc.*[5] In that case, Nabisco added language to the packaging of a new variety of LIFE SAVERS brand candy that read "25% Lower in Calories Than WERTHERS® Original Candy." The owner of the WERTHERS mark claimed infringement and the trial court granted an injunction. However the Seventh Circuit, in an opinion by Judge Easterbrook, reversed, faulting the trial court for granting relief based on a finding of only a "possibility" of confusion. Judge Easterbrook noted in his opinion that "the use is not just permissible in the sense that one firm is entitled to do everything within legal bounds to undermine a rival; it is beneficial to consumers. They learn at a glance what kind of product is for sale and how it differs from a known benchmark." He dismissed the trial court's concerns about the possibility of confusion due to the package reference by observing that "many consumers are ignorant or inattentive, so some are bound to misunderstand no matter how careful a producer is.... If such a possibility created a trademark problem, then all comparative references would be forbidden, and consumers as a whole would be worse off."

31.2.3   The General Nominative Fair Use Doctrine

The situations considered in the two preceding sections—the use of another's trademarks in comparative advertising or in connection with providing repair services or replacement parts—are really two specific instances of a more general phenomenon. Given the prevalence and high visibility of trademarks in our society, it will often be efficient, if not

---

4. 832 F.2d 1317 (2d Cir.1987).   **5.** 59 F.3d 616 (7th Cir.1995).

essential, to use someone else's trademark in order to make any reference to that person or its goods. This situation can confront a wide variety of commercial speakers who might want to refer to or opine about another party. For instance, consumer rating organizations, newspapers and magazines may need to use trademarks in writing stories about specific sellers of goods or services. An individual might want to use another party's trademarks in describing his or her past activities or affiliations. Entertainers or authors may seek to use trademarks for purposes of amusement or cultural commentary. Web site proprietors might want to use third party's trademarks on the Internet to identify the various brands they offer for sale, or to offer a forum for complaints and criticism, or merely as "links" to other web sites of interest.

All of these examples involve what has come to be called "nominative" use of trademarks—nominative, because the mark is being used to name another party. The prevailing approach to nominative use situations is the one formulated by Judge Alex Kozinski in *The New Kids on the Block v. News America Publishing, Inc.*[6] The plaintiffs in that case were a fabulously popular "boy band" who not only used their trademark to identify their musical recordings and concerts, but also used it in connection with a huge variety of promotional products and services. Among those services were various "900 number" calling lines where, in the words of the court, fans could call "to listen to the New Kids talk about themselves, to listen to other fans talk about the New Kids, or to leave messages for the New Kids and other fans." The defendants were two national newspapers—USA Today and The Star—which conducted separate polls asking readers to vote on the most popular or sexiest "New Kid" and to call a 900 number to register their votes. When plaintiffs learned of these activities they filed suit on a variety of theories, including trademark infringement. The district court rejected those theories and granted summary judgment for the defendant newspapers, a ruling affirmed on appeal by the Ninth Circuit.

Judge Kozinski began his analysis by noting that "many goods and services are effectively identifiable only by their trademarks" and that "it is often virtually impossible to refer to a particular product for purposes of comparison, criticism, point of reference or any other such purpose without using the mark." As an example he noted that "one might refer to 'the two-time world champions' or 'the professional basketball team from Chicago,' but it's far simpler (and more likely to be understood) to refer to the Chicago Bulls." Because the person using a mark in this fashion is not trying to make any statement about the source of its own goods or services, he went on to observe that "cases like these are best understood as involving a non-trademark use of a mark—a use to which the infringement laws simply do not apply.... Such nominative use of a mark—where the only word reasonably available to describe a particular thing is pressed into service—lies outside the strictures of trademark law."

6. 971 F.2d 302 (9th Cir.1992).

The opinion then goes on to lay out a three-part test for any party seeking to invoke a nominative fair use defense: "First, the product or service in question must be one not readily identifiable without use of the trademark; second only so much of the mark or marks may be used as is reasonably necessary to identify the product or service; and third the user must do nothing that would, in conjunction with the mark, suggest sponsorship or endorsement by the trademark holder."

Judge Kozinski's first prong is essentially a rule of necessity, limiting nominative fair use to cases where the defendant would otherwise be unable to communicate. The second prong can be characterized as a rule of minimalism, designed to keep defendant's use of the mark confined to the narrowest scope that still permits effective communication. The final part of the test amounts to a requirement of good faith, denying protection under the nominative fair use rubric to anyone who attempts to use a trademark to confuse the public.

The *New Kids* approach seems sound and has the virtue of providing a general theory for all nominative fair use cases regardless of the specific context. It can be faulted, perhaps, for being a bit too stingy with the defense. For instance, we might anticipate litigation over whether certain plaintiffs are "readily identifiable" without use of their trademark. Does one really need to say COCA–COLA when one can say "the World's best selling cola"? A test focusing on whether the usage is a common, convenient and natural form of everyday speech might have provided more latitude for defendants. Similarly, it is not entirely clear why a defendant must limit itself to the minimum necessary for identification if the use of more would not engender any public confusion. For instance, a chart in a consumer testing magazine comparing various brands of athletic shoes does not technically need to use the trademark logos of the various brands alongside the names in order to communicate the findings of the test, but incorporating an illustration of Nike's "SWOOSH" might make the chart more readable without posing any danger of consumer confusion. Despite these criticisms, however, the court's approach has met with a favorable response and has been followed in a number of subsequent cases.

A recent illustration of the *New Kids* approach in action is *Playboy Enterprises, Inc. v. Welles.*[7] The defendant in that case, Ms. Welles, had been selected by PLAYBOY magazine as its PLAYMATE OF THE YEAR in 1981. Many years later, she created a personal website on the Internet. On that site she identified herself as "Playmate of the Year, 1981." She also used the designation in banner advertisements for the site and in the site's "metatags," or hidden code, used by some search engines to identify sites responsive to search queries. When the owner of the PLAYBOY marks filed suit for infringement, Ms. Welles invoked the nominative fair use defense. The Ninth Circuit concluded that she had satisfied all three prongs of the *New Kids* test in using the trademarks to

7. 279 F.3d 796 (9th Cir.2002).

describe her past accomplishments, and that the complaint should therefore be dismissed.[8]

§ 31.3 Descriptive Fair Use

Many trademarks consist of ordinary English words that communicate information. Such words can become trademarks in a variety of situations. If they actually describe the goods or services to which they are appended, they will be considered "descriptive" and only secure legal protection after achieving secondary meaning. On the other hand, if they do not describe the product in question, but merely hint at its attributes or are unconnected with its attributes, they would qualify for immediate protection as either suggestive or arbitrary marks.[1]

In any of these situations, however, the trademark owner of such a mark cannot prevent other firms from using the words in their underlying and everyday English sense to communicate information. All firms remain entitled to use our common language to communicate with the public, in order to promote a competitive and fully informed market. The right to use words in this fashion is usually labeled "descriptive fair use." Some courts have also referred to this as "classic" fair use.

The descriptive fair use concept is endorsed by the Restatement (Third) of Unfair Competition, which provides in section 28 that it is a defense to a claim of trademark infringement that

> the term used by the actor is descriptive or geographically descriptive of the actor's goods, services, or business, or is the personal name of the actor or a person connected with the actor, and the actor has used the term fairly and in good faith solely to describe the actor's goods, services, or business or to indicate a connection with the named person.[2]

The Lanham Act codifies the descriptive fair use concept in section 33(b)(4), which makes it a defense to a claim of infringement that

> the use of the name, term, or device charged to be an infringement is a use, otherwise than as a mark, of the party's individual name in his own business, or of the individual name of anyone in privity with such party, or of a term or device which is descriptive of and used fairly and in good faith only to describe the goods or service of such party, or their geographic origin.[3]

8. The court did find that defendant's use of the abbreviation PMOY 81 repeatedly to create a "wallpaper" background on her site was not necessary to describe herself, and that this use therefore could not qualify as a valid nominative fair use.

§ 31.3

1. See § 27.2 supra.

2. Restatement (Third) of Unfair Competition § 28 (1995).

3. 15 U.S.C.A. § 1115(b)(4) (2000). Defenses codified in this subsection can be asserted against both incontestable registrations, by the terms of the preamble to the subsection, and against contestable registrations, under the language of section § 1115(a).

The descriptive fair use defense does not turn on whether the trademark owner's mark falls into the descriptive category on the continuum by which trademarks are usually analyzed. The focus, instead, is on whether the defendant is using the words to fairly and accurately describe its own goods or services. As the Second Circuit put it, it should make "no difference whether the plaintiff's mark is to be classed on the descriptive tier of the trademark ladder. . . . What matters is whether the defendant is using the protected word or image descriptively, and not as a mark."[4] Any other rule might leave some participants in the market speechless.

A good example is *Sunmark, Inc. v. Ocean Spray Cranberries, Inc.*[5] The plaintiff in that case sold candy under the mark SWEETARTS. The defendant, the dominant seller of cranberry flavored beverages in the U.S., began to advertise its cranberry juice as "sweet-tart." Although plaintiff argued that no fair use defense should be available, because its mark was internally contradictory and not descriptive of its candy, the court felt that this was not the issue. Rather, it focused on whether the phrase was legitimately descriptive of the defendant's juice. Concluding that it was, it found no infringement. Another example is *Wonder Labs, Inc. v. Procter & Gamble Co.*[6] There, plaintiff used the trademark DENTIST'S CHOICE for its toothbrushes. When the defendants began using the phrase "The Dentist's Choice for Fighting Cavities" in advertisements for its CREST brand toothpaste, plaintiff claimed infringement. The court rejected the claim, holding that the defendant was making descriptive fair use of the term in question.

To stay within the scope of the descriptive fair use concept, the defendant must not use the words or symbols in question as a trademark. Although they may feature prominently in advertising or packaging, that will not negate the availability of the defense if they are genuinely used in a descriptive fashion. Of course, as the words become the dominant feature of a given package, a court may justifiably conclude that a line has been crossed and the defendant is impermissibly using the words in their trademark sense. One case where the defendant crossed the line was *Mobil Oil Corp. v. Mobile Mechanics, Inc.*[7] The defendant in that case used the designation MOBILE MECHANICS prominently on signs, letterhead and in advertisements in a way that made it effectively the firm's service mark. Thus, even if it would be

---

4. Car–Freshner Corp. v. S.C. Johnson & Son, Inc., 70 F.3d 267 (2d Cir.1995).

5. 64 F.3d 1055 (7th Cir.1995).

6. 728 F.Supp. 1058 (S.D.N.Y.1990) ("The words are used in their primary sense to describe an important attribute of the CREST product—that it is recommended by dentists. Indeed, CREST has utilized a dentists theme in its advertising since the mid–1960's. The phrase is not used to identify the source of the product. Rather, the CREST mark, prominently displayed in all CREST advertising, clearly serves as the source indicator. 'The dentists' choice' is often followed by explanatory phrases such as 'for fighting cavities' and is always displayed in conjunction with other text. Moreover, the defendant has never used the plaintiff's mark DENTISTS CHOICE without the modifier 'the.' These factors indicate that the defendant's use is not a trademark use but rather is a descriptive or explanatory use.").

7. 192 USPQ 744 (D.Conn.1976).

legitimate to describe its mechanics as being especially "mobile" individuals, the court held that they had infringed the MOBIL mark for gasoline

The descriptive fair use defense also requires that the defendant be acting in good faith. This language has not received much judicial interpretation, but it suggests that evidence of intent to confuse the public or otherwise capitalize on the trademark might negate the defense. At least one court has held, however, that mere knowledge that another firm uses the word, phrase or symbol in question as a trademark is not enough to destroy good faith, nor is there any requirement to secure the advice of counsel before using the words in their descriptive sense.[8]

The real test of "descriptive fair use" is whether the defendant's use avoids generating a likelihood of confusion. If the use creates confusion, it is probably not merely descriptive, and will not to be allowed.[9] Rather than benefitting consumers by providing useful information, the existence of confusion would mean that consumers had been misled, perhaps to their detriment. The commentary to the Restatement pragmatically declares that the fair use defense may remain applicable "even if some residual confusion remains likely" but it notes that the amounts of both actual and likely confusion "are important factors in determining whether a use is fair."[10] The Second Circuit has taken a somewhat different view, declaring that "fair use is a defense under the Lanham Act even if a defendant's conduct would otherwise constitute infringement of another's trademark," and that if "any confusion results, that is a risk the plaintiff accepted when it decided to identify its product with a mark that uses a well-known descriptive phrase."[11] The Second Circuit position seems overly solicitous of the defendant's prerogatives, however, at the expense of the consuming public. In seeking to punish a plaintiff for its poor choice of mark it may tolerate on-going injury to baffled purchasers.

§ 31.4 Other Defenses to Claims of Trademark Infringement

31.4.1 Innocent Infringement

As we have seen in an earlier chapter, intent is not an element of trademark infringement. Thus a claim by a defendant that it was unaware of plaintiff's prior use of the mark in question, that it adopted its mark innocently and in good faith, or that it had no reason to suspect

8. Car–Freshner Corp. v. S.C. Johnson & Son, Inc., 70 F.3d 267 (2d Cir.1995).

9. See, e.g., Zatarains, Inc. v. Oak Grove Smokehouse, Inc., 698 F.2d 786, 791 (5th Cir.1983) ("The holder of a protectable descriptive mark has no legal claim to an exclusive right in the primary, descriptive meaning of the term; consequently, anyone is free to use the term in its primary, descriptive sense *so long as such use does not lead to customer confusion as to the source of the goods or services* [emphasis added].").

10. Restatement (Third) of Unfair Competition § 28, comment b (1995).

11. Cosmetically Sealed Industries, Inc. v. Chesebrough–Pond's USA Co., 125 F.3d 28 (2d Cir.1997).

that any consumer confusion would result from adoption of the mark does not in any way negate liability. As we have also seen, however, wrongful intent is often used by courts as evidence of likelihood of confusion. Consequently an "innocent" party may escape liability in a close case because the court may refuse to find likelihood of confusion. To put the same point another way, while good faith will be a factor in defendant's favor in an infringement analysis, it is never dispositive. There is thus no such thing as a true "innocent infringer" defense.

Courts are generally agreed, however, that the defendant's good faith is relevant to the scope and type of remedy. Where a defendant can show that it has acted in good faith, without any intent to free ride on plaintiff's goodwill, courts will not grant the plaintiff an award of defendant's profits. In addition the Lanham Act contains specific provisions designed to protect printers, publishers and broadcasters who can demonstrate that their acts of trademark infringement were innocent. Thus, an innocent party engaged only in printing the mark for others is subject only to injunctive relief and has no exposure for any damages.[1] If the alleged infringement is in connection with a paid newspaper, magazine, radio or television advertisement and the publisher or broadcaster is an innocent party, again, the sole relief available will be an injunction.[2] Moreover, in this second situation, even an injunction will not be available if it would "delay the delivery of such issue or transmission of such electronic communication after the regular time for such delivery or transmission, and such delay would be due to the method by which publication and distribution of such periodical or transmission ... is customarily conducted in accordance with sound business practice, and not due to any method or device adopted to evade" the law.[3] This last provision is, of course, designed to prevent conflict with constitutional doctrines concerning the prior restraint of expressive communications.

31.4.2 Laches and Acquiescence

Laches is a traditional defense to any request for equitable or injunctive relief, applicable in many contexts besides intellectual property law. Since injunctions are the most commonly sought remedy in trademark infringement cases, it is not surprising that claims of laches have cropped up repeatedly in trademark litigation. Moreover, many courts have held that the laches defense can also be used to defeat a request for profits or damages arising from trademark infringement, even though most monetary remedies are traditionally classified as "legal" rather than equitable.

Simply put, laches is prejudicial delay. To establish the defense the defendant must show that the plaintiff had ample knowledge of defendant's activities concerning the trademark in question, that plaintiff procrastinated in bringing suit, and the defendant has changed its position in the meantime. The usual legal slogan offered in explanation

§ 31.4

1. 15 U.S.C.A. § 1114(2)(A) (2000).

2. 15 U.S.C.A. § 1114(2)(B) (2000).

3. 15 U.S.C.A. § 1114(2)(C) (2000).

of the laches defense is that equity aids only the vigilant, not those who sleep on their rights, or as the Latin buffs like to put it, *"vigilantibus non dormientibus aequitas subvenit."*

The defense is recognized in the Restatement (Third) of Unfair Competition, which provides that "[i]f the owner of a trademark, trade name, collective mark, or certification mark unreasonably delays in commencing an action for infringement or otherwise asserting the owner's rights and thereby causes prejudice to another who may be subject to liability to the owner under the rules stated in this Chapter, the owner may be barred in whole or in part from the relief that would otherwise be available under §§ 35–37."[4] The Lanham Act also recognizes the defense, and declares that it is available even against a federally registered mark that has become incontestible,[5] but the federal statute does not contain a definition of the doctrine.

Unfortunately, there is some terminological confusion in the cases discussing this defense. Some courts use the term "laches" to refer only to the delay component of the defense. Where the delay has caused prejudice, those courts will then say that the plaintiff is "estopped" from asserting its claim, occasionally using the long-form phrase "estoppel by laches."[6] In the view of these courts, then, not all "laches" leads to an "estoppel." Other courts however use the word "laches" as a conclusion meaning that all aspects of the defense have been established and that the plaintiff should be denied some or all of the relief it has requested. Making matters even worse, still other courts sometimes use the term "acquiescence" to mean the same thing, while others reserve the word acquiescence for cases where the plaintiff effectively granted the defendant permission to use the mark.

For reasons of brevity, if nothing else, the following discussion uses the single word "laches" to represent the traditional defense made out by a showing of delay plus prejudice. Where the discussion focuses solely on the issue of delay, we have opted, we hope in the spirit of simplicity, to use the word "delay." This permits us to forgo use of the word "estoppel" in the discussion that follows, though that word appears with regularity in the case law. We will reserve the term "acquiescence" for cases involving not merely delay followed by prejudice, but an express or implied representation by a trademark owner to another user of a similar mark that it does not plan to assert a trademark claim, followed by substantial passage of time and prejudice to that other user, before the owner ultimately changes its mind and decides to file suit.

Obviously, the laches defense bears some similarities to a statute of limitations defense because it focuses on the plaintiff's failure to pursue its rights in a timely fashion. This is an apt moment to note, parentheti-

---

4. Restatement (Third) of Unfair Competition § 31 (1995).

5. 15 U.S.C.A. § 1115(b)(9) (2000) provides that "equitable principles, including laches, estoppel and acquiescence" may be raised as defenses.

6. *See, e.g.,* Kason Industries, Inc. v. Component Hardware Group, Inc., 120 F.3d 1199, 1203 (11th Cir.1997).

cally, that the Lanham Act does not specify any statute of limitations for infringement actions. In large part this is because trademark infringement is a continuing wrong, which occurs again each day that the defendant continues to make use of the plaintiff's mark. When the posture of Lanham Act cases has required the use of a precise statutory standard as a time limit, the federal courts have typically borrowed the closest relevant state law provision of the forum state.[7] It is more common, however, for issues of undue delay to be litigated under the laches doctrine.

Unlike a statute of limitations issue, in determining whether laches is applicable there are few bright line rules. Thus, some courts have declined to find laches despite a delay of as much as 13 years,[8] while others have found the doctrine applicable after a delay of only 3 ½ years.[9] Many courts do use the time period of an analogous state statute of limitations as rough rule of thumb or as a starting point for analysis in determining if delay has been excessive. However, rather than simply looking at the calendar, most courts confronted with a claim of laches attempt to balance the equities and pay close attention to the facts and circumstances of each individual case. More importantly, courts will not deny relief on laches grounds based merely on plaintiff's delay in bringing suit. A finding of related prejudice to the defendant is crucial. Moreover, as Professor McCarthy has pointed out, courts often view the amount of delay by the plaintiff and the degree of prejudice suffered by the defendant as standing in a reciprocal relationship. Thus they might bar plaintiff's claim on laches grounds even after only modest delay, if defendant has suffered severe prejudice, and they might reach the same conclusion in a case involving only slight prejudice, if there has been extreme delay.[10]

The policy basis for the laches defense is not hard to discern. Learned Hand set out the justification for it in characteristic and memorable language back in 1943. He wrote: "Even in 1930 when for the first time it really began to be injured, [plaintiff] did nothing; not a word of protest, or a gesture of complaint escaped it for six years more; and still the . . . [defendant's] business kept increasing. What equity it can have the hardihood now to assert; how it can expect us to stifle a competition which with complete complaisance, and even with active encouragement, it has allowed for years to grow like the mustard tree; why we should destroy a huge business built up with its connivance and

---

7. Island Insteel Systems, Inc. v. Waters, 296 F.3d 200 (3d Cir.2002) ("Because the Lanham Act does not contain an express statute of limitations, we follow the traditional practice of borrowing the most analogous statute of limitations from state law."); Beauty Time, Inc. v. VU Skin Systems, Inc., 118 F.3d 140 (3d Cir.1997) ("The Lanham Act contains no express statute of limitations and the general rule is that when a federal statute provides no limitations for suits, the court must look to the state statute of limitations for analogous types of actions.").

8. Menendez v. Holt, 128 U.S. 514, 9 S.Ct. 143, 32 L.Ed. 526 (1888) (thirteen year delay no bar to injunctive relief).

9. Trustees of Columbia University v. Columbia/HCA Healthcare Corp., 964 F.Supp. 733 (S.D.N.Y.1997).

10. J. Thomas McCarthy, TRADEMARKS AND UNFAIR COMPETITION § 31:2 (2002).

consent: this we find it impossible to understand."[11] As this delightful quotation implies, the required "prejudice" for an invocation of laches is usually established in trademark cases by evidence that the defendant invested significant funds in expanding or building up its business on the assumption that the plaintiff had no objection to the trademarks it was using. The comments to the Restatement are to the same effect, noting that "prejudice in trademark infringement actions usually relate[s] to the potential loss of the good will that has attached to the use of the designation by the defendant. For example, the value of the resources expended by the defendant in advertising and promoting the mark during the period of the plaintiff's delay will be lost in the event of a subsequent injunction barring the defendant's use."[12]

Courts are usually quite hesitant to find the necessary prejudice when the issue is whether to grant the plaintiff injunctive relief. To put the same point another way, it is easier for a defendant to succeed on a laches argument if it is trying to avoid paying damages than it is if it is trying to avoid an injunction. This is because trademark infringement implicates not just the equities between the parties, but issues of consumer protection as well. Penalizing the plaintiff for its delay by denying it damages is one thing, but allowing the defendant to continue to engage in practices that deceive consumers is usually distasteful to most courts and normally against public policy. As the Eleventh Circuit put it a few years ago, "if the likelihood of confusion is inevitable, or so strong as to outweigh the effect of the plaintiff's delay in bringing a suit, a court may in its discretion grant injunctive relief, even in cases where a suit for damages is appropriately barred."[13] Nonetheless, if the delay has been extreme, stretching into decades, if the prejudice is great enough, and especially where the plaintiff's case on the merits is weak,[14] courts do occasionally rely on laches even to deny injunctions.

The strong concern with consumer deception also generates judicial reluctance to deny relief on laches grounds where the defendant is guilty of intentional infringement. As one court put it, only "where the delay is so prolonged and inexcusable that it amounts to a virtual abandonment of the right by the plaintiff"[15] could the balance of equities favor allowing a willful infringer to continue its conduct. An intentional infringer, after all, is deliberately seeking to manipulate consumers to their detriment, and this wrongful intent poses a high risk that it will succeed in that effort. Doctrinally, courts often explain this result by noting that in order to invoke laches a party must be in "good faith," and, of course, an

11. Dwinell–Wright Co. v. White House Milk Co., 132 F.2d 822 (2d Cir.1943).

12. Restatement (Third) of Unfair Competition § 31, comment b (1995).

13. Kason Industries, Inc. v. Component Hardware Group, Inc., 120 F.3d 1199 (11th Cir.1997).

14. "Because laches is an equitable doctrine, its application is inextricably bound up with the nature and quality of the plaintiff's claim on the merits relevant to a prospective injunction." University of Pittsburgh v. Champion Products, Inc., 686 F.2d 1040, 1044 (3d Cir.1982), *cert. denied*, 459 U.S. 1087, 103 S.Ct. 571, 74 L.Ed.2d 933 (1982).

15. Tisch Hotels, Inc. v. Americana Inn, Inc., 350 F.2d 609 (7th Cir.1965).

intentional infringer is the very antithesis of good faith. Again, to quote Learned Hand, "advantages built upon a deliberately plagiarized make-up do not seem to us to give the borrower any standing to complain that his vested interests will be disturbed."[16] Of course, like most legal rules, even this principle has its breaking point. As one court observed, admittedly in dicta, several decades ago, "had there been a lapse of a hundred years or more, we think it highly dubious that any court of equity would grant injunctive relief against even a fraudulent infringer."[17]

There is yet another reason why not every delay gives rise to a defense of laches. In some cases, the defendant's initial scope of activities involving the allegedly confusing trademark may interfere with plaintiff's rights so minimally that the plaintiff is justified in not bothering to file suit. If such a defendant subsequently expands its activities, perhaps by beginning to use the mark in question on new and different products, or in new and different geographic areas, courts typically measure the relevant delay for the purposes of a laches claim only from the time of defendant's newly expanded use. As the Restatement explains "plaintiff in some cases may ... be justified in delaying a protest or the commencement of litigation until the viability of the defendant's infringing business is evident."[18] This situation is sometimes labeled "progressive encroachment."

Acquiescence differs from laches because the trademark owner will have in some way specifically signaled to the defendant that its activities were acceptable before ultimately reversing course and filing suit. It is sometimes said that acquiescence implies active consent to the defendants acts, while laches implies only a passive consent. One federal court has explained that: "Although sometimes used indiscriminately as if they were synonyms, 'laches' and 'acquiescence' are not the same. Laches is a negligent and unintentional failure to protect one's rights while acquiescence is intentional."[19]

The Fourth Circuit provided a useful example of acquiescence when it summarized one of its own prior decisions as follows: "In *Ambrosia Chocolate Co. v. Ambrosia Cake Bakery*,[20] not only was the plaintiff aware that the defendant was using the plaintiff's registered trademark 'Ambrosia' for eight years but also the plaintiff attempted to sell ingredients to the defendant to be used in making 'Ambrosia' cakes to be marketed under that name. The court found this to be 'active encouragement' by the plaintiff to induce the defendant to sell its cakes under the

---

16. My–T Fine Corp. v. Samuels, 69 F.2d 76 (2d Cir.1934).

17. Anheuser–Busch, Inc. v. Du Bois Brewing Co., 175 F.2d 370, 374 (3d Cir. 1949), *cert. denied*, 339 U.S. 934, 70 S.Ct. 664, 94 L.Ed. 1353 (1950).

18. Restatement (Third) of Unfair Competition § 31, comment c (1995).

19. Elvis Presley Enterprises, Inc. v. Elvisly Yours, Inc., 936 F.2d 889 (6th Cir. 1991).

20. 165 F.2d 693 (4th Cir.1947), *cert. denied*, 333 U.S. 882, 68 S.Ct. 914, 92 L.Ed. 1157, (1948).

name 'Ambrosia', and injunctive relief was denied."[21] This course of conduct obviously transcends mere laches because it eliminates any ambiguity about whether the trademark owner is aware of the defendant's activities or proposes to challenge them.

A more recent example of both the laches and acquiescence defenses and of the relevance of the progressive encroachment rebuttal to those defenses came up in the protracted, and still pending, litigation between breakfast food manufacturer Kellogg and oil giant Exxon.[22] Kellogg began using a cartoon tiger as a trademark for its FROSTED FLAKES brand cereal in the early 1950's. You may know him. His name is TONY. In 1959 Exxon began using a cartoon tiger to promote its motor fuel products. Exxon's tiger doesn't have a name and is known, somewhat pathetically, merely as "whimsical tiger."

Kellogg must have known of Exxon's tiger trademark by the mid-sixties, because Exxon used the mark in a national advertising campaign. In addition, in 1965 Exxon secured a federal registration for its cartoon tiger, without any administrative opposition from Kellogg. Indeed when Exxon sought to register its tiger trademark in Germany, it contacted Kellogg and asked it not to oppose the application, and Kellogg agreed. By the mid–1980's Exxon began opening up convenience stores at some of its service stations, called TIGER MART stores, and began using its cartoon tiger trademark to promote the sale of food and beverages at those stores. While there were initially only a few such stores, "Exxon's use of the cartoon tiger to promote food, beverages and convenience stores increased dramatically from 1992 to 1996."

In late 1996 Kellogg filed suit alleging both infringement and dilution and seeking both monetary remedies and an injunction against Exxon's continued use of the mark in connection with food products. Predictably, given the facts, Exxon asserted both laches and acquiescence. Just as predictably, Kellogg attempted to rebut those defenses by raising the progressive encroachment argument. The trial court granted summary judgment for Exxon, finding acquiescence because of what it considered Kellogg's 31–year delay in filing suit, and rejecting the progressive encroachment claim. On appeal, the Sixth Circuit reversed.

The court of appeals began by noting that "implicit in a finding of laches or acquiescence is the presumption that an underlying claim for infringement existed at the time at which we begin to measure the plaintiff's delay .... [A]ny delay attributable to the plaintiff must be measured from the time at which the plaintiff knew or should have known that [the alleged] infringement had ripened into a provable claim." The court said that progressive encroachment "applies in cases where the defendant has engaged in some infringing use of its trademark—at least enough of an infringing use so that it may attempt to

21. Sweetheart Plastics, Inc. v. Detroit Forming, Inc., 743 F.2d 1039, 1046 (4th Cir.1984).

22. *See* Kellogg Co. v. Exxon Corp., 209 F.3d 562 (6th Cir.2000), *cert. denied,* 531 U.S. 944, 121 S.Ct. 340, 148 L.Ed.2d 273 (2000).

avail itself of a laches or acquiescence defense—but the plaintiff does not bring suit right away because the nature of defendant's infringement is such that the plaintiff's claim has yet to ripen into one sufficiently colorable to justify litigation.... [T]he progressive encroachment analysis turns not on the single question of direct competition, but rather, on the likelihood of confusion resulting from the defendant's moving into the same or similar market area and placing itself more squarely in competition with the plaintiff.''

Applying these rules to the case before it, the court noted that Kellogg probably could not have demonstrated any likelihood of confusion during the time that Exxon confined its use of the cartoon tiger to the sale of petroleum products. Thus the delay relevant to any claim of laches or acquiescence should only be measured from the time when Exxon began using the mark on food products. Scrutinizing the record, the court found that there was a genuine factual dispute about when Kellogg was put on notice of Exxon's use of the cartoon tiger in connection with food. Moreover the court held that even if Kellogg knew of such uses by Exxon as early as 1984, when Exxon opened its first TIGER MART store, its failure to bring suit for 12 years was ''not so outrageous, unreasonable and inexcusable as to constitute a virtual abandonment of its right to seek injunctive relief ....'' Having found no acquiescence, it then held it unnecessary to resolve the issue of progressive encroachment, since that issue is only relevant if laches or acquiescence is found.

While the progressive encroachment purportedly at issue in the *Kellogg* litigation involved the defendant's migration from one product line to another, the courts also use the doctrine to negate laches in other situations. For instance, if the defendant changes the format of its trademark from one with only slight resemblance to plaintiff's mark to one that begins to look more and more like the plaintiff's, the plaintiff's delay in suing will not be measured from the date of defendant's first use. Similar considerations apply if a defendant begins as a small, local firm, and then expands its operations geographically to come into conflict with the plaintiff.[23]

Finally, it should be noted that laches arguments take on a different cast when the context is plaintiff's motion for a preliminary injunction. Such a motion is predicated on notions of urgency and irreparable harm. If the plaintiff delays in filing suit, a court may strongly incline towards denying preliminary relief, reasoning that the matter is not really all that pressing and the harm is not all that severe. One empirical study found that a delay of as little as six months will result in a ''significant risk'' that a preliminary injunction will be denied, and that after a year, ''most cases'' denied the preliminary remedy.[24]

23. *See, e.g.,* Tandy Corp. v. Malone & Hyde, Inc., 769 F.2d 362 (6th Cir.1985), *cert. denied,* 476 U.S. 1158, 106 S.Ct. 2277, 90 L.Ed.2d 719 (1986).

24. Robert Raskopf & Sandra Edelman, *Delay in Filing Preliminary Injunction*

Motions: How Long Is Too Long?, 80 TRADEMARK REP. 36 (1990). *See also* Sandra Edelman, *Delay in Filing Preliminary Injunction Motions: A Five Year Update,* 85 TRADEMARK REP. 1 (1995) (''Five years since publication of the original article on this

31.4.3   Abandonment

It is self-evident that if a trademark owner gives up its rights to a mark, it cannot thereafter successfully assert infringement claims against a party who begins a later use of that very same mark. Just as it is not theft for you to take a car that we abandon at the side of the road, it is not infringement for you to use a trademark that we abandon at the side of the stream of commerce. It follows that unlike laches, which forfeits rights only against a single infringer, abandonment forfeits rights against the whole world, and injects the trademark in question into the public domain. After abandonment the abandoned mark may be adopted by any firm that chooses to take it up, and of course, if multiple firms race to appropriate it, it will belong to the first firm to make valid use of it under ordinary rules concerning trademark priority.

Disputed issues of abandonment usually arise either as a defense to a claim of trademark infringement, or as a grounds for cancelling a federal trademark registration. Generally, for a party to be found to have abandoned a mark two elements must combine: The trademark owner must discontinue use of the mark, and it must have no intention to subsequently resume use. These determinations are classified as issues of fact, and the majority of courts have held that they must be established by clear and convincing evidence.[25]

Older cases sometimes referred to an intent "to abandon,"[26] rather than to an intent "not to resume use." An intent-to-abandon standard would require proof that the trademark owner harbored a subjective purpose to relinquish all rights to the mark. Modern authority has moved away from this formula however, and uniformly focuses on the mark owner's intention regarding future use of the mark. An intent to warehouse the mark for some future contingency while refraining from any actual use is thus sufficient to constitute abandonment under current authority. To cite chapter and verse, the Restatement says an abandonment occurs when "the party asserting rights in the designation has ceased to use the designation with an intent not to resume use,"[27] and the Lanham Act says that "a mark shall be deemed to be 'abandoned' when . . . its use has been discontinued with intent not to resume such use."[28]

In most cases where abandonment is an issue, the relevant intent "not to resume" is proved circumstantially, with the necessary inference being drawn from a showing of a sustained period of non-use. Indeed,

---

subject, the lessons remain the same: a delay of three months or less is generally acceptable, but it behooves the movant to offer an adequate explanation to justify delays in the six to twelve month range.").

25. *See, e.g.,* Saratoga Vichy Spring Co. v. Lehman, 625 F.2d 1037 (2d Cir.1980); Pilates, Inc. v. Current Concepts, Inc., 120 F.Supp.2d 286, 295 (S.D.N.Y.2000).

26. *See, e.g.,* Saxlehner v. Eisner & Mendelson Co., 179 U.S. 19, 21 S.Ct. 7, 45 L.Ed. 60 (1900).

27. Restatement (Third) of Unfair Competition § 30(2) (1995).

28. 15 U.S.C.A. § 1127 (2000).

the Lanham Act provides that "nonuse for 3 consecutive years shall be prima facie evidence of abandonment."[29] The Second Circuit has also held that the intent to resume use must be an intent to resume within the "reasonably foreseeable future."[30] Thus while non-use and intent are itemized as discrete aspects of the abandonment doctrine, the evidence in most cases is usually all about the length of non-use and the proper conclusions to be drawn from it.

Since valid trademark use must be "bona fide" and in connection with genuine commercial transactions, mere "token" use to preserve rights in a mark will not negate a finding of abandonment, and an intent to make such token uses in the future is not good enough either. In *Exxon Corp. v. Humble Exploration Co.*[31], the plaintiff had formerly sold petroleum products under the HUMBLE trademark. When it decided to adopt the EXXON mark, it attempted to preserve rights to the HUMBLE designation through what it characterized as a "trademark mainte- nance program," which involved limited sales made through three "name protection companies." The Fifth Circuit held that these sales were insufficient to negate a finding of "intent not to resume use" as a true trademark for the company, and it found the HUMBLE mark abandoned.

Of course, if a trademark owner explicitly declares that it will no longer use a mark, there is no need to rely on circumstantial evidence and an abandonment will readily be found. Thus in *Hiland Potato Chip Co. v. Culbro Snack Foods, Inc.*, where the plaintiff issued a public statement that it would no long use the KITTY CLOVER brand name and would sell all items "under the HILAND label," the court said that it "is hard to imagine how a public declaration of discontinuance of a trademark could be more clear."[32]

Logically enough, where non-use is due to circumstances beyond the control of the trademark owner, courts will not find abandonment. Thus a suspension of sales due to war, labor strife, legal obstacles, or financial setbacks does not give rise to an inference of the legally necessary intent not to resume sales—at least not if the firm resumes sales under the trademark once the difficulties are alleviated. Similarly, intermittent periods of non-use or minimal use will not warrant a finding of abandon- ment if the use of the mark is more or less continuous over time. As in most other areas of trademark law, the precise facts and circumstances are always relevant. Sporadic sales of expensive, custom-built construc- tion equipment might not suggest an abandonment, where comparably sporadic sales of penny candy or bubble gum could.

Some infringement defendants like to point to the plaintiff's failure to police the market or sue other infringers as a basis for a claim that

29. *Id.*

30. Silverman v. CBS, Inc., 870 F.2d 40 (2d Cir.1989) (Failure to use AMOS 'N ANDY mark on entertainment services for 21 years constituted abandonment despite mark owners lingering desire to resume use if social circumstances should permit).

31. 695 F.2d 96 (5th Cir.1983).

32. 585 F.Supp. 17 (S.D.Iowa 1982), *aff'd,* 720 F.2d 981 (8th Cir.1983).

the mark has been abandoned. While the failure to sue infringers might jeopardize a mark owner's ability to protect its mark or prevail in any given lawsuit, it does not technically constitute abandonment.[33] Rather, such a cavalier approach to policing the marketplace is likely to be relevant to issues such as whether the mark has become a generic designation, whether there is sufficient strength in the mark to justify a finding of likelihood of confusion, or whether the plaintiff can make out the irreparable injury necessary to warrant a preliminary injunction.

If a firm stops using a trademark in only one portion of its trading area, an infringement defendant may attempt to argue that there has been a partial abandonment in that area. Where common law rights are at issue, both the cases and the Restatement support the idea of a limited territorial abandonment.[34] If there is a federal registration, however, that registration grants nationwide rights. Use anywhere in the United States will preserve those rights against a claim of abandonment, even though the registrant might go years, or even decades, without using the mark in certain states or regions.[35] Any other rule would undermine the federal trademark registration scheme and destroy incentives to register. On the other hand, a federal registration can be cancelled "in part" if the registrant ceases to use the mark on some, but not all, of the goods specified in the registration, and has no intent to resume.[36]

While the black letter law declares that the key focus in abandonment determinations should be on the future plans of the trademark owner, policy considerations suggest that the mind-set of the consuming public should be equally important. A trademark is a shorthand way that merchants communicate data to the public about the attributes and qualities of their goods and services. If a mark continues to have such significance to the public, a court should hesitate to declare it abandoned. A premature declaration of abandonment would permit other firms to use the mark in ways that, by definition, would confuse the public. On the other hand, where the evidence reveals that the mark has lost all meaning to the public at large—where the goodwill that was once associated with it has entirely dissipated—a finding of abandonment seems entirely in line with the public interest.

The cases also recognize a second type of trademark abandonment. If a party licenses its mark and then fails to supervise its licensees to make sure they observe consistent standards of quality, this too can be found to be an abandonment.[37] This so-called "naked" licensing will

33. *See, e.g.,* Sweetheart Plastics, Inc. v. Detroit Forming, Inc. 743 F.2d 1039 (4th Cir.1984).

34. *See, e.g.,* Youthform Co. v. R.H. Macy & Co., 153 F.Supp. 87 (D.Ga.1957); Restatement (Third) of Unfair Competition § 30, comment a (1995) ("Common law priority in a particular geographic area is . . . lost if the designation has been abandoned by the owner in that geographic area.").

35. Dawn Donut Co. v. Hart's Food Stores, Inc., 267 F.2d 358 (2d Cir.1959).

36. Levi Strauss & Co. v. GTFM, 62 USPQ2d 1394, 1398 (N.D.Cal.2002).

37. *See, e.g.,* Stanfield v. Osborne Industries, Inc., 52 F.3d 867 (10th Cir.1995), *cert. denied,* 516 U.S. 920, 116 S.Ct. 314, 133 L.Ed.2d 217 (1995); Haymaker Sports, Inc. v. Turian, 581 F.2d 257 (CCPA 1978). *See*

inevitably cause the trademark to lose its significance to the public. If one MCDONALD'S restaurant is decorated in red and yellow and sells hamburgers, while a second is decorated in blue and white and sells an assortment of Indian curries, while a third is decorated in green and purple and sells only lasagna, the MCDONALD'S mark would soon be meaningless to consumers. As the Fifth Circuit summarized: "Courts have long imposed upon trademark licensors a duty to oversee the quality of licensee's products.... If a trademark owner allows licensees to depart from its quality standards, the public will be misled, and the trademark will cease to have utility as an informational device. A trademark owner who allows this to occur loses its right to use the mark."[38]

Of course this situation differs from the type of abandonment discussed earlier in this section because the trademark owner in a "naked" licensing situation usually does not have any intent to give up rights to the mark. Semantic purists might want to reserve the word "abandonment" for situations involving voluntary decisions to surrender a mark, and use a different label, such as "forfeiture," for the naked licensing situation. Sadly for them, however, the use of the term abandonment seems firmly entrenched in the case law as a description of the consequence of naked licensing. The details of the doctrine of naked licensing are discussed further in the following chapter.

31.4.4 Unclean Hands and Fraud

Like laches, "unclean hands" is a traditional and general equitable defense. A plaintiff is guilty of unclean hands when it has engaged in some significant misconduct related to the subject matter of the litigation. In such a case, courts will often deny the plaintiff relief. The doctrine is available to trademark defendants both under the Lanham Act and under state law. As we have seen previously, the Lanham Act specifically indicates that traditional equitable defenses are available in infringement suits, even against incontestible marks,[39] and the cases are clear that "unclean hands" is one such defense. The Restatement (Third) of Unfair Competition is even more explicit, declaring that "[i]f a designation used as a trademark, trade name, collective mark, or certification mark is deceptive, or if its use is otherwise in violation of public policy, or if the owner of the designation has engaged in other substantial misconduct directly related to the owner's assertion of rights in the trademark, trade name, collective mark, or certification mark, the owner may be barred in whole or in part from the relief that would otherwise be available under §§ 35–37."[40]

generally Edward K. Esping, Annot., *Granting of "Naked" or Unsupervised License to Third Party as Abandonment of Trademark,* 118 A.L.R. Fed. 211 (1994).

38. Kentucky Fried Chicken Corp. v. Diversified Packaging Corp., 549 F.2d 368 (5th Cir.1977).

39. 15 U.S.C.A. §§ 1115(b)(9), 1116 (2000).

40. Restatement (Third) of Unfair Competition § 32 (1995).

The usual justification offered for the "unclean hands" doctrine is that since the equitable remedy of injunction involves an appeal to the judicial conscience, a court of equity should refuse to come to the aid of a party who is blameworthy. Many legal scholars and more than a few judges have questioned the logic of this justification, but even if the philosophical underpinnings are shaky, the defense continues to be asserted with success in appropriate cases.

The most common form of plaintiff misconduct precluding relief under the unclean hands doctrine is deception of the public in connection with the use of the trademark in question. The Supreme Court held as much a century ago in *Worden v. California Fig Syrup Co.*[41] The plaintiff in that case sold a laxative under the trademark SYRUP OF FIGS. As it turned out, however, there were no figs or fig syrup in this preparation. When the defendant began selling a competing preparation under the same name, the plaintiff sought an injunction. While the lower courts granted the requested relief, the Supreme Court reversed. It noted that "when the owner of a trade-mark applies for an injunction to restrain the defendant from injuring his property by making false representations to the public, it is essential that the plaintiff should not in his trade-mark, or in his advertisements and business, be himself guilty of any false or misleading representation; that if the plaintiff makes any material false statement in connection with the property which he seeks to protect, he loses his right to claim the assistance of a court of equity...."

Of course, a few minutes of reflection reveals that the unclean hands defense can lead to absurd, or at least undesirable results. Trademark litigation, as we have seen repeatedly, implicates not just the rights of the parties, but the public interest as well. When the court denies a plaintiff relief on the grounds of unclean hands, the result is that the public must then endure both the plaintiff's continued deceptive use of its mark, along with the defendant's continued confusing use of a substantially similar mark. In order to avoid consorting with a wrongdoer, the court may very well leave consumers in the worst possible position.

To avoid the illogic of such results, modern cases do not automatically bar relief based on any and all showings of plaintiff misconduct. Rather, they often engage in a comparison or balancing of the misdeeds of the two litigants. If the defendant's wrongs significantly outweigh those of the plaintiff, modern courts sometimes refuse to apply the unclean hands concept, in order to make sure that the greater evil is dealt with. As the Ninth Circuit put it: "In the interests of right and justice the court should not automatically condone the defendant's infractions because the plaintiff is also blameworthy, thereby leaving two wrongs unremedied and increasing the injury to the public.... The relative extent of each party's wrong upon the other and upon the public

41.　187 U.S. 516, 528, 23 S.Ct. 161, 47 L.Ed. 282 (1903).

should be taken into account and an equitable balance struck."[42] In other situations, a showing of unclean hands may cause the court to narrow the scope of the requested injunction, rather than to deny all relief outright.

Courts are also fairly strict in requiring that the misconduct asserted in connection with this defense have a close connection with the subject matter of the litigation. There is no requirement that the plaintiff be as "pure as the driven snow," or have a generally blameless commercial track record. Consequently misconduct that is collateral to the matters at issue in the case is usually disregarded. As one court noted a century ago, "[t]he principle that 'he who comes into equity must do so with clean hand' ... does not repel all sinners from courts of equity, nor does it disqualify any complainant from obtaining relief there who has not dealt unjustly in the very transaction concerning which he complains. The inequity which will repel him must have an immediate and necessary relation to the equity for which he sues."[43]

Predictably, determining whether conduct actually relates to the pending lawsuit can raise close questions. In the late 1970's some chapters of a national organization known as the JAYCEES began to admit women in violation of the group's then existing policies (which have since been changed). In response, the national organization revoked the charters of those chapters, but some of them continued to use the JAYCEES name. When the national group sued the rebellious chapters for trademark infringement, the alleged infringers argued that the discriminatory practices of the organization constituted misconduct sufficiently related to the trademark so as to trigger the unclean hands defense. In one case, the Eighth Circuit agreed and denied relief. In an earlier case, however, the Third Circuit found that there was insufficient connection between the exclusionary practices of the plaintiff and the issues of trademark infringement, so it declined to find unclean hands.[44]

When we turn to the question of "fraud" in trademark law, we are dealing with a rather specialized term of art. This label is usually reserved for situations where a trademark owner has obtained a federal Lanham Act registration based on false representations to the U.S. Patent and Trademark Office, or has made other false filings with the PTO.[45] A party raising a claim of fraud must show that the registrant knowingly or deliberately made the alleged false statements to the PTO, and that the registration would not have issued, but for those false statements. Moreover, the fraud must be proved by clear and convincing evidence, and has been characterized as a "disfavored defense." Given

42. Republic Molding Corp. v. B.W. Photo Utilities, 319 F.2d 347 (9th Cir.1963).

43. Shaver v. Heller & Merz Co., 108 F. 821 (8th Cir.1901).

44. *Compare* United States Jaycees v. Cedar Rapids Jaycees, 794 F.2d 379 (8th Cir.1986), *with* United States Jaycees v.

Philadelphia Jaycees, 639 F.2d 134 (3d Cir. 1981).

45. Such other filings would include affidavits of continued use of the mark, affidavits requesting that the mark be declared incontestable and registration renewal applications.

all these hurdles, allegations of fraud succeed in only a small fraction of the trademark cases where they are asserted.

Many inaccuracies in trademark practice will not rise to the level of fraud because they are either errors based on an honest mistake or arguably founded on a good faith belief in the facts represented. For instance, all Lanham Act applications require an oath that to the best of applicant's knowledge and belief no other party has a superior right to use the mark. Although the applicant may know of other parties using similar marks on related goods, the oath may still reflect an honest opinion that its mark will not generate a likelihood of confusion with those other users, and thus the submission of the required oath cannot fairly be characterized as fraud.

Indeed, even certain deliberate falsehoods will not be fraud if the registration would have issued in any event. Thus a blatant lie about the date of first use of a mark might ultimately make no difference in the registration process, so long as the firm in question used the mark in question at some time before the application was filed, and before any other party did so as well. Such a lie would not be "material" to the registration process. Bear in mind that this narrow approach to fraud in trademark practice is in rather stark contrast to the "inequitable conduct" rules that govern in patent prosecution, and which were treated in some depth earlier in this volume.

The Lanham Act provides that a federal registration for a trademark may be cancelled at any time if it was obtained fraudulently.[16] Elsewhere, the statute indicates that fraudulent procurement of registration is a defense to a claim of infringement of a registered mark, even if the registration in question has become incontestable.[17] It is important to note, however, that even if a party's registration is cancelled and its claim of infringement of the registered mark is dismissed based on a showing of fraud, that party will still have a valid common law trademark. It is still free to sue for infringement of that common law mark both under state law and under section 43(a) of the Lanham Act, and in such case, its fraud at the Patent Office will not bar relief.[48] As one trial court noted, "[t]rademarks are created by use, not registration. Federal registration creates valuable substantive and procedural rights, but the common law creates the underlying right to exclude. Thus, even if a plaintiff's registration is shown to be fraudulently obtained, the plaintiff's common law rights in the mark may still support an injunction against an infringing defendant."[49] Of course, with the cancellation of

46. 15 U.S.C.A. § 1064(3) (2000).

47. 15 U.S.C.A. § 1115(b)(1) (2000).

48. *See, e.g.,* Orient Express Trading Co. v. Federated Dep't Stores, Inc. 842 F.2d 650 (2d Cir.1988); Marshak v. Thomas, 1998 WL 476192, *12 (E.D.N.Y.1998) ("Thomas has raised counterclaims alleging, *inter alia,* that Marshak's mark was fraudulently obtained and thus must be canceled. Even if Thomas were to prevail in canceling Marshak's mark, however, the use of the name The Drifters could still be protected from unfair competition under section 43(a) of the Lanham Act.").

49. Aveda Corp. v. Evita Marketing, Inc., 706 F.Supp. 1419, 1425 (D.Minn.1989). *See also* Orient Express Trading Co. v. Federated Dep't Stores, Inc., 842 F.2d 650 (2d Cir.1988).

the federal registration, the plaintiff would lose all the related benefits conferred by the Lanham Act, such as evidentiary presumptions about its rights to the mark, and in the case of incontestable registrations, the right to cut off certain defenses.

In egregious cases, fraud on the PTO might also constitute misconduct rising to the level of "unclean hands," and where that is the case a plaintiff should and will be denied relief even when purporting to assert common law rights. Such cases are rare, however, because the public interest in being freed from confusion usually outweighs any judicial interest in punishing the trademark owner for lying to the bureaucrats at the Patent Office. Moreover, the Lanham Act contains a separate provision granting a civil cause of action to anyone injured by another person's fraudulent procurement of a federal trademark registration.[50] Thus courts can refuse to treat fraud on the PTO as unclean hands and to enjoin an infringer, secure in the knowledge that anyone who was genuinely injured by the fraud can still have a separate and independent remedy.

§ 31.5   Remedies for Trademark Infringement

31.5.1   Injunctive Relief and Other Equitable Remedies

The usual remedy in a trademark infringement case is an injunction, ordering the defendant to permanently cease using the infringing mark. Indeed, the Ninth Circuit has called it "the remedy of choice."[1] Section 34 of the Lanham Act specifically provides that when a plaintiff proves infringement the court "shall have the power to grant injunctions according to the principles of equity and upon such terms as the court may deem reasonable."[2] Such injunctions are typically nation-wide in scope, even if the defendant engaged in infringing activities in only a limited region of the country. The Lanham Act also empowers the court to require the defendant to file a written report detailing how it has complied with the terms of the injunction. The injunctive remedy under section 34 is available both to plaintiffs who have federally registered marks, and to plaintiffs with unregistered marks, who proceed under the general provisions of section 43(a). A separate provision of the Lanham Act also empowers the court to order "that all labels, signs, prints, packages, wrappers, receptacles, and advertisements in the possession of the defendant" that infringe or dilute "be delivered up and destroyed."[3]

The Restatement (Third) of Unfair Competition reveals that the common law doctrine is the same. It declares, in section 35, that "unless inappropriate ... injunctive relief will ordinarily be awarded against one who is liable to another for ... (b) infringement of the other's trademark."

---

50. 15 U.S.C.A. § 1120 (2000).

§ 31.5

1. Century 21 Real Estate Corp. v. Sandlin, 846 F.2d 1175 (9th Cir.1988).

2. 15 U.S.C. § 1116 (2000).

3. 15 U.S.C.A. § 118 (2000).

Traditionally, any plaintiff seeking an injunction must demonstrate that it has no "adequate remedy at law." A remedy "at law" means, essentially, money. This rule, therefore, requires a plaintiff to show that a monetary award will not suffice to rectify the situation. In trademark cases, once the plaintiff demonstrates infringement, the courts uniformly hold that this standard is automatically satisfied, because the defendant's wrong is a continuing one. As one court put it, the damage from trademark infringement is by its "very nature irreparable and not susceptible of adequate measurement for remedy at law."[4] It would be impractical and unfair to force a trademark owner to keep bringing suits every few months for the on-going damage inflicted by the infringing defendant, while the public became increasingly confused and the value of the mark withered away.

Moreover, the availability of injunctive relief is meant to permit a mark owner to stop the wrongful conduct before any harm has yet occurred. Thus a plaintiff need not prove actual damages in order to obtain an injunction, a proposition that is inherent in the substantive standard for liability that requires only a *likelihood* of confusion, not evidence of actual harm. Even if the defendant voluntarily suspends the infringing activity prior to the litigation, the court may enter an injunction unless the defendant persuades the court that there is no possibility it will resume the infringing conduct.[5]

An injunction need not be "absolute" in its terms. It can be tailored to the situation. Thus, the injunction may permit the defendant to continue using the mark, but only with disclaimers. You may recall that many of the cases considered earlier in this chapter involving repaired or repackaged goods were resolved with qualified orders of this type, mandating precisely how the defendant could refer to plaintiff's mark, and specifying other explanatory information to be included on labels or packages. An injunction may also forbid conduct that, standing alone, might have been permissible, as a method of "fencing in" the defendant and protecting the plaintiff from future harm.[6] It may require the defendant to notify distributors of its lack of affiliation with plaintiff, to undertake corrective advertising, or to recall previously distributed products that bear infringing marks. The precise details of an injunction are a matter for the discretion of the trial court,[7] though appellate courts frequently caution that an injunction should be no more burdensome to

4. International Kennel Club, Inc. v. Mighty Star, Inc., 846 F.2d 1079 (7th Cir. 1988).

5. *See, e.g.,* Elvis Presley Enterprises, Inc. v. Capece, 141 F.3d 188 (5th Cir.1998); Polo Fashions, Inc. v. Dick Bruhn, Inc., 793 F.2d 1132 (9th Cir.1986).

6. Tamko Roofing Products, Inc. v. Ideal Roofing Co., Ltd., 282 F.3d 23 (1st Cir. 2002) (citing McCarthy Treatise).

7. Forschner Group, Inc. v. Arrow Trading Co., Inc., 124 F.3d 402 (2d Cir.1997) (" 'A district court has a wide range of discretion in framing an injunction in terms it deems reasonable to prevent wrongful conduct,' Springs Mills, Inc. v. Ultracashmere House, Ltd., 724 F.2d 352, 355 (2d Cir.1983) (citation omitted), and we will not disturb on appeal the relief granted unless there has been an abuse of discretion.").

the defendant than necessary to provide complete relief to plaintiff and should be closely tailored to the harm that it addresses.[8]

Injunctions are subject to subsequent modification, but usually only on a showing of substantial and unforseen change in circumstances. Quite logically, the defendant is not entitled to re-litigate its liability on the merits by petitioning for modification of an injunction.

Courts may, and frequently do, enter preliminary injunctions in trademark cases. Preliminary injunctions are granted before the trial on the merits, either to preserve the status quo, or to prevent the imposition of harm to the plaintiff while the case is pending. The precise requirements for preliminary injunctions differ from state to state and between the different federal circuits.[9] Generally, to obtain a preliminary injunction in a trademark case the plaintiff must show both probable success on the merits and that it will suffer irreparable injury if the defendant is not enjoined pending trial. Since irreparable harm is usually presumed from a demonstration of likelihood of confusion, the issue at a preliminary injunction hearing often collapses to an inquiry about the merits of the case and the strength of plaintiff's showing of infringement.[10] Some courts also require the plaintiff to show that the balance of hardships favors the plaintiff, and still others explicitly consider the public interest in determining whether a preliminary injunction is appropriate. The delay of a plaintiff in filing suit may lead the court to deny a preliminary injunction, on the theory that the alleged harm is probably not as severe as plaintiff alleges,[11] but delay is not automatically a bar to preliminary relief.[12]

Obviously, from a strategic point of view, an infringement plaintiff who obtains a preliminary injunction has all but won the case. Since the defendant will either have to change the way it marks its goods or services pending trial, or suspend its business operations entirely, ultimate vindication at trial will mean little to such a defendant. Of course, if the defendant is eventually going to be found liable when the case is concluded, it may benefit the defendant to know that as early as possible so that it can adjust its behavior accordingly. One court has even described a preliminary injunction as "an act of kindness to the party enjoined. It cuts him off from a business life which from all the portents, would involve a series of trademark frustrations."[13] We suspect, however, that not all defendants see it that way.

---

8. Tamko Roofing Products, Inc. v. Ideal Roofing Co., Ltd., 282 F.3d 23 (1st Cir. 2002).

9. For a list of the relevant factors in the various federal circuits, *see* J. THOMAS MCCARTHY, TRADEMARKS AND UNFAIR COMPETITION, § 30:32

10. LeSportsac, Inc. v. K–Mart Corp., 754 F.2d 71 (2d Cir.1985) ("Likelihood of confusion is itself strong evidence that in the absence of an injunction [the plaintiff] might face irreparable harm.").

11. *See, e.g.,* Citibank, N.A. v. Citytrust, 756 F.2d 273 (2d Cir.1985) ("Preliminary

injunctions are generally granted under the theory that there is an urgent need for speedy action to protect the plaintiffs' rights. Delay in seeking enforcement of those rights, however, tends to indicate at least a reduced need for such drastic, speedy action.").

12. Vaughan Mfg. Co. v. Brikam International, Inc., 814 F.2d 346 (7th Cir.1987).

13. George Washington Mint, Inc. v. Washington Mint, Inc., 349 F.Supp. 255 (S.D.N.Y.1972).

In some cases, even a preliminary injunction process will be too time consuming to afford the plaintiff effective relief pending trial, perhaps because defendant is likely to disappear before it can be summoned into court for a preliminary injunction hearing. In such cases, the trademark owner may seek a Temporary Restraining Order, or TRO. Not only may such orders be granted on an extremely expedited time schedule, but they may also be granted based on an *ex parte* application—in other words, without any prior notice to the defendant.[14] In such a case, the first the defendant will hear of the action is when the TRO is served. This is obviously very potent medicine. The issuance of TRO's is governed by Rule 65(b) of the Federal Rules of Civil Procedure. Such orders may not last any longer than 10 days, during which time the plaintiff can seek a hearing on a preliminary injunction.

In addition to the general TRO remedy, section 34(d) of the Lanham Act contains specific provisions authorizing the seizure of counterfeit goods based on an *ex parte* application.[15] An applicant for an order under this section must give notice to the U.S. Attorney for the judicial district in which the order is sought, and is required to post monetary security to be used to compensate the defendant if the seizure turns out to be wrongful. This provision sets out seven specific factors that the court must find before such a seizure order will be issued, including the fact that plaintiff will suffer immediate and irreparable injury, that the harm to the plaintiff outweighs the harm to the defendant, and that the defendant is likely to "destroy, move, hide, otherwise make" the infringing items "inaccessible to the court, if the applicant were to proceed on notice to such person." This provision requires a hearing no sooner than 10 days, and not later than 15 days after the seizure. It also creates a damage remedy in favor of the defendant if the seizure is determined to be wrongful.[16]

Failure to obey the terms of an injunction is punishable as contempt. A party seeking a contempt citation must show "that (1) the order the contemnor failed to comply with is clear and unambiguous, (2) the proof of noncompliance is clear and convincing, and (3) the contemnor has not diligently attempted to comply in a reasonable manner."[17] In federal court, the party accused of contempt may not challenge the validity of the underlying order, however, some states do permit such an attack. If the situation at the contempt proceeding suggests that the defendant is acting in bad faith, the court can broaden the injunction to insure that the plaintiff-trademark-owner receives adequate protection.

31.5.2 Monetary Relief

Under section 35 of the Lanham Act, a successful trademark infringement plaintiff may recover both its own damages, the infringer's

14. *See, e.g.,* Fimab–Finanziaria Maglificio Biellese Fratelli Fila S.p.A. v. Kitchen, 548 F.Supp. 248 (S.D.Fla.1982).

15. 15 U.S.C.A. § 1116(d) (2000).

16. For further discussion *see* § 29.6, *supra.*

17. Duracell, Inc. v. Global Imports, Inc., 660 F.Supp. 690 (S.D.N.Y.1987).

profits, as well as the costs of the action.[18] The Restatement (Third) of Unfair Competition has comparable provisions, which reflect the governing principles in suits under state law.[19]

There are several different items that are recoverable as components of a damage award in a trademark case. First and most obviously, any lost sales due to defendant's infringing activities will be included. In addition, plaintiff may recover any losses incurred from selling goods at a discount in order to compete with the infringer. If the plaintiff spent any money on corrective advertising, or in any other efforts to dissipate the confusion in the market place, those sums will also be part of the damage award. And the court can also award damages for any harm to plaintiff's reputation or diminution of its good will attributable to the defendant's conduct.[20]

Plaintiff must offer concrete evidence of the fact of damages. As a practical matter this means that while a showing of *likelihood* of confusion will suffice for injunctive relief, the trademark owner must show *actual* confusion in order to recover damages. The courts, however, tend to be somewhat lenient with regard to proof of the precise amount of damages, often saying that the defendant is the party who should bear any risk of uncertainty created by its own wrongdoing.

Allowing the plaintiff to recover the defendant's profits is based primarily on the notion of unjust enrichment. If the defendant earned money by deceiving the public through the use of a mark confusingly similar to plaintiff's, that money is "ill gotten gain." Virtually all modern opinions hold that in order to recover the defendant's profits, the plaintiff must show that the defendant acted "willfully" or "in bad faith."[21] The Restatement takes this position as well, declaring that profits are only available if "the actor engaged in the conduct with the intention of causing confusion or deception...."

Once damages have been determined, Lanham Act § 35(a) allows the court to enter judgment "according to the circumstances of the case, for any sum above the amount found as actual damages, not exceeding three times such amount." In cases of counterfeiting § 35(b) provides that treble-damages are the norm, unless there are "extenuating circumstances."

Section 35(a) also permits the court to aware reasonable attorney fees to the prevailing parties in "exceptional cases." The statute does not define "exceptional cases." Some legislative history suggests that exceptions cases are those "where acts of infringement can be characterized as 'malicious,' 'fraudulent,' 'deliberate' or 'willful.' "[22] The case law is

---

18. 15 U.S.C.A. § 1117(a) (2000).

19. Restatement (Third) of Unfair Competition §§ 36–37 (1995).

20. *See, e.g.,* ALPO Petfoods, Inc. v. Ralston Purina Co., 913 F.2d 958 (D.C.Cir. 1990); Restatement (Third) of Unfair Competition § 37(1)(a) (1995).

21. *See, e.g.,* SecuraComm Consulting, Inc. v. Securacom, Inc., 166 F.3d 182 (3d Cir.1999); Bishop v. Equinox International Corp., 47 USPQ2d 1949 (10th Cir.1998).

22. S. Rep. No. 93–1400, 93rd Cong. 2d Sess. 2 (Dec. 17, 1974), *reprinted in* 1974 U.S.C.C.A.N. 7132, 7133.

largely to the same effect. As the Tenth Circuit put it, the "Lanham Act does not define what is an 'exceptional' case, but we have determined it occurs when a trademark infringement is malicious, fraudulent, deliberate, or willful."[23] Bear in mind that the attorney fees remedy is not limited to plaintiffs. A successful defendant can also ask for attorneys' fees, usually by demonstrating that the case filed against it lacked a good faith basis or was frivolous. In *Securacomm Consulting, Inc. v. Securacom Inc.*,[24] the court held that "vexatious litigation conduct" justified a fee award in favor of the defendant under the "exceptional cases" standard.

23. *See, e.g.* United Phosphorus, Ltd. v. Midland Fumigant, Inc., 205 F.3d 1219 (10th Cir.2000).

24. 224 F.3d 273 (3d Cir.2000) .

Chapter 32

TRADEMARK ASSIGNMENTS AND LICENSING

Table of Sections

§ 32.1   Assignments

Trademarks are transferable. They can be bought and sold like other business assets. The outright sale of a trademark is known as an "assignment." There is, however, a catch. The law is clear that a trademark can only be sold "with the accompanying goodwill" of the underlying business and that it not permissible to assign a trademark "in gross," which means independently of the associated goodwill.[1] An assignment in gross is null and void.

32.1.1   The Rule Against Assignments in Gross

The rule against assignments in gross is codified in both the Lanham Act and the Restatement (Third) of Unfair Competition. The former

---

§ 32.1

1. *See, e.g.,* United Drug Co. v. Theodore Rectanus Co., 248 U.S. 90, 97, 39 S.Ct. 48, 63 L.Ed. 141 (1918); Marshak v. Green, 746 F.2d 927, 929 (2d Cir.1984) ("a trademark cannot be sold or assigned apart from the goodwill it symbolizes"); Sands, Taylor & Wood Co. v. Quaker Oats Co., 978 F.2d 947, 956 (7th Cir.1992) ("'[T]he transfer of a trademark apart from the goodwill of the business which it represents is an invalid 'naked' or 'in gross' assignment, which passes no rights to the assignee.'").

provides that "a registered mark or a mark for which an application to register has been filed shall be assignable with the good will of the business in which the mark is used, or with that part of the good will of the business connected with the use of and symbolized by the mark."[2] The relevant Restatement section declares that "the owner of a trademark . . . may transfer ownership of the designation to another through an assignment. An assignment of ownership transfers the assignor's priority in the use of the designation to the assignee only if the assignee also acquires the line of business that is associated with the designation or otherwise maintains continuity in the use of the designation by continuing the line of business without substantial change."[3]

To understand this rule, it is important to recall that trademarks are nothing more or less than symbols. They are shorthand ways by which merchants communicate information to the public about the attributes and qualities of goods or services, and sometimes, information about who makes or stands behind those goods as well. If one business wants to transfer to another business the means necessary to make a particular item with particular attributes (such as machinery or blueprints), then, of course, it can transfer the name of that item as well, as part and parcel of the transaction. What it may not do, however, is to transfer the name alone, because to transfer the name alone may confuse the public. As one appellate court put it recently, "[t]he purpose of the rule prohibiting the sale or assignment of a trademark in gross is to prevent a consumer from being misled or confused as to the source and nature of the goods or services that he or she acquires."[4]

Perhaps a silly analogy will be helpful. Assume that you own a pet rottweiler named Spike. The dog is big, and ferocious. Whenever anyone in your neighborhood hears the name Spike they think of your dog—immediately conjuring up an image of its size, its bark, its sharp fangs and drooling saliva. You are free, of course, to sell the dog to any willing buyer, and as part of the transaction, you can allow the purchaser to continue to call the dog Spike. Imagine, however, that you want to sell just the name. You agree with a neighbor who owns a chihuahua that, for fifty dollars, you will stop calling your dog Spike and you will thereafter let him call his dog by that name. You can well imagine that for some time after this transaction your neighbors will be quite puzzled whenever they hear the name Spike. Expecting a ferocious guard dog, they will encounter instead, a distant relative of the former Taco Bell mascot.

The same logic obtains in the case of a trademark. If the company that owns and operates WESTIN brand hotels wants to get out of the hotel business, it can sell the various hotel buildings it owns along with the WESTIN trademark to any willing buyer. Subsequent to such a sale consumers who use the WESTIN trademark to pick a hotel for an

2. 15 U.S.C.A. § 1060(a) (2000).

3. Restatement (Third) of Unfair Competition § 34 (1995).

4. Sugar Busters L.L.C. v. Brennan, 177 F.3d 258 (5th Cir.1999).

upcoming trip will continue to encounter the same hotel buildings in the same locations with the same decor and facilities as they have come to associate with the mark. Consumer expectations will not in any way be thwarted. To consumers, it will be as if the sale never even occurred. On the other hand, if the original trademark owner attempted to sell merely the WESTIN trademark, the buyer might choose to affix it to hotels of an entirely different sort—perhaps smaller and with fewer amenities, perhaps with different and quirky decor, perhaps in only a few out of the way cities. Consumers booking a room at a WESTIN would, on arrival, be baffled and perhaps more than a little angry as well. The key, therefore, to a valid sale or "assignment" of a trademark is continuity in the thing symbolized by the mark before and after the sale, and that is why the law insists on a transfer of "accompanying goodwill" as part of a trademark assignment.

Unfortunately, goodwill is one of those slippery legal concepts like "domicile" or "reasonableness." It is usually defined as the reputation a business has established over time, and its consequent expectation of continued business in the future based on past success. A more customer-centered definition would focus on the propensity of consumers to continue to do business with a familiar name and the favorable attitude that consumers hold towards that name. In grappling with the concept in the context of a tax case, the U.S. Supreme Court did not offer its own definition, but noted that "the Courts of Appeals have consistently held that 'goodwill,' ... refers to 'the expectancy of continued patronage' from existing customers or, alternatively, to the prospect that 'the old customers will resort to the old place.' "[5]

This definition of goodwill seems to raise more problems than it solves. After all, how can a company transfer its "reputation" or its "expectation of continued business" or "the propensity of its customers" to continue to patronize it? While the case law is not entirely explicit on this issue, it does provide at least some guidance.

It is clear that the goodwill is usually conveyed if the assignor transfers the physical assets used to produce the product or render the service known by the relevant trademark. If the owner of local French pastry shop doing business as the CHAMPS ELYSEES bakery were to sell the store, the ovens, and all the other equipment to a new baker, along with an assignment of the CHAMPS ELYSEES trademark, the assignment would be unquestionably valid. In fact, the buyer of the physical assets in such a case would usually insist on the right to use the seller's trademark as part of the deal. After all, the buyer does not want to pay for the bakery only to see the seller re-open a block away under the old and familiar name, and by that maneuver deprive the buyer of the expectation of patronage which was the main reason for the sale.[6]

---

5. Newark Morning Ledger Co. v. United States, 507 U.S. 546, 572, 113 S.Ct. 1670, 123 L.Ed.2d 288 (1993).

6. Indeed, in such cases, it would also be usual for the buyer to ask the seller to agree to a non-competition arrangement as part of the contract of sale, which would be valid provided it is reasonable in scope and duration.

Note that although this transaction involves a clear transfer of goodwill and thus satisfies the prevailing legal rule against assignments in gross, it could nonetheless still result in some deception of the public. After all, the buyer of the pastry shop could be a very poor baker—his fruit tarts might taste much worse than those of the prior owner. Or the new owner might be cheap—he might try to save money by using inferior grades of flour and butter, which would give the products a taste different from what consumers had come to expect. He might change the hours of the store, or even the mix of pastries available. Customers, who have seen no external change in the appearance of the shop nor in the trademark on the window may well be confused as a consequence. The patron who comes looking for almond croissants to discover only chocolate cupcakes is likely to be sorely disappointed.

This example demonstrates that the rule concerning assignments in gross works only approximately to implement to purpose of avoiding public confusion. Nonetheless, while the risks identified in the previous paragraph are real, they are probably not too severe. Presumably, the buyer has a strong incentive to run the business in a manner roughly similar to his predecessor, precisely in order to hold on to the customers. It is that incentive that makes it rational both to treat a transfer of goodwill as some guarantee of post-sale consumer satisfaction, and to treat a sale of physical assets as an adequate transfer of goodwill.

Indeed, modern courts tend to treat the rule requiring goodwill to accompany trademark assignments pragmatically rather than mechanically. Thus, many recent cases hold that it is not necessary to transfer physical assets or to sell the entirety of the business in order to convey goodwill and avoid the pitfall of an assignment in gross. As one opinion put it, a "trademark may be validly transferred without the simultaneous transfer of any tangible assets, as long as the recipient continues to produce goods of the same quality and nature previously associated with the mark."[7] The key is not what the defendant gets as part of the transaction, but rather what the defendant does thereafter, or, as the commentary to the Restatement puts it, "courts now examine not only the content of the assignment but also the nature of the assignee's subsequent use.... The traditional rule requiring an accompanying transfer of 'good will' can thus be seen as a requirement that the assignment preserve the significance of the mark to consumers."[8] As the Seventh Circuit has said, "[t]he central purpose of the technical rules regarding the assignment of trademarks is to protect consumers, and these rules were 'not evolved for the purpose of invalidating all trade-

7. Defiance Button Machine Co. v. C & C Metal Products Corp., 759 F.2d 1053, 1059 (2d Cir.1985), *cert. denied*, 474 U.S. 844, 106 S.Ct. 131, 88 L.Ed.2d 108 (1985). *See also* Visa, U.S.A., Inc. v. Birmingham Trust Nat. Bank, 696 F.2d 1371 (Fed.Cir. 1982) ("A valid transfer of a mark, howev- er, does not require the transfer of any physical or tangible assets. All that is necessary is the transfer of the goodwill to which the mark pertains.").

8. Restatement (Third) of Unfair Competition § 34, comment b (1995).

mark assignments which do not satisfy a stereo-typed set of formalities.' "[9]

Applying these principles to concrete fact patterns, a court might hold that a trademark assignment along with the sale of a secret formula to make the trademarked product was valid even though no physical assets changed hands.[10] The same result would follow if the trademark assignor also conveyed relevant patents or copyrights as part of the transactions. After all, the transfer of formulas or other forms of intellectual property is the essential device that will permit the buyer to make products with the same attributes that consumers have historically associated with the trademark. Brief reflection suggests that in cases involving patented products, even the sale of physical assets as part of a trademark assignment should not be enough to validate that assignment unless the patent is also conveyed, because without the patent there could be no continuity in the qualities of the trademarked item before and after the sale.

In the case of a mark for services, continuity of management might satisfy the requirement for a transfer of goodwill. For example, in *Marshak v. Green*,[11] Marshak had been the manager of the music group known as THE DRIFTERS prior to assignment of that trademark and continued in that capacity after the assignment. Because he continued to offer to the public a group that had the same singing style after the transfer as it did before, the court concluded that the assignment was valid, and not an impermissible assignment "in gross." As one court has noted, since physical assets are less significant in service oriented business, "the transfer of goodwill requires only that the services be sufficiently similar to prevent consumers of the services from being 'misled from established associations with the mark.' "[12] In certain types of personal service businesses where the goodwill of the enterprise is thoroughly bound up with the skill of the person operating the business—for instance a medical or dental practice—there may no way to convey that goodwill, and thus no possibility of executing a valid trademark assignment.

Because the rule about goodwill is designed to protect the public, it is never satisfied by mere incantation. A recitation in a contract assigning a trademark that "goodwill" is also being transferred is not the end of the matter. Courts will look past the self-serving rhetoric of the parties to the underlying reality of the transaction. Moreover, even if there is a transfer of physical assets or other unequivocal token of goodwill, the courts will treat the assignment as void if the assignee then

9. Money Store v. Harriscorp Finance, Inc., 689 F.2d 666, 676 (7th Cir.1982) (quoting Syntex Laboratories, Inc. v. Norwich Pharmacal Co., 315 F.Supp. 45, 54 (S.D.N.Y.1970), *aff'd*, 437 F.2d 566 (2d Cir. 1971)).

10. Mulhens & Kropff v. Ferd Muelhens, 43 F.2d 937 (2d Cir.1930), *cert. de-*

nied, 282 U.S. 881, 51 S.Ct. 84, 75 L.Ed. 777 (1930).

11. 505 F.Supp. 1054 (S.D.N.Y.1981).

12. Visa, U.S.A., Inc. v. Birmingham Trust Nat'l Bank, 696 F.2d 1371 (Fed.Cir. 1982), *cert. denied*, 464 U.S. 826, 104 S.Ct. 98, 78 L.Ed.2d 104 (1983).

uses the mark on products or services of a fundamentally different nature than those previously sold by the assignor. As one court explained, "[i]nherent in the rules involving the assignment of a trademark is the recognition of protection against consumer deception. Basic to this concept is the proposition that any assignment of a trademark and its goodwill (with or without tangibles or intangibles assigned) requires the mark itself be used by the assignee on a product having substantially the same characteristics."[13]

While the assignee of a trademark is thus obligated to purchase goodwill and to continue to use the mark in connection with products of the same basic nature as the assignor, minor alterations in the product will not call the transaction into question or constitute an abandonment of the mark. In *Bambu Sales, Inc. v. Sultana Crackers, Inc.*[14] the plaintiff sold cigarette papers in the United States under the BAMBU trademark as the licensee of a Spanish company. When the Spanish company became insolvent, its liquidators assigned the mark to the plaintiff. Sometime later, the plaintiff sued several defendants for selling counterfeit BAMBU cigarette papers. Those defendants challenged plaintiffs rights in the mark, noting in part that the plaintiff had changed the quality of the paper used from that which had been sold by its Spanish predecessor because its papers were allegedly thinner and more difficult to roll.

The court rejected the challenge, observing that while "[i]t is true that a substantial change in the goods sold under a mark may so alter the nature of the good will symbolized that use of the mark is tantamount to a fraud on consumers and the original right to the mark is abandoned or lost," where the product was "essentially the same before and after the transfer, variations in type or quality will not invalidate the assignment." This seems entirely sound. Merchants frequently change the ingredients or specifications of their trademarked products and most consumers understand that over time such products do not remain unaltered. The key issue is whether the product is sufficiently similar to what consumers have been getting in the past that they will not feel deceived or manipulated.

In addition to the requirement concerning the transfer of goodwill, there are some other facts that can affect the validity of a trademark assignment. First, a corollary of the goodwill rule is that a party may not assign a trademark before it has made use of that mark. Prior to use, there will be no goodwill associated with the mark—actually, under U.S. law, prior to use, there really is no mark at all. Thus, if a firm thinks up a new name, and then decides to sell that name to another party, the other party has effectively paid for something that it could have had for free. A closely related rule is the provision of the Lanham Act that makes it impermissible to assign one's interest in a federal "intent-to-

13. PepsiCo, Inc. v. Grapette Co., 416 F.2d 285 (8th Cir.1969).

14. 683 F.Supp. 899 (E.D.N.Y.1988).

use" registration application prior to making use.[15] Congress included this section to avoid creating a market in abstract trademark rights.

Second, there is no requirement that an assignment at common law trademark rights be in writing.[16] Of course an oral contract over something as important and formal as a trademark would be rare. The rule dispensing with a writing is most important because it enables courts to find a trademark assignment in cases where a party sells its entire business, but the written contract of sale makes no explicit reference to trademark rights. This is sometimes called the "automatic transfer" doctrine.[17] Note, however, that section 10 of the Lanham Act does require a writing to effectuate a transfer of a federally registered mark.[18]

32.1.2 Consequences of Valid and Invalid Assignments

When an assignment conforms to the rules requiring transfer of good will, the assignee steps into the shoes of the assignor.[19] The most important consequence of that fact is that the assignee can claim priority in the trademark dating back to the time of the assignor's first use. For instance, assume Alpha Corporation began using the mark ICY for air conditioners in 1985. In 1995, it assigns the ICY mark, and the related goodwill in its air conditioner business to Beta Corporation. In 1997, Beta learns of another company, Omega, that is using the identical mark on its own competing line of air conditioners. When Beta sues Omega for infringement Omega offers to prove that it began use of the ICY name in 1994, a year before Beta began its own use of that very same mark. Given the assignment, however, that evidence would be irrelevant. Beta stands in Alpha's shoes, and it thus can claim first use as of 1985. It would thus clearly have priority in the mark and it would be entitled to an injunction against Omega.

After a valid assignment, the assignor no longer owns the mark. This is simple fairness. Having successfully sold the asset, it can no longer assert ownership of it. That means that if the assignor continues to the use mark after the transaction, it would be liable both for breach of contract and for trademark infringement. In such a case, the assignor

---

15. 15 U.S.C.A. § 1060(a) (2000). If an ITU applicant uses the mark before the examination process is complete it can file what is known as an "amendment to allege use," or AAU, and that will convert the application to a use-based application under section 1(a) of the Lanham Act. If there is no use until after examination is complete and a notice of allowance has issued, the applicant must then file a "statement of use," or SOU, in order to complete the registration process and obtain the registration. Under section 10 of the Lanham Act, an ITU application cannot be transferred to another party prior to the filing of either an AAU or SOU.

16. Martha Graham School and Dance Foundation, Inc. v. Martha Graham Center

of Contemporary Dance, Inc., 43 Fed.Appx. 408 (2d Cir.2002); Speed Products Co. v. Tinnerman Products, 179 F.2d 778 (2d Cir. 1949).

17. Dovenmuehle v. Gilldorn Mortg. Midwest Corp., 871 F.2d 697 (7th Cir.1989) ("Absent contrary evidence, a business trade name is presumed to pass to its buyer.").

18. "Assignments shall be by instruments in writing duly executed." 15 U.S.C.A. § 1060(a) (2000).

19. Carnival Brand Seafood Co. v. Carnival Brands, Inc., 187 F.3d 1307, 1310 (11th Cir.1999); Premier Dental Products Co. v. Darby Dental Supply Co., Inc., 794 F.2d 850, 853 (3d Cir.1986).

might attempt to escape infringement liability by challenging the validity of the mark—for instance by arguing that it had become generic, or that it was merely descriptive and lacked secondary meaning. There is some slight authority suggesting that in such a situation the assignor will be estopped from making any such argument. This principle seems logical. Having taken money for the assignment previously, it is more than a little inconsistent for the assignor to now claim that what it sold is worthless because the mark is invalid. The assignor's argument amounts to a declaration that it was nothing more than a thief when it previously took the assignee's money in exchange for the alleged trademark rights.

If an assignment is invalid (usually because it is found to be "in gross"), it conveys nothing. In theory, then, the assignor should still own the mark. In the vast majority of cases, however, the assignor will stop using the mark shortly after the assignment. Moreover its agreement to assign is strong evidence of an intent not to resume use of the mark in question.[20] Effectively, therefore, the assignor will be found to have abandoned the mark by its assignment in gross. The assignee, who will likely begin use shortly after the assignment, will be able to claim trademark rights based on its own use, but it can have no claim to a priority dating back before the time it began making sales under the mark. In other words, it cannot claim the priority date of the assignor. In the example above, if the assignment from Alpha to Beta is found to be invalid, Beta's right would date only from 1995, because that is when it first used the ICY mark. That would make Beta a junior user vis-a-vis Omega, who used the mark in 1994, and thus deprive Beta of its rights to the mark. Moreover, prior to its own use, the assignee in an invalid assignment transaction owns nothing, and would lack standing to sue third parties for infringement.

Although an invalid assignment means that the assignee cannot claim priority from the date of the assignor's first use, it still has consequences as between the two parties. The assignor in such a situation cannot sue the assignee for infringement when the assignee begins to use the mark. As the comments to the Restatement put it, "the rule against assignments in gross does not invalidate the agreement as between the parties."[21]

32.1.3   Recordation of Assignments

The Lanham Act establishes a permissive system for recording trademark assignments. There is no requirement to record, and the assignment will generally be valid even if not recorded. As is usual with such schemes, however, recordation provides protection in the event that assignor purports to subsequently assign the same mark to another party who has no notice of the first assignment. This rule is worded in the negative, with the Lanham Act specifying: "An assignment shall be

20. "[A]n assignment in gross followed by a period of nonuse by the assignor may result in abandonment of the assignor's priority in the use of the mark . . . ." Restate-ment (Third) of Unfair Competition § 34, cmt. f (1995).

21. Restatement (Third) of Unfair Competition § 34, comment b (1995).

void against any assignment for valuable consideration without notice, unless the prescribed information reporting the assignment is recorded in the Patent and Trademark Office within 3 months after the date of the subsequent purchase or prior to the subsequent purchase."[22]

Working an example should make the effect of this provision clear. Assume Alpha assigns its registered trademark (and accompanying goodwill) to Beta in February. Further assume that Alpha is unscrupulous, and enters into a second purported assignment transaction involving the very same mark, this time with Gamma, in the month of June. Gamma, in this example, knows nothing of the earlier Alpha–Beta deal and is behaving entirely in good faith. Under the quoted statutory provision, if Beta records its assignment at the PTO any time either prior to June, or within three months after June, Beta will have superior rights to Gamma. If Beta fails to record, however, then Gamma would have the superior rights.

Under recent amendments to the Lanham Act, the actual documents conveying the trademark need not be recorded. The PTO will now also accept "a copy of an extract from the document evidencing the effect on the title," or a "statement signed by both the party conveying the interest and the party receiving the interest explaining how the conveyance affects title" as adequate proof of the transfer.[23] This, of course, permits parties to keep the full details of their business transactions private while still gaining the benefits of the recordation. Congress adopted these amendments to conform U.S. law to the 1994 Trademark Law Treaty.[24]

32.1.4 Security Interests and Bankruptcy Transfers

Many firms need to borrow money to operate. Many lenders will not lend money, however, unless the loan is secured by some valuable asset. In some cases, the most valuable asset owned by the borrower is its trademark. It follows that in many situations, a borrower will want to use its trademark as security for a loan by giving the lender a security interest in that mark. In effect, such an arrangement can be thought of as an "agreement to assign in the event of a default."

Since the grant of the security interest is not itself a trademark assignment, but merely a contingent promise to assign in the future, there need be no simultaneous transfer of physical assets or goodwill at the time the security interest is granted. However, in the event that the trademark owner defaults and the lender seeks to enforce the security agreement, a transfer under the security agreement would be an invalid assignment in gross unless it included an accompanying transfer of goodwill. Thus, to avoid having the security interest in the trademark

---

22.   15 U.S.C.A. § 1060(a) (2000).

23.   37 C.F.R. § 3.25 (2002).

24.   The relevant treaty provision is Article 11 of the Trademark Law Treaty. The legislation conforming U.S. law to the trea-

ty is the Trademark Law Treaty Implementation Act, P.L. 105–330, 112 Stat. 3064 (October 30, 1998). The U.S. formally became a party to this treaty on August 12, 2000.

reduced to a worthless promise, the lender effectively must obtain a related promise in the security interest agreement that goodwill will be transferred along with the mark in the event of default. As noted above, this might be accomplished by also taking a security interest in tangible assets related to the production of the trademarked goods, or in other incidents of goodwill such as formulas and customer lists.

As anyone who has studied the law of secured transactions is aware, in order to "perfect" a security interest, it is necessary to file documents detailing the transaction with the government. This provides notice to other potential lenders about the true financial situation of the borrower and advises them that they may not be able to rely on certain assets to satisfy a debt in the event of a default because those assets have been promised to another creditor. With regard to security interests in federally registered trademarks, one might wonder whether the necessary filing should be made at U.S. Patent and Trademark Office, under the Lanham Act, or whether it should be made in a state office, under the Uniform Commercial Code. The UCC has provisions that defer to federal filing schemes where such schemes are required.[25] The relevant provision of the Lanham Act, however, only deals with recordation of actual assignments, not with the recordations of security interest. Thus, "[c]ase law addressing the issue . . . consistently supports the proposition that the Lanham Act does not pertain to security interests and that Article 9 [of the UCC], therefore, continues to govern the perfection of such interests."[26] To perfect a security interest in a trademark, the relevant documents should thus be filed at the relevant state office, often that of the Secretary of State.

Where a trademark owner goes bankrupt, the trustee in bankruptcy succeeds to all the assets owned by that party. This includes both physical assets and intangibles such as trademarks. As a result, the trustee will be able to convey both the trademark and the related goodwill to any third party willing to pay for it.[27] Trustees are also subject to the rule against assignments in gross, however, and they cannot validly convey the trademarks independently of the goodwill. Where the trustee sells the entire business, it has been held that the trademarks will impliedly pass to the buyer even if no mention is made about trademarks in the contract of sale.[28]

§ 32.2   Licensing

A trademark license is a grant of permission by a trademark owner to another party to sell goods or services under the owner's mark. It does not convey ownership rights in the mark, which remain with the

---

25. Thus, under § 9–302(3)(a) of the UCC, there is an exception to the requirement of a state filing if a "statute . . . of the United States . . . provides for a national registration or . . . specifies a place of filing different from that specified in this division for filing of the security interest."

26. Trimarchi, Personal Dating Servs. v. Together Dev. Corp., 255 B.R. 606, 611 (D.Mass.2000) (citing cases).

27. Haymaker Sports, Inc. v. Turian, 581 F.2d 257 (CCPA 1978).

28. American Dirigold Corp. v. Dirigold Metals Corp.,125 F.2d 446 (6th Cir.1942).

licensor. A license is necessary if, without one, the licensee would liable for infringement if it used the mark on the relevant goods. Trademark licensing arrangements are widespread and enormously important in today's economy. Most restaurants operating under the MCDONALD'S trademark are not owned by the McDonald's corporation, but rather by independent operators who have a license to use its famous trademark, and pay for the privilege. Similarly, most gas stations operating under the EXXON trademark are not owned by Exxon–Mobil, but by independent business people. Even outside the franchising context, trademark licensing is prevalent. Many trademarked toys, packaged foods, drugs and cosmetic products are not manufactured by the mark owner, but rather by a licensee.

Prior to the 1930's, trademark licensing was not very common, and courts were generally hostile to it.[1] In that early era courts felt that a trademark identified the source of goods, and source only. If the ABC corporation owned the trademark ACME for widgets, those courts saw it as logically impossible for it to license the XYZ company to make and sell widgets under the ACME name. Those later widgets could not be genuine ACME, even if ABC supervised every detail of their manufacture, because they did not "come from ABC"—and that was the necessary and only message conveyed to the public if the goods were labeled with the ACME trademark.

A conceptual breakthrough occurred when courts decided that a trademark's chief significance to consumers was as a signal of the attributes of the relevant product or service, rather than as a designation of its source. On this view, the mark ACME means widgets of certain properties, and the consumer is largely indifferent as to who makes them. Another version of this insight is that trademarks can indicate either source or *sponsorship*, so that the mark ACME could mean either "comes from ABC" or made under the sponsorship, supervision, and watchful eye of ABC, but perhaps actually physically put together by someone else. The adoption of the Lanham Act after World War II gave doctrinal support to this new view of the function of trademarks and ushered in an era of widespread trademark licensing along with a generally sympathetic judicial reaction to such schemes.

The parties are free to structure a trademark licensing business arrangement however they see fit. Thus, a license can give the licensee exclusive rights to use the marks either nationwide, or only in a particular territory or from a single location, or the licensor can reserve the right to compete with the licensee or to license other parties to do so. The parties can agree that the licensee is free to sub-license others, or they can specifically forbid sub-licensing. The license can last indefinitely or for a specified term. The parties may agree on any amount and method of payment that they like, though it is customary to tie licensing

§ 32.2

1. For a review of the history *see* K-Mart Corp. v. Cartier, Inc., 486 U.S. 281, 108 S.Ct. 1811, 100 L.Ed.2d 313 (1988) (Brennan, J. concurring and dissenting).

fees to the amount of goods sold or revenues earned from use of the mark. Where there are ambiguities in the terms of a trademark license, ordinary principles of contract law will control any dispute over those terms. While most trademark licenses will be reduced to writing, there is no requirement that they must be, and an oral license agreement is valid.[2] Where necessary, courts may even imply a trademark license based on the dealings of the parties. After a trademark license is terminated, the licensee must stop using the mark. Continued use of a trademark by an ex-licensee is actionable trademark infringement.

32.2.1 Quality Control Requirements and the Dangers of "Naked" Licensing

Just as there is a key requirement for a valid trademark assignment (namely the simultaneous transfer of goodwill), there is a key requirement for a valid license—the trademark owner must supervise the licensee and insure that the licensee observes quality control standards. Licensing without quality supervision of the licensee is usually labeled "naked" licensing, and will result in a finding that the owner of the mark has abandoned its rights. As noted previously, the use of the label "abandonment" in this case is a bit of a stretch, because there is likely no intent on the part of a sloppy trademark licensor to give up its rights. If abandonment properly refers only to an intentional relinquishment of rights, it is a misnomer to use the word in the context of naked licensing, because any licensor, even one who does not engage in quality control, intends to retain the trademark. Nonetheless, the use of the word "abandonment" has become so common in judicial language to describe this situation that it is entirely accurate to refer to the consequence of naked licensing as an abandonment. Substantively, whatever vocabulary you may prefer, the key point to bear in mind is that naked licensing will result in loss of trademark rights.

This basic tenet of trademark licensing applies to both common law marks and those that are federally registered. With respect to the common law situation, the Restatement declares: "The owner of a trademark, trade name, collective mark, or certification mark may license another to use the designation. If the licensor exercises reasonable control over the nature and quality of the goods, services, or business on which the designation is used by the licensee, any rights in the designation arising from the licensee's use accrue to the benefit of the licensor. Failure of the licensor to exercise reasonable control over the use of the designation by the licensee can result in abandonment of the designation...."[3]

The Lanham Act does not have an explicit provision to the same effect, but it has been read as standing for the same proposition. It permits the use of registered marks by related companies "provided such

2. Council of Better Business Bureaus, Inc. v. Better Business Bureau, Inc., 200 USPQ 282 (S.D.Fla.1978).

3. Restatement (Third) of Unfair Competition § 33 (1995).

mark is not used in such manner as to deceive the public."[4] It also provides that use by a "related company" may inure to the benefit of the trademark owner. Finally, it defines a related company as "any person whose use of a mark is controlled by the owner of the mark with respect to the nature and quality of the goods or services on or in connection with which the mark is used."[5] Read together, these provisions impose a quality control obligation on those who license federally registered marks. Thus, both the federal and state case law are to the same effect, requiring quality control as a condition of a valid trademark license, and treating naked licensing as an abandonment of the trademark.[6]

The goal of the quality control requirement is one we have seen repeatedly in all areas of trademark law—the avoidance of public confusion. The key attribute consumers expect when purchasing trademarked goods is consistency. If a trademark licensee provides goods or services identical to those of the licensor, consumer expectations will be met. If, however, the licensee produces goods that differ in significant ways from those the consumer became familiar with before the licensing program began, the consumer will in all likelihood be disturbed. The best way to make sure that does not happen is to require the licensor to keep a watchful eye over the business of the licensee.

Note that neither the black letter rule nor the policy of consumer protection requires that the goods be of any particular quality. A given mark may signal goods of relatively modest quality that may succeed in the market place because they are priced modestly. So long as licensees make goods of the same modest quality as those of the licensor, the purpose of the trademark laws is being fulfilled, and the license should be valid.

In determining whether there has been adequate quality control of a trademark licensee, courts are generally rather lenient. Several opinions, noting the severe consequences that follow from a finding of naked licensing, have held that a party claiming such naked licensing must prove the allegation with clear and convincing evidence, or must satisfy a "stringent" or "high" burden of proof.[7] Other courts have arrived at pretty much the same place by holding substantively, that the required level of quality control is rather slight. As the Fifth Circuit declared in a case involving licensees of the KENTUCKY FRIED CHICKEN mark, "retention of a trademark requires only minimal quality control, for in this context we do not sit to assess the quality of products sold on the open market. We must determine whether Kentucky Fried has aban-

4. 15 U.S.C.A. § 1055 (2000).

5. 15 U.S.C.A. § 1127 (2000).

6. *See, e.g.,* AmCan Enterprises, Inc. v. Renzi, 32 F.3d 233 (7th Cir.1994) ("If the licensor does not maintain adequate quality control, the mark may be deemed abandoned ...."); Haymaker Sports, Inc. v. Turian, 581 F.2d 257 (CCPA 1978) ("Uncontrolled licensing of a mark results in abandonment of the mark by the licensor."); Ritz Associates, Inc. v. Ritz–Carlton Hotel Co., 35 Misc.2d 425, 230 N.Y.S.2d 408, 134 USPQ 86 (Sup.1962).

7. *See, e.g.,* Stanfield v. Osborne Indus., 52 F.3d 867 (10th Cir.1995), *cert. denied,* 516 U.S. 920, 116 S.Ct. 314, 133 L.Ed.2d 217; Exxon Corp. v. Oxxford Clothes, Inc., 109 F.3d 1070 (5th Cir.1997).

doned quality control; the consuming public must be the judge of whether the quality control efforts have been ineffectual."[8]

In evaluating the adequacy of quality control programs, most courts focus on whether the licensor exercised actual control over the licensee rather than on whether the trademark owner had a theoretical or legal right of control. As one trial court explained, "the licensor is not limited by the absence of quality control provisions in the license agreement. If in fact the licensor has made a reasonable inspection of the merchandise bearing the trademark (even though not every item has been inspected) and there is no showing that any of the goods were below the essential quality standards,"[9] no "naked licensing" or trademark abandonment will be found. Explicit contractual provisions concerning supervision or control are thus neither necessary nor sufficient to make the licensing program valid. The question is always what did the trademark owner/licensor do in the way of supervision, not what it was legally entitled to do.

Not surprisingly, the precise details of an appropriate quality control program will vary with the circumstances, the industry, and the nature of the goods. Professor McCarthy observes that the "control that may be sufficient for licensing a soft drink mark for use on T-shirts may be totally inadequate for licensing a pharmaceutical trademark for use on prescription drugs."[10] The Restatement concurs, observing that "cases both under the [Lanham] Act and at common law apply a flexible standard responsive to the particular facts of each case. The ultimate issue is whether the control exercised by the licensor is sufficient under the circumstances to satisfy the public's expectation of quality assurance arising from the presence of the trademark on the licensee's goods or services."[11] There are even cases that hold that the trademark owner may simply rely on the licensee's own self-policing as to quality, at least in situations where there is a track record of consistent quality products, or where the licensor is supplying the components for the goods.[12] Even

8. Kentucky Fried Chicken Corp. v. Diversified Packaging Corp., 549 F.2d 368 (5th Cir.1977).

9. Carl Zeiss Stiftung v. V. E. B. Carl Zeiss, Jena, 293 F.Supp. 892 (S.D.N.Y. 1968). *See also* First Interstate Bancorp v. Stenquist, 1990 WL 300321, *4 (N.D.Cal. 1990) ("the lack of an express contract right to inspect and supervise a licensee's operations is not conclusive evidence of lack of control. . . . However, where the courts have excused the absence of a contractual right of control, they have still required that the licensor demonstrate actual control through some sort of inspection or supervision."). There are, however, cases to the contrary. *See, e.g.*, Cartier, Inc. v. Three Sheaves Co., 465 F.Supp. 123 (S.D.N.Y. 1979) (absence of quality control provisions in licensing agreement rendered license void); Robinson Co. v. Plastics Research &

Development Corp., 264 F.Supp. 852 (D.Ark.1967) ("it is the right to control rather than the actual exercise of control which determines whether or not a licenses is valid.").

10. J. Thomas McCarthy, TRADEMARKS & UNFAIR COMPETITION § 18:55 (2001).

11. Restatement (Third) of Unfair Competition § 33, comment c (1995).

12. *See, e.g.* Land O'Lakes Creameries, Inc. v. Oconomowoc Canning Co., 221 F.Supp. 576, 581 (E.D.Wis.1963), *aff'd,* 330 F.2d 667 (7th Cir.1964). The Restatement endorses this view, in appropriate cases, but not where the licensee is "inexperienced" or where "the goods or services are particularly complex or require careful supervision." *See* Restatement (Third) of Unfair Competition § 33, comment c (1995).

if permissible in the abstract, however, this arrangement should be less likely to pass judicial muster in cases where there are multiple licensees because of the heightened risk of inconsistent product quality if there is no direct oversight by the licensor.

Some courts seem influenced by whether the quality control is regularized, and carried out by skilled personnel, versus whether it is haphazard, sporadic, or conducted by employees with no real expertise in evaluating product quality. Obviously, the tendency is to find that latter types of "quality control programs" inadequate. The absence of any customer complaints or evidence of customer confusion may also be relevant, especially in a close case, as indicative that the licensee has maintained consistent quality. If the arrangement involves an "assignment and license back," the licensee will be the party which originated the trademark and already has a track record of producing goods under that mark. In such cases, a contractual promise by the licensee to maintain its own former standards of quality could be sufficient. Finally, it should be noted that more is not always better where quality supervision of licensees is concerned. An overly zealous quality control program may run afoul of certain antitrust law prohibitions, especially those forbidding "tying arrangements."

The failure of the licensee to conform to quality control requirements that form part of the license agreement is a breach of that agreement, and it will leave the licensee open to liability under contract law principles. If the licensee continues to sell goods marked with the trademark, but which do not conform to required quality control standards, that will also be considered trademark infringement.[13]

There is one form of modern trademark licensing that fits poorly with the traditional requirement of quality control. Many trademark owners license their marks for use on "promotional goods" such as tee-shirts, hats or jackets. The underlying mark usually has nothing to do with clothing. Often it will be the trademark of a professional sports team, or perhaps of a college or university. Increasingly, however, it may be the trademark of a company that makes heavy equipment, food or drugs, or computers. For instance, it would not be uncommon to see baseball caps emblazoned with the JOHN DEERE trademark that is ordinarily used for farm machinery, or to see tee-shirts with word and logo marks for BEN AND JERRY'S ice cream. As we saw in an earlier chapter, modern cases take the view that unauthorized use of trademarks on such promotional goods is infringing, and thus the manufacturers of such goods need trademark licenses to avoid infringement liability.[14]

The authors of the Restatement anticipated this situation. They observed that "[i]f a licensee uses the trademark of a beer or soft drink manufacturer on clothing or glassware, for example, prospective purchasers may be unlikely to assume that the owner of the trademark has

---

13. *See* Franchised Stores of New York, Inc. v. Winter, 394 F.2d 664 (2d Cir.1968).

14. *See* § 29.3.2, *supra*.

more than perfunctory involvement in the production or quality of the licensee's goods even if the manner of use clearly indicates sponsorship by the trademark owner."[15] From this observation they conclude that the quality control measures required in such a case to avoid naked licensing would be quite minimal. Some commentators have gone even further and suggested that no quality control at all should be required in such cases. As one author summarized: "The argument for abolishing the quality control requirement focuses on the fact that in promotional merchandising the consumer does not expect a preordained quality level; therefore, the licensor should not be subject to the unnecessary expense of instituting quality standards without any real benefit to consumers."[16]

Perhaps this goes too far. In our view, policy considerations suggest that the trademark licensor should at least be expected to police the promotional goods to insure that the mark itself is faithfully represented on the promotional items. In other words, it should inspect the tee-shirts to see that the colors of its logo have been accurately reproduced, that the mark is spelled correctly, and that trademark characters look their familiar selves. Second, it seems reasonable to think that the promotional goods should have a quality profile comparable to the quality profile maintained by the trademark owner in its primary industry. Consumers would likely expect that a licensed tee-shirt bearing the ROLLS–ROYCE or TIFFANY trademarks would be a high quality shirt. Finally, once the licensee begins producing the promotional items, whatever their quality, the licensor should take steps to make sure that the quality level remains stable and does not fluctuate. The JOHN DEERE baseball cap purchased in June should be the same quality product as one purchased the previous January.

32.2.2 Licensee Estoppel

Not all trademark licensing arrangements go smoothly. Some even wind up leading to litigation between the licensor and the licensee. In that litigation, the licensee might wish to argue that the licensor's marks are invalid. For instance, the licensee might argue that because there was inadequate quality control, the very licensing arrangement that it was party to actually resulted in an abandonment of the mark and a loss of rights. Several cases have held, however, that the licensee is forbidden to challenge the validity of the trademark. The doctrine is known as licensee estoppel.[17]

In the patent context, the Supreme Court rejected the licensee estoppel doctrine in *Lear v. Adkins*.[18] There, the Supreme Court reasoned that the strong public interest in maximum access to non-patent-

---

15. Restatement (Third) of Unfair Competition § 33, comment c (1995).

16. Lisa H. Johnston, *Drifting Toward Trademark Rights in Gross*, 85 Trademark Rep. 19, 35–36 (1995).

17. Professional Golfers Ass'n of America v. Bankers Life & Cas. Co., 514 F.2d 665, 671 (5th Cir.1975) (citing cases); Westco Group, Inc. v. K.B. & Associates, Inc., 128 F.Supp.2d 1082, 1088 (N.D.Ohio 2001).

18. 395 U.S. 653, 89 S.Ct. 1902, 23 L.Ed.2d 610 (1969).

worthy technology warranted a rule that permitted licensees to challenge patents. Because the policy concerns differ in the trademark context, and because there is no similarly strong interest in invalidating trademarks, courts that have considered the issue after *Lear* have not applied its holding to trademark licensees. Thus, the licensee estoppel rule survives in the trademark context.

Most cases hold that a trademark licensee is only estopped from raising challenges to the trademark that relate to events during the course of the license—such as inadequate quality control. The licensee remains free to challenge the mark based on events that occurred after the termination of the license.[19]

If a licensor violates exclusivity provisions in a trademark licensing agreement, by selling trademarked goods in competition with the licensee, the licensee cannot sue for infringement. This is not because of the estoppel doctrine, but rather because the licensee does not own the trademark. Without title to the mark, it has no standing to complain of infringement. It is not, however, helpless in this situation. It can sue instead for breach of contract, arguing that the licensor has failed to live up to its promises.

---

19. *See, e.g.,* WCVB–TV v. Boston Athletic Ass'n, 926 F.2d 42 (1st Cir.1991); National Council of YMCA v. Columbia YMCA, 8 USPQ2d 1682 (D.S.C.1988).

Chapter 33

TRADEMARKS ON THE INTERNET

Table of Sections

---

§ 33.1   Trademarks and the Internet

In the early days of the Internet, some harbored the dream that it would become a new medium of intellectual exchange and free communication unsullied by the taint of crass commerce. Indeed, prior to 1993, the Internet was limited to non-commercial uses and was funded by the government. In that year, however, the government turned over effective administration of the Internet to a private corporation. Commercial use soon followed.[1] The Internet, or at least that portion of it known as the World Wide Web,[2] is now thoroughly, utterly, and irrevocably commercialized. Although the initial euphoria over the Internet as a new commercial space may have subsided somewhat with the tumbling stock

---

§ 33.1

1. *See* Jessica Littman, *The DNS Wars: Trademarks and the Internet Domain Name System*, 4 J. SMALL & EMERGING BUS. L. 149, 150 (2000).

2. Technically, the World Wide Web is only a portion of the Internet, consisting of those computers supporting specially formatted computer files written in the computer code known as "hypertext mark-up language," or HTML. *See*, http://www.webopedia.com/TERM/W/World_Wide_Web.html

787

market of the early 2000's, it is plain that the use of cyberspace as a venue for transacting business is here to stay.

With commerce comes trademarks. As soon as firms began to offer goods or services over the Internet, they began to use trademarks. Not long thereafter, they began to fight with each over the use of those trademarks. Many of the issues that have come up—and that will come up in the future—involving the use of trademarks on the Internet are routine and familiar trademark disputes. Old wine in new bottles, if you will. For instance, if someone tries to sell cameras over the World Wide Web and calls those cameras KODUCK brand on its web page, when the owner of the KODAK mark brings suit for infringement and dilution, the analysis will be identical to any other trademark controversy.[3] Cyberspace, shmyberspace—there will be liability.

On the other hand, the use of trademarks in connection with e-commerce has generated a variety of new problems unique to the Internet. Most of these problems are outgrowths of the underlying technology or architecture of the Internet itself. In other words, they flow from how web sites are identified and indexed, or from other features of the software that powers the Web. To the extent that the problems are by-products of current technology, they may not be around for long. As computer technology changes, old problems will vanish and new ones will arise. Thus the discussion which follows is in particular danger of being obsolete by the time you read it, and the cautious reader must be alert to that fact.

Perhaps the problem that received the greatest attention in the late 1990's and in the early years of the new century has been the use of trademarks as "domain names"—the names by which a given site or page on the World Wide Web is identified. Other problems relate to the use by Web site owners of other's trademarks as links on their web sites, and to the use of such marks in hidden computer code, not visible to a web surfer, but which can be read by a search engine. Where Web site owners have sold advertising to third parties in the form of banners or "pop-ups" on their site, they have sometimes keyed those advertising messages to the use of another party's trademark word, to the displeasure of the trademark owner. In still other situations, the senders of bulk e-mail have made references to trademarks that they do not own either in the text of their messages or in the "header" of those messages. What follows is a whirlwind tour of these issues and a snapshot of the law that attempts to deal with them as it stands at the dawn of the twenty-first century.

3. One treatise writer has observed that "traditional legal principles apply in determining the existence of trademark rights, priority of use, and likelihood of confusion. In other words, there is no Lanham Act exception for the Internet ...." Jerome Gilson, Trademark Protection and Practice § 7A.01[1].

§ 33.2   The Use of Trademarks in Domain Names

33.2.1   The Domain Name System and "Cybersquatting"

A necessary predicate to understanding the legal disputes that have arisen over domain names is some basic information about how the Internet works.[1] The Internet is a global system by which millions of computers are linked together. Through this linkage they can send each other messages (think of e-mail), they can exchange files (think of Napster), and they each can access the data that has been stored on all the others (think of the World Wide Web). To do any of this, however, you have to be able to find the other computer in this vast network that you are interested in contacting. The Domain Name System, or DNS, is what makes that possible.

Whenever a computer becomes part of the Internet it is assigned a unique address. Formally known as its IP (or Internet Protocol) address, this address is nothing more than a unique string of numbers.[2] Because these numeric strings are hard to remember, the DNS allows words and phrases to function as "synonyms" for IP addresses. These alphanumeric synonyms are more familiarly known as domain names. Each file or other resource at a given domain will have an even more specific designation known as a Universal Resource Locator, or URL.[3] When a user types a given URL into a Web browser, or uses a domain name as part of the address of an e-mail message, the software that drives the Internet "resolves" those words into the numeric string that permits it to go find the target computer. Thus if you want to look up a book in the catalog of the Library of Congress, and type "www.loc.gov" into the appropriate program, you will be instantly (or perhaps not so instantly, depending on your modem) connected with the computers at the Library of Congress.

This system will only work, however, if every computer has a unique domain name and every file has a unique URL. If several computers had the same domain name there obviously would be ambiguities in interpreting a user's commands. The usual analogy is to phone numbers. This requirement of uniqueness means that the DNS requires some form of central oversight, or at least a registration system, to prevent multiple computers from adopting the same domain name. In 1993, the National Science Foundation, the government agency with oversight of the Internet, entered into a five-year contract with a company in Northern Virginia called Network Solution, Inc. (NSI) to serve as the administrator of what was called the Internet Network Information Center (or InterNIC).[4] As a result, anyone who wanted to reserve a domain name

---

§ 33.2

1. A more detailed description of the workings of the Internet can be found in Reno v. ACLU, 521 U.S. 844, 117 S.Ct. 2329, 138 L.Ed.2d 874 (1997) (holding the Communications Decency Act of 1966 unconstitutional).

2. The format of an IP address is a 32–bit numeric address written as four numbers separated by periods. Each number can

be zero to 255. For example, 1.247.16.188 could be an IP address.

3. Thus <www.law.gwu.edu> would be a domain name, while <www.law.gwu.edu /facweb/rschechter> is a URL.

4. The roots of what we now know as the Internet can be traced back to the early 1960's when an organization within the U.S. Department of Defense called the Advanced Research Projects Agency (or ARPA) began developing the software that would

had to sign up with NSI, which had a monopoly on the domain name registration function.

In registering domain names, NSI did not attempt to determine if a requested domain name conflicted with another party's trademark rights. Once it determined that the precise domain name requested had not already been registered to someone else, it granted the registration, and all domain names were granted on a first come first served basis. While the potential for conflict between domain name registrations and trademarks seems obvious in retrospect, neither NSI nor most others gave the problem much thought at the time.[5]

In October, 1998, when the contract with NSI expired, the U.S. government shifted to a "shared registration system." Under that system, multiple firms are now permitted to grant domain name registrations, and they compete with each other based on price and service. NSI (now known as Verisign) continues to maintain the master list of all names to insure that there is no duplication, but otherwise it is just one of the competing registrars. The new system is overseen by a newly formed, not-for-profit corporation known as the Internet Corporation for Assigned Names and Numbers, or ICANN, which is headquartered in the U.S. but governed by a board with representatives from around the world.[6] As of this writing, ICANN has accredited almost 200 domain name registrars.[7]

As part of its effort to manage any conflicts between trademark and domain name rights, ICANN requires all accredited registrars to adopt a uniform dispute resolution policy, and to secure the agreement of those registering domain names that they will abide by this policy. ICANN works closely with the World Intellectual Property Organization, or WIPO, and a variety of other entities interested in both Internet and

permit computers to communicate with each other. The resulting network, which originally linked computers at government agencies and universities, was first known as ARPA Net. In 1990, the U.S. government decommissioned ARPA Net and turned over the administration of the embryonic Internet to the National Science Foundation. In 1993 the NSF, effectively privatized the administration of the Internet by contracting with NSI, after a competitive bidding process. The contract with NSI was designated NSF Cooperative Agreement #NCR–9218742. For general information about the evolution of the Internet see Art Wolinsky, *History of the Internet and the World Wide Web* (1999); Janet Abbate, *Inventing the Internet* (1999).

5. NSI did require domain name applicants to warrant that their proposed domain name did not conflict with anyone's trademark rights, and it did have a dispute resolution policy designed to deal with conflicts, but when disputes became prevalent, it was not particularly effective in dealing with them. For the text of the NSI Dispute Resolution Policy, *see* <http://www.lect-law.com/files/inp08.htm>. For a general discussion of NSI Dispute Resolution practices, *see* J. Thomas McCarthy, TRADEMARKS AND UNFAIR COMPETITION § 25:74.1.

6. The names of the 19 members of the ICANN Board of Directors, with links to their biographies can be found at <http://www. icann.org/general/abouticann.htm.>. Some of these directors are elected by ICANN's three "supporting organizations"—technical groups with expertise in Internet issues. Others were originally elected at large by members of the Internet community world wide but ICANN has amended its by-laws to eliminate the at-large elections. The President of ICANN serves as an ex officio member of the Board.

7. For a list of accredited registrars *see* <http://www. icann.org/registrars/accredited-list.html>.

trademark issues, with the goal of unifying domain name practices around the world and minimizing conflict with trademark law.[8]

For technical reasons, all domain names are grouped into categories known as "top level domains," or TLDs. The TLDs are the familiar generic suffixes that come at the very end of a domain name. The ".com" TLD is certainly the best known, most widely used and most coveted. Others well established TLDs include ".net," ".org," ".edu," ".gov" and ".mil."[9] In addition, there are also over 200 country specific TLDs consisting of two letter abbreviations for the country name, such as .ca for Canada or .fr for France.[10] The relatively small number of generic TLDs (or gTLDs) and the overwhelming popularity of the dot-com designation tended to compound the conflict between the domain name registration practice and trademark rights because it made it difficult for multiple parties with the same or similar trademarks to each use the mark as part of a domain name.

In November, 2000, after lengthy consideration, ICANN approved the introduction of a limited number of additional generic TLDs to make more domain names available. The specific proposal adopted by the ICANN board authorized seven new generic TLDs (.aero, .biz, .coop, .info, .museum, .name and .pro). As the names suggest, some of these new generic TLDs will only be available to specific kinds of entities (.aero for airlines), while others will be open to anyone who applies. The existence of the new TLDs may make it easier for non-competing firms that have similar trademark to each use that mark in a domain name. For instance, the owner of the mark DOMINO for sugar might be able to register "domino.biz" while the owner of the mark DOMINO for pizza might be able to register "domino.info."[11] This is not, however, a solution likely to make the lives of consumers any easier.

In addition, the registrars for these various new TLDs have attempted to adopt procedures that will prevent conflict with trademark rights. On the other hand the proliferation may actually make things more vexing for trademark owners as well. As one commentator has observed:

> As if trademark owners did not have enough concern protecting themselves in the .com, .org, and .net domains, explosive growth in TLDs has dramatically increased the risk of trademark misuse. Mark owners can no longer protect their marks simply by monitoring the three open gTLDs for infringers. First,

8. Further details about the workings of ICANN and its history can be found in Jerome Gilson, Trademark Protection and Practice § 30.03.

9. Prior to 1996, the .com, .org and .net TLDs were reserved for commercial entities, non-for-profit organizations, and computing entities respectively. Thereafter, these distinctions were not enforced in order to permit domain name registrations to be processed more quickly. *See* J. Thomas McCarthy, Trademarks and Unfair Competition § 25:72.

10. These are sometimes denominated ccTLDs (or country-code TLDs) to distinguish them from the generic TLDs like .com.

11. Interestingly, the domain "domino.com" is not owned by either of the companies mentioned in the text, but rather by Domino Systems, a Web site design company. *See* <www.domino.com>.

ICANN approved seven new TLDs in November 2000. Second, there is a continued expansion of commercial activity in country code TLDs (ccTLDs). Third, technical and marketing advances are increasing the viability of alternate TLDs. Finally, multilingual TLDs (mlTLDs) are presently being tested. These mlTLDs have the potential to reach huge segments of the global population previously shutout by an English language based system.[12]

The only safe conclusion that follows from this brief history is that for the foreseeable future, this is likely to be an area where the law will continue to lag a few steps behind the pace of technological change and innovation.

33.2.2 Cybersquatting as Dilution or Infringement

Many companies were slow to realize the commercial potential of the Internet, and thus slow to establish a presence on the World Wide Web. While they were waiting, certain "entrepreneurial" parties frequently were able to register well-known trademarks as domain names for their own web sites. Sometimes such parties collected inventories of dozens or even hundreds of such domain names. (Most of the sites associated with these registered names were either inactive, or contained nothing more than a few words (such as "under construction") or a single picture.) Some of these domain name registrants would subsequently contact the trademark owner and offer to sell the domain name registration to it so that it could operate a web site at a domain name that incorporated its own trademark.[13] Such parties came to be known as "cybersquatters," or "cyberpirates." As the Second Circuit has explained, "[c]ybersquatting involves the registration as domain names of well-known trademarks by non-trademark holders who then try to sell the names back to the trademark owners."[14]

In an effort to reclaim their trademarks from cybersquatters without paying the ransom demanded some trademark owners went to court. In their search for a viable theory, they hit upon claims of trademark dilution. One of the leading cases dealing with such a claim is *Panavision International, L.P. v. Toeppen.*[15] The plaintiff in that case, Panavision, is a well-known maker of professional quality motion picture camera equipment. It has federal trademark registrations for its marks PANAVISION and PANAFLEX. In late 1995 when it attempted to register the domain name "panavision.com" it learned that a Mr. Dennis Toeppen had already registered that name, making it unavailable. As the court noted

---

12. Robert V. Donahoe, *Beyond .Com: What Risk Does the Explosive Growth of Top Level Domains Pose to Your Trademark: Can You Get Any Relief?*, 4 Tul. J. Tech. & Intell. Prop. 59 (2002).

13. Trademark owners often prefer to use a URL incorporating their mark because, as one court noted, "Web users often assume, as a rule of thumb, that the domain name of a particular company will be

the company name followed by '.com.'" Brookfield Communications, Inc. v. West Coast Entertainment Corp., 174 F.3d 1036 (9th Cir.1999).

14. Sporty's Farm L.L.C. v. Sportsman's Market, Inc., 202 F.3d 489, 493, *cert. denied*, 530 U.S. 1262, 120 S.Ct. 2719, 147 L.Ed.2d 984 (2000).

15. 141 F.3d 1316 (9th Cir.1998).

somewhat dryly, "Toeppen's web page for this site displayed photographs of the City of Pana, Illinois."[16] Indeed, Toeppen had secured domain name registrations for over 100 different well-known trademarks.

Panavision, though its attorney, contacted Toeppen and demanded that he cease using their trademark as his domain name. His written response is worth quoting. After declaring that he had the right to the domain name he observed:

> If your attorney has advised you otherwise, he is trying to screw you. He wants to blaze new trails in the legal frontier at your expense. Why do you want to fund your attorney's purchase of a new boat (or whatever) when you can facilitate the acquisition of 'PanaVision.com' cheaply and simply instead?

Toeppen offered to sell Panavision the name for $13,000. Panavision decided to sue rather than pay, and asserted a claim for trademark dilution under the Federal Trademark Dilution Act (or FTDA).[17]

On appeal Toeppen did not challenge the trial court's finding that the PANAVISION mark was famous. Thus, disposition of the case turned on two issues. The first was whether Toeppen was making a "commercial use of the mark in commerce," as required by the FTDA. Citing several district court cases Toeppen argued that the mere registration of a domain name was not a commercial use. The court concluded, however, that Toeppen had done more than "merely register" the PANAVISION mark. As it explained, "Toeppen's 'business' is to register trademarks as domain names and then sell them to the rightful trademark owners. He 'act[s]' as a 'spoiler,' preventing Panavision and others from doing business on the Internet under their trademarked names unless they pay his fee.' This is a commercial use."

The court next considered whether this commercial use diluted plaintiff's mark by diminishing its capacity to identify and distinguish goods—the key substantive requirement of the FTDA. The trial court had found that Toeppen's use of plaintiff's mark as a domain name diminished "the capacity of the Panavision marks to identify and distinguish Panavision's goods and services on the Internet." The Ninth Circuit agreed. It noted that "a significant purpose of a domain name is to identify the entity that owns the web site," and that "potential customers of Panavision will be discouraged if they cannot find its web page by typing in 'Panavision.com,' but instead are forced to wade through hundreds of web sites. This dilutes the value of Panavision's trademark."

While the result in *Panavision* was a victory for the trademark owner, several aspects of the opinion suggested that dilution law might not be an effective tool against cybersquatters in all cases. First, while

---

16. Those curious about Pana, Illinois can visit <http://www.panaillinois.com/ home.htm>.

17. 15 U.S.C.A. § 1125(c) (2000). *See* Chapter 30, *supra.*

the PANAVISION trademark is fairly clearly a famous mark, in many cases, a trademark owner challenging a cybersquatter might not be able to demonstrate the requisite fame. That is precisely what happened in *TCPIP Holding Co., Inc. v. Haar Communications, Inc.,*[18] where the owner of the mark THE CHILDREN'S PLACE for children's clothing stores was unable to secure a preliminary injunction under the FTDA against a party using a virtually identical domain name because the court refused to find its trademark famous.[19]

Second, *Panavision*'s approach to the "commercial use" issue suggests that if the domain name registrant does not offer to sell the name back to the trademark owner (and does not use the web page in question for the sale of goods or services), there would be no commercial use and hence no liability under the dilution law. After this decision savvy cybersquatters presumably would be more discrete than Mr. Toeppen. Rather than broaching the subject of money, they would simply wait for the trademark owner to make an offer.

Third, the conclusion that use of trademark as a domain name lessens the capacity of that name to identify the goods on the Internet is hardly self-evident. While it is true that someone looking for PANAVISION products on-line might begin by typing "panavision.com" into the address line of a Web browser, almost all Web users know that there is a certain hit or miss quality to finding desired locations on the Web. Upon seeing a picture of Pana, Illinois, there is a good chance that most web users would simply go to their favorite search engine and type the word PANAVISION there. In all likelihood, the true home of Panavision would appear on the first page of the search results, and in a few seconds and a few mouse clicks the consumer would be transported there. The court's concern that potential customers will have to "wade through hundreds of web sites" seems a bit overwrought. Moreover, as Professor McCarthy has noted in his treatise, "there is a very poor fit between the actions of a cybersquatter and the federal Anti-dilution Act. The prototypical cybersquatter does not use the reserved domain name as its mark before the public, so there is no traditional dilution by blurring or tarnishment."[20]

Similar observations about the limitations of dilution law in the cybersquatting context were made in a 1999 Senate Report, which observed:

> While the [FTDA] has been useful in pursuing cybersquatters, cybersquatters have become increasingly sophisticated as the

18. 244 F.3d 88 (2d Cir.2001).

19. *See also* Hasbro, Inc. v. Clue Computing, Inc., 66 F.Supp.2d 117 (D.Mass. 1999) (CLUE mark for board game insufficiently famous to obtain dilution relief against similar domain name).

20. J. Thomas McCarthy, TRADEMARKS AND UNFAIR COMPETITION § 25:77. The author of the other leading treatise characterizes the opinion as "push[ing] the Dilution Act envelope very far," and says it "was a major extension of the Dilution Act. It relied on the notion that the lessening of the distinctiveness need not have significant public exposure or have an impact on public perception and need not encompass typical blurring or tarnishment." Jerome Gilson, Trademark Protection and Practice § 7A.07.

case law has developed and now take the necessary precautions to insulate themselves from liability. For example, many cybersquatters are now careful to no longer offer the domain name for sale in any manner that could implicate liability under existing trademark dilution case law. And, in cases of warehousing and trafficking in domain names, courts have sometimes declined to provide assistance to trademark holders, leaving them without adequate and effective judicial remedies. This uncertainty as to the trademark law's application to the Internet has produced inconsistent judicial decisions and created extensive monitoring obligations, unnecessary legal costs, and uncertainty for consumers and trademark owners alike.[21]

This is not to say that the dilution remedy is utterly lacking in utility for trademark owners trying to protect their marks against cybersquatters. Several plaintiffs have succeeded in using the theory since *Panavision*,[22] and it remains available as a weapon in the right situation. Nonetheless it is a path filled with obstacles and left trademark owners very anxious about their ability to combat cybersquatting.

As an alternative some trademark owners have even been able to succeed on a conventional infringement claim against cybersquatters. One very interesting example is *People for the Ethical Treatment of Animals v. Doughney*.[23] People for the Ethical Treatment of Animals, the plaintiff in this case, is a well-known animal rights organization, and the owner of the registered trademark PETA for its various services. In 1995 Doughney, the defendant, obtained a domain name registration for "peta.org." At the time he registered, Doughney told the registrar, NSI, that the entity registering the name was a non-profit educational organization called "People Eating Tasty Animals," even though no such organization then existed. Thereafter, however, Doughney used the Web site at the "peta.org" address as "a resource for those who enjoy eating meat, wearing fur and leather, hunting, and the fruits of scientific research," and labeled the Web page with the designation People Eating Tasty Animals.[24] Doughney claimed that he designed this site as a parody of PETA and its animal rights agenda.

In 1996 PETA complained to NSI, which placed the domain name on "hold." Later that year Doughney was quoted in the media as saying "[i]f they want one of my domains, they should make me an offer."

---

21. S. Rep. 106–140 (Aug. 5, 1999).

22. *See, e.g.,* Ford Motor Co. v. Lapertosa, 126 F.Supp.2d 463 (E.D.Mich.2000); Victoria's Cyber Secret Ltd. Partnership v. V Secret Catalogue, Inc., 161 F.Supp.2d 1339 (S.D.Fla.2001).

23. 263 F.3d 359 (4th Cir.2001).

24. At this writing, a web site by this name exits at "http://mtd.com/tasty/" and contains several links with information about the domain name dispute described in the text. The site, however, does not appear to have been updated in several years. PETA's website can now be found at "http://www.peta.org", as well as at "http://peta.com", at "http://www.peta.net" and "http://www.peta-online.org".

Unable to resolve the dispute, PETA sued in 1999 asserting, among other claims, trademark infringement.[25]

The Fourth Circuit first considered if Doughney had used the mark "in connection with goods or services," which is a threshold requirement for trademark infringement liability under both sections 32 and 43(a) of the Lanham Act.[26] It concluded that he had because, in the court's view, he "need not have actually sold or advertised goods or services on the *www.peta.org* website. Rather, Doughney need only have prevented users from obtaining or using PETA's goods or services, or need only have connected the website to other's goods or services." It concluded that the first condition was satisfied because the use of the domain name would "prevent" Internet users from reaching PETA's own web site. The court reasoned that those who mistakenly arrived at Doughney's site might fail to continue to search for PETA's home page "due to anger, frustration, or the belief that PETA's home page does not exist." The court also noted that Doughney's site contained links to more than 30 commercial operations offering goods and services.

The court then went on to consider if the use of the *peta.org* domain name would create a likelihood of confusion. Apparently, Doughney conceded that it would, but argued that the court should also consider the content of his website, which he claimed was self evidently a parody which would dispel any likelihood of confusion. The court, however, refused to look beyond the domain name itself, stating that "[l]ooking at Doughney's domain name alone, there is no suggestion of a parody. The domain name *peta.org* simply copies PETA's mark, conveying the message that it is related to PETA. The domain name does not convey the second, contradictory message needed to establish a parody—a message that the domain name is not related to PETA, but that it is parody of PETA." Consequently the court affirmed the grant of summary judgement in favor of PETA on the infringement claim.

The *PETA* approach to infringement is very broad. It seems to hold that any use of a trademark in a domain name that might momentarily prevent a web surfer from obtaining the goods or services of a mark owner is both a use "in connection with goods and services" and a use likely to engender confusion, because of the risk that surfers will get frustrated and give up their search. Ironically, the very breadth of the holding may have left some trademark owners uneasy. It is not implausible that a different a court might refuse to find a use in connection with goods if the cybersquatter did nothing but offer political commentary at the site. Similarly, other courts might conclude that a momentary diversion of Web surfers does not really create likelihood of confusion given the efficiency of search engines and ease of hitting the "back" button on a web browser.

---

25. PETA also raised claims under the new federal anti-cybersquatting statute, which is considered in detail in the following section of this chapter.

26. *See* 15 U.S.C.A. §§ 1114(1)(a); 1125(a)(1)(A) (2000).

By the late 1990's, it was becoming apparent that the law was forcing square pegs into round holes by trying to combat cybersquatting under the logic of either the dilution or infringement theories. Consequently, Congress decided to address the problem head-on. The result was the Anti–Cybersquatting Consumer Protection Act, or ACPA, which added a new section 43(d) to the Lanham Act designed to address the problem of cybersquatting explicitly.

33.2.3 The Anti–Cybersquatting Statute

Congress enacted the Anti–Cybersquatting Consumer Protection Act, or ACPA, in late November, 1999. This statute does not displace other claims or causes of action against cybersquatters, such as infringement or dilution.[27] It provides a new and additional cause of action for any trademark owner who can establish that a defendant:

(i) has a bad faith intent to profit from that mark, including a personal name which is protected as a mark under this section; and

(ii) registers, traffics in, or uses a domain name that—

(I) in the case of a mark that is distinctive at the time of registration of the domain name, is identical or confusingly similar to that mark;

(II) in the case of a famous mark that is famous at the time of registration of the domain name, is identical or confusingly similar to or dilutive of that mark....[28]

For ease of discussion, it is profitable to analyze the second condition of liability first. A defendant under ACPA can incur liability for any of three specified acts involving domain names, namely registering them, using them, or "trafficking" in them. The term "domain name" is defined elsewhere in the Lanham Act as "any alphanumeric designation which is registered with or assigned by any domain name registrar ... as part of an electronic address on the Internet."[29] The act of "registering" a domain name is self-explanatory. The "use" of a domain name would presumably be use by a licensee of the party who obtained the registration. The third category obviously contemplates the buying and selling of names in the style of Mr. Toeppen, the defendant in the *Panavision* case.

It is also required, in order to satisfy this prong of the statute, that the domain name in question be identical or confusingly similar to the plaintiff's trademark. This requirement means that the domain name would be infringing if it were used on competitive products in a conventional trademark situation. If the plaintiff's mark is "famous" the statute also says that it is sufficient if the domain name dilutes the mark, but this provision seems superfluous because courts consistently

27. 15 U.S.C.A. § 1125(d)(3) (2000).

28. 15 U.S.C.A.§ 1125(d) (2000).

29. 15 U.S.C.A. § 1127 (2000). The legislative history indicates that this definition was meant to exclude screen names, file names or any other computer-related labels that were not formally assigned by a domain name registrar. *See* H.R. Rep. No. 106–412, at 15 (October 25, 1999).

hold that in order to dilute a mark must be "very" or "substantially" similar to plaintiffs mark, and any domain name that is very similar is, by definition, confusingly similar as well.

Once it is established that the defendant has registered, is using, or is trafficking in a domain name confusingly similar to plaintiff's mark, plaintiff must show that the defendant had "a bad faith intent to profit" from the mark. This is the crux of the statute. To provide guidance to the courts, the statute provides a non-exclusive list of nine factors bearing on the issue of bad faith.

The first four statutory factors are, essentially, indicia of a defendant's good faith. An affirmative finding on these factors will tend to exonerate the defendant. Paraphrasing the statute, this first quartet of statutory factors are: (1) whether the defendant can claim any trademark rights in the designation in question; (2) whether the designation is the actual personal name of the defendant; (3) whether the person previously used the designation in legitimate business activities; and (4) whether the defendant is making a bona fide noncommercial or "fair" use of the designation.

The next four itemized factors point in the opposite direction and are direct indicators of bad faith. Affirmative findings on this group will tend to push the court towards a finding of liability. Again paraphrasing, they are: (5) whether the defendant has an intent to divert consumers from plaintiff's on-line location to a site that could "harm the goodwill represented by the mark, either for commercial gain or with the intent to tarnish or disparage the mark, by creating a likelihood of confusion as to the source, sponsorship, affiliation or endorsement of the site"; (6) whether the defendant offered to the sell the designation without ever having legitimately used it, or has engaged in a past practice of making such domain name sales; (7) whether defendant supplied false contact information when it applied for the domain name; and (8) whether the defendant has registered multiple domain names all of which are similar to the trademarks of other parties. Congress seems to have drafted this second cluster of factors with the likes of Mr. Toeppen, the *Panavision* defendant, in mind.

Finally, factor number (9) is the strength or fame of the plaintiff's trademark.[30] In most cases, the stronger the mark the more likely it is that the defendant acted in bad faith in choosing it as a domain name, and the weaker the mark, the more likely it is that the defendant either never heard of it, or justifiably felt that its use would not impose any hardship on the plaintiff.

The bad faith portion of the statute also contains a "safe harbor" provision. It declares that bad faith intent "shall not be found in any case in which the court determines that the person believed and had reasonable grounds to believe that the use of the domain name was a fair use or otherwise lawful."[31] Professor McCarthy has dubbed this the

30. 15 U.S.C.A. § 1125 (d)(1)(B)(i) (2000).

31. 15 U.S.C.A. § 1125 (d)(1)(B)(ii) (2000).

"pure heart and empty head defense" and counseled that it should be used sparingly.[32] The courts seem to agree, holding that a "defendant who acts even partially in bad faith in registering a domain name ... is not ... entitled to benefit from the Act's safe harbor provision."[33]

The defense, however, seems to us to be a crucial part of the statutory architecture. The reference to "fair use" insulates—or at least should insulate—those who use another's trademark only in its descriptive sense in their domain names. It also should insulate those whose domain names are meant to refer to the trademark owner in non-confusing ways, under the nominative fair use principle. Protection for such parties promotes important policies of free competition and free expression.

The safe harbor provision is also a reminder that not all trademark disputes over domain names involve opportunistic parties acting in bad faith to exploit someone else's trademark. In cases where multiple parties share the same or similar marks for diverse goods in the real marketplace, it is possible that their rights in cyberspace might conflict without any misconduct by either party. For instance, there is both a chain of shoe stores and a chain of health clubs that operate under the BALLY'S mark. Off the Web, they are able to co-exist peaceably because the goods and services they sell are unrelated and the simultaneous use of the same mark by the two of them does not lead to any consumer confusion. On the Web, however, only one firm can have the mark "ballys.com."[34] This is likely to leave the other firm frustrated. But frustration is no indicator of bad faith, and this situation does not implicate any violation of ACPA because whichever firm registers the domain name will have legitimate rights in, and will have previously been conducting business under, the name in question.

Although ACPA has only been on the books for a few years, it has already generated several important decisions. The very first appellate case to interpret the statute was *Sporty's Farm L.L.C. v. Sportsman's Market, Inc.,*[35] and its analysis provides an indication of how courts will approach determinations of "bad faith" under this new statute. Sportsman's Market is a mail order business that sells tools, home accessories and equipment for aviation buffs. In 1985 it obtained a federal registration for its mark SPORTY'S in connection with this business. In the mid–1990's the Hollanders, who owned a mail order scientific instruments business called Omega, decided to enter the aviation catalog

---

32. J. Thomas McCarthy, TRADEMARKS AND UNFAIR COMPETITION § 25:78.

33. Virtual Works, Inc. v. Volkswagen of Am., Inc., 238 F.3d 264, 270 (4th Cir.2001) (where defendant Virtual Works had the intent both to use the domain name "vw.net" for its own business, and also to profit from associations with plaintiff Volkswagen, the safe harbor defense is unavailable).

34. Admittedly, this still leaves "ballys.net" or "ballys.biz" for the other firm, but often the first firm to seek domain name registration will obtain registrations for all similar names in a variety of TLDs to make sure that consumers will locate the Web site regardless of what they type.

35. 202 F.3d 489 (2d Cir.2000), *cert. denied,* 530 U.S. 1262, 120 S.Ct. 2719, 147 L.Ed.2d 984 (2000).

business. They formed a subsidiary which they called Pilot's Depot. Not long after they registered the domain name "sportys.com" with NSI. Mr. Hollander knew of plaintiff's trademark and its business activities when he secured this domain name.

A few months after obtaining this domain name, the Hollanders formed another subsidiary to grow and sell Christmas trees. They named this business Sporty's Farm, and they sold the domain name "sportys.com" to this business for $16,200. At the eventual trial the manager of their Christmas tree operation, Ralph Michael, claimed to have derived the name for the new business from the fact that an uncle of his owned both a farm, and a dog named Spotty, and that as a child he had come to call this farm "Spotty's farm." The appeals court noted, however that there was "no evidence in the record that Hollander was considering starting a Christmas tree business when he registered sportys.com or that Hollander was ever acquainted with Michael's dog Spotty."

When Sportsman's contacted the Hollanders to complain about their registration of the domain name, the Hollanders went straight to court. They filed a declaratory judgment action seeking a ruling that they were entitled to retain the domain name. Predictably, Sportsman's counter-claimed, asserting both infringement and dilution claims. The trial court refused to find infringement because it felt that there was no likelihood of confusion, but it did find dilution. While the case was pending on appeal Congress passed ACPA.

The Second Circuit initially determined that it was proper to apply ACPA to the case. It also had no trouble finding the domain name to be confusingly similar to the trademark despite the fact that the trademark contains an apostrophe while the domain name did not.[36] The court then turned to an analysis of the "bad faith" issue. It reviewed most, but not all, of the factors itemized in the statute and concluded that they pointed in favor of a finding of bad faith. Judge Calabresi did not leave the analysis there, however, observing that the case involved "unique circumstances" fortifying the finding of bad faith. As he saw it:

> It cannot be doubted, as the court found below, that Omega registered sportys.com for the primary purpose of keeping Sportsman's from using that domain name. Several months later, and after this lawsuit was filed, Omega created another company in an unrelated business that received the name Sporty's Farm so that it could (1) use the sportys.com domain name in some commercial fashion, (2) keep the name away from Sportsman's, and (3) protect itself in the event that Sportsman's brought an infringement claim alleging that a "likelihood of confusion" had been created by Omega's version of cybersquatting. Finally, the explanation given for Sporty's Farm's desire to use the domain name, based on the existence of the dog Spotty, is more amusing than credible. Given these facts . . .

36.   As the court notes, apostrophes cannot be used in domain names.

there is ample and overwhelming evidence that, as a matter of law, Sporty's Farm's acted with a "bad faith intent to profit" from the domain name sportys.com as those terms are used in the ACPA.

The court's willingness in *Sporty's* to go beyond the list of statutory factors suggests a pragmatic rather than mechanical approach to the issue of bad faith under ACPA. Given the strong indication in the record that the Hollanders had registered the domain name in question precisely in order to make it difficult for consumers to find Sportsman's on the Web, the conclusion of bad faith seems compelling.

Cases since *Sporty's* have continued to take a realistic, down-to-earth approach to the idea of bad faith under ACPA. A number of courts have pointed to the defendant's failure to make any use of the domain name prior to the start of litigation as weighing in favor of a finding of bad faith—essentially placing heavy reliance on the issue suggested by statutory factor number (3).[37] Other courts have noted that where the plaintiff's trademark is especially famous, the adoption of the mark as part of a domain name particularly smacks of bad faith—an application of statutory factor (9). For instance, in *E. & J. Gallo Winery v. Spider Webs Ltd.*, where the plaintiffs owned the famous ERNEST & JULIO GALLO trademark for wine, the court had little difficulty finding defendant guilty of bad faith for registering the domain name "ernestandjulogallo.com." Another court found it telling that the defendant had failed to investigate the trademark status of its domain name before obtaining registration—a consideration not explicitly appearing in the statutory list. As the judge in that case explained, "[i]t is important to pursue the analysis of the issue of bad faith factor-by-factor.... It is equally important, however, to step back and examine the larger picture to determine whether it is consistent with a finding of bad faith."[38]

Once it proves the requisite bad faith, a successful plaintiff under ACPA is entitled to all the usual Lanham Act remedies, including injunctive relief, monetary awards and attorney fees. If the plaintiff chooses, it may, at any time before final judgement, ask for an award of "statutory damages" instead of actual damages and profits. Such an award can be for any amount between $1,000 and $100,000 per domain name "as the court considers just."[39] In addition, the court can order the transfer of the domain name from the defendant to the plaintiff or the cancellation of the domain name.[40] Moreover, ACPA is retroactive. Language in the statute expressly states that it "shall apply to all domain names registered before, on or after the date of the enactment ...."[41]

37. *See, e.g.,* Shields v. Zuccarini, 254 F.3d 476, 485–86 (3d Cir.2001); E. & J. Gallo Winery v. Spider Webs Ltd., 286 F.3d 270, 276 (5th Cir.2002).

38. Eurotech, Inc. v. Cosmos European Travels Aktiengesellschaft, 213 F.Supp.2d 612 (E.D.Va.2002).

39. 15 U.S.C.A. § 1117(d) (2000).

40. 15 U.S.C.A. § 1125 (d)(1)(C) (2000).

41. Pub. L. No. 106–113 § 3010, 113 Stat. 1536. Sporty's Farm L.L.C. v. Sportsman's Market, Inc., 202 F.3d 489, 496 (2d Cir.2000), *cert. denied*, 530 U.S. 1262, 120 S.Ct. 2719, 147 L.Ed.2d 984 (2000); People for the Ethical Treatment of Animals v. Doughney, 263 F.3d 359 (4th Cir.2001).

However, in cases where the domain name was registered prior to the adoption of ACPA, the sole remedy is injunctive relief and transfer of domain name. Damages are not available in such cases.

There are three other features of ACPA worthy of note. First, an entirely separate section of ACPA provides a remedy against anyone who registers a domain name consisting "of the name of another living person, or a name substantially and confusingly similar thereto, without that person's consent, with the specific intent to profit from such name by selling the domain name for financial gain to that person or any third party...."[42] In this form of cybersquatting, a party might attempt to register the names of actors, athletes, or politicians and hold those URLs hostage until the named individual coughed up a suitable price. Remedies under this provision are limited to injunctive relief, costs and attorney fees. However nothing in this section forbids the registration of another party's name if there is no intent to sell it. Thus, it is permissible to register a domain name consisting of the personal name of a movie star in order to use it as the domain name for a fan club site. This provision also contains a somewhat technical exemption for copyright owners who register a personal name connected with a work in which they hold the copyright. This exception might be applicable if a publishing company registered as a domain name the name of the author of a book in which it held copyright interests, and it then decided to sell that domain name back to the author.

Second, ACPA contains provisions immunizing domain name registrars from liability either to domain name registrants or to trademark owners. The first of these protects the registrar, if sued by the domain name registrant, if it refuses to register a domain name, or if it cancels or transfers a registration in response to a court order or as part of the implementation of reasonable policy designed to prevent conflict with trademark rights.[43] The Uniform Dispute Resolution Procedure (UDRP) put in place by ICANN and described a bit further on in this chapter is an example of such a "reasonable policy." Thus, if a registrar is duly notified that a trademark owner has prevailed in a UDRP arbitration against a domain name registrant, and transfers the domain name in response to that notification, the registrar cannot be held liable for any damages that the domain name registrant suffers. This provision does not, however, protect a registrar which ignores court orders, or which transfers domain names while an action under ACPA is still pending. The second provision shields the registrar from liability for money damages in suits by trademark owners claiming that the registration of a domain name infringes on its trademark rights, unless the registrar has done so with a "bad faith intent to profit from such registration...."[44]

---

42. 15 U.S.C.A. § 1129 (2000). Although this provision is codified immediately following the sections of the Lanham Act in the U.S. Code, the legislation adopting ACPA did not specifically indicate that it should be codified there, and technically the provision is thus not part of the Lanham Act.

43. 15 U.S.C.A. § 1114(2)(D)(ii) (2000).

44. 15 U.S.C.A. § 1114(2)(D)(iii) (2000).

(In such cases, the registrar remains subject to injunctive orders requiring it to transfer or cancel the offending registration.)

Finally, ACPA provides a remedy in favor of a domain name registrant against a party who asserts groundless claims of cybersquatting in order to take control of a desirable domain name—a practice which has come to be known as "reverse domain name hijacking." Specifically, ACPA grants a domain name registrant a right to recover damages against any party who makes knowing and material misstatements in connection with an allegation of cybersquatting, if as a result of those representations the relevant registrar has cancelled or transferred the domain name.[45] In addition, in any such case, the domain name registrant may ask for appropriate injunctive relief, including reactivation of the domain name, or the transfer of the name back to itself. This provision provides a check on abusive use of both ACPA judicial remedies and dispute resolution systems provided by domain name registrars. The statutory standard of a "knowing and material misstatement" may, however, prove difficult for most domain name registrants to establish.

33.2.4   In Rem Actions Under the Anti–Cybersquatting Statute

In the real world, the owner of a trademark might not always be able to litigate directly against a cybersquatter. In some instances, the owner of the domain name may have registered under a false or corporate name, and given only a postal box as an address, making it impossible to locate the owner or to effect service of legal process. In other instances, the owner of the domain name may be located outside the United States, and thus beyond the jurisdiction of the U.S. courts. Congress anticipated these contingencies and included a "back-up" mechanism in ACPA. It permits a trademark owner to proceed *in rem* against the domain name itself, instead of proceeding *in personam* against the cybersquatter.[46]

To invoke *in rem* jurisdiction, the plaintiff must demonstrate to the court's satisfaction either that it "is not able to obtain *in personam* jurisdiction over a person who would have been a defendant in a civil action" or alternatively that despite "due diligence [it] was not able to find a person who would have been a defendant in a civil action."[47] In the latter case, the statute requires the plaintiff to send a notice of the alleged violation to the postal and e-mail addresses on file with the domain name registrar and to publish notice of the action pursuant to whatever terms the court might order after the action has been filed. The case law indicates that the plaintiff must then wait a "reasonable

45. 15 U.S.C.A. § 1114(2)(D)(iv) (2000).

46. This provision is responsive to a previous case holding that *in rem* jurisdiction would be unavailable under the federal dilution statute. *See* Porsche Cars North America, Inc. v. Porsch.Com, 51 F.Supp.2d 707 (E.D.Va.1999). On appeal, that case was remanded for reconsideration under the *in rem* provisions of ACPA which had just become effective. *See* 215 F.3d 1320.

47. 15 U.S.C.A. § 1125(d)(2)(ii) (2000).

time" to see if this publication notice produces results before filing suit.[48] The *in rem* case is to be filed in the district where the relevant domain name registrar is located.

Courts have noted that the *in rem* procedure should be viewed as something of a last resort. As one court put it: "Congress did not intend to provide an easy way for trademark owners to proceed *in rem* after jumping through a few *pro forma* hoops."[49] This seems a sensible approach because in an *in rem* case the domain name registrant is not likely to be present and thus the court will essentially be hearing only one side of the story. The courts have also held, logically enough, that the *in rem* and *in personam* causes of actions under ACPA are mutually exclusive, because in order to proceed under the former basis, the plaintiff must demonstrate the absence of personal jurisdiction, which is the prerequisite of the latter.[50]

Both for constitutional reasons, and because of the statutory language in ACPA, the *in rem* proceeding is available only where the domain name was registered with a U.S. based domain name registrar. Consequently, where a foreign entity registers a domain name with a U.S. registrar, the *in rem* procedure is appropriate, but if that foreign entity registered the domain name with a foreign registrar, and if it had no minimum contacts with the United States, there will be no possibility of either *in rem* or *in personam* jurisdiction here.[51]

Although the *in rem* provisions of ACPA do not specifically refer to the "bad faith intent to profit" standard that governs in *in personam* cases, the courts have held that such a standard is applicable in *in rem* cases.[52] This may pose considerable difficulties in those cases where the *in rem* plaintiff has been unable to identify the true domain name registrant. In these situations, plaintiff may find it impossible to gather evidence on such issues as whether the registrant lacked legitimate rights in the name, whether it has collected a warehouse of domain names, or whether it has an intent to divert consumers (to name a few of the bad faith factors). On the other hand, the very fact that the registrant has provided false contact information is some indication of bad faith. This was the reasoning of at least one trial court, which noted that "[f]ailure to keep one's address current or to leave an accurate forwarding address certainly casts doubt on the bona fides of a registrant. This fact coupled with the similarity of the offending mark may

---

48. Lucent Technologies, Inc. v. Lucent-sucks.com, 95 F.Supp.2d 528, 534 (E.D.Va. 2000).

49. *Id.*

50. Alitalia–Linee Aeree Italiane S.p.A. v. Casinoalitalia.Com, 128 F.Supp.2d 340 (E.D.Va.2001).

51. *See* H.R. Rep. No. 106–412, at 14 (October 25, 1999) ("in rem jurisdiction still

requires a nexus based upon a U.S. registry or registrar [and] would not extend to any domain name registries existing outside of the United States.").

52. *See, e.g.,* BroadBridge Media v. Hypercd.com, 106 F.Supp.2d 505 (S.D.N.Y. 2000); Harrods Ltd. v. Sixty Internet Domain Names, 110 F.Supp.2d 420 (E.D.Va. 2000).

well be sufficient to enable a plaintiff facing a defaulting domain name to obtain an *in rem* judgment against the domain name."[53]

The only remedy available in the *in rem* ACPA action is transfer of the domain name. Given that the court does not have personal jurisdiction over the domain name registrant, it would not be either practical or Constitutional to enter monetary or injunctive orders against that party.

33.2.5 The Uniform Dispute Resolution Procedure

As noted at the beginning of this chapter, ICANN, the entity that currently oversees the domain name registration process, requires all domain name registrars to adopt a dispute resolution policy which is binding on all parties that register domain names with it. Put in place in October, 1999, this policy—known as the Uniform Dispute Resolution Procedure or UDRP—has become a significant non-judicial alternative used by many trademark owners who wish to challenge what they view as illegitimate domain name registrations.[54] In less than three years of operation nearly six thousand disputes affecting nearly ten thousand domain names have been adjudicated under the UDRP.[55]

The UDRP provides for a streamlined, fast-track determination of rights to a domain name through binding arbitration. Under the procedure a mark owner may file an administrative complaint against a domain name registrant with any private dispute resolution service provider which has been approved by ICANN. Currently there are four such approved organizations.[56] The complainant can request to have the matter resolved either by a single arbitrator, known in the relevant jargon as a "sole panelist," or by a three-member arbitration panel. If the complainant elects the single member panel, the respondent has the right to insist on a three-member ·panel instead. The complainant normally pays the costs of the proceedings. However, if the respondent has bumped up the size of the panel from one to three members, the ICANN rules provide that the costs are to be split between the parties.[57]

Proceedings are resolved on the basis of written submissions, with hearings only being held in exceptional cases, and the panel is obliged to decide the case within fourteen days. The complaining party bears the

---

53. Harrods Ltd. v. Sixty Internet Domain Names, 110 F.Supp.2d 420, 426–27 (E.D.Va.2000).

54. *See generally,* <http://www.icann.org/udrp/udrp.htm>. For a thorough history and analysis, *see* A. Michael Froomkin, *ICANN'S "Uniform Dispute Resolution Policy"—Causes and (Partial) Cures,* 67 Brook. L. Rev. 605 (2002).

55. The latest statistics are available on-line at <http://www.icann.org/udrp/proceedings-stat.htm>.

56. These are the World Intellectual Property Organization, or WIPO, the National Arbitration Forum, the CPR Institute for Dispute Resolution, and the Asian Domain Name Dispute Resolution Centre. A fifth dispute resolution service provider, called "eresolutions," ceased operations in November, 2001. It claimed that WIPO had obtained the bulk of the UDRP caseload by deliberately tilting its decisions in favor of trademark owners. For an up to the minute list of approved dispute resolution providers, visit <http://www.icann.org/udrp/approved-providers.htm>.

57. *See,* Rules for Uniform Domain Name Dispute Resolution Policy, ¶ 6 (c), available on-line at <http://www.icann.org/dndr/udrp/uniform-rules.htm#5biv>.

burden of proof, and must establish a violation of the policy by a preponderance of the evidence. Panels will consider judicial decisions from courts around the world as well as prior UDRP panel decisions as precedent on any contested legal issues.

Substantively, the complaining party is entitled to relief under the UDRP if it can prove each of three elements: First, it must show that the domain name in question is identical or confusingly similar to a trademark in which it has rights; second, it must show that the registrant has no rights or legitimate interests concerning that domain name; and third, it must show that the domain name was registered and is being used in bad faith.[58] In connection with this final element, the policy provides a non-exclusive list of four "bad faith factors" which closely resemble several of those in the U.S. Anti-cybersquatting statute discussed previously.[59] If the decision is adverse to the respondent the arbitrator has the power to order either cancellation of the domain name or the transfer of the name from the respondent to the complainant . However an unsuccessful respondent has 10 days in which to seek judicial review of the arbitration ruling and to provide evidence that it has filed suit. The filing of such a suit precludes the domain name registrar from taking any action with respect to the domain name until the law suit is resolved.

The first of the substantive requirements—namely "confusing similarity"—has generated some interesting issues in the decisions thus far. In some cases, the challenged domain name consists of the complainant's trademark plus an additional critical word, such as "sucks," "lemon," "ripoffs," "ihate" or the like. The sites operated at these domain names are usually what are known as "gripe sites," providing a forum for complaints about the allegedly poor products or services of the trademark owner. UDRP panels have come to divergent conclusions concerning whether such domain names are "confusingly similar" to the trademark owned by the complaining party.[60] The majority of decisions have found the requisite confusing similarity. This may ultimately lead to inconsistencies between the UDRP decision making process and U.S. judicial decisions, where the use of the disparaging suffix is likely to be found to negate confusing similarity, and where First Amendment rights may actually protect a domain name registrant's right to adopt such a domain name.[61]

58. UDRP ¶ 4(a) (1999), available online at <http://www.icann.org/dndr/udrp/policy.htm>.

59. *Id.* at ¶ 4(b).

60. *Compare* Lockheed Martin Corp. v. Parisi, WIPO Case No. D2000–1015, 2001 WL 1705134 ("Both common sense and a reading of the plain language of the Policy support the view that a domain name combining a trademark with the word 'sucks' or other language clearly indicating that the domain name is not affiliated with the trademark owner cannot be considered con-

fusingly similar to the trademark.") *with* The Salvation Army v. Info–Bahn, Inc., WIPO Case No. D2001–0463, 2001 WL 1701003 ("A domain name is confusingly similar to a trademark for purposes of the Policy when the domain name includes the trademark regardless of the other terms in the domain name.").

61. *See, e.g.,* Bally Total Fitness Holding Corp. v. Faber, 29 F.Supp.2d 1161 (C.D.Cal.1998) (defendant's use of "ballysucks" as domain name held protected under First Amendment).

Another "confusing similarity" issue arises when parties attempt to register variations on the domain names of highly popular sites so that they can obtain additional web traffic from sloppy typists and poor spellers.[62] Such misspellings of trademarks are almost always found similar to the complainant's mark in the UDRP decisions, an approach which seems to accord with common sense. Panels also find the requisite similarity when the only difference between the parties' names is the use of different TLDs. In other words, "cocacola.net" will be found confusingly similar to" cocacola.com."

Turning to the second substantive element, the UDRP itemizes three specific ways that a responding party can attempt to demonstrate that it has a legitimate interest in the domain name, although that list is specifically declared to be non-exclusive.[63] First, it can show that prior to the dispute it has used, or was preparing to use the name in connection with a *bona fide* offering of goods or services. This would typically be the case where the underlying trademark is one simultaneously used by multiple parties in different lines of commerce in the real world. For instance, if the firm selling DELTA faucets obtained the domain name "delta.com," its prior faucet sales show that it has a legitimate interest in that name sufficient to defeat a protest by Delta Airlines or any other Delta out there that filed a complaint.[64]

Second, proof that the respondent has been commonly known by the name in question also establishes legitimate interests in the name. This is most likely to be relevant where the domain name registrant is an individual rather than a corporate entity or business. Thus in one arbitration, a panel refused to transfer the domain name "strick.com" to the Strick Corporation because the respondent, James Strickland, Jr. established that he had been known by the nickname Strick since he was a child.[65]

Finally, proof that the respondent is making a noncommercial or fair use of the domain name, without intent to divert consumers or tarnish the mark at issue will also suffice to show legitimate interest. While this aspect of the UDRP seems designed to provide protection for parties that use a trademark for a "gripe" or other critical site, not all panels have seen it that way. Some have found that the use of a trademark for a site containing critical commentary will "tarnish" the mark.[66] It would seem that where the respondent signals the critical nature of the web site by

62. For an example, visit "googl.com" (being sure to leave off the final "e" before the "dot").

63. UDRP ¶ 4(c) (1999).

64. *See, e.g.,* Fuji Photo Film Co. Ltd. v. Fuji Publishing Group LLC, WIPO Case No. D2000–0409.

65. Strick Corp. v. Strickland, NAF Case No. 94801, 2000 WL 33674764.

66. *See, e.g.,* Mission KwaSizabantu v. Rost, WIPO Case No. D2000–0279, 2000 WL 33674426. In that case, the complain-

ant was found to have trademark rights a in "KwaSizabantu" in connection with religious activities. Rost, the respondent, registered "kwasizabantu.com", "kwasizabantu.org", and "kwasizabantu.net" and operated web sites critical of the complainant at those sites. The panel held that as a result Rost was "tarnishing the activities associated with the trademark or service mark 'KwaSizabantu'," and that he consequently lacked a "legitimate interest" in the domain name.

including some negative word or phrase in the domain name (e.g., "acmestinks.com"), the critical nature of the site would be quite apparent to all web surfers, and the possibility of confusion of the public would be quite slight. In our view such cases should be decided for the respondent either on the grounds that the domain name is not confusingly similar to the trademark, or on the grounds that the respondent has a legitimate interest in the name as a venue for comment and criticism.[67] Where the domain name consists only of the trademark and a TLD suffix, however, the risk of consumer confusion is considerably greater, and the argument of legitimacy correspondingly weaker.

Panel discussions of the third substantive UDRP factor—bad faith—are quite reminiscent of those we have seen in connection with adjudication of the same issue by U.S. courts, under ACPA. Although the UDRP requires a complainant to prove that the domain name was both registered and "is being used" in bad faith, many panels have found that offering the domain name for sale (either back to the trademark owner, or to one of its rivals) is enough to satisfy this "use" requirement even if the name does not correlate to an active web site.[68] This of course is consistent with the Lanham Act case law discussed earlier in this chapter. Some panels have gone still further and found that merely holding the domain name registration, without either an associated web site or efforts to make a sale, is enough to show that the name is "being used,"[69] but the decision are split on that questions and there are panels going the other way.[70] Thus far, the bad faith element has not proved to be much of a hurdle under UDRP. Complainants have prevailed in the vast majority of arbitrations, though the statistics can be misleading because many complaints are not even contested by the domain name registrant.

A respondent that thinks an arbitration claim against it is baseless may request a ruling from the panel that the complainant is engaging in "reverse domain name hijacking," a practice we encountered previously in considering some of the miscellaneous provisions of the ACPA. The UDRP defines it as "using the Policy in bad faith to attempt to deprive a registered domain-name holder of a domain name."[71] Under the rules, "if after considering the submissions the Panel finds that the complaint was brought in bad faith, for example, in an attempt at Reverse Domain

67. One recent UDRP implied as much, noting: "Respondent's argument would be much stronger and have more merit if the domain name itself included a disclaimer or some other element which clearly told the reader that it was not the site of the owner of the 'Nortel' and/or 'Nortel Networks' marks. For example, an Internet surfer would be unlikely to believe that a site entitled 'nortelnetworkssucks' is sponsored by or affiliated with Nortel Networks. Respondent's domain name includes no such disclaimer or obvious 'warning.'" Nortel Networks Ltd. v. Raynald Grenier, NAF

Case No. FA 0201000104104, 2002 WL 445805.

68. *See, e.g.,* World Wrestling Federation Entertainment, Inc. v. Brosman, WIPO Case No. D99–0001.

69. *See, e.g.,* Phillips Int'l Inc. v. Rao Tella, NAF Case No. FA 0008000095461, 2000 WL 33674989.

70. *See, e.g.,* Netgrocer, Inc. v. Anchor, NAF Case No. FA 0002000094207, 2000 WL 33674612.

71. UDRP Rule 1.

Name Hijacking or was brought primarily to harass the domain-name holder, the Panel shall declare in its decision that the complaint was brought in bad faith and constitutes an abuse of the administrative proceeding."[72] Surprisingly, there are no sanctions levied against a complainant found guilty of reverse domain name hijacking, making invocation of this aspect of the Policy a largely futile exercise, except insofar as it gives the domain name registrant some sense of moral vindication.

Under ACPA, if a domain name registrant loses an arbitration case under the UDRP, it has the right to challenge that decision in the U.S. courts. ACPA gives such a party the right "upon notice to the mark owner [to] file a civil action to establish that the registration or use of the domain name by such registrant is not unlawful under this Act. The court may grant injunctive relief to the domain name registrant, including the reactivation of the domain name or transfer of the domain name to the domain name registrant."[73]

In one of the first appellate decisions applying this section, the successful UDRP complainant argued that it should not apply for two reasons. First, it claimed that because the section refers to suits against "the mark owner" it governed only if the UDRP complainant held a Lanham Act registration for the mark in question. Second, it argued that, because it had no intention of filing a suit against the domain name registrant under ACPA, there was no "case or controversy" between the parties as required by the Constitution. The First Circuit rejected both contentions.[74]

With regard to the first, it said that "it would be very odd if Congress, which was well aware of the international nature of trademark disputes, protected Americans against reverse domain name hijacking only when a registered American mark owner was doing the hijacking." With regard to the second, it noted that there was a genuine controversy between the parties over ownership of the domain name and a clear Congressional intent to provide for judicial review of UDRP decisions.

While the availability of judicial review may serve as a check on abuses of the UDRP arbitration system, there are practical reasons why this check may only be slight. Many trademark owners who bring complaints before UDRP panels are major multi-national companies with deep pockets, represented by expensive legal talent. Many domain name registrants are smaller companies or individuals who find defending the arbitration to be burdensome and who may utterly lack the resources to go to court thereafter, even if they feel they have been treated unjustly. The consequence may be that much "reverse domain name hijacking" will go unpunished.

72. UDRP Rule 15.

73. 15 U.S.C.A. § 1114(2)(D)(v) (2000).

74. Sallen v. Corinthians Licenciamentos, Ltd., 273 F.3d 14 (1st Cir.2001).

§ 33.3   The Use of Trademarks in Meta–Tags

Most Web Sites contain information that is not visually displayed to a web surfer who comes to visit the site. This information—sometimes called "hidden code"—is inserted by the programmer who designs the web page to serve a variety of purposes. Some of this information is included to help search engines more quickly determine whether the web page is relevant to a search request. This hidden code information is usually incorporated into a portion of the Web Page known as a "meta-tag."[1]

Web Site owners might wish to use other parties' trademarks in their meta-tags. For instance, a retailing firm might want to include trademarks of the brands that it sells so that a consumer searching for those brands would be likely to find its website. For example, if Crate & Barrel sells ALL–CLAD brand cookware, it might include want to the ALL–CLAD trademark in a meta-tag. The owner of a non-commercial web site might want to use trademarks in meta-tags if the site offers information or criticism of the trademark owner. For example a web site devoted to the advocacy of gun control might include the trademarks of the NATIONAL RIFLE ASSOCIATION in meta-tags to attract web surfers who use that trademark as a search term. In addition, a firm might wish to list its competitors marks in meta-tags so that parties searching for the competitor will also learn of the existence of their web site. For example, the company that sells ADIDAS footwear might want to use the NIKE trademark in a meta-tag because its web site might make comparisons between its shoes and those sold by Nike.

In some cases, in order to enhance placement in the listings of search results generated by search engines, a company will not merely use someone else's trademark in a meta-tag, but will repeat that trademark dozens or hundreds of times. This can cause some search engines to give that web site a very high "relevancy ranking" and to list it very near the top of the search results. This practice has sometimes been called "cyber-stuffing." The cyber-stuffer expects that its high placement in the search results will lead web surfers to click through to its site. Once there, the Web surfer may decide to remain and even make a purchase there, despite the fact that it is not the site she was originally looking for.

The unauthorized use of marks in meta-tags has given rise to the inevitable trademark disputes. Perhaps the leading case on point is *Brookfield Communications, Inc. v. West Coast Entertainment Corp.,*[2] which condemns the practice, at least in certain circumstances. Brook-

§ 33.3

1. One Web source explains that a Meta–Tag is a "special HTML tag that provides information about a Web page. Unlike normal HTML tags, meta-tags do not affect how the page is displayed. Instead, they provide information such as who created the page, how often it is updated, what the page is about, and which keywords represent the page's content. Many search engines use this information when building their indices." <http://www.webopedia.com/TERM/M/meta_tag.html >.

2. 174 F.3d 1036 (9th Cir.1999).

field, the plaintiff in that case, was a firm that gathered and sold information about the entertainment industry to professionals in that industry. It eventually expanded into the consumer market, offering software that featured a searchable database of entertainment industry related information. It marketed this product under the MOVIEBUFF trademark. In 1996, when it tried to register the domain name "moviebuff.com," it learned that this domain name had already been registered by a video rental chain called West Coast Video. Although the litigation between the parties thus involved rights to the domain name, that is not the issue for which the case is best known. Brookfield also complained that West Coast was using its trademark "moviebuff" in the meta-tags that formed part of West Coast's Web Site, and challenged this practice as trademark infringement.

The Ninth Circuit began its discussion of that aspect of the case by conceding that the risk of confusion flowing from the use of a trademark in a meta-tag was less than that engendered by using the trademark as part of a domain name. It observed:

> when the user inputs 'MovieBuff' into an Internet search engine, the list produced by the search engine is likely to include both West Coast's and Brookfield's web sites. Thus, in scanning such list, the Web user will often be able to find the particular web site he is seeking. Moreover, even if the Web user chooses the web site belonging to West Coast, he will see that the domain name of the web site he selected is 'westcoastvideo.com.' ... [I]t is difficult to say that a consumer is likely to be confused about whose site he has reached or to think that Brookfield somehow sponsors West Coast's web site.[3]

Nonetheless, it still found the meta-tags problematic because they would be likely to cause "initial interest confusion."[4] It elaborated, by noting that:

> Web surfers looking for Brookfield's 'MovieBuff' products who are taken by a search engine to 'westcoastvideo.com' will find a database similar enough to 'MovieBuff' such that a sizeable number of consumers who were originally looking for Brookfield's product will simply decide to utilize West Coast's offerings instead. Although there is no source confusion in the sense that consumers know they are patronizing West Coast rather than Brookfield, there is nevertheless initial interest confusion in the sense that, by using 'moviebuff.com' or 'MovieBuff' to divert people looking for 'MovieBuff' to its web site, West Coast improperly benefits from the goodwill that Brookfield developed in its mark.[5]

The court fortified this analysis with a much cited analogy. It said.

---

3. 174 F.3d at 1062.

4. *See* § 29.2.1, *supra*, for a general discussion of initial interest confusion.

5. 174 F.3d at 1062.

Suppose West Coast's competitor (let's call it "Blockbuster") puts up a billboard on a highway reading—"West Coast Video: 2 miles ahead at Exit 7"—where West Coast is really located at Exit 8 but Blockbuster is located at Exit 7. Customers looking for West Coast's store will pull off at Exit 7 and drive around looking for it. Unable to locate West Coast, but seeing the Blockbuster store right by the highway entrance, they may simply rent there. Even consumers who prefer West Coast may find it not worth the trouble to continue searching for West Coast since there is a Blockbuster right there. Customers are not confused in the narrow sense: they are fully aware that they are purchasing from Blockbuster and they have no reason to believe that Blockbuster is related to, or in any way sponsored by, West Coast. Nevertheless, the fact that there is only initial consumer confusion does not alter the fact that Blockbuster would be misappropriating West Coast's acquired goodwill.[6]

The court was careful to note that a party in West Coast's position would be free to use ordinary descriptive terms in its meta-tags, even if those terms happened to correspond to another firm's trademarks. Thus, West Coast would have been within its rights to include the two separate sequential words "movie buff" in meta-tags, because those are conventional words used to describe someone who likes movies, and would be a relevant way for West Coast to describe the consumers to whom it sought to appeal.[7] In the actual case, however, by using the word "moviebuff" without a space between the words, West Coast was taking a term that had no meaning except as Brookfield's trademark. The court also indicated that West Coast could make comparative statements on its Web Page. As an example it said that West Coast's "web page might well include an advertisement banner such as 'Why pay for MovieBuff when you can get the same thing here for free?' which clearly employs 'MovieBuff'to refer to Brookfield's products. West Coast, however, presently uses Brookfield's trademark not to reference Brookfield's products, but instead to . . . attract people to its web site. . . . That is not fair use."

The analysis in *Brookfield* is not necessarily compelling. The court speaks of a Web searcher being "taken" by a search engine to the site of the party using the challenged meta-tags. Of course search engines do not take surfers anywhere. They merely provide lists of sites, and the surfer gets to decide which, if any, she will visit. Moreover, as the court itself noted, in that list of sites, each URL is clearly displayed. Thus even if West Coast's site appears at the top of the search results because of its massive "cyber-stuffing" of the MOVIEBUFF mark into its meta-tags, any consumer who clicks on the link to West Coast's site would necessarily know that she is going to the West Coast site.

6. *Id.* at 1064.

7. This was the analysis used in Playboy Enterprises, Inc. v. Welles, 279 F.3d 796 (9th Cir.2002), which held that the defendant's use of the trademark PLAYMATE OF THE YEAR in meta-tags was legitimate fair use because it was descriptive of a position she previously had held. The case is discussed in § 31.2.3, *supra*.

Admittedly, consumers might not know the name of the company that owns the MOVIEBUFF mark, and thus might have no way of knowing whether West Coast or Brookfield is really the site they are looking for, and might thus randomly click on the West Coast link and then stay there. However, given that the court concludes that Brookfield, as the owner of the MOVIEBUFF mark, was entitled to the domain name "moviebuff.com" it seems pretty far-fetched to think that surfers will mechanically click on the first site to appear in the search results without even glancing further down the list to notice that there is a site with the URL that matches the trademark. Indeed, the web surfer might first try "moviebuff.com" before even resorting to a search engine, and might only be using a search engine precisely in order to find other companies that are *like* the purveyors of genuine MOVIEBUFF software, but are not that same company.

It is also unclear how the court would analyze a situation in which West Coast placed in its meta-tags the phrase "Our products compete with MOVIEBUFF brand" or "MOVIEBUFF competitor" over and over again. Its language suggests that this would be permissible fair use, yet the effect could be to propel West Coast to the top of search result lists just as effectively as the use of the unmodified trademark would.

Despite these possible criticisms, several subsequent cases have followed *Brookfield* in using the "initial interest confusion" doctrine to hold that the use of another party's trademarks in meta-tags is infringing.[8] Professor McCarthy also approves of the *Brookfield* court's analysis, remarking that "if this sort of deception were legal and every web site routinely inserted attractive and irrelevant meta tags, then meta tags would cease to have any use in navigating the Internet."[9] It may be, however, that as search engines become more sophisticated they will no longer afford much weight to the repeated use of the same word hundreds of times in a meta-tag. Such a technological development would make cyber-stuffing futile and might make the *Brookfield* analysis moot.

§ 33.4   The Use of Trademarks as Keywords for Web Advertising

Anyone who has spent time surfing the web will have encountered advertising. Initially, the typical advertisement consisted of a "banner" ad at the top of a Web page. Such advertising invites the viewer to click

---

8. *See, e.g.,* New York State Society of Certified Public Accountants v. Eric Louis Associates, Inc., 79 F.Supp.2d 331 (S.D.N.Y.1999) (defendant's "use of the . . . 'NYSSCPA' meta-tag caused a likelihood of confusion because it created initial interest confusion"); Eli Lilly and Co. v. Natural Answers, Inc., 233 F.3d 456 (7th Cir.2000), *aff'g,* 86 F.Supp.2d 834 (S.D.Ind.2000) (defendant's "clear intent" in using plaintiff's PROZAC mark among its meta-tags, "whether or not it was successful, was to divert Internet users searching for information on PROZAC® to [defendant's] web site."). *See generally* Chad J. Doellinger, *Trademarks, Metatags, and Initial Interest Confusion: a Look to the Past to Re-conceptualize the Future,* 41 IDEA: J.L. & TECH. 173 (2001).

9. J. Thomas McCarthy, TRADEMARKS AND UNFAIR COMPETITION § 25:69.

on the ad and be directly transported to the web site of the advertiser if he or she is interested in the product or service being advertised. More recently, advertisers have resorted to "pop up" advertising. In this format, a new window opens, often on top of the web page the surfer is visiting, thus obscuring its content. The pop up remains until the surfer either closes the advertising window or clicks on it to check it out.

Like all advertisers, advertisers on the web try to target their message to their audience. One does not need a degree in marketing to know that it would not make much sense to advertise incontinence remedies on the MTV Web site, or skateboards at the site operated by the American Association of Retired Persons (even though a small number of visitors in each case might actually be interested in those products). Where the advertising is placed on a topical web site, it is easy enough for the advertiser to target the audience. Thus products for retirees can be advertised at the AARP site, if the proprietor of the site is willing to take advertising, and everyone will be happy.

The situation for advertisers is a bit more tricky with sites such as search engines or web portals. When a surfer goes to Google.com or Yahoo.com, he or she might fall into any one of a myriad of demographic categories. How then to target the advertising? One way is through the use of keywords. When the surfer enters a search query into the search engine, that search query reveals something about what is on that person's mind. Consequently, an advertiser might contract with the owner of the search engine site to have its banner advertisements appear only when certain words are typed into the search engine. For instance, the marketing folks at Ford Motor might arrange to have their banner advertisement appear whenever anyone types the words "car" or "automobile" into the search engine window. In this situation, the words "car" and "automobile" are called "keywords." Because "car" and "automobile" are generic words, such an arrangement poses no trademark problems. If both Ford and General Motors wanted to purchase the same keywords from Google or Yahoo, the owner of the web site could conduct an auction, sell the keywords to the first party to request them, or do anything else it felt like.

The trademark issue arises when the owner of the search engine site offers to sell someone else's trademark as a keyword. For instance, Yahoo might offer Ford an arrangement under which a Ford banner ad would appear whenever a web surfer typed the word CHEVROLET or BUICK (which are trademarks of Ford's competitor, General Motors). The trademark owner in such a case would argue that the search engine proprietor (Yahoo in the example) is trading on the selling power and goodwill of its mark in order to enrich itself through enhanced advertising revenues. Such a trademark owner might claim that the practice could result in dilution of its mark because it might lessen its selling power.

Thus far, the legal authority on the validity of such a claim is sparse. One of the few cases addressing the situation is *Playboy Enterprises v.*

Netscape.[1] In that case, Netscape, which runs a search engine, keyed over 450 words, including the words "playboy" and "playmate" to advertising for various "adult entertainment" web sites. Plaintiff, the owner of the trademarks PLAYBOY and PLAYMATE for various publications and adult oriented entertainment services brought suit for both trademark infringement and dilution. The trial court denied relief on both grounds, reasoning that because the words "playboy" and "playmate" were ordinary words in the English language, there could be no showing that the defendant had actually used any trademarks belonging to the plaintiff.[2] As it noted, "[a]lthough the trademark terms and the English language words are undisputedly identical, which, presumably, leads plaintiff to believe that the use of the English words is akin to use of the trademarks, the holder of a trademark may not remove a word from the English language merely by acquiring trademark rights in it."

One might accuse the court of more than a little naivete in reasoning that any appreciable number of web surfers entering the word "playboy" into a search engine are looking for generic information about carefree wealthy men with active social lives, rather than for information about the plaintiff's services.[3] Moreover, because the court chose to dispose of the case on the basis of the "ordinary word" status of the keywords in question, it dodged the provocative question of how such a case should be resolved if the keyword was unquestionably and solely a trademark, such as KODAK.

While the use of a trademark as a keyword does necessarily take advantage of the informational content of that trademark, the practice seems to us a reasonable one, roughly analogous to comparative advertising. If a customer patronizing a jewelry store asks to see a BULOVA watch, and the sales person says "Have you considered TIMEX brand?" the suggestion might be based on the notion that customers interested in the first brand might also find the second one attractive (and similarly that such customers might not be in the market for the vastly more expensive ROLEX brand). In that sense, the "information" revealed by the customer's use of the BULOVA mark is deployed by the retailer to sell the product of another firms. However the consumer is free to say "No thank you, I really just want BULOVA." Even more importantly, there is no deception involved in this dialogue. The same seems to be the case with keywords that trigger advertisements. When the consumer inputs CHEVROLET in the search engine and an ad appears touting

---

§ 33.4

1. 55 F.Supp.2d 1070 (C.D.Cal.1999) *aff'd,* 202 F.3d 278 (9th Cir.1999).

2. The court initially denied plaintiff's motion for a preliminary injunction, a ruling which was summarily affirmed on appeal. It is the opinion on that motion that is cited in the previous footnote. In a subsequent opinion, the court granted the defendant summary judgment and dismissed the complaint. *See* Playboy Enterprises, Inc. v.

Netscape Communications Corp., 2000 WL 1308815 (C.D.Cal.2000).

3. Professor McCarthy dryly observes that in his opinion, "it is highly probable that most teenage boys have never even heard of the generic dictionary meaning of 'playboy.'" J. Thomas McCarthy, Trademarks and Unfair Competition § 25:70.1. He might have added that most of them looking for a "playmate" on-line are probably not looking for someone with whom to play board games.

FORD automobiles, the banner ad is merely a suggestion of an alternative. Trademark owners should not be able to erect a moat around their marks to prevent the existence of alternatives from even coming to the attention of consumer.

A somewhat related—but much more pernicious—practice occurs when search engines auction off high placements in lists of search results based on the search words entered by the Web surfer. In this scheme, the potential for consumer deception is considerably greater than with banner or pop-up ads because most web surfers will assume that the search results appearing near the top of a list generated after entry of a keyword are those that are objectively the most relevant to the search, not those belonging to Web Sites that have simply paid for high placement. Where the search engine owner auctions off ordinary English words or generic terms, such as "personal digital assistant," there will be no trademark issues posed by this practice (though it may violate various legal rules concerning consumer protection). On the other hand, where the keyword is the trademark of another firm, such as PALM PILOT, such search engine behavior would seem to raise issues of initial interest confusion at least as serious as those in the meta-tag cases if not more so. At this writing no cases specifically considering this variation of the trademark-keyword problem have been decided. However, in early 2002, a case challenging exactly this practice was filed in federal court in Texas, and it is likely that the next few years will produce some decisions directly addressing this situation.[4]

§ 33.5 The Use of Trademarks in Spam E–Mail Messages

A well-known bane of life on the Internet is the receipt of large numbers of e-mail advertisements, known as "spam" or alternatively as "unsolicited bulk e-mail," or UBE. These messages offering everything from baldness cures to credit cards, to the most lascivious of adult entertainments, are often sent simultaneously to hundreds of thousands of recipients at a time. Scholarly speculation traces this "spam" name to a comedy sketch by the comedy troupe Monty Python: "The prevailing theory on the origins of the term Spam is that it comes from the song in Monty Python's famous 'Spam-loving Vikings sketch.' The Vikings, who were sitting in a restaurant whose menu only included dishes made with Spam, would sing 'Spam Spam Spam Spam Spam Spam' over and over, rising in volume until it was impossible for the other characters in the sketch to converse."[1] Just like those Vikings, e-mail spam can crowd out legitimate messages.

---

4. Mark Nutritionals, Inc. v. Alta Vista Co., Civ. No. SA–02–CA–0087 EP (W.D.Tex.). The complaint can be found online at <http://searchenginewatch.com/sereport/02/02–altavista.doc>.

§ 33.5

1. Joel Sanders, *The Regulation of Indecent Material Accessible to Children on the Internet: Is it Really Alright to Yell Fire in a Crowded Chat Room?*, 39 Cath. Lawyer 125 (1999) (citing, in turn, <http://www.cyber-nothing.org/faqs/net-abuse-faq.html>.).

Spam can raise trademark issues when the sender (or spammer) uses another party's trademark or domain name as its own purported e-mail address, because the recipient will then erroneously interpret who sent the message. This is a classic case of false designation of origin. In *America Online Inc. v. LCGM, Inc.*,[2] AOL alleged that various defendants sent over 92 million spam e-mail messages to AOL customers to promote their various pornographic web sites, despite the fact that AOL's own internal policies barred the use of its system for bulk e-mail. The defendants admitted in discovery that they used special software to evade certain AOL filtering devices meant to block spam. From a trademark perspective, the key allegation in the case was that "defendants forged the domain information "aol.com" in the "from" line of e-mail messages sent to AOL members. . . . Plaintiffs assert[ed] that as a result, many AOL members expressed confusion about whether AOL endorsed defendants' pornographic Web sites or their bulk e-mailing practices.' The defendants essentially admitted this allegation as well.

In the first count of its complaint, AOL asserted a claim under section 43(a) of the Lanham Act for false designation of origin. The district court found that the "recipient of such a message would be led to conclude the sender was an AOL member or AOL, the Internet Service Provider. Indeed, plaintiff alleges that this designation did cause such confusion among many AOL members, who believed that AOL sponsored and authorized defendants' bulk e-mailing practices and pornographic web sites. Finally, plaintiff asserts that these acts damaged AOL's technical capabilities and its goodwill." Citing several earlier spam cases,[3] the court granted summary judgement in favor of AOL.

The court also granted AOL relief on its separate allegation of trademark dilution of the tarnishment variety, noting that AOL had received thousands of complaints about the defendant's practices and observing that "plaintiff's mark will suffer negative associations through defendant's use." The court did not indicate if most of those complaints were based on the pornographic nature of the spam, or more general annoyance at the intrusion of spam regardless of content. Either source of customer irritation, however, does seem to fall squarely within the tarnishment concept.

Of course not all spammers use third party trademarks or domain names in their addresses. By now, most have read the cases condemning such practices and adjusted their conduct accordingly. Consequently, they have now shifted to using cryptic or fictional addresses along with deceptive "subject lines" like "Sorry I Missed Your Phone Call," designed to induce the unwary recipient to open the message. While trademark law is irrelevant in cases of this sort, Internet service providers have sometimes been able to use other, non-trademark, theories to combat spam. Thus, some cases, including the *LCGM* decision discussed

---

2. 46 F.Supp.2d 444 (E.D.Va.1998).

3. The court cited Hotmail Corp. v. Van$ Money Pie Inc., 1998 WL 388389

(N.D.Cal.1998) and America Online, Inc. v. IMS, 24 F.Supp.2d 548 (E.D.Va.1998).

above, hold that the unauthorized sending of large numbers of e-mail messages constitutes a "trespass to chattels."[4] Unfortunately, none of these theories is available to the individual computer user who receives spam, because end users neither own the trademarks that appear in the spam address, nor the computer hardware through which the messages flow.

The public irritation with spam has not escaped the notice of politicians. There have been several bills introduced in Congress to deal directly with spam,[5] and some foreign nations have already adopted anti-spam legislation. About half the states have also passed various forms of anti-spam legislation,[6] including criminal provisions in some cases. There may be serious questions about whether certain of these state statutes conflict with the Commerce Clause of the Constitution that will have to be resolved on a case by case basis, given the wide variation in their provisions.[7] In addition, many software developers are offering increasingly sophisticated spam-blocking features as part of e-mail programs or as stand alone utilities with names such as SpamKiller, SpamCop or iHateSpam, allowing the truly frustrated computer user to resort to a moderately effective form of self-help.

---

4. 46 F.Supp.2d at 451. *See also* Verizon Online Services, Inc. v. Ralsky, 203 F.Supp.2d 601, 606 (E.D.Va.2002).

5. *See, e.g.,* H.R. 95 (107th Cong. 1st Sess.) (January 3, 2001) (proposed "Unsolicited Commercial Electronic Mail Act of 2001"); H.R. 718 (107th Cong. 1st Sess.) (June 5, 2001) (proposed "Anti–Spamming Act of 2001").

6. For a list of relevant state statutes, and links to their full text, *see* <http://www.spamlaws.com/state/index.html>.

7. For a decision rejecting a constitutional challenge to California's state anti-spam law, *see* Ferguson v. Friendfinders, Inc., 94 Cal.App.4th 1255, 115 Cal.Rptr.2d 258 (1st Dist.2002), *review denied* (Apr. 10, 2002).

Chapter 34

INTERNATIONAL ASPECTS OF TRADEMARK PROTECTION

Table of Sections

§ 34.1 Territoriality of Marks and International Ownership

Trademarks are creatures of national laws. They are protected within a given nation only when the claimant has observed the relevant rules of that nation's domestic laws. Consequently, the owner of state or federal trademark rights under U.S. law does not automatically own the right to use its mark on the relevant goods in any other nation, unless it takes steps to conform to that other nation's laws. Moreover, the U.S. trademark owner may actually be precluded from using the mark in a given country if another firm is considered to have superior rights under the domestic laws of that country, even if the U.S. firm was the first to use the mark world-wide and is a much bigger firm with a much larger volume of sales. Similarly, a foreign firm that may have been using a mark for decades in dozens of countries around the world has no automatic rights to that mark in the United States unless it observes the requirements of U.S. law. As the Court of Appeals for the Federal Circuit has observed, "trademark rights exist in each country solely according to that country's statutory scheme."[1]

§ 34.1

1. Person's Co. v. Christman, 900 F.2d 1565 (Fed.Cir.1990).

This principle is sometimes labeled a rule of "territoriality." It is embodied in the Paris Convention, which was first promulgated in 1883 and is the premier international treaty governing international trademark rights. The treaty declares, in Article 6(3), that "a mark duly registered in a country of the Union shall be regarded as independent of marks registered in other countries of the Union, including the country of origin." Over 100 countries, including the United States, have ratified the Paris Convention, and the American courts have consistently concluded that the U.S. has therefore accepted the principle of territoriality of trademarks.

One obvious consequence of the territoriality rule is that where trademark ownership depends on priority of use, as it does in the United States, the only priority that is relevant is priority in domestic commerce. "It is well settled that foreign use is ineffectual to create trademark rights in the United States."[2] Moreover, a firm cannot obtain U.S. priority by promoting a foreign business in the United States—it must actually sell goods or provide services in the U.S. in order to establish U.S. rights.[3] Even if a U.S. firm begins using a mark here with full knowledge of another firm's use of that same mark in a foreign nation, the foreign firm has no rights, and the U.S. user is the party entitled to Lanham Act registration.

A typical example is *Person's Co. v. Christman,* where the defendant had seen the mark PERSON'S used on wearing apparel in Japan, then returned to the U.S. and began using the same mark on apparel in the U.S. domestic market. Some time later, the Japanese firm began selling goods in the U.S. and obtained a Lanham Act registration. The Court of Appeals for the Federal Circuit ruled that the Japanese firm's registration should be cancelled because the U.S. firm was the senior user of the mark in domestic U.S. commerce, notwithstanding the argument of the Japanese firm that the U.S. firm had adopted the mark in bad faith. The court distinguished cases involving bad faith by geographically remote junior users in domestic commerce by noting that "appellant's argument ignores the territorial nature of trademark rights."

While a foreign firm must thus actually market its goods in the United States in order to establish trademark rights here, it need not do so directly, or all by itself. Frequently foreign firms contract with a U.S. firm to serve as their exclusive distributor in the United States. When they do, the sales of that distributor are a sufficient predicate for a claim of U.S. trademark ownership by the foreign firm. Of course, the manufacturer and distributor can alter this arrangement by contract, and specify that the U.S. distributor will be the owner of the U.S. trademark rights, provided that the transaction does not violate the rule forbidding

---

2. La Societe Anonyme des Parfums Le Galion v. Jean Patou, Inc., 495 F.2d 1265, 1270 n. 4 (2d Cir.1974).

3. *See, e.g.,* Buti v. Perosa, S.R.L., 139 F.3d 98 (2d Cir.1998), *cert. denied,* 525 U.S. 826, 119 S.Ct. 73, 142 L.Ed.2d 57 (1998); Linville v. Rivard, 26 USPQ2d 1508 (T.T.A.B.1993), *vacated and remanded on other grounds,* 11 F.3d 1074, 31 USPQ2d 1218 (Fed.Cir.1993).

an "assignment in gross," which was reviewed elsewhere in this text.[4] In the absence of such a contract, however, numerous American cases indicate that the foreign manufacturer—not the distributor—is presumed to be the owner of the mark in the United States.[5] On the other hand, this presumption is rebuttable if the U.S. distributor can show that it is the party that actually possesses the goodwill associated with the product.[6]

The territoriality principle means that the same mark may be simultaneously used by entirely unrelated firms for the same category of goods or services in different nations of the worlds. In such a case, this legal situation supposedly reflects the underlying commercial reality that the mark identifies different sources and different product attributes in each national market. Thus in the case involving the PERSON'S mark described above, the mark in the United States symbolizes the U.S. manufacturer and the goods with the various stylistic and quality attributes associated with that producer, while the mark in Japan would signal the Japanese producer and goods with entirely different traits.

Of course, people do travel between the U.S. and Japan, and as world markets have become more integrated and economic globalization has accelerated, the simultaneous use of the same mark by different firms in different nations poses an increased risk of consumer confusion that was not very likely in former times. Itinerant consumers who travel around the world for business or pleasure are more likely than ever to encounter the same mark in different countries and to be confused about whether the mark signals products of consistent attributes everywhere they see it. Unfortunately, the international legal system has not yet come up with a solution to this problem.

34.1.1 Territoriality and Well–Known Marks

There is one important exception to the rule of strict territoriality and its corollary grant of trademark rights to the firm that first used or registered the mark in each national market. Where a mark is considered "well-known," the leading international trademark treaties require that member countries grant the owner of that mark rights superior to a local registrant or user even if the local party can show priority of registration or use in the country in question. This rule was first

4. *See* § 32.1.1, *supra. See also* Restatement (Third) of Unfair Competition, § 34, comment d (1995), "[A]n assignment of United States trademark rights by a foreign manufacturer to its United States distributor ordinarily will not be regarded as an assignment in gross, even if the transfer occurs after the designation has acquired trademark significance in this country."

5. TMT North America, Inc. v. Magic Touch GmbH, 124 F.3d 876 (7th Cir.1997) (there is a "presumption that, in the absence of an assignment of trademark rights, a foreign manufacturer retains all rights to a trademark even after licensing the use of

the trademark to an exclusive U.S. distributor."); Automated Productions, Inc. v. FMB Maschinenbaugesellschaft mbH & Co., 34 USPQ2d 1505, 1515 (N.D.Ill.1994) ("there is a presumption that in absence of express or implied acknowledgment or transfer by foreign manufacturer of rights in the United States, all rights to trademark remain in the foreign manufacturer.").

6. *See, e.g.,* Sengoku Works Ltd. v. RMC Int'l, Inc., 96 F.3d 1217 (9th Cir.1996), *cert. denied,* 521 U.S. 1103, 117 S.Ct. 2478, 138 L.Ed.2d 987 (1997).

established in the late nineteenth century with the adoption of the Paris Convention, mentioned in the preceding section.[7] In the mid–1990's, the members of the General Agreement on Tariffs and Trade promulgated an agreement known as Trade–Related Aspects of Intellectual Property, or TRIPS, which among its many features greatly strengthened the protection accorded to well-known marks. These treaty provisions reflect the common sense notion that where consumers everywhere in the world associate a given mark with a given producer, it would be deceptive and confusing to allow anyone but that producer to use the mark.

Under TRIPS, the special protection for well-known marks applies to both trademarks and service marks, whereas the Paris Convention provision is limited to goods only.[8] TRIPS also makes it clear that a well-known mark is entitled to protection even if it is used on different types of goods or services than those sold by the mark owner, "provided that use of that trademark in relation to those goods or services would indicate a connection between those goods or services and the owner of the registered trademark and provided that the interests of the owner of the registered trademark are likely to be damaged by such use."[9] This standard is essentially the "likelihood of confusion" test for related goods that is commonly used in U.S. domestic trademark disputes.

The key issue for a trademark owner who seeks to invoke the special protection afforded by these treaties is establishing that its mark is "well-known." In this regard, TRIPS provides that "in determining whether a trademark is well-known, Members shall take account of the knowledge of the trademark in the relevant sector of public, including knowledge in that Member concerned which has been obtained as a result of the promotion of the trademark."[10] This too provides greater protection than the parallel provision in the Paris Convention, which speaks of marks "well-known in that country," since a mark might qualify as well-known to a sector of the public—such as affluent consumers, or business people—in a large nation such as India, China or Brazil, even if the mark is not known in the nation as whole.

It might seem curious that a mark could become known in a nation where the owner of the mark sells no goods or services. Some famous marks, however, may be known in many countries even though the mark owner conducts no business there, by virtue of advertising, references in the news media, or knowledge obtained by international travelers. Unfortunately, there is no international registry of well-known marks, and it can consequently be difficult to predict in advance whether the

---

7. *See* Article 6*bis* of the Paris Convention, which provides: "The countries of the Union undertake, ex officio if their legislation so permits, or at the request of an interested party, to refuse or to cancel the registration, and to prohibit the use, of a trademark which constitutes a reproduction, an imitation, or a translation, liable to create confusion, of a mark considered by the competent authority of the country of registration or use to be well-known in that country as being already the mark of a person entitled to the benefits of this Convention and used for identical or similar goods."

8. *See* TRIPS, Article 16.

9. *See* TRIPS, Article 16(3).

10. Id.

benefits accorded by the Paris Convention and TRIPS to well-known marks will be granted to any specific mark in any particular country. Some nations have attempted to promulgate bright line tests, stating that a mark is "well-known" if it is known by some specific percentage of the public. Other nations, such as Brazil and China, have attempted to deal with this problem by adopting special registers of "famous" or notorious marks.[11] Nonetheless, there is considerable inconsistency on the issue in different legal systems around the world.

Despite the ambiguities in determining which marks are "well-known," the special treatment accorded such marks can be extremely useful to U.S. firms which own truly famous marks with world-wide renown. For instance, if the Coca–Cola company has never used or registered the mark COCA–COLA in Paraguay (an unlikely assumption), it could nonetheless invoke TRIPS to prevent a local Paraguayan firm from obtaining rights to that mark under Paraguayan law, because the fame of the mark requires the administrative agencies and courts of Paraguay to deny a trademark registration application for that mark filed by any other firm, even if that local firm was the first to file for registration in that country.[12] Moreover, if a local firm had "beaten it to the punch" and obtained a Paraguayan registration of the mark, the U.S. Coca–Cola company would be entitled to have that registration cancelled, regardless of whether the Paraguayan firm was using the mark for carbonated beverages, or for some other category of goods, so long as Coca–Cola could demonstrate that consumers in Paraguay would believe there was a connection between the U.S. company and the goods in question.[13] As Professor McCarthy has pointed out, "one common use of the famous marks doctrine is to fight trademark pirates who rush to register a famous mark on goods on which it had not yet been registered in a nation by the legitimate foreign owner."[14]

Foreign firms are, of course, entitled to use the same argument to prevent exploitation of their well-known marks in the United States even if they haven't taken any steps to secure U.S. trademark protection. If a U.S. party were to attempt to register a "well-known" mark of a foreign firm, perhaps arguing that it had made first use in domestic commerce, the U.S. PTO could deny registration on the ground that the mark "falsely suggest[s] a connection with" the foreign owner in contravention of § 2(a) of the U.S. trademark statute. This would also provide a basis for cancellation of the mark pursuant to Lanham Act § 14(3) at any time after registration.

11. *See* Enrique do Amaral, *Famous Marks: The Brazilian Case*, 83 Trademark Rep. 394 (1993).

12. Paraguay is a member of the World Trade Organization, and thus a party to TRIPS. For a list of members, *see* <http://www.wto.org/english/thewto_e/whatis_e/tif_e/org6_e.htm>

13. For an example, *see* Hilton Hotels Corp. v. Belkin & Kalensky, 17 W.W.R. 86 (1955) (B.C.), 1955 WL 40452, where a Canadian court enjoined a Canadian firm from using the mark HILTON for hotel services in Vancouver even though the American owner of the mark had not taken steps to protect the mark in Canada.

14. *See* J. Thomas McCarthy, Trademarks and Unfair Competition, § 29:61.

More generally, Article 10*bis* of the Paris Convention requires all member nations to protect nationals of all other member nations from acts of unfair competition. To implement that obligation, section 44(h) of the Lanham Act grants all the protections of that statute to parties whose country of origin is a treaty partner with the United States. Thus, such parties are entitled to invoke the broad remedial provisions of section 43(a) against any person who uses "any word, term, name, symbol, or device ... which is likely to cause confusion ... as to the affiliation, connection or association of such person with another person, or as to the origin, sponsorship or approval of his or her goods [or] services ...." Certainly where a mark is "well-known," the foreign firm could easily show the requisite confusion and thus enjoin a U.S. firm from using its mark under the unfair competition provisions of section 43(a).

§ 34.2 U.S. Trademark Protection for Foreign Parties

Both the Paris Convention and TRIPS require member nations to adhere to a principle known as "national treatment." This requires each member country to treat foreign parties who apply for trademark protection no less favorably than they treat domestic parties. The national treatment concept can be thought of as a principle of nondiscrimination against foreigners. Consequently, any foreign party seeking U.S. trademark protection is entitled to base its claim on the same activities or representations that would suffice for a domestic firm. For instance, a foreign merchant can begin using the mark in U.S. domestic commerce, and by that act, secure common law rights to the trademark under the laws of the relevant U.S. state or states. Similarly, that foreign merchant can also, based on its use of the mark in domestic U.S. commerce, file for Lanham Act registration. Moreover, a foreign merchant is entitled to seek Lanham Act registration based on an "intent to use" filing, just like a domestic U.S. firm.[1] This treaty obligation of national treatment is given practical effect by the language of the Lanham Act, which speaks consistently in terms of "the owner of a trademark" or "a person who has a bona fide intention to use a trademark" without any reference to the national origin of such parties.

However, neither the Paris Convention nor TRIPS provides any mechanism for the simultaneous protection of trademarks in multiple nations by a single application. As we shall see in the next section, an international agreement, called the Madrid Protocol, attempts to effectuate such a simplified mechanism for simultaneous filings in multiple nations.

The Paris Convention does, however, have one provision that is designed to facilitate the process of protecting a mark in each of several different countries. Once a firm files a trademark application in any nation that is a party to the Convention, that firm is entitled to file in

§ 34.2
1. *See* § 26.2.2, *supra.*

any other member nation within six months and receive the benefit of the earlier filing date.[2] Thus, if a German firm files an application for protection in Germany on March 1st, and then files a U.S. application any time before September 1st, the treaty requires that the U.S. application be treated as if it was filed on March 1st. This six-month grace period gives firms that have begun the process of protecting a trademark in their home country some time to take the necessary steps to secure protection in other nations without losing the benefit of priority associated with the home country filing.

The Lanham Act implements the six-month priority provision of the Paris Convention through the detailed provisions of section 44.[3] The benefits of this section are only available to a person whose "country of origin" is a party to a trademark treaty with the United States.[4] The country of origin is defined as "the country in which [it] has a bona fide and effective industrial or commercial establishment . . . ."[5] Domestic U.S. firms are not entitled to invoke the special benefits of section 44 by going to a foreign nation, getting trademark protection there, and then using the foreign registration as the basis for a claim of priority under the Lanham Act. On the other hand, a firm incorporated in the United States, but with production facilities abroad, is able to take advantage of the provision because its "country of origin" is the foreign nation where those production facilities are located.[6]

Section 44(d) is the provision which substantively implements the Paris Convention six-month priority rule. It provides that if an eligible party has previously filed for trademark registration in any nation that is a party to a relevant treaty, a subsequent U.S. application will be treated as if it was filed on the date of the earlier foreign application, provided the U.S. application is filed within six months of the date on which the foreign application was filed. This priority is only available, however, if the U.S. application conforms exactly to the previously filed foreign application in terms of the details of the mark and the goods for which protection is being sought. In addition, section 44(d) requires that the applicant must include a statement of its bona fide intention to use the mark in U.S. domestic commerce as part of the application.

---

2. Article 4A(1) of the Paris Convention provides: "Any person who has duly filed an application for a . . . trademark, in one of the countries of the Union . . . shall enjoy, for the purpose of filing in the other countries, a right of priority during the periods hereinafter fixed." Article 4C(1) declares that: "The periods of priority referred to above shall be . . . six months for . . . trademarks."

3. Some discussion of these provisions appears earlier in this text, in the chapter dealing with acquisition of Trademark rights.

4. The statute also confers these benefits on parties whose country of origin extends reciprocal rights to nations of the United States by law, even if such country is not a party to a relevant treaty.

5. 15 U.S.C.A. § 1126(c) (2000).

6. Although section 44(i) of the Lanham Act specifies that "citizens or residents of the United States shall have the same benefits as are granted by this section to persons described in subsection (b) of this section," the Trademark Trial and Appeals Board has held that a company located and incorporated only in the United States cannot rely on the special provisions of section 44. *See* In re Eta Systems, Inc., 2 USPQ2d 1367 (T.T.A.B.1987).

To receive the benefit of the early priority date, the foreign application in question need not have been filed in the applicant's country of origin, merely in any country that is a party to a relevant treaty. Thus, if a French firm were to file an application for trademark registration in Brazil on January 15th, and thereafter file an application with the U.S. PTO on April 30th (which is within the 6–month window), the U.S. application would be treated as if it had been filed on January 15th, given that Brazil is a member of the Paris Convention. An early priority date can be especially valuable because under section 7(c) of the Lanham Act, the filing date of an application is also considered to be "constructive use of the mark." Consequently, in this hypothetical situation, the French firm would have superior rights to an American firm that made first use of the mark in U.S. commerce on February 1st as well as against an American firm which filed an "intent to use application" on February 1st, because the French firm would be deemed to have constructively used the mark before both of them—namely on January 15th, which was the date of its Brazilian filing.

Although an applicant eligible to invoke section 44(d) can obtain the benefits of an early priority date, there are no substantive differences between the processing of such an application and any other application under U.S. law. In other words, the application will still be examined to determine if the mark in question is substantively eligible for protection under U.S. law. If the mark contravenes any of the bars to registration itemized in section 2 of the Lanham Act, it will not be registered. Thus, if it is found to be descriptive or to be primarily merely a surname it will only be protected on a showing of secondary meaning; if it is found to be scandalous or immoral, registration would be refused; and so on. To put the same point another way, section 44(d) provides a basis for *filing* a trademark application, but it does not provide an independent basis for the *granting* of a registration.

As we have seen earlier in this text, even if a mark is found eligible for protection under U.S. law, registration does not issue under the Lanham Act unless the applicant has alleged use in interstate commerce in the initial application, or, in the case an intent-to-use application, until the applicant provide a "Statement of Use." However, section 44 goes on to provide another benefit to foreign parties—in effect a separate basis for registration itself. That provision is found in section 44(e) of the statute, which provides that once "a mark [is] duly registered in the country of origin of the foreign applicant [it] may be registered [in the United States].... The application must state the applicant's bona fide intention to use the mark in commerce, but use in commerce shall not be required prior to registration."

Thus, once the foreign applicant obtains registration in its home country, it can secure a U.S. registration even though it has not yet used the mark in the United States. A close reading of section 44(e) will reveal, however, that the foreign registration must have been issued by the applicant's "country of origin." Consequently, in the example above, while the French firm could rely on its Brazilian filing for an early priority date under section 44(d), it would not be able to use a Brazilian registration as a basis for U.S. registration under section 44(e). It would either have to actually use the mark in the U.S. or obtain a *French* registration before the U.S. registration would issue. Once it obtains the French registration, however, it is entitled to Lanham Act registration without any use in the United States.

This basis for registration is highly significant because in many nations, trademark registrations are routinely granted without any requirement of prior use. In the foregoing hypothetical, the French firm might receive its French registration without ever having used the mark in France, or for that matter anywhere in the world. While section 44 makes it clear that use *in U.S. commerce* is not required for an applicant relying on a foreign registration, one might wonder if use elsewhere is, or ought to be required as a matter of domestic law. In the fifty years since Congress adopted the Lanham Act the case law on this question has changed several times.

The current view is that an applicant under section 44 is entitled to registration even if it has never used the mark anywhere in the world. The key case is *Crocker National Bank v. Canadian Imperial Bank of Commerce*.[7] It declares that "the only proper construction of § 44(c), (d) and (e) is that a foreign national qualified under § 44(b) is entitled to an alternative basis for registration of a trademark registered in its country of origin without regard to whether such mark is in use prior to the application's filing date."

Consequently, the special rule of section 44(e) is the sole exception to the otherwise iron-clad principle requiring trademark use prior to federal trademark registration in the United States. Once such a registration issues, however, it is on the same footing as any other Lanham Act trademark registration.[8] Thus, if the foreign firm does not make use of the mark in the United States within a reasonable time after the registration issues, it is vulnerable to a petition to cancel on grounds of abandonment. Indeed, under section 45 of the Lanham Act there is a presumption of abandonment if the mark has not been used within three years. Moreover, section 8 of the statute requires that five years after the mark has been registered, the registrant must file an affidavit attesting that the mark is in use "in commerce," a phrase which means domestic U.S. interstate commerce. Thus even in the absence of a cancellation petition alleging abandonment, the foreign firm must use the mark by the time of the required section 8 filing or the registration will be automatically cancelled.

As noted at the outset of this section, foreign applicants are not limited to section 44(e)—they are free to rely on multiple basis for U.S. registration. Thus, they can predicate an application on *both* the owner-

---

7. 223 USPQ 909 (T.T.A.B.1984).

8. Section 44(f) declares that registrations grounded on section 44 are "independent of the registration in the country of origin" and to "be governed by the provisions of this chapter." 15 U.S.C.A. § 1126(f) (2000). *See also* Imperial Tobacco, Ltd. v. Philip Morris, Inc., 899 F.2d 1575 (Fed.Cir. 1990).

ship of a foreign registration (the section 44(e) basis) and on a conventional "intent to use" in domestic commerce (the section 1(b) basis). This can serve strategic purposes. For instance, if the foreign registration does not issue, or is delayed, the foreign firm can perfect its U.S. registration under section 1(b) by using the mark in the U.S. and filing the requisite "statement of use" without having to wait for matters to be resolved in the relevant foreign trademark office. Similarly if there is some doubt about whether the foreign registration is from the applicant's "country of origin," or if there is a discrepancy between the goods covered in the foreign registration and the U.S. application, the section 1(b) basis for registration would provide a fall-back mechanism to secure protection in the United States.[9]

If a U.S. registration application predicated on a foreign registration is approved by the examining attorney at the U.S. PTO it will be published just like any other proposed mark, and third parties have the right to file an opposition on any available ground. Such grounds can include an attack on the validity of the underlying foreign registration. For instance, an opposer can show that the predicate foreign registration has been subsequently cancelled by administrative or judicial action in the foreign nation.[10] The possibility of such oppositions is yet another reasons why foreign applicants will often couple a request for registration under section 44(e) with a request under the intent-to-use provisions of section 1(b).

Finally, a foreign firm that has never made use of its registered mark in the United States may also face a hurdle if it attempts to sue for infringement. Despite ownership of a Lanham Act registration, such a firm is may not be able to prove a likelihood of confusion until it begins actual sales in the United States. Under the well-established *Dawn Donut* doctrine such a foreign firm would not be entitled to any relief.[11] Of course, if the foreign firm already has a reputation in the United States and is known to American consumers, then the requisite confusion might exist in advance of any sales, and injunctive relief would be appropriate. In most cases, however, a foreign firm with a U.S. trademark registration which is not yet using the mark in the United States is not likely to be able to use that registration offensively against an alleged domestic infringer.

§ 34.3 Foreign Trademark Protection for U. S. Parties

The chief obstacles for U.S. firms seeking trademark protection in other countries are procedural rather than substantive. Under present law, a U.S. firm seeking to protect its trademarks in other nations must

---

9. *See generally,* James T. Walsh, *Tips from the Trademark Examining Operation: The Impact of the TLRA of 1988 on the Filing of Applications Under Section 44 of the Trademark Act,* 80 TRADEMARK REP. 421 (1990); J. THOMAS MCCARTHY, TRADEMARKS AND UNFAIR COMPETITION, § 29:15.

10. *See* Fioravanti v. Fioravanti Corrado S.R.L., 230 USPQ 36 (T.T.A.B.1986).

11. *See* § 29.4, *supra.*

file a separate application in every country where it wishes to obtain trademark rights. There is no "one-stop-shopping." This is, of course, expensive and burdensome. For firms contemplating use of a mark on a global basis, local counsel must be hired in dozens of nations, filings must be made in numerous languages, and administrative and legal fees can be quite substantial. For firms with extensive product lines and multiple trademarks, this cost and the risk of error is enormous.

In 1891 several nations adopted an international agreement known as the Madrid Agreement Concerning the International Registration of Marks to deal with the problem. The Madrid Agreement was designed to permit a trademark owner to simultaneous file for rights in multiple countries through a single filing. Several features of the Madrid Agreement, however, conflicted with U.S. domestic law, and the United States never became a party to that agreement. Indeed, the system established by that treaty was only moderately effective because of the relatively small number of countries that adopted the Agreement.

In 1989, a diplomatic conference promulgated a new document—known as the Protocol Relating to the Madrid Agreement Concerning the International Registration of Marks (or Madrid Protocol)—which was responsive to the various U.S. objections to the original Madrid Agreement. Under the Madrid Protocol, a firm filing for trademark protection in its home country can also indicate that it wishes to protect the mark in other countries that are parties to the Protocol. The national office will forward the application to the World Intellectual Property Organization in Geneva, which would issue an "international registration" for the mark and also forward the application to each national office designated in the application. Each foreign office would then evaluate the application under its own national law, but the applicant would be spared the expense and inconvenience of having to make multiple filings.[1]

The United States signed the Madrid Protocol several years ago, the Senate finally ratified it in October, 2002, and the necessary implementing legislation was finally adopted shortly thereafter.[2] The effect will be to greatly facilitate the efforts of American firms seeking simultaneous protection of their marks in many countries around the globe.

In addition, since 1996 American firms have been able to benefit from the decision of the European Union to establish a single Community Trademark. Any person who is from a country which is a party to the Paris Convention or the World Trade Organization may file an application for a Community Trademark, with the Office for Harmonization in the Internal Market, Trademarks and Designs (or OHIM), located in Alicante, Spain. That office will examine the mark to determine if there are any "absolute" grounds for refusal of registration—such as generic-

§ 34.3

1. For a more detailed discussion, *see* Roger E. Schechter, *Facilitating Trademark Registration Abroad: The Implications of*

U.S. Ratification of the Madrid Protocol, 25 Geo. Wash. J. Int'l L. & Econ. 419 (1991).

2. Pub.L. 107–273, §§ 13401–13403 (November 2, 2002).

ness, or descriptiveness without secondary meaning. It will also search the records of the EU and its member nations to determine if the proposed mark conflicts with a previously registered mark, but such a conflict will not result in a denial. Instead, the holder of the previous registration will be informed and has the opportunity to file an opposition within three months. Once issued, a European Trademark provides protection in all 15 nations of the EU. American firms have made significant use of the Community Trademark—between 25 and 30 percent of the applications handled by that office are from U.S. firms. Moreover, if the EU continues to expand to include additional members, as seems likely, the value and convenience of the Community Trademark will be further enhanced.

While neither a single "global" trademark application process nor a single substantive "global" trademark yet exists, there seems to be significant momentum towards more streamlined forms of multi-nation application, and towards increasing regionalization of trademarks. It may be that in only a few years, world-wide protection might be obtained by securing only three or four registrations, each valid across broad trading areas such as Europe or North America, and that only a single application might be required to obtain those registrations. Such a development might be one of those happy outcomes that both benefits the business community and protects consumer interests at the same time.

§ 34.4   Trans–National Infringement Issues

If a foreign firm sells goods in the United States with a mark confusingly similar to one owned by an American firm, it is plainly guilty of infringement, and this is true even if that foreign firm has rights to the mark in its home country. This is a straightforward application of the territoriality principle reviewed at the start of this chapter. The same result applies if the only activity of the foreign firm is to import the goods into the United States, leaving the sales activity to American wholesalers or retailers.

A number of specific statutory provisions give American trademark owners additional weapons to prevent infringing goods from ever entering the country in the first place. Section 42 of the Lanham Act declares that "no article of imported merchandise which shall ... copy or simulate" a registered trademark may be admitted to entry at any customhouse of the United States.[1] While that provision only refers to "registered" marks, section 43(b) says that any goods that violate section 43 also may not be imported and, as we have seen, section 43(a) protects unregistered marks as well. The actual enforcement mecha-

<hr/>

§ 34.4

1. The same substantive prohibition against importation of goods bearing a registered marks appears as well in 19 U.S.C.A. § 1526(a) (2000), though that provision refers only to marks owned by domestic U.S. persons or companies.

nisms differ somewhat depending on whether the foreign goods are "counterfeits" or whether they are merely infringing.

A counterfeit mark is defined in the Lanham Act as "a spurious mark which is identical with or substantially indistinguishable from a registered mark."[2] In cases involving counterfeits of registered marks that have been previously recorded with the U.S Customs Service, 19 U.S.C.A. § 1526(e) provides that the goods shall be seized and forfeited. The use of the word "shall" makes the seizure requirement automatic and mandatory. Such goods cannot be diverted to another country, nor will they be released if the counterfeit marks are removed. The Customs Service will also inform the owner of the trademark of the seizure and the goods in question must be destroyed unless that trademark owner consents to some other disposition (such as donation to charity). A party attempting to import counterfeit goods is also subject to a variety of civil and criminal penalties. Of course, if the importer feels that the marks have been unjustly deemed counterfeit, it may seek judicial review of the Customs Service's determination in the courts.

Where the goods are counterfeit, but the mark has not been registered with the Customs Service, Customs is still empowered to seize the goods, but in this case, the statutory language in not mandatory. Similarly, in cases involving goods that bear trademarks "confusingly similar" to marks that have been recorded with Customs, rather than outright counterfeit goods, the goods also may be seized.[3] Imported goods that bear marks confusingly similar to marks that have not been recorded with the Customs Service are not barred from importation, but of course the mark owner can then sue for infringement and seek an injunction against their further sale within the United States.

One of the most problematic situations involving trans-national infringement arises when a foreign firm conducts no activities in the United States, but its activities abroad have an indirect effect on the domestic commerce of the United States. The leading case dealing with the problem is *Steele v. Bulova Watch Co.*[4] The plaintiff in that case owned the mark BULOVA for watches. The defendant purchased watch parts in the United States and exported them to Mexico. It them assembled the watches in Mexico and placed the mark BULOVA on them. It sold those watches in Mexico only. It did not import them to the United States or otherwise offer them for sale here. Not surprisingly, however, many of the watches found their way to the United States because Americans in Mexico for business or pleasure purchased them there and then brought them home. When those watches would break, some consumers brought them to American jewelers for repair, thinking that they were genuine American BULOVA brand products. In due course the plaintiff received complaints from the jewelers and filed suit.

2. 15 U.S.C.A. § 1127 (2000).

3. 19 U.S.C.A. § 1595a(c) (2000).

4. 344 U.S. 280, 73 S.Ct. 252, 97 L.Ed. 319 (1952).

Because the defendant in *Steele* was a U.S. citizen, Bulova was able to obtain personal jurisdiction. The question in the case was whether as a substantive matter, his activities in Mexico constituted a violation of U.S. law. The Supreme Court held that they were. Because his Mexican trademark had been held invalid by the Mexican courts the U.S. Supreme Court did not have to deal with the prospect that its ruling might conflict with Mexican law. It found that the effects of defendant's conduct were not confined within the territorial limits of Mexico. It noted that defendant had committed the predicate act of buying the parts for the watches in the U.S. and that his foreign activities impaired plaintiff's trademark rights in the United States.

Subsequent cases have taken slightly different lessons from *Steele*. In the Second Circuit, courts have applied a three part test to determine whether to grant extraterritorial effect to U.S. trademark laws. A plaintiff must show: (1) that defendant's conduct has a substantial effect on United States commerce; (2) that the defendant is a U.S. citizen; and (3) that there is no conflict with valid foreign trademark rights and no valid foreign trademark registration.[5] Thus, where a Canadian company made sales in Canada only, under a mark to which it held valid Canadian rights, an American plaintiff that owned the same mark for the same goods under U.S. law was denied relief notwithstanding the effects on U.S. commerce and the rights of the U.S. party.[6] The Fourth Circuit uses a similar approach, but has characterized the required effect on U.S. commerce as "significant" rather than "substantial."[7] The Ninth Circuit has articulated a balancing test in which the degree of effect on U.S. commerce is compared with the degree of interference U.S. jurisdiction might create with foreign commerce and/or valid interests under foreign law.[8] Bear in mind that in addition to these various substantive tests, the U.S. party must be able to secure personal jurisdiction over the defendant in order to litigate in the U.S. courts, and that in many cases, personal jurisdiction will be unavailable.

Another facet of the international infringement problem involves "spill-over" advertising. For instance, the mark BAYER for aspirin was at one time owned by entirely independent firms in the United States and Germany.[9] Certain German publications advertising the BAYER brand aspirin of the German firm, such as *Der Spiegel*, were available in the United States at sites such as international newsstands and airports. The U.S. mark owner claimed that the German firm should be enjoined from engaging in such advertising activities because they invoked the BAYER brand name in a misleading fashion and violated its rights in the BAYER trademark in the United States. However, the Second Circuit held that an injunction would not be appropriate in such a case. It

5. Vanity Fair Mills v. T. Eaton Co., 234 F.2d 633 (2d Cir.1956), *cert. denied*, 352 U.S. 871, 77 S.Ct. 96, 1 L.Ed.2d 76 (1956).

6. *Id.*

7. Nintendo of America v. Aeropower Co., 34 F.3d 246 (4th Cir.1994).

8. Reebok Int'l Ltd. v. Marnatech Enterprises, Inc., 970 F.2d 552 (9th Cir.1992).

9. A merger in the mid–1990's brought the two independent firms under common ownership.

observed that "not every activity of a foreign corporation with any tendency to create some confusion among American consumer can be prohibited by the extraterritorial reach of a[n] ... injunction," and that "only those foreign uses of the mark ... that are likely to have significant trademark-impairing effects on United States commerce" could be enjoined.[10] This seems a prudent and virtually essential result in a system of territorially based trademark rights. Given modern methods of communication, almost any activities taken by a foreign firm in its home market could come to the attention of U.S. consumers and generate at least some small amount of confusion. A rule making such confusion actionable would amount to an attempt to bar foreign firms from advertising in their own home markets.

A reverse situation can arise when a firm applies infringing trademarks in the United States, but, instead of selling the goods here, exports them to another nation where a U.S. firm owns the local trademark rights. In *American Rice, Inc. v. Arkansas Rice Growers Co-op, Ass'n*,[11] the Fifth Circuit found that conduct of this nature violated U.S. trademark laws because it diverted sales from the plaintiff's domestic export operations. The court observed that "[m]erely because the consummation of the unlawful activity occurred on foreign soil is no assistance to the defendant .... There is also no requirement that defendant's products bearing the infringing marks make their way back into the United States." This is a rather broad reading of American judicial power, of course, and critics have questioned what legitimate interest the United States might have where the only consumers who can be confused by the practices in question are those who live in another nation. On the other hand, the reality is that not every nation of the world has a functioning legal system operating under the neutral rule of law, and where commercial harm is being suffered by an American firm from practices of this sort, its only practical recourse may be in the U.S. courts.

Perhaps the most significant transnational infringement problems in the coming years are likely to involve commerce conducted over the Internet. Given the global reach of the World Wide Web, increasing conflicts in a world of territorially based trademark rights are inevitable. Where a U.S. firm owns a given mark in the United States, and a foreign firm owns a nearly identical mark for the same goods in its home country, each might attempt to establish a presence on the Web. Consumers searching for one might locate the other, place an order, and never realize that they bought from someone other than whom they intended.

One of the few cases to deal with this problem at this early stage in the development of international e-commerce is *Euromarket Designs, Inc. v. Crate & Barrel Ltd.*[12] The defendant in that case opened a retail store in Dublin, Ireland, under the name CRATE & BARREL, selling

10.   Sterling Drug, Inc. v. Bayer, AG, 14 F.3d 733 (2d Cir.1994).

11.   701 F.2d 408 (5th Cir.1983).

12.   96 F.Supp.2d 824 (N.D.Ill.2000).

furniture and housewares. Sometime thereafter, defendant created and registered a website with the domain name "www.crateandbarrel-ie. com." Plaintiff, the U.S. owner of the well-known CRATE & BARREL mark, offered evidence that at least one U.S. resident placed an order for merchandise over defendant's web site, using an Illinois billing address and an Irish shipping address. The district court found the defendant's activities sufficient both to afford personal jurisdiction, and substantively, to constitute a "use in commerce" in violation of plaintiff's U.S. trademark rights.

The *Euromarket* opinion reveals that the plaintiff there was not only the owner of the mark in the United States but also "owns a large number of foreign registrations for the marks, including registrations in Ireland, the United Kingdom, and the European Community." Presumably, therefore, the plaintiff could have obtained relief in an Irish court if it had chosen to litigate there, and in any event, the ruling does not pose any risk of conflict with legitimate foreign trademark rights. If the defendant had superior rights to the mark in Ireland, it is unclear how the case might have been resolved. Under *Steele v. Bulova* and its progeny, the existence of valid foreign trademark rights precludes the application of the Lanham Act to conduct abroad, but one might argue that if the web site is accessible by U.S. consumers sitting in their homes in the U.S. and if payment is made from the U.S., then the conduct is not taking place abroad at all. Professor Graeme Dinwoodie has aptly described the problem:

> [S]ome courts have reasoned that the accessibility in their country of a foreign web site that contains trademarks involves use of those marks in their country. If there were widespread adoption of the principle that prescriptive jurisdiction of a particular country can be premised upon the mere accessibility of a web site in that country, then a producer would be required to clear its trademark use in every country of the world. With respect to future marks, this would significantly increase the cost of trademarks, and hence of goods to consumers. It would convert truly local uses in global uses, giving rise to innumerable conflicts, causing the depletion of available marks, and eviscerating the concept of local use through which trademark law has facilitated co-existence of marks in the past.[13]

The various mechanisms reviewed earlier concerning the resolution of disputes over domain names may help resolve some disputes of the type at issue in the *Euromarket* case, but where different firms own the same mark for different national markets, neither one is likely to be found in bad faith in connection with its use of the mark. Moreover, even where domain names are distinguishable, the use of similar trademarks in the content of a Web Page may mean that search engines will identify both for consumers, with the resulting potential for confusion.

13. Graeme B. Dinwoodie, *Private International Aspects of the Protection of Trademarks*, http://wipo.int/pil-forum/en/documents/pdf/pil_01_4.pdf (2001).

The Standing Committee on the Law of Trademarks, Industrial Designs and Geographical Indications [SCT] of the World Intellectual Property Organization [WIPO] has promulgated a proposal under which use of a trade sign or symbol on the Internet would only constitute use in a particular country if it has a "commercial effect" in that country, and has set out a variety of factors which can be used to determine when such commercial effect exists. Thus, the language of the web page, the currency in which transactions may be conducted, the plans of a party to conduct any physical activities in a given country and whether post-sales services such as warranty repairs are offered in a given country all would be relevant. The SCT proposal also provides that even where a commercial effect is present, liability would be limited until the foreign party received notification from the mark owner. Such a foreign party would be able to avoid liability by promptly taking "reasonable measures which are effective to avoid commercial effect in the Member state."[14] One such measure would be a disclaimer in which the foreign web-site proprietor indicated that it would not engage in transactions with consumers from certain countries.

14. The WIPO SCT Proposal can be found on-line at http://www.wipo.int/ sct/en/documents/session_7/pdf/sct7_2.pdf

*

Appendix

RESEARCHING THE LAW OF INTELLECTUAL PROPERTY

Section 1. Introduction

Intellectual Property: The Law of Copyrights, Patents and Trademarks provides a strong basis for analyzing even the most complex problems involving issues related to intellectual property. Whether your research requires examination of case law, statutes, expert commentary, or other materials, West books and Westlaw are excellent sources of further information.

To keep you informed of current developments, Westlaw provides frequently updated databases. With Westlaw, you have unparalleled legal research resources at your fingertips.

Additional Resources

If you have not previously used Westlaw or have questions not covered in this appendix, call the West Reference Attorneys at 1–800–REF–ATTY (1–800–733–2889). The West Reference Attorneys are trained, licensed attorneys, available 24 hours a day to assist you with your Westlaw search questions. To subscribe to Westlaw, call 1–800–344–5008 or visit westlaw.com at **www.westlaw.com**.

Section 2. Westlaw Databases

Each database on Westlaw is assigned an abbreviation called an *identifier*, which you use to access the database. You can find identifiers for all databases in the online Westlaw Directory and in the printed *Westlaw Database Directory*. When you need to know more detailed information about a database, use Scope. Scope contains coverage information, lists of related databases, and valuable search tips.

The following chart lists Westlaw databases that contain information pertaining to intellectual property, including issues relating to the creation, ownership, transfer, and protection of rights in properties such as computer programs, print media, film, inventions, and biotechnology. For a complete list of intellectual property databases, see the online Westlaw Directory or the printed *Westlaw Database Directory*. Because new information is continually being added to Westlaw, you should also check the tabbed Westlaw page and the online Westlaw Directory for new database information.

Selected Intellectual Property Databases on Westlaw

Database	Identifier	Coverage
Federal and State Materials Combined		
Federal and State Case Law	ALLCASES	Begins with 1945
Federal and State Case Law–Before 1945	ALLCASES–OLD	1789–1944
United States Patents Quarterly	USPQ	Begins with 1926

Database	Identifier	Coverage
State Case Law		
State Case Law	ALLSTATES	Varies by state
Individual State Case Law	XX–CS (where XX is a state's two-letter postal abbreviation)	Varies by state
Federal Case Law		
Federal Intellectual Property–Cases	FIP–CS	Varies by court
Federal Intellectual Property–Supreme Court Cases	FIP–SCT	Begins with 1790
Federal Intellectual Property–Courts of Appeals Cases	FIP–CTA	Begins with 1891
Federal Intellectual Property–District Courts Cases	FIP–DCT	Begins with 1789
State Statutes and Regulations		
State Statutes–Annotated	ST–ANN–ALL	Current data
Individual State Statutes–Annotated	XX–ST–ANN (where XX is a state's two-letter postal abbreviation)	Current data
State Administrative Code Multibase	ADC–ALL	Current data
Individual State Administrative Code	XX–ADC (where XX is a state's two-letter postal abbreviation)	Current data
Federal Statutes, Regulations, and Administrative Materials		
Federal Intellectual Property–U.S. Code Annotated	FIP–USCA	Current data
Federal Intellectual Property–Code of Federal Regulations	FIP–CFR	Current data
Federal Intellectual Property–Federal Register	FIP–FR	Current data
Federal Intellectual Property–Patent and Trademark Office Decisions	FIP–PTO	Begins with January 1987
Federal International Law–International Trade Commission	FINT–ITC	Begins with 1975

Database	Identifier	Coverage
Federal Intellectual Property–Manual of U.S. Patent Classifications	FIP–USPATCL	Current data
Federal Intellectual Property–Manual of Patent Examining Procedure	FIP–MPEP	Eighth edition
Federal Intellectual Property–Trademark Manual of Examining Procedure 2nd Edition	FIP–TMEP2D	Second edition
Federal Intellectual Property–Trademark Manual of Examining Procedure 3rd Edition	FIP–TMEP3D	Third edition
Arnold and Porter Legislative History: General Revision of Copyright Law, 1976	COPYREV76–LH	Full history

Legal Texts, Periodicals, and Practice Materials

Intellectual Property–Law Reviews, Texts, and Bar Journals	IP–TP	Varies by publication
Andrews Intellectual Property Litigation Reporter	ANIPLR	Begins with November 1996
BNA's Patent, Trademark, and Copyright Journal	BNA–PTCJ	Begins with January 1986
E–Commerce Law Report	GLECOMLR	Begins with September 1998
Intellectual Property Quarterly	IPQ	Selected coverage begins with 1997 (vol. 1)
Journal of Intellectual Property Law	JIPL	Full coverage begins with 1993 (vol. 1)
Journal of the Copyright Society of the U.S.A.	JCPS	Selected coverage begins with 1983 (vol. 30)
Journal of the Patent and Trademark Office Society	JPTOS	Full coverage begins with 1994 (vol. 76, no. 2)
McCarthy on Trademarks and Unfair Competition	MCCARTHY	Fourth edition
Patent Law Fundamentals	PATLAWF	Second edition

Database	Identifier	Coverage
Trademark Registration Practice	TMREGPRAC	Second edition

News and Information

Intellectual Property News	IPNEWS	Varies by source
Gale Newsletter Database	GALE–NEWS	Begins with January 1988
Licensing Letter	LICENSING	Begins with December 1991
Licensing of Intellectual Property	LICENSIP	Current data
United Kingdom Current Awareness Intellectual Property	UKCA–IP	Most recent 90 days
Westlaw Topical Highlights–Intellectual Property	WTH–IP	Current data
West Legal Directory® –Intellectual Property	WLD–IP	Current data

Directories

West Legal Directory® –Banking and Finance	WLD–FIN	Current data

Materials from the United Kingdom and Europe

Intellectual Property Law Reports All	IP–RPTS–ALL	Begins with 1991
European Patent Office Reports	EPO–RPTS	Begins with 1979
European Trade Mark Reports	ETR–RPTS	Begins with 1996
European Union Intellectual Property–Legislation	EUIP–LEG	Begins with 1952
Fleet Street Reports	FLEET–RPTS	Begins with 1966
United Kingdom Intellectual Property–Journals	UKIP–JLR	Varies by publication
United Kingdom Intellectual Property–Law in Force	UKIP–LIF	Current data
United Kingdom Intellectual Property–Law in Force	UKIP–TREATIES	Begins with March 1983

Section 3. Retrieving a Document with a Citation: Find and Hypertext Links

3.1 Find

Find is a Westlaw service that allows you to retrieve a document by entering its citation. Find allows you to retrieve documents from anywhere in Westlaw without accessing or changing databases. Find is available for many documents, including case law (state and federal), the *United States Code Annotated*®, state statutes, administrative materials, and texts and periodicals.

To use Find, simply type the citation in the *Find this document by citation* text box on the tabbed Westlaw page and click **GO**. The following list provides some examples:

To Find This Document	Access Find and Type
Two Pesos, Inc. v. Taco Cabana, Inc. 112 S. Ct. 2753 (1992)	**112 sct 2753**
17 U.S.C.A. § 1101	**17 usca 1101**
Sally Beauty Co., Inc. v. Beautyco, Inc. 304 F.3d 964 (2002)	**304 f3d 964**
14 C.F.R. § 1240.105	**14 cfr 1240.105**
Advanced Bionics Corp. v. Medtronic, Inc. 2002 WL 31834909 (Cal. 2002)	**2002 wl 31834909**
NY. Art. & Cult. Aff. § 31.04 (1996)	**ny art & cult aff 31.04**

For a complete list of publications that can be retrieved with Find and their abbreviations, click **Find** on the toolbar and then click **Publications List**.

3.2 Hypertext Links

Use hypertext links to move from one location to another on Westlaw. For example, use hypertext links to go directly from the statute, case, or law review article you are viewing to a cited statute, case, or article; from a headnote to the corresponding text in the opinion; or from an entry in a statutes index database to the full text of the statute.

Section 4. Searching with Natural Language

Overview: With Natural Language, you can retrieve documents by simply describing your issue in plain English. If you are a relatively new Westlaw user, Natural Language searching can make it easier for you to retrieve cases that are on point. If you are an experienced Westlaw user, Natural Language gives you a valuable alternative search method.

When you enter a Natural Language description, Westlaw automatically identifies legal phrases, removes common words, and generates variations of terms in your description. Westlaw then searches for the concepts in your description. Concepts may include significant terms, phrases, legal citations, or topic and key numbers. Westlaw retrieves the 20 documents that most closely match your description, beginning with the document most likely to match.

4.1 Natural Language Search

Access a database, such as Journals and Law Reviews (JLR). In the *Natural Language description* text box, type a description such as the following:

can a patent be obtained for a bacterium

4.2 Browsing Search Results

Best Mode: To display the best portion (the portion that most closely matches your description) of each document in a Natural Language search result, click the **Best** arrow at the bottom of the page.

Term Mode: Click the **Term** arrow at the bottom of the page to display portions of the document that contain search terms.

Previous/Next Document: Click the left or right **Doc** arrow to view the previous or the next document in the search result.

Citations List: The citations list in the left frame lists the documents retrieved by the search. Click a hypertext link to display a document in the right frame.

4.3 Next 20 Documents

Westlaw displays the 20 documents that most closely match your description, beginning with the document most likely to match. If you want to view an additional 20 documents, click the right arrow in the left frame.

Section 5. Searching with Terms and Connectors

Overview: With Terms and Connectors searching, you enter a query, which consists of key terms from your issue and connectors specifying the relationship between these terms.

Terms and Connectors searching is useful when you want to retrieve a document for which you know specific details, such as the title or the fact situation. Terms and Connectors searching is also useful when you want to retrieve documents relating to a specific issue.

5.1 Terms

Plurals and Possessives: Plurals are automatically retrieved when you enter the singular form of a term. This is true for both regular and irregular plurals (e.g., **child** retrieves *children*). If you enter the plural form of a term, you will not retrieve the singular form.

If you enter the nonpossessive form of a term, Westlaw automatically retrieves the possessive form as well. However, if you enter the possessive form, only the possessive form is retrieved.

Compound Words, Abbreviations, and Acronyms: When a compound word is one of your search terms, use a hyphen to retrieve all forms of the word. For example, the term **along-side** retrieves *along-side, alongside,* and *along side.*

When using an abbreviation or acronym as a search term, place a period after each of the letters to retrieve any of its forms. For example, the term **u.s.p.t.o.** retrieves *USPTO, U.S.P.T.O., U S P T O,* and *U. S. P. T. O.* Note: The abbreviation does *not* retrieve *united states patent and trademark office,* so remember to add additional alternative terms to your query such as **"united states patent and trademark office".**

The Root Expander and the Universal Character: When you use the Terms and Connectors search method, placing the root expander (!) at the end of a root term generates all other terms with that root. For example, adding the ! to the root *infring* in the query

patent /s infring!

instructs Westlaw to retrieve such terms as *infringe, infringed, infringing,* and *infringement.*

The universal character (*) stands for one character and can be inserted in the middle or at the end of a term. For example, the term

withdr*w

will retrieve *withdraw* and *withdrew.* Adding three asterisks to the root *elect*

elect* * *

instructs Westlaw to retrieve all forms of the root with up to three additional characters. Terms such as *electing* or *election* are retrieved by this query. However, terms with more than three letters following the root, such as *electronic,* are not retrieved. Plurals are always retrieved, even if more than three letters follow the root.

Phrase Searching: To search for an exact phrase, place it within quotation marks. For example, to search for references to *first sale doctrine,* type **"first sale doctrine".** When you are using the Terms and Connectors search method, you should use phrase searching only if you are certain that the terms in the phrase will not appear in any other order.

5.2 Alternative Terms

After selecting the terms for your query, consider which alternative terms are necessary. For example, if you are searching for the term *code,* you might also want to search for the terms *statute, regulation,* or *ordinance.* You should consider both synonyms and antonyms as alternative terms. You can also use the Westlaw thesaurus to add alternative terms to your query.

5.3 Connectors

After selecting terms and alternative terms for your query, use connectors to specify the relationship that should exist between search terms in your retrieved documents. The connectors are described below:

Use:	To retrieve documents with:	Example:
& (and)	both terms	**disclosure & "capital formation"**
or (space)	either term or both terms	**u.s.p.t.o. "united states patent and trademark office"**
/p	search terms in the same paragraph	**patent /p conceal! /p practic!**
/s	search terms in the same sentence	**patent /s infring! /s jury /s trial**
+s	the first search term preceding the second within the same sentence	**process +s control**
/n	search terms within *n* terms of each other (where *n* is a number)	**notice /3 copyright**
+n	the first search term preceding the second by *n* terms (where *n* is a number)	**computer +4 software application program code language**
" "	search terms appearing in the same order as in the quotation marks	**"fair use"**

Use:	To exclude documents with:	Example:
% (but not)	search terms following the % symbol	**patent /2 infring! % copyright trademark /2 infring!**

5.4 Field Restrictions

Overview: Documents in each Westlaw database consist of several segments, or fields. One field may contain the citation, another the title, another the synopsis, and so forth. Not all databases contain the same fields. Also depending on the database, fields with the same name may contain different types of information.

To view a list of fields for a specific database and their contents, see Scope for that database. Note that in some databases not every field is available for every document.

To retrieve only those documents containing your search terms in a specific field, restrict your search to that field. To restrict your search to a specific field, type the field name or abbreviation followed by your search terms enclosed in parentheses. For example, to retrieve the U.S. Supreme Court case titled *Two Pesos, Inc. v. Taco Cabana, Inc.,* access the United States Patents Quarterly database (USPQ) and search for your terms in the title field (ti).

ti("two pesos" & "taco cabana")

The fields discussed below are available in Westlaw case law databases you might use for researching issues related to intellectual property.

Digest and Synopsis Fields: The digest (di) and synopsis (sy) fields, added to case law databases by West's attorney-editors, summarize the main points of a case. The synopsis field contains a brief description of a case. The digest field contains the topic and headnote fields and includes the complete hierarchy of concepts used by West's editors to classify the headnotes to specific West digest topic and key numbers. Restricting your search to the synopsis and digest fields limits your result to cases in which your terms are related to a major issue in the case.

Consider restricting your search to one or both of these fields if

- you are searching for common terms or terms with more than one meaning, and you need to narrow your search; or

- you cannot narrow your search by using a smaller database.

For example, to retrieve federal cases that discuss the protection of unregistered trademarks by the Lanham Trade–Mark Act, access the Federal Intellectual Property–Cases database (FIP–CS) and type the following query:

sy,di(unregistered "not registered" /s trademark /s lanham)

Headnote Field: The headnote field (he) is part of the digest field but does not contain topic numbers, hierarchical classification information, or key numbers. The headnote field contains a one-sentence summary for each point of law in a case and any supporting citations given by the author of the opinion. A headnote field restriction is useful when you are searching for specific statutory sections or rule numbers. For example, to retrieve headnotes from federal courts of appeals cases that cite 15 U.S.C.A. § 1052, access the Federal Intellectual Property–Courts of Appeals Cases (FIP–CTA) and type the following query:

he(15 +s 1052)

Topic Field: The topic field (to) is also part of the digest field. It contains hierarchical classification information, including the West digest topic names and numbers and the key numbers. You should restrict search terms to the topic field in a case law database if

- a digest field search retrieves too many documents; or
- you want to retrieve cases with digest paragraphs classified under more than one topic.

For example, the topic Copyrights and Intellectual Property has the topic number 99. To retrieve federal cases that discuss the ownership of a copyright for a work made by an employee, access the Federal Intellectual Property–Cases database (FIP–CS) and type a query like the following:

to(99) /p employee /p ownership /p copyright

For a complete list of West digest topics and their corresponding topic numbers, access the Custom Digest by choosing **Key Numbers and Digest** from the *More* drop-down list.

> *Note*: Slip opinions and cases from topical services do not contain the digest, headnote, and topic fields.

Prelim and Caption Fields: When searching in a database containing statutes, rules, or regulations, restrict your search to the prelim (pr) and caption (ca) fields to retrieve documents in which your terms are important enough to appear in a section name or heading. For example, to retrieve federal statutes governing copyrights for computer software, access the Federal Intellectual Property–U.S. Code Annotated database (FIP–USCA) and type the following:

pr,ca(copyright & computer software)

5.5 Date Restrictions

You can use Westlaw to retrieve documents *decided* or *issued* before, after, or on a specified date, as well as within a range of dates. The following sample queries contain date restrictions:

da(2002) & mask-work /s register! registration

da(aft 2000) & trade-mark /s infring! /p web internet

da(2/22/1988) & lanham /3 act

You can also search for documents *added to a database* on or after a specified date, as well as within a range of dates. The following sample queries contain added-date restrictions:

ad(aft 1999) & unexamined "not examined" /s patent /3 application

ad(aft 12/31/2000 & bef 6/1/2002) & "service mark" /s register! registration

Section 6. Searching with Topic and Key Numbers

To retrieve cases that address a specific point of law, use topic and key numbers as your search terms. If you have an on-point case, run a search using the topic and key number from the relevant headnote in an appropriate database to find other cases containing headnotes classified to that topic and key number. For example, to search for federal cases about reissuing patents, use headnotes classified under topic 291 (Patents) and key number 134 (Power to reissue). Access the Federal Intellectual Property–Cases database (FIP–CS) and enter the following query:

291k134

For a complete list of West digest topics and their corresponding topic numbers, access the Custom Digest by choosing **Key Numbers and Digest** from the *More* drop-down list.

> *Note*: Slip opinions and cases from topical services do not contain West topic and key numbers.

Section 6.1 Custom Digest

The Custom Digest contains the complete topic and key number outline used by West attorney-editors to classify headnotes. You can use the Custom Digest to obtain a single document containing the case law headnotes that are related to your legal issue from a particular jurisdiction.

Access the Custom Digest by choosing **Key Numbers and Digest** from the *More* drop-down list on the toolbar. Select up to 10 topics and key numbers from the easy-to-browse outline and click **GO**. Then follow the on-screen instructions.

For example, to research issues involving copyrights, scroll down the Custom Digest page until topic 99, *Copyrights and Intellectual Property*, is displayed. Click the plus symbol (+) to display sub-topics. Click the plus symbol (+) next to the *Copyrights* subtopic to display key number information. Select the check box next to each key number you want to include in your search, then click **GO**. Select the jurisdiction from which you want to retrieve headnotes and, if desired, select a date restriction and type additional search terms. Click **Search**.

Section 6.2 KeySearch

KeySearch is a research tool that helps you find cases and secondary sources in a specific area of the law. KeySearch guides you through the selection of terms from a classification system based on the West Key Number System® and then uses the key numbers and their underlying concepts to formulate a query for you. To access KeySearch, click **KeySearch** on the toolbar. Then browse the list of topics and subtopics and select a topic or subtopic to search by clicking the hypertext links. For example, to search for cases that discuss the doctrine of equivalents, click **Intellectual Property** at the first KeySearch page, then click the **Patents** folder on the next page. Then click **Doctrine of Equivalents** on the next page. The KeySearch page is displayed. Select a source and click **Search**.

Section 7. Verifying Your Research with Citation Research Services

Overview: A citation research service, such as they KeyCite service, is a tool that helps you ensure that your cases are good law; helps you retrieve cases, legislation, or articles that cite a case, rule, or statute; and helps you verify that the spelling and format of your citations are correct.

7.1 KeyCite for Cases

KeyCite for cases covers case law on Westlaw, including unpublished opinions. KeyCite for cases provides

- direct appellate history of a case (including related references, which are opinions involving the same parties and facts but resolving different issues)

- negative indirect history of a case, which consists of cases outside the direct appellate line that may have a negative impact on its precedential value

- the title, parallel citations, court of decision, docket number, and filing date of a case

- citations to cases, administrative decisions, and secondary sources on Westlaw that have cited a case

- complete integration with the West Key Number System so you can track legal issues discussed in a case

7.2 KeyCite for Statutes and Federal Regulations

KeyCite for statutes and federal regulations covers the *United States Code Annotated* (USCA®), the *Code of Federal Regulations* (CFR), and statutes from all 50 states. KeyCite for statutes provides

- links to session laws amending or repealing a statute

- statutory credits and historical notes

- citations to pending legislation affecting a federal statute or a statute from California or New York

- citations to cases, administrative decisions, and secondary sources that have cited a statute

7.3 KeyCite for Administrative Materials

KeyCite for administrative materials includes

- National Labor Relations Board decisions beginning with 1935

- Board of Contract Appeals decisions (varies by agency)

- Board of Immigration Appeals decisions beginning with 1940

- Comptroller General decisions beginning with 1921

- Environmental Protection Agency decisions beginning with 1974

- Federal Communications Commission decisions beginning with 1960

- Federal Energy Regulatory Commission (Federal Power Commission) decisions beginning with 1931 (history only)

- Internal Revenue Service revenue rulings beginning with 1954

- Internal Revenue Service revenue procedures beginning with 1954

- Internal Revenue Service private letter rulings beginning with 1954

- Internal Revenue Service technical advice memoranda beginning with 1954

- Public Utilities Reports beginning with 1974 (history only)

- U.S. Merit Systems Protection Board decisions beginning with 1979

- U.S. Patent and Trademark Office decisions beginning with 1987

- U.S. Tax Court (Board of Tax Appeals) decisions beginning with 1924

- U.S. patents beginning with 1976

7.4 KeyCite Alert

KeyCite Alert monitors the status of your cases or statutes and automatically sends you updates at the frequency you specify when their KeyCite information changes.

Section 8. Researching with Westlaw—Examples

8.1 Retrieving Law Review Articles

Recent law review articles are often a good place to begin researching a legal issue because law review articles serve 1) as an excellent introduction to a new topic or review for a stale one, providing terminology to help you formulate a query; 2) as a finding tool for pertinent primary authority, such as rules, statutes, and cases; and 3) in some instances, as persuasive secondary authority.

Suppose you need background information on the effect of the North American Free Trade Agreement on intellectual property rights.

Solution

- To retrieve recent law review articles relevant to your issue, access the Intellectual Property–Law Reviews, Texts, and Bar Journals database (IP–TP). Using the Natural Language search method, enter a description like the following:

what is the effect of nafta on intellectual property rights

- If you have a citation to an article in a specific publication, use Find to retrieve it. For more information on Find, see Section 3.1 of this appendix. For example, to retrieve the article found at 83 Trademark Rep. 1, access Find and type

83 tmarkr 1

- If you know the title of an article but not which journal it appeared in, access the Intellectual Property–Law Reviews, Texts, and Bar Journals database (IP–TP) and search for key terms using the title field. For example, to retrieve the article *Trademark Parody Unplugged*, type the following Terms and Connectors query:

ti(trade-mark /s parody /s unplugged)

8.2 Retrieving Case Law

Suppose you need to retrieve state cases discussing preemption of state statutes under federal copyright law.

Solution

- Access the State Case Law database (ALLSTATES). Type a Natural Language description such as the following:

federal copyright law preemption of state statutes

- When you know the citation for a specific case, use Find to retrieve it. For example, to retrieve *Kahebie v. Zoland,* 125 Cal. Rptr. 2d 721 (2002), access Find and type

125 calrep2d 721

For more information on Find, see Section 3.1 of this appendix.

- If you find a topic and key number that is on point, run a search using that topic and key number to retrieve additional cases discussing that point of law. For example, to retrieve federal and state cases containing headnotes classified under topic 291 (Patents) and key number 82 (What constitutes abandonment in general), access the Federal Intellectual Property–Cases database (FIP–CS) and type the following query:

291k82

- To retrieve cases written by a particular judge, add a judge field (ju) restriction to your query. For example, to retrieve cases written by Judge Worley that contain headnotes classified under topic 291 (Patents), access the Federal Intellectual Property–Courts of Appeals Cases database (FIP–CTA) and type the following query:

ju(worley) & to(291)

- You can also use KeySearch and the Custom Digest to help you retrieve cases and headnotes that discuss the issue you are researching.

8.3 Retrieving Statutes and Regulations

Suppose you need to retrieve federal statutes addressing the cancellation of trademarks.

Solution

- Access the Federal Intellectual Property–U.S. Code Annotated database (FIP–USCA). Search for your terms in the prelim and caption fields using the Terms and Connectors search method:

pr,ca(trade-mark & cancel!)

- When you know the citation for a specific statute, regulation, or code section, use Find to retrieve it. For example, to retrieve 16 C.F.R. § 1.51, access Find and type

16 cfr 1.51

- To look at surrounding sections, use the Table of Contents service. Click the **TOC** tab in the left frame. To display a section listed in the Table of Contents, click its hypertext link. You can also use Documents in Sequence to retrieve the section following section 1.61 even if that subsequent section was not retrieved with your search or Find request. Select **Docs in Seq** from the drop-down list at the bottom of the right frame and click **GO**.

- When you retrieve a statute that has been amended or repealed, a message appears at the top of the statute:

This document has been updated.

Use KEYCITE.

Click **KEYCITE** to display the amending or repealing legislation.

> Because slip copy versions of laws are added to Westlaw before they contain full editorial enhancements, they are not retrieved with the update feature. To retrieve slip copy versions of laws, access the United States Public Laws database (US-PL) or a state's legislative service database (XX-LEGIS, where XX is the state's two-letter postal abbreviation). Then type **ci(slip)** and descriptive terms, "e.g., **ci(slip) & permissible use**". Slip copy documents are replaced by the editorially enhanced versions within a few working days. The update feature also does not retrieve legislation that enacts a new statute or covers a topic that will not be incorporated into the statutes. To retrieve this legislation, access US-PL or a legislative service database and enter a query containing terms that describe the new legislation.

8.4 Using KeyCite

Suppose one of the cases you retrieve in your case law research is *Two Pesos, Inc. v. Taco Cabana, Inc.*, 112 S. Ct. 2753 (1992). You want to determine whether this case is good law and to find other cases or sources that have cited this case.

Solution

- Use KeyCite to retrieve direct and negative indirect history for *Two Pesos, Inc. v. Taco Cabana, Inc.*

- Use KeyCite to display citing references for *Two Pesos, Inc. v. Taco Cabana, Inc.*

8.5 Following Recent Developments

If you are researching issues related to intellectual property, it is important to keep up with recent developments. How can you do this efficiently?

Solution

One of the easiest ways to stay abreast of recent developments in intellectual property is by accessing the Westlaw Topical Highlights–Intellectual Property database (WTH–IP). The WTH–IP database contains summaries of recent legal developments, including court decisions, legislation, and materials released by administrative agencies in the area of intellectual property. Some summaries also contain suggested queries that combine the proven power of West's topic and key numbers and West's case headnotes to retrieve additional pertinent cases. When you access WTH–IP, you automatically retrieve a list of documents added to the database in the last two weeks.

You can also use the WestClip® clipping service to stay informed of recent developments of interest to you. WestClip will run your Terms and Connectors queries on a regular basis and deliver the results to you automatically. You can run WestClip queries in legal and news and information databases. More information about WestClip is available at **store.westgroup.com/documentation**.

*

Table of Cases

B

G

I

K

Kahn v. General Motors Corp., 135 F.3d 1472 (Fed.Cir.1998)—**§ 18.2, n. 32.**

Kalem Co. v. Harper Bros., 222 U.S. 55, 32 S.Ct. 20, 56 L.Ed. 92 (1911)—**§ 4.3, n. 4; § 4.4, n. 5.**

Karl Storz Endoscopy–America, Inc. v. Fiber Tech Medical, Inc., 4 Fed.Appx. 128 (4th Cir.2001)—**§ 31.1, n. 13.**

Kason Industries, Inc. v. Component Hardware Group, Inc., 120 F.3d 1199 (11th Cir.1997)—**§ 31.4, n. 6, 13.**

Kathawala, In re, 9 F.3d 942 (Fed.Cir. 1993)—**§ 16.2; § 16.2, n. 40; § 17.2, n. 1.**

Katzenbach v. McClung, 379 U.S. 294, 85 S.Ct. 377, 13 L.Ed.2d 290 (1964)—**§ 26.2, n. 29.**

Kearns v. Chrysler Corp., 32 F.3d 1541 (Fed.Cir.1994)—**§ 22.1, n. 3; § 22.2, n. 11.**

Keeler v. Standard Folding Bed Co., 157 U.S. 659, 15 S.Ct. 738, 39 L.Ed. 848 (1895)—**§ 20.1, n. 13.**

Keene Corp. v. Paraflex Industries, Inc., 653 F.2d 822 (3rd Cir.1981)—**§ 28.3, n. 4.**

Kellogg Co. v. Exxon Corp., 209 F.3d 562 (6th Cir.2000)—**§ 31.4, n. 22.**

Kellogg Co. v. National Biscuit Co., 305 U.S. 111, 59 S.Ct. 109, 83 L.Ed. 73 (1938)—**§ 27.3; § 27.3, n. 9, 13.**

Kendall v. Winsor, 62 U.S. 322, 21 How. 322, 16 L.Ed. 165 (1858)—**§ 16.2, n. 36.**

Kentucky Fried Chicken Corp. v. Diversified Packaging Corp., 549 F.2d 368 (5th Cir.1977)—**§ 31.4, n. 38; § 32.2, n. 8.**

Kern v. WKQX Radio, 175 Ill.App.3d 624, 125 Ill.Dec. 73, 529 N.E.2d 1149 (Ill. App. 1 Dist.1988)—**§ 30.2, n. 2.**

Kern River Gas Transmission Co. v. Coastal Corp., 899 F.2d 1458 (5th Cir.1990)—**§ 3.3, n. 13.**

Kewanee Oil Co. v. Bicron Corp., 416 U.S. 470, 94 S.Ct. 1879, 40 L.Ed.2d 315 (1974)—**§ 24.6; § 24.6, n. 3; § 28.5, n. 3.**

Key Mfg. Group, Inc. v. Microdot, Inc., 925 F.2d 1444 (Fed.Cir.1991)—**§ 20.2, n. 47.**

Key Publications, Inc. v. Chinatown Today Pub. Enterprises, Inc., 945 F.2d 509 (2nd Cir.1991)—**§ 4.10, n. 10.**

Kierulff v. Metropolitan Stevedore Co., 315 F.2d 839 (9th Cir.1963)—**§ 21.2, n. 4.**

Kieselstein–Cord v. Accessories by Pearl, Inc., 632 F.2d 989 (2nd Cir.1980)—**§ 4.5; § 4.5, n. 23.**

King v. Mister Maestro, Inc., 224 F.Supp. 101 (S.D.N.Y.1963)—**§ 5.1; § 5.1, n. 14, 25.**

King, Estate of v. CBS, Inc., 13 F.Supp.2d 1347 (N.D.Ga.1998)—**§ 5.1; § 5.1, n. 17.**

King Instrument Corp. v. Otari Corp., 767 F.2d 853 (Fed.Cir.1985)—**§ 22.2, n. 18.**

King Instruments Corp. v. Perego, 65 F.3d 941 (Fed.Cir.1995)—**§ 18.2, n. 27; § 22.2, n. 10.**

Kingsdown Medical Consultants, Ltd. v. Hollister Inc., 863 F.2d 867 (Fed.Cir. 1988)—**§ 19.4; § 19.4, n. 5.**

Kitchens of Sara Lee, Inc. v. Nifty Foods Corp., 266 F.2d 541 (2nd Cir.1959)—**§ 3.1, n. 15.**

K Mart Corp. v. Cartier, Inc., 486 U.S. 281, 108 S.Ct. 1811, 100 L.Ed.2d 313 (1988)—**§ 20.1, n. 32; § 31.1; § 31.1, n. 15, 19; § 32.2, n. 1.**

Knitwaves, Inc. v. Lollytogs Ltd. (Inc.), 71 F.3d 996 (2nd Cir.1995)—**§ 28.1; § 28.1, n. 9; § 28.3; § 28.3, n. 3.**

Kohler Co. v. Moen Inc., 12 F.3d 632 (7th Cir.1993)—**§ 28.1, n. 14.**

Kori Corp. v. Wilco Marsh Buggies and Draglines, Inc., 761 F.2d 649 (Fed.Cir. 1985)—**§ 22.2, n. 20.**

Kotzin, Application of, 47 C.C.P.A. 852, 276 F.2d 411 (Cust. & Pat.App.1960)—**§ 28.1, n. 14.**

Kridl v. McCormick, 105 F.3d 1446 (Fed. Cir.1997)—**§ 16.3, n. 19.**

Kupferberg, Goldberg & Niemark, L.L.C. v. Father and Son Pizza, Ltd., 1997 WL 158332 (N.D.Ill.1997)—**§ 9.5, n. 11.**

L

LaCienega Music.Co. v. ZZ Top, 53 F.3d 950 (9th Cir.1995)—**§ 5.1; § 5.1, n. 20.**

L.A. Gear, Inc. v. Thom McAn Shoe Co., 988 F.2d 1117 (Fed.Cir.1993)—**§ 14.8, n. 6.**

Laitram Corp. v. Rexnord, Inc., 939 F.2d 1533 (Fed.Cir.1991)—**§ 18.2, n. 29.**

Lambert Pharmacal Co. v. Bolton Chemical Corporation, 219 F. 325 (S.D.N.Y. 1915)—**§ 29.1, n. 3.**

Lam, Inc. v. Johns–Manville Corp., 718 F.2d 1056 (Fed.Cir.1983)—**§ 22.2, n. 12.**

Land O'Lakes Creameries, Inc. v. Oconomowoc Canning Co., 221 F.Supp. 576 (E.D.Wis.1963)—**§ 32.2, n. 12.**

Lands' End, Inc. v. Manback, 797 F.Supp. 511 (E.D.Va.1992)—**§ 26.2, n. 14.**

Larry Harmon Pictures Corp. v. Williams Restaurant Corp., 929 F.2d 662 (Fed.Cir. 1991)—**§ 26.2, n. 28.**

Lasercomb America, Inc. v. Reynolds, 911 F.2d 970 (4th Cir.1990)—**§ 9.7; § 9.7, n. 4.**

La Societe Anonyme des Parfums le Galion v. Jean Patou, Inc., 495 F.2d 1265 (2nd Cir.1974)—**§ 34.1, n. 2.**

Latimer, Ex parte, 1889 Comm'r Dec. 13 (1889)—**§ 14.3, n. 1.**

N

O

Y

Z

Table of Statutes

UNITED STATES CODE ANNOTATED

35 U.S.C.A.—Patents

Sec.	This Work Sec.	Note
102	13.1	1
102	13.1	3
102(a)	18.1	
102(a)	19.2	
102(a)	19.3	2
102(b)	18.1	
102(b)	19.4	9
102(d)	19.4	9
102(e)	18.1	
102(e)	19.2	
102(e)	19.3	2
102(g)	1.2	3
102(g)	18.1	
103	1.1	12
103	13.1	1
103	14.3	
103(a)	1.2	8
103(a)	4.5	9
103(a)	13.1	4
111	13.1	5
111(b)	19.2	8
112	1.1	14
112	1.2	3
112	13.1	6
112	13.1	7
112	14.3	
112	24.5	2
112(2)	18.1	
112(4)	18.2	14
113	18.1	2
113	19.2	3
114	18.1	13
115	19.2	2
115	19.3	1
119(b)(2)	19.8	1
119(d)	19.8	2
120	19.2	12
120	19.2	15
121	19.2	19
121	19.4	12
122	19.2	17
122(b)	19.2	20
122(b)(2)(B)(v)	19.2	23
122(c)	19.7	2
131	24.5	7
132	18.1	
132	18.1	19
132	19.2	10
133	19.2	11
134	19.2	13
134	19.2	25
141	19.2	28
145	19.2	27
151	13.1	8
151	19.2	14
154	13.1	9
154	13.1	11
154	16.3	47
154(a)(2)	1.1	16
154(a)(2)	1.2	12

UNITED STATES CODE ANNOTATED

35 U.S.C.A.—Patents

Sec.	This Work Sec.	Note
154(a)(2)	14.9	6
154(b)	19.5	4
154(d)	19.2	21
154(d)	22.2	22
161	1.1	18
161	14.9	2
161	14.9	6
161—164	14.9	
162	14.9	5
171	1.1	17
171	14.8	1
171—173	14.8	
173	14.8	4
181	19.8	8
183	19.8	9
184	19.8	7
184	19.8	11
185	19.8	10
251	19.6	5
251	19.6	6
251	19.6	9
252	19.6	15
253	19.6	3
254	19.6	1
255	19.6	1
256	19.6	2
261	13.1	14
271	1.1	15
271(a)	13.1	10
271(a)	14.2	12
271(a)	20.1	1
271(a)	20.2	1
271(h)	20.1	36
273	24.5	5
273	24.5	9
281	13.1	12
282	13.1	13
282	20.2	3
283	22.1	1
284	22.2	1
284	22.2	4
284	22.2	23
285	22.2	28
286	21.1	
286	22.2	2
287(a)	14.2	14
287(a)	22.2	33
287(c)	14.4	
287(c)	14.4	6
287(c)	22.2	31
288	19.6	4
289	22.2	21
301	19.6	16
301	19.7	3
302	19.6	16
302	19.6	17
302	19.6	18
303(a)	19.6	19
303(c)	19.6	20
304	19.6	21

UNITED STATES CODE ANNOTATED
35 U.S.C.A.—Patents

Sec.	This Work Sec.	Note
305	19.6	22
305	19.6	23
306	19.6	29
307(a)	19.6	26
307(a)	19.6	28
307(b)	19.6	27
311—318	19.6	32
365	19.8	13

STATUTES AT LARGE

Year	This Work Sec.	Note
1790, Ch. 7	13.2	8
1790, Ch. 15	2.2	6
1793, Ch. 11	13.2	10
1836, Ch. 357	13.2	11
1870, Ch. 2	25.2	10
1870, Ch. 230	4.5	11
1870, Ch. 230	13.2	12
1891, Ch. 517	13.2	15
1897, Ch. 391	16.3	53
1909, Ch. 320	2.1	2
1909, Ch. 320	2.2	11
1946, Ch. 540	25.2	16
1952, Ch. 950	13.2	14
1962, P.L. 87–668	8.3	4
1965, P.L. 89–142	8.3	4
1967, P.L. 90–141	8.3	4
1968, P.L. 90–416	8.3	4
1969, P.L. 91–147	8.3	4
1971, P.L. 92–140	1.1	8
1971, P.L. 92–140	4.7	1
1971, P.L. 92–140	10.4	5
1971, P.L. 92–170	8.3	4
1972, P.L. 92–566	8.3	4
1974, P.L. 93–573	4.1	19
1974, P.L. 93–573	8.3	4
1980, P.L. 96–517	4.1	20
1982, P.L. 97–164	13.2	16
1984, P.L. 98–260	4.1	39
1984, P.L. 98–417	20.1	27
1984, P.L. 98–622	17.2	9
1984, P.L. 98–6209	1.1	7
1988, P.L. 100–568	5.1	7
1988, P.L. 100–568	6.4	14
1988, P.L. 100–568	12.2	3
1988, P.L. 100–569	2.2	20
1988, P.L. 100–667	29.8	7
1990, P.L. 101–553	9.7	23
1990, P.L. 101–650	4.8	2
1990, P.L. 101–650	4.8	10
1990, P.L. 101–650	12.2	5
1990, P.L. 101–650	12.2	6
1992, P.L. 102–307	8.3	6
1992, P.L. 102–492	10.2	36
1992, P.L. 102–560	20.1	35
1992, P.L. 102–563	10.4	7
1993, P.L. 103–182	23.4	1
1994, P.L. 103–465	3.2	18

STATUTES AT LARGE

Year	This Work Sec.	Note
1994, P.L. 103–465	8.5	1
1995, P.L. 104–39	C7,Int.	1
1995, P.L. 104–39	7.4	15
1995, P.L. 104–41	17.3	63
1996, P.L. 104–294	24.1	5
1998, P.L. 105–298	2.2	21
1998, P.L. 105–298	8.2	1
1998, P.L. 105–304	1.1	9
1998, P.L. 105–304	2.2	22
1998, P.L. 105–304	5.3	4
1998, P.L. 105–304	7.1	28
1998, P.L. 105–304	7.7	1
1998, P.L. 105–304	9.3	9
1998, P.L. 105–330	32.1	24
1999, P.L. 106–113	13.2	20
1999, P.L. 106–113	33.2	41
2002, P.L. 107–273	30.8	11
2002, P.L. 107–273	34.3	2

POPULAR NAME ACTS

COPYRIGHT ACT OF 1909

Sec.	This Work Sec.	Note
1(c)	7.4	5
4	C4,Int.	1
10	3.2	8
10	5.1	1
11	3.2	8
11	5.3	3
13	5.3	3
19	5.2	
19—21	5.2	
21	5.2	
24	8.1	1
24	8.1	3
24	8.1	4
26	6.2	
26	6.2	2
28	6.4	12
30	6.4	20
209	3.4	7

COPYRIGHT ACT OF 1976

Sec.	This Work Sec.	Note
101	5.1	24
101	7.1	
101	7.2	
101	7.4	
101	7.5	
101	7.6	
102	11.4	
102(4)	11.4	
102(a)	12.2	
102(b)	4.1	
102(b)	11.4	

DIGITAL MILLENNIUM COPYRIGHT ACT

Sec.	This Work Sec.	Note
1201(b)(1)	7.7	
1201(c)(1)	7.7	
1202	7.7	

FEDERAL TRADE COMMISSION ACT

Sec.	This Work Sec.	Note
5	29.8	

HATCH–WAXMAN ACT

Sec.	This Work Sec.	Note
156	20.1	
271(e)	20.1	
271(e)(1)	20.1	

LANHAM ACT

Sec.	This Work Sec.	Note
1(a)	26.2	
1(a)	32.1	15
1(b)	26.2	
1(b)	34.2	
2	27.3	
2	27.5	
2	27.6	
2	34.2	
2(a)	27.5	
2(a)	27.6	
2(a)	30.7	
2(a)	34.1	
2(b)	27.6	
2(c)	27.6	
2(d)	27.4	
2(d)	27.6	
2(d)	29.4	
2(d)	30.7	
2(e)	27.3	
2(e)(3)	27.2	
2(e)(5)	28.1	
2(f)	27.2	
2(f)	27.3	
7(c)	26.2	
7(c)	26.2	61
7(c)	34.2	
8	34.2	
10	32.1	
10	32.1	15
14	27.3	
14(3)	28.1	
14(3)	34.1	
22	29.4	
32	28.5	
32	C29,Int.	
32	C29,Int.	2
33	29.4	
33(a)	29.4	15
33(b)(4)	31.3	

LANHAM ACT

Sec.	This Work Sec.	Note
33(b)(8)	28.1	
34	31.5	
34(d)	31.5	
34(d)(11)	29.6	8
35	30.8	11
35	31.5	
35(a)	31.5	
35(b)	31.5	
42	31.1	
42	34.4	
42(b)	31.1	18
43	C29,Int.	
43	C29,Int.	4
43	34.4	
43(a)	11.3	
43(a)	28.1	
43(a)	28.5	
43(a)	29.7	
43(a)	29.8	
43(a)	31.4	
43(a)	31.5	
43(a)	34.1	
43(a)	34.4	
43(b)	34.4	
43(c)	30.1	
43(c)	30.8	11
43(c)(4)	30.8	1
43(d)	33.2	
44	34.2	
44(b)	34.2	
44(c)	34.2	
44(d)	34.2	
44(e)	34.2	
44(f)	34.2	7
44(h)	34.1	
44(i)	34.2	6
45	29.8	
45	30.3	
45	34.2	

PATENT ACT

Sec.	This Work Sec.	Note
101	15.1	
101	16.3	
101	18.2	
101	19.4	
102	16.1	
102	16.2	
102	16.3	
102	17.1	
102	17.2	
102	17.3	
102	18.2	
102	19.3	
102	19.4	
102	19.6	
102	20.2	
102(a)	16.1	
102(a)	16.2	

INDEX

**INTERNATIONAL UNION FOR THE PRO-
TECTION OF LITERARY AND ARTISTIC
WORKS**—Cont'd
See also Berne Convention, this index

INTERNET
Generally, §§ 7.7.1, 33.2.1
See also Computers and Computer Pro-
grams, this index
Anti-Cybersquatting Consumer Protection
Act, §§ 33.2.3, 33.2.4
Audio Home Recording Act (AHRA), § 10.4
Commercial uses, § 33.1
Consumer deception, use of keywords for,
§ 33.4
Cybersquatting, § 33.2.1
Digital Millennium Copyright Act, this in-
dex
Digital recording and fair use, § 10.4
Dilution
Cybersquatting as, § 33.2.2
Spam, use of marks in, § 33.5
Domain names
Anti-Cybersquatting Consumer Protec-
tion Act, §§ 33.2.3, 33.2.4
Trademarks used as, §§ 33.2, 33.2.1
Uniform Dispute Resolution Procedure,
§ 33.2.5
Fair use doctrine
Generally, § 10.5
Home taping, § 10.4
Fileswapping, § 10.5.1
Infringement
Cybersquatting as, § 33.2.2
ISP liabilities, § 9.3
Spam, use of marks in, §§ 33.4, 33.5
Transnational, § 34.4
Jurisdictional problems, § 33.2.4
Keywords, use of trademarks as, § 33.4
Metatags
Generally, § 33.3
Trademark use in, §§ 31.2.3, 33.3
Napster system, § 10.5.1
Popup advertising, § 33.4
Spam, use of trademarks in, § 33.5
Trademark use generally, § 33
Transnational infringement problems,
§ 34.4
Uniform Dispute Resolution Procedure,
§ 33.2.5

INVENTION AND INVENTORS
Abandoned inventions, §§ 16.2.6, 16.3.2.7
American Inventors Protection Act of 1999,
this index
Concealed inventions, §§ 16.2.6, 16.3.2.7
Conception date, § 16.3.2.3
Derived invention, § 16.3.4
First Inventor Defense Act, § 16.3.2.8
First-to-invent rule, § 16.3.1
Fraudulent inventions, § 15.2
Immoral inventions, § 15.2
Incredible inventions, § 15.2
Joint inventorship, § 19.3

INVENTION AND INVENTORS—Cont'd
Living inventions, § 14.3.2
Prior invention, § 16.3
Proof of inventive activities, § 16.3.2.6
Second inventor awards, § 16.3.2.7
Secrecy, Invention Secrecy Act, § 19.8.3
Suppressed inventions, §§ 16.2.6, 16.3.2.7

INVENTION SECRECY ACT
Generally, § 19.8.3

INVENTIONS AND INVENTORS
See also Patents, this index

LANHAM ACT
See Trademarks, this index

LETTERS, PRIVATE
Generally, § 1.2.1

LITERARY WORKS
See Copyright, this index

LIVE BROADCASTING
See Broadcasting, this index

LIVE PERFORMANCES
Generally, § 7.4
Digital Performance Right in Sound Re-
cordings Act (DPRSRA), § 7.4.5
Fixation requirement, § 3.2
Public display of copyright protected works,
§ 7.5.2

MEDICAL TREATMENT METHODS
See Patents, this index

MENTAL STEPS DOCTRINE
Generally, § 14.5.1

MERGER THEORY
Ideas and expression, § 3.3

MISAPPROPRIATION
Generally, § 11.2
Federal preemption, § 11.4
Fixation, common law protections of un-
fixed works, § 3.2
Passing Off, this index
Remedies, § 24.4
Restatement of Unfair Competition,
§ 11.2.3
Trade secrets, § 24.3

**MONOPOLIES AND RESTRAINTS OF
TRADE**
Patentability standards, relation to, § 17.3.1
Trademarks as fostering, § 25.3

MORAL RIGHTS
Copyright law protections, § 7.6
Copyright protections, § 2.4.2
Shop rights, § 21.2

MUSIC
See Copyright, this index

NAFTA
Patent protections, § 23.4

†

0-314-06599-7

90000

9 780314 065995